Slave Counterpoint

Black Culture in the Eighteenth-Century Chesapeake and Lowcountry

Published *for the* Omohundro Institute of Early American History and Culture, *Williamsburg, Virginia, by the* University of North Carolina Press, *Chapel Hill & London*

Slave Counterpoint
Philip D. Morgan

The Omohundro Institute of Early American History and Culture is sponsored jointly by the College of William and Mary and the Colonial Williamsburg Foundation. On November 15, 1996, the Institute adopted the present name in honor of a bequest from Malvern H. Omohundro, Jr.

© 1998 The University of North Carolina Press
All rights reserved
Manufactured in the United States of America
02 01 00 99 98   5 4 3 2
Library of Congress Cataloging-in-Publication Data
Morgan, Philip D., 1949–
Slave counterpoint : Black culture in the eighteenth-century Chesapeake and Lowcountry / Philip D. Morgan.
    p. cm.
ISBN 0-8078-2409-7 (cloth: alk. paper)
—ISBN 0-8078-4717-8 (pbk.: alk. paper)
1. Slaves—Chesapeake Bay Region (Md. and Va.)—History—18th century. 2. Slaves—South Carolina—History—18th century. 3. Slaves—Chesapeake Bay Region (Md. and Va.)—Social life and customs. 4. Slaves—South Carolina—Social life and customs. 5. Chesapeake Bay Region (Md. and Va.)—Race relations. 6. South Carolina—Race relations. 7. Afro-Americans—Chesapeake Bay Region (Md. and Va.)—History—18th century. 8. Afro-Americans—South Carolina—History—18th century. 9. Plantation life—Chesapeake Bay Region (Md. and Va.)—History—18th century. 10. Plantation life—South Carolina—History—18th century. I. Omohundro Institute of Early American History & Culture. II. Title.
F232.C43M67 1998
975.5′1800496—dc21   97-40316
                        CIP
Maps and graphs drawn by Stinely Associates.
The paper in this book meets the guidelines for permanence and durability of the Committee on Production Guidelines for Book Longevity of the Council on Library Resources.

This volume received indirect support from an unrestricted book publication grant awarded to the Institute by the L. J. Skaggs and Mary C. Skaggs Foundation of Oakland, California.

TO BARBARA, *with love*

Contents

List of Illustrations and Tables, *ix*
Abbreviations, *xiii*
Introduction, *xv*

Prelude. Two Infant Slave Societies, *1*

PART I.
    CONTOURS OF THE PLANTATION EXPERIENCE
1 Two Plantation Worlds, *27*
    Two Landscapes, 29
    Two Plantation Systems, 35
    Two Populations, 58
2 Material Life, *102*
    Housing, 104
    Dress, 125
    Diet, 134
3 Fieldwork, *146*
    Seasons of Labor, 147
    Organization of Labor, 179
    Patterns of Labor, 194
4 Skilled Work, *204*
    Occupational Structures, 205
    The Life Cycle of Skilled Workers, 212
    Drivers and Foremen, 218
    Artisans, 225
    Watermen, 236
    Household Slaves, 244

PART II.
    ENCOUNTERS BETWEEN WHITES AND BLACKS
5 Patriarchs, Plain Folk, and Slaves, *257*
    Masters and Slaves, 261
    Plain Folk and Slaves, 300
6 Economic Exchanges between Whites and Blacks, *318*
    Channels of Communication, 319
    Field Hands and Overseers, 326
    Slaves in the Middle, 334
    Constant Companions, 353
    Trade, 358

7   Social Transactions between Whites and Blacks, 377
       Violence, 385
       Sex, 398
       Recreation, 412
       Religion, 420

PART III.
    THE BLACK WORLD
8   African American Societies, 441
       Africans, 443
       Creoles and Africans, 459
       Creoles, 463
       Blacks and Indians, 477
       Slaves and Free Blacks, 485
9   Family Life, 498
       Structures, 501
       Stability, 512
       Moving and Staying, 519
       The Significance of Kin, 530
10 African American Cultures, 559
       Words, 560
       Play, 580
       Soul, 610

    Coda. Two Mature Slave Societies, 659

    Acknowledgments, 673
    Index, 675

Illustrations and Tables

PLATES

1. *Industry and Idleness*, 6
2. Artifacts, 22
3. *Residence and Slave Quarters of Mulberry Plantation*, 46
4. *Extraordinary Appearances in the Heavens, and on Earth*, 57
5. Ferry Tract Plantation, 104
6. *SW View of the Settlement of Hartford*, 107
7. Fairlawn Plantation, 117
8. Frogmore Plantation, 124
9. Plantation of John Middleton, 150
10. Mortar and Pestle, 154
11. Plantation of John Bull, 158
12. Indigo Culture, 161
13. *Perry Hall Slave Quarters with Field Hands at Work*, 189
14. *Residence of George Heinrick Repold, Lexington Street near Fremont Avenue*, 199
15. Colono Ware Jug, 234
16. Blacks Working on the James River, 237
17. *Portrait of a Man / Virginian Luxuries*, 268
18. *Alic, a Faithful and Humerous Old Servant*, 354
19. *An Overseer Doing His Duty*, 442
20. *The Old Plantation*, 585
21. Drum and Cane, 589
22. *Preparations for the Enjoyment of a Fine Sunday among the Blacks, Norfolk*, 602
23. *A South View of Julianton Plantation, the Property of Francis Levett, Esqr.*, 662

MAPS

1. The Coastal Origins of African Slaves, 66
2. The Distribution of Black Slaves in South Carolina, 1720–1790, 96
3. The Distribution of Black Slaves in Virginia, 1750–1790, 98

FIGURES

1. Adult Sex Ratios among Slaves in the Chesapeake and South Carolina, 1705–1775, 82
2. Female-Child Ratios among Slaves in the Chesapeake and South Carolina, 1705–1775, 83

3 Population Pyramids of Slaves in the Chesapeake, 1709–1791, 88
4 Population Pyramids of Slaves in the Lowcountry, 1758–1780, 90
5 The Months When Slaves Ran Away, 1732–1781, 152
6 Labor to Cultivate and Process Rice, circa 1800, 176
7 Age Profile of Africans and Creoles among Adult Male Slaves on Elias Ball's Comingtee Plantation, 1778, 452
8 Age Profile of Africans and Creoles among Slaves Belonging to Colonel Stapleton on Saint Helena Island, 1810, 453
9 Age Profile of Runaways in the Chesapeake and Lowcountry, 1732–1787, 527

TABLES

1 Plantation Size in South Carolina, 1720–1779, 40
2 Plantation Size in Virginia, 1720–1779, 41
3 Landholding in South Carolina Parishes, 1745–1785, 43
4 Landholding in Virginia Counties, 1768–1778, 44
5 Primary Production of Virginia and South Carolina Plantations, 1730–1776, 50
6 Primary Equipment on Virginia and South Carolina Plantations, 1730–1776, 51
7 Livestock on Virginia and South Carolina Plantations, 1730–1776, 52
8 Secondary and Tertiary Equipment on Virginia and South Carolina Plantations, 1730–1776, 54
9 African Immigration to Virginia and South Carolina, 1700–1790, 59
10 Africans in the Virginia and South Carolina Slave Populations, 1700–1800, 61
11 Coastal Origins of Virginia and South Carolina Africans, 1710s–1770s, 63
12 Origins of South Carolina's African Immigrants and African Runaways, 1730–1782, 68
13 Passage Time from England via Africa to British America, 1720–1798, 69
14 Age and Sex Composition of Slavers to the Chesapeake and Lowcountry, 1710–1774, 71
15 Children among African Immigrants to South Carolina, 1735–1774, and to the West Indies, 1791–1798, 72
16 Months of Arrival of Virginia and South Carolina Slave Vessels, 1700–1774, 74
17 Time between Arrival of Slave Vessel and Sale Dates, Virginia and South Carolina, 1730–1774, 75
18 The Distribution of Africans among Purchasers in the Chesapeake and Lowcountry, 1689–1786, 78
19 Black Population Growth in Virginia, 1700–1800, 81

20 Black Population Growth in South Carolina, 1700–1800, *84*
21 Age at First Conception of Slave Women, 1700s–1790s, *92*
22 Skilled Slaves among Inventoried South Carolina Adults, 1730–1799, *207*
23 Skilled Workers among South Carolina Runaway Slaves, 1730–1799, *208*
24 Occupations of Adult Male Slaves in the Rural Lowcountry, 1730s–1810, *210*
25 Occupations of Adult Male Slaves in the Chesapeake, 1733–1809, *211*
26 Age of Runaway Skilled Workers, 1732–1779, *213*
27 Age of Skilled Male Slaves, 1730–1809, *217*
28 Occupations of Adult Female Slaves on Large Estates in the Lowcountry and Chesapeake, 1757–1809, *245*
29 South Carolina Slave Families, 1730–1799, *500*
30 Household Structures among Slaves in the Chesapeake, 1733–1775, *504*
31 Household Structures among Slaves in South Carolina, 1739–1797, *506*

Abbreviations

AHR	*American Historical Review*
BL	British Library, London
CC	College of Charleston
City Gaz	*City Gazette* (Charleston)
City Gaz and DA	*City Gazette, and [or] Daily Advertiser* (Charleston)
CLS	Charleston Library Society
CW	Research Library, Colonial Williamsburg Foundation, Williamsburg, Va.
Duke	Duke University, Durham, N.C.
Ga Gaz	*Georgia Gazette* (Savannah)
Gaz of State of SC	*Gazette of the State of South-Carolina* (Charleston)
GHQ	*Georgia Historical Quarterly*
GHS	Georgia Historical Society, Savannah
HSP	Historical Society of Pennsylvania, Philadelphia
JAH	*Journal of American History*
Laurens Papers	Philip M. Hamer et al., eds., *The Papers of Henry Laurens* (Columbia, S.C., 1968–)
LC	Library of Congress, Washington, D.C.
Md Gaz	*Maryland Gazette* (Annapolis)
MHM	*Maryland Historical Magazine*
MHR	Maryland Hall of Records, Annapolis
MHS	Maryland Historical Society, Baltimore
NCDAH	North Carolina Division of Archives and History, Raleigh
NYHS	New-York Historical Society, New York
NYPL	New York Public Library
PRO	Public Record Office, London
Royal Gaz	*Royal Gazette* (Charleston)
SC and AGG	*South-Carolina and American General Gazette* (Charleston)
SCDAH	South Carolina Department of Archives and History, Columbia
SCG	*South-Carolina Gazette* (Charleston)
SCG and CJ	*South-Carolina Gazette: And Country Journal* (Charleston)
SCG and DA	*South Carolina Gazette and Daily Advertiser* (Charleston)
SCG and GA	*South-Carolina Gazette and General Advertiser* (Charleston)

SCG and T and MDA	*South-Carolina State-Gazette and Timothy and Mason's Daily Advertiser* (Charleston)
SCG and TDA	*South-Carolina State-Gazette, and Timothy's Daily Advertiser* (Charleston)
SCHM	*South Carolina Historical Magazine*
SCHS	South Carolina Historical Society, Charleston
SC Weekly Gaz	*South-Carolina Weekly Gazette* (Charleston)
SC State Gaz	*South-Carolina State-Gazette* (Charleston)
SPG	Society for the Propagation of the Gospel, London
State Gaz of SC	*State Gazette of South-Carolina* (Charleston)
UNC	University of North Carolina, Chapel Hill
USC	University of South Carolina, Columbia
UVa	University of Virginia, Charlottesville
VaG (C and D)	Clarkson and Davis's *Virginia Gazette* (Williamsburg)
VaG (D and H)	Dixon and Hunter's *Virginia Gazette* (Williamsburg)
VaG (D and N)	Dixon and Nicolson's *Virginia Gazette* (Williamsburg)
VaG (Hunter)	Hunter's *Virginia Gazette* (Williamsburg)
VaG (P and D)	Purdie and Dixon's *Virginia Gazette* (Williamsburg)
VaG (Parks)	Parks's *Virginia Gazette* (Williamsburg)
VaG (Pinkney)	Pinkney's *Virginia Gazette* (Williamsburg)
VaG (Purdie)	Purdie's *Virginia Gazette* (Williamsburg)
VaG (Rind)	Rind's *Virginia Gazette* (Williamsburg)
VaG (Royle)	Royle's *Virginia Gazette* (Williamsburg)
VaG and GA	*Virginia Gazette, and General Advertiser* (Richmond)
VaG and WA	*Virginia Gazette, and [or] Weekly Advertiser* (Richmond)
Va Ind Chron	*Virginia Independent Chronicle* (Richmond)
Va Ind Chron and GA	*Virginia Independent Chronicle and General Advertiser* (Richmond)
VBHS	Virginia Baptist Historical Society, University of Richmond
VHS	Virginia Historical Society, Richmond
VMHB	*Virginia Magazine of History and Biography*
VSL	Virginia State Library, Richmond
W and M	College of William and Mary, Williamsburg, Va.
WMQ	*William and Mary Quarterly*
WPA	Works Progress / Work Projects Administration

Introduction

When Southey was engaged on his *History of Brazil,* Coleridge said to him, "My dear Southey, I wish to know how you intend to treat of man in that important work. Do you mean, like Herodotus, to treat of man as man in general? or do you mean, like Thucydides, to treat of man as man political? or do you mean, like Polybius, to treat of man as man military? or do you mean—" "Coleridge," cried Southey, "*I mean to write the History of Brazil.*"

Most authors have probably shared Robert Southey's exasperation when questioned what their books are about. Just read it, they long to say. Furthermore, when the questions turn philosophical, most historians become uneasy; I am no exception. I have tried to treat slaves, not as slaves political or as slaves military, but as human beings. Accordingly, I have explored the history of slaves in their many roles: as forced immigrants, as workers, as solitaries, as family members, and as churchgoers—to mention a few. I have tried to tell their story as comprehensively as possible—from cradle to grave, from work to play, from private to public, from the mundane details of everyday life to the symbolic dimensions of communal life, from bodily gestures to forms of speech.[1]

My justification for exploring slave life so fully (too fully, some might say, as they stagger under the weight of this tome) is that slavery was no curious abnormality, no aberration, no marginal feature of early America. Most eighteenth-century Americans did not find it an embarrassment or an evil. Rather, slavery was a fundamental, acceptable, thoroughly American institution. In labor recruitment, British America was the land of the unfree rather than of the free. From 1700 to 1780, about twice as many Africans as Europeans crossed the Atlantic to the Chesapeake and Lowcountry. Much of the wealth of early America derived from slave-produced commodities. Between 1768 and 1772, the Chesapeake and Lowcountry generated about two-thirds of the average annual value of the mainland's commodity exports. Slavery defined the structure of these two British American regions, underpinning not just their economies but their social, political, cultural, and ideological systems. As Edmund Morgan and Orlando Patterson among others have demonstrated, the ideal of freedom was intimately, inextricably connected to slavery. Slavery

---

1. Richard J. Schrader, ed., *The Reminiscences of Alexander Dyce* (Columbus, Ohio, 1972), 178.

was the grim and irrepressible theme governing the settlement of these two eighteenth-century regions.[2]

Although slavery was a hemispheric and continental institution, it varied greatly across space. A primary theme of this book, as the title indicates, is spatial comparison. Rather than comparing North America with South America, Virginia with Cuba, the United States with South Africa, American slavery with Russian serfdom, American planters with Prussian junkers, or slave economies in Jamaica and Louisiana, as previous studies have done, I have chosen to compare two regions within the same Anglophone world.[3] Instead of contrasting divergent legal systems, national cultures, and church-state relations—all too readily highlighted in transnational comparisons—these phenomena have been largely held constant, since the Chesapeake and Lowcountry shared basically the same legal and religious structures and were part of the same imperial system. As a result, the impact of different ecologies, settlement patterns, demographic regimes, staple systems, and slaveowners' ways of life—easily ignored in cross-cultural comparisons—are readily discerned. At once very alike, and yet significantly different, Chesapeake and Lowcountry slave societies provide intelligent commentaries upon one another. They are not so dissimilar that comparison is fruitless. Rather, each society looks different in the light of the other; and our understanding of each is enlarged by knowledge of the other.

2. Russell R. Menard, "Migration, Ethnicity, and the Rise of an Atlantic Economy: The Re-peopling of British America, 1600–1790," in Rudolph J. Vecoli and Suzanne M. Sinke, eds., *A Century of European Migrations, 1830–1930* (Urbana, Ill., 1991), 58–77, esp. 61–62; and for all British America, see Philip D. Morgan, "British Encounters with Africans and African-Americans, circa 1600–1780," in Bernard Bailyn and Philip D. Morgan, eds., *Strangers within the Realm: Cultural Margins of the First British Empire* (Chapel Hill, N.C., 1991), 162; John J. McCusker and Russell R. Menard, *The Economy of British America, 1607–1789* (Chapel Hill, N.C., 1985), 108, 130, 174, 199; Edmund S. Morgan, *American Slavery, American Freedom: The Ordeal of Colonial Virginia* (New York, 1975); and Orlando Patterson, *Freedom*, I, *Freedom in the Making of Western Culture* (New York, 1991). See also Nathan I. Huggins, "The Deforming Mirror of Truth: Slavery and the Master Narrative of American History," *Radical History Review*, no. 49 (Winter 1991), 25–46.

3. Frank Tannenbaum, *Slave and Citizen: The Negro in the Americas* (New York, 1947); Herbert S. Klein, *Slavery in the Americas: A Comparative Study of Virginia and Cuba* (Chicago, 1967); Carl N. Degler, *Neither Black nor White: Slavery and Race Relations in Brazil and the United States* (New York, 1971); George M. Fredrickson, *White Supremacy: A Comparative Study in American and South African History* (New York, 1981); Peter Kolchin, *Unfree Labor: American Slavery and Russian Serfdom* (Cambridge, Mass., 1987); Shearer Davis Bowman, *Masters and Lords: Mid-Nineteenth Century U.S. Planters and Prussian Junkers* (New York, 1993); Roderick A. McDonald, *The Economy and Material Condition of Slaves: Goods and Chattels on the Sugar Plantations of Jamaica and Louisiana* (Baton Rouge, La., 1993).

Too often in history one South has served as proxy for many Souths. The design of this work seeks to rebut this homogenizing impulse. By embracing two regional cultures, this book underscores the richness and diversity of black culture. African American culture was no more monolithic than Anglo-American culture. Other regional black cultures certainly existed in early mainland North America: those of New England, New York, French and later Spanish Louisiana, and Spanish Florida, to name a few. But the two major regional black cultures were the Chesapeake and the Lowcountry. The two core colonies within each region—the earliest settled, the most dominant politically, socially, and economically—were Virginia and South Carolina, respectively. The bulk of the documentation has therefore been drawn from these two societies, although, where appropriate, information has been taken from Maryland and northern North Carolina, which constitute part of the Chesapeake region, and from Georgia, East Florida, and southern North Carolina, which form part of the Lowcountry region. On the eve of the American Revolution, nearly three-quarters of all African Americans in mainland British America lived in the Chesapeake and Lowcountry.

The aim of the comparison is not just to increase the "visibility" of one slave society by contrasting it with another. The mere illustration of differences, no matter how enriching, is not the sole goal. Rather, by juxtaposing two roughly equivalent units—that is, two slave societies that were part of the same Anglophone world—while maximizing their differences—that is, two slave societies characterized by different staple crops, settlement patterns, and ecologies—I aim to identify the independent forces that shaped both societies. As Emile Durkheim said many years ago, the comparative method can be an "indirect experiment," without which it would be impossible to move from description to analysis. Or, as Marc Bloch put it, explicit comparisons can allow a historian to take a real step forward "in the exhilarating, never-ending search for causes."[4]

Exploring how slave life differed between regions goes hand in hand with an

---

4. Emile Durkheim, *The Rules of Sociological Method*, trans. Sarah A. Solovay and John H. Mueller, ed. George E. G. Catlin (Glencoe, Ill., 1938), 125; Marc Bloch, "Toward a Comparative History of European Societies," in Frederic C. Lane and Jelle C. Riemersma, eds., *Enterprise and Secular Change* (Homewood, Ill., 1953), 494–521. See also the April issue of *Comparative Studies in Society and History*, XXII (1980); the October issue of the *AHR*, LXXXV (1980); George M. Fredrickson, "Comparative History," in Michael Kammen, ed., *The Past before Us: Contemporary Historical Writing in the United States* (Ithaca, N.Y., 1980), 457–473; Raymond Grew, "The Comparative Weakness of American History," *Journal of Interdisciplinary History*, XVI (1985–1986), 87–101; George M. Fredrickson, "From Exceptionalism to Variability: Recent Developments in Cross-National Comparative History," *JAH*, LXXXII (1995–1996), 587–604.

investigation of what united slaves across regions. Encounters between whites and blacks, for instance, followed many of the same patterns in both the Chesapeake and the Lowcountry. Although they came from highly diverse societies, African newcomers nevertheless shared some cultural principles and assumptions—about how the world worked, how people interact, how to express themselves aesthetically. These shared values were a limited but vital resource upon which an ethnically varied people could all draw. Thus, although slaves worked differently in the Chesapeake and Lowcountry, one by gang labor, the other by task, one by growing tobacco, the other by cultivating rice, they had similar conceptions about the nature of work, shared the same sense of time, moved about the fields in similar ways, and derived the same sense of self-esteem from their work. Likewise, most eighteenth-century Lowcountry slaves spoke a creole language, whereas many Chesapeake slaves spoke standard English, yet these two speech communities were equally inventive in using words, created the same rich metaphorical constructions and forms of imagery, and followed similar grammatical and phonological rules. In documenting two regional cultures, then, this book lays bare the foundations of a black national subculture.

Although a contrapuntal arrangement lies at the heart of this work, it also aims to move to a beat that is insistently sequential. Most previous studies of North American slavery have suffered from a sense of timelessness. They have, in other words, been profoundly ahistorical. In sharp contrast, a major theme of this book is the attention paid to process, to development, to the changes wrought by time. Lowcountry and Chesapeake slave societies passed through various stages of evolution that, for simplicity's sake, might be labeled a frontier phase, a period of institution-building (characterized, above all, by heavy black immigration), and a mature phase (marked, among other things, by the natural growth of the slave population and a routinization of slave life).[5] The picture is, of course, far more complicated. For one thing, these phases did not occur at the same time in the two societies: Lowcountry development lagged behind that of the Chesapeake by at least a generation. The role of the American Revolution and its aftermath also complicates the last stage. Finally, no precise chronological boundaries can be attached to these stages, for, to take but one example, the timing of major demographic changes did not always correspond

5. For Virginia, the approximate dates of these three periods are 1619–1690, 1690–1720, and 1720–1790; for South Carolina, 1670–1710, 1710–1750, and 1750–1790. For two important statements about the importance of time and space, see Ira Berlin, "Time, Space, and the Evolution of Afro-American Society on British Mainland North America," *AHR*, LXXXV (1980), 44–78; and Willie Lee Rose, *Slavery and Freedom*, ed. William W. Freehling (New York, 1982), esp. 18–36.

to significant economic changes.⁶ For this reason, I decided, after much consideration, to eschew a breakdown of this book into rigid chronological sections. Instead, I have taken two synchronic snapshots of these two slave societies: one in infancy, the other in maturity. Sandwiched in between are thematic chapters within which the forces that transformed these societies are explored. Slavery is, after all, the great transforming circumstance of American history.

This book, then, is structural history, rather than anything resembling a traditional narrative, though each chapter contains a rough narrative. Sometimes that narrative can be etched sharply: demographic and occupational changes, for example, can be precisely delimited. At other times, the narrative must be painted with broad brushstrokes: changing master lifestyles and evolving musical styles, for instance, are less susceptible to well-defined chronological markers. My aim has been to delineate broad patterns within which change occurred.

This volume is not, then, divided into stages, nor are the forces, the interplay of which shaped the development of these two slave societies, disentangled for separate presentation. Such a dissection might well aid clarity, but it would destroy historicity. These forces acted in concert: to treat any one in isolation would be to lose sense of the process. As George Kitson Clark put it, the historian "cannot unscramble the eggs of history in order to make up his mind which of them spoiled the taste of the dish that had to be eaten."⁷ However, we can—and should—alert readers to the ingredients of the dish we are about to set before them. Five sets of forces were most influential in determining the shape of Lowcountry and Chesapeake slave societies: the role of staples was absolutely central, but the two regions' ecological and settlement systems, the rate, source, and distribution of the two regions' slave supply, the morphology of the two slave populations, and the planters' different ways of life were hardly less important. Indeed, it is my aim to show how these various sets of pressures interacted and influenced one another to produce two very different slave societies. In other words, the emphasis is on process—the com-

---

6. A detailed analysis of slave life in the Revolutionary era is beyond the scope of this book. Where the documentation in this work extends into the early national period, it is because I am impressed by what I take to be continuations of colonial patterns. For a more detailed investigation of Lowcountry slavery in the Revolutionary era, see my "Black Society in the Lowcountry, 1760–1810," in Ira Berlin and Ronald Hoffman, eds., *Slavery and Freedom in the Age of the American Revolution* (Charlottesville, Va., 1983), 83–142; and for the South as a whole, Sylvia R. Frey, *Water from the Rock: Black Resistance in a Revolutionary Age* (Princeton, N.J., 1991). It is easier to date demographic transitions than, say, changes in planter treatment of slaves, it might be added.

7. G. Kitson Clark, *The Critical Historian* (New York, 1967), 23.

ing together of these forces—rather than on the determining role of any particular one.

This book is divided into three parts, each of which incorporates a major theme. The first establishes the contrasting settings in which Lowcountry and Chesapeake slaves lived out their lives, the second examines the social framework—the patterned encounters between whites and blacks—within which cultural development took place, and the third focuses on the interior world of slaves. This organizational schema derives in part from theoretical premises about how best to explore culture. With no claim to originality, I define culture as the pattern of meanings and ideas that are shared by the members of a society and that guide their behavior.[8] Culture is both behavior or systems of action and ideals or conceptual models for action. An important aspect of this definition is the implied distinction between a social structure and the value system that operates within it. To distinguish between the two, without reifying either, should be the aim. Culture and social structure are categories applied to a process that, in the last resort, consists of individuals dealing with other individuals, of social action. In the case of slaves, this means paying particular attention to the obvious constraints on their actions. Hence the design of this book: society's forms before culture's substance, even though the two are, in reality, interwoven.

The focus of Part I is the key role assigned to land and labor in shaping culture. Under the combined influence of some of the more fertile subdisciplines of social history—historical geography, historical archaeology, the study of the environment, even ecohistory, as it is now known—I have attempted to outline two ecological systems, including everything from land use to material conditions, from climate to physical landscape, and the roles they played in shaping the lives of Lowcountry and Chesapeake slaves.[9] Labor was as impor-

---

8. The point of departure for a definition of culture is Edward B. Tylor, *Primitive Culture: Researches into the Development of Mythology, Philosophy, Religion, Language, Art, and Custom* (New York, 1924 [orig. publ. 1871]), 1, but modified by A. E. Kroeber and Clyde Kluckhohn, *Culture: A Critical Review of Concepts and Definitions*, Peabody Museum of American Archaeology and Ethnology, Papers, XLVII, no. 1 (Cambridge, Mass., 1952); Raymond W. Firth, *Elements of Social Organization* (London, 1951), 27; Clifford Geertz, *The Interpretation of Cultures: Selected Essays* (New York, 1973), 145; Sidney W. Mintz, Foreword, in Norman E. Whitten, Jr., and John F. Szwed, eds., *Afro-American Anthropology: Contemporary Perspectives* (New York, 1970), 10.

9. The work of three schools has been particularly inspiring: the English tradition of historical geography and local history, represented at its best by H. C. Darby and W. G. Hoskins; the American school, represented by Ralph H. Brown, Carville V. Earle, Harry Roy Merrens, and Robert D. Mitchell; and the *Annales* school, presided over by Fernand Braudel. Programmatic statements can also prove useful: see, for example, D. W. Meinig, "The Continuous Shaping of America: A Prospectus for Geographers and Historians," with

tant as land in determining the nature of slave life. Other studies of slave life have depicted the economic role of slaves, their occupational structures, and the like. Though these explorations surely begin by aiming to uncover the work experiences of slaves, too often they end up describing the management priorities of planters. This must be part of the story (and may be too much a part of the present story), but history has often been written from the vantage point of those who have had the charge of running, or attempting to run, other people's lives. The perspective of the workers is too readily neglected. History is not just the actions of ruling groups; it is the sweat, blood, tears, and triumphs of the common folk.

Any attempt to bring history closer to the central concerns of people's lives will undoubtedly fall woefully short of the mark, especially when evidence of personal experience and oral testimony is largely unavailable. A wall of silence divides us from the world of ordinary men and women in the preindustrial world, but this does not justify us in turning a deaf ear to those voices, however small in number, clamoring for our attention. And, in part, behavior can substitute for voices. By keeping at the forefront of our attention the kinds of tasks slaves performed during the year, the rhythms of their work, and the experience of practicing a skill, it is possible to illuminate the dimensions of work most pertinent to the workers themselves. Furthermore, coerced work for others shaped almost every aspect of the slaves' situation. Work was the most important determinant of a slave society.[10]

Slave societies were deeply divided along lines of culture, power, and status but were complicated by the continuous interaction of free and slave. In Part II, I examine the everyday contacts of masters and slaves, whites and blacks. I first explore in general terms how masters and plain white folk interacted with slaves. The core contradiction of slavery guaranteed that masters and bondpeople would engage in varied and complex encounters, for slaves were human beings, though designated as property, and responded in a multiplicity of ways to the demands placed on them. Moreover, the dominant social ethos of eighteenth-century British America, patriarchalism, also encouraged the development of close personal relations between masters and slaves, whites and blacks. Next, I investigate the range and complexity of transactions between

---

comments by Carville Earle and Edward M. Cook, Jr., and response, *AHR*, LXXXIII (1978), 1168–1217.

10. The journal *History Workshop* and the volumes published in the History Workshop series practice the kind of labor history to which I aspire. Also noteworthy is a trend in American labor history in which the reality of work has been the focus, or starting point, of investigation. The work of Alan Dawley, Daniel Walkowitz, David Montgomery, and others, profoundly influenced by E. P. Thompson and Herbert Gutman, has been instrumental in this reorientation.

whites and blacks in key social and economic spheres: work, trade, violence, sex, recreation, and religion.

Previous literature on slave societies has paid remarkably little attention to the humanity or individual variation that can be discerned in the endless encounters between the enslaved and the free. Shifting concentration, in Winthrop Jordan's words, from "the sociology of the slave institution toward an anthropology of the slaves and their masters" is useful, though not without risks. In humanizing the institution of slavery, the scholar can easily understate the sustained exploitation slaves suffered. But an emphasis on routine encounters between master and slave, white and black, has a larger context: it connects to current historiographical trends in working-class life, popular culture, and gender, where attention has focused on the intersection of patrician and plebeian, high and low, male and female. Popularly packaged as upstairs-downstairs history, its real contribution is the search for balance among conflict, confrontation, and contest on one hand and accommodation, cooperation, and negotiation on the other.[11]

Readers may be surprised that there is no chapter on resistance. In a sense, the whole book is a study of resistance. In work and in play, in public and in private, violently and quietly, slaves struggled against masters. Wherever and whenever masters, whether implicitly or explicitly, recognized the independent will or volition of their slaves, they acknowledged the humanity of their bondpeople. Extracting this admission was, in fact, a form of slave resistance, because slaves thereby opposed the dehumanization inherent in their status. In this way, slaves constantly achieved small victories. But their major triumph was the creation of a coherent culture—the subject of this book and *the* most significant act of resistance in its own right. Yet, by carving out some independence for themselves, by forcing masters to recognize their humanity, and by creating an autonomous culture, slaves also eased the torments of slavery, and, in that respect, their cultural creativity encouraged accommodation. Ultimately, then, the struggles between masters and slaves were profoundly ambivalent—another reason why they are explored throughout the book.

At the same time that the enslaved and the free were locked into an intimate interdependence, aspects of slave life assumed their characteristic shape

---

11. Sidney W. Mintz and Richard Price, *An Anthropological Approach to the Afro-American Past: A Caribbean Perspective,* Institute for the Study of Human Issues, Occasional Papers in Social Change, no. 2 (Philadelphia, 1976), 12–19; Winthrop D. Jordan, "Planter and Slave Identity Formation: Some Problems in the Comparative Approach," in Vera Rubin and Arthur Tuden, eds., *Comparative Perspectives on Slavery in New World Plantation Societies,* New York Academy of Sciences, Annals, CCXCII (New York, 1977), 36; Jon F. Sensbach, "Charting a Course in Early African-American History," *WMQ,* 3d Ser., L (1993), 394–405, esp. 400–403.

within, but to some extent separately from, the masters' social and cultural forms. Slave life, as Sidney Mintz and Richard Price have pointed out, "remained in many ways disengaged from the concerns of masters."[12] The exploration of this separate world, the slaves' interior lives, is the subject of Part III. I first consider social relations, particularly the extent of conflict and cooperation among slaves, then examine family and kin ties, and, finally, investigate the major symbolic dimensions of life—language, play, and religion. Although the safe course might have been to confine this part of the book to a behavioral analysis of slave society—the relations between Africans and creoles, between slaves and free blacks, between husbands and wives—I could not ignore the subject of slave values and beliefs.

The change of focus and attendant risks represented by the final chapter, in which values are explored most directly, are well captured by Robert Redfield:

> As soon as our attention turns from a community as a body of houses and tools and institutions to the states of mind of particular people, we are turning to the exploration of something immensely complex and difficult to know.... While we talk in terms of productivity, or of roles and statuses, we are safely and easily out in the light, above ground, so to speak, moving among an apparatus we have ourselves built, an apparatus already removed, by our own act of mind, from the complicated thinking and feeling of the men and women who achieve the productivity or define and occupy the roles. But it is the thinking that is real and ultimate raw material; it is there that the events really happen.[13]

These wise words can be endorsed almost entirely, with one rider. There is a value to tackling the "safe" questions first. It is not just that values and beliefs are "immensely complex and difficult to know" but that their social and institutional roots need first to be uncovered. As Raymond Firth put it, when recalling why his generation of anthropologists (those who sat at the feet of Bernard Malinowski in the 1920s) hesitated before treating religion in depth: "It was not, as has been said, because we were uninterested in the subject, but because we felt it necessary to clarify first the social and economic underpinning of the religious ideas and institutions." For this reason, I make no apologies for devoting much of my study to houses, tools, and social and economic institutions.[14]

My hope is that the combined effect of these three parts will result in a balanced appreciation for the oppressiveness of bondage *and* of the ability of

---

12. Mintz and Price, *Anthropological Approach*, 20.

13. Robert Redfield, *The Little Community* (Chicago, 1960 [orig. publ. 1955]), 59.

14. Raymond Firth, "An Appraisal of Modern Social Anthropology," *Annual Review of Anthropology*, IV (1975), 1–25.

slaves to shape their lives. The realities of the masters' physical power must never be underestimated. Slave victims and damaged individuals there certainly were. Indeed, it would have been nothing short of a miracle if the unbridled domination and naked exploitation inherent in slavery had not created pathologies. The psychic toll will never be easy to gauge, but there can be no doubt of its existence.[15] Yet even a brutal regime could not crush the slaves' unquenchable human spirit. Whatever the constraints, slaves contributed to the making of their history. Not only did they work for their masters, but they labored for themselves; not only did they engage in unrelenting toil for few benefits, but they derived personal satisfaction and political self-assertion from their work; not only were their lives destroyed and disrupted, but they built and rebuilt family structures that sustained them; not only were they exploited, but they engaged in numerous struggles against their exploitation. Slaves actively participated in their destiny *and* were victims of a brutal, dehumanizing system. Subject to grinding daily exploitation, caught in the grip of powerful forces that were often beyond their power to control, slaves nevertheless strove to create order in their lives, to preserve their humanity, to achieve dignity, and to sustain dreams of a better future.

15. For this renewed emphasis, see, for instance, Bertram Wyatt-Brown, "The Mask of Obedience: Male Slave Psychology in the Old South," *AHR,* XCIII (1988), 1228–1252; Clarence E. Walker, *Deromanticizing Black History: Critical Essays and Reappraisals* (Knoxville, Tenn., 1991), xi–xx, 63–72. See also Stanley M. Elkins, "The Slavery Debate," *Commentary,* LX, no. 6 (December 1975), 40–54.

Slave Counterpoint

Youth, what Mans age is like to be doth show;

We may our Ends by our Beginnings know.

—Sir John Denham

Prelude : Two Infant Slave Societies

By the late seventeenth century, Virginia had a plantation economy in search of a labor force, whereas South Carolina had a labor force in search of a plantation economy. A tobacco economy for decades, Virginia imported slaves on a large scale only when its supply of indentured servants dwindled toward the end of the century. By the time Virginia began to recruit more slaves than servants, a large white population dominated the colony. In fact, before the last decade of the seventeenth century, Virginia hardly qualified as a slave society. Only by the turn of the eighteenth century did slaves come to play a central role in the society's productive activities and form a sizable, though still small, proportion of its population. In 1700, blacks formed just a sixth of the Chesapeake's colonial population. By contrast, South Carolina was the one British colony in North America in which settlement and black slavery went hand in hand. From the outset, slaves were considered essential to Carolina's success. With the Caribbean experience as their yardstick, prospective settlers pointed out in 1666 that "thes Setlements have beene made and upheld by Negroes and without constant supplies of them cannot subsist." Even in the early 1670s, slaves formed between one-fourth and one-third of the new colony's population. A slave society from its inception, South Carolina became viable only after settlers discovered the agricultural staple on which the colony's plantation economy came to rest. By the turn of the century, then, the Chesapeake was emerging as a slave society; the Lowcountry, a slave society from its inception, was just emerging as a productive one.[1]

In spite of this fundamental difference, both infant slave societies shared several characteristics. In both societies, seasoned slaves from the Caribbean predominated among the earliest arrivals; early on, the numbers of black men and women became quite balanced; many slaves spent much of their time clearing land, cultivating provisions, rearing livestock, and working alongside members of other races; race relations were far more fluid than they later became. All of these similarities point toward a high degree of assimilation by the slaves of the early Chesapeake and Lowcountry. Many slaves arrived speaking English, could form families and have children (more readily than white servants, for example), worked at diverse tasks, and fraternized with whites both at work and at play.

Nevertheless, as the seventeenth century drew to a close, differences began to outweigh similarities. The Chesapeake imported quite large numbers of Africans long before the Lowcountry; and, by the 1690s, the region had many more slave men than women, whereas the Lowcountry boasted more equal numbers of men and women than ever before—and for many decades thereafter. If these differences seem to point toward a more Africanized slave culture in the Chesapeake than in the Lowcountry, other dissimilarities incline in a different direction and were ultimately more decisive in shaping the lives of blacks in the two regions. Slaveowners in Virginia put most of their new Africans to planting tobacco on small quarters, usually surrounded by whites, whereas their counterparts in South Carolina, though still experimenting with many agricultural products, grouped their slaves on somewhat larger units with little white intrusion. Furthermore, the Lowcountry always was—and increasingly became—a far more closed slave society than the Chesapeake. Lowcountry slaves had less intimate contact with whites and constructed a more autonomous culture than their Chesapeake counterparts.

The origins of the earliest black immigrants to the Chesapeake and Lowcountry were similar. Most came, not directly from Africa, but from the West Indies. Some might have only recently arrived in the islands from their homeland and

---

1. Keith Hopkins, *Conquerors and Slaves*, Sociological Studies in Roman History, I (Cambridge, 1978), 99; and M. I. Finley, *Ancient Slavery and Modern Ideology* (New York, 1980), 79–80 (definition of slave society); Russell Menard, "From Servants to Slaves: The Transformation of the Chesapeake Labor System," *Southern Studies*, XVI (1977), 360–362; William L. Saunders, ed., *The Colonial Records of North Carolina*, I (Raleigh, N.C., 1886), 150; Peter H. Wood, *Black Majority: Negroes in Colonial South Carolina from 1670 through the Stono Rebellion* (New York, 1974), 25, 143. For the epigraph, see Theodore Howard Banks, Jr., ed., *The Poetical Works of Sir John Denham* (New Haven, Conn., 1928), 197.

a few were probably born in the Caribbean, but most were seasoned slaves—acclimatized to the New World environment and somewhat conversant with the ways of whites. Some came with Spanish or Portuguese names; others with some understanding of the English language, none more so perhaps than John Phillip, "Christened in England" in 1612, who acted as a witness in a Virginia court twelve years later; yet others with kinship ties formed in the New World, as with the family of John, Sr., Elizabeth, and John, Jr., who were among the "first fleet" to arrive in South Carolina.[2] Both Lowcountry and Chesapeake received a somewhat gentle introduction, as it were, to New World slavery. Neither experienced a massive or immediate intrusion of alien Africans.

By the late seventeenth century, however, Africans began to arrive, especially in the Chesapeake. From the mid-1670s to 1700, Virginia and Maryland imported about six thousand slaves direct from Africa, most arriving in the 1690s. While the Chesapeake's slave population was being transformed by a predominantly African influx, the Lowcountry did not undergo the same process for another twenty or so years. In the year 1696 the first known African slaver reached South Carolina; a constant trickle of Africans became commonplace only about the turn of the century.[3]

The structures of these two societies' slave populations, much like their origins, were initially similar. By the 1660s in the Chesapeake and by the 1690s in the Lowcountry, a rough balance had been achieved between slave men and women. Although men outnumbered women among the earliest black immigrants to both regions, women apparently outlived men. Moreover, some of the children born to the earliest immigrants reached majority, also helping to account for the relative balance between men and women.[4] When, in 1686,

---

2. Wesley Frank Craven, *White, Red, and Black: The Seventeenth-Century Virginian* (Charlottesville, Va., 1971), 80–103; Edmund S. Morgan, *American Slavery, American Freedom: The Ordeal of Colonial Virginia* (New York, 1975), 154, 305–306; Helen Tunnicliff Catterall, ed., *Judicial Cases concerning American Slavery and the Negro*, 5 vols. (Washington, D.C., 1926–1937), I, 76; Wood, *Black Majority*, 21–22. For the West Indian origins of early blacks to both Virginia and South Carolina, see Elizabeth Donnan, ed., *Documents Illustrative of the History of the Slave Trade to America*, Carnegie Institution of Washington Publication no. 409, 4 vols. (Washington, D.C., 1930–1935), IV, 89, 256.

3. Menard, "From Servants to Slaves," *So. Studies*, XVI (1977), 366–367; Carville V. Earle, *The Evolution of a Tidewater Settlement System: All Hallow's Parish, Maryland, 1650–1783*, University of Chicago Department of Geography Research Paper, no. 170 (Chicago, 1975), 47; Donnan, ed., *Documents of the Slave Trade*, IV, 243, 255n; Donnan, "The Slave Trade into South Carolina before the Revolution," *AHR*, XXXIII (1927–1928), 810n; Wood, *Black Majority*, 100n.

4. Russell R. Menard, "The Maryland Slave Population, 1658 to 1730: A Demographic Profile of Blacks in Four Counties," *WMQ*, 3d Ser., XXXII (1975), 32; Morgan, *American Slavery, American Freedom*, 421; Earle, *Evolution of a Tidewater Settlement System*, 49; Wood,

Elizabeth Read of Virginia drew up her will, she mentioned twenty-two slaves: six men, seven women, five boys, and four girls. Twelve of these slaves had family connections: there were three two-parent families and two mothers with children. An incident involving a free black of Northampton County illuminates a typical Chesapeake slave household at this stage of development. On the eve of the New Year of 1672, William Harman, a free black, paid a visit to the home quarter of John Michael. Harman spent part of the evening and parts of the following two days carousing with Michael's slaves, who numbered at least six adults, three men and three women, only one of whom had been newly imported. The rest had been living with their master for ten years or more.[5]

By the last decade of the seventeenth century, however, Harman would have found it harder to find such a compatible group. By this time, many Chesapeake quarters included at least one newly imported African. In addition, most plantations could no longer boast equal numbers of men and women, because the African newcomers were predominantly men and boys. In fact, evidence from a number of Chesapeake areas during the 1690s indicates that men now outnumbered women by as much as 180 to 100. The impact of this African influx was soon felt. Before 1690, one Virginian planter had boasted of his large native-born slave population; by the first decade of the eighteenth century, another Virginian despairingly found "noe increase [among his blacks] but all loss." In 1699, members of the Virginia House of Burgesses offered an unflattering opinion of these new black arrivals, referring to "the gross barbarity and rudeness of their manners, the variety and strangeness of their languages and the weakness and shallowness of their minds." Prejudice aside, these legislators were responding to the increased flow of African newcomers.[6]

Even as the Africans started arriving, Chesapeake planters put their slaves to more than just growing tobacco. Ever since 1630, when Virginia's tobacco

---

Black Majority, 95, 175. Only 20 South Carolina inventories have survived for the 1690s: 30 men, 28 women, 10 boys, 4 girls, and 9 children were listed (Records of the Secretary of the Province, 1687–1710, 1692–1700, SCDAH.)

5. Will of Elizabeth Read, Feb. 10, 1686, York County Deeds, Orders, Wills, no. 7, 257–259, VSL; J. Douglas Deal, *Race and Class in Colonial Virginia: Indians, Englishmen, and Africans on the Eastern Shore during the Seventeenth Century* (New York, 1993), 339.

6. Craven, *White, Red, and Black*, 99; Earle, *Evolution of a Tidewater Settlement System*, 49; Menard, "Maryland Slave Population," *WMQ*, 3d Ser., XXXII (1975), 32; Allan Kulikoff, "A 'Prolifick' People: Black Population Growth in the Chesapeake Colonies, 1700–1790," *So. Studies*, XVI (1977), 404–405; Darrett B. Rutman and Anita H. Rutman, "'More True and Perfect Lists': The Reconstruction of Censuses for Middlesex County, Virginia, 1668–1704," *VMHB*, LXXXVIII (1980), 55; Richard Beale Davis, ed., *William Fitzhugh and His Chesapeake World, 1676–1701* (Chapel Hill, N.C., 1963), 175; Robert Bristow to John Grason, Sept. 15, 1707, Robert Bristow Letterbook, VSL; W. Noel Sainsbury et al., eds., *Calendar of State Papers*, Colonial Series, *America and West Indies*, XVII, 1699 (London, 1908), 261.

boom ended, the colony's planters had gradually begun to diversify their operations. They farmed more grains, raised more livestock, and planted more orchards. Pastoral farming in particular gained impetus during the last few decades of the seventeenth century when the Chesapeake tobacco industry suffered a prolonged depression. Some planters devoted more attention to livestock than ever before, and large herds of cattle became commonplace. Slaves were most certainly associated with this development. In late-seventeenth-century Charles County, Maryland, there were more cattle in the all-black or mixed-race quarters than in those composed solely of whites. Whether this was coincidental or represented a recognition of black skills in caring for livestock is an open question. What it undoubtedly meant, however, is that some blacks worked closely with stock. In 1697, for instance, at an all-black quarter in Charles County, one old black man and two elderly black women, together with four children, managed a herd of fifty cattle and forty-eight hogs.[7]

The diversified character of the youthful South Carolina economy owed little to the fluctuating fortunes of a dominant staple and more to the harsh realities of a pioneer existence. Many slaves spent most of their lives engaged in basic frontier activities—clearing land, cutting wood, and cultivating provisions. If late-seventeenth-century South Carolina specialized in anything, it was ranch farming—the same activity into which some Chesapeake planters were diversifying. Indeed, some Virginians took advantage of the opportunities presented by the nascent colony. In 1673, Edmund Lister of Northampton County transported some of his slaves out of Virginia into South Carolina. Presumably they had already gained experience, or displayed their native skills, in tending livestock, because Lister sent them on ahead to establish a ranch. The extensiveness of this early cattle ranching economy became apparent when South Carolinians took stock of their defensive capabilities. In 1708, they took comfort in the reliance that could be placed on one thousand trusty "Cattle Hunters."[8]

The multiracial composition of the typical work group suggests yet another similarity between Chesapeake and Lowcountry. In both societies in the late seventeenth century, blacks more often than not were to be found laboring

---

7. Morgan, *American Slavery, American Freedom,* 133–157, 180–195; Russell R. Menard, "The Tobacco Industry in the Chesapeake Colonies, 1617–1730: An Interpretation," *Research in Economic History,* V (1980), 109–177; Lorena Seebach Walsh, "Charles County, Maryland, 1658–1705: A Study of Chesapeake Social and Political Structure" (Ph.D. diss., Michigan State University, 1977), 205–207. For free black ownership of livestock, see T. H. Breen and Stephen Innes, *"Myne Owne Ground": Race and Freedom on Virginia's Eastern Shore, 1640–1676* (New York, 1980), 81–83.

8. Wood, *Black Majority,* esp. 30–31, 95; *Boston News-Letter,* May 17–24, 1708, as quoted in Clarence L. Ver Steeg, *Origins of a Southern Mosaic: Studies of Early Carolina and Georgia* (Athens, Ga., 1975), 106.

PLATE 1. Industry and Idleness. *Handkerchief, detail. Circa 1770–1785. White bound laborers worked alongside blacks in the Chesapeake. Courtesy Colonial Williamsburg Foundation*

alongside members of other races. The South Carolina estate of John Smyth, who died in 1682, included nine Negroes, four Indians, and three whites. All sixteen undoubtedly worked shoulder to shoulder at least some of the time. The picture of Elias Horry working "many days with a Negro man at the whip saw" was hardly an isolated incident in the late-seventeenth-century Lowcountry. Similarly, in late-seventeenth-century Virginia, white servants and slaves—both Indian and black—often worked side by side. An incident involving William Harman, the free black already encountered, underscores the lengths to which work time cooperation extended. In the summer of 1683, Harman's neighbors came to assist him in his wheat harvest. As was the custom, once the task was accomplished, they relaxed together, smoking pipes of tobacco in Harman's house. Nothing unusual in this pastoral scene, one might surmise, except that those who came to aid their black neighbor were whites, including yeomen of modest means and well-connected planters. Harman was not, of course, a typical black man, but his story proves that blacks and whites of various stations could work together, even cooperate, in the late-seventeenth-century Chesapeake.[9]

9. Wood, *Black Majority*, 54–55, 97. The inventory of John Smyth is not an isolated case. At the turn of the century, a tenth of the enslaved laborers on Lowcountry estates were Indian slaves; in a census of 1708, their proportion had risen to a quarter. Even in the 1720s, when black slaves were being imported into the colony in great numbers, 8% of inventoried

In spite of these similarities, the economic situations of these two societies diverged. By the late seventeenth century the Chesapeake possessed a fully fledged plantation economy. No matter what the level of diversification of a late-seventeenth-century Chesapeake estate, therefore, most slaves were destined to spend the bulk of their time tending tobacco. There were some all-black quarters; accordingly, a few slaves acted as foremen, making decisions about the organization of work, the discipline of the laborers, and the like. However, most slaves simply familiarized themselves with the implements and vagaries of tobacco culture. Seventeenth-century South Carolina, by contrast, was a colony in search of a plantation economy. Experiments were certainly under way with rice, which was first exported in significant quantities in the 1690s. In June 1704, one South Carolina planter could bemoan the loss of a Negro slave because the season was "the height of weeding rice." This was still a pioneer economy, however, with no concentration on one agricultural product. Indeed, if South Carolinians were "Graziers" before they were "planters," they were just as much "lumbermen," too. About the turn of the century, a South Carolinian wrote to an English correspondent extolling the virtues of a particular tract of land. If only the proprietor had "twelfe good negroes," the writer asserted, "he could get off it five Hundred pounds worth of tarr yearly." From 1704 to 1706, Daniel Axtell and others operated a tar kiln in which at least four slaves tended the fire, made and carted barrels, and occasionally received cash for their work. On March 30, 1796, for example, Axtell paid five shillings in cash to Nero for minding the kiln.[10] South Carolinians might have been thinking in terms of large profits and sizable labor forces from the first, but, as yet, these were not to be derived from any single agricultural staple.

---

slaves were Indians and mustees. This analysis is based on the Records of the Secretary of the Province, 1692–1731 (14 volumes), SCDAH; and Wood, *Black Majority*, 144. See also Russell R. Menard, "The Africanization of the Lowcountry Labor Force, 1670–1730," in Winthrop D. Jordan and Sheila L. Skemp, eds., *Race and Family in the Colonial South* (Jackson, Miss., 1987), 81–108, esp. 98–101. Indians were a less prominent feature of the Chesapeake labor force, although they were present. Philip A. Bruce, *Economic History of Virginia in the Seventeenth Century: An Inquiry into the Material Conditions of the People . . .*, II (New York, 1895), 105; Deal, *Race and Class in Colonial Virginia*, 346; Gloria L. Main, *Tobacco Colony: Life in Early Maryland, 1650–1720* (Princeton, N.J., 1982), 124, 128–135.

10. Menard, "Maryland Slave Population," *WMQ*, 3d Ser., XXXII (1975), 36; Walsh, "Charles County, Maryland," 204, 206–207; Elizabeth Hyrne to Burrell Massingberd, Mar. 13, 1704, Massingberd Deposit, Lincolnshire County Archives, Lincoln, England; James M. Clifton, "The Rice Industry in Colonial America," *Agricultural History*, LV (1981), 268–269; Wood, *Black Majority*, 29, 108–114; Thomas Smith to Burrell Massingberd, Nov. 7, 1705, Massingberd Deposit; Daniel Axtell Account Book, typescript, 104, SCHS; and Alexander Moore, "Daniel Axtell's Account Book and the Economy of Early South Carolina," *SCHM*, XCV (1994), 280–301, esp. 289–292.

In one final area—the flexibility of early race relations—the Chesapeake and Lowcountry societies also resembled each other. The once-popular view that the earliest black immigrants in the Old Dominion were servants and not chattels is no longer tenable. Rather, from the outset, the experience of the vast majority of blacks in early Virginia was slavery, although some were servants and even more secured their freedom. In fact, the status of Virginia's blacks seems singularly debased from the start, evident in their impersonal and partial identifications in two censuses dating from the 1620s; their high valuations in estate inventories, indicating lifetime service; the practice of other colonies, most notably Bermuda, with which Virginia was in contact; and early legislation, such as a Virginia law of 1640 that excepted only blacks from a provision that masters should arm their households—perhaps the first example of statutory racial discrimination in North American history—or an act of 1643 that included black, but not white, servant women as tithables.[11]

In spite of the blacks' debased status, race relations in early Virginia were more pliable than they would later be, largely because disadvantaged blacks encountered a group of whites—indentured servants—who could claim to be similarly disadvantaged. Fraternization between the two arose from the special circumstances of plantation life in early Virginia. Black slaves tended to live scattered on small units where they were often outnumbered by white servants; more often than not, the two groups spoke the same language; the level of exploitation each group suffered inclined them to see the others as sharing their predicament. In short, the opportunity, the means, and the justification

---

11. Alden T. Vaughan, "The Origins Debate: Slavery and Racism in Seventeenth-Century Virginia," *VMHB*, XCVII (1989), 311–354; Vaughan, "Blacks in Virginia: A Note on the First Decade," *WMQ*, 3d Ser., XXIX (1972), 469–478; Carl N. Degler, "Slavery and the Genesis of American Race Prejudice," *Comparative Studies in Society and History*, II (1959), 49–66; Winthrop D. Jordan, "Modern Tensions and the Origins of American Slavery," *Journal of Southern History*, XXVIII (1962), 18–30; Jordan, *White over Black: American Attitudes toward the Negro, 1550–1812* (Chapel Hill, N.C., 1968), 71–82; Paul C. Palmer, "Servant into Slave: The Evolution of the Legal Status of the Negro Laborer in Colonial Virginia," *South Atlantic Quarterly*, LXV (1966), 355–370; Jonathan L. Alpert, "The Origin of Slavery in the United States—The Maryland Precedent," *American Journal of Legal History*, XIV (1970), 189–221; Joseph Boskin, *Into Slavery: Racial Decisions in the Virginia Colony* (Philadelphia, 1976), 39–44; Whittington B. Johnson, "The Origin and Nature of African Slavery in Seventeenth-Century Maryland," *MHM*, LXXIII (1978), 236–245; Breen and Innes, *"Myne Owne Ground,"* 25–27 (which goes too far in downplaying the 1640 act); George M. Fredrickson, *White Supremacy: A Comparative Study in American and South African History* (New York, 1981), 76–78; Deal, *Race and Class in Colonial Virginia*, 166–169; Robert McColley, "Slavery in Virginia, 1619–1660: A Reexamination," in Robert H. Abzug and Stephen Maizlish, eds., *New Perspectives on Race and Slavery in America: Essays in Honor of Kenneth M. Stampp* (Lexington, Ky., 1986), 11–24; Kathleen M. Brown, *Good Wives, Nasty Wenches, and Anxious Patriarchs: Gender, Race, and Power in Colonial Virginia* (Chapel Hill, N.C., 1996), 116–126.

for cooperation between black slaves and white servants were all present. Racial prejudice, moreover, was apparently not strong enough to inhibit these close ties.[12]

Not only did many blacks and whites work alongside one another, but they ate, caroused, smoked, ran away, stole, and made love together. In the summer of 1681, a graphic example of white-black companionship occurred in Henrico County. One Friday in August, Thomas Cocke's "servants" were in their master's orchard cutting down weeds. The gang included at least two white men, who were in their midtwenties and presumably either servants or tenants, and at least three slaves. After work, this mixed complement began drinking; they offered cider to other white visitors, one of whom "dranke cupp for cupp" with the "Negroes." One of the white carousers, Katherine Watkins, the wife of a Quaker, later alleged that John Long, a mulatto belonging to Cocke, had "put his yard into her and ravished" her; but other witnesses testified that she was inebriated and made sexual advances to the slaves. She had, for instance, raised the tail of Dirke's shirt, saying "he would have a good pricke," put her hand on mulatto Jack's codpiece, saying she "loved him for his Fathers sake for his Father was a very handsome young Man," and embraced Mingo "about the Necke," flung him on the bed, "Kissed him and putt her hand into his Codpiece." Thus, a number of white men exonerated their black brethren and blamed a drunken white woman for the alleged sexual indiscretion. If this was sexism, at least it was not racism.[13]

Black and white men also stood shoulder to shoulder in more dramatic ways. In 1640, six servants belonging to Captain William Pierce and "a negro" named Emanuel belonging to Mr. Reginald stole guns, ammunition, and a skiff and sailed down the Elizabeth River in hopes of reaching the Dutch. Thirty years later, a band of white servants who hoped to escape their Eastern Shore plantations and reach New England put their faith in a black pilot as a guide. In 1676, black slaves and white servants joined together in a striking show of resistance. With Nathaniel Bacon dead and his rebellion petering out, one of the last groups to surrender was a mixed band of eighty blacks and twenty white servants. In the 1680s, a slave named Frank and a servant named Peter Wells, who were drinking in Mrs. Vaulx's parlor in York County, joined forces in fighting two yeoman whites who had insulted the slave by saying

---

12. I am impressed more by the arguments of Jordan, together with Degler, Vaughan, and others, which tend to emphasize the early—though inchoate—existence of racial prejudice, as against those of the Handlins, Edmund Morgan, and T. H. Breen, who tend to minimize racial prejudice by emphasizing the importance of class. Jordan and Morgan provide the most subtle accounts, not easily categorized.

13. Warren M. Billings, ed., *The Old Dominion in the Seventeenth Century: A Documentary History of Virginia, 1606–1689* (Chapel Hill, N.C., 1975), 161–163.

"they were not company for Negroes" and the servant by referring to his lowly status as an indentured tailor. This willingness to cooperate does not mean that white laborers regarded blacks as their equals; it may connote only a temporary coalition of interests. Nevertheless, the extent to which whites, who were exploited almost as ruthlessly as blacks, could overlook racial differences is notable. Apparently, an approximate social and economic (as opposed to legal) parity sometimes outweighed inchoate racial prejudices.[14]

The flexibility of race relations in the early Chesapeake is illustrated most dramatically in the incidence of interracial sex. At first glance, this might seem an odd proposition, for surely interracial sex is largely synonymous with sexual exploitation—particularly of black women. Abuse of slave women undoubtedly occurred in the early Chesapeake, as in all slaveowning societies. At the same time, the evidence of sexual relations between the races suggests that choice, as much as coercion, was involved—as might well have been the case for Katherine Watkins. For one thing, much recorded miscegenation in early Virginia was, not between white men and black women, but between black men and white women. Many white female servants gave birth to mulatto children. The only realistic conclusion to be drawn from this evidence—and Virginia's ruling establishment was not slow to see it—was that "black men were competing all too successfully for white women." In addition, many black women shared relationships of mutual affection with white servant men, and many of their mulatto children were the offspring of consensual unions. In the late seventeenth and early eighteenth centuries, one in six of the Burwell family slaves were mulattoes born to slave women. Finally, there were a number of marriages between blacks and whites in the early Chesapeake. In 1671, for example, the Lower Norfolk County Court ordered Francis Stripes to pay tithes for his wife, "shee being a negro." Occasionally, even a male slave was able to engage the affections of a white woman. The most celebrated example concerns Lord Baltimore's Irish maidservant, Nell Butler, who fell in love with Major Boarman's "saltwater" (or African) slave, Charles. When, in 1681, she informed Lord Baltimore of her intention to marry Charles, he attempted to dissuade her by pointing out that she would thereby enslave herself and her children. For his pains, he learned that "she had rather Marry the Negro under

14. Ibid., 159; Accomac County Orders, 1671–1673, 95, as cited by Deal, *Race and Class in Colonial Virginia*, 324 (see also 179–181); Morgan, *American Slavery, American Freedom*, 327–328; York County Deeds, Orders, Wills, no. 6, 362, VSL. See also Breen and Innes, *"Myne Owne Ground,"* 29–30; Benjamin B. Weisiger III, comp., *Charles City County, Virginia, Court Orders, 1687–1695* (Richmond, Va., 1980), 160; T. H. Breen, "A Changing Labor Force and Race Relations in Virginia, 1660–1710," in Breen, *Puritans and Adventurers: Change and Persistence in Early America* (New York, 1980), 133, 138; and Catterall, ed., *Judicial Cases concerning American Slavery*, I, 80.

them circumstances than to marry his Lordship with his Country." Nell Butler was not alone in the annals of the early Chesapeake in preferring a black partner.[15]

The access slaves had to freedom is a third area that reveals the flexibility of race relations in the early Chesapeake. Some slaves were allowed to earn money; some even bought, sold, and raised cattle; still others used the proceeds to purchase their freedom. This phenomenon may be attributable, in part, to the Latin American background of some of the earliest black immigrants. Perhaps they had absorbed Iberian notions about the relation between slavery and freedom, in particular that freedom was a permissible goal for a slave and self-purchase a legitimate avenue to liberty. Perhaps they persuaded their masters to let them keep livestock and tend tobacco on their own account in order to buy their freedom. Perhaps, however, some of the first masters of slaves were somewhat unsure about how to motivate their new black laborers and assumed that rewards, rather than sheer coercion, might constitute the best tactic. Two blacks who showed an unwillingness to work were given an indenture guaranteeing their freedom in return for four years' labor and seventeen hundred pounds of tobacco. Finally, the confusion that reigned in early Virginia concerning the legal status of the new black immigrants created other paths to liberty: some seventeenth-century Chesapeake slaves even sued for freedom in colonial courts. In 1656, for example, Elizabeth Key, the illegitimate child of a slave woman and a white planter, successfully sued for freedom on the grounds of her paternity, her baptism, and the violation of a contractual agreement to serve a master a period of nine years. The earliest petitions for freedom often stressed baptism as the key rationale; after this loophole was closed in 1667, black petitioners generally charged white masters with breach of contract to effect a manumission. But whatever their origins and precise numbers (which were certainly small), free blacks in late-seventeenth-century

---

15. Morgan, *American Slavery, American Freedom,* 155–156, 333–336; Bruce, *Economic History of Virginia,* II, 110–112; Billings, ed., *The Old Dominion in the Seventeenth Century,* 157–158, 160–163; Ross M. Kimmel, "Free Blacks in Seventeenth-Century Maryland," *MHM,* LXXI (1976), 20; Kimmel, "Slave Freedom Petitions in the Courts of Colonial Maryland" (MS), 19–22, 31–33; Weisiger, comp., *Charles City County,* 54, 96, 200; Fredrickson, *White Supremacy,* 102–103; Deal, *Race and Class in Colonial Virginia,* esp. 180–182; Lorena S. Walsh, "'A Place in Time' Regained: A Fuller History of Colonial Chesapeake Slavery through Group Biography," in Larry E. Hudson, Jr., ed., *Working toward Freedom: Slave Society and Domestic Economy in the American South* (Rochester, N.Y., 1994), 5; deposition of Samuel Abell, Jr., *Mary Butler v. Adam Craig,* General Court of the Western Shore, Court of Appeals, Judgments no. 3, June 1791, MHR. Brown suggests that black men chose white wives because they were not taxable. This is true—and does speak to white society's early devaluation of black women—but the choice white women made is still significant and is evidence of racial fluidity. Brown, *Good Wives, Nasty Wenches, and Anxious Patriarchs,* 126.

Virginia seem to have formed a larger share of the total black population than at any other time during slavery. In some counties, perhaps a third of the black population was free in the 1660s and 1670s.[16]

And, once free, these blacks interacted with their white neighbors on terms of rough equality. At least through the 1680s, Virginians came close to envisaging free blacks as members or potential members of their community. Philip Mongon, a Northampton County free black and former slave, was certainly a full participant in the boisterous, bawdy, and competitive world that was seventeenth-century Virginia. Mongon arrived in Virginia as a slave in the 1640s. While still a slave, he entertained and harbored an English runaway maidservant. Early in 1651, now a free black, he arranged to marry a white woman, a widow. Perhaps the marriage never took place, for, if it did, his bride soon died, and Mongon took a black woman as his wife. However, his contacts with white women were not over: in 1663, he was charged with adultery and with fathering an illegitimate mulatto child whose mother was an unmarried white woman. Mongon gave security for the maintenance of the child. Like many a lower-class white, Mongon was not always deferential to his erstwhile superiors. Accused of hog stealing in 1660, he was able to prove his innocence, but then elicited a fine for his "presumptuous actions" in throwing some hogs' ears on the table where the justices presided. Mongon, like many another Virginian, both borrowed money and extended credit—in his case, primarily with neighbors of another race. He stood up for his rights, as in 1681, when he claimed six hundred pounds of tobacco for dressing the meat for his landlord's funeral dinner. Relations with his neighbors occasionally descended into outright friction. He came to court in 1685 to confess that he "had most notoriously abused and defamed my most loveing friends and neighbours John Duparkes and Robert Jarvis." Two years later, Mongon was a member of an interracial fracas. One Sunday, a number of whites, both tenant farmers and yeomen, both husbands and wives, came to Mongon's house. After much "drinking and carousing as well without doors as within," some of the men began to victimize one of the tenant farmers present. Both Mongon and his

---

16. Morgan, *American Slavery, American Freedom*, 155; Deal, *Race and Class in Colonial Virginia*, 186–187, argues for an Iberian influence; Breen and Innes, *"Myne Owne Ground,"* 72–79; Billings, ed., *The Old Dominion in the Seventeenth Century*, 165–171; Warren M. Billings, "The Cases of Fernando and Elizabeth Key: A Note on the Status of Blacks in Seventeenth-Century Virginia," *WMQ*, 3d Ser., XXX (1973), 467–474; Kimmel, "Slave Freedom Petitions"; Johnson, "The Origin and Nature of African Slavery," *MHM*, LXXIII (1978), 239–240; George M. Fredrickson, "Toward a Social Interpretation of the Development of American Racism," in Nathan I. Huggins et al., eds., *Key Issues in the Afro-American Experience*, I (New York, 1971), 247; Brown, *Good Wives, Nasty Wenches, and Anxious Patriarchs*, 132.

son as well as a number of his guests joined forces to inflict a severe beating on the hapless man. Surely seventeenth-century Virginia could claim the pugnacious, truculent, and enterprising Philip Mongon as one of its very own.[17]

The most celebrated free black family, the Johnson clan, also met with little apparent discrimination. Their activities and opportunities seem not much different from their fellow white planters'. They owned land, paid taxes, and acquired servants and slaves. They went to court, signed legal documents, served as witnesses, and transacted openly with white planters. They not only borrowed money from but extended credit to whites. Although they were excluded from military duties, they might well have voted and served on juries.[18]

The fluidity and unpredictability of race relations in early Virginia gradually hardened into the Anglo-American mold more familiar to later generations. The cooperation between white servants and blacks began to dissolve as the numbers of white servants declined and slaves increased. Moreover, a greater distance between lower-class whites and blacks inevitably arose as more and more black newcomers arrived direct from Africa, unable to speak English and utterly alien in appearance and demeanor. As T. H. Breen has put it, "No white servant in this period, no matter how poor, how bitter or badly treated, could identify with these frightened Africans." There was, of course, more to this distancing than natural antipathies. The Chesapeake ruling establishment did all it could to foster the contempt of whites for blacks. Legislation enacted in the late seventeenth century was designed specifically to this end: no black was to "presume to lift up his hand" against a Christian; no Christian white servant was to be whipped naked, for nakedness was appropriate only for blacks; the property of servants was protected, whereas slaves' property was confiscated.[19]

Legislation was not the only way in which this separation occurred. At midcentury, Lancaster County court appointed Grasher, a black man, to whip offenders who were almost exclusively white, an action that certainly strained

---

17. Morgan, *American Slavery, American Freedom*, 155 (and see 156–157 for a description of Anthony Longo, a kindred spirit to Mongon); this sketch of Mongon's life is taken from Deal, *Race and Class in Colonial Virginia*, 325–336. This study contains a number of equally detailed and fascinating portraits of free blacks. See also Breen and Innes, *"Myne Owne Ground,"* 68–109.

18. Kimmel, "Free Blacks in Seventeenth-Century Maryland," *MHM*, LXXI (1976), 22–25; Breen and Innes, *"Myne Owne Ground,"* 7–18; Deal, *Race and Class in Colonial Virginia*, 217–250.

19. Breen, "A Changing Labor Force," in Breen, *Puritans and Adventurers*, 145; William Waller Hening, *The Statutes at Large: Being a Collection of All the Laws of Virginia . . .* , 13 vols. (Richmond and Philadelphia, 1809–1823), II, 481, III, 448, 459–460; Warren M. Billings, "The Law of Servants and Slaves in Seventeenth-Century Virginia," *VMHB*, XCIX (1991), 45–62; Morgan, *American Slavery, American Freedom*, 311–315, 331–333.

good feelings between blacks and lower-class whites. More than a generation later, an Accomac County planter enlisted his mulatto slave Frank to help beat a white maidservant who was ill and not pulling her weight. At about the same time, a white tenant farmer of neighboring Northampton County invented a scheme to take advantage of the worsening climate for free blacks. He told Peter George, manumitted just six years earlier, that "there was a law made that all free Negroes should bee slaves againe." He promised to look after George's property—three head of cattle and hogs—and encouraged him, by providing his cart, to leave the colony. Three years later, George returned to Virginia and successfully brought suit to recover his livestock. More significant than George's small victory was the growing constriction of status and opportunities for free blacks, a transition that prompted whites of modest means to exploit their black neighbors.[20]

In these and other ways, the slaveowning planter class of late-seventeenth- and early-eighteenth-century Virginia attempted to drive a wedge between servants and slaves, whites and blacks. They were undeniably successful. As slaves grew more numerous in the work force, claims to English customary rights, such as reasonable amounts of food, adequate clothing, and observance of holidays, could more easily be ignored. Onerous work, harsh punishment, and rudimentary conditions became associated primarily with black laborers. In 1672, complaints were heard in Surry County against the "apparrell commonly worne by negroes" that heightened "theire foolish pride"; henceforth, the county court proclaimed, "Noe Negro shall be allowed to weare any white Linninge, but shall weare blew shirts and shifts." Cheap, coarse clothing was to be worn by blacks. Two decades later, the minister of Christ Church in Middlesex County, with the assistance of others, beat his slave Jack to death, at one point giving him "two or three knocks with the Branding Iron about the head." In a matter-of-fact way that speaks volumes about the violence directed against slaves, he stated that "such Accidents will happen now and then." By the end of the seventeenth century, the indentures of white female servants invariably contained a clause that exempted them from field labor. One woman's indenture stated that "she shall do no manner of slaveish work, that is, she is not to work in the ground at the hoe nor further in the tending of a garden or to help plant." A stigma was doubtless attached to working in the fields alongside or

---

20. Lancaster County Deeds, I, 1652–1657, 213, as cited in Robert Anthony Wheeler, "Lancaster County, Virginia, 1650–1750: The Evolution of a Southern Tidewater Community" (Ph.D. diss., Brown University, 1972), 24; Accomac County Wills, 1682–1697, 91a, 93a–96a, as cited in Deal, *Race and Class in Colonial Virginia*, 103–104; Northampton County Orders and Wills, 1689–1698, 116, as cited in Deal, "A Constricted World: Free Blacks on Virginia's Eastern Shore, 1680–1750," in Lois Green Carr, Philip D. Morgan, and Jean B. Russo, eds., *Colonial Chesapeake Society* (Chapel Hill, N.C., 1988), 281–284.

near slaves: some servants even agreed to longer terms to avoid such work. Resistance to authority now came largely from blacks, not from the mixed groups of earlier years. At the same time, the authorities were not reticent in proclaiming the new dangers, thereby fostering a sense of caste consciousness among all whites.[21]

Nowhere were Virginia's rulers more assiduous in separating the races than in the realm of sex. In 1662, they passed a law doubling the fine for interracial fornicators. Almost thirty years later, Virginia took action to prevent all forms of interracial union by providing that any white man or woman who married a black, whether bond or free, was liable to permanent banishment, and by laying down fines and alternative punishments for any white woman who engaged in illicit relations with blacks. This legislation can be ascribed to practical, moral, and religious concerns; but, in part at least, it sprang from deeper anxieties. In Winthrop Jordan's words, the legislators lashed out at miscegenation "in language dripping with distaste and indignation." A Maryland law of 1664 referred to interracial unions as "shamefull Matches" and spoke of "diverse free-born English women . . . disgrac[ing] our nation"; Virginia legislators in 1691 denounced miscegenation and its fruits as "that abominable mixture and spurious issue."[22] This legislation reflected a desire to cordon off the "white, Christian" community—and particularly its female sector. Though never completely successful, the laws gradually had the desired effect, and voluntary interracial sexual relations occurred much less frequently after the turn of the century.

A strenuous attempt to limit the numbers of free blacks began in 1691, when the Virginia assembly forbade masters from freeing slaves unless they were willing to pay for their transportation out of the colony. The law was effective, as Okree, an Essex County slave who had recently secured his freedom, could testify. Okree chose reenslavement rather than exile in order to remain with his slave wife and children. Furthermore, manumissions after 1691 tended to be conditional rather than absolute. Bridget Foxcroft's will, for example, written

---

21. Lois Green Carr and Lorena S. Walsh, "Economic Diversification and Labor Organization in the Chesapeake, 1650–1820," in Stephen Innes, ed., *Work and Labor in Early America* (Chapel Hill, N.C., 1988), 154–161; "Management of Slaves, 1672," *VMHB*, VII (1899–1900), 314; Darrett B. Rutman and Anita H. Rutman, *A Place in Time: Middlesex County, Virginia, 1650–1750* (New York, 1984), 171; Hening, *Statutes at Large*, I, 242; Lancaster County Record Book (Deeds, etc.), VIII, 1687–1700, 26, 274, VSL; Wheeler, "Lancaster County, Virginia," 111–112; Robert Beverley, *The History and Present State of Virginia*, ed. Louis B. Wright (Chapel Hill, N.C., 1947 [orig. publ. 1705]), 271–272; Main, *Tobacco Colony*, 108–109.

22. Hening, *Statutes at Large*, II, 170, III, 86–87; Jordan, *White over Black*, 139, 79–80; Morgan, *American Slavery, American Freedom*, 333–336; Fredrickson, *White Supremacy*, 101–105; Brown, *Good Wives, Nasty Wenches, and Anxious Patriarchs*, 197–201.

in 1704, stipulated that her slave, Betty, be set free for a term of thirty years, after which she was to be placed in the custody of one of Bridget's relations to whom Betty was to pay one ear of corn annually "in . . . acknowledgement of her subjection."[23] With few additions to their numbers, the proportion of free blacks in the total black population declined. Their numbers had always been small: by the third quarter of the seventeenth century, the celebrated and intensively studied free colored population of Virginia's Eastern Shore totaled no more than fifty individuals. But even some of these pulled up stakes in the middle to late seventeenth century, no doubt because of the growing hostility they faced. Those who remained might cling to freedom, but only as a pariah class. Poverty, landlessness, and dissociation from whites increasingly constituted their lot. Occasional amicable relations between free blacks and whites were perhaps still possible, but such associations had to be conducted more furtively than before.[24] By the turn of the century, Virginia, like all the other mainland plantation colonies, was set to become a closed slave society. There was to be no room for an intermediate body of freedpersons.

South Carolina was never at any time an open slave society. And yet seventeenth-century Lowcountry society also had more flexible race relations than its eighteenth-century successor. By comparison with seventeenth-century Virginia, early South Carolinian race relations scarcely seem flexible, but, in the overall history of Lowcountry slave society, the first thirty or so years of slavery constitute something of a privileged era, a time when relations between the races contained an element of spontaneity and unpredictability that they subsequently lost. White servants and black slaves resided on the same plantations in early South Carolina, and where white immigrants might work "comme une esclave," as one Huguenot arrival put it, black newcomers might labor like hired hands. Servants and slaves traded with one another, leading the colony's legislators to pass laws against the practice in 1683, 1687, and again in 1691. In play, as in work, blacks participated rather fully in early Lowcountry life—to the point that their involvement in the trade for strong liquors elicited

---

23. Hening, *Statutes at Large,* III, 87–88; Essex County Court Orders, I, 1692–1695, part 2, 187, 315–316, as cited in James B. Slaughter, *Settlers, Southerners, Americans: The History of Essex County, Virginia, 1608–1984* (Salem, W.Va., 1985), 25; Northampton County Court Orders and Wills, 1689–1710, 189–190, as quoted by Deal, *Race and Class in Colonial Virginia,* 259.

24. Deal, *Race and Class in Colonial Virginia,* 188, 345. See also Breen and Innes, "*Myne Owne Ground,*" 107–109. Deal argues effectively against Breen and Innes that (1) at no time did black Virginians seem likely to "form a free peasantry" and (2) the few gains Eastern Shore blacks had made were whittled away well before 1705, the date Breen and Innes assign as sealing the free blacks' tragic fate. See also Deal, "A Constricted World," in Carr, Morgan, and Russo, eds., *Colonial Chesapeake Society,* 275–305.

official displeasure in 1693. In politics, as in leisure, black involvement led one observer to protest that, in the elections for the assembly in 1701, "Strangers, Servants, Aliens, nay Malatoes and Negroes were Polled." In the first decade of the eighteenth century, white Baptists in South Carolina apparently had enough scruples about slavery, if not sympathy for slaves, to ask for advice from their brethren in England concerning a church member who had castrated a runaway. Some thought such an action was "not becoming" a church.[25]

The degree of cooperation between blacks and lower-class whites was far more attenuated in the Lowcountry than in the Chesapeake—and this, of course, applied to interracial sexual relations as in other spheres. The reason was simple: South Carolina never had a substantial class of white indentured servants. There was therefore little basis for the anxieties about the sexual preferences of white servant women that existed in the Chesapeake. Furthermore, South Carolina had fewer nonslaveholding whites than the Chesapeake and therefore less need or occasion to encourage caste consciousness by outlawing interracial marriages. In the Lowcountry, as in the plantation societies of the West Indies, the yawning social chasm between most whites and most blacks bred a self-confidence about the unthinkability of interracial marriage that was absent in the Chesapeake. Whereas interracial marriage did not have to be prohibited, open concubinage between male planters and female slaves could be treated more casually than elsewhere in North America, precisely because it presented less of a danger to fundamental social distinctions. Nevertheless, in spite of these social realities, sexual relations between whites and blacks probably occurred more frequently in the seventeenth than in the eighteenth century. And, although white servant women were few in early South Carolina, enough of them gave birth to mulatto children that the assembly took notice. In 1717, it legislated against such behavior.[26]

Access to freedom, though never widespread in the Lowcountry, was likewise more extensive in the early than in the late colonial period. From the earliest settlement until the conclusion of the Yamassee War in 1718, black men played a significant role in the defense of the colony, acting not only as messengers, drummers, and pioneers but also as armed militiamen. As early as 1680, an observer touted the fighting qualities of the "many trusty negroes" in the colony. Thirty years later, Thomas Nairne added his testimonial, pointing out that "a considerable Number of active, able Negro slaves were enrolled in

25. Wood, *Black Majority*, 54, 96; Thomas J. Little, "The South Carolina Slave Laws Reconsidered, 1670–1700," *SCHM*, XCIV (1993), 92, 94, 98; William G. McLoughlin and Winthrop D. Jordan, eds., "Baptists Face the Barbarities of Slavery in 1710," *Jour. So. Hist.*, XXIX (1963), 495–501.

26. This paragraph draws heavily on the insights of Jordan, *White over Black*, 137–144; Fredrickson, *White Supremacy*, 108; and Wood, *Black Majority*, 98–99.

the militia." In fact, Nairne continued, any slave "who in the time of an Invasion, kills an Enemy" gained his freedom.[27] A number of such manumissions occurred. Freedom was also occasionally available to those who could purchase it and to those who received it for specific purposes. However, manumissions, for whatever reason, were never numerous in the Lowcountry. Encumbered, conditional freedom, which became the rule in turn-of-the-century Virginia, was the norm from the first in South Carolina. In 1702, for example, a slave named Tickey was guaranteed his release in four years' time *provided* he was not convicted of any insubordination toward his mistress in the interim. Whatever "crude and egalitarian intimacies" arose between the races on the South Carolina frontier, they were always fragile ties, easily rendered asunder.[28]

To compare the infant slave societies of the Chesapeake and the Lowcountry is, in essence, to engage in different ways of measuring time. In fact, three forms of historical time must be kept simultaneously in mind. First, the obvious youthfulness of these two seventeenth-century societies accounts for many of their shared features: both acquired their first slaves from the same places, race relations tended to be flexible in the early years, and whites and blacks often worked alongside one another. To make such a comparison is to employ the time scale common to all social organisms: they are born, develop, and die. What could be more natural, then, but to see the likenesses in these two societies in the youthful stages of their development?

Yet, fundamental differences arose from another facet of historical time—the sheer fact of precedence. Virginia was founded almost three-quarters of a century before South Carolina. From this perspective, to compare Virginia and South Carolina is to compare two societies that, in their historical trajectories, were moving in parallel paths but from different starting points. Virginia acquired slaves, imported Africans, and inserted them into a fully fledged plantation economy much earlier than did South Carolina. This comparison draws on the simplest, most basic form of historical time: the sheer fact of chronological precedence.

Another set of differences comes into view if historical time is conceived in one further way—not which society was founded first, but which was the more developed as a slave society. In this respect, turn-of-the-century Virginia was a late developer while its southern cousin was thoroughly precocious. To make this comparison is to measure these two societies, not by the implacable uni-

27. Wood, *Black Majority*, 124–130; Maurice Mathews, "A Contemporary View of Carolina in 1680," *SCHM*, LV (1954), 158; Thomas Nairne, *A Letter from South Carolina* . . . (London, 1710), 31.

28. Wood, *Black Majority*, 96, 100–102.

formity or fixed divisions of clock-and-calendar time, but by their internal rhythms. In this comparison, the rank order needs to be reversed, with South Carolina being placed ahead of Virginia, for, in 1700, the Lowcountry contained a much larger proportion of slaves and depended more fundamentally on slave labor than its Chesapeake counterpart.

The significance of this juggling act in temporalities lies in our being able not only to situate these two turn-of-the-century slave societies more clearly but also to see in what directions they were pointing. The similarities of youthfulness were most important in defining these two societies in their mid- to late-seventeenth-century phases. At this point, most blacks spoke English, worked alongside whites, and associated fairly easily with them. The cultural distinctions between the two races were muted. The black population was not generally numerous enough to provide the critical mass for autonomous cultural development. Many of the earliest blacks in both the Chesapeake and the Lowcountry assumed the customs and attitudes of their white neighbors and acquaintances.

Furthermore, the early emergence of an assimilationist culture among the slaves of both societies diminished, much more than might otherwise seem possible, the African influences that accompanied the later infusion of African immigrants. In other words, the recently arrived Africans were probably incorporated into an embryonic cultural system that, though creole, nevertheless approximated the Anglo-American model. Later arrivals faced a double challenge. They had to adjust not only to new surroundings but to the rules and customs already worked out by the earliest migrants. The first colonists acted as a "charter group," determining many of the terms under which the newcomers were incorporated.[29]

But the contrasts that were soon evident between these two youthful societies, arising from the timing of their settlements and the rate of their social developments, point in a different direction by the end of the seventeenth century. In the Lowcountry, an assimilationist slave culture had little chance to put down roots before it was swept aside by a rising tide of African slaves. Although these growing numbers of Africans had to adapt to an embryonic cultural system, they swamped it more than they were incorporated within it. Moreover, from the first, Carolina blacks had more freedom to shape their culture than blacks had elsewhere on the North American mainland. Their numbers were not large in the seventeenth century, but most blacks lived in

29. John Porter, *The Vertical Mosaic: An Analysis of Social Class and Power in Canada* (Toronto, 1965), 60; T. H. Breen, "Creative Adaptations: Peoples and Cultures," in Jack P. Greene and J. R. Pole, eds., *Colonial British America: Essays in the New History of the Early Modern Era* (Baltimore, 1984), 205–206.

units made up of more than a few of their fellows; and, in the society as a whole, blacks always formed a significantly large proportion of the population. An important urban center that provided a key gathering place for Lowcountry slaves also emerged quickly. As early as 1698, South Carolina legislators took action against the "great numbers of slaves which do not dwell in Charles Town [who] do on Sundays resort thither to Drink Quarrel Curse Swear and pro-[p]hane the Sabboth." The autonomy of the cowpen and the freedom of movement inherent in stock raising also contributed to the latitude early Carolina blacks enjoyed. It is not difficult to envisage these seventeenth-century Lowcountry slaves incorporating significant elements of their African past into an embryonic African American cultural system. This early Africanization gained momentum, of course, when the floodgates opened in the early eighteenth century and African immigrants poured into the region.[30]

In the Chesapeake, an assimilationist slave culture took much firmer root. To be sure, Africans began to enter the region in large numbers at least by the 1690s. But, in comparison with Lowcountry patterns, they were dispersed more widely, formed a much smaller proportion of the overall population, and for the most part were unable to constitute enclaves within an increasingly black countryside. Of course, they did not abandon their African heritage entirely. The Johnson clan of the Eastern Shore, for example, could hardly have behaved more like typical white settlers. And yet, in 1677, John Johnson, grandson of Anthony Johnson, "the patriarch of Pungoteague Creek," purchased a tract of land that he called "Angola." As T. H. Breen and Stephen Innes put it, "If the Johnsons were merely English colonists with black skins, then why did John, junior, name his small farm 'Angola'?" This small shred of evidence, the authors declare, suggests the existence of a deeply rooted, separate culture, a judgment that, although it likely goes too far, at least points to memories of a homeland being kept alive by at least one third-generation free black (and presumably others).[31]

There is also evidence, both for this clan and for other free black families, and by implication for slaves, of blacks' seeking out other blacks. No doubt, the colony's earliest black residents wove webs of friendship and kinship through which they transmitted cultural values. Racial identity was not necessarily sacrificed even where blacks associated widely with whites. As early as 1672, Surry County "Negroes" were said "to mete together upon Satterdayes and

30. An Act for the Better Ordering of Slaves, no. 168, 1698, MSS Acts, SCDAH. Wood has suggested, for example, that African skills in tending livestock and in growing and processing rice were incorporated into the new African American world (*Black Majority*, 30–31, 59–62, 119–124).

31. Breen and Innes, *"Myne Owne Ground,"* 17–18, 71–72. See, however, Deal, *Race and Class in Colonial Virginia*, 178–179.

Sundayes . . . to consult of unlawful p[ro]jects and combinations." Eight years later, Virginians discovered a "Negro Plott," hatched in the Northern Neck, which they again blamed on the relative autonomy of the black community, particularly "the great freedome and Liberty that has beene by many Masters given to their Negro Slaves for Walking on broad on Saterdays and Sundays and permitting them to meete in great Numbers in makeing and holding of Funeralls for Dead Negroes." Clearly, then, late-seventeenth-century Chesapeake blacks participated in their own social and cultural events.[32]

One way that late-seventeenth-century Chesapeake slaves transmitted values was through their naming patterns. Among the eighty-nine Virginia slaves that Lewis Burwell owned between 1692 and 1710, the vast majority became known at least to their master by English names. Nevertheless, one in nine Burwell slaves achieved something more distinctive: at least five men retained African names, two couples chose an African name for one of their children, and another three parents seem to have combined an English name with a West African naming principle—that is, the father's first name became the son's second name. In this way, African memories were not lost altogether.[33]

A further tantalizing glimpse of possible African influences derives from the decorated clay tobacco pipes produced in the early Chesapeake. Although most known pipe forms were either Native American or European in shape, all three major social groups in the region—Indians, Europeans, and Africans—seem to have made and decorated them. Although many of the decorative techniques (repeated patterns of dots or dashes known as pointillé and rouletted or white inlay) and motifs (hanging triangles, stars, and diamonds) might have been African in inspiration, they also can be traced in prehistoric Indian and European decorative arts traditions. Perhaps African slaves incorporated abstract designs and representational motifs drawn from their home-

---

32. Breen and Innes, *"Myne Owne Ground,"* 103–104, 83–88, 100–102; "Management of Slaves," *VMHB,* VII (1899–1900), 314; H. R. McIlwaine et al., eds., *Executive Journals of the Council of Colonial Virginia,* I (Richmond, Va., 1925), 86. Plots and rumors of resistance, involving black slaves alone, also occurred in Westmoreland County in 1688 ("Punishment for a Negro Rebel," *WMQ,* 1st Ser., X [1901–1902], 177–178), and in Warwick County in 1693 (Affidavits submitted to Sir Edmund Andros from Warwick County, VHS). There is also a cryptic reference to "riotous and rebellious conduct of Mrs. Wormeley's negroes," dating to the fall of 1644, in H. R. McIlwaine, ed., *Minutes of the Council and General Court of Colonial Virginia, 1622–1632, 1670–1676* . . . (Richmond, Va., 1924), 502. Between 1669 and 1699, at least five statutes aimed to curtail slave resistance: Hening, *Statutes at Large,* II, 270, 481–482, 491–492, III, 86, 102–103, 179. Deal, *Race and Class in Colonial Virginia,* 178, 211–212, points to evidence of a shared social life among slaves and free blacks but concludes that "there appears to have been little that was distinctively Afro-American about the culture of the Northampton County blacks."

33. Walsh, "'A Place in Time' Regained," in Hudson, ed., *Working toward Freedom,* 5.

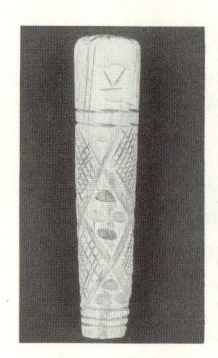

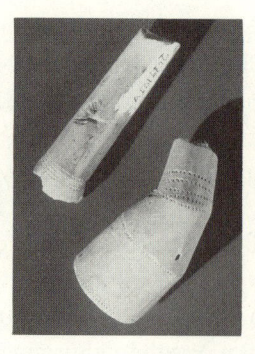

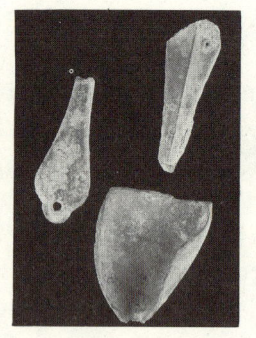

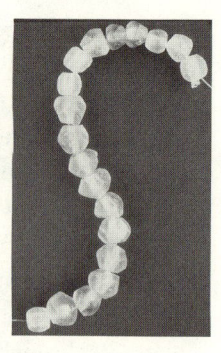

PLATE 2. *Bone Handle; Pipe; Spoon Handle; Beads.* Early eighteenth century. Utopia Quarter in Virginia. African and Euro-American influences blend in these artifacts. Courtesy James River Institute

lands, but most likely the pipes are evidence of a vibrant cultural syncretism in the seventeenth-century Chesapeake. A bone handle discovered at Utopia quarter along the James River in Virginia has been dated to the early eighteenth century, when a large community of Africans was transferred to the site. The bone handle is intricately carved in ways reminiscent of the abstract designs found on many Chesapeake pipes.[34]

Overall, syncretism was more pronounced than African influence in the culture of early Chesapeake slaves, whereas the scales tipped in the other direction in the culture of early Lowcountry slaves. The emergence of an assimilationist cultural amalgam structured later developments in both regions, helping to explain the relative paucity (in New World terms) of African

---

34. Matthew Charles Emerson, "Decorated Clay Tobacco Pipes from the Chesapeake" (Ph.D. diss., University of California, Berkeley, 1988); Emerson, "Decorated Clay Tobacco Pipes from the Chesapeake: An African Connection," in Paul A. Shackel and Barbara J. Little, eds., *The Historical Archaeology of the Chesapeake* (Washington, D.C., 1994); James Deetz, *Flowerdew Hundred: The Archaeology of a Virginia Plantation, 1619–1864* (Charlottesville, Va., 1993), 91–103; Garrett R. Fesler, "Interim Report of Excavations at Utopia Quarter (44JC32): An Eighteenth-Century Slave Complex at Kingsmill on the James in James City County, Virginia" (MS, 1995). For other descriptions of these pipes that posit no or minimal African connections, see Susan L. Henry, "Terra-Cotta Tobacco Pipes in Seventeenth Century Maryland and Virginia: A Preliminary Study," *Historical Archaeology,* XIII (1979), 14–37; David Colin Crass, "The Clay Pipes from Green Spring Plantation (44JC9), Virginia," ibid., XXII (1988), 83–97; L. Daniel Mouer, "Chesapeake Creoles: The Creation of Folk Culture in Colonial Virginia," in Theodore R. Reinhart and Dennis J. Pogue, eds., *The Archaeology of Seventeenth-Century Virginia,* Special Publication No. 30 of the Archaeological Society of Virginia (Richmond, Va., 1993), 105–166, esp. 128–146; and the most authoritative work to date, L. Daniel Mouer et al., "Colono Ware Pottery, Chesapeake Pipes, and 'Uncritical Assumptions,'" in Theresa A. Singleton, ed., *"I, Too, Am, America": Contributions to African American Archaeology* (Charlottesville, Va., forthcoming).

cultural features in eighteenth-century British North American slave life. But the Lowcountry slave world was, from the first, more autonomous than that of the Chesapeake. Carolinian slaves took advantage of this relative measure of latitude to shape a culture more in touch with memories of an African past than Chesapeake slaves could construct. By 1700, the paths on which these two slave societies were embarked had diverged; they moved even farther apart as time passed.

I
Contours of
the Plantation
Experience

The melody of the fields

and woods through Virginia

is greatly beyond the Carolinas.

—Josiah Quincy

1 : Two Plantation Worlds

At the turn of the eighteenth century, the constructed environments of the Chesapeake and Lowcountry were signally unimpressive. In the Chesapeake, abandoned and overgrown tobacco fields, partly cleared fields littered with girdled trees, and throwaway houses "dribbled over the landscape without apparent design" caught the eye. A sense of decay and disorder prevailed. South Carolina's frontier settlements presented an even more hardscrabble and precarious appearance. Scarred and notched trees oozing resin, deer carcasses strewn about Indian traders' camps, scrub cattle roaming at will, and a few failed vineyards and olive groves met the gaze. The landscape reflected South Carolinians' desperate search for a dependable staple.[1]

By the late eighteenth century, Europeans and Northerners alike found the Virginia landscape much more congenial. There were still tobacco fields, but they were now largely cleared and fenced. Imposing mansions and solid yeo-

---

1. Gloria L. Main, *Tobacco Colony: Life in Early Maryland, 1650–1720* (Princeton, N.J., 1982), 153, 141, 44; Darrett B. Rutman and Anita H. Rutman, *A Place in Time: Middlesex County, Virginia, 1650–1750* (New York, 1984), 65–69; Henry M. Miller, "Transforming a 'Splendid and Delightsome Land': Colonists and Ecological Change in the Chesapeake, 1607–1820," *Journal of the Washington Academy of Sciences*, LXXVI (1986), 173–187; Peter H. Wood, *Black Majority: Negroes in Colonial South Carolina from 1670 through the Stono Rebellion* (New York, 1974), 27–33, 55, 108–119.

man houses had replaced shacks. By the second half of the eighteenth century, well-to-do planters who offered their properties for sale boasted of their improvements: ponds, meadows, millraces, quays, orchards, vegetable gardens, even pleasure gardens. The Chesapeake's "excellent farms and charming, large cleared tracts well-fenced and tilled" impressed New Englander Josiah Quincy, who claimed, "Through Virginia you find agriculture carried to great perfection." Only after leaving the Carolinas and reaching the Chesapeake did Lady Liston, a European traveler, encounter a "country [that] now begins to wear a more cultivated appearance." Observers extolled the Chesapeake's extensive production of garden vegetables, its large peach and apple orchards, and its widespread cultivation of small grains. In many ways, the Chesapeake looked more like a land of farms than a plantation landscape.[2]

The Lowcountry prospect was more seductive and less familiar than that of the Chesapeake. When John Farquharson prophesied in 1789 that "the inland part of [South Carolina], when settled, will resemble Europe more than the Sea Coast especially in grain and all Kind of fruit," he merely underlined how distinctive the Lowcountry had become. It possessed few orchards. Some blamed the climate, too warm in summer to support European fruit trees, too cold in winter to allow tropical varieties to thrive. But John Bartram sarcastically "admire[d] the indolence of these people in not planting fig and pomegranates," and William Bartram attributed the lack of fruit trees to planter neglect. The absence of orchards was matched by a notable lack of gardens. "Gardening is not very much in vogue," observed Johann Schoepf, "and is generally left to ignorant negroes." According to David Ramsay, the great profits derived from staple crops accounted for this failure to establish gardens. Only a Southerner, familiar with the proper purpose of plantations, could appreciate the beauty in such a landscape. Thus, George Washington told the governor of South Carolina that "he had no idea that anywhere in America was there such perfection of cultivation as he had seen on the large rice rivers which he had crossed."

2. Camille Wells, "The Planter's Prospect: Houses, Outbuildings, and Rural Landscapes in Eighteenth-Century Virginia," *Winterthur Portfolio*, XXVIII (1993), 1–31, esp. 23, 27, 30–31; Wells, "The Eighteenth-Century Landscape of Virginia's Northern Neck," *Northern Neck of Virginia Historical Magazine*, XXXVII (1987), 4217–4255, esp. 4224–4227; Dell Upton, "New Views of the Virginia Landscape," *VMHB*, XCVI (1988), 403–470; Peter Martin, *The Pleasure Gardens of Virginia: From Jamestown to Jefferson* (Princeton, N.J., 1991); Mark Antony De Wolfe Howe, ed., "Journal of Josiah Quincy, Junior, 1773," Massachusetts Historical Society, *Proceedings*, XLIX (1915–1916), 464, 467; Journals of Lady Liston, January 1798, 5697, 41, Sir Robert Liston Papers, National Library of Scotland, Edinburgh; Harry J. Carman, ed., *American Husbandry* (New York, 1939), 156–157; Johann [von] Ewald, *Diary of the American War: A Hessian Journal*, ed. and trans. Joseph P. Tustin (New Haven, Conn., 1979), 313; Banastre Tarleton, *A History of the Campaigns of 1780 and 1781* (London, 1787), 381; Thomas Anburey, *Travels through the Interior Parts of America . . .*, II (London, 1789), 322–324.

Washington's mention of "rice rivers" was no slip of the tongue. The Lowcountry was a plantation world par excellence.[3]

The transformation of these two landscapes over the course of the eighteenth century resulted from contrasting human adaptations to distinct physical environments. The complex relation between ecosystem and human settlement shaped two plantation worlds in British North America. In exploiting contrasting ecological systems, colonists cultivated different staples and engaged in varying mixes of economic activities. In turn, these contrasting economies generated differing labor demands, which helped govern the magnitude and character of immigration to each region. The pace at which the newcomers arrived, together with the different physical and social settings in which they found themselves, helped regulate the rate of natural increase in the two populations. The peopling, or rather repeopling, of these two regions occurred in contrasting ways, intimately connected to their different environmental and economic constraints and potentials. As a result, two distinct plantation regimes emerged that framed the building of two contrasting slave societies and cultures.

TWO LANDSCAPES

To many eighteenth-century travelers, the natural landscapes of Virginia and South Carolina seemed indistinguishable. Both appeared depressingly monotonous and uniform, a "dull and insipid scene" in Robert Hunter's words. The "face of the country" was low-lying, heavily wooded, and dominated by huge rivers. Trees, water, and flatness were the prevailing images; pines, swamps, and sand flats stretched as far as the eye could see. "No hills nor dales the view diversify," wrote one disenchanted poet, "But one dead Flat fatigues the languid Eye." Even the seaboard's people contributed to the impression of homogeneity. With their feverish, yellow faces, the inhabitants looked prematurely old.[4]

---

3. John Farquharson to Gabriel Manigault, June 24, 1789, Manigault Family Papers, USC; F. A. Michaux, *Travels to the West of the Allegheny Mountains* . . . (London, 1805), in Reuben Gold Thwaites, ed., *Early Western Travels, 1748–1846* (Cleveland, Ohio, 1904–1907), III, 305; John Bartram, "Diary of a Journey through the Carolinas, Georgia, and Florida, from July 1, 1765, to April 10, 1766," ed. Francis Harper, American Philosophical Society, *Transactions,* N.S., XXXIII (1942–1944), 26; Francis Harper, ed., *The Travels of William Bartram* (New Haven, Conn., 1958), 160; Johann David Schoepf, *Travels in the Confederation [1783–1784],* trans. and ed. Alfred J. Morrison, 2 vols. (Philadelphia, 1911), II, 180; David Ramsay, *The History of South-Carolina* . . . , 2 vols. (Charleston, S.C., 1809), II, 127; Archibald Henderson, *Washington's Southern Tour, 1791* (Boston, 1923), 127.

4. Robert Hunter, Jr., *Quebec to Carolina in 1785–1786* . . . , ed. Louis B. Wright and Marion Tinling (San Marino, Calif., 1943), 267–268, 282; Louisa Susannah [Aikman] Wells,

A less panoramic view qualifies the appearance of "dead uniformity" to which so many travelers alluded. Indeed, had more eighteenth-century travelers ventured away from the coast, they would have observed a much larger and flatter coastal plain in South Carolina than in Virginia. A traveler in the Lowcountry had to venture as far as fifty miles from the coast before encountering modest sandhills. One early settler put it well when he described the Carolinian landscape as "soe plaine and Levyll that it may be compared to a Bowling ally." In the Chesapeake, by contrast, it was not necessary to move far inland before encountering an elevated and gently rolling landscape. By the middle of the eighteenth century, Chesapeake society had diversified into at least two subregions, for settlement had by that time become extensive in both tidewater and piedmont. In the Lowcountry, at about the same time, settlement was still confined to a much more extensive coastal plain.[5]

Even the coastal plain of each region was not all of a piece. In the Lowcountry, the inland parts of many parishes exhibited a different appearance from coastal sections. Timothy Ford had in mind the interior of Saint John Berkeley, a parish that straddled both parts of the plain, when he described its topography as one "very frequently interspersed with hills and valleys." In time, inland sections of Lowcountry parishes supported different crops from coastal areas. Nor was the Chesapeake tidewater uniform. Josiah Quincy observed, "When you enter Virginia, and in proportion as you come north, you change the plain for hills, and pitchpine for oaks." J. F. D. Smyth confirmed this impression and

---

The Journal of a Voyage from Charlestown to London (New York, 1968), 77; John Ravenscroft to George MacMurdo, Dec. 15, 1771, Maxwell, MacMurdo, and Newhall Family Papers, National Library of Scotland; J. P. Brissot de Warville, *New Travels in the United States of America, 1788,* ed. Durand Echeverria, trans. Mara Soceanu Vamos and Durand Echeverria (Cambridge, Mass., 1964), 339. For representative views of the landscape, see Frank H. Norton, ed., *Journal Kept by Hugh Finlay . . .* (Brooklyn, N.Y., 1867), 52–53; Schoepf, *Travels in the Confederation,* II, 102–103; Journal of Thomas Owen, Apr. 5, 1735, Birmingham Central Libraries, England; William Ogilvie to Alexander Ogilvie, July 20, 1752, Ogilvie-Forbes of Boyndlie MSS, Aberdeen University Library, Scotland; Rodney Atwood, *The Hessians: Mercenaries from Hessen-Kassel in the American Revolution* (Cambridge, Mass., 1980), 168; Edward Porter Alexander, ed., *The Journal of John Fontaine . . .* (Williamsburg, Va., 1972), 81; Michael Forrest, *Travels through America: A Poem* (Philadelphia, 1793), 40; and Lewis Beebe's Travel Journals, Feb. 11, 1800, microfilm, CW.

5. Langdon Cheves, ed., *The Shaftesbury Papers and Other Records Relating to Carolina . . . ,* SCHS, *Collections,* V (1897), 308; Joseph W. Barnwell, ed., "Diary of Timothy Ford, 1785–1786," *SCHM,* XIII (1912), 185; Baron Ludwig von Closen, *The Revolutionary Journal of Ludwig von Closen, 1780–1783,* ed. and trans. Evelyn M. Acomb (Chapel Hill, N.C., 1958), 178; François Alexandre Frédéric, duke de La Rochefoucault Liancourt, *Travels through the United States of North America . . . ,* 2 vols. (London, 1799), II, 30. Tidewater Virginia measures approximately 11,000 square miles; South Carolina's coastal plain is almost twice as large.

unfavorably compared the "dead flat" of the southern Virginia tidewater with the "extremely broken and hilly" Northern Neck.[6] Significant variations in the two coastal plains followed an east-west axis in the Lowcountry, a north-south axis in the Chesapeake.

The major structural constituents of these two coastal plains produced another striking contrast. In the Chesapeake region, large estuaries, long peninsulas, and offshore bars were the distinctive features. The "noble Chesapeake," as one traveler termed it (that "little Mediterranean," as another exaggerated), and the four great tidal rivers of the Potomac, Rappahannock, York, and James dominated the landscape. The Lowcountry's coastal plain, in contrast, was not dissected by large estuaries, though it was drained by four river systems—the Pee Dee, Santee, Edisto, and Savannah—and it was bordered by sea islands rather than by offshore bars. The tidal shorelines of both colonies were almost identical in length, but the bulk of Virginia's coastal line extended far inland, whereas almost three-quarters of South Carolina's tidal shoreline consisted of islands. In the relation between people and their environment, there are, as Lucien Febvre reminds us, "no necessities, but everywhere possibilities." In this light, the westward thrust of Chesapeake settlement and the littoral pattern of Lowcountry settlement are, at the least, compatible with the contrasting orientations of their respective tidal coasts.[7]

Vegetation in the two regions reflected topographical differences. In the Chesapeake, pines gave way to oaks and hickories on well-drained soils, and in certain parts of the tidewater in the eighteenth century—Prince George County, Virginia, for example—oaks predominated. Furthermore, the Chesapeake piedmont supported a deciduous hardwood forest. Benjamin Henry Latrobe spoke of pines gradually giving way to oaks as he proceeded westward in Virginia in 1796, so that, when he reached Amelia County, "scarce any pines [were to be] seen." Thus, even when allowing for fluidity in vegetational patterns over time, the presence of at least two forest belts—the maritime pines,

---

6. Barnwell, ed., "Diary of Timothy Ford," *SCHM,* XIII (1912), 188; Howe, ed., "Journal of Josiah Quincy," Mass. Hist. Soc., *Procs.,* XLIX (1915–1916), 468; J.F.D. Smyth, *A Tour in the United States of America . . . ,* 2 vols. (London, 1784), I, 177–178. See also Robert Honyman, *Colonial Panorama, 1775,* ed. Philip Padelford (San Marino, Calif., 1939), 2; Jonathan Mason, *Extracts from a Diary Kept by the Hon. Jonathan Mason of a Journey from Boston to Savannah in the Year 1804* (Cambridge, Mass., 1885), 15–16.

7. William Eddis, *Letters from America,* ed. Aubrey C. Land (Cambridge, Mass., 1969), 6; Thomas Balch, ed., William Duane trans., *The Journal of Claude Blanchard . . .* (Albany, N.Y., 1876), 138; William D. Thornbury, *Regional Geomorphology of the United States* (New York, 1965), 32, 38–39; Jean Gottman, *Virginia in Our Century* (Charlottesville, Va., 1969), 444; C. Wythe Cooke, "Geology of the Coastal Plain of South Carolina," *U.S. Geological Survey Bulletin,* no. 867, 1; Lucien Febvre, *A Geographical Introduction to History,* trans. E. G. Mountford and J. H. Paxton (London, 1966 [orig. publ. Paris, 1924]), 236.

interspersed with oaks, and the piedmont hardwoods—created a more diversified vegetation cover and a less uniform outlook in the Chesapeake than in the Lowcountry, where, as Schoepf put it, "the greater part of the fore-country is taken up in pine-forest."[8]

If Chesapeake forests were more diversified, Lowcountry vegetation was more exotic. The noble live oak, the swaying palmetto, the red juniper, the "beautiful deep sands, . . . lofty pines, . . . and twining jessamine flinging its odours far and wide" provided a sensual experience that even the stern Methodist Francis Asbury was unable to resist. When John Bartram encountered this vista, he was "almost ravished of his senses and lost in astonishment." The ubiquitous Spanish moss, hanging from trees in long festoons, added an eerie, otherworldly dimension to the scene. Swampland and its attendant vegetation—cypress, sweet gum, black gum, and tupelo—dominated the Lowcountry landscape much more than in the Chesapeake. The rich hues of this swampland vegetation led one passing traveler to liken the experience to "driving through a Green House." To complete the spectacle, the traveler would continually emerge from thick forest and tangled swamps into patches of treeless marshland or savannas, "a Kind of Natural Lawns."[9]

These contrasting plant covers owed much to climatic differences. Hot summers and mild winters marked Virginia's continental climate. Most Virginia counties lay in the path of warm, moist air currents moving from the south or southwest and of cold, dry air currents moving southward and eastward from the north. These alternating currents often brought sharp weather changes. South Carolina's temperate to subtropical climate was much less

8. Rev. John Jones Spooner, "A Topographical Description of the County of Prince George, in Virginia, 1793," *Tyler's Quarterly Historical and Genealogical Magazine,* V (1923), 4; Edward C. Carter II et al., eds., *The Virginia Journals of Benjamin Henry Latrobe, 1795–1798,* II (New Haven, Conn., 1977), 122; U.S., Census Office, *Report on the Forests of North America . . . ,* by Charles S. Sargent, 10th Census of U.S., 1880, IX (Washington, D.C., 1884), 4, 512, 518; Schoepf, *Travels in the Confederation,* II, 173. For a good general description of southern vegetation, see Timothy Silver, *A New Face on the Countryside: Indians, Colonists, and Slaves in South Atlantic Forests, 1500–1800* (New York, 1990), 14–25.

9. Elmer T. Clark et al., eds., *The Journal and Letters of Francis Asbury,* II (London, 1958), 281; James Edward Smith, comp., *A Selection of the Correspondence of Linnaeus, and Other Naturalists, from the Original Manuscripts,* I (London, 1821), 478; Ewald, *Diary of the American War,* 197; Journals of Lady Liston, Dec. 29, 1797, 5697, 15, Liston Papers; James Glen, *A Description of South Carolina* (London, 1761), in Chapman J. Milling, ed., *Colonial South Carolina: Two Contemporary Descriptions* (Columbia, S.C., 1951), 6. See also Mark Catesby to Dr. Sherard, June 20, 1722, Sherard Letters, Royal Society, London; Francis Moore, *A Voyage to Georgia: Begun in the Year 1735* (London, 1744), in GHS, *Collections,* I (1840), 105; Harper, ed., *Travels of William Bartram,* 19–20, 195–196; E. Merton Coulter, ed., *The Journal of William Stephens, 1741–1743* (Athens, Ga., 1958), 246; and "William Logan's Journal of a Journey to Georgia, 1745," *Pennsylvania Magazine of History and Biography,* XXXVI (1912), 15.

changeable. Maritime tropical air persisted in the Lowcountry for extended periods during the summer, creating extremely oppressive conditions. Annual mean temperatures were at least five degrees Fahrenheit higher than in the Chesapeake, and average annual rainfall was five to ten inches higher. Well might one visitor say, "Carolina is in the spring a paradise, in the summer a hell, and in the autumn a hospital." Lord Adam Gordon, who visited both South Carolina and Virginia in the mid-1760s, was convinced that Virginia was "a more healthy country." He was undoubtedly right. Nowhere in British North America, one historian has observed, was life "more fleeting than in Carolina's funereal lowlands."[10]

Settlers exploited these two ecological systems to cultivate two different staples, which in turn molded two distinct landscapes. Tobacco culture harmonized with the Chesapeake climate. The lengthy frost-free period (about 200 days in the tidewater and 180 days in the piedmont), stretching from early to middle April through middle to late October, permitted the transplanting of tobacco in May and June and its harvesting in July and August. The predominance of fairly well drained soils also facilitated the spread of tobacco culture. In the Lowcountry, an even lengthier growing season (240 days in the inland coastal plain to more than 300 days on the Sea Islands) permitted rice to be planted in mid-March and harvested in September. Extensive swamps, "the Golden Mines of Carolina" in George Milligen-Johnston's words, were also ideal for rice culture. Finally, given that an abundant water supply, rather than a particular climate or soil type, forms the key to successful rice cultivation, the heavy rainfall characteristic of the Lowcountry easily met this requirement. "Rice will grow," Bernard Romans noted, "in any Soil though it loves watery ones best."[11]

These two staples produced two different patterns of land use. Tobacco exhausted the soil rapidly; rice did not. As early as the late seventeenth century,

10. Schoepf, *Travels in the Confederation*, II, 172; Lord Adam Gordon, "Journal of an Officer in the West Indies Who Travelled over a Part of the West Indies, and of North America in the Course of 1764 and 1765," in Newton D. Mereness, ed., *Travels in the American Colonies* (New York, 1916), 407; Peter A. Coclanis, *The Shadow of a Dream: Economic Life and Death in the South Carolina Low Country, 1670–1920* (New York, 1989), 42.

11. U.S., Environmental Data Service, *Climatic Atlas of the United States* (Washington, D.C., 1968), 31–32; U.S., Dept. of Agric., Soil Conserv. Service, *Soil Survey of Goochland County* (Washington, D.C., 1980), 2; U.S., Dept. of Agric., Soil Conserv. Service, *Soil Survey of Beaufort and Jasper Counties, South Carolina*, by Warren M. Stuck (Washington, D.C., 1979), 2, 89; William Gerard De Brahm, *De Brahm's Report of the General Survey in the Southern District of North America*, ed. Louis De Vorsey, Jr. (Columbia, S.C., 1971), 75; George Milligen[-Johnston], *A Short Description of the Province of South-Carolina . . .* (London, 1770), in Milling, ed., *Colonial South Carolina*, 119; Bernard Romans, *A Concise Natural History of East and West Florida . . .* , I (New York, 1775), 126.

tobacco culture's impact on the landscape was well understood, for "as fast as the Ground is worn out with Tobacco and Corn, it runs up again in Underwoods, and in many Places of the Country, that which has been clear'd is thicker in Woods than it was before the clearing." In the Lowcountry, swampland produced a resilient and fertile soil and, because less than one-twentieth of tidewater lands had slopes of more than 2 percent, soil erosion was not a hazard. As a result, the human landscape assumed a more permanent cast. What appeared ephemeral and unkempt in the Chesapeake appeared permanent and orderly in the Lowcountry.[12]

Staples also stamped their imprints on the landscape by shaping settlement patterns. Charleston, the principal town in the plantation colonies of British North America, owed much of its importance to the heavy bulk commodity rice. This staple required forward linkages in the transportation, manufacturing, and service sectors, which could most conveniently be made available in a central urban place. Crèvecoeur visited the city in the 1770s and aptly observed that it was there that "the produce of this extensive territory concentres." A popular saying had "all roads lead[ing] to Charleston." In the Chesapeake, by contrast, tobacco's slight bulk, minimal processing requirements, and particular marketing structure militated against large urban centers. It was only with the marked growth of wheat production after midcentury that towns like Norfolk, Baltimore, Alexandria, and Fredericksburg developed into important urban sites. In spite of the rapidly growing coastal and inland towns, the focus of settlement in the late-eighteenth-century Chesapeake remained the rivers and the bay.[13]

Crops not only helped shape settlement patterns; they defined the plantation regimes of both regions. The two dominant staples—tobacco and rice—created two plantation worlds in the Chesapeake and Lowcountry, respectively. A consideration of the economics of both crops will help explain the contrasting plantation systems of each region.

---

12. Carville V. Earle, *The Evolution of a Tidewater Settlement System: All Hallow's Parish, Maryland, 1650–1783*, University of Chicago Department of Geography Research Paper, no. 170 (Chicago, 1975), 18; Henry Hartwell et al., *The Present State of Virginia and the College*, ed. Hunter Dickinson Farish (Williamsburg, Va., 1940), 8–9; Robert Mills, *Statistics of South Carolina* (Spartanburg, S.C., 1972 [orig. publ. Charleston, S.C., 1826]), 367, 386; D. H. Grist, *Rice* (London, 1959), 148, 258; U.S., Dept. of Agric., Soil Conserv. Service, *Soil Survey of Beaufort and Jasper Counties*, 46.

13. Carville Earle and Ronald Hoffman, "Staple Crops and Urban Development in the Eighteenth-Century South," *Perspectives in American History*, X (1976), 7–78; Jacob M. Price, "Economic Function and the Growth of American Port Towns in the Eighteenth Century," ibid., VIII (1974), 161–172; J. Hector St. John Crèvecoeur, *Letters from an American Farmer*, ed. W. P. Trent and Ludwig Lewisohn (New York, 1925 [orig. publ. 1782]), 222–223.

TWO PLANTATION SYSTEMS

The economics of planting tobacco and rice—whether starting costs, optimum number of workers, capital requirements, profitability, or productivity—were markedly different. These contrasts created larger labor forces and landholdings in South Carolina than in Virginia. Furthermore, the demands of the two staples encouraged specialization in South Carolina and diversification in Virginia.

The costs of establishing a Lowcountry rice plantation were substantial. From Thomas Nairne, who in 1710 calculated that £1,000 sterling would set up a well-equipped rice plantation, to William De Brahm, who in 1772 reckoned that £2,476 was necessary, contemporary estimates follow an upward progression consistent with rising prices. The main component of these high starting costs was the large labor force deemed necessary to begin rice production. Nairne thought that thirty working hands were required, and De Brahm settled on a figure of forty. As James Grant put it to a prospective planter in 1769, "You'll never make yourself whole with less than thirty Negros."[14] A minimum of thirty working slaves, therefore, was the sine qua non for the establishment of a profitable rice plantation, and the rising prices of these indispensable agents of Lowcountry plantations largely accounted for the upward trend in plantation starting costs.

Few comparable estimates for establishing a Chesapeake tobacco plantation exist, but this is instructive, suggesting that the starting costs of a tobacco plantation merited little elaboration. Toward the close of the seventeenth century, Sir Dalby Thomas estimated that eight to nine hands constituted a manageable size for a Chesapeake tobacco plantation, but went no further in estimating costs. Almost a century passed before there was a serious attempt to probe further, and the new calculations are suspect precisely because they were intended as a response to those who said that "fortunes are rarely made by tobacco planters, and that it is much more common to see their estates eat out by mortgages." Indeed, the author of *American Husbandry*, who produced the estimate, took a particularly unrealistic view of his brief by assuming the presence of an overseer on his newly established tobacco plantation. In order

---

14. Thomas Nairne, *A Letter from South Carolina . . .* (London, 1710), 53; John Norris, *Profitable Advice for Rich and Poor* (London, 1712), 93; C[harles] W[oodmason], "The Idigo Plant Described," *Gentleman's Magazine, and Historical Quarterly,* XXV (1755), 258–259; De Brahm, *De Brahm's Report of the General Survey,* 162–163; Carman, ed., *American Husbandry,* 235; Governor James Grant to the Earl of Cassillis, July 22, 1769, Ailsa Muniments, GD 25/9/27, Scottish Record Office, Edinburgh. See also John Murray to Elizabeth Murray, Mar. 6, 1757, Murray of Murraythwaite Muniments, GD 219/287/12, Scottish Record Office; and Mr. Telfair's Answers to Questions about Rice Planting, March 1774, A3/3/19, Countess of Huntingdon's American Papers, Westminster College, Cambridge, England.

to justify the payment of an overseer's wages, he required an outlay of a thousand pounds on twenty slaves. However, as he himself recognized, "It does not follow from hence, that settlers are precluded from these colonies who cannot buy twenty negroes; every day's experience tells us the contrary of this; . . . they begin [by having] no slaves at all, or no more than what they will submit to take care of themselves."[15]

In short, a tobacco plantation could be set up with no slaves at all, or with one or two, and certainly with no more than ten, whereas a rice plantation required at least thirty workers. Environmental constraints help explain this difference in the optimum sizes of tobacco and rice plantations. In the Chesapeake, good tobacco soils occurred in small plots scattered across the region. In order to make the most of the best land and allow it to recover its fertility under sufficiently long fallow, planters tended to restrict their work forces. And even where a planter owned a large amount of land, he dispersed his laborers in small groups to take advantage of the best soil conditions. In the Lowcountry, by contrast, good swampland and tideland were concentrated rather than scattered, and were available in large expanses rather than in small pockets. Large labor forces were therefore possible.[16]

Apart from the availability of the soils required for tobacco and rice, the type of supervision required of the two crops also dictated differing unit sizes. Because tobacco cultivation required close attention from planting through processing, it was most efficiently grown on a small scale. A master or overseer could best supervise only about ten hands. Rice cultivation, in contrast, did not require close supervision. A master or overseer could monitor the performance of a large number of laborers, and indeed many workers could tend and harvest the crop more efficiently than a small number. Contrasting forms of labor management and differing economies of scale helped create different unit sizes.[17]

The capital requirements of the respective staples were also different, and they, too, influenced the size of the respective labor forces. A tobacco producer required little capital equipment—tools, lumber, nails to put up a tobacco shed. Tobacco was an ideal beginner's crop because it could be grown on a

---

15. Sir Dalby Thomas, *An Historical Account of the Rise and Growth of the West-India Collonies* (London, 1690), quoted in Jerome E. Brooks, comp., *Tobacco: Its History Illustrated by the Books, Manuscripts, and Engravings in the Library of George Arents, Jr.*, II (New York, 1938), 531; Carman, ed., *American Husbandry*, 168–177 (quotations on 170, 176).

16. Main, *Tobacco Colony*, 41–42; Lorena S. Walsh, "Slave Life, Slave Society, and Tobacco Production in the Tidewater Chesapeake, 1620–1820," in Ira Berlin and Philip D. Morgan, eds., *Cultivation and Culture: Labor and the Shaping of Slave Life in the Americas* (Charlottesville, Va., 1993), 170–199.

17. Labor organization is explored fully in Chapter 3.

small scale. Rice production, in contrast, had to be undertaken on a large scale to be profitable. A pounding machine, perhaps costing as much as the swampland itself, was a significant capital investment, one made by many planters in the late colonial period. More important, the preparation of land for rice planting was costly. In the late colonial period, Lowcountry planters calculated that it cost eight shillings and six pence to clear an acre of land, a figure that probably applied to planters in both regions. However, to drain, dam, and ditch an acre—an operation confined to Lowcountry planters—cost an additional one pound to four guineas. A laboring force of considerable size was therefore necessary for two reasons: first, to undertake the arduous tasks of draining and damming and, second, to justify the expense by producing large quantities of rice and thereby recouping the heavy investment.[18]

The investment required of the secondary staples of the Chesapeake and Lowcountry—wheat and indigo—reinforced the regional contrast. In the Chesapeake, wheat production required more capital equipment, in the form of draft stock, plows, and carts, than tobacco production. However, the intermittent labor demands of grain production made it the least labor-intensive activity engaged in by either Chesapeake or Lowcountry planters. Some Chesapeake planters even decided that slave labor was a poor investment in grain farming. The Lowcountry's secondary staple, indigo, was certainly less capitalized than the region's primary crop, but it imposed demands beyond anything a Chesapeake planter might expect. A set of indigo vats in the late colonial period ranged in price from less than £10 to £100 sterling. For every seven acres of indigo, a planter needed a series of vats. Average-sized plantations in the mid-1760s had five sets of vats, valued collectively at about £150, the price of a young adult male slave. Indigo plantations also required drying sheds and a regular water supply. Although this was not a particularly heavy capital investment, and certainly indigo plantations were less labor-intensive than rice plantations, there was still a qualitative difference between these demands and those exerted by either of the Chesapeake staples.[19]

---

18. Richard Pares, *Merchants and Planters* (*Economic History Review*, supplement no. 4 [Cambridge, 1960]), 20; Lois Green Carr and Russell R. Menard, "Land, Labor, and Economies of Scale in Early Maryland: Some Limits to Growth in the Chesapeake System of Husbandry," *Journal of Economic History*, XLIX (1989), 407–418; De Brahm, *De Brahm's Report of the General Survey*, 162; Wilbur H. Siebert, ed., *Loyalists in East Florida, 1774 to 1785*, II (DeLand, Fla., 1929), 170, 172–173. According to one loyalist planter, his 200 acres of tideland contained "between 3 and 4 miles of dikes and canals" (ibid., 239).

19. See the section on wheat farming in Chapter 3. On the cost of a set of indigo vats, see G. Moulton to [?], Dec. 20, 1772, Add. MSS 22677, 71, BL; Siebert, ed., *Loyalists in East Florida*, II, 254–255, 257; Carman, ed., *American Husbandry*, 305; John Torrans to James Grant, May 30, Apr. 30, 1769, bundle 552, Papers of General James Grant of Ballindalloch,

The capital requirements of plantations were closely related to the prospective rate of return on investment. In the Lowcountry, early-eighteenth-century planters expected to clear an annual sum of ten pounds sterling per slave; by the third quarter of the century this expectation had increased to between thirty and forty pounds.[20] Expressed another way, a field hand slave was expected to pay for himself in four years in the early part of the century, but in less than two years toward the close of the century. In a good year, Lowcountry planters achieved a rate of return in excess of 20 percent.[21] In the Chesapeake, by contrast, a tobacco planter was happy to clear five pounds for each of his male field hands. At that rate, he would consider himself fortunate if a slave paid for himself in seven years. A 5–10 percent rate of return on his investment was generally the most he could expect. Clearly, these differential returns would influence the number of laborers an individual planter could purchase.[22]

---

sometime Governor of East Florida, in ownership of Sir Evan Macpherson-Grant, Bart., Ballindalloch Castle Muniments, Scotland. For the ratio of indigo vats to acreage, see W[oodmason], *Gentleman's Mag., and Hist. Qtly.*, XXV (1755), 256; Romans, *History of East and West Florida*, I, 138; and Archibald Johnson, "Directions for Making and Curing of Indico," n.d., Papers of General James Grant of Ballindalloch. For the value of vats, see, for example, inventory of Richard Stevens, Apr. 20, 1767, Inventories, WPA (typescript), CLXXIII, 791–792; inventory of Francis Stuart, Aug. 5, 1767, ibid., X, 101–114, SCDAH. Although one observer thought only 1 or 2 slaves were necessary to produce indigo (Carman, ed., *American Husbandry*, 305), others maintained that 20–25 were the optimum number (Schoepf, *Travels in the Confederation*, II, 157; Smyth, *A Tour in the United States of America*, II, 59; Edward Long, *The History of Jamaica . . .* , III [London, 1774], 679).

20. Elizabeth Donnan, ed., *Documents Illustrative of the History of the Slave Trade to America*, Carnegie Institution of Washingtion Publication no. 409, 4 vols. (Washington, D.C., 1930–1935), IV, 273; "Johann Martin Bolzius Answers a Questionnaire on Carolina and Georgia," trans. and ed. Klaus G. Loewald et al., *WMQ*, 3d Ser., XIV (1957), 245; John Murray to Elizabeth Murray, Mar. 6, 1757, and to Sir Robert Laurie, July 12, 1757, GD 219/290/48, Murray of Murraythwaite Muniments; Moulton to [?], Dec. 20, 1772, Add. MSS 22677, 71.

21. Norris, *Profitable Advice*, 58; James Glen to the Board of Trade, July 15, 1751, CO5/373, 155–157, PRO; Dr. Alexander Garden to the Royal Society, May 1, 1757, Guard Book, III, 86, Royal Society of Arts, London; Moulton to [?], Dec. 20, 1772, Add. MSS 22677, 70. In 1768, a Georgia merchant purchased six African men, costing £43 sterling apiece. He noted that they were "fit to be put directly to any work, and if you are a lucky Indico planter they may go near to pay a very considerable part of their cost in twelve months" (John Graham to James Grant, July 30, 1768, bundle 401, Papers of General James Grant of Ballindalloch). See also John Gerar William De Brahm, *History of the Province of Georgia . . .* , ed. George Wymberley-Jones (Wormsloe, Ga., 1849), 51; Ralph Gray and Betty Wood, "The Transition from Indentured to Involuntary Servitude in Colonial Georgia," *Explorations in Economic History*, 2d Ser., XIII (1976), 361–364; and Joyce E. Chaplin, *An Anxious Pursuit: Agricultural Innovation and Modernity in the Lower South, 1730–1815* (Chapel Hill, N.C., 1993), 9.

22. Paul G. E. Clemens, "The Operation of an Eighteenth-Century Chesapeake Tobacco

The sharp contrast in profitability between Lowcountry and Chesapeake plantations can be explained in large part by the differential productivity of rice and tobacco workers. In the early eighteenth century, South Carolinian planters expected to average about 1,000 pounds of clean rice per acre; by the American War for Independence, the average had risen to about 1,500 pounds per acre. At midcentury, a slave hand apparently averaged 2,250 pounds of clean rice a year; later in the century, the yield per slave increased to between 3,000 and 3,600 pounds. In the Chesapeake, by contrast, tobacco output per laborer declined—from an average of about 1,300 pounds in the first decade of the eighteenth century to about 780 pounds by the time of the American Revolution. In other words, per capita output of the primary staple moved in diametrically opposed directions in the two regions, rising by more than 40 percent in the Lowcountry, declining by about the same amount in the Chesapeake.[23]

For all these reasons, more slaves lived on large plantations in South Carolina than in Virginia. As early as the 1720s, more than half of South Carolina's slaves resided on plantations with twenty or more slaves. In the same decade, only 10 percent of Virginia's slaves lived on plantations with twenty-one or more slaves (see Tables 1 and 2). This divergence in plantation size between the two societies grew more marked over time. In South Carolina at midcentury a remarkable concentration had occurred: only about one-tenth of slaves were resident on small plantations (fewer than ten slaves), and about a third were to be found on extremely large units (more than fifty slaves). At about this time, Henry Muhlenberg and Johann Bolzius estimated that blacks outnumbered whites by a ratio of between fifteen and thirty to one. The actual ratio was never more than nine to one. The discrepancy between these observers' impressions and reality may be attributed to the visual impact of these numerous large plantations. And they became more numerous. By the end of the colonial period, the proportion of slaves on large units had increased to about 50

Plantation," *Agricultural History*, XLIX (1975), 517–531, esp. 522; Clemens, *The Atlantic Economy and Colonial Maryland's Eastern Shore: From Tobacco to Grain* (Ithaca, N.Y., 1980), 150–161, esp. 154. Some Chesapeake planters did better than average: see Christine Daniels, "Gresham's Laws: Labor Management on an Early Eighteenth-Century Chesapeake Plantation," *Journal of Southern History*, LXII (1996), 205–238, esp. 213–214.

23. Coclanis, *The Shadow of a Dream*, 97; Lorena S. Walsh, "Plantation Management in the Chesapeake, 1620–1820," *Jour. Econ. Hist.*, XLIX (1989), 395. Walsh's regional figures demonstrate high output in newer regions but dramatically declining yields in older regions. She also demonstrates major productivity gains in Chesapeake grain production. R. C. Nash, "South Carolina and the Atlantic Economy in the Late Seventeenth and Eighteenth Centuries," *Econ. Hist. Rev.*, XLV (1992), 677–702, esp. 687, 689, 698–699, calculates that the volume of exports of the three major South Carolina staples per head of slave population increased by more than 200% between 1710 and 1770!

TABLE 1.
Plantation Size in South Carolina, 1720–1779

	Proportion of Slaves Living on Unit					
	Size of Unit (in Slaves)					No. of
Decade	1–9	10–19	20–29	30—49	50+	Slaves
1720s	24%	18%	29%	18%	12%	3,190
1730s	14	17	22	27	21	3,741
1740s	8	16	20	26	30	10,555
1750s	8	14	15	24	39	17,575
1760s	8	11	14	25	42	20,742
1770s	7	11	11	19	52	20,485

Note: Deviations in totals from 100.0% in tables, expressed or implicit, are due to rounding.

Sources: All extant inventories in the Records of the Secretary of the Province, A–H, and WPA, LV–LXV, LXXVIA; Miscellaneous Records, I, KK, LL, and WPA, LXIV–LXV, LXVIIA, CII–CXXI; and Inventory Books, MM, B, R-Z, &, AA-CC, and WPA, CXXII–CXXVII, CXXXII–CXXXIV, CXLIII–CLXII, LXXXVIIA–B, CLXIX–CLXXIII, CLXXXIV–CLXXXVII, CXC–CXCVIII, SCDAH.

percent and, by 1790, in some regions, to 75 percent. In Virginia, concentration occurred, but at a much less intense pace. Even by midcentury about one-half of the colony's slaves lived on small units, and, by the 1780s, the proportion still stood between one-quarter and one-third.[24]

Variations over space and across time occurred in both regions. In South Carolina, the central inland parishes of Saint James Goose Creek, Saint John Berkeley, and Saint George Dorchester contained extremely large plantations as early as the 1730s. By midcentury, Saint James Goose Creek, which at that time probably boasted a larger proportion of rich householders than any other locality in British North America, had 70 percent of its slaves residing on units with more than fifty slaves. But, after 1750, the truly dynamic areas of the Lowcountry were the regions to the immediate north and south of the central inland region. By 1790, these areas had the heaviest concentration of large plantations. The concentration of large plantations was least marked in the parishes nearest to, and most remote from, Charleston. In the area closest to Carolina's major port town, truck farming opportunities always tended to

24. Henry Melchior Muhlenberg, *The Journals of Henry Melchior Muhlenberg*, trans. Theodore G. Tappert and John W. Doberstein, I (Philadelphia, 1942), 58; "Bolzius Answers a Questionnaire," trans. and ed. Loewald et al., *WMQ*, 3d Ser., XIV (1957), 234.

TABLE 2.
Plantation Size in Virginia, 1720–1779

| | Proportion of Slaves Living on Unit |||| |
| | Size of Unit (in Slaves) |||| |
Decade	1–5	6–10	11–20	21+	No. of Slaves
1700s	39%	19%	32%	10%	287
1710s	30	20	27	23	967
1720s	30	29	27	13	1,332
1730s	28	27	20	25	2,078
1740s	25	25	32	17	2,922
1750s	18	22	29	31	5,291
1760s	15	22	29	33	5,791
1770s	13	22	35	29	6,310

Note: The unit size ranges for Virginia estates are different from those for South Carolina (Table 1) for two reasons: (1) to reflect the smaller size of the former's estates and (2) to allow easy comparisons with other published data on plantation size in the Chesapeake region. See particularly Allan Kulikoff, *Tobacco and Slaves: The Development of Southern Cultures in the Chesapeake, 1680–1800* (Chapel Hill, N.C., 1986), 331, 338.

Sources: Inventories of Amelia, Charlotte, Chesterfield, Essex, Goochland, Halifax, Isle of Wight, Lunenburg, Mecklenburg, Northampton, Orange, Pittsylvania, Prince Edward, Spotsylvania, and York Counties.

keep plantations small. The city was a law unto itself. Few urban residents could boast of households numbering more than twenty slaves. In the northwest parts of the Georgetown region and the backcountry, the least commercialized parts of South Carolina, plantations were also generally small.[25]

In Virginia, the Middle Peninsula and the Peninsula were the first areas to turn heavily toward slave labor. But not until the 1730s and 1740s were a majority of this area's slaves resident on plantations of more than eleven slaves. Even in the 1780s, more than half of all blacks in the area between the Rappahannock and James Rivers lived on quarters with fewer than twenty slaves. Beginning about the second quarter of the eighteenth century, Virginia's most dynamic areas were the central piedmont and Southside. Although most piedmont slaves resided on quarters of eleven or more slaves at an early date—only

25. See Table 1; Philip D. Morgan, ed., "A Profile of a Mid-Eighteenth Century South Carolina Parish: The Tax Return of Saint James', Goose Creek, *SCHM*, LXXXI (1980), 51–65.

a decade or two later than in the oldest tidewater areas—the concentration of large plantations was never high. By the 1780s, when more Virginia slaves resided in the piedmont than in the tidewater, 60 percent resided on quarters with fewer than twenty slaves.[26]

Landholdings within both Virginia and South Carolina also varied significantly over time and across space. Early in a locality's history, landholdings tended to be large, but, as settlement thickened, a marked contraction in size inevitably occurred. This process was continually repeated in both regions as settlement fanned out into new areas. Landholdings thus tended to be larger on the frontier than in more mature areas. In South Carolina, plantation acreages were smallest in the parishes nearest Charleston; in Virginia, the Peninsula had the greatest concentration of small landholdings.

In spite of this universal process, landholdings were almost always larger in South Carolina than in Virginia. This contrast owed much, of course, to the large labor forces required in rice production, but was also due to the amount of land an individual laborer could tend in rice cultivation. In the middle of the eighteenth century, a Lowcountry slave could cultivate between three and four acres of rice; by the late eighteenth century, that average had increased to five acres. With a labor force of between thirty and forty slaves, a planter required between one hundred and two hundred acres of swampland alone to keep his workers profitably employed. A Chesapeake slave, in contrast, was expected to cultivate no more than two acres of tobacco. Even allowing for the extensive fallow periods that tobacco land required, a planter with fewer than ten hands could farm a total of two hundred acres for many years.[27]

In parts of the Lowcountry, the number of acres held by parish residents was staggeringly high. An incomplete listing of landholdings in Saint James Goose Creek, taken in 1745, reveals that three-quarters were more than five hundred acres, and the median was more than nine hundred acres. About forty years later in part of Saint Paul's Parish, about two-thirds of all holdings were more than five hundred acres, and the median was still eight hundred acres. In other areas close to Charleston, notably James Island, landholdings were much smaller. However, even in Christ Church Parish in 1784, the median landholding was more than three hundred acres, and almost a third of all

---

26. See Table 2; Philip D. Morgan and Michael L. Nicholls, "Slaves in Piedmont Virginia, 1720–1790," *WMQ*, 3d Ser., XLVI (1989), 241.

27. The laborer/acreage ratio is based on the observations of 25 18th-century commentators (1712–1796) and about 30 plantation sale advertisements in South Carolina newspapers where the number of field hands and amount of cleared rice acreage are given. See also James M. Clifton, "The Rice Industry in Colonial America," *Agric. Hist.*, LV (1981), 275. The corresponding ratio for the Chesapeake is based on the observations of 10 commentators (1701–1811).

TABLE 3.
Landholding in South Carolina Parishes, 1745–1785

Acres per Landholding	Saint James Goose Creek, 1745 (N=44)	Stono, Saint Paul, 1783 (N=41)	Prince Frederick, 1784 (N=171)	Christ Church, 1784 (N=86)	James Island, Saint Andrew, 1785 (N=32)
1–99	0%	5%	2%	7%	25%
100–200	7	12	27	29	25
201–300	2	2	19	14	22
301–500	16	17	23	19	16
501–1,000	34	24	21	15	12
1,001–2,000	16	22	8	8	0
2,001–3,000	11	10	1	5	0
3,001+	14	7	1	3	0
Total	100	99	100	100	100
Median no. of acres	908	800	350	310	202

Note: Most returns list also the landholdings of an individual outside his parish of residence. Where possible, these have been excluded from the present analysis in order to represent landownership within a particular locality.

Sources: Tax Return of the Parish of Saint James Goose Creek, 1745, loose papers, SPG; Tax Returns of Stono and East Side of Ponpon, St. Paul's Parish, 1783, of Christ Church Parish, 1784, of Prince Frederick Parish, 1784, and of James Island, Saint Andrew's Parish, 1785, SCDAH.

plantations were five hundred acres or more in size (see Table 3). In general, then, most Lowcountry slaves toward the end of the century could expect to live on large holdings. Thus, about two-thirds of the slaves of Saint Paul and a half of those in Christ Church belonged to planters who owned more than a thousand acres.

In stark contrast, the median number of acres owned by freeholders in various Virginia localities was generally no more than two hundred. In some tidewater counties by the late colonial period, two-thirds of planters held fewer than two hundred acres, and nine out of ten held fewer than five hundred acres. In piedmont counties, median landholdings could be twice the size of those in the tidewater, but, even so, most piedmont planters owned between

TABLE 4.
Landholding in Virginia Counties, 1768–1778

Acres per Landholding	Richmond, 1768 (N=236)	Loudoun, 1769 (N=287)	Norfolk, 1771 (N=502)	Lancaster, 1773 (N=284)	Isle of Wight, 1778 (N=122)
1–99	19%	5%	23%	29%	16%
100–200	41	34	43	44	39
201–300	13	18	14	11	20
301–500	14	24	10	8	10
501–1,000	7	14	6	4	9
1,001–2,000	4	3	2	3	8
2,001+	2	1	1	1	0
Total	100	99	99	100	102

Sources: Robert E. Brown and B. Katherine Brown, *Virginia, 1705–1786: Democracy or Aristocracy?* (East Lansing, Mich., 1964), 13–14; abstract from the Isle of Wight Property Book, VSL.

one hundred and two hundred acres by the late colonial period. In general, then, most Virginia slaves resided on smallholdings. In Isle of Wight County, only 14 percent of the slaves belonged to planters owning more than a thousand acres (see Table 4).[28]

These basic realities influenced slave life in two major ways. First, Lowcountry plantations assumed a more insular and inward-looking character than their Chesapeake counterparts. Because Chesapeake plantations were small, in numbers of both workers and acres, plantation boundaries tended to be porous. Second, the relative degree of stability available to slaves differed greatly between Chesapeake and Lowcountry. In South Carolina, the combination of large landholdings, the nonexhaustive nature of the rice crop, and soil properties meant that slaves and their descendants had a greater chance to remain on the same plantation than was the case in Virginia. Lowcountry tideland never wore out, its boosters claimed, and advertisements of plantation sales spoke of enough land being available to keep large labor forces busy for a hundred years

---

28. Even Chesapeake planters who had large amounts of land and large numbers of slaves organized their bondpeople into small working units and dispersed them across their far-flung holdings. For more statistics on median landholding in various Chesapeake counties, see Allan Kulikoff, *Tobacco and Slaves: The Development of Southern Cultures in the Chesapeake, 1680–1800* (Chapel Hill, N.C., 1986), 135, 156.

or more.[29] No such claims were ever heard from Chesapeake planters. Tobacco land could be worked for about three years in succession; it then had to be rested for another twenty. Matters were made worse because marshland was hardly ever used in colonial tobacco cultivation. For these reasons, Chesapeake planters soon looked westward for fresh lands to exploit.[30] Consequently, few Chesapeake plantations offered prospects for long-term stability. Production of the staple crop organized South Carolina slaves into large if isolated units and tied them closely to the coast; in Virginia, it confined them to small though connected units and dispersed them into the interior.

Just as some staples encouraged mobility and others promoted stability, some fostered diversification and others favored specialization. Where profits were low and uneven, planters tended to hedge their bets by turning to other crops and activities. Where profits, however fluctuating, remained high, planters tended to remain committed to their cash crop. Tobacco's low returns encouraged import replacement, the addition of supplementary crops, and pastoral farming; rice's high profits inhibited efforts at diversification.

Most South Carolina plantations produced rice but little else. Lowcountry planters generally had little capacity to produce their own goods or services. Nor did this colony's planters grow a wide range of crops or raise a great variety of livestock. Estates were particularly specialized in the early years of the rice boom—the late 1720s and 1730s. Although there was a movement toward import replacement and agricultural diversification in the depression years of the 1740s and mid-1750s, a resurgence in rice prices and accelerating indigo production guaranteed that the shift was short-lived. Alexander Garden, writing just as the late colonial boom got under way, bemoaned his

29. Gordon, "Journal," in Mereness, ed., *Travels in the American Colonies,* 396; Harper, ed., *Travels of William Bartram,* 30; George Faucheraud, *SCG,* Dec. 15, 1758; Henry Hyrne, ibid., July 10, 1755; Thomas Sacheverell, ibid., Aug. 18, 1758. George Ogilvie waxed enthusiastic about the capacities of the South Carolina "Low Lands calld Swamps [which] are so exceeding Rich that many of them which have been planted above Sixty years without rest or Manure of any kind produce as good Crops as at the first settling and are deemed inexhaustible" (George Ogilvie to Peggie, his sister, June 25, 1774, Ogilivie-Forbes of Boyndlie MSS). Another Scottish immigrant was equally impressed with his newly inherited plantation, particularly "the swamp, which has been cultivated for a number of years without any dung, and may be so for many generations without mising a Rice Crop" (John Martin to his son, John Martin Papers, SCHS). See also P. Purry, *A Description of the Province of South Carolina,* in Peter Force, comp., *Tracts and Other Papers . . . ,* II (Washington, D.C., 1836), tract xi, 5.

30. Edmund Berkeley and Dorothy Smith Berkeley, eds., *The Reverend John Clayton: A Parson with a Scientific Mind* (Charlottesville, Va., 1965), 79; Spooner, "A Topographical Description," *Tyler's Qtly. Hist. and Genealogical Mag.,* V (1923), 7; Carman, ed., *American Husbandry,* 164; Earle, *Evolution of a Tidewater Settlement System,* 25.

PLATE 3. Residence and Slave Quarters of Mulberry Plantation. *Thomas Coram. Circa 1800. A well-established Lowcountry plantation, with solid and symmetrical slave dwellings, though the thatched-roof construction suggests an African influence. Courtesy Carolina Art Association, Charleston*

inability to persuade Lowcountry planters of the benefits of diversification. "Unless evident and immediate profit allure them," he noted in the spring of 1759, "it's impossible by the strongest probable or most rational arguments to draw them from the common path to make the least trial of any thing that is proposed to them."[31]

Although no Chesapeake plantation approximated self-sufficiency, most had more items for home manufactures than their Lowcountry counterparts. Moreover, agricultural production—in range of crops and of livestock—was

31. Dr. Alexander Garden to H. Baker, May 10, 1759, Henry Baker Correspondence, John Rylands Library, Manchester, England. A useful study of the early South Carolina economy is Converse D. Clowse, *Economic Beginnings in Colonial South Carolina, 1670–1730* (Columbia, S.C., 1971). For the fluctuations of the economy after 1730, see Lewis Cecil Gray, *History of Agriculture in the Southern United States to 1860,* I (Gloucester, Mass., 1958 [orig. publ. Washington, D.C., 1933]), I, 277–297, 451–461; and George Rogers Taylor, "Wholesale Commodity Prices at Charleston, South Carolina, 1732–1791," *Journal of Economic and Business History,* IV (1932), 356–377. For the best general overview, see Coclanis, *The Shadow of a Dream,* chap. 3. For an analysis of the inventoried estates of colonial South Carolina and of two counties in Virginia according to two indexes—one measuring potential self-sufficiency, the other measuring the degree of specialization—see Philip D. Morgan, "The Development of Slave Culture in Eighteenth Century Plantation America" (Ph.D. diss., University College London, 1977), 20–31.

more diversified in Virginia than in South Carolina. The long period of stagnation in the tobacco economy, from the 1680s to the 1710s, encouraged the first significant diversification among the region's plantations, but later decades—notably the 1730s and 1760s—added impetus to the trend. Disastrous wheat harvests in the Mediterranean during the mid-1760s and a subsequent rise in European wheat prices greatly accelerated the spread of wheat farming. Diversification reached such a pitch in a few areas of the late colonial Chesapeake that tobacco was dethroned. Wheat became the principal market crop.[32]

This sweeping comparison of the changing economic orientations of plantations in the Chesapeake and Lowcountry obscures two significant variations. First, plantation size cut across the broad regional differences between South Carolina and Virginia, for it was a general rule that the larger the plantation, the greater the diversification. The ownership of large numbers of slaves encouraged or allowed planters to develop home manufactures and diversify agricultural production. Because large plantations were more commonly found in South Carolina than Virginia, the alternatives to rice production for Lowcountry slaves were always more available than the aggregate regional picture might suggest. Second, there were important regional variations within both Chesapeake and Lowcountry. In major sections of the Chesapeake—particularly the Eastern Shore, northern Maryland, and the southeastern tidewater—the shift from tobacco to grains occurred earlier and more fully than in the region as a whole. No marked shift out of staple production occurred in the Lowcountry, except in one localized area—the immediate hinterland of Charleston—where the growth of a major urban market gave rise to market-

---

32. Russell R. Menard, "The Tobacco Industry in the Chesapeake Colonies, 1617–1730: An Interpretation," *Research in Economic History*, V (1980), 141; Gray, *History of Agriculture*, I, 270–272; David Klingaman, "The Significance of Grain in the Development of the Tobacco Colonies," *Jour. Econ. Hist.*, XXIX (1969), 270–271; Jacob M. Price, *France and the Chesapeake: A History of the French Tobacco Monopoly, 1674–1791, and of Its Relationship to the British and American Tobacco Trade*, I (Ann Arbor, Mich., 1973), 668–671; Earle, *Evolution of a Tidewater Settlement System*, 101–141; Clemens, *The Atlantic Economy*, 168–223; Sarah Shaver Hughes, "Elizabeth City County, Virginia, 1782–1810: The Economic and Social Structure of a Tidewater County in the Early National Years" (Ph.D. diss., College of William and Mary, 1975); James Blaine Gouger III, "Agricultural Change in the Northern Neck of Virginia, 1700–1860: An Historical Geography" (Ph.D. diss., University of Florida, 1976); Harold B. Gill, Jr., "Wheat Culture in Colonial Virginia," *Agric. Hist.*, LII (1978), 380–393; Peter Victor Bergstrom, "Markets and Merchants: Economic Diversification in Colonial Virginia, 1700–1775" (Ph.D. diss., University of New Hampshire, 1980); Lois Green Carr, "Diversification in the Colonial Chesapeake: Somerset County, Maryland, in Comparative Perspective," in Carr, Philip D. Morgan, and Jean B. Russo, eds., *Colonial Chesapeake Society* (Chapel Hill, N.C., 1988), 342–388; Russo, "Self-sufficiency and Local Exchange: Free Craftsmen in the Rural Chesapeake Economy," ibid., 389–432.

gardening plantations. Although more Virginia than South Carolina plantations seemed to have engaged in naval stores production, at least from the 1730s onward, one area in each colony concentrated heavily on this activity. In South Carolina, the northwestern section of Winyaw specialized in naval stores; in Virginia, tar and turpentine were the staples of the opposite quadrant, the southeastern tidewater. Both colonies, however, were eclipsed by North Carolina, which became the primary American supplier of naval stores to Britain for most of the eighteenth century.[33]

Although the trend toward diversification of agricultural products and crafts proceeded at different rates within the various subregions of these two slave societies, the broad societal comparison offers a stark contrast. Differences in the changing nature of plantation operations in Virginia and South Carolina structured the work patterns of slaves, determining what combination of crops they grew, what tools they used, and what livestock they tended. The range of plantation activities—whether varied or restricted—profoundly shaped slave life.

Differences in diversification were most evident in the production of provisions. Early in the century, Virginia slaves produced twice as much corn per head as their South Carolina counterparts, and by the Revolutionary era four or even five times as much. In South Carolina, the average amount of corn produced by an adult slave was 17 bushels in the 1730s, 20 bushels in the 1750s, and 22 bushels in the 1770s.[34] In Essex County, Virginia, an adult slave produced an average of 34 bushels of corn in the 1720s, 57 bushels in the 1740s, and 81 bushels in the 1760s. By the Revolutionary era, the average Chesapeake slave produced more than 100 bushels of corn.[35] A number of reasons explain

---

33. John Guerard to Thomas Rock, June 10, 1752, John Guerard Letterbook, SCHS; Fred Shelley, ed., "The Journal of Ebenezer Hazard in Virginia, 1777," *VMHB*, LXII (1954), 412. For more on naval stores, see Gray, *History of Agriculture*, I, 151–160; Sinclair Snow, "Naval Stores in Colonial Virginia," *VMHB*, LXXII (1964), 75–93; and G. Melvin Herndon, "Naval Stores in Colonial Georgia," *GHQ*, LII (1968), 426–433.

34. These estimates are taken from those inventories appraised in the winter months, especially where appraisers noted a whole crop of corn: 14 in the 1730s, 131 in the 1750s, and 92 in the 1770s. Undoubtedly, these totals underestimate the actual amount produced by a field hand, because skilled hands were not always noted and one can never be sure that a whole crop is being appraised. For higher ratios (about 30 bushels per field hand in the 1750s), see inventory of Joseph Wragg, Dec. 3, 1751, Inventories, WPA, CXLIII, 65–67, and inventory of Thomas Waring, Jan. 31, 1754, ibid., CXLIV, 227–229. From occasional inventories and other evidence, it appears that a Lowcountry slave generally tended little more than an acre of provision crops; see, for example, inventory of John Haynes, Sept. 14, 1738, ibid., CV, 308–312; and De Brahm, *De Brahm's Report of the General Survey*, 92.

35. Essex County inventories that permit such calculations number 11 in the 1720s, 12 in the 1740s, and 8 in the 1760s. For equally high or even higher corn per hand ratios, see, for

the disparity. Slaves on Virginia plantations had more dependents than their South Carolina counterparts, and therefore a field hand in the Chesapeake had to cultivate more provisions to feed the children. Rough rice was used as a food for slaves in South Carolina; peas and potatoes were much more in evidence on South Carolina estates than on those in Virginia (see Table 5). Slaves produced more food on their own time in South Carolina than in Virginia, and this independent subsistence was not measured by contemporaries. Most important, Virginia planters raised corn for profit as well as for subsistence, something few Lowcountry planters did.[36]

Contemporaries recognized the difference. Richard Oswald, writing in 1770, marveled at how Virginians raised corn "in such abundance that it becomes the source of plenty in everything else, Poultry, Hogs, feeding Horses and Cattle." Indeed, he thought "Indian Corn is always in that Country the principal object, preferable even to Tobacco—since without plenty of Corn the Country is always In distress." A decade later, Johann Schoepf declared that the "whole compass" of Virginia husbandry rested on an adequate supply of maize. The preferences of Carolinians are nowhere better captured than in the advice Josiah Smith, the manager of two Lowcountry plantations, gave to their owner, George Austin. In 1774, Smith warned against "planting corn at Ashepoo sufficient to serve" it and the other plantation at Pedee. "If more corn is to be raised there than common," he added, "there must of consequence less Rice be planted, and the latter is the most profitable Grain, besides 'twill cost you full 2/6 p. Bushel to be first brought to Charles-Town and then carried to Pedee . . . ; twill therefore be more saving by [being] purchas'd at Pedee, or

---

example, Jerdone Letter Book, 1736–1744, 184, Jerdone Family Papers, W and M; *Thomas Dillon v. Henry Armistead*, Feb. 10, 1744, Caroline County Court Orders, 1740–1746, 254–255, VSL; William Dabney Account Book, 1749–1757, VHS; Philip Grymes's accounts, 1765, Harrison Family Papers, VHS; Jack P. Greene, ed., *The Diary of Colonel Landon Carter of Sabine Hall, 1752–1778*, 2 vols. (Charlottesville, Va., 1965), 389, 900–901. Carter expected his slaves to tend about 9 acres of corn each (ibid., 608, 679, 906). See also Earle, *Evolution of a Tidewater Settlement System*, 128; Clemens, *The Atlantic Economy*, 175; and, most comprehensively, Walsh, "Plantation Management in the Chesapeake," *Jour. Econ. Hist.*, XLIX (1989), 398.

36. For evidence on dependents, see Chapter 9; for food production in the slaves' own time, see the section on diet in Chapter 2. A comparison of corn and wheat exports from South Carolina and Virginia points up the contrast in diversification: see Converse D. Clowse, *Measuring Charleston's Overseas Commerce, 1717–1767: Statistics from the Port's Naval Lists* (Washington, D.C., 1981), 75–77, 86–87; and David C. Klingaman, *Colonial Virginia's Coastwise and Grain Trade* (New York, 1975). Robert Carter of Nomini Hall emphasized to one of his correspondents that "indian Corn and Hogs are part of the Profits of my Plantation," pointing out that there remained in his "Granaries on Potomac River 4500 bushells of Indian Corn" (Robert Carter Letterbook, 1764–1768, 105, microfilm, CW).

TABLE 5.
Primary Production of Virginia and South Carolina Plantations, 1730–1776

	Percentage of Plantations Producing	
Type of Product	Virginia (*N*=1,529)	South Carolina (*N*=4,914)
Rice	0	25
Indigo	0	11
Tobacco	13	0
Wheat	13	2
Corn	29	34
Potatoes	1	9
Peas	8	17
Oats	1	2
Tar, pitch, timber	18	6
Skins	32	11
Wool, cotton	34	9

Note: These are minimum figures, for appraisers generally valued only primary products that were stored. Crops in the field usually went unappraised.

Sources: Inventories of South Carolina (Table 1) and inventories of York and Essex Counties, Virginia (Table 2).

from the Boats that pass your Landing at Georgetown." Smith was not counseling that provisions ought to be neglected but, rather, that grain should be purchased from the backcountry in the case of a poor harvest. This strategy became commonplace among tidewater rice planters in the late eighteenth century.[37]

Even the tools slaves used reflect the degree of diversification of their plantation regime. On specialized rice plantations, slaves spent much of their time in

---

37. Richard Oswald to Governor James Grant, June 8, 1770, bundle 295, Papers of General James Grant of Ballindalloch; Schoepf, *Travels in the Confederation*, II, 89; Josiah Smith to George Austin, Jan. 31, 1774, Josiah Smith Letterbook, UNC; La Rochefoucault Liancourt, *Travels*, I, 597; John Drayton, *A View of South Carolina as Respects Her Natural and Civil Concerns* (Spartanburg, S.C., 1972 [orig. publ. 1802]), 113. The development of tidal river plantations reduced the acreage devoted to provisions. On such plantations less upland acreage was available for cultivating provisions, slave labor was in greater demand to clear swamps and build extensive irrigation systems, and per capita profits were higher than on inland swamp plantations. All these characteristics led to more specialized, less diversified rice plantations.

TABLE 6.
Primary Equipment on Virginia and South Carolina Plantations, 1730–1776

	Percentage of Plantations Owning	
Type of Equipment	Virginia (*N*=1,529)	South Carolina (*N*=4,914)
Axes		
1–9	47	29
10+	2	10
Hoes		
1–9	37	23
10+	8	13
Spades		
1–9	11	14
10+	1	2
Rice/tobacco hooks	19	23
Plows	23	14
Vats	1	20
Fishing gear	9	12
Plantation guns	48	63

Sources: Inventories of South Carolina (Table 1) and inventories of York and Essex Counties, Virginia (Table 2).

irrigation work, handling spades and axes. On diversified Chesapeake plantations, slaves wielded a range of hoes, a function of the varied tasks involved in cultivating tobacco and grain crops (see Table 6). Furthermore, by the late colonial period, from a third to a half of Chesapeake plantations had plows. By contrast, when Ebenezer Hazard traveled through the Lowcountry in 1778, he saw few plows.[38] The greater specialization of Lowcountry plantations produced a more restricted range of agricultural implements than could be found on Chesapeake quarters.

38. Inventory of Joseph Smith, Nov. 20, 1728, Essex County Will Book, no. 4, 280–281, VSL; Morgan, "Development of Slave Culture," 455; Earle, *Evolution of a Tidewater Settlement System,* 122–123; Kulikoff, *Tobacco and Slaves,* 409; H. Roy Merrens, "A View of Coastal South Carolina in 1778: The Journal of Ebenezer Hazard," *SCHM,* LXXIII (1972), 187. Even as late as the first decade of the 19th century, Edisto Islanders were "unacquainted with the plough, the harrow, the scythe, rake, reaping hooks, wagons, sledges and such like implements which are necessary to carry on farming" (Ramsay, *History of South-Carolina,* II, 290).

TABLE 7.
Livestock on Virginia and South Carolina Plantations, 1730–1776

	Percentage of Plantations Owning	
Types of Livestock	Virginia (*N*=1,529)	South Carolina (*N*=4,914)
Cattle		
1–49	78	52
50–99	5	13
100+	1	7
Horses		
1–9	75	57
10–29	2	19
30+	0	3
Hogs		
1–9	22	14
10–29	33	25
30+	17	15
Sheep	42	30
Oxen	11	14
Poultry	84	12

Sources: Inventories of South Carolina (Table 1) and inventories of York and Essex Counties, Virginia (Table 2).

Livestock formed an integral part of the plantation economies of both the Chesapeake and the Lowcountry, but the greater agricultural diversification of the Chesapeake manifested itself in a more extensive animal husbandry. Whereas no fewer than four out of five Virginia plantations owned at least one cow throughout the eighteenth century, a quarter of South Carolina plantations owned no cattle (see Table 7). Almost three-quarters of Chesapeake plantations had hogs, whereas about half of Lowcountry estates had none. Sheep and poultry were more evident on Virginia than on South Carolina plantations. Chesapeake slaves, in other words, worked with a greater variety of domesticated animals than their Lowcountry counterparts.

Although more slaves in Virginia worked with stock, more slaves in South Carolina worked with large herds of cattle. South Carolina was the first North American colony to develop a cowpen complex or system of open-range ranches run by slaves. As John Bartram noted in 1765, there is "commonly 3[,]

4[,] or 5 negroes at A pen to take care of the cattle and horses." As a result, some slaves developed considerable herding skills. Ann Palmer's estate included one slave "not inferior to any in the Province for tending a stock of Horses and Cattle"; two slaves belonging to a Saint John's Parish cowpen were "excellent cattle hunters"; and Edmund Bellinger, when offering his five hundred cattle and fifty steers for sale, mentioned "a very good Negro hunter . . . well acquainted with all the woods where the stock ranges." In addition to knowing the terrain, cowpen keepers became good horsemen. Philander and Paul, for example, were "both very expert in riding." Mounted herdsmen were rare in West Africa, but nightly penning of cattle was an African custom, the construction of wattle fences was reminiscent of Fulani brush pens, and a possible African etymological antecedent for a motherless calf is the term *dogi*, a Bambara word meaning "small." Nevertheless, as Terry G. Jordan has noted, there is "no compelling evidence of meaningful African influence in the cultures and adaptive systems of the various American cattle frontiers." What is clear is that these cowpen keepers, ever on the move, formed a distinct community on the fringes of Lowcountry society, likened by one contemporary to modern Bedouin. Consequently, Cain, a runaway slave who had been a cattle hunter at the Saltketchers, knew "most of the plantations and cowpens in those parts." By contrast, in Virginia it was not a specialist herder who gained employment by driving "cattle from the Northern Neck, to sell in other parts of the country"; rather, appropriately enough, the man was a carpenter and joiner who could "turn his hand" to almost anything.[39]

The pattern characteristic of these two regional economies—one of specialization in the Lowcountry and diversification in the Chesapeake—applies as much to craft operations as to the raising of livestock. The agricultural diversi-

39. Bartram, "Diary," ed. Harper, Am. Phil. Soc., *Trans.*, N.S., XXXIII (1942–1944), 26; Mrs. Ann Palmer's estate, *SCG*, Jan. 31, 1771; *SC and AGG*, Feb. 18, 1779; Edmund Bellinger, *SCG*, Apr. 20, 1752; Lachlan McGillivray, ibid., Apr. 17, 1762; Terry G. Jordan, *North American Cattle-Ranching Frontiers: Origins, Diffusion, and Differentiation* (Albuquerque, N.Mex., 1993), 63, 83, 116–117, 311–312; De Brahm, *De Brahm's Report of the General Survey*, 95; Isaac McPherson, *SC and AGG*, Apr. 18, 1764; Thomas Jones, *VaG or AA*, July 9, 1785. In 1742, Jonathan Bryan lent Johann Bolzius "a skilled negro who readied and somewhat tamed a previously unridden horse that belongs to us" (George Fenwick Jones, "John Martin Boltzius' Trip to Charleston, October 1742," *SCHM*, LXXXII [1981], 107). See also Gary S. Dunbar, "Colonial Carolina Cowpens," *Agric. Hist.*, XXXV (1961), 125–130; James C. Bonner, "The Open Range Livestock Industry in Colonial Georgia," *Georgia Review*, XCVII (1984), 85–92; John S. Otto, "The Origins of Cattle-Ranching in Colonial South Carolina, 1670–1715," *SCHM*, LXXXVII (1986), 117–124; Otto, "Livestock-Raising in Early South Carolina, 1670–1700: Prelude to the Rice Plantation Economy," *Agric. Hist.*, LXI, no. 4 (Fall 1987), 13–24; Mart A. Stewart, "'Whether Wast, Deodand, or Stray': Cattle, Culture, and the Environment in Early Georgia," ibid., LXV, no. 3 (1991), 1–28.

TABLE 8.

Secondary and Tertiary Equipment on Virginia and South Carolina Plantations, 1730–1776

	Percentage of Plantations Owning	
Type of Equipment	Virginia (N=1,529)	South Carolina (N=4,914)
Woodworking	63	51
Spinning	59	27
Leatherworking	33	7
Shoemaking	21	7
Brickmaking	15	10
Blacksmithing	3	6
Tailoring	3	2
Boats, canoes	11	22
Carts, saddles	69	71

Sources: Inventories of South Carolina (Table 1) and inventories of York and Essex Counties, Virginia (Table 2).

fication so evident in Chesapeake plantations extended to the capability for home manufacture and repair. By midcentury, about 60 percent of Virginia estates contained spinning wheels, cards, and woodworking tools. Most planters were in a position to make their own thread and yarn, produce and repair rudimentary domestic utensils, put up fences, cut firewood, and erect simple buildings (see Table 8). Virginia was the leading hemp producer in North America, and some of the crop was made into fabric and rope in the colony. Lumbering was also important in the Chesapeake. According to one observer, "The woods on a tobacco plantation must be in great plenty for the winter employment of slaves else the planters' profits will be less than those of his neighbors." However, plantation self-sufficiency should not be exaggerated, for it was a rare estate that engaged in much blacksmithing, shoemaking, or tailoring. Furthermore, very few Chesapeake plantations employed specialized tradespeople. Rather, perhaps one or two slaves on any estate gained familiarity with craft tools without qualifying themselves for the more specialized role of artisan.[40]

40. Earle, *Evolution of a Tidewater Settlement System,* 101–141; Russo, "Self-sufficiency and Local Exchange," in Carr, Morgan, and Russo, eds., *Colonial Chesapeake Society,* 389–

Although only a minority of South Carolina plantations—and far fewer proportionately than in Virginia—had any significant amounts of craft equipment, a few Lowcountry plantations specialized in craft production on a scale rarely seen in the Chesapeake. When the estate of John Robinson, a butcher who lived four miles from Charleston, was auctioned off in 1740, five slaves, all "Butchers by Trade," formed the prime assets. James Fabian operated a large tanyard in Saint Paul's Parish. In 1768, it contained tanning materials worth more than a thousand pounds, and most of his ten adult male slaves worked as tanners, curriers, and shoemakers. In the same year, Richard Downes put five leatherworkers up for sale. He claimed that one of his tanners was "capable of managing and undertaking the whole care of a tanyard" and that one of his shoemakers had "been entrusted with the care of a shoemaker's shop, without any assistance from any white man." In 1769, William Smith operated a tanyard in Prince George Parish that employed four shoemakers, one leather currier, and a tanner.[41] This level of specialization was rarely equaled on Chesapeake estates.

Transportation, particularly by water, was also more specialized on South Carolina than on Virginia plantations. Although only a minority of planters owned watercraft in either of the two colonies, twice as many Lowcountry as Chesapeake planters owned them (Table 8). The bulk commodity, rice, was best transported by water, whereas tobacco could be efficiently "rolled" across land—as long as the distances were not too great—to the nearest shipping point. For the same reason, watercraft tended to be larger in South Carolina than in Virginia. In the Lowcountry, large planters generally owned schooners and offered packet services to their neighbors. In 1768, one observer estimated that there were "upwards of 130 Boats and Schooners," built and owned in the colony, "threefourths of them decked, carrying from 10 to 50 tons, at four barrels of rice to the ton, employed in bringing the Country Produce to this market."[42]

Canoes were more common on South Carolina than on Virginia planta-

---

432; Gray, *History of Agriculture,* I, 152; G. Melvin Herndon, "Hemp in Colonial Virginia," *Agric. Hist.,* XXXVII (1963), 86–93; Herndon, "A War-Inspired Industry: The Manufacture of Hemp in Virginia during the Revolution," *VMHB,* LXXIV (1966), 301–311; Herndon, "The Significance of the Forest to the Tobacco Plantation Economy in Antebellum Virginia," *Plantation Society,* I (1981), 430–439. On the relative paucity of slave tradesmen on Chesapeake estates, see Chapter 4.

41. Alexander Smith and Robert Raper, *SCG,* July 5, 1740; inventory of James Fabian, Sept. 10, 1768, Inventory Book, X, 385–387, SCDAH; Richard Downes, *SCG,* May 2, 1768; inventory of William Smith, July 13, 1769, Inventory Book, Y, 96–100, SCDAH. See Chapter 4 for a fuller analysis of this development.

42. *SCG,* June 27, 1768.

tions. The expansion of tobacco production into the piedmont revived this form of water transport among some inland Chesapeake planters. One of the pioneers, the Reverend Robert Rose noted in 1749 that his "people were making a Canoe, being the 3d, for carrying Down Tobo"; a year later, his "people" were again "busie in Making Canoes." A local development in Virginia, canoe making was more widespread throughout South Carolina. Estate surveys of Lowcountry plantations indicate that some slaves must have crossed rivers continually to tend fields on opposing banks. Both Virginia and Carolina legislators passed laws outlawing various forms of property ownership among slaves, but only in Carolina were canoes specifically prohibited. The ban could not have been effective, because interrogations of South Carolina slaves suspected of rebellion in 1749 revealed that they had widespread access to canoes. In 1762, the administrator of one Lowcountry estate paid five pounds to a black man for making a canoe in order to retrieve a slave belonging to the plantation. Thirty years later, a manager of a Santee plantation observed that "almost every Man in the plantation has a Canoe." More than twice as many South Carolina runaway slaves fled in boats and canoes as did Virginia fugitives. Waterborne runaways in the Lowcountry made their escape in cypress canoes, often about twenty-five feet long, four feet wide, usually four-oared, and occasionally two-masted, whereas Virginia watercraft tended to be much smaller.[43]

Slaves were more likely to transport staples from the plantation to the shipping point by horse-drawn cart or wagon than by any other means. From the 1730s onward, more than two-thirds of South Carolina and Virginia plantations contained either a cart, a wagon, or cart wheels. Because of the lack of boats on Chesapeake estates, the primary mode of transportation was undoubtedly overland. Perhaps because of more extensive horse ownership on Virginia than South Carolina plantations, more fugitives from Virginia made

43. Ralph Emmett Fall, ed., *The Diary of Robert Rose: A View of Virginia by a Scottish Colonial Parson* (Verona, Va., 1977), 53, 75; compare Thomas Cooper and David J. McCord, eds., *The Statutes at Large of South Carolina,* 10 vols. (Columbia, S.C., 1836–1841), VII, 382, 409, with William Waller Hening, ed., *The Statutes at Large: Being a Collection of All the Laws of Virginia . . . ,* III (Richmond, Va., 1809), 103, 459–460; Philip D. Morgan and George D. Terry, "Slavery in Microcosm: A Conspiracy Scare in Colonial South Carolina," *Southern Studies,* XXI (1982), 121–145; inventory of James Cathcart, May 22, 1762, Inventories, WPA, LXXXVIIA, 277–278; F. DuPont to Gabriel Manigault, Mar. 9, 1792, Manigault Family Papers, USC; William Smith, *SCG,* Oct. 6, 15, 1758, Feb. 1, 1759 (large runaway group). For some good descriptions of canoes taken by runaways, see James Searle, *SCG,* June 17, 1732, Mathurin Guerin, ibid., Oct. 3, 1761, John Rose, ibid., July 20, 1765, Elias Wigfall, ibid., Jan. 12, 1766, Torrans, Poaug, and Co., *SCG and CJ,* Jan. 12, 1768, Nathaniel Bacon-Burwell, *VaG* (Parks), Dec. 17, 1736, and William Flood, ibid. (P and D), Apr. 19, 1770. For escapes by boat or canoe, I count 94 South Carolina runaways between 1732 and 1779 and 37 Virginia runaways between 1736 and 1790 in the respective newspapers.

PLATE 4. *Extraordinary Appearances in the Heavens, and on Earth. Benjamin Henry Latrobe. 1797. Black wagoners before a "most perfect and singular rainbow." Courtesy Maryland Historical Society*

their escape on horseback. By the end of eighteenth century, specialist wagoners were present in the Chesapeake: Lewis, for example, had "been bred to the carting business, and is very expert in driving a cart, and in the management of oxen." Even in South Carolina, where schooners were the main vehicle for transporting rice to Charleston, more slaves were probably part-time wagoners or carters than boatmen. By the end of the eighteenth century, as John Drayton noted, "ox carts, capable of carrying three or four barrels of rice, are, almost, solely the mode of land transportation for the rice planters." Some inland rice plantations employed oxcarts, drawn by three to four yoke of oxen and tended by two to three "negro drivers," to make a round-trip of twenty to twenty-five miles in a day.⁴⁴

Two contrasting plantation regimes inhabited mainland British North America. Large, specialized holdings characterized the rice regime, whereas the

44. I count 44 South Carolina and 55 Virginia fugitives on horseback. Francis Jerdone, *VaG and GA,* Oct. 6, 1790; Drayton, *View of South Carolina,* 141–142. See also Earle, *Evolution of a Tidewater Settlement System,* 142–157; and Kulikoff, *Tobacco and Slaves,* 94–95, 210–214, 409.

TWO PLANTATION WORLDS : 57

keynote of the tobacco region was its variety. Virginia slaves spent more time growing grains, handled a greater range of agricultural implements, generally raised more livestock, and engaged in a wider range of craft activities than their counterparts in South Carolina. However, if Lowcountry slaves followed a more uniform, monotonous routine, they experienced more specialized opportunities than Chesapeake slaves. Large schooners plied South Carolina's waterways, vast cattle-raising operations fringed the hinterland, and specialized craft operations serviced rice and indigo plantations. Slaves constituted the bulk of the work force in all of these activities.

TWO POPULATIONS

Staple production not only created two different plantation systems but also helped shape the volume, pace, and character of the forced migration of Africans and, consequently, the racial composition of each region's population. At the same time, the slave population began—at different times in Virginia and South Carolina—to grow more from natural increase than from immigration. As a result of the differential interaction of immigration and natural growth, the structures of the Chesapeake and Lowcountry populations assumed markedly different configurations.

Patterns of African immigration to Virginia and South Carolina were strikingly dissimilar. South Carolina imported about twice as many Africans as did Virginia, a disparity that assumed even greater proportions because the Lowcountry slave population was always much smaller than that of the Chesapeake. The pace of immigration also varied markedly: Virginia turned to Africans earlier than South Carolina but relinquished its reliance much earlier, too. In addition, South Carolina's Africans were sold more quickly, more centrally, and in larger groups than those in Virginia. Africans were far more evident in the Lowcountry than in the Chesapeake.

Because South Carolina imported far more Africans than Virginia, it was a more important destination for slaving vessels, which also shaped the contours of the slave population. Furthermore, although adults formed the vast majority of slaves brought into both regions, South Carolina received fewer adolescents and children—slaves less preferred by planters—than did Virginia. Finally, as a testament to the colony's importance to slave traders, South Carolina received Africans fairly evenly throughout the year, whereas Virginia's trade was confined to a much shorter period.

Direct importations of slaves from Africa began first in Virginia. During the 1680s, perhaps 2,000 Africans arrived in the colony. This number probably doubled in the 1690s; and, in the first decade of the eighteenth century, im-

TABLE 9.
African Immigration to Virginia and South Carolina, 1700–1790

	No. of African Immigrants	
Decade	Virginia	South Carolina
1700s	7,700	3,000
1710s	6,750	6,000
1720s	12,700	11,600
1730s	15,700	21,150
1740s	12,000	1,950
1750s	9,200	16,500
1760s	9,700	21,850
1770s	3,900	18,850
1780s	0	10,000
Total	77,650	110,900

Notes: Numbers rounded to nearest 50. Some figures, particularly for the first three decades of the eighteenth century, are rough estimates. For example, Virginia's known African immigration in the 1700s was 7,282, which has been revised upward slightly to account for small numbers of unreported imports from some West Indian islands and incomplete reporting for the year 1709. For South Carolina, known immigration in the 1700s was only 206 Africans. From the growth in the slave population in that decade and the sex ratios reported in two censuses of 1703 and 1708, I arrived at the estimate of 3,000. Procedures used in estimating unknowns between 1725 and 1774 in Virginia and between 1750 and 1807 in South Carolina can be found in Philip D. Morgan and Michael L. Nicholls, "Slaves in Piedmont Virginia, 1720– 1790," *WMQ*, 3d Ser., XLVI (1989), 251; and Morgan, "Black Society in the Lowcountry," in Berlin and Hoffman, eds., *Slavery and Freedom*, 89.

Sources: Walter Minchinton et al., eds., *Virginia Slave-Trade Statistics, 1698–1775* (Richmond, Va., 1984); Naval Office Shipping Lists, PRO; newspaper advertisements for African cargoes in South Carolina newspapers; South Carolina Treasury General Duty Books, SCDAH.

ports of slaves averaged at least 750 a year (see Table 9).[45] South Carolina began to receive Africans only at the turn of the century. Imports averaged about 300

45. For late-17th-century Virginia, see Russell Menard, "From Servants to Slaves: The Transformation of the Chesapeake Labor System," *So. Studies,* XVI (1977), 367; Allan Kulikoff, "A 'Prolifick' People: Black Population Growth in the Chesapeake Colonies, 1700–1790," ibid., XVI (1977), 392; and Wesley Frank Craven, *White, Red, and Black: The Seventeenth-Century Virginian* (Charlottesville, Va., 1971), 86–87. Many of the headright claims of the 1690s were deferred from the previous decade, but African imports nevertheless increased substantially from one decade to the next.

a year in the first decade of the 1700s and probably doubled in the 1710s. The character of each colony's slave population thus changed within the space of a generation. By 1710, the slave populations of both colonies contained African majorities, though the smaller black population of South Carolina rendered newcomers more prominent in that colony (see Table 10).

In the 1720s and 1730s, African immigration rose markedly in both colonies. Virginia and South Carolina received about the same number of Africans in the 1720s: an average of about twelve hundred a year. In the next decade, African imports continued to grow in both colonies, but at a much faster pace in South Carolina. The Lowcountry's African imports almost doubled in the 1730s, whereas in Virginia the increase was just over 20 percent. By the late 1730s, South Carolina's reliance on imported Africans gave rise to the popular adage, "Negroes may be said to be the Bait proper for catching a Carolina planter, as certain as Beef to catch a shark." As a partial reflection of these divergent importation trends, South Carolina's slave population still stood at two-thirds African in 1740, whereas in Virginia the proportion had declined to only a third.[46]

The 1740s marked a slowing down of the rate of African immigration into both colonies. South Carolina had gorged so heavily that it fasted almost the whole decade. Fewer than two thousand Africans arrived in the colony in the 1740s. Virginia had indulged less greedily, and its belt-tightening was only modest, although imports of Africans decreased toward the end of the 1740s. As a result, the proportion of Africans declined substantially in both places. At midcentury, perhaps for the first time in the century, Africans were a minority of South Carolina slaves—just over 40 percent—but this was twice the proportion of Africans among Virginia slaves.

The generation before the Revolution saw a continued divergence in the size of the two colonies' slave imports. From midcentury, South Carolina's voraciousness for Africans grew apace. The number of African immigrants rose in each decade; and, in the last five years before the Revolution, the colony imported almost as many Africans as in any previous ten-year period. Virginia's desire for Africans, by contrast, grew progressively more satiated. Indeed, from around midcentury, tidewater planters had little need for new slaves; the demand came almost entirely from the piedmont.[47] Fewer than a thousand Africans a year arrived in the colony throughout the 1750s and 1760s; and, in the last five years before the Revolution, Virginia imported only about

46. *SCG*, Mar. 9, 1738.
47. Morgan and Nicholls, "Slaves in Piedmont Virginia," *WMQ*, 3d Ser., XLVI (1989), 219. Among advertised runaways in Virginia newspapers (1736–1779), I count 44 Africans from tidewater and 75 from piedmont (17% and 31%, respectively, of all slaves with known birthplace), further confirmation of the primacy of piedmont demand.

TABLE 10.
Africans in the Virginia and South Carolina Slave Populations, 1700–1800

	Virginia			South Carolina		
Year	Total Slaves	Africans	%	Total Slaves	Africans	%
1700	13,000	6,500	50	2,400	1,200	50
1710	19,500	10,161	52	5,000	3,366	67
1720	27,000	12,209	45	12,000	6,991	58
1730	40,000	17,530	44	22,700	13,904	63
1740	65,000	22,288	34	39,000	25,556	66
1750	105,000	22,544	21	40,000	16,858	42
1760	140,500	19,236	14	57,000	22,243	39
1770	180,500	15,973	9	82,000	28,933	35
1780	224,000	10,916	5	94,000	31,042	33
1790	293,000	4,740	2	107,000	24,884	23
1800	346,000	678	*	146,150	12,166	8

* Less than .5%

Notes: The number of slaves in each colony is based on my assessment of the best estimates, sometimes modified by analysis of a realistic rate of natural increase of the slave population and estimated African immigration in any decade.

The number of Africans thought to be present in the population in any given year is derived from annual African importations assembled and summarized in Table 9. The number of Africans in 1700 is an educated guess. From thereon, I have calculated surviving African immigrants over the first 10 years by using the low mortality life table outlined in Allan Kulikoff, "A 'Prolifick' People: Black Population Growth in the Chesapeake Colonies, 1700–1790," *Southern Studies,* XVI (1977), 421, that is, .900 to .739 survival rate from 1st to 10th year after importation. If I had assumed higher mortality, the natural growth rates of the two slave populations, as reported in Tables 19 and 20, would have been unrealistically high. I did precisely that in my first estimates of the natural increase of South Carolina's slave population from 1750 to 1810 in my "Black Society in the Lowcountry, 1760–1810," in Ira Berlin and Ronald Hoffman, eds., *Slavery and Freedom in the Age of the American Revolution* (Charlottesville, Va., 1983), 89. Over the remaining period, I assume that .407 survive after 20 years, .204 after 30 years, and .020 after 39 years, with no survivor 40 years after importation.

Sources: U.S., Bureau of the Census, *Historical Statistics of the United States, Colonial Times to 1970,* 2 vols. (Washington, D.C., 1976), 1168; Kulikoff, "A 'Prolifick' People," *Southern Studies,* XVI (1977), 391–428; Peter H. Wood, *Black Majority: Negroes in Colonial South Carolina from 1870 through the Stono Rebellion* (New York, 1974), 144–145; Morgan, "Black Society in the Lowcountry," in Berlin and Hoffman, eds., *Slavery and Freedom,* 89.

one-fifth the number received by South Carolina. On the eve of the Revolution, more than a third of South Carolina's slave population consisted of Africans, whereas in Virginia more than nine of ten slaves were American-born.

The Revolution set the seal on the divergent experiences of the two regions. Virginia had been weaning itself gradually of African supplies in the last years of the colonial era. The process was essentially complete by the onset of the Revolution. Suffering no great wartime loss of black labor, Virginia never again imported Africans. In South Carolina, by contrast, the Revolution interrupted a veritable orgy of African slave-trading. Eschewing fresh supplies of slaves would have been far more difficult, but nonimportation was made impossible by the particularly devastating loss of black labor experienced during South Carolina's vicious Revolutionary war.[48] Consequently, in the 1780s at least ten thousand Africans landed in South Carolina, and, in the following decade, the state's planters bought untold numbers of Africans that had been imported into Georgia. As one Georgian reported in 1784, the "Negro business . . . is to the Trade of this Country, as the Soul to the Body." In the early 1800s, the floodgates reopened with a vengeance when, in one four-year period, forty thousand Africans landed in Charleston—twice as many as arrived in the early 1770s, the previous high-water mark of African immigration. In the early nineteenth century, then, Africans remained a highly visible component of South Carolina's slave population when in Virginia they were almost nonexistent.[49]

Different African ethnic groups predominated in the slave trades to Virginia and South Carolina. In the late seventeenth and early eighteenth centuries, slaves from two regions—Senegambia and the Bight of Biafra—constituted about three-quarters of the Africans arriving in the Chesapeake. By the 1710s and 1720s, the very slaves most detested by Lowcountry buyers—those from the Bight of Biafra, mostly Igbos and usually called "Bites" or "Calabars"— dominated the Virginia trade (see Table 11). Slaves from west-central Africa, in contrast, eclipsed all others in South Carolina's early trade. About ten thousand Africans from Angola arrived in Carolina in the 1730s alone. This predominance of particular African groups—different ones in each region, to be

---

48. On the contrasting wartime experiences of Virginia and South Carolina, see Ira Berlin and Ronald Hoffman, eds., *Slavery and Freedom in the Age of the American Revolution* (Charlottesville, Va., 1983), 49–171; and Sylvia R. Frey, *Water from the Rock: Black Resistance in a Revolutionary Age* (Princeton, N.J., 1991), esp. 108–171. For an insightful contemporary recognition of manpower shortages in South Carolina, see F.H. and E. to John Anderson, May 8, 1784, Slavery Collection, NYHS.

49. Philip D. Morgan, "Black Society in the Lowcountry, 1760–1810," in Berlin and Hoffman, eds., *Slavery and Freedom*, 84–85, 132; Michael E. Stevens, "'To Get as Many Slaves as You Can': An 1807 Slaving Voyage," *SCHM*, LXXXVII (1986), 187–192; "Letters of Joseph Clay, Merchant of Savannah, 1776–1793 . . . ," GHS, *Colls.*, VIII (1913), 194–195.

TABLE 11.
Coastal Origins of Virginia and South Carolina Africans, 1710s– 1770s

Region of Origin	Slaves of Identifiable Origin			
	Virginia			
	1712–1720s (N=11,211)	1730s (N=7,644)	1740–1752 (N=2,876)	1760–1772 (N=3,557)
Senegambia	8%	27%	41%	13%
Sierra Leone	4	0	0	6
Windward Coast	4	0	0	9
Gold Coast	10	4	8	22
Bight of Benin	0	0	0	0
Bight of Biafra	57	33	30	0
Angola	6	37	21	50
Madagascar	11	0	0	0
Total known	100	101	100	100
(Total unknown)	(35)	(47)	(81)	(67)

Region of Origin	South Carolina				
	1730s (N=11,973)	1740s (N=1,229)	1750s (N=13,106)	1760s (N=18,736)	1770s (N=16,882)
Senegambia	12%	15%	43%	22%	30%
Sierra Leone	0	0	4	8	18
Windward Coast	0	11	15	28	14
Gold Coast	2	0	8	14	18
Bight of Benin	0	0	4	3	4
Bight of Biafra	8	33	13	0	2
Angola	77	41	12	25	14
Madagascar	0	0	0	0	0
Total known	99	100	99	100	100
(Total unknown)	(40)	(42)	(24)	(20)	(20)

Sources: Virginia data are based on Minchinton et al., eds., *Virginia Slave-Trade Statistics;* South Carolina data are based on newspaper advertisements for African cargoes, the South Carolina Treasury General Duty Books, SCDAH; South Carolina Naval Office Shipping Lists, PRO; and Elizabeth Donnan, ed., *Documents Illustrative of the History of the Slave Trade to America,* Carnegie Institution of Washington Publication no. 409, 4 vols. (Washington, D.C., 1930–1935), IV, 235–471.

sure—no doubt facilitated sociability and cultural identity in both areas, but more particularly in the Lowcountry, where the Angolan contingent ranked larger in the overall population than Igbos did in the Chesapeake. One South Carolina planter, at least, seems to suggest as much, for, when he advertised for his Angolan runaway in 1737, he pointed out that "as there is abundance of Negroes in this province of that Nation, he may chance to be harbour'd among some of them." No Chesapeake planter, so far as is known, attached significance to the dominance of Igbos among that region's earliest African immigrants.[50]

Over the course of the eighteenth century, the most noticeable trend in the coastal origins of both regions' African immigrants was their growing heterogeneity, a reflection of changes in the regional foci of the British trade on the African coast. In Virginia, Senegambia and Angola came to rival, and indeed surpass, the Bight of Biafra as supplying regions. Senegambia and, to a lesser extent, the Gold Coast and Angola also dominated the Maryland trade in the third quarter of the eighteenth century. In South Carolina, after 1750, Senegambia, the Windward Coast, and, to a lesser extent, Sierra Leone and the Gold Coast overtook Angola as chief suppliers, with the Gold Coast coming to the fore in the 1780s and Angola returning to preeminence in the early 1800s. Georgia followed much the same pattern, with Senegambia dominating the trade in the years before the Revolution, and Sierra Leone and the Gold Coast predominating after the Revolution. In 1783, Benjamin Farrar's 153 Louisiana slaves, who had recently left South Carolina and therefore reflected the composition of Lowcountry estates, comprised a mixture of Africans: 18 "Angolans," 18 from "Guinea" (probably, but by no means certainly, Sierra Leone), 4 "Coromanti" (Gold Coast), 4 "Ibo" (Bight of Biafra), 1 "Maninga" (probably Senegambia), and 1 "Chamba" (Gold Coast).[51] Presumably, as African immi-

50. David Eltis, "The Volume and African Origins of the British Slave Trade before 1714," *Cahiers d'études africaines*, 138–139, XXXV (1995), 617–627, esp. 619; Isaac Porcher, *SCG*, Aug. 13, 1737. Angola is, of course, not a nation, but a large region within which many ethnic groups resided. Perhaps it is no more than coincidence that one of the few slaves to run away from Virginia and reach South Carolina was an Igbo (Workhouse, *SCG*, Sept. 7, 1765).

51. Gwendolyn Midlo Hall, *Africans in Colonial Louisiana: The Development of Afro-Creole Culture in the Eighteenth Century* (Baton Rouge, La., 1992), 283. For Maryland, see Darold D. Wax, "Black Immigrants: The Slave Trade in Colonial Maryland," *MHM*, LXXIII (1978), 36. On the late-18th- and early-19th-century evidence concerning South Carolina, see Morgan, "Black Society in the Lowcountry," in Berlin and Hoffman, eds., *Slavery and Freedom*, 132. For Georgia, see Darold D. Wax, "'New Negroes Are Always in Demand': The Slave Trade in Eighteenth-Century Georgia," *GHQ*, LXVIII (1984), 193–220, esp. 205, 218. The best study of the regional distribution of the overall British slave trade can be found in David Richardson, "Slave Exports from West and West-Central Africa, 1700–1810: New Estimates of Volume and Distribution," *Journal of African History*, XXX (1989), 1–22, esp. 13.

grants into both Lowcountry and Chesapeake came from ever wider areas, it became harder for them to maintain ties.

Although Chesapeake slave traders paid less attention to the coastal origins of their Africans than did their South Carolina counterparts, they did express preferences—or, perhaps, prejudices might be nearer the mark. In 1723, Robert "King" Carter spoke highly of "Gambians" because he thought them "more used to work" than other Africans. He was prepared to give two pounds a head more for them than for "bites." Fifteen years later, John Carter also praised "Gambians," along with Gold Coast slaves, but disparaged Angolans. In 1761, Maryland merchant Thomas Ringold endorsed the high reputation of slaves from Senegambia and echoed "King" Carter's disdain for "Bites."[52] Apparently, Chesapeake traders did not prefer slaves from the regions that seem to have supplied them with most of their Africans. They did, however, seem to favor two regions that provided them with a substantial minority of their slaves.

In South Carolina, planters and merchants endlessly debated the merits of particular African groups. They were unanimous in their detestation of Igbos, raising a chorus of opposition against "Callabars and Bites." The most common explanation for this dislike was that Igbos were, in the words of John Guerard, a Charleston merchant, "too much addicted to destroy them-

---

For attempts to explain these changes, see David Richardson, "The Eighteenth-Century British Slave Trade: Estimates of Its Volume and Coastal Distribution in Africa," *Res. Econ. Hist.*, XII (1989), 151–195; and Richardson, "The British Slave Trade to Colonial South Carolina," *Slavery and Abolition*, XII (1991), 125–172, esp. 136–137. I have retained the distinction between Windward Coast and Sierra Leone, referred to in many South Carolina records, although it is now clear that many so-called Windward Coast slaves were probably from Sierra Leone: Adam Jones and Marion Johnson, "Slaves from the Windward Coast," *Jour. Af. Hist.*, XXI (1980), 17–34.

52. Robert Carter to Micajah Perry, July 13, 1723, Robert Carter Letterbook, July 4, 1723–June 11, 1724, VHS; Carter to John Pemberton, July 23, 1728, Robert Carter Letterbook, May 13, 1727–July 23, 1728, VHS; John Carter to Foster Cunliffe, Aug. 1, 1738, Carter-Plummer Letterbook, UVa; Donnan, ed., *Documents of the Slave Trade*, IV, 40. See also Darold D. Wax, "Preferences for Slaves in Colonial America," *Journal of Negro History*, LVIII (1973), 371–401; and Wax, "Black Immigrants," *MHM*, LXXIII (1978), 35–36. On the whole, Virginia planters exhibited little interest in, or knowledge of, the ethnic origins of their slaves. Possible exceptions include one master's description of his slave's hair as "like a Madagascar's," another who described a native-born slave's countenance as like "a Madegascar," and another's description of his slave's cicatrizations as like "Gold Coast slaves generally are." See Benjamin Needler, *VaG* (Parks), Nov. 5, 1736, Philip Lightfoot, ibid., Mar. 1, 1738; and R. C. Nicholas, *VaG* (P and D), Jan. 15, 1767. Presumably, these masters thought they and others could identify Africans from Madagascar and the Gold Coast by their appearance. It is worth emphasizing that slaves from Madagascar were rare in the British slave trade—another indication of the atypicality of the Chesapeake trade. See Virginia Bever Platt, "The East India Company and the Madagascar Slave Trade," *WMQ*, 3d Ser., XXVI (1969), 548–577.

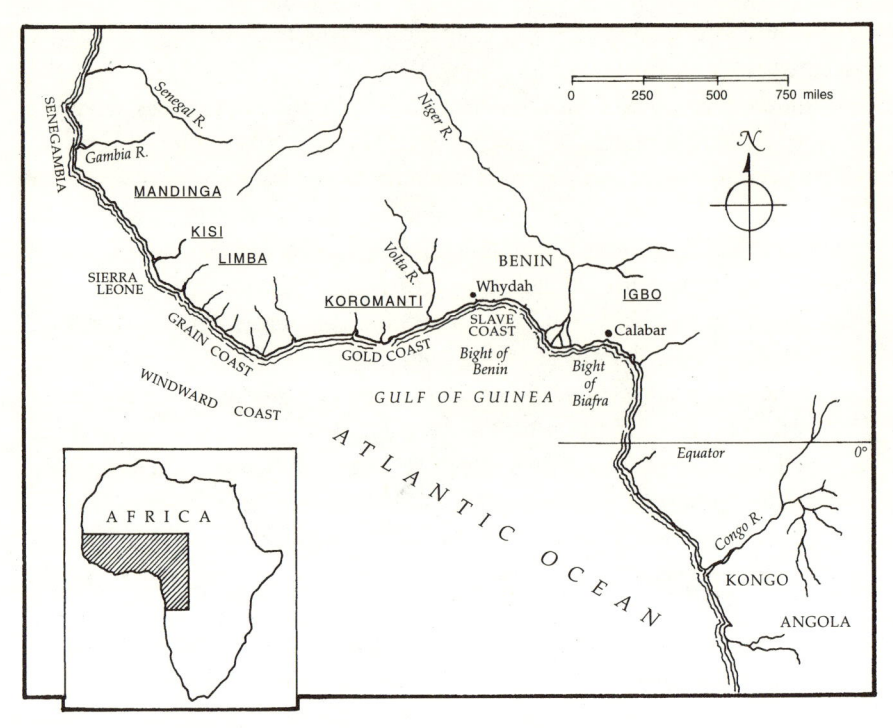

MAP 1. *The Coastal Origins of African Slaves*

selves."[53] Although there was less unanimity on the most desirable regions, slaves from the Gold Coast and Benin were generally the most favorably regarded. Advertisers reserved their highest praise for these regions. Thus, the area around Whydah was described as a "country greatly preferred to any other throughout the West Indies"—a recommendation not lightly disregarded—or simply as "the finest country in Africa." Slaves known as "Coromantees" (Koromanti, from the Gold Coast) were, according to John Bartram, "reconed the best of slaves." Senegambia ran these two regions a close second in the estimation of Lowcountry residents. At one point, Henry Laurens went so far as to regard Gambia "as equal to the Gold Coast"; and slaves from the

---

53. John Guerard to Thomas Rock, Apr. 14, 1752, Guerard Letterbook. The charge is repeated in subsequent letters: see those to William Jolliff, Apr. 30, June [1–7], 1752, and to Thomas Rock, May 27, 1752, ibid. For details on Guerard, see R. C. Nash, "Trade and Business in Eighteenth-Century South Carolina: The Career of John Guerard, Merchant and Planter," *SCHM*, XCVI (1995), 6–29. For other derogatory views of Igbos, see *Laurens Papers,* I, 252, 257, 275, 295, 331, II, 179, 182, 186, 204, 400, 402, 423, 437, 456, IV, 192–193; Josiah Smith to John Smith, Dec. 25, 1771, Josiah Smith Letterbook, UNC. See also Daniel C. Littlefield, *Rice and Slaves: Ethnicity and the Slave Trade in Colonial South Carolina* (Baton Rouge, La., 1981), 8–9.

Windward Coast and Sierra Leone were often promoted as "such as are usually imported from Gambia."[54] In spite of their large contribution to the Carolinian slave trade, slaves from the Angola-Kongo region ranked low on the scale of Lowcountry planter preferences. Henry Laurens described one parcel of "Angola's" as "a very small slender People such as our Planters dont at all like," and John Guerard "wo[ul]d chuse all Men of Gambia or Windward Coast, in failure of wch Angolns."[55]

Is there any basis for these preferences? A comparison of the ethnic origins of incoming Africans and runaway slaves, which is possible for South Carolina, suggests that contemporary opinions were either not that farfetched or assumed the status of self-fulfilling prophecies. At any rate, Igbos were the one group to produce a marked divergence between their known proportions among immigrants and runaways. Forming only 5 percent of known imports, they were 10 percent of all runaways (see Table 12). Perhaps the dislike South Carolinians persistently expressed for slaves from the Bight of Biafra had a basis in fact, or perhaps the low expectations held of this group encouraged them to run away in disproportion to their numbers. Indeed, a disparaging attitude toward slaves from the Bight of Biafra may explain why one Lowcountry owner described his fugitive as "much like an Ebo Negro." By contrast, slaves from the Gold Coast, Senegambia, and Angola—regions preferred or

---

54. Middleton and Brailsford, *SCG,* July 21, 1759; Powell, Hopton and Co., ibid., July 30, 1772; John Bartram to William Bartram, Apr. 9, 1766, Misc. MSS., NYHS; *Laurens Papers,* II, 423; Middleton and Brailsford, *SCG,* Aug. 25, 1758. For other references to the desirability of Gold Coast and Benin slaves, see *Laurens Papers,* I, 295, II, 93, 186; Richard Hill to John Guerard, June 25, 1743, Richard Hill Letterbook, Duke; Donnan, ed., *Documents of the Slave Trade,* II, 516. For other favorable views of Africans from Senegambia, see also Austin and Laurens, *SCG,* Aug. 29, 1754, Aug. 11, 1758. John Guerard usually preferred "Gambian" slaves, for example, Guerard to Henry West, Jr., Dec. 7, 1752, Guerard Letterbook. An English slave merchant thought South Carolina "the only Markett for Gambia Slaves" (William Davenport and Co. to Capt. Samuel Sachevall, Jan. 29, 1755, in Richards Collection, Davenport Letter and Bill Book, 1748, Keele University Library, England, as cited in Littlefield, *Rice and Slaves,* 20).

55. *Laurens Papers,* II, 107; John Guerard to William Jolliff, June [1–7], 1752, Guerard Letterbook. A further indication of the sophistication of Lowcountry purchasers was their realization that a ship from a particular coastal region or carrying a predominant ethnic group might well include slaves from other regions and other ethnic groups. For instance, in advertising for his runaway slave Boston, John Pamor noted that this African had been in the country seven years, "was imported with a cargo of Eboe negroes," but of what country the master "could never make out" (*SC and AGG,* Apr. 10, 1777). More so than in the Chesapeake, Lowcountry masters made ethnic identifications based on appearance. As one example, consider Thomas Radcliffe, Jr., who described his runaway, Sam, as having rather long hair, "being of the Fulla country," suggesting that masters had certain expectations about even the hairstyle of certain ethnic groups (*Royal Gaz,* Jan. 12, 1782).

TABLE 12.

Origins of South Carolina's African Immigrants and African Runaways, 1730–1782

| | Percentage of Slaves of Identifiable Origin ||
Region of Origin	Immigrants (*N*=61,926)	Runaways (*N*=1,164)
Senegambia	27	21
Sierra Leone	8	2
Windward Coast	16	21
Gold Coast	11	13
Bight of Benin	3	1
Bight of Biafra	5	10
Angola	30	28
Miscellaneous	0	3
Total	100	99

Sources: Immigrant figures are based on those in Table 9; the runaway figures, on all runaway advertisements (for both fugitives and captives) in South Carolina newspapers.

tolerated by Lowcountry planters—were not notable runaways, given their proportions in the slave population. In fact, Henry Laurens, in recommending Gambian and Gold Coast slaves to a fellow planter, emphasized that they were "less inclined to wander" than other slaves.[56]

Perhaps a firmer basis for South Carolinian preferences lies in the physique of different African groups. Henry Laurens was unenthusiastic about "Angola's" because they were a "short people." Conversely, he observed that "our Planters almost to a Man are desirous of large strong People like the Gambias and will not touch small limb'd People when such can be had." If a "tall robust people best sute our business," as Laurens maintained, then heights further confirm Lowcountry preferences.[57] Slaves from Senegambia were on average the tallest, with those from Angola the shortest, of the African newcomers.

56. John Champneys, *SCG*, Aug. 30, 1773; Henry Laurens to James Grant, Apr. 20, 1765, 0771/359, Papers of General James Grant of Ballindalloch.
57. *Laurens Papers*, II, 230, 357. An owner of three runaway "Angola" men spoke of their being "all short fellows" (Abraham Swadler, *SCG*, Sept. 19, 1752). See also Workhouse, *SCG and CJ*, Feb. 4, 1766. Interestingly, an Igbo brought to the Charleston workhouse called himself "Little one" (*SCG*, Nov. 30, 1755).

TABLE 13.
Passage Time from England via Africa to British America, 1720–1798

Coastal Region	Virginia, 1725–1769		South Carolina, 1720–1774		Jamaica, 1791–1798
Senegambia	242	(19)	220	(20)	170
Sierra Leone	247	(3)	375	(8)	284
Windward Coast	236	(1)	309	(23)	305
Gold Coast	357	(4)	345	(6)	268
Bight of Benin	—		366	(3)	266
Bight of Biafra	319	(27)	341	(2)	243
Angola	333	(10)	360	(9)	263
Africa	306	(114)	—		—

Notes and sources: Virginia data are based on the date at which bond was posted in England (which can be assumed to be close to the time of departure) and date of entry in the colony. This information is reported in Minchinton et al., eds., *Virginia Slave-Trade Statistics.*

South Carolina data are based on clearing dates for vessels reported in T70/1225 and BT6/3, ff. 100–130, PRO, and Return of Slave Ships Sailing from Liverpool, 1771–1774, Peet Papers, Liverpool University Library, and arrival dates as reported in the Naval Office Shipping Lists and colony newspapers.

For Jamaican data, see Herbert S. Klein, *The Middle Passage: Comparative Studies in the Atlantic Slave Trade* (Princeton, N.J., 1978), 157. Unfortunately, only the Jamaican data allow a consistent breakdown of the three legs of the journey.

The passage times of slaving vessels might also help explain why North American planters preferred slaves from Senegambia to those from Angola and the Bight of Biafra. The journey from England to Senegambia and then on to the New World was the shortest for any coastal region of Africa, on average about seventy to more than a hundred days fewer than for vessels going to and from Angola or the Bight of Biafra (see Table 13). Thomas Ringold placed considerable value on the difference, because Gambian slaves generally arrived "in best helth as the Passage is quick from thence." Conversely, a London firm that sent slaves to Maryland noted that those from Calabar were "very much subject to mortality in their passage."[58]

58. Donnan, ed., *Documents of the Slave Trade,* IV, 40; Higginson and Bird to Col. Edward Lloyd, Sept. 27, 1718, Higginson and Bird Letterbook, microfilm, CW. Passage times could not have been determinative, because long journeys were characteristic of vessels

One final explanation for North American planters' preferences lies in the age and sex of African immigrants. South Carolinians and Virginians generally agreed that male Africans, particularly adults, were most desirable. Charleston merchant John Guerard declared that "our people are all for men," while his fellow slave trader Gabriel Manigault asked for "as many young Men as possible." Charles Steuart of Virginia specified the usual formula: two-thirds of a shipment should be male. Most slave vessels arriving in the two regions met this stipulation, although arrivals to the Chesapeake fell shorter of the ideal than did those to the Lowcountry (see Table 14). Moreover, most slave shipments were overwhelmingly adult, although again Chesapeake cargoes were less so than Lowcountry ones. Children aged under ten to twelve years formed about one-fifth of slave shipments to the Chesapeake but only about one-seventh of those to the Lowcountry.[59]

Within the adult group, however, "men-boys" (those between fourteen and

---

from the Gold Coast, primarily because a long stay on the coast was required to assemble a full cargo. Yet, few complaints were heard of this region's slaves. For passage times and differential mortality, see Jay Coughtry, *The Notorious Triangle: Rhode Island and the African Slave Trade, 1700–1807* (Philadelphia, 1981), 159; Herbert S. Klein and Stanley L. Engerman, "Slave Mortality on British Ships, 1791–1797," in Roger Anstey and P.E.H. Hair, eds., *Liverpool, the African Slave Trade, and Abolition: Essays to Illustrate Current Knowledge and Research*, Historic Society of Lancashire and Cheshire Occasional Series, II (Bristol, 1976), 113–125; Herbert S. Klein, *The Middle Passage: Comparative Studies in the Atlantic Slave Trade* (Princeton, N.J., 1978), 161–162; Richard B. Sheridan, "The Guinea Surgeons on the Middle Passage: The Provision of Medical Services in the British Slave Trade," *International Journal of African Historical Studies*, XIV (1981), 624; David Eltis, "Mortality and Voyage Length in the Middle Passage: New Evidence from the Nineteenth Century," *Jour. Econ. Hist.*, XLIV (1984), 301–308; and Eltis, "Fluctuations in Mortality in the Last Half Century of the Transatlantic Slave Trade," *Social Science History*, XIII (1989), 315–340.

59. John Guerard to William Jolliff, June 7, 1753, Guerard Letterbook; Gabriel Manigault to Messrs. Samuel and William Vernon, Apr. 12, 1755, Slavery Collection, NYHS; Charles Steuart to Messrs. Blackman and Adams, July 5, 1751, Steuart Letterbook, microfilm, CW. On the preference for males, see also John Murray to Adam Smart, Jan. 3, 1756, Letterbook of John Murray, Murray of Murraythwaite Muniments, GD 219/290; *Laurens Papers*, I, 295, II, 348, 357. On the preference for adults, John Guerard claimed that "Grown Slaves dos best" in the South Carolina market, whereas "Young ones sell better in Proportion in the West Indies" (Guerard to Thomas Rock, Apr. 14, 1752, Guerard Letterbook). We know of other Virginia cargoes that had small percentages of men: the *John and Betty* in 1727 sold 37 men, 55 women, and 48 boys and girls (not used in Table 14 because children are not disaggregated), and the *Rose* also in 1727 had only 38 men out of a total of 119 Africans. See Robert Carter to John Pemberton, July 26, 1727, Robert Carter Letterbook, 1727–1728, VHS; and Carter to Pemberton, Sept. 15, 1727, Robert Carter Letterbook, 1727–1728, UVa. The percentages reported in Table 14 compare quite well with the huge 18th-century sample reported in David Eltis and Stanley L. Engerman, "Was the Slave Trade Dominated by Men?" *Journal of Interdisciplinary History*, XXIII (1992–1993), 237–257, esp. 241.

TABLE 14.
Age and Sex Composition of Slavers to the Chesapeake and Lowcountry, 1710–1774

	Chesapeake, 1710–1760			South Carolina, 1720–1774		
Group	Male	Female	Overall	Male	Female	Overall
Adults	52%	29%	81%	56%	29%	85%
Children	11	8	19	9	6	15
Total	63	37	100	65	35	100

Notes and sources: Chesapeake: The sample is 1,536 slaves on 9 ships: in 1710, the *Leopald Gally* with 149 Africans, Lyonel and Stephen Loyde Account Book 1708–1710, Tayloe Family Papers, UVa; between 1717 and 1721, 5 ships and 959 Africans, in Kulikoff, "A 'Prolifick' People," *Southern Studies,* XVI (1977), 399; in 1718, the *Margaret* with 108 Africans, James Carroll's accounts with Bonham and Cassells, Special Collections, Georgetown University Library; in 1723, the *Greyhound* with 172 Africans, in Donnan, *Documents of the Slave Trade,* IV, 100–102; and in 1760, the *Eadith* with 149 Africans, Slaving Account of Brigantine *Eadith,* DX/169/1, 23, Merseyside County Museums, Liverpool.

South Carolina: Data based on the adult-child composition deduced from duty paid on 39,773 slaves (734 slaves in the 1720s, 11,188 in the 1730s, 11,349 in the 1760s, and 16,502 in the 1770s). To secure a sex breakdown of adults and children, I applied the ratios derived from 9 ships (carrying 1,107 slaves) where this information is supplied. These 9 ships brought in small numbers of slaves, with higher than usual proportions of children. Their only usefulness is to establish the male-female ratios among adults and children. The ships are *Orrel* (1751) and *Molly* (1752), *Elizabeth* (1753), *Fortune* (1754), *Pearl* (1755), *Hare* (1756), *Dembia* (1769), *Adventure* (1771), and *Robert* (1773).

eighteen years of age) and "women-girls" (those between thirteen and sixteen years of age), who had a lifetime of labor before them, were said to sell particularly well. Nathaniel Russell of Charlestown declared that "Negroes from 15 to 25 years of Age sute this market best," while Levinius Clarkson demanded "Boys or Men from the Age of 14 to 24." In Virginia there seems to have been, if anything, a greater preference for adolescents. In 1738, John Carter noted that "Men-boys and Women-Girls" are best; Charles Steuart thought those Africans "from 14 to 18 yrs are most saleable"; in 1762, Francis Jerdone believed that young slaves "from 12 to 18 years old [are] always more saleable than older ones"; and, in the following year, William Taylor was most emphatic, declaring that "planters in general chuse men Boys and women Girls before grown slaves."[60]

60. Donnan, ed., *Documents of the Slave Trade,* IV, 451, 456; John Carter to Foster Cunliffe and Samuel Powel, Aug. 3, 1738, Carter-Plummer Letterbook; Steuart to Blackman

TABLE 15.

Children among African Immigrants to South Carolina, 1735–1774, and to the West Indies, 1791–1798

	Percentage of Children (No. of Ships)			
	South Carolina[a]			West Indies[b]
Region of Origin	1735–1739	1765–1769	1772–1774	1791–1798
Senegambia	10.3 (7)	16.1 (23)	8.9 (26)	10.5 (5)
Sierra Leone	—	18.5 (5)	15.7 (15)	22.0 (24)
Windward Coast	—	24.5 (23)	19.4 (14)	14.2 (9)
Gold Coast	9.7 (4)	17.6 (13)	11.3 (12)	12.4 (21)
Bight of Benin	—	16.2 (2)	12.7 (3)	6.0 (1)
Bight of Biafra	16.2 (2)	—	30.3 (1)	14.3 (22)
Kongo-Angola	13.5 (35)	27.3 (11)	14.9 (7)	14.4 (39)
Africa	15.3 (10)	18.0 (13)	15.4 (14)	11.7 (43)
West Indies	16.7 (24)	11.5 (96)	10.1 (102)	—
Total	13.8 (82)	20.3 (186)	13.2 (194)	14.3 (164)

[a] Based on analysis of ships where numbers of slaves and duty paid are both known. After 1740, a three-tier duty was in effect, making it difficult to assess the precise adult-child composition of slave cargoes. Nevertheless, from a comparison of contemporary assessments of the men, women, boys, and girls aboard nine vessels between 1751 and 1773 and the numbers deduced from duty paid, it is clear that only two duties were generally applied: a £10 duty for slaves above 50 inches and a £5 duty for slaves between 38 and 50 inches. One can therefore calculate the proportion of children with a reasonable degree of accuracy.

[b] Klein, *The Middle Passage*, 150.

The age structure of some South Carolina shiploads can be analyzed by African region, and this evidence supplies a further basis both for North American planters' preferences in general and for Virginians' preference for

---

and Adams, July 5, 1751, Steuart Letterbook; Francis Jerdone to Messrs. Buchanan and Simson, Oct. 10, 1762, Jerdone Family Papers, as cited in Calvin B. Coulter, Jr., "The Import Trade of Colonial Virginia," *WMQ*, 3d Ser., II (1945), 307; William Taylor to [?], July 5, 1763, Slavery Collection, NYHS. From the James River in Virginia, John Allen told a Jamaica merchant that he wanted "young" slaves (Allen to Messrs. Peter Furnell and Co., Feb. 15, 1736, John Allen Letterbook, UVa). For further references in South Carolina, see *Laurens Papers*, II, 204, 278, 357, 400, 402, 456. For the age-bands of "men-boys" and "women-girls," see Richard Hill to Capt. William Jeffery, Oct. 17, 1743, Hill Letterbook.

adolescents in particular. Slave shipments from the Gold Coast, Senegambia, and the Bight of Benin generally consisted of fewer children than those from Angola, Sierra Leone, the Windward Coast, and the Bight of Biafra (see Table 15). A buyer's preference for adults made slaves from the former regions particularly attractive. Thus the large share of Virginia's slave trade maintained by the Bight of Biafra and Angola no doubt accounts for the disproportionate number of African children entering that region. Also explicable is the chorus that Chesapeake slave traders raised in favor of young slaves.[61]

Not only the coastal origins of African slaving vessels but their arrival times differed significantly from Virginia to South Carolina. Although the South Carolina slaving season was reputed to extend only from March to October, 12 percent of all slaves direct from Africa and 21 percent of those brought via the Caribbean arrived outside those months (see Table 16). In Virginia, by contrast, the slave trade was concentrated into far fewer months. Just 1 percent of all slaves direct from Africa and 6 percent of those brought via the Caribbean arrived between November and March. And far more of Virginia's slaves arrived during the three summer months than was the case in South Carolina, where arrivals were more evenly dispersed throughout the year.[62]

The speed at which Africans were dispatched to plantations also varied significantly between Lowcountry and Chesapeake. Most slaves who landed in South Carolina were put up for sale within two weeks of arrival. A period of about twelve days (somewhat less earlier in the century, when quarantine restrictions were shorter) generally separated the date of arrival from the date of sale (see Table 17). Sales, once begun, were generally concluded quickly. In 1755, almost a whole shipload of 240 Africans was sold in just thirty-six

---

61. Other demographic evidence supports the notion that the Chesapeake slave trade comprised unusually high proportions of young Africans; see Morgan and Nicholls, "Slaves in Piedmont Virginia," *WMQ*, 3d Ser., XLVI (1989), 211–251. For two important contributions to the issue of regional differences in age and sex ratios, see David Geggus, "Sex Ratio, Age, and Ethnicity in the Atlantic Slave Trade: Data from French Shipping and Plantation Records," *Jour. Af. Hist.*, XXX (1989), 23–44; and David Eltis, "The Volume, Age / Sex Ratios, and African Impact of the Slave Trade: Some Refinements of Paul Lovejoy's Review of the Literature," ibid., XXXI (1990), 485–492.

62. For opinions on the best time to sell Africans and the extent of the slaving season, see Robert Bristow to Thomas Booth, Oct. 30, 1710, Bristow Letterbook, VSL; Robert Carter to [?], May 21, 1728, Carter Letterbook, 1727–1728, VHS; Joseph Wragg to Isaac Hobhouse, July 1, 1736, Jefferies MSS., XVI, 148, Bristol Central Library, Bristol, England; *Laurens Papers*, II, 337, IV, 44; Archibald Dalziel to Andrew Dalziel, Jan. 27, 1773, Letters of A. Dalziel, E 59/34, DK.7 52/30, Edinburgh University, Scotland. Compare Daniel C. Littlefield, "The Slave Trade to Colonial South Carolina: A Profile," *SCHM*, XCI (1990), 68–99, esp. 92–99; Walter Minchinton, "A Comment on 'The Slave trade to Colonial South Carolina: A Profile,'" ibid., XCV (1994), 47–57, esp. 56.

TABLE 16.
Months of Arrival of Virginia and South Carolina Slave Vessels, 1700–1774

	Proportion of Vessels					
	Direct from Africa		From Africa via Caribbean		From West Indies	
Time of Arrival	Va.[a]	S.C.[b]	Va.[c]	S.C.[d]	Va.[e]	S.C.[f]
Winter	.3%	6.2%	5.0%	15.3%	12.8%	36.2%
December	.2	2.1	2.1	4.4	4.2	6.9
January	.1	2.2	0	3.9	2.7	12.6
February	0	1.9	2.9	7.0	5.9	16.7
Spring	22.1	25.7	32.8	42.9	27.4	27.6
March	.3	2.8	0	15.7	4.2	9.6
April	7.1	6.8	13.4	18.5	9.3	5.0
May	14.7	16.1	19.4	8.7	13.9	13.0
Summer	57.0	41.9	50.3	24.5	38.6	22.4
June	18.5	13.8	27.8	7.2	15.0	5.9
July	20.3	15.5	16.5	8.2	13.9	8.4
August	18.2	12.6	6.0	9.1	9.7	8.1
Fall	20.4	26.1	11.9	17.4	21.1	13.6
September	12.9	10.4	8.0	5.8	6.9	1.2
October	7.1	10.1	2.6	6.0	8.6	6.0
November	.4	5.6	1.3	5.6	5.6	6.4
Total	99.8	99.9	100.0	100.1	99.9	99.8

[a] $N = 59,454$ slaves. [b] $N = 66,269$ slaves. [c] $N = 3,117$ slaves. [d] $N = 7,026$ slaves. [e] $N = 4,515$ slaves. [f] $N = 1,193$ slaves.

Notes and sources: All vessels with 40 or more slaves that had a British West Indian island as port of origin, I placed in the column of From Africa via Caribbean. In a number of other cases, sometimes involving vessels with fewer than 40 slaves, there is no ambiguity: an African and West Indian origin are clearly stated. I am, therefore, almost undoubtedly undercounting From Africa via Caribbean. For further confirmation of this procedure, see Kulikoff, "A 'Prolifick People,'" *Southern Studies*, XVI (1977), 392 n. 5; and Susan Westbury, "Slaves of Colonial Virginia: Where They Came From," *WMQ*, 3d Ser., XLII (1985), 228–237.

The Virginia data are from Minchinton et al., eds., *Virginia Slave-Trade Statistics*. For a less complete count, but with similar results, see Herbert S. Klein, "New Evidence on the Virginia Slave Trade," *Journal of Interdisciplinary History*, XVII (1986–1987), 875. The South Carolina data are drawn from newspaper advertisements, South Carolina General Duty Books, Naval Office Shipping Lists, and Donnan, *Documents of the Slave Trade*, IV, 235–471. For a less complete count, again with similar results, see Daniel C. Littlefield, "The Slave Trade to Colonial South Carolina: A Profile," *SCHM*, XCI (1990), 92–93, 96–99; and Walter Minchinton, "A Comment on 'The Slave Trade to Colonial South Carolina: A Profile,'" *SCHM*, XCV (1994), 56.

TABLE 17.
Time between Arrival of Slave Vessel and Sale Dates, Virginia and South Carolina, 1730–1774

Decade	Virginia[a] No. of Vessels	Virginia[a] Average No. of Days[c]	South Carolina[b] No. of Vessels	South Carolina[b] Average No. of Days
1730s	5	8, 15	59	12
1740s	3	11, 17	11	13
1750s	8	10, 13	92	12
1760s	7	19	127	12
1770s	9	19, 37	105	12

[a] Precise date of arrival, rather than date of entry given in the Naval Office Shipping Lists, is known for 1 vessel in the 1730s, 3 in the 1750s (discounting the *Black Prince* of 1752, which is an unusual case), and 2 in the 1760s. On the basis of these known dates, I have assumed that vessels in the 1730s and 1740s arrived on average 3 days earlier than the date of entry; and in the 1750s–1770s, 4 days earlier. See Minchinton et al., eds., *Virginia Slave-Trade Statistics*, 102, 144, 148, 150, 170. The 32 vessels used in this analysis are ones for which reliable sale dates exist.

[b] Precise date of arrival is known for 15 vessels in the 1750s and 16 in the 1760s. On average this was 4 days earlier than the date of entry assumed from or stated in either a newspaper advertisement or Naval Office Shipping List. I have therefore added 4 days to all the spans between arrival and sale.

[c] Two figures are given where we know two sale dates. Many Virginia slavers announced two separate venues, usually one near the coast and the other further inland.

hours.[63] There were variations depending on the length of quarantine, the buoyancy of the economy, the number and health of the Africans, their regional origins, and the seasonal timing of the vessel's arrival. Still, most Africans were resident on their destined plantations within a month of arrival on Sullivan's Island. Two slaves from the Gold Coast, bought at the sale of the *Africa* on July 6, 1772, were declared absent from the backcountry parish of

63. The rigorous application of a 10-day quarantine is noted in John Guerard to Capt. Jon [?], Mar. 4, 1752, and to William Jolliff, May 4, 1752, May 16, 19, 1753, Guerard Letterbook; John Guerard to Benjamin Spencer, Feb. 2, 1756, Spencer Stanhope Muniments, City Library, Sheffield, England; and *Laurens Papers*, II, 223–224, 546. On the quarantine laws, see Cooper and McCord, eds., *The Statutes at Large*, II, 152, 382–385, IV, 11, 78–86. Travelers occasionally saw slaves being quarantined. See T. P. Harrison, ed., "Journal of a Voyage to Charlestown in So. Carolina by Pelatiah Webster in 1765," Southern History Association, *Publications*, II (1898), 143–144; and E. Alfred Jones, ed., "The Journal of Alexander Chesney, a South Carolina Loyalist in the Revolution and After," *Ohio State University Bulletin*, XXVI (1921), 3. For the quick sale in 1755, see *Laurens Papers*, I, 268. As Elizabeth Donnan empha-

Saint Mathew's less than three weeks later. A Charleston merchant's understanding of the most propitious time for a slaving vessel to enter South Carolina indicates how quickly Lowcountry planters expected their Africans to be at work. A slave ship that arrived on the first of May and offered its cargo for sale a fortnight later had, according to John Guerard, "come in at the best Time as the Planters have just Pitch'd their Crops and will give the more as the Negroes will be of Greater Service in hoeing thro' the whole Season." If slaves, sold in mid-May, could be hoeing "thro' the whole Season" (hoeing began in early June), then the dispatch with which slaves were transferred from ship-deck to rice field was indeed impressive.[64]

This rapid transfer owed much to the dominating presence of South Carolina's central port, Charleston. Funneled through this one town, most Africans were sold in one lot. Planters traveled long distances to buy Africans in the city. Charleston merchant Henry Laurens noted that on one occasion forty or fifty purchasers traveled more than seventy miles to attend one of his sales. They went away disappointed because the slaves were in such poor condition, but Laurens maintained that those who traveled the farthest were the keys to "rais[ing] a Sale for if they like the Slaves they wont go back empty handed so far for 10 or £20 in the price." The demand for slaves sometimes became so intense that buyers jostled one another, "pulling and hauling who should get the good Slaves"; some came "very nearly to Blows."[65]

Wrangling over Africans seems not to have occurred in the Chesapeake, where sales took much longer and were more sedate. In the first half of the

---

sized, "One of the marked characteristics of the Carolina trade throughout a large part of the century was the despatch with which large cargoes were marketed" ("The Slave Trade into South Carolina before the Revolution," *AHR*, XXXIII [1927–1928], 816).

64. A diseased cargo could be quarantined for as long as two months; for the role of economic fluctuation, see John Guerard to William Jolliff, June 17, 1754, Guerard Letterbook; and George Appleby to Nathaniel Tregagle, Sept. 1, 1760, Aswarby Muniments, Lincolnshire Record Office, Lincoln, England. Merchants never tired of pointing out that a large shipment sold more quickly than a small one, and one that arrived early in the season generally sold better than one that arrived late: John Savage, *SCG*, Aug. 10, 1772 (the *Africa*'s sale began July 6, and the two Africans absented themselves on July 25); John Guerard to William Jolliff, May 6, 1754, Guerard Letterbook.

65. *Laurens Papers,* I, 281, 308, 350. On Charleston's marketing reach, see also ibid., I, 327, II, 63, 238, IV, 305–306. Apart from occasional sales in Georgetown and Beaufort, almost all Africans were sold in Charleston, except for parts of 1738–1739, 1760–1761, 1763, and 1765, when Ashley River Ferry and other sites were used to avoid city epidemics. See also Daniel C. Littlefield, "Charleston and Internal Slave Redistribution," *SCHM*, LXXXVII (1986), 93–105. For further graphic descriptions of slave sales, see William Brisbane to George Whitefield, Sept. 10, 1753, George Whitefield Papers, LC; and John Graham to Governor Grant, Sept 11, 1769, 0771/401, Papers of General James Grant of Ballindalloch.

century, Virginia slavers generally undertook an initial sale at Yorktown, or a similar lower Peninsula site, and then moved upriver to West Point or other ports. In the third quarter of the century, sites even further upriver were the initial places of sale, most commonly Bermuda Hundred, but also Osborne's Warehouse or Petersburg, which were well inland. Rather than being channeled through one central port, Africans brought to Virginia were transported to numerous riverside wharves for sale. As the century proceeded, it became common for merchants to buy parcels of Africans whom they tramped from one piedmont courthouse to another until all were sold. For these reasons, slave ships to the Chesapeake region took two months or more to complete selling their cargoes. Bristol-based slavers stayed an average of seventy-six days in Virginia, but took a third less time to discharge their cargoes and set off for home in South Carolina.[66] The demoralization wrought on Africans awaiting sale in the Chesapeake can only be imagined. Such protracted procedures no doubt suggest why ethnic origins quickly lost more meaning in this region as compared to the Lowcountry.

Carolina Africans were sold not only more quickly and more centrally than their Chesapeake counterparts but also in larger groups. By midcentury, Henry Laurens began to receive offers from individual planters "to take 20, 30, 40 [Africans]" at a time. Such a practice, as Laurens noted, had not "heretofore been common in our country." Laurens himself accumulated a labor force of about 230 slaves in less than a decade. On two occasions he specified the precise size of his purchases—in June 1764, he dispatched eleven Africans to his Mepkin plantation, and in June 1765, he sent twenty-seven "new Negroes" to his Wambaw plantation—but, presumably, he regularly bought similar or even larger contingents. In 1771, Peter Manigault purchased fifty-five Africans on behalf of Ralph Izard; and, in the following year, John Graham went to Charleston to purchase thirty Africans for James Wright. Five Africans who ran away

---

66. Allan Kulikoff, "The Origins of Afro-American Society in Tidewater Maryland and Virginia, 1700 to 1790," *WMQ*, 3d Ser., XXXV (1978), 233. For a quick sale early in the century, see that of the *John and Betty,* as reported in Walter Minchinton et al., eds., *Virginia Slave-Trade Statistics, 1698–1775* (Richmond, Va., 1984), 62–63. For upriver sites later in the century, see ibid., esp. 148, 150, 166, 176, 184. For examples of Africans' being shunted about the countryside, see Morgan and Nicholls, "Slaves in Piedmont Virginia," *WMQ*, 3d Ser., XLVI (1989), 211–212. Two-thirds of the Africans from the *Eadith,* which arrived in 1761, were bought by merchants—see Slaving Account Book, Merseyside County Museums, Liverpool, England. See also Winthrop D. Jordan, "Planter and Slave Identity Formation: Some Problems in the Comparative Approach," in Vera Rubin and Arthur Tuden, eds., *Comparative Perspectives on Slavery in New World Plantation Societies,* New York Academy of Sciences, Annals, CCXCII (New York, 1977), 38–39. On Bristol slavers, see W. E. Minchinton, "The Slave Trade of Bristol with the British Mainland Colonies in North America, 1699–1770," in Anstey and Hair, eds., *Liverpool, the African Slave Trade, and Abolition,* 39–59.

TABLE 18.
The Distribution of Africans among Purchasers in the Chesapeake and Lowcountry, 1689–1786

	Proportion of Slaves Sold			
No. of Slaves in Purchase	Royal African Company Slaves to Virginia, 1689–1713[a] ($N = 217$)	7 Chesapeake Sales, 1702–1760[b] ($N = 629$)	3 South Carolina Sales, 1751–1756[c] ($N = 186$)	2 South Carolina Sales 1784–1786[d] ($N = 635$)
1	38%	32%	17%	8%
2	25	28	29	14
3	14	11	19	12
4	9	7	9	9
5+	14	22	26	57
Total	100	100	100	100

[a] Allan Kulikoff, "The Origins of Afro-American Society in Tidewater Maryland and Virginia," *WMQ*, 3d Ser., XXXV (1978), 235.

[b] Ibid., counting the *African Galley, Charfield* (weighted), Baylor's sales, and *Prince Eugene,* together with *Leopold Gally, Margaret,* and *Eadith* (also weighted to exclude sales to merchants who then resold Africans in smaller lots). For the sources of the last three sales, see Table 14.

[c] The sales of the *Carolina Merchant* (1751), *Orrel* (1751), and *Hare* (1756) can be found in Donnan, ed., *Documents of the Slave Trade,* IV, 306–309; and *Laurens Papers,* II, 257–258.

[d] The sales of the *Count De Norde* and *Gambia* (1786) can be found in Baillie v. Hartley, Court of Exchequer, 1785, Parish Transcripts, box 3, NYHS; and Donnan, ed., *Documents of the Slave Trade,* IV, 491.

in 1772 reported that their master had bought thirteen men and twelve women from the same vessel. If such large-scale buying was common, the Lowcountry patterns of sale differed markedly from those of the Chesapeake.[67]

67. *Laurens Papers,* I, 262. In 1763, however, Laurens noted that those settling the frontier regions "with a little management will take off almost insensibly a Cargo by one or two in a Lot" (ibid., III, 260). On Laurens's own purchases, see ibid., IV, 319, 634. For more on Laurens, see Philip D. Morgan, "Three Planters and Their Slaves: Perspectives on Slavery in Virginia, South Carolina, and Jamaica, 1750–1790," in Winthrop D. Jordan and Sheila L. Skemp, eds., *Race and Family in the Colonial South* (Jackson, Miss., 1987), 37–79, esp. 54–68. Peter Manigault to Ralph Izard, July 4, 1771, Peter Manigault Letterbook, SCHS; *The Letters*

More precise quantitative evidence, limited as it is, differentiates between the two regions, although the difference is not as great as the occasional spectacular purchases from the Lowcountry would suggest. About a third of African immigrants to the Chesapeake in the late seventeenth and eighteenth centuries were purchased singly, whereas only about one-sixth of those arriving in the Lowcountry in the 1750s and one-twelfth in the 1780s were bought individually. More than half of South Carolina's African immigrants in the 1750s, and three-quarters in the 1780s, were purchased in groups of three or more; in the Chesapeake, by contrast, 40 percent at most were purchased in such groups (see Table 18).[68]

In short, the African presence was far more pervasive in the Lowcountry than in the Chesapeake. Sullivan's Island, close to Charleston, where incoming Africans were quarantined, was indeed "the Ellis Island of black Americans." South Carolina was easily the largest importer of slaves on the mainland. By 1808, when the slave trade was outlawed in the United States, South Carolina had imported about twice as many Africans as Virginia, even though its slave population was much smaller.[69]

A large influx of Africans—mostly male and mostly adult—inevitably made it difficult for a slave population to grow naturally. By the late seventeenth century, before large numbers of Africans arrived, the slave populations of Virginia and South Carolina were on the verge of growing by natural increase. By 1680 in various parts of Virginia and by the 1690s in South Carolina, the sex ratios of the two regions' adult slave populations began to approach parity. With growing numbers of women, the proportion of children in the two

---

of Hon. James Habersham, 1756–1775, GHS, *Colls.,* VI (Savannah, Ga., 1904), 216; Georgetown Gaol, *SCG,* Sept. 24, 1772 (these five shipmates identified their vessel's master as Capt. Dean; on June 30, 1772, Captain Deane of the *New Britannia* put up 220 slaves from Senegambia for sale). Other runaway slaves spoke of being purchased in large parcels: one who spoke "bad English" managed to tell "other negroes that the man who bought him, bought 9 new negroe men and 1 women, most of which ran away" (Workhouse, *SCG,* Nov. 25, 1751, Supplement). Lowcountry planters in East Florida also followed the pattern: David Yeats reported that neighboring planters wished to take 20–30 Africans each (Yeats to Governor Grant, Apr. 10, 1772, 0771/250, Papers of General James Grant of Ballindalloch).

68. Not all slaves were sold slowly or in small lots in the Chesapeake. The *Gally James,* for instance, arrived in the York Customs District on July 13, 1742. See Minchinton et al., eds., *Virginia Slave-Trade Statistics,* 119. Nine days later, John Baylor of Caroline entered a bond of £23.14s. to pay the treasurer of Virginia for the importation of 11 slaves (bond, July 22, 1742, John Baylor Papers, VHS). However, this is the largest individual purchase I have encountered in 18th-century Virginia records, though I have no doubt that a man like Robert "King" Carter purchased Africans on a larger scale.

69. Wood, *Black Majority,* xiv.

populations also began to increase. In southern Maryland, child-woman ratios (expressed as children per 100 women) rose from about 106 in the 1680s to about 140 in 1700; from a much lower figure of 67 in 1703, South Carolina's slave population also achieved a child-woman ratio of 140 by 1720.[70]

The experience of a planter in each region illustrates these possibilities. William Fitzhugh probably bought a few Africans to establish his Northern Neck quarters in the 1670s, but, as early as 1686, he noted that most of his slaves were "country born" and proudly proclaimed that his "Negroes increase being all young, and a considerable parcel of breeders, [so that they will] keep that Stock good for ever." Thenceforth there is no record of his buying slaves; the increase in his slave force from twenty-nine in 1686 to fifty-one in 1703 almost certainly came about from natural increase. In 1694, James Beamer of South Carolina died. His estate included twelve slaves—three men, three women, four boys, and two girls—just the sort of balance of men and women, adults and children, to be expected of a naturally growing complement.[71]

Once African immigration increased in scale, which occurred earlier in Virginia than in South Carolina, a check was placed on these possibilities for natural growth. In the first decade of the eighteenth century, Virginia's slave population experienced almost no natural increase (see Table 19). From late-seventeenth-century levels, adult sex ratios rose markedly, while child-woman ratios fell (see Figures 1 and 2). Similarly, in South Carolina twenty years later, growing numbers of forced African immigrants sent adult sex ratios soaring and child-woman ratios plummeting. The Lowcountry slave population experienced no natural growth in the 1720s (see Table 20).[72]

---

70. The sex ratio of tithable slaves in Northampton County ranged from 103 to 106 in the 1670s (Joseph Douglas Deal III, "Race and Class in Colonial Virginia: Indians, Englishmen, and Africans on the Eastern Shore during the Seventeenth Century" [Ph.D. diss., University of Rochester, 1981], 206). Inventories from Surry County and southern Maryland reveal more balanced adult slave sex ratios c. 1680 than at any other time in the late 17th and early 18th centuries: see Kulikoff, "A 'Prolifick' People," *So. Studies,* XVI (1977), 405; and Russell R. Menard, "The Maryland Slave Population, 1658 to 1730: A Demographic Profile of Blacks in Four Counties," *WMQ,* 3d Ser., XXXII (1975), 32. Only 20 South Carolina inventories have survived from the 1690s: 30 men, 28 women, 10 boys, 4 girls, and 9 children were listed. See Records of the Secretary of the Province, 1687–1710 and 1692–1700, SCDAH. The South Carolina female-child ratios for 1703 and 1708 are reported in Wood, *Black Majority,* 144. For 1720, see Figure 2.

71. Richard Beale Davis, *William Fitzhugh and His Chesapeake World, 1676–1701* (Chapel Hill, N.C., 1963), 84, 93, 104, 105–106, 119, 127, 175, 382; inventory of James Beamer, May 11, 1694, Records of the Secretary of the Province, WPA, LIII, 206–209.

72. It is interesting, however, that the one detailed local census in colonial South Carolina reveals a 128 male-female ratio and 117 child-woman ratio for its slave population—much less imbalanced than the ratios derived from the inventories drawn from the whole colony.

TABLE 19.
Black Population Growth in Virginia, 1700–1800

Period	Population Increase	Surviving New Immigrants	Annual Rate of Natural Increase
1700–1710	6,500	6,210	.2%
1710–1720	7,500	5,680	.9
1720–1730	13,000	10,150	1.0
1730–1740	25,000	12,790	3.0
1740–1750	40,000	9,680	4.7
1750–1760	35,500	7,180	2.7
1760–1770	40,000	7,570	2.3
1770–1775	24,500	3,190	2.4
1775–1780	19,000	0	1.8
1780–1790	69,000	0	3.1
1790–1800	53,000	0	1.8

Notes: Population increase rounded to nearest 500; survivors, to nearest 10. Black population is believed to be 13,000 in 1700 (see Table 10).

As early as the second decade of the eighteenth century, Virginia's slave population began to grow from natural increase, an unprecedented event for any New World slave population. Virginia imported fewer Africans in the 1710s than in the previous decade, and the colony's slave population grew naturally by almost 1 percent a year. By the 1730s—a decade when Virginia imported more slaves than ever before or again in its history—the slave population increased, by natural means, at a remarkable rate of about 3 percent a year. Adult sex ratios reflected the increase in Africans, climbing steeply to 150 in some Virginia counties, and to over 180 in Prince George's County, Maryland. However, the proportion of children increased significantly, too; there were now almost two children for every adult female. Slave women were producing enough children to more than replace adults of the previous generation. Sex ratios among children were roughly equal and were to remain so. Virginian slaveowners began to mention the value of having women in their labor forces. One perceptive clergyman observed the transformation that had occurred

---

See "Names and Number of the Inhabitants of St. George Parish, So. Carolina, Inclosed in Mr. Varnod's Letter dated 21 January 1725," A19/104–108, SPG. My ratios vary slightly from those reported in Wood, *Black Majority,* 164–165.

Sex Ratio (Males per 100 Females)

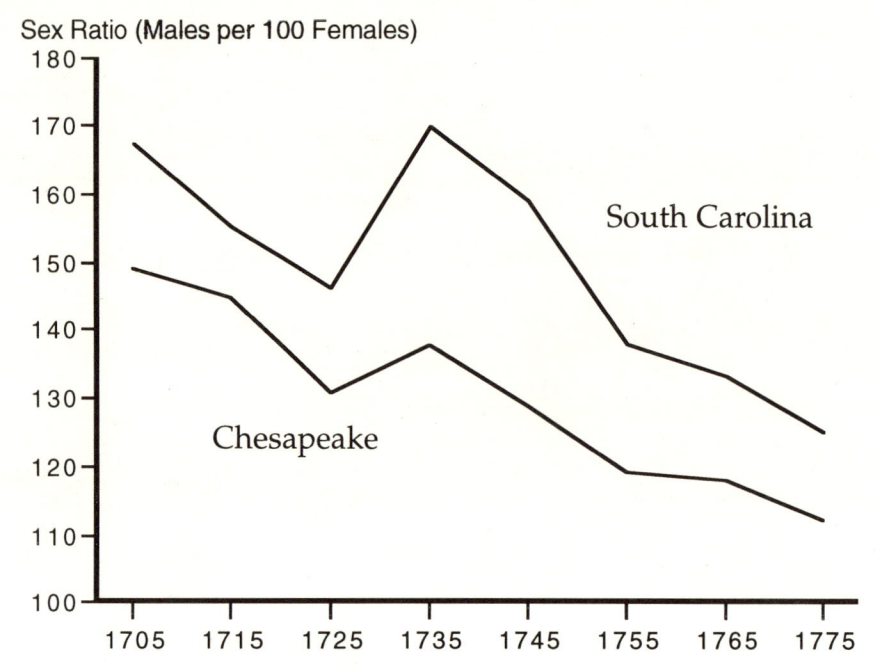

FIGURE 1. *Adult Sex Ratios among Slaves in the Chesapeake and South Carolina, 1705–1775*
Sources: Southern Maryland data, 1700–1729, in Russell R. Menard, "The Maryland Slave Population, 1658 to 1730: A Demographic Profile of Blacks in Four Counties," *WMQ*, 3d Ser., XXXII (1975), 29–54; information from inventories of Middlesex County, Virginia, 1700–1747, kindly supplied by Darrett and Anita Rutman; information from inventories of Amelia, Charlotte, Halifax, Lunenburg, Mecklenburg, Pittsylvania, and Prince Edward Counties, Virginia, 1737–1775, kindly supplied by Michael L. Nicholls; inventories of Chesterfield, Cumberland, Essex, Goochland, Isle of Wight, Loudoun, Northampton, Orange, Spotsylvania, and York Counties, 1700–1779, VSL; all South Carolina inventories, 1700–1779, SCDAH.

among the colony's black population. In 1724, he wrote, "The Negroes are not only encreased by fresh supplies from Africa and the West India Islands; but also are very prolifick among themselves."[73]

In South Carolina, by contrast, a greater influx of Africans and a smaller initial population turned the slowing of the rate of natural increase that had occurred in the 1720s into a negative rate of growth in the following decade. In the 1730s, the adult sex ratio climbed to 170 (its highest point in the century) while child-female ratios plunged drastically. It took another decade, one in

---

73. Kulikoff, "A 'Prolifick' People," *So. Studies*, XVI (1977), 405; deed of gift of Nathaniel Pope, May 26, 1719, Westmoreland County Deeds and Wills, no. 8, part 1, 18; will of Lewis Burwell, Oct. 11, 1710, York County Deeds, Orders, Wills, no. 14, 60–64, VSL; will of John Yeates, 1731, Admiralty and Probate Court of Canterbury, England, as cited in the "Negro in Nansemond" (typescript, UVa); Hugh Jones, *The Present State of Virginia...*, ed. Richard L. Morton (Chapel Hill, N.C., 1956), 75.

Children per 100 Women

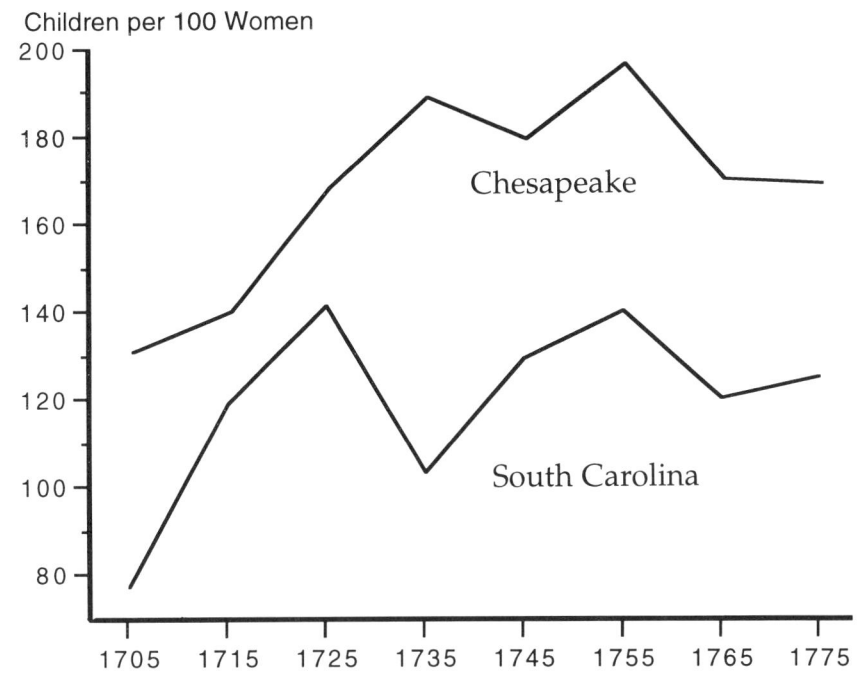

FIGURE 2. *Female-Child Ratios among Slaves in the Chesapeake and South Carolina, 1705–1775*
Sources: See Table 1.

which few Africans were imported, before the Lowcountry slave population recovered its equilibrium. The conjunction, which had occurred in Virginia by the 1730s at the latest, of a considerable African influx and a naturally increasing African American population did not appear in South Carolina until the 1750s at the earliest. Nevertheless, the resurgence of African imports into South Carolina in the quarter-century before the Revolution failed to dampen the slowly rising rate of natural increase of the colony's slave population, which by the 1770s had reached a respectable 1.5 percent. In South Carolina, the number of slave men and women, boys and girls, approached parity in the last twenty-five years of the colonial era, a trend that remained unaffected by massive imports. This Lowcountry transformation also had its contemporary chroniclers. At about midcentury, James Glen observed that, in spite of almost a decade of nonimportation of Africans, the black population of the province increased. By all accounts, he concluded, "the *Negroes* bred from our own Stock will continually recruit and keep [the numbers] up." Similarly, the Reverend James Stuart, resident in South Carolina until 1777, when he left with the British for the West Indies, recalled that he had been a "Rector of a Parish in Carolina, and was ready to advance that many Estates in that District, though

TABLE 20.
Black Population Growth in South Carolina, 1700–1800

Period	Population Increase	Surviving New Immigrants	Annual Rate of Natural Increase
1700–1710	2,600	2,480	.5%
1710–1720	7,000	5,760	2.5
1720–1730	10,000	9,530	.3
1730–1740	17,000	17,130	−.1
1740–1750	1,000	1,580	−.1
1750–1760	17,000	13,390	.9
1760–1770	25,000	17,748	1.3
1770–1775	22,000	15,789	1.5
1775–1780	−10,000	0	−1.9
1780–1790	13,000	15,579	−.2
1790–1800	39,000	16,048	2.1

Notes: Population increase rounded to nearest 500. Population in 1700 is believed to be 2,400 (see Table 10).

more unhealthy than the West Indies, supported themselves, by proper Treatment, independently of the Slave-Trade." A few years later, David Ramsay pointed out that "for forty miles around Charlestown the white inhabitants do not increase by natural generation; but the negroes do." This observation led Ramsay "to think that Providence intended this for a negro settlement."[74]

From about midcentury, the African American population of the Chesapeake accomplished something that its Lowcountry counterpart would not experience for at least another sixty years. It grew *primarily* from natural increase, and at a rapid rate. Virginia's slave population had reached a stability and maturity far in advance of its Lowcountry counterpart. Many a planter

74. Glen, *A Description of South Carolina,* in Milling, ed., *Colonial South Carolina,* 45. Stuart's recollections are reported in Thomas Clarkson to Lord Liverpool, June 25, 1788, Liverpool Papers, Add. MSS 38416; David Ramsay to Benjamin Rush, Jan. 23, 1780, Benjamin Rush Papers, HSP. See also Governor James Grant to Richard Oswald, Oct. 12, 1765, Bound Letter Book, 1764–1766, 0771/659, Papers of General James Grant of Ballindalloch; Questions by Mr. Green, Answers by Mr. Telfair, Mar. 1774, Countess of Huntingdon's American Papers; Siebert, ed., *Loyalists in East Florida,* II, 58; Elias Ball to Elias Ball, Jan. 8, 1788, Ball Family Papers, USC; W[illiam] Faux, *Memorable Days in America . . . ,* in Thwaites, ed., *Early Western Travels,* XI, 71–72.

must have echoed Henry Fitzhugh's quiet satisfaction, registered in a letter to his merchants, that, without imports, "my negroes increase yearly by which I am enabled to settle new quarters and consequently my exports must increase." By the third quarter of the eighteenth century, contemporaries were well aware that most slaves were creoles in the Chesapeake region. In 1770, William Eddis rightly observed that blacks in Maryland were "in general, natives of the country, very few in proportion being imported from the coast of Africa." Similarly, a visitor to Virginia in 1782 noted that "the propagation of the black species is very rapid and very considerable here," so that "most of the Negroes are born in this country."[75]

Such was the impact of this creole predominance that increasingly extravagant (though not outrageous) claims can be heard about the demographic performance of Chesapeake slaves. As early as 1756, the Reverend Peter Fontaine, a minister in Charles City County, believed that black females were "far more prolific than . . . white women." He attributed the difference to the slave women's simple diet and their "being used to labor in the ground." Four years later, another observer wrote that blacks "propagate and increase even faster" than whites. Toward the end of the century, such comments were commonplace. William Beverley believed that blacks were less subject to the agues and fevers that plagued Chesapeake whites; John Leland, a Baptist minister, thought that slaves "populate as fast as the whites do, and are rather more healthy"; and Joshua Evans, a Quaker itinerant, reported a conversation with an elderly man in Maryland who "informed me there was but one white man of his age within 20 miles; and that within the same distance there were more than 20 blacks as old as himself." Evans himself interjected that "in the southern parts, black people are commonly longer lived than the whites, and believe it is owing to their being kept on low diet, than to the blackness of their skin."[76]

A graphic illustration of the difference in the demographic profiles of the South Carolina and Virginia slave populations can be gained from age pyramids of individual plantations. A perfectly stable and closed population will

---

75. Henry Fitzhugh to Messrs. John Stewart and Campbell, July 29, 1766, Henry Fitzhugh Letterbook, Duke; Francis Fauquier to Commissioners for Trade and Plantations, June 2, 1760, CO5/1330, 17–18, PRO; testimony of William Beverley, in Great Britain, Parliament, *House of Commons Sessional Papers of the Eighteenth Century,* LXXXII, *George III, Slave Trade, 1791 and 1792,* ed. Sheila Lambert (Wilmington, Del., 1975), 215; Eddis, *Letters from America,* 35; Marquis de Chastellux, *Travels in North America in the Years 1780, 1781, and 1782,* ed. and trans. Howard C. Rice, Jr., II (Chapel Hill, N.C., 1963), 439.

76. Ann Maury, ed. and trans., *Memoirs of a Huguenot Family . . .* (New York, 1907), 347–348; Andrew Burnaby, *Travels through the Middle Settlements in North-America, in the Years 1759 and 1760 . . . ,* 3d ed. (London, 1798), 150; John Leland, *The Virginia Chronicle . . .* (Norfolk, Va., 1790), 7; testimony of Beverley, *House of Commons Sessional Papers,* LXXXII, 216; diary of Joshua Evans, Nov. 3, 1796, So. Hist. Coll., UNC.

produce a perfectly symmetrical age pyramid. Any significant divergence from this shape suggests a population artificially constructed. Slave populations often exhibit this characteristic, their diagrammatic structures being likened to "lopsided Christmas tree[s]." The more lopsided the tree—the more pronounced the "bulge" in the middle age ranges—the greater the likelihood that the plantation population had been augmented by recently imported Africans. Representative Chesapeake and Lowcountry population pyramids suggest the dimensions of the disparity between the two regions (see Figures 3 and 4). No Lowcountry plantation population that has been uncovered comes near to resembling a perfectly symmetrical pyramid, whereas late-eighteenth-century Chesapeake plantations begin to do so.[77]

How can the demographic performances of these two slave populations be explained? In general terms, as Russell Menard has argued for the Maryland slave population, the key lies in the growing number of native-born women. In Virginia around 1720 and in South Carolina some thirty years later, creole majorities emerged. The preponderance of creole women, who lived longer than their immigrant forebears, were less sickly, less unwilling to have children, and, most important, able to have children at a much younger age, was

77. Michael Craton, *Searching for the Invisible Man: Slaves and Plantation Life in Jamaica* (Cambridge, Mass., 1978), 61. I constructed a number of age pyramids for a variety of Lowcountry and Chesapeake plantations. Those displayed in Figures 3 and 4 are the most graphic, without being unrepresentative. For other age listings in the Chesapeake, see inventories of Paul and Henry Micou [40 slaves], Dec. 2, 18, 1742, Essex County Will Book, no. 6, 408–411, 417, VSL; Notebooks of Rev. Robert Rose [89 slaves], 1752, VHS; lists of slaves, Dec. 1773 through July 1774 [385 slaves], Charles Carroll Account Book, Carroll Papers, MHS; lists of Negroes at Green Spring, etc. [124 slaves], 1774–1775, Lee-Ludwell Papers, VHS; list of Negroes at Green Branch [52 slaves], May 18, 1778, Richard Corbin Papers, microfilm, CW; inventory of Joseph Bass [39 slaves], Mar. 4, 1779, Chesterfield County Will Book, no. 3, 218–220, VSL; list of slaves of Thomas Spriggs [72 slaves], c. 1780s, Mercer Family Papers, VHS; list of Negroes belonging to Samuel Gist [149 slaves], Nov. 12, 1783, VHS; list of slaves belonging to Edmund Randolph, Sept. 23, 1784, Randolph Papers, microfilm, CW; inventory of the estate of George Booth [87 slaves], Jan. 16, 1786, Gloucester County Papers, W and M; appraisement of the estate of Benjamin Harrison [113 slaves], July 1791, Brock Collection, microfilm, CW; inventory of the estate of William Fitzhugh, Apr. 4–5, 1810, conveniently reproduced in Donald Mitchell Sweig, "Northern Virginia Slavery: A Statistical and Demographic Study" (Ph.D. diss., College of William and Mary, 1982), 116–121. For other age listings in the Lowcountry, see the inventory of John Cawood [39 slaves], Jan. 4, 1728, Register of the Secretary of the Province, 1726–1727, WPA, LXIB, 542–552; inventory of George Austin at Pedee [110 slaves], Dec. 6, 1774, Inventories, WPA, XCVIII, 68–71; list of slaves belonging to James Grant [67 slaves], Feb. 3, 1781, 0771/250, Papers of General James Grant of Ballindalloch; a list of Negroes taken at Hampton [432 slaves], May 4, 1793, Butler Family Papers, HSP; appraisement of the Negroes of the estate of Hannah Bull [90 slaves], Dec. 13, 1797, and list of Negroes belonging to Col. Stapleton [112 slaves], Mar. 15, 1810, John Stapleton Papers, USC.

critical in producing rapid rates of natural increase. A closer analysis of this phenomenon can proceed on two levels: first, an examination of appropriate demographic indicators, such as age at first birth of creole mothers, birthspacing intervals, and completed family size; second, a consideration of the underlying social and economic conditions, including such matters as diet, forced migration, sexual mores, and household and family structure. It is impossible, particularly from eighteenth-century sources, to disaggregate this complex of factors and to assess their individual impact; and, in any case, it may be best to see them as thoroughly interrelated.[78]

An important component of natural growth was the childbearing patterns of slave women. Creole women in both the Chesapeake and the Lowcountry began childbearing at extremely youthful ages by early modern European standards (see Table 21). Whereas women in eighteenth-century England began childbearing in their midtwenties, slave women in eighteenth-century North America tended to be in their late teens when they conceived their first child. Moreover, if anything, age at first birth had a downward trend over the course of the eighteenth century. Quite obviously, then, when creole women formed a significant proportion of all slave women, overall slave fertility was enhanced.[79]

Creole women also bore children frequently. In the Lowcountry, the mean birth interval for eighteenth-century slave mothers was about twenty-seven months. In the Chesapeake it ranged between twenty-five and thirty months. John Smyth, a traveler, was not far from the mark when he observed that Virginia slave women gave birth "generally every two or three years." Individual slave women from both colonies illustrate this general pattern: when William Butler of Stono sold a slave family in 1747, he listed the ages of the family's six children, who ranged from two to twelve; when Lucy ran away from her South Carolina master in 1749, she had one "child in her arms, and [was] big of another"; and Judith, aged about thirty and a resident of Williamsburg, was pregnant when she ran away in 1773, although she also carried a twelve-month-

---

78. Menard, "The Maryland Slave Population," *WMQ*, 3d Ser., XXXII (1975), 29–54, esp. 47; Herbert S. Klein and Stanley L. Engerman, "Fertility Differentials between Slaves in the United States and the British West Indies: A Note on Lactation Practices and Their Possible Implications," ibid., XXXV (1978), 357–374; Robert W. Fogel and Stanley L. Engerman, "Recent Findings in the Study of Slave Demography and Family Structure," *Sociology and Social Research*, LXIII (1979), 566–589.

79. For a summary of the comparative data, see Fogel and Engerman, "Recent Findings," *Sociol. and Soc. Res.*, LXIII (1979), 569, 572. See also Cheryll Ann Cody, "A Note on Changing Patterns of Slave Fertility in the South Carolina Rice District, 1735–1865," *So. Studies*, XVI (1977), 457–463. For interesting work on this subject in the 19th-century South, see James Trussell and Richard Steckel, "The Age of Slaves at Menarche and Their First Birth," *Jour. Interdisc. Hist.*, VIII (1977–1978), 477–505; Richard H. Steckel, "The Fertility of American Slaves," *Res. Econ. Hist.*, VII (1982), 239–286.

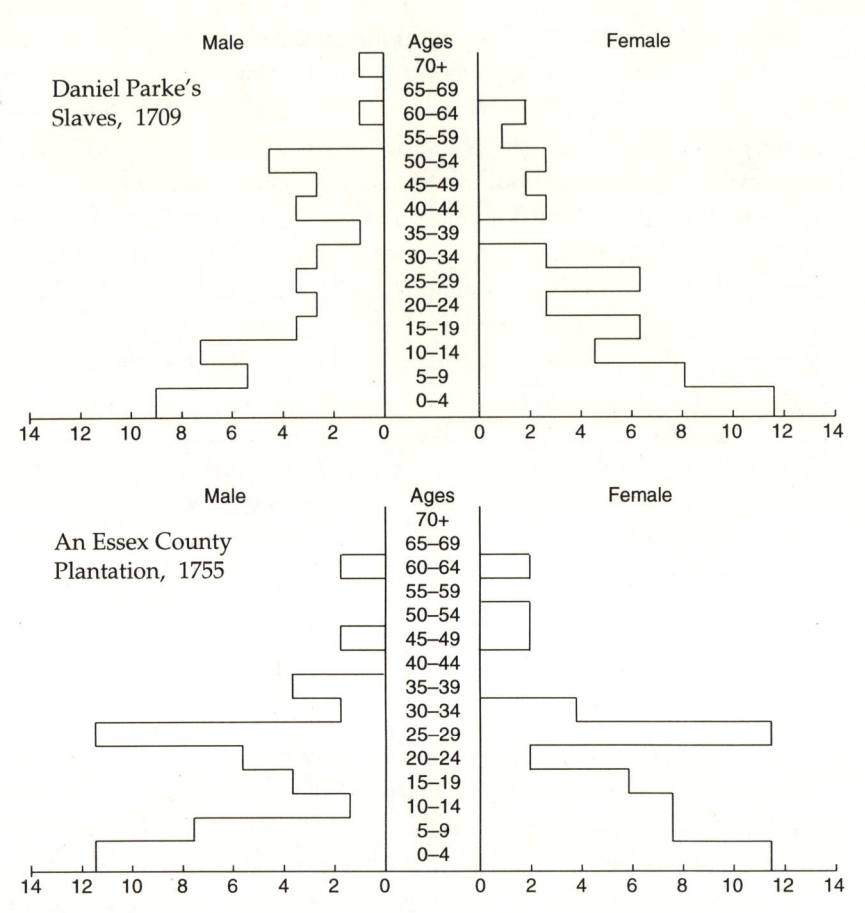

FIGURE 3. *Population Pyramids of Slaves in the Chesapeake, 1709–1791*
Sources: "An Account of all the Negroes and other slaves of Daniel Parke Esq. ...." [111 slaves], Dec. 1709, Emmet Collection, microfilm, CW; inventory of Capt. John Micou [52 slaves], Jan. 15–16, 1755,

old daughter, still "at the breast." Creole slave women in both regions, then, like their European and white American counterparts, and unlike most of their West African forebears, experienced a birth about once every other year, sometimes yearly.[80]

80. Smyth, *A Tour in the United States of America*, I, 47; deed of sale between William Butler and Charles Pinckney, Jan. 1, 1747, Miscellaneous Records, GG, 118, SCDAH; William Randall, *SCG*, Apr. 17, 1749; John Mclean, *VaG* (P and D), May 6, 1773. The South Carolina statistics are based on eight Ball family and seven Ravenel family slave women, who began childbearing in the colonial period and for whom the reproductive cycle can be reconstructed, providing a mean birth interval of 27.1 and 26.5 months, respectively. In addition, other listings that report the ages of a woman and her children provide rudimentary birth intervals by including only those women with three or more children and by discounting

The Custis Slaves, 1771

Robert Carter's Slaves, 1791

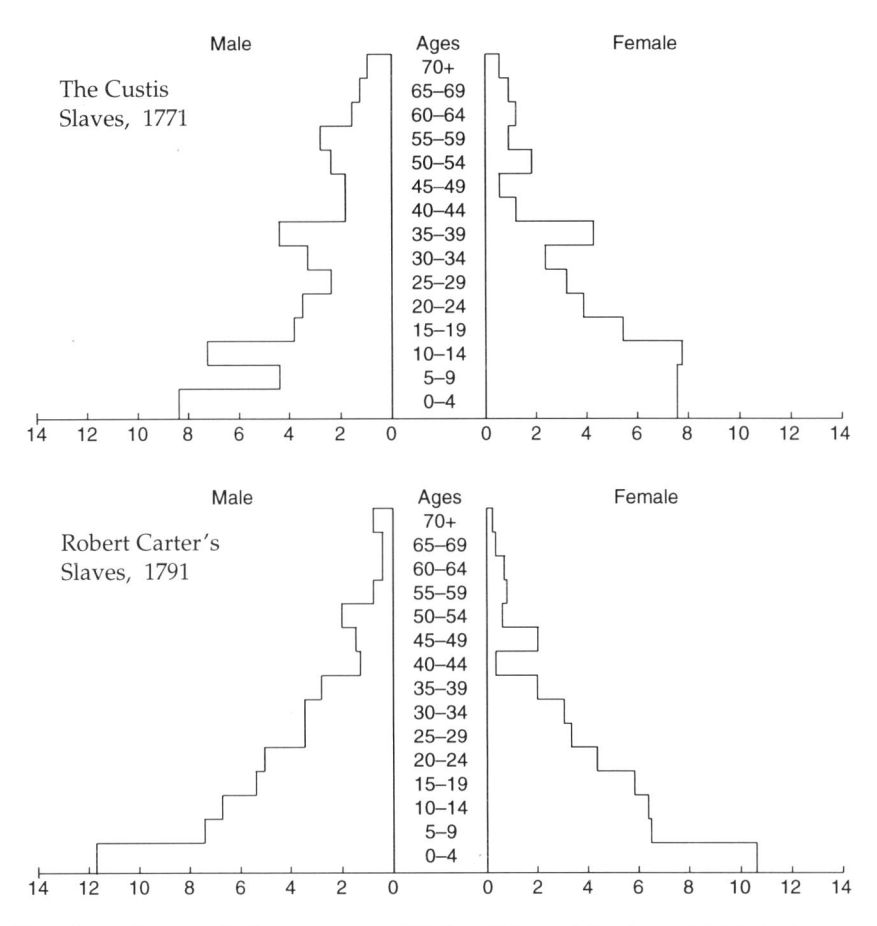

Essex County Inventory Book, no. 10, 133–135, VSL; lists of Negroes belonging to Col. John Parke Custis and George Washington [331 slaves], Dec. 1771, Custis Papers, VHS; list of slaves attached to a deed of emancipation [506 slaves], 1791, Robert Carter Papers, XI, 1–42, Duke.

A creole woman who conceived her first child in her late teens and completed a full reproductive cycle could expect to bear eight or nine children. By no means did all mothers meet this expectation. However, women generally lived longer than men, and the few for whom completed family size can be measured did indeed produce large families. Thus, on four eighteenth-century Chesapeake plantations, the range of completed family sizes averaged from

---

births to mothers over age 35. Using the same data listed in Table 21, the average birth interval was about 36 months (50 observations). I have calculated birth intervals from a variety of piedmont Virginia data (cited in sources to Table 21) and, on the basis of 181 birth intervals, omitting any longer than 60 months, the average was 28 months. See also Kulikoff, "A 'Prolifick' People," *So. Studies*, XVI (1977), 407–408; and Klein and Engerman, "Fertility Differentials," *WMQ*, 3d Ser., XXXV (1978), 368–370.

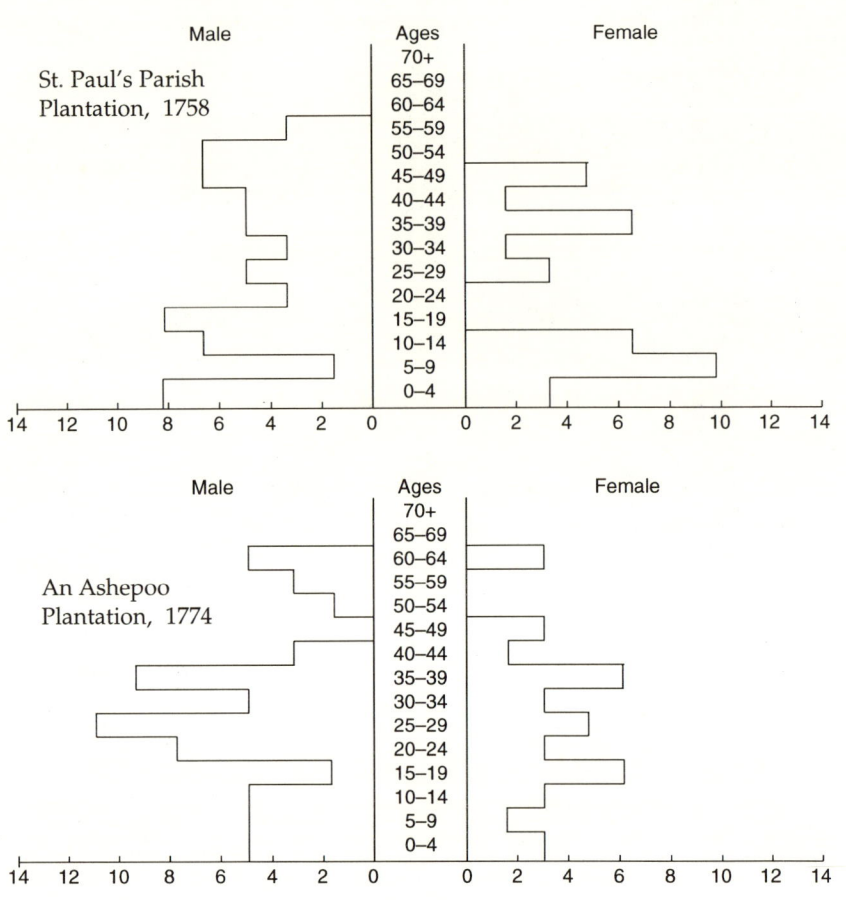

FIGURE 4. *Population Pyramids of Slaves in the Lowcountry, 1758–1780*
Sources: Inventory of Col. Alexander Vanderdussen [61 slaves], Apr. 4, 1758, Inventories, T, 1–2; inventory of George Austin at Ashepoo [64 slaves], Nov. 16, 1774, Inventories, WPA, XCVIII, 65–67;

7.7 to 8.3; and Ball and Ravenel slaves in the Lowcountry reveal an average completed family size of just over 8 persons. In 1789, a South Carolina runaway family that might not have included all members stood at eight persons. But the most extraordinary example of a large Lowcountry family is the one headed by George and his wife, Grace, who in July 1791 gave birth to yet another son. Their master exulted about "this remarkable couple," who had just produced "their 22[d] Child." Hardly a typical couple, but slave families half that size were not unusual—at least by the late eighteenth century.[81]

If reproductive rates of slave women in Virginia and South Carolina were

81. See Kulikoff, "A 'Prolifick' People," *So. Studies*, XVI (1977), 409; Alex Cameron, *City Gaz*, July 8, 1789; Alexander Garden, Jr., to George Ogilvie, July 21, 1791, 10/7/16, Ogilvie-Forbes of Boyndlie MSS.

Prince Frederick's Parish Plantation, 1776

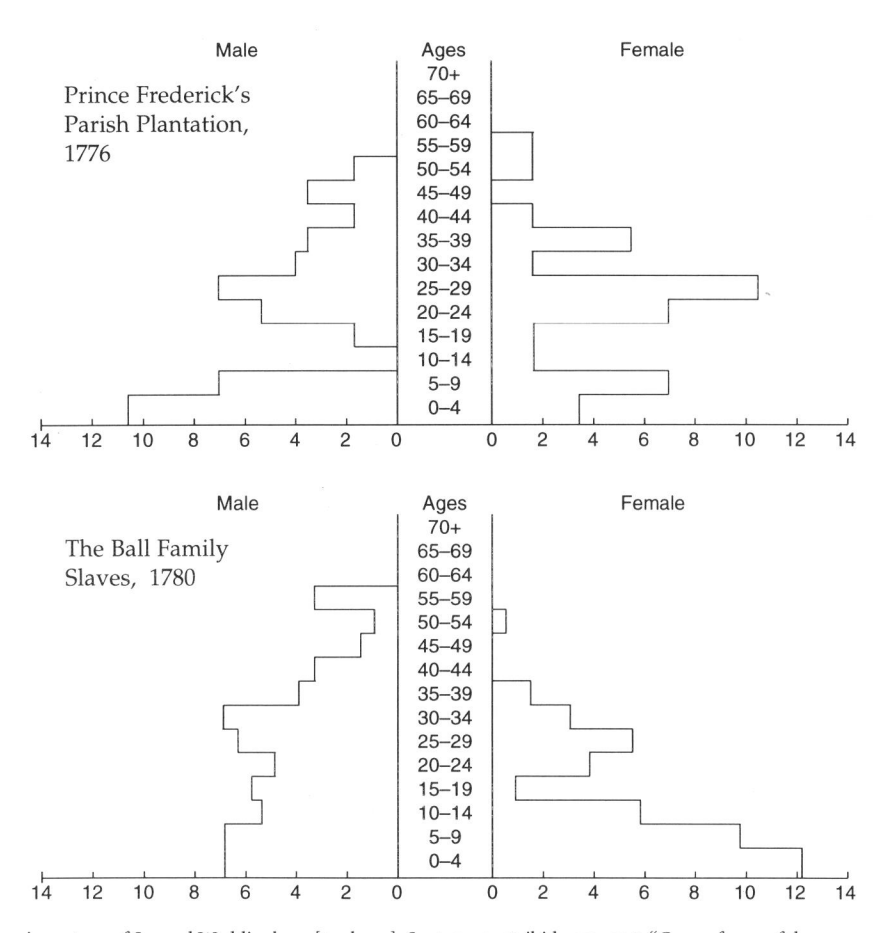

Male | Ages | Female
14 12 10 8 6 4 2 0 | 70+ / 65–69 / 60–64 / 55–59 / 50–54 / 45–49 / 40–44 / 35–39 / 30–34 / 25–29 / 20–24 / 15–19 / 10–14 / 5–9 / 0–4 | 0 2 4 6 8 10 12 14

The Ball Family Slaves, 1780

Male | Ages | Female
14 12 10 8 6 4 2 0 | 70+ / 65–69 / 60–64 / 55–59 / 50–54 / 45–49 / 40–44 / 35–39 / 30–34 / 25–29 / 20–24 / 15–19 / 10–14 / 5–9 / 0–4 | 0 2 4 6 8 10 12 14

inventory of Samuel Waddingham [57 slaves], Sept. 27, 1776, ibid., 223–226; "Copy of ages of the Negroes belonging to my father . . . Mar. 6, 1780," John and Keating Simons Ball Papers, Southern Historical Collection, UNC; and Ball Account Book, SCHS.

similar, mortality rates were not. Rice production undoubtedly forced a harsher work regimen than that of tobacco, and the Lowcountry provided a less favorable environment than that of the Chesapeake. Unfortunately, few eighteenth-century sources allow a precise measure of the difference. Evidence from two eighteenth-century Chesapeake plantations suggests that the death rates of slave children from birth to age four was 327 per 1,000. Only one eighteenth-century source from the Lowcountry permits the calculation of the same rate: it reveals a somewhat higher mortality of 342 per 1,000. It is likely that this small contrast, based on too few cases, understates the difference between the two regions.[82]

82. Kulikoff, "A 'Prolifick' People," *So. Studies,* XVI (1977), 427–428; Peter Gaillard's Book of Accounts, Gaillard Family Papers, SCHS. The Gaillard register of slave births and deaths lists children who survived only a few days (just over half of those dying within the first year

TABLE 21.
Age at First Conception of Slave Women, 1700s–1790s

Birth of Mother	Residence	Mean Age	No. of Cases
	Chesapeake		
1700s–1720s	Virginia and Maryland	18.4	27
1730s–1740s	Maryland	19.1	88
1750s–1760s	Virginia and Maryland	18.2	94
1770s–1790s	Piedmont Virginia	17.5	15
	Lowcountry		
1710s–1720s	South Carolina	19.7	7
1730s–1740s	South Carolina	19.3	25
1750s–1760s	South Carolina	18.8	26
1770s–1780s	South Carolina	17.9	7

Sources: Chesapeake: Lists of Slaves, 1725, 1726, 1732, 1736, Jones Family Papers, LC; Allan Kulikoff, "A 'Prolifick' People: Black Population Growth in the Southern Colonies, 1700–1790," *Southern Studies,* XVI (1977), 407; list of the Negroes at the Green Branch, May 1778, Richard Corbin Miscellaneous Papers, microfilm, CW; Paul Carrington Account Book, VHS; Slave Book, Jerdone Family Papers, VSL; William Bolling Register, 1752–1890, VHS; Stephen Cocke Account Book, 1772–1847, VHS.

Lowcountry: Ravenel Account Book, B1-1, Ravenel Papers, SCHS; Ball Account Book, Ball Papers, SCHS, and John and Keating Ball Books, UNC; inventory of Alexander Vanderdussen, Apr. 4, 1758, Inventory Book, T, 1–2; inventory of Abraham Erhard, Oct. 28, 1758, Inventory Book, T, 76–78; inventory of George Austin, Nov. 16, Dec. 6, 1774, Inventory Book, AA, 42–51; inventory of Samuel Waddingham, Sept. 2, 1776, Inventory Book, AA, 149–151, SCDAH; list of Negroes taken at Hampton, May 4, 1793, Wister Family Papers, Butler Section, HSP.

Diet affected both mortality and fertility rates. In general, it seems obvious that the North American slave diet was sufficient to sustain life; it is inconceiv-

---

were not named, and most of these died within two weeks of birth). Of the 193 children born between 1786 and 1809 to mothers who had at least one child before 1800, 24% died within a year of birth, 6% died between 1 and 3 years, 6% between 4 and 9 years, and 58% survived at least 10 years, with 6% unrecorded. In the 19th century, Richard H. Steckel has found higher infant mortality rates on those plantations that produced rice rather than other crops: Steckel, "Slave Mortality: Analysis of Evidence from Plantation Records," *Social Science History,* III (1979), 86–114, esp. 106. See also John Campbell, "Work, Pregnancy, and Infant Mortality among Southern Slaves," *Jour. Interdisc. Hist.,* XIV (1983–1984), 793–812.

able otherwise that the mainland slave population could have increased so rapidly. Another rough measure of diet's significance is the average height of slaves. On this basis, the North American diet appears more than adequate, for mainland slaves were generally taller than Caribbean slaves, and creoles taller than Africans. Moreover, the diet of Chesapeake slaves was apparently particularly varied and sustaining, for Virginia slaves were on the whole taller than their South Carolina counterparts.[83]

The forced movement of slaves within a region also had significant demographic effects. The relocation of large numbers of slaves obviously disrupted family life and the childbearing patterns of slave women, but, if the relocation was to a healthier environment, the long-term consequences were beneficial—viewed purely in reproductive rates. More Chesapeake slaves were subject to greater internal migration than Lowcountry slaves; by 1790, about half of Virginia's slave population, as compared to only about a quarter of South Carolina's, resided in the piedmont. As a result, Virginia slaves were the victims of a larger scale of family disruptions. But the childbearing patterns of those slaves moved west in the Chesapeake were not affected adversely. In fact, the opposite was true, for the child-woman ratios of piedmont slave women were higher than those for the tidewater. The piedmont was a much healthier environment for slaves, and a rapid rate of natural increase thereby ensued. In this purely demographic sense, the Virginia slave population was in a more advantageous position than that of South Carolina.[84]

---

83. For a discussion of diet in the two regions, see Chapter 2. Information on slave heights—most of it 19th-century—is reported in Fogel and Engerman, "Recent Findings," *Sociol. and Soc. Res.*, LXIII (1979), 573, 585; Richard H. Steckel, "Slave Height Profiles from Coastwise Manifests," *Explorations in Economic History*, 2d Ser., XVI (1979), 363–380; David Eltis, "Nutritional Trends in Africa and the Americas: Heights of Africans, 1819–1839," *Jour. Interdisc. Hist.*, XII (1981–1982), 453–475; the fall issue of *Soc. Sci. Hist.*, VI (1982); Richard H. Steckel, "A Peculiar Population: The Nutrition, Health, and Mortality of American Slaves from Childhood to Maturity," *Jour. Econ. Hist.*, XLVI (1986), 721–741; and Robert W. Fogel, *Without Consent or Contract: The Rise and Fall of American Slavery* (New York, 1989), 138–143. By comparison, colonial data are very sketchy. However, I have compiled age by height data from South Carolina runaway advertisements between 1732 and 1779 (the workhouse jailer perhaps can be relied upon to take reasonably accurate measurements). The average height of native-born males aged 16 to 50 was 67 inches ($N = 292$). For both creoles and Africans, it was 66 inches ($N = 673$). Lathan Algerna Windley reports a corresponding average height of 68.5 inches for Virginia creole men: "A Profile of Runaway Slaves in Virginia and South Carolina from 1730 through 1787" (Ph.D. diss., University of Iowa, 1974), 89, table VII.

84. For the comparisons of tidewater and piedmont within Virginia, see Morgan and Nicholls, "Slaves in Piedmont Virginia," *WMQ*, 3d Ser., XLVI (1989), 211–251. One piece of evidence from the Lowcountry seems to bear out the advantages of an inland over a coastal location. John Graham recalled that annual slave mortality on his inland plantations was

In general, two-parent slave households exhibited higher fertility than single-parent households. In the Chesapeake, however, the plantations with the highest female-child ratios were those formed predominantly or exclusively of adult females. About one-sixth of all adults in the inventoried populations of both York and Essex Counties were resident on such units, but those plantations claimed almost a third of the children in York County and a fifth of those in Essex County. A nineteenth-century study indicates that the percentage of women bearing children was higher on small than on large plantations. Child-woman ratios were highest in divided-residence units, if not single-parent households. Such units were more common in the Chesapeake than in the Lowcountry.[85]

Although the explanation for the differential rates of natural increase of the Lowcountry and Chesapeake black populations rests very largely on impersonal factors, the role of planters cannot be discounted altogether. Certainly, the planters' claims of "good treatment" should be viewed with skepticism; but slaveowners, particularly in the Chesapeake, were quick to see the value in, and then facilitate the supply of, young children, even if they did little to bring the supply about in the first place. Virginia masters were soon advising their overseers to be "kind and indulgent" to pregnant women. Thomas Jefferson rendered the commercial logic of this concern explicit when he stated that masters held "a woman who brings a child every two years as more valuable than the best man on the farm." Ubiquitous payments to midwives and regular distribution of quarts of rum and pounds of sugar to women in childbirth betoken Chesapeake planter interest. Such payments were not as common in Lowcountry plantation accounts. Nor does recognition of the value of slave children appear as early in that region as in the Chesapeake. When, in 1767, the governor of East Florida rejected a slave woman who had been procured for him, Henry Laurens observed, "The Governor does not understand Plantation affairs so well as some of us Southern folks . . . Nancy is a breeding Woman and in ten Years time may have doubled her worth in her own Children." Only by the late eighteenth century were Lowcountry folk coming round to Laurens's view.[86]

---

half the rate of his tidewater plantations: Schedule of Lands and Slaves of John Graham (1781), Miscellaneous Bonds, KK-2, 286–297, and Memorial of John Graham, Georgia Loyalist Claims, A.O. 13/106, as cited in Harold E. Davis, *The Fledgling Province: Social and Cultural Life in Colonial Georgia, 1773–1776* (Chapel Hill, N.C., 1976), 135.

85. Klein and Engerman, "Fertility Differentials," *WMQ*, 3d Ser., XXXV (1978), 364–365; Richard H. Steckel, *The Economics of U.S. Slave and Southern White Fertility* (New York, 1985), 203–206, 226–232; Fogel, *Without Consent or Contract*, 152.

86. Richard Corbin to James Semple, Jan. 1, 1759, Richard Corbin Letterbook, CW; Edwin Morris Betts, ed., *Thomas Jefferson's Farm Book, with Commentary and Relevant*

Although the more rapid natural increase of Chesapeake as against Lowcountry slaves has many explanations, there can be no doubt of the difference. The Chesapeake slave population increased remarkably quickly by natural increase; the Lowcountry slave population eventually achieved a comparable rate, though laggardly. Creoles thus formed a majority of slaves at a much earlier date in the Chesapeake than in the Lowcountry. In fact, creoles were in a majority in Virginia by 1720. By midcentury, they formed about four-fifths of the slave population; and by 1780, nineteen of twenty slaves were creoles. In South Carolina, creoles did not outnumber Africans until midcentury, although by 1780 they formed two-thirds of the province's slave population.

South Carolina possessed not only more Africans and fewer creoles than Virginia but also a greater black presence. "As we advance to the south," observed Annapolis resident William Eddis in 1770, the "multitudes [of Negroes] astonishingly increase, and in the Carolinas they considerably exceed the number of white inhabitants." The difference had long been present. As early as the turn of the century, African American slaves formed almost one-half of South Carolina's population (excluding Indians), and, by 1720, they formed two-thirds. The vast majority of South Carolina's black slaves in 1720 lived in parishes that were more than 60 percent black, and almost half of them lived in parishes that were more than 70 percent black. In 1700, blacks formed but one-sixth of the Chesapeake's population, and, by 1720, they constituted no more than a quarter. In 1720, no Chesapeake county was 60 percent black.[87]

As the century proceeded, blacks assumed greater prominence in both populations, but, by the late eighteenth century, the divergence in the racial composition of the two populations was, if anything, more marked. By 1760, all but three Lowcountry rural parishes were more than 70 per cent black, and, by 1790, eleven of eighteen Lowcountry rural parishes were more than 80 percent black. If in 1737 Samuel Dyssli reckoned that "Carolina looks more like a negro country than like a country settled by white people," by 1780, David Ramsay could speak more authoritatively of "Providence [having] intended this for a negro settlement." When George Ogilvie, an émigré Scot, took up residence at Myrtle Grove plantation on the banks of the Santee River in 1774, the force of these settlement patterns made an immediate impact. "Having no

---

Extracts from Other Writings, Am. Phil. Soc., *Memoirs,* XXXV (Princeton, N.J., 1953), part 2, 46; for payments to midwives, see estate of John Edmonton, June 15, 1739, Essex County Will Book, no. 6, 184; estate of William Parks, June 17, 1754, and of Mark Cosby, Nov. 17, 1755, York County Will Book, no. 20, 323–326, 376–379; William Dabney Account Book, 1749–1757, 15, 16, VHS; Colonel Washington to John Roan, Jan. 10, 1761, Custis Papers; Carter Burwell's Estate Ledger, 1764–1776, Burwell Papers, CW; *Laurens Papers,* V, 370.

87. Eddis, *Letters from America,* 35–36.

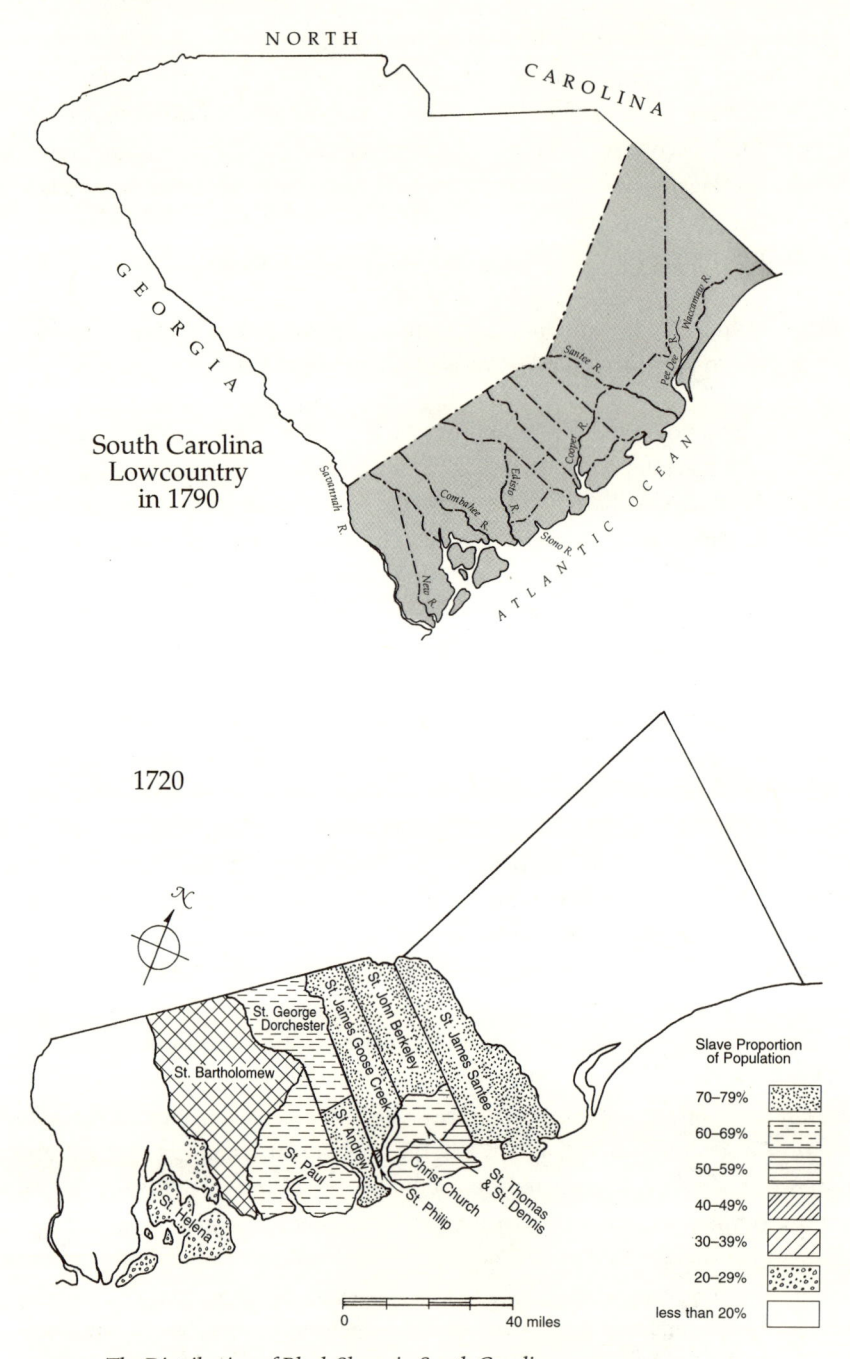

MAP 2. *The Distribution of Black Slaves in South Carolina, 1720–1790*

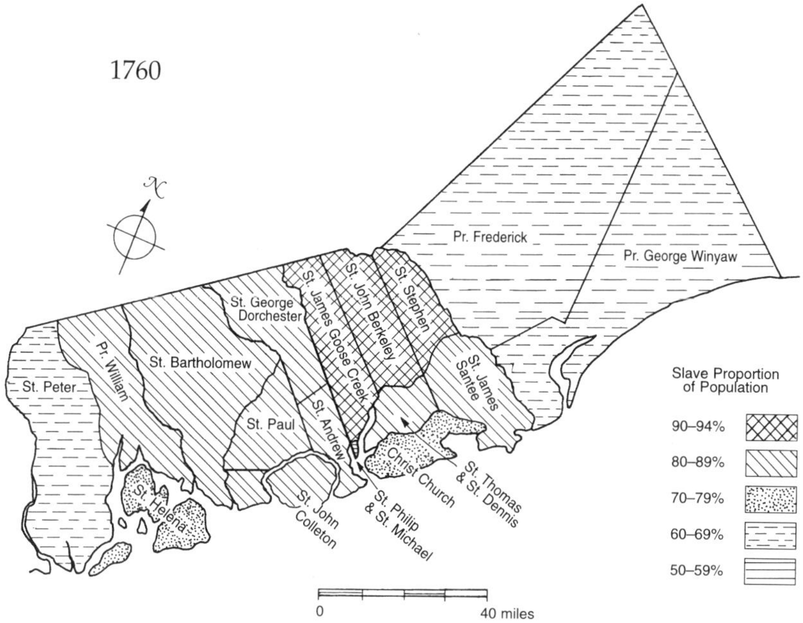
1760
Pr. Frederick
Pr. George Winyaw
St. Peter
Pr. William
St. Bartholomew
St. George Dorchester
St. James Goose Creek
St. John Berkeley
St. Stephen
St. James Santee
St. Paul
St. Andrew
Christ Church
St. Thomas & St. Dennis
St. Helena
St. John Colleton
St. Philip & St. Michael
Slave Proportion of Population
90–94%
80–89%
70–79%
60–69%
50–59%
0
40 miles

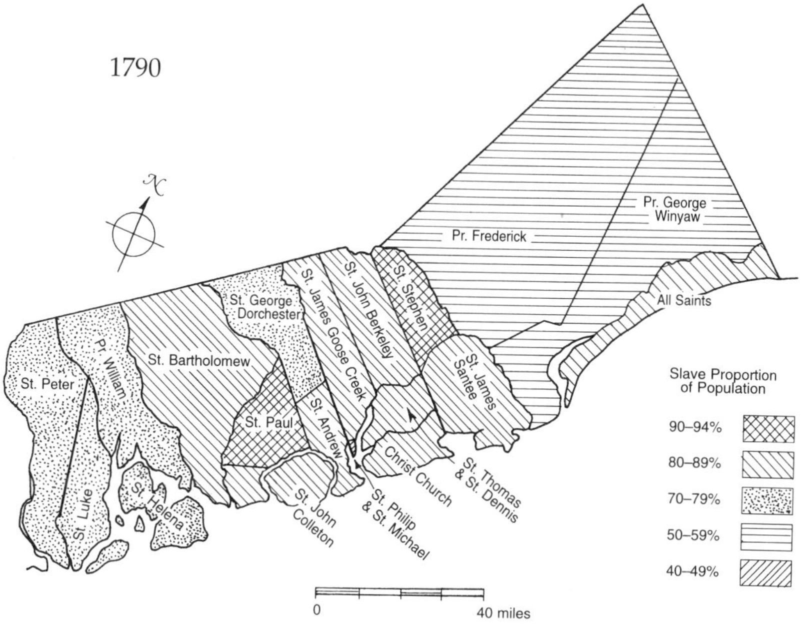
1790
Pr. Frederick
Pr. George Winyaw
All Saints
St. Peter
Pr. William
St. Luke
St. Bartholomew
St. George Dorchester
St. James Goose Creek
St. John Berkeley
St. Stephen
St. James Santee
St. Paul
St. Andrew
Christ Church
St. Thomas & St. Dennis
St. Helena
St. John Colleton
St. Philip & St. Michael
Slave Proportion of Population
90–94%
80–89%
70–79%
50–59%
40–49%
0
40 miles

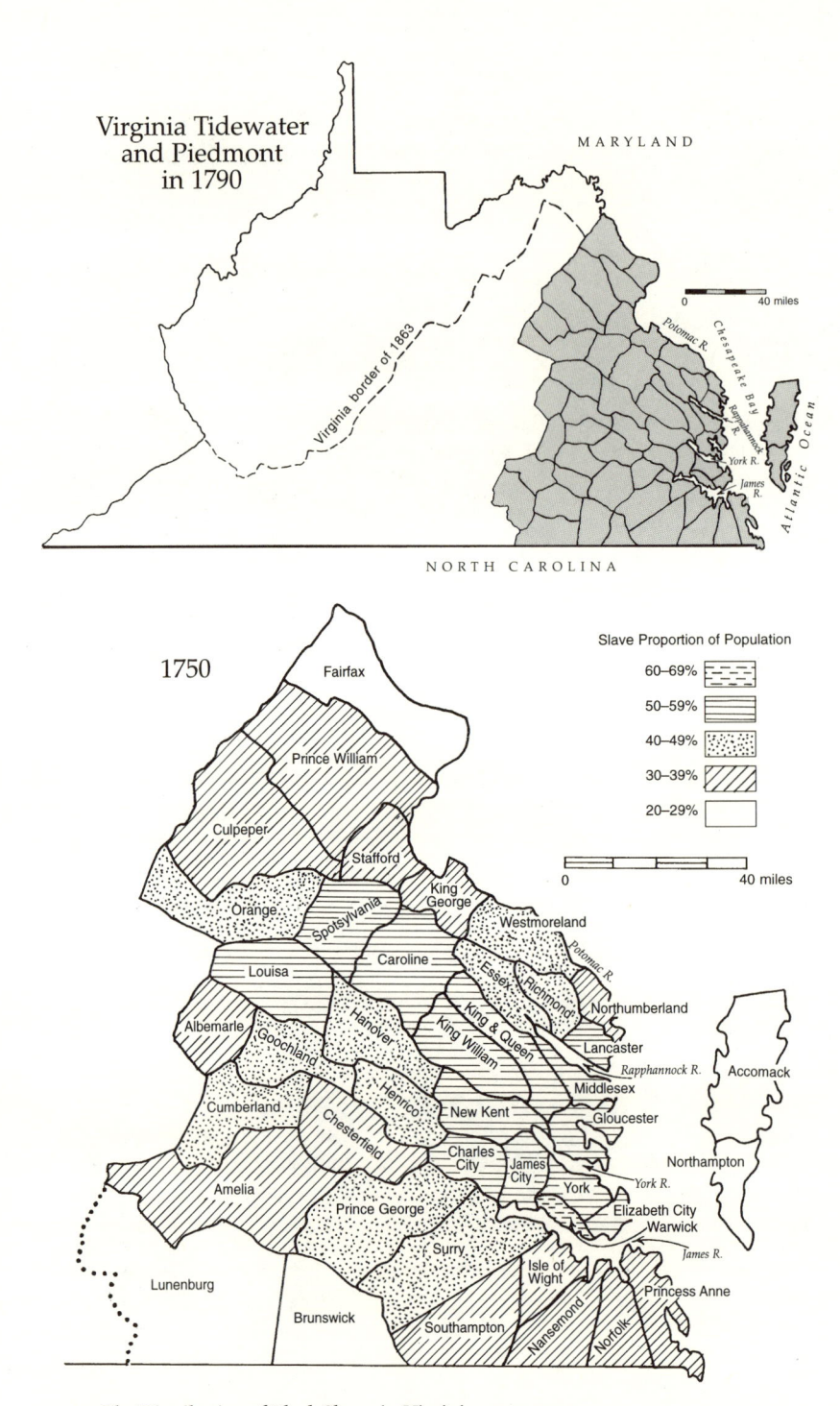

MAP 3. *The Distribution of Black Slaves in Virginia, 1750–1790*

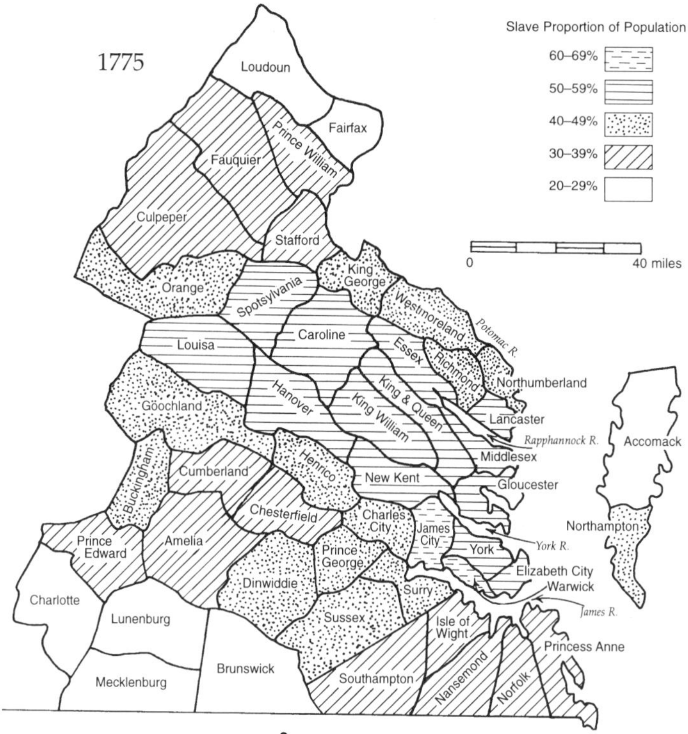
1775
Slave Proportion of Population
60–69%
50–59%
40–49%
30–39%
20–29%
0
40 miles
Loudoun
Fairfax
Prince William
Fauquier
Culpeper
Stafford
King George
Orange
Spotsylvania
Westmoreland
Potomac R.
Caroline
Louisa
Essex
Richmond
Northumberland
Goochland
Hanover
King & Queen
King William
Lancaster
Rapphannock R.
Accomack
Buckingham
Cumberland
Henrico
Middlesex
New Kent
Gloucester
Chesterfield
Charles City
James City
Northampton
Prince Edward
Amelia
Prince George
York
York R.
Elizabeth City
Warwick
Dinwiddie
Surry
Charlotte
James R.
Lunenburg
Sussex
Isle of Wight
Princess Anne
Brunswick
Mecklenburg
Southampton
Nansemond
Norfolk

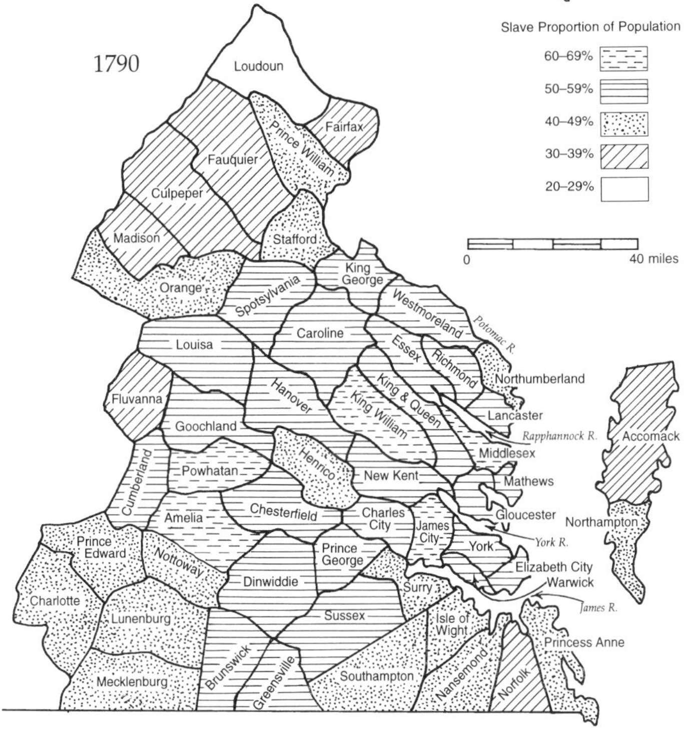
1790
Slave Proportion of Population
60–69%
50–59%
40–49%
30–39%
20–29%
0
40 miles
Loudoun
Fairfax
Prince William
Fauquier
Culpeper
Madison
Stafford
King George
Orange
Spotsylvania
Westmoreland
Potomac R.
Caroline
Louisa
Essex
Richmond
Northumberland
Fluvanna
Hanover
King & Queen
King William
Lancaster
Goochland
Rapphannock R.
Accomack
Cumberland
Powhatan
Henrico
Middlesex
New Kent
Mathews
Amelia
Chesterfield
Charles City
James City
Gloucester
Northampton
Prince Edward
Nottoway
Prince George
York
York R.
Elizabeth City
Warwick
Dinwiddie
Surry
Charlotte
James R.
Lunenburg
Sussex
Isle of Wight
Princess Anne
Brunswick
Greensville
Mecklenburg
Southampton
Nansemond
Norfolk

overseer here just now," he noted, "I slept last night (for the first time in my life) at least four miles distant from any white Person—like the Tyrant of some Asiatick Isle the only free Man in an Island of Slaves." For the most part, then, Lowcountry society was very much a black society. Its demographic characteristics resemble Caribbean rather than other mainland patterns.[88]

A resident in Virginia's slave society was unlikely to feel as isolated as Ogilvie. Josiah Quincy's sigh of relief at leaving Lowcountry South Carolina behind him is almost audible. Now, he noted, "you see husbandmen, yeoman and white laborers scattered through the country, instead of herds of negroes and tawny slaves." Although the number of Virginia counties that were more than 60 percent black increased from one in 1750 to five in 1790, no single Chesapeake county gained an overwhelming majority of blacks in its population. Rather, the area of heaviest slave concentration (never more than two-thirds of a county population) expanded. In 1750, the central band of the densest slave concentration was confined to the area bounded by the Rappahannock and lower James Rivers. By 1790, those boundaries had been broached to include the Northern Neck and, most notably, the central and southern piedmont, the latter known as the Southside. And yet, even in the counties with the largest slave populations, at least a quarter of the households owned no slaves at all. Late-eighteenth-century Chesapeake society was still as much a white society as it was a black one.[89]

An incident that befell William Bartram illustrates the significance of a particular demographic setting. In the late 1770s, Bartram was out riding when he

> Observed a number of persons coming up a head which I soon perceived to be a party of Negroes: I had every reason to dread the consequence; for this being a desolate place, and I was by this time several miles from any house or plantation, and had reason to apprehend this to be a predatory band of Negroes: people being frequently attacked, robbed, and sometimes murdered by them at this place; I was unarmed, alone, and my horse tired; thus situated every way in their power, I had no alternative but to be resigned and prepare to meet them, as soon as I saw them distinctly a mile or two off, I immediately alighted to rest, and give breath to my horse, intending to attempt my safety by flight, if upon near approach they should betray

---

88. R. W. Kelsey, ed., "Swiss Settlers in South Carolina," *SCHM*, XXIII (1922), 90; David Ramsay to Benjamin Rush, Jan. 23, 1780, Rush Papers; George Ogilvie to Peggie, his sister, June 25, 1774, Ogilivie-Forbes of Boyndlie MSS. See also La Rochefoucault Liancourt, *Travels*, I, 592.

89. Howe, ed., "Journal of Josiah Quincy," Mass. Hist. Soc., *Procs.*, XLIX (1915–16), 462. Figure 8 is based on "A General List of Tithables taken in 1750," Chalmers Collection, microfilm, CW.

hostile designs, thus prepared, when we drew near to each other, I mounted and rode briskly up, and though armed with clubs, axes and hoes, they opened to right and left, and let me pass peaceably, their chief informed me whom they belonged to, and said they were going to man a new quarter.[90]

This encounter, so vividly recalled, occurred on the Long Bay, above Georgetown, in South Carolina. That it took place in the Lowcountry, and not in the Chesapeake, was hardly accidental, for there large groups of blacks, with few whites present even for "several miles," were commonplace.

Chesapeake and Lowcountry slaves inhabited different worlds. From a physical environment consisting of a mosaic of different regions to a climate noted for its variability, from a settlement system encompassing mansions and hovels to a predominant staple crop that encouraged agricultural diversification, the Chesapeake was a region of variety and diversity. The Lowcountry, in contrast, as its very name implies, not only presented a uniform face to its inhabitants, both in topography and climate, but also supported a crop that encouraged specialization, not diversity.

These differences framed two contrasting slave regimes. In the Chesapeake, slaves experienced a varied work routine; they cultivated grains, raised livestock, and practiced a wide range of crafts in addition to growing tobacco. They lived on small quarters, surrounded by whites. Chesapeake slaves were the first in the New World to multiply quickly through natural increase. Theirs was as much a farm as a plantation landscape, as much a white as a black world. By contrast, Lowcountry slaves lived in an archetypal plantation environment, dominated by a harsh ecosystem and a demanding primary staple. In large part because of this severe work regime and environment, the slave population of South Carolina failed to reproduce naturally until the second half of the eighteenth century. Yet South Carolina slaves resided on larger plantations, with more blacks and fewer whites around them, and with a greater chance of remaining on the same estate or in the same neighborhood for a longer time than their Virginia counterparts. The specialization that was such a hallmark of the rice regime, furthermore, presented Lowcountry slaves with significant, if necessarily limited, social and economic opportunities. In sum, material conditions and communal autonomy appear to have been inversely related in these two regions.

90. Harper, ed., *Travels of William Bartram*, 298–299.

> The condition of the Carolina negro-slaves is in general harder and more troublous than that of their northern brethren.
>
> —Johann Schoepf

2 : Material Life

Eighteenth-century North American slaves experienced a spartan material existence. They lived in drafty, dark, dilapidated dwellings. Inhabiting cramped quarters, sometimes no more than outbuildings, they spent much of their time huddled about fires, as much outdoors as within. The floors of their houses were usually mere hardened dirt, as were their yards. The smell of decaying food and of domestic animals pervaded their settlements. The slaves' everyday attire was as mean as their dwellings. Masters forced slaves to wear cheap, drab, ill-fitting clothes. The range of materials and styles, together with a widespread resort to dyes, patches, and edging, gave slaves a motley appearance. Many adults and most children went naked and barefoot. And slaves were as poorly fed as they were clothed. Their diet was high in starch, low in protein, and extremely monotonous in content. A peck of corn a week was the standard ration. At midcentury, a South Carolina slave woman provides a revealing glimpse of the harshness of slave life when she recalled how, after an exhausting day in the fields, she arrived at her cabin "pretty late," threw herself on her bed "with all her Cloaths on," and promptly fell asleep. She mentioned no other furniture than a bed, no change of clothes, not even a late evening meal. Richard Parkinson, a perceptive observer, noted that slaves were "both clothed and fed at less expence" than free men; the livelihood of the Southern planter, he continued, was "pinched and screwed out of the negro."[1]

And yet the slaves' bedrock material conditions were not uniform. The status of the master and even of the slave influenced material life. Small planters generally provided their slaves less clothing and flimsier accommodations, although not necessarily less food, than most large planters. Skilled slaves and domestics usually enjoyed more comforts than field hands, even than many poor whites. Status variations were linked to temporal and spatial variations. As plantations grew larger and more slaves escaped field labor over the course of the eighteenth century, the material lives of many slaves improved. And because the number of large plantations and nonfield-workers grew faster in the Lowcountry than in the Chesapeake, Lowcountry slaves benefited the most.

The material conditions of slaves changed significantly over time, independently of variations in status. As colonial societies became more settled, planters built more secure housing, displayed their wealth through their plantation establishment, and in general regularized the material conditions of their laborers. Housing evolved from barracks or quarters to family cabins and duplexes, earthfast structures slowly gave way to more permanent architectural forms, and slave settlements grew more autonomous and communally oriented over time. Although eighteenth-century slaves never wore a uniform, their dress grew more standardized. Similarly, the common elements of the slave diet became widely recognized over the course of the century.

In spite of growing uniformity, material conditions always varied across space; observant whites, in fact, drew sharp regional contrasts. Josiah Quincy thought slaves were "better clothed and better fed" in North, as opposed to South, Carolina. Chesapeake slaves, in Lady Liston's opinion, were "better clothed" than those further south. Johann Schoepf characterized the diet of Lowcountry slaves as "wretched," one reason he judged them worse off than Chesapeake slaves. In extolling the mildness of slavery in his own island, a Bermudian drew a revealing contrast between the Chesapeake and the Lowcountry, attesting to the reputations they had gained. Slave houses in Bermuda were supposedly "far more commodious" than those *"even of"* Maryland, Virginia, and North Carolina, whereas planters in Bermuda were not as harsh as those of South Carolina and Georgia. At pains to associate his island with the Chesapeake and distance it from the Lowcountry, this self-serving planter graphically underlined the gap between the two. Although New World slaves

---

1. Journal of the South Carolina Council, July 13, 1749, 532–535, PRO; Richard Parkinson, *A Tour in America, in 1798, 1799, and 1800* . . . , 2 vols. (London, 1805), I, 27.

PLATE 5. *Plat of Ferry Tract Plantation, May 1795.* Slave houses are arranged ribbonlike. Courtesy South Carolina Historical Society (Charles Town Oversize, 32-39-14)

suffered a similar fate everywhere, territorial distinctions mattered. All slaves led impoverished lives, but variety characterized their material world.[2]

HOUSING

Two countervailing trends characterized eighteenth-century slave housing. On one hand, slave accommodations became more private, substantial, and orderly over time. Single cabins and duplexes gradually supplanted dormitories; houses with sills, brick foundations, and plank floors little by little replaced earthfast dwellings; stratification among both masters and slaves led a few slaves to enjoy better accommodations than most of their peers, even than some free whites; and ribbonlike streets and rectangular compounds slowly superseded randomly distributed huts. In these respects, developments in slave housing mirrored developments in white housing. On the other hand, slave settlements grew more autonomous over time. Slaves often built their own houses, incorporating African influences in both materials and form; slave settlements grew and became more remote from white oversight; and slaves lived as much outside their houses, in their yards and about work buildings, as

2. Mark Antony De Wolfe Howe, ed., "Journal of Josiah Quincy, Junior, 1773," Massachusetts Historical Society, *Proceedings,* XLIX (1915–1916), 463; journals of Lady Liston, January 1798, 5967, 41, Sir Robert Liston Papers, National Library of Scotland, Edinburgh; Johann David Schoepf, *Travels in the Confederation [1783–1784],* trans. and ed. Alfred J. Morrison, 2 vols. (Philadelphia, 1911), II, 220; *Bermuda Gazette,* July 6, 1805, in James E. Smith, *Slavery in Bermuda* (New York, 1976), 166–167.

within doors. Increasingly, slaves lived more communally than their individualistic masters.

In the early years, a single structure generally sufficed to house the few slaves a master owned. Indeed, in the Chesapeake, masters simply allocated slaves to structures that had arisen earlier to house white servants. About 1690, for example, the Clifts plantation in the Northern Neck obtained a new quarter, slightly larger—at nineteen by thirty-six feet—and more elaborate than its predecessor. The building of this structure antedated the blacks' predominance in this plantation's labor force by about fifteen years. Not until the early eighteenth century did the decline of white servants and the increase in blacks make this building home to a number of newly imported Africans.[3]

Dormitories continued to exist throughout the century, most often on small plantations, on estates that were in a formative rather than mature stage, and on units where a number of recently imported Africans were present. In the Chesapeake, the "quarter" became the acknowledged term for such structures, although the word had other, allied meanings. Small outlying plantations, adjuncts of home estates, that were such a feature of tobacco culture, were known as quarters. The term could also denote a slave village or settlement on a plantation; but its most specific meaning, a shortened version of "quartering house," meant a single dwelling that housed either servants or slaves. In this most specific sense, a quarter came to connote a dwelling that housed a number of laborers indiscriminately, as distinct from cabins, which generally lodged a single family.[4] Hugh Nelson had the more precise mean-

---

3. Fraser D. Neiman, *The "Manner House" before Stratford (Discovering the Clifts Plantation)* (Stratford, Va., 1980), 22, 35; Neiman, "Domestic Architecture at the Clifts Plantation: The Social Context of Early Virginia Building," in Dell Upton and John Michael Vlach, eds., *Common Places: Readings in American Vernacular Architecture* (Athens, Ga., 1986), 292–314.

4. Michael Nicholls, "Building the Virginia Southside: A Note on Architecture and Society in the Eighteenth Century" (MS, 1982), 10; Bayly Ellen Marks, "Economics and Society in a Staple Plantation System: St. Mary's County, Maryland, 1790–1840" (Ph.D. diss., University of Maryland, 1979), 49, 53; Orlando Ridout's unpublished compilations, drawn from the Orphan Court Valuations for Queen's Anne County, 1750–1799 (40 quarters), and Federal Direct Tax, Wye Hundred, 1798, Md. (25 quarters), kindly supplied by Edward Chappell; and Carville V. Earle, *The Evolution of a Tidewater Settlement System: All Hallow's Parish, Maryland, 1650–1783*, University of Chicago Department of Geography Research Paper, no. 170 (Chicago, 1975), 137. William Bassett recorded the payment of four pounds for the construction of a "large Quarter 16 × 20" in Blisland Parish, New Kent County (William Bassett Account Book, Aug. 20, 1731, VHS), and Robert W. Carter had "two Negro quarters 20 by 16" built (Robert W. Carter Diaries, Feb. 2, 1768, typescript, CW). For smaller quarters out on the frontier, see the valuations of improvements on the land of John Dixon, Mar. 2, 1730, Spotsylvania Wills, A, 124, VSL, and on the land of Nicholas Davies, Aug. 20, 1745, Goochland Deeds and Wills, no. 5, 26–27, VSL.

ing in mind when he advised his steward to have the Negro "Quarters and cabins... made tight and warm." Clearly, he referred to two kinds of structures. Similarly, Joseph Ball referred to a single building, "the Quarter," for the housing of his slaves, and John Norton described one such structure as a "Barreck." Lists of the real and personal property belonging to the various plantations of Edmund Jenings in King William and York Counties generally distinguished between relatively small "dwelling houses" and relatively large "Quarters." A typical quarter measured about twenty by sixteen feet, but some were as large as fifty by sixteen feet.[5]

As slaves began to form families, or perhaps even earlier if the planter wished to separate African and creole slaves, the single dwelling lost some of its utility. One response was to partition the quarter. In 1740, an observer of South Carolina slave housing noted that there were "often 2, 3 or 4 Famillys of them in one House, lightly partitioned into so many apartments." More typically, however, masters began to assign slaves to separate dwellings. By at least the mid-eighteenth century, most Chesapeake and Lowcountry slaves no longer lived in dormitories. In the Lowcountry, Johann Bolzius described slaves as living "in huts, each family or 2 persons in one hut," and Alexander Garden simply noted that "in all country settlements they live in contiguous houses." In 1762, an anonymous observer provided more detail, describing the slaves' "small houses or huts, much resembling poor peasants thatched houses, to which they have little gardens, and live in families separate from each other." In the Chesapeake, a passing visitor noted the slaves' "Huts or Hovels," where they resided "with their Wives and Families," while the Reverend Hugh Jones simply mentioned that "the Negroes live in small cottages." Whether hut,

---

5. Hugh Nelson to Battaille Muse, Sept. 1, 1779, Battaille Muse Papers, Duke; Joseph Ball to Joseph Chinn, Feb. 18, 1734, Joseph Ball Letterbook, microfilm, LC; John Norton to Battaille Muse, Nov. 4, 1782, Muse Papers; lists of quarters belonging to the Honorable Edmund Jenings, 1712, Francis Porteus Corbin Papers, Duke. In the last source, Rippon plantation had "one 20 foot Quarter" for 9 slaves and Indian Field plantation "one Quarter" for 12 slaves, whereas Skipton plantation had "2 sixteen foot dwelling houses" for 6 slaves. George Washington noted in 1761 that "lightning struck My Quarter and near 10 Negroes in it" (Donald Jackson and Dorothy Twohig, eds., *The Diaries of George Washington*, 6 vols. [Charlottesville, Va., 1976–1979], I, 281, emphasis added). Robert Carter differentiated between quarter and cabins when listing the structures on his plantations in December 1788 (Robert Carter Memorandum Book, 1788–1789, LC). Charles Wall has written that "one-fourth of the Mount Vernon Negroes occupied quarters which were quite barrack-like" ("Housing and Family Life of the Mount Vernon Negro" [MS, 1953], CW). The size of the typical quarter derives from the dimensions of 35 quarters in Saint Mary's County, Md., 1798, from the Federal Assessment, data supplied by Cary Carson, from which comes the 48-by-16-feet quarter.

PLATE 6. SW View of the Settlement of Hartford. *Joseph Purcell. 1722. Part of* Plan of Five Tracts of Land Cal'd Hartford in the Parish of S[aint] Thomas in Berkly County in the Province of South Carolina. *The many outbuildings and separate slave quarters associated with a typical Lowcountry plantation. Courtesy Charleston Museum*

hovel, house, or cottage, slaves in the plantation South usually lived in separate residences, not barracks.[6]

Although separate dwellings became the norm, they might often be outbuildings rather than houses designed exclusively for slaves. The practice of making slaves live in work buildings was more widespread in the Chesapeake than in the Lowcountry because of the small labor forces associated with tobacco production. The one exception to this generalization was Charleston, where most slaves lived above washhouses and kitchens. But the pattern of slaveowning in Charleston was more like the rural Chesapeake than the Carolina hinterland. The number of Chesapeake slaves who lived in outbuildings can be approximated for two counties at the end of the eighteenth century. In 1785, a listing of the buildings belonging to more than two hundred householders in Halifax County, Virginia, suggests that "quarters" housed about one

6. Reverend Alexander Garden to SPG, May 6, 1740, B7/237, SPG; Durand of Dauphine, *Voyage d'un françois exile pour le religion,* ed. Gilbert Chinard (Paris, Baltimore, 1932), 119–120; "Johann Martin Bolzius Answers a Questionnaire on Carolina and Georgia," trans. and ed. Klaus G. Loewald et al., *WMQ*, 3d Ser., XIV (1957), 257; "A Curious New Description of Charles-Town in South-Carolina, and Its Environs . . . ," *Universal Museum,* I (September 1762), 477; [Edward Kimber], "Observations in Several Voyages and Travels in America," *WMQ,* 1st Ser., XV (1906–1907), [148]; Hugh Jones, *The Present State of Virginia . . . ,* ed. Richard L. Morton (Chapel Hill, N.C., 1956), 75.

in ten slaves, cabins more than half, and kitchens and outbuildings the remaining third. In 1798, only 34 of 1,400 households in Saint Mary's County, Maryland, had quarters; cabins were not mentioned, so perhaps the vast majority of this county's slaves made their homes in the lofts of kitchens, corn houses, outhouses, or similar work buildings.[7]

Another variation on the detached cabin was the "double house," a single structure partitioned to form two separate units. Duplexes became more common over time. A South Carolina newspaper advertisement, offering a plantation for sale in 1774, referred to "7 double Negro Houses, all framed on Cills, weather boarded, etc.," and, some twenty years later, a Lowcountry master noted that he wanted a white artisan "to make 2 double Negro Houses" on his plantation. The dimensions and manner of construction varied. In the early 1770s, Christ Church Parish planned to build an earthfast structure in cypress shingles, twenty feet long, ten feet wide, and six feet high, divided into two rooms, with separate entrances, and "a good Pad-lock to each Door." At about the same time, a Lowcountry steward advised an absentee planter to construct more substantial and spacious dwellings. He proposed six buildings, thirty-two by fourteen feet, with sills, a brick foundation, and brick chimneys, which "would cleverly accommodate a dozen family's some of whom are now pretty large." A listing of slaves on this plantation, taken three years later, confirms the steward's description of "pretty large" families, the twelve largest of which averaged between five and six people. A number of slave houses at Tuckahoe, Goochland County, Virginia, probably built in the late eighteenth century, were constructed of two rooms, each with an exterior door, and separated by a central chimney. Similarly, two early-nineteenth-century slave houses located in Saint Mary's County, Maryland, included two rooms about sixteen feet square, separated by a thin wall. The two connected dwellings shared a roof but had separate doorways. Both had fireplaces, so food was undoubtedly prepared separately, but they shared a yard. Many surviving slave dwellings are duplexes and date no earlier than the early nineteenth century.[8]

---

7. Philip D. Morgan, "Black Life in Eighteenth-Century Charleston," *Perspectives in American History*, N.S., I (1984), 190, 193n. 12; Emma B. Richardson, *Charleston Garden Plats*, Charleston Museum Leaflet, no. 19 (Charleston, S.C., 1943); Nicholls, "Building the Virginia Southside," 10–11; Saint Mary's County Federal Tax Assessment, 1798, data supplied by Cary Carson. I assume that slaves did not generally live in their masters' houses. One Chesapeake resident noted that the idea of slaves' living in the same house as whites "cannot be very agreeable to Virginians" (Mary Browne to A. D. Galt, Sept. 13, 1823, quoted in Gerald W. Mullin, *Flight and Rebellion: Slave Resistance in Eighteenth-Century Virginia* [New York, 1972], 52).

8. Roger Pinckney, *SCG*, Oct. 31, 1774; John Colhoun to Mr. Bonneau, Apr. 16, 1798, John Ewing Colhoun Papers, USC; Josiah Smith to George Austin, June 17, 1771, Josiah Smith

The methods and materials used to construct slave houses, like the house forms themselves, changed over time. In the Chesapeake, the earliest slave houses were clapboard structures, set on posts driven directly into the ground at roughly ten-foot intervals. By the mid-eighteenth century, if not before, a more economical and efficient mode of building—log construction—became dominant. In 1774, Landon Carter proposed to one of his tenants that he establish a new quarter. Take four or six hands, Carter ordered, and "knock up a set of log houses" as quickly as possible. The French traveler Jean-Pierre Brissot de Warville noted that George Washington's "three hundred Negroes live in a number of log houses in different parts" of his estate. Harry Toulmin described one of these log houses, viewed near Norfolk in 1793: it was "formed of small pine trees, laid one upon the other and fastened at the end with a notch; but they were not plaistered either on the inside or outside." Indeed, the description "split log" or "round log" was commonly employed of Chesapeake quarters or cabins, an indication of their crude construction. Log and earthfast frame houses continued to be built throughout the eighteenth and nineteenth centuries, but gradually large planters came to value more substantial slave dwellings. These took the form of framed buildings, built on sills, perhaps with brick underpinnings. The large two-room dwellings at Tuckahoe, for example, are framed structures built on sills, with brick chimneys and brick foundations.[9]

Letterbook, UNC; inventory of George Austin, Dec. 6, 1774, Inventories, WPA, XCVIII, 68–71; Dell Upton, "Slave Housing in Eighteenth-Century Virginia: A Report to the Department of Social and Cultural History, National Museum of American History, Smithsonian Institution" (MS, 1982), 11, plates 1–3; Saint Mary's County data kindly supplied by Cary Carson. Other examples of double-pen houses can be seen at the Street, Charlotte County, and the Prestwould Slave House, Mecklenburg County, Virginia. Drawings of these buildings have been supplied by Edward Chappell of the Colonial Williamsburg Foundation. The Prestwould Slave House is a particularly good example of a possible common pattern. In the late 18th century, a single-pen structure was built, measuring 16 by 12 feet. In the early 19th century, this structure was enlarged to form a two-family house. See also Genevieve Leavitt, "Slaves and Tenant Farmers at Shirley Plantation: Social Relationships and Material Culture" (master's thesis, College of William and Mary, 1981), 136.

9. Jack P. Greene, ed., *The Diary of Colonel Landon Carter of Sabine Hall, 1752–1778*, 2 vols. (Charlottesville, Va., 1965), 856 (hereafter cited as *Carter Diary*); J. P. Brissot de Warville, *New Travels in the United States of America, 1788*, ed. Durand Echeverria, trans. Mara Soceanu Vamos and Durand Echeverria (Cambridge, Mass., 1964), 343; Harry Toulmin, *The Western Country in 1793: Reports on Kentucky and Virginia*, ed. Marion Tinling and Godfrey Davies (San Marino, Calif., 1948), 17. On the predominance of log buildings, see Marks, "Economics and Society in a Staple Plantation System," 49–58; Nicholls, "Building the Virginia Southside," 6, 7–8; George W. McDaniel, *Hearth and Home: Preserving a People's Culture* (Philadelphia, 1982), 47; Upton, "Slave Housing in Eighteenth-Century Virginia,"

In the early-eighteenth-century Lowcountry, mud wall—and its extension, *tabby* wall, which was burnt lime or clay, mixed with seashells—palmetto thatch, and wattle-and-daub construction were common building styles. No wonder Johann Bolzius at midcentury estimated the costs of a Lowcountry slave hut as "very minor," reckoning that a planter needed to buy only "a few nails." At about the same time, the appraisers of Alexander Gordon's estate valued his "Negro Cabbins" at four pounds, less than a gun on the same estate. Gradually, however, more solid framed houses superseded the flimsy mud huts. John Mullryne's Combahee River plantation, offered for sale in 1744, possessed "10 good framed Negro Houses" for about fifty to sixty slaves, and Daniel Huger's plantation, put up for sale in 1775, contained "16 very good boarded Negro houses" for a slave force of about sixty. Most late-eighteenth-century duplexes were probably built on sills, sometimes with brick underpinnings.[10]

Over time, Lowcountry slave houses proved somewhat more substantial than their Chesapeake counterparts. Sweeping regional generalizations are hazardous, and it may be invidious to draw distinctions among what were generally little more than hastily built shacks. Nevertheless, the small scale and peripatetic character of tobacco cultivation endowed most Chesapeake slave houses with an especially flimsy and temporary aspect. In 1720, a Virginian noted that the slave houses on his estate were "ready to tumble down"; twelve years later, the governor of Virginia observed that periodic deficiencies in the supply of nails resulted in dilapidated quarters. Wooden chimneys, post construction, and earthen floors were commonplace in Chesapeake slave dwellings. None of these features was absent in the Lowcountry, but larger plantations and greater residential stability meant that Carolina planters turned to brick chimneys, sills or brick foundations, and plank floors more readily than their Chesapeake counterparts.[11]

8–9; and Ridout's compilations. In the early 19th century, a Virginia master who proposed moving slaves from Lancaster County to Amherst County noted that "these negros have been accustomed to hewed-log houses" (Joseph C. Cabell to his brother, Jan. 7, 1808, Cabell Papers, UVa). For frame buildings, see Upton, "Slave Housing in Eighteenth-Century Virginia," 9–11 and plates 1–3 for the Tuckahoe quarters.

10. Steven L. Jones, "The African-American Tradition in Vernacular Architecture," in Theresa A. Singleton, ed., *The Archaeology of Slavery and Plantation Life* (New York, 1985), 199; "Bolzius Answers a Questionnaire," trans. and ed. Loewald et al., *WMQ*, 3d Ser., XIV (1957), 257; inventory of Alexander Gordon, Oct. 1755, Inventories, WPA, CXLV, 435–436; John Mullryne, *SCG*, July 4, 1744; Daniel Huger, ibid., Jan. 23, 1775.

11. John Custis to Bro. March, March 1719/20, John Custis Letterbook, typescript, CW; Governor William Gooch to Board of Trade, May 27, 1732, CO5/1323, PRO. Thomas Jefferson described his slave houses as having "wooden chimnies, and earth floors" (Edwin Morris Betts, ed., *Thomas Jefferson's Farm Book, with Commentary and Relevant Extracts from*

In spite of this broad regional contrast, housing conditions varied from plantation to plantation and even among slaves on individual estates. Within Virginia, observers noted differences in slave housing between piedmont and tidewater and between small and large plantations. On one small piedmont plantation, J. F. D. Smyth encountered six slaves and an overseer living together in a "miserable shell, a poor apology for a house," which contained "no convenience, no furniture, no comfort." By contrast, on the large plantations of the Northern Neck, Isaac Weld found slaves "in general very well provided for" and especially noted that "many of their little huts are comfortably furnished." Housing also varied according to the status of individual slaves. The specifications of a new house for Aron Jameson, a privileged Virginia slave, were that it be a twelve-by-ten-foot framed structure with hardwood sills, brick underpinning, "lathed and filled" walls, loft, raised floor, and outside lock. Many a white Virginian would have coveted such a well-appointed and "tight covered" house. Similarly, many poor whites would have envied the two-roomed dwelling that housed a slave gardener on Landon Carter's Sabine Hall estate.[12]

In part because of the influence of status—whether of the master or of the slave—house sizes ranged widely, but living space per slave did not improve much over the course of the century. The smallest recorded eighteenth-century structure designed for slaves was a seven-by-eight-foot cabin, whereas the largest was a twenty-two-by-fifty-four-foot quarter. But if the quarter housed twenty slaves, as might have been the case, they would have had only the same amount of living space as a single slave in the minuscule cabin. Most cabins probably housed three or four slaves and were typically 150 to 250 square feet in size. At the lower end of the scale was the 144-square-foot house that Landon Carter's carpenters built for Jamy and Jugg. More typical were the twenty-one cabins surveyed on Anne Arundel manor in Maryland. Always smaller than the dwellings for whites that shared the same manorial parcel,

---

Other Writings, American Philosophical Society, *Memoirs,* XXXV [Princeton, N.J., 1953], 6). A visitor to Mount Vernon in 1798 described the slave accommodations as "huts . . . one cannot call them by the name of houses. They are more miserable than the poorest cottages of our peasants. The husband and wife sleep on a mean pallet, the children on the ground; a very bad fireplace" (Julian Ursyn Niemcewicz, *Under Their Vine and Fig Tree: Travels through America in 1797–1799* . . . , trans. and ed. Metchie J. E. Budka, New Jersey Historical Society, *Collections,* XIV (Elizabeth, N.J., 1965), 100. For wooden and clay chimneys in the Lowcountry, see *Laurens Papers,* V, 62, but, in addition to previous references to more solidly built houses, see also John E. Colhoun to Mr. Bonneau, Apr. 16, 1798, Colhoun Papers.

12. J.F.D. Smyth, *A Tour in the United States of America* . . . , 2 vols. (London, 1784), I, 75–76; Isaac Weld, Jr., *Travels through the States of North America* . . . , 2 vols. (London, 1799), I, 84–86; Joseph Ball to Joseph Chinn, Apr. 23, 1754, Ball Letterbook; Greene, ed., *Carter Diary,* 291. See John Norton to Battaille Muse, Dec. 23, 1781, Muse Papers.

they ranged in size from 180 to 256 square feet. Quarters tended to be larger than cabins, but they invariably housed more slaves. Duplexes seem to have provided the most living space—between 225 and 325 square feet per unit—but, because these were constructed only from the late eighteenth century onward, they housed quite large slave families, averaging about five people. Living space per slave probably improved little, if at all, through the eighteenth century.[13]

No matter how cramped and mean a slave dwelling was, at least it usually provided a measure of privacy for its occupants. Most slaves, for example, cooked meals in or around their own homes, rather than having food prepared for them in a common kitchen. The significance of separate slave dwellings surfaced in a dispute between a South Carolina planter and his overseer. The overseer had tried to create a rift between his employer and his charges by suggesting that the slaves "had too much liberty in living in separate houses and advised [the master] to have one House of considerable length built that his slaves might lodge together in it in order to be more restrain'd and kept from stealing and concealing their theft." The overseer hailed from Maryland, where his familiarity with quarters might well have given him the idea for one large building. Another Lowcountry planter, Rawlins Lowndes, might have been inclined to endorse such a plan after a search of one of his slave houses uncovered a large haul of stolen goods: a dozen pewter plates, a dozen china cups and saucers, a milk pot, a butter plate, a china teapot, other items of pottery, and various surveyor's instruments. But Lowndes and other Carolina planters continued the practice of separate slave houses because, on balance, it

13. Joseph Ball to Joseph Chinn, Feb. 19, 1754, Ball Letterbook; Patricia Samford, "The Archaeology of African-American Slavery and Material Culture," *WMQ*, 3d Ser., LIII (1996), 87–114, esp. 93; Greene, ed., *Carter Diary*, 509; Earle, *Evolution of a Tidewater Settlement System*, 137. For representative cabin and quarter dimensions, see in addition to sources reported in notes 4 and 5: Cheryl Davis Hayes, "Cultural Space and Family Living Patterns in Domestic Architecture, Queen Anne's County, Maryland, 1750–1776" (master's thesis, Georgetown University, 1974), 108–109, 114; Churchwardens of Christ Church Parish, *SCG*, June 11, 1772; Robert Carter to Tobert Moore, Oct. 6, 1778, Misc., XI, 60, Duke; Robert Carter Memorandum Book, 1788–1789, LC; Nathaniel Burwell's Assessment, c. 1799–1800, CW; Coffin Point Records, 1800, SCHS. Some have argued that the earliest slave dwellings reveal an African spatial pattern of small, 10-feet or 12-feet squares, later dominated by an Anglo-American pattern of larger 16-feet or 18-feet squares and rectangles, but the evidence is flimsy and contradictory: James Deetz, *In Small Things Forgotten: The Archaeology of Early American Life* (Garden City, N.Y., 1977), 149–150; John Michael Vlach, *The Afro-American Tradition in Decorative Arts* (Cleveland, Ohio, 1978), 133; Vlach, *By The Work of Their Hands: Studies in Afro-American Folklife* (Charlottesville, Va., 1991), 225; Mechal Sobel, *The World They Made Together: Black and White Values in Eighteenth-Century Virginia* (Princeton, N.J., 1987), 112, 117. Leland Ferguson argues that South Carolina slave houses were smaller than Virginia's, but the many examples cited above do not support this claim (*Uncommon Ground: Archaeology and Early African America, 1650–1800* [Washington, D.C., 1992], 73).

served their interests. Separate houses were not only preferred by slaves but offered the master practical advantages, as indicated when one Lowcountry planter ordered the construction of more dwellings on his plantation because he believed that his slaves' recent illnesses derived "in great measure from their being so crowded together."[14]

Masters recognized their slaves' right to a measure of privacy. Robert Carter chastised one of his overseers for whipping a slave because the "offence you [the overseer] charged him with was a matter in his own house." On another occasion, one of Carter's neighbors issued a warrant to search Carter's quarters for stolen tobacco. Carter took issue with his neighbor for taking a pound of spun yarn "out of negroe Willoughby's house, carpenter at my quarter commonly called Gemini," because the yarn "was procured by him honestly." Virginia county courts tried slaves for stealing other slaves' property out of their houses. A Middlesex County court examined Peter for stealing "diverse Goods and Chattels" from Winney's house, and a Richmond County court arraigned Jack for breaking and entering a slave dwelling. Virginia courts, in other words, recognized the slaves' right not just to property but to privacy. Some masters even provided their slaves with padlocks. Slaves at a cabin on Kings Bay Plantation in Georgia had a lock and key; Joseph Ball of Virginia and the churchwardens of Christ Church Parish in South Carolina proposed padlocks for the slave dwellings that they planned to build; and Robert Wormeley Carter's weaver, William, rushed into his house and "bolted his door" when threatened with punishment.[15]

---

14. South Carolina Council Journal, no. 17, part 1, 121, SCDAH; David Youngblood, *Gaz of State of SC*, July 9, 1779; John Channing to William Gibbons, Dec. 20, 1769, William Gibbons, Jr., Papers, Duke. In 1743, there was a bad case of overcrowding at Charlewood Plantation in South Carolina, where only 12 "Tenements" existed for "near 120 slaves." The manager advised that "a few more Negro Houses be built" (Richard Hill to Dr. John Herman, Sept. 8, Richard Hill Letterbook, Duke). Occasionally, communal cooking can be inferred: from an evaluation of seven pounds for "two large pots for negro victuals" (inventory of George Austin, Dec. 6, 1774, Inventories, WPA, XCVIII, 68–73); from the presence of only 1 iron pot for every 10 slaves on James Mercer's Northern Neck quarters in 1771 (Ulrich B. Phillips, ed., *Plantation and Frontier Documents* . . . , 2 vols. [Cleveland, Ohio, 1909], I, 247–250); and from Henry Ravenel's reference to the roof having come off his "Negro Kitchen" (Henry Ravenel Journal, Sept. 15, 1752, B1-1, Ravenel Papers, SCHS). But for the findings of archaeologists, see, for example, Charles H. Fairbanks, "The Plantation Archaeology of the Southeastern Coast," *Historical Archaeology*, XVIII (1984), 2; and Theresa A. Singleton, "An Archaeological Framework for Slavery and Emancipation, 1740–1880," in Mark P. Leone and Parker B. Potter, Jr., eds., *The Recovery of Meaning: Historical Archaeology in the Eastern United States* (Washington, D.C., 1988), 340.

15. Robert Carter to Samuel Straughan, July 6, 1787, Robert Carter Letterbook, VII, 307, Duke; Carter to John Simpson, Apr. 15, 1785, ibid., VI, 137; William Hampton Adams, ed.,

The provision of padlocks indicated that slaves had possessions worth protecting. Most slave houses contained an iron pot for cooking, possibly a frying pan, a pail or iron kettle, and coarse ceramic wares for food preparation and serving. Slaves had bowls and jars rather than plates, suggesting that most meals were one-pot, slow-simmering stews, supplemented with vegetables and sauces served in earthenware and gourd bowls.[16] Furniture was minimal. Some slave huts came with "boarded beds" built into them. Robert "King" Carter, for instance, ordered the construction of "very good" slave cabins, with built-in beds a foot and a half from the ground. However, according to Josiah Henson, late-eighteenth-century Maryland cabins possessed "neither bedsteads, nor furniture of any description." "Our beds were collections of straw, and old rags thrown down in the corners and boxed in with boards; a single blanket the only covering." In 1734, the estate of John Edmondson of Essex County, Virginia, expended thirteen shillings, six pence to provide "4 cow hides for negroes to sleep on." Three years later, when a Virginia quarter burned down, the slaves lost only "their Bed cloathes and Peas and Potatoes," suggesting their limited possessions. In the Carolinas, slaves slept on rush mats, woven by Native Americans early in the eighteenth century and by themselves later in the century. Beds, in short, were optional, whereas minimal furnishings were universal.[17]

Historical Archaeology of Plantations at Kings Bay, Camden County, Georgia, Reports of Investigations, Department of Anthropology, University of Florida (Gainesville, Fla., 1987), 198; Joseph Ball to Joseph Chinn, Nov. 13, 1746, Ball Letterbook; Churchwardens of Christ Church Parish, *SCG,* June 11, 1772; Greene, ed., *Carter Diary,* 845. See also Carter to Andrew Reed, Aug. 19, 1777, Carter Letterbook, III, 154; Carter to Thomas Olive, July 24, 1781, ibid., IV, 93; and Carter to James Clarke, July 28, 1781, ibid., 95. Middlesex County Court Orders, Oct. 5, 1736, VSL; Richmond County Slave Criminal Trials, Oct. 19, 1737, VSL.

16. For pots and pans, see "Churchill Family," *WMQ,* 1st Ser., VII (1898–1899), 186; lists of quarters belonging to Edmund Jenings, 1712, Corbin Papers; estate of John Daniel and Elizabeth Minton, William Robinson Account Book, 1736–1745, microfilm, CW; estate of William Grant, 1739, King George Orphans Accounts, 1740–1761, 18–21, VSL; estate of William Montague, February 1762, Middlesex County Orphans Book, 1760–1820, part 1, 28, VSL; *Laurens Papers,* V, 93; Wilbur H. Siebert, ed., *Loyalists in East Florida, 1774 to 1785,* 2 vols. (DeLand, Fla., 1929), II, 205. For bowls, see William B. Lees and Kathryn M. Kimery-Lees, "The Function of Colono-Indian Ceramics: Insights from Limerick Plantation, South Carolina," *Hist. Arch.,* XIII (1979), 1–13; Theodore Reinhart, *Material Culture, Social Relations, and Spatial Organization on a Colonial Frontier: The Pope Site (44SN180), Southampton County, Virginia,* Department of Anthropology, College of William and Mary (Williamsburg, Va., 1987), 68; James Deetz, "American Historical Archeology: Methods and Results," *Science,* CCXXXIX (1988), 365–367; and Ferguson, *Uncommon Ground,* 36–37, 41, 46–50, 52–55, 84–91.

17. For furniture, see Robert "King" Carter Diary, 1722–1727, Apr. 4, 1727, CW; *An Autobiography of the Rev. Josiah Henson ("Uncle Tom"), from 1789 to 1881,* ed. John Lobb

Nevertheless, as with forms of dwellings, the status of both master and slave created variations in slave possessions. Privileged slaves sometimes acquired flatware, even an occasional piece of porcelain, as well as the odd remnants of tea services. A visitor to one of George Washington's slave huts was impressed by the misery and poverty of the inhabitants, but noted "in the middle of this poverty some cups and a teapot." Archaeological investigations at Mount Vernon's slave quarter confirm this observation. English white salt-glazed stoneware comprised a quarter of the excavated ceramics; teacups, saucers, mugs, small bowls, chamber pots, and plates were all found. The extent of the vessel types suggests that Washington's slaves received the stoneware items as a group rather than piecemeal, probably in the 1770s after the master of Mount Vernon purchased a large quantity of Josiah Wedgwood's creamware. But even some of this creamware found its way into the possession of Washington's slaves. On one group of small to midsized plantations in the Georgia Lowcountry, slaves had some rather expensive ceramics—sometimes even more costly than those found among their masters' possessions. Few of these expensive items seem to have been hand-me-downs, because the correspondence between planter and slave assemblages was only in the most common types of dishes. Either planters were buying transferprinted ceramics, rather than plain creamware or pearlware, for their slaves, or the slaves, particularly the most privileged among them, were acquiring these items. An occasional slave cabin exhibited a few more comforts than normal, as in one Virginia slave dwelling that contained chairs, a bed, an iron and brass kettle, an iron pot, a pair of pot racks, a pothook, a frying pan, and a beer barrel. On another Virginia estate, those slaves who possessed large numbers of chickens traded them for stools.[18]

(London, Ont., 1881), in Robin W. Winks et al., eds., *Four Fugitive Slave Narratives* (Reading, Mass., 1969), 20; estate of John Edmondson, June 15, 1739, Essex County Wills, no. 6, 1735–1743, 184, VSL; Simon Sallard to John Carter, Mar. 1, 1737, Carter Family Papers, VHS; Thomas Anburey, *Travels through the Interior Parts of America . . .* , 2 vols. (London, 1789), II, 7. A number of Virginia inventories refer to "Negro beds," "Negro bedding," "Negro flock bed," "Negro bedtick and coverlet," and the like. More common are references to bedding than to beds. Values, if reported, were low. The most detailed description found to date derives from the inventory of John Jacob, 1730, Northampton County Wills, no. 16, 227, VSL. Jacob's slave complement consisted of two women and six children. The appraisers then listed two "Negro beds," two sheets, two blankets, five coverlets, two boxes, one old chest, three stools, one old chair, and an old table. For mats, see John Lawson, *A New Voyage to Carolina*, ed. Hugh Talmage Lefler (Chapel Hill, N.C., 1967), 195; and Dale Rosengarten, "Spirits of Our Ancestors: Basket Traditions in the Carolinas," in Michael Montgomery, ed., *The Crucible of Carolina: Essays in the Development of Gullah Language and Culture* (Athens, Ga., 1994), 149.

18. Niemcewicz, *Under Their Vine and Fig Tree,* 100; Dennis J. Pogue, "The Archaeology of Plantation Life: Another Perspective on George Washington's Mount Vernon," *Virginia*

Slaves often had storage spaces either inside or adjoining their houses in which to keep food, treasured belongings, and stolen goods. In the Chesapeake, excavations inside slave houses at a number of sites have revealed pits and holes, usually about three feet square though sometimes four by six feet, sometimes lined with bricks or sticks though more often unlined, and generally located near hearths. Archaeologists have unearthed ceramics, coins, tools, and buttons in these root cellars, indicating that slaves used these spaces to store their most personal possessions. The Kingsmill Quarter slaves deposited two mid-eighteenth-century wine bottles bearing the initialed seals of their owner in their root cellar, perhaps to hide the evidence of theft.[19] To date, few root cellars have been found in Lowcountry slave houses. Perhaps Lowcountry slaves stored their produce in sheds attached or standing close to their houses.

Cavalcade, XLI (1991–1992), 76–78; William Hampton Adams and Sarah Jane Boling, "Status and Ceramics for Planters and Slaves on Three Georgia Coastal Plantations," *Hist. Arch.,* XXIII (1989), 69–96; Philip Alexander Bruce, *Economic History of Virginia in the Seventeenth Century: An Inquiry into the Material Conditions of the People . . . ,* II (New York, 1895), 106; Robert "King" Carter Diary, 1722–1727, Apr. 4, 1727.

19. William M. Kelso, *Kingsmill Plantations, 1619–1800: Archaeology of Country Life in Colonial Virginia* (Orlando, Fla., 1984), 104–105, 191, 201; Kelso, "Mulberry Row: Slave Life at Thomas Jefferson's Monticello," *Archaeology,* XXXIX, no. 5 (September–October 1986), 30–34; for a conjectural reconstruction of a shed with a palmetto thatch roof, see Thomas R. Wheaton and Patrick H. Garrow, "Acculturation and the Archaeological Record in the Carolina Lowcountry," in Singleton, ed., *The Archaeology of Slavery,* 248. A lively debate is taking place about the origins of Chesapeake root cellars—whether African, European, American Indian, or, more probably, a creole form that drew on all traditions—for which see Anne Yentsch, "A Note on a Nineteenth-Century Description of below-Ground 'Storage Cellars' among the Ibo," *African-American Archaeology,* IV (1991), 3–4; Douglas Sanford, "A Response to Anne Yentsch's Research Note on Below-Ground 'Storage Cellars' among the Ibo," ibid., V (1991), 4–5; Dan Mouer, "'Root Cellars' Revisited," ibid., V (1991), 5–6; Douglas B. Chambers, "Afro-Virginian Root Cellars and African Roots? A Comment on the Need for a Moderate Afrocentric Approach," ibid., VI (1992), 7–10; Larry McKee, "The Ideals and Realities behind the Design and Use of Nineteenth-Century Virginia Slave Cabins," in Anne Elizabeth Yentsch and Mary C. Beaudry, eds., *The Art and Mystery of Historical Archaeology: Essays in Honor of James Deetz* (Boca Raton, Fla., 1992), 195–213, esp. 205–206; L. Daniel Mouer, "Chesapeake Creoles: The Creation of Folk Culture in Colonial Virginia," in Theodore R. Reinhart and Dennis J. Pogue, eds., *The Archaeology of Seventeenth-Century Virginia,* special publication no. 30 of the Archaeological Society of Virginia (Charlottesville, Va., 1993), 147–152; Richard H. Kimmel, "Notes on the Cultural Origins and Functions of Sub-Floor Pits," *Hist. Arch.,* XXVII (1993), 102–113; Amy L. Young, "Pit Cellars Associated with Slave Houses at Locust Grove: A Unique Upland South Adaptation" (MS, 1994); Donald W. Linebaugh, "'All the Annoyances and Inconveniences of the Country': Environmental Factors in the Development of Outbuildings in the Colonial Chesapeake," *Winterthur Portfolio,* XXIX (1994), 1–17, esp. 9–11; and Samford, "Archaeology of Slavery," *WMQ,* 3d Ser., LIII (1996), 95, 100.

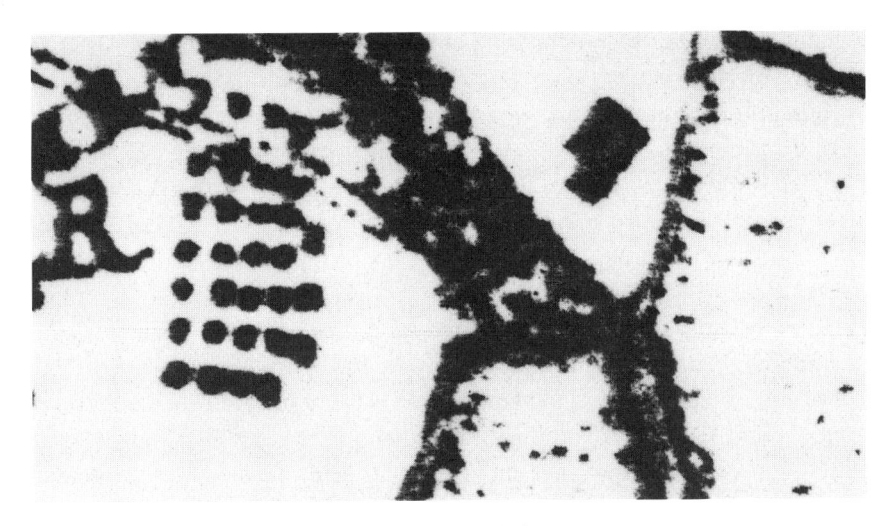

PLATE 7. *Plat of Fairlawn Plantation, Saint John Berkeley, 1789.* Slave houses are arranged in a compound. Courtesy H. A. M. Smith Collection, South Carolina Historical Society (32-33-3)

In addition, whereas Chesapeake slaves obviously made use of lofts, little evidence survives that Lowcountry slaves did the same. When a butter pot was stolen from his dairy, the Virginian Landon Carter had his overseer search all the "holes and boxes" of his house servants. The pot was found in one of their lofts. Landon Carter's father, Robert "King" Carter, had seen the value of lofts, for he ordered one of his quarters to be "lofted not only for the warmth . . . but to lay the peoples corn up in." Perhaps the presence of lofts is another indication of the relative assimilation of Chesapeake slaves. Conversely, when Lowcountry slaves made their palmetto-thatched roofs, they might have seen no need to install lofts, particularly if they had separate storage sheds.[20]

If slaves were, in some sense, masters in their own houses, no doubt this feeling was enhanced when they were personally responsible for their construction. Of course, masters controlled many aspects of the construction of slave houses, supervising size, materials, and location. On the large estates, masters often set their slave carpenters to build slave houses. But, even on large plantations, field hands might fashion their own dwellings. Thus, Philip Fithian observed that on Sundays slaves could often be seen "building and

---

20. Greene, ed., *Carter Diary,* 495; Robert Carter to Robert Jones, Oct. 10, 1727, Robert Carter Letterbook, 1727–1728, UVa. For possible root cellars in the Lowcountry, see John Solomon Otto, *Cannon's Point Plantation, 1794–1860: Living Conditions and Status Patterns in the Old South* (Orlando, Fla., 1984), 38; but for a summary of work on Lowcountry sites that reveal a dearth of trash pits, see Martha A. Zierden, Lesley M. Drucker, and Jeanne Calhoun, *Home Upriver: Rural Life on Daniel's Island, Berkeley County, South Carolina* (Columbia, S.C., 1986), 7-1 to 7-4.

patching their Quarters or rather Cabins." One Sunday he encountered "a number of Negroes very busy at framing together a small House." George Washington commented that the fifty or so slaves at his River Farm quarter were "Warmly lodged chiefly in houses of their own building." Many of the small slave dwellings Johann Schoepf saw in northern Virginia were built "without the assistance of carpenters, patched together by the people themselves and their negroes." Old Dick, living on Spencer Ball's plantation in Fairfax County, Virginia, noted that his master "allowed me to build a loghouse and take in a patch of land where I raise corn and water Melions."[21]

Building their own houses allowed slaves to introduce African elements into their construction. Because the Lowcountry slave population contained more Africans and because the region's climate and construction materials more closely approximated the experience of Africa, Carolina slaves were more successful than Chesapeake slaves in transferring African architectural forms and techniques to the New World. The compoundlike appearance of some Lowcountry slave sites—lines of cabins with yards backing onto one another or "grouped together round something like a farm-yard," which was how Adam Hodgson, an early-nineteenth-century observer, put it—is reminiscent of African (and West Indian) settlements. Similarly, the arc-shaped arrangement of slave dwellings at a Florida plantation and a horseshoe-shaped configuration at a coastal South Carolina site evoke traditional African village layouts. Furthermore, the trench foundations and closely set posts of a number of eighteenth-century slave dwellings on Cooper River sites indicate that they were made of mud. Rammed-earth architecture is widespread throughout Africa, and Lowcountry slaves presumably employed homeland knowledge and skills to build these structures. In the nineteenth century, at least one African-born slave reported building a dwelling with a homeland model in mind. He constructed a twelve-by-fourteen-foot clay-walled hut, with a dirt floor, no windows, and a flat palmetto roof. Mud wall, palmetto thatch, and wattle-and-daub construction were common building styles throughout the Lowcountry. Although there are similar European traditions, all three have more widespread and more

21. Hunter Dickinson Farish, ed., *Journal and Letters of Philip Vickers Fithian, 1773–1774: A Plantation Tutor of the Old Dominion* (Williamsburg, Va., 1943), 96, 202–203; John C. Fitzpatrick, ed., *The Writings of George Washington from the Original Manuscript Sources 1745–1799*, 39 vols. (Washington, D.C., 1931–1944), XXVIII, 178–179, XXXIV, 433–434; Schoepf, *Travels in the Confederation*, II, 33; John Davis, *Travels of Four Years and a Half in the United States of America* . . . (Bristol, 1803), 423. Bernard L. Herman argues that slave housing tells "us more about the plantation owners than the slaves" ("Slave Quarters in Virginia: The Persona behind Historic Artifacts," in David G. Orr and Daniel G. Crozier, eds., *The Scope of Historical Archaeology: Essays in Honor of John L. Cotter* [Philadelphia, 1984], 253–283).

precise African analogues. As late as the early twentieth century, blacks continued to build a variation of the palmetto-thatched hut, with circular walls and conical roofs, on North Carolina's barrier islands.[22]

African influences are less obvious in Chesapeake slave housing. Only Bremo Bluff plantation in Fluvanna County and Four Mile Tree plantation in Surry County provide evidence of mud-walled slave quarters. Moreover, in plan, proportion, and even mode of construction, the buildings on these two sites were European in style. Robert Carter searched on one occasion for a slave, "an Artist, not a Common Labourer," one who "understands building mud walls," but there is no evidence that he had an African in mind. Although it is certainly possible that Chesapeake slaves, like their Lowcountry counterparts, incorporated certain African techniques or models into their house construction—some unusually shaped buildings, such as the Keswick slave quarter or the Waters-Coleman smokehouse in Williamsburg have been attributed to an African influence—the overwhelming predominance of log structures argues for a more thoroughly assimilated slave population.[23]

Even if they used Euro-American techniques, Chesapeake slaves might have conceived of buildings in African ways. One such possibility is suggested by oral traditions, dating to the late eighteenth century, concerning a group of slaves in northern North Carolina. Whenever these slaves, who belonged to a large, extended family, built a house for a member of their white clan, they set a pot on the ground as they laid the foundation. As they worked, they prayed and sang over the pot, "fashioning something of power from their own despair, moving in rhythm around the pot as in a ring shout; pouring emotion

22. Adam Hodgson, *Remarks during a Journey through North America in the Years 1819, 1820, and 1821* . . . (New York, 1823), 116; Sidney W. Mintz, "Houses and Yards among Caribbean Peasantries," in Mintz, *Caribbean Transformations* (Chicago, 1974), 225–250; Theresa Ann Singleton, "The Archaeology of Afro-American Slavery in Coastal Georgia: A Regional Perception of Slave Household and Community Patterns" (Ph.D. diss., University of Florida, 1980), 113; Wheaton and Garrow, "Acculturation and the Archaeological Record," in Singleton, ed., *The Archaeology of Slavery*, 239–259, esp. 243–248; Thomas R. Wheaton, Amy Friedlander, and Patrick H. Garrow, *Yaughan and Curriboo Plantations: Studies in Afro-American Archaeology* (Marietta, Ga., 1983), esp. 98, 107, 193–197, D-1 to D-7; Zierden et al., *Home Upriver*, 4-47 to 4-49, 4-116 to 4-117; WPA, Georgia Writers' Project, *Drums and Shadows: Survival Studies among the Georgia Coastal Negroes* (Athens, Ga., 1940), 179; Jones, "The African-American Tradition," in Singleton, ed., *The Archaeology of Slavery*, 195–213, esp. 199–200; David S. Cecelski, "The Hidden World of Mullet Camps: African-American Architecture on the North Carolina Coast," *North Carolina Historical Review*, LXX (1993), 1–13. For another African-style house in the Lowcountry and a close African parallel, see McDaniel, *Hearth and Home*, 36–37.

23. Robert Carter to John Ballendine, July 7, 1777, Carter Letterbook, III, part 2, 138–139, Duke. Details of the two Virginia sites are on file with the Historic American Buildings Survey, LC, reported in Vlach, *Afro-American Tradition*, 135.

into the pot—then exhaustion. And next day the pot was moved aside and the house was raised up." Legend has it that when certain winds came across the fields, the workers' songs, resonant with despair, hope, and power, rose up again, creating a new structure, as it were, of sound.[24]

The autonomy of slaves was enhanced not only when they built their own houses but when their settlements were distant from the master's oversight. In the Lowcountry, late-eighteenth-century plantation plats indicate that most slave villages were located two hundred yards or more from the master's dwelling, although an overseer's house was often nearby. This average distance between big house and slave settlement tallies exactly with one contemporary observation. "The barn is built about 600 feet away from the house of the master," observed Johann Bolzius, "and the huts of the Negroes are arrayed around the barn, at a little distance from one another so that if fire breaks out in one hut the others are more easily saved." The distance between the residences of masters and slaves seems to have grown over time. By 1771, Charles Woodmason observed that the old "Method" of building houses by swamps so that planters could "view from their Rooms, their Negroes at Work in the Rice Fields" was now "banish'd." Increasingly, masters were "removing their Houses back into the High and dry Lands, remote from the Swamps." Furthermore, because cultivable tideland was often widely scattered within a plantation, separate slave settlements were established near the rice fields.[25] As slave complements grew larger, as masters relocated onto higher lands, and as settlements grew more dispersed, the autonomous, communal focus of Lowcountry slave villages grew more pronounced.

The small size of most Chesapeake plantations inhibited trends favoring the growing autonomy of slave settlements. Certainly large planters erected barriers—terraces, dependencies, piazzas, loggias, fences—to withdraw from and impress the common folk, including their slaves. They planted rows of trees to mask slave quarters, they sited slave houses at a distance from their mansions, and they constructed more orderly streets of houses to impose their sense of hierarchy on their "people" and display their alleged liberality. Yet if a planter as eminent as Thomas Jefferson had to tolerate the sight of his Mulberry Row

---

24. Peter H. Wood, "Whetting, Setting, and Laying Timbers: Black Builders in the Early South," *Southern Exposure*, VIII (1980), 6.

25. "Bolzius Answers a Questionnaire," trans. and ed. Loewald et al., *WMQ*, 3d Ser., XIV (1957), 257; Richard J. Hooker, ed., *The Carolina Backcountry on the Eve of the Revolution: The Journal and Other Writings of Charles Woodmason, Anglican Itinerant* (Chapel Hill, N.C., 1953), 195. The major collections of plantation plats are those of H.A.M. Smith and Theodore Gourdin, SCHS, and of E. McCrady, SCDAH. In addition, the series of colonial plats in the Records of the Surveyor General, SCDAH, are occasionally useful but tend to be no more than boundary surveys.

cabins and their trash-littered slave yards, which were visible from his imposing home at Monticello, most other Virginia masters surely failed to distance themselves all that readily from the residences of their slaves.[26]

Nevertheless, the autonomy of slaves grew as the size of their settlements grew. Even Virginia plantations looked like small villages. As William Hugh Grove journeyed up the York River in the summer of 1732, he observed that each plantation had its kitchen, dairy, barn, stable, storehouse, "and some of them 2 or 3 Negro Quarters all Separate from Each other but near the mansion," making in all "7 or 8 distinct Tenements, tho all belong to one Family." South Carolina plantations tended to have even more buildings than their Virginia counterparts. To form a picture of a South Carolina estate, John Davis described "an avenue of several miles leading through a continual forest, to a wooden house, encompassed by rice-grounds.... On the right, a kitchen and other offices; on the left, a stable and coach-house; a little further a row of negro huts, a barn and yard." The size of the slave settlement—a row of huts, not just one or two huts—was particularly conspicuous. Thus, a Lowcountry planter could have echoed his Chesapeake counterpart when he listed his "Court of offices, Vizt. a good Kitchen and Store house with Lofts, a Hen House, Stable and a large barn and corn house Lofted," but deviated when speaking of his "negro Town of good houses for 70 Negroes." What took John Bartram's eye when he visited a plantation near Willtown in South Carolina were the many slave houses. Similarly, Timothy Ford observed that Lowcountry "negro houses are laid out like a camp and sometimes resemble one." Slave "towns" or "camps" were normal sights in the Lowcountry.[27]

The clustering of slave houses, together with their small size and absence of lighting, meant that domestic life occurred as much out of doors as within them. Fires, both inside and outside, formed a focal point. Archaeological investigations have discovered some slave cabins that had no fireplaces; cooking presumably took place outside. Josiah Henson, conversely, remembered

---

26. William M. Kelso, "Landscape Archaeology at Thomas Jefferson's Monticello," in Kelso and Rachel Most, eds., *Earth Patterns: Essays in Landscape Archaeology* (Charlottesville, Va., 1990), 21. See also Albert Matthews, ed., *Journal of William Loughton Smith, 1790–1791* (Cambridge, Mass., 1917), 64; and Weld, *Travels*, I, 148.

27. Gregory A. Stiverson and Patrick H. Butler III, eds., "Virginia in 1732: The Travel Journal of William Hugh Grove," *VMHB*, LXXXV (1977), 26; Davis, *Travels*, 73–74; Siebert, ed., *Loyalists in East Florida*, II, 251; John Bartram, "Diary of a Journey through the Carolinas, Georgia, and Florida, from July 1, 1765, to April 10, 1766," ed. Francis Harper, Am. Phil. Soc., *Transactions*, N.S., XXXIII (1942–1944), 21; Joseph W. Barnwell, ed., "Diary of Timothy Ford, 1785–1786," *SCHM*, XIII (1912), 145. See also Elkanah Watson, *Men and Times of the Revolution,* ed. Winslow C. Watson (New York, 1856), 48; Johann [von] Ewald, *Diary of the American War: A Hessian Journal,* ed. and trans. Joseph P. Tustin (New Haven, Conn., 1979), 261; and Smyth, *A Tour in the United States of America,* I, 15–16.

how slaves slept so that their "feet [were] toasting before the smouldering fire." Visiting Port Royal Island in 1778, Elkanah Watson noticed how every evening "the negroes, old and young, clustered in their huts, around their pine-knot fires." Slaves "love fire above everything," claimed Johann Schoepf, "and take it with them whatever they are about." Valued for its warmth in winter and deterrence of mosquitoes in summer, "a good fire," declared Joseph Ball, is "the life of a negro."[28]

Gathering around a fire, pipes in hand; singing, dancing, and telling stories in communal yards; congregating in front of a cooking pot—these images probably convey much of domestic life in the slave settlements. With poultry and dogs almost part of the household, slave houses were oriented outward as much as inward. The small plots of ground around slave huts also encouraged slaves to spend much of their free time gardening. This outside activity went largely unnoticed and unremarked on by whites, but, occasionally, the communal participation pressed on their consciousness. One passing traveler complained of the nighttime "chattering of Negroes in their quarters"; another described slaves as "great and loud talkers" who "often sit up after their work is done, over a large fire, even in the heat of the summer"; and yet another was kept awake half the night by "their songs," as slaves shelled Indian corn. Taking a stroll about Nomini Hall plantation, Philip Fithian noted how all the slaves were out and about, so that "we seem like a Town"; on another occasion he observed that the "Neighbourhood seems alive with little Negro Boys playing in every part."[29]

Yards were important places to slaves. Some aspects of daily life outside the slaves' huts were doubtless unattractive. Excavations at various slave sites indicate that slaves threw raw garbage into trash pits near their cabins and sometimes into the root cellars inside their cabins. The stench of rotting food must have pervaded most slave quarters. Yet the experience of Robert "King" Carter indicates a more positive feature of slave yards. Viewing his home quarter one day, Carter upbraided his slave women on the way they kept their yards. By

---

28. Wheaton, Friedlander, and Garrow, *Yaughan and Curriboo Plantations*, 194, 238; *Autobiography of Henson*, in Winks et al., eds., *Four Fugitive Slave Narratives*, 20; Watson, *Men and Times*, 48; Schoepf, *Travels in the Confederation*, II, 153; Joseph Ball to Joseph Chinn, Feb. 18, 1734, Ball Letterbook. See also "Bolzius Answers a Questionnaire," trans. and ed. Loewald et al., *WMQ*, 3d Ser., XIV (1957), 236; David Ramsay, *A Dissertation on the Means of Preserving Health, in Charleston, and the Adjacent Low Country* . . . (New York, 1977 [orig. publ. 1790]), 29.

29. Robert Hunter, Jr., *Quebec to Carolina in 1785–1786* . . . , ed. Louis B. Wright and Marion Tinling (San Marino, Calif., 1943), 273 (and 200); Charles William Janson, *The Stranger in America* (London, 1807), 363; Smyth, *A Tour in the United States of America*, I, 76; Farish, ed., *Journal and Letters of Philip Vickers Fithian*, 98, 226.

regularly sweeping the ground around their houses and the paths that connected their houses and garden plots, they created large grassless areas that were aesthetically unpleasing to Euro-American eyes. Carter owned many African slaves who must have been familiar with hard-baked earthen floors in and around their Old World houses. Some West African figurative brass gold weights from the seventeenth and eighteenth centuries depict sweeping and grass whisk brooms, indicating that the practice was widespread in the region and at a time when slaves were being shipped to the New World. Presumably, they attempted to replicate such an effect in their New World environment. Archaeological investigations of the distribution of ceramic shards at slave settlements also demonstrate that slaves swept their yards clean.[30]

The slaves' domain extended beyond their yards to work buildings. Most slaves lived close to or actually in craft shops, storage houses, and utility buildings. Mulberry Row was the center not just of slave activity at Monticello but also of artisanal labor. At the end of the eighteenth century, this tree-lined road was the site of several slave dwellings, as well as a joinery, a nailery, a weaver's cottage, a smokehouse, a dairy, and a stable. When Philip Fithian witnessed the slaves' cockfights at Nomini Hall, he noted that they occurred at the stables. He viewed the work buildings at this plantation as black areas and recorded with disapproval his pupil Harry Carter's fondness for spending time "either in the Kitchen, or at the Blacksmiths, or Carpenter's Shop."[31]

Lowcountry and Chesapeake slaves shared to some extent in the growing "privatization" that characterized eighteenth-century Anglo-American life. But the growing size of plantations, their increasing remoteness as planters

---

30. Kelso, *Kingsmill Plantations,* 204; Robert Carter Diary, 1722–1728, UVa, as cited by Carter L. Hudgins, "Robert 'King' Carter and the Landscape of Tidewater Virginia in the Eighteenth Century," in Kelso and Most, eds., *Earth Patterns,* 68; Merrick Posnansky, "West Africanist Reflections on African American Archaeology," in Theresa A. Singleton, ed., *"I, Too, Am America": Contributions to African American Archaeology* (Charlottesville, Va., forthcoming); Adams, ed., *Historical Archaeology of Plantations at Kings Bay,* 116. For swept yards among contemporary blacks, see Lydia Mihelic Pulsipher and LaVerne Wells-Bowie, "The Domestic Spaces of Daufuskie and Montserrat: A Cross-Cultural Comparison," *Cross-Cultural Studies of Traditional Dwellings,* VII (1989), 1–28, esp. 9, 13, 20; Richard Westmacott, *African-American Gardens and Yards in the Rural South* (Knoxville, Tenn., 1992), 79–82, 103, 106; Grey Gundaker, "Tradition and Innovation in African-American Yards," *African Arts,* XXVI (1993), 58–71, 94–96; "In Georgia's Swept Yards, a Dying Tradition out of West Africa," *New York Times,* Aug. 8, 1993; and Amelia Wallace Vernon, *African Americans at Mars Bluff, South Carolina* (Baton Rouge, La., 1993), 168–171.

31. Kelso, "Mulberry Row," *Archaeology,* XXXIX, no. 5 (September–October 1986), 28–35; Farish, ed., *Journal and Letters of Philip Vickers Fithian,* 37, 88, 201; Dell Upton, "White and Black Landscapes in Eighteenth-Century Virginia," in Robert Blair St. George, ed., *Material Life in America, 1600–1800* (Boston, 1988), 367.

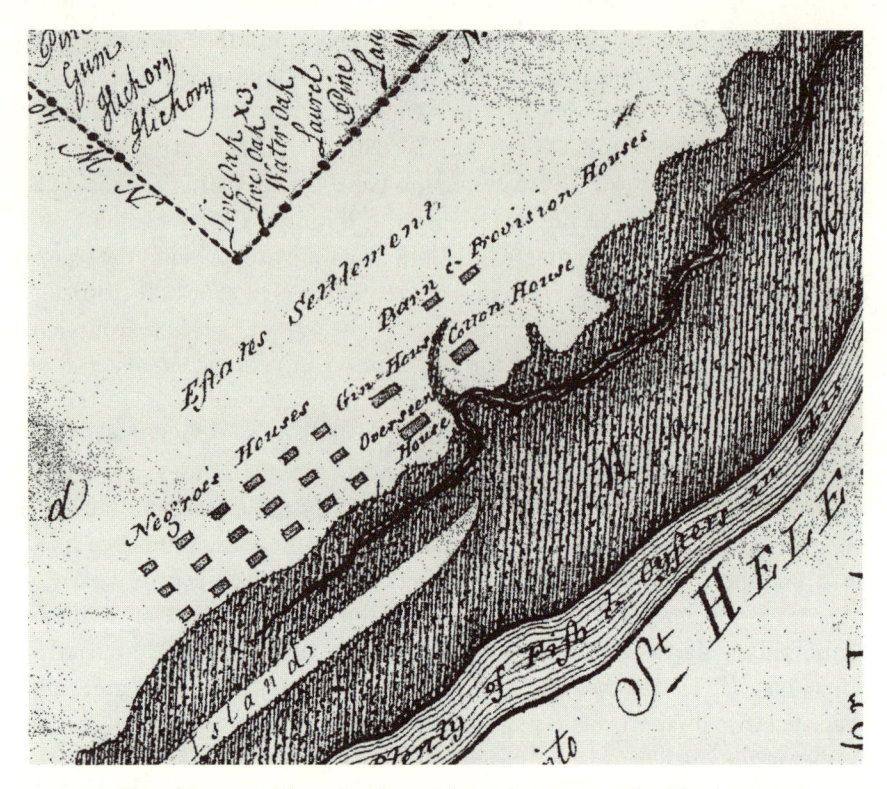

PLATE 8. *Plat of Frogmore Plantation.* Late eighteenth century. A Sea Island cotton plantation, Saint Helena Island, with slaves and overseer living remote from the master. Courtesy John Stapleton Papers, University of South Carolina

distanced their residences from slave settlements, and the apparent preferences of slaves for outdoor activity—trends common to both societies, but felt most fully in the Lowcountry—meant that slave life developed a more communal ethos than did the increasingly individualistic and self-segregated houses of their masters. This characteristic of black life was eventually articulated in architectural form with the nineteenth-century development of shotgun houses, aptly termed houses "without privacy." It has even been suggested that the communal orientation of black life was most influential in disseminating the advantages of the front porch. If the veranda can be attributed at least in part to an African American influence, the black contribution to the southern way of life was even more fundamental than many have acknowledged.[32]

32. For growing privatization and individualism among whites, see Daniel Blake Smith, *Inside the Great House: Planter Family Life in Eighteenth-Century Chesapeake Society* (Ithaca, N.Y., 1980); and Rhys Isaac, *The Transformation of Virginia, 1740–1790* (Chapel Hill, N.C., 1982); Vlach, *Afro-American Tradition,* 123–131, 136–138 (quotation on 123); Vlach, "The

DRESS

Masters realized that minimal provisions in both housing and clothing were necessary to keep their slaves alive and working. With "warm hous's, warm bedding and warm Cloaths," one planter mused, "I cant believe but wee should have fewer mortalitys and I am sure I have done my part." Whether they did their part may be seriously doubted, and slaves occasionally found ways to make the point. Thus, the "poor Negroes" belonging to a Colonel Jones in Virginia, described as "a kind of Adamites, very scantily supplied with clothes," got "even with their master" by making him poor crops, "so that he gets nothing by his injustice but the scandal of it." This action at least suggests that penalties existed when masters economized too severely on slave clothing. It also indicates that the wider community had minimum standards for the slaves' clothing allowance.[33]

What were these standards? William Hugh Grove, who journeyed through Virginia in the summer of 1732, maintained that masters annually provided each slave with a pair of shoes and ten yards of brown linen for two shirts and two drawers. If anything, large planters in the Chesapeake seem to have been more generous than Grove allowed. A pair of shoes, stockings, a suit of clothes (consisting of jacket or waistcoat and breeches for men, of a jacket and petticoat for women), two shirts for men, and two shifts for women formed the typical allocation. Winter and summer suits were usually provided. As a result, each adult slave on the large Chesapeake estates received at least ten yards of cloth a year. Lower down the social scale, scantier allocations were probably the norm. The slave women on one estate in Elizabeth City County, Virginia, for instance, received only about three and a half yards of cloth each year.[34]

Shotgun House: An African Architectural Legacy," *Pioneer America*, VIII (1976), 47–70; and Deetz, *In Small Things Forgotten*, 152. As Upton notes, however, few slave houses reveal the presence of a porch or veranda ("Slave Housing in Eighteenth-Century Virginia," 35). For one slave house that seems to have had an "awning-type extension," see Lesley M. Drucker, "Socioeconomic Patterning at an Undocumented Late Eighteenth Century Lowcountry Site: Spiers Landing, South Carolina," *Hist. Arch.*, XV, no. 2 (1981), 59. Carl Anthony, "The Big House and the Slave Quarters," part 1, "Prelude to New World Architecture," and part 2, "African Contributions to the New World," *Landscape*, XX, no. 3 (Spring 1976), 8–19, XXI, no. 1 (Autumn 1976), 9–15, is an overzealous search for African influences. For sensible, contrary comments, see Mark L. Walston, "'Uncle Tom's Cabin' Revisited: Origins and Interpretations of Slave Housing in the American South," *Southern Studies*, XXIV (1985), 357–373, esp. 358.

33. Robert Carter to [?], fall 1728, Carter Letterbook, 1728–1730, VHS; William Byrd, *The Prose Works of William Byrd of Westover*, ed. Louis B. Wright (Cambridge, Mass., 1966), 349–350.

34. Stiverson and Butler, eds., "Virginia in 1732," *VMHB*, LXXXV (1977), 32. For extensive Chesapeake allocations, see lists of Edmund Jenings's quarters, 1712, Corbin Papers; Joseph

In South Carolina, Johann Bolzius observed that five yards of white or blue "Negro cloth," enough to make a coat and long pants, together with a pair of shoes, formed the typical allocation for a slave man. Women apparently got slightly more than five yards, because their clothing cost a few shillings more than the men's. Every three years, Bolzius noted, slaves received a woolen blanket or bed cover. According to Bolzius, most Lowcountry slaves had but one allocation of clothing, although in the summer some women got a short skirt and a handkerchief to cover their heads and men a pair of pants and a cap. Lowcountry plantation records confirm Bolzius's observation that approximately five yards of cloth formed the annual allocation. Apparently, Lowcountry grandees were less solicitous of their slaves' needs than the Chesapeake gentry.[35]

The amount of cloth allocated to slaves might have differed between the regions, but the fabric was similar. Henry Laurens's injunction to "cloth[e slaves] warm, strong and cheap" was widely followed. Coarse linens from Germany and inexpensive woolens from Britain constituted the most com-

---

Ball to Joseph Chinn, Feb. 18, 1743, Ball Letterbook; Edmund Berkeley Journal, Oct. 25, 1749, Berkeley Family Papers, microfilm, CW; will of Richard Bennett, 1750, "Vestry Book, 1749–1784," Episcopal Church Records, Lower Suffolk Parish, Nansemond County, as cited by Linda Baumgarten, "Clothes for the People: Slave Clothing in Early Virginia," *Journal of Early Southern Decorative Arts,* XIV (1988), 44–45; accounts of Philip Grymes, 1763–1765, Harrison Family Papers, VHS; Robert Carter Waste Book, Nov. 17, 1773, CW; Robert Carter Ledger, Nov. 22, 1773, VHS; Robert Carter Memorandum Book, 1774–1775, November 1774, LC; Carter Memorandum Book, 1788–1789, Dec. 31, 1789; "Negroes to be Cloth'd in Cumber'd," Memo Book, c. 1790–1791, Dr. Thomas Walker Papers, microfilm, CW; Betts, ed., *Jefferson's Farm Book,* 39–41. See also Paul G. E. Clemens, *The Atlantic Economy and Colonial Maryland's Eastern Shore: From Tobacco to Grain* (Ithaca, N.Y., 1980), 152; and Marks, "Economy and Society in a Staple Plantation System," 161. For lesser amounts given out by smaller planters, see Sarah Shaver Hughes, "Elizabeth City County, Virginia, 1782–1810: The Economic and Social Structure of a Tidewater County in the Early National Years" (Ph.D. diss., College of William and Mary, 1975), 243; settlement of James Cosby's estate, Nov. 20, 1732, York County Wills, no. 17, 332–333; and estate of James Backhurst, Mar. 19, 1732, ibid., no. 18, 35–37.

35. "Bolzius Answers a Questionnaire," trans. and ed. Loewald et al., *WMQ,* 3d Ser., XIV (1957), 256. For allocations of five yards, see William Dry's administration of the Rev. Richard Ludlam's estate, Dec. 10, 1728, B1/170, SPG; John Jameson's estate to Edmond Atkin, May 25, 1744, Inventories, WPA, LXVIIA, 57–67; Ball Account Book, Aug. 14, 1755, SCHS; John Lewis Gervais to Henry Laurens, Aug. 7, 1778, Laurens Papers, SCHS; estate of Bernard Elliott to Mrs. Carnes, 1783–1788, Papers of William L. Smith in the Wragg Papers, SCHS; Charles Drayton Diaries, esp. Feb. 7, 1784, Drayton Family Papers, Historic Charleston Foundation; list of Negroes who have taken their cloth, November 1790, Gibbons Papers; Fairfield Plantation Book, Jan. 7, 1792, Pinckney Family Papers, SCHS; Gabriel Manigault to Mr. Owen, Jan. 7, 1794, Manigault Family Letterbook, USC.

mon materials. The planters' quest for the heaviest, most durable cloth resulted in much discomfort for those who had to wear it. William Lee debated the relative merits of "Lancashire Cotton" and "Welch Cotton" solely in terms of which "wd wear as well." John Custis ordered "coars plad stockings . . . sewd strong" for his slaves. James Habersham admired the resourcefulness of a neighbor who imported suits made out of "Sailor Pea" cloth, although Habersham admitted that "this cloth must be too heavy and clumsy for womens wear." Instead, Habersham recalled that "West Country Barge Men have their Jackets made of a very strong, cheap cloth, I believe called Foul Weather and the Color being Drab or something like it I should think wou'd suit our dusty Barns as well as their dusty flour sacks." Cloths with labels that touted their sturdiness—whether Foul Weather, Fearnothing, or Everlasting—were not designed with comfort in mind.[36]

The reliance on overseas suppliers had other negative consequences for the slaves. Undersized, ill-fitting, or plainly inadequate stocks frequently arrived from Britain. Robert "King" Carter complained about the lack of large sizes in the shoes sent his slaves; John Custis wanted stockings that were "long and wide" in the foot instead of ones "so small that they are useless"; and William Beverley returned cloth of such poor quality that even his slaves could not use it. Delays in the arrival of clothing were common. In autumn 1769, Kitty was still wearing "her last winter clothes," and her frostbitten toes were a vivid reminder of her lack of footwear. In December, the administrator of a South Carolina estate observed that the slaves were naked, their winter clothing not having arrived. A Chesapeake planter admonished his agent to supply his slaves "in Good time; and not for the Winter to be half over before they get their winter Cloths, and the summer to be half over before they get their summer Cloths, as the Common Virginia fashion is." Clothing that arrived late in the season or even out of season was common in North America.[37]

---

36. *Laurens Papers,* VIII, 6; William Lee to Richard Lee, July 9, 1770, William Lee Letterbooks, microfilm, CW; John Custis to Jno. Starch, June 25, 1782, John Custis Letterbook, typescript, CW; *The Letters of Hon. James Habersham, 1756–1775,* GHS, *Collections,* VI (Savannah, Ga., 1904), 16; William Hunter, *VaG* (Parks), May 16, 1745; John Briggs, ibid. (Hunter), Feb. 14, 1751; Charles Steuart, ibid. (Hunter), Jan. 24, 1752 (fearnothing jackets); John Thornton, ibid. (Parks), Apr. 24, 1746; and William Heath, ibid. (P and D), Sept. 15, 1768 (everlasting breeches). For specifications on the most appropriate materials for slave clothing, see Thomas Cooper and David J. McCord, eds., *The Statutes at Large of South Carolina,* 10 vols. (Columbia, S.C., 1836–1841), VII, 396; and *Md Gaz,* Oct. 18, 1770.

37. Robert Carter to John Pemberton, Feb. 15, 1724, Robert Carter Letterbook, 1723–1724, VHS; John Custis to Jno. Starch, June 25, 1728, Custis Letterbook; William Beverley to Thomas Backhouse, July 19, 1743, William Beverley Letterbook, microfilm, CW; Jordan

Irregular supplies and random combinations of an array of materials gave slaves a motley appearance. These were no uniformed ranks. In addition to the widespread kersies, Osnaburgs, and cottons, field hands wore clothing made from an extraordinary range of fabrics—from calimanco to camblet, frieze to fustian, and serge to shalloon, to name a few. In addition to imported materials, some slaves, particularly during the Revolutionary era, wore locally made, usually striped, "homespun" cloth. Animal skins, both imported and native-made—whether leather breeches and aprons, buckskin vests, bearskin and beaver coats, swanskin underjackets, or even ermine underwaistcoats—adorned some slaves. Coats came in scores of styles: from double-breasted to riding, from Indian Match to Newmarket, from standard great coats to distinctive, individualized coats like one "with Hearts on the Hips behind, and on the Shoulders, doubled and quilted, with Horn Buttons." One student of slave dress has counted more than one hundred types of coats, about seventy-five kinds of breeches, and fifty forms of buttons. Materials came in a range of colors: blue, red, yellow, and white were most common, but black, brown, green, and gray as well as multicolored checks and stripes were common also. Most slaves were clothed in at least two materials and thereby often two or three colors. But constant wear meant that the colors were rarely vivid. The fabrics worn by slaves were in fact often unbleached, and the term "drab-coloured," used of some slaves' clothing, probably conveys the general appearance.[38]

Slaves enhanced the variety of their clothing by using dyes, patches, and edging. Sancho wore white plain breeches, dyed yellow; Harry a cotton jacket, dyed a dark color; and Will "Negroe Cotton Breeches," dyed purple. John Banister noted that Virginia slaves used "poysonweed" to dye their shirts black. Landon Carter supplied "Patching" for his people's shifts and shirts, and a South Carolina planter expended more than £11, £41, and £48 annually for "thread, Needles for Negroes to mend their clothes." Patched clothes occasionally bore a distinctive individual imprint: Syphax's brown cloth coat had "two patches on the left Side of the Back sewed in with white Thread," and Sterling's

---

Anderson, *VaG* (P and D), Dec. 21, 1769; William Dry's administration of Ludlam's estate, Dec. 10, 1728, B1/170, SPG; Joseph Ball to J. Chinn, Feb. 18, 1744, Ball Letterbook.

38. This discussion of cloths and colors is based on a close reading of all the 18th-century advertisements for South Carolina, Virginia, and Maryland runaway slaves. For the distinctive coat, John Bush, *VaG* (P and D), Apr. 18, 1771. For drab-colored, see, for instance, George Muter, *VaG* (P and D), Sept. 24, 1767; and John Corrie, ibid. (D and H), Nov. 7, 1777. For the most informed studies, see Baumgarten, "Clothes for the People," *Jour. Early So. Dec. Arts*, XIV (1988), 26–70; and Jonathan Prude, "To Look upon the 'Lower Sort': Runaway Ads and the Appearance of Unfree Laborers in America, 1750–1800," *JAH*, LXXVIII (1991–1992), 124–159, esp. 149.

purple jacket had "a piece of cloth put in to widen it at the neck and shoulders." Altering clothes allowed slaves to combine different colors: blue trimmed with red, white patched with blue, red edged with black, and so on. Occasionally, cuffs or collars of one color adorned a jacket or a petticoat of another. Breeches often had knee-bands or were "flourish'd at the Knees."[39]

Most slaves seem to have had their clothes made for them, but occasionally and perhaps increasingly they assumed the task for themselves. Where slaves made their own clothes, less rather than more uniformity undoubtedly resulted. Planters' wives and overseers' wives often made the slaves' clothing, and sometimes a wealthy planter employed a white tailor. As slaves developed kin networks and social relations, however, they asserted control over this process. In 1770, for example, John Channing's male slaves "chose to have the Cloth given them and their Wives or Sisters to cut it out and make them up for them" rather than rely on whites.[40]

Foot and head coverings showed little uniformity. Shoes were either imported—"London fall shoes," "good English Flatts,"—or locally made. Most were "coarse Shoes, such as are usually sold in stores," or "Negro made shoes, with Pegs drove in the Soals," or simply "square Negro shoes," but some were made of leather with wooden heels, some had heels "pegged and nailed with 3d nails, and 2d nails drove through the edges of the soles and clinched," others had "Iron tacked Soles" or were described as "hob-nailed." Occasionally, slaves wore "pumps" ("double-channel'ed Pumps," for instance) or boots ("blue Negro boots," "white Indian boots," or "white negro cloth boots"). In spite of this varied footwear, many slaves, particularly field hands, went barefoot—a practice that might well have been more common in the Lowcountry than in the Chesapeake. Heads were usually covered. Many slaves wore a hat or a cap, most often made of felt, but sometimes of beaver, raccoon, worsted, or gauze. Slaves sported "Negro cloth caps," "Scotch bonnets," "Monmouth caps," "jockey caps," "large slouched," "wide-brimmed," or "flapped" hats, hats with ribbon bands, and, of course, head cloths or bandannas. Headgear

---

39. Col. Richard Randolph, *VaG* (Parks), May 5, 1738; James Newgent, ibid., Mar. 27, 1746; Edmund Walker, ibid. (Hunter), Mar. 12, 1752; Joseph Ewan and Nesta Ewan, *John Banister and His Natural History of Virginia, 1678–1692* (Urbana, Ill., 1970), 202; Greene, ed., *Carter Diary*, 899; J. H. Easterby, ed., *Wadboo Barony: Its Fate as Told in Colleton Family Papers, 1773–1793* (Columbia, S.C., 1952), 20–22; Armistead Churchill, *VaG* (Hunter), June 12, 1752; Hamilton Usher St. George, ibid. (P and D), June 23, 1768. For knee bands, see Jcochim Hardstone, *SCG and CJ,* May 16, 1769 (no knee bands—an unusual feature); Workhouse, ibid., June 25, 1771; James Newgent, *VaG* (Parks), Mar. 27, 1746. Slave inventiveness in dress is discussed in greater detail in Chapter 10.

40. John Channing to William Gibbons, June 26, 1770, William Gibbons, Jr., Papers, Duke.

was not universal, but one owner thought it worth mentioning that his fugitive slave "wore no hat or cap."[41]

Clothing became more standardized through the century. The range of cloths, colors, and garments narrowed over time. In the 1730s, fewer than half of South Carolina's runaway slaves wore primarily "white Negro cloth"; forty years later, almost two-thirds were similarly clothed. In the 1730s, outfits that prominently displayed the colors green, yellow, brown, red, and especially blue were common; forty years later, only blue was a prominent color. Color standardization was less pronounced in Virginia runaways, among whom half wore predominantly white and blue outfits in the first half of the century, rising to almost 60 percent by the 1770s. Early in the century, slave men wore not just jackets and trousers but "frocks" and "Gowns"; by the late eighteenth century, coats and pants were typical. Standardization in attire reached such a pitch in late colonial Virginia that masters simply referred to their slaves as "clothed in the usual manner of laboring Negroes," "clothed in the common dress of field slaves," or wearing "the usual winter clothing of corn field negroes."[42]

Standardization was never complete, however, for three reasons. First, artisans and house servants consistently wore more varied clothing than field hands. As the number of skilled and domestic slaves rose, the range of slave clothing broadened rather than narrowed. Even in the early eighteenth century, there was a clear division between the clothes of artisans and field slaves,

---

41. Shoes and boots (only quotations): William Hunter, *VaG* (Parks), May 16, 1745; Francis Phillips, *Md Gaz,* Sept. 8, 1768; Simon Fraser, *VaG* (P and D), Jan. 23, 1772; Henry Hardaway, ibid. (D and H), Jan. 21, 1775; Hugh Wentworth, ibid. (Parks), Dec. 9, 1737; Charles Duncan, ibid. (P and D), May 6, 1773; William Macon, Jr., ibid. (P and D), Feb. 9, 1769; Jerdone and Holt, ibid. (P and D), Nov. 21, 1771; Col. Richard Randolph, ibid. (Parks), May 5, 1738; John Mecom, ibid. (Hunter), Apr. 10, 1752; Dan Welshuysen, *SCG,* Apr. 1, 1732; Richard Hill, ibid., Feb. 9, 1734; Archibald Blair, ibid., Jan. 22, 1756. Hats and caps (only quotations): Samuel Stevens, ibid., June 16, 1733; Archibald Cary, *VaG* (Hunter), Nov. 14, 1751; John Baptist Boswell, *Md Gaz,* Aug. 24, 1775; James Reid, *SCG,* Sept. 1, 1739; William and John Brown, *VaG* (P and D), July 18, 1771; James Cocke, ibid. (Hunter), Oct. 27, 1757; Inglis and Long, ibid. (P and D), Sept. 27, 1770; Samuel Chase, *Md Gaz,* Dec. 18, 1777. Virginia masters mention fugitive footwear far more than their South Carolina counterparts. This might have been a convention, but, more likely, many Lowcountry slaves went barefoot.

42. Cary Wilkinson, *VaG* (P and D), Mar. 8, 1770; James Buchanan, ibid., Dec. 13, 1770; James Burwell, ibid., Sept. 15, 1768. The analysis of colors is based on the first 400 South Carolina advertisements from the early 1730s and 1770s and on all the Virginia advertisements from the 1730s through the 1750s (57 runaways) and the first 200 advertisements from the early 1770s. A South Carolina planter wrote to a Charleston merchant asking for 300 yards of "Negro Cloth, one piece of which must be Blue, and the rest White," which comports well with the evidence from advertisements for runaways: Robert Hume to John Guerard, Sept. 22, 1748, Misc. MSS, SCHS.

but the gap widened over time. By the late eighteenth century, a few artisans wore jackets with collars and cuffs made from lace or other expensive materials, waistcoats trimmed with gold lace, gold-laced hats, shoes with metal buckles, beaver hats, and superfine cloth coats. Peter, a carpenter, was only somewhat more ostentatious than usual in flourishing a silver watch, silver shoe buckles, and a brown wig. Charles Cox, a slave miller in Anne Arundel County, Maryland, boasted a range of "best" or "Sunday" clothes, each distinguished by a particular style and color of button. As slaves assumed specialized roles over the course of the eighteenth century, they donned the garb of their occupations. Thus, some slaves were identifiable by the "Dress such as Sailors wear," or "such Clothes as Watermen generally wear"; slave blacksmiths donned the emblem of their trade, the leather apron; house servants often wore livery and were generally "neat" and well-groomed; an occasional female house servant had a "great variety" of gowns, jackets, and coats, made of chintzes, cottons, and calicoes.[43]

Second, masters contributed to the variety of slave clothing by rewarding some slaves with extra clothing and facilitating purchases by others. Landon Carter was tightfisted in distributing but one shirt to his slaves and then obliging "them to buy linnen to make their other shirt instead of buying liquor with their fowls." Carter's slaves might well have chosen their own linen and purchased luxuries as well as necessities. Carter also contributed to the differentiation among his slaves by singling out some for special allocations. Henry Laurens indulged his slaves' desire for "finery"—at a price, of course. In one package of clothing sent up to Wambaw plantation, Laurens included "15

---

43. For artisans early in the century, see, for example, Richard Hill, *SCG*, Feb. 9, 1734; Commander of Fort Moor, ibid., June 24, 1734; Nicholas Mathison, ibid., Nov. 23, 1734; Philip Alexander, *VaG* (Parks), Feb. 24, 1738. At midcentury, Bolzius noted that "the skilled Negroes in Charlestown, who are used in the offices and shops or who are mistresses, are very well dressed" ("Bolzius Answers a Questionnaire," trans. and ed. Loewald et al., *WMQ*, 3d Ser., XIV [1957], 236). For late colonial artisans, see, for example, John Thomas, *SCG and CJ*, Sept. 18, 1770; Lionel Chalmers, *SCG*, Apr. 11, 1771; Roger Smith, *SCG and CJ*, Nov. 5, 1771; William Black, *VaG* (P and D), Dec. 13, 1770; Young Parran, *Md Gaz*, Nov. 1, 1764 (Peter); John H. Sprinkle, Jr., "The Contents of Charles Cox's Mill House Chest," *Hist. Arch.*, XXV (1991), 91–93 (Charles Cox). House servants received a better-quality shoe than field slaves: Charleston Account Book, Nov. 28, 1778, Maurice Family Papers, UNC. For sailors, see Stafford Lightburn, Jr., *VaG* (P and D), Mar. 7, 1771; for watermen, see Robert Donald, ibid., Oct. 17, 1771. For blacksmiths and aprons, see John Laforey, *VaG* (Purdie), May 16, 1766; and Francis Jerdone, *VaG and WA*, Apr. 17, 1784. For house servants, see John Grymes, *VaG* (Parks), May 16, 1745; and William Roane, ibid. (P and D), Aug. 17, 1769. For female domestics, see William Roberts, *SCG*, Mar. 27, 1775; Barnard Elliott, *Gaz of State of SC*, Oct. 7, 1778; and Martha Massie, *VaG* (Hunter), Oct. 27, 1752. For livery, see Baumgarten, "Clothes for the People," *Jour. Early So. Dec. Arts*, XIV (1988), 34–37.

very gay Wastcoats . . . at 10 Bushels per Wastcoat"; in another parcel he included "3 Great Coats at 12 Bushels Rough Rice each"; and on a third occasion his package consisted of "6 Dutch caps." Some slaves, like Charles Cox the slave miller, wore white castoffs. Abraham, for instance, could "change his Dress, as he has a variety of Gentlemens old Clothes." Joseph Ball sent his "old Cloaths" from England for his slaves: Will received a gray coat, breeches, and hat; Mingo a "stuff suit"; and Harrison a "Dimmity coat" and breeches, with a knife in the pocket. A Scottish immigrant to Charleston noted that he never had a shirt or stocking mended, but always gave his castoffs to slaves.[44]

Finally, shortcomings in the provision and distribution of clothing, together with the possible preference of some slaves, meant that many slaves were scantily clad, even naked. Travelers to the Chesapeake were often shocked at the appearance of slaves. In 1732, William Hugh Grove noted that slave waiters in the best public establishments had to have their feet washed, an indication that they wore no shoes. A generation later, John Woolman saw Chesapeake slave "men and women [who] have many times scarce clothes enough to hide their nakedness, and boys and girls ten and twelve years old [who] are often stark naked amongst their master's children." In 1777, Ebenezer Hazard observed that "the Virginians, even in the City [of Williamsburg], do not pay proper Attention to Decency in the Appearance of their Negroes." A decade later, Benjamin Henry Latrobe registered his surprise at the sight of naked slave children and bare-breasted girls and women. Mulatto Peter Harlitt was "almost naked" when he ran away one autumn. When Charles Yates put his eighteen-year-old slave Robin, "brought up from his infancy a house servant," into the fields, he observed that the slave's hands and feet were "delicate, having never been used to hard work, or to go without shoes." By implication, field hands often went barefoot.[45]

---

44. Greene, ed., *Carter Diary,* 484 (see also 299, 347, 1040); *Laurens Papers,* V, 20, 61, 73 (see also IV, 148, V, 93, 573, VII, 329); Loftin Newman, *VaG* (P and D), Nov. 7, 1771; Joseph Ball to J. Chinn, June 30, 1749, Sept. 24, 1753, Ball Letterbook; James Steuart to John Steuart, May 7, 1751, Steuart of Dalguise Muniments, Scottish Record Office, Edinburgh. For slaves' being singled out in clothing allocations, see Ball Account Book, Aug. 14, 1755; and J. Channing to W. Gibbons, Aug. 10, 1786, William Gibbons, Jr., Papers. The most striking fact about the purchase of yard goods for the Mallory slaves, Hughes notes, was their unequal allotment ("Elizabeth City County, Virginia, 1782–1810," 242).

45. Stiverson and Butler, eds., "Virginia in 1732," *VMHB,* LXXXV (1977), 22; Phillips P. Moulton, ed., *The Journal and Major Essays of John Woolman* (New York, 1971), 65; Fred Shelley, ed., "The Journal of Ebenezer Hazard in Virginia, 1777," *VMHB,* LXII (1954), 410; Edward C. Carter II et al., eds., *The Virginia Journals of Benjamin Henry Latrobe, 1795–1798,* 2 vols. (New Haven, Conn., 1977), I, 225; George Gordon, *Md Gaz,* Nov. 2, 1748; Charles Yates, *VaG and WA,* Sept. 20, 1783.

In the Lowcountry, the slaves' nakedness or seminakedness was so commonplace that there are precise accounts of the form it took. Johann Bolzius described how, in the summer, Lowcountry slaves "go naked, except that the men cover their shame with a cloth rag. . . . The women have petticoats; the upper body is bare. The children of both sexes go about in the summer just as they left the mother's womb." In 1745, a visitor to the Lowcountry observed that the region's planters gave their slaves "no cloaths but a Breech Clout"; about thirty years later, the overseer of Cypress plantation described his slaves as wearing only "a bit of loin cloth wrapt round their loins," and another traveler was ferried across a South Carolina river by six Negroes, "four of whom had nothing on but their kind of breeches, scarce sufficient for covering." Advertisements for many Lowcountry runaways tell the same story. Descriptions, such as has on "only an Arse-Cloth," "has nothing on but an old rag about his middle," "has nothing on but a piece of check linen about her middle," "a Clout round his Loins," abound. If a house servant dressed "very well, *seldom* without shoes and stockings," presumably field hands *often* went without shoes and socks. In short, like the clothing worn by their African ancestors and by slaves in many other parts of the New World, the essential items of Lowcountry adult dress were the wraparound skirt for women and the breechcloth or waist tie for men.[46]

There were, then, many similarities and a few critical differences in the dress of Chesapeake and Lowcountry slaves. Both sets of slaves wore much the same materials and colors; attire in both regions grew more standardized over time; privileged slaves in each society had access to more extravagant and specialized clothing than other slaves; some fortunate slaves everywhere made occasional purchases or received castoffs to supplement their wardrobes; and significant numbers in both regions appeared naked or seminaked. At the same time, clothing allocations, at least at the level of the larger planter, appear to have been more ample in the Chesapeake than in the Lowcountry; runaway slaves in the Chesapeake had more garments than those in the Lowcountry; and nakedness was more widespread among South Carolina than Virginia slaves.

46. "Bolzius Answers a Questionnaire," trans. and ed. Loewald et al., *WMQ*, 3d Ser., XIV (1957), 236; "William Logan's Journal of a Journey to Georgia, 1745," *Pennsylvania Magazine of History and Biography*, XXXVI (1912), 15; James Barclay, *The Voyages and Travels of James Barclay, Containing Many Surprising Adventures, and Interesting Narratives* (London, 1777), 25; Howe, ed., "Journal of Josiah Quincy," Mass. Hist. Soc., *Procs.*, XLIX (1915–1916), 452; Charlestown Gaol, *SCG*, June 5, 1736; Workhouse, ibid., Oct. 10, 1754; Workhouse, ibid., Nov. 5, 1764; Camden Gaol, ibid., Nov. 8, 1773; Barnard Elliott, *SCG and CJ*, Mar. 8, 1768 (emphases added). For more on nakedness as a cultural preference, see Chapter 10.

DIET

Like dress, the diets of Chesapeake and Lowcountry slaves had much in common and yet diverged significantly. In both regions, maize was the staple food; meat was occasionally available; water and rum rations provided most of the liquid intake; and slaves supplemented rations by hunting, fishing, raising fowl, and cultivating vegetables. Nevertheless, in spite of these similarities, slave diets differed in both variety and nutritional quality between Lowcountry and Chesapeake. Maize and domestic animal rations were less abundant in the Lowcountry than in the Chesapeake; as a result, Lowcountry slaves were forced to grow more vegetables and forage more extensively than their Chesapeake counterparts. If Carolina slaves were less dependent on their masters for subsistence, they were also more overworked and less healthy than Chesapeake slaves.

William Hugh Grove, an observer of the Chesapeake scene in 1732, noted that slaves "are allowed a peck of Indian Corn per week." Virginia plantation records substantiate Grove's observation. Robert Carter reported in 1771 that an annual allocation of fifteen bushels or sixty pecks of corn formed "the common allowance for Negroes who are not fed with Animal food," and ten years later he ordered that his carpenters receive both bacon and one peck of corn weekly. Contemporaries recognized the nutritional value of corn. As early as 1674, one writer observed that corn, rather than wheat, "nourishes labourers better, and brings a far great increase." William Byrd told Mark Catesby that he had at one time obliged his slaves to eat wheat, but they "found themselves so weak that they begged [him] to allow them Indian Corn again." Many years later, George Washington tried the same experiment and "found that though the Negroes, while the Novelty lasted, seemed to prefer Wheat bread as being the food of their Masters, they soon grew tired of it." Washington concluded, "Should the negroes be fed upon Wheat or Rye bread, they would in order to be fit for the same labor, be obliged to have a considerable addition to their allowance of Meat."[47]

In the Lowcountry, the vegetable rations supplied by planters were more varied than in the Chesapeake. Although maize was the primary staple, it did

---

47. Stiverson and Butler, eds., "Virginia in 1732," *VMHB*, LXXXV (1977), 32; "A List of Mills in the Neighbourhood of a Place where the Court of Westmoreland County have Empowered Mr. Thomas Edwards to Build a Mill," n.d. [c. 1771], Carter-Keith Papers, VHS; Robert Carter to William Rains, Sept. 16, 1781, Carter Letterbook, IV, 119, Duke; Shaftesbury Papers, no. 83, 30/24/48, PRO; Mark Catesby, *The Natural History of Carolina, Florida, and the Bahama Islands . . .* , 2 vols. (London, 1731–1743), I, xvii; Carter et al., eds., *Virginia Journals of Latrobe*, I, 170. For other references to the weekly corn allowance, see Robert Carter Corn Book, 1743, UVa; and Hugh Nelson to Battaille Muse, Dec. 22, 1778, Muse Papers. For more on corn's value, see Shaftesbury Papers, no. 83, 30/24/48, PRO.

not dominate the Lowcountry diet. Slaves tended less corn land in the Lowcountry than in the Chesapeake, in part because the discarded parts of Carolina's chief staple, rice, served as a cheap food. Johann Bolzius noted the seasonal variation in the Lowcountry slave diet: "From September to March their food is commonly potatoes and small unsaleable rice, also at times Indian corn; but in summer corn and beans which grow on the plantation." This seasonal variety probably accounts for the conflicting reports of the basic Lowcountry provision. According to George Milligen-Johnston, Indian corn was "the chief subsistence of the Plantation Slaves"; Johann Schoepf thought rice "almost the only food"; a Hessian described calavance peas, or chickpeas, as "one of the principal foods of the Negro, who prefers them to rice"; and André Michaux and others believed that yams formed the chief element in the slaves' diet for a quarter of the year. Whatever the main constituent of the Lowcountry slave diet, the standard weekly ration was one peck of provisions, although some observers noted smaller allowances.[48]

If this was a more varied vegetable diet, it was less ample and nutritious than that of Chesapeake slaves. Maize was, after all, especially sustaining, and, as David Ramsay reported, "the negroes of Carolina give it a decided preference." Grain allocations not only were more meager in the Lowcountry than in the Chesapeake but also tended to be more erratically provided, particularly in the late eighteenth century, when the Lowcountry came to depend on grain supplies from its hinterland. Thus, in 1794, an absentee planter learned that his

48. "Bolzius Answers a Questionnaire," trans. and ed. Loewald et al., *WMQ*, 3d Ser., XIV (1957), 256; George Milligen[-Johnston], *A Short Description of the Province of South-Carolina* . . . (London, 1770), in Chapman J. Milling, *Colonial South Carolina: Two Contemporary Descriptions* (Columbia, S.C., 1951), 137; Schoepf, *Travels in the Confederation*, II, 156–157; Dörnberg, *Tagebuchblätter eines hessischen Offiziers*, II, 2, as quoted in Rodney Atwood, *The Hessians: Mercenaries from Hessen-Kassel in the American Revolution* (Cambridge, Mass., 1980), 165; *Laurens Papers*, VII, 236; Bernhard A. Uhlendorf, trans. and ed., *The Siege of Charleston: With an Account of the Province of South Carolina* . . . (Ann Arbor, Mich., 1938), 34; F. A. Michaux, *Travels to the West of the Allegheny Mountains* . . . (London, 1805), in Reuben Gold Thwaites, ed., *Early Western Travels, 1748–1846* (Cleveland, Ohio, 1904–1907), III, 304; [Francis Moore,] *A New Voyage to Georgia* (London, 1735), GHS, *Colls.*, II (Savannah, Ga., 1842), tract 2, 50; Robert Mills, *Statistics of South Carolina* (Spartanburg, S.C., 1972 [orig. publ. Charleston, S.C., 1826]), 480–481. For a peck a week or a quart daily, see "Bolzius Answers a Questionnaire," trans. and ed. Loewald et al., *WMQ*, 3d Ser., XIV (1957), 257; Alexander Garden to J. Ellis, May 6, 1757, in James Edward Smith, comp., *A Selection of the Correspondence of Linnaeus, and Other Naturalists, from the Original Manuscripts*, 2 vols. (London, 1821), I, 404; John Martin to his son, Dec. 18, 1788, John Martin Papers, SCHS; William Attmore, *Journal of a Tour to North Carolina, 1787*, ed. Lida T. Rodman (Chapel Hill, N.C., 1922), 26–27. Others cite about half this daily allowance: "William Logan's Journal," *Pa. Mag. of Hist. and Biog.*, XXXVI (1912), 15; Miscellaneous Records, VV, 213–214 (1786), SCDAH; Joshua Evans Diary, Feb. 2, 1797, 231–232, UNC.

slaves had "been without a grain of corn for two weeks, living entirely on Fish and Oysters." Three years later, a Lowcountry slave told a traveler, "Me glad it rain; it raise de water in Congoree river, den boats come down, bring corn, Corn very scarce, very deer; den more plenty." Similarly, Daniel Turner was sure his brother in Rhode Island "would be very much surprised to find a rich man unable to buy corn for the support of his negros," but that was the situation in Lowcountry South Carolina in 1805.[49]

Most Chesapeake masters provided their slaves with some meat or other protein, but it was rarely a generous allowance. Thomas Anburey visited a typical plantation where the slaves received a little skimmed milk, "rusty bacon," or salt herring. Half a pound of meat or fish a week became the standard animal protein allowance on large plantations. Chesapeake slaves came to expect a meat ration, as one manager discovered when his gang submitted "a grate Petition . . . for some meat." Virginia's rulers also shared this expectation, though they acknowledged that it was not always met. In commenting on a recent act to try slaves for stealing hogs, Governor William Gooch justified its alleged leniency out of "compassion for servants and slaves who have hard Masters that allow them scarcely any Meat in the Year." Landon Carter was one such master, for he required his slaves to buy his salted pork and only rewarded them "with a bit now and then" for good work. One year, he promised his slaves half a pound of meat for every six crows' heads they caught. Although meat allowances were common, they were generally both scanty and occasional. The exception proves the rule. In 1768, John Mercer acted as a contractor of slave labor for an iron foundry where the rations included an atypical meat allowance of six pounds a week. Once Scipio, Mercer's foreman, heard the news, he said that he would run away unless he was sent to the ironworks.[50]

The composition of the slaves' animal protein was not much better than the amount. Faunal remains at slave sites consist primarily of heads, vertebrae,

---

49. David Ramsay, *The History of South-Carolina* . . . , 2 vols. (Charleston, S.C., 1809) II, 123; P. Butler to Thomas Young, Mar. 25, 1794, Pierce Butler Letterbook, USC; Joshua Evans Diary, Feb. 10, 1797, 233–234; Daniel Turner to his brother, Feb. 20, 1805, Daniel Turner Papers, LC.

50. Anburey, *Travels*, II, 331; Robert Carter to [?], Aug. 27, 1729, Carter Letterbook, 1728–1730, VHS; Ball to Chinn, Feb. 18, 1734, Feb. 21, 1755, Ball Letterbook; Fitzpatrick, ed., *Writings of Washington*, XXXI, 186–187, XXXII, 65, 294, 474–475, XXXIII, 201–202, 303, 336–337; Simon Sallard to John Carter, Nov. 4, 1736, Carter Family Papers; Governor Gooch to Board of Trade, May 10, 1750, CO5/1327, fols. 67–77, PRO, microfilm, CW; Greene, ed., *Carter Diary*, 390, 871; J. Mercer to James Mercer, Jan. 14, 1768, Adams Papers, microfilm, CW. See also Bassett Account Book, Feb. 13, 1743; J. Mercer to B. Muse, Jan. 9, 1780, Muse Papers; Robert Carter Account Book, 1785–1792, 28, VHS; August Wilhelm Du Roi, *Journal of Du Roi the Elder, Lieutenant and Adjutant in the Service of the Duke of Brunswick, 1776–1778* (Philadelphia, 1911), 156; [Anne Ritson], *A Poetical Picture of America* (London, 1809), 36.

ribs, and feet, indicating that slaves received the least desirable parts of the animals. When the managers of one York County estate charged six shillings for "10 heads and Plucks for the Negroes," they were acting typically. Some exceptions have been found to this general pattern. The slave quarters at Shirley plantation reveal a wide range of pig body parts, including choice elements, and there were many good-quality cuts and butchered bones at some of the slave dwellings at Monticello's Mulberry Row. Recovered bones are most often small fragments and are rarely charred, demonstrating that meat was prepared in a pot rather than directly over an open fire. Although hog meat constituted the basis of Chesapeake slaves' animal protein consumption, archaeological investigations have shown that slaves also ate beef and even mutton. In fact, on some Chesapeake plantations, beef contributed more to the slaves' diet than pork. Finally, if Mount Vernon's slave quarter was typical, fish constituted a significant, though never major, part of the slave's protein—the dominant species were small catfish, herring, and bass, and the more desirable sturgeon and large bass were generally absent.[51]

Such protein rations were much stingier in the Lowcountry than in the Chesapeake. Charles Ball, brought up in Maryland, where meat and fish allowances were typical, found conditions very different when he was sold to a plantation in the Lower South. A forty-year-old slave foreman who had lived all his life in South Carolina dramatized the difference when he told Ball that he "never had any meat except at Christmas." Archaeological investigations of many—though not all—Lowcountry sites have also uncovered little evidence of domestic animal protein in the slaves' diet. Perceptive observers such as

51. Diana C. Crader, "The Zooarchaeology of the Storehouse and the Dry Well at Monticello," *American Antiquity,* XLIX (1984), 542–558; Crader, "Faunal Remains from Slave Quarter Sites at Monticello, Charlottesville, Virginia," *ArchaoZoologia,* III (1989), 229–236; Crader, "Slave Diet at Monticello," *Am. Antiq.,* LV (1990), 690–717; Reinhart, *Material Culture,* 86–94; Dennis J. Pogue, "The Archaeology of Plantation Life: Another Perspective on George Washington's Mount Vernon," *Va. Cavalcade,* XLI (1991–1992), 74–83; Pogue and Esther C. White, "Summary Report on the 'House for Families' Slave Quarter Site (44FX762/40–47), Mount Vernon Plantation, Mount Vernon, Virginia," *Quarterly Bulletin of the Archaeological Society of Virginia,* XLVI (1991), 189–206; Stephen Charles Atkins, "An Archaeological Perspective on the African-American Slave Diet at Mount Vernon's House for Families" (master's thesis, College of William and Mary, 1994); Settlement of John Mundell's estate, Aug. 17, 1749, York County Wills, no. 20, 157; Instructions About My Affairs, Feb. 18, 1744, Ball Letterbook. Although archaeologists have found a surprisingly large number of cattle bones at slave sites, leading some to argue that beef contributed the bulk of slaves' meat, it is possible that salt pork, offal, and bacon, which would have left few bones, formed a large part of pork allocations. See also Lorena S. Walsh, "Work and Resistance in the New Republic: The Case of the Chesapeake, 1770–1820," in Mary Turner, ed., *From Chattel Slaves to Wage Slaves: The Dynamics of Labor Bargaining in the Americas* (Bloomington, Ind., 1995), 100.

Johann Bolzius noted that Lowcountry slaves received "meat a few times a year" "if they have benevolent masters," while André Michaux averred that Lowcountry planters "never give [slaves] meat." Michaux concluded that "in the other parts of the United States they are better treated."[52]

Better treated they might have been, but probably no group of slaves could match those of the Lowcountry for the amount of time spent fishing and hunting. Because of the lack of meat supplied by their masters and the amount of time that could be gained for their own affairs through the task system, Lowcountry slaves hunted extensively. Once transported to the Lower South, Charles Ball trapped as many raccoons, opossums, and rabbits as provided for two to three meals a week. Accompanied by his "excellent hunting dog," Ball walked at least ten miles a week, touring his traps. Ball's relationship with his "constant companion" must have been unexceptional; otherwise, why at various times would white South Carolinians have tried to prohibit slaves from owning dogs? A middle-aged slave who ran away from a plantation near Stono was said to be "very expert in hunting." On Christmas Day, 1775, Titus, a recent African immigrant, with "country marks down the sides of his face" and unable to speak a word of English, left his plantation on the lower part of the Santee River. His master thought he must have "lost himself (as he was out a hunting)." In 1765, one Georgia planter complained that in past years slaves had been "killing game" on his land, "highly prejudicial" to his interest. William Bartram saw Jonathan Bryan's slaves return "home with horse loads of wild pigeons . . . which it seems they had collected in a short space of time at a neighbouring Bay swamp . . . by torch light." Lowcountry slaves were also keen fishermen. They poisoned creeks in order to "catch great quantity of fish"; they dammed tidal inlets with reed hedges or logs in order to trap an "abundance of fish, which they in a friendly manner distribute to one another, being by that means continually supplied"; and they caught fish with line and wooden hook.[53]

---

52. Charles Ball, *Fifty Years in Chains* (New York, 1970), rpt. of *Slavery in the United States: A Narrative of the Life and Adventures of Charles Ball, a Black Man* (New York, 1837), 26, 42–44, 107; "Bolzius Answers a Questionnaire," trans. and ed. Loewald et al., *WMQ*, 3d Ser., XIV (1957), 235–236; Michaux, *Travels to the West*, in Thwaites, ed., *Early Western Travels*, III, 304. See also Attmore, *Journal*, 26–27. Archaeological evidence on a lack of meat is found in Wheaton, Friedlander, and Garrow, *Yaughan and Curriboo Plantations*, 293–296.

53. Ball, *Fifty Years in Chains*, 263, 355; John Campbell, "'My Constant Companion': Slaves and Their Dogs in the Antebellum South," in Larry E. Hudson, Jr., ed., *Working toward Freedom: Slave Society and Domestic Economy in the American South* (Rochester, N.Y., 1994), 53–76; Rawlins Lowndes, *SCG*, May 8, 1749; Theodore Gaillard, *SC and AGG*, Apr. 3, 1777; Lachlan M'Gillivray, *Ga Gaz*, Aug. 29, 1765, as quoted in Betty Wood, *Women's Work, Men's Work: The Informal Slave Economies of Lowcountry Georgia* (Athens, Ga., 1995), 45; Francis Harper, ed., *The Travels of William Bartram* (New Haven, Conn., 1958), 297;

Lead shot and gunflints have been found at almost all the Lowcountry (and many Chesapeake) slave sites. In addition to trapping animals, Lowcountry slaves apparently used firearms to hunt for themselves. From faunal remains at different South Carolina and Georgia slave sites, a significant proportion—anywhere from 20 percent to a staggering 90 percent—of Lowcountry slaves' animal diet was composed of wild species, with opossum, raccoon, deer, rabbit, turtle, mullet, and topgaffsail catfish the most frequent constituents. On the eve of the American Revolution, one observer was probably not too far from the mark when he observed that in Carolina a "dextrous negroe will, with his gun and netts, get as much game and fish as five families can eat."[54]

Chesapeake slaves, too, sought to supplement their protein allowances, but their spare time was more circumscribed and their meat rations more ample than for Lowcountry slaves. Some Chesapeake slaves turned to the sea and the rivers for additional supplies. Sometimes masters condoned the slaves' fishing. Thus, George Washington's slaves came one Sunday and "asked the lent of the sein," and a New Kent County planter recorded the amounts of fish that his slaves caught after dark. The slaves' consumption of turtles apparently met with no opposition, because whites were averse to them. But occasionally masters prohibited the activity: one planter stipulated in an agreement with an overseer that the overseer was to "prevent the people from oustering." Chesapeake slaves hunted as well as fished. Richard Parkinson discovered that "partridges [were] chiefly taken by negroes who have a device for snaring whole coveys together in a box," and, in 1763, Colonel James Gordon observed that his "people" had killed about sixty-five pigeons. At Mount Vernon's slave quarter, the bones of such wild fowl as quail, duck, goose, and turkey; such wild animals as deer, squirrel, rabbit, and opossum; and such nonschooling fish as pickerel, gar, and bluegill have all been recovered. Wild animals undoubtedly added variety to the slaves' diet, but, in most Chesapeake slave sites so far excavated, they comprised less than 5 percent of animal bones. Domesti-

---

Cooper and McCord, eds., *Statutes at Large,* III, 270; Peter H. Wood, *Black Majority: Negroes in Colonial South Carolina from 1670 through the Stono Rebellion* (New York, 1974), 122–123; "A Curious New Description," *Universal Museum,* I (September 1762), 477; Barclay, *Voyages and Travels,* 27.

54. John Solomon Otto, "Race and Class on Antebellum Plantations," in Robert L. Schuyler, ed., *Archaeological Perspectives on Ethnicity in America: Afro-American and Asian Culture* (Farmingdale, N.Y., 1980), 9; Charles H. Fairbanks and Sue A. Mullins-Moore, "How Did Slaves Live?" *Early Man,* I (1980), 3–5; Drucker, "Socioeconomic Patterning," *Hist. Arch.,* XV (1981), 62; Fairbanks, "Plantation Archaeology," ibid., XVIII (1984), 2–3, 5; Elizabeth J. Reitz, Tyson Gibbs, and Ted A. Rathbun, "Archaeological Evidence for Subsistence on Coastal Plantations," in Singleton, ed., *The Archaeology of Slavery,* 163–191; Harry J. Carman, ed., *American Husbandry* (New York, 1939), 303.

cated birds, in contrast, were much more significant, comprising as much as a third of the bones at one site, an appropriate reflection of the slaves' renown as the region's "Chicken Merchants." Apparently, so numerous were one slave's poultry that one springtime night saw him, with the aid of another slave who "was holding light," busily counting his chickens.[55]

Just as Chesapeake slaves hunted and fished in order to supplement their meat rations, so they worked in their garden plots to lessen their dependence on maize. As William Hugh Grove observed in 1732, Chesapeake planters allowed slaves "to plant little Platts for potatoes or [?] Indian pease and Cimnells [a squash], which they do on Sundays or [at] night," and a half-century later Thomas Jefferson noted that Virginia slaves "generally" tended a variety of sweet potato and "particularly valued" the potato-pumpkin. In 1737, John Custis noted that his Negroes specialized in making "multitudes of melons." Perhaps these were watermelons, introduced into North America by the slaves. And, in 1781, William Feltman observed that Hanover County slaves raised "great quantities of snaps and collerds." In these ways, Chesapeake slaves added variety to their vegetable and fruit diet.[56]

---

55. Jackson and Twohig, eds., *Diaries of Washington*, I, 261; William Chamberlayne Account Book, Apr. 1800, LC; W[illiam] J. Hinke, ed. and trans., "Report of the Journey of Francis Louis Michel...," *VMHB*, XXIV (1916), 42; Stiverson and Butler, eds., "Virginia in 1732," ibid., LXXXV (1977), 40; agreement between John Hall and John Williams, Dec. 1764, William Henry Hall Papers, Duke; Parkinson, *A Tour in America*, I, 303; "Journal of Col. James Gordon," *WMQ*, 1st Ser., XII (1903–1904), 1. For the small percentage of wild animals at Chesapeake sites, see Henry M. Miller, "Pettus and Utopia: A Comparison of the Faunal Remains from Two Late Seventeenth Century Virginia Households," *Conference on Historic Site Archaeology Papers*, XIII (1978), 158–179; Larry W. McKee, "Delineating Ethnicity from the Garbage of Early Virginians: Faunal Remains from the Kingsmill Plantation Slave Quarter," *American Archaeology*, VI (1987), 34; Crader, "Faunal Remains from Slave Quarter Sites," *ArchaoZoologia*, III (1989), 231; Crader, "Slave Diet," *Am. Antiq.*, LV (1990), 698; and, for domesticated fowl, see Elizabeth J. Reitz, "Vertebrate Fauna and Socioeconomic Status," in Suzanne M. Spencer-Wood, ed., *Consumer Choice in Historical Archaeology* (New York, 1987), 115; and Reinhart, *Material Culture*, 92. For "chicken merchants," see the section on trade in Chapter 6. Petition of Matthew Marable, *VaG* (Rind), June 29, 1769 (slave counting his chickens).

56. Stiverson and Butler, eds., "Virginia in 1732," *VMHB*, LXXXV (1977), 32; Julian P. Boyd et al., eds., *The Papers of Thomas Jefferson*, IX (Princeton, N.J., 1954), 255; Mary Randolph, *The Virginia House-Wife*, ed. Karen Hess (Columbia, S.C., 1984 [orig. publ. 1824]), xxix, 287–288; John Custis to Mr. Collinson, 1737, Custis Letterbook; William Feltman, *The Journal of Lieut. William Feltman* (Philadelphia, 1853), 10. In Carolina, John Lawson listed among the varieties of muskmelon a "guinea melon," presumably from Africa: *A New Voyage to Carolina*, ed. Hugh Talmage Lefler (Chapel Hill, N.C., 1967 [orig. publ. London, 1709]), 81–83. On watermelons, see Ewan and Ewan, *John Banister*, 20. For

Lowcountry slaves cultivated a much greater range of plants, including many more African varieties, in their own plots and gardens than did Chesapeake slaves. A little before he left South Carolina, Mark Catesby noted the introduction of a new variety of yam, "a welcome improvement among the Negroes," since they were "delighted with all their African food, particularly this, which a great part of Africa subsists on." Lowcountry slaves grew other African root crops like the tania, or tannier, and such African grains as millet and sorghum. They introduced sesame—what they called "Benni"—to the region. A late-eighteenth-century history of plants noted that South Carolina slaves made both "soups and puddings" of sesame and used its oil in salads. In 1762, an observer of the "private fields" of Lowcountry slaves saw their "beny-seed," which the bondpeople planted for "their own use and profit." Lowcountry slaves also planted African peppers, which Eliza Lucas referred revealingly to as "negroe pepper." Luigi Castiglioni noted their cultivation of "an annual herb with mallowlike flower . . . , which was brought by the negroes from the coast of Africa and is called okra by them." The fruit, when "boiled with the flesh of veal," he continued, made "very tasty soups." As in other parts of the Americas where Africans were a significant presence, South Carolina slaves grew variously leguminous plants and created rice-and-bean dishes, most famously hoppin' John (constituted usually of rice and red beans or black-eyed peas).[57]

The horticultural skills of Lowcountry slaves merited particular comment. In 1726, Richard Ludlam advised the collection and cultivation of special plants on which the cochineal beetle (an insect used to produce red dye) might feed and grow. Two or three slaves, he noted, could identify and gather as many plants in one day as would then plant a ten-acre field. Janet Schaw was so impressed by how Carolina slaves used their "little piece[s] of land" to grow

---

a general account, see Stacy Gibbons Moore, "'Established and Well Cultivated': Afro-American Foodways in Early Virginia," *Va. Cavalcade*, XXXIX (1989–1990), 70–83.

57. Catesby, *The Natural History of Carolina*, xviii, II, 45; Harper, ed., *Travels of William Bartram*, 297; Bernard Romans, *A Concise Natural History of East and West Florida . . .* , I (New York, 1775), 130; C. Bryant, *Flora Diaetetica; or, History of Esculent Plants* (London, 1783), 345, as cited in William Ed Grimé, *Ethno-Botany of the Black Americans* (Algonac, Mich., 1979), 25; "A Curious New Description," *Universal Museum*, I (September 1762), 477; Elias Ball to Elias Ball, Feb. 26, 1786, Ball Family Papers, USC; Elise Pinckney, ed., *The Letterbook of Eliza Lucas Pinckney, 1739–1762* (Chapel Hill, N.C., 1972), 28; Antonio Pace, trans. and ed., *Luigi Castiglioni's Viaggio: Travels in the United States of North America, 1785–1787* (Syracuse, N.Y., 1983), 171–172. See also Karen Hess, *The Carolina Rice Kitchen: The African Connection* (Columbia, S.C., 1992), 92–113. For a parallel, Edward Long noted that Jamaican slaves specialized in the cultivation of groundnuts, tanniers, "guiney corn," and tobacco and in poisoning fish and catching pigeons (*The History of Jamaica . . .* , 3 vols. [London, 1774], I, 486, II, 719, 761, 769, 788).

vegetables, "rear hogs and poultry, sow calabashes, etc.," that she thought they cultivated them "much better than their Master[s]." The harvesting of gourds, picked from creeping vines rather than small trees (which was the common practice in Africa), is a particularly noteworthy activity, indicating that slaves actively produced their own drinking, eating, and storage vessels. Schaw also believed that Carolina "Negroes are the only people that seem to pay any attention to the various uses that the wild vegetables may be put to." Archaeologists have found evidence of acorns, hickory nuts, walnuts, peach pits, and grape seeds at Lowcountry slave sites.[58]

The liquid diet of both Chesapeake and Lowcountry slaves consisted primarily of water. The Polish traveler Julian Ursyn Niemcewicz claimed that most Virginia planters gave their slaves "only bread, water and blows." A Scottish overseer in South Carolina was surprised that the only drink allowed slaves after meals was "pure water." However, many planters provided occasional rations of rum to their slaves: as a reward at holiday time; as an encouragement to labor, perhaps at harvest or on wet days; and as a tonic for pregnant and sick slaves. Rum rations were large enough to merit planter concern. In 1766, Henry Laurens was amazed to find that more than thirty gallons of rum had been consumed on one of his Lowcountry plantations in less than three months. In spite of his complaints, he still acceded to the request for more by forwarding another ten gallons of sweetened Jamaica rum. At about the same time, a Chesapeake resident thought the expense of providing rum to slaves was sufficient to propose import substitution. He argued that local brandy should replace imported rum. In the late eighteenth century, some abstemious or perhaps just thrifty planters began to eliminate alcohol rations. In 1793, George Washington noted that "others are getting out of the practice of using spirits at Harvest," but, as his "people have always been accustomed to it, a hogshead of Rum must be purchased." Perhaps because of the onerousness of their work, Dismal Swamp Company slaves also began to receive alcohol in the first decade of the nineteenth century. Their ration was as much as a gill (a quarter of a pint) a day, which a company official described as "not too much," provided they behaved. The only real difference in the liquid intake of the two regions' slaves was that in autumn many Chesapeake slaves received a daily pint of cider, which was unavailable in the Lowcountry.[59]

58. Richard Ludlam typescript letter, Jan. 10, 1726, Miscellaneous Letters and Papers from the Charleston Museum, III, USC; [Janet Schaw], *Journal of a Lady of Quality* . . . , ed. Evangeline Walker Andrews and Charles McLean Andrews (New Haven, Conn., 1923), 176–177; Sally Price, "When Is a Calabash Not a Calabash?" *Nieuwe West-Indische Gids*, LVI (1982), 69–82; Drucker, "Socioeconomic Patterning," *Hist. Arch.*, XV (1981), 64.

59. Niemcewicz, *Under Their Vine and Fig Tree*, 101; Barclay, *Voyages and Travels*, 26;

Although Lowcountry and Chesapeake slaves generally drank much the same, their diets differed. Lowcountry slaves depended less on planter rations than their Chesapeake counterparts. Self-subsistence fostered a spirit of self-reliance and encouraged Lowcountry slaves to introduce a wide range of vegetables into their diet, but their overall nutrition undoubtedly suffered. Slaves in South Carolina ate less corn and meat than slaves in Virginia, and they worked harder to supplement their rations. Few Lowcountry slaves starved. An exception was one group of fifteen slaves who ran away from their Goose Creek plantation, "Complaining that they were Ill used and Almost Starved and threatned to hang themselves or cut their throats If they were sent back again." But these slaves were unusual in that they resided on a leased plantation. Where masters were resident—as they generally were in both the Lowcountry and the Chesapeake—there were few complaints of starvation. Nevertheless, slaves ate more poorly in the Lowcountry than in the Chesapeake.[60]

This difference undoubtedly affected the demographic performance of the two slave populations and helps explain why the Chesapeake slave population grew more quickly and earlier from natural increase than did the Lowcountry slave population. The difference also affected slave stature, itself a reflection of demographic well-being, and helps explain why Chesapeake slaves were generally taller than their Lowcountry counterparts. Dietary deficiencies help account for a Hessian's description of a dozen slave men and women on one Lowcountry estate as "all misshapen or disfigured." Similarly, an inadequate diet probably explains why John Smyth thought that Carolinian slaves were "shrivelled and diminutive in size, compared with those in Virginia."[61]

It is easy to dismiss variations in the material life of slaves as trivial or inconsistent. The material conditions of slaves were so impoverished, it can be argued, that it is futile to draw distinctions between them. Certainly, the vast majority of slaves in both the Chesapeake and the Lowcountry were materially worse off

---

Laurens Papers, V, 100; Robert Leroy Hildrup, "A Campaign to Promote Prosperity," *VMHB,* LXVII (1959), 421; Ball, *Fifty Years in Chains,* 42–44. See also John Custis to Robert Cary, 1729, Custis Letterbook; accounts of James Madison, Dec. 26, 1755, Oct. 2, 1757, Feb. 11, May 15, 1759, Mar. 8, 1761, Madison Family Papers, microfilm, CW; diary of Col. Francis Taylor, July 8, 1788, VSL; Fitzpatrick, ed., *Writings of Washington,* XXXII, 470–477; Richard Blow to Samuel Proctor, Jan. 21, 1806, Richard Blow Letterbook, VHS, as cited in Midori Takagi, "Slavery in Richmond, Virginia, 1782–1865" (Ph.D. diss., Columbia University, 1994), 148.

60. Anne King Gregorie, ed., *Records of the Court of Chancery of South Carolina, 1671–1779* (Washington, D.C., 1950), 183.

61. Atwood, *The Hessians,* 165–166; Smyth, *A Tour in the United States of America,* I, 205. See Chapter 1 for the evidence on demographic performance and stature.

than their respective free populations; in that sense, distinctions between them may seem trivial. Certainly, too, the material conditions of slaves rested heavily on the fortunes, decisions, and whims of individual masters; and, in that sense, distinctions between them may seem merely idiosyncratic. But significant variations in slave treatment did occur, and they were patterned, not random.

One variation was status. Slaves of small planters experienced a material life that differed from slaves of large planters. The amount of living space was often restricted on a small estate; accommodation was more likely to be in a work building or single quarter than in a separate cabin. The size and frequency of cloth allocations tended to be more straitened on small than on large plantations. Conversely, the subsistence priorities of many small planters often guaranteed more food to their slaves than those owned by commercially oriented large planters. Material circumstances also varied greatly between privileged slaves and field hands. Artisans and domestics generally lived in better houses, had more possessions, wore better clothing, and ate more adequately than ordinary laborers. Even evidence from the grave offers clues to the distinctions between ordinary workers and domestics. At the Catoctin iron furnace in Maryland, the skeletons of the men—the industrial slave workers—reveal little lead content, because they had no access to lead-glazed ceramic or pewter vessels; but the women had nearly a threefold greater bone lead content because many of them were domestics and so were exposed to lead-containing foodware and products in the white owners' homes.[62]

Material conditions also varied over time. Slave housing evolved in similar ways in both regions—from dormitories to single cabins to duplexes, from earthfast and mud-walled dwellings to frame structures, from isolated encampments to more communal, settled villages. Clothing also became more standardized over time. By the late eighteenth century, a recognizable slave uniform had materialized, even if not all slaves wore it. A core slave diet also became regularized: a peck of corn a week was the standard adult ration, and in time many planters provided a meat or fish allowance. In widely varying degrees, slaves gained the right to hunt, forage, fish, and tend their gardens.

Finally, territorial variations were significant. In general, the material treatment of slaves was better in the Chesapeake than in the Lowcountry. Chesapeake slaves wore more garments and more varied clothes and had more ample and nutritious food than their Lowcountry counterparts. Johann Schoepf was correct when he observed, "The condition of the Carolina negro-slaves is in

---

62. Arthur C. Aufderheide et al., "Lead in Bone," part 3, "Prediction of Social Correlates from Skeletal Lead Content in Four Colonial American Populations (Catoctin Furnace, College Landing, Governor's Land, and Irene Mound)," *American Journal of Physical Anthropology*, LXVI (1985), 353–361.

general harder and more troublous than that of their northern brethren." Conversely, Lowcountry slaves had more control over their domestic lives than Chesapeake slaves. They lived in more communally oriented settlements, grew a wider range of foodstuffs, provided more of their own animal protein, and introduced more direct African influences into their housing, personal possessions, and foodways.[63]

63. Schoepf, *Travels in the Confederation,* ii, 220.

The Planters in General have throve and grown Rich . . . by the help and Labour of their Slaves (for their Lands tho' ever so Fertile are of no use or Profitt without them).

—Richard Hill

3 : Fieldwork

The building of the colonial economies of Virginia and South Carolina rested heavily on the backs of slaves. In the Lowcountry, George Milligen-Johnston thought that African American slaves "with a few Exceptions do all the Labour or hard Work." Johann Schoepf, an observer of plantation life in both Lowcountry and Chesapeake, claimed that "the negroes . . . in Virginia and Carolina are almost the only working people."[1] These reports may be exaggerated, but it would be difficult to overstate both the economic role of blacks in the colonial South and the central place of harsh, unremitting labor in their lives. The endless round of agricultural work occupied the attention of most slaves during most of their waking hours.

Just as the centrality of work in the slaves' experience was common to both regions, the ways that slaves went about their work had much in common. Like all agricultural workers in the preindustrial era, slaves alternated dispatch with deliberateness, speed with slackness. At the same time, their work became

---

1. Richard Hill to Richard Taunton, June 23, 1743, Richard Hill Letterbook, Duke; George Milligen[-Johnston], *A Short Description of the Province of South-Carolina* . . . (London, 1770), in Chapman J. Milling, ed., *Colonial South Carolina: Two Contemporary Descriptions* (Columbia, S.C., 1951), 135; Johann David Schoepf, *Travels in the Confederation [1783–1784]*, trans. and ed. Alfred J. Morrison, 2 vols. (Philadelphia, 1911), II, 40.

more regular over time, as masters sought to fill their days and seasons with full-time employment. Divisions of labor by sex and age were also similar in both regions. An extremely high labor force participation rate—with women, young children, and the elderly dragooned into work—was a defining feature of labor in both regions. Work also informed slave culture in similar ways, ranging from how slaves moved in the fields and how they conceived their work time to how they viewed the fruits of their labors.

And yet the precise requirements of the work demanded of slaves—its pace, intensity, and organization—varied between the Lowcountry and the Chesapeake. The production of different staples—rice and, later, indigo in South Carolina; tobacco and, later, wheat in Virginia—created two contrasting economic worlds. These different primary and secondary crops resulted not only in widely divergent patterns of plantation activities but also in contrasting rhythms of plantation life. Referring to the relation between Virginia and tobacco, one historian claims, "In no similar instance has an agricultural product entered so deeply and extensively into the spirit and framework of any modern community." But much the same can be said of South Carolina and its major product, rice. The connection between the two has led another historian to assert, "Rarely has a single crop ever dominated so completely the energies of a group of agriculturalists." The shaping power of each staple was therefore formidable. And a staple did more than determine work routines; it molded a region's very essence and defined the lives of the region's inhabitants. By dictating dissimilar production schedules, for instance, these dominant crops became the arbiters of time, so that even the social calendars of the respective societies were arranged differently. Marching to different drummers, the two regions moved to different beats.[2]

SEASONS OF LABOR
Rice and Slaves
The destiny of the eighteenth-century Lowcountry was inextricably intertwined with the fortunes of rice. "The only Commodity of Consequence produced in *South Carolina* is *Rice*," observed James Glen in 1761, "and they reckon

2. Philip Alexander Bruce, *Economic History of Virginia in the Seventeenth Century: An Inquiry into the Material Conditions of the People . . .* , II (New York, 1896), 496; Sam B. Hilliard, "Antebellum Tidewater Rice Culture in South Carolina and Georgia," in James R. Gibson, ed., *European Settlement and Development in North America: Essays on Geographical Change in Honour and Memory of Andrew Hill Clark* (Toronto, 1978), 93. See also Peter A. Coclanis, *The Shadow of a Dream: Economic Life and Death in the South Carolina Low Country, 1670–1920* (New York, 1989), 140; T. H. Breen, "Back to Sweat and Toil: Suggestions for the Study of Agricultural Work in Early America," *Pennsylvania History,* XLIX (1982), 241–258; Breen, *Tobacco Culture: The Mentality of the Great Tidewater Planters on the Eve of Revolution* (Princeton, N.J., 1985), esp. 17–23, 40–83.

it as much their staple Commodity, as *Sugar* is to *Barbadoes* and *Jamaica*, or *Tobacco* to *Virginia* and *Maryland*." Throughout most of the eighteenth century, the proceeds of this crop accounted for one-half to two-thirds of the annual value of South Carolina's exports. The occasional advocates for a more diversified Lowcountry economy are the most telling witnesses to the dominance exerted by this grain. In 1747, a propagandist for indigo culture addressed the readers of the *South-Carolina Gazette* in lurid terms about their attachment to rice. He wished, as he put it, to "wean [the planter] from his Bewitchment to Rice, which he has clung to and hugg'd till Draw cansir like it has eaten into his very Vitals." Even after indigo's meteoric appearance on the scene, Dr. Alexander Garden informed one of his correspondents in 1753 that "the Planting of Rice . . . is the slow but sure way of getting rich, thus [planters] have never made themselves fully Master of any one thing but the Management of Rice." No wonder that an East Floridian, in hopes that his colony would one day eclipse South Carolina through a more diversified economy, referred to the rival as a "Rice Thumping Country." In fact, rice was to remain king in the Lowcountry throughout the eighteenth and for much of the nineteenth century.[3]

No mainland crop was so closely associated with black slaves as rice. Johann Bolzius scoffed when he was told, soon after his arrival in the Lowcountry in 1739, that Europeans could not safely plant and manufacture rice. A generation later, when John Bartram was given equally emphatic advice that there was "no raiseing rice" without slaves, the evidence all around him seemed to confirm the opinion. And when Janet Schaw visited the Lowcountry in 1775, she needed no advice, because she could see for herself that "the labour required for [rice] is only fit for slaves, and I think the hardest work I have seen them engaged in." Rice and slaves, as Josiah Quincy discovered, were so closely associated that they even constituted "the general topics of conversation." Johann Schoepf encapsulated the relation when he noted, "Rice is raised so as to buy more negroes, and negroes are bought so as to get more rice."[4]

---

3. James Glen, *A Description of South Carolina* . . . (London, 1761), in Milling, ed., *Colonial South Carolina*, 95; George R. Taylor, "Wholesale Commodity Prices at Charleston, South Carolina, 1732–1791," *Journal of Economic and Business History*, IV (1932), 359; "Patricola," *SCG*, Mar. 2, 1747; Dr. Alexander Garden to Mr. Shipley, Apr. 5, 1753, Eng. MSS 19/vi/143, John Rylands Library, Manchester, England (see also Garden's letter to Royal Society, Apr. 20, 1755, Guard Book, I, 36, Royal Society of Arts, London); Nicholas Sutherland to James Grant, Feb. 29, 1768, bundle 412, Papers of General James Grant of Ballindalloch, sometime Governor of East Florida, in ownership of Sir Ewan-Macpherson-Grant, Bart., Ballindalloch Castle Muniments, Scotland.

4. Extract of a letter from John Martin Bolzius et al., Mar. 13, 1739, in *An Impartial Inquiry into the State and Utility of the Province of Georgia* (London, 1741), in GHS, *Collections*, I (Savannah, Ga., 1840), 190; John Bartram to William Bartram, Apr. 5, 1766, Bartram

One reason for this close association was the length and laboriousness of the rice production schedule. Although there were periods of "dead time," the rice cycle took from twelve to fourteen months to complete. Fernand Braudel correctly observed that "rice holds the record for the man-handling it requires." Similarly, when a Lowcountry master threatened a refractory domestic with "the discipline of a rice Plantation," his was no idle threat. Alexander Garden characterized the methods of eighteenth-century rice planting as "Tedious, Laborious, and slow," and was indignant at the "Labour and the loss of many of their lives" that slaves "Underwent in Satiating the Inexpressible Avarice of their Masters." George Ogilvie's poem *Carolina; or, The Planter,* celebrating Carolina rice culture, acknowledged the enormous labors involved in establishing a Lowcountry plantation, which he likened to the rechanneling of the Euphrates and the building of the pyramids. The onerousness of rice cultivation is perhaps best summarized in Pierce Butler's stipulation for "a Gang of Negroes accustomed to Cultivate Rice." He wanted "no cotton Negroes"; rather, only "People that can go in the Ditch."[5] The rice cycle was the most arduous, the most unhealthy, and the most prolonged of all mainland plantation staples.

If new lands were required, the rice cycle began in January and February. Axes were distributed to male slaves in these months, and, while they cut down "the trees which in some swamps are very numerous," women and boys cleared the ground of bushes and shrubs. It took eight slaves "a day's Task" to cut down the trees in a one-acre plot, but "the lopping and burning [was] nightwork" in which all slaves engaged.[6] March was a time for the preparation of fields and, toward the end of the month, the planting of provisions. The process of rice planting extended from about the beginning of April to early June. The diary of one Black River plantation owner in the Georgetown district affords a more detailed analysis of this ten-week period. On this plantation, rice was first sown on April 2 and last sown on June 9. In that time, nine fields

---

Family Papers, HSP; [Janet Schaw], *Journal of a Lady of Quality . . .* , ed. Evangeline Walker Andrews and Charles McLean Andrews (New Haven, Conn., 1923), 194; Mark Antony De Wolfe Howe, ed., "Journal of Josiah Quincy, Junior, 1773," Massachusetts Historical Society, *Proceedings,* XLIX (1915–1916), 465; Schoepf, *Travels in the Confederation,* II, 182.

5. Fernand Braudel, *Capitalism and Material Life, 1400–1800,* trans. Miriam Kochan (New York, 1975), 97; Ralph Izard to Peter Manigault, Apr. 23, 1769, Ralph Izard Papers, USC; Edmund Berkeley and Dorothy Smith Berkeley, *Dr. Alexander Garden of Charles Town* (Chapel Hill, N.C., 1969), 58; David S. Shields, "George Ogilvie's *Carolina: or, The Planter* (1776)," *Southern Literary Journal,* XVIII (1985–86), 5–134, esp. 53–54; Pierce Butler to François Didier Petit de Villiers, Apr. 6, 1807, Pierce Butler Letterbook, USC.

6. Harry J. Carman, ed., *American Husbandry* (New York, 1939), 275; William Gerard De Brahm, *De Brahm's Report of the General Survey in the Southern District of North America,* ed. Louis De Vorsey, Jr. (Columbia, S.C., 1971), 94.

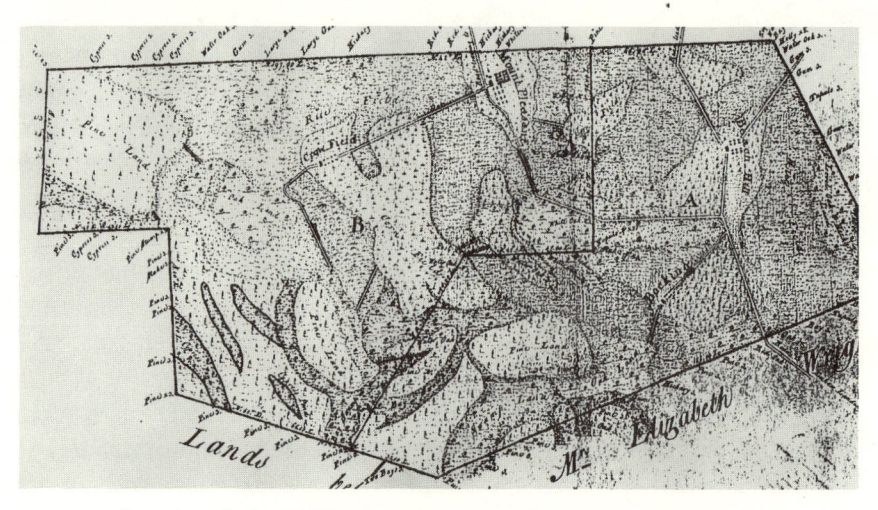

PLATE 9. *Plantation of John Middleton, Saint Luke Parish, March 17, 1784.* An inland swamp plantation, with many dams and roads connecting settlements and rice fields. Courtesy H. A. M. Smith Collection (no. 35) (32-28-6), South Carolina Historical Society

were planted. Of the sixty working days, just twenty-four were devoted to sowing seed; the other thirty-six were spent leveling the ground, trimming and closing ruptures in the banks, and cleaning drains and ditches. A level ground and secure dams were crucial in rice planting, for only then could the flow of water from the reservoir be controlled.[7] Prolonged and heavy manual labor was therefore necessary in preparing the ground for seed.

The actual sowing appears to have involved an amalgam of, perhaps even a conflict between, European and West African planting techniques. Mark Catesby, writing in the early eighteenth century, described rice as being sown "in shallow Trenches made by the hough . . . or in little Holes made to receive it." These "little Holes" were probably made by the slaves' feet, for William Butler, writing in the 1780s, enjoined the "coverers [of the rice seed to] keep

7. Evidence for the timing of operations in rice culture was compiled from the following sources, listed in chronological order: Thomas Nairne, *A Letter from South Carolina . . .* (London, 1710), 10; Ball Account Book, 1741–1742, 172, SCHS; "Johann Martin Bolzius Answers a Questionnaire on Carolina and Georgia," trans. and ed. Klaus G. Loewald et al., *WMQ*, 3rd Ser., XIV (1957), 258–295; Glen, *Description of South Carolina*, in Milling, ed., *Colonial South Carolina*, 15–16; Plantation Journal, 1773, Wragg Papers, SCHS; Bernard Romans, *A Concise Natural History of East and West Florida . . .*, I (New York, 1775), 127; H. Roy Merrens, "A View of Coastal South Carolina in 1778: The Journal of Ebenezer Hazard," *SCHM*, LXXIII (1972), 192; John Ball Account Book, 1780–1784, John Ball, Sr., Papers, Duke; Joseph W. Barnwell, ed., "Diary of Timothy Ford, 1785–1786," *SCHM*, XIII (1912), 182–184; John Drayton, *A View of South Carolina as Respects Her Natural and Civil Concerns* (Spartanburg, S.C., 1972 [orig. publ. 1802]), 117; William J. Ball Books, 1804–1890, UNC. The Black River diary is the Allard Belin Plantation Diary, 1792, SCHS.

their feet out of the Trench and not tread in the Rice, as is commonly done." If trenching was a method Europeans imposed on the slaves, the slaves' West African method of pressing a hole with the heel and covering the rice seed with the foot, to which Catesby and Butler obliquely refer, could not be eradicated. In fact, Sea Islanders were still practicing the heel-and-toe method in the nineteenth century, a testament to the tenacity of African traditions.[8]

From early June to early August, the rice fields (and, when time permitted, provision grounds) were continually hoed. The slaves hoed through the fields three or four times; according to John Drayton, the second hoeing was the most onerous, "for now the grass is handpicked from the roots of the rice." The familiar Carolinian figure of speech, that a planter was "in the grass," referred to a failure to keep rice weed-free, usually owing to a lack of sufficient hands. The work demanded of slaves, particularly in June and July, was thus extremely laborious and repetitive. Unlike farmers in England, who had more leisure during June and July than at any other time, reported one newspaper correspondent in 1758, "the planters of *Carolina* . . . are then in the greatest Hurry." Indeed, June, the month when hoeing began, saw more runaways than any other month, a testament to the harshness of the hoeing regimen (see Figure 5). Planters attempted to avert flight by distributing rum, meat, and clothing. Sometimes they succeeded. Late in July, Josiah Smith informed an absentee owner, "Although the Grass was very bad in all your fields, none of your People had run from it, they being kept to their work by mere dint of Encouragement of a Beef and some Rum, added to lenient treatment by the Overseer."[9]

August and early September provided relief and variety before the slaves

---

8. Mark Catesby, *The Natural History of Carolina, Florida, and the Bahama Islands . . .* , II (London, 1743), xvii; William Butler, "Observations on the Culture of Rice," 1786, SCHS; William R. Bascom, "Acculturation among the Gullah Negroes," *American Anthropologist*, XLIII (1941), 49. In some parts of West Africa, particularly those few areas where an intensive form of wet rice cultivation was practiced, mounding, ridging, and ditching were common; elsewhere, seed was generally broadcast or sown in holes. See Olga F. Linares, "From Tidal Swamp to Inland Valley: On the Social Organization of Wet Rice Cultivation among the Diola of Senegal," *Africa*, LI (1981), 573–575; and Jack R. Harlan et al., "Plant Domestication and Indigenous African Agriculture," in Harlan et al., eds., *Origins of African Plant Domestication* (The Hague, 1976), 16. For trenching as part of the European farming repertory, see Eric Kerridge, "A Reconsideration of Some Former Husbandry Practices," *Agricultural History Review*, III (1955), 30–31.

9. David Doar, *Rice and Rice Planting in the South Carolina Low Country* (Charleston, S.C., 1936), 20; Carman, ed., *American Husbandry*, 276; Drayton, *A View of South Carolina*, 118; *SCG*, Nov. 24, 1758; J. H. Easterby, ed., *Wadboo Barony: Its Fate as Told in Colleton Family Papers, 1773–1793* (Columbia, S.C., 1952), 21; Belin Plantation Diary, June 11, 1797; Josiah Smith to George Austin, July 22, 1773, July 22, 1774, Josiah Smith Letterbook, UNC. See also estate of Abraham Sanders in account with Margaret Sanders, Aug. 3, 1744, Inventories, WPA, CXXIV, 67, SCDAH.

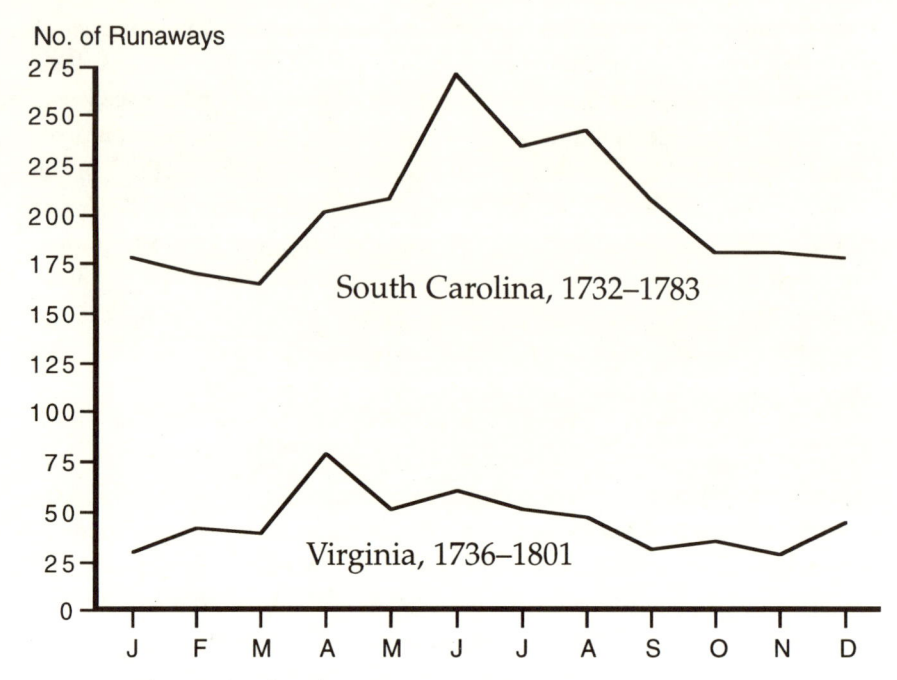

FIGURE 5. *The Months When Slaves Ran Away, 1732–1781*
Sources: Runaway slave advertisements, South Carolina newspapers, 1732–1783; Gerald W. Mullin, *Flight and Rebellion: Slave Resistance in Eighteenth-Century Virginia* (New York, 1972), 192.

were eased back into more months of heavy toil. Late summer was a time to "lay by" the hoes, to let flow the water that had been collected behind dams onto the rice fields, to collect timber, split staves, and cut hoop poles, and, for the slave men, to work on parish roads. In early September, masters provided some slaves with variety of a less pleasant nature, for "2, 3, or more negroes, are constantly kept . . . through every rice field, up to their knees and waists in water, continually hollowing and beating any sounding things to keep these [rice] birds from alighting thereon." Normally, however, slaves were given arms to ward off birds. One overseer petitioned for more ammunition on account of being "compelled to put from 8 to 9 Hands as a guard to the rice."[10]

Rice harvesting began about mid-September. The pace of work intensified, though it was not as taxing as hoeing. Referring to four runaways who had

---

10. Drayton, *A View of South Carolina,* 119; road work in Saint John Parish, Berkeley, generally began on the last Monday in August or the first Monday in September, with four to five days the usual requirement (Records of the Commissioners of the High Roads of Saint John's Parish, Berkeley County, 1760–1853, 3 vols., SCHS; *Gentleman's Magazine, and Historical Quarterly,* XXI [1751], 10; Samuel Dubose to J. E. Colhoun, Sept. 5, 1802, John Ewing Colhoun Papers, USC).

been recently captured, a South Carolina manager noted, "They have since kept to their work, and now have light employment in reaping a very pleasing Crop." When the rice was properly dried, the slaves bound the straw in bundles and housed it in barns or made it into large "ricks" or stacks. On an average-sized plantation, the stacking of rice took a month. After stacking the rice, the slaves threshed it to remove the grains from the stock and then winnowed the grain with the aid of fanner baskets made from coiled black rush or with a "wind fan" to separate the grain from the chaff. Perhaps the collective effort involved in these activities helps explain the decline in the number of slaves who ran away at this season. A contemporary explained it differently. For him, "the negroes [were] inspired with alacrity in beating and preparing the rice by the certainty of their coming in for shares." Slaves ate better at harvesttime, because they then received the rough rice not suitable for export.[11]

Pounding by hand to remove the grain's outer husk and inner film was the most arduous part of the rice cycle. As Dr. Alexander Garden pithily noted, "The worst comes last for after the Rice is threshed, they beat it all in the hand in large wooden Mortars to clean it from the Husk, which is a very hard and severe operation as each Slave is tasked at Seven Mortars for One Day, and each Mortar Contains three pecks of Rice. Some task their Slaves at more, but often pay dear for their Barbarity, by the loss of many . . . Valuable Negroes." Similarly, John English thought pounding "the severest work the negroes undergo and costs every planter the lives of several slaves annually." So exhausting was pounding that contemporaries credited it with increasing slave mortality. Begun in late November or early December, pounding sometimes extended into February if delays occurred or if planters held back their crops for the best market price. Pounding was so protracted that night work was common. As late as February, one planter instructed his overseer that if his rice was not "yet beat out," he wished "to have it sold it in the rough, to save Labour to the Negroes."[12]

Slaves protested. On one plantation where manual pounding continued into February, "the Negroes plagued [the overseer] Greatly by lying up, owing he believes to their beating much Rice by hand." More slaves ran away in early

---

11. Smith to Austin, Sept. 22, 1774, Smith Letterbook; Barnwell, ed., "Diary of Timothy Ford," *SCHM*, XIII (1912), 184. Rice hooks were distributed on one plantation on Sept. 15, 1785 (Fairfield Plantation Book, 1773–1797, SCHS).

12. Garden to Society, Apr. 20, 1755, Guard Book, I, 36; John English to Society, Nov. 15, 1760, ibid., V, 61; Joshua Evans Diary, Feb. 2, 1797, 231–232, UNC; Peter Manigault to John Owen, Feb. 20, 1794, Peter Manigault Letterbook, USC. See also *SCG*, July 14, 1733, for another description of how hard this part of the rice cycle was. One planter reported in early February that he was "pounding out 100 Barrels of Rice and shall keep the Rest in the Rough till it can be Exported" (Stephen Mazyck to Paul Mazyck, Feb. 7, 1776, Wragg Papers).

PLATE 10. *Mortar and Pestle.* Orangeburg County, probably early nineteenth century. For pounding rice. Courtesy South Carolina State Museum, Columbia

spring than in early winter, escaping the more severe weather. An anonymous contributor to the *South-Carolina Gazette* pointed to a possible connection between harsh winter work and sabotage: "I have taken Notice for Several Years past, that there was not one Winter elapsed, without one or more Barns being burnt, and two Winters since, there was no less than five. Whether it is owing to Accident, carelessness or Severity, I will not pretend to determine; but am afraid, chiefly to the two latter." This correspondent, as a more direct warning, referred to a recent incident involving "Mr. James Gray who work'd his Negroes late in his Barn at Night, and the next Morning before Day, hurried them out again, and when they came to it, found it burnt down to the Ground, and all that was in it." In such ways, slaves resisted increased labor demands.[13]

The seasonal cycle that dominated the lives of most eighteenth-century South Carolina slaves was not immutable. By midcentury, machines began to play a much greater role in rice processing. Elaborate wind fans appeared on many estates. But the greatest effort at technological improvement aimed at producing a machine that would, as a South Carolina lower house committee put it, "lessen the Labor and Fatigue of Negroes and other Slaves in this Province in beating and Pounding of Rice." The first plantation sale to mention a pounding mill was in 1754, and only four such notices appeared in the rest of the decade. In the 1760s and 1770s, however, pounding machines, driven by livestock, became regular features in many plantation advertisements, and claims that five to eight barrels of rice could be produced daily were commonplace. Even as early as 1755, Dr. Alexander Garden knew of horse-driven pounding machines that "can pound as much rice in one day as 16 negroes from sun to sun can do." In the 1780s and 1790s, Lowcountry planters built water-powered mills, which were more powerful than those driven by livestock. In the latter half of the eighteenth century, these labor-saving devices substantially improved the lot of many slaves.[14]

Just as the introduction of machines reduced the amount of heavy work required of slaves in the winter months, so tidewater rice cultivation reduced the heavy hoeing required of slaves in the summer months. In the early eighteenth century, irrigated rice was generally produced on "inland swamps."

---

13. Smith to Austin, Jan. 31, 1774, Smith Letterbook; *SCG,* Oct. 14, 1732. On January 25, 1765, Henry Laurens indicated that night work was common, for he wanted his slaves to shell corn in the evenings and mornings, noting that they "have had but little night work yet" (*Laurens Papers,* IV, 571).

14. A wind fan in the late colonial period could be valued as highly as £70, about a quarter of the price of a prime male slave; for example, inventory of Capt. Thomas Ford, June 10, 1767, Inventory Book, X, 94–96, and inventory of Capt. John North, Mar. 9, 1767, Inventories, WPA, CLXXIII, 724–727. On pounding machines, see J. H. Easterby, ed., *The Journal of the Commons House of Assembly, September 14, 1742–January 27, 1744,* Colonial Records of South Carolina (Columbia, S.C., 1954), 207; John Tobler, *SCG,* Apr. 23, 1744; John Lining, ibid., Dec. 5, 1754; Thomas Cooper and David J. McCord, eds., *The Statutes at Large of South Carolina,* 10 vols. (Columbia, S.C., 1836–1841), III, 698, IV, 853; Garden to Society, Apr. 20, 1755, Guard Book, I, 36. For a list of advertisements mentioning pounding machines, see my "Development of Slave Culture in Eighteenth Century Plantation America" (Ph.D. diss., University College London, 1977), 145. See also Lewis Cecil Gray, *History of Agriculture of the Southern United States to 1860,* 2 vols. (Gloucester, Mass., 1958 [orig. publ. Washington, D.C., 1933]), I, 281–283.

Planters stored water from springs and small streams in reservoirs in order to flow it onto their fields when the plants most required moisture, but they could rarely store enough water to flow the fields more than twice. By midcentury, tidewater planters had become aware of the advantages of using the tidal flow of rivers to irrigate rice fields. As early as the late 1730s and 1740s, planters spoke of land on which "the Spring Tide flows" or "in a good Tide's way" or that could be watered "from the River." Tidewater rice plantations had a much greater "command of water," as John Drayton noted, and "the crop [was thereby] more certain, and the work of the negroes less toilsome." Greater control over the water supply meant that planters could, in William Butler's words, dispense with "the slovenly method of flowing fields, and hoeing or chopping thro' the water." Slaves could now hoe in fields that had been fully drained. Moreover, the flowing of water retarded the growth of weeds and grasses while accelerating the growth of rice. Hoeing could then be less frequent. It must have been a tidewater rice plantation that a Virginian witnessed in 1780, for he claimed that "after the ground is once well cleared little cultivation does the ground [need] being soft by continual moisture."[15]

At the same time, however, the reclamation of river swamp, which required large embankments, long canals and irrigation ditches, and impressive sluice gates and trunks, was a massive undertaking. To construct such irrigation works, slaves labored far more intensively than ever, particularly in winter. Joseph Allston, who, according to Pierce Butler, "had the best dams in So. Carolina" because he drove his slaves mightily, tasked his ditchers at six hundred cubic feet a day (the daily task was five to seven hundred square feet in the nineteenth century). Slaves moved at least five hundred cubic yards of river swamp for every acre of rice field in order to construct banks, canals, ditches, and drains. By the end of the eighteenth century, rice banks on the Eastern Branch of the Cooper River—little over ten miles in length—contained more

15. For inland swamps, see petition of Several Inhabitants of the Parish of St. James Santee, May 4, 1743, Journal of the South Carolina Upper House, IX, 103, SCDAH; John Graves, *SCG*, Sept. 5, 1754; Samuel Clegg, *SCG and CJ*, Aug. 9, 1768. For tidewater plantations, see Thomas Smith, *SCG*, July 16, 1737; Joshua Sanders, ibid., Jan. 22, 1741; John Mullryne, ibid., July 4, 1744; Grey Elliott, ibid., Jan. 6, 1762; Jonathan Bryan, ibid., June 7, 1770; William Williamson, ibid., Feb. 28, 1771; John English to Society, Nov. 15, 1760, Guard Book, V, 61; Drayton, *A View of South Carolina*, 116; Butler, "Observations," 1786; James Parker's Journal of the Charlestown Expedition, Feb. 5, 1780, 920 PAR I 13/2, Parker Family Papers, Liverpool City Libraries, England; Douglas C. Wilms, "The Development of Rice Culture in Eighteenth Century Georgia," *Southeastern Geographer*, XII (1972), 45–57; Hilliard, "Antebellum Tidewater Rice Culture," in Gibson, ed., *European Settlement and Development in North America*, 91–115; and Joyce E. Chaplin, "Tidal Rice Cultivation and the Problem of Slavery in South Carolina and Georgia, 1760–1815," *WMQ*, 3d Ser., XLIX (1992), 29–61.

than six million cubic feet of earth. Contemporaries did not exaggerate when they compared these undertakings to building the pyramids. In 1765, John Bartram saw 130 slaves digging a ditch from eight to twelve feet deep and a quarter- or half-mile long. About a generation later, Ben Mazyck lauded his neighbor's new dams and canals: "The most stupendous works I Ever saw of the Kind—and that of 100 of my Negroes would not have completed such in 7 years, which you told me, you did in less than two! I s[ai]d it was substantial, and high Enough to keep Noah's flood from passing over it." No doubt the slaves who accomplished this feat took a somewhat different view of the enterprise. Perhaps their response was like that of laborers on George Austin's Pedee plantation who, in February, "complain'd . . . that they had been bad work'd." They were protesting the harsh driving required in having "the Banks secur'd so as to save the Crop from being hurted by overflowing Tides."[16]

Two other consequences of the shift toward tidal culture were more positive. The most direct result of the new method was the creation of specialized opportunities for some slaves. As one contemporary put it, "the flowing of rice" in tidal culture "is a nice point and cannot be too much attended to." Masters entrusted slaves with this important responsibility. Thomas Middleton, for example, employed two slaves simply to tend the sluice gates on his Combahee plantation. In fact, African slaves might well have transferred to South Carolina the primary mechanism used to regulate water flow in early rice culture: the hollowed log and plug. Sluice valves in West African rice culture were frequently constructed from hollowed silk cotton tree trunks. The

16. Malcolm Bell, Jr., *Major Butler's Legacy: Five Generations of a Slaveholding Family* (Athens, Ga., 1987), 155; Mart A. Stewart, "Rice, Water, and Power: Landscapes of Domination and Resistance in the Lowcountry, 1790–1880," *Environmental History Review*, XV, no. 3 (Summer 1991), 50; Leland Ferguson, *Uncommon Ground: Archaeology and Early African America, 1650–1800* (Washington, D.C., 1992), xxiv–xxv; John Bartram, "Diary of a Journey through the Carolinas, Georgia, and Florida from July 1, 1765 to April 10, 1766," ed. Francis Harper, American Philosophical Society, *Transactions*, N.S., XXXIII (1942–1944), 22; Benjamin Mazyck to J. C. Ball, June 20, 1791, Ball Family Papers, USC; Smith to Austin, Feb. 25, 1772, Smith Letterbook. As John Channing emphasized, "Good Ditches and good Trunks are what are absolutely necessary on a River Swamp plantation" (Channing to Edward Telfair, Oct. 31, 1787, Telfair Papers, Duke). The scale of these dams can be envisaged from one detailed description of an East Florida estate. In 1781, the manager reported that the "best hands" had been making dams and that they were now complete. The upper dam was 300–400 yards long, 20 feet wide, and 4 feet high, with a center ditch 4 feet wide and 2 feet deep, and with two large trunks to let water in. The lower dam was 1,000 yards long, 12 feet wide, and 4 feet high, with a large floodgate in the middle to let water off and with a center ditch of the same dimensions as that of the lower dam. Between the two dams lay 300 acres of clay marsh. Still to construct was a center drain, a mile in length, 6 feet wide, 4 feet deep, banked on each side to a height of 2 feet. David Yeats to James Grant, Sept. 14, 1781, bundle 250, Papers of General James Grant of Ballindalloch.

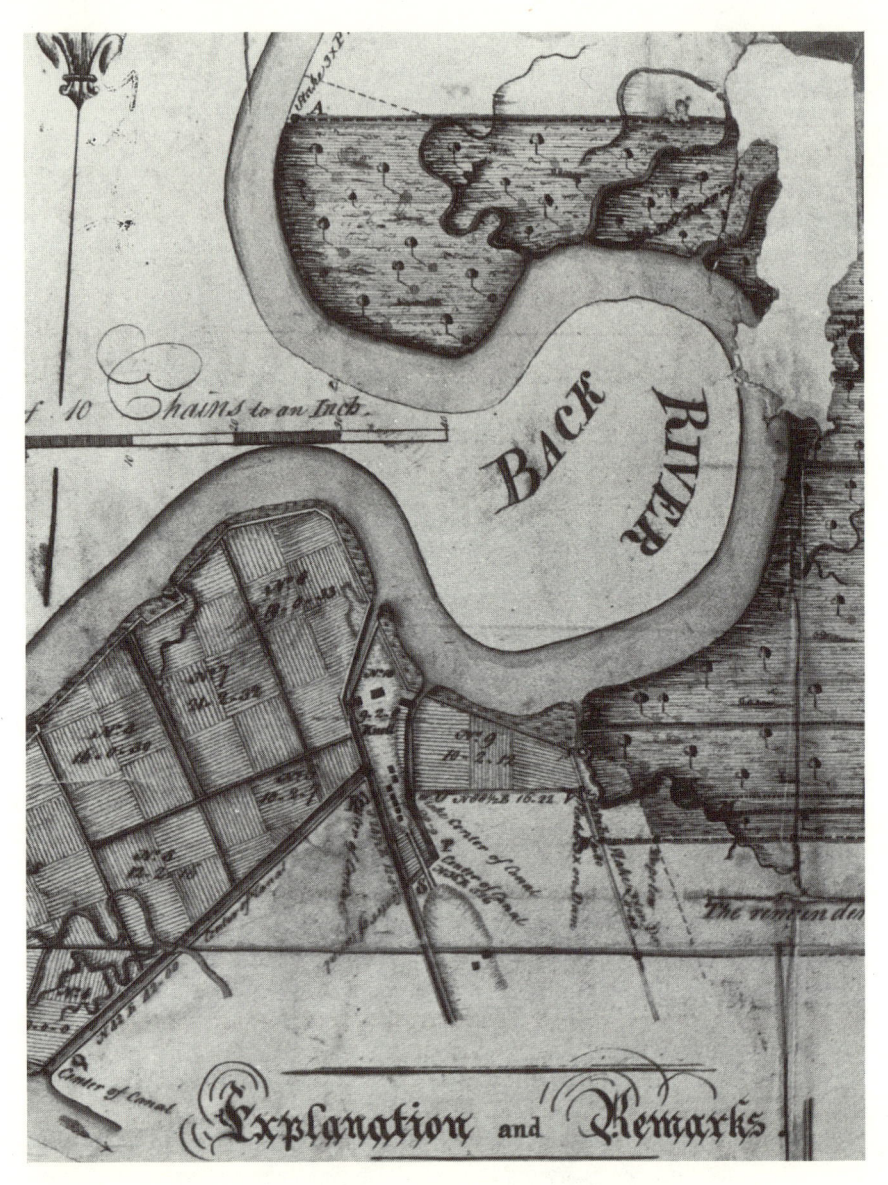

PLATE 11. *Plantation of John Bull, Saint Luke Parish, April 1797.* A tidewater swamp plantation. Courtesy H. A. M. Smith Collection (no. 27) (32-42-9), South Carolina Historical Society

term *trunk* was retained in South Carolina to describe sluice valves long after gates replaced logs. More generally, the development of tidewater rice production meant that rice plantations would be confined to a small area, thereby ensuring stability and cohesion for the slave workforce. The amount of land suitable for tidewater rice cultivation was severely limited by tidal variation, the size and shape of an estuary, and the availability of fresh water. The whole tidewater region did not meet all of these conditions. The principal areas of tidal culture extended along the Waccamaw, Pee Dee, Santee, Ashley-Cooper, Edisto-Ashepoo, Combahee, and Savannah Rivers. As slaves in other regions of mainland North America moved inland, their Lowcountry counterparts became tied ever more closely to the coast.[17]

Indigo: "An excellent colleague Commodity with Rice"

The culture of indigo flourished briefly in the Lowcountry—for little more than a generation—but, in that time, it engrossed the labor of many slaves and made many a fortune. Britain's rapidly growing textile industry and inadequate imperial supplies of the indigo dye help explain why the crop became an attractive proposition in the 1740s. As early as 1745, William Middleton identified the advantage inherent in the crop and the impetus behind its development from South Carolina's perspective. The economic depression of the 1740s, he noted, "has putt us on trying several other things," and because indigo was "not so bulky a Commodity, it will better answer the high Freights we shall be subject to during the war." In 1749, a parliamentary bounty confirmed and augmented the opportunities presented by indigo cultivation. In that year, Alexander Gordon proclaimed Carolina "one of the best Indigo Countrys in the World." A few years later, Dr. Alexander Garden observed that planters were "so Intoxicate[d] with Indigo that . . . nothing else but Indigo, Indigo would be heard of." Exports expanded tenfold in the space of a generation: from more than 100,000 pounds in 1747 to more than 1,000,000 pounds in 1775. Although indigo production recovered after the American Revolution, despite the loss of the British subsidy, it collapsed dramatically in the 1790s owing to growing overseas competition and local problems. Indigo therefore had a short life as a major commercial crop in the Lowcountry, but its contribution to the dynamism of the late colonial economy, and thereby its impact on slave work routines, cannot be exaggerated.[18]

---

17. Butler, "Observations," 1786; a list of the Negroes belonging to the estate of Henry Middleton, 1785, Thomas Middleton Plantation Book, UNC; Judith A. Carney, "From Hands to Tutors: African Expertise in the South Carolina Rice Economy," *Agricultural History*, LXVII (1993), 1–30, esp. 9, 20. For the limits of tidewater rice cultivation, see Hilliard, "Antebellum Tidewater Rice Culture," in Gibson, ed., *European Settlement and Development in North America*, 101–104.

18. Middleton to John Mucklow, Feb. 14, 1745, Zachary Lloyd Collection, Birmingham Central Library, Birmingham, England; Alexander Gordon to [Sir John Clark], July 5, 1749, Clerk of Pencuik Muniments, GD 5023/3/95, Scottish Record Office, Edinburgh; Garden to Society, May 1, 1757, Guard Book, III, 86; Hennig Cohen, ed., "A Colonial Poem on Indigo Culture," *Agricultural History*, XXX (1956), 41–44. For indigo production, see G. Terry

The growing season for indigo was much shorter than that for rice. Sown in early April, indigo was harvested first in early July, with a second cutting usually in late August or early September. Indigo was a more delicate crop than rice and, in Johann Schoepf's words, "require[d] much attention." "There cannot be too great pains taken to prepare land for *Indico*," noted Charles Woodmason, for tree stumps and roots had to be removed completely, a procedure considered unnecessary in rice cultivation. Moreover, the slaves were said to be "always at the hoe" when cultivating indigo, because its fields had to be "daily and hourly attended, otherwise everything planted in them would be quickly choaked" by weeds. Slaves had often to remove caterpillars and grasshoppers from the leaves of the plants, for they could quickly destroy an entire harvest. In other words, a short growing season was, to some extent, offset by the requirement that "an *Indigo* field . . . be a perfect garden, . . . carefully gone over every day."[19]

Sharrer, "Indigo in Carolina, 1671–1796," *SCHM*, LXXII (1971), 94–103; Sharrer, "The Indigo Bonanza in South Carolina, 1740–1790," *Technology and Culture*, XII (1971), 447–455; David L. Coon, "Eliza Lucas Pinckney and the Reintroduction of Indigo Culture into South Carolina," *Journal of Southern History*, XLII (1976), 61–76; and John J. Winberry, "Reputation of Carolina Indigo," *SCHM*, LXXX (1979), 242–250. For broader context, see Kenneth H. Beeson, Jr., "Indigo Production in the Eighteenth Century," *Hispanic American Historical Review*, XLIV (1964), 214–218; and especially Dauril Alden, "The Growth and Decline of Indigo Production in Colonial Brazil: A Study in Comparative Economic History," *Journal of Economic History*, XXV (1965), 35–60. Middleton was correct about freight rates in war years: in 1757, one South Carolina estate with 40 hands made 1,780 pounds of indigo, which, at 5s. per pound, grossed £445 sterling and netted £312 after freight and insurance (30% deduction); the rice crop was 240 barrels, which at £3 per barrel, grossed £720 and netted only £350 after freight and insurance (51% deduction). J. Murray to Sir R. Laurie, July 12, 1757, John Murray Letterbook, GD 219/290, Murray of Murraythwaite Muniments, Scottish Record Office, Edinburgh.

19. On indigo cutting, a Lowcountry inventory taken in late August listed a "small parcel of indico in the mud the produce of 5 vatts and the 2d cutting on the ground" (inventory of Thomas Crosthwaite, Aug. 24, 1756, Inventories, WPA, CLIII, 954–957); another planter's inventory, taken in early October, recorded that there were "8 acres indigo to be cut the second time" (inventory of William Buchanan, Oct. 2, 1758, ibid., CLVII, 93–96); and an overseer wrote to his employer as late as October 18, 1791, informing him that he had only "quit the final cutting of indigo last Friday" (John Couturier to John Calhoun, Oct. 18, 1791, Colhoun Papers). Henry Laurens was undoubtedly correct when he stated that "'tis but seldom people can get through their second cutting before the Frost puts an End to it so that a third cuting is Extreamly rare" (*Laurens Papers*, II, 318). On one occasion, Laurens only finished a first cutting in mid-September (ibid., IV, 670). Schoepf, *Travels in the Confederation*, II, 157; C[harles] W[oodmason], "The Indigo Plant Described," *Gentleman's Mag., and Hist. Qtly.*, XXV (1755), 201–203. The poem on indigo, which circulated in South Carolina in the 1750s, emphasized the dangers posed by "Knotty Grass that choaks the tender Weed"

PLATE 12. *Indigo Culture*. 1770s. From Henry Mouzon's map of Saint Stephen Parish. Courtesy South Carolina Historical Society

The processing of indigo was also quite complex. Indigo planters had to construct sets of vats comprising a steeper (where the plants were placed to ferment), a beater (where the fermented liquid from the steeper was stirred), and a lime vat (containing lime water, which was introduced into the beater to precipitate the sediment). Speed was essential in the preparation of indigo. According to a correspondent of James Crokatt's, "the work should be done with as great expedition as possible; . . . as fast as the plant is cut, it should be carried to the vat." The process was continuous. The plant was fermented in twelve to fifteen hours, and, once the liquid had been drawn off, the vat was refilled. The work was thus repetitive and physically demanding. Daily harvesting, the constant pumping of water into the steeper—"I suppose to fill one Vatt," calculated one planter, "it generally takes two Negroes near an hour and is considered hard labour"—and the "violent, constant stirring and beating" of the fermented liquid lasted from about July to October. Nevertheless, processing ended at about the same time as harvesting, for, after the indigo paste was removed from the vat, it was strained through cloth bags, cut into blocks, and allowed to dry before being packed for export. The indigo cycle was complete by the end of October. Accordingly, the indigo planters of upper Saint John

(Cohen, ed., "A Colonial Poem," *Agric. Hist.*, XXX [1956], 43). See also Samuel Dubose, *Address Delivered at the Seventeenth Anniversary of the Black Oak Agricultural Society . . . to Which Is Attached Reminiscences of St. Stephens Parish* (Charleston, S.C., 1858), 27.

Berkeley, supplied their adult males for the repairing of the parish roads in the first or second week of November.[20]

Because the indigo cycle lasted no more than seven months, a Lowcountry planter could incorporate it into existing routines. Doctor Alexander Garden thought that indigo cultivation could easily be combined with the production of potash, salt, or myrtle wax, because it "takes up and employs but one Season of the year i.e. from March to September." More realistically, by taking only one cutting from the indigo plant, planters could integrate the indigo cycle into their cultivation of rice. Thus, as early in the year as August, James Jamieson informed his merchants that most of his indigo was made and that his rice would "soon begin cutting." In 1757, when accounting for the decline in the Lowcountry's production of naval stores, Henry Laurens explained that most planters had made most of their pitch and tar between the hoeing and harvesting of rice but that this period was now devoted to indigo. Not only did the peak period of indigo cultivation coincide with "dead time" in the rice cycle, but indigo, in Robert Pringle's words, was "planted and made easier with fewer hands than Rice." Many planters set apart some of their laborers to indigo cultivation without compromising their rice crop.[21]

Because indigo cultivation could be "undertaken by Planters of small Capitals," as one contemporary put it, and "on Lands which would not answer for Rice," some planters concentrated exclusively on the crop. Indigo, noted a Georgian, was "lighter Work, and for a weak-handed Planter more profitable than Rice." For these reasons, planters in outlying areas—the upper parts of lowland parishes like Saint John Berkeley, Saint George, and Prince Frederick, as well as the saline-dominated parts of the tidewater such as the more southerly Sea Islands and the East Florida coast—specialized in indigo cultivation. There were whole areas, therefore, where indigo cultivation was the primary activity. Late colonial East Florida, in particular, specialized in indigo culture.

20. [James Crokatt], *Further Observations Intended for Improving the Culture and Curing of Indigo, etc. in South-Carolina* (London, 1747), in H. Roy Merrens, ed., *The Colonial South Carolina Scene: Contemporary Views, 1697–1774* (Columbia, S.C., 1977), 155–156; Plowden Weston to Jonathan Lucas, Aug. 17, 1792, Lucas Family Papers, SCHS; Records of the Commissioners of the High Roads, Nov. 3, 1767, Nov. 1, 1768, Nov. 7, 1769. On the processing of indigo generally, see C. W., "Method of Raising," *Gentleman's Mag., and Hist. Qtly.*, XXV (1755), 256; and Dwight Jackson Huneycutt, "The Economics of the Indigo Industry in South Carolina" (master's thesis, University of South Carolina, 1949).

21. Garden to Society, May 1, 1757, Guard Book, III, 86; James Jamieson to Messrs. Curzon and Seton, Aug. 25, 1774, James Jamieson Miscellaneous Letters, USC; Walter B. Edgar, ed., *The Letterbook of Robert Pringle*, II (Columbia, S.C., 1972), 740; *Laurens Papers*, II, 430; J. H. Easterby and Ruth S. Green, eds., *The Journal of the Commons House of Assembly, March 28, 1749–March 19, 1750*, Colonial Records of South Carolina (Columbia, S.C., 1962), 57.

Focusing on indigo cultivation, which occupied only part of the agricultural calendar, these plantations had to assume a more diversified aspect than those that combined rice and indigo production. Slaves on indigo plantations must have spent almost half of the year growing provisions, rearing stock, and producing naval stores.[22]

Indigo plantations were unpleasant places. The putrid stench of the fermented plants was so offensive that planters usually located their indigo works at least a quarter-mile from their residence. The odor attracted hordes of flies and other insects, facilitating the spread of diseases. Wherever indigo is "long-steeped," noted a South Carolinian, flies "devour Man and Beast"; planters often employed "three or four Negroes with boughs to keep them off." In 1773, the neighbor of an indigo planter urged the South Carolina legislature to compel planters to bury the rotted plants that they ordinarily spread on fields and thereby prevent the swarms of flies that were so troublesome to livestock. Acknowledging that indigo cultivation was associated with "diseases, violent, severe and at times fatal," Samuel Dubose nevertheless claimed to know indigo planters who "acquired fortunes by the natural increase of their negroes."[23]

However unpleasant, indigo plantations required that some slaves become unusually skilled. The processing of rice required little more than the application of physical strength, whereas, according to Henry Laurens, "there is something Extreamly unaccountable in the working of Indigo," inasmuch as no two people could seem to make a dye of the same quality. The skills of indigo making consisted in knowing when to open the taps of the steeper and draw the fermented liquid into the beater, in knowing just how long to beat, and in "curing" the indigo paste so that it did not dry too quickly. Indigo varied greatly, observed the traveler Luigi Castiglioni, depending in large part on "the intelligence of the negroes in its manufacture." For this reason, David Yeats could be sanguine about employing an inexperienced overseer on James Grant's East Florida plantation, because, as he put it, "several of the Negroes

---

22. G. Moulton to [?], Dec. 20, 1772, Add. MSS 22677, 71, BL; Seth J. Cuthbert to Lachlan McIntosh, Aug. 9, 1794, Keith Read Collection, University of Georgia, as cited in J. E. Chaplin, "An Anxious Pursuit: Innovation in Commercial Agriculture in South Carolina, Georgia, and British East Florida, 1740–1815" (Ph.D. diss., The Johns Hopkins University, 1986), 334. On the regional distribution of indigo production, see, for example, Robert Mills, *Statistics of South Carolina* (Spartanburg, S.C., 1972 [orig. publ. Charleston, S.C., 1826]), 471–472, 482. For East Florida indigo, see James Edward Smith, comp., *A Selection of the Correspondence of Linnaeus, and Other Naturalists, from the Original Manuscripts* (London, 1821), I, 527.

23. Beeson, "Indigo Production," *Hisp. Am. Hist. Rev.*, XLIV (1964), 215; Sharrer, "The Indigo Bonanza," *Technol. and Cult.*, XII (1971), 451; *Laurens Papers*, VII, 184; *SCG*, Sept. 27, 1773; Alden, "The Growth and Decline of Indigo Production," *Jour. Econ. Hist.*, XXV (1965), 57; Dubose, *Address Delivered*, 29.

understand the making of [indigo] pretty well." Indeed, "the headmen in this sort of work are commonly Negroes," observed Johann Schoepf, adding that "if they thoroughly understand the management of the indigo, a great value is set upon them." Among William Livingston's twenty slaves was "as good an Indigo maker as any in the Province," and Christopher Jenkins's estate boasted "an extraordinary Indico maker." In his will, dated 1774, Peter Gourdin indicated how much he trusted his indigo maker, Billy, by stipulating that he was not to work in the fields or be answerable to an overseer and should gain his freedom at the death of Gourdin's son. Slave women also earned the admiration of their masters, for Henry Laurens recommended Hagar "for her honesty, care of Negroes, and her great care of Indigo in the Mud." The best testimonial to an indigo maker occurred when a master conveyed his slave's disparaging remarks directly to his white overseer. George, the slave, had secured eighteen pounds of indigo from each vat and reported steeping the plant anywhere from five to seven hours, depending on the time of day. He thought the overseer had "steeped rather too long" and had used too strong a solution of lime water. Quite what the overseer made of this invidious comparison one can only conjecture.[24]

Tobacco and Slaves

Although the eighteenth-century Chesapeake region was always far more agriculturally diversified than the Lowcountry—and became more so over time—tobacco remained its primary staple. Between the end of Queen Anne's War and the beginning of the Revolution, the tobacco trade grew at the rate of about 2 percent a year. There was both a steady growth in production and a modest rise in its price. Benedict Calvert's claim that "Tobacco, as our Staple, is our All, and Indeed leaves no room for anything Else," was exaggerated even for the early eighteenth century, but tobacco was a viable cash crop through the 1770s and remained the mainstay of the Chesapeake economy throughout the colonial period and beyond. By the late 1780s, the tobacco market had recovered from the disruptions of the Revolutionary war, and output matched that of the 1770s. The behavior of some late-eighteenth-century tobacco planters even calls to mind the frenetic, single-minded preoccupation with the crop that characterized their predecessors a century and a half earlier—when Virginia was North America's first boom country. Thus, the author of *American*

---

24. *Laurens Papers,* II, 320, V, 125, 175; Antonio Pace, trans. and ed., *Luigi Castiglioni's Viaggio: Travels in the United States of North America, 1785–1787* (Syracuse, N.Y., 1983), 171; David Yeats to James Grant, Mar. 13, 1780, Papers of General James Grant of Ballindalloch; Schoepf, *Travels in the Confederation,* II, 159; William Livingston, *SCG,* Feb. 2, 1769; Benjamin Jenkins, ibid., Mar. 9, 1765; will of Peter Gourdin, Oct. 4, 1774, Robert N. Gordon Coll., SCHS. See also John Ward's estate, *SCG,* Jan. 11, 1768; and Esther Glaze, ibid., Mar. 9, 1765.

Husbandry observed, in the 1770s, that planters "who meet with very rich forest woodland employ themselves so eagerly on tobacco, as scarcely to raise corn enough for their families." Similarly, when Lady Liston passed through Mecklenburg County in 1798, she found planters "so entirely engrossed by Tobacco that... except the rise and fall of that article, they took little interest in the concerns of the world."[25]

Tobacco, unlike rice, was not invariably associated with slave labor. Most obviously, of course, tobacco was grown successfully in Virginia for almost a century without resort to slaves. Moreover, many nonslaveholding family farmers continued to grow the crop throughout the eighteenth century and beyond. In mid-nineteenth-century piedmont Virginia, for example, tobacco was as much a free-labor as a slave-labor crop. In 1860, almost 90 percent of the free-labor farms as against 80 percent of the slaveholding planters produced tobacco. Furthermore, slaves were rarely the only laborers on the small plantations that were ubiquitous in the Chesapeake. According to William Tatham, the sons "of many planters work in the crop equally with the negroes, nor is there any material distinction observed between them." Looking beyond the Chesapeake provides further evidence that the association between tobacco and slaves was far from axiomatic. As tobacco cultivation spread across the globe in the late sixteenth and seventeenth centuries—whether in England, southwest France, the Netherlands, the valleys of the Rhine and Main, Brazil, or India—it was nearly everywhere the product of the small farmer or peasant. And when tobacco cultivation spread to Kentucky and Tennessee, it continued to be produced by free labor. In 1860, two-thirds of the tobacco crop of those two border states derived from free or small slave farms. The association of tobacco and slaves never matched that of rice and slaves. No one could ever seriously claim that tobacco was a black worker's crop.[26]

25. Paul G. E. Clemens, *The Atlantic Economy and Colonial Maryland's Eastern Shore: From Tobacco to Grain* (Ithaca, N.Y., 1980), 111; Jacob M. Price, *France and the Chesapeake: A History of the French Tobacco Monopoly, 1674–1791, and of Its Relationship to the British and American Tobacco Trade,* I (Ann Arbor, Mich., 1973), 509–567; Benedict Leonard Calvert to the Lord Proprietary, Oct. 26, 1729, in William Hand Browne et al., eds., *Archives of Maryland,* XXV (1905), 602; Carman, ed., *American Husbandry,* 187; journals of Lady Liston, January 1798, 5697, 41, Sir Robert Liston Papers, National Library of Scotland, Edinburgh.

26. James R. Irwin, "Wheat, Tobacco, and Slavery in Piedmont Virginia, 1850–1860" (MS); G. Melvin Herndon, *William Tatham and the Culture of Tobacco* (Miami, Fla., 1969), 104; Joan Thirsk, "New Crops and Their Diffusion: Tobacco-Growing in Seventeenth-Century England," in C. W. Chalklin and M. A. Havinden, eds., *Rural Change and Urban Growth, 1500–1800* (London, 1974), 76–103; H. K. Roessingh, "Tobacco Growing in Holland in the Seventeenth and Eighteenth Centuries: A Case Study of the Innovative Spirit of Dutch Peasants," *Low Countries History Yearbook,* XI (1978), 18–54; Price, *France and the Chesapeake,* chaps. 6, 18; Stuart B. Schwartz, *Sugar Plantations in the Formation of*

Nevertheless, in eighteenth-century Virginia, tobacco cultivation came to be most closely associated with black slaves. During the late-seventeenth- and early-eighteenth-century slump in the Chesapeake economy—a period that saw a greater availability of slaves as a result of developments in the Atlantic slave trade—the areas that were most successful in producing tobacco garnered the lion's share of the incoming Africans. The central counties on the western shores of both Maryland and Virginia—that is, Prince George's, Calvert, and Anne Arundel in Maryland and the tidewater counties between the James and Rappahannock Rivers in Virginia—were the dominant areas of both tobacco production and slave expansion in this period. After about 1720, when slaves became more widely available both through importation and natural increase, this association lost potency. Many small planters in all parts of Virginia, not just the best tobacco areas, acquired a slave or two. However, during the last third of the eighteenth century, when some parts of tidewater Virginia gave up tobacco production altogether, the link between tobacco and slaves again became close. The great expansion of slavery in this period followed the southwestern drift of tobacco production into the piedmont.[27]

In spite of its reputation as a "white man's crop," tobacco could support a slave labor force because of the relatively long cultivation schedule that it imposed. The tobacco cycle was longer than the seven months it took to produce indigo, though shorter than the thirteen months it took to complete the rice cycle. In January and February, Chesapeake slaves cleared new land or old beds for planting. In mid-January, for instance, Landon Carter's slaves burned plant patches; and in mid-February, Robert W. Carter, Landon's son, had his "People burning new ground." In late February and early March, slaves sowed tobacco

---

Brazilian Society: Bahia, 1550–1835 (Cambridge, 1985), 85–86; B. G. Gokhale, "Tobacco in Seventeenth-Century India," *Agric. Hist.*, XLVIII (1974), 484–492; Richard Pares, *Merchants and Planters* (*Economic History Review,* supplement no. 4 [Cambridge, 1960], 21); Joseph M. Hernandez, "On the Cultivation of the Cuba Tobacco," *Southern Agriculturalist,* III (1830), 463; Donald F. Schaefer, "Productivity in the Antebellum South: The Western Tobacco Region," *Research in Economic History,* III (1978), 305–346; Schaefer, "Yeomen Farmers and Economic Democracy: A Study of Wealth and Economic Mobility in the Western Tobacco Region, 1850 to 1860," *Explorations in Economic History,* 2d Ser., XV (1978), 421–437. See also Richard S. Dunn, *Sugar and Slaves: The Rise of the Planter Class in the English West Indies, 1624–1713* (Chapel Hill, N.C., 1972), 49–54; and Fernando Ortiz, *Cuban Counterpoint: Tobacco and Sugar,* trans. Harriet de Onís (New York, 1947), esp. 58.

27. Russell Menard, "From Servants to Slaves: The Transformation of the Chesapeake Labor System," *Southern Studies,* XVI (1977), 382–383; Richard S. Dunn, "Black Society in the Chesapeake, 1776–1810," in Ira Berlin and Ronald Hoffman, eds., *Slavery and Freedom in the Age of the American Revolution* (Charlottesville, Va., 1982), 54–59; Philip D. Morgan and Michael L. Nicholls, "Slaves in Piedmont Virginia, 1720–1790," *WMQ,* 3d Ser., XLVI (1989), 211–251; Schwartz, *Sugar Plantations,* 86.

seed in the newly cleared beds of fine mulch, for the plant was too delicate to be grown in unprotected, open fields. During germination and early growth, the seedlings were susceptible to Virginia's late winter and early spring frosts and had to be covered with oak leaves or pine brush to ward off the chill.[28]

By April, the work demanded of slaves gained momentum. With the danger of frosts removed, weeding and transplanting could begin. Slaves first prepared the fields that were to receive the young tobacco plants. After clearing old or new fields with a "grubbing hoe," they built hills to receive the plants. The worker made hills by drawing the soil around the leg with the aid of a "hilling hoe," and then withdrawing the leg and flattening the top of the hill. By midcentury most planters expected a slave to make about 350 hills a day, each taking less than two minutes. Some slaves responded to the increased pace by running away. More Virginia slaves ran away in April than in any other month (Figure 5). Transplanting was possible only after a shower of rain. Awaiting a "season"—those days when heavy rain occurred—found planters still transplanting in early June. Almost all slaves were pressed into service, for the tedious process had to be accomplished within a relatively short time. Transplanting, weeding, and replanting kept slaves occupied through early summer. If slaves were not weeding or replanting, they were attending to ground worms and tobacco caterpillars, "an endless labour," according to one traveler. Moreover, the tobacco plant, after developing twelve to sixteen leaves, had to be "primed," "topped," and subsequently "suckered."[29]

Hoes were not "laid by" until August, when the first tobacco was ready for harvesting. Judging the ripeness of tobacco was no easy matter. Judge Parker

---

28. Jack P. Greene, ed., *The Diary of Colonel Landon Carter of Sabine Hall, 1752–1778*, 2 vols. (Charlottesville, Va., 1965), 346–347 (hereafter cited as *Carter Diary*); Robert W. Carter Diaries, Feb. 14, 1776, typescript, CW. This account of the tobacco cycle draws on a number of sources, listed in chronological order: A Letter from Mr. John Clayton . . . May 12, 1688 . . . , in Peter Force, ed., *Tracts and Other Papers* . . . , III (Gloucester, Mass., 1963 [orig. publ. 1844]), 17–23; Curtis Carroll Davis, "'A National Property': Richard Claiborne's Tobacco Treatise for Poland," *WMQ*, 3d Ser., XXI (1964), 93–117; Herndon, *Tatham*, 9–67, 107–129; Gray, *History of Agriculture*, I, 215–223; Harold B. Gill, Jr., "Tobacco Culture in Colonial Virginia: A Preliminary Report" (MS, CW, 1972); David O. Percy, *The Production of Tobacco along the Colonial Potomac* (Accokeek, Md., 1979); Breen, *Tobacco Culture*, 46–58.

29. Greene, ed., *Carter Diary*, 423, 681, 684, 686; Percy, *Production of Tobacco*, 20; "Journal of a French Traveller in the Colonies, 1765," part 1, *AHR*, XXVI (1920–1921), 746; William Cabell Commonplace Book, 1774–1776, June 20, 1774, William Cabell Diaries, VHS; J.F.D. Smyth, *A Tour in the United States of America* . . . , 2 vols. (London, 1784), II, 84. "Priming" referred to the removal of the ground leaves, "topping" to the removal of the small leaves and emerging buds at the top of a three-to-four foot high plant, and "suckering" to the removal of the shoots, or suckers, that grew at the junction of the leaves and stem and at the root of the plant.

maintained that a planter had to "have a very skillfull set of cutters, who know well when tobacco is ripe," and William Tatham advised that only "the best and judicious hand" should be employed in this operation. William Woodford's plantation operations were seriously disrupted when his "Negro Tobacco Cutter" ran away for two months. Because not all tobacco plants ripened at once, the harvest lasted from August through September. Once cut and allowed to lie in the field for half a day to aid in handling, the tobacco leaves were piled in a heap and allowed to sweat overnight. The slaves then took the leaves to a tobacco house, drove pegs into the plant stalks, and hung them on high rafters. Taken down, or "struck," from the rafter when cured, and stacked on the floor of the tobacco house, the leaves were covered to await "stripping." Finally, slaves stripped the leaf from its stalk before individually rolling, or "stemming," it and then packing, or "prizing," it into hogsheads.[30]

Harvesting, curing, and packing were delicate maneuvers, requiring close supervision. In August 1750, one Albemarle County overseer noted how cut tobacco "must be turned carefully and often." Nor was this the end of the care that had to be lavished on the crop, for, in processing tobacco, "every plant how meansoever requires an Equal Labour with the very best in the curing, stripping and Packing." Landon Carter, for instance, ordered that every stick of tobacco leaf had to be hung "thick that the Sun may not have too great a power" but then "ought to be thined when housed" so that it would not sweat. Not surprisingly, he found that both his "overseers and negroes think the work too tedious." Richard Corbin, a planter in King and Queen County, described how every morning in September his slaves "struck" as much tobacco as possible. What they stripped in the morning, they stemmed in the evening. Not only were these delicate maneuvers, but they also involved long hours. John Smyth observed slaves laboring from sunrise until late evening during harvesttime. "It is astonishing and unaccountable," he added, "to conceive what an amazing degree of fatigue these poor but happy wretches do undergo, and can support." He further noted that "every night the negroes are sent to the tobacco house to strip" the leaves. All of Landon Carter's slaves who were "well or could move" spent one night hanging "a prodigeous cutting of tobacco in Scaffolds"; on another occasion, "the people stemmed tobacco till the moon went down."[31]

---

30. Herndon, *Tatham*, 124, 24; Catesby Willis Steward, ed., *Woodford Letter Book, 1723–1737* (Verona, Va., 1977), 237. "Striking" referred to the taking down of the tobacco leaves from the rafters of the tobacco house, "stripping" to the severance of the leaves from the plant stalk, "stemming" to the separation of the largest fibers from the web of the leaf, and "prizing" to the actual packing of the hogshead.

31. Ralph Emmett Fall, ed., *The Diary of Robert Rose: A View of Virginia by a Scottish*

Because tobacco was, in John Carter's words, "a very tender plant," it deserved its reputation as "a plant of perpetual trouble and difficulty." Late planting, the tobacco "fly," worms, disease, weeds, excessive moisture left in the leaves, too much pressure applied during packing—all these and more could ruin a crop. Well might Landon Carter liken tobacco planting to "an art to be learned not more by practice than by reasoning justly upon things." Well might tobacco planters distinguish not only between major varieties—Oronoko and sweet scented, for instance—but among strains made in particular regions, neighborhoods, even on individual plantations. And well might this crop generate its own arcane vocabulary—everything from its "seasons" through its "topping," "priming," "suckering," and "striking" to its "stemming" and "prizing." This specialized language spoke to the complexities of producing tobacco.[32]

Although the improvements made in production were confined very largely to the existing state of the "art," some technological changes did affect slave work routines. Because the capital apparatus involved in tobacco production was minimal, there could not be the same radical changes in the methods of its cultivation as were evident in rice culture. Still, the widespread use of carts and, to a lesser extent, plows by the middle of the eighteenth century represented one positive change, so far as the slaves were concerned. Just as tidewater culture meant a less rigorous hoeing regimen in South Carolina, so a greater use of plows and carts reduced the tediousness of preparing ground and handling harvested crops in Virginia.[33]

Social activities in the Chesapeake remained firmly structured around the tobacco calendar. Unlike the Lowcountry, where the intensity of labor on a rice plantation was relieved during late summer, no such summer break was permissible on a Chesapeake plantation. Even the Christian holidays that occurred during the tobacco cycle were not sacrosanct. As "the Crop [was] generally upon Land from the beginning of May till the end of September,"

Colonial Parson (Verona, Va., 1977), 87; H. R. McIlwaine et al., eds., *Executive Journals of the Council of Colonial Virginia*, IV (Richmond, Va., 1930), 47; Richard Corbin to James Semple, Jan. 1, 1759, Richard Corbin Letterbook, microfilm, CW; Smyth, *A Tour in the United States of America*, I, 43–44, II, 136; Greene, ed., *Carter Diary*, 177, 196, 244, 495. For another account that stresses the care taken in sorting and packing tobacco, see William Lee to Cary Wilkinson, May 22, 1771, William Lee Letterbook, Lee-Ludwell Papers, VHS.

32. John Carter to Alderman Perry, Aug. 12, 1733, John Carter Letterbook, 1732–1781, 11, UVa; William Tatham, *Communications concerning the Agriculture and Commerce of the United States of America . . .* (London, 1800), 62; Percy, *Production of Tobacco*, 25–29; Darrett B. Rutman and Anita H. Rutman, *A Place in Time: Middlesex County, Virginia, 1650–1750* (New York, 1984), 40; Breen, *Tobacco Culture*, 64–65.

33. See Chapter 1 for the growing use of carts and plows.

noted Maryland Jesuits, "all hands belonging to or working in the Crop, may be therein employed on all Holidays within the said Term excepting the Ascension of our Lord, Whitsun Monday, Corpus Christie Day and the Assumption of our Lady, on which days no servile works are to be done unless upon ... very urgent necessity." Public duty on the roads occurred in late autumn or winter. Marriages were most often performed between November and February, peaking in December.[34] The social calendars of Chesapeake and Lowcountry revolved around very different production schedules.

Wheat: "A kind of a second Staple"

Wheat in the Chesapeake, like indigo in the Lowcountry, was both a complement to the routines of the dominant staple and a staple in its own right. Grain production expanded vigorously in late colonial Virginia. To cite but one measure, in the years 1738–1742 the ratio of the average annual value of tobacco to grain exports was roughly fourteen to one. Approximately thirty years later, the ratio had fallen to about three to one. By the late colonial period many tobacco planters were growing small grains, and, in some areas, a wholesale shift to wheat cultivation had occurred. In 1772, Roger Atkinson, a Petersburg merchant, proclaimed Virginia the finest "country under the sun" for grain cultivation. Two years later, Charles Yates, a Fredericksburg merchant, observed that most of the planters in his neighborhood "determine to drop planting and turn their Lands to Farming." In the same year, farmers in Stafford County planted such "large fields of Wheat" that they even neglected corn production.[35]

Farming winter wheat (and other small grains) was the ideal complement to the seasonal cycle of tobacco cultivation. Wheat was sown in autumn, after

---

34. "Rules concerning Hollydays," box 4-1/2, Woodstock Records, microfilm, MHR, as quoted in Allan Lee Kulikoff, "Tobacco and Slaves: Population, Economy, and Society in Eighteenth-Century Prince George's County Maryland" (Ph.D. diss., Brandeis University, 1976), 356; Kulikoff, *Tobacco and Slaves: The Development of Southern Cultures in the Chesapeake, 1680–1800* (Chapel Hill, N.C., 1986), 256; Carville V. Earle, *The Evolution of a Tidewater Settlement System: All Hallow's Parish, Maryland, 1650–1783*, University of Chicago Department of Geography Research Paper, no. 170 (Chicago, 1975), 158; Fall, ed., *Diary of Robert Rose*, 50, 97; Greene, ed., *Carter Diary*, 623.

35. David Klingaman, "The Significance of Grain in the Development of the Tobacco Colonies," *Jour. Econ. Hist.*, XXIX (1969), 273; A. J. Morrison, ed., "Letters of Roger Atkinson, 1769–1776," *VMHB*, XV (1907–1908), 353; Charles Yates to Samuel Martin, Apr. 2, 1774, Charles Yates Letterbook, microfilm, CW; Greene, ed., *Carter Diary*, 817. In 1756, the Reverend James Maury of Louisa County noted that "much larger fields of wheat, barley and rye last fall, and of oats this spring, have been sown, and much larger quantities of ground planted with Indian corn, than has ever, heretofore, been known" (Ann Maury, ed. and trans., *Memoirs of a Huguenot Family, . . . from the Original Autobiography of Rev. James Fontaine . . .* [New York, 1853], 407).

tobacco had been harvested, and it was reaped (or mowed) in July, after tobacco had been transplanted. Well might a merchant exclaim that the "article of wheat, a kind of a second staple, is a prodigious addition" to the Chesapeake economy. The great advantage of the crop was that it required little or no maintenance as it grew. Some planters rolled their wheat in early spring, but even that was not essential. The main labor requirement in the wheat cycle was at harvesttime, when reaping with a sickle or mowing with a scythe had to be accomplished quickly before the ripened wheat shed its grain. And so masters offered rewards to make slaves exert themselves; pressed tradesworkers, domestics, and almost every able-bodied hand into service; and hired additional help when necessary. Intense as harvesting wheat undoubtedly was, it lasted little more than a fortnight and could be completed before tobacco was ready for cutting. Wheat was stacked as it was cut; threshing, though laborious, could be undertaken during the slack winter months. This yearly routine interfered little with tobacco production.[36]

The wheat cycle impinged little on tobacco cultivation, but the introduction and widespread adoption of this grain set in motion a chain reaction that markedly increased the specialization and differentiation demanded of the Chesapeake slave workforce. Most obvious, sowing winter wheat necessitated that some slaves learn the art of plowing and sowing. In the 1760s, Landon Carter described his slave Manuel as the "best plowman and mower I ever saw," at the time employing two other plowmen and two plowboys. A more widespread resort to plowing led to a more extensive raising of livestock, particularly oxen and horses. In 1771, six of Carter's Sabine Hall slaves "constantly" tended livestock. Fourteen years later, George Washington counted fifty-seven workhorses and twenty-six oxen on his various quarters; a number of slaves were responsible for their care.[37]

The ramifications of a shift to small grains did not end there. The acquisition of more stock set in train the need for more fodder. To nourish the increased stock, the workforce had to cultivate winter grasses, grow more corn,

36. This account of the wheat cycle draws on Harold B. Gill, Jr., "Wheat Culture in Colonial Virginia," *Agric. Hist.*, LII (1978), 380–393; and David O. Percy, *"English" Grains along the Colonial Potomac* (Accokeek, Md., 1977). For the quotation, see Morrison, ed., "Letters of Roger Atkinson," *VMHB*, XV (1907–1908), 350.

37. Greene, ed., *Carter Diary*, 32, 145, 396, 445, 534; Donald Jackson and Dorothy Twohig, eds., *The Diaries of George Washington*, 6 vols. (Charlottesville, Va., 1976–1979), III, 223–240. Carter noted at one point that two of his plows had been working constantly for 40 working days (Greene, ed., *Carter Diary*, 190). Thomas Jefferson noted four plows at work in 1795 at Monticello (Edwin M. Betts, ed., *Thomas Jefferson's Garden Book, 1766–1824, with Relevant Extracts from His Other Writings*, Am. Phil. Soc., *Memoirs*, XXII [Philadelphia, 1944], 227). Plowboys and plowgirls were common; see, for example, Robert W. Carter Diaries, Dec. 31, 1785.

and make hay. To accomplish these tasks, masters generally divided slave gangs into smaller and more specialized units. In turn, a greater commitment to diversified grain production encouraged the progressive farmer to begin manuring land. And, to transport this manure as well as the hay and harvested wheat, the farmer needed carts. In spring 1758, for instance, two or three slave carters belonging to Sabine Hall spent twenty-five working days making 828 trips in transporting dung to the fields. Mockingly, Landon Carter observed of a neighbor's fields, "More carts and plows I never saw upon any plantation in my life"; but Carter himself, and any other Chesapeake planter who wished to grow grains, had to employ these labor-saving devices. The slaves who operated these carts and plows were but one group singled out for specialized field labor, whereas before there had been virtually none.[38]

Nowhere was this shift toward differentiation and specialization more evident than in the central event of the wheat cycle, the harvest. Mowing with a scythe, or "cradle," was common on large Chesapeake plantations. Because a mower could cut larger quantities of wheat with each stroke than could a reaper and because he left the grain he had cut in more disarray, he required a number of subsidiary workers to keep pace with him. For every two cradlers that George Washington and Thomas Jefferson employed, seven and five gatherers, respectively, accompanied them.[39] To make this "whole machine," as Jefferson termed it, move expeditiously, large Chesapeake planters devised further divisions of labor. George Washington, for instance, hoped to produce "more ease, regularity and dispatch" among his harvesters by a careful allocation of roles and division into gangs. In terms of an eighteenth-century agricultural operation, the high level of organization demanded of wheat harvesters is testimony to the transformation wrought on some Chesapeake slaves.[40]

---

38. Greene, ed., *Carter Diary*, 226, 386, 433. In September 1770, Carter noted that his 11 hay gatherers had to assist his pea-gatherers while yet more slaves carried out other tasks. This led him to complain that "at no work can the hands be kept together but at the hoe" (ibid., 496). The following year he again observed how his increasingly diverse operations gave rise to smaller and smaller groups of slaves (ibid., 576).

39. Jackson and Twohig, eds., *Diaries of Washington*, V, 9; Betts, ed., *Jefferson's Garden Book*, 228. For evidence that scythes and cradles were common on large Chesapeake estates, see William Dabney to Esther Chiswell, July 2, 1749, Dabney Papers, microfilm, CW; Maury, *Memoirs of a Huguenot Family*, 407; Nicholas Cresswell, *The Journal of Nicholas Cresswell, 1774–1777* (New York, 1924), 25; Greene, ed., *Carter Diary*, 311, 318, 584, 764, 1107; Smyth, *A Tour in the United States of America*, II, 113–120; Richard Parkinson, *A Tour in America, in 1798, 1799, and 1800 . . .* , I (London, 1805), 203; Henry C. Knight [Arthur Singleton, pseud.], *Letters from the South and West* (Boston, 1824), 60. In England at this time, the use of scythes was largely confined to certain regions (E.J.T. Collins, "Harvest Technology and Labour Supply in Britain, 1790–1870," *Econ. Hist. Rev.*, XXII [1969], 456–457).

40. Betts, ed., *Jefferson's Garden Book*, 230; Jackson and Twohig, eds., *Diaries of Wash-*

The trend toward specialization and differentiation was most evident in the mechanics of the wheat harvest. Cradling, or mowing, was a specialized and skilled operation. In 1768, George Washington hired four whites to assist his four black cradlers. A year later, he contemplated hiring as few white cradlers as possible and instead confining hired white labor to the task of raking and binding. In other words, he countenanced placing whites in subservient positions to a set of specialized black mowers. It is not clear that he ever did this; but certainly, by the 1780s, his black cradlers were in the majority, eclipsing whites altogether toward the end of the decade. Rubbing shoulders with whites, even eliminating their role, no doubt increased the self-esteem of some blacks, even if the experience was confined to the summer season. Slave mowers were also skilled in a second sense. Most were tradesmen or domestics. Half of the thirty-one mowers George Washington mentioned by name in his diaries were artisans. One mulatto artisan bore a scar on his right knee from a scythe, and the master of Peter, a ditcher, also noted his bondman's ability to "use the sythe in the fields." When wheat rather than tobacco was under cultivation, those skilled slaves who were occasionally put to the field could generally be guaranteed a specialized rather than a menial role.[41]

Harvesting embodied a further aspect of the trend toward differentiation and specialization. Where mowing with a scythe was the chief method of harvesting, a distinct sexual division of labor immediately evolved. The scythe was an exclusively male instrument, and women's role in harvesting was reduced from a position of parity as fellow reaper to one of subservience as gatherer and stacker. In 1795, Thomas Jefferson employed seventeen cradlers, all men; they were assisted by forty-three slaves, most of them women. The increasing separation of male and female workers under a farming regime was not just confined to harvesting, for carting and plowing were generally allocated to men, and operations like fencing, cleaning out stables, and even

---

ington, V, 10, II, 172. The level of synchronization involved in the wheat harvest is captured best in Washington's diaries. He often noted the times at which the harvesters left one field and began in another (ibid., II, 172, V, 5–6).

41. Jackson and Twohig, eds., *Diaries of Washington,* II, 76–81, 172, III, 44, V, 3, 355–356; Robert Gilchrist, *VaG and WA,* Nov. 22, 1783; Vincent Redman, *VaG and GA,* Oct. 27, 1790. See also Greene, ed., *Carter Diary,* 1107; and Edward Miles Riley, ed., *The Journal of John Harrower, an Indentured Servant in the Colony of Virginia, 1773–1776* (Williamsburg, Va., 1963), 50. Self-esteem might have also been bolstered by the rewards offered slaves during the wheat harvest. For these, see account of John Hooe and the estate of J. P. Custis, June 26, 1789, George Bolling Lee Papers, VHS; the accounts of the estate of Abraham Kinnian, July 1751, King George Orphans Accounts, 1740–1761, VSL; Carter Burwell's Estate Ledger, 1764–1776, for years 1769 and 1771, CW; Robert W. Carter Diaries, July 16, 1768. For the profile of the mowers, compare Jackson and Twohig, eds., *Diaries of Washington,* IV, 277–283, with IV, 355, V, 3, 6, 355–356.

leveling ditches became the preserve of all-female gangs. Large planters who turned to a diversified farming regime increasingly organized their workforce into separate gangs of men and women.[42]

To speak of a trend toward differentiation and specialization is almost to underemphasize the transformation that was occurring among late colonial Chesapeake slaves. Another way of characterizing this process is suggested by the terminology used by contemporaries. In the 1750s, Landon Carter referred to his recent assumption of the role of "farmer" and to his adoption of the methods of "English husbandry." Because he continued to raise tobacco, he carefully described himself as both a farmer and a planter. William Nelson noted in 1768 that his son had converted a *plantation* into a *farm* "to produce wheat, corn, etc." When Isaac Weld visited the Northern Neck in 1796, he observed, "Those who raise tobacco and Indian corn are called planters, and those who cultivate small grain, farmers."[43] What was true for masters was also true for slaves. They were undergoing a similar metamorphosis—from plantation hands to farm workers.

In regions of the Chesapeake where little or no tobacco was grown, the slight labor requirements of small grain cultivation meant that slaves had to be put to even more varied tasks than was the case in tobacco- and grain-producing regions. The farm books of Thomas Jones, a resident of Baltimore County, Maryland, in the late eighteenth century, provide a useful insight into these routines. In 1779, the first extant year of his farm journal, Jones had a workforce of twelve adult slaves (aged fourteen or more years). In the early months of the year, his laborers threshed grain, secured wood, broke flax, and attended to newborn calves and lambs. These activities continued into spring, but addi-

42. Betts, ed., *Jefferson's Garden Book*, 228–229; Greene, ed., *Carter Diary*, 465, 570, 571, 577, 755, 919, 1115; Jackson and Twohig, eds., *Diaries of Washington*, V, 109–110, 111, 113, 132, 232–236, 260–266, 268, 276–277, 286, 312–313. Women occasionally plowed: see ibid., V, 209, 225; and William Morgan to B. Muse, Apr. 20, 1779, Muse Papers. A Somerset County, Maryland, planter noted on December 30, 1772, that his slave "Bridget began above 11 oclock to put up 45 Pannell of fence 9 long Stakt and Ridend [?] and was done before night afterward milkt the Cows" (James Wilson Farm Account Book, 1770–1796, MHS). I am indebted to Lorena Walsh for bringing this source to my attention. For the harvest in general, see J. A. Perkins, "Harvest Technology and Labour Supply in Lincolnshire and the East Riding of Yorkshire, 1750–1850," *Tools and Tillage*, III (1976), 56; Eve Hostettler, "Gourlay Steell and the Sexual Division of Labour," *History Workshop*, IV (1977), 95–101; and Michael Roberts, "Sickles and Scythes: Women's Work and Men's Work at Harvest Time," ibid., VII (1979), 3–28.

43. Greene, ed., *Carter Diary*, 131, 145, 163; William Nelson to his son, 1768, Nelson Letter Book, 1766–1775, 75, VSL; Isaac Weld, Jr., *Travels through the States of North America . . .*, 2 vols. (London, 1799), I, 156.

tional time had now to be found for gardening, securing wooden rails and fences, clearing ground, sowing clover and flax, and plowing for oats and barley. In early summer, corn and potatoes were planted and sheep sheared, clover was mowed, hay made, rye reaped, and corn hoed. In middle to late summer, wheat was reaped, flax was pulled, and barley, oats and meadow grasses were mowed; there followed more plowing, the sowing of turnips, rye, and timothy, and the transport of manure to the fields. In autumn, plowing continued, wheat and barley were sown, and threshing, husking, and the collection of wood began. Throughout the year, Jones reported a steady turnover of livestock as they were killed for sale. With such diverse activities, these laborers were indubitably farm workers, not plantation hands.[44]

In parts of the Chesapeake where the shift to diversified farming was most intensely felt, even more creative uses were made of slaves. For instance, in the late-eighteenth-century Lower James region, the movement toward a diversified agriculture gave rise to an extraordinary growth in the practice of slave hiring. In Elizabeth City County, Virginia, as Sarah Hughes has shown, few slaves escaped being hired out; indeed, most had worked outside their home household before assuming adulthood. In other parts of the northern Chesapeake—notably the Eastern Shore of Maryland—the transition from tobacco to grain seems to have been perceived, by some at any rate, as rendering slavery redundant. The wave of manumissions that swept this area in the late eighteenth century is at least in part attributable to the reduced labor demands of grain farmers. Those black laborers who secured freedom, nominal though that might have been, and toiled for an agricultural wage were farm workers par excellence.[45]

The work routines associated with the two major staples of the colonial South were markedly distinct. The rice cycle was the most prolonged, often lasting for more than a year, with two peaks of intense activity at midsummer and midwinter. The tobacco cycle, in contrast, could be completed within a calendar year, with the major period of intense activity confined to the late summer and

---

44. Thomas Jones Farm Books, 1779–1812, MHS. (I thank Lorena Walsh for lending me her detailed notes on this source.)

45. Sarah S. Hughes, "Slaves for Hire: The Allocation of Black Labor in Elizabeth City County, Virginia, 1782 to 1810," *WMQ*, 3d Ser., XXXV (1978), 260–286; Hughes, "Elizabeth City County, Virginia, 1782–1810: The Economic and Social Structure of a Tidewater County in the Early National Years" (Ph.D. diss., College of William and Mary, 1975); Carville V. Earle, "A Staple Interpretation of Slavery and Free Labor," *Geographical Review*, LXVIII (1978), 51–65; Dunn, "Black Society in the Chesapeake," in Berlin and Hoffman, eds., *Slavery and Freedom*, 62–63, 70–71, 75–77.

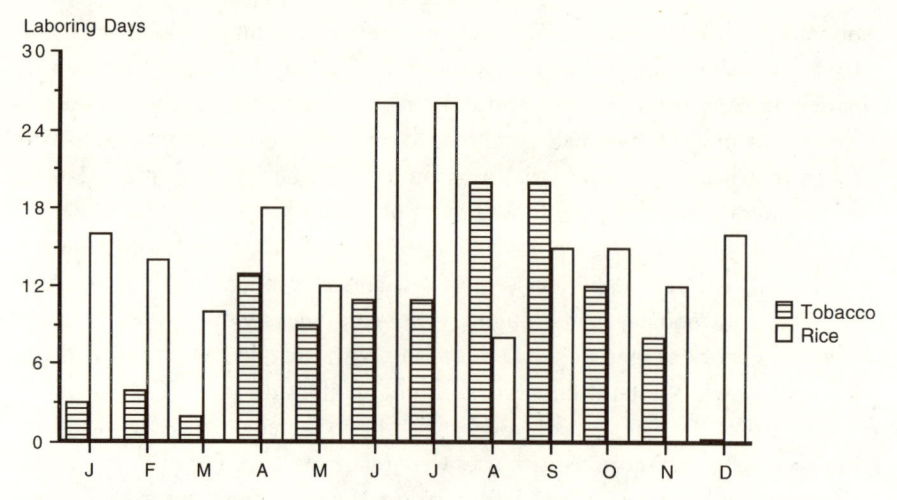

FIGURE 6. *Labor to Cultivate and Process Rice, circa 1800*
Notes and sources: The 113-day estimate for the tobacco cycle is derived from "Copy of a letter from W. E. Nichols of Albemarle . . . concerning the Culture of Hemp, 1811," *Memoirs of the Society of Virginia for Promoting Agriculture* (Richmond, Va., 1818), 19. Nichols estimates the number of days for each operation; I had to distribute those on a monthly basis, which was a somewhat arbitrary procedure. For the 188-day estimate in rice production, see Ralph V. Anderson, "Labor Utilization and Productivity, Diversification and Self-Sufficiency, Southern Plantations, 1800–1840" (Ph.D. diss, University of North Carolina, Chapel Hill, 1974), 49. Also note that on one Georgia rice plantation in the 1830s and 1840s, "the average number of days from planting to harvesting was about 165, but cases of 188 and 148 days are recorded" (Albert V. House, Jr., "The Management of a Rice Plantation in Georgia, 1834–1861, as Revealed in the Journal of Hugh Frazer Grant," *Agricultural History,* XIII [1939], 213). Professor Anderson kindly sent me his estimates of the man-days per acre for the various operations of the rice cycle, based on his analysis of the William J. Ball Books and the John Ball and Keating Simons Ball Books, UNC. I adjusted Professor Anderson's figures so as to represent eighteenth-century realities more accurately. I increased significantly the man-days for threshing and pounding and decreased the days for flooding. I assumed a slave tended three acres of rice.

early fall (see Figure 6). According to early-nineteenth-century estimates, a slave spent about 113 work days tending tobacco but about 188 work days tending rice. The rice cycle was more than a third longer than the tobacco cycle.[46]

Although the rice calendar consumed more work days than the tobacco schedule did, its one redeeming feature was its slack periods, hiatuses when the

---

46. A similar disproportion is evident from more precise late-19th-century estimates. The Census Bureau in 1880 calculated that it took 185 man hours to raise 1,000 pounds of tobacco on two acres (U.S., Bureau of the Census, "Report on the Culture and Curing of Tobacco," comp. J. B. Killebrew, *Agriculture, 1880,* III, 212, as quoted in Carville Earle and Ronald Hoffman, "Staple Crops and Urban Development in the Eighteenth-Century South," *Perspectives in American History,* X [1976], 71–72). It was estimated in 1870 that it took between 248 and 310 man hours to raise between four and five acres of rice (Thirteenth Annual Report of the Commissioner of Labor, 1898, II, 454–455).

staple required little attendance. The intensity of labor in rice cultivation was marked by crests and troughs. The tobacco cycle, by contrast, assumed a plateaulike aspect. As Fernando Ortiz deftly explains, "Tobacco is often smoked to kill time, but in the tobacco industry there is no such thing as 'dead time.'" From planting to harvest, tobacco required consistently applied labor or, in the words of a late-seventeenth-century observer, "continual care and Field-Labour." Even the daily routines of each crop synchronized with these different seasonal rhythms. The rice worker's day might end before sunset; the tobacco worker's day rarely did, for this was the archetypal sunup-to-sundown schedule.[47]

In basic working conditions, Chesapeake slaves were the more favored. The pace of tobacco cultivation might have been unusually steady and painstaking, but it was not particularly arduous or relentless. Tobacco cultivation moved with slow and measured tread. William Byrd's remark to Peter Beckford, though clearly self-serving, was not far off the mark: the labor of Virginia slaves, he claimed, was nothing "other than Gardening and less by far than what the poor People of other Countrys undergo." A Chesapeake slave, after all, was expected to cultivate no more than one and a half to two acres of tobacco—yet one more indication of the care and attention this plant demanded. Tobacco cultivation was also confined to relatively high, dry land even within the tidewater. Its growing conditions, therefore, were reasonably healthy for its workers. Rice, in contrast, was a much less congenial crop. At times, it required a great deal of heavy labor. The Lowcountry field hand cultivated anywhere from three to five acres of rice, more than double the acreage of a tobacco worker. Moreover, the environment most conducive to the successful cultivation of rice shortened the lives of its workers. The proximity of swampland and stagnant water curtailed the lives of many Lowcountry slaves.[48]

To the extent that these disadvantages could be offset, Lowcountry slaves might at least point to some positive social features arising from rice cultivation. Rice created greater opportunities for communal autonomy—in weight of black numbers and long-run residential stability—than did tobacco. Perhaps, too, a sense of satisfaction could be derived from the incorporation of

47. Ortiz, *Cuban Counterpoint*, 56; Sir Dalby Thomas, *An Historical Account of the Rise and Growth of the West-India Collonies* (London, 1690), quoted in Jerome E. Brooks, comp., *Tobacco: Its History Illustrated by the Books, Manuscripts, and Engravings in the Library of George Arents, Jr.*, II (New York, 1938), 531. According to John Taylor, "It would startle even an old planter to see an exact account of the labour devoured by an acre of tobacco" (*Arator: Being a Series of Agricultural Essays, Practical and Political: In Sixty-Four Numbers* [Petersburg, Va., 1818], 171).

48. "Letters of the Byrd Family," *VMHB*, XXXVI (1928), 122. On acreage per laborer and demographic performance of the two slave populations, see Chapter 1.

West African routines and methods into New World work patterns—and this, too, was more available to Lowcountry than to Chesapeake slaves. The heel-and-toe planting technique, the use of rice fanners made to African designs, and the pounding of rice using mortar and pestle—all these activities had direct West African antecedents.[49]

The roles of the secondary staples in these two regions were superficially similar. As new techniques like tidal culture or carts and plows reduced the laboring demands of a region's primary staple, so indigo and wheat cultivation (as well as other forms of diversified agriculture in the Chesapeake) occupied progressively more of the slaves' time in what would otherwise have been increasingly longer "slack" periods. In other words, wheat and indigo played comparable supporting roles to the leading actors in both the Chesapeake and the Lowcountry. Furthermore, in the outlying areas of both regions—the Sea Islands and midcountry of South Carolina and the northern, southern, and western rims of the Chesapeake—these crops assumed center stage. They became starring performers in their own right.

In spite of these similarities, there was an essential difference. Indigo tended to be a plantation crop, just like tobacco or rice; wheat tended to be a farm crop, like any other small grain. A slave spent about seventy-five work days cultivating little more than two acres of indigo. In fact, according to Henry Laurens, "two Acres is a heavy task and in old Lands that are grassy 1½ is full enough." By contrast, a laborer was expected to tend about ten acres of wheat but would spend no more than twenty-five work days in its cultivation. Indigo locked Lowcountry slaves into a typical plantation routine; wheat, in contrast, generally loosened the shackles of the plantation regime, permitting a diversified farm routine to evolve in its stead. The contrast between the two regions was thereby heightened, and any superficial resemblance between the roles of these two secondary staples is placed in perspective.[50]

---

49. Mortars and pestles and rice fanners are only occasionally listed in colonial South Carolina inventories, suggesting that these implements were fashioned by the slaves and not valued by whites. One of the few exceptions was the inventory of one of James Michie's three plantations upon which 34 adults resided. The hoes, axes, shovels, and rice hooks were valued at £26.10s. and the 25 mortars at £6.5s. (inventory of James Michie, Dec. 16, 1760, Inventories, WPA, CLXVI, 734–736). Those slaves who came from intensive wet-rice–producing areas would also have been familiar with more than the hoe-and-digging-stick agriculture prevalent throughout West Africa. They would have known how to handle a shovel (Harlan et al., "Plant Domestication," in Harlan et al., eds., *Origins of African Plant Domestication*, 16; George Peter Murdock, *Africa: Its Peoples and Their Culture History* [New York, 1959], 266).

50. *Laurens Papers*, I, 342. The 75-day estimate represents guesswork, based on the seven-month intensive schedule that indigo culture imposed. If anything, it is an underestimate.

ORGANIZATION OF LABOR

Masters generally organized their labor forces either by gang or by task. Under the gang system, slaves worked in unison, following "each other's tail the day long." Gang members had to keep "up with their leader," the pace set by one or two key laborers, toiling from sunup to sundown under direct and close supervision. Regimentation and discipline were the defining characteristics of ganging. Under the task system, by contrast, slaves were assigned a certain amount of work for the day or perhaps week; when the work was completed, their time was their own. The self-regulated nature of the labor and the absence of direct supervision were the distinguishing characteristics of tasking.[51]

Different crops and economic activities usually lent themselves to one or the other form of labor organization. In the Chesapeake, tobacco became associated with ganging, and in the Lowcountry rice became linked with tasking. Once the two labor systems were in place, masters in both regions extended them to secondary staples, even when, for example, wheat was not obviously eligible for ganging or Sea Island cotton for tasking. Once a system had been tried, tested, and not found wanting, it was often extended to crops not immediately suited to it. Nevertheless, the two forms of labor organization were not hermetically sealed systems. Masters might mix the two, using gangs for some operations and tasks for others; they might abandon one system and wholly adopt the other; or they might modify the archetypal qualities of either ganging or tasking and form a hybrid.[52]

Lowcountry Tasking

The task system was the dominant form of labor management employed on Lowcountry rice plantations. By at least midcentury, the basic "task" unit had been set at a quarter of an acre. Masters subdivided their rice fields into plots measuring 105 feet square, and this basic unit formed the daily task requirement for most planting operations. In recognition of this reality, one Georgia

---

On wheat acreage, see Betts, ed., *Jefferson's Garden Book,* 192. On man-days in wheat, see Earle and Hoffman, "Staple Crops and Urban Development," *Perspectives in Am. Hist.,* X (1976), 71. There were economies of scale in wheat production, and plantations could specialize in the crop. This development, however, was primarily a 19th-century phenomenon.

51. Philip D. Morgan, "Task and Gang Systems: The Organization of Labor on New World Plantations," in Stephen Innes, ed., *Work and Labor in Early America* (Chapel Hill, N.C., 1988), 189–220 (quotations on 189). See also Gray, *History of Agriculture,* I, 550–551.

52. For example, even after tasking became a way of life on Lowcountry rice plantations, ganging occurred in some operations. Ditch-digging probably lent itself more to ganging than tasking, although the task of removing 500–700 square feet became commonplace from the 1820s to the 1860s. Shoring up banks was another operation that was probably best achieved by a gang.

absentee owner in 1786 sent a chain "for running out the Tasks" to his plantation manager. "It is 105 feet long," he noted, "and will save a great deal of time in Laying out the field, and do it with more exactness." Henry Ferguson, an East Floridian who had spent seventeen years in South Carolina and Georgia, specified precisely how much land his slaves had cleared "from the Tasks which he set to his Negroes having measured the Ground frequently for that purpose." He added that "a Task was a quarter of an Acre to weed per day." The measurement assumed such general currency that a plantation could even be advertised as having a swamp "eleven tasks wide." Even with the late-eighteenth-century development of tidewater rice culture, which reduced the heavy hoeing formerly required of slaves and expanded the daily task unit to half an acre, the quarter-acre task remained the measure for a number of planting operations well into the nineteenth century.[53]

Tasking was not confined to the rice field. The readiness with which Sea Island planters extended the task system to Sea Island cotton planting in the 1780s and 1790s suggests prior familiarity. This link argues for an earlier association between indigo cultivation and tasking, for Sea Island planters had primarily been planters of indigo. Other activities were also tasked. The daily quota for pounding was seven mortars, and the quota for fencing was one hundred 12-foot poles; the weekly task of a pair of sawyers was 600 feet of pine or 780 feet of cypress. Unable to deliver a specified number of shingles to a customer, an embarrassed James Habersham discovered that his overseer had simply accepted the slaves' estimate of "their daily work without further examination"—a consequence of allowing woodworking slaves to labor by the task.[54]

---

53. "Bolzius Answers a Questionnaire," trans. and ed. Loewald et al., *WMQ*, 3d Ser., XIV (1957), 258; Butler, "Observations," 1786; one plantation journal recorded completed daily tasks and acres planted, and the quarter-acre task was uniformly applied throughout the planting season (see Plantation Journal, 1773, Wragg Papers); J. Channing to Edward Telfair, Aug. 10, 1786, Telfair Papers; Wilbur H. Siebert, ed., *Loyalists in East Florida, 1774 to 1785*, 2 vols. (DeLand, Fla., 1929), II, 67; *SC and AGG*, Jan. 23–30, 1767 (George Terry of the University of South Carolina kindly supplied me with this reference). On one of Henry Laurens's plantations, the master found "the Tasks Short on each Side which is about ⅕ less than what is the rule in the province 105 feet Square per Task. Godfrey's have only 95, his pole being only 19 feet instead of 21" (*Laurens Papers*, VIII, 291). Charles Drayton was told by his driver, John, that there were "8 tasks from the lane to the terras . . . and eleven from the river, by the lane side, to the row of cedars" (Charles Drayton Diaries, Feb. 10, 1784, Drayton Family Papers, Historic Charleston Foundation). See also Philip D. Morgan, "Work and Culture: The Task System and the World of Lowcountry Blacks, 1700 to 1880," *WMQ*, 3d Ser., XXXIX (1982), esp. 575.

54. Morgan, "Work and Culture," *WMQ*, 3d Ser., XXXIX (1982), 576, 582–583; Butler, "Observations," 1786; Garden to Royal Society, Apr. 20, 1755, Guard Book, I, 36; "Bolzius Answers a Questionnaire," trans. and ed. Loewald et al., *WMQ*, 3d Ser., XIV (1957), 258; De

Staple-crop requirements are crucial in explaining the rise of tasking in the Lowcountry. One key was that rice laborers did not require close supervision. Unlike some plantation staples that required scrupulous care in all phases of the production cycle and were therefore best cultivated by gangs of closely attended laborers, rice was a hardy plant, requiring a few relatively straightforward operations for its successful cultivation. The great expansion of rice culture in seventeenth-century Lombardy, for instance, was predicated, not on a stable, sophisticated, and well-supervised labor force, but on a pool of transient labor drawn from far afield. Nor did rice processing require the strict regimentation and "semi-industrialized" production techniques that attended the cultivation of sugar and necessitated gang labor. Another key was that rice cultivation lent itself to inexpensive and efficient measurement. Drainage ditches provided convenient units for measuring the performance of tasks. Thus, an overseer could inform his employer, "The field in a day or two will be compleatly drean'd, every Task has a drean all around and a number besides has them a Cross." The ubiquity and long-standing history of the quarter-acre task suggest that the planting and weeding stages of the rice cycle provided the initial rationale for the task system; once tasking became established, it was extended to a host of plantation operations.[55]

Other imperatives probably contributed to the attractiveness of tasking, but they were not crucial to its inception. U. B. Phillips claimed that tasking resulted largely from temporary absenteeism: "The necessity of the master's moving away from his estate in the warm months, to escape the malaria, involved the adoption of some system of routine which would work with more or less automatic regularity without his own inspiring or impelling presence." Although the master's desire to escape the swamps in summer should not be underestimated, absenteeism seems an insufficiently powerful agent to account for the emergence of tasking. The example of Caribbean sugar production is pertinent. If the withdrawal of an inspiring master encouraged the development of tasking, why did not sugar planters in the West Indies, where absenteeism began relatively early, adopt the system?[56]

Brahm, *De Brahm's Report of the General Survey*, ed. De Vorsey, 94; *The Letters of Hon. James Habersham, 1756–1775*, GHS, *Colls.*, VI (Savannah, Ga., 1904), 161.

55. Morgan, "Task and Gang Systems," in Innes, ed., *Work and Labor*, 189–220; Ulrich Bonnell Phillips, *American Negro Slavery: A Survey of the Supply, Employment, and Control of Negro Labor as Determined by the Plantation Regime* (Baton Rouge, La., 1966 [orig. publ. New York, 1918]), 247; John Couturier to John E. Colhoun, Jan. 14, 1793, Colhoun Papers.

56. Ulrich Bonnell Phillips, "The Slave Labor Problem in the Charleston District," in Elinor Miller and Eugene D. Genovese, eds., *Plantation, Town, and County: Essays on the Local History of American Slave Society* (Urbana, Ill., 1974), 9. For Caribbean absenteeism, see Dunn, *Sugar and Slaves*, 101–103, 161–163.

Similarly, the experience of some African slaves with rice cultivation probably encouraged a widespread and rapid diffusion of the task system, but it cannot fully explain its origins. By displaying their expertise, one could argue, Africans gained some control over their lives in the Lowcountry, at least to the extent of determining the length of their work days. But this argument is problematic. Lowcountry whites have left little evidence that they recognized African expertise. In 1767, when William Stork promised to find slaves for an East Florida estate, he looked, not to Africa, but to South Carolina or Georgia, for he wished to "choose such as are used to the different Cultivations I begin with as Rice, Cotton, Indigo, etc." Two years later, James Grant stressed the necessity in a new plantation enterprise to procure "some seasoned Negroes ... to teach the new ones, and to help your Overseer, who would not be able to do any work of consequence with a gang of entire new Negros." And it is questionable how much expertise most Africans could have displayed. The coastal regions of Africa that seem to have supplied a majority of slaves to early South Carolina were not rice-producing areas.[57]

Even among the minority of Africans who came from areas where rice was grown, few would have had much direct experience of the rice cultivation practiced in South Carolina. For the most part, women, not men, cultivated rice in Africa, and women were in short supply among incoming slaves. Only

---

57. Dr. William Stork to the Earl of Cassillis, June 14, 1767, Ailsa Muniments, GD 25/9/27, Scottish Record Office, Edinburgh; Governor James Grant to the Earl of Cassillis, July 22, 1769, Ailsa Muniments, GD 25/9/27. Of those slaves imported into South Carolina before 1740 and for whom an African coastal region of origin is known, about 15% were from rice-producing areas. Unfortunately, we know little or nothing about the regional origins of the earliest slave vessels to South Carolina. The first association between an African region and the cultivation of rice comes late in the day and might have been no more than a mercantile gambit. In 1758, the merchant firm Austin and Laurens described the origins of the slave ship *Betsey* as the "Windward and Rice Coast" (*SCG*, Aug. 11, 1758). The most explicit advertisements come even later in the century and smack of enthusiastic merchandising: for instance, *Gaz of State of SC*, May 6, 1784; *State Gaz of SC*, May 30, 1785; and *Evening Post*, July 11, 1785. Significantly, it was a London merchant involved in the African slave trade, although one interested in settling in the Lowcountry, who made one of the earliest and most explicit references to African regional rice cultivation. He thought that if slaves were brought "from the Windward Coast where they cultivate rice they may be soon trained to plantation business." This could, of course, mean no more than that he thought a prior agricultural background useful for a prospective plantation hand (sketch of a plan Richard Oswald of London proposes to follow in setting a plantation in East Florida, May 24, 1764, bundle 517, papers of James Grant of Ballindalloch). For the argument that African expertise was vital to South Carolina rice culture, see Peter H. Wood, *Black Majority: Negroes in Colonial South Carolina from 1670 through the Stono Rebellion* (New York, 1974), 56–62; and Daniel Littlefield, *Rice and Slaves: Ethnicity and the Slave Trade in Colonial South Carolina* (Baton Rouge, La., 1981), 74–114.

in intensive agricultural systems were there significant cooperation between the spouses and a balanced division of labor. Such African agricultural regimes were limited in scope, and few African immigrants to South Carolina came from them. Furthermore, few African rice growers would have been familiar with the irrigated rice culture practiced in South Carolina. Most West Africans grew rice as a dry, upland crop, and those few who grew wet rice relied on the inundations of rivers rather than on extensive irrigation. African slaves undoubtedly contributed strongly to the development of South Carolina's rice economy, perhaps more in the technology of production and processing of rice than in anything else, but, on present evidence, this hardly qualifies them for the role of prime movers in the development of the task system.[58]

African expertise was not crucial to the introduction of the task system, but the role of the labor force was vital in shaping its development. Taskmaster and laborer continually warred over what constituted a fair day's work. After one altercation between a black driver and a group of slaves, the slaves took their case to their master in Charleston. When he asked them "why they could not do their Tasks as well as the rest," they answered that "their Tasks were harder." The master was sympathetic and knowing: "There is sometimes a great difference in Tasks, and Paul told me he remembered that Jimmy had a bad Task that day. I was sorry to see poor Caesar amongst them for I knew him to be an honest, inoffensive fellow and tho't if any will do without severity, he will. I inquired his fault, and Paul told me . . . he had been 2 days in a Task." Hoeing was at issue in this dispute; on another plantation, threshing became a source

---

58. Littlefield, *Rice and Slaves*, 86; *Africa*, LI, no. 2 (1981), special issue, "Rice and Yams in West Africa"; David R. Harris, "Traditional Systems of Plant Food Production and the Origins of Agriculture in West Africa," in Harlan et al., eds., *Origins of African Plant Domestication*, 321; Linares, "From Tidal Swamp to Inland Valley," *Africa*, LI (1981), 571, 575; Thomas Astley, *A New General Collection of Voyages and Travels . . .*, 4 vols. (London, 1745–1747), II, 269, 313, 536; Philip D. Curtin, *Economic Change in Precolonial Africa: Senegambia in the Era of the Slave Trade* (Madison, Wis., 1975), 28–29. Rice fanners in South Carolina were made after African designs, and the mortar and pestle used by Lowcountry slaves bears a striking resemblance to West African models. For memories about rice production among present-day blacks, see Amelia Wallace Vernon, *African Americans at Mars Bluff, South Carolina* (Baton Rouge, La., 1993). As a contrast to my arguments, see Carney, "From Hands to Tutors," *Agric. Hist.*, LXVII (1993), 1–30; and Judith Carney and Richard Porcher, "Geographies of the Past: Rice, Slaves, and Technological Transfer in South Carolina," *Southeastern Geographer*, XXXIII (1993), 127–147. One must not underestimate the inventiveness of white Carolinians. For an early contemporary account of experimentation with rice planting, see "Letters from John Stewart to William Dunlop," *SCHM*, XXXII (1931), 16, 86, 90, 110; and for historians' assessments, see Alexander S. Salley, *The Introduction of Rice Culture into South Carolina*, Bulletin of the Historical Commission of South Carolina, no. 6 (Columbia, S.C., 1919); and James M. Clifton, "The Rice Industry in Colonial America," *Agric. Hist.*, LV (1981), 268–272.

of conflict. Three slaves belonging to George Austin—Liverpool, Moosa, and Dutay—"ran off early in December, for being a little chastis'd on Account of not finishing the Task of Thrashing in due time." By the early nineteenth century, a modus vivendi had apparently been reached on most Lowcountry plantations. One South Carolina planter reckoned: "The daily task does not vary according to the arbitrary will and caprice of their owners, and although [it] is not fixed by law, it is so well settled by long usage, that upon every plantation it is the *same*. Should any owner increase the work beyond what is customary, he subjects himself to the reproach of his neighbors, and to such discontent amongst his slaves as to make them of but little use to him."[59] The requirements of the task system were hammered out just as much in conflicts with the workforce as in the supposedly inevitable march of technological progress.

Labor disputes in the Lowcountry often involved the amount of time a particular task required. A measure of recalcitrance, slow working, feigned sickness, and downright sabotage characterized the slaves' work patterns throughout the New World. Indeed, these weapons were part of the arsenal of any coerced labor force. In the case of tasking, however, there was an inherent incentive to work quickly, at least where the task was clearly defined, so that the laborer's own "time" could be enlarged. Perhaps it was for this reason that a late-eighteenth-century Lowcountry planter could brag that his "people" had "no longer need of a driver's prompting, but perform their work with a spirit that must forever countenance success." Of course, not all Lowcountry workers took advantage of this possibility, but the opportunity did exist. As a result, disputes tended to revolve about the appropriate length of any given task, with the laborers' clear aim being to shorten the daily work requirement.[60]

Lowcountry slaves were also particularly keen to work productive ground, where their labors would bear fruit quickly and efficiently. When Francis Kinlock moved a group of his slaves from a plantation along the Winyaw River in South Carolina to one along the Saint Johns River in East Florida, the transplanted bondpeople were quick to assess the agricultural potential of their new environment. Astonishingly, they "wrote several letters to their friends" back at Winyaw "telling them that every thing ... planted [at Saint Johns] grew very

---

59. Richard Hutson to Mr. Croll, Aug. 22, 1767, Charles Woodward Hutson Papers, UNC; Josiah Smith to George Austin, Jan. 31, 1774, Smith Letterbook; [Edwin C. Holland], *A Refutation of the Calumnies Circulated against ... Slavery ...* (New York, 1969 [orig. publ. Charleston, S.C., 1822]), 53.

60. Alexander Garden, Jr., to George Ogilvie, July 21, 1791, Ogilvie-Forbes of Boyndlie MSS, Aberdeen University Library, Scotland. For general employer-laborer antagonism, see Edmund S. Morgan, *American Slavery, American Freedom: The Ordeal of Colonial Virginia* (New York, 1975), 316–337; and Eugene D. Genovese, *Roll, Jordan, Roll: The World the Slaves Made* (New York, 1974), 285–324.

well, and they are certain by the tryal they have had, that the Land is good." Slaves working by the task were especially interested in the quality of the land that they cultivated.[61]

However onerous tasking could become for some slaves, the system at least allowed slaves a certain latitude to apportion their day, to work intensively on the assigned task and then have the balance of their time. Thus, a forty-year-old slave, blind in one eye, named "Guinea Adam," who was described in a sale notice of 1789 as "light made, industrious and well disposed," could be singled out "for doing his task soon." And, with the institutionalization of the task system, the slave's "time" became sacrosanct. As Daniel Turner pointed out, "Once a slave has completed his task, his master feels no right to call on him." One of the advantages of such a right is neatly illustrated in an incident that befell a Methodist circuit rider named Joseph Pilmore. On March 18, 1773—a Thursday—he arrived at the banks of the Santee River in the Georgetown district of South Carolina. After waiting in vain for the regular ferry, he was met by a few blacks. Presumably they told him that they "had finished their task," for that is how he explained their availability in his journal. He then hired their "time" so that he could be ferried across the river. The actual time was about three o'clock in the afternoon. According to one observer, the slaves "generally" completed their work "by one or two o'clock in the afternoon, and have the rest of the day for themselves." John Drayton thought that the slaves' tasks were reasonable because "when they are diligent in performing them, they have some hours of the day to themselves."[62] Exhausting as task labor

---

61. Francis Kinlock to James Grant, Dec. 26, 1766, bundle 254, Papers of General James Grant of Ballindalloch.

62. Sale of slaves by Thomas Washington to William Clay Snipes, June 6, 1789, Miscellaneous Records, ZZ, 7–9, SCDAH; Daniel Turner to his parents, Aug. 13, 1806, Daniel Turner Papers, microfilm, LC. Equally sacrosanct, at least to some slaves, was the product of their "time." Thus, in 1781, a set of plantation slaves attempted to kill their overseer because he tried to appropriate the corn that they were apparently planning to market (*SC and ACG*, Jan. 20, 1781). Frederick E. Maser and Howard T. Maag, eds., *The Journal of Joseph Pilmore, Methodist Itinerant: For the Years August 1, 1769 to January 2, 1774* (Philadelphia, 1969), 188. Another evangelical preacher also seems to have been the beneficiary of the task system, for George Whitefield noted in his journal in 1740 that "several of the negroes did their work in less time than usual, that they might come to hear me" (George Whitefield, *George Whitefield's Journals* [London, 1960], 444). "A Curious New Description of Charles-Town, and Its Environs . . . ," *Universal Museum*, I (September 1762), 477, which was repeated almost verbatim in ["Scotus Americanus"], *Informations concerning the Province of North Carolina, Addressed to Emigrants from the Highlands and Western Isles of Scotland* (Glasgow, 1773), in William K. Boyd, "Some North Carolina Tracts of the Eighteenth Century," *North Carolina Historical Review*, III (1926), 616 (my thanks to Peter Coclanis for bringing the first of these descriptions to my attention); Drayton, *A View of South Carolina*, 145. This is not to say that

undoubtedly was, then, its prime virtue was that it was not unremitting. Industrious Lowcountry slaves could avoid working from sunup to sundown.

Perhaps the most important consequence of this sharp division between the master's "time" and the slave's "time" was the opportunity it presented slaves to work on their own plots. Tasks were not easily accomplished, of course, and occasionally planters exacted even higher daily requirements, but, as Johann Bolzius noted, the advantage to the slaves of having a daily goal was that they could, once it was met, "plant something for themselves." Indeed, as early as the first decade of the eighteenth century, contemporaries complained that slaves were planting "for themselves as much as will cloath and subsist them and their famil[ies]." During the investigation of a suspected slave conspiracy at midcentury, a Lowcountry planter readily acknowledged that one of his slaves had planted rice "in his own time" and could do with it as he wished. Similarly, a hired artisan occasionally returned to his home plantation to tend "his rice." When Edmund Botsford created a dialogue between two South Carolina slaves, he had the one from the Lowcountry observe to his backcountry friend, "Most everybody have rice of their own, for we all had land to plant, and most everyday we done our task time enough to work for ourselves."[63]

In fact, Lowcountry slaves seem to have had quite large amounts of land available to them. After "their required day's work," Carolinian slaves were, in Bolzius's words, "given as much land as they can handle," on which they planted corn, potatoes, tobacco, peanuts, sugar melons and watermelons, and pumpkins and bottle pumpkins. According to Anthony Stokes, Lowcountry slaves had "a certain limited task every day [that] . . . is not too hard" and had "land enough to plant for themselves." Slaves on one South Carolina plantation, observed the duc de La Rochefoucauld-Liancourt, were "at liberty to cultivate for themselves as much land as they choose." Twenty-five slaves sent to establish a plantation in East Florida cleared five to six acres for their own houses and gardens (giving them about a quarter of an acre apiece). John Drayton referred to the Lowcountry slaves' "gardens" *and* "fields," indicating house-plots and more extensive provision grounds. From one or two o'clock in the afternoon, one observer saw slaves

---

the hours of labor were generally short. The comprehensive Negro Act of 1740 attempted to lay down the maximum amount of daily labor that could be exacted from a slave—that is, 15 hours in spring and summer, and 14 in fall and winter (Cooper and McCord, eds., *Statutes at Large,* VII, 413).

63. "Bolzius Answers a Questionnaire," trans. and ed. Loewald et al., *WMQ,* 3d Ser., XIV (1957), 256; the Instructions of the Clergy of South Carolina given to Mr. Johnston, 1712, A8/429, SPG; testimony of Thomas Akin and Ammon, Feb. 7, 1749, Council Journal, no. 17, part 1, 160, SCDAH; Belin Plantation Diary, July 14, 1797; [Edmund Botsford], *Sambo and Toney: A Dialogue in Three Parts* (Georgetown, S.C., 1808), 34.

working in their own private fields, consisting of 5 or 6 acres of ground, allowed them by their masters, for planting of rice, corn, potatoes, tobacco, etc. for their own use and profit, of which the industrious among them make a great deal. In some plantations, they have also the liberty to raise hogs and poultry, which, with the former articles, they are to dispose of to none but their masters (this done to prevent bad consequences) for which, in exchange, when they do not chuse money, their masters give Osnaburgs, negro cloths, caps, hats, handkerchiefs, pipes, and knives. They do not plant in their fields for subsistence, but for amusement, pleasure, and profit, their masters giving them clothes, and sufficient provisions from their granaries.[64]

Planting for "amusement, pleasure, and profit" was a direct outgrowth of the opportunities presented by a task system.

Chesapeake Ganging

Tobacco was a good candidate for gang labor. Few plantation crops required more care and attention than tobacco. Supervision was vital, and it paid to work a number of hands in order to cover the costs of supervision. Only a tobacco planter would claim, as John Custis did, that his crop had been "under my own eye, and [I] may say I saw almost every plant from the planting to the prizing and striping off." Because tobacco had "all the while . . . carefully to be watched," as Sir Dalby Thomas put it, tobacco plantations were "generally made into small parcells, not above eight or ten hands at a place." The requirements of the staple led tobacco planters to arrange their laborers into small units so that each individual's performance could be closely monitored. With small units, and tobacco laborers cultivating no more than two or so acres apiece, the costs of close supervision were manageable. Where a gang was

---

64. "Bolzius Answers a Questionnaire," trans. and ed. Loewald et al., *WMQ*, 3d Ser., XIV (1957), 259; Anthony Stokes, *A View of the Constitution of the British Colonies in North America and the West Indies* (London, 1969 [orig. publ. London, 1783]), 414; François Alexandre Frédéric, duke de La Rochefoucault Liancourt, *Travels through the United States of North America . . .* , 2 vols. (London, 1799), I, 599; Drayton, *A View of South Carolina*, 147; Siebert, ed., *Loyalists in East Florida, 1774 to 1785*, II, 44; "A Curious New Description," *Universal Museum*, I (September 1762), 477. For other references to the benefits of tasking, see Drayton, *A View of South Carolina*, 145, 147; and Botsford, *Sambo and Tony*, 8, 13. Note also that Allard Belin gave his slaves a Thursday in May "to finish planting their own Crop," thereby indicating that they had been planting in their own time before that day. In another year, he allowed "the Negroes to plant their own crop" on a Thursday and Friday in June (Belin Plantation Diary, May 31, 1798, June 1–2, 1797). A land dispute that reached the Privy Council between Charles Fladger and James Johnston over 185 acres on Little Pedee revealed that "Mr. Fladger's Negroes had all along [for 10 years] planted for themselves a little field on the same land" (Adele Stanton Edwards, ed., *Journals of the Privy Council, 1783–1789*, State Records of South Carolina [Columbia, S.C., 1971], 132).

larger than eight to ten hands, the planter probably followed Landon Carter's method of dividing it into "good, Middling, and indifferent hands," monitoring one laborer's output in each group for one day and then making sure that "all of the same division must be kept to his proportion."[65]

Gang labor was also particularly appropriate where one slave set the pace for all. In tobacco culture, the best hands established the pattern for others. In replanting, for example, expert hands withdrew selected plants from the seedbeds, and less experienced hands transplanted them. In tobacco culture, slave foremen were not so much managers as pacesetters. Landon Carter noted that his "overseers tend their foremen close for one day in every Job; and deducting ⅕ of that day's work, he [the foreman] ought every other day to keep up to that." When the line of female laborers working behind foreman George was found to be weeding too few corn rows a day, Carter promised George "a sound correction" unless he "mended his pace." An individual's place in the gang determined the speed at which he or she worked. When Carter wished to demonstrate to his disgraced gardener that "the hoe [was not] to be his field of diversion," he gave him "the place of my fourth man and have ordered my overseers to keep him to that. I observed it made him quicken the motion of his arm." In this regard, the line of laborers working under the gang system resembled a crew sculling a boat. And, if one foreman, much like the stroke of a crew, established a slower tempo than another, his gang would follow suit. At one point, Carter contemplated joining two gangs to solve this problem, so that "every fellow that does not work as much as the Mangorike fellows and every woman as the Mangorike women shall be whipt to it."[66]

Tobacco cultivation was not extensive, in the sense that a laborer harvested a large crop. Seemingly, then, there was no prohibition against measuring an individual's product by the task. But the quality of the tobacco crop was so variable that there could not be, in Fernando Ortiz's words, "any exact unit of measurement for leaf tobacco."[67] One might count hogsheads, it is true, but the quality of the leaf, just as much as the number of hogsheads, determined the crop's worth. Moreover, tasking a single tobacco laborer made little sense when so much depended on the collective care expended on any one crop. By contrast, everything in rice was measured by neatly demarcated, universal standards, and individuals could be largely left to make their own crops in their own time, with no detriment to the product. In short, the measurement

65. John Custis to Robert Cary, [1729], John Custis Letterbook, typescript, CW; Thomas, *An Historical Account*, in Brooks, comp., *Tobacco*, II, 531; Greene, ed., *Carter Diary*, 502. One June day in 1770, Carter visited one of his gangs three times and on each occasion spent two hours monitoring their progress in turning tobacco hills (ibid., 422).

66. Greene, ed., *Carter Diary*, 376, 430, 451, 502.

67. Ortiz, *Cuban Counterpoint*, 36.

PLATE 13. Perry Hall Slave Quarters with Field Hands at Work. *Francis Guy. Circa 1805. A gang of slaves, working in close unison. Courtesy Maryland Historical Society*

of labor output, as much as the costs of supervision and pace of work, facilitated a gang system.

Once again, then, various staple requirements, particularly how much direct supervision a crop demanded and how easily laborers' output could be measured, largely shaped the prevailing labor arrangement. Apparently, the presence or absence of the master and the slaves' familiarity or unfamiliarity with the crop (many Africans were in fact familiar with tobacco) were not of central significance, particularly in tobacco cultivation, where gang labor antedated slavery.[68]

68. For contemporary observations, see *Books, Manuscripts, and Drawings Relating to Tobacco from the Collection of George Arents, Jr.* (Washington, D.C., 1938), 11–12; Astley, *A New General Collection of Voyages*, II, 56, 306; Robert Norris's evidence given July 27, 1775, Long Papers, Add. MSS 18272, 15–16. For historians' assessments, see Ortiz, *Cuban Counterpoint*, 192–197; Harlan et al., eds., *Origins of African Plant Domestication*, 216, 302; and Curtin, *Economic Change in Precolonial Africa*, 230. A letter from a Bermudan colonist in 1618 mentioned a slave, Francisco, whose "judgement in the caring to tobackoe is such that I had rather have him than all the other negars that bee here" (Wesley Frank Craven, *An Introduction to the History of Bermuda*, 2d ed. (Bermuda, 1990 [orig. publ. in *WMQ*, 2d Ser., XVII, XVIII (1937–1938)], 92). One wonders where Francisco acquired this knowledge. On tobacco in South Carolina: "Bolzius Answers a Questionnaire," trans. and ed. Loewald et al., *WMQ*, 3d Ser., XIV (1957), 236; John Glen to the Board of Trade, Mar. 1753, CO5/374, 147, PRO; "A Curious New Description," *Universal Museum*, I (September 1762), 477; Bernhard A. Uhlendorf, trans. and ed., *The Siege of Charleston: With an Account of the Province of South Carolina* . . . (Ann Arbor, Mich., 1938), 353.

The gang labor practiced on Chesapeake tobacco plantations was far removed from the rigors and regimentation of Caribbean sugar production. Tobacco cultivation required a large measure of judgment and skill. Topping and cutting, for example, demanded attention to each individual plant: all could not be treated in the same way. Similarly, tobacco's delicate leaves were easily damaged by careless handling in harvesting, curing, and packing. Tobacco production was not therefore readily divided into a series of routine, easily repeatable operations. Although transplanting and weeding "could be performed on an assembly line basis," as Robert Fogel puts it, "other operations remained on a handicraft basis." Consequently, gang work in the Chesapeake lacked much of the military precision associated with sugar plantations.[69]

Chesapeake gangs were also much smaller than their Caribbean counterparts and were almost never divided into more than one gang on any one work unit. In fact, because of small workforces, many Chesapeake slaves did not experience much gang labor. Assuming that gang work was not common on plantations with fewer than four slave workers, about a fifth to a quarter of eighteenth-century slaves in Anne Arundel County, Maryland, regularly avoided collective labor. Another quarter or so worked in groups of four to six, where there was probably some mixture of group labor and individual assignments. Gang work was a regular experience for only about half the slaves in this county. Furthermore, on diversified Chesapeake plantations, gang labor was almost a misnomer. Squads or small groups of slaves had to perform a variety of functions; and, although one slave might have set the tempo of the work, there were often so few slaves in a group that the notion of their being driven was probably inappropriate. One Virginia planter's lament, "All hands at work but so much to do and of such various sorts it is hardly possible to keep much at the hoe," was probably typical.[70] In other words, the progressive farmer had to fragment his labor force; in so doing, the advantages of gang labor from the farmer's perspective—the degree of supervision and compulsion that it made possible—were significantly lessened.

Nevertheless, when a Chesapeake planter focused most or much of his production on wheat, as many a planter in the Chesapeake did at the end of the eighteenth century and into the nineteenth century, he could still find a place for ganging. Because wheat required only about twenty-five work days to produce in a year, it was usually considered a farm crop and associated with

---

69. Robert W. Fogel, *Without Consent or Contract: The Rise and Fall of American Slavery* (New York, 1989), 36, 428n.

70. Lois Green Carr and Lorena S. Walsh, "Economic Diversification and Labor Organization in the Chesapeake, 1650–1820," in Innes, ed., *Work and Labor*, 162–165; Greene, ed., *Carter Diary*, 333, 497, also 496, 576.

free labor. Yet, wheat required intensive physical exertion during critical periods of the year, most obviously at harvesttime but also when planting and threshing. Organizing slaves into gangs enabled wheat producers to drive them with greater intensity. Indeed, the larger the slaveowner, the larger the amount of wheat produced per worker. Sufficient economies of scale existed in wheat production to justify ganging.[71]

However idiosyncratic the form of gang labor in the Chesapeake, the central aim of ganging—maximizing labor—meant that this region's slaves had less respite than Lowcountry slaves. Chesapeake slaves worked, in William Tatham's words, "from daylight until the dusk of the evening and some part of the night, by moon or candlelight, during the winter." Stripping tobacco and husking corn were night chores. George Washington unquestioningly assumed that his slaves would "be at their work as soon as it is light, [and] work till it is dark." Lowcountry slaves also worked long hours. In some cases—the combination of a demanding quota and a physically weak slave, for instance—the hours might even have been longer than for Chesapeake slaves. But at least Lowcountry slaves had a fixed amount of work to perform, and, if they could accomplish it expeditiously, their time was their own. Chesapeake slaves, in contrast, had no time of their own during the week, apart from those rare occasions when they were given a "holiday." They were able to work on their own account only on Sundays.[72]

Because working from sunup to sundown was normal in Chesapeake ganging, this region's slaves had no incentive to work quickly, unlike their Lowcountry counterparts. Slow working, malingering, and shirking assumed extensive and ingenious forms on Chesapeake plantations. William Strickland, an English observer of Virginia agriculture in the 1790s, thought "nothing can be conceived more inert than a slave; his unwilling labour is discovered in every step that he takes; he moves not if he can avoid it; if the eyes of the overseer be off him, he sleeps; the ox and the horse, driven by the slave, appear to sleep also; all is listless inactivity; all motion is evidently compulsory." Chesapeake planters were obsessed with what they took to be the feckless, shiftless, and irresponsible character of their slaves. They could not be every-

---

71. James R. Irwin, "Exploring the Affinity of Wheat and Slavery in the Virginia Piedmont," *Expl. Econ. Hist.*, 2d Ser., XXV (1988), 295–322; Lorena S. Walsh, "Slave Life, Slave Society, and Tobacco Production in the Tidewater Chesapeake, 1620–1820," in Ira Berlin and Philip D. Morgan, eds., *Cultivation and Culture: Labor and the Shaping of Slave Life in the Americas* (Charlottesville, Va., 1993), 170–199. See also Robert C. Allen, "The Growth of Labor Productivity in Early Modern English Agriculture," *Expl. Econ. Hist.*, 2d Ser., XXV (1988), 117–146, esp. 137–138.

72. Herndon, *Tatham*, 102; "Washington's Agricultural Notes," *Farmers' Register*, V (1838), 488.

where at one and the same time. When the planter's eye was on them, slaves generally performed adequately; once his back was turned, the work moved slowly. "Where the General is absent," one Virginia planter observed, "Idleness is Preferred to all business."[73]

That gangs had no incentive to reduce the length of any operation—rather, just the opposite—does not mean that they failed to contest the terms of their labor. Just as struggles between masters and slaves in the Lowcountry generated customary tasks, the same processes led to expectations about various gang operations. Measurements tended to be less precise than in tasking, but they did exist. For example, in 1773, Thomas Jefferson noted that a laborer could be expected to hoe a half to one acre of "common bushy land" in a week, working in a gang. Slaves working in groups were especially likely to press their masters on the composition of their gangs. A shorthanded gang was an unhappy one. Landon Carter discovered that the absence of a single slave could seriously disrupt the work of a group. Even if "the most trifling hand is ill but a day or a piece of a day," Carter lamented, "it generally excuses the loss of a whole day's work of the gang."[74]

Unlike Lowcountry tasking, where slaves were left largely alone to grow the crop, master and gang worked closely in Chesapeake agriculture, sometimes leading to friendly exchanges. Thus, when George Washington stood in one of his fields and pondered why a section of corn looked healthier than the rest, he received his answer. "Some of the Negroes," he reported, ascribed it to dunging. Not to be outdone, the planter maintained that intersowing with Irish potatoes had accomplished the feat. Even cantankerous Landon Carter engaged his slaves in agreeable conversation. On one occasion, Carter asked "honest slave Jack Lubbar" about cultivating pea vines. His answer "comfort[ed]" Carter. Slaves might provide more than comfort; they might also educate. When Carter became anxious that rust was attacking his cotton plants, his slaves alleviated his fears with the information that blossoming plants always produced deep, red spots. Slaves also took a real interest in their work. Such seems to be the implication of Carter's remembrance one rain-filled day that "even Sensible slaves say of the winter rains which fell that they wished they might not want some of that rain in the summer."[75]

---

73. G. Melvin Herndon, "Agriculture in America in the 1790s: An Englishman's View," *Agric. Hist.*, XLIX (1975), 509; Greene, ed., *Carter Diary*, 568. Colonel James Gordon gave voice to the universal lament when he noted how he "went about the plantation, found everything amiss almost; the things of this life much disquiet me, my people are so careless" ("Journal of Col. James Gordon," *WMQ*, 1st Ser., XI, (1902–1903), 200.

74. Betts, ed., *Jefferson's Garden Book*, 45; Greene, ed., *Carter Diary*, 588.

75. Jackson and Twohig, eds., *Diaries of Washington*, V, 16; Greene, ed., *Carter Diary*, 470–471, 574–575, 892–893.

Given Landon Carter's personality, discussions easily degenerated into carping criticisms. On one occasion, an old female slave, Sukey, told him that the patch of land she and others were tending "would see a good crop of Tobacco for she knew the ground." Carter disputed this assessment, and Sukey retorted that "she would be hanged if any planter seeing the ground would not say the tobacco stood tollerably well." Carter persisted, telling her that the tobacco was too small. Sukey reiterated that "she knew the ground, knew how it was dunged, and would be hanged if it did not turn out good Tobacco." On another occasion Carter himself was the butt of a slave's criticism, as he discovered when he received a neighboring planter's letter "to tell me Talbot informed him I had but a mean crop."[76]

Overseers also clashed with slaves over agricultural questions. When one white foreman conjectured that a day's cutting would fill a sixty-foot tobacco house, the "old Stagers in the Gang lookt with some contempt at his saying so." Their owner then asked their opinion, which they gave in no uncertain terms, presumably in front of their erstwhile superior. Differences of opinion occasionally led to violence. In the early nineteenth century, a white overseer allocated the day's work to his slave gang. One of the slaves, named Jim, contradicted the overseer and pointed out that some slaves would need to shell corn. The overseer angrily replied that he was in charge and would have to teach Jim some "manners." The two men scuffled. Eventually Jim broke loose, declared that "he would not be whipped for nothing," and went off to work. Not long after, the overseer directed Jim and some other slaves to shell corn. Jim was now in no mood to comply. As the overseer moved toward him, the slave picked up a tobacco fork and brought it down on the white man's head, fracturing his skull.[77]

The difference in available free time between some Lowcountry and Chesapeake slaves, in turn, translated into different economic opportunities. The domestic plots cultivated by Lowcountry slaves merited the terms "little plantations" or "private fields." In the Chesapeake, conversely, these were never more than garden plots. In 1736, Edward Kimber described "the little Spots," which slaves were allowed to "cultivate, at vacant Times." About forty years later, Philip Fithian saw the Nomini Hall slaves "digging up their small Lots of ground allow'd by their Masters for Potatoes, peas etc." Fithian correctly observed why Chesapeake slaves had only small lots, because all "such work for themselves they constantly do on Sundays, as they are otherwise employed on

---

76. Greene, ed., *Carter Diary,* 454–455, 489.
77. Ibid., 487; Trial of Jim, Jan. 14, 1808, Condemned Slaves, box 2, and Executive Papers, VSL, as cited in Philip J. Schwarz, *Twice Condemned: Slaves and the Criminal Laws of Virginia, 1705–1865* (Baton Rouge, La., 1988), 238–239.

every other day." Chesapeake slaves were certainly not reluctant, domestic cultivators. William Tatham noted in 1800 that there were crops "which are *permitted* (and greatly confirmed by custom) to slaves," namely, "potatoes, garden-stuff, pumpkins, melons, a few particular fruit trees, peas, hops, flax, and cotton." The very diversity of this produce is revealing of the "gardening" orientation of this region's slaves, a reflection of the attenuated time and land allowed them.[78]

PATTERNS OF LABOR

The different plants that Chesapeake and Lowcountry slaves cultivated powerfully shaped their lives, influencing everything from daily and seasonal rhythms to basic working conditions, from the variety and nature of work to labor organization. The contrast between the worlds of Chesapeake and Lowcountry slaves could not have been starker, in large part because their lives were intimately and inescapably bound up with different crops. Each region's primary staple was tightly woven into the fabric of its slaves' everyday lives.

Nevertheless, the work experiences of Chesapeake and Lowcountry slaves were not wholly dissimilar. Even the seasonal rhythms, so obviously variant, had at least one feature in common. Slaves in both regions worked hard at some points in the year and avoided work altogether at other times. All slaves experienced a significant reduction in their workload over the winter months. Only so much woodcutting, estate maintenance, and crop processing could be accomplished. Working frozen ground was at times impossible. A willingness to work intensely rather than steadily might have been more pervasive in the Lowcountry than in the Chesapeake, but it was present in both regions. This characteristic may owe something to African culture, but, as Eugene Genovese has persuasively argued, it was a trait much less specifically African than "generally rural, prebourgeois, and especially preindustrial."[79]

---

78. [Edward Kimber], "Observations in Several Voyages and Travels in America," *WMQ*, 1st Ser., XV (1906–1907), [148]; Hunter Dickinson Farish, ed., *Journal and Letters of Philip Vickers Fithian, 1773–1774: A Plantation Tutor of the Old Dominion* (Williamsburg, Va., 1943), 128; Tatham, *Communications concerning Agriculture*, 55. On further references to the size of domestic plots in the Lowcountry and Chesapeake, respectively, see J. Hector St. John Crèvecoeur, *Letters from an American Farmer*, ed. W. P. Trent and Ludwig Lewisohn (New York, 1925 [orig. publ. 1782]), 230, 232; and Doar, *Rice and Rice Planting*, 32; as opposed to Weld, *Travels*, I, 148. See Morgan, "Task and Gang Systems," in Innes, ed., *Work and Labor*, 213, for evidence that this difference between Lowcountry and Chesapeake plots continued into the 19th century.

79. Genovese, *Roll, Jordan, Roll*, 309. The classic description of the characteristic preindustrial attitude toward work is E. P. Thompson, "Time, Work-Discipline, and Industrial Capitalism," *Past and Present*, no. 38 (December 1967), 56–97.

The climate and disease environment of the colonial South also reinforced irregular work patterns. Even the most profit-conscious planter had to bow to the effects of hot, steamy summer days and heavy rains, which inevitably disrupted work routines. Planters sometimes mentioned that their slaves did nothing for a few days in a row, when conditions became particularly oppressive. Illness also took a heavy toll on both regions' labor forces. In August 1780, one Lowcountry overseer, in charge of thirty-five slaves, observed, "The want of medicines, namely pukes and purges . . . has already been the cause of much work being lost, the one half of them are now down with fevers and fluxes." In autumn 1756, Landon Carter had seventy to eighty slaves "laid up," and, the following autumn, he noted that "every monday morning for near 3 weeks," many of his slaves went sick, although never on a Sunday "because they look on that as holy day." In the Lowcountry, the continuity of labor was broken by a simple reduction in the collective output of individual laborers working in the field; in the Chesapeake, the effect was often more subtle, with a group's work rhythms affected by the absence of a single slave.[80]

In spite of the unevenness of agricultural labor, masters in both regions sought to regularize their slaves' work routines. Christmas, Easter, and Whitsuntide became the slaves' only holidays; an occasional "free" day might become available during the year, but only at the master's discretion, and only Sundays were days of rest. Even the Sabbath was not inviolable: masters could declare an emergency—a harvest that was behind schedule or ruptured banks that needed mending—and propel their slaves back into the fields. Slaves sometimes negotiated terms, as in the case of Governor James Wright's twenty field hands, who refused to travel or work on two successive Sundays unless recompensed. Similarly, when time was particularly pressing, masters might extend the slaves' workday into the night, which in turn might lead the slaves to resist. Furthermore, over time masters attempted—though not with uniform success—to keep their slaves busy all year. They chose secondary staples that complemented their primary crops, had their slaves grow corn and other provisions in the interstices of the staple cycle, and then put them to lumbering, collecting firewood, estate maintenance, ground preparation, new construction, and various indoor tasks during winter. Field hands never became "metaphoric clock punchers," but increasingly they toiled year-round.[81]

---

80. Greene, ed., *Carter Diary,* 127, 174, 274, 388. See also ibid., 305, 383–384, 418, 426, 496 (6 of 45 sick), 508 (10 ill), 524 (22 of 30 "pretend to be sick"), 536, 588, 952, 1089; "Journal of Col. James Gordon," *WMQ,* 1st Ser., XI (1902–1903), 201; [?] to Major [?], Aug. 23, 1780, Elliott-Gonzales Papers, UNC.
81. *Letters of Habersham,* GHS, *Colls.,* VI, 190–199; Betty Wood, " 'Never on a Sunday?': Slavery and the Sabbath in Lowcountry Georgia, 1750–1808," in Mary Turner, ed., *From*

Masters in both regions shared similar views about the sexual division of slave labor. Masters were somewhat ambivalent about putting white servant women into the fields, but they had no such reservations about black slave women. In the Lowcountry, Johann Bolzius observed, "A good Negro woman has the same day's work as the man in the planting and cultivating of the fields." John Bartram saw men and women sharing equally in digging a ten-foot-deep ditch, seemingly "alike in their labours as is common in both Carolinas." Visiting Virginia in the early nineteenth century, Henry Knight was surprised at the "novel sight to a New Englander, to see a negro *woman* ride standing up behind a carriage as outtender; or delving on the highways; but more so, to see a woman holding a plough." Slave women rarely plowed, but, in spring 1779, a Virginia overseer wrote to his steward informing him that Peg, one of the plowers, had fallen heavily and would be unable to work for more than a week.[82]

Over the course of the eighteenth century, women came to outnumber men as field-workers. As slave men became the primary beneficiaries of the growth in skilled opportunities that occurred during the eighteenth century, proportionately more slave women worked in the fields. Increasingly, the composition of field laborers was more female than male. Thus, Thomas Jefferson disallowed his overseers from keeping "a woman out of the crop for waiting on them," and only a deathbed legacy from a husband to his wife exempted her favorite slave "from working in the Ground." Just as a larger proportion of women than men worked as field hands, increasingly women performed the least desirable chores, often unaccompanied by men. By midcentury, women bore the main brunt of preparing ground, digging ditches, grubbing swamps, hoeing, and weeding.[83]

But, as masters came to own more slaves, they also distinguished between

---

Chattel Slaves to Wage Slaves: The Dynamics of Labour Bargaining in the Americas (Bloomington, Ind., 1995), 79–96; Fogel, *Without Consent or Contract,* 161–162; Carr and Walsh, "Economic Diversification and Labor Organization," in Innes, ed., *Work and Labor,* 158–160.

82. Lois Green Carr and Lorena S. Walsh, "The Planter's Wife: The Experience of White Women in Seventeenth-Century Maryland," *WMQ,* 3d Ser., XXXIV (1977), 547; J. Douglas Deal, *Race and Class in Colonial Virginia: Indians, Englishmen, and Africans on the Eastern Shore during the Seventeenth Century* (New York, 1993), 113; "Bolzius Answers a Questionnaire," trans. and ed. Loewald et al., *WMQ,* 3d Ser., XIV (1957), 257; Bartram, "Diary," ed. Harper, Am. Phil. Soc., *Trans.,* N.S., XXXIII (1942–1944), 22; Knight, *Letters from the South,* 76; William Morgan to Battaille Muse, Apr. 20, 1779, Muse Papers. See also Jonathan Mason, *Extracts from a Diary Kept by the Hon. Jonathan Mason of a Journey from Boston to Savannah in the Year 1804* (Cambridge, Mass., 1885), 23.

83. Betts, ed., *Jefferson's Garden Book,* 46; Richard Beale Davis, ed., *William Fitzhugh and His Chesapeake World, 1676–1701* (Chapel Hill, N.C., 1963), 382; Carr and Walsh, "Economic Diversification and Labor Organization," in Innes, ed., *Work and Labor,* 176–181.

the workloads of men and women. In the Lowcountry, masters generally counted a slave woman as a three-quarter share, and she was tasked accordingly. In the Chesapeake, large planters divided their workforces into men's and women's gangs. In some operations, clear demarcations arose in the field labor of men and women. In clearing land, for example, men wielded axes, whereas women and boys removed the shrubs. In 1761, a tree felled by Lowcountry slave men killed a slave woman who was standing nearby. Women and children, asserted a Virginian transplanted to the Alabama frontier in the early nineteenth century, were "a dead expense," because the primary need was for axmen. Restoring a plantation, just as much as establishing one, was seen as men's work. Thus, in 1786, a Chesapeake overseer wrote to his employer, asking for more men, "women being of little use in Repairing a Plantation."[84]

Working alongside black women in the fields were boys and girls. Although the age at which a child entered the labor force varied from plantation to plantation, most masters in both Chesapeake and Lowcountry regarded the years of nine or ten as marking this threshold. To be sure, some slave children began working as early as age six or seven, and even younger children were groomed for domestic labor. From about age nine to fifteen, the young slave became a half-share. Black children, unlike their enslaved mothers, do not seem to have been singled out for any more onerous duties than their white counterparts. Those white children who left home to become servants in husbandry in early modern England generally did so at age thirteen to fourteen. However, they had probably been working for neighboring farmers on a nonresident basis from as young as seven.[85]

---

84. Carman, ed., *American Husbandry,* 275; De Brahm, *De Brahm's Report of the General Survey,* ed. De Vorsey, 94; Herndon, *Tatham,* 11, 101–102; distribution of axes to men and hoes to both men and women in Plantation Journal, 1773, Wragg Papers; John Drayton to James Glen, Oct. 11, 1761, Glen Papers, USC; William B. Beverly to Robert Beverly, June 9, 1831, Sept. 13, 1834, Beverly Family Papers, as cited in Steven F. Miller, "Plantation Labor Organization and Slave Life on the Cotton Frontier: The Alabama-Mississippi Black Belt, 1815–1840," in Berlin and Morgan, eds., *Culture and Cultivation,* 155–169; Alexander Brown to Col. Edmund Berkeley, Mar. 11, 1786, Berkeley Family Papers, microfilm, CW. The practice of men's clearing the land and women's cultivating was widespread in Africa (Hermann Baumann, "The Division of Work according to Sex in African Hoe Culture," *Africa,* I [1928], 289–319).

85. In a list of slaves, males were divided into those "that works" and "boys that dont work" (aged 9 or younger) (A list of the Negros in Saint Peter's Parish, New Kent, Oct. 2, 1736, Custis Family Papers, VHS). When the South Carolina Assembly considered a measure for cleaning the streets of Charleston, boys and girls older than 9 were considered eligible (J. H. Easterby, ed., *The Journal of the Commons House of Assembly, November 10, 1736–June 7, 1739,* Colonial Records of South Carolina [Columbia, S.C., 1951], 288). For halfshares, see A List of Slaves belonging to Mr. Edward Ambler sent to Indian Creek, Feb. 12,

Slave children no doubt undertook the same chores that fell to most rural children. David George, who was born in Essex County, Virginia, in about 1740, recollected that the first work he did was fetching water and carding cotton. Presumably, this was at an early age, for he also recalled, "Afterwards I was sent into the field to work about the Indian corn and tobacco, till I was about 19 years old." Johann Bolzius noted how Lowcountry slave children were used for various small jobs, such as hoeing potatoes, feeding chickens, and scaring birds from rice and grain. In the case of tobacco cultivation, a wider-ranging role could be envisaged, for, as Adam Beatty explained, "between the planting and cutting of tobacco, the labor of attending to it is light, but very tedious." Consequently, "weak hands and children can assist and do much of the work." Certainly, this is what the traveler Robert Sutcliff saw in September 1804 when he visited a plantation near Richmond, Virginia. "In one field near the house, planted with tobacco," he counted "nearly 20 women and children, employed in picking grubs from the plant."[86]

Just as masters in both regions had similar attitudes about how their slaves should work in the fields, the slaves themselves went about their fieldwork in similar ways. From cultural preference and custom, and because they were denied beasts of burden, slaves in both regions carried objects on their heads. The most extensive and persistent evidence of head porterage in North America comes from the Lowcountry. In a standard account of pre-Revolutionary rice cultivation, slaves were said to carry the crop out of the fields on their

---

1755, Dabney Family Papers, microfilm, CW; and List of Negroes at Buckingham County, Aug. 1, 1778, Richard Corbin Miscellaneous Papers, microfilm, CW. None of the children aged under 11 years owned by Jefferson in 1774 or Washington in 1799 was listed as a hand, but half of those aged 11 to 12 and nearly all those over 13 worked (Betts, ed., *Jefferson's Farm Book*, 77, 15–18 [facsimiles]; John C. Fitzpatrick, ed., *The Writings of George Washington from the Original Manuscript Sources, 1745–1799*, XXXVII [Washington, D.C., 1940], 256–268). A 16-year-old boy was said to have "been taskable these 3 years past," and a 13-to-14-year-old slave girl had "been in the field some time" (Thomas Washington's sale of slaves to William Clay Snipes, June 6, 1789, Miscellaneous Records, ZZ, 7–9). William Tatham declared that Virginia slave children were "big enough for the plough from ten (though more frequently twelve) years old" (*Communications concerning Agriculture*, 55). Ann S. Kussmaul, *Servants in Husbandry in Early Modern England* (Cambridge, 1981), 70–72. Edmund S. Morgan suggests that slave children were made to start work earlier than free children, but his evidence is inconclusive (*American Slavery, American Freedom*, 310); see, instead, Kulikoff, *Tobacco and Slaves*, 402.

86. "An Account of the Life of Mr. David George, from Sierra Leone in Africa . . . ," *Baptist Annual Register*, I (1790–1793), 473; "Bolzius Answers a Questionnaire," trans. and ed. Loewald et al., *WMQ*, 3d Ser., XIV (1957), 257, 236; Adam Beatty, *Southern Agriculture, Being Essays on the Cultivation of Corn, Hemp, Tobacco, Wheat, etc.* . . . (New York, 1843), 118; Robert Sutcliff, *Travels in Some Parts of North America* . . . (New York, 1811), 50.

PLATE 14. *Residence of George Heinrick Repold, Lexington Street near Fremont Avenue. Baltimore. Henrietta Metta Weachse. Circa 1822. A slave engaged in head porterage in a Chesapeake town. Courtesy Maryland Historical Society*

heads. In 1762, a South Carolina slave woman was "lately seen with a pail of water on her head upon Trott's point." A half-century later, John Lambert saw blacks carrying wood in the same manner. Numerous nineteenth- and early-twentieth-century photographs of Lowcountry blacks portray them carrying firewood, baskets, and jugs on their heads. In the Lowcountry, African Americans widely used the "head tote" basket, a prototypical African form, whereas American Indians generally preferred the "burden basket" strapped to the back and Europeans the cross-handle basket gripped by hand.[87] The practice of bearing loads on the head can still be observed in this part of North America to this day.

But eighteenth-century Chesapeake slaves also engaged in the practice, al-

---

87. Doar, *Rice and Rice Planting*, 20; Thomas White, *SCG*, Jan. 16, 1762; John Lambert, *Travels through Lower Canada and the United States of North America, in the Years 1806, 1807, and 1808*, 3 vols. (London, 1810), III, 18, also II, 378; Dale Rosengarten, "Spirits of Our Ancestors: Basket Traditions in the Carolinas," in Michael Montgomery, ed., *The Crucible of Carolina: Essays in the Development of Gullah Language and Culture* (Athens, Ga., 1994), 150; and Rosengarten, "The Lowcountry Basket in a Global Setting" (paper presented at College of Charleston conference, May 1995). For a pictorial representation of this practice in the mid-19th century, see *Scribner's Monthly*, VIII (June 1874), 129–160; for photographs, see Orrin Sage Wightman and Margaret Davis Cate, *Early Days of Coastal Georgia* (St. Simons Island, Ga., 1955), photograph opp. 123; Edith M. Dabbs, *Face of an Island . . .* (New York, 1971), photographs of Adelaide Washington, "Bringing home some firewood," "Big Dick Middleton," "Cabin on Fuller Place," and Mrs. Green.

though it seems to have died out in the nineteenth century. In 1755, Moravians in North Carolina encountered "a negro servant who followed them back, bringing on his head a basket of potatoes." In Virginia, a pregnant slave was excused carrying "weights on her head or shoulders." Directed to tie a neighbor's seedling peach trees in bundles and bring them home, two slave men did so "on their heads." One Virginia manager was "astonished" to see slave women running more than a mile with baskets of corn on their heads. In 1783, Richmond's public jail required its slave laborers to perform the distasteful task of "carrying upon their heads, the buckets of Excrement and urine three or four times a day to the River." In 1799, Henry Hull saw slaves carrying rails in this manner. And, in the early nineteenth century, Henry Knight was surprised to see Virginia slaves going "twenty or thirty rods, twenty or thirty times every day, to a spring-house, and tote up a tub or huge stone jar, upon their heads, on which they sustain all weights."[88]

An observer of head carrying in the West Indies speculated on its effects on the slaves' body movements. He argued that the habit had "its full and beneficial effect upon the figure of the negroes generally and is the cause of that uprightness of carriage so peculiar to the whole race." We may reject this racial stereotype and yet still speculate whether head carrying—a learned custom—facilitated the "pliability and ease" of movement that this observer described. Scientific investigations have confirmed that Africans who carry heavy burdens on their heads with apparent ease have mastered a walking technique that conserves energy. They have learned to use the body more economically as a pendulum during locomotion. Another West Indian observer commented on the "erect position and firmness of step in walking" that characterized slave women. An erect carriage might also have owed something to the way working women carried their children. In Africa, a mother generally toted her child, who was held by a piece of cloth, on her back, thereby allowing her to work. A Lowcountry resident observed the same behavior in the rice fields. Slave mothers, almost immediately after delivering their children, went to work with their infants "tied on their backs with a bandage."[89]

---

88. Adelaide L. Fries, ed., *Records of the Moravians in North Carolina*, I (Raleigh, N.C., 1922), 144; Greene, ed., *Carter Diary*, 554, 897, 895; William A. Rose to Governor of Virginia, July 2, 1783, *Calendar of State Papers and Other Manuscripts*, III (Richmond, Va., 1883), 504; "Memoirs of the Life and Religious Labours of Henry Hull," *Friends' Library*, IV (1840), 260–261; Knight, *Letters from the South*, 76–77. Landon Carter also mentioned that one of his slaves made 28 "head-baskets" for the corn harvest; these could hold two bushels (Greene, ed., *Carter Diary*, 523, 639).

89. Woodville K. Marshall, ed., *The Colthurst Journal: Journal of a Special Magistrate in the Islands of Barbados and St. Vincent, July 1835–September 1838* (Millwood, N.Y., 1977), 53; "Slight Change in Gait Makes Burden Lighter," *New York Times*, May 30, 1995; C. Richard

Slaves in both regions not only walked in the same way but also conceived of work and time in similar fashion. When they wished to place an incident in the past, they often recalled a natural or social activity with which it was associated. They referred to important seasonal events: before "the Potatoes were all frozen," when "the last great snow" happened, or during "the late gust." They also measured their work according to a lunar division of time. Thus, Sandy, a Virginia slave who had made two crops for his master, spoke of being "absent from his service two moons," while Ned, a South Carolina slave, claimed that "he was stolen from where he was sawing about the last full moon." Most commonly, slaves denoted time by referring to an agricultural activity. Slaves spoke of running away "when they put corn in the ground to plant," "since the planting of corn," "when rice was planting last," and "when he had done cutting rice." One slave recalled that her husband died "at the pulling of corntime." The difference in reckoning time between the European and the African is neatly illustrated by the statement of Robert Wells that two slaves taken up by him "came from the Southward about Midsummer 1773, or, as can be gathered from them-selves, when corn was about three feet high." Some of these slaves could express their thoughts adequately in English, demonstrating that, for many eighteenth-century slaves, a new language had been grafted onto a frame of reference that, in some respects, remained African. It was a frame of reference that reckoned time largely by the agricultural calendar.[90]

In due course, assimilated Africans and native-born slaves came to refer to past time in more European terms. They spoke of events that occurred weeks, months, or years in the past. Christian festivals, so important to their work lives, became important dates. Committed to the Alexandria jail in June, mu-

---

Taylor, "Freeloading Women," and N. C. Heglund et al., "Energy-Saving Gait Mechanics with Head-Supported Loads," *Nature*, May 4, 1995, 17, 52–54; [Trelawney Wentworth], *The West India Sketch Book*, 2 vols. (London, 1834), II, 68; James Barclay, *The Voyages and Travels of James Barclay, Containing Many Surprising Adventures, and Interesting Narratives* (Dublin, 1777), 25; Bascom, "Acculturation," *Am. Anth.*, XLIII (1941), 48.

90. South Carolina Council Journal, no. 17, part 1, 49, 60; William Gregory, *VaG* (Rind), Oct. 19, 1769; John Daniel, ibid., Sept. 22, 1768; Hannah Weaver, *SCG*, Nov. 9, 1767; Workhouse, ibid., Sept. 7, 1765; Workhouse, ibid., Oct. 30, 1762; Printer, ibid., Nov. 11, 1756; Workhouse, *SCG and CJ*, Dec. 30, 1766; John Davis, *Travels of Four Years and a Half in the United States of America* . . . (Bristol, 1803), 237, 413; Robert Wells, *SC and AGG*, Dec. 9, 1774. For other references to agricultural activities, see Workhouse, *SCG and CJ*, Mar. 6, 1770; and John Hutchins, *SC and AGG*, Nov. 19, 1778. For more on time reckoning, see A. Irving Hallowell, "Temporal Orientation in Western Civilization and in a Pre-literate Society," *Am. Anth.*, XXXIX (1937), 660; Paul Bohannan, "Concepts of Time among the Tiv of Nigeria," *Southwestern Journal of Anthropology*, IX (1953), 251–262; and Mechal Sobel, *The World They Made Together: Black and White Values in Eighteenth-Century Virginia* (Princeton, N.J., 1987), 15–67.

latto Charles reported leaving his Cumberland County quarter on New Year's Day; lodged in the South Carolina workhouse in October, African-born Prince said that he had "been runaway since last Christmas." Even when they were most precise about past events, work was usually central to the slaves' measurement of time. Thus, a Virginia slave named James Moore, whose "tongue [was] outlandish," remembered many of the masters and places where he had previously worked. In the "summer of 1774," for example, he recalled that he had "made a crop with mrs. Best on Nansemond River." Similarly, a South Carolina slave named Tom, also an African, recalled a whipping seven years earlier that prompted his flight. After living in the woods for two years, Tom agreed to work for a North Carolina master "for victuals and cloths." He remained there five years, until obliged to pay for his own clothes out of his Sunday earnings. Work and conventional time reckoning went hand in hand.[91]

Just as Tom's sense of injustice at having to work Sundays in order to pay for his clothes inspired him to seek a change of master, so work more generally informed the ideological convictions of slaves. Slaves were well aware that they constituted the bedrock on which their regional economies rested. Nor were they reticent in laying claims to the fruits of their labor. Traveling around the Chesapeake, Richard Parkinson conversed with slaves to understand their view of the world. They declared "their mind very freely," he noted, saying, "Massa, as we work and raise all, we ought to consume all." To underline the point, they continued, "Massa does not work; therefore he has not equal right: overseer does not work; he has no right to eat as we do." Such a perspective explains slaves' attitude to theft. As Edmund Botsford had his fictional South Carolina slave, Sambo, put it: "I hear some black people say, though it been harm to steal from stranger, it been no harm to steal from master."[92]

Field hands in both Chesapeake and Lowcountry shared a great deal. Most obviously, they participated in a preindustrial work regime, using many of the same agricultural implements and working to the dictates of crop rather than clock time. Their work became more regular over the course of the century, although they never became clock-punching automatons. The composition of their labor forces, particularly arranged along gender and age lines, was similar in the two regions. Slaves even moved in the same ways, conceived of work and

91. Michael Gretter, *VaG* (Rind), June 20, 1771; Workhouse, *SCG and CJ*, Oct. 16, 1770; Micajah Wills, *VaG* (Purdie), Oct. 20, 1775; John Ancrum, *SC and AGG*, Apr. 2, 1778. I count 64 slaves, advertised as captured in 18th-century South Carolina newspapers, who used some form of time reckoning. The ratio of unconventional (moons, agricultural activities, and so on) to conventional (years, months, weeks, specific dates) time reckoning was 1:5. For the 23 captured slaves in Virginia, the ratio was 1:7. Despite similarities in both regions, standard time reckoning was more widespread among Virginia slaves.

92. Parkinson, *A Tour in America*, II, 432–433; Botsford, *Sambo and Tony*, 24.

time in like manner, and shared a widespread sense of self-esteem and political assertiveness deriving from their work. These characteristics, however, were what many field hands shared throughout the Americas. The centrality of field labor in the slaves' experience ensured these similarities.

But once the perspective shifts from the general to the particular—especially the pace, seasonal rhythm, and intensity of a work routine—the two regions stand in stark relief. Rice, and to a lesser extent indigo, became known as slave crops; tobacco and even more so wheat were often free whites' crops. These contrasting reputations rested in large part on the much longer production schedules and the far more grueling and unpleasant fieldwork of both rice and indigo as compared to tobacco and wheat. The pace of tobacco cultivation was slow and deliberate; rice cultivation reached breakneck, almost killing speeds. Rice was a roller coaster, tobacco a slow-moving train.

But not all the contrasts were to the disadvantage of Lowcountry slaves. For the most part, technological innovations improved the lot of rice workers by lightening the load of the severest tasks and broadening skilled opportunities, whereas tobacco cultivation changed little over the century. Rice cultivation provided Lowcountry slaves with greater autonomy, more residential stability, and a chance to incorporate more African practices into their work routines than tobacco cultivation did for Chesapeake slaves. Finally, the rice worker's day sometimes ended in the early afternoon; the tobacco worker invariably toiled from sunup to sundown. As a consequence, the opportunity for a slave to work on his or her own account was considerably wider in the Lowcountry than in the Chesapeake.

Many Negroes discover great Capacities.

—Alexander Hewatt

4 : Skilled Work

Staple crops shaped the lives of field hands powerfully and directly, but their impact on slaves who had skills—whether managerial, artisanal, transportational, or domestic—was no less important. To a large extent, the technological, processing, and servicing requirements of the various staple economies determined how many slaves escaped fieldwork. It is important to know how many slaves had skills. It is also important to know what kinds of skills slaves possessed and what kinds of roles they played. Finally, it is most important to know whether the magnitude and composition of the skilled labor force changed over time or varied across space. An occupational structure can reveal much about a social structure.[1]

The numbers and functions of skilled slaves did vary both over time and across space. Over the course of the eighteenth century, the proportion of slaves with skills increased throughout the South, but more rapidly in the Lowcountry than in the Chesapeake. Drivers in the Lowcountry were more numerous and had greater powers than foremen in the Chesapeake. Likewise,

---

1. Herbert G. Gutman, "The World Two Cliometricians Made," *Journal of Negro History,* LX (1975), 99. [Alexander Hewatt], *An Historical Account of the Rise and Progress of the Colonies of South Carolina and Georgia,* 2 vols. (London, 1779), II, 97. "Skilled slave" is construed broadly to include not just craftsworkers but managers, transport workers, and household slaves—that is, the semiskilled and those with specialized roles.

slave craftsworkers threatened to monopolize some trades in South Carolina but never mounted a similar challenge in Virginia. By contrast, Virginia slaves exhibited a greater range of skills than their Carolina counterparts. Among the men, there were more ironworkers, shipwrights, tailors, and millers; among the women, there were more dairymaids, seamstresses, and spinners. Finally, although skilled slaves throughout the South introduced some African influences into their work, the opportunities to do so were greater in the Lowcountry than in the Chesapeake.

In spite of these variations, many characteristics and abilities of skilled workers were much the same across the eighteenth-century South. The life cycle of skilled slaves varied little from Chesapeake to Lowcountry; the same hierarchy of woodworkers—ranging from the prestigious carpenter to the lowly sawyer—existed in both societies; throughout the South, men dominated the available skilled positions; everywhere, women's one real, albeit limited, opportunity to escape the fields was as a domestic; and the kinds of relationships that skilled slaves struck up with field slaves were similar whether in the Chesapeake or Lowcountry. Skilled work, like fieldwork, had variations and uniformities.

OCCUPATIONAL STRUCTURES

Over the course of the eighteenth century, opportunities expanded for North American slaves to learn a skill, assume a managerial position, transport goods, or become a domestic. As staple economies evolved, their technological, processing, and servicing demands required that more slaves be put to nonfield labor. Slaves had to make the barrels, put up the fences, move the products, supervise the field hands, and provide the domestic help that economic growth increasingly demanded.

The expansion of the skilled labor force was most evident in South Carolina. Lowcountry slaves, particularly slave men, escaped field labor on a significant scale. About one in six rural slave men worked outside the fields in the 1730s, rising to one in four by the 1780s and 1790s (see Tables 22 and 23). Occupational opportunities for rural slave women grew much more slowly. In the early eighteenth century, almost all Lowcountry slave women labored in the fields; by the end of the century, only about one in twenty escaped the drudgery of field labor, usually through work as a domestic. Skilled and semi-skilled work was largely male work.[2]

---

2. As is well known, inventories are biased in favor of older and wealthier householders. Nevertheless, there are two reassuring pointers to the representativeness of the inventoried sample. First, the inventories that list skilled slaves are a representative cross-section of all inventories. Second, 65 advertisements of sale, covering the period 1765–1774, are available for inventoried estates that mention no skilled slaves. Of the 3,269 adult slaves offered for

The growth of skilled work in South Carolina can be explained in various ways. First, the most dramatic rise in the proportion of nonfield-workers occurred in the 1780s and 1790s, when average estate size was largest. Thus, the larger the plantation, the more opportunities for skilled work.[3] Conversely, the midcentury dip in the proportion of nonfield-workers reflects Lowcountry planters' response to the depression in the rice economy. They diversified their operations not only by raising more livestock and by branching out into alternative crops but by reducing investments in specialized slave skills. Second, urban growth was important to the expansion of skilled work in South Carolina, for occupational opportunities were considerably greater—by a factor of three to four—in an urban than a rural setting. Slave women, in particular, benefited from the urban demand for their services; by the end of the century, at least a third of the women listed in Charleston inventories held specialized posts.[4] Third, the significant expansion in the occupational opportunities for slave men, which occurred over the course of the century, took place less in crafts than in agricultural management, transportation, and domestic work (see Table 24).

---

sale, about 541 were said to have a skilled or specialized post. If the sale notices are accurate, 1 in 7 slave women and 1 in 3 slave men on these estates were exempt from fieldwork. These exceed the proportions available from the inventoried slave sample.

Sellers undoubtedly exaggerated slave skills. Henry Laurens, for example, found that one of his newly purchased coopers was "a bungler" and observed that many planters "call Negroes Tradesmen at Vendues, merely to run up the price" (*Laurens Papers*, V, 568). Another South Carolina planter was chagrined to find that his recently purchased plowman "says he cannot plough, that he never did plough and has only had the plough horse a little." But note that this last purchaser refrained from calling the seller dishonest, because he acknowledged that "negroes will sometimes deny their qualifications" (Timothy Ford to Henry Izard, Jan. 31, 1808, Ford-Ravenel Papers, SCHS). Furthermore, recourse to the law was always available to masters who had been deceived in their purchases. Jacob Valk gained substantial damages in 1773 when he proved that the slave boy whom he had recently bought was neither "a Cook, a Manager of Horses [nor] a compleat Waiting Man" (Charles Frazer Commonplace Book, 110–111, CC). Although advertisements of sale were undoubtedly exaggerated, there were restraints on wholesale deception.

3. Anecdotal information confirms the high skill levels present on large estates in the latter half of the 18th century. When Henry Laurens established a plantation in the mid-1760s, he advertised for "two negro carpenters, two coopers, three pairs of sawyers, 40 field negroes, young men and women, some acquainted with indico making" (Henry Laurens, *SCG*, Feb. 23, 1765). If a single, skilled indigo maker is assumed, Laurens proposed that, of a male labor force of about 35, 11 (almost one-third) would hold specialized positions. See my "Black Society in the Lowcountry, 1760–1810," in Ira Berlin and Ronald Hoffman, eds., *Slavery and Freedom in the Age of the American Revolution* (Charlottesville, Va., 1983), 97n, for further examples.

4. Philip D. Morgan, "Black Life in Eighteenth-Century Charleston," *Perspectives in American History*, N.S., I (1984), 189–203.

TABLE 22.
Skilled Slaves among Inventoried South Carolina Adults, 1730–1799

	Adult Men		Adult Women	
Decades	No.	% Skilled	No.	% Skilled
Rural Slaves				
1730s	382	15	227	*
1740s	784	13	472	4
1750s	1,647	12	1,200	2
1760s	1,526	14	1,061	3
1770s	2,026	15	1,530	4
1780s	1,185	26	1,182	5
1790s	969	26	971	6
Urban Slaves				
1730s	17	23	18	11
1740s	44	66	26	11
1750s	56	50	49	16
1760s	92	73	67	34
1770s	125	63	98	17
1780s	189	66	119	31
1790s	56	71	51	51

*Less than .5%

Note: For an earlier version of this table, which contains a more detailed breakdown of skills but did not differentiate closely enough between urban and rural residence, see my "Black Society in the Lowcountry, 1760–1810," in Ira Berlin and Ronald Hoffman, eds., *Slavery and Freedom in the Age of the American Revolution* (Charlottesville, Va., 1983), 99, 101, 103.

Sources: Records of the Secretary of the Province, 1730–1736, Inventory Books, II–CC, and Charleston District Inventory Books, A, B, C, SCDAH.

In the early eighteenth century, nearly all Chesapeake slaves worked in the fields. At this time, most Chesapeake plantations were generally too small to support even a few nonfield-workers. In Prince George's County, Maryland, in 1733, an estimated 9 of 10 slave men, and almost every slave woman, worked as a field hand (see Table 25). Even a large Virginia planter like Robert "King" Carter put all but 14 percent of his slave men into the field. In 1733, when his estate was inventoried, only about 1 in 10 of his slave men practiced a craft.

TABLE 23.
Skilled Workers among South Carolina Runaway Slaves, 1730–1799

	Adult Men		Adult Women	
Decade	No.	% Skilled	No.	% Skilled
Rural Slaves				
1730s	384	7	75	8
1740s	432	11	93	4
1750s	617	9	163	1
1760s	1,095	12	157	4
1770s	1,398	14	263	7
1780s	726	19	257	9
1790s	489	23	135	10
Urban Slaves				
1730s	38	21	18	5
1740s	60	43	35	9
1750s	58	38	31	6
1760s	113	50	46	20
1770s	207	43	47	19
1780s	144	41	58	15
1790s	135	44	49	2

Note: For an earlier version of this table, which contains a more detailed breakdown of skills but did not differentiate closely enough between urban and rural residence, see my "Black Society in the Lowcountry," in Berlin and Hoffman, eds., *Slavery and Freedom*, 99, 101, 103.

Sources: Charleston Library Society, *South Carolina Newspapers, 1732–1782*, microfilm. For the years after 1782, see my "Black Society in the Lowcountry," in Berlin and Hoffman, eds., *Slavery and Freedom*, 100, 102, 104.

There were 43 "foremen" on Carter's forty-eight quarters—a further 17 percent of the adult male labor force—but these men undoubtedly worked in the fields and probably did little more than set the pace for their respective gangs. Only 1 of 178 women worked outside the fields, and she was a cook.[5]

5. Chesapeake inventories rarely mention slave skills, and the advertisements for runaways are far more unrepresentative of the broader slave population in Virginia than in South Carolina. The small size of the captive population reported in Virginia newspapers,

After about 1740, occupational opportunities for Chesapeake slaves began to expand. This growth was most evident in the tidewater, with occupational opportunities for piedmont slaves lagging behind those of the seaboard at least up to the American Revolution. The expansion of skills should not be exaggerated. A search of the inventories of five Virginia counties between 1740 and 1779 revealed no more than forty-nine skilled male slaves on twenty-seven separate estates. These skilled slaves were part of labor forces that averaged fourteen adults; estates listing no skilled slaves averaged only five adults. Similarly, among the more than two thousand slaves owned by the gentry in Baltimore County, Maryland, between 1660 and 1776, only twenty-two merited the mention of a skill. Likewise, fewer than 5 percent of plantations in Kent and Talbot Counties before 1760 included slaves characterized as having a skill. In the Chesapeake, particularly Maryland, local merchants and planters could draw upon a large pool of free artisans.[6]

Obviously, the expansion of occupational opportunities for Chesapeake slaves was closely linked to the rise of large plantation units. More than a fifth of all men on five large Chesapeake plantations in the late colonial era worked as craftsmen; and an additional one-sixth of all men on five early national estates worked in semiskilled and domestic positions (Table 25). In fact, it has been estimated that nearly a quarter of all slave artisans and a third of the domestics in Virginia during the 1780s were trained on the plantations of a mere forty gentlemen.[7] Because large units were much more unrepresentative of the average Virginia plantation than was the case in South Carolina, skill levels among slaves were correspondingly lower in the Chesapeake than in the Lowcountry. As late as the eve of the American Revolution, only about 7 percent of the enslaved male labor force in Prince George's County, Maryland, held semiskilled or craft positions (Table 25).

Although skilled occupations were open to fewer slaves in Virginia than in

---

and of advertised runaways as a whole, account for this unrepresentativeness. See Gerald W. Mullin, *Flight and Rebellion: Slave Resistance in Eighteenth-Century Virginia* (New York, 1972), 40, 94–96.

6. The inventories of Chesterfield, Essex, Goochland, Spotsylvania, and York Counties were searched in this investigation. Charles G. Steffen, *From Gentlemen to Townsmen: The Gentry of Baltimore County, Maryland, 1660–1776* (Lexington, Ky., 1993), 55; Jean B. Russo, "Self-sufficiency and Local Exchange: Free Craftsmen in the Rural Chesapeake Economy," in Lois Green Carr, Philip D. Morgan, and Jean B. Russo, eds., *Colonial Chesapeake Society* (Chapel Hill, N.C., 1988), 389–432, esp. 409–410; and Russo, *Free Workers in a Plantation Economy: Talbot County, Maryland, 1690–1759* (New York, 1989), esp. 92–95; Christine Daniels, "'Wanted: A Blacksmith Who Understands Plantation Work': Artisans in Maryland, 1700–1810," *WMQ*, 3d Ser., L (1993), 743–767, esp. 748.

7. Allan Kulikoff, *Tobacco and Slaves: The Development of Southern Cultures in the Chesapeake, 1680–1800* (Chapel Hill, N.C., 1986), 399.

TABLE 24.
Occupations of Adult Male Slaves in the Rural Lowcountry, 1730s–1810

		Proportion		
Occupation	1730s[a]	1760–1770s[b]	1780s[c]	1780–1810[d]
Agricultural	85%	83%	79%	76%
Field hands	85	81	74	69
Drivers	0	2	4	4
Others	0	0	1	3
Tradesmen	15	16	17	14
Carpenters/coopers	9	8	8	7
Sawyers	4	7	5	6
Others	2	1	4	1
Semiskilled	0	0	2	3
Carters	0	0	*	2
Watermen	0	0	1	1
Domestics	0	1	1	8
House servants	0	0	0	4
Waiting men	0	0	1	1
Others	0	1	*	3

*Less than .5%. [a] $N = 382$. [b] $N = 109$. [c] $N = 1,185$. [d] $N = 322$.

Sources: 1730s, 1780s: Records of the Secretary of the Province, 1730–1736, Inventory Books, II–CC, and Charleston District Inventory Books, A, B, C, SCDAH.

1760s–1770s: Appraisement of the Goods and Chattels of Thomas Waties, Dec. 20, 1762, Vanderhorst Collection, SCHS; slaves at Fairfield Plantation, 1773, Fairfield Plantation Book, 1773–1797, SCHS; lists of Charles and George Ogilvie's slaves employed at Myrtle Grove and Belmont Plantations, 1775, Ogilvie-Forbes of Boyndlie MSS, Aberdeen University Library, Scotland.

1780–1810: Lists and Appraisement of Negroes belonging to Major General James Grant, East Florida, Jan. 17, 1781, bundle 250, Papers of James Grant of Ballindalloch, in ownership of Sir Ewan MacPherson-Grant, Bart., Ballindalloch Castle Muniments; schedule of Denys Rolle, Sept. 25, 1783, in Wilbur H. Siebert, ed., *Loyalists in East Florida, 1774 to 1785* (DeLand, Fla., 1929), II, 291–292; lists of Negroes belonging to Thomas Middleton on his plantations at the Combahee and Goose Creek, November 1784, Thomas Middleton Plantation book, UNC; return of the late Countess Dowager of Egmont's and Lord Arden's Negroes on the Plantation Cecilton, East Florida, Jan. 1, 1785, Add. MSS 47054A, BL; list of Negroes belonging to Dr. James Read, Jan. 26, 1786, James Read Papers, UNC; slaves at Fairfield Plantation, Nov. 1, 1789, Fairfield Plantation Book; list of Mr. Stead's Negroes, Mar. 24, 1803, C. C. Pinckney Collection, Duke; list of Negroes belonging to Colonel Stapleton at St. Helena, Mar. 15, 1810, USC.

TABLE 25.
Occupations of Adult Male Slaves in the Chesapeake, 1733–1809

	Proportion				
Occupation	1733[a]	1733[b]	1774[c]	1757–1775[d]	1784–1809[e]
Agricultural	95%	86%	92%	70%	65%
Field hands	90	69	82	70	60
Foremen	2	17	4	*	1
Others	3	0	6	0	4
Tradesmen	4	12	5	21	21
Carpenters/coopers	4	7	3	9	10
Sawyers	0	4	0	2	0
Others	0	1	2	10	11
Semiskilled	0	2	1	3	4
Carters	0	*	*	3	3
Watermen	0	2	*	*	1
Domestics	1	*	1	4	10
House servants	1	*	1	2	6
Others	0	*	0	2	4

*Less than .5%. [a] N = 1,323. [b] N = 243. [c] N = 2,037. [d] N = 409. [e] N = 382.

Sources: 1733 (first column), 1774: Allan Kulikoff, *Tobacco and Slaves: The Development of Southern Cultures in the Chesapeake, 1680–1800* (Chapel Hill, N.C., 1986), 385, 400.

1733 (second column): Inventory of estate of Robert Carter, November 1733, VHS.

1757–1775: List of Negroes belonging to Hon. William Byrd, July 1757, Misc. MSS Collection, LC; list of tithables belonging to George Washington, June 4, 1761, Papers of George Washington, 5th Ser., Financial Papers, microfilm, LC; lists of slaves belonging to Colonel Custis, 1771, Custis Papers, VHS; list of Thomas Jefferson's slaves, 1774, Edwin Morris Betts, ed., *Thomas Jefferson's Farm Book, with Commentary and Relevant Extracts from Other Writings,* American Philosophical Society, Memoirs, XXXV (Princeton, N.J., 1953), 15–18; inventory of Philip Ludwell's estate, 1774–1775, Lee-Ludwell Papers, VHS.

1784–1809: List of Negroes belonging to Edmund Randolph in Charlotte County, Sept. 25, 1784, microfilm, CW; list of slaves belonging to George Washington, Feb. 18, 1786, in Donald Jackson and Dorothy Twohig, eds., *The Diaries of George Washington* (Charlottesville, Va., 1976–1979), IV, 277–283; list of slaves belonging to Robert Carter of Nomini Hall, 1791, Robert Carter Letter Book, XI, 1–15, Duke; appraisement of the estate of Benjamin Harrison, July 1791, Brock Collection, microfilm, CW; a list of John Tayloe's slaves, Jan. 1, 1809, in Richard S. Dunn, "A Tale of Two Plantations: Slave Life at Mesopotamia in Jamaica and Mount Airy in Virginia, 1799 to 1828," *WMQ,* 3d Ser., XXXIV (1977), 52.

South Carolina, the range of skills among Chesapeake slaves was wider, reflecting the greater diversity of plantation life in the Chesapeake. In the late colonial Chesapeake, there were almost as many slave shoemakers, blacksmiths, shipwrights, tailors, bakers, millers, and masons as there were carpenters and coopers. George Mason's memory probably did not deceive him when he recalled that his father in the 1770s "had among his slaves carpenters, coopers, sawyers, blacksmiths, tanners, curriers, shoemakers, spinners, weavers and knitters, and even a distiller."[8]

THE LIFE CYCLE OF SKILLED WORKERS

Acquiring a skill, or assuming a specialized position, set apart a minority of slaves from their fellows. Masters sometimes singled out slaves for privileged posts at remarkably young ages—as early as five or six years. More commonly, they transferred their slaves from the field into nonfield posts at rather late ages: in their middle to late twenties or older. Although some slaves were apprenticed to craftsmen in their teens—the typical pattern among skilled free labor—most slaves entered the nonfield labor force either much earlier or much later than free persons.

The grooming of house servants, particularly personal servants, occurred at the earliest possible age. The phrase "bred from infancy" advertised many an accomplished waiting man and maid. Boys and girls aged anywhere from six up could qualify for the designation "house slave." Boston King, a black Methodist preacher, recollected that he was "six years old" when he "waited in the house upon [his] master" on a Lowcountry plantation. In offering a family of four for sale, a South Carolina master singled out the eldest child, an eight-year-old girl, as "now very useful in a family." Youthful slave children occasionally attended white children only a few years their junior and thereby gained domestic experience. In the Custis household in 1771, a ten-year-old slave boy "wait[ed] on Jacky," while a twelve-year-old girl was "Miss Patey's maid." Runaway domestics were much younger than other nonfield fugitives. About a third of house servants, compared to only one-tenth of craftsmen or water-

---

8. Edmund S. Morgan, *Virginians at Home: Family Life in the Eighteenth Century* (Charlottesville, Va., 1963), 53; Kulikoff, *Tobacco and Slaves,* 398. Eighteen of the 34 slave craftsmen found in the late colonial inventories of the five counties mentioned in note 6 were non-woodworkers. For bakers, see inventory of Col. Richard K. Winterpock, 1764, Chesterfield County Wills, no. 1, 414; and inventory of James Webb, Apr. 17, 1775, Essex County Wills, no. 13, 2–10. For weavers, see inventory of Zachary Taylor, March 1768, Orange County Wills, no. 2, 391; and inventory of Col. Tarlton Fleming, Mar. 3, 1778, Goochland County Deeds, no. 12, 102. For millers, see inventory of Fleming, Mar. 3, 1778, ibid.; inventory of Thomas Graves, June 1768, Spotsylvania County Wills, D, 334; inventory of Elizabeth Scott, February 1770, Isle of Wight County Wills, no. 8, 39; and inventory of Capt. Edward Wilkinson, Mar. 21, 1773, Chesterfield County Wills, no. 3, 41, VSL.

TABLE 26.
Age of Runaway Skilled Workers, 1732–1779

Occupation and Colony (N)	Proportion of Runaways by Age Group				
	15–19	20–29	30–39	40–49	50–59
Woodworkers					
South Carolina (53)	9%	49%	25%	9%	8%
Virginia (41)	6	45	23	22	4
Other tradesmen					
South Carolina (75)	12	45	31	11	1
Virginia (40)	12	35	45	5	3
Watermen					
South Carolina (63)	16	46	24	11	3
Virginia (35)	9	46	37	9	0
Domestics					
South Carolina (58)	36	47	15	2	0
Virginia (47)	28	43	23	6	0

Sources: Charleston Library Society, *South Carolina Newspapers, 1732–1782*, microfilm; Lathan A. Windley, ed., *Runaway Slave Advertisements: A Documentary History from the 1730's to 1790*, I (Westport, Conn., 1983).

men, were in their teens when they ran away (see Table 26). Furthermore, only 5 percent or fewer of runaway domestics were aged thirty or more—much the lowest proportion of other nonfield-workers. Household duties and deportment, masters believed, were best learned at an early age.[9]

Physical maturity, however, sometimes led to a job change for a slave domestic. Hercules "formerly used to wait on his Master in Charlestown" and then became a cooper on a Goose Creek plantation; Adam, still a young man, had "been used to wait in the House for several years" but became a "fine

9. "Memoirs of the Life of Boston King, a Black Preacher," *Methodist Magazine*, XXI (1798), 106; David Denoon, *State Gaz of SC*, July 21, 1788; tradesmen belonging to the Estate and servants in and abt the House, 1771, Custis Papers, VHS; Robert Carter to Mrs. Priscella Mitchell, Dec. 25, 1786, Robert Carter Letterbook, VII, 168, Duke; Elizabeth Hutchings, *SCG*, July 12, 1760; Robert Wells, *SC and AGG*, Dec. 5, 1766; Printer, *SCG*, Sept. 24, 1763; Joseph Nicholson, ibid., Feb. 25, 1764; John Ford, *VaG* (Purdie), Jan. 17, 1777; Gabriel Jones, ibid. (P and D), June 30, 1774; Charles Yates, *VaG and WA*, Sept. 20, 1783; schedule of slaves at the Wateree, June 8, 1790, Drayton Family Papers, Historic Charleston Foundation; will of Samuel Kilpatrick, 1787, Charleston County Will Book, B, 1786–1793, 102–103, SCDAH.

shoemaker." In at least one instance, the slave took the initiative: still young and "chiefly accustomed to House Work," he declared his "aversion to be a Waiting Man" and instead "discover[ed] an inclination to the Carpenter's business." Slaves in their late teens or early twenties were described as ex-domestics. Joe, an African who "used to wait in a house," was eighteen years of age. A seventeen-year-old mulatto named Ben, formerly a waiting man, was relegated to the fields ostensibly for bad conduct, but perhaps his approaching adulthood played a role in his master's decision.[10]

The training of craftsmen and semiskilled workers could also begin early. In 1774, two slave boys, aged nine and eleven, belonging to Charles Carroll, were apprentice wheelwrights, while another fourteen-year-old boy was "learning to be a mason." Two years earlier, a Williamsburg mechanic advertised for two eighteen-year-old runaway "lads" who had been apprenticed to him for seven years and whose contracts were close to expiration. In 1775, Robert Carter of Nomini Hall listed a slave boy of thirteen as a carter, two boys aged fourteen as a miller and a cabinetmaker, respectively, and one of fifteen years as a sailor. A twenty-eight-year-old South Carolina slave was said to have "been a pilot at Winyaw 15 years"; and a cowpen keeper, described as a "remarkable clever fellow capable of taking the Management of any Stocks," probably owed his proficiency to his having "been bred up from his Infancy in this business." An eight-year-old boy served on board Robert Orr's Lowcountry schooner.[11] Heavy responsibilities were thrust on some slaves at young ages.

When a planter referred to the "regular apprenticeship" that his slave had undergone, he usually meant apprenticeship to a white craftsman, and this opportunity generally became available at about age sixteen or seventeen, much as for white youths. Thomas Jefferson thought slaves should "at age 16 go into the ground or learn trades." Robert Wormeley Carter carried out this injunction, almost to the letter. "Sent my Boy Billy to work under Guthrie for

---

10. Robert Hume, *SCG*, Oct. 28, 1732; John Jouet, *VaG* (D and H), Oct. 10, 1777; John Webb and Co., *City Gaz*, July 8, 1799; Archibald Ritchie, *VaG* (P and D), Aug. 6, 1772; Charles Atkins, *Royal Gaz*, June 20, 1780; James Carson, *City Gaz*, June 26, 1797. See also John Cabell, *VaG* (D and H), Dec. 12, 1777; Benjamin Branch, ibid., Mar. 12, 1779; and Kulikoff, *Tobacco and Slaves*, 405.

11. Charles Carroll Account Book, Carroll Papers, MHS; Matthew Tuell, *VaG* (P and D), June 11, 1772; Whites and Blacks living at Nomony Hall in Westmoreland County, Oct. 4, 1775, Carter Family Papers, VHS; Roger Pinckney, *SCG*, Aug. 3, 1767; John Graham to James Grant, June 2, 1767, bundle 401, Papers of General James Grant of Ballindalloch, sometime Governor of East Florida, in ownership of Sir Evan Macpherson-Grant, Bart., Ballindalloch Castle Muniments, Scotland; Robert Orr, *SCG and CJ*, June 7, 1768; list of Negroes at Green Spring, 1774, Lee-Ludwell Papers, VHS. For further South Carolina examples, see M. Allison Carll, " 'Great Neatness of Finish': Slave Carpenters in South Carolina's Charleston District, 1760–1800," *Southern Studies*, XXVI (1987), 94.

one year," he recorded in his diary of 1774; "he is constantly to keep him at his trade, and particularly to learn him to make wheels, I am to cloath him, he is 16 years of age last month."[12] Apprenticeships normally extended three years or more. Ignatius Digges of Prince George's County, Maryland, bound his mulatto slave, Jack, to William Nichols for four years so that he might learn the "Art or Mistery" of carpentry. Nichols contracted to provide meat, drink, clothing, lodging, and tools as well as "permitt the said apprentice to go on Sundays and Hollydas to church." One Virginia planter desired his manager "to put two of the most ingenious and likely young fellows of about 16 or 17 years old prentices for 3 or 4 years to the best country blacksmiths you have."[13]

By about the mid-eighteenth century, most slave artisans—both by the design of the master and through the initiative of slaves—learned their skills from other slaves rather than from whites. In the Lowcountry, the rapid emergence of large plantations, the extensive deployment of black craftsmen, and the general unavailability of white artisans quickened this process. As early as 1743, for example, the estate of one South Carolina planter listed two adult coopers, each with responsibilities toward a pair of "learners." Later in the century, a Lowcountry master even paid a reward of seven pounds to a slave cook for taking a slave boy under his tutelage. The practice of slaves' learning from other slaves, so well developed in the Lowcountry, probably explains Thomas Washington's description of his slave, who possessed "great Mechanical Abilities being a tolerable Carpenter, Cooper, and Bricklayer tho he never served a day to either trade." In the Chesapeake, apprenticeships to slave craftsmen did not become common until the late colonial period, when large

12. Edwin Morris Betts, ed., *Thomas Jefferson's Garden Book, 1766–1824, with Relevant Extracts from His Other Writings,* American Philosophical Society, *Memoirs,* XXII (Philadelphia, 1944), 77; Robert W. Carter Diaries, Dec. 1, 1774, typescript, CW. Robert Carter, however, once apprenticed a slave boy named Henry, aged 12, to a white tailor (Robert Carter Daybook, 1790–1792, Feb. 5, 1792, LC). Henry's age is mentioned in the lists of slaves, 1789–1793, Robert Carter Papers, Duke. In 1791, Henry was 11, the son of Sam Harrison, a 52-year-old waiter, and Judith Harrison, a 46-year-old housemaid. The term "regular apprenticeship" was often used: Benjamin Villepontoux, *SCG,* Oct. 22, 1763; Charles Yates to Capt. George Alison, Feb. 17, 1774, Charles Yates Letterbook, 51, microfilm, CW; Mullin, *Flight and Rebellion,* 87.

13. Articles of apprenticeship between Ignatius Digges and William Nichols, July 31, 1771, MS 446, MHS; William Lee to Cary Wilkinson, May 22, 1771, Lee-Ludwell Papers; apprenticeship agreement between Mary Cary and Nathaniel Hook, Mar. 30, 1717, Virginia Counties Collection, Warwick County Papers, W and M. In October 1781, Thomas Jones, a Maryland planter, bound out his slave Jack, aged 17 years, to a carpenter for four years (Thomas Jones Farm Books, 1779–1812, MHS). In 1797, John Oxendine ordered that his slave boy Billy should be bound out to a trade at age 16 for five years (will of John Oxendine, Jan. 15, 1797, Charleston County Will Book, C, 1793–1800, 394–395, SCDAH).

home quarters had developed. In both regions, the emergence of a robust family life among slaves contributed to the transmission of skills, as slave fathers began to teach their skills to their sons.[14]

Although many domestics and some skilled workers assumed their posts at an early age, age-profiles indicate that a large proportion of slaves holding specialized positions were middle-aged or older. Drivers and foremen were at least in their late twenties before they assumed their posts. Before a slave could be appointed to a supervisory position, he had to acquit himself well, either as a prime field hand or as a responsible craftsman. A quarter of the slaves in their forties on one early-nineteenth-century Virginia plantation and 40 percent of those in their forties, fifties, and sixties on a number of early-nineteenth-century Lowcountry plantations were nonfield-workers (see Table 27). Even among runaway slaves, who were much younger than the general slave population, 40–50 percent of the skilled and semiskilled workers were thirty years or older (Table 26).[15]

Why were skilled workers so much older than the general slave population? First, if a master placed an African in a nonfield position, he was almost always an adult. In attempting to build up his East Florida estate, Richard Oswald, a slave trader, made a rare acknowledgment of indigenous African skills. He directed his "Agents in Africa to send a few, *full grown Men* (not exceeding 10 in Number) in case they can light of such as have been used to the Trades of that country, believing they will soon become useful and handy in a new Plantation." Second, masters more often used American-born slaves for nonfield-work, but few could afford to train such individuals from an early age. They were forced either to purchase trained slaves, usually from their gentlemen neighbors, or "retire" an experienced slave of their own, and in both cases the slave would have been a mature adult. This practice helps explain why only

---

14. Inventory of James St. John, June 22, 1743, Inventory Book, WPA, CXIV, 257–259, 261, SCDAH; H. W. DeSaussure and T. Ford Cash Book, Apr. 1, June 21, 1799, SCHS; Thomas Washington to William Clay Snipes, June 6, 1789, Miscellaneous Records, ZZ, 7–9, SCDAH; Kulikoff, *Tobacco and Slaves,* 403. For the transmission of skills through slave families, see Chapter 9.

15. Runaway advertisements, inventories of estate, and plantation listings provide information on the ages of 15 drivers and foremen. Only 3 were below the age of 40, and only 1 was below the age of 30. He was Esseck, aged 25, "a Jobing Carpinter, Driver eca," listed in the claim of Samuel Bonneau, Sept. 23, 1785, Forfeited Estates Papers, SCDAH. Less precise age material—mention of "old" drivers, for example—supports this conclusion. From advertisements for sale, hire, or running away, Carll documented the ages of 166 slave carpenters in Charleston district between 1760 and 1800. She found that 77% were under age 30, by far the most youthful profile of skilled slaves so far discovered. It may be that sale and hire notices disproportionately featured young artisans (" 'Great Neatness of Finish,' " *So. Studies,* XXVI [1987], 94).

TABLE 27.
Age of Skilled Male Slaves, 1730–1809

	Proportion of Skilled Slaves				
	Chesapeake			South Carolina	
Age Group	1730–1769	1770s, 1791	1810	1758–1776	1800–1810
15–19	1%	12%	9%	8%	0%
20–29	6	30	31	13	13
30–39	6	22	30	13	26
40–49	10	16	24	18	39
50–59	10	16	14	31	38
60+	3	0	0	71	38
Overall	6	23	19	19	24

Sources: 1730–1769: Kulikoff, *Tobacco and Slaves*, 404.

1770s, 1791: Carroll Account Book, 1773–1774, MHS; list of Robert Carter's slaves, 1791, Carter Letterbook, XI, 1–15, Duke.

1810: Slaves belonging to William Fitzhugh, 1810.

1758–1776: Inventory of the estate of Col. Alexander Vanderdussen, Apr. 4, 1758, Inventory Book, T, 1–2; inventory of George Austin's estate, Nov. 16, Dec. 6, 1774, Inventory Book, WPA, XCVIII, 65–71; inventory of Samuel Waddingham's estate, Sept. 27, 1776, Inventory Book, WPA, XCVIII, 223–224.

1800–1810: List of Negroes belonging to James Grant; inventory of the estate of Hercules Daniel Bize, Apr. 22, 1800, Inventory Book of Charleston District, C, 470; conveyance of slaves from Mrs. Mary Turnball to Thomas Cooper Vanderhorst, July 30, 1805, Vanderhorst and Duncombe Collection, Bristol Record Office, England; list of Negroes belonging to Colonel Stapleton, Mar. 15, 1810, USC.

6 percent of the slave men in their twenties and thirties of the predominantly small plantations of eighteenth-century Prince George's County, Maryland, were craftsmen, whereas on large Chesapeake estates the proportion was well over 20 percent (Table 27). Third, skilled slaves were older than most slaves because they survived longer. On most Lowcountry estates, skilled workers formed a third or more of the slaves aged upward of fifty years. Whereas the average age of six skilled slaves belonging to Thomas Spriggs, a Maryland planter, was a remarkable fifty-eight, his nonskilled bondmen averaged thirty-three years of age. Finally, masters retired field hands to specialized posts as their productivity in the field diminished. Of the four men aged sixty years or more on John Stapleton's Saint Helena estate in 1810, three probably began life

as field hands: a former driver aged eighty-two, a "superannuated" gardener aged seventy-nine, and a herdsman and carter aged sixty.[16]

The aging of a skilled or semiskilled slave rarely led to a reversion or conversion to field labor; rather, many skilled slaves mastered more than one trade or assumed other specialized roles during their lives. By the time one Lowcountry mulatto artisan ran away, he was able to "follow the Business of a Tanner, Shoemaker, Sadler, Carpenter, or Wheelwright"; another Lowcountry slave, a good waterman, was also an adept "sawyer and brick-moulder and has been frequently employed in a plantation as a driver"; a third, a "shoemaker by trade," was also "a good fisherman and seinemaker." If anything, Chesapeake tradesmen boasted even more accomplishments. A thirty-year-old blacksmith was also "a compleat wheelwright ... and likewise a good cooper, sawyer, and house-carpenter"; twenty-six-year-old Bob was an "extraordinary" sawyer, a "tolerable good" carpenter and currier, a shoemaker, and a "very good" sailor; young David—a waiting man, hostler, gardener, barber, plowman, and woodworker—clearly merited the accolade of being "a very clever, active brisk Fellow"; and Peter, "by Trade a good House Carpenter," was also a cooper, bricklayer, plasterer, whitewasher, and gardener.[17] Versatility was the hallmark of the eighteenth-century skilled slave.

DRIVERS AND FOREMEN

The most important post on a plantation was that of driver or foreman. However, slave superintendents were not found on all estates, nor were their duties and responsibilities uniformly defined. Rather, a region's staple production and the availability of white overseers largely structured the extent and nature of the managerial opportunities available to slaves.

Chesapeake slaves rarely achieved supervisory status in the eighteenth century. Tobacco production was best accomplished by small groups of laborers. Most units were so small that masters involved themselves and their sons in cultivating the crop. The availability of white laborers also created a sizable pool from which overseers could be drawn. For all these reasons, the need for a slave who did anything more than keep the hands moving was much reduced. As a result, at best one-third of slaves in a typical Chesapeake county worked under

---

16. Richard Oswald to James Grant, May 20, 1767, bundle 295, Papers of General James Grant of Ballindalloch (my emphasis); list of slaves of Thomas Sprigg's estate, c. 1780s, Mercer Family Papers, VHS. Because this list of 77 slaves seems to represent only part of a plantation, it is not used in Table 27.

17. Robert Johnston, *SCG*, Apr. 18, 1774; John Wilson, ibid., Jan. 19, 1760; William Marshall, ibid., Sept. 21, 1767; A. McRae, *Md Gaz*, May 24, 1754; William Trebell, *VaG* (P and D), Apr. 16, 1767; Thomas Gaskins, ibid., Nov. 5, 1772; John West, ibid., Sept. 15, 1774.

black foremen. The term "driver" was not even used in the eighteenth-century Chesapeake. Slaves with supervisory roles were usually designated "foremen" or "captains," occasionally "overseers." None of the estate inventories registered in six Virginia county courts listed a slave foreman, and only one such slave was advertised as a runaway in eighteenth-century Virginia newspapers.[18]

Only on large estates, at least during the first half of the eighteenth century, were Chesapeake slaves employed as foremen. At the turn of the century, Middlesex County's premier family, the Wormeleys, had a quarter named after a slave, presumably to indicate that he supervised that unit. Henry Thacker, in his will of 1704, recommended that his "Doctor Jack" be "Imployed to Look after the rest of the . . . Negroes" with "provisions Equall to an overseer." In 1725, when James Bray, a large planter of York County, made his will, he referred to a number of his quarters by the name of an individual slave. Apparently, Dubblerun, Nero, Debb, and Jacko oversaw the operation of the quarters that bore their names. In the early 1730s, the richest Virginian of his day, Robert "King" Carter, employed forty-three foremen at his many quarters. His son Landon also ran two of his quarters by means of slave overseers.[19]

Not until the Revolutionary era, however, when white out-migration was extensive in tidewater and some piedmont counties and when some slaveholding units had reached manageable sizes, did less wealthy planters begin to follow the gentry's lead. In 1768, apparently for the first time, the grand jury of York County warned five planters for "not keeping [white] overseers on their plantations"; sixteen years later, the Dismal Swamp Land Company of Virginia appointed "one of the old [Negro] fellows" to the position of foreman, because, in the manager's words, "it is difficult to get an overseer there that will do right";

---

18. The inventories found in the court records of York, Essex, Spotsylvania, Goochland, Chesterfield, and Amelia Counties formed my sample. The one runaway overseer, Tom Salter, is mentioned below.

19. Middlesex County Wills, 1698–1713, 113–131, 161, as cited in Darrett B. Rutman and Anita H. Rutman, *A Place in Time: Middlesex County, Virginia, 1650–1750* (New York, 1984), 166, 187; will of James Bray, Nov. 18, 1725, as cited in James P. McClure, "Littletown Plantation, 1700–1740" (master's thesis, College of William and Mary, 1977), 49; inventory of estate of Robert Carter, November 1733, VHS. At the Fork quarter, Jack Lubbar was an "overlooker" in the late 1750s and early 1760s, Fork Jammy was the foreman from the early 1760s onward, and Old Charles succeeded him in 1769 and promptly lost the position to George in 1770, who was in turn replaced briefly by Simon in 1771. At the Mangorike quarter, Jack Lubbar was foreman in the 1730s, and Mangorike Will or Billy held the same position in the 1760s and 1770s. Harry was a foreman for an unnamed quarter in 1757. This information was compiled by searching all the references to these men in Jack P. Greene, ed., *The Diary of Colonel Landon Carter of Sabine Hall, 1752–1778*, 2 vols. (Charlottesville, Va., 1965) (hereafter cited as *Carter Diary*).

and fears of a slave rising in Powhatan County in 1793 were based on evidence that "several of the negro foremen of the different plantations had run away."[20]

These few slave foremen in the eighteenth-century Chesapeake also had circumscribed roles. Setting the pace for a gang of laborers was the Chesapeake slave foreman's primary responsibility. Thus, Landon Carter described his foreman Will as "a most principal hand"; on one occasion, Carter noted how he had watched another foreman working in the corn rows a little ahead of his gang; and, when Jack Lubbar became too old to carry out his supervisory duties, Carter told him to "fall astern of the rest," indicating that he then worked at the hoe. Tom, belonging to George Washington, was a foreman because he was "exceeding healthy, strong, and good at the hoe." A slave named Tom, and "by some called Tom Salter," who "managed several years as an overseer..., under Capt. Robert Downman, at a plantation... on Morattico creek, in Richmond county," was "well made for strength." A slave advertised in the lottery schemes of late colonial Virginia was "a fine gang leader," but his value was placed considerably below that of a number of tradesmen.[21]

A few Chesapeake slaves were more akin to managers than mere gang leaders. Such seems the implication of a description of a Virginia slave as an "Excellent Leader and indeed a good Overseer." A slave advertised for sale in Maryland in 1771 was represented as a shoemaker, mower, sawyer, and one who "perfectly understands the management of tobacco." Perhaps Edmund Bagge of Essex County allowed "Negro Cromwell overseer" to take charge of all aspects of his tobacco production. In 1730, Cromwell, with nineteen shares, apparently made more pounds of tobacco per head than a white overseer, operating with the same number of hands, two years later. Whether Cromwell was then relegated to a mere field hand is unclear. If so, however, Cromwell would probably not have been surprised, for Chesapeake foremen were first and foremost prime field laborers.[22]

In the Lowcountry, the term "driver" was current, and slave supervisors were far more in evidence than in the Chesapeake. In a typical Lowcountry parish around midcentury, at least two-thirds of the adult slaves—twice as

---

20. York County Court Order Book, 1768–1770, June 20, 1768, VSL; John Driver to David Jamieson, June 10, 1789, Dismal Swamp Land Company Papers, Duke; Robert Mitchell to Colo. John Marshal, Sept. 23, 1793, Executive Papers, VSL.

21. Greene, ed., *Carter Diary*, 308, 431, 430, 439, 840; John C. Fitzpatrick, ed., *The Writings of George Washington from the Original Manuscript Sources, 1745–1799*, 39 vols. (Washington, D.C., 1931–1944), II, 437; Henry Lee, *VaG* (P and D), Mar. 9, 1769; Mullin, *Flight and Rebellion*, 84.

22. *Watson and Ux* v. *Cockes*, c. late 1740s, Legal Papers of Nicholas Wythe, 1740–1759, no. 564, UVa; *Maryland Journal, and the Baltimore Advertiser*, Dec. 2, 1777; Edmund Bagge Account Book, 1726–1733, May 1731, April 1733, microfilm, CW.

many as in the Chesapeake—worked under drivers.[23] The contrast with the Chesapeake can be explained by the relatively large and growing size of plantations, the widespread absenteeism of masters, particularly during summer, and the small and declining pool of available white overseers. The difference is evident in the responses of white citizens in each region. In the Chesapeake, few local grand juries complained of the threat posed by widespread black management; in the Lowcountry, the complaints were persistent and vocal. As early as 1726, South Carolina planters were enjoined to employ one white man for every ten slaves. However, as a letter to the *South-Carolina Gazette* in 1742 testified, this act met with much "discouragement" and "various Pretences" aimed at its subversion.[24]

Even more impressive was the openness with which South Carolina planters thwarted these regulations concerning resident whites. Advertising for his four African runaways, Isaac McPherson stipulated that they should be returned "to the driver on the plantation"; when William Hambleton predicted the probable destination of his runaway, delicacy did not prevent him naming the plantation of an illustrious neighbor or from describing it as one where "there is no white man"; and, in disposing of the estate of John Seabrook, George Saxby acknowledged that he had shipped three inferior barrels of indigo because he was "afraid it might be stole[n] by the Negroes, there being no white person at the Plantation." Necessity accounted for this candor. Thus, in 1768, when James Grant requested a Carolinian overseer for his East Florida estate, his agent, John Graham, had to report that he had "sent all over Carolina almost, for Overseers," but could find none.[25]

---

23. For the statistical procedures employed here, see Philip D. Morgan, "The Development of Slave Culture in Eighteenth-Century Plantation America" (Ph.D. diss., University College London, 1977), 117–118.

24. Thomas Cooper and David J. McCord, eds., *The Statutes at Large of South Carolina*, 10 vols. (Columbia, S.C., 1836–1841), III, 272, also VII, 413; letter to editor, *SCG,* Nov. 8, 1742. For persistent complaints, see Grand Jury Presentments for the province, Nov. 23, 1754, South Carolina Council Journal, no. 23, 174–175, SCDAH; Grand Jury Presentments for the province, Mar. 15, 1758, Court of General Sessions Records, SCDAH; several of the inhabitants of the parish of Saint Thomas, *SCG,* Apr. 3, 1762; Grand Jury Presentments for the province, ibid., June 2, 1766; Benjamin Smith and John Weight, *SCG and CJ,* Feb. 12, 1771; Presentments of the Grand Jury of Beaufort District, *SCG,* Jan. 17, 1774, *SC and AGG,* Jan. 16, 1777, and *State Gaz of SC,* May 12, 1777. For the continuation of these complaints into the post-Revolutionary era, see Morgan, "Black Society in the Lowcountry," in Berlin and Hoffman, eds., *Slavery and Freedom,* 119.

25. Isaac McPherson, *SCG,* July 6, 1769; William Hambleton, *SC and AGG,* July 28, 1775; inventory of John Seabrook, Aug. 13, 1750, Inventory Book, WPA, CXXVI, 544–546; John Graham to James Grant, Mar. 1, 1768, bundle 401, Papers of General James Grant of Ballindalloch.

Drivers were ubiquitous, but they were not homogeneous. One identifiable type was a man in his thirties, often single, and able to practice a trade or trades. A tradesman, it seems, was also an eligible driver. Thus, when searching for a northern farmer to be his overseer, Edward Hyrne countenanced the appointment of "cooper Andrew" to the position should his quest fail. The monetary value of driver-tradesmen, such as Elizabeth Rose's "driver and jobbing carpenter" and Benjamin Godin's "cooper and driver," was extremely high. Indeed, Jack belonging to Richard Cochran Ash and John belonging to Samuel Waddingham, both driver-tradesmen, exceeded the appraised value of all other slaves on their respective plantations by large margins. Such drivers were often versatile, none more so than Esther Glaze's driver, who not only understood the "making of indico [but was] also a good cooper, a jobbing carpenter, butcher and market man."[26]

The other type of driver was rather elderly, with a large family, and often rated less than most field hands. Appraisers valued the four drivers belonging to the estates of Alexander Hext and John McKenzie at prices that even female field hands exceeded. A listing of an early-nineteenth-century Lowcountry estate revealed but one driver for 104 slaves (or forty-five taskables), and he was both an old man and a mere half-hand. The wives of many of these elderly drivers often had specialized roles. A number of drivers' wives were either cooks or seamstresses to the plantation slaves. Perhaps the driver's authority was enhanced when his wife was exempt from field labor and when her work—in dispensing communal food or attending to the slaves' clothing—reinforced his position. Such seems to have been the case with the minister Boston King's parents. His father was an African who "had the charge of the Plantation as a driver for many years," and his mother "was employed chiefly in attending upon those who were sick, having some knowledge of the virtue of herbs, which she learned from the Indians. She likewise had the care of making the people's clothes, and on these accounts was indulged with many privileges which the rest of the slaves were not."[27]

---

26. [Elizabeth Poyas], *The Olden Time of Carolina* (Charleston, S.C., 1855), 88; inventory of Elizabeth and Margaret Rose, July 21, 1769, Inventory Book, Y, 114–115; inventory of Benjamin Godin, June 21, 1749, Inventory Book, WPA, CXXIV, 170–185; inventory of Richard Cochran Ash, June 6, 1770, Inventory Book, Y, 289–291; inventory of Samuel Waddingham, Sept. 27, 1776, Inventory Book, WPA, XCVIII, 223–224; Esther Glaze, *SCG*, Mar. 9, 1765. See also inventory of James Michie, Dec. 16, 1760, Inventory Book, WPA, CLXI, 734–736; James Donnom and Thomas Bee, *SCG and CJ*, Jan. 1, 1771; inventory of John Bulline, May 21, 1772, Inventory Book, &, 88–89; inventory of James Simmons, June 1, 1775, ibid., 567–569; and inventory of Elizabeth Lessene, Aug. 14, 1775, Inventory Book, WPA, XCIXA, 66–71.

27. Inventory of Alexander Hext, Feb. 4, 1771, Inventory Book, Y, 382; inventory of John McKenzie, Aug. 9, 10, 1771, Inventory Book, WPA, CLXXXIV, 105–112; list of slaves, c. 1806,

The families of married drivers were often the largest on the plantation. George Austin's driver, George, was fifty-five years of age and had five children living with him; Jehu Elliott's driver had two wives and also boasted five children; Ralph Izard's driver headed a family group of eleven slaves. Having a family might have helped secure the driver his post, because it probably indicated stability and maturity to the master. A Georgia planter acknowledged the advantage that family status conferred when, after purchasing a South Carolina gang, he singled out "the two fellows with the families [who were] born on [the] plantation" as the ones best "capable of the Management of a plantation themselves." At the same time, a driver was better able to support a large family than other slaves. Certainly, mere aging did not disqualify a driver from fulfilling his functions; indeed, as a patriarchal head of a large family, his authority appears to have waxed rather than waned. Such slaves, possessing an authority that derived as much from their age and patriarchal status as from the mandate of the estate, formed a significant proportion of Lowcountry drivers.[28]

Drivers were significant authority figures in slaves' lives. Will, a recent African immigrant, could not "tell his Master's name," but reported his driver's name as Mingo. Another African, "by what can be learnt of the workhouse negro who can talk with him," observed that his master had two plantations, "that on the one he came from the driver's name [was] Robin and on the other the driver's name [was] Scipio." Two slaves from Calabar described their master—rather unflatteringly—as a "lusty man with a big belly," but they knew the name of their driver. One slave even supplied a snippet of personal information about his driver, remarking that "the fellow who overlooks them is lame in one knee and named Bosue or Boatswain." Even an infirm driver could do

---

Ford-Ravenel Papers, SCHS. For elderly drivers with large families, see, for example, inventory of John Edwards, Nov. 8, 1770, Inventory Book, Y, 337–341; inventory of Joseph Fabian, June 23, 1773, Inventory Book, &, 273–276; and inventory of Daniel Ravenel, Sr., 1775, ibid., 623. A 1779 listing of the slaves belonging to the Bethesda Orphanage included a 45-year-old driver named Adam and his wife, Susan, who "mends and makes the childrens cloaths" (A 3/2/2, A 3/2/4, Countess of Huntingdon's American Papers, Westminster College, Cambridge, England). One of George Austin's slaves who "managed the planting" had a wife who was "employed in the making of butter and raising of poultry" (Josiah Smith, Jr., *SCG and CJ*, Apr. 26, 1768). "Memoirs of Boston King," *Methodist Mag.*, XXI (1798), 105–106.

28. Inventory of George Austin, Nov. 16, 1774, Inventory Book, WPA, XCVIII, 65–67; inventory of John Elliott, Mar. 27, 1762, ibid., LXXXVIIA, 242–243; inventory of Ralph Izard, Mar. 21, 1761, ibid., CLXVI, 124–125 (and 827–840 for other Izard driver with large families); John Graham to James Grant, Mar. 1, 1768, bundle 401, Papers of General James Grant of Ballindalloch. See also inventory of James Postell, Aug. 4, 1773, Inventory Book, &, 287–288; inventory of Hugh Thomson, Dec. 21, 1774, ibid., 480–483; inventory of Dr. Thomas Caw, Mar. 8, 1773, Inventory Book, WPA, CLXXXVI, 498–502; inventory of John Izard, Apr. 4, 1781, ibid., C, 381–384.

his job; and, if by no other means than making his name known, the Lowcountry driver registered an impression on most slaves. Masters might remain shadowy figures, but drivers could not be ignored. Indeed, one South Carolina owner, in advertising for five runaways, acknowledged, "As they are all new negroes, they may not be able to tell their own or their master's names, their overseer's name is *John Hopkins,* and the negro driver's *Tom,* which they probably may know."[29]

Some drivers made their presence felt by acting in a harsh and vindictive manner. A disturbance on Richard Hutson's plantation in 1767 involved an unusual three-way power struggle. A group of field hands who came to town in order to complain to Hutson "said they had nothing to say against [their overseer], but that Paul [the driver] had a spight against them and endeavored to set [the overseer] against them." Because "all their complaint was against Paul and he was in Town," Hutson confronted his driver, who "acknowledged the greater Part of it." Occasionally, these plantation power struggles erupted into violence. One slave who ran away at planting time left "on account of ill usage from a negro driver called Peter." An African fugitive mentioned that his plantation was "directed by a driver named Prince, who abused and imposed on him." Undue severity from black managers led Henry Laurens to recommend the replacement of "cow skins" with "switches," because the former were "generally esteem'd bad weapons in the hands of a Negro driver." Violence between driver and field hand did not flow in one direction only. In 1775, Jemmy ran away from his plantation at the Saltketchers "after beating his driver." Six years later, field hands on a Johns Island plantation attacked their drivers "with hoes, axes and poles."[30]

But it seems unlikely that most drivers were irrevocably estranged from their fellow slaves. It is difficult to see how they could have been effective managers otherwise. Their absence from the ranks of runaway slaves suggests that their situation rarely became intolerable. The advanced years of many drivers indicate that their authority rested on more than naked threats or brute

---

29. Workhouse, *SCG,* May 24, 1760, Oct. 30, 1762; Workhouse, *SCG and CJ,* May 27, 1767, Dec. 2, 1766; Daniel Ravenel, ibid., Feb. 25, 1772. See also Workhouse, ibid., Feb. 4, 1766; ibid., Jan. 13, 1767; ibid., July 4, 1769; ibid., Sept. 12, 1769; ibid., Apr. 17, 1770, supplement; ibid., May 8, 1770; Henry Laurens, *SC and AGG,* Dec. 19, 1776; John McPherson, *Columbian Herald, or the Independent Courier of North-America* (Charleston), June 15, 1786; and Workhouse, *State Gaz of SC,* Mar. 27, 1794.

30. Richard Hutson to Mr. Croll, Aug. 22, 1767, Charles Woodward Hutson Papers, UNC; the Printer, *SCG,* Nov. 11, 1756; Elias Horry, *Charleston Courier,* Mar. 23, 1805; *Laurens Papers,* V, 200; James Donnom, *SC and AGG,* June 16, 1775; a Correspondent, ibid., Jan. 20, 1781. In another power struggle, it appears that the drivers and two white overseers allied in opposition to a new general manager (Arthur Middleton to Mr. Butler, Sept. 1783, Arthur Middleton Papers, SCHS).

force. Henry Laurens, for example, described one of his drivers, old Cuffy, as "kind and wise." A black patroon, or skipper, on a trip up the Cooper River in 1749, spoke of the hospitality of the plantation drivers who put him up in their houses on successive nights. More than likely, then, most drivers sought alliances among the field hands and fellow slaves.[31]

The most spectacular example of cooperation between driver and field hands has, as its central figure, a slave named Andrew. When the British held Savannah during the Revolutionary war, he "carried off all Mrs. Graeme's Negroes that were then in Prince William's Parish; and Mrs. Graeme could not get them back, until she made terms with Andrew." Some fifteen years later, driver Andrew had lost nothing of his former authority, for he was then described as the "most influential fellow in the gang" of slaves from "Ca Ira" plantation, belonging to J. and W. B. Mitchell. In March 1796, he led away the entire gang, some seventy slaves; eight months later, only one slave had been apprehended, although evidence of their camps had been found a mere quarter of a mile from a plantation mansion in Prince William Parish (Andrew's home during the war); and Andrew himself had been sighted fishing in full view of that plantation. By year's end, the Mitchells had become so exasperated at the influence of this adroit pied piper of slaves that they offered a thousand-dollar reward for the gang's return.[32]

Drivers and foremen appear to have had firm roots in the slave community. This sense of allegiance might have been particularly strong among Virginia foremen, who were generally no more than prime field hands. But even though the South Carolina driver was more of a manager, he also had to establish close ties with his workforce. Occasionally, this close relationship exploded into recriminations and open violence, but for the most part drivers identified and allied themselves with their charges.

ARTISANS

Just as large planters tended to employ slave foremen and drivers, so they aimed for a measure of autarky in crafts. In the Lowcountry, James Grant observed how "in established Plantations, the Planter has tradesmen of all kinds of his Gang of slaves and 'tis a Rule with them, never to pay Money for what can be made upon their Estates, not a Lock, a Hing or a Nail if they can avoid it." In the Chesapeake, Isaac Weld noted: "The principal planters . . . have nearly everything they can want on their own estates. Amongst their slaves are found taylors, shoemakers, carpenters, smiths, turners, wheelwrights, weavers,

---

31. *Laurens Papers*, VIII, 399; South Carolina Council Journal, no. 17, part 1, 78–79. Running away, or rather lack of running away, by drivers and foremen is documented in Chapter 6. Andrew, noted in note 32, below, is an exception.

32. J. and W. B. Mitchell, *City Gaz*, Nov. 10, 30, 1796.

tanners, etc." If the intent was much the same, the only difference was in the greater range of skills available on large Chesapeake estates.[33]

Another difference was how extensively slaves monopolized crafts in the two regions. As early as 1734, the ruling authorities of South Carolina expressed concern at how "many Negroes are now train'd up to be Handicraft Tradesmen, to the great discouragement of Your Majestys White Subjects." Thirteen years later, a Lowcountry resident reported: "So it goes through all Carolina; the negroes are made to learn all the trades and are used for all kinds of business. For this reason, white people have difficulty in earning their bread there." Slaves filled, but never monopolized, craft positions in the Chesapeake. Few complaints were heard, either from white artisans or on their behalf, about slaves' dominating trades. In Talbot County, Maryland, for instance, more than eight hundred independent craftsmen found employment between 1690 and 1760. Although these numbers declined over time, the cause was less competition from slaves than the growing skills of ordinary planters. The slave tradesmen owned by the occasional large planter and the part-time craftsworkers owned by small planters, Jean Russo observes, had "no more than a limited impact" on independent artisans. Even though coopering and shoemaking were declining trades for free craftsmen, the demand for wheelwrights, blacksmiths, and tanners remained steady, whereas employment for house carpenters, bricklayers, and joiners expanded modestly over time.[34]

33. James Grant to the Duke of Athole, Feb. 12, 1768, bundle 2, Letterbook, Papers of General James Grant of Ballindalloch; Isaac Weld, Jr., *Travels through the States of North America...*, 2 vols. (London, 1799), I, 147. For more references to widespread slave skills, see "Johann Martin Bolzius Answers a Questionnaire on Carolina and Georgia," trans. and ed. Klaus G. Loewald et al., *WMQ*, 3d Ser., XIV (1957), 218–261; Governor James Glen, An Attempt Towards an Estimate of the Value of South Carolina..., March 1751, Records in PRO Relating to the Value of South Carolina, XXIV, 303–330, SCDAH, and conveniently reprinted in H. Roy Merrens, ed., *The Colonial South Carolina Scene: Contemporary Views, 1697–1774* (Columbia, S.C., 1977), 177–191, esp. 183; *The Letters of Hon. James Habersham, 1756–1775*, GHS, Collections, VI (Savannah, Ga., 1904), 101; and Johann David Schoepf, *Travels in the Confederation [1783–1784]*, trans. and ed. Alfred J. Morrison, 2 vols. (Philadelphia, 1911), II, 221.

34. The Humble Remonstrance of Your Majesty's Governor, Council and Assembly of South Carolina, Apr. 9, 1734, in Elizabeth Donnan, ed., *Documents Illustrative of the History of the Slave Trade to America*, Carnegie Institution of Washington Publication no. 409, IV (Washington, D.C., 1935), 288; Yates Snowden, "Labor Organization in South Carolina, 1742–1861," University of South Carolina, *Bulletin*, XXXVIII (1914), 7; Russo, "Self-sufficiency and Local Exchange," in Carr, Morgan, and Russo, eds., *Colonial Chesapeake Society*, 389–432; and Russo, *Free Workers in a Plantation Economy*. For another excellent county study, see Christine Marie Daniels, "Alternative Workers in a Slave Economy: Kent County, Maryland, 1675–1810" (Ph.D. diss., The Johns Hopkins University, 1990). Thad W. Tate has contrasted, to good effect, the different responses of white artisans to the threat of black

The availability of white craftsmen in the Chesapeake and their scarcity in the Lowcountry seems to have resulted in different apprenticeship practices. In the Lowcountry, if a planter wished to place his slave under a white artisan, he had to pay a large sum for the privilege. In 1769, Daniel Slade summoned William Coachman to court for failing to pay him thirty-five pounds for instructing Coachman's slave Matthias in the trade of house carpentry. Three years later, the estate of one South Carolina planter paid John Fullerton a hundred pounds "for undertaking to learn Boy Dick the Carpenters Trade." In Virginia, conversely, the relation of supply and demand was often reversed. There, white artisans could pay for the services of slaves whom they instructed.[35]

The first trade to which slaves were assigned in any numbers was woodworking. In fact, until about the middle of the eighteenth century, almost all slave tradesmen were woodworkers, for theirs was the one craft that staple production required on a significant scale. In both the Lowcountry and the Chesapeake, barrels and hogsheads, schooners and flats, cabins and quarters had to be provided in large numbers. A hierarchy of skills quickly emerged within the woodworking fraternity. The elite carpenters fetched the highest prices, carried out the most varied and skilled tasks, and enjoyed a measure of itinerancy, whereas sawyers were but a step above field hands. Sawyers might graduate to carpentry, but not easily. Thus, a master who rated his slave a "good sawyer" also mentioned that he "handles his tools so well in the coarser branches of that trade" that he might make "a tolerable country carpenter." The three most valuable slaves inventoried in colonial South Carolina were all carpenters.[36]

By the late eighteenth century, some slaves had become master carpenters. In 1785, one Lowcountry owner described his carpenter as "capable of taking charge of any number of negro carpenters." In the late-eighteenth-century Chesapeake, George Washington appointed a head slave carpenter who made plantation implements, built simple structures, and directed other carpenters. Some slave carpenters developed highly specialized skills. A skilled coachmaker, housewright, carver, wheelwright, and painter, James was "as good a

---

competition in Charleston and Williamsburg (*The Negro in Eighteenth-Century Williamsburg* [Williamsburg, Va., 1965], 40–41).

35. *William Coachman v. Daniel Slade,* Court of Common Pleas, Judgment Rolls, box 82A, 1769, no. 66A, SCDAH; account book of the Estate of John Cordes, May 17, 1772, WPA, typescript, 55, CC; John Baylor Ledger, Sept. 19, 1739, Aug. 11, 1742, Baylor Family Papers, microfilm, CW.

36. Negro sale, *SCG*, Mar. 9, 1767; James Fitch, ibid., June 1, 1765; inventory of Edward Fenwicke, Aug. 1775, Inventory Book, &, 627–628; inventory of James Postell, Aug. 4, 1773, ibid., 287–288. The three carpenters listed in these two inventories were valued at £2,000, £1,800, and £1,250, respectively.

joiner as any in Virginia." David, another Virginia tradesman, made chairs and, perhaps as a consequence, was "a proud trafficking fellow." A South Carolina woodworker earned the ultimate accolade for being a "master in several branches of the mechanical business, a compleat cabinet-maker, house-carpenter, wheelwright, and boat-mender."[37]

Sawing was the least valued woodworking skill. One Lowcountry sale notice, after describing the carpenters, coopers, and wheelwright, turned to "the field slaves [among whom] is a great proportion of as fine sawyers as any in the parish." Another Carolina master described his two runaways as "both sawyers and plantation slaves." Just as sawyers and field hands were sometimes lumped together, so sawing was thought an appropriate task for newly imported Africans. The six sawyers who ran away from their Lowcountry master in 1763 included one native-born and five Angolan slaves. But sawyers were generally more than glorified field hands. A Lowcountry overseer retained the services of two sawyers required by his employer because he "could not do without sawing and they was but three On the place that Sawd." Similarly, an East Florida planter bemoaned his lack of sawyers, though he owned many slaves, because few of his "People were broke in to sawing"; another listed his eight sawyers as tradesmen; and a third had a number of highly capable sawyers, including Caesar, who was "a sawyer, squarer—understands keeping saws in order and all branches of lumber." Slave sawyers could be in demand in Virginia, too, because Landon Carter hired two of them in one year.[38]

In the Lowcountry, most rural tradesmen who were not woodworkers were either leatherworkers or, more occasionally, bricklayers, brickmakers, and blacksmiths. Even as early as the 1730s, bricklaying slave families had emerged in the Lowcountry. On the eve of the Revolution, some masters owned many bricklayers. Few could surpass Edward Fenwicke, who employed six bricklayers and a blacksmith at his Johns Island plantation in 1775. Slaves not only laid but also made bricks. A slave who ran away from a brickyard in Christ Church Parish in 1767 was able, as his master pointed out, to "mould bricks." A

---

37. Conyers and Holmes, *State Gaz of SC*, May 23, 1785; Fitzpatrick, ed., *Writings of Washington*, XXXII, 263, XXXIII, 244; William Fitzhugh, *VaG or AA*, June 26, 1784; John Rodes, ibid., Nov. 13, 1784; James Witter, *SCG*, Mar. 20, 1784.

38. John Dutarque, *SCG*, Nov. 28, 1771; Andrew Deveaux, *SCG and CJ*, Apr. 7, 1772; Henry Smith, *SCG*, Nov. 19, 1763; John Couturier to John Colhoun, Jan. 14, 1793, John Ewing Colhoun Papers, USC; Dr. Turnbull to James Grant, Oct. 27, 1769, bundle 253, Papers of General James Grant of Ballindalloch; Siebert, ed., *Loyalists in East Florida*, II, 291; return of Egmont's and Arden's Negroes, Jan. 1, 1785, Add. MSS 47054A, BL; Greene, ed., *Carter Diary*, 967. In two listings of Thomas Pinckney's slaves taken in 1777, one described nine of his men as sawyers, and the other omitted to mention this occupational designation at all. Presumably, these nine slaves doubled as field hands (Lists of Negroes, Mar. 5, 1777, Thomas Pinckney Papers, LC).

generation later, owners touted the productivity of their slave brickmakers: John Dupont's brickmaker could make five thousand bricks a day, whereas James Kennedy's manufactured between five and six thousand a day.[39]

Charleston supported by far the most specialized craft concerns in the Lowcountry. Most South Carolina shipyards were located either in or near the city, and almost all were large employers of slave labor. In 1747, shipwright John Daniel employed eight slaves as ship carpenters, as did one of his successors, Alexander Russell, a quarter-century later. By 1776, John Langresh had built a large cooperage in the city, employing four "tight" coopers, six "common" or "ordinary" coopers, and even a cooper who doubled as a barber. In addition to these unusually large craft shops, the city hosted a wider range of trades than was available in the countryside. The city's grand jurors thought it "a very great GRIEVANCE" that "the manufacturing of Candles and Soap in Charles Town" was "generally left to Negroes by Night as well as by Day." The few slave tailors, butchers, bakers, and barbers who lived in the Lowcountry were generally to be found in the city, and the more esoteric trades of silversmithing, gunsmithing, harness-making, and chairmaking were confined to urban workers, some of them slaves.[40]

As urban growth and economic diversification gained momentum in the Chesapeake after about 1750, craft opportunities for slaves expanded. As in the

---

39. George Mitchell, *SCG*, Oct. 13, 1739; inventory of Edward Fenwicke, 1775, Inventory Book, &, 627–628; William Hopton, *SCG and CJ*, Aug. 25, 1767; John Dupont, *City Gaz*, Mar. 18, 1791; James Kennedy, *Columbian Herald*, July 7, 1788. For brickmaking, see Lucy Bowles Wayne, "Burning Brick: A Study of a Lowcountry Industry" (Ph.D. diss., University of Florida, 1992), esp. 51, 55; and Bradford L. Rauschenberg, "Brick and Tile Manufacturing in the South Carolina Low Country, 1750–1800," *Journal of Early Southern Decorative Arts*, XVII (1991), 103–113.

40. Inventory of John Daniel, Dec. 2, 1747, Inventory Book, WPA, CXXIII, 303; inventory of Alexander Russell, Mar. 6, 1771, ibid., CLXXXIV, 19–21. For more on shipyards, see inventory of Mary Yerworth, Aug. 16, 1756, ibid., CLIII, 922–924; and inventory of David Brown, June 10, 1765, Inventory Book, X, 40–41. Inventory of John Langresh, Jan. 31, 1776, Inventory Book, WPA, XCIXA, 89–90. For sample references to the four trades (tailor, butcher, baker, and barber) that were particularly common in an urban setting, see inventory of Alexander Smith, Nov. 12, 1745, Inventory Book, WPA, CII, 391–394; inventory of Abraham Crouch, Dec. 23, 1763, ibid., CLXIX, 12–14; inventory of John Kelly, Nov. 20, 1766, ibid., CLXXII, 665–666; and Robert Wells, *SCG*, June 9, 1763, and John Bothwell, *SC and AGG*, May 8, 1767, respectively. The grand jury presentments are in *SCG*, Oct. 31, 1774. For more esoteric trades: silversmith (inventory of Andrew Dupey, Sept. 10, 1743, Inventory Book, WPA, CXV, 317–318); gunsmith (John Dodd, *SCG*, Oct. 11, 1770); harnessmaker (Hans Ernest Hoff, ibid., Mar. 10, 1759); chairmaker (John Fisher, *SC and AGG*, Feb. 21, 1781); cabinetmaker (John Pacerow, *Gaz of State of SC*, Aug. 12, 1778); sailmaker (Eaton Rudolph, *SCG*, July 7, 1777); painter and glazer (Rawlins Lowndes, *SCG and CJ*, Jan. 30, 1770); chimney sweep (inventory of Ann Air, May 18, 1764, Inventory Book, WPA, CLXX, 162–167).

Lowcountry, shipyards began to make an appearance in the Chesapeake during the 1750s, with a pronounced concentration in the area around Norfolk. In fact, by the end of the colonial period, the Chesapeake region had replaced Philadelphia as the shipbuilding center second in importance to New England. Most Chesapeake shipwrights appear to have been significant employers of skilled black labor. Thirty-year-old Billie, "by trade a ship-carpenter," was so "proficient in that business as not only to repair but to build all sorts of small craft." Slave blacksmiths and leatherworkers became more widespread throughout the Chesapeake in the late colonial era, and the development of small-scale extractive service and craft industries such as mining, milling, ropemaking, saltmaking, and glassmaking also gave rise to new opportunities for slave workers.[41]

The development that typified the scale of diversification in the late colonial Chesapeake, one without parallel in the Lowcountry, was the growth of ironworking. Most blacks who worked in the few early Chesapeake ironworks of the 1720s and 1730s appear to have been relegated to such menial tasks as woodcutting. At an early date, however, slaves were envisaged as constituting the bulk of the labor force of these new establishments. In 1732, Alexander Spotswood told William Byrd that 120 slaves were needed to operate an ironworks successfully. Moreover, Spotswood "had contrived to do everything with his own people, except raising the mine and running the iron," but "believed that by his directions he could bring sensible negroes to perform those parts of the work tolerably well." Forty years later, Charles Carroll, part owner of the Baltimore Company ironworks, advised the purchase of "35 or 40 young, healthy and stout country born negroes" to replace the free wage laborers in order that the "Business . . . be carried on with more alacrity and fewer disappointments."[42]

Owners of Chesapeake ironworks followed the example and advice of men like Spotswood and Carroll. An iron furnace in Baltimore County, Maryland,

---

41. Joseph A. Goldenburg, *Shipbuilding in Colonial America* (Charlottesville, Va., 1976), 65, 118–120; Thomas Lawson, *VaG* (Rind), Feb. 9, 1769; Mullin, *Flight and Rebellion*, 94–96, 156, 185; Benjamin Harrison, *VaG* (P and D), Oct. 18, 1770; Edward Wilkinson, ibid., May 28, 1767. The Custis estate in 1771, Washington household in 1786, and Robert Carter's plantation in 1791 all had a slave miller. For sources, see Table 25.

42. Louis B. Wright, ed., *The Prose Works of William Byrd of Westover: Narratives of a Colonial Virginian* (Cambridge, Mass., 1966), 348, 358. For an early reference to the menial labor of slaves in ironworks, see [Fayrer Hall], *The Importance of the British Plantations in America to This Kingdom . . .* (London, 1731), 76; Charles Caroll to [Company], Dec. 8, 1773, as cited in Bernard Bailyn, *Voyagers to the West: A Passage in the Peopling of America on the Eve of the Revolution* (New York, 1986), 253. On South Carolina ironworks, see Ernest M. Lander, Jr., "The Iron Industry in Ante-Bellum South Carolina," *Journal of Southern History*, XX (1954), 337–355.

before midcentury employed one and a half times more slaves than white servants. By 1764, the proprietor of the Occoquan Ironworks in Virginia wrote to his agents in Scotland in search of "two good Forgemen to teach Negro Prentices"; and, later that decade, the most valuable slaves offered for sale in the various lottery schemes published in Virginia newspapers were "forgemen," "hammermen," and "finers" (finishers of iron). In 1766, three slaves ran away from a forge in Chesterfield County, Virginia. Stephen was a carpenter, and the other two were "fire-men," both of whom had "scars on their arms, from burns which they got by melted cinders flying on them when at work." One historian has counted about sixty-five ironworks in the late colonial Chesapeake, giving employment to perhaps as many as forty-five hundred slaves.[43]

The skill levels that characterized this sizable workforce far exceeded those of any other slave work group. In fact, ironmasters generally grouped more slaves in one unit than all but the largest Chesapeake planters. In Baltimore County, Maryland, in 1773, ironworks accounted for the six largest slaveholdings and 12 percent of the entire adult slave population. More than three-quarters of the seventy-four workers employed at the Snowden Ironworks in Anne Arundel County, Maryland, in 1768 were slaves, and 85 percent of the black men labored in specialized roles. Twenty-one years later, James Russell, a loyalist, listed his slaves at the Nottingham Ironworks in Baltimore County, Maryland. At the furnace he reported 27 workers, including 5 slave founders, 2 tillers, 2 blacksmiths, and an unspecified number of colliers; at the forge were 44 workers, including 16 slave forgemen, 3 blacksmiths, 2 carpenters, and, again, an unspecified number of colliers. Of course, not all Chesapeake ironworks placed most slaves in skilled posts: the majority of slaves at the Northampton Ironworks in Maryland were woodcutters. Nevertheless, the leading Chesapeake ironworks of the day, Oxford, belonging to David Ross and located in Campbell County, Virginia, operated almost exclusively with slave labor. By the early nineteenth century, its slave labor force stood at more than two hundred, and "the range of skills possessed by the slave workers," Charles Dew declares, "made them one of the most remarkable industrial slave labor forces ever assembled."[44]

---

43. John Lee Webster (Bush Town, Maryland, Iron Works), Feb. 23, 1747, LC; John Semple to Messrs. James Russell and Mollison, June 21, 1764, Currie-Dal. Miscellaneous Bundle 20, box 2, microfilm, CW; Mullin, *Flight and Rebellion,* 85; Archibald Cary, *VaG* (Purdie), Mar. 7, 1766; Ronald L. Lewis, *Coal, Iron, and Slaves: Industrial Slavery in Maryland and Virginia, 1715–1865* (Westport, Conn., 1979), 7, 21–26.

44. Steffen, *From Gentlemen to Townsmen,* 53; Kulikoff, *Tobacco and Slaves,* 415; valuation of slaves at the Nottingham Iron Works, Nov. 11, 1789, the Russell Papers, American Papers, 120/32, House of Lords, London; Charles G. Steffen, "The Pre-Industrial Iron Worker: Northampton Iron Works, 1780–1820," *Labor History,* XX (1979), 93–95; Charles B. Dew,

Could ironworkers, and other slave tradesmen, directly apply learned African skills in their New World occupations? The odds were against it, if for no other reason than that planters generally preferred to train native-born slaves for skilled work. Moreover, masters were not inclined to credit Africans with any previously acquired skills. Typical perhaps was Henry Laurens's condescension concerning the alleged blacksmithing abilities of a newly imported African slave. "If he [h]as wrought any time in his country," Laurens noted skeptically, "he will soon be improved in his knowledge by practice under a White Man." Even Richard Oswald, who had extensive contacts on the African coast and knew firsthand the extent of indigenous skills, asked his African agents only to look out for African tradesmen; he made no direct request for specific skills.[45]

Even though African craftsmen were not accorded the respect they deserved, black immigrants created artifacts in North America within a framework that owed much to their native cultural ideas. In due course, the traditions they created were transmitted to their creole descendants, who, in turn, extended them through their innovations. Although the full history of this creative and dynamic process remains to be told, elements of the story are beginning to be understood. Blacksmithing was, in fact, one trade into which slaves incorporated African influences. A wrought-iron figure of a man, legs spread apart, arms bent and reaching forward, discovered at the site of a blacksmith's shop and slave quarters in Alexandria, Virginia, has been dated to the late eighteenth century and has been described as "one of the rare objects which link American Negro Art to Africa." Even a modern-day black blacksmith, Philip Simmons of Charleston, reveals connections to an earlier and broader African American tradition, most noticeably in his belief that his designs are products of "visions" and by his use of improvisatory techniques.[46]

Slave basketmakers, particularly in the Lowcountry, created artifacts that

---

"David Ross and the Oxford Iron Works: A Study of Industrial Slavery in the Early Nineteenth-Century South," *WMQ*, 3d Ser., XXXI (1974), 195. See also Michael Warren Robbins, "The Principio Company: Iron-Making in Colonial Maryland, 1720–1781" (Ph.D. diss., George Washington University, 1972), 110–120.

45. Henry Laurens to James Grant, July 22, 1765, bundle 359, and Richard Oswald to James Grant, May 20, 1767, bundle 295, Papers of General James Grant of Ballindalloch.

46. John Michael Vlach, *The Afro-American Tradition in Decorative Arts* (Cleveland, Ohio, 1978), 108–109; Vlach, *Charleston Blacksmith: The Work of Philip Simmons* (Athens, Ga., 1981), esp. 108–110; and Vlach, *By the Work of Their Hands: Studies in Afro-American Folklife* (Charlottesville, Va., 191). See also Robert Farris Thompson, "African Influence on the Art of the United States," in Armstead L. Robinson et al., eds., *Black Studies in the University* (New Haven, Conn., 1969), 122–170; Mary A. Twining, "African–Afro-American Artistic Continuity," *Journal of African Studies*, II (1976), 576–577; and Gregory Day, "Afro-Carolinian Art: Towards the History of a Southern Expressive Tradition," *Contemporary Art / Southeast*, I (1978), 10.

had even broader African associations. In Africa, both sexes made baskets, with men making the larger work baskets and women the smaller, fancier household baskets. A similar distinction seems to have persisted in early South Carolina, where the fanner, or winnowing, basket would have been the most important work basket and where some men at least were specifically valued for their basketmaking skills. Thus, in 1789, Charles Drayton noted that one of his male slaves had gone "to make baskets" at another of his plantations. Two years later, a "Negro Man, who is a good jobbing carpenter and an excellent basket maker," was put up for public auction. At the turn of the century, Caesar, belonging to Mr. Stead, was described as a "good baskett Maker." The one known basketmaker in eighteenth-century Virginia was an African man who spoke "bad English" and who was "remarkable for making baskets." In 1774, William Gibbons, a Savannah River rice planter, paid widely fluctuating prices—from three shillings to eight pounds, nine shillings—for slave baskets, which may well reflect the difference between large work and small household baskets. Close stylistic parallels link the coiled rush baskets of South Carolina with parts of Africa, notably Senegambia. Although they exhibit influences of Native American coiled designs and perhaps European wickerware, the baskets made by Lowcountry slaves were remarkably similar in design and shape to certain regional baskets in Africa. "Even in their recent innovations," Dale Rosengarten has noted, "African-American baskets have more in common with African baskets than with neighboring Native American traditions." The one European tradition of coiled basketmaking that took hold in America was the German, but there was little contact between Germans and slaves in the Lowcountry. Two- or three-storied baskets have been cited as an example of the African "additive approach to design," a linear repetition of units, also evident in African American strip quilts. Particular basket shapes—notably the rice fanner, or winnowing tray, and the "head tote basket," both constructed without handles—have specific African analogues.[47]

47. Charles Drayton Diary, Oct. 28, 1789, Drayton Family Papers, Historic Charleston Foundation; *City Gaz and DA,* Feb. 15, 1791, as cited in Dale Rosengarten, *Row upon Row: Sea Grass Baskets of the South Carolina Lowcountry* (Columbia, S.C., 1986), 44; list of Mr. Stead's Negroes, Mar. 24, 1803, C. C. Pinckney Collection, Duke; Robert Rakestraw, *VaG* (D and N), Feb. 26, 1780; William Gibbons' Account Book, 1765–1782, GHS. Sixteen slaves managed to stay at large by picking black moss, making baskets, and taking their handiwork to town in boats (*Charleston Courier,* May 28, 1825, cited in Michael P. Johnson, "Runaway Slaves and the Slave Communities in South Carolina, 1799 to 1830," *WMQ,* 3d Ser., XXXVIII [1981], 436). For other accounts of specialist basketmakers, see Mary E. Wilkinson Miller, *Slavery Days in Georgia* (Richland, Ga., n.d.), 28–29; and Alice R. Huger Smith, *A Carolina Rice Plantation of the Fifties* (New York, 1936), 71. For interpretations of style, see Gerald L. Davis, "Afro-American Coil Basketry in Charleston County, South Carolina," in Don Yoder,

PLATE 15. *Colono Ware Jug.* Circa 1670–1825, Bluff Plantation. Courtesy South Carolina Institute of Archaeology and Anthropology, University of South Carolina

Slave potters also found work in the eighteenth-century mainland South, particularly in the Lowcountry. More "Colono Ware has been found in South Carolina," observes Leland Ferguson, than in all the other southeastern colo-

---

ed., *American Folklife* (Austin, Tex., 1976), 151–184; Vlach, *Afro-American Tradition*, 7–19; Mary A. Twining, "Harvesting and Heritage: A Comparison of Afro-American and African Basketry," *Southern Folklore Quarterly*, XLII (1978), 159–174; Day, "Afro-Carolinian Art," *Contemp. Art / Southeast*, I (1978), 10–21 (quotation on 19); and, for the best work, Dale Rosengarten, "Spirits of Our Ancestors: Basket Traditions in the Carolinas," in Michael Montgomery, ed., *The Crucible of Carolina: Essays in the Development of Gullah Language and Culture* (Athens, Ga., 1994), 133–157; and Rosengarten, "The Lowcountry Basket in a Global Setting" (paper presented at College of Charleston conference, May 1995). Melville J. Herskovits made one interesting reference to Sea Island baskets in *The Myth of the Negro Past* (New York, 1941), 147.

nies combined. The many unfired shards and fired lumps of clay that have been recovered at slave settlements in early South Carolina suggest on-site manufacture by slaves. Lowcountry slave production of their own Colono ware no doubt explains why in 1773 "a large quantity of Earthen ware, etc, was seized from Negro Hawkers" in Charleston. Some stylistic similarities—both in vessel form and in decoration—between Colono ware and Africa also point to slave manufacture. Yet not all ceramic experts are convinced of these connections. Matthew Hill, for example, is impressed by the decorative impoverishment and ethnically undiagnostic character of most Colono ware. He concludes: "Colono ware is remarkable . . . not for being distinctively African, but for being distinctively non-European." The impoverishment may be attributed in part to the small number of older African women in the transatlantic slave trade, for, in Africa, potting was generally a female occupation, and skills came with maturity. Still, clearly individual Africans and their descendants made pottery styled on generalized mental images drawn from their homelands. Thus the nineteenth-century slave potters of Edgefield district, South Carolina, who produced conventional Anglo-American stoneware, also appear to have drawn on African aesthetic ideas for some products. They created face vessels, or mask pitchers, that have been linked to sculptural techniques employed in the region of Angola. More important than any formal parallels are broad artistic principles that lie at the heart of these creations and that may well be African in origin, most significantly their creators' multimedia approach and shaping of eyes and mouths with kaolin inserts. These techniques have little or no precedent in Anglo-American ceramics.[48]

48. Leland Ferguson, "Looking for the 'Afro' in Colono-Indian Pottery," in Robert L. Schuyler, ed., *Archaeological Perspectives on Ethnicity in America: Afro-American and Asian American Culture History* (Farmingdale, N.Y., 1980), 14–28; Ferguson, *Uncommon Ground: Archaeology and Early African America, 1650–1800* (Washington, D.C., 1992), 8–9, 36 (quotation), 41–55, 82–107; *SCG*, May 17, 1773; Matthew H. Hill, "Ethnicity Lost? Ethnicity Gained? Information Functions of 'African Ceramics' in West Africa and North America," in R. Auger et al., eds., *Ethnicity and Culture: Proceedings of the Eighteenth Annual Chacmool Conference* (Calgary, 1987), 135–139 (quotation on 138); Patrick H. Garrow and Thomas R. Wheaton, "Colonoware Ceramics: The Evidence from Yaughan and Curriboo Plantations," in Albert C. Goodyear III and Glen T. Hanson, eds., *Studies in South Carolina Archaeology: Essays in Honor of Robert L. Stephenson*, Anthropological Studies 9, Occasional Papers of the South Carolina Institute of Archaeology and Anthropology (Columbia, S.C., 1989), 175–184 (evidence of uneven thicknesses of vessels and lack of decoration); Marla C. Berns, "Art, History, and Gender: Women and Clay in West Africa," *African Archaeological Review*, XI (1993), 129–148; Robert Farris Thompson and Joseph Cornet, *The Four Moments of the Sun: Kongo Art in Two Worlds* (Washington, D.C., 1981), 157–165; and Vlach, *Afro-American Tradition*, 76–94. See also Kenneth E. Lewis, *The American Frontier: An Archaeological Study of Settlement Pattern and Process* (New York, 1984), 134–136; Thomas R. Wheaton and

Important as African slaves were to ironworking, basketmaking, and pottery, woodworking was the trade to which most Lowcountry Africans were put in the eighteenth century. The birthplaces of more than a hundred South Carolina woodworkers were mentioned in colonial runaway advertisements. A significant proportion, just over a quarter, were Africans. No doubt they were responsible for fashioning even that most utilitarian of objects—the rice mortar—so as to resemble the shape of, and incorporate decorative motifs from, African drums. Blacks in coastal Georgia were famous for a distinctive woodcarving tradition—walking sticks embellished with reptile and human figures. One cane found in Savannah was "topped by a carved human head and decorated with numerous crosshatching marks," common features of African Georgian woodcarving, "but, in addition, along the side of the shaft [was] a mask form with long spiraling horns and eyes set on sharp, raking angles, strongly reminiscent of an Ogoni mask from Nigeria."[49]

Although some skilled slaves maintained links to an African past, others, particularly those at the top of the craft hierarchy, were inevitably brought into close contact with Anglo-American traditions. Perhaps singled out when young, apprenticed to a white man, kept apart by the nature of their work, by itinerancy, by privileges, and even by advanced years, some artisans could hardly be blamed for feeling distanced from fellow blacks. Perhaps it was to avoid this isolation that one of Landon Carter's skilled slaves got himself demoted to the field. "He was so pleased in being turned to the hoe," noted Carter, "that he came this morning to tell me he was going and the rascal took his row next to hindmost man in my field." Such was the pressure that the possession of a skill entailed.[50]

WATERMEN

The number of watercraft planters owned declined over the eighteenth century, but the proportion of specialist watermen among slaves increased. The growing size of plantations was largely responsible for this seeming paradox, for large plantations supported large watercraft more easily than did small ones. Therefore, although there were fewer vessels per head as the century

---

Patrick H. Garrow, "Acculturation and the Archaeological Record in the Carolina Lowcountry," in Theresa A. Singleton, ed., *The Archaeology of Slavery and Plantation Life* (New York, 1985), 248–251; and John A. Burrison, "Afro-American Folk Pottery in the South," *So. Folklore Qtly.*, XLII (1978), 175–199.

49. Vlach, *Afro-American Tradition*, 9, 20–21, 27–43 (quotation on 29). See also Robert Farris Thompson, "Siras Bowens of Sunbury, Georgia: A Tidewater Artist in the Afro-American Visual Tradition," *Massachusetts Review*, XVIII (1977), 490–500. Few runaway woodworkers in the Chesapeake were said to be Africans.

50. Greene, ed., *Carter Diary*, 397.

PLATE 16. *Blacks Working on the James River.* Benjamin Henry Latrobe. 1798–1799. Courtesy Virginia State Library

progressed, slave crews became appreciably larger. This development was most noticeable in South Carolina. In the late colonial era, decked schooners with sails and rigging, a capacity of one to two hundred barrels, and a complement of as many as five boatmen began to replace pettiaugers able to convey only about forty to fifty barrels and employing no more than three slaves. Boats tended to be smaller in the Chesapeake, but, as William Tatham observed of the flats commonly employed in the tobacco trade, they were "managed by negroes, who became very dextrous in their profession as fresh water sailors; and many of them excellent skippers, and good river pilots."[51]

Growing numbers of slave boatmen also owed much to the regularizing of transportation networks through the century in both the Chesapeake and the Lowcountry. Whether this took the form of more regular ferries, the standardized provision of local canoes, or the establishment of coastal packets and inland services, slaves constituted the basic manpower. Canoe services were literally in the hands of slaves, and more than one traveler testified to their proficiency. When Edward Kimber visited Virginia in 1746, he traveled in "a very small and dangerous Sort of Canoa, liable to be overturn'd by the least Motion of the Sitters in it." He added that the "Negroes manage them very

---

51. G. Melvin Herndon, *William Tatham and the Culture of Tobacco* (Miami, Fla., 1969), 211. For South Carolina boats, their capacity, and their value, together with number of boatmen, compare the inventories of Edward North, Nov. 30, 1743, Inventory Book, WPA, CXIV, 312–314, and of Isaac Hayne, 1752, ibid., CXXXIII, 279–283, with inventories of Walter Izard, Feb. 20, 1759, ibid., CLVIII, 239–241, of Daniel Crawford, July 11, 1760, ibid., CLX, 611–629, of John Mayrant, Aug. 11, 1767, Inventory Book, X, 163, and of Thomas Caw, Mar. 8, 1773, Inventory Book, WPA, CLXXXVI, 498–505. Most impressive were the estates of Thomas Lind, 1771, Inventory Book, &, 94–99, and Katherine Lind, *SCG*, Nov. 28, 1771, and estates of John Marley, Mar. 12, 1772, Inventory Book, WPA, CLXXXVII, 709–712, and of George Wood, *SCG*, Mar. 15, 1773.

dextrously with a Paddle." Some thirty years later, Hugh Finlay went from Purrysburg to Savannah "in a wooden canoe rowed by three Negroes," who impressed their passenger with their traveling speed. They covered the distance of twenty-four miles in just over four hours.[52] Schooner services linking inland towns to coastal ports or connecting contiguous coastal towns depended on slaves. A Camden merchant in the late eighteenth century referred to a boat coming up from Charleston that had "only negros on board"; a visitor to Norfolk mentioned the custom of hiring scows for transporting goods between that Virginia port and neighboring Portsmouth, a practice that also included "hiring Negroes [who] were employed to run them"; and the duc de La Rochefoucauld-Liancourt noticed that the crews on the Savannah-Charleston packets in the early national era were composed largely of slaves.[53]

Transatlantic shipping also became more frequent and predictable over the course of the eighteenth century, and opportunities increased for slaves to work aboard ship. But maritime slavery was never extensive, for most slaveowners feared the loss of control that seafaring inevitably involved. The mobility and worldliness of sailors were for the most part corrosive of bound labor. Nevertheless, many ships trading to and from the Chesapeake and Lowcountry had the occasional slave aboard. Some merchants hired slaves or put their own to work at sea; some captains took their slaves aboard their vessels; and slaves themselves took the initiative by escaping to ships where they could often find employment with few questions asked. No doubt the slave who hired himself without a license to a ship captain would have escaped notice had he not

---

52. [Edward Kimber], "Observations in Several Voyages and Travels in America," *WMQ*, 1st Ser., XV (1906–1907), 217; Frank H. Norton, ed., *Journal Kept by Hugh Finlay . . .* (Brooklyn, N.Y., 1867), 54. For more on canoes paddled by slaves, see Baron Ludwig von Closen, *The Revolutionary Journal of Baron Ludwig von Closen, 1780–1783*, ed. and trans. Evelyn M. Acomb (Chapel Hill, N.C., 1958), 159; Frederick E. Maser and Howard T. Maag, eds., *The Journal of Joseph Pilmore, Methodist Itinerant: For the Years August 1, 1769 to January 2, 1774* (Philadelphia, 1969), 147, 181, 191–192; Antonio Pace, trans. and ed., *Luigi Castiglioni's Viaggio: Travels in the United States of North America, 1785–1787* (Syracuse, N.Y., 1983), 121. A Lowcountry slave boy told a melancholy tale of being in a canoe—along with five other blacks, two whites, and an Indian—that overturned in an inlet near Cape Romain. One white and four blacks drowned instantly. The slave boy, one white, and the Indian reached an island. Significantly, perhaps, it was the slave boy who managed to negotiate a creek, a marsh, and a hike of 14 miles to fetch help (Deposition of Peter Shepherd [relating the slave boy's tale], July 30, 1732, Miscellaneous Records, I, 440–441).

53. John Chesnut to Robert Henry, Apr. 15, 1794, John Chesnut Letterbook, LC; Kenneth Roberts and Anna M. Roberts, trans. and ed., *Moreau de St. Méry's American Journey [1793–1798]* (Garden City, N.Y., 1947), 66–67; François Alexandre Frédéric, duke de La Rochefoucault Liancourt, *Travels through the United States of North America . . .* , I (London, 1799), 618.

drowned trying to disentangle the ropes around the ship's rudder. His master then took the master to court claiming heavy damages. In both South Carolina and Virginia, slave sailors from other colonies jumped ship, and many local fugitives escaped to an oceangoing vessel.[54]

Although slaves never dominated eighteenth-century North American oceangoing vessels, all-slave crews increasingly manned South Carolina's river and coastal boats. By 1744, white patroons were so alarmed at the growing threat to their jobs that they petitioned the colony's legislature for relief. The petition had no apparent effect, because blacks continued to dominate South Carolina waters. Five years later, for example, the South Carolina Council investigated an alleged slave conspiracy hatched in an area served by the Eastern Branch of the Cooper River. In the course of its inquiry, the council unwittingly uncovered evidence of the slaves' dominance of that river's traffic. The slaves of the plantation at the center of the alleged conspiracy were familiar with eight boat crews that plied between Charleston and adjacent estates. Five were all-black crews with slave patroons at the helm, whereas only three boats were in the hands of white patroons. In 1762, residents of a Cooper River parish complained of the "divers boats plying there having only slaves go in them."[55]

Black watermen in the Chesapeake were more likely to work alongside whites than their Lowcountry counterparts. In 1730, the governor of Virginia referred to the prevalence of mixed crews, composed "for the most part [of] Planters with Negros and other Servants," that manned "the small Shallops which are constantly employed in the Bay and in transporting the country's commoditys from one River to another." A half-century later, Robert Carter observed, "Barges infest some plantations situate on the water of Potomac River—from the mouth upwards about 30 miles but no higher—the crews are partly White and Blacks." The desirability of mixed crews was finally enshrined

---

54. *John Clark* v. *James Boone,* Oct. 7, 1746, Court of Common Pleas, Judgment Rolls, box 30A, no. 38. The role of slave sailors in rescue work is illustrated in Walter B. Edgar, ed., *The Letterbook of Robert Pringle,* II (Columbia, S.C., 1972), 490; and John Guerard to Thomas Rocke, Mar. 4, 1753, John Guerard Letterbook, SCHS. For a significant innovation by a black sailor, see David MacPherson, *Annals of Commerce . . . ,* III (London, 1805), 374. For the best work on maritime slavery, see W. Jeffrey Bolster, *Black Jacks: African American Seamen in the Age of Sail* (Cambridge, Mass., 1997).

55. Petition of Masters or Patroons or Pettiaugers of small coasting vessels, Jan. 27, 1744, Journal of South Carolina Commons House of Assembly, IV, 556, SCDAH; Philip D. Morgan and George D. Terry, "Slavery in Microcosm: A Conspiracy Scare in Colonial South Carolina," *So. Studies,* XXI (1982), 130–134; Several of the inhabitants of the parish of St. Thomas and St. Dennis, *SCG,* Apr. 3, 1762. See also Robert Raper to John Colleton, May 22, 1760, Robert Raper Letterbook, microfilm, SCHS.

in law when, in 1784, the Virginia legislature enacted that not more than one-third of a crew should consist of slaves.[56]

Some slave watermen used their skills to supply their masters and other whites with fish. By the early eighteenth century, an identifiable group of "fishing Negroes" had emerged in South Carolina, particularly in Charleston. In the 1730s, Moses was a well-known fisherman in town, "often employed in knitting of Nets"; three years later, a city resident warned the black fraternity from carrying her slave, Lancaster, "a Fishing"; and, in 1750, a slave, who had been a runaway upward of two years, was apparently "harboured by his father Robin, a noted fisherman in this town." Also at midcentury, Dr. Alexander Garden's botanical investigations led him to seek the assistance of several fishermen in the city. This proved frustrating, he reported, because "most or indeed all of them are negroes, whom I find it impossible to make understand me rightly what I want."[57]

As Garden suggests, by midcentury, blacks had established a virtual monopoly on town fishing. A South Carolina act of 1770 establishing a separate fish market in the city of Charleston explicitly acknowledged the preeminent role of blacks. "The business of Fishing," it declared, "is principally carried on by Negroes, Mulattoes, and Mestizoes." According to one white observer two years later, slaves were able "at their pleasure to supply the town with fish or not." He charged that they could "exact whatever price they think proper for that easily-procured food." As a result of their stranglehold over supply, the price of drumfish had risen almost tenfold in recent years. The demeanor of a runaway slave who was "carrying on the fishing business between town and James-Island" merely confirmed the worst suspicions of "The Stranger." According to his owner, this slave's "insolent behaviour to several, since absent, is known."[58]

---

56. Governor Gooch to Board of Trade, July 23, 1730, CO5/1322, PRO; Robert Carter to Richard Lemon, July 11, 1782, Carter Letterbook, V, 27; William Waller Hening, ed., *The Statutes at Large: Being a Collection of All the Laws of Virginia . . .*, XI (Richmond, Va., 1823), 404.

57. Kennedy O'Brien, *SCG*, Nov. 5, 1737; David Arnett, ibid., Nov. 5, 1737; Elizabeth Smith, ibid., Dec. 25, 1740; John McQueen, ibid., Jan. 15, 1750; Dr. Alexander Garden to Mr. Ellis, Mar. 25, 1755, in James Edward Smith, comp., *A Selection of the Correspondence of Linnaeus, and Other Naturalists, from the Original Manuscripts,* I (London, 1821), 349. See also Peter H. Wood, *Black Majority: Negroes in Colonial South Carolina from 1670 through the Stono Rebellion* (New York, 1974), 201; and John Raven to William Moultrie, May 3, 1764, William Moultrie Papers, USC. For slaves' fishing on their own account, see Chapter 2.

58. "The Stranger," *SCG*, Sept. 24, 1772; Paul Hamilton, *SC and AGG,* Nov. 18, 1780. A complaint from two free black fishermen came before the Charleston Board of Police in 1780. A white pilot had "threatened to run them down in their Canoe" for infringing on his livelihood by bringing in a schooner from Savannah. They claimed that the pilot's "menaces" prevented them "from following their occupation of Fishermen and supplying the Town with Fish" (Board of Police Minutes, July 11, 1780, CO5/519, fols. 12–14). When Josiah

The independent character of slave fishermen might have rested, in part, on their de facto ownership of watercraft. "The Stranger" observed that slaves dominated the fishing business because they were "permitted to keep boats, canows, etc." An inventory of one Charleston household listed three slave fishermen but no boats or canoes, suggesting that the slaves had their own access to the sea. A runaway slave who was "possessed of a canoe" was thought to be fishing in and around the city. In 1778, during the fire of Charleston, Elkanah Watson observed how "every vessel shallop, and negro-boat was crowded with the distressed inhabitants." Perhaps these "negro-boats" were aptly termed, indicating that blacks owned them.[59]

Whether in their own or their masters' boats, Lowcountry slave fishermen were successful. Writing in the 1730s, James Sutherland claimed to have "known two Negroes take between 14 and 1500 Trouts above 3 feet long." A half-century later, Samuel Kelly visited Charleston and noted that the most popular local fish was a blackfish, caught with hook and line, by slaves in canoes. According to Kelly, the slaves arrived at the fishing ground south of the Charleston bar about daylight and returned to town with the sea breezes about midday. A bounty went to those with the largest catches. During the Revolutionary war, a British cruiser seized twenty-five African-Americans who were fishing off Charleston Bar one Sunday. One of those captured, a slave named Ishmael, passed up ten shillings a day for domestic work in order to fish—an indication of how lucrative the activity was. Ishmael supported a slave woman out of his earnings. Early in the nineteenth century, a French visitor to Charleston described how he found himself "in the midst of twenty-five dug-outs, each containing four Negroes who were having excellent fishing." Every ten minutes, they hauled a twelve-to-fifteen-pound fish into one of their canoes.[60]

Limited marketing opportunities, the absence of a major urban center, and competition from whites explain why the Chesapeake's slaves never established

---

Smith proposed selling a schooner belonging to George Austin's estate, he planned to employ "old Primus" in "supplying the Family with a little Fish now and then" because "he will not incline to tarry at either" of Austin's plantations—another indication of the independent-minded waterman (Josiah Smith to George Austin, Jan. 31, 1774, and to George Smith, June 8, 1781, Josiah Smith Letterbook, UNC).

59. "The Stranger," *SCG*, Sept. 24, 1772; inventory of Daniel Chopard, Aug. 3, 1770, Inventory Book, Y, 306–307, and his estate, *SCG*, Aug. 30, 1770; Henry Osborne, *City Gaz*, Apr. 7, 1794; Elkanah Watson, *Men and Times of the Revolution*, ed. Winslow C. Watson (New York, 1856), 45.

60. James Sutherland to [?], c. 1730s, Coe Papers, SCHS; Crosbie Garstin, ed., *Samuel Kelly: An Eighteenth Century Seaman* (London, 1925), 55; Baron de Montzlun, "A Frenchman Visits Charleston, 1817," ed. Lucius Gaston Moffatt and Joseph Médard Carrière, *SCHM*, XLIX (1948), 136. For early accounts of slave fishing skills, see Wood, *Black Majority*, 123.

the monopoly over the trade their Lowcountry counterparts managed. In 1775, for instance, Will, a slave blacksmith, absented himself while oystering near the mouth of the Potomac River. His master thought that he had been enticed away either by a pilot boat or by a large, flat-bottomed oystering boat in the vicinity. Significantly, these two boats were manned by two and three whites, respectively. In April 1788, Robert Carter provided one of his overseers with three hands, only one of whom was a fisherman, so that they might spend a whole week in "drawing the seine in the waters about Nomony." Chesapeake slaves went fishing for their masters, but they never dominated the trade.[61]

Yet Chesapeake slaves demonstrated their fishing expertise. In 1782, two slaves of the Westover estate told the marquis de Chastellux how they caught sturgeon. Because this fish usually slept near the riverbed at midday, they went in a small boat, taking "a long rope, at the end of which is a sharp hook, which they trail along like a sounding line. As soon as they feel this line stopped by some obstacle they pull it sharply towards them, so as to hook the sturgeon." Chesapeake slaves also drugged fish. An "old negro" told Benjamin Henry Latrobe: "It is very common for the negroes, when the tide retires, and in the low country leaves lakes or ponds of water full of fish, to throw in a Basket full of bruised Asmart and stir it about. The Fish soon come to the Surface in a torpid state and are easily taken."[62]

Was this an African influence? The drugging of fish was well known in West Africa, but the practice was common to Indians too, so it may have multiple origins. In 1726, the South Carolina Assembly charged that "many persons in this Province do often use the pernicious practice of poisoning the creeks in order to catch great quantity of fish," and significantly imposed a public whipping on any slave convicted of the act. Lowcountry slaves commonly used a second technique that also might have had African and Indian antecedents. According to one observer in 1762, "Those living upon the rivers, by stopping of creeks with reeds and small canes tied closely together, on the ebbing of the tide, take abundance of fish." A few years later, another Lowcountry resident saw the same method. Describing slaves as being "very expert in catching fish," he observed them "artfully" closing up creeks with "reed hedges, or logs of wood," in order to trap fish. This witness also described a third method, by which slaves made "lines of very strong grass to which they affix a small piece

---

61. James Lyle, *VaG* (P and D), Dec. 29, 1774; Robert Carter to William Dawson, Apr. 7, 1783, Carter Letterbook, VIII, 106; *Laurens Papers*, XI, 346; George Turberville, *VaG* (Purdie), Mar. 15, 1776.

62. Marquis de Chastellux, *Travels in North America, in the Years 1780, 1781, and 1782*, ed. and trans. Howard C. Rice, Jr., II (Chapel Hill, N.C., 1963), 432; Edward C. Carter II et al., eds., *The Virginia Journals of Benjamin Henry Latrobe, 1795–1798* (New Haven, Conn., 1977), I, 272.

of wood, sharpened at both ends, but thick in the middle; they bait this in such a manner that the fish must take it both ends, and when once they shut their mouths upon it, they cannot again extricate themselves from it, and so are catched."[63]

Occasional links connect the slaves' boating prowess with their African background. A Virginia master acknowledged that his runaway boatman was of "the Ibo Country," where he had "served in the capacity of a Canoe Man." Possibly, this slave, like other Africans, employed homeland methods in fashioning New World dugouts. The provisions proposed for a group of *grumetes* that Richard Oswald planned to bring to South Carolina from Bance Island in Sierra Leone also recognized prior African skills. Acting on Oswald's behalf, Henry Laurens observed to his South Carolina agent that "some of those Gramatas who are Water Men may probably chuse to reside in Charles Town on the Salt Water and with their own Consent you may Sell or hire out all such." Some masters, then, were aware of their African slaves' familiarity with boats and canoes.[64]

Indirect evidence suggests other links between Africa and American watermen. Masters were not averse to assigning recently arrived Africans to boats. One Lowcountry crew comprised "four negro men . . . put on board the schooner . . . as mariners, to sail the schooner coastwise from Ponpon to Charlestown. OAK, PONPON, and HAZARD can speak very little English and may not be able to tell their masters name; AFRICA can speak English but stammers, and stops in his speech." In 1774, a South Carolina manager purchased "a very active good Tempered Fellow of the Congo country with his son" and immediately put them on a schooner. Revealing the typical prejudices of an eighteenth-century South Carolinian, he cast aspersions on their former idle way of life, but then admitted that "they prove very handy and take to their work with a seeming kind of Pleasure." Another African slave was "very fond of the water." The alacrity with which some African slaves took to the water, their familiarity with navigating boats between ocean and inland rivers and swamps, and their

63. Cooper and McCord, eds., *Statutes at Large,* III, 270; Wood, *Black Majority,* 122–123; "A Curious New Description of Charles-Town in South-Carolina, and Its Environs . . . ," *Universal Museum,* I (September 1762), 477; James Barclay, *The Voyages and Travels of James Barclay, Containing Many Surprising Adventures, and Interesting Narratives* (Dublin, 1777), 27. See also Richard Price, "Caribbean Fishing and Fishermen: A Historical Sketch," *American Anthropologist,* LXVIII (1966), 1366, 1372.

64. Richard Booker, *VaG* (Rind), Dec. 24, 1772; Henry Glassie, "The Nature of the New World Artifact: The Instance of the Canoe," in *Festschrift für Robert Wildhalper . . .* (Basel, Switzerland, 1973), 153–170; R. Smith, "The Canoe in West African History," *Journal of African History,* XI (1970), 515–533; *Laurens Papers,* IX, 395, but see V, 475. *Grumetes* were African associates of European traders on the West African coast. Though many were Christians, as Laurens notes in this case, they were "Slaves to all intents and purposes."

penchant for singing, as one traveler put it, "their plaintive African songs, in cadence with the oars," are a true measure of the influence of homeland experiences.[65]

The readiness of masters to place Africans aboard boats suggests that the post did not convey great prestige. True, watermen and fishermen enjoyed unusual mobility, and their daily routines had none of the monotony of field labor. Yet boatmen regularly rubbed shoulders with field hands while loading and unloading their cargoes, and many fishermen no doubt also doubled in the field. Only deep-sea sailors and urban fishermen lived in a world far removed from the experiences of ordinary plantation slaves.

HOUSEHOLD SLAVES

During the eighteenth century, increasing prosperity and larger plantations ensured that progressively more slaves escaped the fields into household work. In 1769, the Westover estate of William Byrd III was a spectacular example, for one-fifth of the 79 men (5 house servants, 5 gardeners, 3 stablemen, 2 butchers, and a cook) and a staggering two-thirds of the 36 women (12 housemaids, 4 washerwomen, 3 dairymaids, 2 cooks, and 2 poultrywomen and bakers) on this home estate were domestics. Almost half of the adult slaves at Westover were household workers. By the late eighteenth century, the number of domestics on large estates in the Lowcountry was equally impressive. As he traveled through South Carolina in 1786, Timothy Ford was amazed at "the multiplicity of servants." In the "higher classes," he noted, "every body must have a vast deal of waiting upon"; dinners were enjoyed in proportion to the number of attendants who "surround the table like a cohort of black guards." A recent arrival to Georgetown described his sister's comfortable life: she "lives very genteel," he reported, "having 3 or 4 negro's to wait at Table and a man to attend the House."[66]

As Ford noted, large household complements were confined to the "higher classes." On most plantations, even by the late eighteenth century, no more than about 1 percent of the male workforce served in a domestic capacity. Only

65. Joseph Glover, *SCG*, Mar. 15, 1770; Josiah Smith to George Austin, June 17, 1771, Smith Letterbook; Thomasin White, *SC and AGG*, Apr. 16, 1779; Watson, *Men and Times*, 52. For African boat songs and their early African American derivations, see Dena J. Polachek Epstein, *Sinful Tunes and Spirituals: Black Folk Music to the Civil War* (Urbana, Ill., 1977), 6, 71–72, 166–167, 254; and Chapter 10. For other examples of African boatmen, see James Lyle to Neil Jamieson, Dec. 6, 1774, Neil Jamieson Papers, LC; and William Martin, *SCG*, Jan. 19, 1738.

66. An Exact List of William Byrd's Negroes at Westover, Aug. 11, 1769, Charles City County Records, 1766–1774, 191, VSL (this listing is not used in Table 27, because it does not include all of Byrd's slaves); Joseph W. Barnwell, ed., "Diary of Timothy Ford, 1785–1786," *SCHM*, XIII (1912), 142–143; John Martin to John Martin, Feb. 16, 1788, John Martin Papers, SCHS.

TABLE 28.
Occupations of Adult Female Slaves on Large Estates in the Lowcountry and Chesapeake, 1757–1809

	Proportion			
	South Carolina		Virginia	
Occupation	1760–1770s[a]	1780s[b]	1757–1775[c]	1784–1809[d]
Agricultural	98%	86%	89%	76%
Domestic	2	11	10	10
House servant	2	3	9	4
Washerwoman	0	3	*	2
Cook	0	2	*	1
Other	0	3	0	3
Housewifery	0	3	2	14
Dairymaid	0	1	1	2
Seamstress	0	2	1	12

* Less than .5%. [a] $N = 64$. [b] $N = 236$. [c] $N = 322$. [d] $N = 313$.
Sources: South Carolina: see Table 24. Virginia: see Table 25.

large estates had a significant number of male household workers, occasionally approximating 10 percent of slave men (Tables 24 and 25). A similar pattern existed for slave women. In the early eighteenth century, virtually all worked in the fields; by the end of the century, perhaps 5 percent at best worked in the house. On large estates, however, the proportion rose to as high as one-fourth (see Table 28).[67]

The elite house slaves were the personal manservants, or waiting men. Ben accompanied his South Carolina master to England and on his return spoke "very good English." By the late colonial era, South Carolina had an identifiable group of waiting men, for a master suspected that his twenty-year-old fugitive was "harboured in the Kitchens or back Buildings of some Gentlemen in or near Charlestown as his acquaintance among Gentlemen's Waiting-Men is very general." As waiting men became more numerous, they became more specialized. Thus, Ned, described as a waiting man and noted for his skills as a

67. The figure of 5% is an educated guess, based on inventories of estates, runaway advertisements, and advertisements of sale.

hairdresser and butcher, gained most of his fame as a groom. He was well known throughout South Carolina, Georgia, and North Carolina "as a keeper of race horses." He looked the part: his master described him as "handsome and well made," with "a good countenance, a full and manly look."[68]

Virginia manservants were, if anything, even more worldly-wise. Nineteen-year-old George, "genteel and well made" and "as complete a waiting boy as perhaps any on the continent," spoke excellent English, wore fine clothes, and even carried a brace of pocket pistols. Eighteen-year-old Robin, who had visited England as a waiting boy, had "delicate" hands and feet and was "very fluent in speech." But few could compare with thirty-year-old Bacchus, who cut a fine figure in his "blue Plush Breeches," "fine Cloth Pompadour Waistcoat," white shirt, neat shoes with silver buckles, and "fine Hat cut and cocked in the Macaroni Figure." In the summer of 1774, he ran off, probably to Williamsburg. He could plausibly pretend to be there "upon Business," because his master frequently sent him to the capital. He knew his way around "the lower Parts of the Country," since he "constantly rode" with his master. He left with a purse of dollars, apparently stolen from his trusting owner. He even had the audacity to change a five-pound note. Passing as free under the name of John Christian, Bacchus aimed for Great Britain, "from the Knowledge he has of the late Determination of Somerset's Case."[69]

If a few men stood at the apex of the domestic hierarchy, the vast majority at the base were women. Eighteenth-century household work was primarily women's work. In fact, by the late colonial period, the household activities of slave women were extensive enough to merit a twofold division. Some were employed, as always, in truly domestic activities: cooking, childcare, cleaning. Others became involved in housewifery: dairying, raising poultry, marketing, and the manufacture and repair of cloth and clothing. The development of housewifery was most pronounced in the Chesapeake, where diversification extended much further than in the Lowcountry.[70]

The most notable shift toward housewifery in the Chesapeake region was the rise of textile production, a development normally associated with the Revolution. John Harrower, the English tutor to a Virginia family, noted in 1775 that slaves had begun to process the first crop of flax grown on Belvidere plantation near Fredericksburg in order to make "coarse linnen for shirts to the Nigers." He also claimed, "Before this year, there has been little or no

68. Edward Thomas, *SCG*, Apr. 26, 1735; Wellins Calcott, *SC and AGG*, Oct. 5, 1772; John McPherson, *City Gaz*, Aug. 24, 1795, supplement.

69. Hamilton Ballantine, *VaG* (D and H), May 22, 1779; Charles Yates, *VaG and WA*, Sept. 20, 1783; Gabriel Jones, *VaG* (P and D), June 30, 1774.

70. Carole Shammas, "Black Women's Work and the Evolution of Plantation Society in Virginia," *Labor History*, XXVI (1985), 5–28.

linnen made in the colony." In general terms, Harrower was correct, but textile production did not develop overnight. Through the eighteenth century, planters increasingly added equipment for carding wool and spinning yarn for homemade stockings, caps, and gloves in their households, and presumably some black women became adept at using them. Certainly, on large estates, groups of slave women were manufacturing cloth before the Revolution. Landon Carter's slaves were spinning and weaving in the 1750s. In the following decade, George Washington owned a spinner and a seamstress and then built a manufactory, hiring one white and five black spinners. In 1769, William Lee, an absentee Virginia planter, recommended that his "People" be cloathed "with their own Manufactures." Two years later, he was eager to have his flock of sheep augmented so that there would be enough raw material, along with flax and cotton, to clothe all his slaves. He also ordered that "some of the Girls and infirm old women be taught to spin flax, and kept constantly at it, as flax grows very well in every part of Virginia and is much more worth your regard than cotton."[71]

However widespread these pre-Revolutionary ventures were, the war undoubtedly accelerated the domestic production of cloth. Before the war began, Robert Carter of Nomini Hall had foreseen the need to produce his own cloth; at war's end, he was employing ten weavers, four of them slave women, and twelve female spinners at the "Linnen and Woolen Factory" on his Aries quarter.[72] In 1775, William Cabell bound out his slave girl Aggy for six years in order that she might be taught "the art of Weaving." Four years later, a visitor to Virginia claimed that spinning was now "the chief employment of the female negroes." After the war, most planters reverted to buying their cloth, but some continued to use their skilled black female spinners and weavers until

---

71. Edward Miles Riley, ed., *The Journal of John Harrower, an Indentured Servant in the Colony of Virginia, 1773–1776* (Williamsburg, Va., 1963), 121. For spinning wheels, see Chapter 1. Greene, ed., *Carter Diary*, 212, 253, 362, 383–384; W. W. Abbot et al., eds., *The Papers of George Washington*, Colonial Series, 10 vols. (Charlottesville, Va., 1983–1995), VI, 282, VII, 507–508, VIII, 154–156; William Lee to Richard Henry Lee and Francis Lightfoot Lee, Mar. 15, 1769, and to Cary Wilkinson, May 22, 1771, William Lee Letterbook, Lee-Ludwell Papers.

72. Mary Beth Norton, *Liberty's Daughters: The Revolutionary Experience of American Women, 1750–1800* (Boston, 1980), 164. Biographical information is available for some of the women employed at Aries quarter. In 1782, 4 "winders" were listed (Kate, aged 65; Sally, 16; Alice, 15; and Mary, 14). At this point, old women and young girls were drafted to the workforce. Seven years later, 12 spinners were listed, and, from this and subsequent lists, their ages were: Rose, 60; Sarah, 48; Phillis, 46; Bab, 34; Sally, 27; Alice, 26; Jemima, 24; Becky, 23; Lucy, 22; Betty, 21; Betsy, 19; and Sally, age unknown (notice that the ages of Sally and Alice in 1789 have mysteriously increased). The workforce was now much more mature. See Robert Carter's agreement with Daniel Sullivan, Jan. 1, 1782, Carter Family Papers; Robert Carter Memorandum Book, 1788–1789, 105, LC; and lists of slaves in Carter Letterbook, XI.

machine-made American textiles became available following the War of 1812. In 1784, for example, Edmund Randolph employed four spinners, one weaver, one loom assistant, and a spinner-seamstress, all aged between sixteen and twenty-five, on his plantation in Charlotte County, Virginia.[73]

In the Lowcountry, the shift to housewifery was much less extensive. Small-scale domestic production of cloth began before the Revolutionary war. In 1755, for example, Dr. Alexander Garden noted that some South Carolina planters grew cotton and employed "some old superannuated negroe wenches that can no longer serve in the field to make some homespun . . . for some other favourite negroes clothing." The war accelerated these developments. In December 1775, Ralph Izard gave "orders for a considerable quantity of cotton to be planted for clothing [his] negroes." The following year, James Akin promised to pay Martha Chubb a hundred pounds a year for four years to have eight of his slave girls taught to spin and weave and another fifty pounds to have a girl knit. One Lowcounty planter transformed his plantation into a cloth manufactory in the space of three months. By early 1777, so an exhortatory newspaper feature claimed, he had "30 Hands constantly employed from whom he gets 120 Yards of a good wearable stuff made of Woolen and Cotton every week. He had only one white Woman to instruct the Negroes in spinning and one Man to instruct in Weaving. He expects to have it in his Power not only to clothe his own Negroes, but soon to supply his Neighbours." Such dramatic responses to wartime exigencies lost much of their rationale once peace arrived. Still, some never forgot the wartime lessons, for, when Lady Liston passed through the rice-growing area of southern North Carolina in 1797, she observed, "It is customary for these people to keep one or two female slaves brought up to weave."[74]

The origins of a distinctive African American quilting tradition may well lie in the growing involvement of slave women in textile production. At an eighteenth-century South Carolina plantation site near the Congaree River where many African-Americans are known to have lived, archaeologists have found a ceramic spindle-whorl made from fired clay, which suggests an Afri-

73. William Cabell Diary, V, Apr. 20, 1775, VHS; Thomas Anburey, *Travels through the Interior Parts of America . . .* , II (London, 1789), 246; Norton, *Liberty's Daughters,* 165; list of Negroes belonging to Edmund Randolph, Sept. 23, 1784, microfilm, CW; G. Melvin Herndon, "A War-Inspired Industry: The Manufacture of Hemp in Virginia during the Revolution," *VMHB,* LXXIV (1966), 301–311.

74. Dr. Alexander Garden to the Royal Society, Apr. 20, 1755, I, 36, Royal Society of Arts, London; Anne Deas, ed., *Correspondence of Mr. Ralph Izard, of South Carolina . . .* , I (New York, 1844), 174; *Ann Akin* v. *Martha Chubb,* Court of Common Pleas, Judgment Rolls, box 110B, 1784, no. 2A; *SC and AGG,* Jan. 30, 1777; journal of Lady Liston, December 1797, 5697, 12, Sir Robert Liston Papers, National Library of Scotland, Edinburgh.

can spindle-spinning technique, using a distaff, spindle, and whorl, with the whorl placed in a dish or potsherd or against the ground. Black women wove wide-loom textiles both in Africa and in North America and were no doubt responsible for transmitting a number of African design principles into African American textiles. The key elements in African American quilting that can be traced to an African aesthetic include the use of strips as the dominant design element and chief construction technique; large-scale designs; highly contrasting colors, particularly the preference for red; offbeat patterns to create an irregular, asymmetrical effect; and multiple rhythmic design, achieved by varying strip width, color contrast, and patch shapes.[75]

Lowcountry slave women also engaged in dairying and raising poultry. As early as the 1730s, an old slave woman served as a "Milk-woman." In the late colonial era, Eliza Pinckney described in detail the activities of her household slaves. At least two of her five female domestics were employed in housewifery. "Mary-Ann understands roasting poultry in the greatest perfection you ever saw," Eliza reported, "and old Ebba the fattening of them to as great a nicety. Daphne makes me a loaf of very nice bread. You know I am no epicure, but I am pleased they can do things so well, when they are put to it.... I shall keep young Ebba to do the drudgery part, fetch wood, and water, and scour, and learn as much as she is capable of Cooking and Washing. Mary-Ann Cooks, makes my bed, and makes my punch, Daphne works and makes the bread, old Ebba boils the cow's victuals, raises and fattens the poultry.... Peggy washes and milks." Later in the century, Mrs. Alice Izard commended her dairymaid Chloe for keeping an excellent dairy and providing plentiful supplies of milk and butter. But such activities seem to have been confined only to the large estates.[76]

---

75. Mark D. Groover, "Evidence for Folkways and Cultural Exchange in the Eighteenth-Century South Carolina Backcountry," *Historical Archaeology*, XXVIII (1994), 52–55; Maude Southwell Wahlman and John Scully, "Aesthetic Principles in Afro-American Quilts," in William Ferris, ed., *Afro-American Folk Art and Crafts* (Jackson, Miss., 1983), 79–97; Robert Farris Thompson, *Flash of the Spirit: African and Afro-American Art and Philosophy* (New York, 1983), 207–223; Vlach, *Afro-American Tradition*, 43–67; Gladys-Marie Fry, *Stitched from the Soul: Slave Quilts from the Ante-Bellum South* (New York, 1990), 31, 37, 44–45. See also Maude Southwell Wahlman and Ella King Torrey, *Ten Afro-American Quilters* (Jackson, Miss., 1983); Maude Southwell Wahlman, *Signs and Symbols: African Images in African-American Quilts* (New York, 1993).

76. John Whitfield, *SCG,* Sept. 4, 1736; Harriott Horry Ravenel, *Eliza Pinckney* (New York, 1896), 245; Alice Izard to Ralph Izard, Dec. 11, 1794, Ralph Izard Papers, USC. By comparison, dairying seems to have been quite extensive even on Robert Carter's outlying quarters. In 1781, an overseer's wife complained of the lack of female help "to milk and churn" because three slave women were absent. Carter responded that Negro Sally and Judy were experienced and could serve in that capacity. Bett the "butter maker" was resident at

Lowcountry slave women surpassed their Chesapeake counterparts in one area of housewifery—marketing—in large part, because their region contained a major urban center. Charleston was the largest town in the Southern colonies, and slave women were in the vanguard of those exploiting its marketing potential. Typical were John Stanyarne's Bella, "well known in Charles Town, being almost every Day at Market selling divers Things"; Margaret Remington's Phillis and Elsey, "well known in town, having been used to sell oysters for these 13 years past"; and Eliza Hill's Peg, who "walked the streets with a tray on her head with peaches." Slave women hawked cakes, tarts, and bread about the city streets; others peddled milk, garden produce, and fruit; one even sold sand. So ubiquitous did such women become that the Charleston grand jury complained in 1768 of the "many idle Negro Wenches, selling dry goods, cakes, rice, etc. in the markets," and eleven years later it denounced "the excessive number of Negro Wenches, suffered to buy and sell about the streets, corners and markets of Charlestown." In 1778, one observer "counted in the market and different corners" of Charleston "sixty-four Negro wenches selling cake, nuts, and so forth."[77]

Even more important than the variety of articles black women marketed was their monopoly of the business. In 1772, a "Stranger" commented at length on the black women to be found around Charleston's Lower Market,

> who are seated there from morn 'til night, and buy and sell on their accounts, what they please in order to pay their wages, and get as much more for themselves as they can; for their owners care little how their slaves get the money so they are paid. These women have such a connection with and influence on, the country negroes who come to that market, that they generally find means to obtain whatever they choose, in preference to any white person; thus, they forestall and engross many articles, which some hours afterwards you must buy back from them at 100 or 150 per cent advance. I have known those black women to be so insolent as even to wrest things out of the hands of white people, pretending they had been bought before, for their masters or mistresses, yet expose the same for sale again within an hour afterwards, for their own benefit. I have seen country ne-

---

another of Carter's quarters (Robert Carter to Mrs. Easter Sutton, Oct. 16, 1781, Carter Letterbook, IV, 133, and to George Newman, Jan. 4, 1788, ibid., VIII, 164).

77. John Stanyarne, *SCG*, Nov. 10, 1746; Margaret Remington, ibid., Nov. 25, 177; Eliza Hill, *City Gaz*, Sept. 2, 1793; Presentments of the Grand Jury of the Province, *SC and AGG*, Jan. 29, 1768; Presentments of the Grand Jury of Charlestown District, ibid., Dec. 3, 1779; ibid., Feb. 19, 1799. See also Elizabeth Bullock, *SCG*, Dec. 6, 1751; Leonard Graves, *SCG and CJ*, Jan. 27, 1767; Frederick Smith, *Royal Gaz*, Dec. 26, 1781; and my "Black Society in the Lowcountry," in Berlin and Hoffman, eds., *Slavery and Freedom*, 123.

groes take great pains, after having been spoken to by those women, to reserve what they choose to sell to them only, either by keeping the articles in their canoes, or by sending them away, and pretending they were not for sale, and when they could not be easily retained by them-selves, then I have seen the wenches as briskly hustle them about from one to another that in two minutes they could no longer be traced.

By the late colonial era, then, black women had assumed an important role in the town's economic affairs, not unlike the place traditionally held by female entrepreneurs in the trading centers of certain parts of Africa. Perhaps a link existed between an African background and slave marketing, explaining why, for example, the responsibility was given to one slave woman aged "about 45 years, Angola born and speaks very bad English." Even more remarkably, this woman managed to remain at large as a runaway for at least six months, going "about the country, within 10 miles of Charlestown, selling cakes, etc. and pretending to have permission from [her owner], and sometimes hires herself to free negroes." Female higglers were obviously everyday sights in and around the city.[78]

The presence of a large urban market in South Carolina created specialized opportunities for men as well as women. Bacchus sold fruit and vegetables, Quaco veal, and Hector cakes in Charleston. Most butchers and fishermen in the city were slave men. As early as 1733, black "Hucksters of corn, pease, fowls, etc.," many of them men, were found both "Night and Day on the several Wharfes . . . buy[ing] up many Articles necessary for the support of the Inhabitants," which they then resold at "exorbitant price[s]." In addition, many hawkers who lived in the surrounding countryside were men. Colonel Rivers's marketman apparently harbored a runaway slave woman on James Island. Another James Island resident, John Hearne's Caesar, "traded at the market" for years. A thirty-three-year-old slave, June, another James Island slave, was "well known in Charles Town by his being the principal market man to his master for many years." In fact, an identifiable group of island peddlers had emerged by the late colonial period. Thus, when an owner advertised for his runaway boatman in 1767, he could surmise that he would "associate with some of

78. "The Stranger," *SCG*, Sept. 24, 1772; Elizabeth Bourquin, ibid., May 23, 1761. For a cautious assessment of this possible "Africanism" in the West Indian context, see Sidney W. Mintz and Douglas Hall, "The Origins of the Jamaican Internal Marketing System," *Yale University Publications in Anthropology*, no. 57 (New Haven, Conn., 1960), 23–24, but compare Hilary McD. Beckles, "An Economic Life of Their Own: Slaves as Commodity Producers and Distributors in Barbados," in Ira Berlin and Philip D. Morgan, eds., *The Slaves' Economy: Independent Production by Slaves in the Americas* (London, 1991), 31–47; and Betty Wood, *Women's Work, Men's Work: The Informal Slave Economies of Lowcountry Georgia* (Athens, Ga., 1995), 80–100.

the island Negroes, who frequent the markets." But market men also came from further afield. An Ashley River resident advertised for her runaway slave, Harry, who was "well known in town, where he usually attended the market." In 1792, Gabriel Manigault, resident in Saint James Goose Creek, directed his slave Cudgo "to go to Town with vegetables, once a week, as usual."[79]

Initially, the small towns of the Chesapeake created limited opportunities for slave marketing. Places like Yorktown, Williamsburg, and Annapolis were only moderate consumers of dairy products, meat, and perishable goods. But slaves peddled many of these products. In 1781, for example, forty-four-year-old Pheby was "seen frequently in Williamsburg about the market, selling cakes, oysters." By the latter half of the eighteenth century, urban expansion in such places as Baltimore, Norfolk, Richmond, Alexandria, and Fredericksburg provided new opportunities for slave marketing. Richard Parkinson, who raised produce for the Baltimore market at the end of the eighteenth century, observed that black hucksters were superior to white ones. They "can sell more, and frequently at a higher price than a white man," because the blacks associated with one another so that the black "marketman has ten customers to the white man's one; and both buyer and seller have a share in the produce." According to Parkinson, slaves were much employed in selling hay and all kinds of farming produce in local towns and cities. They frequently made a little money on the side and, Parkinson noted, "generally return drunk from market."[80]

Although the expansion of marketing opportunities was part of a general expansion of the domestic sector, what is most impressive in the final analysis is the limited character of household work even on late-eighteenth-century plantations. The slave societies of the Chesapeake and Lowcountry were not organized for the promotion of housewifery or for the enhancement of domesticity. They were in the business of producing staples. As a southerner declared during a late colonial congressional debate on nonimportation, slave women were "best employed about Tobacco." Most planters echoed these sentiments. Consequently, masters confined household work for the most part to less physically strong slaves—women and young slaves. Thomas Jefferson prohibited his overseers from keeping "a woman out of the crop for waiting on

---

79. Thomas Walters, *SCG*, June 11, 1744; Richard Hill, ibid., July 1, 1745; Mr. Drouillard, *City Gaz*, June 5, 1797; Presentments of the Grand Jury for Charlestown, *SCG*, Mar. 30, 1734; John Forrester, ibid., May 7, 1763; John Hearne, *SCG and CJ*, Sept. 25, 1770; Malory Rivers, *SC and AGG*, Aug. 27, 1779; Joseph Rivers, *Royal Gaz*, Oct. 3, 1781; Joseph Glover, *SCG and CJ*, July 7, 1767; Margaret Ladson, *SCG*, Oct. 19, 1765; Gabriel Manigault to Mrs. Manigault, Nov. 20, 1792, Manigault Family Papers, SCHS.

80. Robert Sanford, *VaG or WA*, Jan. 19, 1782; Richard Parkinson, *A Tour in America, in 1798, 1799, and 1800* . . . , II (London, 1805), 433–434. See also Morris Birkbeck, *Notes on a Journey in America* (Ann Arbor, Mich., 1966 [orig. publ. London, 1817], 11.

them"; and only "superannuated women" or "children till 10 years" were to serve as nurses for slave infants. Three slave women were listed as house servants on John P. Custis's estate: one was seventy, another fifteen, and the third ten. The two slave women listed as house servants at the Bethesda Orphanage in Georgia in 1771 were described as "old but assist in washing, cutting fire wood, other necessary business about the House."[81] The typical eighteenth-century house servant was either an old woman or a young girl.

Most domestics, then, had much in common with the vast majority of plantation slaves. Their numbers were few, they often lived in outbuildings close to field hands, and they were as likely to work in the stables and gardens as in the house. The work of a washerwoman was no more glamorous than that of a field hand. The significant exceptions were the manservants, who lived in another world: they traveled widely, dressed opulently, and even spoke differently. And, as housewifery expanded, some women and a few men learned skills that inevitably distanced them from field hands. For the most part, however, most domestics lived very near the world of the ordinary plantation slave.

Skilled slaves had much in common. Most were men; woodworkers predominated; and they came to their posts sometimes early, more often late, in life. The vast majority were not far removed from field hands: drivers and foremen worked alongside them, sawyers were but a step from them, boatmen and fishermen rubbed shoulders with them, and most domestics lived with them. Skilled slaves and domestics were sometimes drafted into the fields; most drivers and a number of other nonfield-workers had been field hands when younger. However close to field hands, all skilled slaves shared one obvious characteristic that separated them from field laborers: for the most part, they avoided the drudgery, monotony, and onerousness of wielding a hoe. Other privileges followed from this basic difference: some secured specialist training, others enjoyed substantial freedom of movement, many received extra perquisites, most lived longer. In association with, and in separation from, field hands, skilled slaves found a common identity.

In spite of the uniformities, the ranks of skilled slaves encompassed significant variations. The responsibilities assumed by a capable driver far outweighed those devolving on a mere gang leader; the broadened horizons of the

---

81. L. H. Butterfield et al., eds., *The Diary and Autobiography of John Adams,* II (Cambridge, Mass., 1961), 216, as cited in Norton, *Liberty's Daughters,* 164; Edwin Morris Betts, ed., *Thomas Jefferson's Farm Book, with Commentary and Relevant Extracts from Other Writings,* American Philosophical Society, Memoirs, XXXV (Princeton, N.J., 1953), 76–77; account of the Negroes of the great house, York County, Dec. 20, 1771, Custis Papers; account of Negroes now at and belonging to the Orphan House, c. 1771, A 3/2/2, Countess of Huntingdon's American Papers.

mobile, jobbing carpenter were far removed from the plantation-bound orbit of the sedentary sawyer; the highly developed skills of an urban craftsman far exceeded the reach of an ordinary plantation tradesman; the experience of working on an all-black crew was far different from that of laboring on a mixed crew; and the waiting man's privileged existence was a far cry from the prosaic world of the washerwoman. There was no typical skilled work experience.

The size, character, and composition of skills also varied markedly across space. Opportunities for skilled men were always greater in the Lowcountry, both in the countryside and city, than in the Chesapeake. By the end of the century, perhaps one in four slave men in the Lowcountry and no more than one in six in the Chesapeake had escaped the fields. Moreover, the more specialized South Carolina economy gave greater opportunities to drivers, specialist urban tradesmen, larger and less racially mixed boat crews, and female hawkers than did the Virginia economy. In addition, basketmakers, potters, woodworkers, and fishermen found greater scope to incorporate African techniques into their crafts in the Lowcountry than in the Chesapeake. Conversely, more diversified Chesapeake estates gave rise to a greater range of skilled tradesmen—notably, ironworkers, blacksmiths, and shipwrights—and to a higher proportion of female workers, particularly those engaged in housewifery. The overall opportunities for skilled work were greater in the Lowcountry, but the range of skilled activities was broader in the Chesapeake.

II
Encounters between Whites and Blacks

No one from being a person

can become a thing.

—John Davis

5 : Patriarchs, Plain Folk, and Slaves

The free and the unfree engaged in endless and varied encounters. To comprehend these kaleidoscopic contacts between masters and slaves, whites and blacks requires complex formulations. However cruelly whites exploited blacks, their fates were intricately intertwined. However much masters treated their slaves as chattels, the humanity of their property could not be ignored or evaded. However total the masters' exercise of power, negotiation and compromise were necessary to make slavery function. However sincerely planter patriarchs stressed mutuality and reciprocity, their authority ultimately rested on force. However sentimentally and benevolently some late-eighteenth-century masters viewed slaves, their relentless denial of rights to bondmen increasingly placed slaves outside society. However unequivocally daily existence brought blacks and whites together, growing race consciousness and class distinctions thrust them apart. However deep a chasm opened between whites and blacks, channels of communication arose to bridge it. However fundamentally slavery was the result of interaction between master and slave, nonslaveholders intruded to shape the institution's character. The intricacy of eighteenth-century white-black relations defies easy definition.

The core contradiction of slavery—treating persons as things—accounted for much of the complexity of master-slave relations. Although slaves were defined legally as property and thereby subject to unparalleled dehumanization, they were also human beings, simultaneously called on to respond in a multiplicity of ways to the demands placed on them. Bought and sold like cattle, bequeathed and inherited like furniture, won and lost like lottery prizes, slaves nevertheless were flesh-and-blood human beings with whom working relationships had to be established, negotiations arranged, and accommodations reached. Slaves suffered a deprivation of freedom so extreme as to be likened, in Orlando Patterson's words, to "social death," yet they were also part of society. In spite of the barbarity with which many masters treated their slaves, the bonds of common humanity served as the ligaments of a shared social order. Perceptive contemporaries were aware of this interdependence. In 1743, Commissary James Blair of Virginia observed that slavery "had become a molding power, leaving it a vexed question which controlled society most, the African slave or his master." Modern commentators have deepened Blair's insight. Masters and slaves, blacks and whites, in C. Vann Woodward's words, "shaped each other's destiny, determined each other's isolation, shared and molded a common culture." Eugene Genovese began his magisterial *Roll, Jordan, Roll* with the following statement: "Cruel, unjust, exploitative, oppressive, slavery bound two peoples together in bitter antagonism while creating an organic relationship so complex and ambivalent that neither could express the simplest human feelings without reference to the other."[1]

The dominant social ethos and cultural metaphor of seventeenth- and early-eighteenth-century Anglo-America, patriarchalism, embodied the ideal of an organic social hierarchy. Invoking the Great Chain of Being, one Virginia lawyer argued in 1772: "Societies of men could not subsist unless there were a subordination of one to another.... That in this subordination the department of slaves must be filled by some, or there would be a defect in the scale of order." Deeply ingrained assumptions about the workings not only of society but also of politics elevated the role of father to mythic heights. From this perspective, patriarchs anchored a social system based on the protection that the powerful offered the weak, just as monarchs defined a political system where royal power defended the people in return for their obedience and loyalty. Indeed, masters might draw a precise parallel, as Henry Laurens once did when he reflected, "Never was an absolute Monarch more happy in his Subjects than at the Present time I am." Suffusing the thought of the age, the patriarchal outlook was an austere code, emphasizing control, obedience, discipline, and severity.

1. Orlando Patterson, *Slavery and Social Death: A Comparative Study* (Cambridge, Mass., 1982), 38–45; Blair, as cited in Sydney E. Ahlstrom, *A Religious History of the American People*, I (New Haven, Conn., 1972), 245; C. Vann Woodward, *American Counterpoint: Slavery and Racism in the North-South Dialogue* (Boston, 1964), 5; Eugene D. Genovese, *Roll, Jordan, Roll: The World the Slaves Made* (New York, 1974), 3. The epigraph derives from John Davis, *Travels of Four Years and a Half in the United States of America . . .* (Bristol, 1803), 92.

Yet patriarchalism also involved protection, guardianship, and reciprocal obligations. It defined the gentleman planter's self-image and constituted the ideals and standards by which slaveholding behavior was judged.[2]

Other discourses, other ways of thinking about slaves, made inroads on the patriarchal ideal. Slaves were chattel, and masters thought of and acted toward them using the language of property. Anglo-American masters were also profit-conscious, operated in a market economy, and employed the language of commercial capitalism. The importance of money in defining personal relations in colonial North America can never be exaggerated. Nevertheless, for much of the eighteenth century, neither the discourse of property nor the discourse of capitalism overrode, though they certainly encroached on, the masters' sense of slaves as dependents. Being part of a household cushioned slaves from the full force of free-market commercialism. Harsh profit-and-loss purgatives had not yet voided the body politic of its traditional notions of duty, mutuality, and patriarchal care.

Nevertheless, patriarchalism was reformulated over the course of the eighteenth century. Masters began to speak less of duties and obligations, more of individual rights, particularly property rights. Slaves were more and more defined as people without rights; and, because they were viewed increasingly as property, they were said to enhance their owners' independence. Whereas the patriarchal ethos held that even the lowliest person was part of an organic society, the denial of rights could place the slave completely outside society. In part because slaves were being seen as perpetual outsiders, masters could emphasize solicitude rather than authority, sentiments rather than severity, in their governance. This shift in emphasis was partly a response to political events but also resulted from the development of a more affectionate family life, the rise of evangelicalism, the growth of romanticism, and the increase of humanitarianism. It was a reflection in the realm of ideas of broad-gauged changes affecting Revolutionary America. Austere patriarchalism slowly gave way to mellow paternalism.

At the same time as the inclusiveness of patriarchal ideology was being undermined, the everyday world of masters and slaves, whites and blacks became more fractured. Over the course of the eighteenth century, a rapidly growing slave population, increasingly independent living quarters, larger plantations, and an influx of Africans distanced blacks from whites. These forces were more intensely experienced in the Lowcountry than in the Chesa-

---

2. *Robin* v. *Hardaway,* 1 Va. (Jeff.), 58, 62–63 (1772), as cited in A. Leon Higginbotham, Jr., and Barbara K. Kopytoff, "Racial Purity and Interracial Sex in the Law of Colonial and Antebellum Virginia," *Georgetown Law Journal,* LXXVII (1989), 1969; Harold C. Syrett et al., eds., *The Papers of Alexander Hamilton,* 27 vols. (New York, 1961–1987), III, 605–608.

peake, for master-slave relations were more impersonal and usually harsher in the Lowcountry than in the Chesapeake. Thus, although masters and slaves always interacted less closely and intimately on Lowcountry rice estates than on Chesapeake tobacco plantations, the gap between these two regional patterns widened as the century progressed. Nevertheless, people everywhere in mainland North America increasingly aligned themselves according to the color of their skins. The articulation of a racist ideology, which intensified in the late eighteenth century, contributed to the growing cleavage that separated whites and blacks.[3]

The duality of growing separation and common bonds applied as much to the relationship of plain white folk and blacks as it did to large planters and their slaves. Because in the late seventeenth century poor whites associated closely and openly with slaves, the growing gap between them was notable. Relations between poor whites and blacks were also part of a larger tangled web that enmeshed patriarchs, plain folk, and slaves. The existence of a large group of plain white folk, for example, encouraged planters to seek their support and recognition. To the degree that nonslaveholders honored slaveholders, they enhanced the large planters' social legitimacy. Slaves in turn saw proud, free white men defer to powerful masters, reinforcing in their eyes the authority of large planters. Paradoxically, the ties established between patriarchs and plain folk could strengthen those between grandees and slaves.

My aim in this chapter is to provide a way of conceptualizing the social dynamics of white-black relations in the eighteenth-century South, to provide an overview for succeeding Chapters 6 and 7, which explore the exchanges and transactions of quotidian life. If a single message can be gleaned, it is that southern society was bedeviled by a perennial conflict of irreconcilable opposites, the most fundamental of which was inherent in the very notion of human bondage. Consequently, masters and slaves, whites and blacks were bound together in amicable and antagonistic, cooperative and conflictual, harmonious and hostile ways. The contradictions varied over time: patriarchalism and later paternalism were changing ideological attempts to resolve or mediate these contradictions. They varied across space: relations between masters and slaves, whites and blacks were always more intimate in the Chesapeake, more distant in the Lowcountry. And, finally, they varied according to the dynamic interplay of race and class: in part, relations were bipolar—be-

3. Compare the whole thrust of Mechal Sobel's *World They Made Together: Black and White Values in Eighteenth-Century Virginia* (Princeton, N.J., 1987), which ignores these trends; for example: "Ultimately, an ideology based on white superiority did divide poor whites from blacks; however, a very long history and black and white interaction preceded the marked separation of the nineteenth century" (45).

tween whites and blacks—but they were also triangular—between masters, plain folk, and slaves. Encounters between blacks and whites, masters and slaves overflowed with complexities and teemed with ambiguities.

MASTERS AND SLAVES

The inherent contradiction of treating a person as property lay at the heart of slavery. In theory, the slave was a thing, a piece of property, a beast of burden, and could be treated with all the impersonality accorded a mere possession, an extension of the master's will. The slave's existence was wholly contingent on the master's volition. Yet slaves continually demonstrated that they had wills of their own, that they were sentient, articulate human beings, that they were members of society as well as capital assets. In reality, masters implicitly, if not always explicitly, recognized the humanity of their slaves. The slave could never become the thing he or she was supposed to be.[4]

The slaves' status as chattel was at the root of the callousness and dehumanization they faced, setting them apart from other compulsory laborers. Slaves experienced a more encompassing denial of rights than did other forced laborers. The slave suffered not only loss of control over labor-power but also loss of control over person. This deprivation of freedom was so extreme as to be qualitatively distinct from all other forms of unfreedom. Further, the slave was an outsider. Uprooted from one society and introduced into another, slaves were denied the most elementary of social bonds. A defining characteristic of slaves was their legal "kinlessness" or "natal alienation."[5] If brutality in human relations is common and if societies always inflict gross injustices on those who have nothing to offer but their labor, what singles out slaves is the sheer nakedness of the exploitation to which they were subject.

Whenever North American colonists felt most abused, they likened their condition to slavery or compared their fate to that of blacks. Nor was this merely a rhetorical ploy of upper-class colonists. In 1668, a Virginia maidservant who had been raped by her master claimed that he "would make her worse than a negro by whoring her." A widow in Charles County, Maryland,

---

4. There is a sharp difference of opinion about the importance of the concept of property to a definition of slavery. For the view that it is unimportant, see, among others, Igor Kopytoff, "Slavery," *Annual Review of Anthropology*, XI (1982), 207–230, esp. 219–221; and Patterson, *Slavery and Social Death*, esp. 18–34. Perhaps the best counterargument comes from the late Moses I. Finley. See, for example, his *Ancient Slavery and Modern Ideology* (Harmondsworth, Eng., 1983), 73–75. I find Finley's position most useful for a study of New World slavery. I have also been influenced by David Brion Davis, *The Problem of Slavery in Western Culture* (Ithaca, N.Y., 1966); and Sidney W. Mintz and Richard Price, *An Anthropological Approach to the Afro-American Past: A Caribbean Perspective*, Institute for the Study of Human Issues, Occasional Papers in Social Change, no. 2 (Philadelphia, 1976), 13.

5. Finley, *Ancient Slavery*, 74–75; Patterson, *Slavery and Social Death*, 5–6.

in the late seventeenth century, complained of the treatment her son had received when in the household of Ralph Shaw. She alleged that Shaw used her son as "a servant or rather a white Negro clothing him in such things as Negroes are usually Clothed and Putting him under an overseer to make tobacco and corne instead of going to Schoole." Work became associated with servile drudgery, leading a Lowcountry resident to declare, "Where there are Negroes, a white Man despises to work, saying, *what, will you have me a Slave and work like a Negroe?*" Convicts likened their situation to slavery, and one claimed that slaves were "better used."[6]

Yet, as this last comment suggests, the slaves' status as perpetual property—the primary source of their more systematic dehumanization as compared to other forced laborers—could work to their advantage. A slave might be treated with greater consideration than a servant or convict precisely because he or she was a capital asset. A white overseer charged with murdering a white maidservant in late-seventeenth-century Virginia saw himself as a victim of exactly such reverse discrimination. He had been made a scapegoat, he alleged, for a mulatto, whom his employer wanted to "clear . . . because he was a slave for his life." Even while acknowledging that some Virginia masters "use their Negros no better than their Cattle," Governor William Gooch made a claim that would be heard with resounding regularity down the years. "Far the greater Number [of slaves]," he asserted, "having kind Masters, live much better than poor Laboring Men in England." Such claims of humane treatment of individual slaves by individual masters, however accurate and however widespread, go no way to lessening the inhumanity of slavery as an institution, for the indictment of slavery rests, not on the issue of treatment, but on its denial of freedom. But they do go some way to pointing up one of the many ironies of slavery—

---

6. Accomac County Orders, 1666–1670, 112, in J. Douglas Deal, *Race and Class in Colonial Virginia: Indians, Englishmen, and Africans on the Eastern Shore during the Seventeenth Century* (New York, 1993), 111; Charles County Court, V, no. 1, fol. 410, X, no. 1, fol. 375, in Lorena Seebach Walsh, "Charles County Maryland, 1658–1705: A Study of Chesapeake Social and Political Structure" (Ph.D. diss., Michigan State University, 1977), 139; Allen D. Candler, comp., *The Colonial Records of the State of Georgia*, 26 vols. (Atlanta, Ga., 1904–1916), V, 476, in Winthrop D. Jordan, *White over Black: American Attitudes toward the Negro, 1550–1812* (Chapel Hill, N.C., 1968), 129–130; *Account of the Ordinary of Newgate*, June 4, 1770, 43, in A. Roger Ekirch, *Bound for America: The Transportation of British Convicts to the Colonies, 1718–1775* (Oxford, 1987), 151; Elizabeth Sprigs to John Sprigs, Sept. 22, 1756, in Merrill Jensen, ed., *English Historical Documents: American Colonial Documents to 1776*, vol. IX of David C. Douglas, ed., *English Historical Documents* (New York, 1955), 489. More generally, see Bernard Bailyn, *The Ideological Origins of the American Revolution* (Cambridge, Mass., 1967), 232–246; and Jack P. Greene, "'Slavery or Independence': Some Reflections on the Relationship among Liberty, Black Bondage, and Equality in Revolutionary South Carolina," *SCHM*, LXXX (1979), 193–214.

namely, that the humane treatment of some slaves was predicated on the very source of their most systematic dehumanization: their propertied status.[7]

Because law distills some of any society's most cherished values, it provides a graphic demonstration of the degradation to which slaves were subject. One of the first Virginia acts relating to slaves concerned their punishment. Passed in 1669, the act was appropriately entitled "An act about the casuall killing of slaves." It declared that, in case a slave died from a beating administered for insubordination, the master or his agent was to be exonerated, "since it cannot be presumed that prepensed malice (which alone makes murther ffelony) should induce any man to destroy his owne estate." Andrew Burnaby considered this immunity enjoyed by masters the most repugnant feature of Virginia society, tantamount to an open season on slaves.[8]

As Virginia's commitment to slavery deepened, a specialized form of justice—or, more appropriately, injustice—arose to deal with slaves. After 1692, a slave who committed a capital offense was denied the "sollemnitie of jury" or right of appeal and could be convicted on the evidence of his or her own confession "or the oaths of two witnesses or of one with pregnant circumstances." Whereas free persons charged with capital offenses had to be brought to the capital for trial ("'tis a maxim," declared an act of 1656, "that no deliberation can be too much pondered that concernes the life of the meanest man"), no such concern was extended slaves, who were tried in their respective counties. Slaves were made even more vulnerable in 1705, when the slave code awarded owners the full value of an executed bondman, whereas the act of 1723 reduced the number of necessary "credible witnesses" to one. By the first

---

7. Accomac Wills and Orders, 1682–1697, 91a, 93a–96a, in Deal, *Race and Class in Colonial Virginia*, 104; Governor Gooch to the Bishop of London, May 28, 1731, Fulham Palace Papers, XV, SR 650, microfilm, CW. William Eddis thought that white servants in North America "groan[ed] beneath a worse than Egyptian bondage." Because blacks were "a property for life," they were, in his estimation, "almost in every instance, under more comfortable circumstances than the miserable European" (Eddis, *Letters from America*, ed. Aubrey C. Land [Cambridge, Mass., 1969], 38).

8. William Waller Hening, *The Statutes at Large: Being a Collection of All the Laws of Virginia . . .* , 13 vols. (Richmond, Va., and Philadelphia, 1809–1823), II, 270; Andrew Burnaby, *Travels through the Middle Settlements in North-America, in the Years 1759 and 1760 . . .* , 3d ed. (London, 1798), 22–23. See also John Clayton to Lords Commissioners for Trade and Plantations, Dec. 20, 1716, CO5/1318, fols. 95–98, microfilm, CW; Marion Tinling, ed., *The Correspondence of the Three William Byrds of Westover, Virginia, 1684–1776*, I (Charlottesville, Va., 1977), 297; and William M. Wiecek, "The Statutory Law of Slavery and Race in the Thirteen Mainland Colonies of British America," *WMQ*, 3d Ser., XXXIV (1977), 258–280. A study that stresses the legal importance of the slave as property in ways compatible with my analysis, but treating the relationship at much greater length and with greater sophistication, is Thomas D. Morris, *Southern Slavery and the Law, 1619–1860* (Chapel Hill, N.C., 1996).

quarter of the eighteenth century, the basic criminal law of slavery was in place. Although the law was uniform and not arbitrary (owners could defend their slaves in court either personally or through a lawyer), the slave was subject to a rapid, harsh, and singular justice.[9]

South Carolina's slave code took shape, if anything, even more quickly and was even harsher in intent than that of Virginia. Carolina's special courts (of two justices and three freeholders) were created two years earlier than those in Virginia, and the policy of reimbursement for executed slaves was introduced a decade earlier. Moreover, whereas Virginia moved over time to make its special courts less severe—in 1748, for instance, a slave was to be acquitted if the court was divided; in 1772, a sentence of death required unanimity from four justices—South Carolina moved in the opposite direction. A law of 1696 specified that murder cases involving slaves needed to be based not just on an examination of "all evidences, proofs and testimonies" but also on "violent presumption and circumstances"; and, in 1714, majority verdicts were made permissible in capital cases, whereas only three persons were required to decide noncapital crimes. No free person could be executed for killing a slave in eighteenth-century South Carolina; in Virginia, it was at least a theoretical possibility.[10]

Punishments were also more stringent further south. For striking a white man in Virginia, a slave received thirty-nine lashes by the act of 1705, reduced to thirty lashes forty-three years later. In South Carolina, an act of 1714 made the same offense punishable by death, lessened to a "severe whipping" and the loss of an ear for a first offense eight years later. But this lowered sentence was a minor concession, for the death sentence was still reserved for any action that "bruised, wounded, maimed or disabled" a white person. South Carolina law was also brutally specific concerning the type of physical punishment to be administered. Explicit provisions in the South Carolina code for nose slitting, "gelding" (though permissible in Virginia before 1769, when it was reserved only for cases of rape), and ankle-cord cutting were absent from the pages of Virginia's statute books. In the eighteenth century, at least seven South Carolina slaves were burned alive for alleged crimes. As late as 1830, a South

---

9. Hening, ed., *Statutes at Large*, I, 398, III, 102–103, 269–270, IV, 127. As an indication of the sort of "justice" often meted out to slaves, the views of one white Virginian are pertinent. He returned home from court angry because "we had a Jury on those Negroes and one Damn'd Fool hung the Jury, a clearer case never was; there was many Lawyers present and at least 30 bystanders and they were to a Man in our favour—we are to have another Tryal next Friday" (Bowler Cocke to William Cocke, Feb. 22, 1791, Armistead-Cocke Papers, W and M).

10. Thomas Cooper and David J. McCord, eds., *The Statutes at Large of South Carolina*, 10 vols. (Columbia, S.C., 1836–1841), VII, 343, 355 (misdated 1712), 358, 365–366; Hening, ed., *Statutes at Large*, VI, 106, VIII, 523. For more on the murder of a slave, see Morris, *Southern Slavery and the Law*, 165–171.

Carolina slave faced execution by fire. In Virginia, by contrast, only two slaves are known to have been burned to death, the second in 1746. Well might Josiah Quincy exclaim, when he visited South Carolina in 1773, that the "Legislators [have] enacted laws touching negroes, mulattoes and masters which savor more of the policy of Pandemonium than the English constitution."[11]

Once again, however, the slaves' propertied status mitigated the full rigor and severity of the law. In South Carolina, for example, the public treasury was deemed incapable of supporting the full reimbursement for executed slaves. In 1714, the maximum sum allowable was only fifty pounds. In 1740, it was raised to two hundred pounds precisely so that "owners of slaves may not be tempted to conceal the crimes of their slaves to the prejudice of the public." But two hundred pounds was insufficient compensation for a prime field hand, and some slave crime was concealed on this account. A visitor to South Carolina in 1772 claimed that one could see "daily instances of the most execrable villains being sold, or sent off the province, or no farther than Winyaw, even for the horrid crime of administering poison which is an evil of the first magnitude." Most losses fell on tradesmen, he argued, because wealthy slaveowners saw to it that their slaves never came to trial. In the following year, the grand jury of Georgetown district echoed the visitor's complaint by again pointing to the "insufficiency of the valuation of negroes and other slaves that are executed, by which means, many notorious Villains are not brought to Justice." Similar complaints were heard in Virginia. According to Landon Carter, Virginia justices were disinclined to try too many felony cases or to hand down too many death sentences because of the amount of compensation chargeable to the public. During the Revolutionary war, one magistrate acquitted a slave of treason on the grounds that he was a chattel, and thereby a noncitizen. Propertied status occasionally had advantages.[12]

---

11. Hening, ed., *Statutes at Large*, III, 459, VI, 110, VIII, 358; Cooper and McCord, eds., *Statutes at Large*, VII, 343, 360, 366–367, 377; Lowry Ware, "The Burning of Jerry: The Last Slave Execution by Fire in South Carolina?" *SCHM*, XCI (1990), 100–106; Philip J. Schwarz, *Twice Condemned: Slaves and the Criminal Laws of Virginia, 1705–1865* (Baton Rouge, La., 1988), 15, 92; Mark Antony De Wolfe Howe, ed., "Journal of Josiah Quincy, Junior, 1773," Massachusetts Historical Society, *Proceedings*, XLIX (1915–1916), 457. On "gelding," see Adam Culliatt, *SCG*, Apr. 14, 1757; Workhouse, *SCG and CJ*, Jan. 26, 1768 (this captured fugitive reported that his master castrated him and another slave); and Journal of South Carolina House of Representatives, Dec. 19, 1794, 221, available in Willam S. Jenkins, ed., *Records of the States of the United States of America*, microfilm series (Washington, D.C., 1949). To my knowledge, no evidence of castrated slaves survives from 18th-century Chesapeake runaway advertisements, but, between 1740 and 1785, four Virginia slaves were sentenced to castration for the attempted rape of a white woman (Schwarz, *Twice Condemned*, 157).

12. Cooper and McCord, eds., *Statutes at Large*, VII, 366, 403; "The Stranger," *SCG*, Sept. 17, 1772; Georgetown District Grand Jury presentments, ibid., Dec. 27, 1773; Jack P. Greene,

Informal attempts to protect slaves from the rigors of the law are difficult to discover, for obvious reasons, but sometimes they come to light. In the Lowcountry, Robert Raper informed Thomas Boone in 1770 that he had sent his slave man Abraham to Pon Pon because he had committed two or three robberies in the vicinity of his Cooper River plantation and "was very near being hanged." In the following year, two of Governor James Grant's boatmen robbed a store in Saint Augustine, East Florida. Grant's manager had initially hoped to keep the affair private, but the storekeeper demanded a search warrant and discovered most of his stolen property. The manager offered a handsome reimbursement, but the storekeeper "was advised by people in town not to make it up," provoking the manager to bewail "the disposition of the Mobility." Chesapeake slaves also benefited from private arrangements designed to evade the law. In 1729, a ship captain had arranged, with various masters of slaves involved in a robbery of his storehouse, to take back the stolen goods and avoid a trial. The Virginia Council charged him with compounding the felony. A less blatant example of protection occurred one winter when Vincent Marmaduke ignored a magistrate's warrant committing a runaway slave named Tom to the Westmoreland County jail. As he explained, "The weather at that time being very Cold, I thought proper to Keep him out of Gaol and from the good behaviour of sd fellow since, I shall continue him out of Gaol." Tom had then been in Marmaduke's employ for four months.[13]

A defining characteristic of slavery was its highly personal mechanisms of coercion; the whip, rather than resort to law, was its indispensable and ubiquitous instrument. Virginians, as Edmund Morgan has pointed out, were casual and matter-of-fact about the lashings and dismemberings they meted out to their slaves. Thomas Jones could happily tell his wife of having "chear'd" a slave with thirty lashes on Saturday and another thirty on Tuesday. In Charles County, Maryland, in 1772, a small planter killed a slave by hanging him from the beams of his house for six hours, by whipping him one hundred times with

---

ed., *The Diary of Colonel Landon Carter of Sabine Hall, 1752–1778*, 2 vols. (Charlottesville, Va., 1965), 676 (hereafter cited as *Carter Diary*); Benjamin Quarles, *The Negro in the American Revolution* (Chapel Hill, N.C., 1961), 129. See also Thomas Wright, *SCG*, Oct. 30, 1762, for a master's unhappiness at his slave's "unjust" punishment.

13. Robert Raper to Thomas Boone, July 3, 1770, Robert Raper Letterbook, West Sussex Record Office, England, microfilm, SCHS; David Yeats to James Grant, Aug. 31, 1771, bundle 250, Papers of General James Grant of Ballindalloch, sometime Governor of East Florida, in ownership of Sir Evan Macpherson-Grant, Bart., Ballindalloch Castle Muniments, Scotland; H. R. McIlwaine et al., eds., *Executive Journals of the Council of Colonial Virginia*, IV (Richmond, Va., 1930), 198; Vincent Marmaduke to Robert Carter, Mar. 2, 1782, Carter Family Papers, VHS.

more than thirty birch rods, and by inflicting wounds six inches long and half an inch deep on his back, shoulders, sides, and stomach. A jury acquitted the planter of murder. Absolutely chilling are the sentiments committed to a diary by a young Virginia girl after a slave had killed her cat. "A vile wretch of new negrows," she raged, "if he was mine, I would cut him to pieces, a son of a gun, a nice negrow, he should be kild himself by rites." Robert "King" Carter boasted of curing a runaway by taking off his toes. If anything, Carolina masters gained an even worse reputation than their Virginia counterparts. In the early eighteenth century, the Reverend Francis Le Jau witnessed a slave woman burned alive and a slave man put into "a hellish Machine" shaped like a coffin. Masters in his neighborhood, Le Jau observed, "hamstring, maim, and unlimb those poor Creatures for small faults." In 1711, an English immigrant spoke encouragingly to her relatives back home of the advantages of the Carolina environment. Craftsmen or husbandmen can succeed, she predicted, provided they "get a few slaves and can beat them well to make them work hard." Eighty years later, another immigrant to the Lowcountry noted that on first arrival he "could not bear to see a negro corrected" but that within five years "he could bear to flay one of them alive." The estates of South Carolina planters contained the instruments of coercion: mouthpieces, pairs of "iron negro fetters," and "Negro spurs." The famous scene, so movingly rendered by Crèvecoeur, of a slave suspended in a cage, preyed on by birds and insects, and barely alive, derived, appropriately enough, from South Carolina.[14]

14. Edmund S. Morgan, *American Slavery, American Freedom: The Ordeal of Colonial Virginia* (New York, 1975), 312–315; Thomas Jones to his wife, Oct. 22, 1736, "Jones Papers," *VMHB*, XXVI (1918), 285; Jean B. Lee, *The Price of Nationhood: The American Revolution in Charles County* (New York, 1995), 68; "Diary of a Little Colonial Girl," *VMHB*, XI (1903–1904), 213; Robert Carter to Robert Jones, Oct. 10, 1727, Robert Carter Letterbook, 1727–1728, UVa; Francis Le Jau to SPG, Mar. 22, 1709, A4/142, Feb. 20, 1712, A7/395–398, Feb. 23, 1713, A8/346–348, SPG; St. Julien R. Childs, "A Letter Written in 1711 by Mary Stafford to Her Kinswoman in England," *SCHM*, LXXXI (1980), 4; George W. Corner, ed., *The Autobiography of Benjamin Rush: His "Travels through Life" Together with His Commonplace Book for 1789–1813*, American Philosophical Society, Memoirs, XXV (Princeton, N.J., 1948), 219–220; J. Hector St. John Crèvecoeur, *Letters from an American Farmer*, ed. W. P. Trent and Ludwig Lewisohn (New York, 1925 [orig. publ. 1782]), 242–245; and for a similar account to that of Crèvecoeur, see George Fenwick Jones, "The 1780 Siege of Charleston as Experienced by a Hessian Officer: Part Two," *SCHM*, LXXXVIII (1987), 72. For typical inventories listing mouthpieces, etc., see those of William Ritch, June 28, 1751, Inventory Book, WPA, CXXXII, 55–56; of Silas Kerslake, Feb. 4, 1754, ibid., CXLIV, 164–165; of William Eding, Apr. 20, 1756, ibid., CLIII, 889–891; of Capt. William Lawton, Dec. 19, 1757, ibid., CLV, 310–315; of John Hogg, 1759, ibid., CLIX, 371–373, SCDAH. For customary violence by masters, see Harold E. Davis, *The Fledgling Province: Social and Cultural Life in Colonial Georgia, 1773–1776* (Chapel

PLATE 17. Portrait of a Man / Virginian Luxuries. *Artist unknown. Circa 1810. Double-sided painting. The obverse of a portrait of a man, this hidden side represents the seamy side of Virginia life. Courtesy Abby Aldrich Rockefeller Folk Art Center, Williamsburg*

And yet precisely because a slave entered into no contractual relationship with his or her master but was instead subject to direct personal domination, so he or she could be more readily considered part of the household. The slave was not simply a factor of production with whom an employer maintained a limited relationship—a condition that was becoming familiar to some laborers in eighteenth-century British America—but was a part of the master's household. Not for nothing were slaves termed *famuli* in the ancient world. They were the original *familia*, a group of *famuli* living under the same roof. Anglo-American masters were party to this tradition. They referred to their slaves as their "people," as their "folks," or as part of their "family." Slaves were almost uniformly known by familial, not formal names—Jack for John, Matt for Matthew, Sukey for Susanna, and so on—and they largely lacked surnames. As Michael Zuckerman has argued of William Byrd: "His attachments were never confined within the sealing circle of spouse and fledglings. On the contrary, they were diffused far and wide among a heterogeneous plantation commu-

---

Hill, N.C., 1976), 131; Mrs. Elizabeth Sindrey Estate Account Book, 1705–1721, October 1708, SCHS; Louis B. Wright and Marion Tinling, eds., *The Secret Diary of William Byrd of Westover, 1709–1712* (Richmond, Va., 1941), 2, 46, 112, 113, 117, 119, 419.

nity, conceived in its entirety as his family and explicitly so described." Seen from this vantage point, slavery was but one of a number of subordinate statuses in the Anglo-American world—one that rested on a personal rather than an impersonal basis.[15]

It is easy to deride these personal ties. Orlando Patterson has claimed: "No authentic human relationship was possible where violence was the ultimate sanction. There could have been no trust, no genuine sympathy, and while a kind of love may sometimes have triumphed over the most perverse form of interaction, intimacy was usually calculating and sadomasochistic." As much as one might like to believe this, too much evidence contradicts it. An inhumane institution like slavery could still encompass within it warm and caring human relationships. Charles Ball, who experienced slavery, is an excellent witness. Indeed, Patterson might enlist him as an ally, for Ball once declared that there "never can be any affinity of feeling between master and slave." Yet Ball also recollected "instances of the greatest tenderness of feeling" on the part of masters toward their slaves and described one mistress as "a true friend to me." Strong personal ties, a measure of trust, even sympathies did arise between many a master and slave. True, there was always the ever-present threat of violence, but these human associations were no less authentic for that.[16]

A spectacular example concerns John Gibb of Queen Anne County, Maryland. In 1740, he provided for the manumission of his nineteen slaves, giving each a share of his clothing and land. Gibb's niece, Janet Cleland, contested the will and won a ruling in her favor from the Maryland Prerogative Court. The nineteen slaves in turn appealed this decision. Cleland claimed that the slaves had taken advantage of their master during his last illness. They had refused to work unless he provided for their freedom. Gibb's executors disputed this claim and instead made the telling observation that the master had trusted his slaves far more than his niece. Depositions from neighbors confirmed elements

---

15. György Diósdi, *Ownership in Ancient and Preclassical Roman Law* (Budapest, 1970), 19, 22–23, 30; *Oxford English Dictionary*, s.v. "family"; Ann Kussmaul, *Servants in Husbandry in Early Modern England* (Cambridge, 1981), 7; Frederick Cooper, *Plantation Slavery on the East Coast of Africa* (New Haven, Conn., 1977), 2. On planters' referring to their "folks," etc., see, for example, Gerald W. Mullin, *Flight and Rebellion: Slave Resistance in Eighteenth-Century Virginia* (New York, 1972), 23–24; and Sobel, *The World They Made Together*, 163. On the use of familial names, see Newbell Niles Puckett, "Names of American Negro Slaves," in George Peter Murdock, ed., *Studies in the Science of Society* (New Haven, Conn., 1937), 478–481; Darrett B. Rutman and Anita H. Rutman, *A Place in Time: Explicatus* (New York, 1984), 101; Michael Zuckerman, "The Family Life of William Byrd," in his *Almost Chosen People: Oblique Biographies in the American Grain* (Berkeley, Calif., 1993), 97–144, esp. 113–114.

16. Patterson, *Slavery and Social Death*, 12; Charles Ball, *Fifty Years in Chains* (New York, 1970), rpt. of *Slavery in the United States: A Narrative of the Life and Adventures of Charles Ball, a Black Man* (New York, 1837), 53, 298–299.

of both stories. There were certainly strong bonds between master and slave, but the central question revolved about whether the bondpeople had won their master's respect, even love, or whether they had been able to manipulate a weak man to the point that he favored them at the expense of his kin (who, at the time the will was made, included his brother and a nephew as well as the niece). Either possibility is, of course, surprising. Perhaps most surprising, however, is that the jury of lawyers who heard the appeal overturned the court ruling. Apparently, they believed the slaves. Of course, if manumission rates are a barometer for gauging the level of concern for slaves, then emotional attachments between masters and bondpeople may seem extremely shallow.[17]

But feelings of compassion, even friendship, could exist between master and slave without manifesting themselves in a manumission document. Elias Ball, a loyalist in exile, wrote to his brother in South Carolina thanking Old Tom for his gift of Indian corn and expressing concern that the slave did "not get the things I sent him. I gave them to the Capt . . . and he brought them back which realy vext me much not for the value but the disappointment to the old man. Have sent them out again in the hopes he may now receive them." Another loyalist couple, James and Margaret Parker, of Norfolk, Virginia, agonized over what to do with their slaves when they realized that they faced long-term exile. Margaret spoke of her "grief" at the thought of her "poor creatures" finding "masters that would not use them as well as we have done." James thought their slaves should be hired "as I cannot bring myself to think of selling the poor creatures who have served us so well. . . . I would rather suffer a little myself as sell them for any consideration to a Tyrant who would use them cruely."[18]

Viewed from the perspective of personal relationships, slavery can assume the appearance of the most extreme form of service, differing only in degree,

---

17. Proceedings of the Special Court of Delegates, 1751, MHR, cited in Ross M. Kimmel, "Slave Freedom Petitions in the Courts of Colonial Maryland," MS, 27–29. On the unavailability of manumission in both Virginia and South Carolina, see David W. Cohen and Jack P. Greene, eds., *Neither Slave nor Free: The Freedmen of African Descent in the Slave Societies of the New World* (Baltimore, 1972), 4, 10; Ira Berlin, *Slaves without Masters: The Free Negro in the Antebellum South* (New York, 1974), 46–47; Theodore Stoddard Babcock, "Manumission in Virginia, 1782–1806" (master's thesis, University of Virginia, 1974); Larry Darnell Watson, "The Quest for Order: Enforcing Slave Codes in Revolutionary South Carolina, 1760–1800" (Ph.D. diss., University of South Carolina, 1980), 164; Richard S. Dunn, "Black Society in the Chesapeake, 1776–1810," and Philip D. Morgan, "Black Society in the Lowcountry, 1760–1810," in Ira Berlin and Ronald Hoffman, eds., *Slavery and Freedom in the Age of the American Revolution* (Charlottesville, Va., 1983), 74–75, 115–117.

18. Elias Ball to Elias Ball, Jan. 26, 1788, Ball Family Papers, USC; Margaret Parker to James Parker, c. 1782–1783, 920 PAR I 22/21, Parker Family Papers, Liverpool Central Libraries, England.

not in kind, from that of the poor in England or of servants in North America. The English poor, as Edmund Morgan has pointed out, were considered "vicious, idle, dissolute," addicted to "every Kind of Vice." They were confined to workhouses and put to work for the general good. There was even talk in eighteenth-century Britain of enslaving them. Contempt for the poor approximated that shown blacks "even to the extent of intimating the subhumanity of both."[19] In British America similar views were expressed about white servants. They were "filth and scum," "miserable Wretches," "insolent young Scoundrels." They were shiftless, irresponsible, disloyal, and dishonest. They often met with brutal and savage treatment, not far removed from that extended to blacks. Indeed, seventeenth-century planters treated their servants sufficiently like commodities to make wholly explicable their ease in dealing with slaves. The similarities in the treatment of slaves and servants, and in attitudes toward slaves and the poor, help explain how the overwhelming majority of Anglo-Americans took slavery for granted.[20]

And yet much as the poor or servants were viewed and treated like slaves, the attitudes and treatment were not equivalent. Consider those humans who were said to display beastlike qualities. Those on the margins of respectable society— the poor, servants, the Irish, the insane—were often likened to animals. Even children could be compared to wild, untamed colts and women to breeding sows. But no group attracted more discourses on their animal nature or experienced an everyday treatment so close to animal domestication as did black slaves. Many eighteenth-century treatises dwelled on the supposedly brutish nature and beastlike sexuality of blacks. The routine activities of slavery reinforced the allegedly animal-like qualities of slaves. Masters generally bought slaves at market, often branded them, and sometimes gave them names normally reserved for dogs and horses. Masters sometimes bought metal neck collars for their slaves much as they did for their pets. They bridled, haltered, padlocked, and even dismembered and castrated their delinquent slaves as if they were domesticated livestock. The punishment for running away on the plantation of William Byrd II was the "bit," treating slaves much like horses. Masters sold fugitive slaves "as they ran," much as they did cattle on the hoof. Symbolic of this equation between slaves and livestock was the exchange effected by two South Carolinians. When Daniel Lesesne asked John Parker to put in a bid for his slave boy Jamey, Parker obliged by offering either fifty pounds sterling or

19. Morgan, *American Slavery, American Freedom,* 320, 325. See also J. H. Plumb, *In the Light of History* (London, 1972), 102–113.
20. Morgan, *American Slavery, American Freedom,* 236; Darrett B. Rutman and Anita H. Rutman, *A Place in Time: Middlesex County, Virginia, 1650–1750* (New York, 1984), 130.

his sorrel horse. Lesesne decided to take the horse. Other bargains were available in a slave society. Masters sometimes entered into partnership to purchase a half or a lesser fraction of a human being. It was even possible to win a slave in a card game, much like gambling on horses at the track.[21]

Visitors to North America were often struck by the similarities in how slaves and animals were viewed and treated. What Edward Kimber found "really shocking" in Virginians was their display at slave marts, where "Buyers handle [their intended purchases] as the Butchers do Beasts in Smithfield, to see if they are proof in Cod, Flank and Shoulders." Likewise, David M. Erskine saw a parallel in the Virginian practice of hiring out blacks much "as horses are in England." If anything, matters were even worse in the Lowcountry. In South Carolina, Luigi Castiglioni discovered, blacks "are scarcely reputed to be human beings." He met one Lowcountry master who asserted that blacks were "a kind of animal closer to monkeys than to man." Crèvecoeur observed that Carolinians looked on their slaves "with half the kindness and affection with which they consider their dogs and horses," whereas Benjamin West thought that a South Carolina planter would "shoot a Negro with as little emotion as he shoots a hare."[22]

21. Keith Thomas, *Man and the Natural World: Changing Attitudes in England, 1500–1800* (London, 1983), esp. 36–50, 92–117; Jordan, *White over Black*, 28–40, 54, 156, 228–234, 238; Wright and Tinling, eds., *Secret Diary*, 46, 199; William Gregory, *VaG* (P and D), Oct. 22, 1772; James French, ibid. (D and H), Oct. 31, 1777; James Narvell, *SCG*, Sept. 10, 1763; William Thompson, ibid., July 7, 1777 (sale "on the run"); deposition of John Parker, Sept. 28, 1787, Miscellaneous Records, XX, 9, SCDAH; inventory of John Wyatt, Feb. 21, 1798, Charleston County Inventories, C, 326–327, and inventory of Patrick Martin, Jan. 30, 1799, ibid., 358 (buy fraction of a slave); John Torrans to James Grant, May 30, 1769, bundle 552, Papers of General James Grant of Ballindalloch; Charles William Janson, *The Stranger in America* (London, 1807), 360; Julia Cherry Spruill, *Women's Life and Work in the Southern Colonies* (Chapel Hill, N.C., 1938), 95 (slaves won in gambling).

22. [Edward Kimber], "Observations in Several Voyages and Travels in America," *WMQ*, 1st Ser., XV (1906–1907), [149]; letter of Oct. 18, 1798, David M. Erskine Travel Diary, UVa; Antonio Pace, trans. and ed., *Luigi Castiglioni's Viaggio: Travels in the United States of North America, 1785–1787* (Syracuse, N.Y., 1983), 164–165; Crèvecoeur, *Letters from an American Farmer*, 242–245; James S. Schoff, ed., *Life in the South, 1778–1779: The Letters of Benjamin West* (Ann Arbor, Mich., 1963), 33. See also Burnaby, *Travels through the Middle Settlements*, 54; Baron Ludwig von Closen, *The Revolutionary Journal of Baron Ludwig von Closen, 1780–1783*, ed. and trans. Evelyn M. Acomb (Chapel Hill, N.C., 1958), 187; John C. Van Horne, ed., *Religious Philanthropy and Colonial Slavery: The American Correspondence of the Associates of Dr. Bray, 1717–1777* (Urbana, Ill., 1985), 129; Robert L. Brunhouse, ed., "David Ramsay, 1749–1815: Selections from His Writings," American Philosophical Society, *Transactions*, N.S., LV, pt. 4 (1965), 61; Henry Melchior Muhlenberg, *The Journals of Henry Melchior Muhlenberg*, trans. Theodore G. Tappert and John W. Doberstein, 2 vols. (Philadelphia, 1942–1958), II, 674–675; David Hackett Fischer, *Albion's Seed: Four British Folkways in*

Ambiguities and contradictions were intrinsic to slavery. The fundamental contradiction—that slaves were at one and the same time property and human beings—made for deeply ambivalent relations between masters and bondpeople. Masters and slaves were the opposite extremes of a magnetic field, poles apart and yet holding one another in suspension, each defining the other. As much as masters and slaves distrusted each other, they also needed each other, watched each other, and moderated each other's behavior. This is not to say that the slave societies of the Chesapeake and Lowcountry crackled with tension or that slaveholders were stretched on a rack of anxiety. Problems obviously arose in the attempt to define persons as things. There was confusion, for example, whether slaves should be considered real or personal property. There might have been confusion in the minds of Elizabeth City County justices about how to charge Sam and Peter, who apparently helped a mulatto woman escape from her owner; they settled on an action for theft rather than for kidnapping. Slave codes were themselves a testament to the essential contradiction of slavery. Slaves were simultaneously defined as chattel and denied positive protection by the law, yet they were held morally responsible for their actions. Most members of slave societies, however, simply accepted the ambiguity inherent in property endowed with a soul. Their societies repeatedly demonstrated a capacity to survive and absorb severe contradictions.[23]

Patriarchalism

One of the reasons why slavery with all its attendant ambiguities could be readily assimilated into the early modern Anglo-American world was a long-standing patriarchal tradition that had clearly defined the relationship between master and servant. Manuals of household government in sixteenth- and seventeenth-century England spoke of servants as they did of wives and children. All were subservient members of the family, living under the authority of the paterfamilias. Gentlemen were not to let their care stop at their own children. "Let it reach to your menial servants," they were instructed, for "though you are their master, you are also their father." The relationship between master and servant received the highest ideological sanction in the concept of patriarchalism. Patriarchal doctrines can be found, as one historian

---

America (New York, 1989), 402. In the U.S. Constitution, noted John Leland caustically, "a slave is possessed of 3 fifths of a man and 2 fifths of a brute" (*The Virginia Chronicle* . . . [Norfolk, Va., 1790], 9).

23. Elizabeth City County Orders, 1747–1755, 461, as cited in Schwarz, *Twice Condemned,* 135; Davis, *Problem of Slavery,* 248–251; Jordan, *White over Black,* 103–104; M. Eugene Sirmans, "The Legal Status of the Slave in South Carolina, 1670–1740," *Journal of Southern History,* XXVIII (1962), 462–473; Gaines M. Foster, "Guilt over Slavery: A Historiographical Analysis," ibid., LVI (1990), 665–694.

has argued, in all strata of thought in seventeenth-century England, "from well-ordered and self-conscious theories . . . to the unstated prejudices of the inarticulate masses." A deep respect for rank and hierarchy infused the very marrow of the early modern British American world, and at its core lay the authority of the father-figure in his household.[24]

Many eighteenth-century masters of slaves conspicuously defined themselves in light of this venerable tradition. None more so perhaps than William Byrd II, who in a famous passage took a quasi-spiritual view of his role, likening himself to a biblical patriarch amid his bondmen and bondwomen. Similarly, it required little imagination for a South Carolina planter to "fancy [him]self one of the Patriarchs of old . . . being surrounded with near 200 Negroes who are guided by my absolute Command." As the most dependent members of the patriarchal family, slaves were, according to the Reverend Thomas Bacon of Maryland, "an immediate and necessary part of our household." He emphasized that "next to our children and brethren by blood, our servants, and especially our slaves, are certainly in the nearest relation to us." A Jesuit priest echoed his Anglican counterpart when he stated, "Charity to Negroes is due from all[,] particularly their Masters." As members of Christ, he continued, black slaves were "to be dealt with in a charitable, Christian, paternal manner."[25]

24. William Darrell, *The Gentleman Instructed* (London, 1727), part 1, 87, cited in Jean Hecht, *The Domestic Servant Class in Eighteenth-Century England* (London, 1956), 75; Gordon J. Schochet, *Patriarchalism in Political Thought: The Authoritarian Family and Political Speculation and Attitudes, Especially in Seventeenth-Century England* (New York, 1975), 5; Gordon S. Wood, *The Radicalism of the American Revolution* (New York, 1992), 11–92; Jay Fliegelman, *Prodigals and Pilgrims: The American Revolution against Patriarchal Authority, 1750–1800* (New York, 1982). I have explored patriarchalism in a little more depth, and cite some of the relevant literature, in an essay, "Three Planters and Their Slaves: Perspectives on Slavery in Virginia, South Carolina, and Jamaica, 1750–1790," in Winthrop D. Jordan and Sheila L. Skemp, eds., *Race and Family in the Colonial South* (Jackson, Miss., 1987), 37–79. A related culture—the monarchical—is explored in Richard L. Bushman, *King and People in Provincial Massachusetts* (Chapel Hill, N.C., 1985), which I found highly instructive.

25. William Byrd to the Earl of Orrery, July 5, 1726, *VMHB*, XXXII (1924), 27; George Lockey to M. Harford, Apr. 5, 1804, Correspondence of John Lloyd, Gloucestershire Record Office, England; Thomas Bacon, *Sermons Addressed to Masters and Servants and Published in the Year 1743 . . . and Now Republished . . . by the Rev. William Meade* (Winchester, Va., [1813]), 3; memorandum of Father George Hunter, Dec. 20, 1749, in the Maryland Province Archive of the Society of Jesus, 202.A.7, as cited in Lee, *The Price of Nationhood*, 67–68. See also Edmund Botsford in Anne C. Loveland, *Southern Evangelicals and the Social Order, 1800–1860* (Baton Rouge, La., 1980), 189; and Frank Cundall, ed., *Lady Nugent's Journal of a Voyage to, and Residence in, the Island of Jamaica . . .* (London, 1907), 204. As late as 1802 in a South Carolina tort case, a judge was still arguing that the positions of slave and servant were analogous: Morris, *Southern Slavery and the Law*, 358.

Plantation owners in the eighteenth-century South were especially prone to think of themselves as all-powerful father figures. Plantation America was a remarkably underinstitutionalized world. An attenuated social and economic infrastructure enhanced the authority of the household head. Moreover, household authority expanded rather than contracted over the colonial period in the South. Even though early modern Britain and Western Europe are generally thought to have had a more hierarchical social structure than colonial America, Carole Shammas rightly notes that "a notably higher proportion of people in the Americas," particularly in plantation America, "fell into the category of legal dependents." Not accidentally, "the first thing" Robinson Crusoe did "in the advancement" of his New World plantation was to purchase "a negro slave, and an European servant"; he soon had prospects of becoming "a rich and thriving man" in his "new Plantation." Crusoe was later shipwrecked en route to Africa to acquire more slaves. Marooned, Crusoe establishes "two plantations." Crusoe is generally good to Friday, but, as Christopher Hill points out, the first word he taught him was "Master." Eventually, Crusoe acquires both native and foreign labor and begins to envisage himself in monarchical terms. Since the "whole country" was his property, Crusoe mused, he had "undoubted right of dominion," and since "my people," as he significantly termed them, were "perfectly subjected," he was "absolute lord and lawgiver." The family was the foundation of the plantation social order, and its head was lord, master, a monarch in miniature. In a sequel, Crusoe returns bearing goods, to be told he "was a father" to his people. He himself was "pleased" with "being the patron of those people I placed there, and doing for them in a kind of haughty majestic way, like an old patriarchal monarch; providing for them, as if I had been father of the whole family, as well as of the plantation." Defoe had shrewdly caught the tenor of idealized plantation life.[26]

Patriarchalism cannot be dismissed as mere propaganda or apologetics—although, like all ideological rationalizations, it contained its share of self-serving cant; rather, it was an authentic, if deeply flawed, worldview. Its familial rhetoric was not just a smokescreen for exploitation, because patriarchalism offered no guarantee of benevolence. It was no sentimental self-image, but rather a harsh creed. Patriarchs in ancient Rome exercised the right to dispatch wives, children, and slaves. In Virginia, a law of 1669 allowed masters the Roman "power of the father" over the life and death of a slave, but later

26. Daniel Scott Smith, "Genealogy, Geography, and the Genesis of Social Structure: Household and Kinship in Early America" (MS, 1985); Carole Shammas, "Anglo-American Household Government in Comparative Perspective," *WMQ*, 3d Ser., LII (1995), 104–144; Daniel Defoe, *The Life and Strange Adventures of Robinson Crusoe*, 3 vols. (New York, 1903 [orig. publ. 1719), I, 40–41, 170, 272, II, 117, 186; Christopher Hill, "Robinson Crusoe," *History Workshop*, X (1980), 16.

legislation balanced the interests of the state, masters, and white nonslaveholders with minimal protections for slaves. Although the despotic powers of masters were moderated, the cruel and authoritarian core of patriarchalism helps explain why patriarchs could ignore the enormity of what they did to their slave families. Fathers, after all, do not normally sell their children. But when patriarchs spoke of their family, both white and black, their protective domination contained little of the warmth or tenderness associated with modern familial relations.[27]

Eighteenth-century patriarchs might rationalize what they did to slaves by drawing analogies—however farfetched—with their treatment of their more immediate family. Denial of property to slaves was one obvious demonstration of the bondpeople's dependence on masters. Like children, masters could argue, adult slaves were to be reliant on patriarchs. One Virginia county court case likened a slave man's legal and social status to coverture, the dependent status accorded married white women. In 1690, Sambo escaped punishment for shooting a horse before the Norfolk County court because he was "under covert." Conversely, when a slave living under the master's protection violated that trust by murdering or poisoning the patriarch, the courts often specified that he or she was guilty of petit treason. A slave's killing his master was like a wife's killing her husband. Lèse-majesté to the patriarch was the equivalent of treachery toward the father-king.[28]

Patriarchalism rationalized the severity that lay at the heart of the slave system. True, the patriarch was obliged to provide for his slaves, but in return the slaves had to obey. When they did not, they could expect the swift retribution of a wrathful and unforgiving father figure. Patriarchalism was an austere code. Households were above all to be "well regulated." Governance, authority, rigid control, adjudication, unswerving obedience, and severe discipline were the dominant watchwords. The master ought, in Henry Laurens's words, to "carry a steady command" and exude "easy authority." A "sullen Slut" of a slave could be "easily kept down," he advised an overseer, "if you exert your

27. Hening, *Statutes at Large*, II, 270; Kathleen M. Brown, *Good Wives, Nasty Wenches, and Anxious Patriarchs: Gender, Race, and Power in Colonial Virginia* (Chapel Hill, N.C., 1996), 322–324.

28. Norfolk Deed Book, no. 5, part 2 (Orders), Jan. 15, 1690, 163, VSL, as cited in Brown, *Good Wives, Nasty Wenches, and Anxious Patriarchs*, 183; Rhys Isaac, *The Transformation of Virginia, 1740–1790* (Chapel Hill, N.C., 1982), 20; Schwarz, *Twice Condemned*, 81–82n, 92; William Blackstone, *Commentaries on the Laws of England*, 4 vols. (Philadelphia, 1771–1772), IV, 204. For representative works that, in my view, wrongly see patriarchalism or paternalism as a sham, see Marvin L. Michael Kay and Lorin Lee Cary, *Slavery in North Carolina, 1748–1775* (Chapel Hill, N.C., 1995), esp. 4–5, 53–58, 105–107, 323–324; and Norrece T. Jones, *Born a Child of Freedom, Yet a Slave: Mechanisms of Control and Strategies of Resistance in Antebellum South Carolina* (Middletown, Conn., 1989).

Authority." When demeanor failed, the master inevitably turned to force. Single out a couple of the more stubborn slaves, Laurens recommended, and "chastise them severely but properly." The power to judge, rebuke, and inflict punishment was the most awesome trust placed in the hands of a patriarch. Robert Carter of Nomini Hall, like other masters, on occasion delegated that authority to underlings. These surrogate masters often abused the powers entrusted to them, which in Carter's case provoked a pained response couched in the highest moral tones. He informed his employee that from henceforth only the master would "hear and consider the fault or faults that may be aledged against any of my Negroes—so that I my-self am to be their future judge, and to direct the manner of the punishment, if on the tryal the accusation be well founded." Similarly, William Byrd "gave audience" to his slaves, and when they submitted "a petition" to him, he "did them right."[29]

Masters fulfilled one aspect of their roles as patriarchs by serving as de facto judges, administering a form of plantation justice—and Laurens's and Carter's choice of language exemplifies this role-playing—but masters also buttressed their position by assuming official posts as magistrates. In court, their discretionary capacities equaled their punitive powers in importance. An awesome sovereign power was in practice softened by the prerogative of clemency, by the grace of mercy. In eighteenth-century Virginia, gentlemen slaveholders ordered hangings for only about one-fifth of the slaves tried in their county courts for poisoning and theft. Even some slaves sentenced to hang escaped that punishment: both Hannibal of York County and Manuel of Richmond County evaded the hangman's noose on at least three occasions. Will, who stood before Mecklenburg County judges on a charge of plotting an insurrection, was found guilty, yet was sentenced to thirty lashes because the judges took "into consideration [his] extream youth." The gentry's authority and reputation as persons of magnanimity were no doubt enhanced—at least among slaves—by such extensions of mercy. Even more was this true when whites openly complained of the justices' discretionary actions. Citizens of Botetourt County, for example, were opposed to the reprieve of a slave sentenced to hang for robbery, attempted poisoning, and recruiting slaves to join Lord Cornwallis. Magnanimity toward slaves did not always endear the gentry to fellow whites.[30]

---

29. *Laurens Papers*, III, 205, IV, 633, V, 227, VIII, 617; Robert Carter to Thomas Olive, May 8, 1781, Robert Carter Letterbook, IV, 75, Duke; Zuckerman, "Family Life of Byrd," in *Almost Chosen People*, 117.

30. Schwarz, *Twice Condemned*, 96, 123; trials of Mar. 8, 1774, Apr. 17, 1780, York County Court Order Books, 1772–1774, 529, 1774–1784, 271–272, VSL (Hannibal); Gwenda Morgan, "The Hegemony of the Law: Richmond County, 1692–1776" (Ph.D. diss., The Johns Hop-

Masters also augmented their patriarchal authority in the way they administered "justice." However unjust the legal framework set up to deal with slave offenders, magistrates often attempted to give slaves a fair trial. They maintained the appearance of impartiality and fairness, acquitting slaves when evidence was insubstantial and witnesses were suspect. Of the two thousand or so slaves prosecuted for crime in colonial Virginia county courts, 30 percent were acquitted. Masters followed legal procedures. Thus, in 1790, Edmund Randolph took up the case of a New Kent County slave tried for theft. The bondman had entered a house in the daytime through an open door, and he had stolen a considerable sum of money. He was sentenced to death. Randolph protested the sentence on the grounds that no proof of a break-in existed. He acknowledged that "very respectable and sensible men" had tried the case, but, quite simply, they had "mistaken the law." Increasingly, attorneys defended slaves, and able slaves could, on occasion, defend themselves. Moses was "heard in his own defence" and acquitted in an Essex County court. An attorney recalled that in a James City County court case the slaves "were undefended, but asked themselves many questions of the witnesses, which, as well as I remember, were answered strongly against them."[31]

Patriarchs did not expect their slaves to be content or submissive; the myth of the happy and docile slave was not an eighteenth-century invention. Few patriarchs were as emphatic as one Maryland planter who claimed to have "never known a single instance of a negro being contented in slavery," but most anticipated that their dependents would be contentious, disgruntled, and dissatisfied. Provoked beyond measure, John Channing declared his slaves "an unreasonable set of beings"; Landon Carter's welling frustrations led him, in almost his last breath, to brand slaves as "devils"; Henry Laurens, like other masters, railed at individual slaves, calling them variously "a vile Scoundrell," an "eye Servant and a great Rogue," and an "impudent gipsey." But, as Edmund Morgan has pointed out, "these were the complaints that masters in every age have made against their servants." At the same time, eighteenth-century masters rarely underestimated their slaves' capacity to rebel. Henry Laurens's ad-

---

kins University, 1980), 154 (Manuel); trial of Will, Aug. 19, 1785, Mecklenburg County Court Order Book, 1784–1787, 392, VSL; Memorial of Sundry of the Inhabitants of Botetourt County, January 1781, in William P. Palmer, ed., *Calendar of Virginia State Papers and Other Manuscripts, 1652–1781 . . .* , I (Richmond, Va., 1875), 477–478.

31. Schwarz, *Twice Condemned*, 50; Edmund Randolph to Governor of Virginia, July 14, 1790, Miscellaneous MSS, Chicago Historical Society, microfilm, CW; trial of Moses, Jan. 20, 1783, Essex County Orders, 1782–1783, 386, VSL; attorney for James City County Court, July 26, 1793, Executive Papers, VSL. For an interesting case of a slave represented by a famous attorney, see Accomac County Court Order Book, 1774–1777, 377, 393.

vice to a prospective slave trader was: "Be very careful to guard against insurrection. Never put your Life in their power for a moment. For a moment is sufficient to deprive you of it and make way for the destruction of all your Men and yet you may treat such Negroes with great humanity." Matters did not improve much once the slaves were ashore. Laurens thought East Florida a dangerous place, for without good neighbors, he argued, your slaves might be "tempted" to "knock you in the head and file off in a body." Eighteenth-century masters spoke of their slaves as the enemies within their "bowels," their "internal" or "intestine enemies," their "dangerous Domestics," an "inveterate enemy." South Carolinians told Ebenezer Hazard that the reason for "the *severity* with which the Negroes are treated is that it is necessary in order to break their spirits." Slaves were "always on the point of rebellion," the Reverend Henry Muhlenberg learned.[32]

Patriarchs also assumed that slaves naturally sought liberty. This assumption was the basic argument a South Carolinian used when he petitioned for compensation for his executed slave. In 1742, the slave had tried to run away and had engaged others to accompany him, but, according to his master, "with the sole design of obtaining Liberty, a desire so naturally implanted in the minds of all Men and That seldom any other consideration has been found sufficient to root it out, and as this desire of Liberty is founded on the General Law of Nature, the attempts in slaves to obtain it are punishable by the laws of particular Countries, yet the Crime taken simply has ever been deemed only an Evil prohibited; and never ranked amongst those termed Evils in themselves by the best civilians as well as common Lawyers." With money at stake, a master

---

32. Corner, ed., *The Autobiography of Benjamin Rush,* 151; John Channing to William Gibbons, June 4, 1770, William Gibbons, Jr., Papers, Duke; Greene, ed., *Carter Diary,* 1149; *Laurens Papers,* II, 123, IV, 602, V, 125, VI, 438; Morgan, *American Slavery, American Freedom,* 319; James Edward Smith, comp., *A Selection of the Correspondence of Linnaeus, and Other Naturalists, from the Original Manuscripts,* I (London, 1821), 492 (enemies within "bowels"); Richard J. Hooker, ed., *The Carolina Backcountry on the Eve of the Revolution: The Journal and Other Writings of Charles Woodmason, Anglican Itinerant* (Chapel Hill, N.C., 1953), 94, 121 ("internal enemies"); Ann Maury, ed. and trans., *Memoirs of a Hugenot Family . . .* (New York, 1907), 347 ("intestine enemies"); George Milligen[-Johnston], *A Short Description of the Province of South-Carolina . . .* (London, 1770), in Chapman J. Milling, ed., *Colonial South Carolina: Two Contemporary Descriptions* (Columbia, S.C., 1951), 136 ("dangerous Domestics"); Henry Lee, *Memoirs of the War in the Southern Department of the United States,* I (Philadelphia, 1812), 234n ("inveterate enemy"); H. Roy Merrens, "A View of Coastal South Carolina in 1778: The Journal of Ebenezer Hazard," *SCHM,* LXXIII (1972), 192; Muhlenberg, *Journals,* II, 658; William Byrd to Peter Beckford, Dec. 6, 1735, and to Lord Egmont, July 12, 1736, "Letters of the Byrd Family," *VMHB,* XXXVI (1928), 121, 220–221. See also Jordan, *White over Black,* 110–122.

might resort to almost any legal stratagem, but in this instance the master confidently based his argument on natural law.[33]

Reciprocal obligations and duties between master and servant were the essence of patriarchalism. Henry Laurens thought very much in these terms. In more reflective moments, he spoke of his slaves as "those poor Creatures who look up to their Master as their Father, their Guardian, and Protector, and to whom their is a reciprocal obligation upon the Master." To protect and guard was, of course, to invoke a powerful and ancient image of the master's role. Landon Carter did much the same when he recreated, with some embellishment, no doubt, the "dismal" scene when lightning struck Sabine Hall. At the center of the ensuing bedlam stood the calm, undaunted patriarch, with "poor slaves crowding round and following their master, as if *protection* only came from him." Carter drew his own moral: "God was merciful, and I hope it will not be misplaced on anyone who saw this sight at least."[34] God looked kindly on patriarchs.

A patriarch who failed to live up to his obligations could be held accountable by his slaves. When a report circulated in South Carolina that absentee Ralph Izard, then the owner of more than five hundred adult slaves, had been put in London's debtors' prison, Henry Laurens, the manager of his affairs, could not believe it. Nevertheless, when the rumor "reached the Ears" of Izard's slaves, Laurens was unable in all conscience to "contradict the Story." Rather, he "recommended Strongly to them to work" hard so that they might bail their master out of jail. Apparently, this exhortation had the desired effect at least on some of Izard's slaves. But others, "who think themselve more judicious than their fellows," Laurens noted sarcastically, believed that Izard's plight was his own fault. Indeed, they claimed that their master "don't deserve Negroes." A master who could not provide support relinquished his claims to his slaves' obedience. Inadequate supplies of clothing spurred many of Izard's slaves to desert his plantations and to travel to Charleston, where they made their complaints. Izard's slaves proved more troublesome to Laurens in the two years he had managed Izard's estate than in the twenty years he had managed his own. The only way to rectify matters, Laurens advised, was for Izard to appear in person before his slaves. The restoration of respect would require the presence of the patriarch.[35]

Patriarchal responsibilities were not lightly borne. Landon Carter went

---

33. Petition of Michael Jeans, Jan. 12, 1743, South Carolina Council Journal, CO5/441, fols. 448–449, PRO. The Revolutionary crisis led some masters to a more acute recognition of this point; see, for example, William T. Hutchinson et al., eds., *The Papers of James Madison* (Chicago and Charlottesville, Va., 1962–), VII, 304.
34. *Laurens Papers*, VIII, 617–618; Greene, ed., *Carter Diary*, 751 (emphasis mine).
35. *Laurens Papers*, XI, 331–332, 349–354.

riding one day "to unbend" his mind "from this prodigeous concern" of caring for slaves. "It is a hard task to do our duty towards [our slaves] as we ought," admitted another Virginian, "for we run the hazard of temporal ruin if they are not compelled to work hard on the one hand—and on the other, that of not being able to render a good account of our stewardship in the other and better world if we oppress and tyrannize over them." Governor Francis Fauquier took an even loftier view of the obligations of stewardship when he came to write his will. With respect to his slaves, he wrote: "I hope I shall be found to have been a Merciful Master to them and that no one of them will rise up in Judgment against me in that great day when all my actions will be exposed to public view. For with what face can I expect Mercy from an offended God, if I have not myself shewn mercy to those dependent on me."[36] Patriarchal obligations could embrace the notion of Christian stewardship.

A more mundane obligation was to provide sustenance. The master as provider was a powerful self-image for eighteenth-century patriarchs. When, in a bad harvest year, John Carter was pressed to provide corn for his poor white neighbors, he pointed out where his primary obligations must reside. "I shall always be ready to assist [my neighbors] as well as I can," he declared, "but my Care must be first directed to my own Slaves, and those of my near Relations." Self-interest had much to do with this response, of course, but the notion of guardianship raised this response above the level of sheer selfish calculation. It was a self-image easily idealized. Masters liked to conceive of slaves feeding at their tables or feeding from their hands. Perhaps for this reason, managers told owners that their slaves thanked them or were grateful for, say, the annual allocation of clothes. Patriarchs elevated the well-being of their slaves to a noble cause.[37]

After sustenance, perhaps the next most important obligations and duties concerned work. Slaves were, of course, duty-bound to work diligently at their master's pleasure. As one manual of household government put it, servants were to be "only concerned in *one* matter, to do the work that lies before them." But the master could not simply work his slaves as he wished. There were limits, admittedly minimal, beyond which a master could not go, unless he wished to forfeit community approval. Grand jury presentments and the levy of fines for Sunday working testify to one important communal sanction.

36. Ibid., II, 632–633; Peter Fontaine, Jr., to John Fontaine, June 7, 1754, in Maury, ed. and trans., *Memoirs,* 364; "Francis Fauquier's Will," *WMQ,* 1st Ser., VIII (1899–1900), 175–176.

37. John Carter to Landon Carter, Aug. 12, 1737, Carter Family Papers, UVa; George Seaman to Lady Pitcalny, Mar. 1, 1756, Ross of Pitcalnie Muniments, Scottish Record Office, Edinburgh; Henry Pattillo, *The Plain Family's Assistant* . . . (Wilmington, Del., 1787), 22 (slaves feeding); Robert Raper to John Colleton, Dec. 6, 1759, and to Margaret Colleton, Nov. 15, 1768, Raper Letterbook.

One young planter was so upset at the claim that he had acted in a "barbarous" manner by working slaves on the Sabbath that he publicly disavowed the charge in a South Carolina newspaper.[38]

At its most elevated, the patriarchal ethos was an uplifting creed, with the master offering to protect, guard, and care for his dependents, but, at its worst, it consisted of little more than sanctions, punishments, "menaces and imprecations."[39] These extremes, these contrasting patriarchal dispositions, are captured well in a particularly intense and unusual master-slave relationship. In 1754, an absentee planter named Joseph Ball decided to return his slave waiting man, Aron, then resident in England, to Virginia. Ball specified in detail the conditions under which Aron would live once he arrived back in the Old Dominion. He was to be "used kindly," not put immediately to hard labor, but employed on odd jobs. Precise instructions were given for the construction of a "framed House," and Aron was to inherit an old bedstead that had belonged to the master. All the slave's "Household Goods and other things in his own Custody" were to be lodged in this new dwelling. He was to be allowed his own meat, fat, and milk rations as well as the privilege of raising fowls. Aron was even to "have the Liberty of a Horse to Ride to Church."

In a subsequent letter, responding to the news of the slave's safe return, the underside of patriarchal protection emerged. Ball gave instructions to a relative in case Aron

> offers to be unruly or Strike his Overseer[.] [He] must be tyd up and Slasht Severly, and pickled. I suppose if you go to do it, he will Resist you: for he Resisted me twice. If you have occasion to slash him get two or three Good White Men to help; and give it him heartily at once, and if he should Runaway, he must wear a Pothook about his neck, and if that won't bring him under, he must wear Iron spaneals upon his Legs till you are pretty sure he will be orderly; for as he is my slave he must and shall be obedient, but if he be orderly use him kindly. Shew him this letter.

This was accompanied by a personal letter to Aron that, after reiterating the same threats, ended on a more dignified note. "If I hear a Good Character of you," Ball observed, "I will send you some of my best old cloths and other

---

38. William Fleetwood, *The Relative Duties of Parents and Children, Husbands and Wives, Masters and Servants, Consider'd in Sixteen Sermons: With Three More upon the Case of Self-Murther* (London, 1705), 385; Barnaby Cockfield, *SCG*, Dec. 8, 1758. For Sabbath working, see Court of General Sessions Journal, 1769–1776, Oct. 19, 1769, 20, and Feb. 18, 1773, 221, SCDAH; Charles City County Court Order Book, 1737–1751, Nov. 1, 1739, 105, VSL.

39. Davis, *Travels*, 99. A missionary in Georgia declared that "no white People will have any thing to say to [blacks] but to abuse them with bitter Execrations and cruel Blows" (quoted in Van Horne, ed., *Religious Philanthropy and Colonial Slavery*, 130).

things. Take warning and don't Ruin youself by your folly. I red your Letr. If you will be good I shall be yr Loving Master." The eighteenth-century Virginia patriarch could quite naturally alternate offers of love, when the slave was obedient, and threats of a "pickling," when the slave proved "unruly."[40]

Perhaps the patriarchal temper is best seen at times of crisis, and there was no greater in the eighteenth century than the Revolutionary war. Two vignettes, one from South Carolina, the other from Virginia, capture the patriarchal mode in extremis. First, let us eavesdrop on Henry Laurens, a man destined to play a major role in America's Independence movement but who, on a hot and humid Saturday evening in June 1775, had dependence more on his mind. He called together all his brother's slaves and, as he later related it, "admonished them to behave with great cicumspection in this dangerous times, set before them the great risque of exposing themselves to the treachery of pretended friends and false witnesses if they associated with any Negroes out of [his brother's] family or [his own]. Poor Creatures they were sensibly affected, and with many thanks promised to follow my advice and to accept the offer of my Protection." The patriarchal compact was fully explicated here: warnings and an offer of protection on one side, promises and a seeming acceptance of protection on the other. At the center stood the awe-inspiring paterfamilias—or so Laurens liked to think.[41]

A year later, on another Saturday in summer, Robert Carter amassed his slaves living at Coles Point quarter, situated on the Potomac River. The gathering was in response to the recent arrival of the British fleet. Carter informed his slaves that "the King of Britain had declared war agst the people" of the thirteen colonies and named them. Lord Dunmore was the commander of the opposing forces, Carter continued, and his fleet could be seen from a nearby point. He explained that many people in Britain disapproved of the dispute and refused to enlist as soldiers and that the king had resorted to foreign mercenaries. His history lesson even extended to a disquisition on the origin of "titles [and] appellations of dignity, given to some white people in Great Britain." He was not afraid to confront the issue of Lord Dunmore's proclamation or to mention that some slaves had responded to Dunmore's offer, although he did so only to raise the specter of sale to the West Indies.

The climax came when Carter posed the following question: "Do any of ye dislike the present conditions of life, as do wish to enter into Lord D[un-m]o[re']s Service, and trust to the consequences?" His slaves made the appropriate reply: "We all fully intend to serve you our master and we do now

---

40. Joseph Ball to Joseph Chinn, Apr. 23, 1754, and to Chinn and Aron, Aug. 31, 1754, Joseph Ball Letterbook, microfilm, LC.
41. *Laurens Papers*, X, 162–163.

promise to use our whole might and force to execute your Comands." With this resounding confirmation of the patriarchal bargain, Carter proceeded to practical details. If the British did land on Coles Point, all heads of households were to take their wives, children, and acquaintances to "private places" and await the master's "directions, tending for your imediate Relief." Much of this encounter is merely an elaboration of the earlier scene between Laurens and his South Carolina charges. Yet this Chesapeake master differed significantly in acknowledging his slaves' powers of reasoning and in assuming their receptivity to political argumentation. Here truly was an enlightened patriarch.[42]

The Emergence of Paternalism

The emergence of a more enlightened patriarchalism in the second half of the eighteenth century was not confined to Robert Carter. Patriarchal doctrines and strategies were transformed more generally in at least three major directions. First, although late-eighteenth-century masters continued to stress order and authority, they were more inclined to emphasize their solicitude toward and generous treatment of their dependents. Second, no self-respecting patriarch would speak cloyingly of his kindness toward his slaves, but gradually masters began to express such sentiments and came in return to expect gratitude, even love, from their bondpeople. Their outlook became far more sentimental. Third, patriarchs rarely boasted of the submissiveness or docility of their bondpeople, but gradually masters began to create the fiction of the contented and happy slave. This shift in patriarchal strategies—greater softness, more reciprocity, less authoritarianism—had complex origins. In part it was a response to political and military events, but it owed far more to broader developments—a more affectionate family environment, the rise of evangelicalism, romanticism, and humanitarianism, and a growing emphasis on private property rights. Gradually it blossomed in the nineteenth century into full-blown paternalism.

Late-eighteenth-century masters sometimes appealed to rather than threatened their slaves. This change of emphasis may be attributed in part to the temporary disruption of the masters' power caused by the Revolutionary crisis. During wartime and in the early postwar years, in particular, masters often had little control over their slaves. Threats were useless; exhortations became commonplace. Thus, there was the spectacle of a South Carolina slave, resident in Saint Augustine in 1784, telling his master's envoy that he was prepared to return home "willingly . . . but not at present." The master's spokesman was reduced to hoping that he "might be able to persuade him" to return earlier than the slave intended. Or there was Maria Byrd's Wat, a Virginia slave who

42. Robert Carter Daybook, XIII, July 12, 1776, 175–180, Duke.

had aided the British during the war and resided in New York in the spring of 1783. Byrd assured Wat that he could "come home with Safety." She had heard that he "wishes much to return, and his wife and Children are very anxious to see him"; these were her "inducements for wishing him to come back." She was prepared to overlook past actions; indeed, she was even prepared to engage Wat's services in recovering her other lost slaves. For these "good offices," Wat would receive a "handsome" reward. She did not expect that any of her absent slaves would "return willingly whatever they may pretend to." But "to make them more happy if they are sent me," she wanted them to know that no slaves, to her knowledge, had been punished on their return and that her slaves "may rely on the best usage."[43]

The seeming loyalty of many other slaves who did not flee their masters during the Revolutionary war, however, contributed to the growing myth that slaves might be content in their condition. In the summer of 1776, Henry Laurens proudly recorded that his slaves "to a Man are strongly attached to me . . . hitherto not one of them has attempted to desert." These claims of loyalty may be more important for what they say of the owners' perceptions than what they record of the slaves' behavior. But, after the war had ended, Laurens contrasted the "faithless" behavior of his white servants with the "fidelity" of his slaves, "a very few instances excepted." As a result, he noted, "we are endeavouring to reward those and make the whole happy." Making them happy was a prescient remark. Late in life, Laurens took great pride in his various labor-saving experiments that reduced the arduousness of his slaves' labor. These "improvements," he maintained, "are the pleasure of my life, more particularly as they contribute to bring my poor blacks to a level with the happiest peasants to be found in Europe"—a refrain that would echo down the corridors of Southern history.[44]

A more caring attitude toward slaves also arose as the strength of their family ties became recognizable to masters and as family life in general became more egalitarian and affectionate. In 1764, James Habersham was "affected" by the death of one of his slave women, not just because she had been a favorite of his late wife or because she had nursed two of his daughters, but because she had left behind an "inconsolable" husband. Eight years later, he recalled that

---

43. John Douglass to J. Owen and J. L. Gervais, Apr. 14, 1784, J. L. Gervais Papers, USC; W. Byrd to Neil Jamieson, April 1783, Neil Jamieson Papers, LC. Two letters dated Nov. 2 and Nov. 8, 1782, in the Peter Horry Papers, Peter Force Collection, LC, also describe fruitless negotiations with slaves who had left with the British. One slave told an envoy "with an air of Insolence [that] he was not Going back with" him.

44. Henry Laurens to John Laurens, Aug. 1, 1776, Miscellaneous MSS, CLS; Henry Laurens to William Bell, Apr. 25, 1785, Laurens Papers, microfilm, SCHS. See also Anne Deas, ed., *Correspondence of Mr. Ralph Izard, of South Carolina . . .* , I (New York, 1844), 154.

he had buried almost eighty slaves during his lifetime and in each case had "acquiessed in the Dispensation of divine Providence." However, he found it impossible to "divest myself of Humanity," as he put it, at the events surrounding a recent slave death. It concerned a slave boy bitten by a rabid dog. "The Cries and Intreaties of the Mother begging her Child to be put to Death," wrote the shaken master, "the dreadfull shreiks of the Boy, and his more than pretty Behaviour in his taking leave of all around him, has rung such a Peal in my Ears, that I never can forget." Late-eighteenth-century masters seemed much more respectful of slave family ties than their predecessors. Gangs were often sold "in families" rather than individually, and many a prospective purchaser stated a preference for family units. When a South Carolina slave patroon became "dissatisfied and desirous of being sold," his master was quick to assure prospective buyers that the man's wife had also to be sold "for a principle of humanity *alone*," because "they were very unwilling to be separated."[45]

When slaves had been part of a planter family for years—a possibility that grew more likely by the second half of the eighteenth century—the ties between whites and blacks could be especially close. John Moultrie was happy that his overseer was "humane" to his slaves, because they had "been so long in my family I have a respectful attachment for them as my fellow Creatures." Similarly, Peter Horry recollected that Susie and Rachel, two of his slaves, had been "born on my Plantation and brought up by my hands." He described their relationship in familial terms: the former acted toward him "as a Mother"; the other "as a Sister." In 1787, sixty residents of Georgetown, South Carolina, petitioned on behalf of the Cuttino family, who were "very distressed at the prospect of having a servant [Abraham, a slave] executed who has been in the Family a considerable time and for whom they entertain a certain degree of Affection." In the same year, the close ties that James Mercer had established with his slave Christmas led to a rupture. Mercer decided to sell his waiting man because "he has treated me ungratefully in my late sickness"—indicating that gratitude was now expected of slaves. But, even in the sale, Mercer claimed to be acting in a humanitarian way, for he lowered the price by twenty pounds as an inducement to another member of the Mercer clan to purchase the slave. In this way, Mercer "would still give [Christmas] choice in a master," because he presumed that the slave "wou'd prefer one of the family."[46]

45. *The Letters of Hon. James Habersham, 1756–1775*, GHS, Collections, VI (Savannah, Ga., 1904), 23, 163; John Webb and Co., *City Gaz*, Dec. 15, 1800. This subject is explored in greater depth in Chapter 9.

46. John Moultrie to Isaac Ball, Aug. 17, 1815, Ball Family Papers; A. S. Salley, ed., "Journal of General Peter Horry," SCHM, XXXVIII (1937), 117–118; petition of Georgetown residents, Apr. 4, 1787, Thomas Pinckney Papers, LC; James Mercer to John Francis Mercer,

A shift toward romantic sentimentalism, which was closely linked to a more affectionate family life, helped created a climate in which slaves could be viewed more sympathetically. In 1775, a Virginia almanac printed a story about two friends, black slaves, who fell in love with the same slave woman, on the island of Saint Christopher in the British West Indies. All three were said to be notably handsome. Finding no way to resolve their dilemma, the two friends killed their loved one, then, overcome with grief and despair, killed themselves. Blacks, in other words, could be attractive, tragic figures, and could suffer like white people. A Virginia master made the same discovery when he was awakened one night "by a most piteous lamentation." His slave boy had called out in his sleep for his "mammy." The master chided himself for regarding the boy "as insensible when compared to those of our complexion." A Methodist preacher had a similar revelation during a church investigation of sexual harassment of a young black woman. The preacher "was delighted" at the woman's story, so modest was her language and so strong the "proof of her chastity." But a "truly Melting" scene followed the excommunication of the accused, a "poor black man." His twelve-year-old daughter "ran to him caught him round the neck and wept as if her Very heart would break." As the preacher put it, this drama "was calculated to awaken some of the finest feelings of human nature."[47]

The heightening of religious sensibilities, particularly through the rise of evangelicalism, awakened more kindliness on the part of masters toward their slaves. Patriarchalism could, of course, embrace the notion of Christian stewardship. A Virginia grandee like William Lee desired that his "people" be "treated as human beings whom Heaven has placed under my care." Evangelicals, however, tried to elicit a more active response toward slaves. They spoke "very affectionately" on slaves' behalf in order to engage their masters' "tender feelings" toward them. By "melting," "softening," or "piercing" the heart of a master, sympathy could be won for the slave. The evangelical Presbyterian Henry Patillo believed that masters should consider their slaves "as [their] humble friends." Because masters and slaves generally grew up together, Patillo continued, the masters ought to "feel, then, a kind of brotherly affection for" their bondpeople.[48]

Mar. 3, 1787, Mercer Family Papers, VHS. See also Richard Walsh, ed., *The Writings of Christopher Gadsden: 1746–1805* (Columbia, S.C., 1966), 314.

47. *Virginia Almanac,* 1775, microfilm, CW; Henry St. George Tucker to his father, St. George Tucker, Feb. 17, 1804, in Mary Haldane Coleman, comp., *Virginia Silhouettes: Contemporary Letters concerning Negro Slavery in the State of Virginia . . .* (Richmond, Va., 1934), 9–10; Marjorie Moran Holmes, "The Life and Diary of the Reverend John Jeremiah Jacob" (master's thesis, Duke University, 1941), 152 (entry, Sept. 4, 1802).

48. William Lee to Mr. Ellis, June 24, 1778, "Notes on 'Green Spring,'" *VMHB,* XXXVII (1929), 299; William McKendree, "Diary of Bishop McKendree from 7 May 1790 to 18

How many masters responded to such appeals is difficult to know. The cultivation of an evangelical sensibilty did not inevitably produce sympathy for the slave. But the late-eighteenth-century diaries of evangelical preachers are dotted with examples of the fruits of their appeals. Thomas Coke met a Virginia Methodist in the 1780s who was "as kind to his negroes as if they were white servants." Francis Asbury related how a "tyrannical" old master on his circuit was suddenly "much softened" so that his "whole plantation, 40 or 50 [were] singing and praising God." James Meacham made a slaveowner feel "much distress" for whipping his slave. Even when the impact cannot be gauged, what catches the attention is how strongly some evangelicals interposed themselves between master and slave. Thus, when Thomas Haskins came across a master who had his runaway slave in tow, making him travel barefoot on a wintry day, his "heart was afflicted at the scene." Nor did he remain quiet. He "spoke with compassion for the poor creature to his master—who seemed tolerable pliant—I told him he was a part of God's Creation, and that he ought not to use him so." Appeals to the sensibility of slaveowners might only have entrenched slavery more firmly by making it less cruel, but some slaves seem to have benefited in the short run by being treated more humanely.[49]

This rise of humanitarianism called into question the worst excesses of planter cruelty, and, in response, Virginians (if not South Carolinians) ameliorated some aspects of their slave code. Thus, in 1769, Virginia's legislators agreed that the dismemberment of slaves was often disproportionate to the offense and "contrary to the principles of humanity." They forbade any court to order the castration of a bondman except for attempted rape of a white woman. Three years later, the assembly warned justices about issuing proclamations against slaves unless they were fugitives and doing mischief. No slave was to be put to death unless at least four justices upheld the verdict. In 1775, the *Virginia Gazette* drew attention to the death sentence passed on a white master for beating his slave boy to death. The report emphasized, "This man has justly incurred the penalties of the law, and we hear will certainly suffer,

---

February 1791," Feb. 12, 1791, MS, Vanderbilt Divinity School, Nashville, Tenn.; Elmer T. Clark et al., eds., *The Journal and Letters of Francis Asbury,* 3 vols. (London, 1958), II, 109; [David Rice], *Slavery Inconsistent with Justice and Good Policy* (Lexington, Ky., 1792), 11; James D. Essig, *The Bonds of Wickedness: American Evangelicals against Slavery, 1770–1808* (Philadelphia, 1982), 42; Pattillo, *Planter's Assistant,* 22. This subject is explored in greater depth in Chapter 7.

49. *Extracts of the Journals of the Late Rev. Thomas Coke . . .* (Dublin, 1816), 69; Clark et al., eds., *Journal of Asbury,* III, 160; James Meacham, "Journal," Mar. 4, 1790, Duke; Thomas Haskins's journal, Jan. 26, 1785, VI, 16, LC. See also Sam L. Straughan to Robert Carter, Sept. 27, 1786, Carter Family Papers, VHS.

which ought to be a warning to others to treat their slaves with moderation." In 1786, only a unanimous court of oyer and terminer could condemn a slave to death. One student of slave trials in eighteenth-century Virginia has concluded that pardons increased dramatically and hanging for property crimes decreased markedly in the late eighteenth century.[50]

Amelioration of slave laws accompanied shifts in community sentiment. In the late eighteenth century, groups of whites first began to request pardons for slaves on humanitarian grounds. In 1787, ninety-two inhabitants from three Southside counties felt strongly enough about the death sentence passed on two slaves found guilty of stealing to petition for mercy. They argued that the slaves were now sincerely penitent and had learned their lesson. Indeed, they continued, the slaves' actions "seemed *only* to have been perpetrated to satisfy hunger." Even more striking is the support of fifty-six residents from Prince George County, Virginia, on behalf of a slave under sentence of death for killing a white. They claimed that the slave had freely confessed to the deed and that, without his confession, it would have been difficult to prove that a murder had been committed. Furthermore, they thought that his master was "bloody-minded and cruel" and that the slave had only acted on his master's orders. In marked contrast, the slave "declar'd his Abhorrence of his Master's Principles and Practices in the plainest Terms and declar'd if he could avoid it, He would never live with Him again."[51] Some whites, at least, could regard a slave the superior of a master in respect of moral judgment.

Perhaps the most remarkable glimpse of the new community sentiment occurred in Sunbury, Georgia. In 1791, twenty-two white women, drawn from some of the wealthiest families of Liberty County and linked through intermarriage and membership in two Congregational churches, signed a petition on behalf of a mulatto slave man named Billy who had been condemned to death. Their arguments derived less from their sympathy for Billy than from their feelings for his mother, Patty, who was free and living in Saint Augustine. These elite white women claimed to "sincerely feel" for a fellow, albeit black,

---

50. Hening, ed., *Statutes at Large*, VIII, 358, 522–523, XII, 345; *VaG* (P and D), Apr. 21, 1775; Schwarz, *Twice Condemned*, 22–23. For humanitarianism in general, see Thomas L. Haskell, "Capitalism and the Origins of the Humanitarian Sensibility," *AHR*, XC (1985), 339–361, 547–566; and Norman S. Fiering, "Irresistable Compassion: An Aspect of Eighteenth-Century Sympathy and Humanitarianism," *Journal of the History of Ideas*, XXXVII (1976), 195–218. For more localized treatment, see Joyce E. Chaplin, "Slavery and the Principle of Humanity: A Modern Idea in the Early Lower South," *Journal of Social History*, XXIV (1990–1991), 299–315.

51. Petition from residents of Dinwiddie, Prince George, and Surry Counties, July 24, 1787, Executive Papers (emphasis added); petition from residents of Prince George County, Nov. 16, 1786, ibid.

mother whose behavior had always been exemplary. They admired Patty's "Industry and Saving," most evident in her efforts to acquire the sum necessary to secure her son's freedom. Finally, Patty's patriotism was a mark in her favor; she had extended "much kindness" to Georgians and Carolinians—perhaps including some of the fathers, husbands, and sons of these same white women— held prisoner in Florida during the Revolutionary war. As good republican women, these daughters of Columbia could empathize with a hard-working, respectable, respectful, and virtuous mother, who just happened to be black.[52]

In advertising for their runaways, Virginia masters chart changing sensibilities. At midcentury, a master noted perfunctorily that his slave "ran away without any Cause." By the later eighteenth century, in contrast, some masters tended to write more self-consciously about their treatment of slaves. One master declared that he had always been "tender" of his bondpeople "and particularly attentive to the good usage of them." He desired that his two runaways "receive such moderate correction as will deter them from running away for the future." But even moderate punishment could be avoided, it would seem. Edward Cary's two fugitives had never been "ill used at [his] hands." Stafford Lightburn claimed that his runaway slave had never been punished and, indeed, had never complained, "neither had he any Cause to be dissatisfied at his Treatment." Before long, masters were speaking of their indulgence toward their slaves. James Mercer asserted that his slave had "lived little short" of freedom and had been "too much indulged." Never been punished, no cause for complaint, remarkably indulged—such was the self-justificatory litany of a number of masters in the late eighteenth century.[53]

Masters in both late-eighteenth-century Chesapeake and Lowcountry were especially sensitive about their reputations and even their own "feelings." After tinkering with his grain ration and encountering "eternal complaint" from his slaves, George Washington insisted that they get ample corn in large part so that he would not have his "feelings again hurt" and that he would not "lye under the imputation of starving" his slaves. When Edward Lloyd IV, a Maryland planter, faced a public attack for being a "Cruel and hard Task Master who neither feeds nor Cloaths sufficiently his Black Family of People," he went to great lengths to justify his conduct, making a public address to the citizens of

52. Betty Wood, "White Women, Black Slaves, and the Law in Early National Georgia: The Sunbury Petition of 1791," *Historical Journal*, XXXV (1992), 611–622. Billy was reprieved, but apparently not because of the white women's petition.

53. James Newgent, *VaG* (Parks), Mar. 27, 1747; Ro. C. Nicholas, ibid. (P and D), Jan. 14, 1767; Edward Cary, ibid. (Rind), Aug. 10, 1769; Stafford Lightburn, Jr., ibid. (P and D), Mar. 7, 1771; James Mercer, *VaG*, Mar. 19, 1772. For the refrain, see James Walker, ibid. (Rind), Jan. 10, 1771; Peterfield Trent, *VaG* (P and D), Dec. 1, 1774; Robert Brent, ibid. (D and H), Nov. 18, 1775; Pitmon Kidd, *VaG and WA*, May 1, 1784; Joseph M'Caughey, ibid., Oct. 8, 1789.

his home county, which he accompanied with more than a score of affidavits from current and former stewards and overseers. Similarly, Pierce Butler was "mortified" when some of his slaves absconded. He wanted them told "how much it hurts me." He recommended an attitude of "paternal kindness" to his manager. By "tenderness in sickness" and "mildness in health," he thought the "situation of slavery" could be made "less burdensome." Indeed, he even thought good treatment might elicit "a smile of content" from his slaves. He declared: "Their reasonable and rational comfort—happiness I will not term it—is near and dear to me."[54]

In the Lowcountry, there was little amelioration of the slave code, but, by the late eighteenth century, masters began to go to greater lengths to justify their actions. When John Channing left his estate in the hands of another in 1786, he declared that he wanted his slaves "treated as reasonable creatures, that is, with humanity and kindness" as long as "they behave well." Fifteen years later, John Ball told his son, "Our first charitable attentions are due to our slaves." Masters ought, he continued, to "strive to make the bitter portion of slavery . . . comfortable." When John Huger made out his will in 1803, he requested his heirs "to regard my Negroes as humble friends, and their own fellow Creatures, and to treat them with all the humanity and compassion, and to give them all the indulgence which existing circumstances can admit of." Occasionally, in advertising for a runaway, a master might now point out that the fugitive had left "without reason or provocation" or with no "Mark of a Lash." Masters began to include offers of forgiveness or a "kindly" reception if an absentee would return voluntarily within a set time. Sale notices occasionally mentioned that the slave was being sold because of his or her preferences. Some notices coupled both offers. Thomas Whitesides proclaimed that if Jemmy and Athy "will return home they will be pardoned, and have tickets to look for a new master." In place of the blood-curdling advertisements calling for a runaway's head that graced the pages of early-eighteenth-century newspapers, a more resigned note was struck in many a notice at the end of the century. One master, for example, eschewed a practical in favor of a poetic description: "Charity is gone! Thrice has she departed from my habitation, notwithstanding her abode was comfortable, and her labour with me light. . . . It is supposed she has left the busy city in disgust, and retir'd to rural quiet, on

---

54. John C. Fitzpatrick, ed., *The Writings of George Washington from the Original Manuscript Sources, 1745–1799*, 39 vols. (Washington, D.C., 1931–1944), XXXII, 434–438, 470–477; Edward Lloyd IV, Treatment of Slaves, 1793, roll 40, Lloyd Papers, MHS, as cited in Lorena S. Walsh, "Work and Resistance in the New Republic: The Case of the Chesapeake, 1770–1820," in Mary Turner, ed., *From Chattel Slaves to Wage Slaves: The Dynamics of Labour Bargaining in the Americas* (Bloomington, Ind., 1995), 101, 117; Pierce Butler to Colonel McPherson, July 19, 1798, and to William Page, Oct. 10, 1798, Jan. 11, 1799, Pierce Butler Letterbook, HSP.

the banks of Stono, to enjoy the company of the sable nymphs and swains, who there cultivate the luxuriant pearly grain." Rather than be prosaic, this master invoked an elegiac vision of pastoral bliss.[55]

Even a late-eighteenth-century notice that called for the head of a runaway (such advertisements were frequent in colonial South Carolina) now went to great lengths to justify the decision:

> Bristol . . . ran away from John G. Blount esq. some years ago, and after weeks of persuasion and many fair promises prevailed on the subscriber to purchase him upon an expressly stipulated condition that . . . if he ran away after drawing me into a loss by inducing me to purchase and then absconding, he would be satisfied to forfeit his head. . . . He has now left my service without the slightest provocation, without having ever been whipped in it, without undergoing the most laborious and disagreeable part of duty, . . . and under peculiar circumstances of treachery and provocation—I do therefore, in consequence of the above mentioned solemn assurances made to him, and with his consent, offer a reward of FIFTY DOLLARS— . . . [for] his Head.[56]

If a slave lost his head in the Revolutionary era, it would at least be at his consent!

Manumission documents also reflect this new humanitarian spirit. Too much should not be read into the terminology employed in testatory manumissions, for they were often formulaic and generally made no mention even of the surface motives involved. However, insofar as colonial wills mentioned the motivation for freeing a slave, references to "honesty and fidelity," "long and faithful services," or "many faithful services" were the constant refrain. By

---

55. John Channing to Edward Telfair, Aug. 10, 1786, Edward Telfair Papers, Duke; John Ball, Sr., to John, Jr., Oct. 6, 1801, Ball Family Papers, SCHS; will of John Huger, Oct. 12, 1803, Charleston County Will Book, 1800–1807, 431–436, SCDAH; James Reid, *SCG*, Nov. 14, 1761 ("without reason"); Rene Peyre, ibid., Nov. 14, 1743 ("Mark of Lash"); Thomas Whitesides, ibid., Nov. 7, 1761 (other examples: John Forbes, ibid., Oct. 2, 1762; and William Roberts, *SC and AGG*, May 22, 1776); Charles Simmons, *State Gaz of SC*, Dec. 7, 1793 (Charity). For forgiveness, see James Michie, *SCG*, Apr. 16, June 20, 1754; Solomon Milner, ibid., Mar. 25, 1756; Christopher Holson, ibid., Jan. 6, 1757; Robert Boyd, ibid., Jan. 5, 1759; Thomas Tucker, ibid., Feb. 17, 1759; John Snelling, ibid., Feb. 2, 1760; James Roulain, ibid., Nov. 15, 1770; Peter Valton, ibid., Feb. 28, 1771; George Smith, Jr., *SCG and CJ*, Dec. 3, 1771; and Zachariah Ladson, ibid., Mar. 31, 1772. These offers became much more numerous in the late 18th century. For this evidence and for examples of sale notices mentioning slave preferences, see Morgan, "Black Society in the Lowcountry," in Berlin and Hoffman, eds., *Slavery and Freedom*, 114.

56. Benjamin Smith, *Times* (Charleston), June 1, 1803.

the Revolutionary era, conversely, references to "love," to "good will and great regard," to "natural affection," to "great respect and Gratitude" vied with the earlier predominant style.[57]

Two eighteenth-century masters anticipated the more sentimental appeal to feelings that became more commonplace in the succeeding century. Consider, first, the unlikely case of Landon Carter, who in many respects fully lived up to the patriarchal mode of domination. He seemed always to be threatening, cajoling, and punishing his slaves for actual or suspected transgressions. At the same time, he could invoke a shared humanity between master and slave. "As a human creature," he said of one of his sick slaves, "I had all imaginable care taken of him." When told that his sick slaves were mending, he could "hope in God they are; for though they can be no loss to such an advanced age [Carter was then sixty-one], Yet they are human creatures and my soul I hope delighteth in releiving them." He "begged," "prayed," and "talked a great deal in a most religious and affectionate way" with a slave in order to effect a reformation of character. He could be the "forgiving" father, pardoning a fellow "creature out of humanity, religion, and every virtuous duty."[58]

Or consider Henry Laurens, in many ways a stern patriarch, but one whose concern for slaves went beyond protection. He desired his overseers not just to guard but to "take care of" and "be kind to" his slaves. When an overseer made it clear that he did not like a particular slave, Laurens enjoined him to remember that "he is a human Creature whether you like him or not." Indeed, Laurens insisted that his slaves be treated with "Humanity." Recalling his own actions toward his waiting man, Laurens emphasized that he had "treated him with all that humanity which a Man for his own Sake ought to extend to every Criature in Subjection to him." Indeed, he had been "indulgent" toward him. A prospective separation of some of his slave families provoked an uncharacteristic outburst: "Slaves are still human Creatures," he exclaimed, "and I cannot be deaf to their cries least a time should come when I should cry and there shall be none to pity me." Extending pity, invoking a common humanity, appealing to a religious benevolence—here is a new constellation of ideas and

---

57. For the new language, see, for instance, deeds of manumission of Joseph Creighton, Dec. 14, 1773, Miscellaneous Records, RR, 300; of Mary Glen, May 31, 1777, ibid., SS, 137–138; and of Joseph Bell, Aug. 21, 1788, ibid., ZZ, 123. My analysis is based on a reading of all the manumission documents in the Miscellaneous Record Series, together with occasional wills, between 1700 and 1790 in SCDAH. See also Sobel, *The World They Made Together*, 145.

58. Greene, ed., *Carter Diary*, 589, 636, 778, 941. For a similar argument, see Rhys Isaac, "Communication and Control: Authority Metaphors and Power Contests on Colonel Landon Carter's Virginia Plantation, 1752–1778," in Sean Wilentz, ed., *Rites of Power: Symbolism, Ritual, and Politics since the Middle Ages* (Philadelphia, 1985), 275–302.

values, revolving around a greater recognition of emotion, sentiment, and feelings. Laurens went even further, for, in 1785, he assured Alexander Hamilton that the lash was now forbidden on his estate; no slave was a beggar, for they enjoyed property, good lodging, food, and clothing; indeed, his slaves were his "watchmen" and his "friends"; in return, all his slaves knew that if they behaved so badly as to merit a whipping, it meant that they "don't love me" and deserved to be sold. Laurens now thought in terms of his slaves' love, and the penalty for its denial was sale.[59]

Enlightened patriarchalism had limits. Where it collided with self-interest and commercial advantage, the slave invariably lost. According to one early-nineteenth-century observer, Georgia slaves were "considered nothing more than perishable property, and interest not principle clothes and feeds them." Similarly, in the early nineteenth century, a South Carolina master was willing to speak cynically of the conflict between his slaves' desire for freedom and his property rights. He described the motivations of his runaways and his own response in this way: "Liberty is sweet and in that they are right—property is comfortable and if I can stop them, I will also be right."[60]

A sense of the flexibility and ultimate rigidity of enlightened patriarchalism is unwittingly captured in the self-justifying remarks of a loyalist slaveholder. "In this land of Nominal freedom and actual Slavery," he had been able, he admitted, to "justify the keeping my fellow beings in bondage" by alleviating the "too common weight of the[ir] chains." He explained that he "scarce used the rod except for theft and other crimes" and, for his slaves' "encouragement," provided ample supplies of corn, meat two or three times a week, and a regular and adequate clothing allowance. Not that his "slaves are used better than any others," he acknowledged, for "some Masters I know, and I hope there are many, treat theirs with the utmost humanity." At the same time, however, he was proud of how he had secured his slaves' respect. "By selling a few, who proved obstinately bad," he had "brought the others to consider their being sold" as the "greatest punishment I can inflict." He had found that the "greatest incitement to their duty" lay in their "hopes of living and dying my property without being separated from their families, connexions, and friends." It hardly became this generous-spirited master—and, presumably, by the lights of eighteenth-century Anglo-American masterdom, he was exactly that—to rail at the possibility that his slaves might be confiscated and be "subject to the

---

59. *Laurens Papers,* IV, 596, 666, V, 379, VIII, 617–618, IX, 316–317, 576; Henry Laurens to Alexander Hamilton, Apr. 19, 1785, Laurens Papers, USC.

60. Richard K. Murdoch, ed., "Letters and Papers of Dr. Daniel Turner: A Rhode Islander in South Georgia," *GHQ,* LIII (1969), LIV (1970), 478; Charles Harris to William Page, Mar. 1, 1808, William Page Papers, UNC.

most humiliating circumstance of human nature—that of being sold like the *Brutes that perish.*"[61]

As this master implies, humane treatment did not have to conflict with economic benefit, nor did modes of control have to be crudely coercive. Masters employed a variety of positive incentives to achieve their aims. In fact, compassion could maximize profits and enhance the masters' investment in their slaves. The threat of sale was perhaps even more effective than the whip in keeping slaves in line. When the duc de La Rochefoucauld-Liancourt visited the Lowcountry in the late eighteenth century, he encountered planters willing to laud the advantages of their new approach. One "excellent master to his negroes" claimed, "against the opinion of many others, that the plantations of mild and indulgent masters thrive most, and that the negroes are more faithful and laborious" than those who belonged to severe masters.[62]

Paradoxically, masters felt that they could show more indulgence toward their slaves as they increasingly placed them outside civil society. As North Americans affirmed the absolute value of individual liberty, the only effective way to justify slavery was to exclude its victims from the community of man. When all free inhabitants were seen as enjoying certain unalienable rights, slaves had to be defined as lacking all rights. Moreover, as liberty was predicated on the acquisition and maintenance of private property, so slaveowners' rights to their slaves became inviolable. Slaves enhanced the independence of their owners. Arbitrarily deprive someone of his or her possessions, and that person became a slave. Whereas the patriarchal ethos held that even the lowliest person was part of an organic society, the denial of rights to slaves and the conception of private property as a basic natural right placed slaves outside society altogether. Ironically, as slavery became more firmly entrenched, masters could show more benevolence toward their dependents.[63]

In thoroughgoing patriarchal households, the subjection of slaves was absolute and unquestioned. The master was first cause, prime mover, almost a demigod. Restraint, order, and authority were constant watchwords. Gradually, however, new values infiltrated this patriarchal citadel. Masters began to view themselves less as harsh taskmasters grandly presiding over their estates and more as benefactors providing for their dependents. They preferred to see their relationship with their slaves grounded less in the tradition of divine right than in voluntary, consensual terms. Austere, rigid patriarchalism gave

---

61. George Ogilvie to Alexander Ogilvie, Apr. 25, 1778, Ogilvie-Forbes of Boyndlie MSS, Aberdeen University Library, Scotland.

62. François Alexandre Frédéric, duke de La Rochefoucault Liancourt, *Travels through the United States of North America . . .* , 2 vols. (London, 1799), I, 601.

63. James Oakes, *Slavery and Freedom: An Interpretation of the Old South* (New York, 1990), 57, 67, 70, 72, 77; Jordan, *White over Black*, 350, 366.

way to warm, mellow paternalism. By the early nineteenth century, William Moultrie reflected on the changes that had occurred. "I am very much pleased to see the treatment of the slaves in the country is altered so much," he observed, particularly noting the "tenderness and humanity" now extended to slaves. Slavery would soon be viewed as a benign institution; slaves would, in George Fitzhugh's exaggerated words, be enveloped in "domestic affection"; before long, it would be the master for whom pity would be invoked as "the greatest slave" of all.[64]

Intimacy and Distance

Just as the nature of master-slave relations changed over time, so it varied across space. Chesapeake whites always interacted more closely and openly with blacks than their Lowcountry counterparts. Although the flexibility of race relations in seventeenth-century Virginia did not persist into the eighteenth century, the greater openness of race relations in the Chesapeake as against those of the Lowcountry still held true. Thus, at the end of the eighteenth century, a visitor to the Chesapeake heard claims from residents that their slaves were "more intelligent [best translated as "assimilated"] than those of more southern states" and, most significantly, that "they are said to be greatly attached to their families and their masters." Of course, this was self-serving, but the close and regular contact between masters and slaves was a fact of life in the Chesapeake and must, in many cases, have fostered such sentiments. By contrast, David Ramsay observed that "the distance between a slave and his master" was "great" in South Carolina.[65]

A Virginia-born slave named Peter personifies, in exaggerated fashion, perhaps, this close identification between master and bondman. In 1769, Peter, then aged forty-four, fled his Charles City County master, William Gregory. He carried off his and some of his wife's clothes, a gun "of an uncommon large

---

64. Fragment from early 1800s, folder 38, box 3, William Moultrie Papers, USC, cited in Joyce E. Chaplin, *An Anxious Pursuit: Agricultural Innovation and Modernity in the Lower South, 1730–1815* (Chapel Hill, N.C., 1993), 127. The best study of 19th-century paternalism is Genovese, *Roll, Jordan, Roll*, esp. 3–7. For an interesting essay that implicitly recognizes the difference between patriarchalism and paternalism, but without doing the distinction full justice, see Paul Conner, "Patriarchy: Old World and New," *American Quarterly*, XVII (1965), 48–62, esp. 54–55 for quotations of Fitzhugh. For more recent explorations, see Brown, *Good Wives, Nasty Wenches, and Anxious Patriarchs*, chap. 10; and Alan Gallay, "The Origins of Slaveholders' Paternalism: George Whitefield, the Bryan Family, and the Great Awakening in the South," *Jour. So. Hist.*, LIII (1987), 369–394.

65. Kenneth Roberts and Anna M. Roberts, trans. and eds., *Moreau de St. Méry's American Journey [1793–1798]* (Garden City, N.Y., 1947), 59; Brunhouse, ed., "David Ramsay," *Am. Phil. Soc., Trans.*, N.S., LV, pt. 4 (1965), 60–61.

size," and a fiddle, which he "much delighted in when he gets any strong drink." In fact, Peter was "remarkably fond" of liquor, which made him "very talkative and impudent." Peter was a true Virginian. Gregory suspected that his "sly artful rogue" aimed for Amelia County, where he would seek out Mrs. Tanner, Peter's former owner. Apparently, she had sold Peter to Richard Hayles, who in turn sold him to Gregory. But Peter held to a different version of events. He "often told the other Negroes that if ever [Gregory] used him ill he would go to his old mistress, as she never sold him to Mr. Hayles, but only lent him during pleasure, and that he would go to her, and be protected." Perhaps Peter placed too much trust in Mrs. Tanner, but equally William Gregory might have placed too much trust in a bill of sale. Such were the self-delusions produced by the proximity of master-slave relations in the Chesapeake.[66]

An even more unusual relationship between master and slave involved another Virginia bondman named Peter. In 1790, he ran away from his Richmond County master, Vincent Redman. A "cunning, artful fellow," Peter was in his midtwenties, about five feet, ten inches tall, weighing about two hundred pounds, a ditcher by trade, a Baptist by faith, and "fond of conversing on religion." In about 1786, Peter had been sold by a Mr. Harris or Harrison, an Irishman, to William Graham of Northumberland County, who in turn sold him to William Siffel. Redman had never clapped eyes on Peter, for he purchased him from Siffel as a runaway in December 1789. It happened that, at about the time Peter absconded, his first master, the Irishman, had also eloped. Redman now saw the connection: "It is suspected that those two fellows have joined themselves together again, and if a second sale has not already taken place, that it is their design for Peter to be sold as often as they find it convenient." In short, Peter was in cahoots with his former master to defraud would-be owners of slaves.[67]

As this case suggests, the close ties between a master and slave in the Chesapeake might have been wholly pragmatic. Indeed, intimacy arose very largely from the basic demographic and economic features of Chesapeake life. Small plantations, fairly equal numbers of whites and blacks, a close working relationship between master and slaves constituted the typical Chesapeake setting, one conducive to close and regular contact between the free and the unfree. Moreover, from Fernando Ortiz's vivid description of the distinction between tobacco and sugar plantations in Cuba, it is evident that the particular quality of master-slave relations owed a great deal to the crop with which a society was primarily associated. Whereas sugar was an impersonal industry, "the personal

66. William Gregory, *VaG* (P and D), May 4, 1769.
67. Vincent Redman, *VaG and GA,* Oct. 27, 1790.

element," as Ortiz characterized it, "always predominated in tobacco growing, and there was a patriarchal, intimate quality about its work."[68]

The production of rice, in contrast, resembled the anonymous, impersonal sugar industry. With large numbers of relatively isolated slaves, Africans ubiquitous, masters often absent for long periods, and nonslaveholding neighbors few, Lowcountry blacks had much less regular contact with whites than their Chesapeake counterparts. Charles Ball, who experienced slavery firsthand in both regions, drew a revealing contrast. In the Chesapeake, a member of the slaveowner's family might take a young slave under his or her wing, an advantage of the "master and his family living at home." In the Lowcountry, by contrast, "many a slave has been born, lived to old age, and died on a plantation, without ever having been within the walls of his master's domicil." In varying ways, two South Carolina masters offer insights into the impersonal quality of a large plantation enterprise. One planter described his situation as being surrounded by hundreds of slaves and "a couple of overseers who are the only White Faces and scarcely white, on the Place except my own—and yet all orderly and regular." So well regulated was his plantation that he compared his situation favorably to an English farmer who has "as much trouble in farming with 20 or 30 People as we have here with 6 Times the Number." Another was more impressed by the difficulties that arose in managing such a large group of blacks. He could never assemble his gang on the field at the same time, he said, because "they don't understand Roll calling."[69] At variance as these two accounts are, they both testify to the lack of intimacy and impersonal, regimented quality that characterized large-scale plantation enterprises.

South Carolina slaves, particularly recent African immigrants, often knew little of their masters. Perhaps it is coincidence (John was, after all, an extremely popular name among eighteenth-century whites), but a number of South Carolina fugitives referred to their master as "Johnny." Other slaves were more impressed by their master's physique. Polydore and Cato knew no more of their master than to say he was "a very big man"; Carolina said "his master's name is Porcher, is a big man, and has negroes enough"; and Charley most unflatteringly described his master as having "a large Belly." Perhaps Toby was confused about his ownership, for he was under the impression that he had two masters, "the one in the country, the other in town, and that one of them is named Peter." Tom was only a little more knowledgeable, saying "he has an

---

68. Fernando Ortiz, *Cuban Counterpoint: Tobacco and Sugar,* trans. Harriet de Onís (New York, 1947), 65.

69. Ball, *Fifty Years in Chains,* 58, 280; George Lockey to [M. Harford], Apr. 5, 1804, Correspondence of John Lloyd; M. D. Rolle to Col. Laurens, c. 1765, encl. in a letter by James Grant, May 4, 1765, in Bound Letter Book of James Grant of Ballindalloch, bundle 659, Papers of General James Grant of Ballindalloch.

old mistress, but cannot tell her name, two young masters, named Billy and Johnny, Billy he says lives in town." Perhaps it took the isolated world of South Carolina rice plantations for a slave to imagine that he or she might gain redress from the colony's ruler. At any rate, one bondman ran away from his plantation, reached the governor in Charleston, and there complained of his master. In an effort to reach out to a recognizable person, this slave suffered a spell in the city workhouse for his pains. South Carolina slaves experienced a less personal, intimate, everyday association with masters than their Chesapeake counterparts.[70]

Intimacy was not always beneficial, of course, as occasional glimpses of demeanor and gesture on the part of Chesapeake slaves suggest. Consider the old slave who complained to his master about his food allowance. He adopted a "humble posture" and "sat himself down on the Floor clasp'd his Hands together, with his face directly to Mr [Robert] Carter, and then began his Narration." If the slave played a ritualized game, it was one where the master largely made the rules. Or consider the slave carpenter who, when commanded to align his fencing more evenly, "stoopt down like falling," leading his master to wonder whether this "was the Negroe's foolish way of hearing better." Perhaps the slave exaggerated a submissive pose so that it bordered on a gesture of defiance, but the willingness to appear foolish must have taken its toll. Finally, consider a traveler's observation that Virginia slaves cringed and crouched before masters; even a slave's dog cowered, he claimed, "as if ashamed of his owner."[71]

The more distanced relationship many Lowcountry slaves had with their

---

70. Workhouse, *SCG*, June 14, 1760; Workhouse, *SCG and CJ*, May 6, 1766; William King, *SC and AGG*, Nov. 24, 1775; Alexander Macullagh, ibid., Dec. 30, 1774 (Johnny as master); Workhouse, *SCG*, June 29, 1765 (Polydore and Cato); Workhouse, *SCG and CJ*, July 4, 1769 (Carolina); Workhouse, ibid., Dec. 8, 1772 (Charley) [for another "big man," see Workhouse, *SCG*, Feb. 28, 1761, and for another master with a large "belly," see Chapter 4, n. 29]; Workhouse, *SCG and CJ*, Sept. 9, 1766 (Toby); Workhouse, ibid., Sept. 24, 1771 (Tom); Workhouse, *SCG*, Feb. 19, 1753 (complaint of governor). This last slave knew the location of his plantation and his master's name. He was unlikely, therefore, to have been a recent immigrant, though no information is given about his birthplace. For other imprecise references to masters, see Workhouse, *SCG and CJ*, Sept. 17, 1771; Georgetown Gaol, ibid., Nov. 19, 1772; Workhouse, ibid., May 4, 1773; Workhouse, ibid., Sept. 24, 1771; Robert Wells, *SC and AGG*, Dec. 9, 1774; Workhouse, *SCG*, Nov. 14, 1775; William King, *SC and AGG*, Nov. 24, 1775. For runaway slaves' mentioning drivers, see Chapter 4. For runaway slaves' mentioning an overseer's name (Christian name only), see Workhouse, *SCG*, Aug. 18, 1757; Workhouse, ibid., Apr. 4, 1761; and Workhouse, *SCG and CJ*, June 3, 1766.

71. Hunter Dickinson Farish, ed., *Journal and Letters of Philip Vickers Fithian, 1773–1774: A Plantation Tutor of the Old Dominion* (Williamsburg, Va., 1943), 170; Greene, ed., *Carter Diary*, 378 (see also 369); Henry C. Knight [Arthur Singleton, pseud.], *Letters from the South and West* (Boston, 1824), 80. See also Ball, *Fifty Years in Chains*, 58.

masters seems to have lessened the intense pressures their Chesapeake counterparts felt. Visitors to Lowcountry plantations encountered slaves who were anything but deferential. In 1743, two Moravians on their way to Charleston crossed the Santee River but realized that they would not make their destination before nightfall. They called at a "house... full of negroes, who would not receive" them. Joseph Pilmore had a similar experience thirty years later. Traveling along Long Bay, he called at a house for refreshment, but "the Master was from home," and "the Negroes would not let me have anything, so I was obliged to go on as well as I could." Most revealing, perhaps, was the response of an old South Carolina slave woman to the appearance of two visitors at her master's plantation. Significantly, the visitors arrived to find all the whites absent and only the slaves in attendance. The black woman greeted them in her own inimitable style, exclaiming, "Too much buckra come here today, for true!"[72]

The difference in tone between slavery in the Lowcountry and in the Chesapeake echoes the difference between patriarchalism in the early eighteenth century and enlightened patriarchalism in the late eighteenth century. Although there was more brutality in Lowcountry than Chesapeake slavery, and in colonial than in late-eighteenth-century slavery, at least there was also more latitude for the slave. As slavery became softer, more openly solicitous of the slave, so it grew tighter, with less room for autonomy. Willie Lee Rose has summarized the difference as a shift from a time when slaves were seen as "luckless, unfortunate barbarians" to one when they were seen "as children expected never to grow up." That shift was not just temporal but spatial. It occurred earlier and more powerfully in Virginia than in South Carolina.[73]

PLAIN FOLK AND SLAVES

In general, the distance between plain white folk and black slaves grew progressively wider throughout the course of the eighteenth century. In the middle to late seventeenth century, black slaves and the poorer sections of the white community, particularly servants, associated closely and openly. By the turn of the eighteenth century, however, cooperation and alliances between white servants and black slaves began to dissolve, in part because of actions taken by the planter class, in part because servant numbers declined, and in part because the black population became more numerous and alien. Most of these processes remained at work well into the eighteenth century. Yet, the rul-

72. Extracts from the Diary of Leonhard Schnell and Robert Hussey, of Their Journey to Georgia, November 6, 1743–April 10, 1744, in Rev. William J. Hinke and Charles E. Kemper, "Moravian Diaries of Travels through Virginia," *VMHB*, XI (1903–1904), 386; Frederick E. Maser and Howard T. Maag, eds., *The Journal of Joseph Pilmore, Methodist Itinerant: For the Years August 1, 1769 to January 2, 1774* (Philadelphia, 1969), 177; Davis, *Travels*, 107.

73. Willie Lee Rose, *Slavery and Freedom*, ed. William W. Freehling (New York, 1982), 23.

ing class was never completely successful in wooing lower-class whites to their cause; the importation of twenty thousand convicts into the Chesapeake during the eighteenth century meant that servant ranks were never negligible—at least in that region; and, as the black population creolized, so it again became possible for lower-class whites and blacks to identify with one another. The gap between lower-class whites and blacks widened in the second half of the eighteenth century, but more slowly than before.

Common Bonds

The growing divide that separated lower-class whites from blacks had its limits. However much the ruling class attempted to separate the races, plain white folk and slaves still shared their lives in ways impermissible for a planter-patriarch and his bondpeople. Slaves and plain white folk not only lived nearer to one another but were more likely to work alongside one another, speak the same dialect, have their children play together, commit crimes jointly, and run away together. Contacts between plain white folk and slaves were also more regular and frequent in some places than others. They were more evident in the Chesapeake than in the Lowcountry; in both regions, they were more evident on the periphery and in towns than in plantation heartlands. Contacts between plain white folk and slaves also fluctuated over time. Even though the gap between the two gradually widened over the eighteenth century, the Revolutionary crisis proved that some poor whites and slaves could still cooperate.

Shared labor helped create common bonds. The duc de La Rochefoucauld-Liancourt thought that the small planters of Virginia treated their slaves better than did large planters because they "share[d] with them the toils of the fields." He added, "Although they do not clothe and feed them well, yet [they] treat them . . . as well as they do themselves." One of Henry Laurens's slaves, Sampson, a recent African immigrant, offers similar testimony from South Carolina. Absenting himself from Laurens's Mepkin plantation only a few days after his arrival, Sampson went to the Santee and, in Laurens's words, "fell in with a poor worthless fellow who entertained him near 8 months." Fearful that he would be discovered, the white man sent Sampson back to Laurens. But Sampson was no longer the same man, for, during his absence, he had "learned to make Indigo or at least to work at it and to speak tolerable good English." What is more, when Laurens returned Sampson to Mepkin, he immediately ran off again "to his former range which proves," his master acknowledged, "that he had not been unkindly treated there."[74]

In addition to their work, plain white folk and blacks shared even the items they wore and the language they spoke. When Devereaux Jarratt, of modest

---

74. La Rochefoucault Liancourt, *Travels*, II, 69; *Laurens Papers*, IV, 645.

slaveholding stock in Virginia, wanted to "be counted somebody," he got himself "an old wig, which, perhaps being cast off by the master had become the property of his slave, and from the slave it was conveyed to me." A nonelite white man had no reservations about wearing an item that had previously adorned the head of a black slave. Plain folk and blacks also shared a patois. Ebenezer Hazard observed that "the common country people" of South Carolina "talk very much like Negros," while the "better sort" used only "a little of that dialect." Similarly, another Lowcountry traveler encountered an illiterate German overseer and his wife, who "by living with the Negroes . . . had become so accustomed to the swearing and cursing . . . that they had to do themselves violence to refrain from it during my presence."[75] Those who lived together swore together.

From cradle to grave, plain white folk and black slaves lived near one another. Thus, although a patriarch's child might occasionally play with slaves of the same age, such contact was almost inevitable for the children of plain white folk. Charles Drayton became aware of such activity when his slave boy Jack, waiting on an overseer at an outlying plantation, came to Drayton Hall with a broken arm and dislocated shoulder, the product of his "idly riding about the fields with the ov[erseer's] son." Growing up in a poor white home might mean sharing living space with blacks, certainly living close to them, sharing much the same diet and clothes. Death, too, might bring lowly white and slave together, as in the scene described by a visitor to Maryland's Eastern Shore: "Last evening at dark the corps [of overseer Nathan Cullins] was put in a plain coffin, and conveyed to the grave, by four negroes, and one carrying a spade and shovel—No other person attended." A white overseer went to his grave unrecognized, except by the blacks with whom he labored.[76]

Proximity of estate created a measure of intimacy, a regularity of contact, even shared bonds between plain white folk and slaves, but did it create mutual sympathies? Did poor whites and slaves identify with one another? One of the best, but by no means conclusive, types of evidence concerns the criminal record. It is hard to imagine that the partners to a crime were not also partners in much else besides.

Instances of interracial criminal cooperation in Virginia, though never extensive, were constant. In 1720, Mary Turner, a white servant of Middlesex County, was arraigned for helping three slaves steal a hog; in the same decade,

75. *The Life of the Reverend Devereaux Jarratt . . . Written by Himself . . .* (Baltimore, 1806), 26; H. Roy Merrens, "A View of Coastal South Carolina in 1778: The Journal of Ebenezer Hazard," *SCHM,* LXXIII (1972), 181; George Fenwick Jones, "John Martin Boltzius' Trip to Charleston, October 1742," ibid., LXXXII (1981), 103–104.

76. Charles Drayton diary, Feb. 24, 1793, Drayton Family Papers, Historic Charleston Foundation; Miscellaneous MSS, Apr. 2, 1800, microfilm, CW.

Jacob and two white women of Lancaster County were convicted of stealing tobacco and provisions. Half a century later, in Southampton County, William Parsons and Pierce, a slave, apparently combined to steal a horse, whereas, in 1780, in the Blue Ridge County of Amherst, a slave man and a white man were caught at their camp in the woods after breaking into a neighboring farm and plantation owner's home.[77]

Criminal contact between plain white folk and slaves was much less frequent in South Carolina than in Virginia. Most Lowcountry parishes contained only a few white nonslaveholders and a large number of middling to large slaveowners. Still, even in the heart of the rural Lowcountry, lower-class whites and slaves occasionally cooperated in crime. In 1735, the governor of South Carolina ordered the provost marshal to apprehend "several white persons and Blacks [who] have committed many Outrages and Roberys and ly in the Swamp at the Head of Wando River." Four years later, a white servant and black slaves belonging to a Captain McPherson murdered a white man. Ten years after Stono, an alleged conspiracy involving more than a hundred slaves and sixteen lower-class whites came to light in an area served by the eastern branch of the Cooper River. Although the evidence for a full-fledged conspiracy proved weak, lower-class whites seemingly identified closely with slaves. One overseer reportedly tried to arouse slave resentment against the hardships of their lives by asking "how they could be satisfied with Eating Homminy, Potatoes and Such Victuals and . . . how they could work in the Sun without Shirts." Other lowly whites employed more utopian arguments. Run away with us, a lower-class white allegedly told the slaves, and you will be "baptised as the white People are."[78]

Because of their acute vulnerability, poor white women were particularly prone to accusations of interracial fraternization, especially in the Chesapeake, where their numbers were always much greater than in the Lowcountry. In 1721, Katherine Jones of Norfolk was accused of "consorting" with slaves in another man's kitchen. A couple of decades later, a grand jury in Lancaster County

---

77. Middlesex County Court Orders, Dec. 6, 1720, VSL; Lancaster County Court Orders, 1721–1729, 104, 128, VSL; Southampton County Court Orders, 1772–1777, 370–371, VSL; Amherst County Court Orders, 1773–1782, 408–410, VSL. See also Richmond County Criminal Trials, Sept. 4, 1718, VSL; York County Court Orders, May 9, 1735, July 19, Nov. 13, 1736, VSL; Fairfax County Court Orders, Aug. 19, 20, 1771, 234–236, VSL; Northampton County Court Orders, 1722–1729, 145, VSL; and Robert Beverley, *VaG or AA,* July 9, 1785. And see Sobel, *The World They Made Together,* 51.

78. South Carolina Council Journal, May 29, 1735, CO5/437; Hugh Bryan to the Public, Mar. 1739, SCHS; South Carolina Council Journal, no. 17, part 1, 72, 121. For more on this interracial conspiracy, see Philip D. Morgan and George D. Terry, "Slavery in Microcosm: A Conspiracy Scare in Colonial South Carolina," *Southern Studies,* XXI (1982), 121–145.

accused an unmarried or widowed white woman of "feasting and harboring negroes." In the same year, Sarah McBoyd of the same county stood charged with failing to go to church, leading a "Loose life," and "harbouring negroes and servants." In 1770, a Sussex County master accused Anne Ashwell, "a woman of infamous character," of having "dealings" with his fugitive slave Davy and of advising him to run away. Self-respecting white men cast poor white women not just as economically marginal but as sexually reprehensible.[79]

The most spectacular example of cooperation between lower-class white women and a slave occurred on the Eastern Shore. In 1724, a runaway slave named Caesar managed to remain at large for a number of months. He found as much, if not more, support among lower-class whites as among his fellow blacks. A free black couple admitted to feeding him on three occasions, but the wife refused to make him a shirt from some linen he had stolen. Similarly, although Caesar received food and occasional shelter from slaves on at least three plantations, his wife also refused to make him a shirt and even told her mistress about his proposal. By contrast, the wife of a yeoman white farmer exchanged a gourd of cornmeal for Caesar's "harthberries," and Alice Cormack, an illiterate, poor white widow was even more accommodating. Although she knew that Caesar had been outlawed, Alice gave the fugitive food, drink, and a place to sleep. In turn, she and her three children shared the fresh pork, game birds, and ears of corn that he brought to the house. She made a shirt for her son and an apron for her daughter with some of the linen that Caesar gave her. Naturally, she "often charged [her children] to say nothing of the said Caesars coming there." She eventually received twenty-five lashes and a month in prison for her "great misdemeanor" in harboring and entertaining a runaway slave.[80]

The closest associations between lower-class whites and blacks probably occurred on the fringes of the plantation heartland—in a backwater area like the Eastern Shore or in the backcountry of South Carolina. Backcountry bandit gangs, for instance, were often interracial. In 1767, a slave who escaped from a Savannah River plantation "was seen ... on Savannah River in company with Timothy Tyrrell, George Black, John Andrews, Anthony Distow, Edward Wells

---

79. Norfolk Orders, Appraisements and Wills, Nov. 17, 1721, 39, and Lancaster County Court Order Book, no. 8, June 11, July 9, Dec. 10, 1742, 347, 350, 369, VSL, all cited in Brown, *Good Wives, Nasty Wenches, and Anxious Patriarchs,* 239, 289; John Verell, *VaG* (P and D), Sept. 6, 1770.

80. Depositions of Caesar, Alice Cormack, Francis Cormack, Edmund Cormack, Anne Cormack, Thomas Carter, Elizabeth Carter, Hope Steel, Nell, Little Tom, and Great Tom, Sept. 4–8, 1724, Northampton County Loose Papers, no. 8, 1724, Northampton County Court House (information kindly supplied by Douglas Deal).

and others, all horse thieves." In the same year, an overseer on a Lowcountry plantation, an Irishman, ran away with three of his employer's creole slave men, all of whom spoke "very good English," as well as with several other slave men from neighboring plantations. They were thought to be making either for another colony or "at least to the back parts" of South Carolina. All were armed, suggesting a high degree of cooperation in this interracial escape. The overseer was eventually caught and appeared in court alongside several inland bandits, with whom the slaves had no doubt associated. Most of the small farmers and planters who harbored fugitives acted largely out of self-interest. When advertising for his two African fugitives, a Lowcountry master explained, "It is a customary thing for the back settlers of this province, to take up new negroes, and keep them employed privately." But, presumably, the fugitives found their situation improved or they would not have headed and remained inland in such numbers.[81]

Cooperation between plain white folk and slaves was also extensive in the city. In 1782, many residents of Richmond complained to the state legislature about a large ring of slaves who regularly stole goods under the leadership of white men. Edmund Randolph estimated that the "formidable gang of blacks and whites" numbered fifty. They had "perpetrated some of the most daring and horrid thefts." Similarly, one of the largest robberies in eighteenth-century Charleston, involving goods worth two thousand pounds, occurred through the collaboration of urban whites and blacks. Lower-class whites and slaves shared more than crime in the city. Charleston's public authorities denounced a Mr. Gordon as "a Mountebank" and "a public Nuisance and Deluder of the lower and Ignorant Part of the Community" because his "Exhibitions not only lead white People but great Numbers of slaves to Idleness and Dissipation." Apparently, Joseph Tobias had a similar effect on the three runaway slaves that he harbored, for "by keeping the evil and vicious company of the said Joseph," these three bondmen had "contracted a habit of Laziness Idleness and wickedness." There were other Charlestonians like Tobias. The master of one runaway slave declared, "There are certain despicable characters in this city who harbor and encourage the desertion of negroes from their owners and by furnishing them with tickets in their master's name render their recovery extremely difficult." Although slaves could take advantage of these opportunities, there were always risks. One fugitive slave woman, who hired herself to a soldier's wife in

81. William Williamson, *SCG and CJ*, Sept. 29, Oct. 27, 1767 (and see *SC and AGG*, July 17, 1767); Thomas Fuller, ibid., Aug. 18, 1767, and notice, ibid., Feb. 12, 1768; Robert Dearington, *SCG and CJ*, June 17, 1766, and *SC and AGG*, Nov. 6, 1767. See also Rachel N. Klein, *Unification of a Slave State: The Rise of the Planter Class in the South Carolina Backcountry, 1760–1808* (Chapel Hill, N.C., 1990), 62–63, 69–72, 98–99.

Charleston's new barracks, found her service terminated when she fell sick, for the white woman "would not keep her."[82]

Just as lower-class whites harbored black fugitives, so the roles were sometimes reversed. In 1729, a white man was caught stealing sheep in Richmond County, Virginia. When apprehended, he said he was destined for Mr. Churchill's "Negro quarter." He denied stealing various other goods found in a hollow tree nearby, saying that they belonged to one of Churchill's slaves. In recounting his past movements, he described how he had "lived in the quarter along with the negroes for three or four months last past, and that the sd negros Supplyed him with meale and hominy."[83] Probably a white criminal's best means of support lay in the slave quarters.

A constant trickle of runaway groups in Virginia was interracial. Most groups comprised white servants, occasionally convicts, even more occasionally free artisans, and black slaves. No doubt some of these lower-class whites aimed to make capital of their fellow fugitives. In 1769, a Hobbes Hole master feared that David Randolph, a cooper who had served his time in Philadelphia, aimed to return northward with his sixteen-year old slave, Billy, in order to profit from his sale. But, in a number of cases, blacks and whites appear to have joined common cause. In 1752, a mulatto slave blacksmith went off with a white servant man from Middlesex County. As a measure of their cooperation, they "took a Gun with them." In 1768, two English convicts and a black slave lad went off on horseback together from their master in Loudoun County. Masters spoke of slaves going off "in company" or "together" with whites. As slaves, they were always vulnerable, of course, but then, again, a black slave could always accuse the servant of man-stealing.[84]

Even more occasionally, Lowcountry slaves ran off with whites. In 1735, two Irish servant men fled in company with two slave men. A generation later, a Scottish carpenter absconded from a plantation on the Combahee River along with six slaves—two men and four women. Perhaps the harsh conditions and extreme prejudice experienced by white servants, particularly if they were not

82. Petition of Henrico County citizens, June 8, 1782, Legislative Petitions, Henrico County, VSL; Hutchinson et al., eds., *Papers of James Madison*, V, 91–92 (see also Schwarz, *Twice Condemned*, 125, 134); *SCG*, June 21, 1735; presentments of the Grand Jury of Charleston, *SCG*, Feb. 28, 1774; Charles Fraser Commonplace Book, 59 (and see 49), CC; Henry Gibbes, *State Gaz of SC*, Mar. 4, 1790; Workhouse, *SC and AGG*, June 10, 1768.

83. Richmond County Slave Criminal Trials, June 20, 1729, VSL.

84. John Brockenbrough, *VaG* (Rind), June 15, 1769; Armistead Churchill, ibid. (Hunter), June 12, 1752; William Carr Lane, ibid. (Rind), May 12, 1768. I count 30 interracial groups among advertised Virginia runaways, involving 38 whites (mostly servants) and 31 black slaves. There are other examples of whites' aiding runaways, for example, Jane Vobe, *VaG* (P and D), June 30, 1768; John Stratton, ibid., Jan. 23, 1772; Josiah Riddick, ibid., Aug. 13, 1772; Richard Hipkins, ibid. (Pinkney), Jan. 12, 1775.

English, encouraged them to throw in their lot with blacks. It is also possible, of course, that these whites decoyed away the slaves in the hope of selling them. Particularly suspicious, perhaps, are those white overseers who "carried away" or "enticed away" slaves. One overseer's wife ran off with a slave boy whom it was thought she planned to sell. Sampson and Scipio, two Africans, encountered a couple of unscrupulous whites who later tried to sell them. Although slaves could be exploited by lower-class whites, they were far from passive victims. Hannah, a creole who had previously passed as free, was unlikely to have been the dupe of Joseph Johnson. She had invited him into her cabin the night before her flight. Similarly, the slave man, his free Indian wife, their two-year-old child, his slave mother, and a mulatto boy, who went off in a canoe from Winyaw, seem to have acted voluntarily. After all, they told some slaves at a plantation on the Pee Dee River that they aimed to visit relatives near Charleston. Perhaps the white man who accompanied them was simply hitching a ride. In yet other cases, whites and blacks appear to have entered into an alliance. Handy and Fortune, for instance, were seen in a camp with a white man.[85]

The reluctance of plain white folk to share in the policing of the slave system does not prove that they were sympathetic toward blacks, but it does indicate that white solidarity could not be automatically assumed, even as the gap between the races widened. In 1705, a refusal to assist a sheriff in conveying runaways to jail was made a punishable offense in Virginia, but a number of subsequent court cases demonstrate that white reluctance was difficult to eradicate. Nor was patrolling any more popular. In 1771, one Virginia slaveowner complained to another that his "people" were "rambling about every night" because the patrollers failed to do their duty. Even when captains of companies appeared in order to encourage others, their actions met with no response. In early 1775, Joseph Glover, commander of a South Carolina regiment of foot, reported that the general mobilization included a commitment to patrol duty. However, by September, "the Patrol Service" had "stagnated" because lower-class whites had lost interest in it. Officers observed, Glover reported, "that

---

85. Bryan Reily and John Carmichael, *SCG*, Mar. 21, 1735 (Irishmen); John Burn, ibid., July 21, 1757 (Scotsman); George Smith and John Waring, ibid., July 6, 1767 (overseer's wife); Workhouse, *SCG and CJ*, Oct. 25, 1768 (Sampson and Scipio); Samuel Jenkins, *SCG*, July 18, 1761 (Hannah); Joseph Allston, ibid., Feb. 20, 1762 (slave family); Francis Lejau, ibid., July 17, 1762 (Handy and Fortune). For slaves' being "stolen" or "carried away" by lower-class whites, usually overseers, see Thomas Ellery, *SCG*, May 21, 1737; Robert Snow, ibid., Dec. 4, 1755; Benjamin and Joseph Waring, ibid., Mar. 10, 1757; Benjamin Payton, ibid., Dec. 4, 1762; Edmund Bellinger, ibid., May 11, 1765; Isaac Neavel, ibid., May 4, 1769. Instances of white servants' running away with slaves are rare in South Carolina. Apart from the example given above, I have come across only two other instances: John Edwards, ibid., May 22, 1736, and William Marshall, ibid., Sept. 21, 1767.

they must be subservant to their mens humours." Even when they did patrol, the lower orders were not always as conscientious as the gentry would have liked. In 1745, Charleston's grand jury reprimanded a member of the town watch for "entertaining seamen and Negroes at unseasonable Hours." A generation later, the practice had apparently magnified, for the grand jury complained about "the number of Licenses which are annually granted to Watchmen, or their Wives, to keep Dram-Shops, whereby it becomes their Interest to encourage Negroes, and others to frequent their Houses." During a house search, a patroller in North Carolina desired, a slave woman later told her mistress, "to be very fond of her, tho' she had her Husband hid under Bed." Some plain white folk seem not to have taken their police duties seriously. Occasionally, whites even undermined their own patrols. In 1796, at least one white resident of Richmond, Virginia, rescued several blacks taken into custody by the patrol.[86]

The possibility that slaves and lower-class whites would cooperate is evidenced by the establishment's constant fear of such a liaison. There was, of course, a striking precedent in Virginia history. In the late seventeenth century, about 10 percent of Virginia's black males formed part of Nathaniel Bacon's "giddy multitude" of servants and poor freepersons in their opposition to the colony's rulers. Most illuminating was the absence of contemporary comment about the mixed racial character of this force, which suggests that Virginia's gentry took the cooperation of slaves and poor whites for granted. No subsequent large-scale class confrontation with an interracial component ever again occurred in the Chesapeake. But the gentry never rested easy. The Revolutionary crisis, in particular, aroused acute fears. The Committee of Inspection for Dorchester County, Maryland, became alarmed at "the malicious and impudent speeches of some among the lower class of whites [which] have induced [the slaves] to believe that their Freedom depended on the success of the Kings

86. Hening, *Statutes at Large*, III, 460; for transgressions of this law, see Richmond County Slave Criminal Trials, Mar. 4, 1744, and York County Court Orders, Feb. 20, 1764; John Tayloe to Landon Carter, Mar. 31, 1771, Carter Family Papers, microfilm, UVa; Holt Richeson to the governor, June 5, 1792, Executive Papers, box 74, VSL; Return of the Officers and the whole of the men . . . , Sept. 22, 1775, Glover Papers, SCHS; presentments of the Grand Jury for the province, *SCG*, Apr. 15, 1745; ibid., Oct. 29, 1772; J. Blair to Miss Blair, June 29, 1783, James Iredell Papers, Duke; *Commonwealth* v. *Archelaus Hughes*, Richmond Suit Papers, box 20, September, October, December 1796 bundle, VSL, as cited by James Sidbury, *Ploughshares into Swords: Race, Rebellion, and Identity in Gabriel's Virginia, 1730–1810* (New York, 1997). Barnard Elliot suffered from the uncooperativeness of a lower-class white, for he learned that his runaway slave had been captured by a white sailor and taken to an Elliott plantation, where the overseer refused to "take the fellow and pay for apprehending him." More than a month after this incident, no news had turned up of the sailor and his fugitive (*SCG and CJ*, Mar. 8, 1768).

Troops." John Simmons of that county was reported to have said "that the Gentlemen were intending to make us all fight for their lands and Negroes, and then said Damn them (meaning the Gentlemen) if I had a few more White people to join me I could get all the negroes in the county to back us, and they would do more Good in the night than the white people could in the day." In Williamsburg, the York County justices examined Thomas Cox for trying to "raise a Conspiracy and Insurrection" among the local slaves. Other poor whites had to defend themselves from similar accusations.[87]

The same fears and, to some extent, realities threatened the peace of mind of South Carolina's gentry. The disposition of urban and backcountry plain folk gave the most cause for alarm. In early 1775, white Methodists in Charleston were reprimanded for sponsoring black preachers who proclaimed radical messages. In the summer, two whites, "poor wretches," were convicted of spreading the "good news" that Negroes, Roman Catholics, and Indians were to receive British arms. In the fall, city authorities became alarmed at the existence of an interracial marauding band operating on Sullivan's Island and, in December, sent an expedition against them. Several blacks were shot, and four white men, three white women, and four black men were brought to the city as prisoners. In the backcountry, loyalists attempted to arouse the populace to their side by fostering resentment against Lowcountry planters. In the summer of 1775, Colonel Thomas Fletchall, a prominent loyalist, played on this theme in a public address by saying that any backcountry resident who assisted Lowcountry planters against their slaves "would be a Fool"; one member of the audience responded, "They will not get a man from here." At about the same time, rumors flew that slaves in North Carolina planned to rebel and make for "the Back Country where they were to be received with open arms." In 1778, Moses Kirkland, a South Carolina loyalist, sanguinely anticipated that Lowcountry slaves would soon "be ready to rise upon their Rebel Masters." His sympathies were apparently with the slaves, for he referred to the "Fiends," the "hard Task-masters" who ruled over those "poor slaves."[88] Such expressions, if widely circulated, would have sent shock waves throughout the Lowcountry.

87. Committee of Inspection for Dorchester County, May 23, 1775, and Deposition by John Mollineux against John Simmons, May 1775, Gilmor Papers, IV, 14, MHS; examination of Thomas Cox, July 17, 1775, York County Court Orders, 1774–1784, 95; Schwarz, *Twice Condemned*, 183. A particularly fascinating case occurred in the 1790s in Richmond, Virginia. In 1792, Jacob Valentine, imprisoned for debt, had a sexual affair in jail with a free black woman with whom he had a child. Five years later, he spent another stint in jail for allegedly encouraging an insurrection among the city's slaves. The case is explored in Sidbury, *Ploughshares into Swords*.

88. John Edwards to the Countess of Huntingdon, Jan. 16, 1775, A3/6/10, Countess of Huntingdon's American Papers, Westminster College, Cambridge, England; presentments of the Grand Jury, *SCG*, Mar. 27, 1775; "Journal of the Second Council of Safety," SCHS,

Growing Antipathies

Although white solidarity could never be assumed in eighteenth-century Virginia or South Carolina, and although a surprising level of cooperation between lower-class whites and blacks persisted through the century, the trend was in the opposite direction. Proximity of estate induced some plain white folk to throw in their lot with slaves, but more often it spurred most to put as much distance as possible between themselves and bondpeople. The eighteenth century was a crucible in which the deep and increasingly reciprocal contempt felt between lower-class whites and blacks was forged. That contempt had not emerged in fully polished form by 1800, but the essentials were in place.

The gentry helped foster lower-class contempt for slaves by aligning plain folk on their side. At the end of the seventeenth century, gentlemen busily created a legal framework that gave advantages to lower-class whites at the expense of blacks. Throughout the eighteenth century, as Edmund Morgan has shown in Virginia, the status of plain white folk rose. In part, this improvement was inadvertent, a consequence of a broadly based, rising prosperity; but ruling class efforts to reduce taxes and to involve plain folk in the political process worked to the same end. More directly relevant to their interests as slaveholders, the gentry held out inducements to lower-class whites in order that they might support and police their respective slave societies. The gentry was not uniformly successful where patrolling was concerned, but the capture of runaways seems to have been a particularly rewarding activity. Eighteenth-century Virginia county court records list several thousand claims for the capture of runaways. The vast majority of claimants were individuals outside the gentry, whereas almost two-thirds of the captured blacks belonged to members of the gentry.[89] The ruling class had recruited plain white folk to support its interests.

Ironically, the very people who collectively welcomed and helped foster the antipathy of lower-class whites toward blacks were the first to deplore the casual brutality that this policy often entailed. Thus, a Virginia slaveholder, who in the abstract must have been only too glad to see lower-class whites and slaves at loggerheads, expressed outrage at the conduct of the seamen of a public cruiser, who had frequently "insulted" his slave ferrymen. The real

---

Collections, III (1859), 62–63, 75, 84, 89, 103, 105, 145; Oliver Hart diary, Aug. 14, 1775, Oliver Hart Papers, USC; William L. Saunders, ed., *The Colonial Records of North Carolina,* 10 vols. (Raleigh, N.C., 1886–1890), X, 94–95; Randall M. Miller, "A Backcountry Loyalist Plan to Retake Georgia and the Carolinas, 1778," *SCHM,* LXXV (1974), 213. See also Drayton, *Memoirs,* I, 411.

89. Morgan, *American Slavery, American Freedom,* 338–362; Morgan, "The Hegemony of Law," 162.

outrage came, however, when they casually fired on his boatmen, killing one, "who was," the master noted sanctimoniously, "in his duty crossing the river." Similarly, a visitor to Norfolk saw a slave woman "behave a little impertinently" toward a constable who "dragged her to the side of the street and began to box and kick her in a most cruel and unmerciful Manner." Significantly, the constable's extreme behavior provoked a number of people to intervene and prevent him "from Continuing his barbarity."[90] The well-to-do were squeamish spectators at the sport their policies had created.

The gentry behaved just as hypocritically in South Carolina. For the most part, the prominent citizens of Charleston berated the laxness of their public watchmen. But, at times, the watchmen proved too effective, as in 1772, when they were accused of "beating and abusing Negroes sent on Errands by their Masters with Tickets." Twenty years later, the grand jury of Charleston district, with no sense of irony, complained that most patrollers were overseers "who frequently maltreat the slaves, and commit other excesses." Gentry unctuousness is well displayed in an early-nineteenth-century North Carolina lawsuit that complained of the frequent beatings of blacks "by men of dissolute habits, hanging loose upon society, who being repelled from association with well-disposed citizens, take refuge in the company of coloured persons and slaves who they deprave by their example, embolden by their familiarity, and then beat, under the expectation that a slave does not resent a blow from a white man."[91]

The resentments of poor whites toward slaves were spontaneously generated, not just encouraged from above. After all, many poor whites accurately perceived that slaves posed a threat to their livelihoods. In the Lowcountry this menace was most acute in Charleston, where a variety of white artisans expressed indignation at competition from black workers. Over the course of the eighteenth century, shipwrights, chimney sweeps, house carpenters, bricklayers, cordwainers, master coopers, and master tailors banded together in turn to complain that blacks were taking their jobs. Their inability to halt this process was hardly designed to make them look kindly on their black counterparts. In the countryside, skilled and semiskilled white labor increasingly felt the pressure of black competition as native-born slaves assumed positions ranging from boatman to blacksmith, wheelwright to wagoner. The nature of rural life, however, made it difficult for white laborers to organize and protest.

90. Petition of James Hunter, Nov. 7, 1776, Miscellaneous Legislative Petitions, VSL; Dick Journal, Mar. 10, 1808, UVa.

91. Presentments of the Grand Jury, *SCG,* Jan. 25, 1772; House of Representatives Presentments, Jan. 20, 1794, SCDAH; Chief Justice Taylor in *State* v. *Hall* (1823), as cited in Duncan J. MacLeod, *Slavery, Race, and the American Revolution* (Cambridge, 1974), 151.

One exception was a group of South Carolina patroons who in 1744 complained of "several Planters and others in this Province, who did order, permit and appoint their Negro Slaves to be constantly employed to go as Masters or Patroons of their Pettiaugers or small vessels without any White man on board to take any charge or care of such vessels, which hindered the Petitioners from being constantly employed there."[92]

If plain white folk could befriend slaves and yet just as easily persecute them viciously, this ambivalence was not solely a white prerogative. Slaves sometimes turned against their erstwhile allies. They might, for example, be instrumental in the arrest of poor whites. In 1723, two York County planters claimed expenses for the capture of a runaway white servant through the combined efforts of their slaves. Sixteen years later, a witness in a Virginia county court case reported that at four o'clock in the morning he had heard "an uproar without amongst the People" and had found that his slaves had apprehended a white man who was robbing their meat house. In 1790, two whites visited the Nomini Hall estate in Lancaster County and asked directions of Robert Carter's overseer. Because it was night, the overseer was suspicious, but he let them pass. They made their way to the granary, where Carter's slave Solomon "got up and took his axe in his hand, went out and called them to, and asked them to go into his House, and warm themselves. . . . [T]hey accepted of his invitation—Solomon gave them some Bread, made them a good Fire, they laid down on some boards and fell asleep—Solomon suspecting they were the men that lately escaped from Northumberland Jail" went to the overseer and rounded up a number of slaves sufficient to arrest his two unsuspecting visitors.[93] Friendly, trusting slaves were not always what they seemed.

Slaves adopted even subtler methods to provoke hostility from plain white folk. An overseer employed by Landon Carter complained that Carter's waiting man, Nassau, had "refused to bleed him." When Carter confronted the slave, Nassau denied the story, saying the overseer had "only asked a vomit of him and he gave him one." Nassau was then sent to the sick man on his "honor

---

92. See Philip D. Morgan, "Black Life in Eighteenth-Century Charleston," *Perspectives in American History*, N.S., I (1984), 204; Loren Schweninger, "Slave Independence and Enterprise in South Carolina, 1780–1865," *SCHM*, XCIII (1992), 114; J. H. Easterby, ed., *The Journal of the Commons House of Assembly, September 14, 1742–January 27, 1744*, Colonial Records of South Carolina (Columbia, S.C., 1954), 556. In 1725, British ironworkers angrily declared that they would not teach blacks their trade, for they were "murdering Rogues." No doubt such feelings were intensified in North America, where blacks were far more of a threat. See Ekirch, *Bound for America*, 162–163.

93. York County Court Orders, May 6, 1723, 199; Richmond County Slave Criminal Trials, Nov. 24, 1739; Robert Carter to John Roberts, Mar. 12, 1790, Carter Letterbook, IX, 110–111.

not to touch a drop of Spirits" and with instructions to use both blister and lancet if necessary. Apparently, Nassau broke his promise and got drunk; perhaps that helps explain why the overseer died two days later. Slaves persecuted by word as well as by action. Morgan Godwyn observed that slaves contemptuously taunted the Irish with the claim "that if the Irishman's country had first lighted in the Englishman's way, he might have gone no further to look for Negro's." As Eugene Genovese has remarked, it was probably slaves who coined the term "po'r white trash."[94]

Slaves occasionally turned the tables on lower-class whites through force. Slaves directed many more acts of personal violence against lower-class whites than against their masters. Almost all of the twenty-four whites known to have been murdered by slaves in Virginia between 1740 and 1785 were men of lowly status. Similarly, plain white folk were the primary targets of slave assaults. The justices of Essex County court adjudicated a number of such cases. Cornelius Selor complained that two slaves belonging to Thomas Cooper Dickinson had "much abused and beaten him"; Vall, a slave belonging to Jacob Satur, lifted "up his hand agt Thomas Cornbee"; and Jack was whipped "for beating and wounding" Edward Wright. In fact, most victims of slave crime, whether aimed against persons or property, were whites of lowly status.[95]

In 1773, a poor white woman—either a servant or an overseer's wife—was the focus of a remarkable incident that occurred on William Richardson's Bloom Hill plantation in the High Hills of Santee, South Carolina. This "Irish Wench," as Richardson referred to her, "had rob'ed several of the Negroes and was chastised for it"—not by the master, but by the slaves. "The Negroes in their Defense," continued Richardson, "say they only moderately whipt her," and they attributed her subsequent miscarriage to other causes. The woman herself denied that she had been cruelly punished, and the slaves escaped lightly. A severe reprimand and "threats of severe punishment if ever they commit the like" again were their only retribution.[96] Some white victims merited little sympathy from their social superiors.

Lower-class whites brought actions against slaves not only for the violent crimes they had committed but also for those they might commit. Fear of a

---

94. Greene, ed., *Carter Diary*, 946–947; Morgan Godwyn, *The Negro's and Indians Advocate, Suing for Their Admission into the Church* . . . (London, 1680), 35–36; Genovese, *Roll, Jordan, Roll*, 22.

95. Schwarz, *Twice Condemned*, 142; Essex County Court Orders, Sept. 19, 1721, Mar. 15, 1725, Dec. 15, 1777. For violence against overseers, see the section on field hands and overseers in Chapter 6.

96. Emma B. Richardson, ed., "Letters of William Richardson, 1765–1784," *SCHM*, XLVII (1946), 8. Another South Carolinian was fined £100 for "making negroes under his care whip a white person" (*SC and AGG*, Jan. 29, 1768).

slave led a number of plain white folk in Virginia to turn to their county courts for protection. A Mr. Edmondson of Middlesex County "swore the peace" against a slave of Ralph Wormeley and a slave belonging to Miss Thatcher, whereupon the sheriff took them into custody until a bond of one hundred pounds each was given for their good behavior. A similar case involved another Middlesex County slave who was charged with hog stealing by George Blakely. Obviously uneasy, Blakely got the slave "bound to his good behaviour, to keep the peace," not just toward George and his son Robert but toward "all other his Majestie's Liege People." After Toby, a Caroline County slave, had been whipped for assaulting two white men, one of the victims testified that he still feared Toby's capacity to commit bodily harm, arson, or "other injuries." Finally, Dick, belonging to the estate of Richard Johnson in York County, was imprisoned on suspicion of poisoning John Dudley and others. A month later, Dudley wanted "leave to swear the peace against Dick" because he feared the slave's ability to "do some hurt or prejudice" to his person or property. In this case, the gentlemen of the court refused Dudley's request that Dick be kept in the county jail until bond was entered.[97]

Like Dudley, some lower-class whites probably felt that slaves often got off lightly for their transgressions. How must William Compton have felt when he learned that the slave who had inflicted on him a "felonious stabbing . . . with a large knife under his left shoulder" suffered no more than a whipping? Or how did Benjamin Burck, who lay "in danger" from knife wounds inflicted by a slave, react to the news that his assailant had been released from custody on his owner's surety? It was even possible for a slave to be found innocent of killing his overseer, as happened in late-eighteenth-century Alexandria. And although humanitarians could take heart at this outcome—an antislavery Methodist asked rhetorically, "Surely a black man should have the right to defend his life as well as a white man?"—overseers no doubt thought differently. A slave might even evade both legal action and punishment for an assault on a lower-class white. One of Landon Carter's slaves, Fork Jamy, fought back against his overseer after a switch had been laid across his shoulders. They "had a fair box." The master then ordered his bondman to return to work, as if nothing had happened, though he did note that "it seems nothing scared him."[98] What the overseer thought of this turn of events is quite another matter.

Just as some slaves escaped harsh punishment for assaulting, wounding, per-

---

97. Middlesex County Court Orders, Mar. 7, 1748, Feb. 7, 1758; Caroline County Court Orders, Aug. 8, Sept. 12, 1735; York County Court Orders, Jan. 15, 1732.

98. Essex County Court Orders, Nov. 21, 1738; Richmond County Slave Criminal Trials, Sept. 4, 1728; Journal of Ezekiel Cooper, Jan. 22, 1791, photocopy, Lovely Lane Museum, Baltimore; Greene, ed., *Carter Diary,* 754.

haps even killing lower-class whites, the reverse was almost uniformly true. Masters, of course, were the ultimate beneficiaries in either case. Lower-class whites were not likely to look kindly on blacks who avoided retribution for their violent acts, although the relative immunity at law enjoyed by plain white folk bound them to their white superiors. In only one known case in eighteenth-century Virginia and South Carolina was a lower-class white hanged for murdering a slave. More typical was the reasoning of Virginia's rulers as they considered the appeal of Andrew Bourne, an overseer, found guilty of whipping a slave to death. They decided to recommend a pardon, less on the merits of the appeal, but out of fear for the repercussions of a death sentence. To hang a white man for the death of a slave, argued Governor Gooch, would "make the Slaves very insolent and give them an occasion to contemn their masters and overseers." A chilling entry in John Mercer's ledger probably indicates how a slave death was normally handled. In the accounts for 1746, William Graham, Mercer's overseer at Bull Run quarter, was simply debited £35 sterling for the Negro he "made hang himself." South Carolina whites convicted of killing slaves were generally fined £350 currency in the late 1760s and early 1770s, although, when they were unable to pay, the half due the public treasury was usually suspended (the other half due the informer was usually not waived).[99] In other words, the public could afford to be magnanimous toward lower-class whites.

Perhaps the most subtle way the well-to-do engaged the support of the less well-off was in effecting a disassociation between their own class interest and the broader societal interest. Their administration of the law is a perfect illustration. Most slaves prosecuted for crimes were the property of the gentry, whereas their accusers were more frequently plain white folk. The impact of this pattern on lower-class whites is not hard to imagine. The gentry's seeming willingness to permit the trial of its slaves—even if the resulting punishments were not always as severe as many whites would have liked—sustained the image of an open and even-handed justice. Although the colonial gentry made most of the legal code, and administered all of it, they were able, like their English counterparts, to project the law as an authority higher than themselves, to which all were subordinate.

Relations between plain white folk and slaves are instructive in two important ways. The rift that progressively opened between the two was portentous for North America's future. Throughout the eighteenth century, whites gradu-

---

99. *VaG* (P and D), Nov. 23, 1739, is the one case; McIlwaine et al., eds., *Executive Journals*, IV, 206; Governor Gooch to the Secretary of State, June 29, 1729, CO5/1337, fols. 132–133, CW; "Virginia Council Journals, 1726–1753," *VMHB*, XXXIV (1926), 209; John Mercer Ledger, 1746, microfilm, CW; John Drayton, *SC and AGG*, Jan. 29, 1768; Court of General Sessions Journal, 1769–1776, 17, 20, 72, 102, 104, 135, 195, 307, 309, 324, SCDAH; Court of Oyer and Terminer, Jan. 21, 1771, Miscellaneous Records, PP, 252, SCDAH.

ally moved toward a sense of communal solidarity and purpose through their debasement of blacks. White unity was never fully achieved, but Chesapeake and Lowcountry slave societies moved steadily to a position where, functionally, they rested on a rationale of racial superiority. At the same time, lower-class whites had an ameliorative effect on the character of the two emerging slave systems. Where a large group of plain folk existed, as preeminently in Virginia, but to a lesser degree also in South Carolina, masters courted their support and generally received their recognition. The master class thus gained in legitimacy and respect, and the society as a whole could afford to have pretensions to culture and civilization. By contrast, the absence of a substantial class of nonslaveholding whites, as in many slave societies of the Caribbean and Dutch East Indies, helps explain why slavery in these places became so brutal and degrading to slaves and masters. Lower-class whites played a vital role in determining the nature of any slave society.

Encounters between whites and blacks in the eighteenth-century South were never simple or straightforward. As much as masters treated slaves as chattels, they were unable to ignore their inescapable humanity. As much as they devised barbarous laws to hamstring their slaves, they also sought ways to mitigate the impact of legislation. As much as they subjected slaves to personal domination, they also offered them personal protection. As much as they inflicted unspeakable cruelties on slaves, they also established warm and caring relationships with them. As much as they viewed slaves as animals, they never doubted slaves' desire for liberty and capacity to rebel. As much as they spoke the language of commercial capitalism, they also talked of reciprocal obligations and mutuality. As much as plain white folk and slaves became implacable foes, they also continued to share much and to cooperate. White-black relations in the eighteenth century were riven with ambiguities.

These paired polarities were not immutable. For most of the eighteenth century, control and discipline were the masters' watchwords. To be sure, masters acknowledged their obligations to provide and protect, but they were also quick to judge and punish. They were often brutal, whipping and dismembering their slaves almost at will. Yet, at least these severe taskmasters viewed slaves as integral parts of society, as members of their households. But new ways of thinking gradually emerged. By the late eighteenth century, masters began to augment their threats with appeals, temper their severity with solicitude, expect not just obedience but gratitude, and manumit not just for faithful service but out of respect and regard for their slaves. At the same time, masters who saw themselves less as taskmasters than as benefactors increasingly viewed slaves, not as organic members of society, but as outside civil society altogether. Just as the masters' worldview became more exclusive, so the everyday world of whites and blacks became more fissured. The distance between plain white folk and black slaves, for example, grew wider through the eighteenth century.

White-black relations not only changed over time; they also varied across space. Whites always interacted more closely with blacks in the Chesapeake than in the Lowcountry. Sharing field labor with their slaves, plain white planters, who were more numerous in Virginia than in South Carolina, generally treated their bondpeople with greater consideration than large planters did. Poor white women, again most numerous in the Chesapeake, had the least to lose by associating closely with slaves and were particularly prone to accusations of interracial fraternization. The closest contacts between lower-class whites and blacks occurred on the perimeter of plantation heartlands—in towns, in the backcountry, and in backwater regions.

This broad overview of the social dynamics of slavery in the eighteenth century has emphasized the immense shaping power of whites over slaves' lives. Interracial relations have been viewed largely from the perspective of whites, focusing on how masters conceptualized their relations with whites and how plain white folk interacted with blacks. We have seen that slaves, far from being powerless, probed the limits of obedience and sometimes held their own against lower-class whites. But the full story of this active and reciprocal relationship can be uncovered only by investigating the everyday transactions of blacks and whites in a variety of arenas.

There is, in fact, a mutual

dependence between the master

and his slave.

—Charles Ball

6 : Economic Exchanges between Whites and Blacks

Relations between masters and slaves, whites and blacks acquired meaning only through countless human transactions. Too frequently, slavery is seen from an institutional perspective, and too often the treatment of slaves is inferred only from statute law, intellectual treatises, or dominant social attitudes. Such perspectives need to be supplemented with explorations of actual behavior, of the extensive daily contacts that occurred across the racial divide. The everyday encounters—the boundary-crossing, melding, jostling, downright collisions—of whites and blacks form the subject of this and the next chapter.

The growing divide that separated whites from blacks should not obscure an equally important development—the emergence of channels of communication across racial lines. Relations between the two races were conducted more at arm's length over the eighteenth century, but various ligatures bridged the gap. Over time, relations between masters and slaves, blacks and whites became routinized at key connecting points.

Because slavery was first and foremost an economic enterprise, masters and slaves, whites and blacks had to interact simply to get the job done. A principal avenue of encounter, then, was created by the communication and delegation of command. But this communication was never straightforward. Although power originated at the top of the system, it could not be exercised without accounting for the nature of the response from below. This active and reciprocal relationship was evident in all economic transactions, from running an errand to managing a field gang.

CHANNELS OF COMMUNICATION

A seemingly trivial but nevertheless recurrent economic activity—errand running or message taking—illustrates the complexity of even the simplest economic transaction. It would be easy to envisage the relationship of master and messenger as uncomplicated: the master calls in the slave, gives directions, hands over the object to be delivered or list of items to be picked up, and the order is executed. In practice, of course, simply by entrusting slaves with valued communications or possessions—large sums of money, for example—the transaction had already become less impersonal. Why else, for example, would a slave, entrusted with a valuable object, make "promises" to deliver it safely?[1]

Moreover, a confidence, once extended, could always be betrayed. When a peahen, which Henry Laurens had secured for an English correspondent, did not survive the trip from plantation to town, the master did not doubt the cause. It was the fault, he raged, of a "vile Scoundrell of a Negro [who] kill'd it on the Journey." Messengers and errand boys found other ways to annoy—by varying their itinerary or by "forgetting" to undertake parts of their mission. It might have been little more than literary convention, but it speaks to the initiative of slaves when letters between slaveholders were hurriedly concluded with a nod to the restless slave, only too impatient to begin the journey. Certainly, more than convention was involved when Henry Laurens's Scipio, on a trip from Charleston to Georgia, peremptorily "Saddle[d] his Horse" and took his leave before Lachlan MacIntosh could respond to one of Laurens's requests. After prolonging what was to have been a two-day stay into a week, Scipio suddenly discovered the virtues of haste.[2]

---

1. Dudley Digges to William Dabney, Dec. 18, 1758, Dabney Family Papers, UNC. For examples of these transactions, see John Symmons to Edmund Berkeley, Nov. 2, 1768, Berkeley Family Papers, microfilm, CW; Robert Carter to George Turberville, Dec. 24, 1774, Robert Carter Letterbook, II, 157, Robert Carter Papers, Duke; William Washington Account Book, 1779, LC; George Weedon Account Book, January 1780, CW; James Macleod to M. Page, July 21, 1790, Mann Page, Jr., Papers, microfilm, CW. Merchant account books indicate that slaves transported large and valuable consignments between store and plantation. See, for example, James Poyas Merchant Day Book, 1764–1766, SCHS; King William Court House Store Ledger, 1773, microfilm, CW; George Buckner Ledger, 1781–1797, VSL. Dr. Alexander Garden even sent a slave overseas to gather fish specimens (James Edward Smith, comp., *A Selection of the Correspondence of Linnaeus, and Other Naturalists, from the Original Manuscripts*, I [London, 1821], 331).

2. *Laurens Papers*, II, 123, VII, 228. For changes of itinerary or lapses of memory, see ibid., III, 481, 508–509, IV, 633; Jack L. Cross, ed., "Letters of Thomas Pinckney, 1775–1780," *SCHM*, LVIII (1957), 72; and Robert Carter to Col. John Taylor, July 14, 1789, Carter Letter-

Masters went much further in their conception of the messenger's role than simply entrusting slaves with valued objects or messages. For one thing, not all communications were written. Confiding in a slave messenger gave him or her an opportunity to engage in inadvertent or deliberate distortion. Certainly one Virginia overseer thought himself the victim of deception when he demanded of his employer, "Ther may not be any mor messages sent by Tom osterman [because] I have found him to be so treachrous I cannot put any confidence in anything he sais."[3]

Even with written communications, messengers were expected to elaborate on events. Eliza Lucas learned that her friend Mrs. Pinckney was unwell, not from the letter she had received, but from the bearer, her slave Togo. Slaves often took the initiative on such occasions. Dudley Digges wrote that a slave messenger of his told him the following: "I don't know whether truly or not that there is Tobacco enough [on one of Digges's quarters] to make one or two [more] Hhds." The opportunity to embellish a story or supply information allowed the slave a fleeting moment at center stage, with whites hanging on every word. Denial of information, in contrast, was no doubt perversely pleasurable. One South Carolina slave, according to an exasperated Eliza Pinckney, would not "utter a sentence more than he is commissioned to do for the world. I asked him many questions, particularly about [her son-in-law's] wound and whether it was still bad but I could not get anything out of him more than it was a scratch, though Harriet [her daughter] calls it a deep Gash." Control of the word gave otherwise defenseless slaves a measure of power.[4]

Not just individual masters but the state had to confront the problems of using slaves as messengers. Public mail services, established in the southern colonies in the late colonial period, employed slave riders. The fact that slaves could, in the words of Hugh Finlay, "take no oath" had to be overlooked. Although dehumanized in this way, the slave who carried the public mail between Fredericksburg and Gloucester in Virginia forced whites to recognize

---

book, VIII, 306–307. For hurried conclusions to letters, see Hugh Nelson to B. Muse, Mar. 29, 1779, Battaille Muse Papers, Duke; Robert Carter to John Sutton, Feb. 24, 1781, Carter Letterbook, IV, 47; and Robert Taylor to N. Jamieson, Apr. 3, 1781, Neil Jamieson Papers, LC.

3. Solomon Nash to Robert Carter, May 3, 1788, Carter Family Papers, VHS. For a useful oral message, see Virgil Maxcy Diary, Aug. 1, 1801, NYPL.

4. Elise Pinckney, ed., *The Letterbook of Eliza Lucas Pinckney, 1739–1762* (Chapel Hill, N.C., 1972), 34; Dudley Digges to William Dabney, Mar. 5, 1759, Dabney Papers, microfilm, CW; Eliza Pinckney to [D. Horry], Mar. 9, 1768, Pinckney Family Papers, SCHS. For other elaborations, see "Journal of Col. James Gordon," *WMQ*, 1st Ser., XI (1902–1903), 198; John Howard to Dr. William Cabell, June 6, 1771, N. F. Cabell Collection, VSL; Richard Hutson to Isaac Hayne, Sept. 2, 1776, Charles Woodward Hutson Papers, UNC; Robert Carter to Col. John Taylor, July 14, 1789, Carter Letterbook, VIII, 306–307.

his humanity. Once, while performing his duties, he was waylaid by two white men, but "with the utmost fortitude and intrepidity resisted the said attack for which he received many dangerous wounds." His "valour" prompted a number of white citizens to petition for his emancipation.[5]

Slave messengers made whites acknowledge their humanity in another way. Because slaves were often the bearers of stray scraps of information, they were directly responsible for many rumors and panics that periodically swept slave societies. Often these rumors were harmless, as with the "wild and uncertain accounts" of comets in the sky regaled to one master. More serious was one southern woman's alarm "at the news of the small pox being in Town." Her fears, she noted, "are not quite removed as we have never had any certain accounts, none but what Negroes brings, and you know my Dear their is no depending upon what they say." But depend they must. Thus, Eliza Wilkinson described vividly the "confusion and distress" produced by the news of the imminent arrival of the British. The information derived from a "negro wench, who had been out visiting" one Sunday morning. Furthermore, slaves relayed information selectively. Eliza Wilkinson later complained of hearing nothing about the patriot forces under General Benjamin Lincoln, "unless from disaffected people, and negroes, and they were always the most disheartening accounts that one did hear." A slave society's susceptibility to rumor in turn made whites acutely aware of the significance of manipulating surface appearances. Even at moments of crisis, masters had, according to Charles Lee, to assume an "air of dignity and superiority." Outward appearances are usually of great significance in nonliterate societies, but in slave societies they were paramount.[6]

Taking messages and running errands, therefore, constituted one channel of communication that involved masters and slaves in a complex web of interlocking relations. The effects of this seemingly straightforward activity extended far beyond the economic realm. Its repercussions were felt in social, cultural, and even political terms.

Much the same was true of another basic economic concern—the health of slaves. Masters took a keen interest in their slaves' well-being for obvious pecuniary reasons. Some of their actions involved no more than the imper-

---

5. Frank H. Norton, ed., *Journal Kept by Hugh Finlay* . . . (Brooklyn, N.Y., 1867), 90; Legislative Petitions, Middlesex County, Dec. 7, 1798, VSL. See also Robert Bolton, *Ga Gaz*, June 2, 1763.

6. Jack P. Greene, ed., *The Diary of Colonel Landon Carter of Sabine Hall, 1752–1778*, 2 vols. (Charlottesville, Va., 1965), 440–441(hereafter cited as *Carter Diary*); Penelope Dawson to Miss Blair, Mar. 8, 1779, James Iredell, Sr. and Jr., Letters, Duke; Caroline Gilman, ed., *Letters of Eliza Wilkinson* . . . (New York, 1839), 13, 17; Charles Lee to R. H. Lee, Apr. 5, 1776, Lee Family Papers, UVa.

sonal prescription of drugs or the careful recounting of sums outlaid on their chattels' welfare. They were safeguarding a valuable asset. When one of Henry Laurens's slaves contracted smallpox, Laurens hurried to the plantation because he "could not trust so important a point wholly to the discretion of the Overseer." The "point" he had most in mind was "the great danger [to] my own Interest and the terrour of all the neighbourhood." Moreover, there is also more than a hint that some masters viewed slaves as experimental objects. Dr. Alexander Garden spoke proudly of the progress he had made in treating smallpox patients "partly by some *bold trials* on a negro" of his own. Landon Carter used harsh drugs on his slaves that he would not countenance for his own children.[7]

At the same time, masters involved themselves too personally and with too much care in treating slave illnesses for their behavior to be dismissed as mere calculating regard for pieces of property. William Byrd II, Michael Zuckerman has argued, showed "greater solicitude for his slaves than for his immediate family." Byrd's concern cannot be ascribed simply to self-interest; indeed, he often considered himself complicit in their sickness and implored God for forgiveness for his sins so that his "people" might be "restore[d] . . . to their health." Another great Virginia slaveholder like Robert Carter of Nomini Hall did not feel it beneath his dignity to examine his slaves personally. When one of them was thrown from a horse, Carter concluded that some of his ribs were broken only after he had carefully "felt his body." To see Landon Carter closely monitoring symptoms and dispensing medicines, as he did on numerous occasions, is to know that much of his self-image depended on these tasks. On one occasion, Carter declared that his soul "delighteth in releiving" his slaves' illnesses. Even when a master delegated his authority to an overseer, he might well enjoin his employee, as George Washington did, to "take all necessary and proper care of the Negroes committed to his management, treating them with humanity and tenderness when sick." Plantation wives often assumed the role of plantation doctor. Mary Willing Byrd was described by one traveler as taking "great care of her Negroes, mak[ing] them as happy as their situation will admit, and serv[ing] as their doctor." She had even made "some interest-

---

7. *Laurens Papers,* III, 237; Smith, comp., *A Selection of the Correspondence of Linnaeus,* I, 483 (emphasis added); Greene, ed., *Carter Diary,* 731. Masters sometimes used medicine as a punishment (Maude H. Woodfin, ed., and Marion Tinling, trans., *Another Secret Diary of William Byrd of Westover, 1739–1741: With Letters and Literary Exercises, 1696–1726* [Richmond, Va., 1942], 123). More generally, see Robert Nesbitt Medical Account Book, 1796–1804, USC; Wyndham B. Blanton, *Medicine in Virginia in the Seventeenth Century* (Richmond, Va., 1930); Blanton, *Medicine in Virginia in the Eighteenth Century* (Richmond, Va., 1931); and Diane Meredith Sydenham, "Practitioner and Patient: The Practice of Medicine in Eighteenth-Century South Carolina" (Ph.D. diss., The Johns Hopkins University, 1979).

ing discoveries about their sicknesses." So close an attention did John Custis pay to a group of newly purchased, and diseased, Africans that he caught, as he believed, "a Negro distemper endemicall to Afrike."[8]

A more impersonal quality to health care in the Lowcountry can be inferred from the emergence of hospitals, both on plantations and in Charleston, a function of larger holdings and a wealthier planter class than was present in the Chesapeake. Consequently, individual plantations could more realistically support hospitals, and urban entrepreneurs could see a market in providing institutionalized health care for the large numbers of slaves either passing through or residing in the city. The scale of the operations and the attempts to appeal to planters, who in the Chesapeake generally took care of their own slaves, suggest that a distinction can be drawn between the two regions. In the Lowcountry, private hospitals were in existence by the 1740s, and at least seven were functioning in the early 1760s. There is no evidence of such hospitals in the eighteenth-century Chesapeake, where personal care was ubiquitous.[9]

Whether health care was extended personally or impersonally, its very availability created opportunities for slaves to take the initiative. Most obvious, slaves could feign an illness to escape work. Masters were often inclined to grant bondpeople the benefit of the doubt. Slaves requested particular doctors or changes of locale. Robert Carter acceded to the desire of his carpenter Daniel to see a man in the neighboring county who might cure his nosebleeds. Daniel Horry wrote from Santee to his mother-in-law in Charleston, informing her that one of his slaves who had "been a long time complaining of a violent pain in his Head and Eyes but no fever, imagines that the change of Air and a Jaunt to ChsTown will recover him." Horry humored his slave, gave him a fortnight's leave, and maintained a vestige of authority by suggesting a visit to

---

8. Michael Zuckerman, "The Family Life of William Byrd," in his *Almost Chosen People: Oblique Biographies in the American Grain* (Berkeley, Calif., 1993), 119–121; Robert Carter to Dr. Timothy Harrington, Oct. 30, 1787, Carter Letterbook, VIII, 23; Philip D. Morgan, "Three Planters and Their Slaves: Perspectives on Slavery in Virginia, South Carolina, and Jamaica," in Winthrop D. Jordan and Sheila L. Skemp, eds., *Race and Family in the Colonial South* (Jackson, Miss., 1987), 51; Greene, ed., *Carter Diary*, 636; Worthington Chauncey Ford, *Washington as an Employer and Importer of Labor* (Brooklyn, N.Y., 1889), 33; Marquis de Chastellux, *Travels in North America in the Years 1780, 1781, and 1782*, ed. and trans. Howard C. Rice, Jr., II (Chapel Hill, N.C., 1963), 431–432; John Custis to Peter Collins, 1742, John Custis Letterbook, typescript, CW. Africans introduced a more virulent strain of malaria into the plantation colonies than had come with the English from Europe.

9. For slave hospitals, Oliphant and Mackie, *SCG*, Mar. 6, 1749; *Laurens Papers*, Jan. 31, 1756; account book of Henry Laurens, Sept. 26, 1772, 491, CC; Peter Donald, *SC and AGG*, June 24, 1774; and Elizabeth Donnan, ed., *Documents Illustrative of the History of the Slave Trade to America*, Carnegie Institution of Washington Publication no. 409, IV (Washington, D.C., 1935), 443.

Dr. Garden to see whether medicine might help. Another possible diplomatic illness (or was it stress?) is signified in an overseer's answer to a query about Hazard's seizures. "I never heard," the overseer wrote, "that Hazard had any fits but Once afore he was sold and then he had 4 or 5 fits at one time, and I don't know that he had any after untill the time he was burnt—tho' he certainly can tell you. The reason for his being low spirited I think is because he does not wish to live down that way."[10] It is impossible now to assess whether this illness was genuine. But, then again, the master had the same quandary.

Slaves took the initiative in another sense by becoming specialists in their own right. Slave doctors found themselves in demand to treat not only their fellow bondpeople but also neighboring whites, occasionally even their masters. Landon Carter was bled by his body servant, Nassau, "the best bleeder about," who performed the same service for other lesser planters, lower-class whites, and occasionally his master's children. For a while, Landon Carter even employed Isaac Haynes, a white clerk who had trained as an apothecary, to assist Nassau. So proficient was Nassau that he claimed, much to Carter's annoyance, that "on every recovery it is his doings." Other slaves also nursed whites back to health. One South Carolina account recorded a payment of two pounds, six shillings for the hire of a "Negro wench" during a planter's sickness.[11]

The clearest case of blacks' ministering to whites was during or immediately after childbirth. Black midwives, or "grannies," delivered everybody from humble slave mothers to the wives of the most eminent patriarchs. When his wife's delivery was delayed, William McCarty of Virginia wrote to a relative on his wife's behalf, "begg[ing] that you will let Winney stay till it is over." In wealthy families, the involvement of black women often persisted beyond the birth of a child. Robert Carter's wife, for example, summoned two slave women with "a good breast of milk" to Nomini Hall to suckle the great planter's child. Philip Fithian, along with other visitors to the South, was

10. Robert Carter to Randall Kirk, Sept. 12, 1785, Carter Letterbook, VII, 17; Daniel Horry to Eliza Pinckney, Apr. 4, 1781, Pinckney Family Papers; John Couturier to John E. Colhoun, Sept. 21, 1793, John Ewing Colhoun Papers, USC. See also Richard Hutson to Isaac Hayne, Jan. 15, 1766, Hutson Papers, UNC; and Robert Carter to Clement Brooke, Nov. 11, 1776, Carter Letterbook, III, 78.

11. Greene, ed., *Carter Diary*, 411, 505–506, 521, 667, 758, 769, 781, 793, 794, 797, 811, 946–947, 952, 993, 1111 (quotation); inventory of Maurice Jones, May 22, 1772, Inventory Book, &, 59–61, SCDAH. Robert Carter's chief medical aide, Tom Coachman, also performed services for slaves and local whites (Benjamin Dawson to Robert Carter, July 21, 1778, Carter Family Papers; Robert Carter to Dr. Timothy Harrington, Jan. 12, 1787, Carter Letterbook, VII, 172–173; John Peck to Robert Carter, Feb. 23, 1787, Carter Family Papers; Robert Carter to Newyear Branson, Nov. 10, 1787, Carter Letterbook, VIII, 39–40; Robert Carter to Sol. Nash, Mar. 1, 1788, ibid., 91–92; Elder William Dawson to Robert Carter, July 21, 1788, Carter Family Papers). The practice of slaves' ministering to other slaves is treated in Chapter 10.

surprised to "find it is common here for people of Fortune to have their young Children suckled by the Negroes!" It took a Carolina lady to point out one of the virtues of the practice. In a conversation in England with the Princess of Wales, Eliza Pinckney emphasized that Carolina children were nursed within the household, not put out, as was common in English upper-class circles. Even this spirited justification could not deflect the English women from dwelling on the idea of "suckling blacks," even leading one of the company to stroke the cheeks of Eliza's daughter and to wonder aloud how it had "made no alteration" in her complexion.[12]

Complexions might remain untouched, but the intimacy of black nurse and white child had far-reaching effects. For John Davis, close attachments flowed from the intimacy of black nurse and white child. "Each child has its *Momma*," he claimed, "whose gestures and accent it will necessarily copy, for children, we all know, are imitative beings. It is not unusual to hear an elegant lady say, *Richard always grieves when Quasheehaw is whipped, because she suckled him*." Davis's observations were not romantic speculations. David Greene freed Sue "because she suckled his wife in her infancy," and John Rutherford freed Titchy for "having carefully attended my Children during their Infancy." In 1784, Benjamin Guerard purchased his old nanny, a mulatto woman named Bess, so that he could liberate her out of "the great respect and Gratitude due from me most Justly to her, she having carried me in her arms when a very infant as my dry nurse." As Davis also mentioned, white accents could be traced to the intimate contact between black nurses and white children. Josiah Quincy detected influences along age and gender lines: white children "contracted a negroish kind of accent, pronounciation, and dialect," which they gradually lost as adults, although women were still "vastly infected" with black speech patterns. As a result, Quincy claimed, parents talked to "their very young children . . . as though they were speak[ing] to a new imported African."[13]

---

12. William McCarty to George Turberville, Oct. 5, 1784, Joseph Downs MSS, microfilm, CW; Robert Carter to Richard Dozier and Jeriah Bonham, Nov. 25, 1778, Carter Letterbook, XII, 75–76; Hunter Dickinson Farish, ed., *Journal and Letters of Philip Vickers Fithian, 1773–1774: A Plantation Tutor of the Old Dominion* (Williamsburg, Va., 1943), 52; John Davis, *Travels of Four Years and a Half in the United States of America* . . . (Bristol, 1803), 93; Harriott Horry Ravenel, *Eliza Pinckney* (New York, 1896), 151–152. For more on slaves as midwives and nurses, see Greene, ed., *Carter Diary*, 306, 514, 840; Memorandum Book, July 25, 1772, William Ennals Papers, LC; Robert Carter to Bennett Neal, Sept. 15, 1781, Carter Letterbook, IV, 118–119, and to Presly Self, Dec. 22, 1785, ibid., VII, 20; account with Old Pegg the Granny, 1784–1787, William A. Washington Ledger of Accounts, 1776–1796, fol. 78, LC; "Letters of Rev. Jonathan Boucher," *MHM*, VII (1912), 6.

13. Davis, *Travels*, 93–94; will of David Greene, South Carolina Wills, XVII, 726, cited in Larry Darnell Watson, "The Quest for Order: Enforcing Slave Codes in Revolutionary

Seemingly straightforward economic transactions like the taking of a message or the care of a sick worker had far-reaching consequences. The master's monopoly of power was constrained not only by the need to achieve certain results, in production and profit, but also by the slaves' clear recognition of the master's dependence on them. This general truth can best be explored by investigating the interpenetration of white and black worlds at two key points of intersection: the workplace and the marketplace.

FIELD HANDS AND OVERSEERS

Over the course of the eighteenth century, there was a growing separation of blacks and whites at the workplace. As plantations grew in size and as masters established new outlying quarters or separate plantations, the close working relationship between master and slave, characteristic of frontier days, became less common, particularly in the older, more mature areas of both Chesapeake and Lowcountry. This development was always more intensely experienced in the Lowcountry than in the Chesapeake, but to some extent all seaboard slaves increasingly spent more time working beyond the purview of their masters.

This lack of intimacy was obviously compounded wherever overseers were employed. Even in late-eighteenth-century Virginia, where plantation operations never approached the impersonal and anonymous quality of the rice country, as many as one-half of the slaves in various tidewater areas lived on units headed by overseers. In late-eighteenth-century South Carolina, the proportion was much higher.[14] Overseers, therefore, represented, or rather personified, a major channel of communication between master and slave.

The position of overseer was fundamentally weak. Most occupants were young, single men—not individuals calculated to inspire trust from mature, well-established planters. The masters' lack of confidence in overseers as well as the ambitiousness of many of these young men on the make ensured a high turnover rate. Rarely did an overseer hold the same post for more than a year

---

South Carolina, 1760–1800" (Ph.D. diss., University of South Carolina, 1980), 167; manumission to Tithy, Mar. 27, 1782, Miscellaneous Records, TT, 127, SCDAH; Benjamin Guerard's deed of manumission to Bess, Apr. 22, 1784, ibid., UU, 94–96; Mark Antony De Wolfe Howe, ed., "Journal of Josiah Quincy, Junior, 1773," Massachusetts Historical Society, *Proceedings*, XLIX (1915–1916), 456–457.

14. This assumes one overseer for two-thirds of units with more than 20 slaves. See Allan Kulikoff, *Tobacco and Slaves: The Development of Southern Cultures in the Chesapeake, 1680–1800* (Chapel Hill, N.C., 1986), 409–410. For an early-18th-century request to have overseers on Chesapeake quarters, see Darrett B. Rutman and Anita H. Rutman, *A Place in Time: Middlesex County, Virginia, 1650–1750* (New York, 1984), 175. Because plantations were larger in South Carolina than in Virginia, it seems likely that more Lowcountry than Chesapeake slaves worked under overseers.

or two. Henry Laurens, for example, employed twenty-five overseers on five plantations between 1763 and 1774; the average length of service was twenty months. Abraham Schad was in Laurens's employ for the longest period—six years—whereas James Laurens lasted just six weeks. None of the ten overseers employed by Thomas Jefferson between 1786 and 1800 served more than two years. As William Bolling remarked in the early nineteenth century, overseers "all seem to wear out after a while and to require changing."[15]

Masters intervened in the affairs of their outlying plantations, thereby undermining their overseers' authority, especially when punishment of a slave was at issue. Henry Laurens's injunction to an overzealous overseer was to "submit to make less Rice and keep my Negroes at Home in some degree of happiness" rather than to produce "Large Crops acquired by Rigour and Barbarity." Robert Carter of Nomini Hall went much further in trying to restrain one of his overseers, Thomas Olive, who had ordered a slave whipped but then faced resistance from Abraham, the slave foreman. In the presence of both master and foreman, Olive incautiously inquired "if he had not full power and authority to beat, strip and whip all the Negroes." Carter emphatically refuted the claim, and Abraham, together with two other slaves from the quarter, witnessed the public humiliation of his erstwhile superior. Perhaps this explains why five slaves ran away from Olive's quarter the following day and why, a month later, two slave boys came to Carter and reported further whippings by their overseer. Olive lost his post at the end of the year.[16]

If masters had intervened only to safeguard their slaves' physical welfare, they would have created enough problems for their overseers. But they did not stop there. Robert Carter involved himself in an altercation over one of his slave's proprietorial rights. In 1781, one of Carter's overseers helped himself to a slave's pot; the slave immediately absented himself, "without obtaining Permission," his master acknowledged, in order to register his complaint; Carter listened to him and unhesitatingly took his side, noting that "these people did not consent to hire this Pot to me," and then described the overseer's actions as "arbitrary." Even a seemingly innocent intervention by a master might prove troublesome for an overseer. When James Mercer informed one of his slaves that he would soon be put to work on a boat, the bondman immediately did

---

15. *Laurens Papers,* III–X; Kulikoff, *Tobacco and Slaves,* 410; Philip D. Morgan, "Slave Life in Piedmont Virginia, 1720–1800," in Lois Green Carr, Philip D. Morgan, and Jean B. Russo, eds., *Colonial Chesapeake Society* (Chapel Hill, N.C., 1988), 467; Ulrich Bonnell Phillips, *Life and Labor in the Old South* (Boston, 1929), 223, 238 (quotation).

16. *Laurens Papers,* VIII, 635; Robert Carter to the trustees in behalf of the Creditors of Robert Bladen Carter, Sept. 9, 1784, and to George Howe, Sept. 10, 1784, Robert Carter Letterbook, VI, 31–32; Robert Carter Daybook, Nov. 15, 1784, XVI, 33–34, LC (see previous problems with Olive, May 8, 1781, Carter Letterbook, IV, 75).

"everything with reluctance," his overseer asserted, "frequently absenting himself in the busiest time." The overseer now had to manage a constantly "grumbling" slave. Even interventions aimed at bolstering an overseer's authority might have the opposite effect. John Norton called his overseer and slaves together and informed his "People that [he] must have large Crops made and ordered that the people in any instance to do their Duty." All well and good, apparently, but he then pointed out the consequences of their disobedience: "They should suffer for descharging" their overseer.[17] This acknowledgment was probably too blunt a recognition of slave power to reassure the overseer.

Simply by entertaining the complaints of his slaves, a master effectively undermined his overseer's authority. Masters struck poses of impartiality, announced that they would not be a party to the tittle-tattle of plantation gossip, yet listened, often sympathetically. Disclaimers that slaves "are not legal Evidences," as James Mercer admitted, or that "it is not altogether proper to attend to the Tales of Negroes," as John Norton acknowledged, were then followed by testimonials to the reliability of slave witnesses. Thus, Mercer "almost constantly found negroes tell Truth enough of distant overseers," and said of one slave complainant, "I know he informed me as well as he knew . . . I cannot therefore admit he could be lying," whereas Norton observed that, when he "made inquiries" of his slaves, "it is their business to give me a true acc[oun]t." Even when masters trod warily in adjudicating between overseers and slaves, they often sided with their bondpeople. Thus, Robert Raper, agent for John Colleton's plantation affairs in South Carolina, seemed eminently evenhanded when he informed the overseer of Colleton's Wadboo plantation that three slaves were "full of complaints of ill usage, whether right or wrong I cannot tell." But he then recalled a similar incident only a few months earlier, when he had found another set of complaints "to be Reasonable, which you could not, did not deny in my house, when told of it." Even a thick-skinned overseer must have recognized that his credibility was being questioned.[18]

Masters did not just listen to slaves because they found them reliable witnesses; their own self-image guaranteed their receptiveness. Thus, when a Virginia steward attributed the neglect and destruction that had occurred at a quarter to "the authority taken from the overseer by hearing every tale that deceitful negroes will advance," the master did not defend the integrity of

17. Robert Carter to Thomas Olive, July 24, 1781, Carter Letterbook, IV, 93; Seto. Betton to Col. John Mercer, Sept. 19, 1791, Mercer Family Papers, VHS; John H. Norton to B. Muse, Dec. 17, 1787, Muse Papers.

18. James Mercer to B. Muse, Dec. 6, 1788, John H. Norton to B. Muse, June 30, 1786, and James Mercer to B. Muse, May 18, 1780, Muse Papers; Robert Raper to Mr. Swainston, Feb. 25, 1764, Robert Raper Letterbook, microfilm, SCHS.

blacks, but pointed to his higher duty. "No man who possessed the principles of Justice and Humanity," he observed gravely, "would ever deny those who are dependent on him (whether slave or freeman) the privilege of making known their grievances to him." Adopting a similar sanctimonious tone, Frances Tucker objected to her overseer's cruelty on the grounds that her "miserable creatures" should not become "a prey to the worst part of mankind."[19]

Overseers were undermined not just from above but from below. Before the quiet but steady campaigns of their slaves, one Virginian aptly observed, Chesapeake overseers "tire as corn fields do." Put more forcefully by Hugh Washington, "There is no such thing as satisfying [slaves] in regard to their overseers." Dissatisfaction led on occasion to open subversion. In 1737, a Virginia steward faced a "Desturbance with the Overseer and People" at Richneck quarter. The slaves had "lived so long" with a previous overseer that they would work only "as They Pleas'd." After the new overseer applied "some small Correction," the slaves "abused him very much" and complained to their master, who then dismissed the overseer. Eleven years later, slaves on another Virginia estate gained the upper hand over their overseer. The steward reported to his employer that the slaves essentially refused to be managed, doing only "what they please." The overseer was a good man, he continued, but the "Negroes there has used him so ill, he would not stay if I would give him the Whole Crop." He would have made a third more corn and tobacco, the steward estimated, if the slaves had "worked like other Negroes." Some slaves did as they pleased and abused their overseers. No wonder Joseph Ball's injunction was not just, "Let not the overseers abuse my People," but also, "Nor let them abuse their Overseers."[20]

Slaves occasionally attacked their overseers. In the Chesapeake, overseers no doubt drew little comfort from an incident that occurred in James City County. An overseer, provoked by a slave woman's impertinent language, struck her; she retaliated by hitting the overseer so many times "with fists and switches" that he died. Overseers presumably also thought twice before attempting to apprehend slave fugitives after pondering the following newspaper reports. In the first, an overseer apprehended two runaways, a husband and a

---

19. Thomas Fairfax to B. Muse, Apr. 3, 1794, Muse Papers; Robert C. Nicholas to Charles Dabney, Sept. 4, 1773, Dabney Papers; Mary Haldane Coleman, comp., *Virginia Silhouettes: Contemporary Letters concerning Negro Slavery in the State of Virginia* . . . (Richmond, Va., 1934), 3–4.

20. Greene, ed., *Carter Diary*, 302; Hugh Washington to B. Muse, May 21, 1786, Muse Papers; Simon Sallard to Richard Chapman, Jan. 25, 1737, UVa; Francis Willis to Robert Bristow, Sept. 9, 1748, Robert Bristow Letter Book, microfilm, CW; Joseph Ball to Joseph Chinn, Feb. 18, 1744, Joseph Ball Letterbook, LC.

wife, only to have his field hands "violently" rescue them and set them free. Another fugitive escaped by "cutting his overseer in several Pieces [places?] with a knife." Perhaps the most dramatic incident occurred in Hanover County about Christmas 1769, when a new steward and his deputy tangled with a set of plantation slaves who had allegedly been treated with so "much lenity and indulgence" that they had become "extremely insolent and unruly." Events soon escalated from a fight between a single slave and his overseer to a pitched battle between forty or fifty slaves "armed with clubs and staves" and a dozen white men armed with guns. The struggle "continued somewhat desperate" before the gunmen killed three blacks and wounded another five. No wonder, when the owner of twenty slaves at Jericho plantation advertised for an overseer, he required the successful applicant to "have Activity and Courage enough to Correct an insolent or lazy slave."[21]

Lowcountry overseers had even more reason than their Chesapeake counterparts to fear slaves. In 1733, a slave killed an overseer with an ax; forty years later, an overseer died "in consequence of the bruises he received" in attempting to capture a fugitive; the following year, a group of slaves newly arrived from Africa went on the rampage in Saint Andrew Parish, Georgia, slaughtering their overseer in the field, killing three more whites, and wounding others before being taken. Particularly chilling, no doubt, was the pose of a slave belonging to Silas Miles who, after killing his overseer's wife, "appeared openly with his Gun and boasted of what he had done." In 1781, a riot on one Lowcountry estate merited a lengthy and bloodcurdling description: one slave "attempted to cut [the overseer's] throat with a rice hook, another to beat out his brains with his own musket, while the others were mauling him with his powder horn and sticks."[22]

Perhaps most revealing of the insecurity of Lowcountry overseers was the offhand way that Henry Laurens responded to the loss of Richard Oswald's employee, Samuel Huey. In describing his successor—a man named Johnson, probably of mixed Indian and African descent—Laurens casually mentioned the manner of Huey's removal. Johnson would have to "behave above the rank of common Carolinian fugitives," predicted Laurens, if he were "to save his

21. Deposition of R. Janaders, attorney for James City County, July 26, 1793, Executive Papers, VSL; Joseph MCalland, *VaG* (Rind), May 23, 1771; George Narsworthy, ibid. (P and D), Apr. 18, 1771; ibid. (Rind), Jan. 25, 1770; ibid. (D and H), Nov. 18, 1775. See also Robert Tyler, *Md Gaz*, Dec. 8, 1774, where a slave ran away "for having resisted his overseer, by throwing him down, throating him and striking him sundry times with his fist"; two others fled at the same time "for refusing to assist their overseer."

22. *SCG*, Aug. 25, 1733; ibid., Oct. 4, 1773; *Ga Gaz*, Dec. 7, 1774; South Carolina Council Journal, no. 22, Feb. 23, 1753, 3–4, SCDAH; *SC and AGG*, Jan. 20, 1781.

Scalp a whole Year." He would have to "be discreet and carry a steady command otherwise the Blacks will *drown him too*."[23] Apparently, the drowning of an overseer by his slaves merited no great surprise in the eighteenth-century Lowcountry.

The methods Lowcountry slaves used to undermine their overseers are illustrated in a series of incidents that occurred at Charles Drayton's Jehosse plantation in 1800. On February 1, Thomas Merchant assumed the superintendence of the plantation. A little more than a month later, a slave woman came to Drayton complaining of the new overseer's "licentiousness and threatnings." Two weeks later, Philip the driver followed suit. Drayton supported his overseer against his slaves, noting, "There appears a combination to endeavour to get the overseer turned off, He being more intelligent and industrious than suits their disposition." Philip received a whipping and demotion to the field. The contest continued. In late March, six field hands absconded and remained absent for about two weeks. Drayton decided to pay the plantation a visit in order to reestablish authority. A day later, the ex-driver, Philip, described as "the leader of the plot," ran off with seven other slaves. Hunters managed to capture two of Drayton's fugitives, but the rest eventually returned of their own volition. Little more was heard from Jehosse until October, when Drayton received a letter announcing his overseer's death. The slaves had failed to have Merchant dismissed, but perhaps his troubles had contributed to his untimely death.[24]

Another tussle of wills took place at William Read's Ricehope plantation in the same year. Read made his way there "on the disagreeable business," as he candidly put it, "of restoring my Negroes to order or turning away my overseer." He arrived to find seven of his prime slave men in the woods, some of them absent eight weeks, and an apathetic overseer "dismayed or despairing to recover them." Read remained inactive for a few days in hopes that his slaves would return to state their grievances. When this strategy failed, he took the offensive, hunting them on foot, often up to his knees in water. When news spread that Read had requested the assistance of his neighbors with their hunters and dogs, the fugitives returned "two or three at a time." They made their case against their overseer, but Read, a self-described "prejudicial Judge," punished them and put them back to work. The whole "disturbance" Read attributed to the overseer's diligence in following the slaves "thro' their work" and to "the artful measures and bad disposition" of a gang that he had inte-

---

23. *Laurens Papers,* V, 227 (emphasis added). Laurens also once noted that another of his overseers "seems to be held in contempt by the negroes," which led him to muse, "and I am afraid of Some fatal accident": ibid., XI, 487.

24. Charles Drayton diary, Mar. 7, 21, Apr. 8–9, 12–13, Oct. 23, 1800, Drayton Family Papers, Historic Charleston Foundation.

grated into his own. Read "persuaded" the overseer to stay, but whether he easily overcame his "dispondence" may be doubted.[25]

The nature of the complaints brought by slaves against their overseers tied their masters' interests even more closely to their own. Slaves were just as likely to accuse their overseers of abusing their masters' trust as to complain of overwork or cruelty to themselves. Thus, in 1727, slaves belonging to Robert "King" Carter charged their overseer with fattening his horses at their master's expense, helping himself to their master's timber, using their labor to cultivate his corn, keeping a female slave to tend his wife, making others do his washing each week, requiring hay and water to be brought to him each morning, and "never work[ing] himself." When John Lewis Gervais went to Wright Savanna plantation in 1772 to look into the conduct of overseer William Godfrey, a slave named Sam came forward to tell him how seed rice had been used for domestic rather than for planting purposes, how the blacks had been "working for Mr. Godfrey," and how Godfrey had appropriated a barrel of small rice for his own recently established plantation. When slaves complained of overseers to masters, they invariably spoke of being employed on illegitimate tasks or of misappropriation of the master's property. They knew full well where their masters' interests ended and those of the overseer began. Perhaps slaves felt the misuse of the master's property as a personal insult; more probably, they calculated that the quickest route to a master's sympathy was to arouse his proprietorial instincts. The significant point, however, is that slaves were aware of such a distinction. Once again, direct and focused action by slaves undermined an overseer's position.[26]

Although overseer and workforce were, more likely than not, pitted against one another, occasionally they worked together. Indeed, they might even like one another. Robert Carter of Nomini Hall observed that one of his overseers and wife were so "careful of the negroes" that the slaves "appeared to have an affection for both him and her." More probably, a pragmatic alliance was reached between overseer and workforce, with the slaves dictating many of the terms. In 1748, Francis Willis, a steward of Robert Bristow's plantations, reported that the slaves at Fleetsbay plantation went short on clothes and rations but did not complain of their overseer, because "they are allowed to live Lazy." A couple of decades later, another Virginia steward ascribed the problems encountered on one Louisa County quarter to the previous overseer, who "was

---

25. William Read to Jacob Read, Mar. 12, 1800, Read Family Papers, SCHS. See also Elizabeth Izard to Henrietta Izard, Nov. 13, 1799, Middleton Papers, Middleton Place, S.C.

26. Robert "King" Carter Diary, 1722–1727, Apr. 4, 1727, microfilm, CW; *Laurens Papers*, VIII, 289 (see also V, 90–91). For more complaints, see Carter Daybook, Sept. 29, 1776, XIII, 204, XVI, 33–34; and James Mercer to B. Muse, Dec. 6, 1778, Muse Papers.

so good natured to the Negroes under him that he suffered them to Impose on him very much." In fact, "the Negroes were almost free." Under the new overseer, the slaves were "very unwilling to give up the priviledges they were allowed.... Indeed they seem to be determined to Maintain them." And, in 1784, an almost identical situation was reported for another piedmont quarter. "The Negroes [were] very difficult to manage," observed the steward, "owing to the Great Indulgence as they have had ... [they] work at their own discretion—they are given to complaints which they are too much indulged in to make them Either happy to themselves or Invisible to their Masters."[27] Complaints were often generated when the old modus vivendi was disrupted.

Overseers often pursued the line of least resistance and followed their slaves' lead. Thus, George Washington complained of experienced farmers from England who were "perfectly acquainted with every part of a farmer's business" but who failed to practice it in British America. In spite of their impressive qualifications, these farmers, in Washington's experience, found it "a little troublesome to instruct the Negros" and, failing to compel them to adapt to Euro-American ways, "slided" into the slaves' ways of working. The proof of the argument, Washington maintained, was how easily these English newcomers adopted customary hoop poles rather than using "proper flails" for the threshing of grain and allowed the slaves to tread out grain rather than use the new barn's threshing floor. Progressive European techniques were no match for colonial realities, which were as much human as they were environmental.[28]

In general, however, an overseer normally generated hostility from the workforce. It was undoubtedly irritating for masters to keep searching for overseers and to be burdened with slave complainants. Yet, it was to the master's advantage to have the slaves' resentments deflected onto an intermediary, for this enhanced the master's authority. This major channel of communication between master and slave was therefore double-edged: it represented a way for field hands to assert their rights but at the same time easily drew them into a more complete dependence on their masters for the amendment of their complaints.

The gap that opened in the eighteenth century between many masters and field hands had mixed consequences for blacks. A close working relationship—and the benefits that might attend it—was now denied many. At the same time,

---

27. Robert Carter's testimonial to Youell Rust, July 22, 1784, Carter Daybook, XVI, 23; Francis Willis to Robert Bristow, Jan. 1, 1748, Bristow Letter Book; Charles Dabney to [?], 1770, Dabney Papers; Battaille Muse to George William Fairfax, c. 1784, Muse Papers. Apparently, a Maryland slave and his overseer (and another white man's wife) ran away together (Elizabeth Rawlings, *Md Gaz*, Mar. 19, 1789).

28. John C. Fitzpatrick, ed., *The Writings of George Washington from the Original Manuscript Sources, 1745–1799*, 39 vols. (Washington, D.C., 1931–1944), XXXIV, 103.

field-workers could take consolation in being spared the tensions and pressures that proximity to whites induced. And at least they had some influence. If they could not bring easily recognized skills, as artisans did, into their struggles with whites, field hands could at least exert their sheer weight of numbers. Collectively, field hands did influence events, particularly where they were pitted against insecure overseers. Their actions reveal, especially in the nature of their complaints against overseers, a perception of their powers in a situation where white authority was diffused.

SLAVES IN THE MIDDLE

To get the job done, slaves had to be given specialized responsibilities. Before long, a complex system of differentiation based, among other things, on the sex, age, intelligence, and experience of the slaves, as well as on the demands of the various staple economies, had emerged in all plantation societies. This, in turn, had important repercussions for the relationship of master and slave. Although encounters between masters and field hands were hardly straightforward, a slave's elevation to a special position inevitably made the relationship with a master more complex, demanding, and—most important from the slave's perspective—susceptible to manipulation. Four categories of slaves who mediated between masters and slaves are worth singling out for closer analysis: the elderly, watermen, supervisors, and craftsmen. These were slaves in the middle, mediating either directly or indirectly between the worlds of master and slave, meeting whites on an intermittent but more regular basis than ordinary field hands.

Eighteenth-century Anglo-America was a young person's world. Elderly people were rare and, in part as a result, tended to be respected. Even old black field hands could aspire to this privileged status. Faced with selling some of his bondpeople, Edmund Jenings was particularly concerned that the infirm and elderly, who deserved "Relaxation from Labor," secure their just reward. Landon Carter's lament that he no longer met honesty from his dependents did not extend to his elderly slaves. It was just that his "honest ones" were now too old to be of much use in the field, whereas his "young ones" were "all rogues." Particularly as a master aged, he came to value the people with whom he had shared so much of his adult life.[29]

In fact, some slave families produced respected elderly slaves across generations. In 1732, Robert "King" Carter owned a slave "Old Gumby," who lived

---

29. Edmund Jenings to Mr. Bruce, Mar. 29, 1756, Jenings Papers, VHS; Greene, ed., *Carter Diary*, 591. On old age in general, see David Hackett Fischer, *Growing Old in America* (New York, 1977), 4, 26–76. Relations that elderly blacks had with other slaves are explored briefly in Chapter 8.

with his wife and a son at Wolf House Quarter. Perhaps Gumby derived from Gambia, indicating the old man's ancestral homeland. If so, he bequeathed an African connection to his children, for they all had Gumby as a surname—an indication of the old man's importance. In 1732, Old Gumby seems to have been a grandfather, for Tom Gumby, apparently his eldest son, was married to Caty and had three children: Mary, a young woman, Dick, aged thirteen, and one-year-old Martha. Another son, David Gumby, also lived on the estate. "King" Carter and later his sons and grandsons relied on Tom Gumby to carry messages, and, in the 1760s, Tom served "King" Carter's grandson in Williamsburg. By 1774, when the grandson, Robert Carter, now lived at Nomini Hall, where he employed a new tutor, Philip Fithian, Tom and Caty were still together and were now the oldest slaves on Carter's plantations. They were in at least their seventies, perhaps their nineties. They lived in a small house about three hundred feet from a large garden just north of the mansion where they tended vegetables and kept chickens. Their family was vital to them. They asked Fithian to draw up a list of their children with their ages, for which the tutor had "as many Thanks" as he had "blessings before now from a Beggar for sixpence." Tom often told stories about his family and, in a manner associated with the elderly, "leaving some of his Narrations half untold, beginning others in the middle having entered into the true Spirit of loquacity." On one occasion, he told a tale, presumably set in Africa, of "his Grandfather's Uncle harpooning a Porpoise." Tom Gumby was the patriarch of an African American family, much like his father before him, who could readily trace his history to Africa.[30]

Masters showed their elderly slaves respect by caring for them. In 1770, Henry Laurens described Cudjoe as "a quiet orderly old Man, not able to do much Work and therefore is never drove to Labour, but suffer'd to go on in his own way." Allocated more clothes and shoes than any other slave, Cudjoe "seems to be so perfectly satisfied with his situation" that Laurens believed "he has no Desire to change it." Four years later, Landon Carter offered his valediction to a "very old slave and fellow creature Jack Lubbar," his "good and faithful servant," who was "as honest a human creature as could live." Carter could only guess at Jack's age; all he knew for certain was that some forty years earlier he had found Jack "too old a man to keep as a foreman." Gradually, Carter lightened Jack's workload, until, in his characteristically self-regarding words, his slave lived "quite retired under my constant kindness." However,

---

30. Inventory of estate of Robert Carter, November 1733, VHS; Farish, ed., *Journal and Letters of Philip Vickers Fithian*, 177–178; John Randolph Barden, "'Flushed with Notions of Freedom': The Growth and Emancipation of a Virginia Slave Community, 1732–1812" (Ph.D. diss., Duke University, 1993), 84–88.

even then, this "good old man" remained as active as ever, growing food in a well-provisioned garden, catching fish, trapping beavers and other river animals, attending church, and continuing to be as "erect and fast a Walker as almost any man in the Parish." Jack was a yardstick against which even a master might measure his achievements. Unlike Carter's unhappy experience as a father, Jack had been "blessed with his children's company." Finding Jack "prudently working amongst his melon vines" one day, Carter observed him closely and inquired why he had not hilled his peas. Jack answered, "The Prudence of Experience, Master." Carter had followed a similar method, so this answer comforted him.[31]

Respect for elderly slaves derived in part from quite practical reasons—the slaves' value, for example, as repositories of information. In a dispute about some land that Ralph Izard's grandfather had allegedly given a neighbor, Izard asked Henry Laurens to question "the old Negro Joshua at Goose Creek or Robin [who] can inform you more about it than I can." Landon Carter "sometimes divert[ed]" himself by talking to his old people about the worming and topping of tobacco. He also listened to the "old Stagers" in his field gangs, because their knowledge of agricultural matters was often superior to that of their white overseers. In 1777, when Robert Carter was trying to locate a pair of millstones that had been imported twenty years earlier, he asked his overseer to "make enquiry of the ancient Negroes," who would know where to look.[32]

Masters also made practical use of trusted elderly slaves by placing them in positions of responsibility. In 1768, when Henry Laurens needed somebody to visit Mepkin plantation and watch over the new indigo crop, he sent "Old Man Stepney" on a month's loan. As Laurens told the overseer, Stepney "is very honest and if you will speak to him, he will not allow anybody within his sight to rob you." Not surprisingly, the loss of such a valuable ally was not easily borne. When John Moultrie's "most faithfull and valuable old black servant George" died, Moultrie observed that it was a loss he did not "expect to retrieve." Moultrie's additional reflections indicate the closeness of his ties to his faithful, elderly slaves. "I must expect my good old servants will go," he observed resignedly; "it suits me in mind that I must beat a march myself one of these days."[33]

---

31. *Laurens Papers*, VII, 329 (see also III, 203, IV, 148, IX, 262–263); Greene, ed., *Carter Diary*, 834, 836, 840–841, 574–575. Carter's memory was selective about Jack (ibid., 295, 299, 301, 303).

32. Ralph Izard to Henry Laurens, June 4, 1775, Henry Laurens Papers, SCHS; Greene, ed., *Carter Diary*, 454, 487; Robert Carter to the overseer at Mr. John Currie's plantation, May 5, 1777, Carter Letterbook, III, 125.

33. *Laurens Papers*, IV, 661 (see also V, 175–176, 702, VII, 566, VIII, 67–68, 96); John Moultrie to James Grant, Nov. 3, 1772, Papers of General James Grant of Ballindalloch,

A master's reliance on elderly slaves created a situation that could be manipulated by these erstwhile dependents. The old slave who complained of his overseer to Robert Carter might have calculated that maturity lent his words authority. Certainly other slaves assumed precisely this on another Virginia plantation, for they prevailed on the oldest among them to make a complaint. On occasion, elderly slaves used their privileged position to lead the opposition. In 1784, one Virginia steward despaired of reforming a particular gang of slaves because "the old ones will never be broke to Labour." In the same year, the manager of the plantation belonging to the Bethesda Orphanage in Georgia made the same complaint. The "old Slaves" were essentially worthless, he argued: "I had equally as much trouble to bring them to work kindly as I had with the New Negroes." He had been obliged "many times to take the hoe into [his] Own hands by way of instruction." One slave apparently attempted to gain a little leverage by claiming to be much older than he was, an action that points to the respect accorded the elderly in the eighteenth century. When sold, fifty-seven-year-old Abraham insisted that he was in fact eighty. Whether he was hoping for lenient treatment, for the sale to be voided, or perhaps most simply for the esteem that came with age is unclear. His new master deferred to Abraham at least to the extent of reporting that the slave seemed "willing and Contented enough, But time can only Explain how he may turn out."[34]

As repositories of plantation traditions, as respected and venerable figures, as knowledgeable workers, and perhaps above all as longtime acquaintances, elderly blacks made their voices heard and their actions felt in their dealings with masters. Rather than being cast on the scrap heap, elderly slaves wielded influence with their masters, usually amicably, but occasionally antagonistically.

Another group of slaves who came into infrequent but privileged contact with masters and other whites were boatmen. These slaves led rather autonomous lives, often spending days away from their masters, seeing life beyond the normal horizons of the plantation slave. Consider Tony, a South Carolina patroon, or skipper, who described a typical trip up the Cooper River with his customary crew of Jemmey, Scipio, and Worster. He arrived at Samuel Wragg's Dacon plantation one Saturday, delivered a letter to the overseer by three o'clock in the afternoon, loaded about ten barrels of rice that evening, and

---

sometime Governor of East Florida, in ownership of Sir Evan Macpherson-Grant, Bart., Ballindalloch Castle Muniments, Scotland.

34. Farish, ed., *Journal and Letters of Philip Vickers Fithian*, 170; Charles Dabney to [?], 1770, Dabney Papers; Battaille Muse to George William Fairfax, c. 1784, Muse Papers; Joseph Law to Rev. Joseph Cook, Aug. 14, 1784, A3/12/16, Countess of Huntingdon's American Papers, Westminster College, Cambridge, England; William Brown to Robert Carter, Nov. 22, 1785, Carter Family Papers.

slept in the house of Kingroad, Wragg's black overseer. Sunday was an off day, and that night he slept at Joseph Wragg's plantation in the house of Gibby, his black overseer. He finished loading his boat by noon on Tuesday and set off for town. On this occasion, he had not visited James Akin's plantation—he had not been there since "the Yellow Fever was in Town"—but he admitted knowing most of that plantation's slaves and "frequently" stopping there. Black patroons inhabited a largely black world, spending days away from their base, among fellow slave crewmen, striking up an acquaintance with many plantation slaves, and sometimes sleeping in their houses.[35]

The resourcefulness and self-reliance exhibited by Lowcountry patroons and Chesapeake pilots elicited effusive testimonials. In South Carolina, Robert Boyd's slave was "inferior to none employed in the coasting business"; John Alleyne Walter's slave Shadwell had been for a "long time a patroon of a schooner and is well acquainted with all the rivers and inlets to the southward of Charles Town"; Robert William's slave knew all the rivers south of Charleston "as far as Savannah in Georgia." Likewise, Chesapeake masters sang the praises of their black watermen: Solomon Haynes was "an exceeding good pilot," and another skipper was "well acquainted with the Bay and most of the Rivers in Virginia and Maryland." Patroons and pilots enjoyed considerable freedom of movement and came to know their regions intimately.[36]

In the Chesapeake, slave watermen often worked alongside whites, and

---

35. South Carolina Council Journal, no. 17, part 1, 78–79. The many days each month that slave boatmen spent out of their masters' sight is graphically depicted in Charles Drayton's diary, where Drayton regularly listed the itineraries of his two slave patroons, Tim and Wadmelaw. Two of the more specific entries, relating to Tim, read: "Informed that Tim arrived in town the 19th from Coosawhakhie—the rice not being ready, he was detained there 3 days—coming into the dock he was overset by accidents, loosing her rudder and oars and the chief of the rice" [Mar. 23, 1784]; and "Tim says he was wind bound at the mouth of Stono branch from the 6th. Had on board a runaway wench. Roguery, idled the voyage" [Mar. 9, 1793] (Charles Drayton Diary, Drayton Family Papers). Josiah Smith once noted that George Austin's schooner took a full month in getting from Charleston to Pedee (about 50 miles, as the crow flies), because of contrary winds and bad weather (Josiah Smith to George Austin, Jan. 31, 1774, Josiah Smith Letterbook, UNC).

36. Robert Boyd, *SCG*, Oct. 1, 1764; John Alleyne Walter, *SC and AGG*, Dec. 8, 1775; Robert Williams, Jr., *SCG*, Dec. 24, 1763; James Scrosby, *VaG* (P and D), Nov. 3, 1768; James Hunter, *VaG* (P and D), Apr. 11, 1771. See also Charles Lee, ibid. (Rind), Feb. 9, 1769; Robert Donald, ibid. (P and D), Aug. 24, 1769; Alexander Vanderdussen, *SCG*, Jan. 22, 1737; George Logan, ibid., July 29, 1745; John Gordon, ibid., Sept. 10, 1763; Richard Beresford, ibid., Sept. 12, 1761; Thomas Bee, *SCG and CJ*, Nov. 11, 1766; William Coachman, ibid., Oct. 6, 1767; John Marley, ibid., Sept. 20, 1768, Mar. 20, 1770; John Mitchell, *SC and AGG*, Apr. 24, 1771; Anthony Bourdeaux, *City Gaz*, Aug. 24, 1797; Joseph Addison, *Charleston Courier*, Mar. 12, 1807; and James Gordon to Elias Ball, Jan. 7, 1792, Ball Family Papers, USC.

accepted social distinctions were sometimes jettisoned. John Hoomes's brig, which traveled between Portsmouth and other Virginia ports in the 1780s, employed large numbers of blacks and whites on a monthly basis. The rough equality in wages between the two groups is one indicator of the narrowness of the gap that separated free and enslaved on board ship. Further evidence of leveling occurred aboard Robert Carter's sloop. In 1775, Alexander Jones, a mariner, offered his services to the master of Nomini Hall; Carter at first refused because he thought Jones "might expect better fair [sic] than any people [he] had on board the sloop." Jones secured the position when he assured his future employer that "he would be perfectly satisfied to eat, lodge, and be clothed, as that gang were." The white and black crew of a schooner carrying passengers and mail from Norfolk to Hampton made the most of the opportunity to "make a perquisite offering the Passengers a dinner and liquor." One passenger complained bitterly of the scantiness and high prices of the fare. The egalitarianism generated by shared working conditions could be taken too far, as when one sloop's crew, comprising two whites and two blacks, was charged with murdering a white man in Richmond County. The victim had been put on board to look after a customer's cargo and had apparently threatened the crew's illegitimate practices.[37]

The more frequent all-slave crews and more densely black countryside of the Lowcountry meant that this region's boatmen had even more autonomy than their Chesapeake counterparts. Complaints of trafficking between slave boatmen and plantation slaves were unending. In 1737, the Charleston grand jury fulminated against "Negroes going in Boats and Canoes up the Country trading with Negroes in a clandestine manner." A generation later, a Savannah River resident reported a theft from his plantation and attributed it to the "common practice for trading boats and others to land their people, and remain whole nights and days on the plantation." In 1767, inhabitants from many parts of South Carolina objected to the comptroller of customs's issuance of permits, "several of which are to common Negro slaves," thereby affording "a shelter for illicit traffick." Four years later, Provost Marshall William Pinckney served notice that he would enforce the law requiring owners of coastal vessels to have at least one white person on board; this action testified to a growing problem, for disregard of the law had caused plantations along the Ashepoo River to be "frequently plundered and robbed." To prevent such

37. Disbursements of the Brig Mars, 1780–1781, John Hoomes Papers, Duke; Carter Daybook, May 5, 1775; unidentified author, MS Diary, Mar. 23, 1796, MSS 5:1, 3–4, VHS; Richmond County Slave Criminal Trials, June 29, 1734, VSL. See also Alexander McKenzie Day Book, April 1749, microfilm, CW; and Jenifer and Hooe Journal, 1775–1785, and Ledger, 1775–1777, microfilm, UVa.

activity, Henry Laurens warned his overseers "to prevent an intercourse between Boat and Plantation Negroes."[38]

Henry Laurens's experiences with boatmen emphasize the latitude that the position encouraged. According to Laurens, Abraham, a boatman, was "so very sly and artful" that it needed all his master's "skill . . . to counteract him." In July 1763, Abraham failed to board Laurens's schooner before it left Georgetown, because "he thought that [Captain] Smart cou'd not come away without him." About a year later, Laurens lost patience and prepared to sell his errant boatman. Of particular concern to him were "some pernicious connexions that [Abraham] has made with slaves in Charles Town," an indication of the independence of this slave's social network. But Laurens did not sell Abraham; instead, he promoted him. By the summer of 1765, "Captain Abraham" was a patroon in his own right—and his master's troubles multiplied. In that same year, Laurens suspected his newly appointed patroon of, in turn, selling wood, trading with slaves, and harboring stolen provisions.[39]

Laurens's entanglements with boatmen were not confined to his slaves. In the fall of 1763, he prepared to receive an expected consignment of turpentine, only to be told by "the Negro Patroon of Watboo Boat" that the cargo was destined for another. When the goods began to spoil on the wharfside, Laurens made inquiries and discovered the error—or perhaps deception. In February the following year, in spite of his increased wariness about the assumed powers of patroons, Laurens reluctantly complied with a request for salt, even though it lacked written authorization, simply because Diamond, the skipper, "insists upon it." Later that same year, Laurens reported to a correspondent that he had spoken to Watboo Johnny, who "promises to bring down your Pitch this trip." For slave patroons to make pronouncements, demands, and promises when confronted with an imposing man like Laurens indicates the striking extent of their independence.[40]

Watermen displayed their independence most obviously when they ran away. Although they constituted no more than 1 or 2 percent of adult workers on plantations, slave watermen formed a quarter of all the nonfield runaways advertised in both South Carolina and Virginia newspapers. The explanation is

38. *SCG*, Nov. 5, 1737; John Stevens, *Ga Gaz*, June 27, 1765; remonstrance of divers inhabitants of the Province of South Carolina to Mark Robinson, November 1767, Garth Papers, SCHS; William Pinckney, *SCG*, Apr. 30, 1771; *Laurens Papers*, IV, 633.

39. *Laurens Papers*, III, 508–509, IV, 298–299, 616, 633, 661, V, 3, 11. Laurens's relations with boatman (and occasional tradesman) Scaramouch are also instructive: see ibid., V, 86, VII, 566, 573, VIII, 67, 355, X, 487, XI, 386–387, XIV, 39, 86, 291; account book of James Laurens, 1767–1773, Nov. 4, 1768, CC; and account book of Henry Laurens, 1766–1773, September 1768, Sept. 5, 1770, February, Mar. 5, 31, May, Sept. 7, 1772, CC.

40. *Laurens Papers*, IV, 6, 168, 196.

not hard to find. Watermen had access to a means of escape, gained an unparalleled knowledge of the countryside, and formed a network of supportive acquaintances. One Lowcountry master had trouble predicting the whereabouts of his boatman, who had twenty years' service to his credit. He named a couple of plantations where the waterman might be lurking but then noted forlornly that "he has many acquaintances especially those in coasting schooners." A Chesapeake master was at a similar loss, for his waterman had "a wife at almost every landing on *Rappahannock, Mattapony,* and *Pamunkey* Rivers." Furthermore, slave watermen assisted other slaves who wished to escape. Thus, a washerwoman in Charleston was thought to have "gone into the Country, being acquainted with many Boat Negroes," and Daniel was carried from Williamsburg to Portsmouth "by a craft conducted by negroes."[41]

But a boatman's best opportunity to escape slavery was to make for the open seas. In 1777, Abraham, who was employed in a Lowcountry schooner, ran away and hired himself out as a free seaman. On discovering that he was advertised as a runaway "by the beat of drum," he left Charleston, intending to make his way to Saint Augustine. Embarking on a sloop for Port Royal, he was discovered by the black patroon, who handed him over to a white master of a packet sloop. But Abraham was not so easily captured, for he then stole a boat from the sloop and escaped to Saint Helena Island. Abandoning the boat, he apparently planned to make the rest of his journey on foot. Perhaps he reached his destination, for his master then lost his trail. In 1771, Sam, a mulatto sailor in the Chesapeake, ran off after distributing stolen broadcloth to his crewmates "in order to bribe them to secrecy." On Christmas Day, in Norfolk, he told a suspicious resident that he was part of a crew lately wrecked on the coast. With such a story, his master warned, "some Person in want of Hands might be induced to engage him."[42]

During the Revolutionary war, such ingenuity made skilled watermen a valuable asset and a potential liability. In 1775, with British ships close at hand, a licensed harbor pilot in Charleston, Thomas Jeremiah, described by the colonial governor as "a Free Negroe of considerable property, one of the most valuable and useful men in his way, in the Province," was hanged for allegedly plotting an insurrection. Jeremiah's importance either induced him to envisage a role for blacks in the coming war, one in which he would have "the

---

41. Morgan, "Black Society in the Lowcountry, 1760–1810," in Ira Berlin and Ronald Hoffman, eds., *Slavery and Freedom in the Age of the American Revolution* (Charlottesville, Va., 1983), 101–104; Mullin, *Flight and Rebellion*, 94; James Bolton, *SC and AGG*, May 12, 1775; John Holiday, *VaG* (P and D), Apr. 21, May 5, 1768; Benjamin Villepontoux, *SCG and CJ*, May 25, 1773; Edward C. Travis, *VaG* (Purdie), July 10, 1778.

42. James Parson, *SC and AGG*, Aug. 21, 1777; Stafford Lightburn, *VaG* (P and D), Mar. 7, 1771.

Chief Command," or it made him the best available scapegoat for patriot forces who wanted both to intimidate other black harbor pilots and to promote military preparedness.[43] Black pilots in Virginia also aroused patriot suspicions, and a number were executed. A slave pilot belonging to John Taylor of Richmond County, Virginia, was condemned to death for "Traiteriously Adher[ing to] the Enemies of the Commonwealth"; Sancho, belonging to a Caroline County master, met the same fate for "giving Intelligence and acting in capacity of a pilot, to some of the British forces"; and, in 1781, a runaway slave, formerly of Gloucester County, was arrested while operating as a spy and pilot for the British. In South Carolina, Louisa Susanna Aikman described how she escaped from Charleston to British ships by paying "a hundred dollars Congress" to a black pilot.[44]

Masters entrusted watermen with great responsibilities. Put in charge of expensive vessels and valuable cargoes, boatmen spent much time away from the scrutiny of masters and so had to make many important decisions for themselves. They traveled widely, broadened their horizons, established extensive social networks with plantation slaves, and enjoyed the camaraderie of their fellow boatmen. Most enjoyed the opportunity to make a little money by trading with rural slaves. A sizable number of slave watermen made the most of their advantages by escaping from their masters.

Most slave foremen and drivers came into greater contact with masters than boatmen, and their autonomy, particularly in the Chesapeake, was more circumscribed. The primary function of most Virginia slave foremen was to keep the hands moving. Control of most facets of crop production remained in the hands of white men, whether masters, stewards, or overseers. Generally speaking, therefore, foremen had limited room for maneuver, although not all

---

43. For more on Jeremiah, see Philip D. Morgan, "Black Life in Eighteenth-Century Charleston," *Perspectives in American History*, N.S., I (1984), 213. For an earlier example of the potential liability (and ultimate loyalty) of a slave pilot, see Thomas Cooper and David J. McCord, eds., *The Statutes at Large of South Carolina*, 10 vols. (Columbia, S.C., 1836–1841), VII, 419–420. The crucial role played by slave pilots was also pointed up during the war. In July 1777, the South Carolina Navy Board resolved that Negroes on board armed vessels of the state would no longer be insured by the public. Presumably, this order was rescinded, for in September the board noted that, if Negroes were not insured on pilot boats, "the owners will take them from on board and the boats will by that means be rendered useless" (South Carolina Navy Board Minutes, July 3, Sept. 5, 1777, Peter Force Collection, Ser. 7E, box 62, LC).

44. Petition of Mann Page, June 7, 1781, Prince William County, Legislative Petitions, VSL; petition of William Evans, Nov. 22, 1785, Caroline County, Legislative Petitions; petition of William Evans, Oct. 27, 1790, Gloucester County, Legislative Petitions; Louisa Susannah [Aikman] Wells, *The Journal of a Voyage from Charlestown to London* (New York, 1968), 2.

rested content with simply following orders. Thus, foremen varied the work pace: Landon Carter's George heard that he was to be given a plow and accordingly slowed his gang, until told to "look well into the dispatching of his business." They decided priorities: George put his gang to weeding tobacco rather than drawing young plants for replanting. Occasionally, they blatantly disobeyed authority: one foreman refused to discipline a field hand; another, whose "Usage has bin so Easy heartherto," did almost nothing his steward told him; a youthful Jack Lubbar engaged in drinking bouts that resulted in dead cattle, broken fences, and destroyed cornfields; and George Washington's Davy cut lambs out of season for his own use, a practice that his master chose to overlook because of his usefulness as a foreman. Chesapeake foremen sometimes overstepped the bounds set by their masters, but those bounds were tightly restricted.[45]

Because drivers in South Carolina were more often managers than mere gangleaders, they were valued for their ability to take decisive and independent action. Working without supervision merited great praise. In 1768, John Graham purchased a slave who for two years had managed a plantation without an overseer and was "perhaps one of the most valuable Negroes" in either South Carolina or Georgia. Put up for sale as part of an estate of a hundred slaves six years later, two "fine Drivers" received accolades for their "sole Management" of a plantation and for making "as large Crops to the Hands under their Care, as any Managers whatsoever." According to his master, Dembo handled "the planting business as well without a Superintendent as with one." The loss of such competent deputies was a major setback. John Thomas, in petitioning for compensation for his executed slave, referred to him as a "capital Fellow" on whom "he principally depended for the conducting of the whole of his Plantation Business." Similarly, John Green spoke of his great misfortune at losing his manager, "the only Slave he could place Confidence in."[46]

Lowcountry masters often compared their black drivers favorably to white overseers. Few white men had "a more general or better knowledge of plant-

---

45. Greene, ed., *Carter Diary,* 295, 299, 408, 579; Seto. Betton to Col. John Mercer, Sept. 6, 1791, Mercer Family Papers, VHS; Simon Sallard to John Carter, Apr. 15, 1737, Simon Sallard Papers, UVa; Washington to Pearce, Dec. 18, 1793, in M. D. Conway, ed., *George Washington and Mount Vernon,* Long Island Historical Society, Memoirs, IV (Brooklyn, N.Y., 1889), 13–14, 20.

46. John Graham to James Grant, Mar. 1, 1768, Papers of James Grant; William Williamson, *SCG,* May 16, 1774; Joseph Clark to William Page, Jan. 7, 1808, William Page Papers, UNC; petition of John Thomas, Feb. 3, 1783, Journal of the House of Representatives, SCDAH; petition of John Green, Nov. 25, 1794, Senate Petitions, SCDAH. For other such testimonials, see Daniel Crawford, *SCG,* Jan. 25, 1748; Josiah Smith, Jr., *SCG and CJ,* Apr. 26, 1768; John Joor, *SCG,* Nov. 5, 1772; Henry Hyrne, *Gaz of State of SC,* Mar. 24, 1785; and *Columbian Herald, or the Patriotic Courier of North-America* (Charleston), Mar. 26, 1789.

ing" than his driver, averred one master. After some years of evaluating the performance of a slave driver and a white overseer who managed adjoining plantations, Henry Laurens declared that the white man was "wretched," not even "the tythe in virtue" of his driver. Ralph Izard became aware of the relative value of black drivers when he learned that his plantations had been subject to "considerable embezzlement." The one exception, the plantation where he made the "most to the hand and really a good Crop," was where there was "no overseer, but only a Black Driver." Izard was advised to transfer more authority from white to black managers.[47]

Drivers assumed wide-ranging responsibilities in carrying out their jobs. One driver applied successfully to a neighbor for a loan of corn by promising on "behalf of his master" to return it as soon as possible. Another slave driver authoritatively estimated flood damage and calculated the prospective crop. In purchasing a gang of slaves, a Lowcountry planter naturally "consulted with Moses the driver as to the apportioning the negroes into tasks." Moses informed his new owner, among other things, that "Joe the son of Sancho, was apt to fly the course when pressed to work." Reckoning up with his furnishing merchant for corn, Thomas Pinckney noted that his "Driver insists upon it that there is a mistake of no less than 550 bushels in the last year's account." Pinckney himself kept no record, but his driver itemized and dated the errors: "500 bushels charged in February '91 and 50 bushels too much in the parcel delivered in Dec. '90." Either this driver kept accounts or his memory was so well attuned to his master's interest that he could recall grain deliveries made some fifteen months earlier.[48]

By proving their worth, drivers inevitably drew close to their masters. The successful management of Daniel Ravenel's Santee plantation rested on a driver who was "very faithful and assiduous in executing his master's wishes." On the rare occasions when master and driver needed to confer, the driver would travel to Charleston, the carpet in the hall of Ravenel's townhouse would be taken up, and a map of the plantation would be chalked out for the driver's study and understanding. The bounds to which a driver's fidelity extended is indicated in a newspaper report of 1774. Four white men accosted a driver who was conveying a runaway back to his plantation. After the driver refused to sell the horse that he rode, the white "Banditti" whipped the fugi-

---

47. Alexander Rose, *Gaz of State of SC*, Dec. 20, 1784; Laurens Papers, VI, 445, VIII, 399 (see also VIII, 635); C. C. Pinckney to Ralph Izard, Dec. 26, 1794, Manigault Family Papers, SCHS.

48. John Ball to N. Harleston, Aug. 7, 1790, Ball Family Papers; C. C. Pinckney to Thomas Pinckney, Sept. 13, 1794, Pinckney Family Papers, LC; Timothy Ford to Henry Izard, Jan. 31, 1806, Ford-Ravenel Papers, SCHS; Thomas Pinckney to [?], Mar. 1792, Thomas Pinckney Papers, USC.

tive, wounded the driver, who "lay senseless, a considerable Time," and rifled his pockets "of every thing he had." Loyalty sometimes came at a heavy price.[49]

Drivers and foremen were conspicuously absent from the ranks of runaway slaves; only four were ever advertised as fugitives in eighteenth-century South Carolina newspapers, and only one was posted in Virginia newspapers. Even during the chaos of the Revolutionary war, drivers rarely took advantage of the situation to abscond. This might have been proof of their loyalty to whites or, at least, of their unwillingness to relinquish an advantageous post, but equally it might have reflected a sense of responsibility toward, and identification with, their charges. Standing their ground and asserting their authority, rather than abandoning their fellow slaves, seems to have been an overriding concern for most drivers.

The desire to maintain or strengthen a sphere of influence was the ostensible cause of a dispute between two drivers on the Pinckney plantations in the late eighteenth century. Much of the contention revolved about the issue of who would make the greater crop. The white manager noted at one point, "As to your Drivers they are often quarreling and jarring with each other which is a disagreeable business to me at times but I believe their jealousy of each other serves to keep them Honest."[50] More to the point, perhaps, it kept them on the plantation.

Drivers extracted concessions for their seeming loyalty. When a Lowcountry planter rented his driver "to instruct and direct" another's slaves in "how to plant," he did not simply order him away. Rather, the planter told the slave that "he wou'd oblige me to go there." The driver, however, was uneasy, thinking his master "wanted to sell him *softly*," or without his consent. The master "perfectly understood his meaning and assured him that [he] had no Intention to part with him." At least a driver had to be reassured. Even where the driver exceeded his authority, he might escape lightly. An absentee Georgia planter informed his agent that he always gave Saby the driver leave now and then to kill a hog for his own consumption "by way of encouragement, when he behaved to my satisfaction." Saby, however, not only preempted his master's right to reward him but began taking hogs to Savannah to sell them. The master's rather lame response was to query Saby's need to go "so often to Savannah on pretence of business." A driver could even disgrace himself and yet still be difficult to remove. One Lowcountry manager observed that, if his

---

49. Samuel Dubose, *Address Delivered at the Seventeenth Anniversary of the Black Oak Agricultural Society . . . to Which Is Attached Reminiscences of St. Stephens Parish* (Charleston, S.C., 1850), 7; Roger Pinckney, *SCG*, May 30, 1774.

50. C. C. Pinckney to Thomas Pinckney, May 25, 1792, William Frazer to Mrs. Harriott Horry, Oct. 8, 1792, William Frazer to Thomas Pinckney, Feb. 5, 1793, Pinckney Family Papers, LC.

driver acted dishonestly once more, he would have "to degrade him from his present office . . . into that of a Common Field hand," but he later admitted that the plantation could not "well do without him."[51]

Drivers, much like watermen, were men-in-between. Singled out for a specialized role, they were inevitably distanced from their fellow slaves and brought into close, if occasional, contact with whites. Unlike watermen or artisans, however, they lacked marketable skills; they could not go to sea or to town or to a new plantation neighborhood and readily find a market for their services. Their position was a function of a particular economic system. Drivers and certainly foremen saw masters more often than watermen, and the interests of superintendents and masters coincided in important respects. Thus, despite their greater responsibilities—their management of many fellow slaves—drivers were more dependent both on a system and the lords of it than were boatmen. Men-in-between they might have been, subject to stresses in mediating between white and black they certainly were, but drivers and foremen were not suspended between two worlds. The driver generally stood fast and traveled little. If they were less independent than artisans, they were also less isolated.

Like drivers, proficient tradesmen earned the respect of their masters. One Virginia planter held his artisan "in great Esteem," as one of the best brickmakers in the colony, a good bricklayer, and as good a sawyer as any. John Tayloe reckoned that Billy's ingenuity was such that he was capable of "almost any sort of Business," evident in his employment as a foundry worker, stonemason, and miller. Similarly, Peter Deadfoot, according to his master, could "turn his hand to anything," for he was an indifferent shoemaker, a good butcher, a good plowman and carter who understood the training of oxen, an excellent sawyer and waterman, and "one of the best scythemen, either with or without a cradle, in America." Peter also had the appearance of a superior slave: he was a "clean-limbed . . . genteel handsome fellow."[52]

Because his master thought so highly of him, Peter naturally enough gained "a great share of pride" in his abilities. Likewise, Sam, a carpenter, said to be "very clever at his work," could hold his head high when others praised his new pounding machine as exceeding "all Expectations." It could produce five barrels of rice a day "with Ease." When Robert Carter received a query about

51. *The Letters of Hon. James Habersham, 1756–1775,* GHS, *Collections,* VI (Savannah, Ga., 1904), 242; John Channing to Edward Telfair, Oct. 31, 1787, Edward Telfair Papers, Duke; Josiah Smith to George Austin, June 14, 1775, Smith Letterbook.

52. Petition of Edward Voss, May 17, 1777, Legislative Petitions, Spotsylvania County, VSL; John Tayloe, *VaG* (P and D), Apr. 1, 1774; Thomas Mason, ibid. (Rind), Sept. 22, 1768.

supplying armaments during the Revolutionary war and deferred to the specialized knowledge of his "Negro Smiths," they no doubt took pleasure in informing him that a "Buk iron . . . is a proper Iron for forging Bayonets." White respect helped foster black self-assurance.[53]

Respect for a tradesman's talents translated into increased material benefits. Extra clothing, supplemental food, and the opportunity to travel off the plantation were advantages that came the way of most artisans. When Ralph Izard's carpenter was taken ill, he received "every attention" from a physician and had his request for "a bottle of wine, and some sugar" immediately honored. Henry Laurens paid not just a neighbor for the use of his carpenters but also the tradesmen themselves in both money and rum for working on a Sunday. In his will of 1774, Peter Gourdin explicitly ordered that his slave Billy "shall not be put to any field work, but be kept a jobbing on the plantation and in the proper Season to tend the Indigo works about the Vatts as in my life time, and further that he shall not be under the power and authority of any Overseer that shall or may be put on the Plantation after my decease."[54]

In the Chesapeake, the privileges accorded ironworkers far exceeded those of any other tradesmen. Ironmasters supplied more and better provisions than most planters. An investigation of sixteen adult skeletons dating to the late eighteenth century from Catoctin Furnace in Maryland found not only that the men outlived the women but that male ironworkers outlived nineteenth-century plantation workers. Although the skeletal evidence indicated heavy lifting at relatively young ages, the superior longevity of the men no doubt derived in large part from superior nutrition. The "overwork" system allowed ironworking slaves to acquire cash or goods for surpassing daily or weekly production quotas or for working on Sundays and holidays. Company store accounts indicate that many slave ironworkers purchased extra linen, clothing, and bedding to improve their own and their families' quality of life. Members of the same slave family frequently worked alongside each other; and skilled slave ironworkers, perhaps more than other groups of artisans, were able to pass their skills on to their children.[55]

---

53. *Laurens Papers,* IX, 269; Robert Carter to Capt. John Turberville, Jan. 22, 1780, Carter Letterbook, XVII, 39.

54. Ann Izard to Ralph Izard, Feb. 16, 1795, Ralph Izard Papers, USC; *Laurens Papers,* IV, 660; will of Peter Gourdin, Oct. 4, 1774, Robert N. Gordon Collection, SCHS.

55. Jennifer Olsen Kelley and J. Lawrence Angel, "The Workers of Catoctin Furnace," *Maryland Archaeology,* XIX (1983), 2–17; Kelley and Angel, "Life Stresses of Slavery," *American Journal of Physical Anthropology,* LXXIV (1987), 199–204; Angel and Kelley, "Health Status of Colonial Iron-worker Slaves," ibid., LX (1983), 170–171; Charles B. Dew, "David Ross and the Oxford Iron Works: A Study of Industrial Slavery in the Early Nineteenth-

The extension of privileges by the master could easily become the assertion of rights by the artisan. If one of the advantages for a skilled slave was the opportunity to travel, he might attempt to maintain control over his movements. The "bargaining" that occurred on such occasions is captured in a letter from one master to another, which was conveyed

> by old Cupid Brickmaker-General. [T]he old gentleman (whether from a prudent regard to his health or from whatever other motive, I cannot say) was at first very averse to going. I at first tried threats and menaces, but found they were not likely to succeed for his health began to decline very fast and I believe it would have continued to do so, had I not changed my Rhetoric to the persuasive kind, and I believe you will find it your Interest to adopt the same method of proceeding for he's as capricious as the God whose name he bears. I have told him that he will not be there long so beg you will give him all the dispatch in your power.

The master had his way, of course, but not without compromise. Presumably, James Habersham engaged in similar persuasion when he loaned his young cooper to the Bethesda Orphanage in order that he might "make Rice Barrels and teach two of [the] People in that Business." Habersham reported having "trouble enough to make him go there, for I do not chuse to make use of force and violence."[56]

When more permanent moves were afoot, a tradesman might be more assertive. In 1768, Henry Laurens purchased a cooper for the "extravagant" price of £650. He planned to ship him to East Florida, whereupon the artisan "declar'd he wou'd not go out of the Province." Laurens thought it expedient "to indulge this fellow for fear of Accidents, as one bought for Doctor Stork lately under the same declaration ran away and it cost me much trouble and expence to get him again and now I must endeavour to sell him to avoid a second Flight." Rawlins Lowndes was not even given the "choice" presented Laurens. When he purchased a slave bricklayer, the man promptly "absconded and secreted himself," his master plaintively noted, "without so much giving me an opportunity of speaking to him since he became my Property." A skilled slave might also be able to escape or at least postpone an impending sale. Trying to negotiate the purchase of a baker for a friend, Thomas Newton had eventually to report that the deal had fallen through, because the slave had

---

Century South" *WMQ*, 3d Ser., XXXI (1974), 198–199, 206–214; Ronald L. Lewis, *Coal, Iron, and Slaves: Industrial Slavery in Maryland and Virginia, 1715–1865* (Westport, Conn., 1979), 117, 199–127; Robert S. Starobin, *Industrial Slavery in the Old South* (New York, 1970), 101.

56. Richard Hutson to Isaac Hayne, Oct. 7, 1773, Hutson Papers; *Letters of Habersham*, GHS, *Colls.*, VI, 242.

"made the Matter up with his master (who is old and infirm and easily prevailed on) not to sell him." In Newton's account, a weak master was at the mercy of a strong-willed slave. He could only hope that it would "not be long before they wrangle again," because such a baker could not be found anywhere else in Virginia.[57]

Tradesmen engaged in battles not only over where they would work but even over the design and quality of their work. While out riding one day, Landon Carter took issue with the way a slave carpenter was fencing his garden. Dismounting, Carter "measured the ground off" to the slave in order to demonstrate the exact placement of the posts. When Carter returned from his ride two hours later, nothing further had been done; and when the irate master demanded of his slave the reason for the lack of progress, the answer was "because it would not answer his design." On another occasion, Carter complained of his inability at "making my Carpenters understand me." Carter had ordered some makeshift repairs to an old tobacco house; his carpenters, probably out of willfulness, but perhaps out of a sense of pride in their craft, saw fit to fashion new plates, posts, sills, and rafters. One of the carpenters had insisted that this be done and, as Carter noted, "spent a week more in doing it his way." The master was right on the mark when he remarked that "each rascal will be a director."[58]

Craftsmen also battled their masters by running away. Carpenters, the most itinerant woodworkers, were also the likeliest of their craft to run away. In both Virginia and South Carolina, the numbers of carpenters and coopers were roughly equal, but carpenters outnumbered coopers heavily among advertised runaways. Bristol, a skilled woodworker, exemplifies the association between itinerancy and flight. In July 1762, armed with "a monthly ticket" that permitted him to "work out," Bristol ran away from his master and evaded capture for about eighteen months. In that time, his owner calculated that he must have lost three hundred pounds to those people who had "harboured, entertained, and employed" his tradesman. In late 1763, Bristol either returned or was caught, but he fled almost immediately and remained at large at least another twelve months. Thirteen years later, now in his fifties, Bristol escaped yet again and, appropriately enough, was thought to be passing for "a free fellow." When craftsmen fled, they often took along the tools of their trade. One "very good shoemaker" carried away not only a full set of tools but some lasts and four pairs of recently made shoes. George, "a good cooper and tolerable good carpenter," took along his broadax, gimlets, and a pair of car-

---

57. *Laurens Papers,* V, 70; Rawlins Lowndes, *SCG and CJ,* Aug. 22, 1766; Thomas Newton to Robert Bolling, Dec. 20, 1771, Robert Bolling Papers, VHS.

58. Greene, ed., *Carter Diary,* 369, 568.

penter's compasses. These slave artisans no doubt aimed to earn their living by their trades and thereby pass as free.[59]

Learning to live with a capricious and truculent artisan was a trial, but masters were, of course, the final arbiters. Just as the master singled out a slave for training as a craftsman, so he could always reduce the artisan to his former condition. As the slave was made, so he could be unmade. And yet this ultimate deterrent was much less powerful in practice. Skilled slaves were just too valuable to discard wantonly. The loss of a youth's labor while he underwent a three-to-four-year apprenticeship argued strongly for making allowances to a mature artisan's whims. The lack of white tradesmen and the high costs of those who were available meant that there were few alternative sources of skilled labor. The degree to which skills were passed down within slave families also suggests how much the original choice of the master was later usurped, at least in part, by the slaves.[60]

Perhaps nothing epitomizes better the ambivalent relationship that most masters had to their skilled slaves than the capsule character sketch Henry Laurens compiled of his thirty-five-year-old slave Abraham. In ledgerlike fashion, Laurens listed both the slave's "good qualities" and "his bad ones." Among the good were woodworking, boating, whitewashing, plastering, and horsemanship skills, together with a healthy, strong constitution and a willingness to work hard to avoid "chastisement." Among the bad were his constant deceptions, pilfering, womanizing, ingratitude, disobedience "to any Man that uses him well and does not keep him close to work," and feigned illnesses. This balance sheet graphically portrays what most masters felt about their skilled slaves. The biography was written not for Laurens's edification alone; rather, it was intended to be useful to the person handling Abraham's sale. Significantly, however, Laurens changed his mind, and Abraham continued in his service.[61]

When a tradesman was offered for hire, a master's problems generally mounted. For one thing, the self-esteem natural to a tradesman was enhanced as he moved about, worked for a variety of whites, and saw how he was valued.

---

59. Samuel Lavington, *SCG*, Dec. 11, 1762; William Walter, ibid., Dec. 17, 1763, Dec. 24, 1764; John Allen Walter, *SC and AGG*, Apr. 10, 1776 (Bristol); Robert Gilchrist, *VaG and WA*, Nov. 22, 1783 (shoemaker); Josiah Foster, *VaG or AA*, Oct. 30, 1784 (George). In the inventories of 10 colonial Virginia counties, I found mention of 11 carpenters, 9 coopers, and 4 sawyers. Among advertised runaways between 1736 and 1779, there were 33 carpenters, 13 coopers, 14 sawyers, and 19 woodworkers with multiple skills. In South Carolina inventories between 1730 and 1799, there were 394 coopers and 359 carpenters, but among advertised runaways, 163 carpenters and 84 coopers.

60. Dependence on artisans is the subject of a letter from Colonel Theodorick Bland, Sr., to Theodorick Bland, Jr. (Apr. 28, [1794], Bland Papers, VHS).

61. *Laurens Papers*, IV, 299.

If artisans often took pride in their price tag—one runaway told his captor that he was "a cooper and sa[id] his master gave £700 for him"—this was even more the case with the hired artisan, who was repeatedly reminded of his monetary value. When Robert Carter was prepared to pay three times the hiring price of a common laborer for a slave bricklayer, because this was "a reasonable difference between him an artist, and a common field hand," it is difficult to imagine that the contrast escaped the bricklayer's notice. Or, again, when he offered to pay the same monthly hire, "the highest I pay," for a slave as for a white master bricklayer and stonemason, the slave was unlikely to remain oblivious of the compliment. The potential impact of such positive evaluations is captured in Landon Carter's denunciation of his slave bricklayer. According to Carter, this artisan was "more [lazy] as he works abroad, for the people treat him so much like a gentleman, that he can't fancy himself otherwise when he gets home."[62]

The considerable independence of the hired artisan is exemplified in the behavior of a carpenter named Billy, who worked on a periodic basis at the Sandy Island plantation in the Georgetown district of South Carolina in the late eighteenth century. Billy often failed to show up at Sandy Island, sometimes because of sickness or alleged sickness. At other times, he absented himself to attend to his affairs. One Friday evening, he went back to his mistress's plantation in order "to hoe his rice" and returned the following Monday morning. Weekend trips home were common. On one occasion, he left on a Saturday evening and did not return until 11 A.M. on Tuesday. Apart from long weekends, which could stretch from Saturday to Thursday, Billy occasionally visited Georgetown. He once went for three days to get some files. Billy guarded his privileges jealously. His employer noted: "Billy said New Year's day his Mistry allowed him as his day. I must pay him for that day's work which I did." He was also particular about working conditions. On one occasion, his employer observed, with more than a hint of acerbity, "Monday the 15th Janry it rained all day so Mrs Keiths Billey would not work."[63]

If the artisan hired his own time, he might be able to drive advantageous bargains and pocket additional income. One South Carolina mistress cautioned her neighbors not to engage her sawyer without her permission, because he "frequently hires himself out and defrauds me of his hire." In Eliz-

---

62. Workhouse, *SCG and CJ,* Mar. 7, 1769; Robert Carter to John Ballentine, July 7, 1777, Carter Letterbook, III, 138–139; Robert Carter to Griffin Garland, Sept. 29, 1775, ibid., 38; Greene, ed., *Carter Diary,* 754. Even children took pride in their prospective value (Eugene D. Genovese, *Roll, Jordan, Roll: The World the Slaves Made* [New York, 1974], 506).

63. Allard Belin Plantation Diary, May 2, 15–17, 26, Nov. 19–21, 1792; Feb. 24, Mar. 4–8, 11, May 26, June 5–6, 12–13, July 1–4, 14–17, 29, Aug. 2, 5–8, 19, Oct. 9, 28, Nov. 1, Dec. 22–29, 1797; Jan. 15, Feb. 4, Mar. 8, 19–20, 31, Apr. 9, May 25–28, June 9, July 8, 27, Aug. 4–9, Sept. 3–4, 15–19, Oct. 5, 8, 18, 19–20, 21, Nov. 5, 19, 1798, SCHS.

abeth City County, Virginia, a slave shoemaker named Hampton hired out his time and submitted accounts to his customers similar to those of free craftworkers. He received sums far in excess of those usually paid hired slaves in estate settlements. Artisans did not necessarily earn extra money simply by plying their trade. One Virginia carpenter would "at the time of cutting grain . . . be in the field and not at his bench, for he was extremely fond of that business and generally gets from 6 to 8 shillings per day by it."[64]

Skilled town slaves were able to earn quite large sums through "self-hiring," a widespread urban phenomenon. As early as 1712, South Carolina's legislators attempted unsuccessfully to halt the practice whereby urban slaves "do what and go whither they will, and work where they please," on condition that they bring in an agreed sum of money. As befits its much less precocious urban development, the Chesapeake region did not see attempts to prohibit slaves from "hiring their own time" until the late eighteenth century. In 1782, residents in and nearby the rapidly growing town of Richmond complained that those slaves who hired "themselves" led "Idle and disorderly" lives. Access to money explains why some self-hired slaves could purchase themselves for staggeringly large sums. In Charleston in 1770, Leander purchased himself for nine hundred pounds. His white intermediary observed how this amount "was delivered to [him] by . . . Leander from time to time as Monies which he had by his great care dilligence and industry in his business Trade or Occupation of a Butcher for several years last past got together and Earned." The latitude enjoyed by self-hired slaves posed problems for masters. Consider the consternation of a Savannah resident whose slave woman hired out her time in Charleston; she had "been so long her own Mistress" that she would return only "with great reluctance." Or consider the embarrassment of Thomas Sacheverelle, who allowed his slave bricklayer Thom to hire out his time. Customers had extended credit to Thom for articles he had purchased; to "free himself from such debts," the slave had defrauded his master of "a good deal of money." Another Charlestonian decided to sell his skilled slave because he was "obliged to hire him out, and the fellow having the handling of so much money, has of late been several times in liquor."[65]

64. Catherine Finlay, *SCG*, Apr. 14, 1759 (see also Executors of Mr. Baker's estate, ibid., Sept. 3, 1737); Sarah Shaver Hughes, "Elizabeth City County, Virginia, 1782–1810: The Economic and Social Structure of a Tidewater County in the Early National Years" (Ph.D. diss., College of William and Mary, 1975), 239; and see also Hughes, "Slaves for Hire: The Allocation of Black Labor in Elizabeth City County, Virginia, 1782 to 1810," *WMQ*, 3d Ser., XXXV (1978), 260–286; L. A. Pauly, *Va Ind Chron*, May 7, 1788.

65. Douglas Egerton, *Gabriel's Rebellion: The Virginia Slave Conspiracies of 1800 and 1802* (Chapel Hill, N.C., 1993), 26; Cooper and McCord, eds., *Statutes at Large*, VII, 352–365; Henrico County Legislative Petitions, June 8, 1782, VSL; Jacob Willeman's deed of manumis-

Artisans were accomplished, privileged slaves, only too willing and able to assert their independence, but they also comprised a large percentage of all those runaways who were said to stutter, stammer, or have uncontrollable hand or facial movements. These traits have been interpreted variously: either as evidence of inner personal turmoil or as an attempt to convey emotions of anger and resentment too intense to be articulated easily. Eugene Genovese has suggested that stammering lends support to "theories that associate stuttering with a sense of isolation, with fathers vague or distant, with domineering mothers, and with an inability to cope with authority." However, perhaps the sense of isolation peculiarly characteristic of artisans can serve as a more persuasive explanation of stammering than a more ubiquitous one that stresses the absence of father-figures.[66]

The artisan was suspended between the two worlds of master and slave. Brought into regular and recurrent contact with the world of masters, the artisan was yet not part of it. Though a slave, he was denied the compensating, close companionship of his peers. Most artisans had to live with the contradiction of a measure of freedom and a heightened awareness of the constraints of being black. This confusion expressed itself in halting speech. This contradiction best explains the paradox of the plantation artisan—resourceful when on his own, often experiencing difficulties when answering whites.

CONSTANT COMPANIONS

Yet other privileged slaves were brought into an almost uninterrupted working relationship with whites. Although patriarchs considered all their slaves as part of their "family," those who lived and worked in the same house as their owner became family in a more meaningful sense. Eugene Genovese has characterized the atmosphere of the nineteenth-century Big House as a battlefield. "If closeness bred affection and warmth," he argues, "it also bred hatred and violence; often it bred all at once, according to circumstances, moods and momentary passions."[67] Most eighteenth-century slaves, even

---

sion to Leander, Oct. 11, 1770, Miscellaneous Records, OO, 385–386 (see also George Flagg's deed of manumission to Friday, July 21, 1773, ibid., PP, 568–569; Alexander Hewat's deed of manumission to Diana, Apr. 16, 1777, ibid., SS, 49–50); "Letters of Joseph Clay, Merchant of Savannah, 1776–1793 . . . ," GHS, *Colls.*, VIII (1913), 212; Thomas Sachaverelle, *SCG*, Oct. 6, 1759; Bartholomew Carroll, *City Gaz*, June 24, 1800. See also Francis Robertson, *SC State Gaz*, Mar. 2, 1798; *Laurens Papers*, IX, 414; and Morgan, "Black Life in Charleston," *Perspectives in Am. Hist.*, N.S., I (1984), 187–232, esp. 191–194.

66. Genovese, *Roll, Jordan, Roll*, 646–647. See also Gerald W. Mullin, *Flight and Rebellion: Slave Resistance in Eighteenth-Century Virginia* (New York, 1972), 80–81, 98–103; and Kenneth M. Stampp, *The Peculiar Institution: Slavery in the Ante-Bellum South* (New York, 1956), 381.

67. Genovese, *Roll, Jordan, Roll*, 361.

PLATE 18. Alic, a Faithful and Humerous Old Servant. *Benjamin Henry Latrobe. Perhaps wearing cast-offs, the favored manservant. Courtesy Maryland Historical Society*

household workers, never saw the inside of a Big House. They saw more of the garden, the kitchen, or the stable. Yet, a few personal servants belonging to the richest planters anticipated the experience of nineteenth-century domestics.

The intimacy of household service had advantages. Masters cared for their personal servants in ways that transcended anything they might have felt for their other slaves. Robert Carter refused to visit a fellow Baptist during cold weather because he did not want to endanger the health of his waiting man. House slaves were frequent recipients of their masters' cast-offs. A new suit of clothes went to Shrews-Berry, a waiting man serving South Carolinian

John Laurens at Valley Forge. Addressing Shrews-Berry in remarkably intimate terms, John's father inquired of his "old friend" whether a sturdy linen coat, waistcoat, and breeches would "be acceptable"; if so, the slave would receive the requisite cloth and should then "consult his Taylor." The arrangement seems more suited to a lord and his butler in a metropolitan setting. In his letters to his niece, John Randolph sent regards to his old house slave, Mammy Aggy, and answered her inquiries about her kinfolk. Of body servant John, Randolph wrote, "I have not a truer friend."[68]

But the same intimacy that produced occasional favors also led to greater cruelty, both mental and physical. Unlike crop hands, domestics could not find protection in numbers and anonymity. Unlike the work of artisans, watermen, or drivers, their performance was subject to unrelenting scrutiny. A household slave's privacy was easily invaded. William Byrd II whipped a husband for beating his wife, a woman for being a man's "whore," and another woman for allowing a man to lie on her bed. Sadistic masters could readily vent their furies on household servants. William Byrd's wife wrestled with a young slave girl and was adept with a branding iron. A visitor to the Mason household saw whippings "for every little offence most cruelly." In South Carolina households, according to John Davis, slaves were "execrated for every involuntary offence." Such an atmosphere caused emotional disturbances, as is indicated by the behavior of Byrd's slave Eugene, who was whipped "for pissing in bed." Eugene's further punishment—being made "to drink a pint of piss"—is also an indication of how easily master-slave relations assumed a warped, inhuman cast in a domestic setting.[69]

Masters complained of myriad petty provocations from their domestics. Philip Ludwell's evening was spoiled when he encountered his waiting man Sawney in dirty clothes, "a pipe in his mouth, and fast asleep." Wakened and threatened with punishment, Sawney responded in a "very provoking" fashion, leading Ludwell to ponder the ingratitude of a slave who received "ten pds a year." All the more annoying were recollections of Sawney's taking meat from the dishes he served and drinking liquor behind his master's back. Anaka,

68. Robert Carter to Elder William Hazard, Jan. 3, 1783, Carter Letterbook, V, 89; *Laurens Papers*, XIII, 365, 388; Greene, ed., *Carter Diary*, 751; Robert Dawidoff, *The Education of John Randolph* (New York, 1979), 52–53. For consideration toward personal servants, see Pierce Butler to Roger P. Saunders, Sept. 6, 1790, Pierce Butler Letterbook, 1790–1794, USC; and Robert Raper to John Colleton, July 8, 1763, Raper Letterbook.

69. Louis B. Wright and Marion Tinling, eds., *The Secret Diary of William Byrd of Westover, 1709–1712* (Richmond, Va., 1941), 15, 22, 38, 46, 53, 84, 113, 117, 119, 205, 224, 290, 307, 412, 419, 494, 564; Martha von Briesen, ed., *The Letters of Elijah Fletcher* (Charlottesville, Va., 1965), 14 (see also 25–26); Davis, *Travels*, 100. For violence in the household, see Robert Carter to Messrs. Scott, Pringle, Cheap and Co., Apr. 29, 1767, Carter Letterbook, II, 41–42.

William Byrd's servant, not only drank Byrd's wine but replaced it with water. George Washington estimated that his servants stole two glasses of wine to every one he consumed. Venus did "everything in her power to provoke" her master to remove her from the household and send her to an outlying quarter, and eventually won her wish. Other house slaves used no more than a harsh tongue and some privileged information in their campaigns against masters, but perhaps they were no less effective for that. One house slave, for instance, was heard to "say that his Mistress, Mrs Motley, was the Greatest Drunkard in the Country and that if the Sea was Brandy she would Drink it up."[70]

No slave knew his or her master better than a personal attendant; consequently, no slave possessed greater opportunities to exploit this knowledge. Landon Carter's personal body servant was a slave named Nassau. Nassau was Carter's constant companion, his alter ego, almost part of his identity. Virtually a surrogate master, Nassau inspected crops, counted and branded livestock, and administered the occasional whipping, but, primarily, he acted as the plantation's chief medical aide both to slaves and to lower-class whites. Carter and Nassau shared a great deal. The master came to know that his slave fervently disliked snakes; the two of them discussed and often disagreed on medical diagnoses; one Sunday found the two of them walking about the home fields exchanging observations on the quality of the tobacco. Carter obviously valued his assistant's judgment, recording faithfully, "Dr Nassau says he has seen much tobacco, and never saw any stand better."[71]

If Nassau's responsibilities were great, so were his frailties. He was, in fact, a chronic alcoholic. On one occasion, Nassau had "not been sensibly sober one evening since this day fortnight." On another, he crawled about the room at night, not knowing "a chamber pot from a bottle of water." Carter did not just threaten Nassau; he "begged him, Prayed him, and told him the consequences if he neglected the care of one of the sick people." Their conversations even led Carter to examine his own conduct. "I confess I have faults myself to be forgiven," he acknowledged, "but to be every day and hour committing them, and to seek the modes of committing them [that is, searching out liquor] admits of no Plea of frailty." And yet Nassau continued to drink "in spight" of Carter, even as the master dimly understood, "in order to spight him."[72]

The battle between sober patriarch and drunken body servant was a long-

70. Philip Ludwell to H. Corbin, Dec. 22, 17[??], Peckatone Papers, VHS; Wright and Tinling, ed., *Secret Diary*, 42; Conway, ed., *George Washington and Mount Vernon*, 35–36; Thomas Jones to Elizabeth Jones, July 22, 1728, Roger Jones Family Papers, LC; deposition of Reuben Pain, May 9, 1787, Executive Papers. For a more serious domestic misfortune, see Samuel Fothergill to his wife, Feb. 13, 1755, Crosfield MSS, Friends House, London.

71. Greene, ed., *Carter Diary*, 583, 628, 651, 665, 793, 1036.

72. Ibid., 778, 940, 953.

running saga, bordering on farce. In 1768, Carter put Nassau up for sale because he could no longer be "trusted" and after efforts to cure him of his drunkenness through "persuasion" had obviously failed. Not for the last time, Carter relented, and Nassau continued in his employ. But the bouts of drunkenness persisted—as did the master's vacillations. Two years later, Carter engaged in one of many self-deceptions: "I have been learning to do without [Nassau]," he noted, "though it has been but very badly yet I can bear it and will." In 1773, he vowed never to pass over another instance of Nassau's drunkenness. Two years later, the most dramatic scene occurred. In sheer frustration at finding Nassau "dead drunk," the sixty-five-year-old patriarch "offered to give him a box on the ear." Nassau "fairly forced himself against" his master, who managed to tumble him into the cellar and tie him up. After Nassau "called on God to record his solemn Vow that he never more would touch Liquor," Carter forgave him. Almost exchanging blows one minute, appealing to God in forgiveness the next—such were the demands of the master–body servant relationship. No reformation was wrought, of course. Nassau continued to drink, and Carter, though bitter at his servant's "forfeit[ing] his solemn Promise before heaven," could still not bear to part with him. A few months before Carter's death in 1778, Nassau was his usual contrary self: one day reassuring his master that the heavy rains would not ruin the corn and turnips, the next getting so drunk as "to contradict boldly every time" Carter spoke. Only death would part Carter and Nassau.[73]

Henry Laurens's body servant was a slave named Scipio. Before the fall of 1771, when Scipio accompanied Laurens to England, he is a shadowy figure, glimpsed traveling back and forth between Laurens's various plantations and Charleston, taking messages, delivering essential supplies, and the like. Little personal information is available. Once in England, he comes into clearer focus. Apparently, on his initiative, he changed his name to Robert Scipio Laurens. He and Laurens's son James shared the experience of being inoculated against smallpox; he traveled about England on his own, delivering essential messages; he "rambl[ed] . . . in the fields" with the master's children; he accompanied young James on his holidays; he saw to callers while Laurens wrote letters home. He was, in short, a valued member of the household. "No stranger," Laurens observed, "can serve me as acceptably as [Robert] can." Sharing so much time together, Laurens came to know Robert's personal

---

73. Landon Carter, *VaG* (Rind), Mar. 3, 1768, as cited in Mullin, *Flight and Rebellion*, 78; Greene, ed., *Carter Diary*, 492, 778, 941, 953, 1145. Nassau ran away at least twice in 1777 (ibid., 1128; and Outlawry concerning Nassaw, Oct. 19, 1777, Carter Family Papers, microfilm, UVa) and also on August 16, 1778, the last time Carter mentions him in his diary, but Nassau either returned or was captured, for he is listed in Carter's inventory of estate.

habits, even his "grunt[ing] according to his way," as he moved about the kitchen.[74]

But this relationship did not always run smoothly. For every time Robert "behav[ed] well," he committed a misdemeanor. Much like Landon Carter, Laurens claimed to "have been particularly Indulgent by exempting him from punishment for Capital faults, from a Consideration of Instances of past Merits admitted, and the security of his own promises of amendment." Laurens brought Scipio "to England in consequence of his *own* Intreaties, founded upon his *own* apprehensions that he Should not be So well used if I left him behind me, and ten Thousand promises of attachment and good behaviour." Much like Nassau, Robert's frailties continued to unfold. The denouement came when Robert stole some bacon, which, as Laurens pointed out, "a Negro counts a Crime, to be Cancelled by a flogging." Unfortunately, the burglary occurred in England, not South Carolina. Liable to be hanged or transported to the West Indies, "foolish and Rascally" Robert's life seemed set fair to end "in deep Tragedy." Laurens's last words on Robert reflect his disillusionment: "He is a sad Rascal, unprincipled, ungrateful, and never will be better."[75]

To be in an uninterrupted working relationship with whites brought with it special privileges and unusual pressures. Personal slaves often drank, ate, even slept with whites. The psychic toll that this intimacy exerted—manifest in the master's carping criticisms, casual violence, and intrusiveness, the warped and tragicomic relationships of the Byrd and Carter households, Nassau's drunkenness, and Scipio's sad end—was enormous. The servant's confident and articulate exterior often masked excruciating pain and stress. A seemingly straightforward economic transaction was nothing of the kind.

TRADE

It may seem farfetched to conceive of trade as an essential basis for encounter between blacks and whites. How could a population that was enslaved, landless, legally propertyless, and largely powerless exchange anything? Yet, as Orlando Patterson has pointed out, "in all slaveholding societies the slave was allowed a *peculium*," which "may be defined as the investment by the master of a partial, and temporary, capacity in his slave to possess and enjoy a given range of goods." Moreover, as Patterson also notes, slaves were "frequently allowed to trade and engage in business," using their possessions.[76]

Masters permitted slaves to produce and exchange goods because it served

---

74. *Laurens Papers*, IV, 632–633, 664–665, VI, 181–182, VII, 219, 228, VIII, 1, 4, 16, 26–27, 47, 156, 286, 335, 342–343, 639.

75. Ibid., VIII, 227, 232, 658, IX, 316–318, 347.

76. Orlando Patterson, *Slavery and Social Death: A Comparative Study* (Cambridge, Mass., 1982), 182.

their own interests to do so. To have slaves produce part of their provisions helped ensure that they avoided hunger. Trading within the "family" allowed the master to display his benevolence, to make the system a little more humane for his slaves. Last, but not least, trading made economic sense. Provision grounds, noted one Lowcountry resident, meant that "the expence the master is at in supporting his negroes is but very small." The master probably bought his slaves' products below market price, and the slaves at least gained access to some cash or small luxury items. As the German missionary Johann Bolzius noted, Lowcountry slaves turned "their crops into money." Landon Carter touched on most of these motives when reflecting on what to do with his salted pork:

> I think I now see a good way of selling it, and Perhaps at a greater Price than others have got for theirs. My Poor Slaves raise fowls, and eggs in order to exchange with their Master now and then; and, though I don't value the worth of what they bring, Yet I enjoy the humanity of refreshing such poor creatures in what they (though perhaps mistakenly) call a blessing. Indeed, I hope this is a good way of selling what I may have to spare out of my own sumptuous fare, and not to injure the small profits which I am content with.[77]

Altruism and disdain for money vied with profit making and neighborly competition.

As Carter indicates, Chesapeake slaves commonly raised poultry for exchange. Isaac Weld, who traveled through Virginia in 1796, commented that the slaves' "flocks of poultry [were] numerous." A few years later, William Tatham observed that "there are very few [slaves] indeed who are denied the privilege of keeping dunghill fowls, ducks, geese, and turkies." Chesapeake slaves not only raised chickens extensively but also dominated the poultry trade. In 1779, James Mercer ordered his steward to hold in reserve at least a half of his bacon to have some bartering power with the "Negroes who are the general Chicken Merchants." Two years later, when the agent provisioning the French ships of war searched for fresh meat, he had to purchase fowl from slaves. Such was the monopoly of blacks that a contributor to the *Virginia Gazette* urged planters to break their stranglehold. "Why is a fowl more disgraceful in the sale of it at market," he asked, "than a pig, a lamb, a mutton, a veal, a cow or an ox?"[78]

77. E. Merton Coulter, ed., *The Journal of Peter Gordon, 1732–1735* (Athens, Ga., 1963), 58; George Fenwick Jones, "John Martin Boltzius' Trip to Charleston, October 1742," *SCHM*, LXXXII (1981), 104; Greene, ed., *Carter Diary*, 1095.

78. Isaac Weld, Jr., *Travels through the States of North America . . .* , I (London, 1799), 148;

Although part-time production by Chesapeake slaves centered on poultry raising, their industry manifested itself in other ways. In fact, the only product denied them was tobacco. But not until 1798 was the practice of cultivating tobacco "as the peculiam of the negroes" stopped on Thomas Jefferson's estate. Jefferson stated the obvious reason: "There is no other way of drawing a line between what is theirs and mine." The rest of the Chesapeake's repertoire of diversified agriculture was available to slaves. A traveler to Mount Vernon observed not only the slaves' chickens but also their vegetable plots. Slaves sold their garden crops. In fact, when George Washington had his workers planting sweet potatoes, he ran short and had to purchase some from the slaves of a neighbor and from his own "old Negroe fellow Jupiter." On occasion, John Mercer bought between one and four bushels of peas, potatoes, and corn from three of his slave men. Robert Carter directed that two bushels of peas and three bushels of "Irish Potatoes" be purchased from his slaves. Baroness Von Riedesel, stationed near Charlottesville during the Revolutionary war, noted how slaves brought them "everything they had in the way of poultry and vegetables." Tom Gumby offered eggs, apples, potatoes, and watermelon to the tutor Philip Fithian in exchange for listing his children. Accounts of a Jesuit estate in Saint Mary's County, Maryland, in the early nineteenth century show cash payments to slaves for garden produce and oysters. According to the manager, slaves earned from eighty to one hundred dollars a year in this way. In general, Virginia masters, William Tatham observed, allowed their slaves "the privilege of cultivating cotton, melons, potatoes, vegetables, flax, hops, fruits, etc."[79]

William Tatham, *Communications concerning the Agriculture and Commerce of the United States of America* . . . (London, 1800), 54–55; James Mercer to B. Muse, Apr. 8, Jan. 9, 1779, Muse Papers; deposition respecting Capt. Libly, Nov. 6, 1781, John Page Papers, microfilm, CW; *VaG*, Mar. 29, 1770, as cited in Mullin, *Flight and Rebellion*, 61. For more on poultry raising, see Greene, ed., *Carter Diary*, 602; Col. Francis Taylor Diary, Aug. 15, 1787, VSL; Julien Ursyn Niemcewicz, *Under Their Vine and Fig Tree: Travels through America in 1797–1799* . . . , trans. and ed. Metchie J. E. Budka, New Jersey Historical Society, Collections, XIV (Elizabeth, N.J., 1965), 101; Carter Daybook, Dec. 20, 1773, XIII, 15–16; Burwell Papers, 1749–1750, 43, 45, CW.

79. Thomas Jefferson to Thomas Mann Randolph, June 14, 1798, Thomas Jefferson Papers, as cited in Barden, "'Flushed with Notions of Freedom,'" 190; Robert Carter to William Brickey, Jan. 6, 1779, Carter Letterbook, III, pt. iii, 86; Farish, ed., *Journal and Letters of Philip Vickers Fithian*, 184–185, 199, 206; Niemcewicz, *Under Their Vine and Fig Tree*, 100; Donald Jackson and Dorothy Twohig, eds., *The Diaries of George Washington*, 6 vols. (Charlottesville, Va., 1976–1979), V, 145; John Mercer Ledger Book B, "Negro Accounts," microfilm, CW; Marvin L. Brown, Jr., ed., *Baroness von Riedesel and the American Revolution* . . . (Chapel Hill, N.C., 1965), 82; Bayly Ellen Marks, "Economics and Society in a Staple Plantation System: St. Mary's County, Maryland, 1790–1840" (Ph.D. diss., University of

In addition to garden crops, Chesapeake slaves supplied their masters with fish, oysters, baskets, mats, bowls, trays, sieves, rails, leather, and staves. When one of the owners of the Dismal Swamp Land Company demanded some boards, the manager reported that the only ones ever available were "what the Negroes get in their own time on Sundays and Nights." He then communicated the slaves' stipulations as to size and price. One planter recorded annual payments of between one and five pounds to a number of his slaves for their supply of shells (probably oyster shells). At between two shillings and three shillings, six pence per hogshead, these slaves must have been kept busy to earn these sums. As Virginia plantations diversified into domestic cloth manufacture in the late eighteenth century, the region's slaves saw a new opportunity. In 1775, William Cabell provided hats to those of his slaves who supplied him between two and three pounds of picked cotton; two years later, Edmund Wilcox paid a slave fifteen shillings for five pounds of picked cotton and another ten shillings for "breaking and swingeling flax"; and, in 1779, Charles Dabney bought 26½ pounds of cotton from his slave Bob. The part-time production of Chesapeake slaves mirrored the diversified economic activities of Chesapeake plantations.[80]

The most common of exchanges in the Lowcountry, as in the Chesapeake, consisted of provisions, fish, poultry, and small livestock. In 1728, Elias Ball paid his slave Abraham one pound, fifteen shillings for eighteen fowl (Abraham added one free of charge). In the same year, this master paid two pounds to Maree for a hog and, seven years later, seven pounds to Johny for two hogs. In the 1760s, Henry Ravenel frequently purchased corn, fowl, hogs, and catfish from his slaves. During this decade, he recorded more than a hundred transactions with about twenty-five individuals. On June 23, 1780, Philip Porcher drew

---

Maryland, 1979), 161; G. Melvin Herndon, *William Tatham and the Culture of Tobacco* (Coral Gables, Fla., 1969), 104–105. See also Davis, *Travels,* 423.

80. Robert W. Carter Diaries, Dec. 29, 1765 (apples), May 1, 1768 (sieves), typescript, CW; Edmund Wilcox's miscellaneous accounts, VI, 1761–1764 (ducks, chickens, shells), and miscellaneous cash expenditures and receipts, XI, 1770–1778 (chickens, fish, picked cotton, breaking flax), Hubbard Papers, CW; William Ennals Memo Book, Sept. 27, 1771, Apr. 23, July 19, Aug. 1, 28, Sept. 22, Oct. 11, 1773, Jan. 15, Mar. 5, Apr. 19, 1774 (fowl, turkeys, chickens, mats, tray, bowl, eggs, oysters), LC; James Parker's "Virginia Almanack," 1771, 920 PAR I/6 (tanned leather and staves), Parker Family Papers, Liverpool City Libraries, England; diary of William Cabell, Sr., Jan. 22, Feb. 12, 1775 (cotton), VSL; Charles Dabney Commonplace Book, Jan. 8, 1779 (cotton), Dabney Family Papers, VHS; Thomas Jones Farm Books, April 1786 (baskets), MS 517, MHS (courtesy of Lorena Walsh); John Driver to David Jameson, May 2, 1790 (boards), Dismal Swamp Land Company Papers, Duke; estate of John Smelt, Oct. 28, 1790, Deeds and Wills, Book 34 (rails), cited by Hughes, "Elizabeth City County, Virginia, 1782–1810," 239. See also Michael Mullin, *Africa in America: Slave Acculturation and Resistance in the American South and the British Caribbean, 1736–1831* (Urbana, Ill., 1992), 139.

up his tally with his slaves. He had bought more than seventy chickens from seven women and six men.[81]

Nor were exchanges between Lowcountry masters and slaves confined to standard provision goods. Henry Ravenel paid five pounds for a canoe made by his slave Pearoe; Lucretia sold him a basket; two slaves brought him honey; Hector supplied rails and Somerton myrtle wax. The provision of myrtle wax and baskets also appears in other Lowcountry plantation accounts. In 1778, the Lowcountry partnership of Torrans and Rose paid thirty pounds to a slave for a breeding sow and nine pounds to four slaves for a pair of ducks and scantling for a fowl house. When a Lowcountry planter transferred his slaves from one plantation to another, he informed the recipient that the slaves "have with them some flax of their own to dispose of, so I hope you may purchase it of them." In Goose Creek, South Carolina, in the late eighteenth century, a traveler saw slaves collecting Spanish moss. Masters apparently allowed their slaves to sell it "to the upholsterers of Charleston who stuff with it mattresses and chairs."[82]

Yet master-slave exchanges in the Lowcountry differed from those in the Chesapeake in two major ways. First, because rice was both a provision and a staple, Lowcountry slaves were permitted to grow the primary crop of their region. Unlike slaves in the British West Indies and the Chesapeake, who were prohibited from growing their respective staples, slaves in the Lowcountry grew rice. This concession was not always manifest in the colony's legislation. Indeed, in 1714, the legislature went so far as to prohibit slaves from planting "for themselves any corn, peas or rice." Although this stark ban appears definitive, later legislation suggests its ineffectiveness—so much so that, by 1751, legislators bowed to the inevitable. By outlawing the sale of slaves' rice and corn to anybody other than their masters, they implicitly recognized the right of slaves to cultivate such crops.[83]

Whatever the law, Lowcountry planters always accepted the slaves' right to grow rice on their own time. In 1733, Elias Ball stored more than 20 bushels of rice belonging to four of his slaves. Three years later, he paid £57 to twenty-two

---

81. Ball Account Book, Jan. 26, Apr. 7, 1728, February 1735, fols. 74–75, 97, SCHS; Henry Ravenel Day Book, 1748–1777, SCHS; Philip Porcher Account Book, June 23, 1780, USC.

82. Ravenel Day Book, June 26, 1765 (canoe), Feb. 15, 1766 (basket), October 1766 and November 1769 (honey), Jan. 24, 1767 (rails), Dec. 11, 1769 (mirtle wax); Account Book, New Distillery, Dec. 18, 1778, January 1779, Maurice Family Papers, UNC; George Lucas to Charles Pinckney, Jan. 30, 1746, Pinckney Family Papers, LC; François Alexandre Frédéric, duke de La Rochefoucault Liancourt, *Travels through the United States of North America . . .* (London, 1799), I, 593. See also Bethesda Orphanage Accounts, June 4, 1776, A 2/3, no. 5, Countess of Huntingdon's American Papers.

83. Cooper and McCord, eds., *Statutes at Large,* II, 22–23, III, 398, 489, VII, 11, 368, 423.

slaves for 152 bushels of their rice. In 1744, he even marketed their rice, for he recorded the sale of "6 bbs of Negro Rice." In the investigation of a slave conspiracy in South Carolina in 1749, Ammon declared that he planted rice "himself in his own time and by his Masters allowance and leave," which his master acknowledged to be true. A decade later, the administrators of Dr. David Caw's estate paid £5 to a neighbor's slaves for their seed rice. In 1769, Henry Laurens paid £158 to his Wambaw slaves for "their Rice," and four years later he sent cloth, handkerchiefs, felt hats, and threads, worth more than £40, to his Wright Savanna slaves for "Rice and Corn of their own which they sold to the Overseers." Just after the Revolutionary war, John Ball borrowed 20 bushels of seed rice from one slave and 6 bushels from another, for which he promised to pay twenty shillings per bushel. At the end of the eighteenth century, William Grimes, a newcomer to the Lowcountry, recalled raising for himself "a small crop" of rice. He estimated the ground at twenty rods' length—about a hundred yards. At his first try, and following the example of other slaves, he made enough rice to sell it in Savannah for five or six dollars.[84]

A second difference concerns the scale of these transactions in provisions. The accounts of a number of Lowcountry estates record sizable payments to slaves for their produce. Around midcentury, the administrators of James Hartley's estate made three separate purchases from slaves: in 1758, they paid £71 for 191 bushels of corn, in the following year, £10 for 13 bushels, and in the next year, £43 for 86 bushels. At about the same time, the managers of Dr. Caw's estate settled payments of £27 for "corn, Fowles and Rice [the Doctor] had from [his slaves] himself," another £9 for rice the slaves had "delivd their Masters before his Death," and £30 after his death for corn they had purchased. In 1778, another Lowcountry estate paid £132 for 64 bushels of corn purchased from eight slaves. Eight years later, the Gibbons estate in Georgia recorded a purchase of 31 bushels of corn from the slaves of a neighboring plantation. In 1806, an overseer on a Georgia estate paid a hundred dollars to some slaves for their corn; once the cash had been distributed and trust established, others approached him offering their corn for sale.[85]

---

84. Ball Account Book, October 1733, fol. 187, Jan. 21, 1736, fol. 170, November 1744, fol. 168; South Carolina Council Journal, no. 17, part 1, 160; administration of David Caw's estate, Dec. 25, 1760, Inventories, WPA, LXXXVIIA, SCDAH; account book of Henry Laurens, March 1769, March 1773, fols. 217, 508, CC; Account Book, April 1783, John Ball, Jr., Papers, Duke; William Grimes, *Life of William Grimes, the Runaway Slave, Brought down to the Present Time* (New Haven, Conn., 1855), 46.

85. Administration of James Hartley's estate, Aug. 31, 1758, Mar. 30, 1759, July 7, 1760, Inventories, WPA, LXXXVIIA; administration of Caw's estate, Apr. 10, July 12, 1759, Feb. 3, 1761; Maurice Family Papers, November and December 1778; corn bought of Zuberbuler's Negroes, 1786, William Gibbons, Jr., Papers, Duke; Peter Massie to James Hamilton, May 11,

Payments to Lowcountry slaves at least reflected approximate market demand. The fluctuating prices fetched by the slaves' corn, ranging from seven shillings to more than two pounds a bushel, indicate that bondpeople were not placed beyond the pale of this market economy. Bargaining, however asymmetrical, was open to them. Henry Laurens advised one of his overseers, "Purchase of your own Negroes all that you know Lawfully belongs to themselves at the lowest price that *they will sell it for.*" On another occasion, Laurens dispatched "sundry articles sent to be dispos'd among the Negroes for their Rice at the prices mark'd to each article." Slaves were apparently keen, discriminating traders, because Laurens registered his hope that the slaves would accept these "without too much fuss and trouble that I may not be discouraged from being their Factor another year." He added that at seven shillings, six pence per bushel, he was paying "full value."[86]

Although masters in both Chesapeake and Lowcountry often bartered with their slaves, more often than not they paid cash for their slaves' produce. Even when a master offered items of clothing to his slaves, he generally specified their cash value. Thus, in 1782, James Mercer of Virginia offered linen at two shillings, six pence the yard to "pay the Negroes some debt I am said to owe them for Chickens." Henry Laurens followed the same practice, but his slaves also received money. If not, how could he have expected his country slaves to pay their own ferriages when making jaunts to Charleston? The records of Chesapeake planters list frequent cash payments to slaves for their poultry: in 1762, Nimcock belonging to Dr. Edmund Wilcox earned seven shillings, six pence for his twelve ducks; and three years later, Robert Wormeley Carter paid his slave Peg two shillings, six pence for six chickens. In some cases, planters made small cash advances to guarantee supply. In 1771, William Ennals of the Eastern Shore of Maryland paid his slave Nero fifteen shillings for fowl already received and another five for the prospect of turkeys. In 1783, Richard Henry Lee paid one of his slaves two shillings more than he owed him in order that he might have two dozen partridges or four pullets.[87]

Exchanging provisions or other products with masters did not exhaust the slaves' opportunities to earn money. Small sums came their way in exchange for the performance of a variety of small services: from ferrying people across a

---

1806, James Hamilton Papers, University of Georgia, cited in Joyce E. Chaplin, *An Anxious Pursuit: Agricultural Innovation and Modernity in the Lower South, 1730–1815* (Chapel Hill, N.C., 1993), 126–127.

86. *Laurens Papers*, IV, 616, V, 41 (my emphasis). See also ibid., V, 29, 61, 93.

87. James Mercer to B. Muse, Jan. 6, 1782, Muse Papers; *Laurens Papers*, IV, 657; Edmund Wilcox's miscellaneous accounts, VI, June 23, 1762; Robert W. Carter Diaries, May 14, 1765, July 16, 1768; William Ennals Memo Book, Sept. 27, 1771; Richard Henry Lee Memo Book, Dec. 21, 1783, CW. See also Ravenel Day Book, May 1764, January 1768.

river to directing a lost traveler, from putting out fires to refloating grounded boats, from killing a wolf to finding a lost horse, from saving on expenses to turning in a runaway, from transporting a desk to sweeping a church. The opportunity presented slaves living near a regular fording point is suggested by one traveler who had just crossed the James River in a Negro "scow." He contrasted his good fortune to that of "two men, who had been waiting a considerable time to get across but had not interest sufficient to prevail with the Negroes."[88]

Some slaves had more chance to earn money than others. Household servants probably had the greatest access to cash. When gentlefolk visited, they often offered gratuities to their host's domestics. One Charleston master claimed that one of his servants had purchased her freedom "with money of his own, as he had more than once been pilford of his money while she was about the house." Robert W. Carter, Landon's wayward son, even borrowed money from his household slaves. Artisans put their talents to their own use. Robert Carter believed that his carpenters "surely must depend on a great deal of their Time in making Pails and Piggins and churns for Merchandizing." He also learned that his "smith does a great many jobs for neighbours." In Georgetown, South Carolina, according to one witness, slaves made "mats, brooms, piggins and pails for sale."[89]

---

88. Frederick E. Maser and Howard T. Maag, eds., *The Journal of Joseph Pilmore, Methodist Itinerant: For the Years August 1, 1769 to January 2, 1774* (Philadelphia, 1969), 191; Elkanah Watson, *Men and Times of the Revolution,* ed. Winslow C. Watson (New York, 1856), 39 (helping travelers); Charles Pinckney Account Book, July 21, 1753, LC; "Narrative of George Fisher, Commencing with a Voyage from London, May, 1750, for Yorktown in Virginia and Ending in August, 1755, on His Return from Philadelphia to Williamsburg," WMQ, 1st Ser., XVII (1908–1909), 152 (putting out fires); William Manson Day Book, July 21, 1771, Sol Feinstone Collection of the American Revolution, no. 876, microfilm, CW (refloating of boats); Cooper and McCord, eds., *Statutes at Large,* II, 216 (killing wolves); diary of William Cabell, Sr., Jan. 24, 1778, VHS (lost horse); administration of the estate of Francis Le Jau, Sept. 6, 1766, Inventories, &, 234–243, SCDAH (transporting desk); St. Johns Berkeley Vestry Minutes, Aug. 14, 1754, SCDAH (closing and sweeping church); Robert W. Carter Diaries, Dec. 1784 (saving on expenses); Edmund Wilcox's miscellaneous cash expenditures and receipts, XI, June 1, 7, 1772, April 1777; and John Christian Grininger to J. E. Colhoun, July 30, 1791, John Ewing Colhoun Papers, UNC (turning in runaway); Robert Hunter, Jr., *Quebec to Carolina in 1785–1786* . . . , ed. Louis B. Wright and Marion Tinling (San Marino, Calif., 1943), 257–258 (quotation).

89. Josiah Smith to Alexander Taylor, Mar. 3, 1773, Smith Letterbook; Robert W. Carter Diaries, Jan. 30, July 16, 1768, Jan. 18, Apr. 16, 1769 (see also, for tips to household slaves, June 20, 1769, Nov. 16, 17, 1776, Apr. 19, 1777); Robert Carter to Benjamin Grayson, July 13, 1731, Robert "King" Carter Letterbook, UVa; Edmund Botsford notes on slavery, Edmund Botsford Papers, Baptist Historical Collection, Furman University, Greenville, S.C., as cited in Edward Anthony Pearson, "From Stono to Vesey: Slavery, Resistance, and Ideology in South

Even humble slaves benefited from unexpected windfalls. One slave acquired his freedom by sharing in the "prize" money paid his master for taking an enemy vessel. Another was on hand when General Christopher Gadsden offered a reward of two guineas to anybody who could rescue the occupants of a capsized canoe. The slave threw himself into the water, reached one of the four drowning men, and earned his prize. Black children in Savannah, Georgia, seized an unusual opportunity during the Revolutionary war, when the town was under siege and ammunition scarce. They went up and down the streets picking up the "spent balls," for which each received seven pence. Twenty field-workers received five shillings so that they might more "cheerfully" travel to an outlying plantation and acquiesce in the loss of two successive Sundays (they traveled on the Sabbath so that they could put in a full week's work).[90]

Earning small sums of money and trading within the "family" generally met with a master's approval or, at least, acquiescence. Yet, slaves never rested content with these legitimate outlets for their industry; they sought other, perhaps more lucrative, avenues for trade. This was anathema to slaveowners, who inevitably associated extraplantation trading with theft. Slaves, of course, had other views. What masters labeled theft, slaves considered legitimate access to the fruits of their well-earned labors to do with as they wished. Charles Ball, who knew both the Chesapeake and the Lowcountry, declared that he "was never acquainted with a slave who believed that he violated any rule of morality by appropriating to himself any thing that belonged to his master, if it was necessary for his comfort." The slaves' right to the products of their labor extended to the right to trade this produce off the plantation.[91]

Carolina, 1739–1822" (Ph.D. diss., University of Wisconsin–Madison, 1992), 184. For payments to house slaves, see John Mercer Ledger, "Domestick Expenses," September 1725, microfilm, CW; diary of Robert Carter, Aug. 1727, microfilm, CW; John Saunders' Notebook, Feb. 28, 1751, NCDAH; Carter Burwell Account Book, 1749, 44, Burwell Papers; Phillips P. Moulton, ed., *The Journal and Major Essays of John Woolman* (New York, 1971), 60; Henry Melchior Muhlenberg, *The Journals of Henry Melchior Muhlenberg,* trans. and ed. Theodore G. Tappert and John W. Doberstein, 2 vols. (Philadelphia, 1942–1958), II, 597.

90. Mary Heskett's certification of freedom to Tom, Oct. 1, 1753, Miscellaneous Records, II, 554; *Columbian Herald,* May 12, 1785; Elizabeth Lichtenstein Johnston, *Recollections of a Georgia Loyalist,* ed. Rev. Arthur Wentworth Eaton (New York, 1901), 57; *Letters of Habersham,* GHS, *Colls.,* VI, 190–191. When Robert Carter purchased the blacksmith, General, and his wife and three children, he gave the skilled slave six shillings, presumably as an encouragement (Robert W. Carter Diaries, December 1784).

91. Charles Ball, *Fifty Years in Chains* (New York, 1970), rpt. of *Slavery in the United States: A Narrative of the Life and Adventures of Charles Ball, a Black Man* (New York, 1837), 299; Alex Lichtenstein, " 'That Disposition to Theft, with Which They Have Been Branded':

As early as 1686, South Carolina passed an act to prohibit trading with servants or slaves on account of recent "indirect bargaines between freemen, servants and slaves, amongst themselves, whereby some evilly disposed have adventured privately to embezzle, wast and sell divers of their master's goods." By 1714, trading off the plantation had reached such proportions that a slave informant earned a reward of two pounds for proving that stolen goods had been sold by a fellow bondman. A generation later, hawkers and peddlers were numerous enough in South Carolina to merit a licensing system. Apparently, these men traveled "from one plantation to another, both by land and water," selling rum, sugar, and other wares in exchange for the slaves' "hogs, fowls, rice, corn and other produce." Not surprisingly, this was seen as a "great prejudice" to the slaves' masters.[92]

But licensing did little to mute criticism. In the early 1770s, repeated complaints were heard against "the many people [who] have been suspected and detected in corrupting and seducing our Negroes to Rob and Steal and of buying and receiving stolen goods." Between 1772 and 1774, ten whites in Wilmington in the Cape Fear region of North Carolina were charged with selling rum illicitly to slaves. In 1775, the Beaufort grand jury fulminated against the "abominable" clandestine trade between petty traders and slaves involving "several hundred Bushels of Corn, and other Provisions." In the same year, from the opposite end of the colony, Georgetown district planters observed that this "dealing" between whites and slaves had "grown to an enormous Heighth." In 1796, South Carolina's General Assembly again attempted to prevent shopkeepers and traders from unauthorized trading with slaves—that is, without the slaveowner's permission—on penalty of a two-hundred-dollar fine. And yet at the turn of the century, large plantation owners on the north side of the Combahee River opposed the establishment of a public landing place because it would attract the "many pedling boats which frequent the river," enabling them to remain near "large and productive rice plantations for the purpose of trading with the negroe slaves."[93]

Moral Economy, Slave Management, and the Law," *Journal of Social History*, XXI (1987–1988), 413–440.

92. Cooper and McCord, eds., *Statutes at Large*, II, 22–23, III, 395–399, 456–461, VII, 365–368, 385–397. Almost every law regulating the militia or the market, as well as slaves, contained provisions that prohibited "dealing" or trading with bondpeople. As late as 1796, an act was passed prohibiting shopkeepers, traders, and others from buying directly or indirectly from slaves either "corn, rice, peas, or other grain, bacon, flour, tobacco, cotton, indigo blades or anything else" (ibid., VII, 434–435).

93. Court of General Sessions Journal, Jan. 15, 1770, 43, SCDAH; presentments of Grand Jury for Beaufort District, *SCG and CJ*, June 13, 1775; presentments of Grand Jury for George-Town District, *SCG*, June 23, 1775; memorial of Nathaniel Hayward et al. to House

The persistence—indeed escalation—of these planter complaints indicates that South Carolina slaves were not easily dissuaded from trading off the plantation. Because Lowcountry plantations were so isolated, it is difficult to see how the practice could have been curtailed. Overseers were unlikely policemen. In 1742, when a traveler approached a South Carolina plantation hoping to purchase two quarts of corn, the overseer directed him to the slaves. One slave obliged the traveler, but only for a half-crown of local paper currency, or almost five pence sterling. Much later in the century, another traveler remarked that food for horses, whether rough rice or maize, was hard to come by in South Carolina, but that "when I could buy it from Negroes, I was never destitute, that is why I always carried some small change." The overseer who followed his employer's bidding courted disaster. In 1781, one plantation's slaves attempted to kill their overseer when he tried to take the corn they intended to market. In early-nineteenth-century Colleton County, a local trader substantial enough to employ a clerk was found guilty of buying cotton illegally from slaves. The clerk informed on his employer, saying that he had been directed to pay a shilling per pound for the cotton and that he had made purchases "several times" even though the slaves had no tickets to sell. Local lower-class whites probably saw nothing wrong in a small trade with blacks. In 1749, a white boatman acknowledged exchanging a pig for a slave's deerskin. In the early nineteenth century, a Baptist church in western South Carolina considered a case of a member's wife "tradeing . . . for corn" with a slave. The moral was clear. Nobody could be counted on to refrain from trading with slaves.[94]

Trading off the plantation elicited almost as much complaint in the Chesapeake as in the Lowcountry. As early as the late seventeenth century, Virginia masters began complaining of "ill disposed persons" who either "deal[t]" or had "commerce" with their slaves. In 1768, a Virginian complained bitterly of white "traffickers" who engaged in "clandestine" trade with slaves for cotton,

---

of Representatives, Dec. 4, 1806, General Assembly Petitions, 1806–1892, SCDAH. See also Marvin L. Michael Kay and Lorin Lee Cary, *Slavery in North Carolina, 1748–1775* (Chapel Hill, N.C., 1995), 117.

94. Jones, "John Martin Boltzius' Trip to Charleston, October 1742," *SCHM*, LXXXII (1981), 104; C. S. Sargent, ed., "Portions of the Journal of André Michaux . . . 1785 to 1796," American Philosophical Society, *Proceedings*, XXVI (1889), 108 (my translation); *SC and AGG*, Jan. 20, 1781; *State* v. *James Pendergrass*, November 1802, Thomas Waties Papers, USC; South Carolina Council Journal, no. 17, part 1, 85; minutes of the Shoal Creek Baptist Church, Oconee County, Apr. 4, 1804, Baptist Historical Collection, Furman University. In 1793, three Catawba Indians were prosecuted in Lancaster County Court "for trading with Negroes" (Pardon from Governor William Moultrie, Mar. 28, 1793, Miscellaneous Records, EEE, 46–47; information kindly supplied by James Merrell).

beans, peas, and fowl. These traders employed free blacks, an "idle scatterloping people," on commission to purchase the slaves' commodities. Two years later, a correspondent to the *Maryland Gazette* informed its readers, "In the Neighbourhood where I live, it is almost impossible to raise a Stock of Sheep or Hogs, the Negroes are constantly killing them to sell to some white people, who are little better than themselves, purely to raise Money to buy fine Cloaths." In 1779, one Virginia master believed that trafficking by his slaves was so extensive that he advised his manager to tell the "overseer to keep the keys of the folks' cornhouse or else they will sell it, and starve themselves."[95]

Prosecutions of local whites for "dealing" with slaves were common in the Chesapeake. Alleged to have sold rum to slaves, George Fisher, a merchant in Williamsburg, turned the tables on his accuser, Mayor John Holt. He then broadened his attack to include John Greenhow, another Williamsburg merchant, "infamously remarkable for trafficking with Negroes in wine, or any other commodity, Sundays not excepted." Fisher's counterattack was effective, and the charges against him were dropped. Another urban resident was less fortunate. According to a white witness, John Richardson of Norfolk bought tanned leather and staves from slaves. The countryside was no more immune to such transactions. In 1756, John Nelson of Cumberland County faced a charge of "dealing with [a] Negro," and, twenty years later, John Sutton, a Lancaster County tenant, was accused of buying corn from a slave. As in South Carolina, Baptist church members could not be trusted. In 1799, Sister Hines of Yeopim Baptist Church in Chowan County, North Carolina, was accused of "Trading with Negroes Unlawfully." A slave member of a Baptist church in the Shenandoah Valley even sold bacon out of "pity" to a poor white man.[96]

---

95. J. Douglas Deal, *Race and Class in Colonial Virginia: Indians, Englishmen, and Africans on the Eastern Shore during the Seventeenth Century* (New York, 1993), 181–182; B——, E——, *VaG* (Rind), Mar. 17, 1768; *Md Gaz*, Oct. 18, 1770, as cited in Kulikoff, *Tobacco and Slaves*, 340; James Mercer to B. Muse, Apr. 8, 1779, Muse Papers. See also Mechal Sobel, *The World They Made Together: Black and White Values in Eighteenth-Century Virginia* (Princeton, N.J., 1987), 51; Governor Gooch to Secretary of State, Feb. 28, 1729, CO5/1337, fols. 130–131, British Records, microfilm, CW; trial of Harry, James, and Stepney, Oct. 28, 1734, King George County Orders, 1721–1734, 678, as cited in Philip J. Schwarz, *Twice Condemned: Slaves and the Criminal Laws of Virginia, 1705–1865* (Baton Rouge, La., 1988), 76; Mullin, *Africa in America*, 154.

96. "Narrative of George Fisher," *WMQ*, 1st Ser., XVII (1908-1909), 148–149; James Parker's "Virginia Almanack," 1771 920 PAR 1/6, Parker Family Papers; John Fleming Ledger, January 1756, microfilm, CW; Carter Daybook, c. 1775, XIII, 116; minutes of the Yeopim Baptist Church, Chowan County, Aug. 23, 1799, Wake Forest University, Winston-Salem, N.C.; minutes of Waterlick Baptist Church, Shenandoah County, May 19, June 16, 1787, VBHS. Not all trade with white traders was illegitimate. Thirty-one slaves belonging to 15

The ease with which passing travelers, not just local whites, traded with Chesapeake slaves illustrates the hopelessness of the planters' position. In 1777, a white family, en route from North Carolina to Maryland, stopped near one of Robert Carter's quarters, buying corn and meal from old Tom and Breacky, two of Carter's slaves. Even circumspect Moravians could enter into trading arrangements with slaves. One Sunday in autumn 1755, a number of the brethren halted at a plantation near Fredericksburg and all day encountered a constant "stream of visitors, white and black," before they retired at about eight o'clock. However, "about ten [they] were awakened by a crowd of negroes who came with chickens, beans, chestnuts and apples for sale." After reassuring themselves that the produce was not stolen, the Moravians bought the slaves' wares.[97]

Slaves were not dependent solely on neighboring whites or passersby in their search for trading opportunities; they could also trade among themselves. In the Lowcountry much of this trade was between plantation slaves and boatmen and was universally condemned. But other transactions met with no overt disapproval. Thus, in 1749, a South Carolina master acknowledged that he allowed one of his slaves to cultivate rice and then do with it as he wished. The slave sold a barrel of his rice to his brother, who resided on a plantation fifteen miles away; he transported it one weekend by canoe. In the same year, another South Carolina slave unconcernedly told authorities of traveling to a neighboring plantation because a slave there "owed him some money." Apparently, Philip Porcher expressed no outrage when he learned that his slave George had engaged in trade with Joe belonging to Job Marion. George got a pair of stockings, two jackets, and two pairs of trousers in return for a blanket. The transaction came to light only when it was discovered that Joe had stolen these items of clothing from his fellow slaves.[98]

In the Chesapeake, whites associated economic transactions among slaves with theft of white property. The vast majority of slaves accused of crimes in the courts of eighteenth-century Virginia faced charges of robbery. Slaves stole primarily cloth and clothing, food and livestock, and, to a lesser extent, liquor and cash. No doubt, much of this loot circulated within the slave community. In 1750, an Amelia County slave named Lemas offered to sell stolen goods to a

---

owners traded, with their master's permission, at a store in the Virginia piedmont: Mullin, *Africa in America*, 152.

97. Robert Carter, Mar. 9, 1777, Carter Daybook, XIV, 34–35; Adelaide L. Fries, ed., *Records of the Moravians in North Carolina*, I (Raleigh, N.C., 1922), 142.

98. South Carolina Council Journal, no. 17, part 1, 160; Philip Porcher Account Book, May 23, 1776. On watermen and field hands, see Chapter 4.

slave named Caesar. A generation later, a Richmond County master reported a robbery in which he suspected his own groom, who allegedly intended to exchange stolen rum for another slave's watch.[99]

The trading horizons of many slaves therefore stretched far beyond the confines of their households. Although masters were probably their slaves' best customers, a wider community, of lower-class whites and fellow blacks, unknown travelers and familiar neighbors, beckoned alluringly for any slave with produce to exchange. In fact, those slaves who could get to town had the best opportunities to reach a broader community of prospective buyers.

Many slaves on Charleston's neighboring islands and inland rivers thus came regularly to town in order to sell their produce. A runaway woman confined to prison in 1731 kept "up a Constant Communication with some Country negroes who at Sundry times have furnished her with Rice and other provisions." Forty years later, the traffic was so heavy that planters on Charlestown Neck complained of "the great Number of NEGROES who are continually passing and repassing, selling Vegetables, etc. without Tickets." Even as the patriots encircled Charleston, in August 1782, a dozen to twenty slaves, in Governor John Mathews's estimation, ventured out of town each night to Goose Creek and up the Cooper River and returned with supplies. Consequently, he noted, "The Chs Town markets are now daily supplied with the greatest plenty of Everything they want." As soon as peace was restored, the governor attempted to curtail the Sunday visits of "Country Negroes" who sold their "Truck" on the town wharves. So ineffective was he that an ad hoc market day arose for the "negroes belonging to the neighbouring plantations." They came to the city on the Sabbath and held a public market on South-Bay. In 1798, two fugitives, a father and son who hailed from Goose Creek, supported themselves by "going backwards and forwards to town by land and water"; they were seen "three or four times in the lower Market selling what they have plundered from neighbouring Plantations."[100]

---

99. Schwarz, *Twice Condemned*, 39, 131 (70% of 18th-century slave crime and 75% of all felony and misdemeanor convictions in the middle to late 18th century involved theft); trial of Lemas, Nov. 15, 1750, Amelia County Court Minutes, unpaginated, VSL; Moore Fauntleroy Crandall to Landon Carter, July 10, 1774, Landon Carter Papers, UVa. For an example of a legal exchange among slaves, see minutes of the Buck Marsh Baptist Church, Frederick County, Aug. 3, 1799, VBHS.

100. South Carolina Assembly journal, Apr. 2, 1731, CO5/432; John Robinson et al., *SCG*, Oct. 8, 1772; Governor Mathews to Gen. Marion, Aug. 1782, Peter Horry Papers, Peter Force Collection, LC; journal of South Carolina House of Representatives, Aug. 6, 1783, SCDAH; Presentments of the Grand Jury for the District of Charlestown, *State Gaz of SC*, June 20, 1791; James W. Gadsden, *City Gaz*, Aug. 21, 1798. See also John Milner, *SCG*, June 29, 1763;

The overwhelmingly rural character of Virginia restricted the opportunities for its slaves to engage in marketing. However, as towns grew in size in the second half of the century, slave participation in urban markets increased. In 1768, a correspondent to the *Virginia Gazette* observed that "at present there is no place so likely to purchase cotton, beans, pease, fowls, etc. as at [the] pretty towns" of Virginia. But he was less happy about the origins of this produce, which he attributed to the licenses some masters gave slaves to sell their vegetables and livestock, thereby creating "factors" for the slaves' stolen goods. In 1782, the newly formed Fredericksburg Council acted swiftly to prohibit slaves from selling anything in town without written consent. Two years later, when slaves committed a rash of robberies of merchants' stores in Petersburg, some whites voiced the suspicion that "a combination among the slaves" helped them fence the stolen goods. In 1787, the inhabitants of Dumfries complained of the numbers of "country peoples and Negroes being permitted to bring provisions and carry to private Houses or hawk about the streets." They proposed that "the Market people" should be confined to a recently built market house. And, by the end of the century, Richard Parkinson could marvel at the numbers of slaves who were "good marketmen" and who sold "more, and frequently at a higher price, than a white man."[101]

By the early nineteenth century the slave presence in the urban markets of the Chesapeake region seems to have been more readily accepted. A visitor to Alexandria in 1805 observed how, on market days, many black slaves "come out of the country with fruit, vegetables, etc. and some, even girls of 10 or 12 years of age, are seen walking the streets with baskets on their heads, without any clothing." This same traveler heard about a slave, resident on a plantation near Baltimore, who marketed his owner's produce in the city. This slave had "the care of receiving and bringing home the money; by which means it frequently happens that large sums of money pass through his hands." The slave performed this service so well that the master "scarcely ever ventures to employ any other person for these purposes." In June 1807, a visitor to Washington, D.C., observed how the wild strawberries, which grew with abandon in the

---

Paul Edwards, ed., *The Life of Olauda Equiano; or, Gustavus Vassa the African, 1789*, 2 vols. (London, 1969), I, 254, 266–268. Specialized marketeers, as opposed to rural slaves bringing their own produce to market, are discussed in Chapter 4.

101. B——, E——, *VaG* (Rind), Mar. 17, 1768; Fredericksburg Council Minutes, 1782–1811, 10–11, in William Harold Siener, "Economic Development in Revolutionary Virginia: Fredericksburg, 1750–1810" (Ph.D. diss., College of William and Mary, 1982), 317; M. P. Palmer et al., eds., *Calendar of Virginia State Papers and Other Manuscripts*, 11 vols. (Richmond, Va., 1875–1893), II, 632 (see also Henrico County Orders, Apr. 30, 1784); Legislative Petitions, Prince William County, Nov. 19, 1787, VSL; Richard Parkinson, *A Tour in America, in 1798, 1799, and 1800 . . .* , II (London, 1805), 33.

neighboring countryside, were "brought every Morning to market in profusion by the Negroes."[102]

Because some Lowcountry slaves cultivated crops intensively on their own time and then traded that produce extensively, a few of them acquired more substantial items of property. In 1714, the South Carolina legislature attempted to deny the slaves' claim to "any stock of hogs, cattle or horses." The directive apparently fell on deaf ears, for, in 1722, it became lawful to seize any hogs, boats, or canoes belonging to slaves. The later act referred to the "great inconveniences [that] do arise from negroes and other slaves keeping and breeding of horses"; not only were these horses (and cattle) to be seized, but the proceeds of their sale were to be put to the support of the parish poor. The irony of using slave property to sustain white paupers was presumably lost on South Carolina legislators but perhaps not on the slaves. Once again, legislative intentions seem to have been thwarted, for, in 1740, more complaints were heard about those "several owners of slaves [who] have permitted them to keep canoes, and to breed and raise horses, neat cattle and hogs, . . . for the particular and peculiar benefit of such slaves."[103]

In spite of these acts, slaves remained singularly reluctant to relinquish their claims to horses, because they were a symbol of white male mastery and obviously aided mobility. In 1772, the Charlestown District grand jury was still objecting to "Negroes being allowed to keep horses . . . contrary to Law." Eight years later, an unusually efficient parish patrol confiscated five horses from slaves living at Dean Hall plantation. In 1788, a slave named Will exchanged his horses for his freedom. A witness to the exchange heard Will's master, Lewis Dutarque, say to

> old fellow Will that he had been a faithful servant to him and if he had a mind to purchase his freedom he should obtain the same by paying him three hundred pounds old currency and says he will you have two Horses which will nearly pay me. I will allow you hundred pounds old currency for a Roan Gelding and forty five currency for your Gray for which the fellow Will readily consented to the proposals and Mr. Dutarque took possession of the Horses and the fellow Will was to pay the Balance as soon as he could make it up. Mr Dutarque also borrowed of the fellow Will a small Black mare which he lost and he said she was worth six Guineas and would allow him that price for her.

102. Robert Sutcliffe, *Travels in Some Parts of North America* . . . (New York, 1811), 98, 195; Dick Journal, June 26, 1807, UVa.
103. Cooper and McCord, eds., *Statutes at Large*, VII, 368, 382, 409.

One begins to wonder how many horses Will had. Horse trading might even have been possible within the slave community, if a notice placed in a South Carolina newspaper in 1793 is any indication: "On Sunday last was apprehended by the patrol in St. George's parish, a certain negro man who calls himself *Titus* and his son about 10 year who is called *Tom;* he was trading with the negroes in that neighbourhood, and he had in his possession 2 horses . . . one poultry cart, and several articles of merchandise, consisting of stripes, linens, and handkerchiefs."[104]

As the contents of this cart indicate, slaves aspired to own property other than livestock. Clothing or pieces or fine linen were attractive items for many slaves. The parish patrol that was so effective in 1780 seized linens and cottons as well as guns, china, glass, and saddles from slaves "at different plantations." Henry Laurens supplied his slaves with "gay wastcoats," "Great Coats," "Dutch Caps," "pieces of Blue Stroud," hats, and iron pots. Another popular item of exchange was tobacco pipes, for, as Henry Muhlenberg noted, "slaves love tobacco." Indeed, in 1799, one South Carolinian complained that he was unable to buy a fashionable tobacco pipe because "there are none but negro pipes now imported, which are too short to be serviceable." The most dramatic example of property ownership and then exchange by an eighteenth-century Lowcountry slave involved, not horses, canoes, fine clothing, or pipes, but men. According to a deed of manumission, a slave named Sampson, "by his Industry and the Assistance of Friends," had purchased and "procured in his owne Right and property and for his owne Use" another slave named Tom. Sampson then exchanged his slave Tom for "fifty years of his [that is, Sampson's] life time and Servitude (to come)."[105]

Masters had to take account of the value that slaves attached to the small amounts of property they had managed to acquire. When Henry Laurens proposed to remove a group of slaves from his Santee plantation to a newly established plantation in Georgia, he emphasized to his manager that it would "quiet their Minds much if you will see all their Little Estates packed up." The

---

104. Charleston District Grand Jury Presentments, *SCG*, Jan. 25, 1772; *SC and AGG*, Nov. 1, 1780; declaration of John Blake, Apr. 25, 1788, Miscellaneous Records, VV, 473; *State Gaz of SC*, Oct. 26, 1793. For hog ownership by slaves, see William Feltman, *The Journal of Lieut. William Feltman . . .* (Philadelphia, 1853), 37.

105. *SC and AGG*, Nov. 1, 1780; *Laurens Papers*, V, 20, 61, 73, 93; Muhlenberg, *Journals*, II, 675; Judith Dwight Martin, ed., "The Letters of Charles Caleb Cotton, 1798–1802," *SCHM*, LII (1951), 19; Mr. Isaac Bodett's Release to a Negro for Fifty Years, Nov. 13, 1728, Records of the Secretary of the Province, Book H, 42–43, SCDAH. By the late 18th century, deeds of manumission sometimes included the following clause: "with all his goods and chattels, Lands and tenements by him already bought or hereafter to be bought" (Sarah Smith's deed of manumission, Sept. 7, 1790, Miscellaneous Records, YY, 312–313; Edward Weyman Jr.'s deed of manumission, Feb. 18, 1791, ibid., ZZ, 324–325).

manager received orders to itemize the "estates" and "give the strongest assurances that each Man's property shall be safely deliver'd." The advantage of choosing married men, Laurens noted, was that their wives "will give an Eye to their respective goods." When Eliza Pinckney desired her slaves to move out of range of the marauding British army during the Revolutionary war, the slaves refused because they were so "attached to their homes and the little they have there." A Lowcountry owner was perhaps right to be sanguine about an unsuccessful hunt he had launched for a group of seven absentees. He was, after all, "convinced these runaways would not go far, being connected at home, and having too much property to leave." John Drayton was close to the mark when he asserted that South Carolina slaves were "protected in the property which they ... acquire."[106]

Chesapeake slaves seem to have had less personal property than their Lowcountry counterparts. The less time available for work on their own plots and the institutionally weaker market setting no doubt account for the difference. But Chesapeake slaves could not be denied entirely. In the late seventeenth century, some Virginia slaves had obviously acquired livestock, for an act of 1692 provided for the confiscation of "all horses, cattle and hoggs marked of any negro or other slave marke, or by any slave kept." However, although this stipulation was repeated in 1705, suggesting that the practice persisted, no further legislation was deemed necessary.[107]

Only toward the end of the eighteenth century do small scraps of information surface to indicate that some slaves managed to evade the laws' restrictions. During the Revolutionary war, a slave named old Sarah left Norfolk and went over to the British; she loaded her possessions, which included a sow and piglets, onto a small boat. In 1786, the grand jury of Elizabeth City County cited Mary Mallory for letting a goat belonging to her slave "run at large." Fourteen years later, at the estate sale of William Brown in the same county, "Old Jack" bought a red cow for five pounds. Reflecting on his experiences as a slave in late-eighteenth-century Maryland, Charles Ball recollected that some expert fishermen caught and sold as many fish and oysters as enabled them to buy coffee, sugar, and other luxuries, notably Sunday clothes, for their families. Similarly, at the end of the century, William Tatham claimed that nearly all Chesapeake slaves "have their favourite dog, many are allowed to raise hogs, and I know numbers who have their horses, and ride to church every Sunday,

106. *Laurens Papers,* V, 99–100; Eliza Pinckney to Thomas Pinckney, May 17, 1779, Pinckney Family Papers, SCHS; William Read to Jacob Read, Mar. 22, 1800, Read Family Papers; John Drayton, *A View of South Carolina as Respects Her Natural and Civil Concerns* (Spartanburg, S.C., 1972 [orig. publ. 1802]), 145.

107. William Waller Hening, *The Statutes at Large: Being a Collection of All the Laws of Virginia . . . ,* III (Philadelphia, 1823), 103, 459–460.

with their wives, in very decent apparel." Even a twelve-year-old boy, in transit from one quarter to another, was permitted "to bring whatever belongs to him." But perhaps the best indication that slave property rights were recognized is that some slaves were even prosecuted in Virginia county courts for stealing, as one indictment put it, "the proper Goods, Chattles and money" of other slaves.[108]

Trade held out advantages for both masters and slaves. From the perspective of the slaveowners, they received additional provisions, probably at bargain prices, they were able to display their benevolence, and they offered a measure of latitude to their bondpeople that theoretically made them more content. Slaves, for their part, were allowed to acquire a few possessions, express a measure of individual initiative, promote their self-esteem, and to some extent benefit both economically and socially. Part-time production and subsequent exchanges created, in other words, a minor "peasant breach in the slave mode of production."[109]

It was, as we have seen, a wider breach in the Lowcountry than in the Chesapeake. This was not always an advantage. Lowcountry masters might well have exploited their slaves' part-time output, by forcing them to make up shortfalls in their allotted rations. Conversely, Lowcountry slaves at least learned to take care of themselves in a commercial world. Marketing and part-time production among slaves, as with other seeming opportunities in slave life, proved to be deeply ambiguous.

108. WPA, Writers' Program, *The Negro in Virginia* (New York, 1940), 19; Elizabeth City County Order Book, 1784–1788, 305–306, as cited in Hughes, "Elizabeth City County, Virginia, 1782–1810," 238; estate sale of William Brown, Oct. 2, 1800, Elizabeth City County Deeds and Wills, book 12, 135, as cited ibid., 239; Ball, *Fifty Years in Chains,* 43; Tatham, *Communications concerning Agriculture,* 54–55; Robert Carter to Newyear Branson, Aug. 22, 1788, Carter Letterbook, VIII, 170. For the trials, see Richmond County Criminal Trials, Oct. 19, Nov. 9, 1737, Nov. 15, 1753; Middlesex County Court Order Book, Oct. 5, 1736; and A. Spotswood to the Governor, November–December 1793, Executive Papers.

109. Tadeusz Lepkowski's phrase is referred to by Sidney W. Mintz, "Was the Plantation Slave a Proletarian?" *Review,* II (1978), 94.

I know not which to pity the

most—the master or the slave.

—Francis Asbury

7 : Social Transactions between Whites and Blacks

Transactions between masters and bondpeople were enormously wide-ranging. Many a white child came into the world in the arms of a black nurse; many a master went out of it on the backs of black pallbearers.[1] Masters' dependence on and exploitation of their slaves was both comprehensive and far-reaching, from the most public to the most private of activities, from the most elemental to the most tangential of roles. Conversely, the slave's existence was inextricably shaped by the master's will and power. However hard they struggled to break free, slaves could never escape the long shadow cast by the master. This mutual dependence took a frightening toll on everyone. Nothing and no one escaped the effects of slavery, an institution forged in the heat of continual, inescapable, face-to-face encounters.

From public places to private spaces, slaves were ubiquitous. They could intrude on society's most elevated ceremonial occasions. In 1719, celebrations of the anniversary of the king's coronation in Williamsburg involved the firing of the great guns; unfortunately, the slave gunner lost his arm. The privacy of the home was no more sacrosanct. Janet Schaw took pleasure in getting up

---

1. For the role of black nurses and midwives, see Chapter 6. For black pallbearers, see will of Philip Rootes, Aug. 13, 1746, in Beverley Fleet, ed., *Virginia Colonial Abstracts,* IV, *King and Queen County Records concerning Eighteenth Century Persons* (Baltimore, 1961), 79; and will of William Sanders, Aug. 4, 1775, Guignard Family Papers, USC.

early because there would be no "yelping Negroes with their discording voices to grate my ears and disturb my thoughts." A South Carolina resident advised against building stairs of cedar, for the wood was "too brittle . . . at least where Negroes go up and down." He also noted composing a letter to the loud snores of his waiting man. Slaves gave their masters no peace.[2]

Whites even encountered slaves in their dreams. According to one minister, a woman of his acquaintance who had a withered arm dreamed three nights successively that if she applied to a Methodist preacher her arm would be restored. Blocking her path, however, was "a Negro Man (as she thought) who, by persuasion, threats and lyes turn'd her back." Conversely, the slave in Lachlan Bain McIntosh's religious vision played a more positive role—a portent of the master's fate. The apparition of Jesus Christ first spoke to McIntosh's slave, July, telling July that he would soon die. It then pointed to McIntosh, saying he would be "call'd" the following day. More prosaically, Frederick George Mulcaster, a young Scottish planter in East Florida, had a wish-fulfillment reverie, in which he was standing "in a Hall and beneath me was Indigo Rice Cotton etc., in great abundance [and] at my command my slaves . . . instantly gathered the crop and put it on Board Vessels." Most dramatically, when nine of Landon Carter's slaves fled to the British in 1776, both he and his daughter dreamed about them. In the father's case, he envisioned them "most wretchedly meager and wan," begging him to intercede for a pardon on their behalf. Carter had to dream on, for the slaves never returned.[3]

Just as blacks invaded the masters' unconscious world, so they intruded on their everyday world. Slaveowners populated their figures of speech with slaves: humble as slaves, yellow as a mulatto, looking skyward "like a Negro weeding corn," sleeping in one's clothes "like a Negro." These derogatory similes reveal the impact of blacks on the everyday consciousness of whites. Blacks also inscribed themselves on the landscape. Masters named fields and quarters after slaves and transferred African locations to North America. John Ball (or one of his ancestors) named an area within his plantation as Gold

---

2. Petition of John Tyler to the Governor, May 6, 1721, Colonial Papers, VSL; [Janet Schaw], *Journal of a Lady of Quality* . . . , ed. Evangeline Walker Andrews and Charles McLean Andrews (New Haven, Conn., 1923), 169; *Laurens Papers,* IV, 98, X, 222.

3. Marjorie Moran Holmes, "The Life and Diary of the Reverend John Jeremiah Jacob" (master's thesis, Duke University, 1941), 135; Memoranda Book, Sept. 22, 1807, Lachlan Bain McIntosh Papers, GHS, cited by J. E. Chaplin, "An Anxious Pursuit: Innovation in Commercial Agriculture in South Carolina, Georgia, and British East Florida, 1740–1815" (Ph.D. diss., The Johns Hopkins University, 1986), 144; F. George Mulcaster to [?], Nov. 6, 1768, Manigault Family Papers, USC; Jack P. Greene, ed., *The Diary of Colonel Landon Carter of Sabine Hall, 1752–1778,* 2 vols. (Charlottesville, Va., 1965), 1064 (hereafter cited as *Carter Diary*).

Coast Hill; Cumberland County, Virginia, had its Guinea Road, Little Guinea Neck, Great Guinea Creek, Angola Road, and Angola Creek. Even a slave's features made an impression. Henry Laurens was so taken with the appearance of his gardener that he had his picture drawn; a newly arrived guest at Mount Vernon, in contrast, promptly turned on his heels, "disgusted" at seeing "an old Negroe there resembling his own Image." Whether their impact was pleasing or not, slaves could at least take satisfaction in registering their presence.[4]

For the master, much of his self-image depended on the possession of slaves. According to William Byrd II, slaves served to "blow up the pride" of "white people." This was as true of the urban tradesmen who owned one or two slaves as of the great planter. Timothy Ford observed that many Charleston mechanics "bear nothing more of their trade than the name," precisely because they were the proud owners of slaves. They were always "followed by a negro carrying their tools," and barbers were "supported in idleness and ease by their negroes who do the business." Gentlemanly status was equally predicated on slaveowning. Ford found that "a person can no more act or move without an attending servant than a planet without its satellites." A gentleman out riding without servants was a contradiction in terms. Slaves formed the advance guard, the "ensigns" of a gentleman's "rank and dignity." Indeed, a recent immigrant to South Carolina in 1749 discovered that "they say here when they talk of a Man's being Rich he has so many Negroes."[5]

Because social respect was inextricably connected to slaveownership, wealthy families made sure their young children had slaves at an early age. In 1728, Robert "King" Carter proposed to buy three slave girls to distribute

4. *Laurens Papers*, III, 553 (humble), V, 702 (picture); Josiah Smith to George Austin, Jan. 30, 1773, Josiah Smith Letterbook, UNC (yellow); Sam Briggs to Randolph Barksdale, July 22, 1789, Peter Barksdale Letters, Duke (skyward); John C. Fitzpatrick, ed., *The Writings of George Washington from the Original Manuscript Sources, 1745–1799*, 39 vols. (Washington, D.C., 1931–1944), I, 17 (sleeping); Account or Planting Book, 1780–1784, Apr. 2, 1781, John Ball, Jr., Papers, Duke; Cumberland County Court Order Book, 1758–1762, 286, 1774–1778, 483, 524, 1779–1784, 21, 166, VSL; Donald Jackson and Dorothy Twohig, eds., *The Diaries of George Washington*, 6 vols. (Charlottesville, Va., 1976–1979), I, 222. See also Darrett B. Rutman and Anita H. Rutman, *A Place in Time: Middlesex County, Virginia, 1650–1750* (New York, 1984), 164, 166; and Mechal Sobel, *The World They Made Together: Black and White Values in Eighteenth-Century Virginia* (Princeton, N.J., 1987), 93–94.

5. Marion Tinling, ed., *The Correspondence of the Three William Byrds of Westover, Virginia, 1684–1776*, 2 vols. (Charlottesville, Va., 1977), II, 488; Joseph W. Barnwell, ed., "Diary of Timothy Ford, 1785–1786," *SCHM*, XIII (1912), 142, 189–190; James Steuart to Thomas Steuart, Oct. 17, 1749, GD38/2/7/96, Steuart of Dalguise Muniments, Scottish Record Office, Edinburgh. See also Henry Melchior Muhlenberg, *The Journals of Henry Melchior Muhlenberg*, trans. and ed. Theodore G. Tappert and John W. Doberstein, 2 vols. (Philadelphia, 1942–1958), II, 664; and John Hammond Moore, ed., "The Abiel Abbot Journals: A Yankee Preacher in Charleston Society, 1818–1827," *SCHM*, LXVIII (1967), 68.

to each of his three male grandchildren. In 1792, Robert Stafford, a two-year-old boy living on Cumberland Island, Georgia, received a mulatto slave boy named Peter, also about two years of age, from his uncle. According to Johann Schoepf, at age fifteen, a well-bred Virginian acquired "a horse and a negro," the two adjuncts of gentlemanly self-presentation, "with which he riots about the country, attends every fox-hunt, horse race, and cock-fight, and does nothing else whatever." In Baltimore County, Maryland, slaveowners who deeded slaves as gifts routinely picked black boys of roughly the same age as their sons, "perhaps hoping," Charles Steffen notes, "to groom a lifelong companion and trusted servant." Whites learned to command at an early age.[6]

Countless observers realized that youthful command took an emotional toll on whites as well as blacks. Charles Wesley was strongly opposed to the practice of giving a white child a slave of the same age "to tyrannize over, to beat and abuse out of sport." Similarly, John Lambert noted that South Carolina planters appropriated one or two young slaves to each of their children so that white Carolinians "are nurtured in the strongest prejudices against the blacks, whom they are taught to look upon as beings almost without a soul, and whom they sometimes treat with an unpardonable severity." The process by which young white children learned to dehumanize blacks began early. For Elkanah Winchester, "Little children are taught, from their cradles, . . . to exercise the most brutal cruelties upon [slaves] without the least pity"; for the duc de La Rochefoucauld-Liancourt, "The little white man learns, even before he can walk, to tyrannize over the blacks." But the most powerful indictment came from Thomas Jefferson. In a famous passage, he described how "the parent storms, the child looks on, catches the lineaments of wrath, puts on the same airs in the circle of smaller slaves, gives a loose to his worst of passions, and thus nursed, educated, and daily exercised in tyranny, cannot but be stamped by its odious peculiarities." George Mason was right on the mark when he observed, "Every Master is born a petty tyrant."[7]

---

6. Robert "King" Carter to [?], May 21, 1728, Robert Carter Letterbook, 1727–1728, VHS; John E. Ehrenhard and Mary R. Bullard, *Stafford Plantation, Cumberland Island National Seashore, Georgia: Archaeological Investigations of a Slave Cabin* (Tallahassee, Fla., 1981), 4; Johann David Schoepf, *Travels in the Confederation [1783–1784]*, trans. and ed. Alfred J. Morrison, 2 vols. (Philadelphia, 1911), II, 95; Charles G. Steffen, *From Gentlemen to Townsmen: The Gentry of Baltimore County, Maryland, 1660–1776* (Lexington, Ky., 1993), 88. See also *Laurens Papers,* IV, 363; and Robert Carter to Priscilla Mitchell, Dec. 25, 1786, Robert Carter Letterbook, VII, 165, Duke.

7. *The Journal of the Rev. Charles Wesley . . .* (Taylors, S.C., 1977 [London, 1909]), 68; John Lambert, *Travels through Lower Canada and the United States of North America, in the Years 1806, 1807, and 1808,* II (London, 1810), 393; Elhanan Winchester, *The Reigning Abominations, Especially the Slave Trade . . .* (London, 1788), 24 (see also 22); François Alexandre

But there was a more benign side to contact between some white children and slaves. In the 1770s, William Richardson, a South Carolina slaveowner, advised his wife to keep a close eye on their four-year-old son, Billy, because "some of the little Negroes that Billy is fond of playing with, go often down to the Pond to play and that it is not impossible that some accident . . . may happen." Billy obviously liked playing with black children, and his father countenanced the fraternization, provided it was monitored. A few years earlier, Richardson's young daughter Nancy pleaded "in favour" of three household slaves who were about to be punished. Her appeal had the desired effect. Due to depart for an English school, a young Richard Henry Lee had daily fights with "a stout negro boy" in preparation for his anticipated boxing bouts with English youths. A young white man and his slave even went to their deaths together: a planter's son, accompanied by a slave, traveled by canoe down the Ashley River to Charleston, where he was to attend school. Neither completed the journey. Their bodies were ultimately found, "sticking in the Mud in the said River, their Arms clasping one another."[8]

Whether the contacts between white and black children were benign or malignant, there can be no doubt that growing up in a slave society meant learning to rely on slaves. In fact, adult masters clearly proclaimed their dependence on their slaves—particularly where money was involved. In claiming compensation for the loss of his "valuable waterman," one humble Virginia master had no hesitation in declaring that he had thereby been "deprived of his chief support in maintaining a large Family." Similarly, the mainstay of a South Carolina resident was his capable house painter and glazier, who had become "the chief support of [his] poor Family wch without such assistance must soon be reduced to Indigence and want."[9]

Frédéric, duke de La Rochefoucault Liancourt, *Travels through the United States of North America . . .* , 2 vols. (London, 1799), I, 557; Adrienne Koch and William Peden, eds., *The Life and Selected Writings of Thomas Jefferson* (New York, 1944), 278; Max Farrand, ed., *The Records of the Federal Convention of 1787*, rev. ed., 4 vols. (New Haven, Conn., 1937), II, 370. See also diary of Jonathan Evans, July 24, 1797, UNC; *Laurens Papers*, III, 356; Kenneth Roberts and Anna M. Roberts, trans. and eds., *Moreau de St. Méry's American Journey [1793–1798]* (Garden City, N.Y., 1947), 54; Tinling, ed., *The Correspondence of the Three William Byrds*, I, 32, II, 682.

8. Emma B. Richardson, "Letters of William Richardson, 1765–1784," *SCHM*, XLVII (1946), 17, 10; Richard H. Lee, *Memoir of the Life of Richard Henry Lee, and His Correspondence with the Most Distinguished Men in America and Europe . . .* , 2 vols. (Philadelphia, 1825), I, 7; *SCG*, Jan. 22, 1737, cited in Peter A. Coclanis, *The Shadow of a Dream: Economic Life and Death in the South Carolina Low Country, 1670–1920* (New York, 1989), 111.

9. Legislative Petitions, Gloucester County, Dec. 23, 1800, VSL; petition of Michael Jeans, South Carolina Council Journal, Jan. 12, 1743, CO5/441, fols. 448–449, PRO; petition of Col. John Thomas, Journal of South Carolina House of Representatives, Feb. 3, 1783, SCDAH.

But eighteenth-century masters were even willing to declare their dependence on their slaves gratuitously, publicly, even humiliatingly. Thus, a South Carolina master, in advertising for his runaway slave, managed to strike a note of maudlin self-pity and exaggerated anger that would be humorous were it not pathetic. "As this inhuman creature, when she went away," the master whined, "left myself extreme ill in one bed, her mistress in another, and two of my children not one able to help the other, she must be conscious of some very atrocious crime." Similarly, a Virginia master grew self-righteous because his slave had become "very idle during my present Indisposition" and then had run away in order to seek freedom, "though he has lived little short of it with me, having been too much indulged." Masters did not hide their misplaced trust.[10]

As masters relied on slaves, so slaves returned the favor. The set-piece that seemed to convey the depths of the slaves' attachment to their masters was the scene—the stuff of which plantation legends are made—when the long-absent patriarch returned home to the warm greetings of joyful dependents. Even if such occasions are interpreted as ritualized events, with a certain amount of role-playing on all sides—William Drayton, for example, lightheartedly asked of a friend who had just returned home how he found "being kiss'd and Slabber'd" by the "Masters, Misses, Negroes, Dogs and Cats of your Family"—some receptions seem too effusive to be explained away as a set of cynical maneuvers. Henry Laurens, for instance, was obviously moved by the welcome he received when he returned to his Charleston home in 1774 after an absence of three years in Europe:

> I found no body here but three of our old Domestics Stepney Exeter, and big Hagar, these drew tears from me by their humble and affectionate Salutes and congratulations my Knees were Clasped, my hands kissed my very feet embraced and nothing less than a very, I can't say fair, but *full* Buss of my Lips would satisfy the old Man [Stepney] weeping and Sobbing in my Face—the kindest enquiries over and over again were made concerning Master Jacky, Master Harry, Master Jemmy [Laurens's children, still in Europe]—they encircled me held my hands hung upon me I could scarcely get from them—Ah said the old Man, I never thought to see you again, now I am happy—Ah, I never thought to see you again.

As much as he tried to make a joke about the "fair" kiss on his lips, Laurens was clearly moved. He finally broke his "way through these humble *sincere friends* thanking them a thousand times for such marks of their affection and pro-

---

10. Stephen Hartley, *SCG*, Oct. 13, 1757; James Mercer, *VaG* (P and D), Mar. 19, 1772. See also Thomas Ringgold, *Md Gaz*, Mar. 20, 1755; Gabriel Jones, *VaG* (P and D), June 30, 1774; Robert Brent, *VaG* (D and H), Nov. 18, 1775.

ceeded to Broad Street."[11] These were, of course, urban domestics, hardly typical eighteenth-century slaves.

Yet fifteen years later, much the same happened in the depths of the Virginia countryside when Thomas Jefferson returned from France. According to his daughter Martha, Jefferson's slaves "collected in crowds" around his carriage well before it reached Monticello, "and almost drew it up the mountain by hand." The shouts of greeting reached a climax when they reached the top. And when Jefferson stepped from the carriage, "they received him in their arms and bore him to the house, crowding around and kissing his hands and feet—some blubbering and crying—others laughing." Black folklore was a little at variance with Martha's account. According to the "lips of old family servants who were present as children," the carriage horses had been unharnessed and the vehicle dragged to the front door at Monticello by "strong black arms." Jefferson was literally borne back home on the strong backs of his slaves.[12]

Similar welcomes greeted humble planters, too. When Devereux Jarratt, a common planter and minister, returned home, "his brothers and their wives, and all the black people on the plantation, seemed overjoy'd" at his coming. Edmund Botsford, another minister of humble status, encountered an effusive reception when reunited with his slave. As Botsford described it, his "poor negro was almost frantic upon seeing once more his kind master. He jumped, hallowed, fell down, embraced his master's feet, and in every possible way gave vent to his joy." Homecomings were opportunities for slaves to display their attachment to masters, whether the estates were large or small.[13]

As these scenes suggest, many slaves identified closely with their masters. When Landon Carter had his son's weaver whipped, the slave invoked the protection of his own master, who "would not have let him be served so." Similarly, fugitive Peter's destination was predictable, for "he often told the other Negroes that if ever [his present master] used him ill he would go to his old mistress . . . and be protected." Slaves allied with masters not just for protection but in opposition to outsiders. A gang of slaves ridiculed a tenant recently discharged by their master; do not worry, they mocked, if our master's

---

11. William Henry Drayton to Peter Manigault, Nov. 16, 1756, Manigault Family Papers; *Laurens Papers,* X, 2–3 (my emphasis).

12. Sarah N. Randolph, *The Domestic Life of Thomas Jefferson* (Charlottesville, Va., 1871), 152–153. For similar homecomings, see St. George Tucker's Journal to Charlestown, Apr. 14, 1777, Tucker-Coleman Papers, typescript, CW; William Moultrie, *Memoirs of the American Revolution,* 2 vols. (New York, 1802), II, 355–356; Robert Dawidoff, *The Education of John Randolph* (New York, 1979), 52.

13. Devereux Jarratt, *The Life of the Reverend Devereux Jarratt . . . Written by Himself . . .* (New York, 1969 [orig. publ. Baltimore, 1806]), 42; Charles D. Mallary, *Memoirs of Elder Edmund Botsford* (Charleston, S.C., 1832), 58.

horses eat your grain, because it no longer belongs to you. Imagine the bombshell when a slave disclosed to his master that a "Friend" had seduced his master's wife; the frenzied slaveholder, with the assistance of his slaves, promptly cut off the cuckolder's ears. A Virginia master and his slaves even went on a rampage together, killing one white man and wounding another. The affinity of slave and master knew no bounds.[14]

The supreme test of slave loyalty, however, came during the Revolutionary war. Many slaves during this long, drawn-out conflict had opportunities to throw off their allegiance to masters and decamp to the British. Many did. However, most did not—for a variety of reasons, most strategic—and a significant minority went further and actively demonstrated their allegiance. Thus a Georgia loyalist recalled that her father was able to escape from patriot forces when a favorite slave "contrived to amuse the soldiers in different ways" in order to delay them. One Lowcountry plantation was spared a visit from enemy because a neighbor's slave "disuaded [the British] from it by saying it was not worth while, for it was only a plantation belonging to an old decrepit gentleman, who did not live there; so they took his word for it and proceeded on." The slave received "many blessings" from the owners "for his consideration and pity." A slave driver exhibited such fidelity that "during the invasion of the country [he] never went off with the British, and had the address to prevent any going who were under his care."[15]

Because slaveholders' expectations concerning the loyalty of their slaves were not high on the eve of the Revolutionary war, they suffered no "moment of truth" akin to the trauma, the deep shock experienced by slaveholders during the Civil War, when so many slaves proved faithless. In fact, if anything, the reverse was true in the earlier civil war. Revolutionary slaveholders were generally surprised and gratified by their slaves' actions, even though only a minority could be said to have demonstrated "loyalty." An advertisement offering a South Carolina gang of forty slaves for sale suggests the sense of wonder, for what made them valuable was "that not one ever quitted their owner," even

14. Greene, ed., *Carter Diary*, 845; William Gregory, *VaG* (P and D), May 4, 1769; Anne King Gregorie, ed., *Records of the Court of Chancery of South Carolina, 1671–1779* (Washington, D.C., 1950), 123; *SCG*, July 24, 1738; J. F. Mercer to R. Sprigg, Aug. 6, 1794, Mercer Family Papers, VHS. For a series of slave crimes that seemed to have been instigated by masters, see trial of Dick, July 26, 1748, and related episodes, Accomac County Court Order Book, 1744–1753, 265, 283, 332–333, 339, VSL (Philip Schwarz first alerted me to this case).

15. Elizabeth Lichtenstein Johnston, *Recollections of a Georgia Loyalist*, ed. Rev. Arthur Wentworth Eaton (London, 1901), 45; Caroline Gilman, ed., *Letters of Eliza Wilkinson* . . . (New York, 1839), 13 (see also 67–71); Colcock and Gibbons, *SCG and GA*, June 10, 1783. See also John Postele to Major Hyrne, June 2, 1781, South Carolina, Peter Force Collection, series 7E, box 62, LC; *Laurens Papers*, XI, 223–224, 254.

when the state "was in confusion, and invested by the British Army." Similarly, a Lowcountry manager informed his absentee employer that his two plantations had suffered remarkably little: not a single slave had been lost "either per force or by their own acord but on the contrary they have behaved exceeding well, faithfully attending to their work, though pinched by cold." In gratitude for "their fidelity," the manager planned to reward them with an extra suit of summer clothing and a personal visit, for "the poor Creatures I am told are desirous of seeing Me." These claims of loyalty may smack of a desperate need to believe in the slaves' constancy, but clearly the behavior of some slaves provided confirmation. If the overwhelming response of mid-nineteenth-century slaveholders to their slaves' actions in the Civil War was one of betrayal, that of late-eighteenth-century slaveholders was one of surprise.[16]

Masters and slaves depended on one another, and the burdens of that dependence were enormous. Masters often succumbed to the corrupting temptations of untrammeled power; slaves were frequently drawn into a tragic complicity in their own fate. At one end of the scales was the raw horror of an institution that condoned cruelty, violence, rape, and even murder; at the other was the tragic involvement of many slaves in their own oppression. Many masters tried to treat their slaves humanely, but their efforts were doomed to fail, for at bottom the relationship violated humanity. Conversely, many slaves acted generously toward their masters, but "ten thousand recollections," to use Jefferson's words, "of the injuries they have sustained" inevitably corroded their magnanimity, creating unfathomable depths of bitterness. Masters and slaves created a world that "could shimmer with mutual affection or . . . shatter in mutual antagonism." Plantations were arenas of shared companionship and intense warfare, friendly cooperation and savage conflict.[17]

VIOLENCE

Because slavery bound whites and blacks together in bitter antagonism, violence was always an important part of their relationship. Yet whites were often complacent about the prospect of collective slave violence, and this was

---

16. Frances-Susanna Pinckney, *Gaz of State of SC*, Nov. 27, 1783; Josiah Smith to George Appleby, June 5, 1783, Smith Letterbook. See also Maurice A. Crouse, ed., "Papers of Gabriel Manigault, 1771–1784," *SCHM*, LXIV (1963), 2; M. Pope to J. Jacob, Aug. 25, 1775, British Museum transcripts, LC; Anne Deas, ed., *Correspondence of Mr. Ralph Izard, of South Carolina . . .*, I (New York, 1844), 154. For slaveowners during the Civil War, see Eugene D. Genovese, *Roll, Jordan, Roll: The World the Slaves Made* (New York, 1974), 97–112; and Leon F. Litwack, *Been in the Storm So Long: The Aftermath of Slavery* (New York, 1979), esp. chaps. 1–3.

17. Thomas Jefferson, *Notes on the State of Virginia*, ed. William Peden (Chapel Hill, N.C., 1954), 138; Elizabeth Fox-Genovese, *Within the Plantation Household: Black and White Women of the Old South* (Chapel Hill, N.C., 1988), 27.

evident not just in their response to potential rebellions but in their policing of slaves and in the access slaves had to firearms. Eighteenth-century American slave societies were not police states constantly on the brink of violent rebellion. Sporadically, however, white fears about potential slave rebelliousness assumed near-hysterical proportions. The fury of slaveowners lay just below the surface like a smoldering volcano, always about to erupt. This rhythm—long periods of laxity alternating with short bursts of frenzy—needs explanation. The everyday violence committed by masters on their slaves and occasional acts of retaliation by slaves will help provide the answers by exposing the raw nerves of slavery.

Eighteenth-century masters never doubted that slaves were capable of violence or that they might rebel. As it happened, however, no Anglo-American mainland region had to face a large-scale slave insurrection in the eighteenth century. The one incident that came close was the Stono revolt of 1739, in which about sixty slaves in South Carolina killed approximately twenty whites and destroyed much property. By New World standards, however, this was a small-scale revolt of short duration. In spite of the lack of prolonged or widespread slave rebelliousness, both Chesapeake and Lowcountry slave societies experienced periods of sheer panic when an insurrection seemed imminent. At the prospect of collective slave violence, eighteenth-century public opinion oscillated between protracted stretches of near-complacency and brief spasms of near-paranoia.[18]

An incident that occurred in Virginia at the end of the eighteenth century neatly captures this divided state of mind. Passing the door of a magistrate in Madison, Virginia, Charles Janson, a stranger, heard the justice's raised voice "and the strokes of the cow-skin" being applied to one of the slaves of the justice of the peace. At every blow, the magistrate "urged the obstinate creature to confess to something which he appeared anxious to discover." Eventually the justice extracted the information he feared: "The negroes were planning an insurrection." As the neighboring whites assembled in a state of armed readiness, their "fears were wrought up to a high degree of alarm." Their anxieties were understandable, Janson observed, for "we counted our ranks at twelve or fifteen" whereas the slaves "could form a phalanx of as many hundreds within the circle of a few miles."

Six whites paid a visit to a quarter some two miles away, where the leaders of the insurrection were supposedly to be found. As his companions entered the

18. Peter H. Wood, *Black Majority: Negroes in Colonial South Carolina from 1670 through the Stono Rebellion* (New York, 1974), chap. 12; John K. Thornton, "African Dimensions of the Stono Rebellion," *AHR*, XCVI (1991), 1101–1113.

loghouse, Janson stood guard outside and saw a slave appear on the roof and jump to safety. Within the quarter were an old couple and their daughter. The man who made his escape was the girl's lover. These were hardly the leaders of a conspiracy. Returning empty-handed, Janson found that other raiding parties had been more successful. After a "strict examination" of various captured slaves, however, Janson concluded, "Nothing appeared to confirm our suspicions." When asked why they had been out so late, some slaves replied that they had been out hunting raccoons and opossums; others had been visiting their friends and relations. Janson "really believed" their stories. The magistrate did not, because "he had never known an instance of so many being out of their quarters at such a time." Janson responded that it was between two and three o'clock in the morning and, perhaps, no search of this nature had ever been conducted before. But the magistrate prevailed, and the slaves were severely flogged.

Four or five nights later, Janson was at the house of a friend, Mr. Gilpin, a newcomer to the area, when they "were greatly alarmed by an uncouth Singing of the negroes about a mile distant." They listened attentively "and fancied the noise drew near." While the host's family slept, "in great consternation we sallied out, myself with my loaded gun and Mr Gilpin with his mounted bayonet. We first ascended a rising ground to determine with more precision from what quarter the alarm proceeded. Convinced that our surmises were just, apprehending an attack, and conceiving that it was the negro war-song," the two headed for the local tavern to raise an alarm. The party playing cards were "greatly surprised" at seeing the armed men. And when they heard the reason, "they burst into a laugh, informing us that it was only a harvest-home of the negroes, in one of the quarters." The two would-be heroes "now felt ashamed," although their neighbors "greatly commended [their] activity," for which they became more respected in the community.

This sequence of events provides a revealing glimpse into the swirling, conflicting maelstrom that engulfed so many slaveholding communities when a slave insurrection seemed imminent. At one moment, local residents believed the worst. Only an outsider, it seems, thought otherwise. However unjustified, the floggings served their purpose. Not only were blacks given a sharp lesson, but whites reaffirmed their solidarity. After all, the whippings were "executed by the white men, in turns." A few days later, the outsider again found himself out of step with community opinion. With the recent incident fresh in his mind, he was only too susceptible to new fears. This time, the locals were skeptical. They scoffed at his alarm. The outsider had not yet adjusted to the rhythms of the slaveholding community: first, a short burst of intense suspicion, more than likely out of proportion to the real dangers; second, a cathartic show of force; and, finally, a return to normalcy or near-complacency. To the passerby, there seemed no logic to this process; to a slaveowning community, such inconsistencies were second nature.[19]

A similar inconsistency was the hallmark of contemporary observations about the potential rebelliousness of slaves. Eighteenth-century whites knew that their slaves were not truly submissive. And yet they could still sound a note of complacency—particularly if they were Virginians. Thus William Byrd, who could be positively apocalyptic about the prospect of a slave rebellion, yet spoke confidently of harboring no fears where slaves were concerned. Byrd and other Virginians pinpointed a major reason for their assurance. In the words of Charles Steuart, black numbers were "not so large as to give any uneasiness, and the country is under so proper regulation that we have no apprehension of an Insurrection." Even after Lord Dunmore had, as Archibald Cary put it, pointed "a dagger to [the whites'] throats, thro' the hands of their slaves," this Virginia patriot could still claim, "We have, however, no apprehension on that score."[20]

For Arthur Lee, this blithe self-confidence would only hasten the day of doom. He explained himself as follows:

> Since time, as it adds strength and experience to the slaves, will sink us into perfect security and indolence, which debillitating our minds, and enervating our bodies, will render us an easy conquest to the feeblest foe. Unarm'd already and undisciplined, with our Militia laws contemned, neglected or perverted, we are like the wretch at the feast; with a drawn sword depending over his head by a Single hair; yet we flatter ourselves, in opposition to the force of reason and conviction of experience, that the danger is not imminent.[21]

But the sword never fell. And the opinions of eighteenth-century whites concerning the dangers presented by their slaves came to alternate between even longer periods of complacency and even shorter bursts of fear.

The uneven performance of Chesapeake patrols is symptomatic of the fluctuating nature of white concern. On his appointment as a patroller in Princess Anne County, Virginia, in 1767, Edward James received orders "at least one night in every week to visit all negro Quarters," to break up all "unlawful

---

19. Charles William Janson, *The Stranger in America* (London, 1807), 402–405. See also Bertram Wyatt-Brown, *Southern Honor: Ethics and Behavior in the Old South* (New York, 1982), chap. 15, which judiciously probes insurrectionary scares.

20. For Byrd's comments, see Chapter 5, n. 25; Charles Steuart to Walter Tullideph, Sept. 23, 1751, microfilm, CW; Archibald Cary to R. H. Lee, Dec. 24, 1775, Lee Family Papers, UVa.

21. Richard K. MacMaster, ed., "Arthur Lee's 'Address on Slavery': An Aspect of Virginia's Struggle to End the Slave Trade, 1765–1774," *VMHB*, LXXX (1972), 156–157.

Assemblys," and to apprehend all slaves who lacked a pass. In spite of these extensive responsibilities, James claimed for only thirteen nights' work in 1767 and but two nights' labor in 1768. Not exactly a rigorous policing system; rather, a highly irregular one. The same general laxness and alternating annual rhythms are evident elsewhere. In 1755, twelve Middlesex County whites patrolled an average of nine nights each; the following year, six patrollers averaged three nights each. In 1757, the Sussex County patrol met just about once a week, but only from the beginning of July to the end of September. On some nights, they "found several Negroes," presumably slaves wandering off their plantations without passes; at other times, they whipped slaves by their owners' "consent." In 1763, the same county patrol met less than once a week, but over a longer period—from April to early November. Each night they traveled on average to about seven slave quarters. This spotty itinerary and half-yearly activity—during late fall, winter, and early spring, patrollers stayed at home—indicates a less than draconian police system.[22]

Most of the time, policing was no more diligent in South Carolina. In 1756, a provincial grand jury confidently reported, "In several parts of the country the people have not been mustered these two years, and few will take trouble to ride patrol in any part of the country." This complaint was only a pointed variation on a persistent refrain: grand juries warned of "the want of a patrol duty being duly done" or an "almost total neglect of patrol duty." Yet, as in the Chesapeake, an extraordinary incident could galvanize a community, as happened at Christmastime in 1765, when some Charleston blacks, in the words of Henry Laurens, "mimick'd their betters in crying out 'Liberty.'" As a result, Laurens reported, patrols rode "day and Night for 10 or 14 days in most bitter weather," although, as it happened, "there was Little or no cause for all that bustle."[23]

Whites were no more consistent in their attitude toward slaves' possession of firearms. Certainly, masters denied guns to most of their slaves, and both Virginia and South Carolina passed laws restricting bondpeople's access to

22. Order from Edward H. Moseley, County Lieutenant, Oct. 4, 1767, and County of Princess Anne to Edward James, 1767 and 1768, Edward Wilson James Papers, UVa; Middlesex County Orders, 1752–1758, 324–325, 383–385, VSL; Freemans and Payne Patrol Accounts, July 7–Sept. 29, 1757, Sussex County Court Papers, 1758, VSL; Patrol Journal, Apr. 30–Nov. 6, 1763, ibid., 1763–1764.

23. Charleston Grand Jury presentments, *SCG*, May 1, 1756; for succeeding complaints, see Court of General Sessions, Mar. 15, 1758, Apr. 22, 1769, Jan. 21, 1771, Oct. 19, 1773, SCDAH; Provincial Grand Jury presentments, *SCG*, June 2, 1766; *SC and AGG*, Jan. 29, 1768; and *Laurens Papers*, V, 53–54. See also Senate Presentments, Nov. 26, 1799; Liberty County, Ga., 1787, Duke. For more on lax policing in Charleston, see Philip D. Morgan, "Black Life in Eighteenth-Century Charleston," *Perspectives in American History*, N.S., I (1984), 217–221.

guns. Nevertheless, the Virginia law of 1723 banning guns to slaves made an exception for frontier regions. And the South Carolina law of 1722 permitted a plantation owner to license one slave to carry a gun for the hunting of game and vermin and the slaughtering of cattle. Even this stipulation was unnecessary if a white man accompanied the slave when hunting. In addition, the legislature made an exception where the slave carried his master's arms either to and from muster or to and from a plantation. Moreover, no limit was placed on those slaves' "keeping off rice-birds and other birds in the day time within the plantation," provided the guns were lodged at night in the master's dwelling. Slave watchmen on Lowcountry plantations usually carried guns.[24]

Even more important, slaves had much greater access to guns than statutes allowed. In the Chesapeake, one county court fined several masters for selling weapons to their slaves. Two of Landon Carter's slaves took "Guns loaded with small shot" to catch a runaway, and one of them shot the fugitive in the leg. On another occasion, Carter complained that hogs were jumping over his fences, even though he had "guns out every night after them." Slaves with guns did not always do their master's bidding. One slave faced trial for shooting a horse and cow and wounding a white man; another faced excommunication from his church for shooting his master's dog. Perhaps the best insight into the general distribution of arms among Chesapeake slaves was a discovery made by Eastern Shore residents on the eve of the Revolution. They collected about "eighty Guns, some Bayonets, swords, etc." from their slaves.[25]

---

24. William Waller Hening, *The Statutes at Large: Being a Collection of All the Laws of Virginia* . . . , 13 vols. (Richmond, Va., and Philadelphia, 1809–1823), III, 459, IV, 131, XII, 182; Thomas Cooper and David J. McCord, eds., *The Statutes at Large of South Carolina*, VII (Columbia, S.C., 1837), 345, 353–354, 372–373, 422. In North Carolina, licensing was the law. Thus, a planter petitioned his county court "to grant him Liberty for his Negro slave by name Derry to Carry a gun on his own Plantation" (application of James Hathaway, Mar. 13, 1804, Chowan County Slave Papers, NCDAH).

25. Lancaster County Court Order Book, no. 7, 1721–1729, 140, cited in Robert Anthony Wheeler, "Lancaster County, Virginia, 1650–1750: The Evolution of the Southern Tidewater Community" (Ph.D. diss., Brown University, 1972), 143; Greene, ed., *Carter Diary*, 289, 613; Granville County Court, Oct. 4, 1776, Treasurer's and Comptroller's Records, Miscellaneous Group, box 8, NCDAH; Court of Oyer and Terminer, Apr. 23, 1784, Executive Papers, box 34, VSL; minutes of Black Water Baptist Church, Southampton County, June 21, 1793, photostat, VSL; Committee of Inspection for Dorchester County, Maryland, May 23, 1775, Gilmor Papers, IV, 14, MHS. Only about 1% of runaway slaves in either Virginia or South Carolina had weapons. Between 1736 and 1790, 16 advertisements for Virginia fugitives mention that they carried weapons (15 guns, 1 sword). One group of six slaves was "armed with Guns"; another group of twelve stole "some guns"; Peter took along a gun of "uncommon large size," George a brace of pocket pistols, and Prince a brass-barreled holster pistol: Robert King et al., *VaG* (Hunter), May 24, 1751 (group of six); John Payne, *Maryland Journal, and the Baltimore Advertiser*, June 27, 1780 (group of 12); William Gregory, *VaG* (P and D),

It was public policy in early South Carolina to arm slaves. In principle, the colony never abandoned the enlistment of slaves, and, even as late as 1747, the assembly passed a law to draft slaves during emergencies, but, in practice, slaves were never mobilized after 1715. Yet the private arming of slaves continued well past this date. In Charleston, numbers of slaves were often seen carrying firearms. In 1754, at one muster, slaves carried home their masters' firearms, "which they charged and discharged several times as they went along the streets to the great Terror of many Ladies." Thirteen years later, the city grand jury complained that masters let their slaves keep their guns "during divine service." In 1772, the same body observed more generally that "Negroes were being allowed to . . . carry Fire-Arms." On the frontier, the private enlistment of slaves was still necessary. In 1788, Edward Rutledge noted that Indians had raided various outlying Georgia plantations and that the farmers had in turn "armed their Negroes."[26]

The chief reason for whites' complacency toward potential slave violence, the ineffectiveness of patrols and watches, and the use of firearms by slaves was the overwhelming coercive powers available to individual masters and the white community in general. In an emergency, masters could depend on a large adult white male population to come to their rescue. White supremacy was a more effective authority than any patroller or watchman could ever be. The best witnesses to the formidable array of masters' powers were the slaves

---

May 4, 1769 (Peter); Hamilton Ballantine, ibid. (D and N), May 22, 1779 (George); James Marsden, ibid. (Purdie), Aug. 21, 1778 (Prince).

26. Wood, *Black Majority*, 124–130; Cooper and McCord, eds., *Statutes at Large*, IX, 645–663. In 1743, the South Carolina Council debated a plan for the defense of the province in the case of invasion, in which blacks were to be armed and enlisted in companies that were always two-thirds white (South Carolina Council Journal, no. 10, Apr. 14, 1743, 158); 12 years later, the same body thought it might be a good idea, in case of Indian attack, to arm "the most Trusty of our Slaves" (ibid., Mar. 7, 1755); Parish Transcripts, box 3, NYHS; *SCG*, Oct. 17, 1754; presentments of the Grand Jury of Charlestown, *SCG and CJ*, Nov. 17, 1767, and *SCG*, Jan. 25, 1772; William L. McDowell, Jr., ed., *Documents Relating to Indian Affairs, May 21, 1750–August 7, 1754*, Colonial Records of South Carolina, 2d Ser. (Columbia, S.C., 1958), 370 (my thanks to James Merrell); Edward Rutledge, Jr., to John Rutledge, Apr. 8, 1788, Rutledge Papers, UNC. Between 1732 and 1782, 26 advertisements for South Carolina fugitives mention that they carried guns (also in three cases a cutlass and in another a Dutch knife). Tim, an "Angolan," was captured with a gun; London, another African, carried a gun, a shot pouch, and some powder and shot; and a group of four took three guns and a cutlass. Sometimes the descriptions of the weapons were highly specific: Nero, a "Coromantee," had "a holster pistol of Wilford's make," and Bob had "one of Wilson's fowling-pieces." Workhouse, *SCG*, Sept. 13, 1742 (Tim); Arthur Bull, ibid., July 24, 1755 (London); John Forbes, ibid., Aug. 20, 1763 (group of four); John Mouret, *SC and AGG*, June 5, 1777 (Nero); John Brailsford, ibid., Dec. 3, 1779.

themselves. The few extant narratives of eighteenth-century slaves speak eloquently of the barbarities they suffered.

James Carter, born a slave in Virginia, began the "Small Jernal" of his life by recounting the tragedy that befell his brother Henry. Raised in the "Family of Mrs. Lucy Armistead of Caroline County," Henry Carter reached age twenty-two before being sold to George Buckner. So cruel was Buckner's reputation that Henry immediately ran off. Discovered crossing a river, Henry was stoned to death by an overseer. James recorded in touching detail how his family scoured the riverbanks until they found his brother's body, which they brought home for a family burial.[27]

David George, born in Surry County, Virginia, about 1740, began the account of his life by recalling the cruelties visited on his family:

> My oldest sister was called Patty: I have seen her several times so whipped that her back has been all corruption, as though it would rot. My brother Dick ran away, but they caught him, and brought him home; and as they were going to tie him up, he broke away again; then they hung him to a cherry-tree in the yard, by his two hands, quite naked, except his breeches, with his feet about half a yard from the ground. They tied his legs close together, and put a pole between them, at one end of which one of the owner's sons sat, to keep him down, and another son at the other. After he had received 500 lashes, or more, they washed his back with salt water, and whipped it in, as well as rubbed it in with a rag; and then directly sent him to work in pulling off the suckers of tobacco. I also have been whipped many a time on my naked skin, and sometimes till the blood has run down over my waist band; but the greatest grief I then had was to see them whip my mother, and to hear her, on her knees, begging for mercy.[28]

The punishments were harsh enough, but the humiliation was even worse.

Boston King was rather more fortunate than either Carter or George. Both his parents held responsible posts on Richard Waring's South Carolina plantation. His father was a driver much "beloved by his master," his mother a nurse and seamstress. King's hardships began when he was apprenticed to a tradesman in Charleston. He assumed charge of the artisan's tools, and, whenever

---

27. Linda Stanley, ed., "James Carter's Account of His Sufferings in Slavery," *Pennsylvania Magazine of History and Biography*, CV (1981), 335–339.

28. "An Account of the Life of Mr. David George, from Sierra Leone in Africa . . . ," *Baptist Annual Register*, I (1790–1793), 473. George gave his birthplace as Essex, but this was probably a transcription error, because the other details he mentioned suggest that he was born in the part of Surry that later became Sussex County: Grant Gordon, *From Slavery to Freedom: The Life of David George, Pioneer Black Baptist Minister* (Hantsport, Canada, 1992), 7–11.

they were lost or misplaced, his master "beat [him] severely, striking [him] upon the head, or any other Part without mercy." When the workshop was burglarized, the master blamed King, whom he flogged "in a most unmerciful manner," so that he was unable to work for a fortnight. On another occasion, the craftsman "tortured" King "most cruelly," and he missed work for three weeks. Only when his owner intervened did King's treatment improve.[29]

If life in Charleston could be cruel, a Lowcountry plantation could be a living hell. Warwick Francis's reminiscences of the barbarities suffered by slaves in the South Carolina countryside are gruesome in the extreme. He first recounted how Dr. Aron Jelot tied a slave boy

> on a wooden spit so near the fire that it Scorch him well and basted with Salt and Water the same as you would a pigg. I have seen this same Aron Jelot took a pinchers and clap it to a mans tooth the Soundest in his head about one hour and a half and then draw it out the two persons was his own Slaves. I have seen the same A Jelot shoot a man Down the same as You would a Buck. This was about Nine or ten o'clock at night. I have also seen Joseph Belseford in the same County chain two of his slaves and make them Walk on a plank at a mill pond and those 2 got drownd and the said Joseph Belseford gave a man 360 lashes and then wash them down with Salt and Water and after that took brand that he branded his Cattel with and make the Brand red hot and put it on his buttocks the same as you would brand a creater.
>
> I have seen John Crimshire oversear on Barnet Elicot [or Elliot] estate a man whose name is Tom had 300 Lashes and put on the pickit with his Left Hand tied to his left toe behind him and his Right hand to post and his Right foot on the pickets till it worked through his foot. John Draten I have Seen him take his Slave and put them in a tierce and nailed spikes in the tierce and Roale down a Steep hill.
>
> The crueltity and punishment of the Slave which I have seen would not permit me to make mention but for Lashes 300 or 400 a[nd] to be Washed Down with Salt and Water is but Slite punishment[.] Many poor Women which I have Seen likely to be Deliver the child and oblige to wear a mouth peace and Lock out the Back part of it the keys the Driver keeps and are obliged to Worke all Day and at Night Put in Clos Houses.
>
> I have Seen them with a thim Screw Screwed till the Blood gushed out of their Nails. This I have Seen at Isaac Macpersons . . . this is what I have said I am an Eye Witness to it is not what I have heard. Time will not permit me to go further.

29. "Memoirs of the Life of Boston King, a Black Preacher," *Methodist Magazine*, XXI (1798), 105–107.

A number of the planters Francis mentioned lived in the Stono region of South Carolina, lending his account a ring of authenticity.[30]

The physical appearance of many runaway slaves also points to widespread cruelties practiced on individual plantations. About two hundred slave fugitives advertised in colonial South Carolina newspapers were branded, usually with the master's initials but occasionally with his surname. Masters applied brands most commonly to the breast or shoulder, but slaves were also branded on the forehead, cheek, and buttocks. About another hundred runaways went off with iron clogs (weighing, in some instances, about eight to twelve pounds) or spurs on their legs, iron collars or pot hooks (often with three or more protruding prongs) around their necks, their arms pinioned together, their hands cuffed, or their head in an iron contraption. Finally, another seventy-five bore the marks of a whipping, had some toes removed, had cropped ears, or had been castrated. In all, at least one in seventeen of the fugitives advertised in colonial South Carolina newspapers exhibited the physical scars of oppression. A similar proportion of Virginia runaways displayed maltreatment. But whippings accounted for about half of the physical scars and brandings for another third. Rare were the Virginia runaways who had irons fastened to their legs or an iron collar attached to their neck. No Virginia runaway slave was described as suffering castration, although a few had lost toes or had had their ears cropped.[31]

Slaves suffered so much personal violence at the hands of masters that they might be expected to have reciprocated. Yet, just like large-scale insurrections, prosecutions of slaves for crimes of violence, ranging from assault to murder, were infrequent. A study of slave trials in Richmond County, Virginia, from 1721 to 1776 reveals that only 4 of 55 cases involved murder and attempted murder and in just 2 cases were the victims white. My analysis of slave trials in eight Virginia counties from 1710 to 1785 indicates that acts of violence by slaves

---

30. Testimony of Warwick Francis, 1812, Paul Cuffee Collection, New Bedford Public Library, Mass. (reprinted in Ellen Gibson Wilson, *The Loyal Blacks* [New York, 1976], 23–24). Francis lived in the Horse-Savannah / Stono area of Colleton County, where Barnard Elliott, John Drayton, and Isaac McPherson all resided.

31. Among South Carolina runaways, I count 188 brandings, 70 leg irons, 14 chains, padlocks, spurs, or collars, 2 arms pinioned, 1 handcuffs, 1 headpiece, 61 whip marks, 3 toes removed, 3 castrations, 1 broken arm, and 1 gunshot wound. In all, this number represents just over 6% of all colonial South Carolina's advertised fugitives. Among Virginia fugitives, I count 40 whippings, 26 brandings, 10 leg irons or iron collars, 2 toes removed, and 5 ears cropped, representing about 7% of Virginia's advertised runaways. Presumably, not all masters mentioned the physical scars of their slave runaways. Yet, the fugitive population probably included a disproportionately large number of slaves who had experienced physical punishment. It is difficult, therefore, to know how representative this group is of the larger population.

against whites numbered only 47 of a total of 449 prosecutions. The most comprehensive study of eighteenth-century slave crime—Philip Schwarz's investigation of all Virginia county court cases involving slaves—concludes that "less than one-tenth of 1 percent" of Virginia's slave population in the mid-eighteenth century "resorted to killing white people." More whites than blacks were found guilty of murdering white people. Acts of violence by slaves that ended up in court were rare, crimes against property far outnumbered crimes against persons, and most slave crime was committed individually rather than collectively. All of this might seem to support the contention that masters had little to fear from their slaves.[32]

Some contemporaries said as much. St. George Tucker asserted that the murder of a master or mistress was a highly unusual event in eighteenth-century Virginia. Such crimes occurred so seldom that he was "inclined to believe as many cases happen in England of masters or mistresses murdered by their servants, as in Virginia." The duc de La Rochefoucauld-Liancourt, who visited South Carolina in 1796, reported, "Lawyers and judges have informed me that the white inhabitants commit more criminal offences, in proportion to their numbers, than the negroes." Although he acknowledged that "some masters may perhaps, from avaricious motives, shelter their slaves from punishment," he judged: "This can only take place in regard to crimes perpetuated in the midst of plantations. Few people assaulted, robbed or injured by the negroes would refrain from prosecuting them, merely to save their masters."[33]

Reassuring though such reflections and statistics might prove, a murder did not, as Eugene Genovese has pointed out, "have to occur often: one nearby, perhaps no closer than a neighboring county and perhaps only once in a decade to make a deep impression on masters as well as slaves." The unpredictability of such occurrences was particularly disturbing. A "most shocking murder" committed in Orangeburg, South Carolina, by a slave belonging to John Meyer was found sufficiently newsworthy to be publicized in the *London Gazette*. Apparently, the slave murdered Mrs. Meyer, the Meyers' daughter of

---

32. Gwenda Morgan, "The Hegemony of the Law: Richmond County, 1692–1776" (Ph.D. diss., The Johns Hopkins University, 1980), 145–146. My sample is based on a study of York, Essex, Middlesex, Richmond, Caroline, Chesterfield, Charles City, Louisa, and Elizabeth City County court orders; Philip J. Schwarz, *Twice Condemned: Slaves and the Criminal Laws of Virginia, 1705–1865* (Baton Rouge, La., 1988), 144–145. See also Rutman and Rutman, *A Place in Time,* 486; Arthur P. Scott, *Criminal Law in Colonial Virginia* (Chicago, 1930), 321; Gerald W. Mullin, *Flight and Rebellion: Slave Resistance in Eighteenth-Century Virginia* (New York, 1972), 61–62; Thad W. Tate, *The Negro in Eighteenth-Century Williamsburg* (Charlottesville, Va., 1972), 99–102.

33. St. George Tucker to Belknap, June 29, 1795, Massachusetts Historical Society, *Collections,* 5th Ser., III (1877), 409; La Rochefoucault Liancourt, *Travels,* I, 566.

sixteen years, and a suckling infant. He then dressed himself in his master's best clothes and set fire to the house. John Meyer, who was away in Charleston at the time, could think of no reason for his slave's behavior. Virginians must have pondered the same question when they learned that the sole slave belonging to Benjamin Hyde suddenly turned on his master, killing him and his whole family. Or they might have paused over a notice in the *Virginia Gazette* of 1778 reporting that eight Elizabeth County slaves strangled their master in bed and were "two hours about it." No one was safe. In 1780, the minister of Wappetaw congregation in South Carolina was murdered by one of the parsonage slaves.[34]

To travel any distance in the Anglo-American plantation colonies was to have one's complacency shaken, even if momentarily. In 1765, a Frenchman arrived in Williamsburg to be greeted by the spectacle of three slaves hanging from the gallows. In 1771, when Oliver Hart passed through Amherst County, Virginia, the local news was of a horrid murder committed some years earlier. A slave had killed four people outright and wounded another two. Hart even saw "some of the Blood still remaining on one of the Doors." Three years later, near Piscataway, Maryland, Nicholas Cresswell saw one-quarter of a slave body chained to a tree. The man had murdered his overseer. In 1781, at the Guilford County court house in North Carolina, William Feltman saw a slave head stuck on a sapling on one side of the road, and the man's right-hand side on a sapling on the opposite side. Talking with the residents could be even more alarming. A traveler in Virginia in 1800 met a gentleman who assured him "that more than 500 Masters and overseers had been murdered by the negroes within the limits of his knowledge and memory." It is impossible to reconcile this hearsay observation with the recorded prosecutions of murders committed by slaves and other contemporary observations. It was undoubtedly an exaggeration, but it is evidence of at least one white person's perceptions.[35]

A white person probably had more reason to fear for personal safety in South Carolina than in Virginia. Between 1735 and 1755, when Virginia's slave

---

34. Genovese, *Roll, Jordan, Roll*, 616–617; *London Gazette,* May 10, 1763, in Belfast Newspaper file, USC; Albemarle Parish Register, Sussex County, Virginia, Jan. 14, 1754, in *WMQ*, 1st Ser., XIV (1905–1906), 3; *VaG* (P and D), Nov. 6, 1778; Josiah Smith to Rev. J. J. Zubly, Aug. 22, 1780, Smith Letterbook. See also Schwarz, *Twice Condemned*, 137–164; and Marion Dargan, "Crime and the Virginia Gazette, 1736–1775," *University of New Mexico Bulletin*, Sociological Series, II, no. 1 (May 31, 1934), 3–61, esp. 13–15.

35. "Journal of a French Traveller in the Colonies, 1765," part 1, *AHR*, XXVI (1920–1921), 745; Oliver Hart diary, Dec. 1, 1769 (see also Jan. 16, 1770), Oliver Hart Papers, USC; Nicholas Cresswell, *The Journal of Nicholas Cresswell, 1774–1777* (New York, 1924), 20; William Feltman, *The Journal of Lieut. William Feltman* . . . (Philadelphia, 1853), 30; Miscellaneous MSS, HSP, June 10, 1800, II, 7, microfilm, CW.

population was at least twice as large as South Carolina's, the number of compensations for executed slaves was half as large. Between 1786 and 1815, compensations for executed slaves in South Carolina were a little more than half of those in Virginia, but the disproportion in the size of the two black populations was widening rather than diminishing. A dominating black majority, more isolated plantations, and less acculturated slaves all contributed to a more threatening environment in the Lowcountry than in the Chesapeake.[36]

The knife-edge that Lowcountry planters trod between economic gain and personal safety is captured well in the comments of an East Florida planter who was rapidly building up his estate in the 1760s. "I am sensible the progress ought to be gradual," he reflected judiciously, "that there should (with a view to safety) be an addition of strength of whites, before I can venture to increase the number of Negros." At the same time, the imperative to buy more slaves was almost impossible to resist, because "the life of the settlement and the profits arising from it must depend upon the Negro." The situation of William Bartram, who also established a plantation in East Florida in the 1760s, was a vivid reminder of these dangers. According to Henry Laurens, who visited Bartram, here was "a gentle mild Young Man, no Wife, no Friend, no Companion, no Neighbor, no Human inhabitant within nine miles of him," except for his slaves, and one of them threatened his life.[37]

The precariousness of life in the Lowcountry is suggested in some particularly gruesome and graphic incidents. One South Carolina master described how his "stout young Negroe man" armed himself with a "Scymeter," broke into his house, threatened to get a gun, and defied anyone to take him alive. The master managed to shoot the slave, but he could be forgiven for being uneasy thereafter. Beaufort residents were no doubt reassured when a slave was gibbeted for the murder of Charles Perry. Before his execution,

36. Compare John Donald Duncan, "Servitude and Slavery in Colonial South Carolina, 1670–1776" (Ph.D. diss., Emory University, 1972), 708–710, with Timothy Everett Morgan, "Turmoil in an Orderly Society: Colonial Virginia, 1607–1754: A History and Analysis" (Ph.D. diss., College of William and Mary, 1976), 290. For the early national years, compare Larry Darnell Watson, "The Quest for Order: Enforcing Slave Codes in Revolutionary South Carolina, 1760–1800" (Ph.D. diss., University of South Carolina, 1980), 99, and Philip D. Morgan, "Black Society in the Lowcountry, 1760–1810," in Ira Berlin and Ronald Hoffman, eds., *Slavery and Freedom in the Age of the American Revolution* (Charlottesville, Va., 1983), 117, with Schwarz, *Twice Condemned*, 56. Schwarz's early national Virginia figure is for all executions, whereas the corresponding figure for South Carolina is just for compensations for executions. The South Carolina figures, therefore, are artificially low.

37. Richard Oswald to James Grant, Mar. 15, 1767, bundle 295, Papers of Governor James Grant of Ballindalloch, sometime Governor of East Florida, in ownership of Sir Evan Macpherson-Grant, Bart., Ballindalloch Castle Muniments, Scotland; Francis D. West, "John Bartram and Slavery," *SCHM*, LVI (1955), 116; *Laurens Papers*, V, 153–154.

however, the slave "disclosed a scene equally shocking," one in which he and eight other blacks had planned to murder two other of the town's "Gentlemen" and make off with a schooner to Saint Augustine. A notice in the *South-Carolina Gazette* asked the owner to retrieve his gun and shot pouch taken from a slave, who "was gibeted last spring for murdering people near the Congarees." No wonder a Lowcountry resident might say, "Instances of Negroes murdering, scorching, and burning their own masters or overseers are not rare."[38]

The response of whites to the prospect of slave violence has been aptly likened to listening to static on an old radio. The background noise was always present; it would never quite go away. Similarly, whites were never free from anxiety, never entirely convinced of their slaves' intentions. Fear always lurked beneath the surface of these brittle societies. And yet Anglo-American planters could also go for long periods without paying the noise much attention. The listener could even get accustomed to the static, essentially not notice its presence. Whites congratulated themselves on the control they exercised over their slaves, were generally lax about patrolling, and often appeared recklessly complacent. Yet, if the static became louder or if the listener got a headache, the noise could become overwhelming and drown out all other sounds. Indeed, the hearer might became obsessive about it. In the same way, once whites fixated on the prospect of slave violence, they became prey to all sorts of imaginary fears. Perhaps this helps explain why insurrectionary scares came in clusters.[39]

SEX

Wherever whites and blacks congregated, sexual liaisons resulted. Even mundane, daily encounters had a sexual dimension. Slaves, after all, in contrast to whites, often wore little or no clothing. Admittedly, their seminudity might well have impressed a passing visitor more than their masters, who no doubt accustomed themselves to such things; but it is doubtful whether the shock registered by travelers could be ignored entirely. William Feltman, for instance, was surprised that the feelings of Virginia women were not hurt when they were attended by virtually naked "young boys of about Fourteen and Fifteen years Old." Feltman added, "I can Assure you It would Surprize a

---

38. South Carolina Commons House Journal, Dec. 18, 1766; *SCG*, Aug. 29, 1754; Peter Taylor, ibid., Sept. 1, 1759; "Johann Martin Bolzius Answers a Questionnaire on Carolina and Georgia," trans. and ed. Klaus G. Loewald et al., *WMQ*, 3d Ser., XIV (1957), 234.

39. Robert M. Weir, *Colonial South Carolina: A History* (Millwood, N.Y., 1983), 202. Insurrectionary scares clustered in the 1740s and 1790s. See Winthrop D. Jordan, *White over Black: American Attitudes toward the Negro, 1550–1812* (Chapel Hill, N.C., 1968), 110–122, 391–399.

person to see these d——d black boys how well they are hung." In an imaginary dialogue with a Virginia mistress, Benjamin Henry Latrobe expressed similar sentiments. "What do you think, Madam," inquired the visitor, "of the naked little boys and girls running about every plantation. What do you think of the Girls and Women, waiting upon your daughters in presence of Gentlemen with their bosoms uncovered. What think you of the known promiscuous intercourse of your servants, the perpetual pregnancies of your young servant girls, shamefully exhibited to your children, who well know, that marriage exists not among them?" The mistress of the plantation quickly dismissed the questions. "Oh but who minds the blacks," she argued. "Our Girls never think of these things."[40] To shrug off pertinent questions so hastily may suggest unease. One wonders, for example, Did white men "never think of these things"? Moreover, the conversation ignored the most obvious demonstration of the relevance of these questions—the presence of mulattoes.

The proportion of mulattoes in the black population provides a clue, albeit a rough one, to the incidence of interracial sex. Unfortunately, reliable statistics on the mulatto population are unavailable for the eighteenth century. The only listing that differentiates between "Negroes" and "Mulattoes" is the Maryland census of 1755. Apparently, 8 percent of Maryland's slaves were of mixed racial origin in that year. Great significance cannot be attached to this figure, for British colonists were notoriously indiscriminate about degrees of racial intermixture. They were inclined to lump slaves of mixed racial ancestry with other blacks. One colonial planter even described his slave as a "Mulatto or Negro man." For what they are worth, contemporary perceptions suggest quite large mulatto populations. An observer of mid-eighteenth-century Virginia reckoned that "the country swarms with mulatto bastards"; Johann Bolzius thought it all too common in midcentury South Carolina for "white men [to] live in sin with Negresses" so that mulatto children abounded "in large numbers"; and a generation later Ebenezer Hazard judged that "the number of Mulattoes in the four southernmost states" is clear "proof of a viciated taste in their inhabitants." But, if, as seems likely, there were proportionately more mulattoes in the eighteenth century than later, the difference cannot be measured precisely.[41]

40. Military journal of Lt. William Feltman, June 22, 1781, HSP, as cited by Jordan, *White over Black*, 159; Edward C. Carter II et al., eds., *The Virginia Journals of Benjamin Henry Latrobe, 1795–1798*, I (New Haven, Conn., 1977), 225.

41. Robert V. Wells, *The Population of the British Colonies in America before 1776: A Survey of Census Data* (Princeton, N.J., 1975), 146, 149; Julien Legge's deed of sale, Apr. 19, 1755, Miscellaneous Records, KK, 163, SCDAH; Peter Fontaine to Moses Fontaine, Mar. 30, 1757, Maury Papers, as cited in Robert E. Brown and B. Katherine Brown, *Virginia, 1705–1786: Democracy or Aristocracy?* (East Lansing, Mich., 1964), 68; "Bolzius Answers a Question-

What also seems clear, though equally impervious to precise measurement, is that mulattoes formed a higher proportion of the black population in the Chesapeake than in the Lowcountry. The more evenly matched black and white populations of the Chesapeake provided more opportunities for racial intermixture than the heavily imbalanced black-white ratios of the Lowcountry. The duc de La Rochefoucauld-Liancourt, who visited both regions in the late eighteenth century, had no doubts about the difference. "In Virginia," he noted, "mongrel negroes are found in greater number than in Carolina and Georgia." He attributed this in part to "the superior antiquity of the settlement of Virginia."[42] In fact, however, the proportion of mulattoes among the Chesapeake's black population was probably higher in the earlier as opposed to the later part of the eighteenth century.

Restrictions on interracial sex promulgated in the Chesapeake in the middle to late seventeenth century were not immediately effective. In 1671, Norfolk County court ordered Francis Skiper, a white resident, to pay levies and tithes on his wife, "shee being a negro," but apparently eschewed any other legal harassment. A generation later, a mulatto slave woman petitioned for her freedom on the grounds that she had lived "without disguise" with a white man, had borne a child by him, had had herself and her child baptized, and had been promised marriage by her white lover before his death. Her petition was granted. A number of Virginia whites also petitioned their council to repeal a prohibition on interracial marriage in the late seventeenth century. In early-eighteenth-century Maryland, a white woman persisted in her common law marriage to a slave, despite the penalties, and bore him seven children. In the first decade of the eighteenth century, a Northern Neck planter, Stephen Loyde, openly recorded the birthdates of his two illegitimate children. As he noted in his diary, both were born "of Rachel a negro woman." Late in the century, Robert Carter of Nomini Hall took an interest in the legal status of Thomas Clarke, a mulatto, then detained in servitude. This led Carter to reconstruct the history of the Clarke family in Westmoreland County. It happened that Thomas was the grandson of Sarah Clarke, a white woman who came to Westmoreland as an indentured servant in 1729. She gave birth to "two

---

naire," trans. and ed. Loewald et al., *WMQ*, 3d Ser., XIV (1957), 235; H. Roy Merrens, ed., "A View of Coastal South Carolina in 1778: The Journal of Ebenezer Hazard," *SCHM*, LXXIII (1972), 190. About 1 in 6 of 251 fugitives, who came primarily from the Lowcountry to Spanish Florida in the late 18th century, were listed as mulattoes. Mulattoes are known to have taken flight more readily than the broader population, but perhaps the high proportion also owes something to a precise interest in racial origins among Spanish investigators. See Jane Landers, "Spanish Sanctuary: Fugitives in Florida, 1687–1790," *Florida Historical Quarterly*, LXII (1984), 296–313, esp. 307.

42. La Rochefoucault Liancourt, *Travels*, II, 82.

Mulatto bastard Children during her servitude," both of whom were free by 1775. Thomas was the eldest son of Sarah's daughter.[43]

However, by midcentury, the incidence of interracial sex, particularly between black men and white women, but perhaps also between white men and black women, seems to have declined, as social sanctions against the practice gradually took effect. Thus, sixteen white women were convicted of bearing mulatto bastards in Prince George's County, Maryland, in the 1720s and 1730s; but this number was more than halved in the next two decades. Too much should not be read into individual plantation listings, but the difference between the number of mulattoes among William Fitzhugh's slaves at the turn of the century (8 of 51) and those belonging to Robert "King" Carter a generation later (3 of 734) is striking. In the late-eighteenth-century Chesapeake, a traveler reported that a man's reputation could be ruined by fathering a mulatto child. He "would be scorned, dishonored; every house would be closed to him; he would be detested." Another traveler noted that public opinion was firmly against miscegenation, so much so that "no white man is known to live regularly with a black woman." The intensity of social disapproval against miscegenation contradicts Joel Williamson's assertion that colonial Virginia "supported conditions nearly ideal for the proliferation of a large mulatto population."[44]

Public condemnation was often the fate reserved for those who committed infractions of the new moral code. In this racially charged sexual atmosphere, well in evidence by the early eighteenth century, one white woman accused another of being "a Negro whore and Negros strumpet [who] . . . would have Jumpt over nine hedges to have had a Negroe." In 1767, the Reverend Patrick Lunan of Nansemond County found himself roundly condemned for drink-

---

43. Norfolk County Wills and Deeds E (Orders), Aug. 15, 1671, 73, VSL, cited in Kathleen M. Brown, *Good Wives, Nasty Wenches, and Anxious Patriarchs: Gender, Race, and Power in Colonial Virginia* (Chapel Hill, N.C., 1996), 126; Legislative Petitions, Lancaster County, 1697, as cited in Philip Alexander Bruce, *Economic History of Virginia in the Seventeenth Century: An Inquiry into the Material Conditions of the People . . .* , II (New York, 1896), 110; H. R. McIlwaine, ed., *Legislative Journals of the Council of Colonial Virginia*, I (Richmond, Va., 1918), 262; Allan Kulikoff, *Tobacco and Slaves: The Development of Southern Cultures in the Chesapeake, 1680–1800* (Chapel Hill, N.C., 1986), 387; Letterbook of Stephen Loyde, July 3, 1709, Aug. 15, 1710, Tayloe Family Papers, VHS; Robert Carter Daybook, Jan. 18, 1775, XIII, 65–66, Duke.

44. Kulikoff, *Tobacco and Slaves*, 386–387, 395; Richard Beale Davis, ed., *William Fitzhugh and His Chesapeake World, 1676–1701* (Chapel Hill, N.C., 1963), 378–379, 381–382; inventory of Robert "King" Carter, November 1733, VHS; Ferdinand-M. Bayard, *Travels of a Frenchman in Maryland and Virginia*, ed. and trans. Ben C. McCrary (Williamsburg, Va., 1950), 20; Robert Sutcliffe, *Travels in Some Parts of North America . . .* (New York, 1811), 53; Joel Williamson, *New People: Miscegenation and Mulattoes in the United States* (New York, 1980), 35.

ing, quarreling, fighting, swearing, "exposing his private parts" to public view, and, last but not least, his solicitation of "Negro and other women to commit the crimes of fornication and adultery with him." Two years later, when Mary Skinner bore a black child, her husband, a prominent gentleman of Calvert County, Maryland, proclaimed his disgust at her "pollut[ing]" his bed. In 1785, the members of the Hartwood Baptist Church in Stafford County, Virginia, registered their strong displeasure at the behavior of Susan Leftrage. In their eyes, "such an Evil person" had to be excommunicated and expelled from membership because she had "swerved intirely from the line of truth and brought public scandal on our holy profession by commiting fornication by cohabiting with a negro." Ten years later, Captain James West of Maryland called off his proposed marriage to Peggy Whitaker when he discovered that Peggy's sister had a mulatto or black husband.[45]

As these incidents suggest, cases of interracial cohabitation or marriage, though never numerous in the eighteenth-century Chesapeake, recurred. In spite of a Virginia law that stipulated six months' imprisonment and fine of ten pounds for any white person entering into an interracial marriage, some whites went ahead and faced the consequences. In 1738, a Northampton County white, Tamar Smith, served the prison term and paid the fine so that she could marry a mulatto man, Edward Hitchens. A half-century later, when Robert Ayres, a Methodist circuit rider, passed by Old Town, Virginia, he met a white woman who had married a black slave. In 1764, Bolling Stark acknowledged the disappearance of his slave man Bob, "decoyed away by a white woman who, it seems had a child by him, and who disappeared about the time he runaway." John Custis so favored his mulatto child, Jack, born of slave woman "young Alice," that he threatened to disinherit his only legitimate son in Jack's favor. Perhaps his respect for community opinion prevailed, for he did not carry out his threat, although he did provide for Jack's manumission and for his "handsome" maintenance.[46]

---

45. *Anne Batson v. John Fitchet and wife Mary*, Northampton County Loose Papers, 1731, as cited in Douglas Deal, "A Constricted World: Free Blacks on Virginia's Eastern Shore, 1680–1750," in Lois Green Carr, Philip D. Morgan, and Jean B. Russo, eds., *Colonial Chesapeake Society* (Chapel Hill, N.C., 1988), 279–280; complaint against Rev. Patrick Lunan, Fulham Palace Papers, miscellaneous typescripts, CW; Walter Skinner, *Md Gaz*, Oct. 12, 1769; Hartwood Baptist Church, June 25, 1785, VBHS; William Faris diary, Dec. 31, 1795, MHS, as cited in Daniel Blake Smith, *Inside the Great House: Planter Family Life in Eighteenth-Century Chesapeake Society* (Ithaca, N.Y., 1980), 132n.

46. J. Douglas Deal, *Race and Class in Colonial Virginia: Indians, Englishmen, and Africans on the Eastern Shore during the Seventeenth Century* (New York, 1993), 180; journal of Robert Ayres, Apr. 9, 1788, microfilm, Duke; Bolling Stark to George MacMurdo, Dec. 15,

Affectionate interracial unions also occurred among the Wright family in piedmont Virginia. In 1779, Thomas Wright bought a 390-acre plantation in Bedford County. Among his slaves was a "very black" woman, Sylvia, who had already given birth to two children and was pregnant with another. Almost a year after moving to the new plantation, Sylvia bore Thomas Wright's mulatto son Robert. Thomas Wright and Sylvia lived together openly as man and wife, and she gave birth to three more mulatto children between 1784 and 1793. Thomas was said to be "much attached" to Sylvia. He eventually freed her, her children (including those not his), and provided for her after his death. Thomas's attitude toward his children was equally loving. In 1791, Thomas decided to free "his Robin," as he called eleven-year-old Robert, told friends that the boy would be his heir, and gave him a horse to ride to school, where his closest companions were white boys. The proud father even boasted that his son—usually described as a "light" or "bright" mulatto—was one of the "strongest negro fellows" in the county. After Thomas's death in 1805, Robert Wright inherited his father's plantation and six adult slaves, and a year later married a white woman. Robert's marriage was contrary to law but aroused no controversy among his neighbors. Although the marriage did eventually fail, it was happy for the first eight years, with Robert "kind and affectionate" to his wife and she bringing him "great domestic comfort and felicity." Three white male neighbors declared that Robert "allways treated his wife with kindness." As Thomas Buckley puts it, the story of the Wright family suggests "a level of openness in interracial sexual relationships and a degree of white acceptance of miscegenation that challenge historical generalizations and traditional stereotypes."[47]

Of course, there were always masters who preyed on slave women. William Byrd II approached slave and servant women indiscriminately. One night he asked a slave girl to kiss him; another time, he felt the breasts of a black girl; even as a sixty-seven-year-old he could be found "playing the fool with Sally." Virginia masters learned these lessons at a young age. In the spring of 1774, Robert Carter's eighteen-year-old son Ben reportedly took a young maid named Sukey into the stable "and there for a considerable time lock'd" themselves together. Six months later, the Carter household "whispered" with ru-

---

1764, Maxwell, MacMurdo, and Newhall Family Papers, box 3, National Library of Scotland, Edinburgh; Josephine Zuppan, "The John Custis Letterbook, 1724 to 1734" (master's thesis, College of William and Mary, 1978), 34–35; Ivor Noel Hume, *All the Best Rubbish* (New York, 1974), 189; Sobel, *The World They Made Together*, 150–152.

47. Thomas E. Buckley, S.J., "Unfixing Race: Class, Power, and Identity in an Interracial Family," *VMHB*, CII (1994), 349–380 (quotations on 350, 354, 355, 363).

mors that Ben had broken into the nursery in order to "commit fornication with Sukey (a plump, sleek, likely Negro Girl about sixteen)."[48]

The life of Thomas Jefferson offers insight into the twisted web created by sexual relations between generations of blacks and whites. After his third wife died in 1761, John Wayles, Jefferson's father-in-law, allegedly took Elizabeth, or Betty, Hemings, the mulatto child of an English sea captain and an African woman, as his concubine. Apparently, Wayles and Hemings had six children between 1762 and 1773, this last the year of Wayles's death at the age of fifty-eight. Jefferson's refusal to defend himself against the scurrilous attacks concerning his connection to the Hemings family seemingly stems from his reluctance to reveal that they were his own beloved wife's half-brothers and half-sisters. Furthermore, Sally Hemings, the last child born to John Wayles and Betty Hemings in 1773, probably became the mistress of Peter Carr, Jefferson's favorite nephew and surrogate son. It seems likely that their intimacy, begun when both were in their early twenties, lasted at least fifteen years and resulted in five children. Peter Carr's marriage to Hetty Smith, the daughter of a prominent Baltimore family, in the same year that Sally conceived their second child might have fostered jealousy on Sally's part, which later led her to repudiate Carr's paternity of her children. Such, in Douglass Adair's words, were the "circumstances that knotted the lives of the Wayles, the Hemingses, the Carrs, and the Jeffersons into the tangled web of love and hatred, of pride and guilt, of love and shame." And such may well explain Jefferson's explosive condemnation of slavery, especially his description of the "whole commerce between master and slave" as the "perpetual exercise of the most boisterous passions." In spite of Jefferson's oft-stated aversion to miscegenation and regardless of his possible personal involvement, he headed a household and a family in which interracial sex had been and was still commonplace. He lived, as Lucia Stanton notes, "surrounded by its examples."[49]

Precisely because community disapproval of miscegenation was so intense

---

48. Louis B. Wright and Marion Tinling, eds., *The Secret Diary of William Byrd of Westover, 1709–1712* (Richmond, Va., 1941), 90, 425; Wright and Tinling, eds., *William Byrd of Virginia: The London Diary (1717–1721), and Other Writings* (New York, 1958), 484; Maude Woodfin, ed., and Marion Tinling, trans., *Another Secret Diary of William Byrd of Westover, 1739–1741: With Letters and Literary Exercises, 1696–1726* (Richmond, Va., 1942), 157, 168; Hunter Dickinson Farish, ed., *Journal and Letters of Philip Vickers Fithian, 1773–1774: A Plantation Tutor of the Old Dominion* (Williamsburg, Va., 1957), 115, 241–243, 246, 248.

49. I have relied heavily on the highly judicious and insightful "Jefferson Scandals," in Douglass Adair, *Fame and the Founding Fathers: Essays by Douglass Adair*, ed. Trevor Colbourn (New York, 1974), 160–191; and Lucia Stanton, " 'Those Who Labor for My Happiness': Thomas Jefferson and His Slaves," in Peter S. Onuf, ed., *Jeffersonian Legacies* (Charlottesville, Va., 1993), 147–180, esp. 152, 173–174. I think the case for the paternity of Sally's children is stronger for Peter Carr than for Jefferson, although I realize that definitive proof is lacking.

by the second half of the eighteenth century, Virginians tended to respond calmly rather than hysterically to alleged rapes committed by slaves on white women. Before 1740, the eight Virginia slaves tried for rape were all convicted, but, from 1740 to 1785, 30 percent of the fifty-one slaves tried for rape were found not guilty, and another 12 percent were punished only with a whipping. Of the sixty rape sentences (by black men on white women) that came before the Virginia executive in the late eighteenth and early nineteenth centuries, almost half included either recommendations for mercy from the justices or petitions for pardon from the community. In 1803, the justices of King and Queen County, who had sentenced a slave for rape, recommended a pardon on the grounds that the victim "by her own confession" acknowledged having three mulatto children "begotten by different negro men." Perhaps sexism outweighed racism here, but it does indicate that the alleged sexual aggressiveness of black men did not automatically rule out other considerations—particularly gender and class concerns, for naturally all the alleged victims were women, and most appear to have been lower-class—in late-eighteenth-century Virginia.[50]

Miscegenation was probably even less widespread in the Lowcountry than in the Chesapeake, but more commonly accepted. This seeming paradox is simply explained. South Carolina's black majority made for fewer sexual contacts across racial lines than Virginia's white majority. At the same time, South Carolinians viewed open concubinage quite casually precisely because it presented little danger to fundamental social distinctions. The chasm between white and black opened wide in South Carolina, and the presence of a small mulatto population was unlikely to bridge it. A matter-of-fact acceptance of interracial unions explains why a leading South Carolina planter petitioned to act as the guardian of a mulatto slave child who had been granted "her Freedom and fifteen Negroes" by her white father. It also explains why the white heirs of Benjamin Williamson decided to manumit three mulatto children whom they openly acknowledged to be Williamson's "Issue."[51]

---

50. Schwarz, *Twice Condemned*, 39, 82, 157, 206; James Hugo Johnston, *Race Relations in Virginia and Miscegenation in the South, 1776–1860* (Amherst, Mass., 1970), 257–260. In an atmosphere somewhat rawer and cruder than Virginia, whites did not always act calmly. Thus, when Phill was convicted of raping a white woman in North Carolina in 1762, he was sentenced not only to be hanged but then to have "his private parts cut off and thrown in his face": Marvin L. Michael Kay and Lorin Lee Cary, *Slavery in North Carolina, 1748–1775* (Chapel Hill, N.C., 1995), 85.

51. Petition of James Coachman, June 6, 1770, William Bull Papers, Duke; indenture agreed to between the heirs of Benjamin Williamson, June 18, 1774, and subsequent deed of manumission, Nov. 21, 1774, Miscellaneous Records, WW, 77–78. See also deposition of Paul Trapier, Mar. 24, 1784, ibid., VV, 63.

Visitors to the Lowcountry were shocked by the openness with which white men consorted with black women. In 1737, a Swiss settler in South Carolina railed at the "swinishness" of his neighbors, for "if a white man has a child by a black woman, nothing is done to him on account of it." Thirty years later, a New Englander observed that "the enjoyment of a negro or mulatto woman is spoken of as quite a common thing: no reluctance delicacy or shame is made about the matter." Some visitors, however, adapted rapidly to the region's mores. "I assure you," wrote one recently arrived Englishman to his friend at home, that "one is obliged to be exceeding Severe with the Sooty race, from a native Obstinacy and Idleness which pervades them[.] Its true there are exceptions for some deserve every attention that can be paid them." No wonder Francis Bayard believed that the inhabitants of the Carolinas and Georgia were "less scrupulous" about interracial affairs than their Chesapeake counterparts.[52]

This casualness is not to say that there was universal acceptance of interracial unions in the eighteenth-century Lowcountry. In 1743, the grand jury of South Carolina emphatically denounced "the too common practice of CRIMINAL CONVERSATIONS with Negro and other slave wenches in this Province, as an Enormity and Evil." But these criticisms were often class-related. In 1763, for example, Henry Laurens dismissed an overseer for his "familiarity" with a slave woman in part because it was "wrong and unwarrantable in itself" but, more important, it seems, because it was "extremely offensive to me and very hurtful to my Interest, as it must tend to make a good deal of Jealousy and disquiet among my Negroes." Seven years later, Laurens revealed the extent of his moral scruples when he reemployed an overseer who had previously given in his notice "for no other Cause but my kind and friendly Admonition against keeping a Wench in the House in open Adultery." Similarly, a Georgia planter was apparently less upset that his overseer had engaged in sexual relations with his slaves than that during his "four month stay he infected every negroe wench on the plantation with a foul, inveterate and highly virulent disease." Another social group that sometimes elicited criticism for dalliances with black women was ministers. In 1756, the vestry of Saint Helena Parish accused their clergyman of "indecent familiarities" with Mrs. Cattell's "Negro Wench." A vestryman in Saint Bartholomew Parish opposed more clerical power be-

---

52. R. W. Kelsey, "Swiss Settlers in South Carolina," *SCHM*, XXIII (1922), 90; Mark Antony De Wolfe Howe, ed., "Journal of Josiah Quincy, Junior, 1773," Mass. Hist. Soc., *Proceedings*, XLIX (1915–1916), 463; L. Dalton to Mr. Gibbs, 1796, Miscellaneous MSS, LC; Bayard, *Travels of a Frenchman*, 20. See also John S. Ezell, ed., and Judson P. Wood, trans., *The New Democracy in America: Travels of Francisco de Miranda in the United States, 1783–84* (Norman, Okla., 1963), 14.

cause it might lead his rector to "stay at home drinking his Bottle with his negroe woman" instead of officiating at church.[53]

On the whole, however, interracial sex in the Lowcountry was not just countenanced but rather regarded with amusement. Lowcountry residents could afford to be flippant about racial intermixture. Black slaves were in a firmly subordinate position, and the mulatto population was never likely to be sizable. A supporter of the plan by the governor of East Florida to purchase slaves pointed out that a "few likely young wenches must be in the parcell, and should their Husbands fail in their duty, I dare say my friend Sweetinham and other publick spirited Young Men, will be ready to render such an essential service to the Province as to give them some help." The public mood of Charleston concerning miscegenation is captured in a number of lighthearted contributions to the local newspaper in the 1730s. Some seventy years later, the mood had changed little, for John Davis met some gentlemen on his travels who were "laughing over their nocturnal adventures in Mulatto Alley at Charleston."[54]

The Lowcountry capital undoubtedly saw the most openly displayed interracial liaisons in British North America. As was to be expected of a port, prostitutes (most of whom were probably black) were widely available. A runaway slave man, for example, was said to be "intimate with abundance of black prostitutes" in town, and a slave woman was thought to be harbored in "these houses where sailors frequent." Visitors to Charleston were generally appalled at the level of racial intermixture. Johann Bolzius longed "to get out of this sinful city . . . [where] the Europeans commit dreadful excesses with the Negro girls" with "little or no shame." Henry Muhlenberg found "many slaves who are only half black, the offspring of those white Sodomites who commit fornication with their black slave women." The one visitor who is on record as being surprised by the relative "privacy" with which interracial "conversations" were conducted was from the West Indies, where concubinage was both extensive and even more openly countenanced than in South Carolina.[55]

If Charlestonians generally adopted a relaxed, tolerant view of miscegena-

53. *SCG*, Mar. 28, 1743; *Laurens Papers*, III, 248, VII, 376, 380; Kenneth Baillie, Sr., *Ga Gaz*, Sept. 26, 1765; A. S. Salley, Jr., *Minutes of the Vestry of St. Helena's Parish, South Carolina, 1726–1812* (Columbia, S.C., 1919), 78–83; Florence Gambrill Geiger, ed., "St. Bartholomew's Parish as Seen by Its Rectors, 1713–1761," *SCHM*, L (1949), 192.

54. John Graham to James Grant, July 19, 1765, bundle 401, Papers of Governor James Grant of Ballindalloch; Jordan, *White over Black*, 146–150; Wood, *Black Majority*, 234–238; Duncan, "Slavery and Servitude," 284; John Davis, *Travels of Four Years and a Half in the United States of America . . .* (Bristol, 1803), 355.

55. James Reid, *SCG*, Nov. 14, 1761; Margaret Peronneau, *SC and AGG*, Oct. 15, 1779; George Fenwick Jones, "John Martin Boltzius' Trip to Charleston, October 1742," *SCHM*, LXXXII (1981), 101; Muhlenberg, *Journals of Muhlenberg*, I, 58; G. Moulton to [?], Jan. 23, 1773, Add. MSS 22677, 75, BL.

tion, the privileges that some black women assumed for their favors were far more disturbing. Sexual exploitation of black women produced no unease; the aspirations of these same black women proved profoundly disquieting. Ebenezer Hazard drew precisely this implication from Charleston's "black dances," to which "many of the first gentlemen (so called) attend" and at which many of the black women "dress elegantly, and have no small acquaintance with polite behaviour." During the Revolutionary war, a Charlestonian found no better illustration of the "shame and perfidy [to which] the officers of that once great nation (Britain) has arriv'd" than their attendance at "an Ethiopian Ball," where female slaves "dress'd up in the most pompous manner." In 1795, a public investigation followed a "Negro dance" that the Charleston Guard discovered. Most unsettling was the presence of a white magistrate; indeed, as one of the black women was taken into custody, she handed him "her Head Dress and Bonnet and desired him to take Care of it for her."[56]

The expectations of black women in Charleston extended far beyond the dance floor. More tangible benefits could be realistically entertained from their liaisons with whites. George Dick, a mariner, left all his property to Jenny Dick, a free black who lived with him as his servant, and to Alexander Dick, his natural son. Abraham Newton, a self-styled Charleston "gentleman," bequeathed his whole estate to Rose Peronneau, a free black woman, because of the "very great Care, Tenderness and Attention" she displayed in tending him through an illness. The mulatto mistress of Captain Davis of Savannah "had the custody of all his Cash, as well as Books." She was instrumental in having one of Davis's employees, a ship's master, fired. If a slave mother gained nothing for herself, she might yet entertain hopes for her children. In the early eighteenth century, a mulatto slave woman bore a white butcher a daughter. The slave's mistress, a Mrs. Frost, refused to sell the girl to the butcher, who died in 1740. But his plans for his progeny did not expire with him, though they had to wait twenty-six years, until Frost died, before his executors could purchase his daughter, set her free, and bestow on her £350, the balance of his estate. If her mother was still alive, she might have taken solace from having a daughter who was free.[57]

56. Merrens, "A View of Coastal South Carolina in 1778," *SCHM*, LXXIII (1972), 190; Daniel Stevens to John Wendell, Feb. 20, 1782, Mass. Hist. Soc., *Procs.*, XLVIII (1915), 342; depositions of Peter S. Ryan, William Johnson, James Allison, James McBride, and Henry Moses, Nov. 7, 1795, General Assembly, Governor's Messages, no. 650, Nov. 24, 1795, 9–30, SCDAH.

57. Will of George Dick, Oct. 24, 1773, Charleston County Wills, XV, 1771–1774, 609–610, SCDAH; will of Abraham Newton, Apr. 8, 1790, ibid., XXIII, 1786–1793, 635; William Stephens, *A Journal of the Proceedings in Georgia Beginning October 20, 1737* . . . , in Allen D.

Black women in the rural Lowcountry occasionally benefited from their intimate relations with whites. In 1749, a planter in Saint Bartholomew Parish bequeathed to his "friend," James Bond, the right to purchase his three enslaved children. Two years later, Bond, styling himself a "planter," bought the Negro woman Peggy and her three children from his friend's estate for a thousand pounds. Two years after this purchase, Bond freed his family out of his "love and affection" for them and acknowledged that Peggy had been his wife "for many years past." In 1756, Bond made his will, stipulating that his estate should be divided into four equal parts and entrusting this task to his wife, Peggy. Another marriage of a slave woman to a white man was recognized in a manumission document. A mulatto slave woman named Elizabeth who belonged to Captain Thomas Broughton was permitted to "intermarry with one Henry Clusteny by whom she had Issue one Daughter," also named Elizabeth. In 1754, the wife gained her freedom because of "her good and faithful services, the request of Elizabeth [and] the desire of her husband."[58]

In the Chesapeake, such favors were perhaps less common and certainly less openly acknowledged. An exception was Ryland Randolph, who, in the 1780s, freed his house servant Aggy and her two children on account of his "great affection" for them. He bequeathed them "all his Household furniture of every kind including Gold and Silver," provided for their passage to England, and established a trust fund of three thousand pounds sterling for them. Not even acknowledged members of his family were so generously treated. Far more typical, no doubt, was the fate that befell a slave woman who had five children by an Alexandria merchant. Nicholas Cresswell, who visited the household in 1776, marveled at the man's callousness in seeing "his own flesh and blood in this horrid situation," daily "wanting the common necessaries of life." Johann Schoepf caustically remarked on the "great-mindedness of the Virginians"

Candler, comp., *The Colonial Records of the State of Georgia*, IV (Atlanta, Ga., 1906), 344–345; Robert Raper to Thomas Boone, Mar. 5, 1770, Robert Raper Letterbook, West Sussex Record Office, England, microfilm, SCHS. See also Elias Ball's deed of sale to William Ellis, July 9, 1746, and William Ellis's deed of manumission to William, Oct. 28, 1746, Miscellaneous Records, GG, 75–76; and Michael Dougherty's deed of manumission to Isaac Dougherty, June 14, 1758, ibid., LL, 53.

58. Will of John Peter, Jan. 2, 1749, Will Book, NN, 164; Tabitha Peter's sale of Negroes to James Bond, May 2, 1751, Miscellaneous Records, II, 182; James Bond's deed of manumission, Feb. 14, 1753, ibid., 381–382; and will of James Bond, Dec. 4, 1756, Will Book, RR, 518. I find no manumission document for a James Bond. I therefore assume that he is white, especially given the wording of John Peter's will (Nathaniel Broughton's deed of manumission, Oct. 19, 1754, Miscellaneous Records, KK, 290–291). The only reference to a Henry Clusteny notes that he lives at Mrs. Child's plantation, perhaps as the overseer (Charlestown Gaol, *SCG*, Oct. 12, 1738).

who failed to "speak of the cases, not rare, of mulattoes out of negresses by gentlemen, who then sell their own children to others as slaves."[59]

Most sexual contacts between whites and blacks, in other words, reflected only physical needs and opportunities in societies where whites possessed a disproportionate share of power. This was nowhere more blatantly expressed than by John Ross, a resident of East Florida, who in 1766 bought a black woman and child for seventy pounds. In justifying his purchase, he reproached his father for suspecting him "of any other connexion with such a wench than that of having got some children by her." After all, he continued in jocular vein, "I am not yet old enough for dotage, although my head and beard are become pretty gray." However, the son then explained that he would like to have the purchase price transferred to his account "not because I would choose, if it were in my power to give either the mother or children their freedome at present—but only because I would wish to have that in my power as soon as possible, for fear of accidents, I mean to myself." In short, Ross's apparent callousness masked at least a measure of responsibility to his New World family. And, in fact, he made good on his promises, for, in 1782, he freed his two daughters, paid for their passage to Scotland, where they were educated at his expense and under the eye of their paternal grandfather.[60] Personal sentiment insinuated even the most heartless relationship.

Miscegenation always gave rise to a tangled web of competing emotions and tensions. Slaves themselves might even take the initiative in forcing this to the attention of whites. In 1775, a mulatto girl accused her master, Mr. Walton, a Baptist of Southside Virginia, of "offering the Act of uncleaness" to her. She "often hinted to [her master's] Daughters that [he] was the Father" of her prospective child. When Walton attempted to correct her for making this allegation, "she faced him in it, and declared she believed he was the father of it, if any one was; tho' she knew not that any person had carnal knowledge of her but supposed it might be done while she was asleep but that she knew of his coming and offering such things at times to her." Even more damning was the testimony she gave "at the time of her extremity in childbearing [when] she was charged by the midwives then to own the truth and clear her Master, if clear, and as her extremity was more than common, they told her it might be a Judgement of God upon her, and that she might die; but all could not prevail upon her she confidently affirmed what she had said she then said." However, when

---

59. Will of Ryland Randolph, Henrico County Wills, 1781–1787, 179, cited in Gerald Steffens Cowden, "The Randolphs of Turkey Island: A Prosopography of the First Three Generations, 1650–1806" (Ph.D. diss., College of William and Mary, 1977), 462; Cresswell, *Journal*, 165; Schoepf, *Travels in the Confederation*, II, 92–93.

60. John Ross to his father, March 1776, Leith Ross Muniments, Scottish Record Office, Edinburgh.

the child was born, it proved to be "a negro without any doubt." Even then, four white members of Walton's church still doubted him, and some weeks passed before they "relinquished" their "difficulties" concerning the case.[61]

If miscegenation was a source of tension in slave societies, too often it resulted in tragedy. Ben, a Virginia slave, was one such victim. In the late eighteenth century, Ben took a neighboring planter's house servant for his wife; like many another slave husband in the Chesapeake, he visited her weekly. Then, for no apparent reason, Ben was barred from seeing his spouse. It soon became common knowledge that her master allowed a neighboring white man to visit her. Some time later, these two whites had a disagreement; and Ben, seeing an opportunity, applied to see his wife again. In return for renewing the old arrangement, the master of Ben's wife encouraged him to harm his white usurper. Ben stole his master's gun and shot his white rival. The pathology of slavery also seems evident in the early-eighteenth-century trial of "old Caesar," charged with the attempted rape and buggery of a four-year-old white girl.[62]

Children suffered from the tensions to which the issue of interracial sex gave rise. In 1754, a thirteen-year-old South Carolina slave boy was convicted of "having carnally and unlawfully known" a ten-year-old white girl. At the trial it was accepted that this encounter had occurred with the girl's consent. However, the court felt that an example had to be set, even of a boy of such tender years. It is debatable whether any serious sexual misdemeanor occurred in this instance. In any event, the master whose property was at stake did not rest his case on this possibility. Rather, he claimed that the girl had already "been Injured by others." He was then challenged to support his "allegation . . . of the Girl's having been deflowered by any other Negro," so that the governor might reduce the punishment of his slave.[63]

The capacity of slavery to poison the relations of otherwise decent men and women was nowhere more evident than in the realm of sex. Some sexual encounters were marked by tenderness, esteem, and a sense of responsibility, but most were exploitative and unspeakably cruel—nothing more than rapes by white men of black women—a testament to the ugliness of human relations when people are treated as objects. Similarly, although some whites took a relaxed view of miscegenation, most saw it as potentially explosive, because it threatened to close the gap between the free and the enslaved and produced a group of people whose position was deeply ambiguous. Love and cruelty, affection and callousness, composure and frenzy—such were the contradictory

---

61. Minutes of Meherrin Baptist Church, Lunenburg County, 1775, photostat, VSL.

62. Executive Papers, *Commonwealth* v. *Ben*, Jan. 12, 1801, VSL; trial of "old Caesar," Nov. 3–4, 18, 1724, Spotsylvania County Court Order Book, 1724–1730, 29, 36–37, VSL.

63. South Carolina Council Journal, Apr. 16, 1754. The outcome of this case is unknown.

strands in the twisted emotional knot that bound whites and blacks in the sexual arena.

RECREATION

When work was done, blacks and whites sometimes played together. Fraternization across the racial divide did not mean that slaves were treated equally at play or that interracial conviviality was common throughout British America. More often than not, whites tolerated blacks at festive gatherings simply because they were slaves and therefore relegated to a subordinate position. Nevertheless, blacks made their presence felt by mixing openly with whites in a variety of recreational settings. The extent of this contact varied from region to region. In the Lowcountry, overwhelming black numbers proved less conducive to leisure-time encounters than the more balanced white and black populations of the Chesapeake.

Perhaps the pastime that saw slaves most firmly in a dependent role was hunting. In 1739, John Clayton of Gloucester County, Virginia, observed that shooting deer was a favorite diversion of his neighbors, who sent "their servants w'th dogs to drive 'em out and so shoot 'em running." In the Lowcountry, the killing of deer by torchlight was a favorite amusement. As described by Elkanah Watson, it was a particularly unsportsmanlike practice: "A negro precedes the sportsmen, bearing a piece of burning pitch pine; the foolish animal, fascinated by the light, remains stationary, with his head erect, and his eyes steadily fixed on the blaze. The glare of his eyes expose him to the sportsman's aim, who approaches the deer as near as he pleases." Even in hunting, blacks might occasionally take the initiative. Joseph Bell hunted on the Ball plantation in South Carolina. On one occasion, he pursued a buck that took to the river to escape. However, a slave who saw the chase fetched Cupid, "who immediately went and got a shot, and laced [the buck] from stern to stem; for all that, he made shift to get up as far as Silkhope Orchard, and there he lost him." Cupid then went to Bell, borrowed his dogs, put them on the scent, and found the deer, which by then was dead. Perhaps, too, as Stuart Marks has observed, "plantation masters in their youth might slip out at night against parental injunctions to run 'coon and 'possum with slaves," but these cooperative ventures ended once the masters reached adulthood.[64]

If hunting expeditions generally relegated blacks to a firmly subordinate position, holidays put them in the public eye as extremely visible members of

---

64. "Virginia Game and Field Sports . . . , 1739," *VMHB*, VII (1899–1900), 172–174; Elkanah Watson, *Men and Times of the Revolution*, ed. Winslow C. Watson (New York, 1856), 41; Anne Simons Deas, *Recollections of the Ball Family of South Carolina* . . . (Summerville, S.C., 1909), 76; Stuart A. Marks, *Southern Hunting in Black and White: Nature, History, and Ritual in a Carolina Community* (Princeton, N.J., 1991), 28.

the interracial crowd. The black presence was most notable in the Chesapeake. Thus, a visitor to Maryland's Eastern Shore in 1800 observed that blacks "made much" of holidays, although "many of the lower class of people assemble with them, forming a mixt multitude and a scene of confusion." What ensued, the traveler complained, was much drinking, gambling, swearing, and fighting, particularly "gouging [which] is by no means uncommon." At Whitsuntide, this same traveler "found great numbers, white and black, assembled." At Queenstown, Maryland, he "dined where 100s and 100s of blacks were assembled—wonderfully interspersed with whites young and old Gaming—Fiddling, Dancing, drinking, cursing and swearing formed one of the most tumultuous scenes I ever beheld."[65]

That slaves "made much" of holidays is one of the best testaments to cultural diffusion. When traveling through the Carolinas, an exasperated Johann Schoepf had to kick his heels "for full four days" in Edenton waiting to cross Albemarle Sound, because the ferryman "had allowed the negroes to go across the Sound with the boat for a holiday." The testy traveler proclaimed, "No people can be so greedy after holidays as the whites and blacks here, and none with less reason, for at no time do they work so as to need a long rest." Indeed, he continued, "It is difficult to say which are the best creatures, the whites here or their blacks, or which have been formed by the others; but in either case the example is bad." It was impossible, in other words, to disentangle the complex ways in which the two races shaped one another in their love of holidays—as in so much else.[66]

During holidays but at almost any other time, too, alcohol was a significant medium of interracial exchange. In the Lowcountry, it circulated most readily in Charleston. As early as 1693, the governor of South Carolina complained of the presence of "very disorderly houses" in the town where "strong liquors" were sold to the lower orders of white society and to "Great numbers of Negroes" who were drawn from the surrounding countryside, "knowing they can have drinck . . . for mony or what else they bring." By midcentury, the problem had grown. In 1742, an advertisement for a runaway slave mentioned a sighting at a tavern; two years later, the city grand jurors named twelve establishments that had been caught "retailing liquors to Negroes"; in 1752, a master threatened to prosecute any person who sold liquor to his slave butcher; eleven years later, a writer to the *South-Carolina Gazette* claimed that the dramshop owners who retailed liquors to slaves "have raised by it in a few years considerable fortunes from the most indigent circumstances." In 1770, about one in ten of all the dwellings in Charleston was a licensed tippling

---

65. Journal of a Traveler, Feb. 11, June 2, 1800, Miscellaneous MSS, HSP, microfilm, CW.
66. Schoepf, *Travels in the Confederation*, II, 117–118.

house; presumably, others operated illegally. Well might an owner offer his house servant for sale for "too frequently getting to the Dram-Shops (these too numerous Pests that are a Scandal to this Town, and bid fair to ruin every Black Servant in it)."[67]

How much fraternization between blacks and whites occurred in these urban dramshops it is impossible to say. But apparently slaves were not just served surreptitiously at a back entrance; rather, they entered the houses themselves. The "Stranger" reported that in Charleston "at all times, nay, even at noon-day, many dram-shops are crowded with negroes." A complaint against watchmen and their wives for keeping dramshops pointed out that it was in "their interest to encourage Negroes, and others to frequent their Houses, and consequently to protect such disorderly Persons in their Male-Practices." In 1741, a mistress who objected to her hired slave's failure to turn over his wages was told that the money was lost "either by Gaming or spend[ing] among the lettle Punch-Houses." Three years later, Charleston's authorities attempted to curtail the practice of urban blacks' playing at dice and other games *within* the city punch-shops. Charleston blacks certainly played Anglo-American games, many of them probably associated with punch-shops. Thus, in 1773, Josiah Quincy saw blacks in the Lowcountry capital playing huzzle-cap and pitch penny, and in the same year the Beaufort grand jury complained of blacks' playing trap-ball and fives on Sunday.[68]

Alcohol and its attendant delights were more readily available in town than in the countryside, but the rural Lowcountry was hardly "dry." Masters made rum available as a reward for hard work. Others apparently went further. In 1717, one South Carolina mistress was accused of selling alcohol to her slaves. Even slaves had designs as suppliers. In 1764, Henry Laurens thought that his slave "Amos has a great inclination to turn Rum Merchant." And if liquor was not available from masters, there were other sources. In 1749, drinking bouts involving slaves and nonslaveholding whites came to light in the parish of Saint Thomas and Saint Dennis. On one occasion, a planter's wife thought that an

---

67. Governor's Message, Apr. 10, 1693, Miscellaneous Records of the Secretary of the Province, 1692–1700, 46–47, SCDAH; James Mathewes, *SCG*, June 5, 1742; presentments of the Grand Jury, ibid., Apr. 15, 1745; Samuel Smith, ibid., Jan. 1, 1752; ibid., Mar. 19, 1763; Sampson Neyle, ibid., Apr. 11, 1771. On the number of dramshops, see Carl Bridenbaugh, *Cities in Revolt: Urban Life in America, 1743–1776* (New York, 1955), 227, 358; and Weir, *Colonial South Carolina*, 123, 170.

68. "The Stranger," *SCG*, Sept. 24, 1772; Charleston Grand Jury presentments, ibid., Oct. 29, 1772; Elizabeth Smith, ibid., Oct. 17, 1741; South Carolina Council Journal, Mar. 20, 1744, CO5/388; Howe, ed., "Journal of Josiah Quincy," Mass. Hist. Soc., *Procs.*, XLIX (1915–1916), 455; *SCG*, May 24, 1773; *SCG and CJ*, May 18, 1773.

overseer and his three white friends had provided two gallons of rum for her slaves. A number of slaves talked of being "treated" by neighboring plain folk. Ordinaries were dotted about the rural Lowcountry. Williamsburg township, located in Georgetown district, contained a number of "tippling and gaming Houses" that were thought to be "dealing with and enticing Negroes." In 1772, there were "many small Tippling-Houses along the Public Roads" in Orangeburg district.[69]

Slaves in the rural Chesapeake also had ready access to liquor. Occasionally, even a master hosted a session of heavy drinking. In 1716, a Lancaster County planter permitted "a great concours of negroes to assemble at his plantation and there to revel and drink in a very disorderly manner." More often, lower-class whites were the suppliers. In Elizabeth City County, a white woman was accused of keeping "a disorderly House" in which she "entertains and Harbours negros and idle, disorderly persons." Landon Carter's waiting man, Nassau, bought liquor from a neighboring farmer, Robin Smith; carpenter Guy purchased rum from a nearby overseer; and Carter himself bitterly complained of the prevalent "night shops" to which his slaves resorted. In 1792, a tavernkeeper exchanged a pint each of rum and brandy with "Negro Bobb" for a dozen chickens. As towns developed in the Chesapeake, slaves gravitated to them in their search for alcohol. In 1786, Robert Hunter visited Tappahannock on election day and found most of the inhabitants, "black as well as white," drunk. A year later, James Mercer of Fredericksburg decided to sell his house servant, Christmas, because he could not be kept from liquor.[70]

As in the Lowcountry, Chesapeake slaves fraternized with whites, particularly in gambling. York County court in Virginia accused Anne Brathewaite of keeping "a disorderly House" where she "harbour[ed] and entertain[ed] slaves and suffer[ed] them to game at Cards." In 1769, a Maryland overseer became too friendly with the slaves under his charge, for during the "holidays" he

---

69. Gregorie, *Records of the Court of Chancery,* 178–201; *Laurens Papers,* IV, 616; Philip D. Morgan and George D. Terry, "Slavery in Microcosm: A Conspiracy Scare in Colonial South Carolina," *Southern Studies,* XXI (1982), 140; Georgetown District Grand Jury presentments, *SCG,* May 31, 1773; Orangeburg District Grand Jury Presentments, ibid., Nov. 26, 1772. For liquor as a reward, see Chapter 3.

70. Lancaster County Orders, no. 6, 1713–1721, 154–162, as cited in Wheeler, "Lancaster County," 110; Elizabeth City County Order Book, 1747–1755, Nov. 7, 1750, 201, VSL; Greene, ed., *Carter Diary,* 419–492, 648–649; anonymous account book, Westmoreland County, Virginia, 1792–1795, UNC, in Kym S. Rice, *Early American Taverns: For the Entertainment of Friends and Strangers* (Chicago, 1983), 72; Robert Hunter, Jr., *Quebec to Carolina in 1785–1786 . . . ,* ed. Louis B. Wright and Marion Tinling (San Marino, Calif., 1943), 249; James Mercer to John F. Mercer, Mar. 3, 1787, Mercer Family Papers. See also "Journal of Col. James Gordon," *WMQ,* 1st Ser., XI (1902–1903), 112.

played "at Cards with Negroes who had come to the plantation." A generation later, a Baptist church in the northern piedmont of North Carolina charged a white member of "rusling [wrestling] with a negro at the fishing place for money." The rapidly growing towns of the late-eighteenth-century Chesapeake were especially notable for interracial conviviality—blacks and nonelite whites drank and danced together. One white storekeeper who served liquor to slaves in Richmond also played "Five Corns" with them at "two Cents per Game."[71] Apparently, some whites and blacks enjoyed each other's company in their off-duty moments.

Part of the popularity of the main spectator sport of colonial North America—horse racing—was the drinking and gambling it inspired. As early as 1710, Virginia legislators attempted to curb the number of "booths, arbours and stalls" that were set up at such public places as race fields where "servants and negroes" were entertained. Three-quarters of a century later, William Attmore saw horse races near New Bern, North Carolina, where the "betting . . . , quarrelling, wragling, Anger and swearing" made the most lasting impression. He saw "white Boys and Negroes eagerly betting 1/-, 2/-, a quart of Rum, a drink of Grog etc., as well as Gentlemen betting high." Anne Ritson spoke of the blacks' "gaming spirit" at the twice-annual Norfolk horse races:

> From ev'ry quarter they can come;
> With gentle, simple, rich, and poor,
> The race-ground soon is cover'd o'er;
> Negroes the gaming spirit take,
> And bet and wager ev'ry stake;
> Males, females, all, both black and white,
> Together at this sport unite.[72]

Black spectators were an integral part of the eighteenth-century horse race. In 1752, the grand jury of Northumberland County, Virginia, accused five white men of holding "a disorderly meeting with negroes"—a horse race one Sunday afternoon. On two weekdays in October 1786, George Washington

---

71. York County Court Order Book, June 19, 1775, VSL; Kulikoff, *Tobacco and Slaves,* 411; Flat River Primitive Baptist Church, Person County, November 1791, Wake Forest University, microfilm, NCDAH; *Francis Tyree* v. *Hurt,* Richmond Suit Papers, box 54, May 1810 bundle, VSL, as cited in James Sidbury, *Ploughshares into Swords: Race, Rebellion, and Identity in Gabriel's Virginia, 1730–1810* (New York, 1997).

72. Hening, *Statutes at Large,* III, 335–336; Lida Tunstall Rodman, ed., *Journal of a Tour to North Carolina by William Attmore, 1787,* James Sprunt Historical Publications, XVII, no. 2 (Chapel Hill, N.C., 1922), 17–18; [Anne Ritson], *A Poetical Picture of America* (London, 1809), 79–80.

recorded in his diary that "most of [his] People had gone to the races." Five years later, a black Baptist church member in northern North Carolina who was accused of "frequenting Races [and] shooting matches" declined to see evil in his actions. Indeed, he even claimed to have conducted "business" at horse races. John Bernard heard a "tornado of applause from the winner's party" at the end of one Virginia horse race, "the niggers in particular hallooing, jumping and clapping their hands in a frenzy of delight, more especially if the horses had happened to jostle and one of the riders been thrown off with a broken leg." Blacks were obviously enthusiastic participants at horse races.[73]

Perhaps the performance of black jockeys elicited a partisan response from the black members of the crowd, for black riders undoubtedly became common in southern horse races. In the 1770s, John Harrower, an immigrant servant, no sooner stepped onto Virginia soil than he attended a race where two boy jockeys were pitted against one another, one black and one white. The jockeys at the New Bern races witnessed by William Attmore were all "young Negroes of 13 or 14 years" who generally rode bareback. In 1796, Isaac Weld attended races near Petersburg, where the horses were "commonly rode by negro boys, some of whom," he noted patronizingly, "are really good jockeys." Some black jockeys in fact gained considerable renown. A runaway slave belonging to John Taylor was an excellent hostler, a "remarkable good Racekeeper and Rider," and known "at all the race grounds of consequence." His owner acknowledged that he might be anywhere in Virginia or the Carolinas if he chose to "make his living in the line of his old profession."[74]

South Carolina had horse races, but on a lesser scale than in the Chesapeake. Some members of the gentry, however, maintained fine stables. On the eve of the Revolutionary war, the estate of Edward Fenwicke of Johns Island included a string of race horses valued at fifty-six hundred pounds and "Toney a Jockey," appraised at eight hundred pounds. Only rarely did the mixed company at horse races elicit much comment. In 1783, for example, South

---

73. Northumberland County Court Order Book, Nov. 13, 1752, 362–363, in Lawrence George Herman, "Presentments of the Grand Jury of Northumberland County, Virginia, 1744–1770" (master's thesis, College of William and Mary, 1976), 28; Jackson and Twohig, eds., *Diaries of Washington*, V, 50; minutes of Flat River Primitive Baptist Church, Person County, November 1791; John Bernard, *Retrospections of America, 1797–1811*, ed. Mrs. Bayle Bernard (New York, 1887), 155–156.

74. Edward Miles Riley, ed., *The Journal of John Harrower, an Indentured Servant in the Colony of Virginia, 1773–1776* (Williamsburg, Va., 1963), 40; Rodman, ed., *Journal of Attmore*, 17; Isaac Weld, Jr., *Travels through the States of North America . . .* , I (London, 1799), 185–186; John Taylor, *VaG and GA*, July 15, 1795. See also Thomas Jefferson, *VaG* (P and D), Sept. 14, 1769.

Carolina's governor complained of "the Great Number of Whites as well as Blacks taking pleasure in the Roads, even unto making of Horse Racing, and retailing of liquors on the course."[75]

Cockfighting was another spectator sport associated most closely with the Chesapeake. Because blacks were the area's "chicken merchants," it would be surprising if they were not actively engaged in the sport. They even arranged cockfights among themselves. One Sunday before breakfast, Philip Fithian, the tutor at Nomini Hall, "saw a Ring of Negroes at the stable, fighting cocks." Another of Fithian's observations—an assessment of the character of Harry Willis, Robert Carter's nephew—underlines the association between blacks and cockfighting. "Harry's genius," Fithian despaired, "seems towards Cocks, and low Betts, much in Company with the waiting Boys." Certainly, slaves constituted an important element of any cockfighting crowd. On Easter Monday, Fithian noted that the Nomini Hall blacks were enjoying a two-day holiday at "Cock Fights through the County." Ten years later, Elkanah Watson, attending a cockfight in Southampton County, described how the "roads, as we approached the scene, were alive with carriages, horses, and pedestrians black and white, hastening to the point of attraction."[76]

Virginians, it was said, "will dance or die." And they danced distinctively—in a manner influenced by their slaves. According to Andrew Burnaby, the Virginia jig, which he described as a dance lacking "any method or regularity," was "a practice originally borrowed, I am informed, from the Negroes." Fithian provides an invaluable glimpse into how this cultural transfer might have taken place. One Sunday evening at Nomini Hall, "the Negroes collected themselves into the School-Room and began to play the *Fiddle,* and dance." Fithian immediately dispersed the group upon finding Robert Carter's son Benjamin and his nephew Harry part of the company. Harry was even "dancing with his coat off." Black dancing not only proved attractive to white adolescents; it could also impress white adults. In the summer of 1743, at a "merry-making" in Northampton County, North Carolina, a white man compared the dancing styles of a number of whites unfavorably to that of his slave. One of the disparaged whites predictably retorted, "Any man who would compare a Negro to a white man was no better than a negroe himself." The discussion became heated and ended in a brawl—testimony, indeed, to the influence of black slaves.[77]

---

75. Inventory of Edward Fenwicke, 1775, Inventories, &, 627–628; Journal of South Carolina House of Representatives, Aug. 6, 1783, SCDAH. See also Carl Bridenbaugh, *Myths and Realities: Societies of the Colonial South* (New York, 1965), 81.

76. Farish, ed., *Journal and Letters of Philip Vickers Fithian,* 121–122, 128, 177, 250; Watson, *Men and Times,* 261.

77. Andrew Burnaby, *Travels through the Middle Settlements in North America,* in the

Blacks shaped white dances in another way—by supplying the music. Nicholas Cresswell described the accompaniment to a Virginia jig as a "Negro tune." Black fiddlers played at many Virginia dances. As early as the 1690s, an Eastern Shore slave fiddled at a white dance. More than a century later, George Washington paid twelve shillings to Harry Piper for his "slave Charles playing the fiddle" at an Alexandria ball. Another Virginia planter gave ten shillings to Moses, one of his slaves, so that he might buy a fiddle and a further one shilling, three pence for new strings; and, on the following New Year's Eve, he paid two shillings, six pence to another of his slaves for "playing the fiddle." In the 1780s, Lucinda Lee mentioned dancing to the music of Harry, a fiddler, and Luigi Castiglioni discovered that Chesapeake whites "dance all night to the music of the violin of a negro." Indeed, a slave named Dick related how, on a "moonlight night," his master loved to listen to his banjo playing and watch the slave women dance. Furthermore, Dick's master "could shake a desperate foot at the fiddle" and outperform others at "a *Congo Minuet.*" At a barbecue in Saint Mary's County, Maryland, in 1774, "a great number of young people met together with a Fiddle and Banjo played by two Negroes." This is a particularly appropriate illustration of cultural fusion, with the African American banjo assuming its place alongside the Anglo-American fiddle. Some blacks became proficient performers in the Euro-American style. One Virginia slave, for instance, could sing "Scotch songs."[78]

The same two-way process of cultural diffusion occurred in the Lowcountry. Just as in Virginia, colonial South Carolina boasted its black fiddlers and French horn players. The slave Noah, for example, was "well known in Charles-Town and throughout the province for his playing on the fiddle, and is the fellow who some time ago used to play at the young ladies' and gentleman's dancing-school." Slaves supplied the music found in taverns and at assemblies. Many whites were only too happy to attend the "Negro Dances" for which Charleston was famous. Whites could even be co-opted into participating in an African American cultural event. In 1807, in Edgefield district (a locale that undoubt-

---

Years 1759 and 1760 . . . (London, 1798), 26; Farish, *Journal and Letters of Philip Vickers Fithian,* 61, 62; Northampton County Court Records, August 1743, NCDAH (my thanks to Roger Ekirch for this reference).

78. Cresswell, *Journal,* 30, 53; Philip Alexander Bruce, *Social Life of Virginia in the Seventeenth Century* . . . (Richmond, Va., 1907), 181–183; Jackson and Twohig, eds., *Diaries of Washington,* III, 74; Martin Cockburn Ledgers, June 22, Sept. 13, 1772, Dec. 31, 1773, LC; Emily V. Mason, ed., *Journal of a Young Lady of Virginia, 1782* (Baltimore, 1871), 65; Antonio Pace, trans. and ed., *Luigi Castiglioni's Viaggio: Travels in the United States of North America, 1785–1787* (Syracuse, N.Y., 1983), 196; Davis, *Travels,* 414; John Aylett, *VaG* (P and D), Nov. 3, 1775. For more on black music and dance, viewed as an aspect of black culture rather than as an influence on whites, see the section entitled Play in Chapter 10.

edly contained many recently imported Africans) a white member of a Baptist church was disciplined for "beating the Drum for the Negroes to dance."[79]

Popular recreations were not ephemera in a play world of little consequence. Rather, they served a variety of important social functions. Most notable, perhaps, public sporting occasions like cockfights and horse races tended to cut across racial and class lines, drawing followers from all ranks. In some cases, the gentry promoted these public events, in part to court popularity and in part to reinforce the dependence of the lower orders. Second, sporting occasions and particularly holiday revels served as a welcome release from everyday constraints. Ordinary social restraints were temporarily relaxed; a certain amount of license was permitted. What was not countenanced, but could not be halted, was the more regular fraternization among slaves and lower-class whites that occurred in drinking establishments. Third, other popular pastimes—especially dancing, music making, and the celebration of holidays—fostered social cohesiveness and cultural fusion. Finally, yet other amusements, particularly horse races but also musical diversions and cockfighting, allowed common people to acquire prestige and self-respect. Black fiddlers and jockeys were undoubtedly men of substance in the black community, and some made their mark in white society. Recreation, in short, was woven into, and derived its meaning from, the total social fabric. It was not an epiphenomenal activity.

RELIGION

The vast majority of eighteenth-century Anglo-American slaves lived and died strangers to Christianity. In general, Anglican ministers were not zealous proselytizers of black slaves. And the few who were sympathetic to the slaves' needs faced almost insurmountable odds, ranging from the vast territorial extent of the average parish to the institutional weaknesses of the church. The most formidable barrier, however, to the Christianization of the slaves was the resistance posed by masters and bondpeople alike. It took the rise of evangelicalism in the middle to late eighteenth century to effect a gradual change in the disposition of both slaveholders and slaves. By the last two decades of the century, large numbers of slaves were being exposed to the Christian message.

Although most eighteenth-century Anglo-American slaves stood outside the fold of Christianity, more Chesapeake than Lowcountry bondpeople were encouraged to breach its mysteries. After all, at least a number of Anglican ministers in Virginia and Maryland periodically baptized sizable numbers of

---

79. Elias Bate, *SCG*, Nov. 8, 1751; Davis, *The Fledgling Province*, 192; "The Stranger," *SCG*, Sept. 17, 1772; minutes of the Big Stephen Creek Baptist Church, Edgefield District, February 1807, Furman University, Greenville, S.C.

slaves. From 1722 to 1728, the minister of All Hallow's Parish, Maryland, baptized more than 100 slaves; from 1724 to 1732, the minister of North Farnham Parish in Richmond County, Virginia, baptized more than 350 blacks. Furthermore, moderate successes were more readily achieved as the century proceeded. In 1732, one Anglican minister counted 14 blacks who "could answer for themselves and repeat the Catechism very distinctly"; two years later, he was passing out books to the black slaves "he thought most diligent and desirous to learn to read"; in 1738, the new incumbent of a parish in Goochland County baptized almost 200 blacks on his first trip through his domain; a year later, the inhabitants of a parish in Cecil County, Maryland, observed, "Most people are careful to have their sensible negroes baptized, and their Negro children." Virginia's capital seems to have undergone the most intensive proselytization. In the third quarter of the eighteenth century, almost 1,000 slaves received baptism. In 1770, the Anglican minister of Gloucester County reported that baptism was actually "in Fashion" among his black parishioners, both "Infant and adult Negroes."[80]

In the Chesapeake, Anglicans gradually made headway among slaves, but, in the Lowcountry, their efforts were Sisyphean in their futility. The fortunes of black conversion in the parish of Saint George Dorchester, South Carolina, are a case in point. In the early eighteenth century, the combination of relatively assimilated slaves and an energetic cleric resulted in scores of baptisms. In the mid-1720s, the missionary sponsored by the Society for the Propagation of the Gospel reported that about one in ten of the parish's 1,300 slaves were Christians. As Africans poured into the parish in the 1730s, however, this proportion

---

80. Negroes and Mulattoes that have been Baptized, Married, and Buried in and near the Parish of All Hallows in Maryland by Rev. Joseph Colebatch, 1722–1729, Fulham Palace Papers, III, 126–131, Lambeth Palace Library, London; a list of the Negroes Instructed and Baptized by John Garzia, Parish of North Farnham, Richmond County, Virginia, Mar. 4, 1724–July 9, 1732, ibid., XII, 194–197, and also Richmond County Papers, W and M; Adam Dickie to [?] Newman, June 27, 1732, Fulham Palace Papers, XII, 182–183; Adam Dickie, Sept. 3, 1734, CR 1/18, SPCK archives, microfilm, CW; Anthony Gavin to Bishop Gibson, Aug. 5, 1738, Fulham Palace Papers, XII, 273–274; William Stevens Perry, ed., *Historical Collections Relating to the American Colonial Church*, IV (Hartford, Conn., 1878), 194, 201, 206, 208, 218, 229, 304–307, 316–317 (for significant baptisms of slaves), 320 (quotation); Tate, *Negro in Eighteenth-Century Williamsburg*, 73–75; Rev. Thomas Baker to John Waring, Apr. 23, 1770, in John C. Van Horne, ed., *Religious Philanthropy and Colonial Slavery: The American Correspondence of the Associates of Dr. Bray, 1717–1777* (Urbana, Ill., 1985), 289. There were other overtures to blacks: Thomas Story, *A Journal of the Life of Thomas Story . . .* (Newcastle, 1747), 157; Jonathan Boucher, ed., *Reminiscences of an American Loyalist, 1738–1789* (Boston, 1925), 57–59; Mary O. Klein, "'We Shall Be Accountable to God': Some Inquiries into the Position of Blacks in Somerset Parish, Maryland, 1692–1865," *MHM*, LXXXVII (1992), 399–406.

dwindled rapidly, so that in 1741, only 3 percent, at best, of its 3,347 slaves were Christian. By midcentury, the SPG missionary reported that there were almost no Christian blacks in the parish at all. John Wesley was distraught at the state of Christianity among Lowcountry slaves. He conversed with one slave woman, who had been "many times instructed" in Christianity but seemed not to have learned the rudiments of the faith; another woman, who had lived in a minister's family from childhood, knew nothing of Christianity; and the one slave he encountered "who was tolerably well instructed in the principles of Christianity" complained that he was "buried in the woods" with no church nearby. In 1762 one clergyman estimated that there were only about five hundred black Christians in South Carolina—just 1 percent of the slave population. When the Moravian John Ettwein visited South Carolina in 1763, he became "very uneasy," not just because few blacks were Christians, but because the prospects for conversion were so bleak. Henry Laurens, with whom Ettwein corresponded, did not even try to dispute this assessment. Lowcountry planters, he acknowledged, thought "the ading House to House and laying Field to Field" a more "profitable event" than "the saving of Souls." In 1765, the Reverend Isaac Amory paid too much attention to his black parishioners and was driven from his post within the year. With a few exceptions—in 1766, about 11 percent of the slaves in the parish of Saint James Goose Creek were said to be Christians—the proportion of slaves baptized into the Anglican church was minuscule.[81]

Similar obstacles faced Anglican proponents of slave conversion in the Chesapeake. In 1732, the Reverend Adam Dickie reported that he had upset some planters in his Virginia parish by showing an "over active Zeal in Instructing and Baptizing Negroe Slaves" and noted that he now examined black candidates for baptism separately because "white People thought it a Mighty Scandal to have their Children repeat the Catechism with Negroes." A generation later, the Reverend James Maury encountered opposition from a churchwarden and members of his congregation because he allowed "Whites and Blacks to be baptized together." Put immediately on the defensive, Maury noted that the blacks had "behaved modestly and orderly, neither crowding

---

81. Rev. Francis Varnod to SPG, Apr. 3, 1728, A21/17–18; Rev. Stephen Roe to SPG, Dec. 28, 1741, B10/174; Rev. William Coles to SPG, Jan. 4, 1749, B16/147; W. Reginald Ward and Richard P. Heitzenrater, eds., *The Works of John Wesley* (Nashville, Tenn., 1988), XVIII, 169, 180–181, 501–503; Charles Martyn to Bishop of London, Apr. 11, 1762, Lambeth Palace Library; *Laurens Papers*, III, 356–357, 374; Richard J. Hooker, ed., *The Carolina Backcountry on the Eve of the Revolution: The Journal and Other Writings of Charles Woodmason, Anglican Itinerant* (Chapel Hill, N.C., 1953), 62; Frederick Dalcho, *An Historical Account of the Protestant Episcopal Church in South Carolina . . .* (Charleston, S.C., 1820), 361–362; James Harrison to SPG, Aug. 8, 1766, SPG. See also Rodney Atwood, *The Hessians: Mercenaries from Hessen-Kassel in the American Revolution* (Cambridge, Mass., 1980), 166.

nor jostling their Betters." Revealing his own prejudices, Maury speculated that objections could not have arisen from the "unsavoury Effluvia" from "African constitutions," because masters tolerated that smell daily. Further, he argued, if slaves were excluded on such grounds, why not poor whites? If not exactly a ringing endorsement of interracial baptism, Maury's defensiveness may be explained by the fate that befell the Reverend Alexander Rhonnald. In the late 1750s and early 1760s, the "Grandees" of Elizabeth City and Norfolk Counties, Virginia, "vilified and branded" him "as a Negro Parson" because he baptized an unusual number of slaves, instructed them from the pulpit, and encouraged them to take baptism. Chastened by his experience, Rhonnald learned his lesson and blamed "Negro Children" for being "very dull and stupid" and telling tales on their teacher. As a result, Anglican conversions of slaves were, at best, sporadic.[82]

The first evangelical inroad made among blacks in either Chesapeake or Lowcountry occurred in the unlikeliest of places—the frontier parish of Saint Helena in South Carolina. After George Whitefield's tour of South Carolina in 1740, the prominent Bryan family, along with neighboring whites like William Gilbert and Robert Ogle, were sufficiently aroused to begin proselytizing blacks. In 1742, their actions in drawing blacks from "different Plantations" in "frequent and great Assemblies" came to the attention of the South Carolina legislature. Sensational accounts soon began to circulate about the nature of Hugh Bryan's message. A report to the Georgia trustees claimed that he had ordered the slaves not to "go to work but go and seek Christ . . . to which they reply'd in the Height of Joy and Transport, Christ was a very good Master, if he would get 'em a Holy Day, they would seek him every day." The slaves apparently then "went running in the Wood, for some time till their Masters were oblig'd to take them under Discipline." However, a more sympathetic observer reported in the fall that several slaves on both Jonathan Bryan's and neighboring plantations were "honestly converted to God." Indeed, they loved "their master and mistress so well that they do not desire freedom and show great loyalty in their work." The alleged neglect of their work was clearly contradicted by the "very great blessing that he has just had in his fields."[83]

---

82. Rev. Adam Dickie to Mr. Newman, June 27, 1732, Fulham Palace Papers, XII, 182–183; Rev. James Maury to [Rev. Dawson], Oct. 10, 1759, photostat, UVa; Rhonnald to John Waring, Sept. 27, 1762, in Van Horne, ed., *Religious Philanthropy and Colonial Slavery,* 180–183.

83. South Carolina Commons House Journal, Feb. 16, 17, 23, Mar. 3, 1742; Thomas Bosomworth to the Georgia Trustees, Mar. 10, 1742, in Allen D. Candler, comp., *The Colonial Records of the State of Georgia,* 26 vols. (Atlanta, Ga., 1904–1916), XXIII, 231; Jones, "John Martin Boltzius' Trip," *SCHM,* LXXXII (1981), 107. See also *Boston Weekly Post-Boy,* May 3, 1742; Harvey H. Jackson, "Hugh Bryan and the Evangelical Movement in Colonial South Carolina," *WMQ,* 3d Ser., XLIII (1986), 594–614; Leigh Eric Schmidt, "'The Grand

Far more threatening than the slaves' supposed neglect of their work was the claim that Hugh Bryan was promoting a slave insurrection. The grand jury of the province asserted that Bryan had been guilty of various "Enthusiastic Prophecy's" about "the destruction of Charles Town and the deliverance of the Negroes from their Servitude." According to Eliza Pinckney, Bryan foretold that "Charles Town and the Country as farr as Ponpon Bridge should be destroyed by fire and sword, to be executed by the Negroes." He also had apparently tried to work miracles, "lived for several days in the woods barefooted and alone with his pen and Ink to write down his prophecies till at length he went with a wan[d] to divide the waters." When this failed, Bryan sloughed off the mantle of Moses and volunteered that he had been suffering from "a Delusion of Satan," although he denied ever suggesting that the bondpeople throw off the yoke of slavery. Hugh Bryan lived, apparently without incident, for another eleven years, becoming a "worthy member" and deacon of the Stony Creek Independent (Presbyterian) church, located in Saint Helena Parish. The revival had some positive impact. Jonathan Bryan had some of his slaves baptized at Stony Creek church; and Andrew Bryan, a famous black preacher, was one of his former slaves.[84]

The controversy provoked by the Bryan affair no doubt contributed to the evangelical movement's later lack of progress in South Carolina. A further setback occurred in the backcountry when in 1756, Jacob Weber, a Swiss settler, established an enthusiastic cult among the German and Swiss settlements of Saxe Gotha and Dutch Fork. The trinity of leaders included "a colored preacher" named Dauber, who represented the Holy Ghost. Weber, who played at God, accused Dauber's Holy Spirit of being "neither hot nor cold but lukewarm," and he and his followers murdered him. They then turned on the erstwhile Jesus Christ and killed him. In 1761, Weber was executed for his crimes. Not until just before the War of Independence were evangelical efforts renewed to great effect—and, once again, they sparked a considerable counterreaction. In the mid-1770s, at least two blacks associated with Methodism were preaching in Charleston: Thomas, a slave of John Edwards, a Methodist preacher in town, and David Margate, trained in England and sent to the Lowcountry by the countess of Huntingdon. In late 1774 or early 1775, David set off a storm of

---

Prophet,' Hugh Bryan: Early Evangelicalism's Challenge to the Establishment and Slavery in the Colonial South," *SCHM*, LXXXVII (1986), 238–250.

84. South Carolina Council Journal, Apr. 10, 27, 1742, CO5/441; Elise Pinckney, ed., *The Letterbook of Eliza Lucas Pinckney, 1739–1762* (Chapel Hill, N.C., 1972), 30; Mrs. R. W. Hutson, "Register Kept by the Rev. William Hutson of Stoney Creek Independent Congregational Church and Circular Congregational Church in Charlestown South Carolina, 1743–1760," *SCHM*, XXXVIII (1937), 21–36; Allan Gallay, *The Formation of a Planter Elite: Jonathan Bryan and the Southern Colonial Frontier* (Athens, Ga., 1989), 30–54.

protest that almost caused his lynching. At the house of Patrick Hinds, a noted bootmaker in town, David delivered an inflammatory speech to a group of assembled blacks in which he compared slaves to Israelites, proclaimed himself a second Moses, and prophesied deliverance from slavery. Incensed local residents pointedly emphasized that David's role "was to preach a Spiritual Deliverance" to black slaves, "not a temporal one."[85]

But David's removal from Charleston did not quell South Carolina's fear of evangelical fervor. Rather, a white rather than a black person became the object of suspicion. In the summer of 1775, the South Carolina Council of Safety accused John Burnett of Saint Bartholomew Parish of assuming too "strong a tincture of enthusiasm which led him many months ago to read and pray to negroes in the woods, and in private places, without the knowledge or permission of their masters." Burnett was finally released with a severe caution, but the lesson was clear. To extend evangelical religion to slaves was to risk opprobrium, not to mention life and limb, in the eighteenth-century Lowcountry.[86]

Another notable evangelical inroad in South Carolina occurred in the Pee Dee region during the Revolution. In 1775, Elhanan Winchester, who had already written an antislavery address, became pastor of the Welsh Neck Baptist Church. Once his opposition to slavery became known and after he "began to adopt a more open and general method of preaching," slaves flocked to hear him. Winchester in turn told the slaves that "Jesus Christ loved them, and died for them, as well as for us white people." Apparently, the results of his teaching were dramatic, for the slaves "did not even give sleep to their eyes," as they put

---

85. Richard Maxwell Brown, *The South Carolina Regulators* (Cambridge, Mass., 1963), 19–20; John Edwards to the Countess of Huntingdon, Jan. 11, 18, 1775, A3/6/9–10, William Piercey to the Countess of Huntingdon, Nov. 28, 1774, A4/1/9, and Mar. 25, 1775, A4/2/6, Countess of Huntingdon's American Papers, Westminster College, Cambridge, England; presentments of the Grand Jury, *SCG*, Mar. 27, 1775; James Habersham to the Countess of Huntingdon, Apr. 19, 1775, and to Robert Keen, May 11, 1775, *The Letters of Hon. James Habersham, 1756–1775*, GHS, *Collections*, VI (Savannah, Ga., 1904), 238–244; Boyd Stanley Schlenther, "'To Convert the Poor People in America': The Bethesda Orphanage and the Thwarted Zeal of the Countess of Huntingdon," *GHQ*, LXXVII (1994), 225–256, esp. 244–245. There were a few isolated instances of evangelical success between the Bryan affair and the Revolution, for instance, John Gano, *Biographical Memoirs of the Late Rev. John Gano* . . . (New York, 1806), 66–67, 68–69. In the mid-1770s, John Marrant had some success in proselytizing about 30 blacks on a plantation outside Charleston, although he also encountered much white opposition: see *A Narrative of the Lord's Wonderful Dealings* . . . (London, 1785), 30–33, as cited in John Saillant, "'Wipe Away All Tears from Their Eyes': John Marrant's Theology in the Black Atlantic, 1785–1808" (MS, 1996).

86. "Journal of Council of Safety for Province of South Carolina," SCHS, *Collections*, II (1858), 37, 43, 50–51, 70–72.

it, "until they had settled every quarrel among themselves" and dignified their unions by engaging in a "form of marriage." Within a few months, Winchester had baptized a hundred slaves, two-thirds men and one-third women. Just before he left the church in autumn 1779, the black members formed "a church by themselves," although it later reintegrated into the Welsh Neck Church.[87]

The first sustained evangelical movement among Anglo-American slaves took place in Virginia at midcentury. Centered in Hanover County and inspired by the charismatic Presbyterian Samuel Davies, the revival radiated outward, first to neighboring piedmont counties and then to the Northern Neck. In 1751, Davies reported that 100 slaves attended his services and that he had baptized 40 in the past three years. Four years later, the numbers had increased to 300 and 100, respectively. His efforts then gained momentum, for, in 1757, Davies claimed to have baptized 150 black adults in the past year and a half and to have 60 black communicants in attendance. Similar successes were reported in other areas influenced by Davies and his disciples. In 1760, Colonel James Gordon, a staunch Presbyterian, observed that his Lancaster County church boasted "a pretty large company of the common people and Negroes"; near Christmas, he noted the presence of about 75 blacks; and, three years later, he counted 115 white and 85 black communicants. In 1778, at a meetinghouse in Lancaster County, two Presbyterian clerics administered the sacrament. Robert Carter and his waiting man, Sam Harrison, both received communion, perhaps side by side. The influence of the early Presbyterian revival was long-lived. Well into the nineteenth century, slaves who had been taught by Davies were teaching other slaves. A dispersal of his tutelages into Charlotte County, Virginia, was particularly influential.[88]

Perhaps most surprising about this Presbyterian success among the slaves was its rigorous and conservative nature. Davies and his disciples thought it part of their mission to teach the slaves to read. They distributed books among them. As late as 1843, one writer commented that he had "seen persons, born in Africa, who were baptized by Mr Davies . . . and . . . seen in their hands the

---

87. Elhanan Winchester, *The Universal Restoration, Exhibited in Four Dialogues between a Minister and His Friend* . . . (Philadelphia, 1792), viii–x; Minutes of the Welsh Neck Baptist Church, June 27, 1779–Aug. 29, 1779, microfilm, Duke. See also John Scott Strickland, "Across Space and Time: Conversion, Community, and Cultural Change among South Carolina Slaves" (Ph.D. diss., University of North Carolina, 1985), 192–193.

88. Philip D. Morgan, "Slave Life in Piedmont Virginia, 1720–1800," in Carr, Morgan, and Russo, eds., *Colonial Chesapeake Society,* 472–473; "Journal of Col. James Gordon," *WMQ,* 1st Ser., XI (1902–1903), 199, 205, XII (1903–1904), 9; Religious Daybook, 1777–1779, XII, 10, and Nomony Hall Daybook, 1776–1778, XIV, 2, Robert Carter Papers, Duke, as cited in John Randolph Barden, " 'Flushed with Notions of Freedom': The Growth and Emancipation of a Virginia Slave Community, 1732–1812" (Ph.D. diss., Duke University, 1993), 254–255.

books given to them by this eminent preacher." Davies was also demanding of his converts. He acknowledged that he was "affraid of discouraging them . . . by imposing high Forms of Admission to Baptism," but equally he underlined his caution at not "swelling the number of proselites with only nominal Christians." He admitted that he had been obliged to exclude many blacks from baptism because they thought it either a fashionable communal rite or, more ominously, a means to "be upon an Equality with their Masters." Davies strenuously opposed these misinterpretations of his message. Indeed, one observer of Davies's actions reported that the planters were impressed "by the visiable Reformation wrought by his preaching among the Slaves, whose Sobriety and diligence excited their Curiosity." Only a willful distortion of Davies's teaching could overlook its fundamentally conservative intent. The fact that one such misreading occurred—in 1758, Colonel Edwin Conway of Lancaster County accused Davies of fomenting unrest among the slaves—is a testament to the obstacles that faced any wholesale conversion of blacks.[89]

Evangelical successes among the slaves gained impetus as less conservative groups—first the New Light Baptists and then the Methodists—began to make their influence felt. The Virginia New Lights established their first beachhead in the Southside. In 1767, a female slave runaway from Buckingham County was said to "pretend much to the religion the Negroes of late have practised"; later that year, a slave who was "a great Newlight preacher" ran away from neighboring Prince George County. The Baptists' influence soon extended northward, though it was confined at first to piedmont counties. Thus, in 1769, James Ireland noted that, in Culpeper County, "the poor negroes have been stripped and subjected to stripes" for listening to Baptists; in the early 1770s, a nineteen-year-old mulatto who had been "a preacher ever since he was 16 years of age" ran away from Chesterfield County; at about the same time, an address to the Anabaptists imprisoned in Caroline County claimed that slaves were being drawn "from the obedience of their Masters"; and in the same county in 1774, a master described his runaway shoemaker as "a Baptist and I expect he will shew a little of it in Company."[90]

Although the heart of Baptist strength through the 1770s remained the Southside, the influence of evangelicalism began to spread throughout the colony. In the early 1770s, it had penetrated the tidewater. In 1771, William Lee was disturbed that a "wandering new light preacher" had established contact

89. Morgan, "Slave Life in Piedmont Virginia," in Carr, Morgan, and Russo, eds., *Colonial Chesapeake Society,* 473; Edwin Conway to Thomas Dawson, Mar. 3, 1758, William Dawson Papers, LC.

90. Stephen Dence, *VaG* (P and D), Mar. 26, 1767; George Noble, ibid., Oct. 1, 1767; Lewis Peyton Little, *Imprisoned Preachers and Religious Liberty in Virginia . . .* (Lynchburg, Va., 1938), 163, 259; Seth Ward, *VaG* (P and D), Feb. 27, 1772; John Evans, Sr., ibid., July 21, 1774.

with his slaves in James City County. He had heard that most of them were in fact "crazy with their New light and their new jerusalem." To counter these incursions, he ordered that all his slaves be encouraged "to go every Sunday to their Parish church by giving those, who are the most constant attendants at church, a larger allowance of food, or an additional shirt more than the rest." In addition to inducements, Lee ordered "very exemplary and solemn" punishments for any slave caught stealing on behalf of "these vagabond preachers, for I think," he declared, "*that* is generally the consequence of their preaching." Opposition from tidewater planters mounted as the decade progressed. In 1778, inhabitants from King William County complained that Baptists, "the leaders of whom are Men of immoral and dissipated Lives," were seducing their "negroes from their Duty." A year later, Essex County petitioners sought a prohibition against "all licentious and Itinerant Preachers collecting or assembling of negroes and others at unseasonable times."[91]

In the last two decades of the eighteenth century, Methodists and Baptists began to convert extraordinarily large numbers of blacks throughout the Chesapeake. The nature of their success merits explanation. Part of the reason lay in both denominations' emphasis on an untutored, spontaneous religious response. As William Spencer, a Methodist preacher on the Surry circuit, put it, "My Soul is happy when I preach to people that are engaged but when I get among formalists, or half-hearted Christians, my Soul is troubled, and I am bowed down." Spencer went on to draw a direct comparison between the "engaged" and the "half-hearted" in racial terms: "In general the dear black people, that profess Religion are much more engaged than the whites." Admittedly, this favorable evaluation of black responsiveness probably arose as much from lordly condescension toward the allegedly childlike slaves as from sympathy for the oppressed. But at least the comparison was often drawn in the slaves' favor. And many evangelical preachers made it. William Colbert observed that, at one Methodist love feast, "very few spoke among the whites but the blacks spoke with life and power"; Freeborn Garrettson thought that a black boy he met on the Brunswick circuit in Virginia "exceeded all the youths [he] had ever seen for a gift and power in prayer"; even the otherwise stern Francis Asbury was amused when he encountered a master who gave "an old Negro woman her liberty because she had too much religion for him."[92]

---

91. William Lee to Cary Wilkinson, 1771, Lee Family Papers, VHS; petition from King William County residents, Nov. 21, 1778, and from Essex County, Oct. 22, 1779, Legislative Petitions, VSL.

92. William Spencer diary, Jan. 1, 1790, VHS; Spencer diary, July 27, 1790, CW; journal of William Colbert, Jan. 18, 1801, microfilm, Garrett Theological Seminary, Evanston, Ill.; Nathan Bangs, *The Life of the Reverend Freeborn Garrettson* (New York, 1830), 54; Elmer T.

Evangelical preachers often put their high opinion of black responsiveness to good use. They appealed to the slaves in their audience so that they might ignite an unresponsive gathering. Only when the Reverend Thomas Rankin called on a Maryland congregation "to look toward that part of the chapel where all the blacks were" stretching "out their hands and hearts to God" did the meetinghouse seem to shake with a "mighty power" and many of the congregants become "so overcome, that they were ready to faint." One Easter Sunday in southern Maryland, William Colbert labored for "a considerable time" to engage his audience. Finally, he "endeavoured to cry aloud and spare not." His efforts first struck a chord among the black members of his audience, who "began to shout aloud—two of them fell on the ground and began to wallow whilst others were praying for them." Then "the power of God" became "manifest in the house among the white people." A day later, Colbert was even more explicit about his methods. Again, he found himself preaching to "a hardened congregation"; but, this time, he was strategically placed "at the door of a partition: the black people were behind me and the white before." As he put it, "I wanted to see a move among them, therefore I exerted myself, and sure enough there was a move, for the blacks behind began to shout aloud jump and fall." In 1788, Robert Ayres presided over a quarterly meeting in Virginia: "The first thing I saw Remarkable was a Negro woman standing (as I think) on one of the seats, and begin to Cry and Tremble, and presently fall backwards, which together with the alarm of the Exhortation set the Whole Congregation in an uprore. Some fell to the floor, some into a Trance, some fainted, and many crying to God for mercy, caused the Numerous Spectators to stand 'and wonder' . . . while many grew pale and some began to Tremble."[93] Blacks could, and often did, take the initiative in evangelical meetings—often at a preacher's behest.

The results, however, were not always what the preacher expected. Extreme religious behavior on the part of blacks could provoke hostility from fellow white evangelicals. Certainly, as evangelicalism became more respectable, some preachers became uneasy at blacks' uninhibited response. At a Methodist meeting by the Patuxent River in Maryland in 1790, the preacher James Riggins took exception to the behavior of the "black people [who] began to shout and jump about." He claimed "that the devil was among them and told the people to go out from among them." However, other evangelicals, at least before the

---

Clark et al., eds., *The Journal and Letters of Francis Asbury*, 3 vols. (London, 1958), I, 655–656. For other examples, see Sobel, *The World They Made Together*, 182–183.

93. Rev. P. P. Sandford, comp., *Memoirs of Mr. Wesley's Missionaries to America: Compiled from Authentic Sources* (New York, 1843), 231; journal of Colbert, Apr. 4, 5, 1790; journal of Robert Ayres, Nov. 30, 1788, microfilm, Duke.

turn of the century, were reluctant to reach such conclusions. William Colbert certainly feared the impact of black "noice" on whites, but he consoled himself with the thought that there was "a power in it." Jeremiah Norman realized that the cries of torment emitted so readily by blacks might offend whites, but, he rationalized, "the devil always get angry at the weakening of His Kingdom." Similarly, John Kobler argued that those who objected to Negro "hollering" only took "the Shadow for the Substance."[94] For the most part, then, although evangelical preachers were beginning to register unease at the unrestrained quality of black evangelicalism, they were not generally prepared to condemn it out of hand—at least not before the end of the eighteenth century.

Some black evangelicals influenced whites even more directly: they preached to them. The most famous black preacher was "Black Harry," or Harry Hoosier, who often rode with Francis Asbury. Richard Dozier, a Baptist, resident in the Northern Neck, heard Hoosier and other black preachers. He was most impressed by a slave named Lewis who belonged to a Mr. Brockenbough of Essex County. In 1782, Dozier heard Lewis preach to four hundred people; five years later, he heard him speak to three hundred, observing that "his gift exceeded many white preachers." Dozier recorded Lewis's death in his journal and noted admiringly that he "preached just before he expired." In the 1790s, Richard Parkinson noted that "the lower class of people" who worked for him "said, that they had known a black fellow give a better sermon than they ever heard from a white man." In the same decade, a couple of predominantly white Baptist congregations in Virginia even appointed black ministers: William Lemon to a church in Gloucester County and Jacob Bishop to another in Portsmouth.[95]

If white evangelicals were prepared to extend the gift of preaching to some blacks, others were also prepared to adopt a radical stance toward the white opponents of black conversion. Until the 1790s, many Baptist and Methodist preachers actively opposed slavery. Perhaps none matched James Meacham, who spoke of his "burning fury" at the "blood and oppression" faced by blacks. He consoled himself with the thought that he would "see many a poor

---

94. Journal of Colbert, July 4, 1790, Oct. 29, 1791; diary of Jeremiah Norman, Apr. 8, 1800, Stephen B. Weeks Collection, Duke; journal of John Kobler, July 7, 1791, Lovely Lane Museum, Baltimore.

95. *Extracts of the Journals of the Late Rev. Thomas Coke* . . . (Dublin, 1816), 47; Clark, ed., *Journal and Letters of Asbury*, I, 360, 413; journal of Colbert, Sept. 15, 1804, Jan. 19, 20, 26–27, 1805; George A. Phoebus, comp., *Beams of Light on Early Methodism* (New York, 1887), 27; J. S. Moore, "Richard Dozier's Historical Notes, 1771–1818," *Virginia Baptist Register*, XXVIII (1989), 1402, 1414, 1415, 1416, 1417, 1424, 1426, 1427, 1429, 1430, 1436, 1439; Luther P. Jackson, "Religious Development of the Negro in Virginia from 1760 to 1860," *Journal of Negro History*, XVI (1931), 175–177; Richard Parkinson, *A Tour in America, in 1798, 1799, and 1800* . . . , II (London, 1805), 459.

slave raised up in God and Heaven" while "their cruel bloody oppressive Masters will sink and burn in Hell fire for ever and ever." When William Colbert heard that blacks were being kept from Methodist meetings by "their Lordly Masters," he expostulated, "Surely the Curse of God hangs over the head of such oppressors." Another Methodist preacher reacted to the news that one of his congregation had branded a runaway slave with the apocalyptic warning, "They will be sick of hot Irons in a coming day." Evangelical preachers were also partial to tales with a simple but radical moral. Ezekiel Cooper recorded one when visiting Kent Island, Maryland, in 1789: "Here I was told of an awful fact which was about five years ago, viz., an overseer who was very cruel to the negroes for some matter tied up a poor slave to whip him in an unmerciful manner after whipping some time the poor negro expecting to die finding no friend to relieve, he lifted up his cries to God for mercy, finding none with man and immediately the overseer fell dead on the spot."[96] The evangelical preacher was prepared to believe that the slave's religious fervor could exert its own power—even, on occasion, in this world.

Another indication of the radical stance of evangelicalism—at least in the context of late-eighteenth-century Chesapeake society—was the implicit egalitarianism that often characterized evangelical disciplinary proceedings. Although, in general, evangelical church discipline buttressed white authority, disciplinary meetings were rarely a rubber stamp for a master's whim. In 1780, a Baptist church in Nansemond County, Virginia, heard charges of "disobedience and harsh language" brought by a master against his slave, but the slave counterattacked by accusing his master of "misconduct." Both were expelled and later restored to membership. Fourteen years later, Brother John Sanders complained of his slave, Brother Mingo, in the same church. None of his charges was proved; indeed, they were called "slanders." Two months later, both master and slave appeared before the church and "Declared a Reconciliation Between themselves." At about the same time and in the opposite corner of the state, the members of the Zoar Baptist Church of Berkeley County maintained a strict impartiality when a difference arose between Sister Marmaduke and Sukey, a black member. "Much was said on both sides," the church minutes note, "which the church attended to with regret." Finally, they were both restored to fellowship when "sister Marmaduke appeared to forgive the injury which Sukey had done her (considering she might have done some part of the offence, and omitted some Duties, through ignorance), and as

---

96. "Meditation and Exercises of James Meacham," Nov. 24, 1788, Jan. 12, 1789, James Meacham journals, Duke; "Journal of James Meacham," *Trinity College Historical Society Papers*, IX (1912), esp. 68, 78–79; journal of Colbert, June 6, 1794; Kobler journal, July 15, 1791, 108–109; journal of Ezekiel Cooper, Nov. 11, 1789, Lovely Lane Museum.

Sukey professed to have had a sense of her error, and to have repented of her misconduct."[97] Such evenhandedness must have impressed slaves.

The experience of a small number of black Moravians in piedmont North Carolina provides a fascinating case study of the extent and ultimate limits of spiritual egalitarianism in early America. The first black Moravian in North Carolina seems to have been Sam, who, when baptized in 1771, received the name "Johannes Samuel." In the 1780s and 1790s, about a score of other blacks joined Johann Samuel and his wife, Maria, in the North Carolina Moravian Church. Although only a handful of blacks became Moravians in the late eighteenth century—indeed, black Brothers and Sisters were at best a quarter of the African-American population of Wachovia—the degree of interracial fraternization in Moravian congregations was remarkable. Black and white Moravians washed each other's feet, celebrated choir festivals together, experienced communal lovefeasts, sat on the same church benches, sang and prayed in German, faced the same disciplinary system, and were buried alongside one another in God's Acre, the Moravian graveyard. Most dramatic was the baptismal ceremony: especially in the early years, when there were few black Moravians, whites sponsored blacks or acted as godparents, they blessed blacks with the laying on of hands, and, most remarkably, they extended the kiss of peace to them. At a time when most whites viewed blacks with contempt, the Moravian kiss was an emblem of acceptance, inclusion, and welcome. Symbolic of interracial exchanges were the conch shells that white Moravians blew to summon their members, a practice they probably learned from Africans. But for all the familiarity and reciprocity, the incorporation of blacks into the Moravian church was also a way for owners to discipline and control their slaves. The tightrope was never easily trod. According to a report of 1776, some Brethren who were "too friendly with the Negroes" were afterward "amazed at their freshness." Joking with their slaves one minute, Moravian owners "beat them like dogs" the next. Although the Moravian Elders expected humane treatment from slaveowners, they expected nothing less than obedience from slaves.[98]

The evangelicals' drive to control the personal lives of church members undoubtedly had a double-edged impact on the slaves. On one hand, white norms and sanctions intruded into their lives as never before; on the other, blacks now had some protection against whites who offended against church standards. This interference was real and can be gauged by the anger of one

---

97. Minutes of South Quay Baptist Church, August, October 1780, January 1781, Mar. 1, May 3, 1794, photostat, VSL; minutes of Zoar Baptist Church, Oct. 19, 25, 1793, VBHS.

98. This paragraph draws on the excellent study by Jon F. Sensbach, *A Separate Canaan: The Making of an Afro-Moravian World in North Carolina, 1763–1840* (Chapel Hill, N.C., 1997), 55, 80–84, 94, 105, 120, 125–126, 132, 153, 155, 178, 201.

Baptist slaveholder who, when disciplined for the way he behaved toward his slaves, retorted that "people had better look more at home, and that he did not hold himself accountable to any one for his conduct towards his own people, and that he should treat them as he thought proper." This view was simply incompatible with the evangelical code as it was propounded in the late eighteenth century. Another indicator of evangelical intrusiveness can be found in James Meacham's reprimand of a white man before a mixed audience. At a Methodist meeting, "a poor black man began to get happy with shouting," which provoked "a poor young backslider . . . to laugh at him." Meacham intervened and "sharply reproved [the white man] and asked him if he was not ashamed and told him if it was me I would go out at the dore if I could not behave no better—he gave me a silly look, grited and gnashed his Teeth and out he went." That such a humiliation of a white person could take place before slaves was a striking reversal of societal norms. Nor would masters have welcomed the sentiment Francis Asbury committed to his journal: "I know not," he wrote pointedly, "which to pity most—the slaves or their masters."[99]

Some evangelical preachers were prepared to confront their own prejudices toward blacks. They were not always able to overcome them, but their honesty did them some credit. Thus James O'Kelly recounted how one day there were several slaves "and a very discreet white woman (as I thought)" at the communion table. Afterward he "inquired what humble genteel white woman that was among the blacks." When the blacks informed him that she was a slave, he described how his soul was "wounded," how he "sought out a secret place to weep and bewail my sister." He could not be comforted. "At last," he observed, "I discovered my prejudice in favor of mine own colour, and herein do confess my infirmity and prejudice of education." James Meacham similarly subjected himself to self-examination when, mounted on a horse, he passed by a "poor black Bro on foot." He asked himself whether it was his "duty to get down and walk and let my black bro. ride." He wondered whether, had the pedestrian been white, "perhaps my heart would submit to give him my seat." Meacham did not dismount, but he proclaimed his "love [for] my poor Black Brethren" and claimed "none but God alone knows the secret feelings of my poor heart concerning them poor outcasts of men."[100]

Some evangelicals were prepared to risk their lives to extend religion to slaves. In some cases, this danger was perhaps more rhetorical than real. In 1788, Philip Bruce observed that the wholesale conversions wrought on blacks

---

99. Minutes of Zoar Baptist Church, June 1, 1799, VBHS; journal of James Meacham, Aug. 20, 1789, Duke; Clark et al., eds., *Journal of Asbury,* I, 615.

100. James O'Kelly, *Essay on Negro Slavery* (Philadelphia, 1789), 19; journal of James Meacham, Nov. 14, [?], Eli Washington Caruthers Papers, Duke.

in the Portsmouth area gave "huge offense to the rich and great," who, he imagined, would "tear [the Methodists] to pieces," if they dared. Bruce proclaimed himself ready to "offend one half the world to save the other." In other cases, the danger was real enough. In 1776, Freeborn Garrettson was beaten up in Baltimore County, Maryland, for extending the hand of fellowship to blacks. In 1789, the authorities in King William County, Virginia, notified evangelicals that all slaves found at night meetings would be seized. The Methodists and Baptists of the county not only encouraged slaves to ignore the warning, they even sent a message to the captain of the patrol, informing him that "they wood protect the negroes if they said a word wood beat them." Indeed, they made good on their promise, throwing one patroller out of one of their meetings and overpowering the others.[101]

In spite of the inclusive tendencies of Chesapeake evangelicals toward slaves, their antislavery stance was shortlived. Exclusionary forces grew more important over time. From the beginning, blacks might be turned out of a crowded evangelical meeting to make room for whites. In 1772, in Norfolk, Virginia, Joseph Pilmore saw whites station men at the doors to keep all blacks out "till all the white people were got in." Over time, whites and blacks alike began to express preferences for separate meetings. Over time, too, white evangelicals made their accommodations with slavery. As James D. Essig notes, "Success removed the circumstances which had helped to make antislavery commitment possible." By the last decade of the eighteenth century, most evangelical churches had reversed or markedly diluted their antislavery stances. Whatever blacks had contributed to white religion, whites no longer felt a need for it. Mixed congregations gave way to separate institutions.[102]

The same process occurred among the Moravians of piedmont North Carolina. By the last decade of the eighteenth century, the integrated communitarianism of the late colonial and the Revolutionary years had begun to unravel. Some white Brethren began to object to common seating arrangements, church officials began limiting interracial contact at work and at play, and, in 1797, when a slave girl sought to attend the meeting of single women, the women "all walked out." As Jon Sensbach notes, "Nothing symbolized these

101. Philip Bruce to Thomas Coke, Mar. 25, 1788, in *Arminian Magazine,* II (November 1790), 563–564; journal of Freeborn Garrettson, c. 1776, 17–18, microfilm, Duke; Holt Richeson to Gov. Randolph, Sept. 5, 1789, Executive Papers, VSL.

102. "Journal of Col. James Gordon," *WMQ,* 1st Ser., XII (1903–1904), 8; Frederick E. Maser and Howard T. Maag, eds., *The Journal of Joseph Pilmore, Methodist Itinerant: For the Years August 1, 1769 to January 2, 1774* (Philadelphia, 1969), 149–150; James D. Essig, *The Bonds of Wickedness: American Evangelicals against Slavery, 1770–1808* (Philadelphia, 1982), 116, and see 62–72, 115–126, 133–134.

changes more vividly than the fate of the kiss of peace." In the early nineteenth century, the Moravian Elders no longer deemed it "seemly to give Negroes the kiss of peace in a public service." By 1810, the last black was buried among white Brethren.[103]

Evangelicalism met with much less success and even more opposition in the late-eighteenth-century Lowcountry. Ezekiel Cooper's impressions of Charleston, which he visited in 1792, were cryptic but pointed. "Very little religion, either among the clergy or laity," he observed, "but luxury, fashion, and abomination in abundance." Four years later, Francis Asbury echoed his colleague's remarks and lamented "the superficial state of religion among the white people" of the state. At the same time, Asbury speculated that, if the Methodists "had entered here to preach only to the Africans, we should probably have done better." A year later, Asbury noted optimistically that "the slaves soon see the preachers are their friends, and soften their owners toward them." More realistically, he then observed that "there are thousands here of slaves who if we could come to them would embrace religion." There was the rub. Evangelicals found it extraordinarily difficult to gain access to slaves in a society dominated by worldly and suspicious slaveholders. Perhaps this lack of access to evangelicals explains one Georgia slave's apparent cynicism when he told a Moravian missionary that "he would rather belong to the Moravian Brethren than to the High Church because the latter was always preaching about work and labor, whereas the former preached faith without works, and he was tired of working."[104]

Not surprisingly, towns were the only Lowcountry places where evangelicals achieved real success in the late eighteenth century. Urban slaves were certainly more assimilated than their rural counterparts and were thereby responsive to evangelicals; but, even more to the point, they were much less easily controlled by their masters. In the middle to late 1780s, "truly Amazing" reports of black participation in Methodist meetings began to emanate from Charleston. "Hundreds" of blacks were said to attend their services; one minister reported that "to hear them tell what God has done for their Souls ... would almost create a Heaven in your soul." In the mid-1790s, the Methodist "Society of Blacks" in Charleston numbered five hundred. In Georgetown, at the same time, the Hammett wing of the Methodist church reported more than three hundred black members. And Savannah hosted one of the largest Baptist churches in the South—formed exclusively by blacks. In 1794, it boasted almost

---

103. Sensbach, *A Separate Canaan*, 178–217 (quotation on 201).
104. Phoebus, comp., *Beams of Light*, 149; Clark et al., eds., *Journal of Asbury*, II, 78, III, 160; Muhlenberg, *Journals of Muhlenberg*, II, 638.

four hundred members, by far the largest congregation in the Georgia Baptist Association.[105] Asbury was correct. Where evangelicals could establish contact with slaves, they converted many.

In spite of these successes, evangelicals in the late eighteenth century faced insurmountable obstacles. In 1793, William Hammett, the leader of a breakaway Methodist church in Charleston, came face to face with the harsher realities of Lowcountry slaveholding. A slaveowner wrote him about her "servant Peggy [who] has done everything bad except beating me"; in retribution, she asked Hammett to deny Peggy the sacrament. Hammett replied that he was "sorry to be informed that any person who partakes of my holy ordinances under my care should act improperly, as it is what I never admit of.... But as I do not judge prematurely in these cases, I beg the accused and her accuser may be brought before me and shall act accordingly." Because no specific charges had been leveled, Hammett reasoned that he had to investigate, but "however well intended my lenity was," he continued, "my name was cast out as evil and my note handed about thro' the highest circles of the community, and the worst construction put upon it, ... even that I put the Maid and Mistress on a footing, and of course intended to introduce equality which would overset slavery." Hammett learned his lesson well. He established his own plantation and stocked it with slaves. As one former colleague acidly put it, "No one was more strenuous against slavery than he, while destitute of the power of enslaving."[106]

The failures and successes of white evangelicals in reaching out to blacks in the Lowcountry and the Chesapeake, respectively, are but one example of significant regional variations in the extent and character of interracial social transactions. There were fewer religious contacts, fewer sexual encounters (though more open cohabitations), fewer opportunities for recreational fraternization, and more cruel acts of violence across the racial divide in South Carolina than

105. John Cossom to the Countess of Huntingdon, Mar. 25, 1785, A3/12/19; Thomas Hill to the Countess of Huntingdon, Apr. 12, 1788, A3/12/20; Oliver Hart to J. Hart, Apr. 18, 1785, Hart Papers; *Extracts of Journals of Thomas Coke*, 248; Albert Deems Betts, *History of South Carolina Methodism* (Columbia, S.C., 1952), 69; Rev. Albert M. Shipp, *The History of Methodism in South Carolina* (Nashville, Tenn., 1883), 320. See also journal of George Wells, Sept. 11, Dec. 3, 1791, Lovely Lane Museum.

106. Journal of William Hammett, May 10, 1793, USC; *Extracts of Journals of Thomas Coke*, 217. When Hammett broke away from the orthodox Methodists in the early 1790s, he persuaded 24 whites and 35 blacks to join him (Thomas Morrell to Ezekiel Cooper, Feb. 20, 1792, Ezekiel Cooper Collection, XV, no. 36, Garrett Theological Seminary). Another interesting insight into the opposition faced by Methodists is the treatment meted out to the Reverend George Dougherty in 1800 (James Harper to Ezekiel Cooper, 1800, in Clark et al., eds., *Journal of Asbury*, II, 266).

in Virginia and Maryland. The gap between the races was wider in the Lowcountry than in the Chesapeake.

Yet, in spite of these variations, in both regions the social lives of blacks and whites were inextricably intertwined. The two races fought, had sex, played, and prayed together. Everyday contacts across the color line were commonplace. They occurred in public and in private, among children and adults, even in dreams. Blacks made their presence felt in matters both large and small—from masters' declarations of their dependence on their slaves to inscriptions on a landscape, from acts of loyalty and disloyalty during the Revolutionary war to popular figures of speech. So intimately bound together were black and white, unfree and free that their encounters could not fail to produce unlimited permutations of human emotions, infinitely subtle moral entanglements. The eighteenth-century South was not the segregated place it later became in the nineteenth and twentieth centuries.

As much as blacks and whites came together, however, they remained apart. Truces punctuated the open and violent struggles; demographic and cultural restraints inhibited interracial sex; recreation brought blacks and whites together intermittently; and barriers to evangelical access to slaves were formidable. Boundaries were fluid and imprecise, but boundaries they were, and behind them whites and blacks developed distinctive social and cultural forms. Reciprocal influences across the racial divide should not be exaggerated; claims that much of Anglo-American culture was at heart African are no more persuasive than suggestions that African American culture was at heart European. How best to characterize African American society and culture forms the subject of Part III.

III
The Black World

When you see how the people live, and still more how easily they die, it is always difficult to believe that you are walking among human beings. All colonial empires are in reality founded upon that fact. The people have brown faces—besides, there are so many of them! Are they really the same flesh as yourself? Do they even have names? Or are they merely a kind of undifferentiated brown stuff, about as individual as bees or coral insects? They rise out of the earth, they sweat and starve for a few years, and then they sink back into the nameless mounds of the graveyard and nobody notices that they are gone.—George Orwell

8 : African American Societies

In his short essay on Marrakech, Orwell described a fundamental characteristic of highly exploitative societies: the invisibility of the laboring population. As he acknowledged, "All people who work with their hands are partly invisible, and the more important the work they do, the less visible they are." But Orwell believed that this phenomenon was compounded wherever the laborers had dark skins. In hot climates, he argued, "one's eye takes in everything except the human beings." It takes in the parched soil, the exotic vegetation, the striking vistas, but it always misses the laborer "hoeing at his patch. He is the same colour as the earth, and a great deal less interesting to look at."

Orwell's reflections, spurred by a visit to Morocco, apply just as powerfully to another place and time—the slave plantations of the New World two centuries earlier. Few visitors to this eighteenth-century world shared Orwell's compassion; for them, the black laborers were, as he put it, "next door to invisible." Consider, for instance, Benjamin Henry Latrobe, a perceptive, intelligent, and humane observer. He acknowledged the existence of blacks, to be sure. He even peopled some of his sketches with them. But, in some of these representations, the black figures are barely recognizable as human beings. Their facial features are blurred. The artist has not depicted them as individuals.[1]

---

1. George Orwell, *The Collected Essays, Journalism, and Letters of George Orwell*, ed. Sonia Orwell and Ian Angus, I (Harmondsworth, Eng., 1970), 427, 429.

PLATE 19. An Overseer Doing His Duty. Sketched from Life near Fredericsburg. *Benjamin Henry Latrobe. 1798*

The invisibility accorded slaves was one of the few advantages they possessed as they attempted to order their lives. They could develop social ties to some extent apart from, and largely unknown to, their owners. It was just as well that slaves had this measure of latitude to shape their own lives, for in other respects the obstacles they faced were enormous. After all, slaves did not arrive in the New World as communities of people; they had to *create* communities. The slave trade irrevocably severed numerous social bonds that had tied Africans together. Unable to transport their institutions, slaves were forced to rebuild a society in the New World. They brought a few building blocks with them, but they had to fashion the foundation and framework of their new lives from scratch. Their organizational task was immense; they forged a social life only under the most severe handicaps.

Conflict among slaves was inevitable. Apart from all the pressures associated with the institution of slavery—the divide-and-rule strategies of masters, the inability of slaves to create strong communal institutions—there were the social strains intrinsic to varied peoples thrown together. Romantic interpretations of black life often overlook the evidence of divisiveness and too easily speak of a cooperative ethos and communal solidarity magically present in slave quarters. As Bertram Wyatt-Brown notes, "We simply cannot continue expatiating on the riches of black culture without also examining the social and psychological tensions that slavery entailed." Such oversight does a disservice to the impediments slaves faced as they attempted to give their lives coherence.[2]

In spite of the evidence of conflict, slaves learned to cooperate, to establish codes of behavior, to regularize social relationships among themselves—in short, to do all the things necessary to order their lives even as they confronted continuing disruption and disorder. A number of demographic and economic changes—the emergence of creole majorities, of black majorities in some places, of larger plantations, and of a social and economic hierarchy—facilitated the search for regularity by encouraging contact and communication among them. But black actions, not just impersonal forces, were primarily responsible for the growing cohesion of slave communities. Slaves were shapers of their destiny in the face of all the handicaps imposed by slavery.

An exploration of community formation among slaves must, then, encompass conflict and cohesion, mutuality and divisiveness. Antagonism, hostility, and mistrust rent the harmony of slave quarters; slaves, like other Americans, exhibited atomistic, individualistic behavior. Numerous fissures cleaved through black communities—notably, the stratification associated with the workplace and the modest yet real economic differentiation of the marketplace. And yet these divisions were not so deep that blacks failed to develop a strong sense of themselves as a separate people. Oppression and racism helped create unity among slaves, helped forge a sense of common identity. Racial camaraderie was at least as strong as class hostility. Rather than rehearse the story of conflict and cohesion at the workplace, this chapter focuses on five key social relationships hitherto unexplored: encounters among Africans, between creoles and Africans, among creoles, between blacks and Indians, and between enslaved and free blacks. Such an investigation demonstrates, at the very least, that African Americans were not "undifferentiated brown stuff" and, more ambitiously, that critical networks of their social relations can be uncovered.

AFRICANS

The Middle Passage exacted a harrowing toll on bodies and minds. Many Africans died en route to the New World, and all immigrants arrived physically debilitated. On average, about a sixth of a slaver's complement failed to survive the transatlantic crossing, although this figure varied tremendously depending

---

2. Bertram Wyatt-Brown, "The Mask of Obedience: Male Slave Psychology in the Old South," *AHR,* XCIII (1988), 1230. See also Clarence E. Walker, *Deromanticizing Black History: Critical Essays and Reappraisals* (Knoxville, Tenn., 1991), esp. xii–xiv.

on the coastal region of origin, the date of departure, and the duration of the voyage. Dr. Alexander Garden was Charleston's port physician in the 1750s and 1760s and was in a good position to know the state of health of many African immigrants. His comments are worth quoting in full:

> There are few ships that come here from Africa but have had many of their Cargoes thrown overboard; some one-fourth, some one-third, some lost half; and I have seen some that have lost two-thirds of their slaves. I have often gone to visit those Vessels on their first Arrival, in order to make a Report of their State of Health to the Governor and Council, but I have never yet been on board one that did not smell most offensive and noisome, what for Filth, putrid Air, putrid Dysantries (which is their most common Disorder) it is a wonder any escape with Life.[3]

Arrival in the New World only heightened the odds against survival; Africans were now exposed to a new disease environment. Perhaps as many as a quarter of Virginia's new arrivals died within their first year of arrival. Chesapeake planters well knew the risks they took in purchasing Africans. In 1686, William Byrd purchased two Senegambian slaves who carried smallpox, killing three of his slaves and making fifteen others sick. Robert Bristow, an absentee slaveowner in London, badgered his Virginia correspondents about his losses. In 1711, for instance, he lamented the "mortality which rages so much in the Country." A quarter-century later, Dr. Roderick Gordon of King and Queen County tempered his optimism about his economic prospects by emphasizing, "Our Estates are precarious because they depend chiefly on slaves, who are

---

3. Edmund Berkeley and Dorothy Smith Berkeley, *Dr. Alexander Garden of Charles Town* (Chapel Hill, N.C., 1969), 124. For gruesome incidents and contemporary comment about loss in transit, see Elizabeth Donnan, ed., *Documents Illustrative of the History of the Slave Trade to America,* Carnegie Institution of Washington Publication no. 409, 4 vols. (Washington, D.C., 1930–1935), IV, 270, 373; testimony of R. Norris, Add. MSS 18272, fol. 18, BL; William Colhoun to his sister, July 20, Oct. 3, 1770, William Colhoun Letters, TD 301/6/1–3, Strathclyde Regional Archives, Glasgow, Scotland; *Laurens Papers,* I, 267; and Walter Minchinton et al., eds., *Virginia Slave-Trade Statistics, 1698–1775* (Richmond, Va., 1984), 144. For loss in transit to Virginia, see ibid., 48, 160, 162, 170, 172, 186; and Thomas Harrison to his wife, July 31, 1752, DDO 11/57, Lancashire Record Office, Preston, England. Of the 1,205 slaves shipped from Africa in these slavers, 19% died in transit. I have assembled comparable information for 25 South Carolina–bound voyages between 1723 and 1773. The number of voyages is small, and the resulting information can only be suggestive; but for vessels from Senegambia, the loss of Africans was reported at 15% (13 voyages, range 1–38%); from Sierra Leone, 5% (4 voyages, range 3–19%); Windward Coast, 31% (1 voyage); Gold Coast, 16% (4 voyages, range 1–28%); Bight of Benin, 16% (1 voyage); and Angola, 7% (2 voyages, range 5–7%). The overall loss on 4,574 Africans shipped from the coast was 14%.

very mortal in this country." Even those who survived were often sick, particularly in the fall of their first year.[4]

In the Lowcountry, the odds of an early death were probably even greater than in the Chesapeake, rising to the loss of perhaps a third of arrivals within the first year. Many deaths occurred as sales proceeded. City authorities in Charleston grew anxious at the number of bodies thrown from slavers. In 1769, the governor complained of the stench produced by the "large number of dead negroes, whose bodies have been thrown into the river [and] are drove upon the marsh opposite to Charles Town." In the spring of 1807, a number of jury inquests on bodies found floating in the harbor drew attention to the "custom too prevalent in this port" of throwing bodies overboard to avoid paying burial fees. The arbitrariness with which death struck is well captured by one Lowcountry master who "lost not less than sixteen fine Negroes in as many Months," though sometimes only one in a hundred died, leading him to reflect on the "kind of Lottery" that occurred when purchasing "new Negroes." An African slave named Martha can stand as one example of the risks to which African slaves were subject. Wracked by "asthma," from which she suffered "by her own discourse long enough before She came out of her own Country," Martha died before performing a day's work as a New World slave.[5]

The mind-numbing trauma of the Middle Passage defies easy comprehension. Some newcomers recalled a recent branding on board ship. The memory of so many days at sea undoubtedly explains the description that some Africans gave of their master's residence as being near the "Big Water" or "great water."

---

4. Marion Tinling, ed., *The Correspondence of the Three William Byrds of Westover, Virginia, 1684–1776,* I (Charlottesville, Va., 1977), 65–66, 68; Robert Bristow to Thomas Booth, Sept. 5, 1711 (see also letters of Sept. 15, 1707, Jan. 25, 1708, Oct. 30, 1710), Bristow Letterbook, CW; Dr. Roderick Gordon to Arthur Gordon, Aug.1, 1736, Miscellaneous Bundle RH 15/1/95/32, Scottish Record Office, Edinburgh. See also Thomas Bluett, "The Capture and Travels of Ayuba Suleiman Ibrahima," in Philip D. Curtin, ed., *Africa Remembered: Narratives by West Africans from the Era of the Slave Trade* (Madison, Wis., 1967), 41; and, for seasonality, Allan Kulikoff, *Tobacco and Slaves: The Development of Southern Cultures in the Chesapeake, 1680–1800* (Chapel Hill, N.C., 1986), 326–327; and Darrett B. Rutman et al., "Rhythms of Life: Black and White Seasonality in the Early Chesapeake," *Journal of Interdisciplinary History,* XI (1980–1981), 36–37.

5. Proclamation of Lord Charles-Greville Montagu, *SCG,* June 8, 1769; *Charleston Courier,* Apr. 8, 21, 22, 1807; John Graham to Governor Grant, June 13, 1767, bundle 401, Papers of General James Grant of Ballindalloch, sometime Governor of East Florida, in ownership of Sir Evan Macpherson-Grant, Bart., Ballindalloch Castle Muniments, Scotland; "Journal of the Proceedings of Mr. William Dry, appointed administrator of the estate of the late Rev. Mr. Richard Ludlam," Dec. 23, 1728, A/21/170, SPG. A workhouse announcement for a recent African immigrant described him as "very low in flesh, and in a miserable condition for want of sustenance" (*Charleston Courier,* Feb. 2, 1807).

One newcomer, arriving at Charleston, was unable to stand after his long confinement. "It was more than a week after I left the ship," he noted, "before I could straighten my limbs." Other new arrivals, hardly able to speak any English, could yet identify the name of their ship's captain or the merchant who had handled their sale—another indication of the indelible impression that the Middle Passage and the auction block made on their minds. Yet others succumbed to utter despair and committed suicide. One "poor pining creature hanged herself with a piece of a small Vine," another with a small piece of cord.[6]

If they lived long enough to be purchased, Africans underwent a period of painful adjustment. Some plainly did not wish to adjust, perhaps returning to the site of their sale in a forlorn attempt to find a return passage. Indeed, some Africans explicitly spoke of returning home—and acted on their words. In Virginia, a thirty-year-old African made at least "three attempts, as he said, to get to his country," and two recent immigrants joined other slaves near Petersburg, "being persuaded that they could find the Way back to their own Country." In South Carolina, five "Angolans" pursued "an East course as long as they could, thinking to return to their own country that way." Another group of five—four men and a woman—commandeered a small paddling canoe on the Ogeechee River. The men soon put the woman ashore, telling "her they intended to go to look for their own country, and that the boat was not big enough to carry her with them."[7]

Disoriented and alienated, many Africans yet demonstrated a significant measure of camaraderie. Most cooperated when they ran away. If runaway advertisements are a reliable guide, just over half the African fugitives in Virginia and South Carolina ran away in pairs or in larger groups. In Virginia, the typical African fugitive ran away, at best, with one other African; in South Carolina, exactly half the Africans who ran away together left in groups of

---

6. Workhouse, *SCG*, June 29, 1765, and Workhouse, *SCG and CJ*, Oct. 12, 1773 (brandings); Camden Gaol, *SCG*, Oct. 24, 1774, Henry Patrick, *SC and AGG*, July 7, 1775, and William Rees, *Charleston Courier*, Aug. 30, 1805 ("great water" and "big water"); Charles Ball, *Fifty Years in Chains* (New York, 1970), rpt. of *Slavery in the United States: A Narrative of the Life and Adventures of Charles Ball, a Black Man* (New York, 1837), 186; William McLaughlin, *SCG*, Sept. 24, 1772 (when captured in early September, five Africans recalled their captain's name, three months after their arrival); Workhouse, ibid., Nov. 27, 1762 (sale of the *Marlborough* began Aug. 31, the slave was captured Nov. 24, and then reported the merchant house that handled his sale); Workhouse, ibid., Nov. 19, 1763 (sale of the *Upton* began Aug. 11, the slave was captured Nov. 17, and then reported both the merchant house and locations of sale); *Laurens Papers*, VII, 192; *Charleston Courier*, Jan. 7, 1807.

7. Jordan Anderson, *VaG* (P and D), Oct. 20, 1768; George Robertson, ibid., Sept. 12, 1771; David Williams, *SCG and CJ*, Nov. 21, 1769; Joseph Weatherly, *SC and AGG*, Jan. 27, 1775. For Africans returning to the site of their sales, see Aaron Truehart, *VaG* (Parks), Sept. 26, 1745; and Mr. Wragg, *SCG*, Jan. 22, 1737.

three or more, and bands of six, seven, or eight fugitives were fairly common. Evading capture was also somewhat easier in South Carolina than in Virginia. In South Carolina, four "Senegambians" remained at large for at least ten months in 1754; in 1773, after about a year in the colony, a number of Africans belonging to William Flud had absconded twice and seem to have spent as much time off as on his Santee plantation. Conversely, the African fugitive in Virginia faced a much bleaker existence, as is suggested by Robert "King" Carter's optimism concerning a recently captured "new negro woman." Now that "she hath tasted of the hardship of the woods," he predicted, "she will go near to stay at home where she can have her belly full." A single, isolated African fugitive, far more common in Virginia than in South Carolina, had a hard time scavenging off the land.[8]

Sometimes Africans from the same coastal region or of a similar ethnic background collaborated. In Virginia, two "Senegambians" ran away from their Hanover County master in 1745, and two "Ibos" quit the service of their King William County master in 1773. In South Carolina, the ethnic collaborations were more spectacular. In 1761, seven "Coromantees" and a "Calabar" ran away from an estate in Prince William Parish; eight years later, five recent immigrants "of Angola country" absconded from their Welch Tract residence. Overall, a quarter of the runaway groups advertised in colonial South Carolina newspapers consisted of Africans who shared regional origins. Perhaps most remarkable, in South Carolina, Africans of similar ethnicity established or renewed ties with one another even when they lived on separate plantations. In 1775, an African fugitive who had "been many years in the province" apparently headed toward a plantation "where he *frequently* used to visit a countryman of his." A decade later, two recent immigrants escaped in a four-oared boat along with "two new negroes (countrymen of theirs)" resident on a neighboring plantation. In 1807, a runaway "Mandingo" slave was "supposed to be secreted by some of his country people" on another plantation. It was not easy to maintain ethnic ties across plantation boundaries, but it was certainly not impossible—at least in the Lowcountry.[9]

---

8. Daniel Heyward, *SCG*, Jan. 22, 1754; William Flud, ibid., Nov. 1, 1773; Robert Carter to Robert Jones, Oct. 10, 1727, Robert Carter Letterbook, 1727–1728, VHS. Carter had much experience of African fugitives, for he referred to 33 runaways in the period 1725–1727 alone, many of whom must have been Africans. On one occasion, 7 African men went off in a canoe five days after arrival, but they were soon recaptured (Robert Carter Diary, July 12, 17, 25, 1727, VHS). Another major exception to the small size of African runaway groups in the Chesapeake is the group of 14 who ran off while awaiting sale (John Burnley, *VaG* [P and D], Aug. 19, 1773). In South Carolina between 1732 and 1779, I count 331 of 663 African fugitives and captives in groups of 3 or more.

9. Margaret Arbuthnott, *VaG* (Parks), Oct. 10, 1745; Joseph Hillyard, ibid. (P and D),

Over time, however, Africans from one ethnic group increasingly cooperated with those of another ethnic group. From the 1730s to the 1770s, runaway groups composed of a single African ethnicity declined from a third to a quarter of all groups, whereas those formed by individuals of different African origins rose from 3 to 13 percent. In 1770, the warden of the workhouse reported the capture of two women who called themselves Binsaw and Cumba, one a "Mondingo," the other a "Congo," and two men from the "Malimbo" and "Kishey" country, respectively. The following year, an African couple ran away, with their one-year-old infant: the husband was from Angola, the wife from Calabar. By necessity or choice, Africans increasingly associated with members of other ethnic groups.[10]

Another association that became important to Africans in the New World was that among shipmates. A number of runaway groups consisting of slaves described as "lately come in the country" or "lately imported" or simply as "new" likely comprised former shipmates. In Virginia, concrete evidence of the shipmate bond is rare. A good example, however, concerns a few of the 240 Africans imported in the snow *Yanimarew* in the summer of 1770. One month after being purchased and taken to Amherst County, Charles ran away. Meanwhile, in Richmond, three men from the same ship fled their master. They apparently sought out the companionship of their former shipmates (perhaps Charles was among them), for their master reported, "It is imagined that they were seen some time ago (along with three others of the same cargo) on Chickahominy, and it is supposed they are still lurking about the skirts of that swamp." But the sale of Africans individually or in small groups to dispersed plantations throughout the Chesapeake made the maintenance of shipmate ties difficult.[11]

In South Carolina, shipmates had an easier time maintaining contact. Some ran away from the same plantation, such as three Senegambians who eloped three weeks after disembarking the *Princess Carolina,* or the four Angolans,

---

Oct. 7, 1773 (these are the *only* known Virginia examples where Africans from the same region ran away together); Thomas Middleton, *SCG,* Dec. 5, 1761; David Williams, *SCG and CJ,* Nov. 21, 1769; Daniel Bourget, *SCG,* Aug. 19, 1745, and Apr. 18, 1748; Thomas Ladson, *SC and AGG,* Feb. 17, 1775 (emphasis added); James and Edward Penman, *SCG and DA,* July 26, 1785; *Charleston Courier,* Aug. 14, 1807. See also Dr. Samuel Stevens, *SCG,* June 16, 1733; and Charles Daily, *Columbian Herald, or the Patriotic Courier of North-America* (Charleston), May 23, 1785.

10. Workhouse, *SCG and CJ,* Apr. 17, 1770, supplement; Workhouse, ibid., June 19, 1770 (two groups reported); Workhouse, ibid., Oct. 23, 1770; John Gaillard, *SCG,* Mar. 21, 1771.

11. John Jacobs, *VaG* (Rind), Feb. 7, 1771; James Buchanan, ibid. (P and D), Dec. 13, 1770. For African groups that might well have comprised shipmates, see, for example, Peyton Smith, ibid. (Parks), Oct. 22, 1736; Maj. John Bolling, ibid., June 10, 1737; William Hunter, ibid., May 16, 1745; William Randolph, ibid. (Hunter), Oct. 20, 1752; and Peter Jones, ibid. (P and D), Dec. 7, 1769.

part of a complement of 360 slaves shipped in the *Shepherd*, who returned to the site of their sale two months after their purchase. Shipmates separated from one another also renewed contact. Thus, in 1774, two young men from the Grain Coast ran off with "five or six wenches of the same cargo" belonging to a neighboring plantation, and, eleven years later, Robin ran away to a shipyard because it employed some slaves "purchased out of the same ship" as himself. Two shipmates brought to the Charleston workhouse in 1759 identified their master and then declared that he owned "a negro wench named Betty and that she came out of the same ship with them." In 1774, Homidy, a "Guinea negro," and Polidore, a "Congo," absconded from their Goose Creek plantation; their master thought they would stick together because "both came here in one ship about 18 months ago." This ready recognition of the shipmate tie suggests its importance.[12]

Very occasionally, African kin ties, usually between siblings, survived the Middle Passage. Three slaves from Angola who ran away from a Wando Neck plantation in 1734 included two brothers; in 1779, two African runaways, one aged about twenty-five and the other twenty-three, were brothers who belonged to the same planter and had worked at the same jobs (first on a schooner and then in a rum distillery); and, six years later, two Senegambian brothers ran away together. One runaway group reveals that even generational ties sometimes remained intact. Two Africans lodged in the New Bern jail in 1767 said they were father and son; the father, aged forty-five, spoke "broken English," whereas his young son spoke "better English."[13]

Some Africans made a greater commitment to long-term cooperation when they attempted to establish an autonomous *maroon* (from *cimarrón*, meaning escaped or runaway, in a New World context) settlement. In the Chesapeake, African numbers were never overwhelming, whites predominated, and the topography was not particularly conducive to maroon settlements. In the early

---

12. John Lawson, *SCG*, Sept. 11, 1736 (the advertisement mentions that these Africans were bought from Mr. John Guerard out of a cargo imported by Capt. Coe; John Coe brought 148 Africans from Gambia in the *Princess Carolina* and offered them for sale Aug. 25, 1736); Mr. Wragg, ibid., Jan. 22, 1737 (these 4 Angolans arrived in the ship *Shepherd* and were probably purchased in early November—the sale began on Nov. 2, 1736; two months later they were back at Wragg's lot in town); Roger Pinckney, *SCG*, Oct. 31, 1774; Charles Morgan, *SCG and DA*, Oct. 18, 1785; Workhouse, *SCG*, Aug. 11, 1759; George Parker, *SCG and CJ*, Oct. 11, 1774. For another example of shipmates with different ethnic backgrounds, see Workhouse, ibid., Oct. 12, 1773.

13. James Paine, *SCG*, Feb. 9, 1734; John Smyth, *Gaz of State of SC*, Oct. 13, 1779; George Savage, *SCG and DA*, Aug. 30, 1785; *SC and AGG*, Oct. 30, 1767. In 1783, a 40-year-old African and his wife "of the same country" ran away. Both were said to speak "bad English," suggesting that they were recent immigrants, but whether they were married in Africa or in South Carolina is unclear (Daniel Cannon, *SC Weekly Gaz*, Mar. 15, 1783).

eighteenth century, Africans attempted to establish a few settlements on the frontier, but they were short-lived. In the Lowcountry, more Africans, a black majority, and extensive swamplands were greater encouragements to maroon bands. Furthermore, the proximity of Spanish Florida provided a ready sanctuary for Lowcountry fugitives. In 1738, a large contingent—perhaps seventy slaves—fled from South Carolina to Saint Augustine, attracted no doubt by the founding of a new frontier town named Gracia Real de Santa Teresa de Mose populated by freed slaves. A small but steady stream of Lowcountry slaves aimed their flight for Saint Augustine. By what they took with them, a number of African runaway groups in South Carolina indicate that they had independence firmly in mind. Carrying axes, hoes, and blankets, a number of African groups revealed a determination to cope with their new environment.[14]

Some of these Lowcountry groups established settled camps. A vivid account of an expedition mounted against a band of Savannah River maroons in November 1765 provides a graphic description of a quasi-permanent settlement. The expedition first encountered a large canoe that, according to their guide, was manned by the maroons' "head or leading man." They then encountered three blacks who took to the swamp. Proceeding at least four miles through a swamp in which they were often up to their waists in water and mud, they came to the "town," where

> they discovered two Negroes on a Scaffold one Beating a Drum and the other hoisting Colours, but on their resoluteing coming up they Jump'd off the scaffold and betook themselves to flight after discharging their guns without doing them any mischief, that on their arrival at the Town which was then totally deserted they found it a square consisting of four Houses 17 feet long and 14 feet wide, that the kettles were upon the fire boiling rice and about 15 bushels of rough rice, Blanketts, Potts, Pails, Shoes, Axes, and many other tools all which together with the Town they set fire to.[15]

---

14. James Paine, *SCG*, Feb. 9, 1734; Daniel Ravenel, *SCG and CJ*, Feb. 25, 1772; Elias Ball, ibid., Oct. 14, 1766. For maroons aiming for Spanish Florida, see John J. TePaske, "The Fugitive Slave: Intercolonial Rivalry and Spanish Slave Policy, 1687–1764," in Samuel Proctor, ed., *Eighteenth-Century Florida and Its Borderlands* (Gainesville, Fla., 1975), 1–12; Jane Landers, "Spanish Sanctuary: Fugitives in Florida, 1687–1790," *Florida Historical Quarterly*, LXII (1984), 296–313; and Landers, "Gracia Real de Santa Teresa de Mose: A Free Black Town in Spanish Colonial Florida," *AHR*, XCV (1990), 9–30. See also the pardon for Peter, who attempted to reach Saint Augustine, Dec. 3, 1761, Miscellaneous Records, LL, 421, SCDAH.

15. Roderick McIntosh to Isaac Young, Nov. 18, 1765, enclosed in Governor Wright to Lt. Gov. of South Carolina, Nov. 25, 1765, Council Journal, no. 32, 674–675, SCDAH. For a description of another small camp, located at the head of a creek, with a small canoe, fish, and grains in the runaways' possession, see Josiah Smith to George Austin, July 22, 1774, Josiah Smith Letterbook, UNC.

The military organization of this township, together with its regular layout and signs of residential stability, make it a notable example of *marronage* in mainland British America.

Lowcountry whites mounted similar expeditions in the same year and subsequent years in other parts of the region. The resemblances in an account of one such expedition, undertaken in 1786, with the expedition of twenty-one years earlier are uncanny. A party of militia and members of the Savannah light infantry mounted an attack against a maroon group, estimated at more than a hundred strong, that had established a secure camp on an island seventeen miles up the Savannah River. After a number of bloody skirmishes, this group of maroons also "quitted precipitately" when the whites approached. They had on hand enough rough rice to beat out twenty-five or more barrels, sixty bushels of corn, and four acres of unripened rice. They had fourteen or fifteen boats and canoes. Their camp measured 700 yards in length and 120 yards in width, contained a four-foot-high breastwork of logs and cane, and consisted of twenty-one houses. This band, like many others, had planned on a long stay.[16]

In the Chesapeake, the vast majority of Africans neither fled with shipmates nor attempted to set up independent communities, and they left little trace. Their "invisibility" is easily explained. Africans were a minority of Virginia slaves by the early eighteenth century, and their proportion declined markedly throughout the century. Slaveholdings were generally small, and the occasional large plantation often garnered a number of Africans, so most recent immigrants would be fortunate indeed to end up sharing the same residence. Even on a large estate, the overwhelming majority of immigrants lived on quarters with numerous native adults and children.[17]

African names soon disappeared in Virginia. According to a study of slave names in Middlesex County in the late seventeenth and early eighteenth centuries, fewer than 5 percent of slaves had African names. The proportion throughout Virginia declined rapidly thereafter. Rare indeed were the two

---

16. *Charleston Morning Post, and Daily Advertiser,* Oct. 26, 1786; trial of Negroe Man Slave named Lewis, the property of Oliver Bowen, Telamon Cuyler Collection, box 71, file Georgia Slavery Trials, University of Georgia Library, cited in Sylvia R. Frey, *Water from the Rock: Black Resistance in a Revolutionary Age* (Princeton, N.J., 1991), 226–227; Betty Wood, "'Until He Shall Be Dead, Dead, Dead': The Judicial Treatment of Slaves in Eighteenth-Century Georgia," *GHQ,* LXXI (1987), 391–392. For continuing small maroon encampments, see Loren Schweninger, "Slave Independence and Enterprise in South Carolina, 1780–1865," *SCHM,* XCIII (1992), 116–117.

17. See Chapter 1; and Kulikoff, *Tobacco and Slaves,* 332–333. John Thornton's claim that "most slaves would have no shortage of people from their own nation with whom to communicate and perhaps to share elements of common culture" is untrue for the Chesapeake (*Africa and Africans in the Making of the Atlantic World, 1400–1680* [Cambridge, 1992], 197).

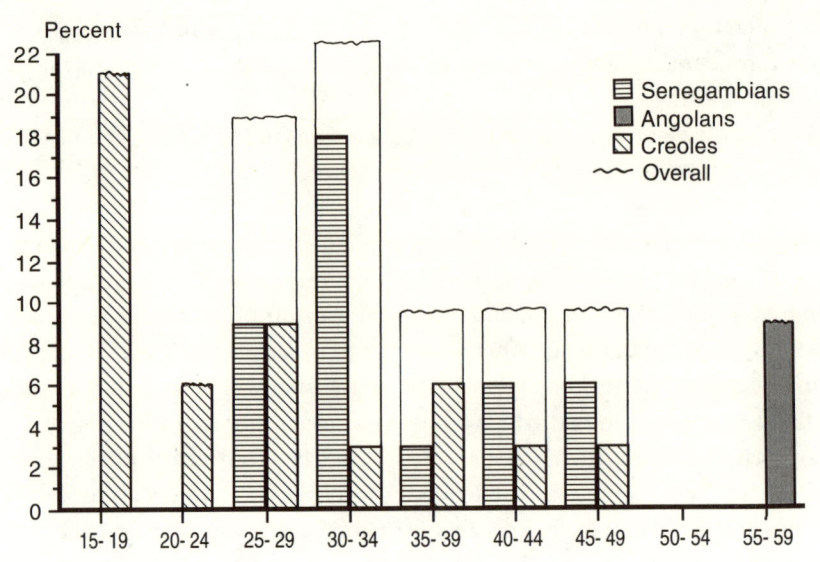

FIGURE 7. *Age Profile of Africans and Creoles among Adult Male Slaves on Elias Ball's Comingtee Plantation, 1778*
Source: Ball Family Account Book, SCHS.

plantations in mid-eighteenth-century Goochland County that listed eleven African names in all (Jolloff, Quaw, Fatima, Congo, Cudgo, Shantee, Cudjee, Bussee, Jallapa, Jubah, and Abanah); if all of these individuals were Africans, they accounted for about a third of the adult slaves on each estate. Ethnic designations as well as African names were sparse. In 1782, "Ebo" Billy and Billy "Congo" belonged to William Daingerfield, but they were heavily outnumbered by the other 140 Daingerfield slaves who betrayed no African antecedents in their names. African names were also infrequent among Virginia slave runaways. In 1767, a runaway from Lunenburg County preferred to be known as Fooser; four years later an African runaway from Williamsburg went by the name of Quomony; and, as late as 1790, an African resident of Surry County was known as Mungo. Perhaps more telling, however, was the "outlandish" slave who, like these others, retained his African name but compromised with Anglo-American expectations. He sometimes called "himself John Quash."[18]

18. Darrett B. Rutman and Anita H. Rutman, *A Place in Time: Explicatus* (New York, 1984), 100; "Tithables in Southam Parish in the County of Goochland for the year 1746 taken by George Carrington," Goochland County tithable lists, VSL. By midcentury a smattering of African names appears in inventories and tax lists—fewer than 1% of all slave names. For the inventory of Daingerfield, see Spotsvylania County Will Book E, 1772–1798, 447–451, VSL. The 30 slaves with an ethnic designation represent a fraction of all slaves listed in

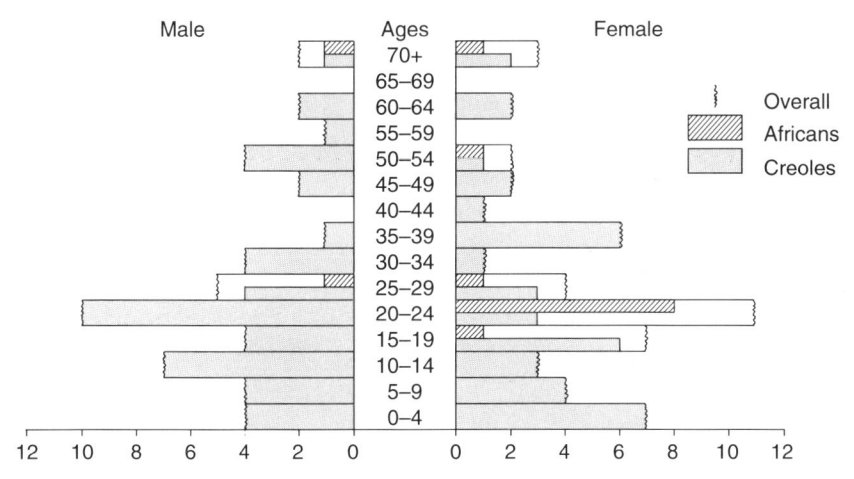

FIGURE 8. *Age Profile of Africans and Creoles among Slaves Belonging to Colonel Stapleton on Saint Helena Island, 1810*
Source: List of Negroes belonging to Col. Stapleton . . . , Mar. 15, 1810, USC.

On Lowcountry plantations, the African presence was more notable. In 1778, the 34 slave men resident on Elias Ball's Comingtee plantation were equally divided between native-born and African-born. The 3 oldest men were from Angola, all estimated at age fifty-five, whereas another 14 from "Gambia" predominated among men in their early thirties and forties (see Figure 7). The youngest African was only twenty-seven, whereas all men in their late teens and early twenties were creoles. If authority followed age, then these African men should have been disproportionately influential. Thirty years later, Colonel Stapleton of Saint Helena Island owned 112 slaves. Three Africans—seventy-nine-year-old Sambo, a former gardener, eighty-year-old Dorinda, "a cripple crawling upon hands and knees," and fifty-year-old Dido from "Moroco"—were no doubt survivors from the eighteenth-century era of African immigration. Another 27 Africans—a quarter of the total complement and fully half of the prime slaves (aged twenty to fifty)—were recent immigrants, survivors of the last great flourish of the African slave trade into Carolina (see Figure 8). Almost all of these newcomers were in their twenties; 2 were broth-

---

inventories. For what it is worth, five African coastal regions are represented: 37% apiece for Senegambia ("Gambia," "Mandingo," and "Bambra," or variations thereof, are used) and Angola ("Golahs" and "Congos"), 20% for the Bight of Biafra ("Ebos" and a "Callibar"), and 3% apiece for the Bight of Benin (a "Pawpaw") and Madagascar or Eastern Africa (a "Malagawyow"). Bennidick Alderson, *VaG* (P and D), Sept. 17, 1767; Andrew Estave, ibid., June 20, 1771; B. Middleton, *VaG and GA,* Sept. 29, 1790; Bourne Price, *VaG* (D and H), Nov. 8, 1776.

ers; a remarkable number (20 in all) had paired off in marriage; 4 of these couples had produced at least 1 child; only 1 African man had found a creole wife; 5 men and 1 woman were single. These Africans, perhaps in large part because of the demographic structure of this plantation, looked inward for their most important social ties.

On these and other Lowcountry plantations, African names were more common among creoles than among recent immigrants. At Comingtee, only one African man (Quash) but two creoles (Quau and Quaco) had African names. Similarly, creoles with African names (Coomba, Dembo, and Minda) outnumbered Africans with homeland names (Mamoody and Sambo) on Colonel Stapleton's plantation. Of the 208 slaves belonging to the estate of Daniel Huger, 10 percent of the 96 adults, 13 percent of the 27 boys and girls (many if not most of whom must have been creoles), and 15 percent of the 85 children (almost certainly all creoles) had African names.[19] The pattern seems clear: although some African immigrants were able to retain their names, more often they bequeathed homeland names to their children in an effort to honor tradition and family ties.

Throughout the eighteenth century, Africans in South Carolina maintained symbolic ties to their native country through their naming patterns. At midcentury, about one in five slaves belonging to Benjamin De St. Julien, to Elisha Ball, and to Benjamin Godin had African names. Although no late-eighteenth-century estate matched these levels, at least one in ten slaves on plantations belonging to Daniel Huger, to Thomas Elliott, and to George Austin had an African name. Moreover, not just the number but the range of African names was impressive in South Carolina. In Virginia, the standard African names—Cudjo, Cuffee, Quamina, Quash, Sambo—predominated, whereas in South Carolina they were joined by more unusual names, such as Balipho, Bendar, Dubau, Fulladi, Moosa, Noko, Okree, Sogo, Yanki, and Yarrow.[20] Furthermore, African ethnic or regional designations—Jack Gambia or John Gola, for in-

---

19. Inventory of Daniel Huger, Jan. 30, 1755, Inventory Book, WPA, CXLV, 470–486, SCDAH. One wonders how "Stay now William," an African on Colonel Stapleton's plantation, arrived at his name. Was Stapleton perhaps making a reference to William's prior propensity to absent himself, or was William signaling his reconciliation to the new home?

20. Inventory of Benjamin De St. Julien, c. 1756, ibid., CLIII, 966 (57 slaves); inventory of Elisha Ball, Nov. 8, 1751, ibid., CXXXII, 133–139 (101 slaves); inventory of Benjamin Godin, May 24, 1749, ibid., CXXV, 191–197 (147 slaves); inventory of Daniel Huger, ibid., CLXII, 937–956 (453 slaves); inventory of Thomas Elliott, Mar. 28, 1761, ibid., 882–899 (490 slaves); and inventory of George Austin, Nov. 16, Dec. 6, 1774, ibid., XCVIII, 65–71 (175 slaves). These proportions are at the higher end of those reported in South Carolina inventories. Unusual names from South Carolina runaway advertisements include Binsaw, Bola, Bungee, Dembo, Dibbee, Fodee, Gamone, Gychie, Jowler, Mamado, Mambee, Mamena, Manfo, Movery, Pombo, Saffran, Sirrah, Sungoe, Wofe, Yalfa, and Zango.

stance—were more than occasional on some South Carolina plantations: 10 of 148 slaves belonging to Noah Serre conveyed their ethnic identity in their names, as did 5 of 83 belonging to Joshua Grimball.[21]

Perhaps most significant, many Africans in South Carolina continued to use a "country name" *after* their masters had christened them. This evidence obviously complicates patterns of naming based on lists drawn up by masters. Even the most Anglicized list of names could conceal the continued use of African names among the slaves. In some cases, as Peter Wood has pointed out, African and Anglo-American names coexisted because they sounded alike. Alexander Wood reported that his slave went "by the Name of Cooper Joe or Cudjoe"; a recent African immigrant brought to the Charleston workhouse gave his name as "Tom or Tomboe." But since most African and Anglo-American names were not readily convertible, a newcomer often had to struggle to retain a homeland name. A surprising number were successful. Thus, two Angolan slaves named after the biblical heroes Moses and Sampson continued to be known as Monvigo and Goma. Bristol held to his African name Cuffee, John to Footabea, London to Appee, March to Arrow, and Charlestown to Tamoo. One slave woman's retention of an African name led to much confusion when she became part of a marriage settlement. Her former overseer testified that the slave named both Affey and Occoe was indeed one and the same person. He recalled that the slave's owners "oftner called her by [the name Affey] than by the Name of Occoe." More significant, perhaps, is that Occoe, like many another slave, ensured that whites knew the name she presumably preferred.[22]

The most dramatic example of African self-identification occurred during the Stono Rebellion. The instigators were twenty "Angolan" slaves—from the

---

21. Inventory of Noah Serre, Feb. 11, 1746, ibid., CIII, 551–568 (3 "Golas," 3 "Ebos," 3 "Echaws" or "Itchaws" [?], and 1 "Coromantie"), and inventory of Joshua Grimball, Jan. 13, 1758, ibid., CLVI, 350–354 (3 "Angolas" and 2 "Gamboas"). In all, I count almost 200 ethnic identities in the slave names reported in inventories, broken down as follows: 45% Angola, 40% Bight of Biafra, 8% Senegambia, 3% Gold Coast, and 3% Bight of Benin.

22. Alexander Wood, *SCG*, Sept. 22, 1746 (for a similar example, see Paul Pritchard, ibid., Apr. 3, 1775); Workhouse, ibid., Sept. 27, 1772; Daniel Bourget, ibid., Apr. 18, 1748; Mary Bailey, ibid., Mar. 17, 1747; Henry Laurens, ibid., Aug. 27, 1753; Arthur Bull, ibid., July 24, 1755; James Parsons, ibid., Jan. 29, 1763; John Delahowe, ibid., May 14, 1778; deposition of Samuel Evans, June 10, 1778, Miscellaneous Records, VV, 451. For other examples of dual names, see Workhouse, *SCG*, Aug. 17, 1765; James Laurens, ibid., Sept. 20, 1773; George Gray, ibid., Sept. 27, 1773; John Savage, *SC and AGG*, June 3, 1774; Joseph Lawton, ibid., Nov. 18, 1774; Josiah Allston, *SCG and CJ*, Mar. 11, 1766 (particularly interesting because the two African runaways retained the Islamic names of Mahomet and Mousser); William Remington, *SCG*, Sept. 12, 1768; Jeoichum Hardstone, *SCG and CJ*, May 16, 1769; Paul Porcher, *SCG*, June 7, 1773; and George Parker, *SCG and CJ*, Oct. 11, 1774.

Kongo kingdom. Perhaps, as John Thornton has suggested, former soldiers provided the nucleus of the rebels. Their seizure of a supply of guns, which they seem to have handled adroitly, suggests prior experience with weapons. Their marching under banners to the accompaniment of drums is also reminiscent of African practices. Finally, when the rebels "set to dancing," they were not necessarily acting shortsightedly but, rather, engaging in a form of military exercise, much like drill in Europe. For Kongo soldiers, "dancing was a form of training to quicken reflexes and develop parrying skills." In Kongo, dancing a war dance was virtually synonymous with declaring war.[23]

In the long run, however, Africans, even in the Lowcountry, were aliens in a strange land. Many found themselves completely isolated. One "Angolan" man, found on the high seas off the coast of South Carolina, lay "in a small canoe half-full of water in a wretched helpless condition"; another recent immigrant, hauled out of a swamp after swimming across the Santee River, was "almost perished with hunger, very much crippled in his feet and legs"; an elderly Angolan arrived at the workhouse in tattered rags, saying he had been in the woods for two years; and the Cherokees captured a runaway who spoke very little English, though he had been absent "two summers," who reported that his companion had "died in the woods by eating a snake." The sense of bewilderment and frustration at not being able to communicate with fellow slaves or whites is personified by an African "of the Horobania country" who, when asked to report his own or his master's name, could only mouth "a word like Fisher, which cannot be understood, whether he means that for his own or his master's name"; he languished in the Cheraws district jail for well over a year.[24]

Africans in the Chesapeake were even more alienated. None was more so than the African, recently imported, who "taking Notice of his Master's giving another Correction for a Misdemeanor, went to a Grindstone, and making a Knife sharp cut his own Throat, and died on the spot." The typical experience for the eighteenth-century African in Virginia must have been rather like that recounted by Olaudah Equiano, who spoke eloquently of his sense of isolation on arrival in the colony:

23. John K. Thornton, "African Dimensions of the Stono Rebellion," *AHR*, XCVI (1991), 1101–1113. For another kind of dance by Jamaican maroons, see Michael Mullin, *Africa in America: Slave Acculturation and Resistance in the American South and the British Caribbean, 1736–1831* (Urbana, Ill., 1992), 50–51.

24. Walter McAuley, *SCG*, Dec. 15, 1758; John Cantey, ibid., May 11, 1765; Workhouse, ibid., Feb. 25, 1765; Printer, ibid., Sept. 6, 1768; Cheraws District Gaol, *SC and AGG*, July 22, 1774. For other examples of bewilderment and frustration, see James Holmes, ibid., Mar. 24, 1775; and John Mills, ibid., Mar. 31, 1775.

> We were landed up a river a good way from the sea, about Virginia count[r]y, where we saw few or none of our native Africans, and not one soul who could talk to me. I was a few weeks weeding grass, and gathering stones in a plantation; and at last all my companions were distributed different ways, and only myself was left. I was now exceedingly miserable, and thought myself worse off than any of the rest of my companions; for they could talk to each other, but I had no person to speak to that I could understand.[25]

Equiano might have been mistaken only in his assumption that his fellow Africans had companions with whom to talk. More than likely, they did not.

But Equiano never forgot Africa, as he later vividly recollected in his autobiography. The pool of homeland memories was always deeper than surface appearances might suggest. These remembrances might amount to nothing more than a reminder of an important event. In South Carolina, Malinke Ben had a large scar on his left arm produced by a knife, Toby a blotch on his right cheek from a dog bite, Anthony a hole near his eye from a bullet, and a "Jalunka" (Dyalonke) slave a great bump in the small of his back, the result of a fall. All remembered receiving these wounds in their "own country." In Virginia, Charles had a couple of broken front teeth, which he said "was done by a Cow in his Country."[26] As insignificant as these connections to a homeland might seem in themselves, they were reminders of a valued past. These, and many other memories, were a resource on which Lowcountry and Chesapeake slaves could draw.

Homeland divisions continued in the New World. Differences among Africans were particularly noticeable and persistent in the Lowcountry. In 1740, Alexander Garden observed the "many various Ages, Nations, Languages" within the "Whole Body of Slaves." Differences were known to produce hostilities. Some Lowcountry Africans bore palpable reminders of homeland conflict: Jack had a "large blotch under his lower lip, occasioned by fighting in his own country," and Joe had a great scar in the small of his back, the result of a knifing in Africa. James Barclay's experiences on a South Carolina rice plantation in the 1770s indicate that African memories were not short-lived.

---

25. *VaG* (Hunter), July 10, 1752; Paul Edwards, ed., *The Life of Olauda Equiano; or, Gustavus Vassa the African, 1789,* I (London, 1969 [orig. publ. 1789]), 90.

26. Workhouse, *SCG,* Jan. 17, 1761; Workhouse, ibid., Feb. 28, 1761; Workhouse, *SCG and CJ,* Oct. 14, 1766; Workhouse, *SCG,* Aug. 26, 1765; Joseph Hillyard, *VaG* (P and D), Oct. 7, 1773. For further examples, see Workhouse, *SCG,* Nov. 4, 1756; Workhouse, ibid., Mar. 3, 1764; Workhouse, *SC and AGG,* Dec. 19, 1768; Camden Gaol, *SCG,* Dec. 12, 1774. Slaves' appearance is explored in Chapter 10.

"There are some provinces from whence they are brought," Barclay observed, "whereof the people have a violent antipathy to one another, and [when] they are brought over here, the same antipathy subsists." In particular, Barclay continued, "those of Gully or Gulli [Angola] and Iba [Igbos] are the chief. The one will say to the other, 'You be Gulli Niga, what be the use of you, you be good for nothing.' The other will reply 'You be Iba Niga; Iba Niga great 'askal [rascal].'"[27]

Even in the late eighteenth century, the deep strains that divided African from African were evident, as an exchange between the traveler William Attmore and a slave immigrant illustrates:

> ATTMORE, How came you brought from yr. Country.
> POLYDORE, I went with many more to attack a town, where they were too strong for us, they killed a great many, and took 140 of us prisoners, and sold us—
> ATTMORE, Had you not better have left them alone and remained in peace at home?
> POLYDORE, No—My Nation always fight that Nation—
> ATTMORE, And what would [you] do if you return'd to your Country now, wou'd you be quiet?
> POLYDORE, No—I go there, and fight 'em worse than ever.[28]

Apparently, absence had not made the heart grow fonder.

In the Chesapeake, conflict among Africans was less evident and confined to the early eighteenth century. African marriage customs provided a source of tension on Edmund Jenings's Selsdon quarter in King William County. In 1712, Roger hanged himself in an old tobacco house for "not any Reason," an uncomprehending master observed, except his "being hindred from keeping other negroes mens wifes beside his owne." After about 1740, however, the tidewater received few Africans, and the piedmont, the destination of most Africans for the next thirty years, dispersed its African influx widely. As a result, Africans rarely generated the numbers sufficient to maintain homeland rivalries and antipathies.[29]

---

27. Alexander Garden to the SPG, May 6, 1740, B7/235; Workhouse, *SCG,* Aug. 15, 1761; Workhouse, ibid., Mar. 3, 1764 (see also Workhouse, ibid., June 15, 1765); James Barclay, *The Voyages and Travels of James Barclay, Containing Many Surprising Adventures, and Interesting Narratives* (Dublin, 1777), 26.

28. William Attmore, *Journal of a Tour to North Carolina, 1787,* ed. Lida T. Rodman (Chapel Hill, N.C., 1922), 45.

29. List of Edmund Jenings's slaves at Selsdon quarter, Jan. 4, 1712, Francis Porteus Corbin Papers, Duke. For more on the piedmont, see Philip D. Morgan and Michael L. Nicholls, "Slaves in Piedmont Virginia, 1720–1790," *WMQ,* 3d Ser., XLVI (1989), 211–251; and Morgan,

As Africans became less numerous in both regional populations, their differences must have seemed increasingly incongruous, even irrelevant. This process occurred earlier in Virginia than in South Carolina. But, from the first, many Africans in both regions dramatically overcame ethnic differences by cooperating in maroon bands, by running away together, by marrying. An even more notable social bond that emerged among Africans was the tie between shipmates. Whether the shipmate attachment became as significant a principle of social organization in North America as in other parts of the New World—where it extended beyond the original tie to encompass the children of shipmates—is unlikely, but its existence is a testament to the creativeness and cooperativeness of Africans in the New World. Last, perhaps the most important way differences among Africans became irrelevant was the necessity for extensive contact with creoles.[30]

CREOLES AND AFRICANS

Creoles and Africans did not always get along. An occasional glimpse can be caught of tensions between native and newcomer in the early Chesapeake. In 1728, Robert "King" Carter, aware of "a great many new hands" in his gangs, warned his overseers to take particular care that the "old hands," no doubt largely native-born, did not abuse the immigrants. One African who arrived in the Chesapeake at about this time needed no such protection. He "always expressed great contempt for his fellow slaves." He viewed them, "as he said, a mean and vulgar race." Africans did not always defer to creoles. Conversely, a child of African parents might feel embarrassment at his origins. In the narrative of his life, David George, who was born in Virginia, mentioned the names of his parents—John and Judith—but precious little else, except to point out that they "had not the fear of God before their eyes." With this note of disapproval, George preferred to draw a veil over their lives.[31]

Tensions among creoles and Africans persisted longer in the Lowcountry than in the Chesapeake. In the beginning, the African majority was more powerful. Thus, in 1710, the Reverend James Gignilliat reported that, when a slave was baptized, all the other slaves, predominantly Africans, "do laugh at

---

"Slave Life in Piedmont Virginia, 1720 to 1800," in Lois Green Carr, Philip D. Morgan, and Jean B. Russo, eds., *Colonial Chesapeake Society* (Chapel Hill, N.C., 1988), 433–484.

30. For the importance of shipmates generally, see Sidney W. Mintz and Richard Price, *An Anthropological Approach to the Afro-American Past: A Caribbean Perspective,* Institute for the Study of Human Issues, Occasional Papers in Social Change, no. 2 (Philadelphia, 1976), 22–23.

31. Robert Carter to [?], fall 1728, Robert Carter Letterbook, 1728–1750, VHS; Ball, *Fifty Years in Chains,* 21; "An Account of the Life of Mr. David George, from Sierra Leone in Africa . . . ," *Baptist Annual Register,* I (1790–1793), 473.

'em and render 'em worse and worse." Thirty years later, the Reverend Lewis Jones found that the seed of Christianity "Sown in the young Ones," or native-born, "seems to be Choak'd by their conversation with the Elder uninstructed Negroes," or Africans. But creoles soon dominated in the Lowcountry as in the Chesapeake, and, inevitably, the objects of laughter began to shift. At midcentury, Scipio, an accomplished waterman, boasted of his ability to "go before Gentleman, for he had waited before on his Master in the Council Chamber, and was used to it" and described one of his crew members as "a Fool" who "did not know how to Talk before White People." By the early nineteenth century, creoles could adopt a less strident, more condescending tone when referring to those less conversant with white ways than themselves. A traveler overheard a native black Carolinian "observe, on seeing a drove of newly imported negroes going out of Charleston to a plantation in the country—'Ah! dey be poor devils, me fetch ten of dem, if massa swap.'" The self-confident creole took pity on the newcomers.[32]

Continuing friction among Africans and creoles should not obscure how they learned to cooperate. In the Chesapeake, creoles were a majority on most plantations and neighborhoods by the early eighteenth century; they set the tone and tenor of slave life in the region remarkably early. Africans learned the ropes from them. Instructive is the pair of runaways who fled their Surry County home. Bristol, an "outlandish Fellow," ran away in the company of Bob, a ferryman, an "artful, designing, and exceedingly smooth tongued" mulatto who possessed "an immoderate Stock of Assurance." The master predicted that Bristol would "entirely submit to, and confide in, his Companion's Counsels." Similarly, even in a Maryland parish that in the late 1730s had seen an influx of Africans, the leader of the approximately two hundred slaves allegedly involved in a plot to kill all white men was a creole.[33]

Bacchus, an African, best personifies how quickly newcomers adjusted to their Chesapeake surroundings, largely because of their close association with creoles. In 1771, this seventeen-year-old, who went by a number of names, including an African one (Juba) and two English ones akin to it (Jemmy and James), was just beginning to grasp English, speaking it in a "broken" fashion. In the next couple of years, he ran away at least four times, faced four separate criminal charges, was branded in the hand, heard himself pronounced guilty

---

32. Rev. James Gignilliat to the SPG, May 28, 1710, A5/119; Rev. Lewis Jones to SPG, Dec. 27, 1743, B11/226; South Carolina Council Journal, no. 17, part 1, 98, SCDAH; John Lambert, *Travels through Lower Canada and the United States of North America, in the Years 1806, 1807, and 1808*, II (London, 1810), 414.

33. John Hartwell Cocke, *VaG* (P and D), Postscript, May 19, 1774; Kulikoff, *Tobacco and Slaves*, 329–330; Mullin, *Africa in America*, 44. Where ethnic background is known, Africans and creoles comprised one in four runaway groups.

and sentenced to hang in two county courts, but evaded the hangman's noose on both occasions. By late 1773, his mastery of an alien language had apparently improved, for he now spoke "somewhat broken" English, but his understanding of English ways had progressed by leaps and bounds. He was sufficiently conversant with white ways to pass as a free black. Bacchus learned of the Somerset Case (the famous legal decision of 1772 that was widely but erroneously perceived to outlaw slavery in England) and imagined that he would be free if only he could get to that country, "a Notion now too prevalent among the Negroes," his master noted. The source of Bacchus's information might well have been his companion, another of his master's fugitives, a twenty-seven-year-old woman named Amy, probably a creole, because she hired herself as a free black in Portsmouth under the name Sukey Jones. That news of the Somerset Case had reached the ears of a humble African like Bacchus in piedmont Virginia, some three thousand miles away, speaks well not only of his initiative and resolve but more particularly of the political education he had acquired in the Chesapeake. No doubt, his primary teachers were creoles.[34]

Although the lessons largely flowed from creoles to Africans, the reverse also occurred. Charles Ball, born in Maryland about 1780, was fortunate enough to know his African grandfather, "old Ben," who had been brought to Calvert County a half-century earlier. Ball recalled that his father, after he had been forcibly separated from his wife (Ball's mother), consoled himself by spending "nearly all his leisure time with my grandfather, who claimed kindred with some royal family in Africa, and had been a great warrior in his native country." After his father fled to escape sale, Charles had only his grandfather to "claim kindred." He learned of his grandfather's "strange and peculiar notions of religion" and marveled at how, even at age eighty, the half-acre he cultivated on his own account produced "a large portion of his subsistence." Charles Ball's African grandfather became the significant other in his early life.[35]

In Charleston, even the most sophisticated creole slaves lived cheek by jowl with Africans. Urban settings promoted acculturation, and, in Charleston more than anywhere else, creoles could congregate. But they rubbed shoulders with Africans. Creoles met African women in the marketplace, played the popular African dice game papaw, and saw "frequent" African-style funeral

---

34. Trials of Bacchus, Jan. 15, 1771, Jan. 1, 1772, Mar. 17, 1773, Surry County Criminal Proceedings against People of Color, Surry County Court House (information kindly supplied by Kevin Kelly); trials of same, July 21, Sept. 18, 1773, Chesterfield County Court Order Book, no. 5, 1771–1774, 305, 347, VSL; John Austin Finnie, *VaG* (P and D), July 4, 1771, Sept. 30, 1773. For other examples of highly assimilated Africans in the Chesapeake, see Michael Sherman, *VaG* (Parks), Nov. 21, 1745; David Pattison, ibid. (P and D), Feb. 15, 1770; Thomas Roberts, ibid., June 27, 1771.

35. Ball, *Fifty Years in Chains*, 19, 21, 22.

processions. They introduced Africans to the delights of grogshops, to Sunday recreations, and to work opportunities. They cooperated, as did Mulatto Betty and African Molly, two runaways, who were seen "lurking about town" together. Urban Africans adapted quickly. Titus was "very cunning and artful"— the standard description of a creole—even though he spoke "bad English." Perhaps he learned from his more acculturated acquaintances his ability to "pass for a fool."[36]

Rural creoles in South Carolina associated closely with Africans at work, at home, in flight, even in dress. Creole Sampson labored alongside five other sawyers, all from Angola. Native-born Jack married Sapho "of the Guiney country." A creole family of husband, wife, and daughter ran away with a Calabar and an Angolan. Creoles were often the dominant partners. Native-born Reo "persuaded" Isaac, an African, to run away. Peter of "Angola country" spoke very good English when he fled; one reason might have been his association with Jamaican-born Tom, who was "very sensible [and] artful." The master predicted that Peter would "accompany Tom wherever he goes"; and the duo ran away twice more that same year. Rumor had it that the native-born slave who persuaded twelve Angolan slaves to run away with him "was taking them back to their own country." This native leader knew what the newcomers wanted to hear. By example, if nothing else, creoles taught Africans to modify their appearance. Igbo Beckey assimilated to the point that she "look[ed] more like a country born" slave; "Angolan" Peter could "pass for country born."[37]

Forcibly moved from the Chesapeake to the Lowcountry in about 1805, Charles Ball's contacts with Africans greatly expanded. Rather than his single grandfather, he now encountered "a great many African slaves," many newly arrived, with whom he became "intimately acquainted." Their range of religious beliefs impressed him: he met "Mohamadans," worshipers of many gods, and believers in witchcraft and conjuration. One of the "Mohamadans," who prayed "in a language I did not understand," told him an elaborate animal

---

36. Thomas Phepoe, *SC and AGG*, Nov. 29, 1780; Charles Atkins, *Royal Gaz*, June 20, 1780. For the urban activities alluded to in this paragraph, see Philip D. Morgan, "Black Life in Eighteenth-Century Charleston," *Perspectives in American History*, N.S., I (1984), 187–232.

37. Henry Smith, *SCG*, Nov. 19, 1763 (Sampson et al.); John Ernest Poyas, ibid., Sept. 17, 1763 (Jack and Sapho); William Smith, ibid., Oct. 13, 1757 (the family et al.); Plowden Weston, *SC and AGG*, Feb. 26, 1778 (Isaac and Reo); Joseph Wigfall, *SCG*, Apr. 18, 1769, *SCG and CJ*, Aug. 22, 1769, and ibid., Oct. 24, 1769 (Peter and Tom); William Boyd, *Charleston Courier*, Dec. 28, 1807 (13 slaves); Peter Guerry, *SCG and CJ*, Dec. 5, 1769 (Beckey); Abraham Hayne, *SC and AGG*, Aug. 27, 1778 (Peter). Overall, 1 in 10 of all creole runaways in South Carolina fled in company with 1 or more Africans. For other examples of highly assimilated Africans, see Thomas Chisham, *SCG*, Sept. 21, 1747; Plowden Weston, *SC and AGG*, Feb. 26, 1778; James Dunwoody, ibid., Feb. 25, 1779; and James Clarke, ibid., Oct. 28, 1780.

story, featuring camels and lions, as a way to explain his own capture and transportation to North America. Ball recalled a weekend feast to celebrate "the laying by of the corn and cotton" at which the old folks "recited the stories of former times." Most of the tales concerned events in Africa "and were sufficiently fraught with demons, miracles, and murders, to fix the attention of many hearers."

Not all was harmonious. Ball met a former Maryland creole slave, like himself, who had been compelled to marry. Her husband was, in her condescending words, "a native of Africa, and still retains the manners and religion of his country." A priest in his former nation and the proud possessor of many wives, the immigrant had trouble adjusting to his lowly status in South Carolina and often maltreated his native-born wife. This troubled marriage symbolized what, for Ball, was the most significant division on his new South Carolina plantation: the rift of incomprehension between the African, "indignant" about enslavement, "revengeful" toward whites, uninterested in material comforts, and bent on returning to Africa after death, and the creole, who was "not so impatient of slavery" and whose "heart pants for no heaven beyond the waves of the ocean."

Yet Ball's close contacts with Africans, his respect for their religions, his recollection of their stories, his inclusion in their feasts, and particularly his account of how he entered into "the participation of the felicity of [this plantation] community" demonstrate that racial solidarity could overcome divisions between native and newcomer.[38]

CREOLES

The emergence of a creole majority facilitated cohesiveness among slaves. Once sex ratios became more balanced, slaves found it much easier to find mates; a major source of tension was thereby greatly reduced. Similarly, once numbers of children and old people began to populate the slave quarters, the barracks atmosphere associated with concentrations of adult men dissipated. Furthermore, for all the pain that slavery entailed, creoles at least did not have to undergo the traumas of capture, enslavement, and overseas migration. They had a distinct advantage over Africans in growing up in their environment. They knew no other home. They were raised with whites and knew their ways.

No slave population in the plantation world of British North America was as familiar with white ways as that of the Chesapeake. In describing their creole slaves, Virginia masters employed a battery of flattering adjectives. Native-

---

38. Ball, *Fifty Years in Chains*, 157, 164–165, 167–186, 201, 203, 219, 263–265. For a creole son who showed much respect for his African parents, see "Memoirs of the Life of Boston King, a Black Preacher," *Methodist Magazine*, XXI (1798), 105–106.

born slaves were brisk, lively, smart, sharp, sensible, shrewd, subtle, ingenious, and artful. Some slaves were even said to be "genteel." Creoles generally spoke fluently and were often described as smooth-tongued or fair-spoken. A few could read and write; one knew a number of "indecent and Sailor songs"; another spoke "Scotch and [sang] Scotch songs"; some loved cockfighting, cardplaying, and horse races, three notable regional pastimes; yet others grew fond of the major product of the region, so that one slave "always had a great Quid of Tobacco in his mouth," another was a great taker of snuff, and an elderly couple wore down their teeth by incessant pipe smoking.[39] In short, many native-born slaves seemed thoroughly at home, which is not really surprising because they knew no other.

This is not to imply, of course, that Virginia creoles were passive and content with their lot. Indeed, their masters also exploited a rich vocabulary that bespoke a far more negative view of the native-born. All too often they described creoles as bold, audacious, impertinent, saucy, sly, knavish, cunning, crafty, insinuating, slippery, dissembling, and deceitful. Consider mulatto Argyle, resident in Hampton, who loved to drink, was "very bold in his Cups," but, even more ominously, was "dastardly when sober." Or sixteen-year-old George, born on Maryland's Eastern Shore, who was "very smart in Conversation, and an insinuating Rascal, as would appear from his cozening the Post Rider out of his Mail about 15 Miles" north of Urbanna. Or twenty-year-old Anthony, who was "very cunning and comical in his behavior," indicating perhaps an early attempt to use humor to dupe white folks. Thoroughly conversant with white mores, creoles proved extremely irritating to their masters. Creole slaves were more likely than Africans to subvert authority with stealth.[40]

Perhaps the most common way in which Virginia creoles, like Africans, vexed their masters was to run away. Unlike Africans, however, creoles generally ran away alone. This was especially true in Virginia, where three-quarters of creole fugitives absconded singly. Creoles might have realized that a fugitive stood a better chance of escape by relying on his or her own resources, rather than by joining a more conspicuous group. The minority who engaged in cooperative action, however, sometimes combined resources in daring ways.

---

39. Hamilton Ballantine, *VaG* (D and N), May 22, 1779, and Thomas Mason, ibid. (Rind), Sept. 22, 1768 (genteel); John Draper, ibid. (P and D), Jan. 20, 1774, and John Aylett, ibid. (Purdie), supplement, Nov. 17, 1775 (songsters); Charles Grymes, ibid., Oct. 13, 1774, and Anne Tomkins, ibid., Sept. 1, 1775 (cockfighting and cardplaying); William Heath, *VaG* (P and D), Sept. 15, 1768, and Henry Delony, ibid., Aug. 3, 1769 (horse races); Henry Armistead, *VaG* (Parks), May 9, 1745, Peter Royster, ibid. (D and H), July 31, 1779, and Robert Ruffin, ibid. (P and D), Sept. 24, 1772 (use of tobacco).

40. Jacob Wray, *VaG* (D and H), Nov. 4, 1775; Bennett Browne, ibid., May 16, 1777; Thomas Jones, ibid. (P and D), Jan. 29, 1767.

In spring 1751, six Eastern Shore natives—two brothers and four mulattoes belonging to three separate masters—armed themselves with guns, broke into several houses, and took a canoe to cross the bay. Sixteen years later, three slaves—two brothers and their mother—fled after the elder brother, "a great Newlight preacher," had been severely whipped in Sussex County "for stirring up the Negroes to an insurrection." These concerted and defiant actions were all the more alarming to whites, we may conjecture, precisely because they were undertaken by slaves well versed in white ways.[41]

Even the majority of creoles who ran away alone relied heavily on other creoles for support. One southern Maryland woman, "a great Rambler," ran thirty miles to the place she had once lived, but then apparently indulged herself "a little in visiting her old Acquaintances" throughout the colony. It must have been particularly galling to proud Landon Carter to discover that two of his creole runaways had been "harboured . . . all the while they were out" by his own gardener and that they had hidden in his kitchen vault "the day [his] militia were hunting for them." Even when captured, fugitives could rely on the power of the slave community. Billy and Lucy, who absconded from their Cumberland County plantation in early 1771 to be supported by John Walker's slaves in adjoining Albemarle County, were apprehended by Walker's overseer. But he in turn was no match for his supposed charges when they rose up and "violently" rescued the two runaways. The couple remained at large three months later. Glasgow managed to support his runaway wife, who was accompanied by her seven-year-old child (also named Glasgow), long enough so that she gave birth to their second child.[42]

The few glimpses caught of Lowcountry creoles before midcentury suggest a much less acculturated native-born population than that of the Chesapeake. Two slaves born in South Carolina were even said to speak "broken English," a term reserved for Africans in Virginia but indicative of the widespread "Gullah," or creole language, in the Lowcountry. In the first half of the century, the occasional Lowcountry creole merited the adjectives "clever" or

41. Robert King, James Pettigrew, and William Andrews, *VaG* (Hunter), May 24, 1751; George Noble, ibid. (P and D), Oct. 1, 1767.

42. *Md Gaz*, Nov. 11, 1756, as cited in Kulikoff, *Tobacco and Slaves,* 379; Jack P. Greene, ed., *The Diary of Colonel Landon Carter of Sabine Hall, 1752–1778,* 2 vols. (Charlottesville, Va., 1965), 291–292 (see also 601) (hereafter cited as *Carter Diary*); Joseph Calland, *VaG* (Rind), May 23, 1771; Jennings Pulliam, *VaG and WA,* Sept. 25, 1784. For "friends" supporting Virginia runaways, see Peterfield Trent, *VaG* (P and D), Dec. 1, 1774; and Nathan Yancey, *Va Ind Chron and GA* (Davis), Sept. 23, 1789. Robert Carter of Nomini Hall wrote in exasperation at not being able to capture six "outlying" slaves (a married couple, their two grandchildren, and two men). "Whenever we attempt to collect them," he observed, "they hide themselves," although they were always "skulking" about his plantations (Robert Carter to George Newman, July 15, 1788, Robert Carter Letterbook, VIII, 141–142, Duke).

"crafty," "sensible" or "subtle," but the richness of characterization employed of Virginia slaves is missing. Only after midcentury do we begin to hear of native-born slaves like Stepney, who "can very readily invent a plausible tale if questioned," or Toby, who was "cunning, artful, and bold." Gradually, the vocabulary broadened: after midcentury, we learn of sober, upright, knowledgeable, and sedate-looking slaves or, more frequently, of roguishly inclined, arch, obstreperous, saucy, or cunning ones.[43]

The one creole group in the Lowcountry that matched, perhaps even exceeded, the sophistication of Chesapeake slaves was the population of Charleston. Urban creoles played such Anglo-American games as huzzle-cap, pitch penny, trap-ball, and fives; one understood "French cookery"; another, nicknamed the "Lawyer," owing to his "constant attendance on the Courts," was overheard delivering a legal opinion in the streets. Urban creoles looked different: they often wore "gay" clothes; one wore "goggles" to compensate for weak eyes; another sported a watch on a chain; still others wore wigs. The insouciance of the urban slave is captured in one master's claim that his fugitive could be "very easily caught, as he is very lazy [and] sleeps pretty late." Insolence more aptly characterizes another, who was sold "for no other fault than being too much her own mistress. If locked out at ten o'clock, she jumps the fence and forces a window open to get into the house." But the ultimate in self-possession must be reserved for "negro man [who] stole into the house No 2 St. Michael's alley, and, while the family were at supper in the adjoining room began to pack up every thing that was portable; but perceiving himself seen by a young girl, he told her that he was come for his master's great coat, and gave her a hat to carry into the next room, while he leisurely walked down stairs and escaped."[44]

Creole runaways in the Lowcountry fled in groups, either with fellow creoles or with Africans, more frequently than they did in the Chesapeake. Only half of Lowcountry creoles, as opposed to three-quarters of their Chesapeake counterparts, ran away alone. The reason may well be that Lowcountry creoles

43. The creole language spoken by Lowcountry slaves is explored in Chapter 10; for descriptions of native-born slaves before 1750, see Job Rothmahler, *SCG*, July 13, 1734, or John Fenwicke, ibid., Aug. 8, 1743, or Isaac Nicholls, ibid., July 29, 1745; Rawlins Lowndes, ibid., Sept. 30, 1756 (Stepney); Godin Guerard, *SCG and CJ*, Oct. 18, 1768 (Toby); for descriptions of creoles after 1750, see James Riddle, ibid., June 14, 1768, or Thomas Eustace, *SCG*, Oct. 11, 1770, or Miles Brewton, ibid., Feb. 28, 1771.

44. Mark Antony De Wolfe Howe, ed., "Journal of Josiah Quincy, Junior, 1773," Massachusetts Historical Society, *Proceedings*, XLIX (1915–1916), 455; Rogers, Barker, and Lord, *City Gaz*, Mar. 29, 1797; *SCG*, Nov. 9, 1734, and Ribson Hutchinson, ibid., Sept. 16, 1732; Samuel Warner, *SC and AGG*, Apr. 18, 1764; Laval, *State Gaz of SC*, Aug. 2, 1793; M. Russell, *City Gaz*, July 24, 1800; ibid., Apr. 3, 1788. More generally, see Morgan, "Black Life," *Perspectives in Am. Hist.*, N.S., I (1984), 187–232.

were less acculturated and felt less able to strike out successfully on their own; or, perhaps, living on large plantations with many slaves about them, they could mount cooperative actions more easily. In any event, groups composed only of creoles were quite common: a third of all native-born runaways fled in such company.[45]

Just as striking as groups running away was the capacity of creoles in South Carolina to support native-born fugitives. Even when a runaway's movements were known and publicized, he or she might evade capture. Jacob had been often seen on the "broad Path," and at Stono and Wappo, but he remained free because he was "secreted by other slaves." Close acquaintances were important sources of support. According to their masters' conjectures, Harry was "harboured by some of his friends" at three separate plantations, and Dinah was supported by Robert Cochran's slaves because she had "a very good friend" among them. Masters even named individual slaves, almost always creoles, thought to be harboring their fugitives. By sustaining runaways, the creole community signaled its cohesive capacities and carved out, however sketchily, some independence.[46]

As much as the act of running away united slaves, it could divide them. Some slaves might have resented the extra work that befell them when another was absent. Slaveowners also offered rewards for information and capture. It seems a reasonable assumption that creoles would have been the most likely to respond. A fifth of the captives advertised in the *South-Carolina Gazette* in the 1730s were seized by other slaves; this proportion fell to 10 percent in the next decade and to a negligible amount thereafter. Perhaps the greater cohesiveness of an increasingly creolized slave community helps explain this sharply declin-

---

45. In South Carolina, 30% of creoles ran away in groups with other creoles, 11% with Africans, and 6% with unknown others; the other 53% ran away alone. In Virginia, the comparable proportions are 16%, 5%, 3%, and 76%, respectively.

46. "Johann Martin Bolzius Answers a Questionnaire on Carolina and Georgia," trans. and ed. Klaus G. Loewald et al., *WMQ*, 3d Ser., XIV (1957), 234; Edward Lightwood, *SCG*, Aug. 27, 1748 (Jacob); Roger Saunders, ibid., Apr. 27, 1738 (Abram); Elizabeth Ladson, *SC and AGG*, Mar. 5, 1778 (Harry); Brian Cape, ibid., Oct. 23, 1777 (Dinah); Thomas Doughty, *SCG*, May 26, 1777 (August). For named individual slaves said to be harboring runaways, see Thomas Radcliffe, ibid., Mar. 10, 1746; Elizabeth Timothy, ibid., July 8, 1756; Thomas Clifford, ibid., Mar. 10, 1759; and Mary Gordon, *SCG and CJ*, Oct. 7, Dec. 2, 1766. Many advertisements named plantations whose slaves were said to be harboring runaways. About 350 fugitives were noted as having been absent for six months or more at the time of advertising. Two South Carolina planters, assessing the relative strengths of their gangs over a three-year period, recognized that one of them had been particularly unfortunate in having a number of runaways, and "many were out for 5 or 6 months at a time" (lists of slaves belonging to Charles and George Ogilvie, 1775–1777, Ogilvie-Forbes of Boyndlie Papers, Aberdeen University Library, Scotland).

ing trend, but a change in the nature of the reporting also contributed, because, after midcentury, almost all captives tended to be advertised by the workhouse jailer, whose notices followed a standard format and excluded information about mode of arrest. The slaveowners' desire to drive wedges between slaves remained undiminished, of course. Thus, a master who confiscated clothes and two horses from runaways gave notice that the owner of the property should give a "reasonable gratuity" to the captors—his own slaves.[47]

The law was another arena in which masters encouraged slaves to betray one another. Again, it seems reasonable to presume that their opportunities were greatest with creole or well-assimilated slaves. In crimes committed by groups of slaves, one member might try to save his or her skin by incriminating fellow slaves. Thus, a South Carolina slave named Peter secured a promise of a pardon for turning king's evidence against two other slaves accused of enticing blacks to leave the province. In Virginia, slaves occasionally gave "evidence for the King" against other slaves. In 1743, two male slaves, one resident in Williamsburg and the other in James City County, were accused of the theft of two horses and other property. The urban slave—no doubt the more assimilated—got off scot-free by giving evidence against his rural cousin, who was sentenced to death. In 1754, Sam, one of three slaves accused of a crime in Elizabeth City County, testified against his two compatriots, who were then both sentenced to hang.[48]

In yet other cases, slaves who were not on trial acted as witnesses against accused bondpeople. Occasionally, they were identified as "Christian Negro Slaves," again a reasonable indication that they were well-assimilated, probably creole, slaves. Whether slave witnesses came forward voluntarily is impossible to say. Masters could certainly exert a variety of pressures to "encourage" testimony from their bondpeople. Yet, some slaves were accused of giving false testimony against their fellows, so the process was no charade. There is little

---

47. *SCG and CJ*, Mar. 24, 1767. For other examples of rewards, see Ellery, *SCG*, July 13, 1734; Gadsden, ibid., July 2, 1737; Isaac Porcher, ibid., Aug. 13, 1737; and Alexander M'Elroy, ibid., Nov. 22, 1742. Forty-two of 230 captives in the 1730s were taken up by blacks, 23 of 235 in the 1740s, and then only 7 in succeeding decades. On legislative practice concerning rewards for slaves capturing runaways, see Thomas Cooper and David J. McCord, eds., *The Statutes at Large of South Carolina*, 10 vols. (Columbia, S.C., 1836–1841), VII, 342–347.

48. *SCG*, Jan. 10, 1743; trial of Bradford and Sophy, Nov. 20, 1743, York County Court Order Book, no. 19, 241–242; trial of Hampton, Sam, and Scipio, May 27, 1754, Elizabeth City County Order Book, 1747–1755, 430. For other examples of slaves' turning king's evidence, see trial of Toney and Harry, May 27, 1754, Middlesex County Court Order Book, 1752–1758, 156–157; trial of Sam and Caesar, Dec. 12, 1754, Elizabeth City County Order Book, 1747–1754, 461; trial of Joe, Robin, and Sam, July 1771, Halifax County Pleas, no. 7, part 1, 201–202; and trial of Sawney, Tom, Bernard, and Moses, Dec. 21, 1772, Essex County Court Order Book, no. 28, 427.

evidence to support one historian's assertion that "slaves sometimes refused to testify against their fellows, especially when slaves stole goods from whites." Indeed, in Virginia county courts, slave witnesses were most commonly found in cases involving the theft of whites' property by slaves.[49]

The largest groups of slave witnesses, however, were present at trials involving black, not white, victims. In 1756, five slave witnesses belonging to four masters gave evidence against Frank, accused of assaulting a slave boy on the king's highway. In 1772, six slaves belonging to four masters were instrumental in proving the guilt of Harry for "preparing and administering poisonous medicines to Jack and Dick." Perhaps large numbers of slaves were pressed into testifying when the case involved slaves alone. Who else would have known what happened? Yet, the renegade who harmed fellow slaves could expect little sympathy. The community mobilized, rallied round, and ostracized the transgressor of group norms.[50]

Slaves who stole from bondpeople were shown little mercy. Some masters even had slaves who stole from other slaves tried in county court for their crimes. In some cases, the slave was accused of entering a "Negro Quarter" and taking goods that belonged to the master but were presumably used by the slaves. In others, the slave's property itself was the issue. Jack Russell allegedly stole property worth ten shillings belonging to David, as David himself claimed in court; Peter faced a charge of stealing "divers goods and chattels" belonging to Winney; and Daniel was accused of carrying away the "proper Goods, Chattles and money" belonging to Harry. These victims might have encouraged their masters to prosecute. A disaffected South Carolina slave

---

49. Kulikoff, *Tobacco and Slaves*, 344. References to slave witnesses have been found in the records of 14 Virginia county courts: 40 cases involved the theft of whites' property; 3 concerned alleged poisonings of whites; in 7, the alleged victims of the crime were slaves; and in the 7 remaining cases, the victims or nature of the crime was unspecified. For references to "Christian slave witnesses," see trial of Nat, Mar. 3, 1751, York County Court Order Book, no. 20, 399; trial of Josiah, June 20, 1751, ibid., 429–431; trial of Will, June 8, 1775, Caroline County Court Order Book, 1772–1776, 585; and trial of Simon, Apr. 9, 1776, Middlesex County Court Order Book, 1772–1782, 434. For slaves accused of giving "false testimony," see trial of Simon and Guy, July 2, 1729, Richmond County Criminal Trials, 1710–1754, 151–152; trial of Jamey, July 25, 1754, Brunswick County Court Order Book, no. 5, 270; trial of Adam, Mar. 2, 1761, Spotsylvania County Minute Book, 1755–1765, 194; and trial of General, Oct. 20, 1772, Essex County Court Order Book, no. 28, 406. County clerks seem to have noted the presence of witnesses (and their race) haphazardly. It is impossible, therefore, to generate meaningful statistics on the number of cases in which slaves testified against other slaves.

50. Trial of Frank, July 7, 1756, Charles City County Court Order Book, 1751–1757, 420; trial of Harry, Mar. 4, 1772, Amelia County Court Order Book, no. 11A, n.p. See also trial of Daniel, July 16, 1761, Caroline County Court Order Book, 1759–1763, 243; and Kulikoff, *Tobacco and Slaves*, 344.

upset a whole plantation. In 1796, Leath, belonging to John Ewing Colhoun, was "caught in one of the negro-houses robbing." He received a whipping for his offense, but the very next day he broke open two more houses. His fellow slaves, the manager reported, "were very unhappy and unwilling to go to work," wondering where Leath would strike next. The last straw came when Leath attempted to brain the driver with a hoe, at which point an exasperated manager shipped him off to Colhoun. Sell Leath to the Spanish, the manager advised, or he would shoot him. Presumably, Leath's fellow slaves felt little sympathy for his plight.[51]

Internal divisions undermined most slave rebellions and conspiracies. Slave informers thwarted many a revolt; and many a slave conspirator turned state's evidence, implicating a comrade. Consider two of the major acts of resistance by slaves in eighteenth-century North America. In 1739, sixty or more slaves, among whom "Angolans" were prominent, rebelled at Stono in South Carolina; less well known are the thirty-one slaves who received rewards for opposing them. It would be surprising if many of these thirty-one were not creoles or well-assimilated slaves. July, belonging to Thomas Elliott, "was very early and chiefly instrumental in saving his Master and his Family" and "at several Times bravely fought against the Rebels, and killed one of them." When the Stono rebels marched on Mr. Rose's "resolving to kill him," he "was saved by a Negroe, who having hid him went out and pacified the others." Their rewards included suits made of blue strouds, trimmed with red, and adorned with brass buttons. These trusty slaves would at least look well assimilated.[52]

51. Trial of Jack Russell, August, Sept. 2, 1761, Goochland County Court Order Book, no. 9, 3, 21; trial of Peter, Oct. 5, 1736, Middlesex County Court Order Book, 1732–1737, 77; Peter C. Hoffer and William B. Scott, eds., *Criminal Proceedings in Colonial Virginia: [Records of] Fines, Examinations of Criminals, Trials of Slaves, etc., from March 1710 [1711] to [1754] [Richmond County, Virginia]*, American Historical Association, American Legal Records, X (Athens, Ga., 1984), 244–246; John Lewis Gervais to John Ewing Colhoun, Apr. 14, 1796, John Ewing Colhoun Papers, USC. For entry of a slave quarter and the theft of goods belonging either to the master or to the slaves, see Hoffer and Scott, eds., *Criminal Proceedings*, 180–182, 222–223; trial of Tom, July 1748, Orange County Court Order Book, no. 5, 15; trial of Tom and Brister, Nov. 6, 1766, ibid., no. 7, 397–398; trial of Ned, Feb. 21, 1775, Cumberland County Court Order Book, 1774–1778, 314; trial of Cesar, Mar. 28, 1760, Amelia County Court Order Book, no. 5, 292–293; and trial of Coy, July 3, 1759, Lunenburg County Court Order Book, no. 6, 13. For examples of slaves' stealing slave property, see trial of David, Dec. 15, 1775, Brunswick County Court Order Book, no. 13, 99; trial of Amey, Jan. 4, 1777, Lunenburg County Court Order Book, no. 13, 480; Stephen Dence, *VaG* (P and D), Apr. 2, 1767; and Landon Carter, ibid. (D and H), Feb. 25, 1775.

52. Peter H. Wood, *Black Majority: Negroes in Colonial South Carolina from 1670 through the Stono Rebellion* (New York, 1974), 308–326; Mullin, *Africa in America*, 43; J. H. Easterby,

In 1800, a slave named Gabriel, a blacksmith, allegedly conspired with hundreds, perhaps thousands, of entirely creole slaves and free blacks to take Richmond, Virginia. The revolt did not materialize because a number of blacks—notably, Pharoah and Tom, belonging to Mosby Sheppard—betrayed it. Pharoah, in particular, had a stake in the status quo, in that he apparently hired his own time and sold goods at market. He bought several articles of clothing on credit from his master and subsequently paid the debt with cash. He had something to lose from an unsuccessful revolt and something to gain by informing on the conspiracy: he and Tom secured their freedom and sixty-dollar annual dividends from separate thousand-dollar trust funds donated by several Richmond merchants. In addition to informers, Gabriel's conspiracy reveals a number of slaves who were reluctant to join the planning, who joined and then backed out, who rejected the insurrectionaries' overtures, and who received pardons for testifying against other conspirators. As far as can be determined, none of the primary informers suffered retaliation of even ostracization for his collaboration.[53]

Slaves, of course, occasionally fought in everyday situations. One Sunday evening in Charleston, two hundred slaves met on the green; one drank too much, drew a knife, and struck another in the neck. On another occasion, three urban slaves were charged with "fighting in the Publick Street." Jenny sported a black eye, Cato and Aaron missed part of an ear, and Joe had a gash on his back, all courtesy of other slaves. The scar that disfigured sixteen-year-old George had been produced by a fellow boy's teeth marks, suggesting that serious fighting began early in life. Moody put out the eye of Jack, Harry stabbed Tim in the stomach, and Jeffrey wielded a stick against Colly. For sheer brutality, the attack on James seems difficult to surpass: his two assailants, Ned and Harry, "with hands and feet, fists, sticks, whips, [and] switches . . . [did] whip, cut, slash, beat, bruise, and wound" him. James died from the assault.[54]

---

ed., *Journal of the Commons House of Assembly, September 12, 1739–March 26, 1741,* Colonial Records of South Carolina (Columbia, S.C., 1952), 50, 63–65.

53. My understanding of Gabriel's conspiracy has benefited from reading Douglas R. Egerton, *Gabriel's Rebellion: The Virginia Slave Conspiracies of 1800 and 1802* (Chapel Hill, N.C., 1993); and especially James Sidbury, *Ploughshares into Swords: Race, Rebellion, and Identity in Gabriel's Virginia, 1730–1810* (New York, 1997). See also Colonial Papers, Mar. 19, 1709, VSL.

54. Charleston News, *SCG*, Oct. 28, 1732; trial of Billy, Prince, and Harry, Jan. 30, 1770, Miscellaneous Record Book, OO, 205, SCDAH; William Hort, *SC and AGG*, May 8, 1776 (Jenny); William Dixon, *VaG* (P and D), Nov. 25, 1773 (Cato); Joseph M'Caughey, *VaG and WA*, Oct. 8, 1789 (Aaron); Jacob Valk, ibid., Feb. 5, 1778 (Joe); Workhouse, *City Gaz*, May 13, 1797 (George); Benjamin Bucktrout, *VaG* (P and D), Sept. 23, 1773, and trial of Moody,

Combatants often divided on the basis of gender. Ben cut the throat of Winney, Will cracked Peggy's skull, Sarah died from wounds inflicted by Abram, Cudjo murdered Iris and Beck with a hominy pestle, and Davy killed Nanny and "so badly used" Pendar that she ran away to her master, only to die from her "weak and sickly" condition. Each of these couples or trios resided on the same or adjacent quarters. Proximity bred deep tensions that welled up in violence. Perhaps the imbalance of the sexes, the denial of full family responsibilities to slave men, or plain misogyny helps explain the anger and frustration evident in such actions. Some disputes among men originated in differences over women. Jerry of Robert Carter's Forest quarter managed to defuse conflict when, on a Wednesday night, three slave men (two belonging to neighboring planters and a third to Forest) arrived at his house "very much disposed to fight on acct of negro Mary," who lived with Jerry. Occasionally, women turned the tables on men. In Prince George County, a slave woman named Nutty was accused of murdering Sam; in Amelia County, Hannah confessed her threat, delivered "in a passion," to kill Eaton; and, in Elizabeth City County, Hannah stabbed Pompey with a knife.[55]

In spite of the evidence of internal conflict, serious slave crime against persons was not widespread in the colonial South. Indeed, it would have been surprising, given the harsh powers arrogated by whites, had slaves engaged in massive internecine violence. Thirty murder cases involving only slaves—the total for twenty-four Virginia counties between 1710 and 1790—does not seem,

---

Aug. 30, 1773, York County Judgements and Orders, 1772–1774, 362; Hoffer and Scott, eds., *Criminal Proceedings in Colonial Virginia*, 123 (Harry); trial of Jeffrey, Apr. 25, 1777, Cumberland County Court Order Book, 1774–1778, 398; trial of Ned and Harry, July 7, 1794, Executive Papers, July–August 1794, VSL. The loss of South Carolina's court records dealing with slave crime hampers this investigation. Only fragmentary survivals—in the newspapers, the miscellaneous record series, or in personal papers—remain. See, for instance, one planter's estate accounts that included a note of the expenses in going to "Green Point to get Prince and Diana try'd for the Death of Bess" (Estate Accounts of James Hartley, July 24, 1759, Inventories, WPA, LXXXVIIA, 220).

55. Hoffer and Scott, eds., *Criminal Proceedings in Colonial Virginia*, 88–89 (Ben); trial of Will, Oct. 14, 1730, York County Court Order Book, no. 17, 112; trial of Abram, Middlesex County Court Order Book, 1769–1771, 431; trial of Cudgo, Sept. 10, 1753, Cumberland County Court Order Book, 1752–1758, 19–20; trial of Davy, Dec. 15, 1741, Goochland County Court Order Book, no. 5, 17–18; Robert Carter to Samuel Straughan, July 6, 1787, Carter Letterbook, VII, 307, Duke; William Gooch's Commission appointing Justices, Prince George County, Aug. 23, 1749, Single MSS, W and M (Nutty); trial of Hannah, September 1775, Amelia County Court Order Book, no. 13, 325; trial of Hannah, Feb. 9, 1726, Elizabeth City County Deeds, Wills, and Orders, 1704–1730, 191. For further cases of males' killing females, see Essex County Court Order Book, 1770–1772, 425; and Chesterfield County Court Order Book, 1704–1730, 191.

in and of itself, to betoken serious internal conflict within the slave community. How much more violence was committed within the confines of individual plantations and never came to light is impossible to determine. Nevertheless, as many slaves appeared before Virginia courts accused of murdering other blacks as they did of killing whites. In other words, serious slave crime, though apparently never large-scale, appears to have been as much internally directed against blacks as outwardly aimed at whites.[56]

Crimes against persons were rare, but group crimes were not. The extent to which bondpeople engaged in concerted actions that placed them at considerable risk is an extreme example of their willingness to cooperate against powerful odds. Just under half of all slaves prosecuted in a number of Virginia county courts committed their alleged crimes in pairs or larger groups. Occasionally, groups of as many as six to eight slaves were accused of committing a crime together. In 1733, for example, six slaves belonging to three planters in Goochland County were charged with murdering a white man. Fourteen years later, eight slaves belonging to seven masters were said to have conspired against "Christian White People" in Orange County. As these cases suggest, a large proportion of group crimes—more than half, in fact—involved slaves belonging to separate masters. Cross-plantation alliances were the norm, not the exception.[57]

Another potential friction in the slave community was the generational differences that accompanied an increasingly creolized population. Age did not always bring respect: Joe, an African, beat up an elderly black woman; Jack Lubbar, so old that he was almost blind, asked to be removed from overlooking

---

56. The county court order books on which this analysis is based came from Albemarle, Amelia, Brunswick, Caroline, Charlotte, Chesterfield, Culpeper, Cumberland, Elizabeth City, Essex, Fauquier, Goochland, Halifax, Loudoun, Louisa, Lunenburg, Mecklenburg, Middlesex, Orange, Pittsylvania, Prince Edward, Prince William, Spotsylvania, and York Counties, all at VSL (Michael Nicholls kindly shared his Southside data). I count 60 murder cases, in exactly half of which the victims were black. Black victims were rare in assault and rape cases: 17 white and 5 black victims in assaults, 19 white and 1 black victim in the case of rape. Whether these disparities reflect a differential incidence in the committal of crimes or a differential concern on the part of whites is impossible to say. See also Philip J. Schwarz, *Twice Condemned: Slaves and the Criminal Laws of Virginia, 1705–1865* (Baton Rouge, La., 1988), 89–90, 142, 152. Poisoning cases, as we shall see, were similar to murder cases in being quite equally divided between white and black victims.

57. Trial of Champion, Lucy, Sampson, Harry, George, and Valentine, June 25, 1733, Goochland County Court Order Book, no. 3, 199–200; trial of Sambo, Frank, Peter, Tom, Jack, Tom, Simon, and Jack, May 31, 1747, Orange County Court Order Book, no. 4A, 65. Of 1,289 slaves accused of crime in 24 Virginia counties, 44% were reported to have committed their crimes in groups. Where ownership of slaves brought before the courts in a group action is known (i.e., 553 slaves), 308, or 56%, belonged to different masters.

Fork quarter because his great-grandchildren abused him. More often than not, however, it did bring respect, as even Jack Lubbar could attest. He seems always to have retained the affection of his children. While at Fork quarter, he inspired his charges to produce unusually large crops. Old Cudjoe, in Henry Laurens's employ, also derived economic benefit from the activities of younger slaves. In his case, he made "larger Crops of Rice and Corn *for himself* than the most able Young Negroes." The reason, Laurens observed, was that the younger slaves assisted Cudjoe, "for they all Respect and Love him." Cudjoe was an outsider, belonging to another master, and serving in a supervisory capacity; yet, he managed to elicit the love of Laurens's slaves, in large part no doubt because of his age. Slaves were noted for the respect they exhibited toward one another, particularly their elders. In 1807, a visitor to the nation's young capital noted "the politeness which the Negroes observe among themselves." In addressing one another, slaves commonly used "Yes Sir" and "No Ma'am," the visitor remarked in surprise, while "the common titles of respect," such as "Gentleman" and "old Lady," were very much in vogue. The Caribbean practice of applying family names—such as "old daddy," "buddy," "sissy," and particularly "aunty" and "uncle"—to nonfamily also occurred on the mainland. It betokened respect particularly toward the elderly.[58]

As further indications of the deference generally exhibited by younger slaves to their elders, consider three snapshots—two from the Lowcountry, one from the Chesapeake. In 1749, the South Carolina Council, in its investigation into an alleged slave conspiracy, took testimony from a slave named Tony. Referring to a meeting at a neighboring plantation, Tony observed "that as he was a Young fellow he kept out in the Yard where they were playing on the Bangio for the most part" while the old men talked in one of the slave houses. Although Tony's testimony no doubt aimed at exonerating himself, he suggests that weighty matters were the preserve of the elderly and young men knew their place. Two years later, the SPG missionary in the parish of Saint James Goose Creek reported some success in the proselytization of slaves. To show their gratitude, the slaves "sent six of the[ir] Old Men with a Present of Poultry." That the slave community should entrust this mission—itself an indication of courtesy—to the elderly shows the respect in which that group was held. A similar implication can be drawn from an encounter between master and slave in Virginia. In 1769, an elderly slave named George presented a complaint to Charles Dabney. When Dabney looked into the matter, he learned that fellow blacks had prevailed on George to serve as their spokesman. Because "he was

58. Charles Atkins, *Royal Gaz*, June 20, 1780; Greene, ed., *Carter Diary*, 834, 836, 840–841; *Laurens Papers*, III, 203; [Trelawny Wentworth], *The West India Sketch Book*, II (London, 1834), 201; Dick Journal, July 20, 1807, UVa.

the oldest Negro on that plantation," they calculated that a "complaint from him wou'd be listened to." Apparently, young slaves trusted their elders in matters of importance.[59]

Just as slaves developed generational ties that had the potential to divide, so residential loyalties could lead to conflict. In 1772, "some differences" arose between slaves belonging to neighboring Georgia planters. One master supported his bondpeople by whipping a number of his neighbor's slaves, but one of his own slave men, "not satisfied" with his master's actions, followed his example and "beat" one of the neighbor's slave girls when she came on an errand. On other occasions, slaves took the initiative without waiting for a master's cue. In 1782, in Orange County, Simon, belonging to John Alston, threatened to kill Frank, a slave of Richard Benehan. Simon spoke proprietorially, referred to *his* "Side of the River," and told Frank to stay away. In a similar dispute, threats grew into violence. A slave named Duff, a driver, warned a black sailor named John never to visit *his* plantation. Indeed, one slave testified that he heard Duff say that "he hated to see" John and "would drive him off." Undeterred, John appeared "about first cock crow" one Sunday and, in the ensuing struggle, killed Duff with a butcher's knife.[60]

Slaves even developed residential loyalties within estates. Among Landon Carter's slaveholdings in the Northern Neck of Virginia, Rhys Isaac has detected that "membership in different settlements was the basis of accepted factional divisions." Thus, in one dramatic incident, runaway Simon the oxcarter drew support from family and friends, all of whom lived on Carter's "home quarter," whereas slaves from Mangorike, Fork, and Lansdowne quarters either denounced members of the home quarter confederacy or helped search for Simon and his fellow fugitive, Bart. Indeed, Mangorike Will, the foreman of Mangorike quarter, went to great lengths to seize Simon. One day he noticed smoke coming from trees by the side of a cornfield; he returned at night, searched long and hard, and finally came upon the fugitive, whom he captured after a "small struggle." Arresting a fellow slave might have been easier when the bonds of comradeship were weak, as when the protagonists lived on separate quarters.[61]

59. South Carolina Council Journal, no. 17, part 1, 101; Rev. Robert Stone to SPG, Mar. 22, 1751, B17/186; [?] to Charles Dabney, c. 1769, Dabney Papers, microfilm, CW.

60. Archibald Bullock to John Houston, 1772, Archibald Bullock Papers, photostat, GHS; Negro George's deposition against Alston's Simon, Dec. 3, 1782, Cameron Family Papers, UNC; trial of John belonging to Walter Holman, July 13, 1749, South Carolina Council Journal, no. 17, part 1, 531–535; Council Proceedings, July 13, 1749, Parish Transcripts, box 2, NYHS.

61. Rhys Isaac, *The Transformation of Virginia, 1740–1790* (Chapel Hill, N.C., 1982), 328–341 (quotation on 341). Four years after this incident, Simon the runaway turned slave-

Although some slaves identified with their plantations and locales in opposition to other slaves, the growing density of black populations, the improved communications of local neighborhoods, the relocations and sales of slaves, and the slaves' propensity for visiting encouraged the establishment of social ties beyond plantations. Envisaging a division of an estate and the establishment of a new plantation, a South Carolina agent recommended that the site be located nearby; otherwise, it would "be very hard upon the old Negroes to be moved such a Distance from all their Friends." Visiting, it was foreseen, would occur between the slaves of the two plantations. In this and other ways, social networks knit together slaves from many residences, so that bondpeople came to have a sense of place that extended beyond their home lots. Even place-names reflected this reality. Thus, early-eighteenth-century Middlesex County contained its "Negro Road," and Cumberland County had its Guinea Road and Guinea Creek. These were probably paths, watersheds, and waterways most often traveled by blacks, linking dense settlements into neighborhoods. They are reminders of the growing interconnectedness of black community life in the eighteenth century.[62]

Communication among slaves is one example of this growing interconnectedness. In 1775, two Georgia planters told John Adams of their fears for the loyalty of Lowcountry slaves. They predicted that a thousand well-equipped British troops, proclaiming freedom to slaves, would have twenty thousand black recruits within two weeks. As they explained, "Negroes have a wonderful art of communicating intelligence among themselves; it will run several hundreds of miles in a week or fortnight." Perhaps this was an exaggeration de-

---

catcher. He captured a slave boy named Ambrose, who, significantly, appears to have lived off the home quarter at the Fork, for on July 20, 1770, a report reached Carter that his fugitive spent "every day in Fork Jammy's house" (Greene, ed., *Carter Diary*, 446–451).

62. Peter Manigault to Ralph Izard, Aug. 19, 1765, Peter Manigault Letterbook, SCHS; Darrett B. Rutman and Anita H. Rutman, *A Place in Time: Middlesex County, Virginia 1650–1750* (New York, 1984), 164; Cumberland County Court Order Book, 1758–1762, 286; ibid., 1774–1778, 483, 524; ibid., 1779–1784, 21, 166. For communications, the accounts of Lowcountry ferries are useful: during 10 months in 1777, at least 250 slaves (thousands if all the "boys" and "grooms" were slaves, as they almost certainly were) can be positively identified as using one ferry, and during 6 months in 1788, 24 named slaves made 83 crossings, 49 on foot and 34 on horseback, at another ferry. See the Strawberry Ferry Ledger, 1777, microfilm, USC; and John Coming Ball to John Saunders, Mar. 18–Sept.17, 1788, Ball Family Papers, SCHS. For long-distance trips between masters' far-flung quarters in the Chesapeake, see Dudley Digges to William Dabney, Dec. 18, 1758, Mar. 5, 1759, and Mary Ambler to Charles Dabney, Dec. 20, 1769, Dabney Papers; accounts of Peyton Randolph's estate with A. Cary, Jan. 14, 1770, microfilm, CW; John Sutton to Robert Carter, Oct. 18, 1784, Carter Family Papers, VHS; and Thomas Oliver's permit to Bobb and George, Oct. 29, 1771 (with notations by innkeepers on costs), photostat, CW.

signed to dramatize their plight, but Lowcountry whites well knew the self-sustaining powers of the slave community. Their fears were not unjustified.[63]

Creolization was a double-edged sword, encouraging both conflict and cooperation, atomized and collective behavior. Creoles ran away on their own far more than Africans, but they also depended far more on other slaves to support them; greater reliance on other slaves in turn heightened the chances of betrayal. Thoroughly conversant with the divisive pressures of slavery, creoles yet worked together to mount occasional conspiracies and commit a significant proportion of their crimes. But they also succumbed to those same pressures, fighting among themselves, stealing from one another, and incriminating one another, although, in toto, internecine violence was not rife. As the slave population creolized, generational differences and local identities divided the native-born, and yet respect for elders and the development of neighborhood networks united them. In general, social differentiation clearly created tensions among creoles, but it also allowed them to bring more order and predictability into their world. Conflict and cooperation marched hand in hand.

BLACKS AND INDIANS

Indians were important players in the triracial world of the early South. White colonists hoped to use Indians in a divide-and-rule policy. If Indian and black antipathies could be fostered, whites would more easily dominate both peoples. The goal was, not to foster a division within the black community, but to keep that community demoralized and disinclined to engage in interracial cooperation.[64] Thus, whites recruited blacks to fend off Indian attacks and employed Indians to catch runaway slaves and to deter maroons. The policy

---

63. Charles Francis Adams, ed., *The Works of John Adams . . .* , 10 vols. (Boston, 1850–1856), II, 428.

64. What follows does not purport to be a comprehensive analysis of black-Indian relations in the Chesapeake and Carolinas. I have relied heavily on the available secondary literature, which remains sketchy. I regard James H. Merrell, "The Racial Education of the Catawba Indians," *Journal of Southern History*, L (1984), 363–384, as the best account of the evolution of one Indian group's attitudes toward blacks. Kathryn E. Holland Braund, "The Creek Indians, Blacks, and Slavery," ibid., LVII (1991), 601–636, is also useful. Review essays that provide a guide to the literature include James H. Merrell, "The Problem of Slavery in Cherokee Culture," *Reviews in American History*, VII (1979), 509–514; and Susan A. Kenney, "Exploring the Dynamics of Indian-Black Contact: A Review Essay," *American Indian Culture and Research Journal*, V, no. 3 (1981), 49–57. For a guide to the literature on Chesapeake Indians generally, see J. Frederick Fausz, "The Invasion of Virginia: Indians, Colonialism, and the Conquest of Cant: A Review Essay on Anglo-Indian Relations in the Chesapeake," *VMHB*, XCV (1987), 133–156. The most useful books—one confined to a single Indian group, the other attempting a general survey—are Theda Perdue, *Slavery and the Evolution of Cherokee Society, 1540–1866* (Knoxville, Tenn., 1977); and J. Leitch Wright, Jr., *The Only Land They Knew: The Tragic Story of the American Indians in the Old South* (New York, 1981).

enjoyed some success. Allegedly, Virginia Indians hated and despised "the very sight of a Negroe," and Carolina Indians had a "natural aversion to the Blacks." Blacks seemed to reciprocate these sentiments. According to a South Carolinian, blacks held a "natural Dislike and Antipathy" toward Indians. Perhaps actions spoke as loud as words. A runaway black slave named Fortune made his "Escape"—his characterization—from the Catawbas. Another black fugitive, who appears to have lived among Indians voluntarily, spoke of "growing tired of that life." He, like Fortune, voted with his feet.[65]

White claims of mutual hostility between Indians and African Americans are no substitute for understanding the changing context that shaped social interaction and cultural contact between red and black. Time, place, numbers, and rank were the key factors in shaping black-Indian encounters. By 1700, blacks were numerous and Indians scarce in Virginia (the ratio was three to one), whereas the reverse was true in South Carolina (eighteen Indians for every black). Although blacks soon outstripped Indians in South Carolina, the ratio was still less than three to one by 1730, whereas in Virginia it was then an overwhelming fifty-five to one. Relations between the races also varied greatly according to the status of members from each side. Most blacks that Indians encountered were slaves, although a significant minority were free or passing as free. Blacks, conversely, confronted a greater range of categories among Indians, who could be slaves, tributaries, or members of independent nations. Finally, Indians and blacks interacted differently depending on whether they lived near one another or far apart, whether they met in the heart of the plantation belt or on the frontier. This is not the place to offer a detailed portrait of each Indian group's relations with blacks. Rather, what follows is little more than a sketch of the varied and changing contours of black-Indian relations in the two regions.[66]

65. Hugh Jones, *The Present State of Virginia . . .* , ed. Richard L. Morton (Chapel Hill, N.C., 1956), 50; Adolph B. Benson, ed., *Peter Kalm's Travels in North America* (New York, 1937 [orig. publ. 1770]), 208; Brickell, *The Natural History of North-Carolina* (Dublin, 1737), 263; George Milligen[-Johnston], *A Short Description of the Province of South-Carolina . . .* (London, 1770), in Chapman J. Milling, ed., *Colonial South Carolina: Two Contemporary Descriptions* (Columbia, S.C., 1951), 136; Isaac Barksdale, *SCG*, Aug. 30, 1748; Alexander Macullagh, *SC and AGG*, Dec. 30, 1774. For other "escapes"—from the Creeks and Cherokees, respectively—see George Livingston, *SC Weekly Gaz*, Nov. 28, 1783; Benjamin Du Pre, *Charleston Courier*, May 11, 1807. For the use of blacks in the military against Indians and Indians as runaway-slave catchers, see William S. Willis, "Divide and Rule: Red, White, and Black in the Southeast," *Journal of Negro History*, XLVIII (1963), 157–176.

66. Peter H. Wood, "The Changing Population of the Colonial South: An Overview by Race and Region, 1685–1790," in Wood et al., eds., *Powhatan's Mantle: Indians in the Colonial Southeast* (Lincoln, Nebr., 1989), 38. For context, in addition to Merrell, "The Racial Educa-

Two incidents drawn from turn-of-the-century Virginia illustrate the importance of context. In 1692, "some Strange Indians"—presumably, non-Virginia Indians—raided William Byrd's plantation, killing a white servant woman and kidnapping a mulatto boy and woman, the last of whom was later sold. Although by this time Indians numbered no more than two thousand in tidewater and piedmont Virginia, powerful nations moved back and forth along the edge of settlement, where they still posed a potent threat to whites and blacks alike. At least these Indians, however, were not so motivated by racial hatred as to kill all people with black ancestry. A decade later, North Carolina authorities objected to the "pernicious Practices" of two Virginia free blacks who traded "with the Indians to the Southward." Most objectionable was their "stirring up the Indians called the Windaws to cutt of and carry away diverse of the Indians called Wawees living under the Government of South Carolina." Roles, then, might be reversed. In a world that Indians still dominated, free blacks might exert influence, particularly if they came with goods to exchange. On the early frontier, relations between blacks and Indians were fluid, with class as important as race.[67]

An equality of status and residential proximity encouraged intimate associations. Some Indians in the Chesapeake—often imported from elsewhere—became slaves alongside blacks. They cooperated. In 1695, an Indian and two black slaves in Henrico County, Virginia, committed a burglary together. Fifteen years later, Virginia authorities decapitated and quartered the bodies of two ringleaders of a slave conspiracy: one was black, the other Indian. Throughout the century, white masters referred to "dark mulatto" slaves of "the Indian breed" or to Negroes "mixed with the Indian"—evidence of another form of intimacy among Indian and black slaves. Indeed, one key way in which Indians became invisible to whites was through their intermixture with blacks and their subsequent classification as "Negroes."[68]

---

tion of the Catawba Indians," *Jour. So. Hist.*, L (1984), 363–384, see William G. McLoughlin, "Red Indians, Black Slavery, and White Racism: America's Slaveholding Indians," *American Quarterly*, XXVI (1974), 367–385.

67. H. R. McIlwaine et al., eds., *Executive Journals of the Council of Colonial Virginia*, 6 vols. (Richmond, Va., 1925–1966), I, 262, II, 351–352. Later in the 18th century, whites feared that free Indians and blacks might make common cause in frontier Virginia. In 1763, a Shenandoah Valley slaveowner claimed that the Indians in his region were "saving and Carressing all the Negroes" they took in raids. He feared a general insurrection (George Reese, ed., *The Official Papers of Francis Fauquier, Lieutenant Governor of Virginia, 1758–1768*, 3 vols. [Charlottesville, Va., 1980–1983], II, 998).

68. Wright, *The Only Land They Knew*, 91, 273; Henrico County Deeds and Wills, 1688–1697, 557–558, as cited in Helen C. Rountree, *Pocahontas's People: The Powhatan Indians of*

The dwindling communities of Chesapeake Indian "tributaries" also mixed closely with blacks. Although many of these Chesapeake Indians would later claim to have practiced endogamy, their earlier behavior was rather more flexible. Thus, the two Nansemonds who in 1742 and 1797 got certificates to authenticate their "purity" were conveniently ignoring an earlier Nansemond man who had married a manumitted mulatto. Intermarriage was common: "mulatto" Jim of Cumberland County was the son of a free Indian man and an African American woman; Frank, a black slave, skulked about the Pamunkey Indian reservation, where he had a wife; a free Indian woman in Albemarle County and her black slave husband in neighboring Amherst County ran away together; Thomas Jefferson claimed that the Mattaponys had "more negro than Indian blood in them." Intermarriage was not the only form of close contact. Eastern Shore Gingaskins openly provided "an Asylum for free Negroes." Mandingo words were incorporated in what purported to be the Nanticoke language. In the increasingly harsh racial climate of the late eighteenth and nineteenth centuries, tributary Indians would attempt to distance themselves from blacks, but this represented a repudiation of earlier behavior.[69]

Virginia through Four Centuries (Norman, Okla., 1990), 140; Christian F. Feest, "Virginia Algonquins," and Douglas W. Boyce, "Iroquoian Tribes of the Virginia–North Carolina Coastal Plain," in William C. Sturtevant, gen. ed., *Handbook of North American Indians*, XV, *Northeast*, ed. Bruce G. Trigger (Washington, D.C., 1978), 257–258, 263, 286–287; Governor Francis Fauquier to the Lords of Trade, Aug. 1, 1765, CO5/1331, fols. 21–22, PRO. For descriptions of slaves with reputed Indian and black ancestry, see William Cuszens, *VaG* (P and D), July 15, 1773; Dorothy Jones, ibid. (Rind), Nov. 11, 1773; Edmund Ruffin, ibid. (Pinkney), Jan. 6, 1776; Daniel Hardaway, ibid. (D and H), Aug. 1, 1777; Henry Skipwith, *VaG or AA*, Dec. 21, 1782; Abraham Fontaine, ibid., Apr. 16, 1785; John Jones, *VaG and WA*, May 21, 1785; and Drury Thweatt, ibid., June 25, 1785. In the colonial inventories of Amelia, Chesterfield, Essex, Isle of Wight, Northampton, Orange, Spotsylvania, and York Counties are just 20 Indian slaves and servants: 9 men, 8 women, 1 boy, and 2 girls (in the other county records I searched I found no reference to Indians). Most were found on estates with black slaves. Indians rarely appear in tidewater inventories after 1730; their occasional presence is then confined to the piedmont. Perhaps the most interesting estates are those of John Clay and Henry Clay, Sr., c. 1761, of Chesterfield County. In John Clay's estate, 14 Negroes, 5 mulattoes, and 3 Indians were listed; in the estate of Henry Clay, Sr., 16 Negroes, 9 mulattoes, and 1 Indian. See Chesterfield County Will Book, no. 1, 1749–1765, 344, 351. Some of the mulattoes might well have been the products of black and Indian unions. See also Jack D. Forbes, *Black Africans and Native Americans: Color, Race, and Caste in the Evolution of Red-Black Peoples* (Oxford, 1988), 88, 199–208.

69. Rountree, *Pocahontas's People*, 161, 163, 180, 337n; Paul Michaux, *VaG* (P and D), Nov. 26, 1772; *VaG*, Sept. 12, 1771, as cited in Wright, *The Only Land They Knew*, 259; Patrick Rose, *VaG* (D and H), Aug. 3, 1776; Thomas Jefferson, *Notes on the State of Virginia*, ed. William Peden (Chapel Hill, N.C., 1954), 96. On endogamy after 1800, in addition to Rountree's

In eighteenth-century South Carolina, Indian slaves were sufficiently numerous to maintain a measure of cultural identity. At the turn of the eighteenth century, enslaved Indians were a significant presence on Lowcountry plantations. A quarter of the colony's slaves were Indians in 1708. Although this proportion quickly dwindled—twelve years later, only one in ten slaves in the parish of Saint Thomas and Saint Dennis was a native American—Indian slaves were more in touch with their heritage and better able to interact among themselves than their Chesapeake counterparts. Thus, some Indian slaves in the Lowcountry ran away to visit other Indian relatives even in the late colonial period: in 1756, Ned, a resident of Johns Island, was thought to be making for Wadmelaw Island, where he had family; fourteen years later, Dick of Ashepoo headed for Silver Bluff on the Savannah River to visit his kinfolk. Indian slaves also engaged in cooperative actions: in 1774, Will encouraged his fellow Indian Hannah to run away with him, and three Indian slave men of Saint Thomas Parish passed as free, harbored by fellow Indians. Most interesting is Simon Flowers, a bound servant threatened with reduction to slavery by an unscrupulous master. When captured in 1766, he reported that his mother and father were free Indians named Tom and Betty Flowers and that his mother and two brothers resided at Santee, where he had been born. The marks on his cheeks were put there by his father, who used a needle and gunpowder—a ritual branding applied to all the young children of the family. Preserving this measure of their cultural traditions, some Indian bondpeople were able to distance themselves from black slaves.[70]

---

book, see Christian F. Feest, "Nanticoke and Neighboring Tribes," and "Virginia Algonquians," in Sturtevant, gen. ed., *Handbook of North American Indians*, XV, *Northeast*, ed. Trigger, 248, 263; Theodore Stern, "Chickahominy: The Changing Culture of a Virginia Indian Community," American Philosophical Society, *Proceedings*, XCVI (1952), 191; and Frank W. Porter III, "Behind the Frontier: Indian Survivals in Maryland," *MHM*, LXXV (1980), 42–54. On intermixture, see Helen C. Rountree, "The Termination and Dispersal of the Nottoway Indians of Virginia," *VMHB*, XCV (1987), 197–198; D. G. Brinton, "On Certain Supposed Nanticoke Words, Shown to Be of African Origin," *American Antiquarian and Oriental Journal*, IX (1887), 350–354. The Moravian missionary who noted these words (the numerals 1–10) encountered Nanticokes between 1741 and 1751, a time when recently arrived Africans could be expected to have escaped into the group.

70. Wood, "The Changing Population of the Colonial South," in Wood et al., eds., *Powhatan's Mantle*, 38; William Townsend, *SCG*, Jan. 22, 1756 (Ned); William Pinckney, ibid., Nov. 22, 1770 (Dick); Thomas Jervey, *SCG and CJ*, Oct. 4, 1774 (Will and Hannah); Robert Collins, ibid. (Joe, John, and Will); Workhouse, ibid., Nov. 4, 1766 (Simon Flowers). On Indian slaves in individual parishes and the colony at large, see Verner W. Crane, *The Southern Frontier, 1670–1732* (New York, 1981 [orig. publ. Durham, N.C., 1928]), 112–113, 194; Wood, *Black Majority*, 144, 155; Wright, *The Only Land They Knew*, 152. For information

Indian slaves in the Lowcountry increasingly faced the same imperatives as their Chesapeake counterparts: declining numbers and growing contacts with a burgeoning black population. The sexual composition of the African and Indian slave trades encouraged intimacy, for, among Indian newcomers, women outnumbered men by as much as five to one, whereas the ratio was reversed, though less markedly, among African forced migrants. John Wright's slave complement, listed in a mortgage of 1715, renders these gross statistics in human terms, for he owned fifteen men, all black, and seventeen women, thirteen of them Indian. Interracial unions were almost inevitable on such a plantation. Indian and black slaves committed crimes and ran away together. In 1728, Dick, the one Indian slave, and Philip, the one skilled black slave, belonging to the estate of the Reverend Richard Ludlam in Saint James Goose Creek combined to rob their master. A few runaway groups in the late colonial era included Indians (or people with Indian ancestry) and blacks. Thus, three runaways, claiming to be brothers, were described as two "dark Negroes" and one "yellow," being "somewhat of the Indian breed"; a "black negro" man ran off with his mother, his Indian wife, their two-year-old child, and a mulatto boy; and a slave named Bastian, described as a "mustee [or rather Indian breed]," ran off with his "very black" creole wife, Lucy.[71]

Tributary Indians in Lowcountry South Carolina put more distance between themselves and blacks than their counterparts in the Chesapeake. Early in the eighteenth century, settlement Indians, still a notable presence in the Lowcountry, vented their hostility at the invasion of their land on black slaves. Three incidents are symptomatic: a Kiawah murdered a black slave belonging to Samuel Eveleigh; an "Indian Man of the Cusso Nation did without any manner of Provocation willfully Shoot dead a Negro Man Slave" as he worked

---

on Indian slaves derived from inventories, wills, and other records, see William Robert Snell, "Indian Slavery in Colonial South Carolina, 1671–1795" (Ph.D. diss., University of Alabama, 1972), 130–132, app. 8.

71. Wright, *The Only Land They Knew*, 148–149 (on slave trades), 258 (for reference to John Wright's mortgage to Samuel Wragg et al., June 15, 1714, Charleston County Wills, no. 45, SCDAH); Journal of the Proceedings of Mr. William Dry, A21/160–170, 210–230 [in addition to Dick and Philip, Ludlam owned at his death another 4 men, 5 women, and 1 boy, all described as Negroes]; John Persu, *SCG*, Feb. 13, 1762 (3 brothers); Joseph Allston, ibid., Feb. 20, 1762 (Craig et al.); William Gibbes and Benjamin Simons, ibid., Feb. 16, 1769 (Bastian and Lucy). See also Andrew Williamson, ibid., Apr. 12, 1773. Of course, one cannot discount white parentage for some children born to Indian slaves in the Lowcountry. Perhaps this explains why a Goose Creek planter freed 3 "halfbreed" children: Dukey Cox and George Cox, born to Indian Jenny, and Minerva Watkins, born to Indian Moll. Perhaps these surnames derived from the children's white fathers. See the manumission of Alexander Wood, Sept. 12, 1753, Miscellaneous Records, II, 551–552. George Galphin, the famous Indian trader, fathered children with a number of his Indian and black slave women.

on John Stone's plantation; and a group of Indians simply helped themselves to seven turkeys that two slaves had in their possession. As early witnesses to the degradation inherent in racial slavery, settlement Indians could hardly be expected to treat blacks more sympathetically than did whites. By the late colonial period, the few remaining tidewater Indians had come to terms with a slave system that now dominated their ancestral lands. In 1761, an "Indian Doctor" received one pound from a Lowcountry estate for treating a slave woman. Nine years later, a Lowcountry Indian, perhaps an Etiwan, captured a runaway African in Ferguson's Swamp and presumably took his reward. Providing services to the regnant institution, settlement Indians secured a niche for themselves and kept apart from blacks.[72]

Powerful Indian groups on the periphery of Lowcountry settlement were less familiar with the racial slavery developing in Carolina than were tributary Indians, and their relations with blacks could afford to be more pragmatic. Many frontier nations harbored runaway slaves. In the first decade of the eighteenth century, the Tuscaroras sheltered Harry, who supervised the building of one of their forts. In 1724, a South Carolina official encountered an escaped Carolina slave who assumed "a Bould Maner" in the Apalachicola square ground. At midcentury, a "half-Breed" Cherokee encouraged six black slaves to run away with him by promising them freedom. Three of the fugitives later told the Cherokees that "the white People was coming up to destroy them all." The report gained credence when "the old Warriour of Keewee said some Negroes had applied to him, and told him that there was in all Plantations many Negroes more than white People, and that for the Sake of Liberty they would join them." Only the liberal distribution of ammunition dampened this inflammatory talk. A slave man named Wanny passed as free for about six years among the Chickasaws. In 1771, a black slave who spoke Creek ran off in the direction of that nation.[73]

---

72. Gene Waddell, *Indians of the South Carolina Lowcountry, 1562–1751* (Spartanburg, S.C., 1980), 240, 267; Dec. 13, 1724, Ball Account Book, fol. 186, SCHS. The one extant Lowcountry census, taken in 1726, lists two free Indians—Nero had no family, Sam Pickins was listed with a woman and four children. They were lumped with three free black households at the end of the census. Whether this grouping betokened familiarity between free blacks and Indians is unclear. See "Names and Number of the Inhabitants of St. George's Parish, Jan. 21, 1726," A19/104–108, SPG. For other references to Indian hostility toward blacks, see Wood, *Black Majority*, 261–263. The late colonial incidents can be found in Accounts of David Caw's Estate with Robert Hume, Aug. 6, 1761, Inventories, WPA, LXXXVIIA, 18; and *SCG and CJ*, Aug. 7, 1770.

73. "Journal of John Barnwell," *VMHB*, VI (1898), 44–45 (and see South Carolina Upper House Journal, no. 6, part 1, June 6, 1735, 143–144, for other reports of Tuscaroras' harboring runaways); "Captain Fitch's Journal to the Creeks, 1725," as cited in Braund, "Creek Indians,

Frontier nations were not always accommodating. Over time, they increasingly bowed to white wishes and handed over runaways. In 1756, the "Cussitaw" Indians captured an African runaway near Saint Mark's Fort; three years later, the Cherokees returned a West Indian–born slave runaway to white authorities; and, in 1768, an Indian in the Cherokee nation reported the capture of Caesar, an African, who had arrived at his home. As late as 1783, the Catawbas were capturing runaway slaves. Frontier nations assessed arrivals among them case by case. In 1752, Catawba headmen were "very angry" that a "Negro Fellow" had arrived among them in order to trade. They "told him to be gone with his Goods," but he refused. At the same time, a "free Negro" lived among them, was considered a Catawba, and spoke their language. Apparently, much depended on the incomer's attitude as well as his status. Some of the blacks that interior tribes encountered were the slaves of white traders, and no doubt the views of their owners rubbed off. As early as the 1730s, a Muscogulge view of life after death consigned poor hunters to a netherworld of thorns and thickets ruled by a black man. Although frontier nations were not always friendly toward blacks, they were less openly hostile than settlement Indians.[74]

Eighteenth-century whites failed to make blacks and Indians implacable enemies. Rather, Indian-black relations were complex, pragmatic, and fluid. In the Chesapeake, Indian numbers declined so rapidly that close contacts, almost amalgamation, characterized native relations with blacks. Even tributary Indians in the Chesapeake mixed intimately with blacks. In the Lowcountry, some Indian slaves preserved a measure of autonomy, although increasingly they intermarried, committed crimes, and ran away with their black counterparts. Settlement Indians in the Lowcountry had little choice, it seems, but to offer tacit support to the slave regime, and their resentment showed in occasional acts of vengeance toward blacks. Indians on the frontier exhibited a broad range of responses toward blacks, oscillating between friendship and hostility, between sheltering and returning runaways, between welcoming and rejecting what blacks had to offer. Blacks in both Chesapeake and Lowcountry

---

Blacks, and Slavery," *Jour. So. Hist.*, LVII (1991), 611; William L. McDowell, Jr., ed., *Documents Relating to Indian Affairs, May 21, 1750–August 7, 1754*, Colonial Records of South Carolina, 2d Ser. (Columbia, S.C., 1958), 83, 103; William Drayton, *SCG*, July 28, 1767 (Wanny); John Stuart, *SC and AGG*, Jan. 21, 1771.

74. Braund, "Creek Indians, Blacks, and Slavery," *Jour. So. Hist.*, LVII (1991), esp. 608–612; George Galphin, *SCG*, July 1, 1756; James Beamer, ibid., June 2, 1759; Printer, *SCG and CJ*, Sept. 6, 1768; John Sandford Dart, *SCG and GA*, June 10, 1783; McDowell, ed., *Documents*, 210 (this is an oft-cited example of early racial hostility on the part of an Indian group, but the full context of this incident indicates that it was not color to which the Catawbas objected: see Merrell, "Racial Education," *Jour. So. Hist.*, L [1984], 372); William Glen to Peter Mercier, Nov. 9, 1751, Council journal, Dec. 13, 1751, as cited ibid., 364.

had little reason, therefore, to feel demoralized because of a supposedly intransigent Indian foe; indeed, the minority of blacks who sought interracial cooperation with Indians often achieved their ends.[75]

SLAVES AND FREE BLACKS

James Madison claimed that, once free, "a freedman immediately loses all attachment and sympathy with his former fellow slaves." Free blacks separated themselves from slaves in many ways: they signaled their freedom by adding a surname or assuming a new name; they relocated; they put their families on a more secure footing; they created associations—schools, fraternal orders, and churches—to strengthen their community life; they bought and sold property, even held slaves; and they resorted to the courts to protect their hard-won gains. The dissociation of free blacks and slaves was extensive. Nevertheless, Madison exaggerated when he claimed that free blacks lost all attachment to slaves. Many, perhaps most, free blacks did not relocate; most young free blacks worked alongside slaves as bound servants; for most of the eighteenth century, free blacks were too few to separate themselves markedly from slaves; somatically, free blacks and slaves grew more alike in the late eighteenth century; the tenuousness of the free black's lot narrowed the gap between freedom and slavery; free blacks actively sought the company of slaves; and bonds of kinship tied freed persons to slaves. The gap between slave and free was wider in the Lowcountry than in the Chesapeake, but it was not wide enough anywhere that most free blacks lost sympathy for slaves.[76]

Some free blacks separated themselves from slaves both physically and communally. A number of free blacks resided on the fringes of the plantation heartland—in backwater areas like the Eastern Shore of Virginia and Maryland, on the frontier, or in a town—where they were surrounded by whites and somewhat distant from slaves. Over time, free blacks tended to congregate, creating identifiable neighborhoods. A web of social, economic, and political ties gradually bound free blacks more closely. Free blacks intermarried, acted as guardians for their orphans, and thus knit together their families. Economic networks grew denser as free blacks employed one another, lent and borrowed money among themselves, and posted security for one another. Grievances

---

75. Implacable hostility between the two groups was more common in the 19th century, especially because many Southeastern Indians came to practice some kind of black slavery. Seminole-black relations are the major exception to this rule.

76. William T. Hutchinson et al., eds., *The Papers of James Madison*, II (Chicago, 1962), 209. The best study of free blacks is Ira Berlin, *Slaves without Masters: The Free Negro in the Antebellum South* (New York, 1974). The prologue looks briefly at the colonial period, and chap. 2 describes name changes and institution building among eastern seaboard free blacks in the Revolutionary era.

and conflicts inevitably accompanied the closer ties: suits for debt, trespass, theft, assault, and battery also rose among free blacks. Yet, in spite of these internal strains, the free black community grew more cohesive. Free blacks, for example, began to organize concerted political action.[77]

Economic success also distanced free blacks from slaves. A few, admittedly exceptional, free blacks vaulted into the property-holding middle class. When Edward Nicken died in 1735, his possessions were more valuable than half the white estates of Lancaster County, Virginia. Three years later, Azaricum Drighouse, a free mulatto resident of Northampton County, died possessed of an estate appraised at more than a hundred pounds, which placed him among the wealthiest one-third of white decedents on the lower Eastern Shore. In 1777, John Goodbe, a free black of Saint John Parish, South Carolina, deeded all his property to his loving wife, Betty Carter. She inherited his house, all his hogs, three horses, seven sheep, and fourteen cattle—a modest but by no means inconsequential estate by the standards of the day.[78]

To succeed, free blacks generally established close relations with whites, further removing themselves from the orbit of slaves. Thus, when the Banneker family purchased a 100-acre tract in southwestern Baltimore County, then the frontier of Maryland, the Ellicotts were their patrons. This white family took a particular interest in the fortunes of the eldest Banneker son; in part because of the support, Benjamin Banneker later gained fame as a mathematician, astronomer, and author of six almanacs. In 1754, on another part of the Chesapeake frontier—Augusta County, Virginia—Edward Tarr purchased a 270-acre farm, where he established a smithy. He was the only blacksmith for miles around, and he served an extensive white clientele. Tarr spoke German, was literate, and had a Scottish wife; he participated vigorously in the social and economic life of his predominantly white neighborhood. So far as is known, Talbot Thompson was the only slave in eighteenth-century colonial Virginia to secure freedom through self-purchase. He established a successful sail-making business in Norfolk. So dependent was he on his customers that during the Revolution he and his wife threw in their lot with the British and left Virginia. Thomas Cole, Sr., of Charleston, a free mulatto bricklayer, had

---

77. Douglas Deal, "A Constricted World: Free Blacks on Virginia's Eastern Shore, 1680–1750," in Carr, Morgan, and Russo, eds., *Colonial Chesapeake Society*, 275–305; Kathleen M. Brown, *Good Wives, Nasty Wenches, and Anxious Patriarchs: Gender, Race, and Power in Colonial Virginia* (Chapel Hill, N.C., 1996), chap. 7, esp. 236–241; John H. Russell, *The Free Negro in Virginia*, Johns Hopkins University Studies in Historical and Political Science, XXXI, no. 3 (Baltimore, 1913), 112–113.

78. Deal, "A Constricted World," in Carr, Morgan, and Russo, eds., *Colonial Chesapeake Society*, 275, 290; Brown, *Good Wives, Nasty Wenches, and Anxious Patriarchs*, 226; John Goodbe's deed, Nov. 6, 1777, Miscellaneous Records, SS, 304.

two prominent white Charlestonians purchase his wife and two children. The two whites then transferred the family to Cole, and he paid back the purchase price with interest. In one final context—piedmont Virginia—Christopher McPherson rose from working in a store to serving as clerk to the High Court of Chancery (and even a stint in Philadelphia as an enrolling clerk to Congress). He met Thomas Jefferson and James Madison and could count on some of the most prominent men in the state to write testimonials on his behalf. Few men, whatever their skin color, had as many patrons as McPherson.[79]

The pinnacle of economic success in a slave society was to own slaves, and free black slaveowners were probably no more altruistic than their white counterparts. Anthony Johnson of Northampton County, Virginia, perhaps the earliest African American to own a slave on the mainland, aggressively defended his property rights when he won a suit against a white man for detaining his slave. Alexander Gowan, a free black resident of Saint Bartholomew Parish, South Carolina, experienced the most common frustration of slaveownership: his slave Primus ran away. Perhaps for that reason, Gowan sold Primus to a white woman. Black slaveowners were not above exploiting their human chattel for profit, as Sabinah, a free black woman of Charleston, proved when she used her 3 slaves as security to procure a loan. In late-eighteenth-century South Carolina, only 59 free blacks, 3 percent of all free blacks in the state, were slaveowners, but they owned 357 slaves in all. Many of them were no doubt bent on accumulating more slaves. Edward Tanner of Saint John Berkeley increased his complement from 3 to 7 between 1790 and 1800.[80]

---

79. Silvio A. Bedini, *The Life of Benjamin Banneker* (New York, 1972); Robert J. Hurry, "An Archaeological and Historical Perspective on Benjamin Banneker," MHM, LXXXIV (1989), 361–369; Turk McCleskey, "The Radical Challenge of Edward Tarr: The Free Black as Freeholder on Virginia's Colonial Frontier," paper delivered at the Southern Historical Association Meeting, 1992; Michael L. Nicholls, "Straddling Hell's Boundaries: Profiles of Free People of Color in Early Virginia" (MS, 1991); manumission of Ruth, Tom, and Barbary, May 5, 1763, Miscellaneous Records, LL, 603–604; Edmund Berkeley, Jr., "Prophet without Honor: Christopher McPherson, Free Person of Color," VMHB, LXXVII (1969), 180–190.

80. T. H. Breen and Stephen Innes, *"Myne Owne Ground": Race and Freedom on Virginia's Eastern Shore, 1640–1676* (New York, 1980), 13–15; SCG, Dec. 6, 1768; Jacob Valk, ibid., Oct. 10, 1771; Larry Koger, *Black Slaveowners: Free Black Slave Masters in South Carolina, 1790–1860* (Jefferson, N.C., 1985), 18, 40, 209–210. Isaac Ball's administration of the estate of Edward Tanner, which illustrates aspects of Tanner's career stretching from 1773 to 1816, is in John Ball, Sr., Papers, Duke. A number of masters gave slaves to newly manumitted blacks, who presumably used them for profit: appointment of guardian for Molly, June 6, 1770, Miscellaneous Records, OO, 310; Stephen Deane's deeds of gift to Fanny Deane and Mary Keast, Feb. 15, 18, 1779, ibid., TT, 85–86; Frederick Brindley's deed of manumission, Feb. 12, 1782, ibid., 103; Joseph Bell's deed of gift to John Bristol, Aug. 21, 1788, ibid., ZZ, 102. For

Before the Revolution, skin color demarcated most freedpeople from slaves, and free mulattoes pointed up the chasm that separated them from slaves by openly standing up to whites. In 1755, John Cousins, a member of the Cousins clan of free mulattoes of Goochland County, Virginia, allegedly threatened "to beat and prejudice" a white resident. In nearby Orange County, two free mulattoes, Reuben and Peter Lanter, self-styled "Planters," encountered a suspected runaway with whom they fought and "scrimage[d]." The supposed fugitive was a white planter. The Lanters stood their ground in court and made no apologies. In 1771, George Vane, a free mulatto of Charleston, assaulted James Simpson, a white resident. Sentenced to one month in prison and a twenty-five-pound fine, Vane petitioned for a pardon. His appeal must have been persuasive, for the penalty was commuted to a ten-pound donation for the poor.[81]

Some free mulatto families passed as white. Gideon Gibson, a free mulatto, is a famous case in point. His daughter married an English settler and, after the Englishman's death, remarried one of the wealthiest white men in South Carolina. Gibson's son, Gideon, Jr., became a leader in the Regulator movement. When the son's status as a white person was challenged, Henry Laurens came to his defense. An even more spectacular example is James Pendarvis, who lived in Saint Paul's Parish and owned about 150 slaves. He was the eldest son of Joseph Pendarvis, a white planter, and Parthena, his slave mistress. James married a white woman, Catherine Rumph Pendarvis, and both of their daughters married white men. Thomas Cole, Jr., son of a prominent mulatto bricklayer of Charleston, married Sarah Lary, a white or light-skinned mulatto. Sarah

---

contractual arrangements between free blacks and slaves, see manumission of Tony, June 5, 1759, ibid., LL, 177–178; deed of sale between William Johnson and Conrad Keckely, Aug. 1, 1778, ibid., QQ, 290; manumission of Robin, Dec. 16, 1789, ibid., WW, 346–347; deed of sale between Catherine Mazyck and Leander Fairchild, Oct. 27, 1790, and manumission of Nancy and Leander, Nov. 9, 1790, ibid., ZZ, 254–25. The census of 1790 does not exist for Virginia, so no statistics of slaveowning, comparable to those for South Carolina, can be determined. However, Carter Woodson estimated that, in 1830, fewer than 2% of the state's free blacks were slaveowners. Others believe his count to be too high. Certainly, the proportion would have been much lower, to the point of insignificance, 40 years earlier. For more on this subject, see Philip J. Schwarz, "Emancipators, Protectors, and Anomalies: Free Black Slaveowners in Virginia," *VMHB*, XCV (1987), 317–338.

81. Investigation of John Cousins, March 1755, Goochland County Court Order Book, no. 7, 1750–1755, 512; investigation of Reuben and Peter Lanter, Oct. 11, 1755, Orange County Court Order Book, no. 6, 1754–1763, 178; trial of George Vane, June 28, 1771, Miscellaneous Records, OO, 614. In 1755, 80% of Maryland's free blacks were identified as mulattoes. See "Number of Inhabitants in Maryland," *Gentleman's Magazine, and Historical Chronicle*, XXXIV (1764), 261; and Berlin, *Slaves without Masters*, 3. It would be surprising if the composition of Virginia's or South Carolina's free blacks was much different.

was, according to a witness, "born Free" and educated in Newport, Rhode Island. She was the daughter of John Lary, fisherman, and his wife, Flora, who was the daughter of "a White Person altogether Free."[82]

Fascinating as these dramatic examples are, they represent the exceptions. Most free blacks were not far removed from slaves—either in station or in residence. This proximity between freedperson and slave was particularly evident in the Chesapeake, where most free blacks lived humbly in the countryside. A list taken in 1778 of forty-seven blacks on Hugh Nelson's estate in Fauquier County lumped "old Nell a free Negro" with the forty-six slaves. Indeed, for a large part of their lives, many free blacks worked as bound servants, alongside slaves. Consider Jesse Donaldson, a native of Somerset County, Maryland, who was born in 1759, the "Bastard Son of Sarah Donaldson a Free Mulatto." At birth, Jesse, in accordance with existing law, was bound (although his certificate refrained from using that term and instead spoke of his being "sold") for thirty-one years to James Wilson, who ten years later sold the remaining balance of Jesse's time to John Glasgow. In 1780, Jesse, now more than a thousand miles from his Maryland home, finally received his freedom. Some young men grew restive at the protracted wait for liberty. In 1766, twenty-three-year-old mulatto Sam Howell of Cumberland County attempted to gain his release from bondage, first through his county court and then by approaching the king's attorney in Williamsburg. On both occasions, he was rebuffed and told to serve his thirty-one years; he then took the law into his hands, became a fugitive, and passed for a free man. Significantly, his master advertised for the return of his "slave." Four years later, twenty-year-old Solomon ran away from his Caroline County residence. As his master pointed out, Solomon "will be free at 31, but he pretends to be free now." Instead of precipitating their freedom, Sam Howell and Solomon probably extended their servitude.[83]

For most of the eighteenth century, free blacks in Virginia were too few to create a marked divide from slaves. No census of their numbers survives for the

82. Winthrop D. Jordan, *White over Black: American Attitudes toward the Negro, 1550–1812* (Chapel Hill, N.C., 1968), 171–172; Koger, *Black Slaveowners*, 13–14, 109–110; deposition of Catherine West, Oct. 29, 1784, Miscellaneous Records, VV, 223–224. For other members of the Cole and related Raper clans that definitely passed as white, see Koger, *Black Slaveowners*, 15.

83. List of Negroes . . . belonging to the Estate of Hugh Nelson, Esq. in Fauquier County, Dec. 9, 1778, Battaille Muse Papers, Duke; John Glasgow's certificate of emancipation to Jesse Donaldson, July 10, 1785, Miscellaneous Records, WW, 243 (Sarah Donaldson is not listed among the 61 free blacks identified as living in the county between 1745 and 1755, although a Mulatto Sarah lived there [Thomas E. Davidson, "Free Blacks in Old Somerset County, 1745–1755," *MHM*, LXXX (1985), 151–156]); Wade Netherland, *VaG* (Purdie), May 2, 1766 (Howell); Benjamin Hubbard, ibid. (P and D), Sept. 1, 1774 (Solomon).

colonial era, but St. George Tucker estimated the group at about two thousand in 1782. If true, this number represents less than 1 percent of blacks in the state. The proportion was not likely to have been higher earlier in the eighteenth century. Contemporaries recalled that before the Revolution "the number of free negroes was so small that they were seldom to be met with." After the Revolution, the number of free blacks in Virginia grew considerably. From a thousand or two before the Revolution, the free black population climbed to about thirteen thousand in 1790 and to twenty thousand in 1800. However, even in 1800, fully 95 percent of blacks in Virginia remained enslaved. The truly explosive growth in the Chesapeake free black population occurred in Maryland. Maryland's free black population "skyrocketed" after the Revolution, as Richard Dunn notes, numbering twenty thousand, or 16 percent of the state's black population in 1800.[84]

Although the free black population of the Chesapeake expanded after the Revolution, its members did not grow apart from slaves. Some masters were no longer manumitting one or two mulattoes but rather freeing all or many of their bondpeople. The free black population therefore "darkened" in the 1780s and 1790s. In somatic terms, slaves and free blacks became more alike. Furthermore, the relatively small size of Chesapeake towns limited the migratory possibilities of recently manumitted blacks. For the most part, then, Chesapeake free blacks remained in their old neighborhoods. They often worked alongside slaves, many of whom were being hired out, as tidewater planters responded to the new demands of grain cultivation. A hired slave embraced some of freedom's attributes, if not its substance. In another way, therefore, the gap between free black and slave narrowed rather than widened.[85]

In colonial South Carolina, the number of free blacks was minuscule. There are no estimates of their numbers before 1790, when they stood at eighteen

---

84. St. George Tucker, *A Dissertation on Slavery* (Philadelphia, 1796), 72, and petition from Petersburg, Dec. 11, 1805, Legislative Papers, VSL, as cited in Berlin, *Slaves without Masters,* 4, 48. The proportion of free blacks in Maryland's black population rose from 4% to 7% between 1755 and 1790. A similar growth curve probably occurred in Virginia. If so, then approximately 1% of Virginia's blacks were free in 1755, for in 1790 the proportion stood at 4%. This conjecture is supported by data from Maryland on the eve of the Revolution: in Talbot County, free blacks constituted fewer than 4% of the black population, indicating no growth, and perhaps a slight decline, in that group between 1755 and 1776. See Richard S. Dunn, "Black Society in the Chesapeake, 1776–1810," in Ira Berlin and Ronald Hoffman, eds., *Slavery and Freedom in the Age of the American Revolution* (Charlottesville, Va., 1982), 62. For population figures, also see Berlin, *Slaves without Masters,* 46–47.

85. Berlin, *Slaves without Masters,* 30–31, 41; Ira Berlin, "Time, Space, and the Transformation of Afro-American Society in the United States, 1770–1820," in Elise Marienstras and Barbara Karsky, eds., *Autre temps, autre espace: An Other Time, An Other Space: Etudes sur l'Amérique pré-industrielle* (Nancy, France, 1986), 142–146.

hundred persons, less than 2 percent of the state's black population. Many of these eighteen hundred had only recently gained their freedom, for masters freed more slaves in the 1780s than in the previous three decades. The size of this group expanded modestly in the 1790s—by the turn of the century just over three thousand free blacks existed in the state—but these still represented just 2 percent of the state's blacks. In terms of numbers alone, then, the gap between slavery and freedom was always small in eighteenth-century South Carolina.

But appearance and residence meant that the gap between slavery and freedom was wider in the Lowcountry than in the Chesapeake. Because post-Revolutionary manumissions in South Carolina continued to be selective and paternal—sometimes literally so—the state's freedpeople were predominantly of mixed racial origin. In addition, Charleston received many, perhaps most, of the light-skinned *gens de couleur* who fled Saint Domingue in the 1790s. Unlike the Chesapeake, then, the somatic contours of the Lowcountry's free black population continued to diverge from that of slaves. Indeed, rather than using the expressions "free Negroes" or "free blacks" common among Chesapeake residents, both whites and blacks came to use the appellation "free people of color" to denote the distinctive pigmentation of the region's free blacks. Even distinctions among browns and blacks arose within the free black group. Furthermore, unlike the free blacks of the Chesapeake, this small population of free blacks tended to live in an urban center, not in the countryside. In 1790, a majority of the state's free blacks probably lived in Charleston and its environs. This large body of urban free blacks could not be expected to have much in common with plantation slaves.[86]

But what of the sizable minority of Lowcountry free blacks who lived in the countryside? Would they have had regular contact with slaves? Apparently so, for many of them lived on plantations, alongside slaves. In late-eighteenth-century Saint James Goose Creek, "Free Harry" lived at Mr. George Parker's plantation, and a free black woman, mother of Peter Holmes, lived on the estate of Mr. Coachman. When Joseph Huggins of Craven County freed his slave woman Rebecca and her children in 1759, he allowed her to "have the house wherein she now Lives and a Quarter of an Acre of Land adjoining to it." Because "their maintenance on the plantation" was conditional on their good

---

86. Berlin, "Time, Space, and the Transformation of Afro-American Society," in Marienstras and Karsky, eds., *Autre temps, autre espace,* 136–142; Berlin, *Slaves without Masters,* 31, 35–36, 48–49, 58; Marina Wikramanayake, *A World in Shadow: The Free Black in Antebellum South Carolina* (Columbia, S.C., 1973), 21–22; Robert L. Harris, Jr., "Charleston's Free Afro-American Elite: The Brown Fellowship Society and the Humane Brotherhood," *SCHM,* LXXXII (1981), 289–310; Philip D. Morgan, "Black Society in the Lowcountry, 1760–1810," in Berlin and Hoffman, eds., *Slavery and Freedom,* 116.

behavior, Rebecca and her children had not left the constraints of slavery far behind. Twenty-five years later, Joseph Allston was rather more generous when he freed his mulatto man Dandy together with his five children (one of whom was named after his father), for he provided eight guineas annually for the freedman's services, access to two milk cows, and provisions. However, Allston required Dandy to remain at one of his plantations for seven years. Free blacks in the countryside, often by the circumstances of their manumission as well as by their continued residence on plantations, tended to remain close to the world of slaves.[87]

Robin, a free black resident of Saint John Berkeley also did not leave slavery far behind. Elias Ball, his former master, referred to him as "my" freedman. Robin continued to live on Ball's plantation as his driver. He received a salary of twenty pounds a year between 1793 and 1795, when he was discharged "merely from some complaints the Negroes [made] against him," only to be reinstated and kept in Ball's employ into the nineteenth century. Their relationship was that of patron and client. In December 1795, Ball acted as a conduit for a neighboring planter, paying Robin for curing a slave woman of venereal disease; seven years later, Ball charged Robin for clothing for his son. Robin depended on his former master but also worked closely with the slaves, serving as their driver and doctor. Although his relations with slaves were once acrimonious, it is hard to imagine that Robin would have retained his position if he had alienated the vast majority of the people with whom he lived and worked.[88]

The ever-present threat of reenslavement made a free black's lot particularly precarious and narrowed the gap between freedom and slavery. When passing

---

87. John Collins, *SC and AGG*, Feb. 13, 1777, and *SCG*, June 16, 1777 (Free Harry or Henry); Laurence Mayer, *SCG*, Sept. 5, 1771 (mother to Peter Holmes); Joseph Huggins's deed of manumission, Mar. 2, 1759, Miscellaneous Records, LL, 490; Joseph Allston's deed of manumission, June 2, 1784, ibid., WW, 256.

88. Elias Ball's "Account with my freedman Robin," Jan. 1, 1793 through Oct. 19, 1803, Ball Memorandum Book, c. 1788–1812, SCHS. When Lowcountry masters spoke of rural free blacks, either in their own accounts or in runaway advertisements, they generally did so as if they were still slaves. If the free black had a surname, it was not always recognized. Moreover, some free blacks themselves eschewed surnames: an advertisement for a captured African woman thought to be a runaway stated that she had been in the possession of "an old negro who calls himself Free Peter, two or three years, and pretends to own her as his property, but cannot shew any title to her" (Workhouse, *SCG and CJ*, July 27, 1773). See also the list of free black slaveowners in Koger, *Black Slaveowners*, 209–210. Also noteworthy is that a fifth of the 61 free blacks identified as residing in Somerset County, Maryland, at mid-century had no surname but either took or were given the appellation "Free," "Negro," or "Mulatto" (Davidson, "Free Blacks in Old Somerset County," *MHM*, LXXX [1985], 152–153).

through Orange County, Virginia, Rose Severally and her son George were arrested and thrown into jail on suspicion of being runaway slaves. Although they were eventually freed, the experience must have been humbling. Sam, who gained his freedom in 1772 and later served in Lord Dunmore's expedition against the Indians, was in 1775 reduced again to slavery for attempting to inveigle away a number of slaves to "Indian country." Like Sam, Sarah Greene of Fairfax County lived at liberty for many years, but then two of her children were sold as slaves, and she and another two children faced the same threat because she lacked the legal document that proved her freedom. Thomas Gibbes, Jr., "born free," as a number of Carolina planters testified, was sold into slavery by his unscrupulous employer. Free blacks brought suit in court to prove that their masters "kept and detained" them as slaves.[89]

Free blacks cooperated with slaves in ways that whites found especially alarming. They committed crimes together. A 1709 slave conspiracy in three southeastern counties of Virginia apparently involved free blacks; one freedman, for instance, "entertained" slaves at his house. In 1754, three blacks were brought before a Goochland County court to answer a charge of poisoning Obadiah Smith and his wife, Mary. Two were slaves, the third a free mulatto named Frank Cousens. All were acquitted, but Smith swore that he went in danger of his life from Cousens, who had to post bond; in Smith's mind, Cousens was the leader. Because slaves and free blacks often resided on the same plantation, they ran away together. Thus, in 1770, three blacks ran away from William Flood's Westmoreland County plantation: Ned and Frank were slaves, but Henry Cooke was free. And, of course, some slave runaways headed

---

89. Investigation of Rose Severally, Aug. 27, 1756, Orange County Court Order Book, no. 6, 1754–1763, 260; Gabriel Jones, *VaG* (Purdie), June 16, 1775 (Sam); petition of Sarah Greene, Dec. 3, 1784, Fairfax County, Legislative Petitions, VSL; affidavits and depositions in support of Thomas Gibbes, March 1762, Miscellaneous Records, PP, 261–264; Michael L. Nicholls, "Passing Through This Troublesome World: Free Blacks in the Early Southside," *VMHB*, XCII (1984), 59; complaint of Moll, Jan. 23, 28, 1743, Orange County Court Order Book, no. 3, 1741–1743, 312, 323; and other freedom suits, Goochland County Court Order Book, no. 8, 1757–1761, 175; Louisa County Court Order Book, 1760(72)–1774, 95; Chesterfield County Court Order Book, no. 6, 1774–1784, 264; and John Fleming Ledger, 1754–1766, August 1756, microfilm, CW; William Holt, *VaG* (P and D), supplement, Sept. 5, 1766; John Hardaway, ibid. (Rind), May 31, 1770. For the tenuous position of free blacks, see also C. Ashley Ellefson, "Free Jupiter and the Rest of the World: The Problems of a Free Negro in Colonial Maryland," *MHM*, LXVI (1971), 1–13; deposition of Caleb Davis and court proceedings, Frederica, Georgia, 1738–1747, Miscellaneous Records, GG, 177; deposition of Robert Oswald, July 24, 1753, ibid., II, 526; depositions from Elizabeth Gilbert and William Carr, St. James Parish, Georgia, Oct. 15, 1768, ibid., NN, 409–410; and Russell, *The Free Negro*, 100.

for the households of sympathetic free blacks. In Richmond, a number of free blacks were convicted of running "disorderly" houses, where slaves congregated to drink, dance, and gamble.[90]

A close and, on occasion, incendiary relationship existed between free blacks and slaves in the Webb family of Northampton County, Virginia. Jane Webb, born in the early 1680s and freed about 1700, married a slave in 1703. She lived with her slave husband on the plantation of his master. Jane was a determined and forthright woman. In 1726, after failing to secure the release of two of her children from service to her husband's owner, she blurted out in court, "If all Virginia Negros had as good a heart as she had they would all be free." Jane lived to a ripe old age but never again troubled the courts. However, she did bequeath some of her spirit to her children. Twenty-four years after Jane's outburst, her son Abimilech Webb, who had been one of the two children detained by his father's master, was even more outspoken. While husking corn with a white laborer, he predicted that the county's blacks would soon secure their freedom. When asked how, he replied, "With their own indeavour and godalmightys assistance or blessing, for what would it be for the Negroes to go through this County in one night's time." Whipped like his mother before him, Abimilech Webb felt the force of an increasingly racist society. Perhaps this progressively harsh climate, together with his particular family background, accounts for his vision of collective action by all blacks, both free and slave.[91]

In South Carolina, even urban free blacks developed close relations with slaves. Some freedpeople were suspected of hiring slave runaways. One Lowcountry master claimed that his Angolan washerwoman "sometimes hires herself to free negroes," while an Angolan needlewoman had "been employed by free Negroes and others" when absent without permission. A mulatto slave carpenter named Harry, absent from his master for eight months but then sighted in King Street, Charleston, was thought to be harbored by a "free carpenter, as he is intimate with numbers of them." In these cases, a trade brought a slave and free blacks into close contact. It is not difficult to imagine

---

90. Colonial Papers, Mar. 20, 1709, in Brown, *Good Wives, Nasty Wenches, and Anxious Patriarchs*, 216; trial of Squire, Myrtilla, and Frank Cousens, Apr. 1, 1754, Goochland County Court Order Book, no. 7, 1750–1757, 380–381, 409, 489; William Flood, *VaG* (P and D), Apr. 19, 1770. For slaves supposedly harbored by free blacks, see Matthew Mayers, ibid., Oct. 25, 1770; William Rose, *VaG and WA*, Nov. 22, 1783; Lawrence Baker, ibid. (Nicolson), Apr. 26, 1787; John Pryor, *VaG or AA*, May 10, 1786; and James Johnston, *Va Ind Chron and GA*, Jan. 13, 1790. For free black and slave life in Richmond, the best work is Sidbury, *Ploughshares into Swords*.

91. Deal, "A Constricted World," in Carr, Morgan, and Russo, eds., *Colonial Chesapeake Society*, 275–305.

how their relationship might be mutually beneficial, with the free black gaining additional labor and the slave pocketing more in earnings than any master would have allowed. But free blacks ran great risks by these actions, as John McLeach, a free mulatto of Charleston, could testify. In 1781, a court of justices and freeholders found McLeach guilty of "having harboured and entertained a run-away Negro woman" named Silvia. McLeach had two weeks to pay the large fine of fifty pounds sterling and court costs; otherwise, he was to be sold at public outcry "for the most Money that can be got." Slavery stared this free black in the face.[92]

A worse fate befell Thomas Jeremiah, another free black resident of Charleston. Jeremiah had made impressive economic strides in the colonial capital. As a fire fighter, fisherman, and harbor pilot, he accumulated a fortune reputed at more than a thousand pounds sterling. The governor of South Carolina described him as man "of considerable property, one of the most valuable and useful men in his way in this province." According to a more jaundiced observer, he was "a forward fellow, puffed up by prosperity, ruined by Luxury and debauchery and grown to an amazing pitch of vanity and ambition." His dizzying ascent halted abruptly in the summer of 1775, when Jeremiah was sentenced to death for plotting an insurrection. In spite of his wealth, had Jeremiah sided with the slaves? Did he say, as another black reported, that "the war was come to help the poor Negroes"? Predictably, perhaps, Jeremiah denied the charge; less predictably, many prominent whites, including the governor, believed the denial; but there was damning black testimony and apparent perjury from the defendant. If the truth eludes us, the significance of Jeremiah's story is no less important. In a very real sense, his fall can be attributed to his unusually elevated and precarious position within Charleston society. Either this induced him to envisage a role for blacks, one in which he would have "the Chief Command," in the imminent war between Britain and the colonies; or it made him the best available scapegoat for patriot forces who wanted both to intimidate other black harbor pilots and promote military preparedness. Either Jeremiah sided with slaves or he learned—painfully and tragically—that he was as vulnerable as any slave.[93]

A free black might scale impressive economic heights, but bonds of kinship tied even the most successful freedperson to the slave community (in Jeremiah's case, this connection came back to haunt him, for the chief prosecution

---

92. Elizabeth Bourquin, *SCG*, May 23, 1761; Peter Timothy, *SCG and CJ*, May 20, June 9, 1766; James Troup, *City Gaz*, Apr. 22, 1800; court of Justices and Freeholders, Aug. 25, 1781, Miscellaneous Records, TT, 23.
93. Morgan, "Black Society in the Lowcountry," in Berlin and Hoffman, eds., *Slavery and Freedom*, 213.

witness was his wife's brother). Most often, familial ties bound free and enslaved blacks together in cooperative ways. In Virginia, Stepney Blue, a slave, and his wife, Easter Roberts, a free black, both of York County, ran away together; Sam, a mulatto slave in King William County, aimed his course for Hampton, where his father, Joe Hill, a free black, lived; and Jane Bell, a mulatto servant, persuaded Charles Lee to buy her remaining years of service and agreed to serve an extra year so that she could live with her husband, who was Lee's slave. In South Carolina, a number of slaves ran to visit their free mothers: Jacob ran away to Free Peg, who lived at Mr. Ladson's plantation on the Ashley River, while Jack headed for Saint Helena, where his mother, Julie, a free black, resided, and mulatto Peggy left Port Royal Island for Charleston, where her mother, a free woman named Nelly, lived. Free blacks commonly purchased slave relatives in order to free them.[94]

Women headed many free black households, and they remained especially close to the world of slaves. Many free black women were married to slaves. They often worked alongside or with slaves. Mary Roberts and Elizabeth Armfield, two mulatto women of York County, acted as midwives to slaves. Free black women had business dealings with slaves: Cris Younhocon, a free black woman of Lancaster County, confessed to receiving goods from Robert "King" Carter's slaves. Finally, free black women often became familiar with exploitative and abusive masters. Forced by poverty to bind out their children to white masters, many free black mothers later resorted to the courts to protect their sons and daughters from treatment that was not far removed from that accorded slaves.[95]

Even though the numbers of free blacks increased through the eighteenth century, particularly in the last two decades, the gap between free and slave

---

94. Nathan Yancey, *VaG* (P and D), Sept. 29, 1774; Samuel Garlick, *VaG and WA*, Nov. 1, 1783; Lancaster County Court Order Book, no. 8, 85, as cited in Robert Anthony Wheeler, "Lancaster County, Virginia, 1650–1750: The Evolution of a Southern Tidewater Community" (Ph.D. diss., Brown University, 1972), 144; Rawlins Lowndes, *SCG*, Aug. 25, 1757; John Lampart, ibid., Mar. 14, 1761; Elizabeth Roupell, *City Gaz*, Feb. 3, 1798. For other kinship ties, see Hamilton Jones, *VaG* (D and H), Jan. 28, 1775; John Hudson, ibid. (Pinkney), Jan. 20, 1776; William Rose, *VaG and WA* (N and P), Nov. 22, 1783; William Scott, *SCG*, Dec. 30, 1760; William Brisbane, *City Gaz*, July 11, 1798; Henry Bell, *State Gaz of SC*, Aug. 14, 1786; [unidentified master], *Columbian Herald*, Mar. 26, 1789 (Exmouth et al.); Bing's deed of manumission, June 4, 1754, Miscellaneous Records, KK, 98; deed of sale between John Edwards and Mathew Daniels, July 7, 1757, and Mathew Daniels's deed of manumission, July 12, 1757, ibid., LL, 254; Robert Smith Timothy's deed of manumission to Beckey, Dec. 3, 1789, ibid., ZZ, 102–103; Sam's deed of manumission, Oct. 22, 1790, ibid., 244.

95. York County Orders and Wills, no. 18, Nov. 17, 1735, 237–238; York Grants and Inventories, Aug. 15, 1763, 315; Lancaster County Court Orders, no. 5, Mar. 9, 1709, 206; all cited in Brown, *Good Wives, Nasty Wenches, and Anxious Patriarchs*, 237, 240.

generally remained narrow. Ironically, in the region where free blacks were least numerous, the Lowcountry, a greater rift opened between slaves and freedpersons. A fragment of the black population, generally light-skinned residents of Charleston, charted a path toward assimilation and separation from the large mass of black, rural field hands. The Brown Fellowship Society, an exclusive mulatto benevolent society, established in 1790, embodied these aspirations. Because many of these urban free coloreds were skilled, they tended to be quite well off. In the Chesapeake, conversely, where free blacks were most numerous, the "darkening" of the freedpeople and their continued residence in the countryside served to minimize the divergence of interests that a transition from slavery to freedom inevitably wrought.

Various fault lines ran through black communities. Africans had little or no reason to see themselves as one people at first. Only gradually, if at all, did members of disparate African nations learn to cooperate on North American soil. Africans and creoles often viewed each other with mutual incomprehension, although over time they, too, sometimes found ways to overcome their differences. The emergence of a predominantly creole population facilitated cohesion and cooperation, because slaves born into slavery had much in common. Nevertheless, collective activity was in some ways made even more difficult, for creoles learned that it was sometimes better not to cooperate with their comrades if they were to succeed either in or out of slavery. Some blacks intermingled with Indians, creating a triracial group that in some ways further fragmented the black community. More commonly, however, most Indians who mixed closely with blacks seem to have been incorporated into black society; rarely was the reverse the case. Finally, although slaves and free blacks had many reasons—from skin color to economic standing—to dissociate from one another, common interest in the face of white oppression usually brought them together.

   Overall, then, although considerable strains and stresses tugged at the cohesion of black societies, there were no irrevocable fractures. A sense of group identity encompassing different African nations, Africans and creoles, Indians and blacks, and free and enslaved blacks arose within black communities. Blacks came to share a belief that they were a separate people in large part because they established networks of social relations that, though never harmonious, were marked by mutuality. The key social network that tied together involuntary immigrants, natives and newcomers, native and black Americans, and free and enslaved blacks was the family. As the central institution of black life, it deserves separate investigation.

The uncertainty of distinguishing one [slave] from another after several Generations, no Registers of their Genealogy being kept, and none of them having Sirnames were great Mischiefs to Purchasers, Strangers and Creditors.—Francis Fauquier

9 : Family Life

In the face of formidable obstacles, eighteenth-century slaves struggled to create and maintain families. Contemporaries were well aware both of the hurdles in the way of successful family formation and of the slaves' efforts to overcome them. Thus, in 1757, John Woolman observed that Chesapeake slaves were marrying "after their own way," even as he emphasized the lack of recognition masters accorded such unions. Similarly, Johann Bolzius, an observer of the Lowcountry scene at midcentury, reported that slaves "have to take as their wives or husbands whomever their masters give them without ceremonies," though he also recognized that slaves "love their families dearly and none runs away from the other."[1]

We would like to know the family structures of slaves. However, as Governor Fauquier of Virginia noted, few genealogical registers for slaves were probably ever produced, and fewer have survived.[2] Instead, the historian of the colonial slave family must rely largely on cross-sectional information in which family and household structures can be glimpsed at particular times. Invento-

---

1. Phillips P. Moulton, ed., *The Journal and Major Essays of John Woolman* (New York, 1971), 65; "Johann Martin Bolzius Answers a Questionnaire on Carolina and Georgia," trans. and ed. Klaus G. Loewald et al., *WMQ*, 3d Ser., XIV (1957), 236.

2. Governor Francis Fauquier to the Lords of Trade, Jan. 10, 1763, CO5/1330, fol. 178, PRO.

ries of estate and, less frequently, plantation listings are the most common sources. Some estate appraisers, more particularly in South Carolina than in Virginia, saw fit to note family connections among slaves. This information provides a fairly wide coverage of the slave population, thereby minimizing a major drawback of generational records—their sheer atypicality. Furthermore, even if the kin ties of particular plantation slaves cannot be traced through time, at least the family and household structures of different plantations can be compared from decade to decade, enabling a rudimentary evolutionary analysis.[3]

Yet, the definition of the slave family presents significant problems. To speak of married couples even where listings mention husbands and wives or to assume that a woman listed with her children constitutes a variant of the "simple family" may be too large a deductive leap. More neutral categories, such as coresidential union or perhaps coresidential consensual union, might be more accurately substituted for "married couple." Serial polyandry, rather than a widowed or separated status, might conceivably explain the situation of a woman listed with children. We cannot forget that slaves lacked that legally sanctioned sexual monopoly in a partner that is a defining characteristic of marriage, although they undoubtedly did make and maintain marriagelike associations. The problem of applying terminology that presupposes freedom to relationships that were grounded in slavery must always be borne in mind.[4]

No slave family could ever feel secure, for planter intrusion was an omnipresent threat. Not only did slave marriages lack legal sanction, but they could always be broken by sale, gift, and bequest. When planters moved long distances or opened up inland plantations, they inevitably separated slaves

---

3. The drawbacks of cross-sectional data are significant. Those inventories or plantation listings that group slaves into "families" tend to refer only to immediate kin ties. The "simple family"—that is, a married couple or married couple with offspring, or a widowed, separated, or unmarried person with children—predominates (Peter Laslett and Richard Wall, eds., *Household and Family in Past Time* . . . [Cambridge, 1972], 23–24). More distant kin ties were probably not common, but the way listings were constructed made their recognition unlikely. Many appraisers grouped slaves by sex and age, listing men first, then women, and so on, ignoring family ties altogether, even if they existed; but, in a minority of cases, it seems plausible to picture appraisers assembling slaves outside their huts and recording names and connections accordingly. In such situations, appraisers probably paid more attention to household composition than to distant family links, or even to relatively close ones if they involved separate households. The disadvantages of stopping "history at a given point" are outlined by Herbert G. Gutman in *The Black Family in Slavery and Freedom, 1750–1925* (New York, 1976), 96–99.

4. Peter Laslett, *Family Life and Illicit Love in Earlier Generations* (Cambridge, 1977), 233–260; Stephen Gudeman, "Herbert Gutman's *The Black Family in Slavery and Freedom, 1750–1925:* An Anthropologist's View," *Social Science History*, III (1979), 56–65.

TABLE 29.
South Carolina Slave Families, 1730–1799

	1730s	1740s	1750s	1760s	1770s	1780s	1790s
2-parent families							
No.	84	336	668	895	1,504	822	764
No. of children	65	480	1,150	1,175	2,247	1,363	1,369
1-parent families							
No.	14	83	204	270	445	344	427
No. of children	23	161	353	534	941	660	936
Extended families							
No.	0	0	11	16	29	75	98
No. of members	0	0	25	77	97	398	556
Solitaries	245	781	1,653	1,952	3,027	1,318	1,289
Total slaves[a]	515	2,177	4,721	5,798	9,765	5,727	6,105
Proportion of slaves in families	52%	64%	65%	66%	69%	77%	79%

[a] Counting two slaves as parents for each two-parent family (no.×2), and subsuming all parents in extended families under "members."

Note: This table comprises only slaves listed in inventories that specify kin ties.

Sources: Records of the Secretary of the Province, H (1730–1731) through Inventory Book, CC, and Charleston Direct Inventory Books, A, B, C, SCDAH.

from family members. A slave's domestic affairs were never immune from a master's watchful eye. A slave husband, Cumberland, of the Northern Neck in Virginia, surely understood as much, for his master had him whipped for "abusing his wife." When Cumberland still "behaved in a very unruly manner," his master ordered him "to prison, which seemed to frighten him." Conversely, a slave wife, Sally, of South Carolina must have bemoaned her doubly cruel fate: she received not only a "Horse whipping" from her master for her "impertinent behaviour" but also "a terrible beating from her Husband," which "laid [her] up." Even her master sympathized with her plight, observing, "Poor Devil she gets disciplined on all sides."[5]

In spite of this double dose of discipline, the master acknowledged that nothing could "reduce" Sally's "spirit to order." In many ways, she personifies the realities of slave family life in eighteenth-century British America. Slaves faced almost overwhelming odds as they attempted to create and maintain families. Yet no matter how trying the circumstances, how painfully fragile the bonds that were created, many slave couples attempted, not always successfully, to live as husband and wife, to remain faithful to one another, to bring up their children according to standards of their own making, and to recognize wider kin. To understand both dimensions of this story—the impediments to family life and the slaves' spirited commitment to overcoming them—must be our goal.

STRUCTURES

During the eighteenth century, South Carolina slaves increasingly organized themselves into families. In the 1730s, only 6 percent of all inventoried slaves were grouped in families, but, by the 1790s, the proportion had risen to 30 percent. These percentages, however, undoubtedly understate the presence of families among the colony's slaves, for some appraisers overlooked family ties. On those inventoried plantations where at least some kin ties were noted, the proportion of slaves involved in families rose from just over half in the 1730s to four-fifths by the 1790s (see Table 29).

As many studies of slave households elsewhere in the New World have demonstrated, the two-parent family form predominated. Throughout the eighteenth century, half of all slaves in South Carolina inventories that noted kin ties were grouped in two-parent households. Single-parent and extended households became more numerous over time (comprising about a third of slaves by the 1790s), whereas solitaries declined markedly from almost half of all slaves in the 1730s to a fifth in the 1790s.[6]

---

5. "Journal of Col. James Gordon" *WMQ*, 1st Ser., XII (1903–1904), 3; William Read to Jacob Read, Nov. 25, 1795, Read Family Papers, SCHS.

6. B. W. Higman, "The Slave Family and Household in the British West Indies, 1800–1834," *Journal of Interdisciplinary History*, VI (1975–1976), 261–287; Higman, "African and Creole Slave Family Patterns in Trinidad," *Journal of Family History*, III (1978), 163–180; Michael Craton, "Changing Patterns of Slave Families in the British West Indies," *Jour. Interdisc. Hist.*, X (1979–1980), 1–36; Richard Graham, "Slave Families on a Rural Estate in Colonial Brazil," *Journal of Social History*, IX (1975–1976), 382–402; Cathy Duke, "The Fam-

Virginia inventories, by contrast, reveal few kin connections. Indeed, in the eighteenth-century inventories of ten counties, few direct references to a marriage tie can be found, and even mother-child relationships are infrequently mentioned.[7] Perhaps there was no custom of observing family connections by Chesapeake appraisers; perhaps, of course, the region's slaves failed to create meaningful family ties. That slaves did not form families seems unlikely in view of considerable other evidence. Rather, the explanation appears to lie in the small size of quarters in the Chesapeake. If many of the adults on small quarters were forced to find mates on other plantations, estate appraisers were bound to ignore such connections. This seems a plausible solution to the lack of family relationships recorded in Chesapeake inventories.[8]

To gain some impression of the presence of slave families and common household forms among Chesapeake slaves, it is necessary therefore to resort to extremely imperfect proxies. Allan Kulikoff's educated guess is that, in 1776, about 20 percent of the slaves on small units in Prince George's County, Maryland, appear to have lived in two-parent households, a third in single-parent households, and fully 40 percent in households with no family. Almost three-quarters of the men and just over two-fifths of the women apparently lived with neither spouse nor children. Other, even more imperfect proxies can be derived by examining the composition of households by gender and age over time. In the early eighteenth century, most Chesapeake slaves were grouped on plantations where men so outnumbered women that marriages were out of the question for the majority. By midcentury, however, at least half, and in some cases two-thirds, of adult slaves resided on units with evenly balanced numbers of men and women. This is not to say that these men and women did in fact marry one another, but at least opportunities for companionship rose as the century progressed. Similarly, a detailed study of Charles County, Maryland, has shown that, by 1782, about half of all slaves were grouped on plantations

---

ily in Eighteenth-Century Plantation Society in Mexico," in Vera Rubin and Arthur Tuden, eds., *Comparative Perspectives on Slavery in New World Plantation Societies,* New York Academy of Sciences, Annals, CCXCII (New York, 1977), 226–241; David L. Chandler, "Family Bonds and the Bondsman: The Slave Family in Colonial Colombia," *Latin American Research Review,* XVI, no. 2 (1981), 107–131; Ann Patton Malone, *Sweet Chariot: Slave Family and Household Structure in Nineteenth-Century Louisiana* (Chapel Hill, N.C., 1992), 14.

7. The inventories of Amelia, Chesterfield, Essex, Goochland, Isle of Wight, Loudoun, Northampton, Orange, Spotsylvania, and York Counties between 1700 and 1779 were searched.

8. In the Chesapeake, wills are more likely to refer to slave family ties than inventories; unfortunately, reporting is sporadic, and it is a rare will that mentions a significant proportion of slaves on any one estate.

where a full range of daily contacts between young and old, male and female, parent and child, and perhaps even grandparent and grandchild could occur.[9]

What tentative conclusions can be drawn from this initial comparison of household structures on Lowcountry and Chesapeake plantations? First, early in the century, family life was extremely tenuous for most slaves in both regions. Second, by midcentury, the demographic environment became much more conducive to family formation, and perhaps a majority of slaves knew some form of family life. Last, by the late eighteenth century, the most common household form for slaves appears to have been a two-parent one in the Lowcountry and a single-parent one in the Chesapeake. To explore these comparisons more graphically, it is necessary to focus on individual plantations or groups of plantations.

The household structures of slaves belonging to two planters who died in the 1730s provide a useful starting-point. Although these two units were exceptionally large for their time and place, the contrast that they offer on the familial experiences of Chesapeake and Lowcountry slaves is instructive. Robert "King" Carter, who died in 1733, had amassed a slave force beyond the wildest dreams of his contemporaries; yet the actual size of many of his quarters would have been familiar to his neighbors. His forty-eight quarters averaged fifteen slaves each; by differentiating between his large and small units (taking fifteen as a dividing line), we can separate out the more atypical groupings (see Table 30). On Carter's small quarters, two household types predominated: those formed entirely of solitaries and those comprising two parents and a few children. A large number of the men on Carter's small quarters were presumably Africans; 57 percent of the adult males lived alone or with other unrelated men, a reflection of the extreme shortage of women on these units. On larger quarters, the numbers of men and women were much more evenly balanced; here, solitaries were somewhat less in evidence, whereas two-parent families were numerous, though so were mother-headed households.[10]

If an African's opportunities for family life were bleak in the early-eighteenth-century Chesapeake, they were dismal in the Lowcountry. The estate of

---

9. Allan Kulikoff, *Tobacco and Slaves: The Development of Southern Cultures in the Chesapeake, 1680–1800* (Chapel Hill, N.C., 1986), 371–372; Philip D. Morgan and Michael L. Nicholls, "Slaves in Piedmont Virginia, 1720–1790," *WMQ*, 3d Ser., XLVI (1989), 211–251; Jean Butenhoff Lee, "The Problem of Slave Community in the Eighteenth-Century Chesapeake," *WMQ*, 3d Ser., XLIII (1986), 352. Lee emphasizes the half that could not share this full range of contacts.

10. Robert Carter refers to buying "near four score Slaves" after losing a great number of slaves to an epidemic. See Robert Carter to Micajah Perry, June 2, 1727, Robert Carter Letterbook, 1727–1728, VHS.

TABLE 30.
Household Structures among Slaves in the Chesapeake, 1733–1775

Household Type	Proportion			
	Men	Women	Children	Total
Robert Carter's Virginia Quarters of 15 or Fewer Slaves, 1733[a]
	N = 100	N = 56	N = 79	N = 235
Husband-wife	11%	20%	0%	9%
Husband-wife-children	28	45	54	41
Single-parent	3	4	13	6
Extended	1	7	3	3
Solitary	57	25	30	40
Total	100	101	100	99
Robert Carter's Virginia Quarters of 16 or More Slaves, 1733[a]
	N = 144	N = 122	N = 232	N = 498
Husband-wife	12%	14%	0%	7%
Husband-wife-children	31	38	48	41
Single-parent	5	25	38	25
Extended	2	1	0	1
Solitary	50	21	14	26
Total	100	99	100	100
7 Small Virginia Estates, 1744–1775[b]
	N = 12	N = 18	N = 33	N = 63
Husband-wife	17%	11%	0%	6%
Husband-wife-children	8	5	6	6
Single-parent	0	56	82	59
Solitary	75	28	12	29
Total	100	100	100	100

504 : THE BLACK WORLD

TABLE 30.
Continued

Household Type	Proportion			
	Men	Women	Children	Total
6 Large Chesapeake Estates, 1740–1788[c]				
	N = 289	N = 233	N = 529	N = 1,051
Husband-wife	10%	13%	0%	6%
Husband-wife children	33	40	53	45
Single-parent	6	21	24	19
Extended	7	11	8	9
Sibling	1	1	3	2
Solitary	42	14	11	20
Total	99	100	99	101

[a] Carter distributed his 734 slaves on 48 quarters, with 1 woman attached to the Lancaster County vestry. Robert Carter inventory, November 1733, Robert Carter Papers, VHS.

[b] Inventory of William Keith's estate, June 4, 1744, York County Inventory Book, no. 19, 291–292; inventory of Henry Reeves's estate, May 16, 1749, Essex County Inventory Book, no. 8, 237–238; inventory of Robert Crawley's estate, Jan. 3, 1760, York County Inventory Book, no. 21, 1–2; inventory of Anne Singleton's estate, Feb. 23, 1765, York County Inventory Book, no. 21, 237–238; sale of Leonard Hill's estate, Aug. 19, 1765, Essex County Inventory Book, no. 12, 179; inventory of James Shedd's estate, Apr. 15, 1774, Loudoun Will Book, B, 214–216; inventory of James Burwell's estate, Oct. 9, 1775, York County Inventory Book, no. 22, 348–351, all in VSL.

[c] Jones Family, 1740; Bolling, 1758; Jerdone, 1770; Deed of Trust, Dec. 9, 1772, William Byrd; Edmund Randolph, Charlotte County, 1784; Robert Carter, 1788.

Thomas Lynch, who died in 1739, was less imposing than that of King Carter; but his plantation labor forces were larger, averaging twenty-eight slaves, a typical unit size for this region. His plantations were almost devoid of children, who comprised less than 10 percent of all his slaves. Moreover, in spite of a relatively equal adult sex ratio, almost three-quarters of the men and two-thirds of the women were listed as solitaries. Recently imported Africans presumably predominated on these plantations, for only a quarter of the adults had found partners and only 5 percent lived in two-parent households with children (see Table 31).

The gap that separated the familial experiences of Lowcountry and Chesa-

TABLE 31.
Household Structures among Slaves in South Carolina, 1739–1797

Household Type	Proportion			
	Men	Women	Children	Overall
Colonel Thomas Lynch's South Carolina Plantations, 1739[a]				
	N = 98	N = 79	N = 18	N = 195
Husband-wife	23%	29%	0%	24%
Husband-wife-children	4	5	55	9
Single-parent		1	6	
Solitary	72	65	39	66
Total	99	100	100	100
7 Large Lowcountry Estates, 1753–1797[b]				
	N = 302	N = 318	N = 480	N = 1,100
Husband-wife	20%	19%	0%	11%
Husband-wife-children	39	37	55	46
Single-parent	4	21	31	21
Extended	6	9	7	8
Siblings	4	0	1	2
Solitary	27	13	5	13
Total	100	99	99	101
4 Small South Carolina Estates, 1772–1776[c]				
	N = 47	N = 30	N = 34	N = 111
Husband-wife	8%	13%	0%	7%
Husband-wife-children	13	20	35	22
Single-parent	0	27	56	24
Solitary	79	40	9	47
Total	100	100	100	100

[a] Lynch distributed his 195 slaves on 7 plantations. Inventory of Colonel Thomas Lynch, 1739, Inventory Book, WPA, CV, 282–293, SCDAH.

[b] Pinckney, 1753; Henry Ravenel, 1756; Pinckney, 1777; Morel, 1777; Middleton, 1784; P. Butler, 1793; Bull, 1797.

[c] Inventory of James Miles, Feb. 12, 1774, Inventory Book, Z, 535–537; inventory of William Young, Apr. 22, 1772, Inventory Book, &, 62–68; inventory of Joshua McPherson, Aug. 13, 1774, Inventory Book &, 454–455; inventory of John Pelot, July 27, 1776, Inventory Book, &, 619–620, SCDAH.

peake slaves in the early eighteenth century narrowed substantially over the century. By the last half of the century, the proportion of slaves involved in two-parent, single-parent, and extended households seems to have been much the same on large estates in both regions (Tables 30 and 31). The two-parent household form was dominant, although about a fifth of slaves were involved in single-parent families and just under a tenth in extended households. The similarities in household structure on large estates in both regions are thus striking. At the same time, the few differences seem to suggest a more favorable family environment in the Lowcountry. There, fewer solitaries and more numerous two-parent households (with and without children) existed. On large estates, at least, Lowcountry slaves seem not just to have caught up with developments in the Chesapeake but to have surpassed them.

On smaller estates, the differences in the familial experiences of slaves in the two regions were somewhat more marked. The predominant household form differed in each region. In South Carolina, it was solitaries, in Virginia, single-parent families (Tables 30 and 31). In this respect, South Carolina slaves were worse off than their Chesapeake counterparts, with more of them living in households composed of singles. Nevertheless, coresident two-parent families were more widespread on small estates in South Carolina than in Virginia—thereby providing further confirmation of the importance of estate size, because small estates in the Lowcountry were larger than those in the Chesapeake.

In general, then, the evidence points to the advantages of large plantations over small ones in terms of slave family formation. In particular, large plantations facilitated coresident unions among slaves. Because plantations were considerably larger in the Lowcountry than in the Chesapeake, this is one major way in which the Lowcountry slaves were favored. Impressionistic evidence confirms the difference. When Chesapeake masters sought to purchase slaves, they knew that most would have formed connections off their places of residence and accordingly refrained from mentioning the value of purchasing whole family units. By the second half of the century, at any rate, Lowcountry masters could realistically expect to buy groups of slaves arranged into coresident families. When Henry Laurens proposed a purchase of slaves in 1770, he could anticipate buying "twenty working hands, Men and Wives for the Field." In the same year, Edward Telfair advised a friend to purchase a particular plantation that was up for sale, because the slaves were "all Family Negroes and behaves well."[11]

If the prevalence of coresident unions was the most positive feature of

---

11. *Laurens Papers*, VII, 344; Edward Telfair to Mr. Cowper, Jan. 1, 1770, Telfair Papers, Duke. See also Robert Norris and Co., *State Gaz*, June 23, 1788; Francis Levett, *SC State Gaz*, Sept. 28, 1797; John Chesnutt to Col. John Hoomes, Dec. 9, 1800, J. Chesnutt Letterbook, LC.

family life among Lowcountry slaves, the most negative was the high proportion of households formed of solitaries. The Lowcountry region's heavy reliance on imported Africans, which resulted in a severe imbalance between men and women, meant that many adult slaves, even in the last half of the eighteenth century, found it difficult to find a mate. This problem was more acute on small plantations, but many slaves from large plantations undoubtedly faced shortages in persons of the opposite sex. In 1764, for example, Henry Laurens received a request for prospective wives from the men on his Mepkin plantation. He promised to serve these "Gentlemen" as opportunity arose. A year later, a division of Laurens's Wambaw plantation meant that once again Laurens had to supply "Young women for those who lately lost their wives."[12]

The settling of East Florida in the late colonial period is a vivid reminder of the problem of solitaries that faced some Lowcountry slaves, even on large plantations. Thus, in 1767, Richard Oswald, an absentee planter and slave trader, notified the governor that he was sending a number of African women for his estate, because "it might be of bad Consequence if the Men Slaves now on the Plantation remained longer unprovided with Wives." Two years later, another absentee owner ordered slave women for his plantation so as "to render the Negroes I now have happy and contented, which I know they cannot be without each having a wife." He predicted that this provision of women "will greatly tend to keep them at home and to make them Regular and tho the women will not work all together so well as the Men, Yet Amends will be sufficiently made in a very few years by the Great Encrease of Children who may easily [be] trained up and become faithfully attached to the Glebe and to their Master." In 1781, the governor himself heard that his plantation had too few women. Not only did he lose by the "Negroes not increasing," his agent pointed out, but the labor of the "young fellows" was intermittent, because many absented themselves, complaining "what must they do for a wife."[13]

In the Chesapeake, the apparent prevalence of the single-parent *residential* arrangement masked an important *familial* relationship. Single-parent households often involved cross-plantation marriages. This was so common that the term "broad marriage" came into wide currency in the Chesapeake to describe slaves marrying "abroad," or off their home plantation. Passing visitors became aware of this custom, as when a traveler to Virginia in 1779 observed that

---

12. *Laurens Papers,* IV, 148, 625.

13. Richard Oswald to James Grant, May 20, 1767, MSS 0771/295, Papers of General James Grant of Ballindalloch, sometime Governor of East Florida, in ownership of Sir Evan Macpherson-Grant, Bart., Ballindalloch Castle Muniments, Scotland; the Earl of Egmont to James Grant, May 14, 1769, 0771/264; David Yeats to James Grant, Feb. 3, 1781, 0771/250. See also John Tucker to James Grant, Apr. 10, 1769, 0771/412.

"sometimes the [slave] man belongs to one master, while the woman is owned by another." Charles Ball lived the experience when he married Judah, who belonged to a neighboring planter in Calvert County, Maryland. He visited her house every week and "became as well acquainted" with her master as with his own. Masters generally did not like the practice: the slave with attachments off the home plantation aroused suspicion. Thomas Jefferson described the practice as "imprudent" and rewarded his slaves who married within his plantation "family." But, despite planter concern, small plantations, ubiquitous estate divisions and sales, the constant shuffling of slaves from one quarter to another, and the growing practice of slave hiring helped create many divided-residence families among Chesapeake slaves.[14]

Inevitably, the law had to come to terms with this widespread social convention. A fundamental feature of the slave code was the prohibition of slave movements off home plantations. However, in a court case of 1799, a judge permitted one major exception—that is, where the slave had "general leave" to be absent. Significantly, the one example he cited concerned "a negro [who] has a wife" on another plantation. Indeed, according to Richard Parkinson, an even more surprising breach of customary legal practice ensued from "broad marriages." In Virginia in the late 1790s, Parkinson observed, "It is an usual practice for the negroes to go to see their wives on the Saturday night." Moreover, according to Parkinson, husbands often borrowed horses and rode "from ten to fourteen miles" in order to visit their spouses. This practice was "looked upon as so slight an offence" that Parkinson "never heard" of a slave "being brought to justice for it." Joseph Ball, for example, allowed his slave Black Joe to live at his Little Falls quarter provided it was not more than twenty-five

---

14. August Wilhelm Du Roi, *Journal of Du Roi . . .* , trans. Charlotte S. J. Epping (New York, 1911), 157–158; Charles Ball, *Fifty Years in Chains* (New York, 1970), rpt. of *Slavery in the United States: A Narrative of the Life and Adventures of Charles Ball, a Black Man* (New York, 1837), 30; Edwin Morris Betts, ed., *Thomas Jefferson's Farm Book, with Commentary and Relevant Extracts from Other Writings*, American Philosophical Society, Memoirs, XXXV (Princeton, N.J., 1953), part 2, 26; and Betts, ed., *Thomas Jefferson's Garden Book, 1766–1824, with Relevant Extracts from His Other Writings*, Am. Phil. Soc., Memoirs, XXII (Philadelphia, 1944), 450. On hiring, see Sarah Shaver Hughes, "Elizabeth City County, Virginia, 1782–1810: The Economic and Social Structure of a Tidewater County in the Early National Years" (Ph.D. diss., College of William and Mary, 1975), 263–265. For planter concerns, see John Sutton to Robert Carter, Apr. 3, 1782, Carter Family Papers, VHS; Jack P. Greene, ed., *The Diary of Landon Carter of Sabine Hall, 1752–1778*, 2 vols. (Charlottesville, Va., 1965), 348, 648 (hereafter cited as *Carter Diary*); Robert Carter to Newyear Branson, Apr. 18, 1785, Robert Carter Letterbook, VI, 138, Duke; Jefferson to [?], Oct. 12, 1792, Edgehill-Randolph Papers, microfilm, CW; Mill Swamp Baptist Church, Isle of Wight County, June 13, 1794, Oct. 17, 1795, photostat, VSL.

miles from the home of Joe's wife and made a horse available so that he might ride over to his wife's residence. Ball's solicitude had distinct limits: Joe's visits were to be no more frequent than once a month.[15]

The development of extended households on large estates in both regions constituted a major improvement in slaves' lives. In the late-eighteenth-century Lowcountry, grandparents occasionally lived with adult sons or daughters, some households contained adult siblings, and others occasionally included in-laws. Because consistent natural increase among slaves occurred earlier in the Chesapeake than in the Lowcountry, Chesapeake blacks were eventually surrounded by more kin than their Lowcountry counterparts. It is hard to imagine a Lowcountry slave, for instance, matching the experience of a Chesapeake resident like Fanny, who, as early as the 1770s, lived on a quarter surrounded by five children, nineteen grandchildren, nine great-grandchildren, four children-in-law, and three grandchildren's spouses. Even in late colonial North Carolina, where slavery had been late developing, one elderly slave couple lived on a plantation with their four children, eleven grandchildren, four great-grandchildren, and one great-great-grandchild.[16]

The piedmont region of Virginia provides an illuminating illustration of the extensiveness of kin networks among slaves. On the face of it, this area seems an unlikely place to look for dense kin ties among slaves. From the 1720s onward, tidewater planters transferred many of their bondpeople beyond the fall line, which undoubtedly disrupted family ties, and a major influx of Africans in the third quarter of the eighteenth century further hampered family formation. Surely such a youthful population, containing so many newcomers, exhibited truncated family structures? Although stunted families were undoubtedly widespread, piedmont slaves built and rebuilt their kin networks so rapidly that extended kin structures were clearly discernible by the late eighteenth century.

Consider the slaves belonging to Peyton Randolph. In the 1750s, Randolph, like many another tidewater planter, transferred a number of his young slaves to a quarter more than a hundred miles from his home plantation. These

---

15. Louisa County Court, May 1799, Garrett Minor Papers, LC; Richard Parkinson, *A Tour in America, in 1798, 1799, and 1800* . . . , II (London, 1805), 448; Joseph Ball to J. Chinn, Aug. 30, 1746, Joseph Ball Letterbook, LC.

16. Inventory of Rev. William Hutson, June 2, 1761, Inventory Book, V, 5–8; inventory of Benjamin D'harriette, Mar. 2, 1756, Inventory Book, R(2), 445–449; inventory of Ralph Izard, February–March 1761, Inventory Book, T, 507–522, SCDAH; Kulikoff, *Tobacco and Slaves*, 365–367, 370; "Lean by Thomas Pollock to Jacob Mitchell," Mar. 27, 1770, Pollock Papers, NCDAH, as cited in Marvin L. Michael Kay and Lorin Lee Cary, *Slavery in North Carolina, 1748–1775* (Chapel Hill, N.C., 1995), 169.

teenagers and young adults left kin behind when they moved west. The imbalance between men and women meant that large age differentials (of about ten years) separated spouses, when they were fortunate enough to marry. But a generation later, some of the children of the original migrants had reached maturity and established families of their own. Nanny, for instance, left kin behind when she came to the piedmont as a twenty-five-year-old mother of four. But, by 1784, at least two of her three daughters had given birth, and Nanny was now a grandmother to four children, one of whom bore her name. Sarah's experience paralleled that of Nanny. About twenty when she relocated to the piedmont, Sarah was already the mother of three children; she gave birth to at least three more in her new home. By 1784, two of her daughters had married and had borne one child apiece. Nanny and Sarah were matriarchs of rapidly growing clans.[17]

By the end of the eighteenth century, the building and rebuilding of kin ties had produced dense kin networks for some piedmont slaves in both town and countryside. Thus, a Petersburg slave, sentenced to die in 1793 for robbery, gained the support of many of the town's white residents because of the effect that they calculated his death would have on his large family. The petitioners referred to the criminal's "numerous" relatives, all of whom, and particularly his "weeping broken hearted parents," earnestly desired a pardon. In deepest rural Bedford County, in the southwestern part of the piedmont, an old couple belonging to Thomas Jefferson was surrounded by a bevy of grown children, in-laws, and grandchildren. The quarter was virtually one extended family.[18]

Although the household structures of Chesapeake and Lowcountry slaves grew more alike over time, significant differences remained. Over the eighteenth century, family life became more robust in both societies; by century's end, most slaves in both regions lived in simple families. On large estates especially, there was little difference in the familial experiences of Lowcountry and Chesapeake slaves: most lived in two-parent households. But more Lowcountry than Chesapeake slaves lived in coresident two-parent households and households composed of solitaries, whereas more Chesapeake than Lowcountry slaves lived in divided-residence two-parent, one-parent, and extended households.

---

17. Inventory of the estate of Peyton Randolph, 1776, and a list of Negroes belonging to Edmund Randolph in Charlotte, Albemarle, and James City Counties, Sept. 23, 1784, Randolph Family Papers, microfilm, CW.

18. Petition of 31 Petersburg residents, n.d., Executive Papers, June–August 1793, VSL; Mary Beth Norton, Herbert G. Gutman, and Ira Berlin, "The Afro-American Family in the Age of Revolution," in Ira Berlin and Ronald Hoffman, eds., *Slavery and Freedom in the Age of the American Revolution* (Charlottesville, Va., 1983), 182.

STABILITY

No slave family was truly stable. All slave relations were contingent, held together by threads that a master might cut at any time. All slaves knew someone who had been sold from a family; even those who avoided sale almost certainly faced a change of ownership at least once, perhaps when a master deeded slaves to a son or daughter upon marriage, more commonly when one master died and another assumed charge. To be sure, some slave unions were long lasting; many slave children knew both their parents; over the course of the eighteenth century, masters grew more sensitive to the desires of their slaves and attempted to minimize familial disruption either by sale or bequest. Nevertheless, examples of constancy in slave families must be understood within a context that recognizes the essential insecurity of *all* slave marriages.

In the Chesapeake, small holdings and a proliferation of heirs meant that slave families faced severe disruption when a master died. The nineteen slaves belonging to Thomas Thorpe's estate in Essex County had to be divided among nine heirs; the estate of Peter Dishman, another Essex County planter, consisting of sixteen slaves, had to be divided among eight heirs. When so few blacks had to be distributed among so many whites, the devastation wrought on slave kinship networks can readily be imagined.[19] Even where a family core was maintained in an estate division, many families lost at least one member. When William Fitzhugh's estate was divided among his six heirs in 1703, four of his nine slave families suffered the removal of two or more children, although no husband and wife were separated. In George Mason's will of 1773, twenty slave siblings were listed; six were kept together, and fourteen were separated.[20]

When a division loomed, masters occasionally granted slaves some latitude in choosing their new owner. In 1740, Charles Wise of York County willed that his slave man George should be sold by his executor but granted him "the liberty of choosing his master," and, in 1766, a Charles County, Maryland, mistress allowed her only slave, Cate, to "go to which of my Sisters she shall chuse to go to." Governor Francis Fauquier of Virginia set perhaps the most exalted example of masterly solicitude. In 1767, he willed that his slave children were not to be separated from their mothers and that all his slaves, then

---

19. Division of Thomas Thorpe's estate, July 18, 1774, Essex County Will Book, no. 12, 587–588; division of Peter Dishman's estate, June 21, 1773, ibid., 533. See also division of Henry Reeve's estate, June 13, 1730, Essex County Will Book, no. 4, 373–383; division of George Newbill's estate, Apr. 9, 1741, ibid., no. 7, 523–526; and division of Augustine Boughan's estate, June 1771, ibid., no. 12, 414–417.

20. Richard Beale Davis, ed., *William Fitzhugh and His Chesapeake World, 1676–1701* (Chapel Hill, N.C., 1963), 378–382; Robert A. Rutland, ed., *The Papers of George Mason, 1725–1792*, 3 vols. (Chapel Hill, N.C., 1970), I, 147–161.

numbering about seventeen, were to have six months to choose their new masters. Indeed, he stipulated that they were to be maintained by his estate while they decided on their new owners, who were then to be allowed to purchase the "willing slaves" at 25 percent below market price. Such instances, involving exceptional masters and favored slaves, were rare.[21]

On the large, albeit atypical, estates of the Chesapeake region, slaves were less subject to family disruption than on small plantations. Landon Carter expected stability of his slave couples, as suggested by his reaction to the promiscuous behavior of one woman, "the oddest creature in all my gang," for being so "sallatious and ill tempered withall that no husband will keep to her long." More typical, it seems, was Mary Adam at Rings Neck, who had five children by George Ball's Adam. All the children but one inherited Adam's constitution, for they all died at about age thirty-five. Significant familial traits, indicative of constancy, impressed Carter on other occasions. Family continuity also characterized large plantations in the more newly settled piedmont region. John Bolling of Chesterfield County owned 135 slaves at his death in 1758, of whom about 80 percent were listed in family units. Only two of the two-parent and one of the single-parent families had a child removed in the estate division. On this estate, at least, the integrity of family units was respected. Later in the century, on the Jefferson plantation farther west, marital relations among slaves, which can be viewed through successive censuses, were nearly always lifelong.[22]

Over the course of the eighteenth century, masters of large numbers of slaves gradually came to profess an unwillingness to separate families. In the early eighteenth century such expressions were rare and pragmatic. In 1723, Robert "King" Carter proposed purchasing some slaves because they were "very much related to several of my families of slaves." By midcentury, such expressions were more common and more idealistically couched. Thus, in 1746, when Francis Willis gave his wife a slave woman and child, he attempted to purchase the slave's husband, with whom she had had several children, in the hope that they "may never be parted." As Willis explained to the owner of

---

21. Will of Charles Wise, Sept. 25, 1740, York County Wills, no. 18, 658; Charles County Wills, Lib. AD5, fol. 344, as cited in Lee, "The Problem of Slave Community," *WMQ*, 3d Ser., XLIII (1986), 356; will of Barbara Jones, rec. Jan. 22, 1795, Elizabeth City County Deeds and Wills, no. 34, as cited in Hughes, "Elizabeth City County," 228; will of Francis Fauquier, Mar. 26, 1767, York County Wills, no. 21, 396–404.

22. Greene, ed., *Carter Diary*, 385, 555, 604, 609, 865; *Thomas Bolling complt. v. John, Robert, Edward, and Archibald Bolling*, June 1758, Chesterfield County Court Order Book, no. 2, 1754–1759, 432–434; Norton, Gutman, and Berlin, "Afro-American Family," in Berlin and Hoffman, eds., *Slavery and Freedom*, 177.

the husband, "I am very unwilling I should be the Instrument of the Concern, or rather Inhumanity, that will naturally arise at their being separated." When, in 1768, Daniel Dulany sold some slaves, he refused to sell them separately even though the prices would thereby have been higher, because he "could not think of separating Husbands and Wifes, and tearing young Children away from their Mothers." His "distress" at splitting families would have been "intolerable," he claimed.[23]

Separating older children from their parents, as Dulany implies, gave masters less concern. In 1771, John Page foresaw a time, just "a few years hence," when he would be "better able to sell Negros" because "a great Number of young ones will be grown up." In 1800, a Chesterfield County master was even more forthright. In his will, he divided his slaves between a son and a daughter. He emphasized, "No man and wife shall be separated, nor shall any child be separated from its mother, except as are old enough to have a care of themselves." Adolescents could be separated from families without much soul-searching.[24]

On occasion, even the most concerned master felt that separations, even of young children from parents, could not be avoided. In 1757, Peter Randolph advised William Byrd III to sell his "Young Negroes, for it will by no Means answer to sell the Workers." Acknowledging that the "only objection to this scheme is that it will be cruel to part them from their Parents," Randolph refused to let sentiment override economic sense. "What can be done," he asked rhetorically; the young ones "alone can be sold without great Loss to you, and at present they are a Charge." In 1785, Charles Ball, then only four years old, experienced the disintegration of his immediate family. His master died, and the heirs apparently decided to sell the estate at public vendue to meet their debts. Charles's mother, brothers, and sisters "were all sold on the same day to different purchasers," never to see each other again. "Young as I was," Charles recalled a half-century later, "the horrors of that day sank deeply

23. Robert Carter to Micajah Perry, July 13, 1723, Miscellaneous Typescripts, 1606–1769, CW; Francis Willis, Jr., to Charles Carter, Feb. 3, 1746, Carter Family Papers; Daniel Dulany to [?], Dec. 18, 1768, Daniel Dulany Papers, LC. See also Brett Randolph to Robert Beverley, Mar. 18, 1801, Beverley Papers, W and M; C. Blagrove to Mrs. L. Blagrove, Nov. 7, 1806, Pelham Letters, CW; Samuel Johnston to Nathaniel Duckinfield, June 30, 178[?], folder 102, Hayes Collection, UNC, cited in Alan D. Watson, "Impulse toward Independence: Resistance and Rebellion among North Carolina Slaves, 1750–1775," *Journal of Negro History*, LXIII (1978), 318–319.

24. Frances Norton Mason, ed., *John Norton and Sons, Merchants of London and Virginia* . . . (Richmond, Va., 1937), 199; will of George Woodson, July 27, 1800, Chesterfield County Will Book, no. 5, 324.

into my heart, and . . . the terrors of the scene return with painful vividness upon my memory."[25]

In spite of the increased sensitivity to the familial ties of slaves, a significant number of masters continued to divide both by sale and bequest. Between 1782 and 1810, the sales of 166 slaves in Elizabeth City County indicate that a few were sold in family groups of husband and wife, mother, daughter, and even grandchildren, and a number of women were sold with their children. More often, however, adults and children were sold separately; furthermore, very young children, aged six or younger, were separated from their parents. A study of testatory practices in Charles County, Maryland, observes that those slaveowners who disclosed family ties among slaves more often than not kept husbands and wives as well as mothers and children together. Nevertheless, a casual attitude to the taking of children from mothers is evident in gifts and bequests. One owner gave her niece an infant so young it had not yet been named; masters occasionally disposed of children still in the womb or pondered what to do with a woman's "future increase"; the division of one estate allowed that an infant boy could "suck its Mother till twelve Months old" but that mother and child were then to be separated. Some masters entered into oral arrangements concerning gifts of young slaves—a testament to the off-hand manner in which slave families were disrupted.[26]

The hiring of slaves, which became widespread at least in parts of the tidewater Chesapeake toward the end of the century, also had a major impact on the stability of slave families. Between 1774 and 1776, Edward Cary rented out the services of eighteen-year-old Kate to three different masters—the first in Williamsburg, the next two in Gloucester—in successive years. Kate married a Williamsburg man, presumably in 1774, and, after a year or two in Gloucester, ran away and returned to the colonial capital to be with her husband. Between 1784 and 1786, only a minority of slaves in Elizabeth City County lived and worked in the same household for three successive years. Maintaining a

25. Peter Randolph to William Byrd, Sept. 20, 1757, VHS, as cited in Gerald Steffens Cowden, "The Randolphs of Turkey Island: A Prosopography of the First Three Generations, 1650–1806" (Ph.D. diss., College of William and Mary, 1977), 191; Ball, *Fifty Years in Chains*, 17–18.

26. Hughes, "Elizabeth City County," 189–196 (sales of 44 men, 45 women, another 16 women sold with 1 or 2 children, 16 boys, and 22 girls), 196–200 (bequests); Lee, "The Problem of Slave Community," *WMQ*, 3d Ser., XLIII (1986), 356, 359; Lee, *The Price of Nationhood: The American Revolution in Charles County* (New York, 1994), 73–74; inventory and division of John White's estate, 1729, Northampton County Wills and Inventory Book, no. 16, 183, 195–196; will of William Davis, 1732, York County Wills, no. 18, 33–34; Goochland County Court Order Book, no. 11, July 1768, 230; Cumberland County Court Order Book, 1767–1770, Jan. 25, 1769, 274.

stable family life under such circumstances must have been almost impossible. Moreover, the practice of hiring out children apart from their families also increased; by 1810, about one of nine slave children was removed from his or her parents to work in another master's household.[27]

Until about midcentury, the high death rates, the imbalance of sexes, and the large numbers of Africans necessarily produced many more transitory unions among Lowcountry slaves than among their Chesapeake counterparts. One observer in the early eighteenth century railed against the "perpetual" changing of wives and husbands, "the constant and promiscuous cohabiting of slaves of different sexes and nations together," that characterized family life in South Carolina. Henry Laurens, a witness to divorce petitions reaching England's House of Lords, was reminded "of our Negroes throwing away one wife and taking another." In the second half of the century, however, creolization facilitated family continuity on Lowcountry plantations just as it did in the Chesapeake. So stable were most unions among Ravenel family slaves that a register of their 160 births, stretching from 1730 to 1805, apparently noted all incidences of illegitimacy, of which there were just nine. Lucretia accounted for six illegitimate children: only her last recorded child was deemed legitimate. Three other slave women had one illegitimate child each (their first recorded child in each case); all then settled into long-lasting unions.[28]

The larger size of Lowcountry plantations (and smaller average number of heirs) meant, further, that estate divisions and sales could more readily respect the integrity of slave families than was the case in the Chesapeake. An occasional advertisement for a slave sale made this design explicit. The one condition placed on a midcentury sale of twenty to thirty slaves belonging to a Johns Island plantation was that "those in families will be disposed of altogether." Actual divisions reveal that this concern was often honored. Thus, the four-way division of Mary Bull's estate in 1772, consisting of 403 slaves grouped into 89 nuclear or extended families, appears not to have separated one family member. Even purchasers of estates respected the integrity of slave families. In 1773, Thomas Caw's estate, including his 137 slaves, was offered for sale. Twenty-nine separate purchasers bought the slaves, but there is no evidence that any of the families, of which there were 32, suffered disruption. In fact,

---

27. Edward Cary, Jr., *VaG* (Purdie), Nov. 29, 1776, Apr. 11, 1777, supplement (Cary's chronology is inconsistent in these two advertisements); Hughes, "Elizabeth City County," 260; Hughes, "Slave for Hire: The Allocation of Black Labor in Elizabeth City County, Virginia, 1782 to 1810," *WMQ*, 3d Ser., XXXV (1978), 260–286. See also Lee, "The Problem of Slave Community," *WMQ*, 3d Ser., XLIII (1986), 355–356.

28. Rev. Francis Le Jau to SPG, Sept. 15, 1708, A4/125, SPG; *Laurens Papers*, VIII, 239; Ravenel Account Book, B1-1, Ravenel Papers, SCHS.

George Porter bought a man and his mother, and Isaac McPherson bought a man and woman who were brother and sister. Of the 22 solitaries, 10 were skilled slaves, most of whom resided in Charleston and probably had families belonging to other masters. One prospective Lowcountry purchaser advertised for 20 or 30 native-born slaves "in large families, the more so the more agreeable," and another would not purchase "any gang where any of the slaves have been separated from their families."[29]

If anything, large planters in the Lowcountry protested even more ardently about avoiding the separation of slave families than their counterparts in the Chesapeake. George Ogilvie, a loyalist, spoke of his "unexpressible mortification" at having to sell as "happy and contented a gang as any in America." He could "not endure the thoughts of having families [torn] asunder" and eventually found his slaves such masters as they "wished." He secured one purchaser for 57 slaves and sold the other 20 in "separate families." Henry Laurens spoke of the "inhumanity" of "separating and tareing asunder" slave families. In his will, William Sanders left his wife two thousand pounds sterling, which, if she preferred to have in slaves rather than in cash, must be taken "in families." Richard Oswald changed his mind about selling his 170 East Florida slaves, because "he felt a Reluctance to separating the families however advantageous a Sale in that way might have proved to his Interest." Pierce Butler committed to keeping together a slave family because he felt "a moral duty to a black as well as to a white person."[30] Large planters in both Chesapeake and Lowcountry voiced similar sentiments, but the volume was a little louder in Carolina.

Unlike Chesapeake masters, most Lowcountry owners bequeathed slaves in groups rather than separately. From 1746 to 1763, South Carolina masters deeded 590 slaves, four-fifths in groups—15 percent in groups that included at least one woman and her children and 67 percent in groups that mixed men and women and boys and girls. This does not mean that those slaves deeded in

29. Samuel Eveleigh, *SCG,* Jan. 1, 1754; on the small number of heirs, compare white household sizes in Upper and Lower Souths: Philip J. Greven, Jr., "The Average Size of Families and Households in the Province of Massachusetts in 1764 and in the United States in 1790: An Overview," in Laslett and Wall, eds., *Household and Family,* 545–560; division of Mary Bull's estate, Jan. 1772, Inventory Book, Z, 177–187; inventory and sale of Thomas Caw's estate, Mar. 8–10, 1773, ibid., 345–350; Robert Norris and Co., *State Gaz of SC,* June 23, 1788; Francis Levett, *SC State Gaz,* Sept. 28, 1797.

30. George Ogilvie to Alexander Ogilvie, Aug. 21, 1778, 10/5/7, Ogilvie-Forbes of Boyndlie Papers, Aberdeen University Library, Scotland; *Laurens Papers,* IV, 595; will of William Sanders, Aug. 4, 1775, Guignard Family Papers, USC; Henry Laurens to John Lewis Gervais, Aug. 16, 1783 (about Richard Oswald), typescript, Henry Laurens Papers Project, Columbia, S.C.; Pierce Butler to Mrs. Izard, Feb. 25, 1797, Pierce Butler Papers, HSP. See also Margaret Williams to James Spears, Feb. 30, 1783, Miscellaneous Record Book, VV, 213–214, SCDAH.

groups suffered no family disruptions—many certainly did, but presumably the chances were minimized when exactly half of all deeded slaves were transferred in groups of five or more. The ages of children were rarely mentioned, but, in one case at least, there was no apparent prohibition against separating a young child from her mother, for Mary Hancock of Saint Paul Parish gave her niece a slave boy named Stephen who was a mere one and a half years old.[31]

In South Carolina, slave sales follow a similar pattern to deeds of gifts in being composed mostly of groups. Between 1753 and 1763, 580 slaves were sold in South Carolina. Almost three-fourths were sold in groups: 13 percent were sold in family groups (61 mothers and their children, with 5 apparently unrelated slaves and 7 in a couple of two-parent families), and 60 percent were sold in groups that mixed men and women and boys and girls. In the case of sales, just under half of all slaves were purchased in groups of five or more slaves. Moreover, upon their sale, slaves were more than twice as likely to stay in their locale as to be moved to a new parish. Masters rarely mention the precise age of a slave to be sold. But, if known ages are representative, then masters were much readier to separate adolescents from their mothers than young children. Five youths, ranging in age from ten to sixteen, were sold separately, as compared to only one child, a three-year-old.[32]

If runaway slave advertisements are any clue, a significant minority of slaves in both Chesapeake and Lowcountry experienced at least one change of ownership, with the Lowcountry revealing a more widespread turnover. A third of runaways listed in colonial South Carolina's newspapers and a fifth of those mentioned in colonial Virginia newspapers had former owners. Too much should not be made of this comparison, for masters were under no obligation to report a slave's former masters. Some might have thought the information irrelevant. Even so, the scale of turnover is striking, particularly when the extreme youthfulness of the fugitive population is considered. Most changes of ownership occurred relatively early in a fugitive's life. The figures, therefore, understate ownership turnover among the larger slave population. As for the

31. Mary Hancock's deed of gift, Oct. 10, 1758, Miscellaneous Records, LL, 100, SCDAH; analysis of all the deeds of gift and marital agreements in Miscellaneous Record Books, KK, LL (covering the period 1746–1763).

32. George Eiland's deed of sale, Nov. 6, 1755, Miscellaneous Record Book, KK, 250–251 (10-year-old boy); Samuel Strother's deed of sale, May 30, 1757, ibid., 485 (12-year-old boy); Thomas Buer's deed of sale, Feb. 12, 1759, ibid., LL, 142–143 (16-year-old boy); James Laden's deed of sale, July 11, 1760, ibid., 372 (14-year-old boy, native of Gambia); John Stevenson's deed of sale, Aug. 10, 1761, ibid., 405 (12-year-old "country born" girl); John Collins's deed of sale, July 15, 1760, ibid., 402 (3-year-old boy); analysis of sales in Miscellaneous Record Books, KK, LL. The locations of purchasers and sellers are mentioned in more than half the cases: 214 slaves were sold within the same parish, and 107 were sold to a master in a new parish.

effect on slave families, only an educated guess is possible. Perhaps many slaves remained in the same neighborhood even when changing owners. A fifteen-year-old boy named July had three changes of ownership in his short life but remained in the same parish. Yet the odds surely were that a sale or a bequest would separate a slave from some loved ones and familiar surroundings.[33]

Although slave families became more stable over time in both the Lowcountry and the Chesapeake, the course of family stability followed different trajectories in the two regions. In both societies, slave families seem to have enjoyed greater stability over time, as masters came to recognize the usefulness, if not the legitimacy, of slave family life. Similarly, in both regions family continuity was greater on large than on small estates. But in the first half of the century, heavier immigration, more Africans, and a younger slave society meant that slave families were harder to create and maintain in the Lowcountry than in the Chesapeake. During the third quarter of the eighteenth century, however, and certainly by its last quarter, larger plantations and less disruptive sales and bequests facilitated greater continuity among South Carolina slave families than among those in Virginia. These differential improvements, however, were always constrained by severe limits. Every slave family floated, in Willie Lee Rose's evocative phrase, "on the precarious raft of [a master's] good will." If obstacles were encountered—a financial crisis, a loss of favor, the master's demise—a family could founder. At each wreckage, slaves were made painfully aware of the perils they faced.

MOVING AND STAYING

The degree to which slaves were mobile affected the stability of their families. Two complementary propositions deserve investigation. On one hand, if slaves were relatively immobile, in the sense of not being moved long distances once on North American soil, then the development of extensive kin connections ought to have been enhanced. On the other hand, if slaves were relatively mobile, in the sense of the ability to move off a plantation, then they ought to have been able to visit relations and establish ties beyond the confines of their estates. Slave family life, then, can be understood only within the larger context of internal migration and local mobility.

Many eighteenth-century slaves lived for long periods in the same locality. In the Chesapeake, well-to-do slaveholders, who owned most slaves, were less mobile than their poorer neighbors. For instance, between 1736 and 1749, more

33. In colonial South Carolina, slightly more than 1,150 runaways were said to have had two or more masters; the Virginia figures are derived from Lathan Algerna Windley, "A Profile of Runaway Slaves in Virginia and South Carolina from 1730 through 1787" (Ph.D. diss., University of Iowa, 1974), 133, who reports 286 slaves as having former owners, or 22% of 1,276 fugitives; Thomas Ladson, *SCG and CJ,* Mar. 29, 1774 (July).

than two-thirds of Amelia County's original settlers left the county. Yet only a quarter of the slaveholders left, and they took about the same proportion of the county's slaves with them. In other words, the vast majority of the slaves remained in the county during this thirteen-year period. In Prince George's County, Maryland, only about one in ten of the migrants who left between 1733 and 1743 owned slaves. Also in Maryland, in Montgomery County's last tobacco frontier, between 1776 and 1783, about three-quarters of the slaves stayed on the same plantations. Two-thirds of those who remained in Prince Edward County between 1782 and 1792 held slaves, whereas only two-fifths of the outmigrants were slaveowners. Because poorer whites generally moved more readily than their wealthier counterparts, and because wealthy planters owned most slaves, blacks were almost certainly more sedentary than lower-class whites. This does not mean that all slaves were immune to the westward movement characteristic of so many Americans; it does mean, however, that slaves were one of the least mobile sectors of the population—in the eighteenth century, at least.[34]

In colonial South Carolina, too, many slaves lived and died in the same parish. The one locality for which it is possible to measure persistence and outmigration—admittedly, in the most rudimentary fashion—is the parish of Saint John Berkeley. On the basis of annual lists of masters owning adult male slaves, about 40 percent of slaveholders disappeared between 1762 and 1772. Some certainly died without issue during the decade, but the rate of outmigration for established residents must have been high. However, the masters who made an appearance on the first, but not the second, list held only a quarter of the parish's adult male slaves. Even though many slaveholders disappeared, then, as many as three-quarters of the male slaves might have remained in the parish between 1762 and 1772.[35]

Other evidence supports the conclusion that slaves were relatively immobile. A highly imperfect and indirect proxy for the rate of internal migration among eighteenth-century North American slaves is a regional growth rate. If

---

34. Michael Lee Nicholls, "Origins of the Virginia Southside, 1703–1753: A Social and Economic Study" (Ph.D. diss., College of William and Mary, 1972), 112–115; Kulikoff, *Tobacco and Slaves*, 92–93, 96–99, 145–148, 159–160; Todd H. Barnett, "Tobacco, Planters, Tenants, and Slaves: A Portrait of Montgomery County in 1783," *MHM*, LXXXIX (1994), 184–203, esp. 194.

35. Records of the Commissioners of the High Roads of St. John's Parish, Berkeley, 1760–1853, SCHS. Between 1762 and 1772, I count 37 slaveholders as possible outmigrants; they reported 289 slave men in 1762. Eight slaveholders also disappeared between 1762 and 1772, but their family names remained in the parish, so I assume that their 106 slaves descended to other family members and stayed within the parish. The remaining 47 masters who are present on both lists report 740 slaves in 1762 and 940 slaves in 1772.

some regions were growing much faster than others, it seems a reasonable presumption that some slaves were being shifted from one to the other. In late colonial South Carolina, the Santee and Georgetown regions to the north of Charleston, the Beaufort region to the south, and the backcountry region to the west experienced the largest upsurges in their black populations. Indigo culture spread rapidly throughout the Sea Islands and inland regions during these years, and the shift to tidewater rice culture impelled a search for virgin coastal soils. Recently imported Africans supplied the bulk of this growing demand for labor, but a few thousand slaves—it is impossible to be more precise—were moved from the Ashley-Cooper River region to the more distant and rapidly growing settlements. Although slavery was growing most rapidly in the backcountry in the late colonial era, about nine of every ten slaves remained in the Lowcountry on the eve of the American Revolution. The institution made substantial inroads into the interior only in the last few decades of the eighteenth century; by 1800, a third of South Carolina's slaves lived in the backcountry. For most of the eighteenth century, therefore, slavery spread north and south but always hugged the coast.[36]

Even in the Chesapeake, where forced migration was far more substantial than in the Lowcountry, only a minority of slaves was required to move. Whereas rice and indigo tied Lowcountry slaves to the coast, tobacco's insatiable thirst for new land impelled a rapid dispersion of Chesapeake slaves into the interior. The first trickle of slaves into the piedmont occurred in the 1720s; within a generation, the trickle had become a stream, so that, by 1755, about forty thousand slaves resided in the region; over the course of another generation, the stream became a deluge as the number of slaves almost tripled. Virginia emerged from the Revolutionary war with more slaves living in the piedmont than in the tidewater. Between 1755 and 1782, about twenty thousand tidewater slaves—about a fifth of the region's bondpeople—were transferred west of the fall line.[37]

Compared to nineteenth-century southern slaves, relatively few eighteenth-century African Americans were forced to move long distances. Only when the expansion of cotton took hold in the last decade of the eighteenth century did large numbers of tidewater slaves have to trek great distances westward. The migration associated with the expansion of tobacco production into the piedmont region of the Chesapeake and of rice and indigo cultivation into the far

36. On the proportion of slaves in the Lowcountry in the second half of the 18th century, see my "Black Society in the Lowcountry," in Berlin and Hoffman, eds., *Slavery and Freedom*, 85.

37. Morgan and Nicholls, "Slaves in Piedmont Virginia," *WMQ*, 3d Ser., XLVI (1989), 211–251; Philip D. Morgan, "Slave Life in Piedmont Virginia, 1720–1800," in Carr, Morgan, and Russo, eds., *Chesapeake Society*, 435–437.

reaches of Lowcountry and inland Carolina should not be minimized, for these two migration streams (the tidewater migration more consequential than the Lowcountry movement) undoubtedly disrupted the lives of many eighteenth-century blacks. However, in the eighteenth century at least, neither region experienced a wholesale uprooting of slaves.[38]

Rather, over time, a growing number of slaves spent their childhood and much of their adult life in the same locale. Perhaps none more so than Sam and Philander, who, as their master put it, were "both born in my kitchen" and had not strayed far from it by the time they reached thirty. Or Peg, aged about fifteen or sixteen, who, according to her master, "was born where I live, and never was 5 miles from home." Masters commonly spoke of slaves' being "born and bred" or "bred and raised" in particular locales. Colin Campbell described his slave Solomon in the archetypal terms of the day as one who "was born in my family." By the late colonial period, some slaves could trace their antecedents back many decades within the same plantation family, as witness John Moultrie's refusal to sell his faithful servants "brought up for several generations in our family." Belonging to a particular "family of negroes" is a strong indication of growing family continuity. Many slaves displayed strong attachments to particular neighborhoods: some ran away to avoid being moved; others, once sold, returned to their old haunts almost immediately; and yet others sold long distances hankered for old surroundings.[39]

Evidence from two Chesapeake neighborhoods can illustrate how slaves, by staying put, were able to create dense networks of affiliation. Because many of the Burwells entailed slaves and attached groups of slaves to particular tracts, by midcentury more than three hundred Burwell slaves resided on a handful of family plantations and quarters all within a five-mile radius of Carter's Grove, just east of Williamsburg, Virginia. Some of these slaves, Lorena Walsh notes, "shared family connections . . . as close as those of the Burwell clan on whose land they lived and labored." Even when the Burwells began moving their

---

38. Kulikoff, *Tobacco and Slaves,* 359–360; Allan Kulikoff, "Migration in the Age of the American Revolution," in Berlin and Hoffman, eds., *Slavery and Freedom,* 143–171.

39. Jonathan Scott, *SC and AGG,* Jan. 19, 1776 (Sam and Philander); Richard Hipkins, *VaG* (Pinkney), Jan. 12, 1775 (Peg); Francis Pelot, *SCG and CJ,* Feb. 8, 1774 ("born and bred"), H. Dixon, *VaG* (P and D), Feb. 11, 1768 ("bred and raised"); Colin Campbell, *VaG* (Rind), June 30, 1768; John Moultrie to James Grant, June 17, 1783, Papers of General James Grant of Ballindalloch, 0771/261; David Yeats to James Grant, Aug. 7, 1776, ibid., 0771/250; William Richardson to Thomas Hutson, Aug. 28, 1780, Hutson Family Papers, SCHS, and Wilbur H. Siebert, ed., *Loyalists in East Florida, 1774 to 1785* (DeLand, Fla., 1929), II, 134 (to avoid a move); Philip Tidyman, *SCG,* Mar. 14, 1774 (immediate return); James Scott, *VaG* (Purdie), May 1, 1778, Peterfield Trent, *VaG* (P and D), Dec. 1, 1774, Cuthburt Bullitt, ibid. (Rind), Nov. 8, 1770 (hankerings).

slaves westward in the mid-1760s, they generally moved them to the same area. At about the same time, a few hundred slaves in southern Maryland had their own sense of generational continuity. This clan—the Butlers—traced its origins to the marriage between a white servant woman and an African man about a century earlier. The descendants of the original couple had been distributed among numerous white family members, but most continued to live within striking distance of one another in Charles and Saint Mary's Counties. Although slave families were often split up, they still lived close enough that many of them could visit one another. A hundred years later, they recalled details of the original wedding ceremony, clearly preserving and transmitting their family history.[40]

Most eighteenth-century slaves, then, did not make long treks westward. Indeed, compared to the lower orders of early modern England or the nonslaveholders of eighteenth-century British America, eighteenth-century African American slaves appear rather *immobile*. English servants generally changed jobs and locales every year; the yeoman farmers and poor whites of colonial North America moved long distances readily. These two groups moved voluntarily, of course, and were spared forced family separations. Nevertheless, in terms of sheer mobility, lower-class whites often tramped long distances, whereas slaves largely stayed put, at least when on North American soil. Indeed, when one historian, familiar with the extensive servant mobility characteristic of early modern England, took a look at the situation of American slaves, he pronounced them "servants forbidden to move." In the nineteenth century, Frederick Douglass drew a significant contrast between the "attachment to place" exhibited by slaves and by free people. Those who were free "to come and go, and to be here and there," Douglass contended, developed no "extravagant attachment to any one place." The slave, in contrast, "was a fixture, he had no choice, no goal but was pegged down to one single spot, and must take root there or die." Douglass was more right than he knew, for his

---

40. Lorena S. Walsh, "A 'Place in Time' Regained: A Fuller History of Colonial Chesapeake Slavery through Group Biography," in Larry E. Hudson, Jr., ed., *Working toward Freedom: Slave Society and Domestic Economy in the American South* (Rochester, N.Y., 1994), 1–32 (quotation on 12); petition of *Mary Butler* v. *Adam Craig,* 1784, Papers of the General Court for the Western Shore, 1787, MHR. The case has been analyzed by Norton, Gutman, and Berlin, "Afro-American Family," in Berlin and Hoffman, eds., *Slavery and Freedom,* 190–191, and most fully by Lorena S. Walsh, "Rural African Americans in the Constitutional Era in Maryland, 1776–1810," *MHM,* LXXXIV (1989), 335. The rash of freedom suits that occurred in the Chesapeake in the late 18th and early 19th centuries is especially revealing of familial memories, with some able to trace descent over many generations. For one example, see Eric Robert Papenfuse, "From Recompense to Revolution: Mahoney v. Ashton and the Transfiguration of Maryland Culture, 1791–1802," *Slavery and Abolition,* XV (1994), 38–62.

observation held particularly true for the eighteenth century, when most slaves sank deep roots in particular locales.[41]

If eighteenth-century slaves generally stayed put, they were not confined to their plantations. Slaves moved off their home quarters far more readily than a perusal of slave codes, with their strictures about passes and patrols, would ever suggest. Visiting neighboring slaves on weekends, at night, even during workdays was much more common than the stereotypical picture of isolated plantations allows. If slaves were remarkably *immobile* in the sense of internal migration, they seem to have been remarkably *mobile* in the sense of short-distance, local movements. This local mobility could pave the way for more prolonged absences.

Sunday visiting was widespread among eighteenth-century slaves. In the Chesapeake, whites grumbled about the "continual concourse of Negroes on Sabboth and holy days" and the "great Crowds of Negroes that assemble together." In the Lowcountry, such complaints were muted, probably because, with far fewer whites around, Sunday visiting went largely unnoticed. Thus, the South Carolina Council learned only indirectly of a group of slaves setting out one Sunday afternoon, traveling fifteen miles in two canoes, and reaching another plantation "soon after dark." Along the way, these would-be revelers met a number of slaves belonging to different plantations and invited them to a dance. Significantly, a prime mover in the expedition was a slave who had a brother at the plantation where the dance was being held.[42]

Slaves did not confine their jaunts to the weekends, for, as Ebenezer Pettigrew shrewdly observed of his slaves, "Night is their day." The construction of a road, leading close by his door, led one Maryland planter to complain of the many "Negroes and other loose persons, going the said Road at all Hours of

---

41. Laslett, *Family Life and Illicit Love,* 259; Frederick Douglass, *Life and Times of Frederick Douglass, Written by Himself...* (New York, 1855), 97.

42. William Hand Browne et al., eds., *Archives of Maryland* (Baltimore, 1883–), XXXVIII, 48, and Somerset County Judicials, 1707, 1711, MHR, as quoted in Russell R. Menard, "The Maryland Slave Population, 1658 to 1730: A Demographic Profile of Blacks in Four Counties," *WMQ,* 3d Ser., XXXII (1975), 37; Browne et al., eds., *Archives of Maryland,* XLIV, 647, as quoted in Carville V. Earle, *The Evolution of a Tidewater Settlement System: All Hallow's Parish, Maryland, 1650–1783,* University of Chicago Department of Geography Research Paper, no. 170 (Chicago, 1975), 161; *The Journal of Nicholas Cresswell, 1774–1777* (New York, 1924), 18; correspondence of the President, Mar. 21, 1709, CO5/1316, fol. 167; Lunenburg County, Nov. 21, 1763, VHS; Jasper W. Cross, "John Miller's Missionary Journals—1816–1817: Religious Conditions in the South and Midwest," *Journal of Presbyterian History,* XLVII (1969), 234; South Carolina Council Journal, no. 17, part 1, 47–168, SCDAH; Philip D. Morgan and George D. Terry, "Slavery in Microcosm: A Conspiracy Scare in Colonial South Carolina," *Southern Studies,* XXI (1982), 121–145.

the Night." A Virginia planter discovered that his "people" were "rambling about every night" when his horses revealed the tell-tale effects of hard riding. Another Virginia master complained of the "night walking" of one of his slaves for the purposes of "drinking and whoring." A Savannah River planter described the many slaves who visited his plantation "by land and water in the night-time," some of whom were "so audacious as to debauch his very house wenches." When one of his carpenters went lame, Landon Carter devised a telling punishment: "I have forbid him coming home to his wife at night," he noted smugly, "and shall have him watched for they cannot work for me cannot without great deceit walk 2 or 3 miles in the night." Under cover of darkness, slaves played, danced, visited "night shops," traded, and committed crimes, but above all they rambled about, visiting friends and relatives. These nightly peregrinations were a fact of life. Richard Parkinson's lament that "though you have them slaves all the day, they are not so in the night" must have been echoed by many a planter.[43]

Any picture of the eighteenth-century landscape must make room for knots of slaves shepherding livestock, running errands, taking goods to market, venturing into the countryside, attending weekend meetings, and visiting at night. Even an occasional slave on horseback or a number of slaves in a canoe would not be out of place. Eighteenth-century plantations might have aspired to self-sufficiency, but they were never self-contained. Indeed, perhaps blacks ought to be accorded a significant role in that venerable Southern institution, plantation visiting. When, in 1758, smallpox hit the DeSaussure household, which also served as a tavern, the governor of South Carolina dispatched a party of soldiers with particular orders "to prevent any Negro or Negroes belonging to DeSaussure from going out of the Bounds of his Plantation, and any other Negro or Negroes from coming to them." Eighteenth-century residences, in other words, were notable for their openness, their permeability; and this extended to blacks as much as to whites.[44]

Rambling at night, caballing at weekends, even occupational mobility could all pave the way for prolonged absences. The practice of "petit marronage"— repetitive or periodic truancy—was rife throughout the plantation colonies. A

---

43. Sarah McCulloh Lemon, ed., *The Pettigrew Papers,* I (Raleigh, N.C., 1971), 398; Anne Arundel County Judgments, 1B, no. 4, fols. 394–395, as quoted in Earle, *Tidewater Settlement System,* 161; John Tayloe to Landon Carter, Mar. 31, 1771, Carter Papers, UVa; Edward Miles Riley, ed., *The Journal of John Harrower, an Indentured Servant in the Colony of Virginia, 1773–1776* (Williamsburg, Va., 1963), 92; and George Weedon's Account Book, June 12, 1775, CW; Greene, ed., *Carter Diary,* 348, 396–397, 442, 579, 583, 927, 1063; Patrick Mackay, *Ga Gaz,* Sept. 22, 1763; Parkinson, *A Tour in America,* II, 420.

44. Governor Lyttleton to Capt. John Stewart, July 11, 1758, Governor Lyttleton Letterbook, 152–153, photostat, SCDAH.

considerable number of advertised runaways were said to be visiting acquaintances, friends, or relatives. In South Carolina, those attempting to maintain contact with family and friends outnumbered those attempting to pass as free by about four to one. Although this predominance was not matched in the Chesapeake, about half of the advertised runaways in southern Maryland and more than a third in Virginia were also said to be attempting to stay with friends or kinfolk. Visiting, rather than any simplistic equation of running away with resistance, merits investigation. Visiting is most significant for revealing the range, strength, and tragic dimensions of kin attachments under slavery. In many runaway advertisements, masters can be heard surmising why their slaves left, whom they had gone to see, what they hoped to gain. Much can be learned about the deepest concerns and heartfelt aspirations of slaves.[45]

The predominance of men among runaways can be explained in part by the absence of binding family ties and the attractions of finding mates. Men far outnumbered women among advertised runaways: by more than four to one in South Carolina, by eight to one in Virginia, and by ten to one in southern Maryland. Moreover, about two-thirds of the male runaways from all three colonies were in their twenties and early thirties (see Figure 9). Men were much less "faithfully attached to the glebe," as one master put it—or, to put it another way, less encumbered by children—than women. Furthermore, it was surely no accident that the ages most highly represented among male runaways coincided with those years when they were in search of mates. Some women ran away for the same reasons—one fifteen-year-old was thought "to have gone a courting," while Phillippa went "a-sweethearting at Jacksonburgh, where her mother Amey lives"—but the shortage of women always made it more likely that men would be the most active searchers of mates. An overseer in East Florida penetrated to the heart of the matter when he observed to his owner that a shortage of young women on the plantation induced the young men to absent "themselves after the wenches in town." Similarly, the author of a proposal for draining parts of the Dismal Swamp envisaged a gang of slaves

---

45. For the predominance of visiting in South Carolina, see my "En Caroline du Sud: marronage et culture servile," *Annales: Economies, sociétés, civilisations,* XXXVII (1982), 574–590, a revised and translated version of which is "Colonial South Carolina Runaways: Their Significance for Slave Culture," in *Slavery and Abolition,* VI (1985), 57–78 (also accessible in Gad Heuman, ed., *Out of the House of Bondage: Runaways, Resistance, and Marronage in Africa and the New World* [London, 1986], 57–78), and "Black Society in the Lowcountry," in Berlin and Hoffman, eds., *Slavery and Freedom,* 130. For southern Maryland, see Kulikoff, *Tobacco and Slaves,* 379. For Virginia, see Mullin, *Flight and Rebellion,* 108, 129. But, in Virginia, masters often reported the former master or residence of a runaway; this was usually meant to indicate probable destination. Adding these numbers to those said to be visiting makes the Virginia runaway destinations much more comparable to those from Maryland than first appears.

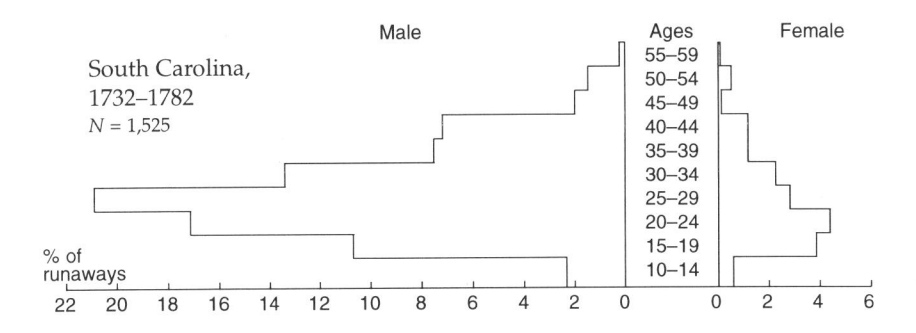

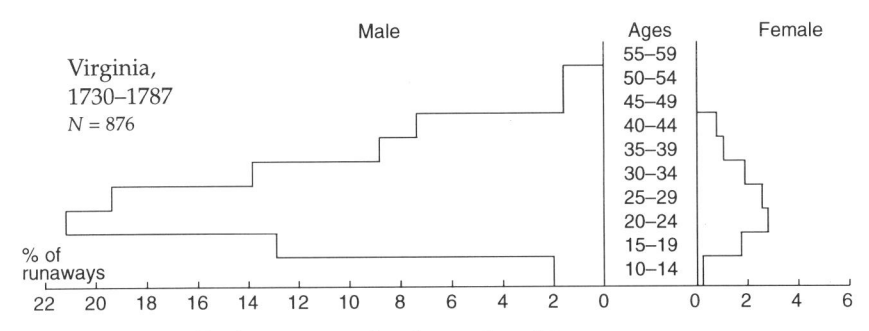

FIGURE 9. *Age Profile of Runaways in the Chesapeake and Lowcountry, 1732– 1787*
Sources: South Carolina: fugitives and captives advertised in South Carolina newspapers, 1732–1782, microfilm edition of Charleston Library Society.
   Virginia: Latham Algerna Windley, "A Profile of Runaway Slaves in Virginia and South Carolina from 1730 through 1787" (Ph.D. diss., University of Iowa, 1974). I estimated the sex breakdown of each age category.

in which the men would have wives because families would keep the men "at home, and prevent their rambleing abroad anights."[46]

Runaway slaves also speak directly—and painfully—to the subject of broken family ties. Of the colonial South Carolina runaways whose intentions were specified by masters, 30 percent were thought to be visiting relatives from whom they had been separated. Where a relative was identified precisely, the most common aim was to reunite with a wife or a husband. Cuffee's flight was, his mistress acknowledged, "occasion'd by his Wife and Child's being sold from him"; the very evening that an African woman named Patt ran away she was seen in company with her husband; an iron collar with two protruding prongs failed to deter Rose from fleeing to her husband, to whom "she [was]

---

46. Earl of Egmont to James Grant, May 14, 1769, Papers of General James Grant of Ballindalloch, 0771/264; Workhouse, *SCG*, Aug. 17, 1765; George Cuhun, *SC and AGG*, Nov. 5, 1778; David Yeats to James Grant, Feb. 3, 1781, Papers of General James Grant of Ballindalloch, 0771/250; A Description of the Dismal Swamp, n.d. [late 18th–early 19th century], Vernon-Wager MSS, Peter Force Collection, LC.

very much attached." Running away to visit parents was also common, and some of these flights indicate the early age at which parents and children could be separated. Thus, twelve-year-old Jack was "supposed to be harboured by his father Cupid," from whom he had been torn; fifteen-year-old August had been put up for sale at least twice in his short life, but he had not forgotten his mother and other relatives, who still belonged to his first owner and to whom he ran away. Some parents even ran away to visit young children: perhaps the master of Sue, a mother in her early twenties, felt a pang of guilt when she ran away to see her child at another master's plantation, for he put it about that she would be forgiven if she returned of her own accord. Most commonly, slaves were said to have many relations from whom they had been separated. Sold at public vendue on July 6, 1767, Ned ran away twice within the next four months in order to reunite with his mother, wife, and children, who remained at his former residence.[47]

Of those fugitives said to be visiting relatives, a larger proportion in the Chesapeake than in the Lowcountry were thought to be rejoining a spouse. The pervasiveness of cross-plantation marriages in the Chesapeake probably accounts for this difference. Authorized visits of one spouse to another encouraged more prolonged absences. Thus, Davy, who belonged to John Verrell of Sussex County, had "leave to go to see his wife, who lives at Mr. Cornelius Lostin's, in this county," but then decided to extend his stay and "lurk ... about in that neighborhood"; similarly, Aberdeen of Chesterfield County, who had a wife belonging to John Parke Custis back in King and Queen County, where he used to live, was thought to have run away to her, "as he would sometimes stay a Month there when [his master] gave him Liberty to go and see his Wife." Where ownership of a slave couple was divided, marriages were easily broken and running away became the only way to be reunited.[48]

---

47. Peter Timothy (for Catherine Cattell), *SCG*, Mar. 13, 1749 (Cuffee); Stephen Drayton, *SC and AGG*, Nov. 20, 1769 (Patt); S. Spurr, *City Gaz*, June 20, 1797 (Rose); John Lampert, *SCG*, Aug. 23, 1760 (Jack); William Burrows, ibid., May 16, 1774, Supplement (August); John Milkigan, *City Gaz*, Feb. 14, 1798 (Sue); Peter Sanders, ibid., Nov. 24, 1767 (Ned). Between 1732 and 1782, masters in South Carolina specified intentions for 1,056 runaways; 323, or 31%, were thought to be visiting relatives. Of these 323, 32% were thought to be visiting a spouse, 18% a parent, 7% a brother or sister, 2% a son or daughter, and the remaining 41% a number of relatives, referred to either specifically or vaguely as "several" or "many."

48. John Verrell, *VaG* (P and D), Sept. 6, 1770; William Black, ibid. (D and H), Dec. 5, 1777. See also Baylor Banks, *Va Ind Chron and GA*, Mar. 10, 1790; William Skipwith, *VaG* (Hunter), Feb. 28, 1755; Walker Taliaferro, ibid. (Rind), Oct. 5, 1769; William Alexander, ibid. (D and N), May 1, 1779; James Mason, *VaG* (C and D), Aug. 28, 1779. Between 1736 and 1779 masters in Virginia specified intentions for 370 runaways; 110, or 30%, were thought to be visiting relatives. Of these 110, 54% were thought to be visiting a spouse, 14% a parent, 6% a brother or sister, 3% a son or daughter, and the remaining 23% a number of relatives.

Many absentees were able to spend time, often long periods, with their kinfolk. Topsam was especially persistent. In the spring of 1749, then aged ten, he lurked about Hobcaw near Charleston in the company of his parents, who were also fugitives. Topsam's master had recently died, and he and his parents no doubt feared separation. Their fears were realized, for, six months later, Topsam was the property of John Cattell and again a fugitive, probably revisiting his parents. Almost twenty years elapsed before Cattell resorted to a further advertisement for Topsam. Not that Topsam, now twenty-eight years old, had been inactive in the intervening years, for his master referred to him as a habitual runaway; indeed, on one occasion, Topsam had apparently spent thirteen months at a plantation belonging to a Mr. Whiteside. In May 1767, therefore, Cattell expected Topsam to make for that same plantation; eight months later, Topsam was still at large and at Whiteside's, or so his master believed. The Whiteside plantation was located at Hobcaw, the site of Topsam's childhood flight. And Cattell had a good idea who was harboring his slave: none other than Topsam's father, Bristol, who had been purchased by Whiteside when Cattell bought Topsam. In May 1770, Topsam had an even more daunting journey ahead of him, for he now lived in Georgia as the property of Josiah Tatnell, who had purchased him from Cattell. Tatnell predicted that Topsam would return to South Carolina and, in particular, to the Cattell plantation. In July, sure enough, Topsam turned up in Charleston but was expected to make his way to Hobcaw, "where he has some relations." Topsam was nothing if not predictable: his filial bond had survived twenty years, several sales, and long geographic distance.[49]

Over time, slave kinship networks expanded, and masters consequently had trouble pinpointing the whereabouts of many of their runaways. The master of twenty-three-year-old Tom, a resident of Caroline County, Virginia, named four sites in four counties ranging from the mid-reaches of the Potomac River to the mouth of the Rappahannock River, where he "may meet with some Assistance" from his "many relations." Abraham, who ran away from Manchester in Chesterfield County, was thought to be harbored either by his wife at one quarter or by several relations at another in King William County or by other relations at two separate plantations in Hanover County. The wife of a runaway married couple in South Carolina had a mother and sister at William Bull's plantation on the Ashley River, a sister at Thomas Holman's, several relations at Doctor Lining's, and a brother at Mr. William Elliott's. The master thought that there was "great reason" to believe they were being harbored but by whom it was difficult to say. Increasingly, masters began to refer less to

---

49. The Printer, *SCG*, Apr. 17, 1749; John Cattell, ibid., Oct. 23, 1749; *SCG and CJ*, Aug. 4, 1767, Jan. 12, 1768; Josiah Tatnell, ibid., May 22, July 3, 1770.

specific relatives who might support their runaways but more generally to "a numerous Stock of Relations" scattered throughout the province.[50]

Visiting had its origins in innumerable tragic family separations, but it reflected slaves' determination to overcome those separations as best they could. The practice owed much to the sexual imbalances on Lowcountry plantations, to the small size of Chesapeake quarters, and most particularly to estate sales and divisions that scattered kinfolk across the land. Slaves were forced to visit in order to maintain contact with relatives. And yet this enforced scattering of kinfolk led many slaves, like the three runaways belonging to one South Carolina master, to have "a long train of acquaintances and relations" both nearby and distant upon whom they could count for support. The emergence of these kinship and friendship networks served to succor and sustain those in need, to supply a sense of order, predictability, and belonging in a world that otherwise seemed capricious and alien.[51]

THE SIGNIFICANCE OF KIN

It is one thing to have kinfolk around, but it is another entirely to recognize and regulate relationships with them in such a way as to demonstrate their significance. When slaves can be shown to be aware of, and openly making use of, kin ties, it is possible to speak of a kinship system coming into being and of its being passed from one generation to the next. Visiting is important, then, because it provides one measure of the quality of kinship relationships among slaves. To explore further the meaning attached to kin, four relationships are worth investigating in more detail: husbands and wives, parents and children, siblings, and extended kin. By way of conclusion, the possible African influences on this emerging kinship system can then be assessed.[52]

Although slave unions were put under extraordinary pressure by slavery, marriage was a vital institution in the slave community. In general, slaves chose their own marital partners. When Henry Laurens sent one young woman to his Mepkin plantation, he told the overseer to allow her "to be a Wife to whome she shall like the best amongst the single men." Slaves acted not only independently but with dispatch. Two "New Negroes," bought in South Carolina and destined for an East Florida plantation, "chose each other for man and wife" before they arrived. As she was being transferred from one of John

---

50. Thomas Jones, *VaG* (Rind), Feb. 6, 1772; Edward Johnson, ibid. (D and H), May 23, 1777; Thomas Tucker, *SCG*, Feb. 17, 1759; Brian Cape, ibid., Jan. 25, 1772. Better communications and more far-flung kin may help explain the greater distances traveled by runaways over time.

51. John Dawson, *Gaz of State of SC*, Oct. 3, 1779.

52. Laslett, *Family Life and Illicit Love*, 260.

Carter's quarters to another, a Virginia girl fell ill and "before there was another opportunity of sending her" got one of the "Negro fellows for her husband." The rather perfunctory nature of slave courtship is also suggested in an incident on Robert Carter's estate. One Monday, Abraham of Dickerson Mill quarter visited Gemini quarter and "prevailed" with Milly "to go with him" back to his quarter "he calling Milly his wife." Carter consented to the transfer. In fact, masters rarely interfered. David Ross spoke for many when he declared that his "young people might connect themselves in marriage, to their own liking," although he added, "with consent of their parents who were the best judges." Most young slaves, then, acted voluntarily; rarely were they forced into marriage by a master; they required a master's consent but apparently parental consent, too.[53]

Particularly common in the Chesapeake was the slave who came to a master to ask permission to marry another owner's slave. In 1789, Frank did precisely this, asking "leave" of his master, Colonel Francis Taylor of Orange County, to "have Miss M. Conway's Pat for a Wife." Taylor employed Frank as his messenger and errand-runner, a valuable slave whose wishes ought to be respected if possible and who already traveled off the plantation. Thus Taylor "did not object," particularly when Frank told him that he "had the necessary consent" from Miss Conway. Frank must have anticipated his master's approval, because he had already arranged the wedding for the following evening.[54]

The ceremonial element of slave marriages was necessarily constrained. The origins of the nineteenth-century custom of "jumping the broomstick"—as a way of signifying a marriage—may well lie in the eighteenth century, but no trace of its existence has been found. One of the few firsthand observations is rather dismissive of any ritualistic quality to slave marriages. John Brickell, the historian of early North Carolina, explained that slave marriages were "generally performed amongst themselves, there being very little ceremony used upon that Head." However, he noted one common feature: "The Man makes the Woman a Present, such as a *Brass Ring* or some other Toy, which if she accepts of, becomes his Wife; but if ever they part from each other which frequently happens, upon any little Disgust, she returns his present." James

---

53. *Laurens Papers*, IV, 148; John Bartram to William Bartram, Apr. 5, 1766, Bartram Family Papers, HSP; John Carter to George Carter, July 6, 1737, Carter-Plummer Letterbook, UVa; Robert Carter Journal, 1784–1789, Jan. 13, 1785, 30, LC (six years later, the couple was still together, parents to four children, one aged four, twins aged three, and the last a six-month-old infant named after his father); Ross to Robert Richardson, Apr. 30, 1812, David Ross Letterbook, 1812–1813, VHS, as cited in Charles B. Dew, "David Ross and the Oxford Iron Works: A Study of Industrial Slavery in the Early Nineteenth-Century South," *WMQ*, 3d Ser., XXXI (1974), 211.

54. Diary of Colonel Francis Taylor, Jan. 30, 1789, VSL.

Barclay, who acted as an overseer on a Lowcountry plantation in the early 1770s, also detected little ceremony, but much conviviality, in slave marriages. Marriages took place at night in his neighborhood, and a couple with many acquaintances might draw "several hundred" slaves from surrounding plantations. The owner often allowed a hog or two, the slaves served land tortoises and rum bought from their Sunday earnings, and the whole night was spent "eating and drinking, singing, dancing, and roaring."[55]

If slave courtships and weddings appeared perfunctory, the same cannot be said of the slaves' view of marriage. When the colony of Virginia demanded a female slave replacement for every man sent to aid South Carolina in the Yamassee War of 1715, Carolinians rejected the request on the grounds that slave husbands might rebel. In 1723, the governor of Virginia thought that transportation would be an effective punishment for the ringleaders of a slave conspiracy because "separation from their wives and children is almost as terrible to them as death itself." A Maryland slave, destined to be taken to Virginia to satisfy a debt, spoke in exactly these terms. He had such "a great Affection" for his family that he "declar'd Several times that he will Loose his life, or had rather Submit to Death then go to Virginia to leave his Wife and Children." When his removal appeared imminent, he asserted that he "had much rather be hang'd than come to Virginia." The loss of a chosen partner was the occasion for grief. When the wife of one of James Habersham's male slaves died, the husband was "inconsolable." Slaves clearly took marriage very seriously.[56]

Within and without marriage, slave women were strong figures. They often brought up their children alone; in that sense, many slave families were matrifocal. Women worked alongside men in the fields, even predominated in some field gangs, which might well have inclined them to think themselves the

55. John Brickell, *The Natural History of North Carolina* (Dublin, 1737), 274; James Barclay, *The Voyages and Travels of James Barclay, Containing Many Surprising Adventures, and Interesting Narratives* (Dublin, 1777), 27; Gutman, *Black Family,* 270–284.

56. Records in the British Public Record Office Relating to South Carolina, 1663–1782, VI, 262–263, SCDAH, as quoted in Wood, *Black Majority,* 128–129; Hugh Drysdale to Commissioners for Trade and Plantations, June 29, 1723, CO5/1319, fol. 115, PRO; Adams to Washington, Mar. 15, 1775, Papers of George Washington, 4th Ser., microfilm, reel 33, Manuscript Division, LC, and Lund Washington to George Washington, Jan. 17, 1776, in possession of the Mount Vernon Ladies' Association, as cited in Lee, "The Problem of Slave Community," *WMQ,* 3d Ser., XLIII (1986), 357; *The Letters of Hon. James Habersham, 1756–1775,* GHS, *Collections,* VI (Savannah, Ga., 1904), 23. See also Betts, ed., *Jefferson's Farm Book,* part 2, 19; Edwin Morris Betts and James Adam Bear, Jr., eds., *The Family Letters of Thomas Jefferson* (Columbia, Mo., 1966), 131; Henry Lee to Col. Robert Goode, May 17, 1792, Executive Letterbook, 1792–1794, 4–5, VSL; and John Sutton to Robert Carter, Apr. 3, 1782, Carter Family Papers.

equals of men. The self-reliance and self-sufficiency of many slave women impressed white contemporaries. Henry Laurens attributed the transgressions of his slave March, who apparently had "a placid and obliging disposition," to his recent "Union" with Mary, a woman of "very great abilities" but who had long been "the bane" of Laurens's "Negro families." Not only had she "corrupted and ruined March," but she had schooled Cuffee, one of her sons, to follow in her footsteps. James Barclay marveled at the hardiness of slave women, many of whom turned out to work the day after childbirth, bearing their infants on their backs. Because slave men lacked much of the power that flows from the ownership and distribution of property, often failed to gain recognition as fathers, and were largely denied the role of provider, a picture of relative equality between the sexes under slavery may be plausible.[57]

If slavery bred strong women, however, it hardly emasculated black men. For one thing, as Jacqueline Jones has argued, the state of powerlessness that affected all slaves renders "virtually meaningless the concept of equality as it applies to marital relations." Furthermore, the male monopoly on most skilled and privileged positions cannot be ignored. Lorena Walsh, speaking of the late-eighteenth-century Chesapeake, wryly observes that black women indeed "shared the doubtful advantages of greater equality with black men—usually the equal privilege of working with hoes and axes in the tobacco, corn, and grain fields." In fact, as men gained opportunities for more varied work, more women spent time in monotonous drudgery. In large part because of their greater work opportunities, men traveled more than women. In divided-residence households, husbands, not wives, were the routine visitors. The growing importance of two-parent, male-centered households is indisputable. The naming practices of families, explored below, suggest the importance of the father and husband. Finally, in most rebellions and conspiracies that did materialize in early America, men rather than women dominated. Virtually no black woman, for example, was implicated in Gabriel's conspiracy in Virginia, and indeed one male conspirator required a recruit not to divulge their secrets to a woman.[58]

---

57. *Laurens Papers*, VIII, 89, 101, 290, XI, 487, 492, 561–562, 565, XIII, 539–540, XIV, 134, 181; Barclay, *Voyages and Travels*, 25.

58. Jacqueline Jones, *Labor of Love, Labor of Sorrow: Black Women, Work, and the Family from Slavery to the Present* (New York, 1985), 42; Lorena S. Walsh, "The Experiences and Status of Women in the Chesapeake, 1750–1775," in Walter J. Fraser, Jr., R. Frank Saunders, Jr., and Jon L. Wakelyn, eds., *The Web of Southern Social Relations: Women, Family, and Education* (Athens, Ga., 1985), 13. For other critiques of slave women as dominant, see Christie Farnham, "Sapphire? The Issue of Dominance in the Slave Family, 1830–1865," in Carol Groneman and Mary Beth Norton, eds., *"To Toil the Livelong Day": America's Women at Work, 1780–1980* (Ithaca, N.Y., 1987), 68–83; and Elizabeth Fox-Genovese, *Within the*

Slave husbands tended to be older than their wives. In the eighteenth-century Chesapeake, eight of ten husbands were older than their wives by an average of nine years. In the few cases in which wives were older than husbands, the age gap was much smaller—an average of four years. Similarly, in the eighteenth-century Lowcountry, seven of ten husbands were older than their wives by an average of eight years, two of ten wives were older than husbands by four years, and in one of ten marriages the spouses were the same age. Such large age differences owed much to the imbalance of the sexes in these two eighteenth-century societies, although African customs might also have played a role, for large age gaps between spouses were commonplace in many African societies. Whatever the origins, the major implication seems clear. In North America (and in Africa, too, it might be added), authority clearly followed age. For better or ill, then, slave husbands were in a more powerful position than their wives.[59]

Masters, in fact, often saw slave husbands as domineering. Perhaps these observations owed something to the patriarchal assumptions of the day, but their very pervasiveness suggests some basis in life. In Virginia, thirty-seven-year-old Charles "took" his nineteen-year-old wife with him when he ran away; Will "carried" away his wife and young child; fifty-year-old Tony and his forty-year-old wife, Phillis, were expected to make for Lancaster because that is

---

Plantation Household: Black and White Women of the Old South (Chapel Hill, N.C., 1988), esp. 48–50. On the masculine world of Gabriel's conspiracy, I have benefited from reading James Sidbury, *Ploughshares into Swords: Race, Rebellion, and Identity in Gabriel's Virginia, 1730–1810* (New York, 1997).

59. The age difference between husbands and wives comes from two sources: plantation listings and runaway slave advertisements. In Virginia, the ages of husbands and wives were reported for 74 couples in the records of the Jones family (1730s), Paul Carrington, Edmund Randolph (1784), Robert Carter (1788), and William Fitzhugh (1810), and for 13 runaway couples in newspaper advertisements between 1736 and 1789. Of these 87, 73 husbands were older than wives by 8.6 years, 12 wives were older than husbands by 4.4 years, and 2 couples were the same age. Similarly, Kulikoff found that on three late-18th-century Maryland plantations, 47 husbands were on average 6.8 years older than their wives (*Tobacco and Slaves*, 374n). In the Lowcountry, the ages of husbands and wives were reported for 151 couples in the plantation listings of Alexander Vanderdussen, George Austin, Samuel Waddingham, Pierce Butler, Hannah Bull, and Colonel Stapleton and for 21 runaway couples in the newspaper advertisements between 1732 and 1799. Of these 172, 126 husbands were older than wives by 8.1 years, 32 wives were older than husbands by 4.4 years, and 14 couples were the same age. The evidence from South Carolina indicates some narrowing of the age difference over time. For remarking on the African evidence, and noting correctly that age differences were much smaller in the 19th century, see Stanley L. Engerman, "Studying the Black Family," *Jour. Fam. Hist.*, III (1978), 96, although also see Wayne K. Durrill, "Slavery, Kinship, and Dominance: The Black Community at Somerset Place Plantation, 1786–1860," *Slavery and Abolition*, XIII (1992), 9; and Malone, *Sweet Chariot*, 169–170, 230.

where *he* wished to return. A master of an African couple, a twenty-year-old man and a sixteen-year-old woman, "imagine[d]" that the wife was "entirely governed" by the husband. Even when the wife was older, the husband apparently assumed the dominant role, for twenty-one-year-old Mack "carried with him" his thirty-three-year-old wife, Molly. Likewise, in South Carolina, husbands appear to have been the dominant partners: Cupid "inticed" his wife to run away; Toby came to Samuel Bonneau's plantation and removed his wife and young child; Binah's husband "persuaded her" to abscond with him.[60]

African beliefs concerning the respective roles of husbands and wives probably contributed to the upper hand held by men. In the Lowcountry, Charles Ball encountered a creole woman named Lydia, who had been "compelled" to marry an African. Her husband was atypical in that he "had been a priest in his own nation, and had never been taught to do any kind of labour." He also claimed to have "had ten wives in his own country, who all had to work for, and wait upon him." As a result, he "refused to give" Lydia "the least assistance in doing anything." Although this African man's view of marriage was probably unusual, it was not singular: Ball noted that Lydia was just "one of the women whose husbands procured little or nothing for the sustenance of their families." Her husband's stipulation that she "do all the little work that it was necessary to perform in the cabin; and also to bear all the labour of weeding and cultivating the family patch or garden" was one apparently shared by other of his countrymen.[61]

Some slave men adopted a cavalier attitude to matrimony itself. When Robert Carter sent three young men to the Baltimore Company ironworks in 1783, he described them to the manager as "all men of gallantry, Polygamists, and they may now want Physick proper in the venereal disease." Similarly, when twenty-one-year-old Jack of Dinwiddie County ran away to Prince George

---

60. Joseph Jones, *VaG* (P and D), May 14, 1767 (Charles); Francis Jerdone, *VaG and WA*, Apr. 17, 1784 (Will); Cuthburt Bullitt, *VaG* (Rind), Nov. 8, 1770 (Tony); William Watt, ibid. (P and D), Sept. 10, 1772 (two Africans); Josiah Garey and Lucy Clark, *VaG and WA*, Oct. 30, 1784 (Mack); William Lloyd, *SCG*, Dec. 11, 1756, supplement (Cupid); Samuel Bonneau, *SC and AGG*, July 30, 1778 (Toby); E. McClellan, *City Gaz*, July 13, 1797 (Binah).

61. Ball, *Fifty Years in Chains*, 157, 263–264. This African husband, "a morose, sullen man," "often beat and otherwise maltreated his wife." The overseer "refused to protect her, on the ground, that he never interfered in the family quarrels of the black people." Perhaps, for the same reason, there were few recorded 18th-century rapes by black men on black women. An exception was 19-year-old Christopher, who was found guilty of raping Sarah and sentenced to hang but was later pardoned. Westmoreland County Orders, 1776–1786, 57, VSL; and Robert Carter to Governor Patrick Henry, June 3, 1778, and to Clement Brooke, July 27, 1778, Carter Letterbook, III (3), 35, 45, Duke. For another case, also in Westmoreland, see Thomas D. Morris, *Southern Slavery and the Law, 1619–1860* (Chapel Hill, N.C., 1996), 306.

County in 1777, he was "supported and concealed . . . by several Negro Women whom he calls his Wives; his greatest Favourite amongst them belongs to Robert Bates." In South Carolina, the Reverend Francis Le Jau had trouble with a slave man who "had vowed to keep to his lawful Wife" (the reference to "lawful," a significant comment in itself) but "thro' love for another Man's wife . . . has been quite distracted and furious." Rather than trying to deal with the man, Le Jau significantly attempted to keep the "Adultress" away from him. Other slave men apparently used their privileged occupational status to their advantage. Cambridge was a boatman and had "a wife at almost every landing on Rappahannock, Mattapony, and Pamunkey Rivers"; Billy Barber was a much-traveled waiting man who lived in Urbanna but had a wife in Norfolk and in Hampton as well as in his hometown. Male promiscuity may conceivably reflect an assertion of masculinity in the face of feelings of inadequacy, but it hardly contradicts the domineering demeanor otherwise noted of slave men.[62]

Consider a young slave named Nero who formed liaisons with a number of women in the late-eighteenth-century Lowcountry. In March 1779, John M'Illraith advertised for two runaways from his plantation at Four Holes: Nero and a young woman named Marianne. At about the same time, Martin Pfeniger, also of Four Holes, declared his twenty-year-old woman Bynah missing. In early April, Pfeniger resorted to the advertisement columns yet again to announce the departure of his twenty-four-year-old woman, Cloe, who had been seen with Nero. Finally, a third owner from Four Holes, Thomas Caton, made sense of these seemingly separate scraps of information when he advertised for a twenty-four-year-old woman who had left him in May. According to Caton, the precocious mulatto Nero had "deluded or led away" all these women, "and it is supposed and partly proved by account, that the said fellow supports and provides for them all." For the past six months, Nero and his female companions had been seen at James Island, Sullivan's Island, Saint James Goose Creek, and Charleston. Quite who provided for whom is made less clear when Caton observed that these slaves found employment by washing and ironing for white folk. This was women's work, so perhaps Nero lived off the labors of his consorts.[63]

Finally, although slavery in general denied slave families the ability to func-

---

62. Robert Carter to Clement Brooke, Jan. 7, 1783, Carter Letterbook, V, 91–93, Duke; James French, *VaG* (D and H), Oct. 31, 1777 (Jack); Rev. Francis Le Jau to the SPG, July 10, 1711, A6/103, 318–319; John Holladay, *VaG* (P and D), Apr. 21, 1768 (Cambridge); Bennett Browne, ibid. (D and H), July 15, 1775 (Billy Barber).

63. John M'Illraith, *Gaz of State of SC*, Mar. 17, 1779; Martin Pfeniger, *SC and AGG*, Mar. 18, May 29, 1779; Thomas Caton, ibid., Sept. 10, 1779. For other examples of creole slaves with more than one wife, see James Kennedy, *State Gaz of SC*, Feb. 18, 1790; and Allard Belin, *City Gaz,* May 10, 1797.

tion as self-subsisting units, men were occasionally able to look out for their families. Slave ironworkers in the Chesapeake purchased small luxuries and domestic items for their wives. During the 1730s, one skilled hand at the Baltimore Company ironworks in Maryland used his overwork pay to purchase a bed, two blankets, and a rug for his wife and children. In 1797, a slave named Phil, who worked at John Blair's foundry in Virginia, bought shoe leather and seven and a half yards of ribbon for his wife. Even ordinary field hands could provide for their womenfolk. Charles Ball's father came to see his family on a Saturday night, always bringing "some little present," such as "apples, melons, sweet potatoes, or, if he could procure nothing else, a little parched corn." North Carolina slaves "allowed to plant a sufficient quantity of *Tobacco* for their own use" and to gather snake-root used the proceeds to purchase "*Linnen, Bracelets, Ribbons,* and several other Toys for their Wives and Mistresses." Slave men were not totally bereft of the ability to provide small favors for their women.[64]

What is important to notice, however, no matter which sex provided these small domestic items, is their existence at all. The ability of even unskilled slave families to acquire a little property that they could call their own was important. Consider Caesar and Kate, both born in Virginia in the early 1730s. Neither possessed a skill, although both were "smooth tongued, and very sensible." Of what their domestic life consisted we cannot know, except for two small details. The first may suggest that they enjoyed smoking tobacco together after a long day of field labor, for both had "Teeth somewhat worn with Pipes." The second is more telling, for in 1772, when they decided to abscond together from their home in King William County, they were thought likely to go by water at least part of the way, for they took with them a "Variety of Clothes, and Articles for House keeping not very portable." Even families divided by ownership could own property in common. A slave couple who lived apart in piedmont Virginia still shared possessions, for the wife was convicted of receiving stolen goods from her husband and storing them in his chest, which was in her custody. Similarly, when Jemmy absented himself from the fields one day, wearing only his shirt and trousers, "which were of very good rolls, much wore," by rights his master ought to have been able to provide a good description. However, Jemmy then went to a neighboring plantation, and carried off "other clothes, together with his wife, and a boy of 12 to 14 years old, with all the luggage." Two South Carolina fugitives—Bess and Berwick—were

---

64. Inventory of Ben Tasker at Baltimore Co., 1737, Carroll-Maccubbin Papers, MHS, and Ledger of John Blair, 1795–1797, W and M, as cited in Ronald L. Lewis, "Slave Families at Early Chesapeake Ironworks," *VMHB,* LXXXVI (1978), 172; Ball, *Fifty Years in Chains,* 18; Brickell, *Natural History of North Carolina,* 275.

seen passing through Ponpon on a Monday morning, each on horseback, with their clothes, blankets—and pets! Housekeeping items, substantial furniture, luggage, even pets: slaves would not be denied a semblance of domesticity.[65]

Much more important than taking along a few domestic items, fugitives took family members with them. Many runaways aimed to visit a spouse, but just as significant were those who ran away *with* a spouse. About one in ten of the fugitives advertised in South Carolina and Virginia newspapers ran away with family members. Half of these family groups consisted of a husband and wife, sometimes with children. Although groups were conspicuous and slow-moving, the desire to keep a family together overrode the dangers. Indeed, by the late eighteenth century, slaves even risked moving in larger groups. Thus, in 1784, Polidore and his wife, Betty, together with their three young children, another couple, Cyrus and his wife, Charity, and a woman named Hannah with her son, Job, fled Charleston, apparently hoping to make their way together to Camden. A year later, Robin and his wife, Charity, together with their two young sons and another couple, Jack and his wife, Hannah, all fled the same plantation in Charlotte County, Virginia, apparently with forged passes and in hopes of passing as free people.[66]

Slaves went to extreme lengths to maintain their marriages. Poignantly and expressively, slaves tell us what was dearest to their hearts. None spoke more eloquently than Chesapeake slaves, who faced even more forced separations than their Lowcountry counterparts. When James belonging to Fleet Coxe heard that his wife and two children were about to be removed to Frederick County, he visited her master and proposed that he be exchanged for another male slave so that he might accompany his family. After Christopher Collins bought a slave woman named Judy, he received repeated visits from her husband, Tobit, who made "several applications to me to endeavour to keep him and his wife together." Indeed, Collins observed in a letter written to Tobit's

65. Robert Ruffin, *VaG* (P and D), Sept. 24, 1772; trials of Deborah, Nov. 23, 1743, Feb. 20, 1744, Orange County Court Order Book, 1743–1746, 22–23, 47–48; Augustine Moore, *VaG* (Purdie), June 23, 1775; Roger Pinckney, *SC and AGG*, Mar. 9, 1772. For other slaves with pets, see John Harrison, ibid., May 22, 1776; and Charles Harris, *SCG*, July 14, 1777. For a slave's conveying many of his clothes to his wife's home on another plantation, see John Hales, *VaG* (D and H), Apr. 1, 1775.

66. George Bedon, *Gaz of State of SC*, Apr. 15, 1784; John Olives, *VaG or AA*, Sept. 24, 1785. Between 1732 and 1779, I count 403 South Carolina runaways as members of family groups—12% of all advertised fugitives. Of these, 48% consisted of spouses alone or with children (24% alone, 24% with children), 43% mothers and children, 4% father and children, 4% siblings, and 2% extended family groups. In Virginia between 1736 and 1779, I count 78 members of family groups—7% of all advertised fugitives. Of these, 51% consisted of spouses alone or with children (36% alone, 15% with children), 20% mothers and children, 20% siblings, and 8% extended family groups.

master, "He is now here pressing me." Sam, a carpenter on Robert Carter's Cancer plantation, deserted his post to be near his wife, who belonged to Charles Carter. Sam's complaint that it was "a hard case to be separated from his wife," together with the intercession of his overseer, carried the day, and Carter acceded to the transfer.[67]

When Charles Ball first learned that he would be sold from Maryland to Georgia, his first thoughts were of his wife and children. As he put it, "My heart died away within me." Shocked and numbed, "I felt incapable of weeping or speaking," he later recollected, "and in my despair I laughed loudly." Hands bound, Ball set out southward that same day, his request to see his family one last time rudely denied. On his journey he dreamed of his wife and children "beseeching and imploring my master on their knees not to carry away from them." Ball had only his memories to keep alive his sense of family affiliation. And, in time, those memories inevitably dimmed. Symbolic perhaps was the day he decided to lay aside his old straw hat, the one "my wife had made for me in Maryland," so as to "avoid the appearance of singularity" among his fellow cotton hands. The discarding of this concrete reminder of family feeling—an important way for slaves to affirm family ties—probably weighed on Ball more than even he knew and accounted for his recollection of the event many years later.[68]

Lowcountry slaves were equally distraught at the thought of family separation. When seven or eight slave families were on the verge of being "torn to pieces," Henry Laurens predicted "*great distraction* among the whole." Similarly, when Thomas Wright, on his deathbed, decided to bequeath a slave to his friend, he determined not to do it in the presence of the slaves, "observing that it might occasion *some uneasiness*" among them. The news of a prospective separation was like a stone thrown into a lake: the ripples of concern extended far and wide. And once a separation had occurred, Lowcountry slaves, like their Chesapeake cousins, strove to put right the damage. Two planters in the Cheraws district agreed to an exchange of slaves in order to reunite a wife and her husband. The impetus for the exchange apparently came from below, because one master agreed to it "for Peace sake." In 1764, William Simpson, a resident of Savannah, was "disobliged" by one of his male slaves, which induced him to sell the man along with his son. During the next three years, the bondman wrote "to his wife frequently, and appear[ed] by his letters

---

67. Robert Carter to Fleet Cox, Jan. 2, 1788, Carter Letterbook, VIII, 61, Duke; Christopher Collins to Robert Carter, Jan. 11, 1788, Carter Family Papers; Robert Carter to John Pound, Mar. 16, 1779, Letterbook, III (3), 110. See also Erasmus Gill to Duncan Rose, Jan. 24, 1801, Haxall Family Papers, VHS.

68. Ball, *Fifty Years in Chains*, 36, 39, 147.

to be in great distress for want of her." Believing sufficient punishment had been wrought, Simpson inquired of the new owner whether the two slaves had behaved well enough "to intitle them to any favour or indulgence." If so, Simpson offered to sell the man's wife and four other children in order to reunite the family. Ending on a moralistic note, unbefitting his earlier action, Simpson declared, "A separation of those unhappy people is adding distress to their unfortunate condition."[69]

The lengths to which slaves went to keep marriages together testifies to the strength of the bond between husband and wife. Slaves invariably chose their partners, underwent some form of ceremony to signify a marital union, and showed great distress when forced separations occurred. Women were not submissive: they often raised children alone, they did the same kind of work as men, and they were—often had to be—self-reliant. Men were not emasculated: they monopolized skilled posts, they were generally much older than their wives, they often domineered and sometimes exploited their womenfolk, but most often they headed families and tried as best they could to support them. For the most part, slave men and women took marriage very seriously.

They also took their responsibility as parents seriously, even though the realities of slavery always made caring for children difficult. Crèvecoeur, for instance, argued that slaves "have no time, like us, tenderly to rear their helpless offspring, to nurse them on their knees, to enjoy the delight of being parents. Their paternal fondness is embittered by considering, that if their children live, they must live to be slaves like themselves." Perhaps the distance that slave parents had often to place between themselves and their children accounts for one slave couple's willingness to part with their son Primas, "and he with them," when their master, then resident in London, requested the services of a boy as a personal servant. Perhaps also the opportunities involved in metropolitan service and proximity to an influential master outweighed the pains of separation. Some slave parents might have become so embittered at their offsprings' prospects that they took their children's lives. In 1760, Jenny of King George County was tried for murdering her daughter; thirteen years later, the Brunswick County court found Sall guilty of killing her child; and, in 1779, the Caroline County court tried Patt for the same offense, although she was even-

69. *Laurens Papers*, IV, 595; Thomas Wright's deed of gift, Oct. 28, 1775, Miscellaneous Record Book, RR, 349; depositions of William Davis and William Allston, Oct. 24, 1777, Miscellaneous Records, RR, 452–453; William Simpson to Governor James Grant, June 15, 1767, Papers of General James Grant of Ballindalloch, 0771/243. See also David Yeats to James Grant, Apr. 6, 1774, ibid., 0771/370.

tually acquitted. To be sure, accusing slave mothers of crimes, in the context of the far larger crime of slavery, reflected the authorities' hypocrisy. An old slave woman's answer to a question about how many children she had was a most effective riposte. She replied that she had "five to her present Mistress and three to her last—the father was left out of the question."[70]

Although a measure of callousness and passivity was almost inherent in a parent-child relationship under slavery, most slave parents were loving and caring. They might well have been bitter, but not generally toward their children. Charles Ball encountered a slave mother who carried her young child all day on her back, while working with the hoe, because she could not bear hearing the child's cries if left at the end of the row. When a slave child died at Nomini Hall, the parents were so distraught, so overwhelmed with "overflowing Grief," that they did not appear at the funeral. The response of "an old, stooped, worn-out Negro" on a Georgia plantation to the Reverend Henry Muhlenberg's suggestion that the minister become the owner of the old man's "half-grown daughter" also revealed strong parental feelings. Although Muhlenberg promised to treat the girl as his "own child," the father "showed by his fearful countenance and gestures that he would rather lose his own life than be separated from his daughter." His conscience pricked, a chastened Muhlenberg confided to his journal that he had never intended to carry out the proposal.[71]

By their actions, many runaway slaves demonstrate that they, too, were not about to be separated from their children. Families that included quite old children sometimes ran away together. The record for the largest eighteenth-century fugitive family goes to forty-five-year-old Bacchus and his thirty-five-year-old wife, Betty, who, in 1789, fled in a six-oared canoe, apparently making their way to Georgia. They took with them six offspring: twenty-year-old Andrew, eighteen-year-old Sarah, fifteen-year-old Little Bacchus, twelve-year-

---

70. J. Hector St. John Crèvecoeur, *Letters from an American Farmer,* ed. W. P. Trent and Ludwig Lewisohn (New York, 1925 [orig. publ. 1782], 228; Robert Raper to Thomas Boone, Mar. 15, 1770, Robert Raper Letterbook, West Sussex Record Office, microfilm, SCHS; Governor Fauquier's appointment of the Justices in King George County, Oct. 11, 1760, photostat, CW; Court of Oyer and Terminer, Brunswick County, Jan. 11, 1773, Colonial Papers, VSL; Caroline County Court Order Book, 1777–1780, Jan. 14, 1779, 147, VSL; Dick Journal, Dec. 18, 1808, UVa. I have found only one South Carolina slave trial that refers to a mother's alleged murder of her child (in this case, her bastard) (trial of Mellum, Sept. 18, 1754, Miscellaneous Record Book, KK, 90–91).

71. Ball, *Fifty Years in Chains,* 151; Hunter Dickinson Farish, ed., *Journal and Letters of Philip Vickers Fithian, 1773–1774: A Plantation Tutor of the Old Dominion* (Williamsburg, Va., 1957), 239, 241; Henry Melchior Muhlenberg, *The Journals of Henry Melchior Muhlenberg,* trans. Theodore G. Tappert and John W. Doberstein, 2 vols. (Philadelphia, 1942–1958), II, 675.

old Bess, seven-year-old Kate, and two-year-old Grace. More common than two-parent families with children were single parents, usually mothers, and children. Occasionally, women like Jenny, "very big with child," summoned the resolve to elope: she left with a toddler in tow. These pregnant women perhaps wanted to be near their husbands when the baby was born. Mothers sometimes ran off with large numbers of children. Twenty-six-year-old Lucy gathered up her four children—two boys, aged eight and six, and two younger girls—for the long trek from Saint Thomas Parish in South Carolina to Savannah in Georgia, where she had sisters and other relations. Only one fugitive slave was reported to have left children behind when running away: she was a forty-year-old woman named Hannah, the mother of two young children and a resident of Charleston. However, she might not have abandoned her offspring, because she was "frequently" seen in the city as a runaway. Few single fathers ran away with children. Forty-year-old Bow, who fled Charleston with his twelve-year-old son Sandy, and forty-six-year-old Bristol, who took along his thirteen-year-old son, also named Bristol, for the trip from Horse Savannah to Johns Island, were the exceptions. Most male fugitives were unencumbered by children, in part because these men were too young to have married.[72]

As adults, slaves maintained ties to their parents. About nine of every ten slaves said to be visiting parents in both Virginia and South Carolina were adults, and most (like other fugitives) were in their twenties or early thirties. Jemmy was typical: age twenty-eight, a resident of Charleston, purchased as a boy from a Black River plantation where his parents still resided, and thought likely "to pay them a visit during his absence." Quite elderly slaves turned to their parents for support. Thirty-six-year-old Saucy, a Maryland slave, made his capture that much harder by changing his clothing, courtesy of his father, who lived on a quarter fourteen miles away. In South Carolina, forty-year-old Robin was thought to have gone to a plantation where his mother and other relations lived, while fifty-two-year-old Hesther, her master concluded, had

---

72. Alex Cameron, *City Gaz*, July 8, 1789 (this family had escaped in a canoe in 1781 [Mrs. Holmes, *Royal Gaz*, Aug. 15, 1781]); Allen Freedman, *VaG* (Purdie), Apr. 11, 1777 (Jenny); James Akin, *SC and AGG*, Aug. 16, 1780 (Lucy); Christopher McDonald, *SCG and TDA*, Dec. 15, 1798 (Hannah); John Edwards, *SCG*, Apr. 17, 1762 (Bow); John Haly, ibid., Aug. 4, 1766 (Bristol). Of the 1,004 women listed as both fugitives and captives in South Carolina newspapers between 1732 and 1782, 113, or 11%, were accompanied by their children (78 with 1 child, 24 with 2, 9 with 3, and 2 with 4). In Virginia newspapers between 1736 and 1779, only 7 of 112 women, or 6%, were said to have been accompanied by children. I have found 8 cases of a father's running away with 1 or more sons—all are from colonial South Carolina newspapers. For the pattern in Georgia, which was much like South Carolina's, see Betty Wood, "Some Aspects of Female Resistance to Chattel Slavery in Low Country Georgia, 1763–1815," *Historical Journal*, XXX (1987), 610.

long prepared her "jaunt" to mother and family. The parental bond was obviously vital for many adult slaves, even at advanced ages. Most runaways who were said to be visiting a parent ran to a mother, but slightly more than a third were thought to be running either to fathers or to both parents.[73]

The few slaves who penned autobiographies in the eighteenth century spoke fondly of their parents. Boston King, a South Carolina slave, especially respected his African father, who never swore in front of others and prayed with his family every night. "To the utmost of his power," King recalled, "he endeavored to make his family happy, and his death was a very great loss to us all." James Carter, a former Virginia slave, recalled conversations with his parents when searching for his fugitive brother, who had been killed by his overseer. His mother, for instance, had addressed him as follows: "Do my Son try and get home by sun set we may hear of your brother and you can help your father to get him home." In the early nineteenth century, Carter observed that his mother, then aged sixty-four, had just been freed, no longer being "of any service" to the Armistead family. He had attempted to purchase his father, then aged sixty-seven, in order that he might "go and Live with [his] Mother." Carter obviously retained strong ties of affection to his parents.[74]

Younger children, by word and deed, reveal similarly strong attachments to parents. In 1740, Robert Pringle, a Charleston merchant, decided to sell his girl Esther, who was a good house servant, because "she had a practice of goeing frequently to her Father and Mother, who Live at a Plantation I am concern'd in about Twenty Miles from [Charles]Town." Esther's frequent visits are eloquent reminders of the pain young children felt at being separated from parents, pain put into words by a Virginia slave boy named Bob. In the early 1800s, St. George Tucker replaced his waiting man, Johnny, with the boy Bob. Tucker traveled around Virginia as a lawyer, and Bob was separated from his mother, who lived in Williamsburg. The boy wrote to his mother; once he awakened Tucker by calling out in his sleep as he dreamed about his "mammy"; and on

---

73. John Strobel, *City Gaz*, July 11, 1799 (Jemmy); Samuel Wortington, *Maryland Journal and Baltimore Advertiser*, Aug. 7, 1781 (Saucy); William Ekells, *Gaz of State of SC*, Sept. 3, 1778 (Robin); Peter Spence, ibid., Aug. 26, 1778 (Hesther). In colonial South Carolina, there were 80 cases (counting any group as one case) of slaves who were thought to be visiting a parent or parents. Of these 80, 89% were adults above 16 years of age; 65% were said to be visiting a mother, 20% a father, and 15% both parents. In Virginia from 1736 to 1779, there were 24 such cases: 92% were adults; 63% were said to be visiting a mother, 29% a father, and 8% both parents.

74. "Memoirs of the Life of Boston King, a Black Preacher," *Methodist Magazine*, XXI (1798), 105–106; Linda Stanley, ed., "James Carter's Account of His Sufferings in Slavery," *Pennsylvania Magazine of History and Biography*, CV (1981), 336–338.

another occasion, he greeted a returning Tucker by saying, "I am mighty glad to see you, Sir, . . . I couldn't have been gladder to see anybody but my mammy and my sister." Bob's "affectionate temper" toward his mother touched the heart of his master.[75]

Masters were quick to recognize slave parents, mothers in particular, as protective and caring of their children. Landon Carter wondered whether slave mothers were not too indulgent toward their offspring. He believed that slave children were prone to sickness from being allowed to "press their appetites" and eat "loads of Gross food." Thus, when, in 1774, a slave mother came "bellowing" about her six-year-old girl "all swelled up to the eyes," Carter suspected that she had "been stuffing Potatoes [down her child] for some time." The master of Sabine Hall also engaged in a tussle of wills with his "Suckling wenches" about the frequency and duration of their absences from the field to attend to their infants. They wanted five feeding times, he only three. He was also aware that the death of a child was not easily passed off, for he observed that Winny was much "affected" by the loss of her daughter. Other members of the Carter clan came to understand the strong attachments that bound slave mothers to their children. In 1778, for example, Robert Carter of Nomini Hall sent a young woman and her two small children to the Baltimore Company ironworks because she would "not agree that her children stay with her relations." Twelve years later, the same master faced an angry mother who complained that her son and another boy who lived with her had been beaten unnecessarily by an overseer. Carter ordered the overseer to correct more moderately in the future and to "make a proper allowance for the Feelings of a Mother."[76]

Nor could masters ignore the important role of fathers. Landon Carter's plowman, a slave named Manuel, broke open the hut in which his daughter Sarah had been confined and freed her. On another occasion, the master of Sabine Hall lamented the roguery of his slave Johnny and "all his family bred under him," a comment that hardly suggests powerless slave fathers. On the Nomini Hall estate, carpenter George remarried but did not forget his child of a former marriage. When, in 1781, his former wife died, he asked his master to let his seven-year-old daughter Betty live with him and his new wife. Earlier on the same estate, Philip Fithian, the resident tutor, admitted Dennis, "the Lad

---

75. Walter B. Edgar, ed., *The Letterbook of Robert Pringle*, I (Columbia, S.C., 1972), 247; Mary Haldane Coleman, ed., *Virginia Silhouettes: Contemporary Letters concerning Negro Slavery in the State of Virginia . . .* (Richmond, Va., 1934), 9–10.

76. Greene, ed., *Carter Diary*, 194, 218, 496, 865; Robert Carter to Clement Brooke, July 27, 1778, Carter Letterbook, III (3), 46, Duke; Robert Carter to Newyear Branson, Feb. 13, 1790, ibid., X, 93.

who waits at Table," into school at his father's request. These fathers were important figures in their households.[77]

Some slave parents, and particularly fathers, could pass on to their children one important possession—their skill. They made the most of the opportunity. Woodworking was the most common trade in which a son might follow his father, but others gradually opened up even to mothers and their children. England and his two sons—twenty-one-year-old Prince and nineteen-year-old Prosper—were bricklayers. Two of George Washington's young ditchers were sons of Boatswain, the head ditcher. Bess, in her seventies, still practiced midwifery, along with daughter Flora, who was in her late forties, on the Pinckney plantations. By the late eighteenth century, slave families with a range of skills were beginning to emerge. Although some skilled slaves might have been passive recipients of masters' favors, others were active agents in passing on their trades to their children. Thus, when his son turned twelve and of working age, John Thomas, a slave blacksmith who resided on Robert Carter's Nomini Hall plantation, asked that his son be transferred from an outlying quarter to join him in the smith shop. Carter fell in with John's "scheme." A North Carolina cooper, put up for sale with his fifteen-year-old son, who had been "bred to the same work," continually called out, "Who buys me must buy my son too."[78]

Some parents were apparently so successful in passing on their skills to their children that a few families came to monopolize privileged positions on some plantations. When one Chesapeake planter transferred slaves from one quarter to another, he mentioned at least six skilled slaves who were part of just two families. There was "an old fellow called Charles and his son Anthony who have been employed always at the carpenters business," as well as Charles's

---

77. Greene, ed., *Carter Diary*, 385, 777; Robert Carter to Samuel Carter, Mar. 10, 1781, Carter Letterbook, IV, 48, Duke; Farish, ed., *Journal and Letters of Philip Vickers Fithian*, 184, 240. See also Mechal Sobel, *The World They Made Together: Black and White Values in Eighteenth-Century Virginia* (Princeton, N.J., 1987), 163.

78. Joseph Wragg, *SCG*, Oct. 13, 1739; Donald Jackson and Dorothy Twohig, eds., *The Diaries of George Washington*, IV (Charlottesville, Va., 1978), 277–283 (see also John C. Fitzpatrick, ed., *The Writings of George Washington from the Original Manuscript Sources, 1745–1799*, 39 vols. [Washington, D.C., 1931–1944], XXXVII, 256–268); C. C. Pinckney Plantation Book, LC; Robert Carter to Newyear Branson, Aug. 22, 1788, Carter Letterbook, VIII, 170, Duke; Johann David Schoepf, *Travels in the Confederation [1783–1784]*, trans. and ed. Alfred J. Morrison, 2 vols. (Philadelphia, 1911), I, 148. For father and son woodworkers, see will of Lewis Burwell, York County Deeds, Orders, and Wills, no. 14, 60–64; inventory of Robert Carter, November 1733, Carter Papers, VHS; Greene, ed., *Carter Diary*, 367; *Laurens Papers*, IV, 579; and diaries of Charles Drayton, Mar. 14, 1792, Drayton Family Papers, Historic Charleston Foundation.

wife, Betty, who was a house servant and assisted "in overlooking some spinning, her Girls knit, and do Needle Work," together with "Mulatto Milly who was the principal Spinner" and one of her children, who could "spin and work at her Needle." On the Carroll estate in Maryland, in 1773, more than half the tradesmen under age twenty-five learned their trades from kinsmen who were also skilled mechanics.[79]

Fathers passed not only their skills but also their names to their children. Many South Carolina slave families bear out the common practice of naming a son for a father. The first slave families on record in the Carolinas—dating to 1670 in South Carolina and to 1709 in North Carolina—both had sons named for fathers. Among Ball family slaves in the eighteenth century, one in six named a son for a father, whereas fewer than one in ten named a daughter for a mother. Similarly, three of the thirty-three families on the Ravenel plantations named sons for fathers, but only one named a daughter for a mother. On the Pinckney estate, five of a possible nine families (those in which names of fathers and sons are known) transmitted the name of a father to a son, whereas only one of a possible eleven families bequeathed a mother's name to a daughter. Over the course of the colonial period, slave families in South Carolina inventories were four times as likely to pass on a father's name to a son as a mother's name to a daughter, and five times as likely by the 1760s and 1770s.[80]

A similar pattern can be discerned among Virginia slaves, although it grew less pronounced over time. A listing of the Jones family slaves, taken in 1740,

---

79. John Norton to B. Muse, Dec. 23, 1781, Battaille Muse Papers, Duke; Kulikoff, *Tobacco and Slaves*, 373; Dew, "David Ross and the Oxford Iron Works," *WMQ*, XXXI (1974), 212–213; Lewis, "Slave Families," *VMHB*, LXXXVI (1978), 177; Norton, Gutman, and Berlin, "Afro-American Family," in Berlin and Hoffman, eds., *Slavery and Freedom*, 181–182.

80. John C. Inscoe, "Carolina Slave Names: An Index to Acculturation," *Journal of Southern History*, XLIX (1983), 529–530; Ball Account Book, Ball Family Papers, SCHS; John and Keating Simons Ball Books, Southern Historical Collection, UNC; Ravenel Account Book, B1-1, Ravenel Papers; C. C. Pinckney Plantation Book. There were 304 cases of naming children for parents in colonial South Carolina inventories. In the 1730s and 1740s, the ratio of sons named after fathers as compared to daughters after mothers was less than 3:1 (29:11). In the 1760s and 1770s, the ratio had increased to more than 5:1 (164:33). See also Gutman, *Black Family*, 345–346; Cheryll Ann Cody, "There Was No 'Absolom' on the Ball Plantations: Slave-Naming Practices in the South Carolina Low Country, 1720–1865," *AHR*, XCII (1987), 563–596; and Inscoe, "Generation and Gender as Reflected in Carolina Slave Naming Practices: A Challenge to the Gutman Thesis," *SCHM*, XCIV (1993), 252–263, who emphasizes that the majority of slave families did not name sons for fathers, though he recognizes that names of slave mothers were very infrequently passed on to daughters. For other marked differentials between naming sons for fathers more frequently than daughters for mothers, see Kay and Cary, *Slavery in North Carolina*, 163; and Jerome S. Handler and JoAnn Jacoby, "Slave Names and Naming in Barbados, 1650–1830," *WMQ*, 3d Ser., LIII (1996), 685–728.

indicates that five families named a son for a father (of a possible twenty-one cases in which fathers and sons were named); no family named a daughter for a mother (of a possible twenty cases). In his diary, Landon Carter mentioned in passing that four of his male slaves shared a name with a son; he failed to observe a comparable pattern among his female slaves. Three of William Byrd's slave families, listed in 1772, named sons for fathers; again, no daughter assumed the name of her mother. Even a slave family divided by ownership—perhaps because it was divided by ownership—exhibited this pattern. Thus, when thirty-three-year-old Beck and her seven-year-old son Glasgow, formerly the property of a York County master but since sold to a Hanover County resident, ran away, it should have surprised no one that they were later seen in Hampton, where the head of the family, also named Glasgow, lived. Although the sample sizes are small, on some late-eighteenth-century estates the practice of naming children for parents seems to have become bilateral. At least as many daughters were named for mothers as sons for fathers.[81]

Two explanations may be offered for these patterns. First, naming sons for fathers rather than daughters for mothers may be partly an imitation of white practices. The available evidence suggests that whites did indeed name sons for fathers—on a much greater scale than among slaves—but they also named daughters just as frequently for mothers. If slave practices are considered imitative, then only late-eighteenth-century Virginia slaves approach correspondence to white patterns. Second, the sheer fact of slavery explains the differential naming of sons for fathers as opposed to daughters for mothers. Masters recognized the kinship relationship of a mother to her offspring, not that between a father and his children. Slaves named sons for fathers as their way of asserting that a child had relatives through both paternal and maternal lines. The practice also, of course, points to a more influential role for fathers than a matriarchal view of slave family life would permit.[82]

No doubt there were irresponsible and embittered slave parents, but most were protective and caring. Slave parents assiduously bequeathed the few things they had to their children—their knowledge, their skills, their names.

---

81. Jones Family Papers, microfilm, CW; among Landon Carter's slaves, foreman George, Joe, and carpenters Ralph and Toney all passed their names on to one of their sons (Greene, ed., *Carter Diary,* 159, 219, 749–750, 1072); deed of trust between William Byrd and Peyton Randolph and Benjamin Harrison, Dec. 9, 1772, Charles City County Records, 1766–1774, 471–472, VSL; Jennings Pulliam, *VaG and WA,* Sept. 25, 1784. Two late-18th-century Chesapeake slave lists in which the incidence of sons named for fathers roughly equaled daughters named for mothers are those of Edmund Randolph, 1784, and Robert Carter, 1787–1788.

82. Cody, "There Was No 'Absalom,'" *AHR,* XCII (1987), 563–596; Gutman, *Black Family,* 93–95, 180–181, 189–191; Gudeman, "Gutman's *Black Family,*" *Soc. Sci. Hist.,* III (1979), 61.

They cared for their infants in the fields, made sure they got enough food, grieved over their death, and feared separation from them. And the children responded to their parents' efforts. They spoke kindly of their parents and ran away to visit them. Slavery severely tested the link between parent and child but never broke it.

The bond between siblings seems to have been particularly strong among slaves. Brothers and sisters played a significant role in some slaves' lives well into adulthood. Thus, Bristol, a young man, who ran away from his master in the Cape Fear region of North Carolina in December 1765, was still at large twenty months later and thought to be in the Northern Neck of Virginia, supported by his three brothers. Peter, in his midtwenties, absented himself from his master for more than a year, roaming widely throughout the Southside region of Virginia, and he ran away again only five days after being captured. He was thought to be with a brother in Surry County or with "several brothers and sisters in North Carolina." Twenty-two-year-old South Carolina slave Will, absent for six weeks before his master advertised for him as a runaway, was thought to have taken refuge with either of his two sisters or a brother in order "to get provisions." A network of brothers and sisters was obviously helpful to the slave runaway.[83]

Even slaves well advanced in years retained close ties to brothers and sisters. Thirty-five-year-old Maria was spotted at a plantation on the Santee River where she had a brother; Jenny, also in her middle to late thirties, was seen going in a wagon from Charleston to inland plantations where two of her brothers resided; forty-year-old Dickey left Saint Stephen Parish and was observed at Dr. Fausseaux's plantation in adjoining Saint John Parish, the residence of his brother. Most notable was fifty-year-old Peter, "somewhat grey, but particularly so in his side locks," a former driver and patroon, who absented himself on March 24, 1796, and remained at large seventeen months later. He had a wife at Goose Creek, where it was thought he spent most of his time, but he had also been seen in Savannah, where he had a sister.[84]

Some siblings made particularly strenuous efforts to renew acquaintances.

---

83. George Moore, *VaG* (P and D), July 9, 1767; Samuel Sherwin, ibid. (Rind), May 9, 1771; Thomas Legare, Jr., *City Gaz*, Feb. 12, 1799; Theodore Gaillard, Sr., ibid., Aug. 23, 1799. For siblings running away together, see John Nelson, *VaG and WA*, Aug. 6, 1785; and Thomas Barksdale, *SCG*, Sept. 22, 1798.

84. Robert Johnston, *SCG*, July 9, 1763; William Sams, *SC and AGG*, Dec. 24, 1778; John Sinkler, *State Gaz of SC*, May 11, 1786; Anthony Bourdeaux, *City Gaz*, Aug. 24, 1797. See also Benjamin Singellton, *SCG and CJ*, June 23, 1772; John Austin Finnie, *VaG* (P and D), July 4, 1771; and John Lewis, ibid. (Purdie), July 10, 1778.

In 1772, a twenty-two-year-old Virginia-born slave named Kit ran away from his master in Northampton County, North Carolina, and joined up with his brother Tom, who lived in Prince George County, Virginia. Together, they stayed out at least a year and, according to their owners, "committed many Outrages" on or near the Rappahannock River. Similarly, in August 1798, Peter ran away from Charleston, and his master had no doubt about his intentions, for, the previous fall, Peter had made his way to Santee, near Murray's Ferry, where his family resided, and from there to the Canal, where they were working. Peter had followed his old track, his master concluded, because "his brother, named Fortune, was seen with him in town, a noted run-away, belongs to Archibald Campbell, near Murray's Ferry."[85]

Masters recognized and often made use of slaves' strong sibling bonds. When Toby's state of health was pronounced "helpless," his master, Robert Carter, transferred him to Billingsgate quarter so that he could be "under the Care of his Sister Judith, who lives there." John Channing observed that his slave men preferred to have their wives *or* sisters make up their clothes. When masters separated adolescents from their families and transferred them to new quarters, they often kept siblings together. A number of households on the larger Chesapeake and Lowcountry plantations, in particular, consisted of siblings.[86]

Strong sibling bonds were important to extended family networks. As Herbert Gutman has suggested, they may represent an adaptation of "West African kinship beliefs where particular adult siblings ('mother's brother' and 'father's sister') retained important social functions in families headed by brothers and sisters." At any rate, the role of aunts and uncles in the lives of nieces and nephews appears to have been prominent; even cousins could occasionally be seen cooperating with one another.[87]

Extended kin not only grew more numerous over time, but slaves also increasingly recognized and made use of extended kin in their families. Far more pervasive than naming sons for fathers, for example, was the slave practice of naming children for extended kin. As slaves named for kin, inevitably their pool of names narrowed. This took time, for, in the early formation of any slave plantation, the pool tended to be large, since masters aimed to give each

---

85. Samuel Meredith, Sr., *VaG* (P and D), Apr. 21, 1772; Robert Giles, *City Gaz*, Sept. 19, 1798.
86. Robert Carter to Richard Dozier, Dec. 7, 1778, Carter Letterbook, III (3), 78, Duke; John Channing to William Gibbons, June 26, 1770, William Gibbons, Jr., Papers, Duke; and see Tables 30 and 31.
87. Gutman, *Black Family,* 200–201.

slave a distinctive name that would facilitate easy identification. In 1727, Robert "King" Carter told his overseers to "take care that the negros" recently purchased "always go by the names we gave them." So often were the new names repeated that he was convinced that "every one knew their names and would readily answer to them." Over time, however, as slaves assumed the right to name within families, the pool narrowed considerably. Before 1780, 423 slaves were named in the Ball family record, but 259 shared a name with another slave. In Chesapeake estates by the second half of the eighteenth century, the pool of names tended to be even smaller. Landon Carter mentioned the names of 165 of his slaves in his diary, of which 106, or 64 percent, shared a name (there were 8 Toms, 6 Sarahs, and 6 Bettys). As slaves named for kin, so masters began to use modifiers (place names, ethnic designations, skin color, former owners, and size) to differentiate slaves who shared names. Perhaps that is why they also began to note surnames among their slaves.[88]

The pattern of naming children for extended kin became much the most important way in which the pool of slave names narrowed. Thus, among Ball family slaves in South Carolina, more than 60 percent of families reused the name of a paternal and maternal grandfather for their sons, whereas 71 percent transmitted the name of a maternal grandmother to a daughter. Among Ravenel family slaves, naming for extended kin was widespread. Gibby and Nanny, for example, had twelve children. One child was given the same name as Nanny's brother, two were named for Gibby's sisters, and one shared the same name as Gibby's mother. Savey and Sarry had six children. Two sons were named after uncles (paternal and maternal), two daughters were named for aunts (again, in both lines), while a fifth child took the name of Sarry's mother. Three other Ravenel slave families passed on the names of grandparents to grandchildren. Among Gaillard family slaves, where two-generation kinship networks have been constructed, seven children were named for parents, as opposed to seventy for more extended kin. In 1808, Charles Cotesworth Pinckney listed his slaves, one of whom was Old Anthony. He was the son of Isaac and Molly. Old Anthony had two daughters, Rinah and Molly, the latter named for her grandmother. Rinah named one of her sons Anthony for her father, while Molly named her son after her great-grandfather Isaac, born almost a century earlier. The predominant pattern among eighteenth-century South Carolina slaves was the naming of children for more distant kin in both

---

88. Robert Carter to Robert Jones, Oct. 10, 1727, Carter Letterbook, 1727–1728, VHS; I have made my own calculations from the Ball family papers located in the SCHS and UNC, but see also Cody, "There Was No 'Absalom,'" *AHR*, XCII (1987), 563–596; and Greene, ed., *Carter Diary*. In all, Henry Laurens named 147 slaves in his correspondence; only 35, or 24%, shared a name with another slave (*Laurens Papers*, III, 203, IV, 319, and account book of Henry Laurens, 1766–1773, April 1771, 377, CC).

paternal and maternal lines. Presumably, they wished to link their children to a more distant and, in many cases, an African past.[89]

The greater kinship density present among Chesapeake, as against Lowcountry, slaves is reflected in an even more tightly knit pattern of kin naming. On the Carroll plantations of Anne Arundel County, Maryland, sixty-one slaves were named for blood relatives: nineteen bore the names of grandparents, sixteen of uncles and aunts, nine of great-grandparents and granduncles or aunts, as opposed to only seventeen for parents, usually the father. Similarly, among Jefferson family slaves at the turn of the century, thirty carried the names of uncles and aunts, twenty-five the names of grandparents, two the names of granduncles, and four the names of great-grandparents, as opposed to twenty-three who assumed their parents' names. By naming their children predominantly for more distant kinfolk, Chesapeake slave parents linked new to past generations. As Gutman has observed, "Slavery had not obliterated familial and social memory."[90]

Extended kin played a particularly active role in a number of Chesapeake slave families. In a dispute between a slave girl and an overseer that came to the attention of Landon Carter, the girl's grandmother manufactured a story to discredit the white manager. The girl begged Carter not to let it be known that she had confessed to the influence of her "Granny," who "would whip her for it." Carter's refusal to remove the girl from under the overseer's charge prompted the grandmother to take revenge by turning loose all of Carter's cattle. She also had the "impudence" to tell Carter that the overseer "starved" her granddaughter. When a mother at Robert Carter's Cancer plantation wanted a nurse for her two-year-old child, Carter arranged for the baby's seventy-one-year-old grandfather to be transferred and "live at Suckey's house he to have the care of both his grand Children." Seventeen-year-old John fled Williamsburg, making for a plantation in Warwick where not just his father but also his grandmother resided.[91]

---

89. Ball, Ravenel, and Pinckney sources are listed in note 80, above; the Gaillard data come from Cheryll Ann Cody, "Naming, Kinship, and Estate Dispersal: Notes on Slave Family Life on a South Carolina Plantation, 1786–1833," *WMQ*, 3d Ser., XXXIX (1982), 192–211. For a precise African analog for naming children after grandparents, see John Thornton, "Central African Names and African-American Naming Patterns," *WMQ*, 3d Ser., L (1993), 727–742, esp. 740–742. For a likely matrilineal emphasis in naming children for kin, see Handler and Jacoby, "Slave Names and Naming in Barbados," *WMQ*, 3d Ser., LIII (1996), 685–728.

90. Norton, Gutman, and Berlin, "The Afro-American Family," in Berlin and Hoffman, eds., *Slavery and Freedom*, 180, 183; Gutman, *Black Family*, 93.

91. Greene, ed., *Carter Diary*, 760, 762; Robert Carter to Charles Haynie, Apr. 21, 1784, Carter Letterbook, V, 201, Duke; Robey Coke, *VaG* (Purdie), July 25, 1777; Kulikoff, *Tobacco and Slaves*, 377.

More remote kin—in-laws, cousins, uncles and aunts, nephews and nieces—cooperated in the Chesapeake, indicating that distant ties could be meaningful. Thus, Landon Carter's slave Tom was reluctant to work in his master's garden, because he did not wish to replace his father-in-law. A decision by two slaves to attend a Baptist meeting without their master's approval was probably made a little easier because the two could rely on each other; they were, after all, cousins. In 1781, when two slaves—Carter Jack, aged about thirty-five, and London, about fifteen—ran away, their master assumed not unnaturally that the adult instigated this flight; Jack also happened to be London's uncle. When one of Robert Carter's slaves gained his freedom, he petitioned his former master to have his wife and twelve-year-old niece come and live with him. He promised to "make an allowance" for both members of *his* family.[92]

Extended kin ties, if less pervasive in the Lowcountry than in the Chesapeake, became of increasing importance to that region's slaves as the century wore on. As early as 1753, a young woman named Doll who ran away from a plantation in Horse Savannah was thought to be harbored by her relations in Charleston, one of whom was an aunt belonging to Mr. Thomas Else. Three years later, twenty-one-year-old Ketch ran away to visit either his father on James Island or his grandmother in Saint George Dorchester. In the decade before the American Revolution, Sam sought support from an aunt and several cousins among Jonathan Scott's slaves, Toby headed for Willtown, where he had an uncle, Jack was "probably" among some of his in-laws, and an apprentice mulatto boy named Richard Collis was thought to have made for Ponpon, where his brother-in-law resided.[93]

By the second half of the century, extended family groups occasionally ran away together in South Carolina. Thus, in 1762, a twenty-three-year-old black male slave named Crack ran away with his free Indian wife, their two-year-old child, and his fifty-year-old mother. In 1783, forty-year-old Clarinda turned up at a plantation in Cheehaw to be with her husband, who had taken her as his wife in Virginia during the Revolutionary war. Clarinda had her twenty-one-year-old daughter Sarah and her sixteen-year-old son Charles in tow, together with her grandchild, Sarah's child in arms. Most remarkable was the four-generational family group that ran away from a Charleston master in 1785:

---

92. Greene, ed., *Carter Diary,* 547, 575, 842, 854 (see 731 for the mention of a young boy's grandfather and uncle); Robert Carter Daybook, Apr. 22, 1778, XV, 15–16, Duke; Robert Pleasants to General Arnold, Jan. 30, 1781, Robert Pleasants Lettercopy Book, W and M; Robert Carter Daybook, 1790–1792, Aug. 27, 1792, LC; Gutman, *Black Family,* 200–202.

93. Andrew Letch, *SCG,* June 12, 1753 (Doll); Jonathan Copp, ibid., Jan. 22, 1756 (Ketch); Francis Roche, *SCG and CJ,* Oct. 20, 1767 (Sam); John Chapman, ibid., July 26, 1774 (Toby); William Hort, ibid., July 25, 1775 (Jack); Richard Lamput, *SCG,* Oct. 24, 1775 (Richard Collis).

an elderly woman named Jenny, her thirty-five-year-old daughter Dido, her granddaughter Tissey, and her great-granddaughter, Tissey's suckling child.[94]

The important role of extended kin in slaves' lives may derive in part from African beliefs. The slaves' propensity for thinking in kinship forms—the use of familial terms, particularly "aunt" and "uncle," in addressing nonkin or the important role of fictive kinfolk where kin were absent altogether—corresponds with what is known about basic assumptions concerning kinship in West African societies. Two sets of beliefs, as Sidney Mintz and Richard Price have emphasized, were particularly central: "the sheer importance of kinship in structuring interpersonal relations and in defining an individual's place in his society" and the vital "importance to each individual of the . . . lines of kinsmen, living or dead, stretching backward and forward through time." Conversely, the circumstances of eighteenth-century slavery kept some slaves rooted to the same spot and scattered others across the land, both of which either surrounded slaves with kin or gave them access to far-flung kin networks. How much traditional beliefs, as opposed to or in combination with the exigencies of slavery, produced the slaves' distinctive stress on the role of kinship, and particularly extended kin, is hard to assess.[95]

Similarly, the age gaps between husbands and wives and the close bonds between siblings and sibling families may owe something to African influences. Yet, slavery itself—whether the sexual imbalances of the slave trade that led inevitably to a pattern of older husbands and younger wives or the disruption of families that led siblings to bond together and masters to place older siblings together in households—may just as easily explain these traits. In these instances, perhaps the compatibility of homeland beliefs and the imperatives of slavery combined to produce these behavioral patterns.

One distinctive family form—polygyny—was transferred across the Atlantic, but only partially and incompletely. Though it was never widespread, polygyny was more common among Lowcountry slaves than among any others in British North America. Early in the eighteenth century, the Reverend Francis Le Jau warned South Carolina slaves that "the Christian Religion dos not allow plurality of Wives." Some bondpeople continued to ignore the minister's admonition throughout the century. In 1772, Mary Bull's estate listed a slave man Pompey with "his wife Alvira, and five children, Flora, July, Lisbon, Sue

94. Joseph Allston, *SCG*, Feb. 20, 1762 (Crack et al.); Charles Skirving, *SC Weekly Gaz*, Mar. 8, 1783 (Clarinda et al.); Charles H. Simmons, *State Gaz of SC*, Aug. 8, 1785 (Jenny et al.).

95. Gutman, *Black Family*, 91, 154, 194, 217–220; Sidney W. Mintz and Richard Price, *An Anthropological Approach to the Afro-American Past: A Caribbean Perspective*, Institute for the Study of Human Issues, Occasional Papers in Social Change, no. 2 (Philadelphia, 1976), 34.

and Monmouth and another wife Ackey." Seven years later, James Parson's Bob headed a household that consisted of "his wife Nelly and their children Caesar and Sibbey, his other wife Elsey and child Bob." Such arrangements do not seem to have been a privilege conferred solely on skilled slaves. Whereas Jehu Elliot's driver had two wives, as did Isaac Godin's carpenter, two of the field hands on Hugh Thomson's plantation had two wives apiece, as did other field hands on a number of other estates. Henry Laurens mentioned his field hand Mathias's two wives only when one, in a fit of jealousy, poisoned the other.[96]

Instances of polygyny were much less common in the Chesapeake. The few cases that have materialized come, as might be expected, from the early eighteenth century, when Africans were more numerous. Thus, in the 1740s, a few men on the Eastern Shore of Maryland seem to have lived with more than one woman, and one of the 243 men—a foreman—belonging to Robert "King" Carter in 1733 had two wives. More indirectly, it has been suggested that slave women in turn-of-the-century Maryland might have nursed infants for three or four years, a common practice in polygynous societies. However, this is indirect evidence at best; what is more impressive is the speed with which Chesapeake slave women approximated Anglo-American nursing patterns, in the same way presumably as they rejected polygynous marriages.[97]

Another marriage pattern may also have had African antecedents. Slaves appear to have shared particular exogamous beliefs that dictated their selection of marital partners. Unlike whites, slaves seem to have had a taboo against marriage between cousins. Admittedly, no precise West African origins have been identified for this pattern, but it is difficult to see the behavior as originating in the exigencies of slavery or under Anglo-American influence, particularly when marriages between cousins were increasingly common among both gentry and plainfolk throughout the eighteenth century.[98]

96. Rev. Francis Le Jau to SPG, Oct. 20, 1709, A5/49, SPG; inventory of Mary Bull, Jan. 16, 1772, Inventory Book, Z, 177–187, SCDAH; inventory of James Parson, Nov. 9, 1779, ibid., BB, 190–201; inventory of Jehu Elliott, Mar. 27, 1762, ibid., V, 180–184; inventory of Isaac Godin, Jan. 22, 1778, ibid., CC, 320–326; inventory of Hugh Thomson, Dec. 21, 1774, ibid., &, 480–483. It is difficult, in other cases, to know whether African tradition or forced separation accounted for a male slave's having more than one wife.

97. "Eighteenth Century Maryland as Portrayed in the 'Itinerant Observations' of Edward Kimber," *MHM*, LI (1956), 327; Robert Carter inventory, 1733, Carter Papers, VHS; Menard, "Maryland Slave Population," *WMQ*, 3d Ser., XXXII (1975), 41; Herbert S. Klein and Stanley L. Engerman, "Fertility Differentials between Slaves in the United States and the British West Indies: A Note on Lactation Practices and Their Possible Implications," *WMQ*, 3d Ser., XXXV (1978), 369–371.

98. Gutman, *Black Family*, 88–91; Kulikoff, *Tobacco and Slaves*, 252–255, 374. But for a skeptical assessment of the African origins of the slaves' supposed taboo against cousin marriage, see Engerman, "Studying the Black Family," *Jour. Fam. Hist.*, III (1978), 89–91.

In general, then, it cannot be claimed that African influence was fundamental to African American familial development. What is more interesting is that slaves created a distinctive form of family life, irrespective of the derivation of particular influences. There is no better example of this than the naming patterns of slaves. As we have seen, some African names were retained, but they were never more than a fraction of the names employed by eighteenth-century slaves. Yet, at the same time as slaves were employing standard Anglo-American names, they were naming in ways that were distinctive, whether it was the naming of sons for fathers far more than of daughters for mothers or the naming for extended kin in particularly tight-knit ways.

Also distinctive was the relative absence of the white pattern of necronymic naming among slaves. Among South Carolina slaves, this practice has been discovered only among the more assimilated house slaves and artisans in the nineteenth century. In the Chesapeake, three newborn Jefferson slaves bore the names of recently deceased siblings, and a blood cousin carried the name of a dead kinsman. Landon Carter's personal body servant, Nassau, used the name Nat twice for his sons: the first died in 1757, and the second seems to have begun working alongside his father in the early 1770s, suggesting that Nassau reused the name at the first opportunity. That the practice can be found in the Chesapeake at all is evidence of the greater assimilation of that region's slaves to white practices, but it should be emphasized that it was never more than a minor occurrence.[99]

Another distinctive pattern, forced on slaves as much as anything else, was the absence of surnames. Last names were least common in the Lowcountry. Only a few of the more acculturated South Carolina runaways had surnames. Two bricklayers, a mustee and a mulatto, belonging to Christopher Holson, were known as William Saunders and Jack Flowers, respectively; a Charlestonian master advertised for his runaway "Jack, sirnamed Ryan"; and a mulatto fugitive named Jemmy took the name James Freeman, an indication of the status to which he aspired. A new name obviously meant much to a slave: in 1756, Frank ran away and assumed the name John Williams; six years later he ran away again, also as John Williams. Overall, however, only 1 percent of advertised runaways in South Carolina newspapers were said to have surnames. Last names were just as scarce among slaves in plantation listings and inventories. Jack and Tom Stuard were the only bondpeople with surnames

---

99. Cody, "There Was No 'Absalom,'" *AHR*, XCII (1987), 595; Norton, Gutman, and Berlin, "The Afro-American Family," in Berlin and Hoffman, eds., *Slavery and Freedom*, 183; Greene, ed., *Carter Diary*, esp. 159, 345, 348–349, 373. The relative absence of necronymic naming among 18th-century slaves argues against its African origin, a point of view supported strongly by Inscoe, "Generation and Gender," *SCHM*, XCIV (1993), 260; and Gutman, *Black Family*, 193–194.

among John Peacom's 65 slaves; Dick Williams, a field hand, was similarly conspicuous among John McKenzie's 210 slaves, as were Jack Outerbridge and Jack Green among Thomas Godfrey's 112 slaves. Only three of the few hundred bondpeople mentioned by Henry Laurens had a surname: Andrew Dross and Jemmy Holmes were mariners, and Scipio became Robert Scipio Laurens when he was taken to England as a waiting man.[100]

Slaves with surnames were somewhat more widespread in Virginia. There, one in ten runaways was known either to have a surname or to be using one in passing as free. Thus, Charles Bruce matter-of-factly advertised for his fifty-year-old "Negro fellow called Harry Spencer," and Anthony Martin referred to his slave Will, who, when absent, added a surname and a little more dignity to his forename by passing as William Cousins. Slaves clearly took the initiative in assuming surnames. Robert Rawlings advertised for his runaway "negro fellow by the name of GEORGE, but calls himself GEORGE LEWIS," Alexander Baugh for his slave Ben, who "calls himself Ben Sharp," Edward Carter for his "likely Negro man, who calls himself John Cellars," Thomas Walker for his man Frank "but frequently calls himself Frank Waddy." Surnames, though never widespread, dotted the pages of inventories and plantation listings in the Chesapeake. Three slaves with the surname Parrott (together with Will Coley, Jack Tooth, Sue Miller, and Jack Sambo) belonged to James Burwell's estate in York County; three mulattoes with the surname Bond were the only slaves on John Gildy's estate in Essex County; four slaves, all with separate surnames, lived on John Spotswood's estate in Spotsylvania County; and four Stewarts (as well as Barton Cocheno) belonged to Colonel Richard Jones's estate in Amelia County. On large estates in Virginia by the turn of the century, many slaves possessed surnames. There were Carys, Johnsons, Newmans, Smiths, and at least seven Joneses among Robert Carter's slaves, while Samuel Harrison and his wife, Judith Harrison, so liked their surname that they named one of their sons Harrison. On William Fitzhugh's plantations in 1810, forty-two of ninety-four adults shared surnames: Carters, Tripletts, Douglasses, and Bossees were present on most of his quarters.[101]

100. Christopher Holson, *SCG*, July 21, 1757; Joseph Tobias, ibid., Aug. 4, 1758; Thomas Whitesides, ibid., Nov. 7, 1761; Thomas Smith, ibid., May 29, 1756, Nov. 13, 1762 (there were 64 runaway slaves with surnames in colonial South Carolina newspapers); inventory of John Peacom, Dec. 8, 1752, Inventory Book, WPA, CXXXIV, 491–494; inventories of John Mackenzie, June 19–Aug. 10, 1771, ibid., CLXXXIV, 102–114; inventory of Thomas Godfrey, Aug. 20, 1776, ibid., CXCII, 110–115; *Laurens Papers*, VII, 231, VIII, 1, 34, 37, 60, 348, 370, 412, 612. I am skeptical about the argument that West African traditions were reflected in the adoption of surnames: Handler and Jacoby, "Slave Names and Naming in Barbados," *WMQ*, 3d Ser., LIII (1996), 685–728.

101. Charles Bruce, *VaG* (P and D), May 21, 1767 (Harry Spencer); Anthony Martin, ibid.,

Most interestingly, however, few slaves shared a surname with their current owner. Highly exceptional were Jenny Carter, belonging to Landon Carter, and Robert Laurens, belonging to Henry Laurens. Significantly, both these slaves were personal servants, closely identified with their masters. Slaves generally followed a more independent and inventive path: George took the surname America; John thought in monetary terms and became John Twopence; Sharper in fragrant terms, becoming Henry Perfume; a mariner in religious terms, becoming John Baptist; Jack Dismal might have named himself after the swamp; Tim became James Traveller, highly appropriate for a fugitive. In other cases, slaves assumed the last name of a former, often their first, owner. Thus, a mulatto sailmaker formerly named Cubbina, who was sold by Joshua Lawson of the island of Saint Christopher to Thomas Mace and then to Josiah Smith of South Carolina, adopted the name John Lawson when he decided to pass as a free man. A Jamaican-born slave named Gloucester who served as hostler and cook to the Fox family in Gloucester County, Virginia, and whose services were then rented out in the city of Richmond, took the name John Baker when he ran away. Apparently, his first Virginia master was Dr. John Baker, with whom "he lived some years in Williamsburg." Taking the name of an earlier owner was, as Genovese and Gutman have emphasized, a way for slaves to recapture their history, to establish a link to a family of origin, and to forge a social identity separate from that of successive owners. A South Carolina slave, born in 1852 and able to trace his ancestry to an African great-grandfather, spoke eloquently of these concerns when he said: "I do not know the name my great grandfather bore in Africa, but when he arrived in this country he was given the name Clement, and when he found he needed a surname—something he was not accustomed to in his native land—he borrowed that of the man who

---

June 21, 1770 (William Cousins); Robert Rawlings, *VaG and WA,* Sept. 4, 1788 (George Lewis); Alexander Baugh, *Va Ind Chron and GA,* July 7, 1790; Edward Carter, *VaG* (Rind), Oct. 31, 1771 (John Cellars); Thomas Walker, Jr., *VaG or AA,* July 12, 1783 (Frank Waddy) (there were 107 slaves with surnames among Virginia fugitives); inventory of James Burwell, Mar. 10, 1718, York County Deeds, Orders, and Wills, no. 15, 421 (42 slaves); inventory of John Gildy, Feb. 21, 1726, Essex County Wills and Inventories, no. 4, 202; inventory of John Spotswood, Dec. 5, 1758, Spotsvylania County Will Book, D, 88; inventory of Col. Richard Jones, November 1780, Amelia County Will Book, no. 3, 5 (48 slaves). The best data on slave names in the Robert Carter material come from his manumission document of 1791, Duke; and for the Harrison family, see "Valuation of Nomony Hall," in Robert Carter's Memo Book, 1788–1789, LC; see also John Randolph Barden, " 'Flushed with Notions of Freedom': The Growth and Emancipation of a Virginia Slave Community, 1732–1812" (Ph.D. diss., Duke University, 1993), 352–353, where the author notes 56 family names emerging from the Nomini Hall community as they were manumitted; for Fitzhugh, see Donald Mitchell Sweig, "Northern Virginia Slavery: A Statistical and Demographic Study" (Ph.D. diss., College of William and Mary, 1982), 116–121. See also Sobel, *The World They Made Together,* 159.

brought him. It was a very good name, and as we have held the same for more than one hundred and fifty years, without change or alteration, I think, therefore, we are legally entitled to it."[102]

That it was a South Carolina and not a Virginia slave who recalled an African great-grandfather is indicative of the difference in familial experiences of the two areas' bondpeople. More solitaries, the existence of polygyny, fewer surnames, and the absence of necronymic naming all point to a more widespread African presence in South Carolina than in Virginia. There were other differences, too. Coresident two-parent households were more widespread in the Lowcountry, divided-residence and one-parent families more widespread in the Chesapeake. Chesapeake slaves enjoyed greater kinship density than their Lowcountry cousins, but they also faced more family disruptions through sale, bequest, estate division, and forced migration. Slave family life was far from uniform throughout the plantation South.

Nevertheless, slaves everywhere experienced similar pressures and responded in similar ways. Although enslavement denied slaves essential familial choices and essential knowledge about their pasts, they never accepted that denial. As Edmund Morgan shrewdly observed, "Human nature has an unpredictable resiliency, and slaves did manage to live a life of their own within the limits prescribed for them." If the limits were constricting, they were never "so close as to preclude entirely the possibility of a private life." Many slaves were prevented from enjoying much of a family life, particularly early in the eighteenth century, and many others had their family lives disrupted by masters. But by the late eighteenth century, more than half of the slaves in both Lowcountry and Chesapeake had formed families. That so many lived as faithful husband and wife, as devoted parent and child, and as supportive extended kin, even under the most trying circumstances, is remarkable. The immediate family and the enlarged kin group were, in Gutman's words, "central binding institutions within slave communities." They helped shape and support a separate culture.[103]

---

102. Greene, ed., *Carter Diary*, 810 (Jenny Carter); Thomas Watkins, *VaG* (Purdie), Apr. 11, 1766 (George America); Robert Beverley, ibid. (D and H), Apr. 11, 1777 (John Twopence); John Edloe, ibid. (Purdie), Mar. 10, 1775 (Henry Perfume); Paris Boillat, *SCG*, June 27, 1774 (John Baptist); Robert Burwell, *VaG* (P and D), Feb. 18, 1773 (Jack Dismal); Catesby Jones, *VaG and WA*, Oct. 25, 1783 (James Traveller); Thomas Mace, *SCG and CJ*, May 13, 1766 (John Lawson); John Fox, *Va Ind Chron and GA*, July 28, 1790 (John Baker); Eugene D. Genovese, *Roll, Jordan, Roll: The World the Slaves Made* (New York, 1974), 445–447; Gutman, *Black Family*, 230–256, esp. 252.

103. Edmund S. Morgan, *Virginians at Home: Family Life in the Eighteenth Century* (Charlottesville, Va., 1952), 66; Gutman, *Black Family*, 260.

From the days of their introduction into the colonies, Negroes have taken, with the ruthlessness of those without articulate investments in cultural styles, whatever they could of European [culture], making of it that which would, when blended with the cultural tendencies inherited from Africa, express their own sense of life—while rejecting the rest.

—Ralph Ellison

10 : African American Cultures

African American social development varied greatly between the Chesapeake and Lowcountry. Two remarkably different African American societies inhabited the same continent and adjoined one another. Different combinations of African immigrants, coming from dissimilar backgrounds, arriving in contrasting regional settings—shaped most notably by disparate ecologies, staple crops, settlement patterns, and demographic forces—created two distinctive social and cultural configurations. Just as there were many Souths, so there were many African American societies.

Nevertheless, these two regional groupings of black people still had much in common. In addition to their common enslavement and their location within the same Anglophone world, African involuntary migrants to British North America possessed a common cultural heritage, if not a collective culture. Coming from highly diverse societies, African newcomers shared some cultural principles and assumptions—about how the world worked, how people interacted, and how to express themselves aesthetically. This normative bedrock Melville Herskovits has labeled a "grammar of culture." It provided a limited but vital resource on which an ethnically diverse people could draw, a broad framework within which so much else had to be elaborated, a scaffolding on which a whole new structure could arise.

An investigation of the major symbolic dimensions of slave life—language, play, and religion—will speak to both themes. Additional differences in the two regional cultures will surface, but the focus on interior beliefs will facilitate the discovery of a number of shared values. The outlines of the two regional cultures will be etched in even sharper relief, but the foundations of a single ethnic subculture will also be uncovered. To change metaphors, a contrapuntal arrangement need not obscure the existence of harmonies.[1]

WORDS

Language is central to culture. It is the means by which a people communicates, expresses values and beliefs, and bequeaths a cultural heritage. But the precise relation of a language and a culture is harder to specify. Language may frame a culture. It may serve as the living representation of a people's way of life, enabling them, in George Steiner's words, to keep secret the "inherited, singular springs of their identity." From this perspective, the disappearance or destruction of a language signals an assault on group identity and the replacement of one cultural system by another. The loss of an indigenous tongue means the loss of much of the culture that was inextricably bound up with it. Particularly might this be true, of course, with a people who suffered the trauma of enslavement and transportation to the New World and, in the words of one linguist, a "catastrophic" and "unparalleled" break in their linguistic traditions. But a language may also refract rather than reflect a culture. After all, some linguistic groups cut across cultural boundaries, some cultures contain within them diverse languages, and some cultural groups have maintained much of their heritage even with the total loss of their original language. As Ernest Gellner has observed, "changing one's language" is not necessarily "the heart-breaking or soul-destroying business which it is claimed to be in romantic nationalist literature." Whether language loss is stressful or not, language itself is undoubtedly an active force in society, used by some as a means of control and by others as a means of self-defense. Clearly, the relation of language and culture is complex and needs to be explored with care.[2]

Africans arriving in North America spoke a bewildering variety of indige-

---

1. Melville J. Herskovits, *The Myth of the Negro Past* (New York, 1941), 81. See also Sidney W. Mintz and Richard Price, *An Anthropological Approach to the Afro-American Past: A Caribbean Perspective*, Institute for the Study of Human Issues, Occasional Papers in Social Change, no. 2 (Philadelphia, 1976); and Sally Price and Richard Price, *Afro-American Arts of the Suriname Rain Forest* (Berkeley, Calif., 1980). Ralph Ellison, *Shadow and Act* (New York, 1964), 255 (I have substituted the word *culture* for *music* in the original, because Ellison's point is of general import).

2. George Steiner, *After Babel: Aspects of Language and Translation* (London, 1975), 232; Gillian Sankoff, "The Genesis of a Language," in Kenneth C. Hill, ed., *The Genesis of Language* (Ann Arbor, Mich., 1979), 24; Ernest Gellner, *Thought and Change* (London, 1964), 165. An excellent introduction to this complex subject can be found in Peter Burke and Roy Porter, eds., *The Social History of Language* (Cambridge, 1987), 1–20.

nous languages. One of the least densely populated continents in the world, Africa is *the* most linguistically complex. Today about sixteen hundred languages are spoken in Africa, and eleven hundred of those are confined to a belt that encompasses most of the territory that supplied slaves to British North America. This band, running south of and parallel to the Sahara Desert, has been appropriately labeled the "Sub-Saharan Fragmentation Belt" and is an area of extraordinary linguistic intricacy. European explorers and traders soon learned that languages differed at almost every point of call. Consequently, most new arrivals to British America were unable to converse with one another in a native language. Mutual unintelligibility was a consequence of the heterogeneity of African immigrants and of the deep fragmentation of their linguistic heritage.[3]

Nevertheless, African languages, though multiple, shared affinities. The differences among West African languages are mainly lexical. Their structures—their grammatical, phonological, and semantic systems—are often quite similar. Many Africans have become experienced in operating different sets of vocabulary while retaining many of the structural rules of their first language.[4] In addition, certain languages—Wolof and Manding, in particular—had a disproportionately large influence during the era of the slave trade, because most other parts of the West African coast and hinterland were (and are) more linguistically fragmented than Senegambia and its hinterland, the home of these two languages. It has been argued that "the Mandinka language," in particular, "early became the *lingua franca* . . . from the mouth of the Gambia to the upper Niger." Certainly, as David Dalby has stated, Manding was "the most geographically extensive language in western West Africa." Bilingualism or multilingualism was therefore already common before slaves left Africa for the New World.[5]

---

3. David Dalby, "The Language Map of Africa," appendix to chap. 12, in UNESCO, *General History of Africa*, I, *Methodology and African Prehistory*, ed. Ji Ki-Zerbo (London, 1981), 309–315; and for the maps themselves, see David Dalby, *Language Map of Africa and the Adjacent Islands* (London, 1977). See also Richard Ligon, *A True and Exact History of the Island of Barbadoes* (London, 1673), 46. Cf. John Thornton, *Africa and Africans in the Making of the Atlantic World, 1400–1680* (Cambridge, 1992), 186.

4. David Dalby, "Black through White: Patterns of Communication in Africa and the New World," in Walt Wolfram and Nona H. Clarke, eds., *Black-White Speech Relationships* (Washington, D.C., 1971), 99–138, esp. 107. On language families in West and Central Africa, see Joseph H. Greenberg, *The Languages of Africa* (The Hague, 1966).

5. J. F. Ade Ajayi and Ian Espie, *A Thousand Years of West African History: A Handbook for Teachers and Students* (Ibadan, Nigeria, 1965), 142; David Dalby, "The African Element in American English," in Thomas Kochman, ed., *Rappin' and Stylin' Out: Communication in Urban Black America* (Urbana, Ill., 1972), 172; Ian F. Hancock, "Manding Lexical Behavior in Sierra Leone Krio," in Ivan R. Dihoff, ed., *Current Approaches to African Linguistics*, I

Linguistic developments on the coast of Africa, moreover, also laid the basis for the later evolution of black languages in the New World. Pidgins, or functionally restricted languages employed by speakers of different languages usually for trading, emerged among the indigenous coastal peoples. The first pidgins borrowed heavily from the Portuguese lexicon but contained many grammatical and phonological features of West African languages; later, they gave rise to an English-derived Proto-Pidgin, based heavily on English "nautical language." Once a pidgin became the primary language of a speech community, it was transformed through relexification into a creole. A Guinea Coast Creole English, it has been argued, developed in West Africa, particularly in the Senegambia region. This Afrogenetic theory posits an African-derived grammar underlying the systems of all Atlantic creoles. By some or all of these means, significant linguistic interchange occurred even before Africans left the coast.[6]

In sum, through the shared structural principles of most African languages, the multilingualism of many of the continent's inhabitants, the development of pidgins, and perhaps even the development of a Guinea Coast Creole English, the basis for mutual intelligibility among Africans was undoubtedly much greater than the sheer number of separate African languages might suggest. Moreover, all these possibilities point to Africans' being less powerless in linguistic encounters with Europeans than their slavery might imply. Africans were able to strip away a European morphological system and recast it in a

---

(Dordrecht, Holland, 1983), 247–261. A South Carolina runaway boy from Senegambia was said to speak "the Jollof [Wolof] language" (Charles Mayne, *SCG,* Jan. 29, 1756). Mervyn C. Alleyne, *Comparative Afro-American: An Historical-Comparative Study of English-based Afro-American Dialects of the New World* (Ann Arbor, Mich., 1980), authoritatively traces the structural similarities of creoles to West African languages.

6. Keith Whinnom, "The Origin of the European-based Creoles and Pidgins," *Orbis,* XIV (1965), 509–527; J. L. Dillard, "Creole English and Creole Portuguese: The Early Records," in Ian F. Hancock, ed., *Readings in Creole Studies* (Ghent, Belgium, 1979), 261–268; Morris Goodman, "The Portuguese Element in the American Creoles," in Glenn G. Gilbert, ed., *Pidgin and Creole Languages: Essays in Honor of John E. Reinecke* (Honolulu, 1987), 361–405; Ian F. Hancock, "A Provisional Comparison of the English-based English Creoles," *African Language Review,* VIII (1969), 7–72; Hancock, "The Domestic Hypothesis, Diffusion, and Componentiality: An Account of Atlantic Anglophone Creole Origins," in Pieter Muysken and Norval Smith, eds., *Substrata versus Universals in Creole Genesis,* Papers from the Amsterdam Creole Workshop, April 1985 (Amsterdam, Philadelphia, 1986), 71–102; Frederic G. Cassidy, "The Place of Gullah," *American Speech,* LV (1980), 3–16; Elizabeth Tonkin, "Some Coastal Pidgins of West Africa," in Edwin Ardener, ed., *Social Anthropology and Language,* Association of Social Anthropologists Monograph, no. 10 (London, 1971), 129–155; Anthony Naro, "The Origin of West African Pidgin," in Claudia Corum et al., eds., *Papers from the Ninth Regional Meeting of the Chicago Linguistic Society* (Chicago, 1973), 442–449.

familiar mold. They grafted a European vocabulary onto West African grammatical structures that had much in common.[7]

Lowcountry slaves spoke a wide range of African languages. The jailer of the Charleston workhouse employed as interpreter a slave who spoke Manding; when an Angolan slave was brought to jail, "other negroes in the house" had to translate. A rural South Carolina master learned how long two Africans caught near his plantation had been absent from one of his own slaves, "who is of their country." John Graham, a Savannah merchant, included a young girl in a group consigned to an East Florida planter on the mistaken assumption that she had a sister among them only to find out from "Tom who speaks her language" that he had made a mistake. Some of these slaves able to converse in an African language might not have been speaking their first language. Thus, one of the slave interpreters employed by the Charleston jailer could converse in both Manding and Bambara. Similarly, two Lowcountry slaves, who had been in the province two years and spoke enough English "so as to be understood," conversed primarily in "Bombra," or Bambara, but one of them could also speak "the Fulla language."[8]

Chesapeake masters were largely oblivious of the specific languages spoken by Africans. They knew they existed, but, by the middle of the eighteenth century at least, they could be pardoned for thinking them inconsequential. It took an exceptional event like an anticipated revolt in Prince George's County, Maryland, in 1740 to bring the existence of African languages to their attention. This plot gained credence when a slave woman claimed to have heard "several of [the] Negroes talking in their Country language." Or it took the

---

7. This claim that Atlantic creoles were based on the grammatical forms of African languages does not rule out the possibility that they were also based on universal human grammars found in innate mental structures common to all languages. See in particular Derek Bickerton, *Roots of Language* (Ann Arbor, Mich., 1981), for a powerful argument for the role of "universals," and for two good collections on the debate: Muysken and Smith, eds., *Substrata versus Universals in Creole Genesis;* and Salikoko S. Mufwene, ed., *Africanisms in Afro-American Language Varieties* (Athens, Ga., 1993). For a useful bibliography, see C. Jourdan, "Pidgins and Creoles: The Blurring of Categories," *Annual Review of Anthropology*, XX (1991), 187–209; and for the best overall survey, John A. Holm, *Pidgins and Creoles*, I, *Theory and Structure* (Cambridge, 1988), and II, *Reference Survey* (Cambridge, 1989).

8. Workhouse, *SCG,* Feb. 2, Aug. 30, Nov. 22, 1760, Oct. 30, 1762, Mar. 26, 1763, Apr. 27, 1765; John Mullryne, ibid., June 24, 1734; John Graham to James Grant, Jan. 25, 1769, 0771/401, Papers of General James Grant of Ballindalloch, sometime Governor of East Florida, in ownership of Sir Evan Macpherson-Grant, Bart., Ballindalloch Castle Muniments, Scotland; Workhouse, *SCG,* Nov. 1, 1759; John Savage, *SC and AGG,* June 3, 1774. For other references to African languages, see William Healy, *SCG,* Jan. 3, 1771; Charles Ferguson, *State Gaz of SC,* Nov. 6, 1786; Elias Horry, *Charleston Courier,* Mar. 23, 1805; and David Suares, ibid., July 24, 1806.

presence of an observer in a region such as the piedmont of Virginia where Africans could still be found in significant numbers late into the century. Thus, in 1764, the Reverend James Marye, Jr., reported from Orange County, "There are great Quantities of those Negroes imported here yearly from Africa, who have Languages peculiar to themselves." The dwindling numbers of Africans in the late colonial Chesapeake, particularly in the tidewater region, account for the residents' silence on the languages that they spoke.[9]

How quickly Africans learned the rudiments of English is complicated. Much depended on the age of the immigrant, degree of contact with creoles and whites (which varied most importantly across space, over time, and according to work assignments), predisposition to learn the new language, and linguistic abilities. Moreover, an assessment of this process is filtered through the ears of contemporaries, who are more often than not insensitive to the nuances of slave speech.

Missionaries provide useful clues to Africans' acquisition of English. In the Lowcountry, their testimony ranges from the Reverend William Pierce, who claimed that saltwater blacks soon learned English, to the Reverend Thomas Hasell, who believed that those "brought hither from their own Country, except a few that come very young, seldom or never speak good English." The weight of opinion supported Hasell rather than Pierce. In the early eighteenth century, the Reverend Francis Le Jau faced a predicament when asked to grant baptism to a pious slave, who even "after having been above twenty years in this Province . . . can hardly speak even common things, so as to be understood." At midcentury, after spending three years ministering to Africans in Georgia, the Reverend Joseph Ottolenghe emphasized the problems in getting "them to understand what the Meaning of Words is." In the Chesapeake, too, Africans were sometimes said to be slow learners. In 1764, the Reverend James Marye declared that Africans had to spend "many years" in North America "before they understand English." Even then, he continued, "great Numbers . . . never do understand it, well Enough to reap any Benefit from what is said in Church." This comment might have been self-serving, justifying Marye's lack of interest in proselytizing blacks, but it no doubt bore some relation to reality.[10]

9. Stephen Bordley to Matthias Harry, Jan. 30, 1740, Bordley Letterbook, MHS; Rev. James Marye, Jr., to Rev. John Waring, Sept. 25, 1764, in John C. Van Horne, ed., *Religious Philanthropy and Colonial Slavery: The American Correspondence of the Associates of Dr. Bray, 1717–1777* (Urbana, Ill., 1985), 219.

10. W. Pierce to Countess of Huntingdon, Mar. 25, 1774, A 4/2/9, Countess of Huntingdon's American Papers, Westminster College, Cambridge, England; Rev. Thomas Hasell to SPG, Mar. 12, 1712, A7/400–401, SPG; Rev. Francis Le Jau to SPG, Mar. 12, 1715, A10/95; Joseph Ottolenghe to [Rev. John Waring], Nov. 18, 1754, Oct. 4, 1759, in Van Horne, ed.,

Masters' descriptions of the speech patterns of their African slaves provide further insight into the acquisition of a new language. Generally, Africans who had spent less than a year in the Lowcountry spoke little or no English. After four months' residence in South Carolina, four Africans were apparently unable to pronounce their new names. The captors of Toby, who spoke "very little English," concluded that he must have been about "9–12 months in the country." Nor did proficiency in English improve for many Africans after the first year. Sylvia, said to be from "Gulla country" and a Lowcountry resident for two years, spoke "a few words of English badly." Many Africans with three to four years' residence in the Lowcountry exhibited minimal command of English. Others never achieved proficiency. Middle-aged Paris had lived for a decade in South Carolina, "notwithstanding which, he spoke very bad English and is scarcely able to distinguish his owner." Even Africans who had learned Anglo-American skills were sometimes said to speak English poorly or hardly at all. Indeed, many masters thought that most Africans betrayed their origins as soon as they opened their mouths. Thus, Charles spoke "English remarkably well, but may easily be distinguished from one born in this Province by his Speech," and Colly was "African born, consequently speaks bad English."[11]

Yet a few Africans learned English adeptly and quickly in the Lowcountry. It helped enormously if they were young on arrival. Thus, Cordelier from Angola spoke good English, "having been in the province from a boy," and York, from "Coromantee country," spoke "as good English as a country born" slave, "having been brought here young." For one young African, it is possible to chart his progress in learning English. Ned arrived from Angola in his midteens. In 1741, he ran away; two years later, aged about seventeen, he absconded again, then speaking "broken" English; by the following fall, he spoke "tolerable good English"; and, two years after that, "good English when he pleases." Young Africans were often quick learners, but Lowcountry masters clearly saw them as exceptional.[12]

In the Chesapeake, Africans seem to have mastered English rather more quickly than in the Lowcountry. To be sure, Chesapeake Africans, like their

---

Religious Philanthropy and Colonial Slavery, 116, 138; Rev. James Marye, Jr., to Rev. John Waring, Sept. 25, 1764, ibid., 219.

11. Daniel Ravenel, *SCG*, Feb. 25, 1772 (four Africans); Stribling and Buchannan, *State Gaz of SC*, Aug. 16, 1787 (Toby); Steuart and Barre, *Columbian Herald, or the Patriotic Courier of North-America* (Charleston), Aug. 29, 1785 (Sylvia); Samuel Richbourg, *SCG and CJ*, Feb. 2, 1773 (Paris); John Champneys, *SCG*, Aug. 30, 1773 (Charles); George Evans, Jr., *SC and AGG*, Mar. 12, 1778 (Colly).

12. Nathan Tart, *SCG*, Nov. 8, 1751 (Cordelier); Isaac Waight, *SCG and CJ*, Feb. 11, 1772 (York); Joseph Batsford, *SCG*, Oct. 10, 1741, Apr. 18, Oct. 3, 1743, Oct. 22, 1744, John Gordon, ibid., Oct. 18, 1746 (Ned).

Lowcountry counterparts, seem rarely to have lost all traces of their distinctive linguistic heritages. Thus, Tomboy retained "much of his country dialect, though imported young," and Will, though resident in Virginia for "many years," was "easily discover[ed]" to be an African by his speech. Still, Africans in the Chesapeake generally learned English more rapidly and extensively than in the Lowcountry. Some Africans, resident in Virginia for no more than two years, spoke "pretty good English." Furthermore, some Chesapeake Africans mastered English. Few matched Ayre, who, "although an African, affects to pronounce the English language very fine, or rather to clip it," but others elicited comments about their "very good English."[13]

In South Carolina, many Africans and later native-born slaves, even when ostensibly speaking their master's language, spoke something other than Standard English. In describing exceptional slaves who spoke English well, this region's masters inadvertently provide information on the speech of *most* slaves. Thus, Rachel, a mulatto, spoke English "a little more properly than Negroes do in general"; Ben, a native of Carolina, spoke "plain and tolerably free from the common negro dialect"; and a teenage boy, who had a mustee complexion, spoke "English free from the negro accent." A Baptist minister's quandary as to the language best employed in an instructional text designed for blacks is further testament to this distinctive "lowcountry Lingo," as he termed it. He decided on Standard English rather than "the Negro stile" in ways that anticipate modern debates on this subject. From his "acquaintance with the Negroes," he explained, "there is a great diversity in their manner of expressing themselves. Many words they will pronounce their own way, let them be spelt as they may. Those of them who can read, learn to read by our common spelling, and would be at a loss to read their own lingo as we would spell it." The distinctiveness of black speech is further emphasized by one master who described his five slaves as speaking "very good (Black English)." Most significant, Lowcountry masters mentioned native-born slaves who spoke "bad" or "broken" English, descriptions they usually reserved for Africans.[14]

---

13. Alex Spark, *VaG* (Rind), Aug. 10, 1769 (Tomboy); Leighton Wood, Jr., *VaG or AA*, June 22, 1782 (Will); Thomas Lawson, *VaG* (D and H), Jan. 23, 1778 (Ayre). For quick learners among recent immigrants, see Lewis Burwell, *VaG* (Parks), Apr. 21, 1738; William Hunter, ibid., May 16, 1745; Samuel Du-Val, *VaG* (Hunter), Mar. 28, 1755. For Africans speaking "good English," see John Ravenscroft, ibid. (Parks), June 6, 1745; William Winston, Jr., ibid. (Hunter), Nov. 7, 1754; Daniel Parke Custis, ibid., Dec. 12, 1755; William Black, ibid., (D and H), Dec. 5, 1777.

14. Paul Hamilton, *Gaz of State of SC*, Nov. 1, 1784 (Rachel); James Kennedy, *State Gaz of SC*, Feb. 18, 1790 (Ben); Elias Smerdon, *City Gaz*, Mar. 26, 1794 (teenage boy); Edmund Botsford to Dr. Richard Furman, Oct. 15, 1808, Botsford Papers, Baptist Historical Collection, Furman University, Greenville, S.C.; The Printer, *SCG*, Mar. 30, 1734.

The distinctiveness of Lowcountry black speech is further underscored by its unintelligibility to whites. Eliza Pinckney knew a slave who understood English "very well" but who spoke it so badly that she could not understand him. John Glen described his elderly slave Daniel as "generally [having] much to say tho' he is not easily understood, unless by those who have been used to him." Another Lowcountry master alerted his fellows to a specific misunderstanding that might arise from his slave's speech: the slave's name was Christopher but "may be taken for Cato by his way of expression." Visitors encountered more severe obstacles than residents. In 1780, a band of Hessians on Johns Island sought guidance from a slave boy who claimed to know the way to Stono ferry. From his age and familiarity with the environment, the lad was probably a native Carolinian, but Johann Ewald, one of the Hessians, found him "extremely hard to understand." Five days later, they discovered the universality of the problem. They were unable to talk with blacks because of their "bad dialect." Indeed, another Hessian officer, Carl Bauer, observed that "most of the field Negroes do not understand the English language at all."[15]

The survival of a creole language in parts of the Lowcountry down to the twentieth century is a vital clue to its presence—and more widespread presence, presumably—two centuries earlier. In fact, twentieth-century analyses of Gullah throw light on the creole's early origins, revealing that particular African linguistic areas were disproportionately influential in its formation. In the 1940s, Lorenzo Dow Turner discovered 251 African words that were regularly used in conversation among speakers of Gullah. Turner's informants knew the meaning of these words, unlike the more than 3,000 personal names whose meaning had been lost or the 92 words heard in stories, songs, and prayers that were sustained only by memory and were confined to these set pieces. The words that were current in modern Gullah can be compared against African words that come close in form and meaning. On this basis, fully 40 percent of the 251 words were from the Angola-Kongo region (99 words alone from the Kongo language), whereas Senegambia and Sierra Leone together contributed 38 percent. The two areas that supplied South Carolina with most of its slaves in the eighteenth and early nineteenth centuries also supplied most of its traceable African vocabulary.[16]

---

15. Eliza Pinckney to Mrs. D. Horry, 1768, Pinckney Family Papers, SCHS; John Glen, *City Gaz*, Jan. 17, 1798; Rawlins Lowndes, *SCG*, June 7, 1760; Johann [von] Ewald, *Diary of the American War: A Hessian Journal*, ed. and trans. Joseph P. Tustin (New Haven, Conn., 1979), 197, 199; George Fenwick Jones, "The 1780 Siege of Charleston as Experienced by a Hessian Officer," part 2, *SCHM*, LXXXVIII (1987), 73.

16. Lorenzo Dow Turner, *Africanisms in the Gullah Dialect* (Chicago, 1949); Cassidy, "Place of Gullah," *Am. Speech*, LV (1980), 3–16; Cassidy, "Sources of the African Element in Gullah," in Lawrence D. Carrington et al., eds., *Studies in Caribbean Language* (Saint Au-

Of the African words retained in Gullah, many were specialized—whether for animals, plants, musical instruments, or magical beliefs—but there were at least three other, more general categories. First, some words described basic, everyday activities or items: *bumbu* for "to carry in the hands," *nam* for "to eat," *nini* for "female breast," *tima* for "to dig," and *tutu* for "excrement." Second, kin terms or nouns denoting age and sex were quite common: *da* for "mother, an elderly woman," *dindi, do,* and *li* for "child," *na* for "mother," and *tata* for "father." Finally, interjections and exclamations, so important to the expression of emotions, were retained: *ban!* for "It is done!" *dede* for "exactly," *kange* for "an exclamation indicating shock," and perhaps most common of all, *ki*. When John Smyth came upon his slave asleep in a canoe, the bondman began his excuse, exclaiming "Kay massa." Similarly, when General William Moultrie returned unexpectedly to his plantation at the end of the Revolutionary war, his slaves "gazed at [him] with astonishment, . . . saying, 'God bless you, massa! we glad for see you, massa!' and every now and then some one or other would come out with a 'ky!' " *Ki* or *kie* is an exclamation, indicating great surprise, heard throughout the African American world and among Gullah informants in the twentieth century.[17]

---

gustine, Trinidad, 1983), 75–81; Cassidy, "Some Similarities between Gullah and Caribbean Creoles," in Michael Montgomery and Guy Bailey, eds., *Language Variety in the South: Perspectives in Black and White* (University, Ala., 1986), 30–37; Cassidy, "Gullah and the Caribbean Connection," in Michael Montgomery, ed., *The Crucible of Carolina: Essays in the Development of Gullah Language and Culture* (Athens, Ga., 1994), 16–22; P.E.H. Hair, "Sierra Leone Items in the Gullah Dialect of American English," *African Language Review,* IV (1965), 79–84; Salikoko S. Mufwene, "The Linguistic Significance of African Proper Names," *Nieuwe West-Indische Gids,* LIX (1985), 149–166; Mufwene, "Africanisms in Gullah: A Re-Examination of the Issues," in Joan H. Hall, Nick Doane, and Dick Ringler, eds., *Old English and New: Essays in Language and Linguistics in Honor of Frederic G. Cassidy* (New York, 1992), 156–182; and Mufwene and Charles Gilman, "How African Is Gullah, and Why," *Am. Speech,* LXII (1987), 120–139.

17. Turner, *Africanisms,* 190–204; J.F.D. Smyth, *A Tour of the United States of America . . .* (London, 1784), I, 121; William Moultrie, *Memoirs of the American Revolution . . . ,* 2 vols. (New York, 1802), II, 356. For modern Gullah speakers' use of ki, see T. J. Woofter, Jr., *Black Yeomanry: Life on St. Helena's Island* (New York, 1930), 54; Guy B. Johnson, *Folk Culture on St. Helena Island, South Carolina* (Chapel Hill, N.C., 1930), 57; and Patricia Jones-Jackson, *When Roots Die: Endangered Traditions on the Sea Islands* (Athens, Ga., 1987), 44. For its use among other New World blacks, see Bolingbroke, *A Voyage to the Demerary . . .* (London, 1807), 96, 105; William Dickson, *Letters on Slavery* (London, 1789), 75, 156; Michael Mullin, *Africa in America: Slave Acculturation and Resistance in the American South and the British Caribbean, 1736–1831* (Urbana, Ill., 1992), 50, 156; Frederic G. Cassidy, "OK—Is It African?" *Am. Speech,* LVI (1981), 271; and F. G. Cassidy and R. B. Le Page, eds., *Dictionary of Jamaican English* (Cambridge, 1967), 259.

In addition, translations, or calques, rather than direct loans, were quite common in Gullah. The English language often uses abstract words to describe modes of human behavior; African words represent the same conduct often by reference to parts of the body. Thus, Gullah-speakers translated English abstract words into African-style equivalents: *bad-mouth* (to curse), *sweet-mouth* (to flatter), *crack one's breath* or *crack teeth* (to speak), *long eye* (envy), *eye-water* (tears). Similarly, Gullah-speakers use phrases that describe something literally or concretely: *day clean* (daybreak), *a-beat-on-iron* (mechanic), *wide mouth* (catfish). Finally, African languages often repeat words to intensify their meaning, and this practice turns up in Gullah: *fillfill* (to fill entirely), *trutru* (very true), *whitewhite* (very white).[18]

Although an African influence was not negligible in the lexicon of Lowcountry slaves, it was a more powerful presence in other areas of their language, particularly grammar. Unfortunately, few depictions of eighteenth-century slave speech have survived; the few relics aimed more to poke fun at, than provide a faithful record of, the slaves' syntax. Nevertheless, as illustrations of a different syntactical system, these fragments are useful. Thus, in the 1770s, James Barclay reckoned that a slave might commonly say when flogged, "Da buccary no be good fatru." In 1783, Hugh Crow claimed to have heard a black, who attended the sale of indentured Irish servants in Charleston, laughingly cry out, "One dollar more for 'em da; I have 'em, negra buy buckra now!" to which another replied, "Three bit more for 'em da; I have 'em, negra buy buckra now!" Eleven years later, a South Carolina newspaper carried an anecdote about a burial. The four bearers were slaves, none of whom had been given the customary gloves. "About midway from house to churchyard, Cuffee turned slyly round and thus accosted his brother bearer: 'Caesar, you got-e grove?' 'No. Ask Cato.' 'Cato, you got-e grove?' 'No. Ask Toney.' 'Toney, you got-e grove?' 'No; dam a grove me got!' 'Well, then,' says Cuffee, 'Fring he down an' let he go besel!'" Five years later, John Connolly struck a jocular note when advertising for his runaway slave Stephen, requesting him to come back, "when his cruise is out"; otherwise, Stephen would "get what Paddy gave the drum." To which a later notice replied, "Oho! Massa Conly, mee tink you paddy; you sa you beet me like one paddy beet him drum, if I no comb homb myself. We poor Nega la, no kitche no habbee; how paddy beet me den?" In the

---

18. Turner, *Africanisms*, 232–236; Jones-Jackson, *When Roots Die*, 140–141. For calques, see Richard Allsopp, "Africanisms in the Idiom of Caribbean English," in Paul F. A. Kotey and Haig Der-Houssikian, eds., *Language and Linguistic Problems in Africa,* Proceedings of the Seventh Conference on African Linguistics (Columbia, S.C., 1977), 429–441; Jeffrey Hirshberg, "Towards a Dictionary of Black American English on Historical Principles," *Am. Speech,* LVII (1982), 167–168, 175.

same year, John Davis encountered a slave woman who exclaimed, "Too much buckra come here, for true!"[19]

These depictions contain many African features. Not least, of course, is the word, *buckra* or *backra,* derived from Efik *mbakara,* meaning "he who surrounds or governs," which in turn became associated with "white man." Far more important, however, is the verbal and pronominal system that underlies these and other examples of early black American speech. The use of "me" as a subject pronoun as in "grove me got" or "mee tink you paddy," or "he" and "em" as object pronouns, as in "'Fring he down an' let he go" or "I have 'em," was common in creole and reflects a simpler, more efficient use of pronouns in African grammars. Even more distinctive perhaps, and a link to many languages spoken along the West African coast, is the grammatical rule that verb stems are not inflected to indicate either person or tense, as in "Da buccary no be good." Indeed, as with "We poor Nega la," the verb "to be" is often omitted altogether, particularly when present tense is indicated.[20]

The existence of modern Gullah suggests a more widespread creole in earlier times; by the same token, does the absence of a creole in the modern

19. James Barclay, *The Voyages and Travels of James Barclay, Containing Many Surprising Adventures, and Interesting Narratives* (Dublin, 1777), 26, and see also 25, 28; Hugh Crow, *Memoirs of the Late Captain Hugh Crow, of Liverpool . . .* (London, 1830), 9; *State Gazette of SC,* Sept. 25, 1794, reprinted in "Note on Gullah," *SCHM,* L (1949), 56–57; John Connolly, *City Gaz,* June 25, 1799, and Stephen's answer, ibid., June 27, 1799; John Davis, *Travels of Four Years and a Half in the United States of America . . .* (Bristol, 1803), 107. For similar examples of black speech in plays, see Richard Walser, "Negro Dialect in Eighteenth-Century American Drama," *Am. Speech,* XXX (1955), 269–276. The expression "for true," cited by Barclay and Davis, is commonly found in Jamaican English. Barclay mentions a slave's telling him "stand off obsia," also commonly found in Jamaican English. See Cassidy and Le Page, eds., *Dictionary of Jamaican English,* 84, 186. For an interesting poem that seems to have been written in Jamaican Creole but was conceivably written in Gullah, see Donald R. Kloe, "Buddy Quow: An Anonymous Poem in Gullah-Jamaican Dialect Written circa 1800," *Southern Folklore Quarterly,* XXXVIII (1974), 81–90.

20. For more technical accounts of creole grammatical principles, see William A. Stewart, "Continuity and Change in American Negro Dialects," in Robert H. Bentley and Samuel D. Crawford, eds., *Black Language Reader* (Glenview, Ill., 1973), 55–69; J. L. Dillard, *Black English: Its History and Usage in the United States* (New York, 1972); John R. Rickford, "The Question of Prior Creolization in Black English," in Albert Valdman, ed., *Pidgin and Creole Linguistics* (Bloomington, Ind., 1977), 191–215; Rickford, "Ethnicity as a Sociolinguistic Boundary," *Am. Speech,* LX (1985), 99–125; John Holm, "Variability of the Copula in Black English and Its Creole Kin," ibid., LIX (1984), 291–309; Edgar W. Schneider, *American Earlier Black English: Morphological and Syntactic Variables* (Tuscaloosa, Ala., 1989). For less technical discussions, see Eugene D. Genovese, *Roll, Jordan, Roll: The World the Slaves Made* (New York, 1974), 434–435; and Charles Joyner, *Down by the Riverside: A South Carolina Slave Community* (Urbana, Ill., 1984), 197–202. For *backra,* see Turner, *Africanisms,* 191; and F. G. Cassidy, "Another Look at *Buckaroo,*" *Am. Speech,* LIII (1978), 49–51.

Chesapeake point to its nonexistence in earlier times? Although such logic is clearly faulty—the absence of a creole in the modern Chesapeake may be explained by that region's lack of isolation as compared to the Sea Islands of South Carolina and Georgia—the question is extremely difficult to answer. Its intractability is suggested by a similar debate concerning the status of Barbadian slave speech. Unlike many other British West Indians, present-day Barbadians speak a form of Standard English, not a creole. Indeed, some scholars claim that a stable creole failed to establish itself among Barbadian slaves at any point in the island's history. As early as 1700, Ian Hancock argues, both blacks and whites on that island spoke "a local metropolitan, rather than creolized variety of English." Conversely, Frederic Cassidy, while acknowledging the tradition of superior English spoken in Barbados, attributes it, not to the lack of a creole, but rather to its rapid *decreolization*. The evidence that Cassidy and others adduce seems the more persuasive. Through the eighteenth century at least, most Barbadian slaves spoke a creole. Decreolization was undoubtedly rapid and extensive, but whether it had progressed to more than a minority of the island's slaves by 1800 may be doubted.[21]

Provided Cassidy's interpretation is correct, should it be inferred that a stable creole materialized in Virginia, much as in Barbados? The answer must be no, for, although the demographic profile of the Barbadian population approximated Virginia's more closely than any other British Caribbean colony, the contrast was still striking. Despite the presence of more whites than any other British Caribbean island, Barbados still had a formidable black majority, received a constant and large influx of Africans throughout the eighteenth century, and grouped slaves on large plantations. Indeed, were we to transpose Hancock's view of early Barbados to Virginia, it might assume more credence. Perhaps a local form of Standard English was the common form of speech for most slaves in the eighteenth-century Chesapeake?[22]

---

21. Compare Cassidy, "The Place of Gullah," *Am. Speech,* LV (1980), 3–16; Ian F. Hancock, "Gullah and Barbadian—Origins and Relationships," ibid., 17–35; and Cassidy, "Barbadian Creole—Possibility and Probability," ibid., LXI (1986), 195–205. See also Audrey Burrowes, in collaboration with R. Allsopp, "Barbadian Creole: Its Social History and Structure," in Carrington et al., eds., *Studies in Caribbean Language,* 38–45; John D. Roy, "The Structure of Tense and Aspect in Barbadian English Creole," in Manfred Görlach and John A. Holm, eds., *Focus on the Caribbean* (Amsterdam, 1986), 141–156; John R. Rickford, "The Creole Residue in Barbados," in Hall et al., eds., *Old English and New,* 183–201; and Rickford and Jerome S. Handler, "Textual Evidence on the Nature of Early Barbadian Speech, 1676–1835," *Journal of Pidgin and Creole Languages,* IX (1994), 221–255.

22. John Holm, "The Atlantic Creoles and the Language of the Ex-Slave Recordings," in Guy Bailey et al., eds., *The Emergence of Black English: Text and Commentary* (Amsterdam, 1991), 231–248 (quotations on 244–246); Michael Montgomery, Janet M. Fuller, and Sharon

The absence of a creole language among early Chesapeake slaves gains some support from linguistic analyses of black speech in the nineteenth- and twentieth-century South. Many linguists have found significant discontinuities between Gullah and the speech of other southern blacks. Apart from "a few isolated areas such as coastal South Carolina and Georgia," John Holm argues, "there is still no unambiguous evidence that the English of North American blacks was ever completely creolized." Most likely, Holm continues, "blacks in most parts of the American South spoke a semi-creole from the beginning." An analysis of nineteenth-century letters written by African-Americans found little or no creole influence; these semiliterate blacks used vernacular varieties of English. Similarly, Edgar Schneider has taken issue with the claim that "a supraregionally uniform 'Plantation Creole,' supposedly spread all over the South, ever existed." The speech of ex-slaves, he argues, was predominantly dialectical English in character.[23]

But instances of mutual unintelligibility between whites and blacks and of distinctive black speech patterns can be found in the Chesapeake region. As in the Lowcountry, statements about the radical divergence between white and black speech might suggest the existence of a creole language. Thus, in 1748, a missionary reported that blacks had "a language peculiar to themselves, a wild confused medley of Negro and corrupt English, which makes them very unintelligible except to those who have conversed with them for many years." Similarly, John Smyth was unable to understand his own boy attendant and found that many Virginia blacks spoke "a mixed dialect between the Guinea and English." Other remarks might suggest only dialectical differences between white and black speech. Thus, Landon Carter described a slave of his who spoke "readily, and without restraint, seeming to aim at a stile above that used generally by slaves, though something corrupt," and John Leland observed that black "language is broken, but they understand each other and the white may gain their ideas." An alleged letter written by a Maryland slave to his master

---

DeMarse, "'The Black Men Has Wives and Sweet Harts [and Third Person Plural -s] Jest like the White Men': Evidence for Verbal -s from Written Documents on Nineteenth-Century African American Speech," *Language Variation and Change,* V (1993), 335–357; Edgar W. Schneider, "Africanisms in the Grammar of Afro-American English: Weighing the Evidence," in Mufwene, ed., *Africanisms in Afro-American Language Varieties,* 209–221; Schneider, "The Origin of the Verbal -s in Black English," *Am. Speech,* LVIII (1983), 99–113; Schneider, *American Earlier Black English.*

23. Richard S. Dunn, *Sugar and Slaves: The Rise of the Planter Class in the English West Indies, 1624–1713* (Chapel Hill, N.C., 1972), esp. chap. 7; Jerome S. Handler and Frederick W. Lange, *Plantation Slavery in Barbados: An Archaeological and Historical Investigation* (Cambridge, Mass., 1978), esp. chap. 2.

had some creole features. For example, a creole usage of pronouns is indicated in Toby's wife "[Re]member he luff to you masser."[24]

Because no creole, if it existed, has survived in the Chesapeake, it is impossible to trace African roots in the same way as in South Carolina. As with American English more generally, most of the direct African loanwords in use among eighteenth-century Virginia slaves were presumably largely zoological, botanical, and culinary—words like *cooter* (turtle), *pojo* (heron), *banana, yam, cola, pinder* (peanut), and *goober* (peanut). In the 1820s, a traveler in Virginia recognized that *tote* was an African word in use among slaves. No African region can be identified as supplying a large proportion of words to Chesapeake black English.[25]

Although black speech in the Chesapeake, therefore, had certain distinctive characteristics, some of which derived from Africa, most observers were more impressed by the ability of Chesapeake slaves to speak Standard English, or its near equivalent. On the basis of residence in Virginia from 1716 to 1721, Hugh Jones claimed that the "Native Negroes generally talk good English without idiom or tone, and discourse handsomely upon most common subjects." John Davis, while noting pidgin and creole forms of speech, quoted a number of Virginia slaves in Standard or near-Standard English. In 1796, Benjamin Latrobe "observed that better English is spoken by the common people, and even by the Negroes in Virginia than by the lower orders in any county of England with which I am acquainted." Even if many Chesapeake blacks at first spoke a creole or semicreole, apparently most had shifted quite rapidly toward speaking English dialects.[26]

In more grudging fashion, Chesapeake masters also testified to the linguistic proficiency of their native-born slaves. Most common was the description "smooth-tongued," which, though not offered as a compliment, spoke well of

---

24. Rev. Philip Reading to Rev. Samuel Smith, Oct. 10, 1748, in Van Horne, ed., *Religious Philanthropy and Colonial Slavery,* 100 (this missionary worked in Delaware, adjoining the Chesapeake); Smyth, *A Tour in the United States of North America,* I, 39, 78–79, 88, 121; Landon Carter, *VaG or AA,* Dec. 18, 1784; John Leland, *The Virginia Chronicle . . .* (Norfolk, Va., 1790), 12; Toby Chew to his master, *Md Gaz,* July 7, 1747. See also Creed Haskins, *VaG* (P and D), Mar. 22, 1770; and Peter Pelham, ibid., Aug. 4, 1774.

25. Dalby, "The African Element," in Kochman, ed., *Rappin' and Stylin' Out,* 170–186; M. M. Matthews, *Some Sources of Southernisms* (University, Ala., 1948); Henry C. Knight [Arthur Singleton, pseud.], *Letters from the South and West* (Boston, 1824) 82.

26. Hugh Jones, *The Present State of Virginia . . .* , ed. Richard L. Morton (Chapel Hill, N.C., 1956), 80 (see also 75); Davis, *Travels,* 407; Edward C. Carter II et al., eds., *The Virginia Journals of Benjamin Henry Latrobe, 1795–1798,* 2 vols. (New Haven, Conn., 1977), I, 125; Donald Winford, "Back to the Past: The BEV / Creole Connection Revisited," *Lang. Variation and Change,* IV (1992), 311–357.

the slaves' ability to manipulate the dominant language. Some slaves had mastered the art to an impressive degree: John Wilson was "sober and smooth in his discourse"; Joe had "a fine smooth address"; and Davy spoke "softly and civilly." The ultimate compliment went to George Quacca, who had "a masterly speech," but Jacob also had similar aspirations, for he liberally sprinkled the words "moreover and likewise" in his conversation.[27]

As Chesapeake slaves migrated out of their region in ever increasing numbers in the last quarter of the eighteenth century, their new purchasers described their speech as "Virginian." In some cases, the new masters located the accent more precisely. Thus, King, "being born and hired on the Borders of Virginia," was said to have "the Accent peculiar to the lower sort of those People," whereas Jack spoke "the language of a Back Country Negro." More often, however, the ascription was general: Elijah, described as Virginia-born, spoke "with the accent of that country"; nineteen-year-old Sealy brought from Baltimore into South Carolina spoke "the Virginia language"; Will and Sarah appeared "by their dialect to be Virginians"; and William had "the Virginia accent."[28] Many Chesapeake slaves had an identity closely bound up with their region.

Such an identity and such an ability to speak Standard English, or a dialectical variant thereof, also manifested itself among native-born Lowcountry slaves. There, too, masters report slaves speaking "very correct" or "proper" English, although this usually exhausted the repertory of their compliments. Missionaries, such as the Reverend Thomas Hasell, observed that those slaves "born and brought up among us are both Civilized and speak English as well as our selves." By the second half of the eighteenth century, some Carolina slaves had distinctive regional accents. Thus, Scipio had "been much accustomed to the Back Woods, which is known by his speech," and Dinah, from Ninety-Six district, spoke "the back-country dialect." Other slaves, particularly those who worked as sailors on the high seas—frequent visitors to Charleston and other

---

27. William Black, *VaG* (P and D), Dec. 13, 1770 (John Wilson); John Gordon, *VaG* (Purdie), May 29, 1778 (Joe); Robert Beverley, *VaG or AA*, July 9, 1785 (Davy); George Hope, *VaG and WA*, Nov. 5, 1785 (George Quacca); David Hoops, *VaG* (D and H), Mar. 30, 1776 (Jacob). For a few of many examples of "smooth-tongued" slaves, see William Broadnax, *VaG* (Hunter), Mar. 20, 1752; William Skipwith, ibid., Feb. 28, 1755; Francis Willis, Jr., ibid., Oct. 10, 1755; and Richard Eggleston, *VaG* (Royle), Nov. 4, 1763. Fugitives were most likely to be slaves who had attained a relative mastery of Standard English.

28. Stephen Drayton, *SCG*, Apr. 11, 1774 (King); Andrew Fornea, *State Gaz of SC*, Apr. 18, 1785 (Jack); Peter Lepoole, *SC and AGG*, Aug. 21, 1776 (Elijah); Randal Eldredge, *City Gaz*, Aug. 17, 1790 (Sealy); William Rouse, *SCG and T and MDA*, Oct. 17, 1796 (Will and Sarah); Roger Smith, Jr., *City Gaz*, July 15, 1797 (William). A traveler to North Carolina heard of a settlement of Highlanders who still spoke Gaelic, as did their slaves: Journals of Lady Liston, Dec. 1797, 5697, 12, National Library of Scotland, Edinburgh.

Lowcountry ports—were fluent speakers of a variety of European languages. All of these forms of linguistic assimilation, however, were much less pronounced in the Lowcountry than in the Chesapeake.[29]

Although significant differences existed between these two regional speech communities, slaves in the Chesapeake and Lowcountry used language in similar ways. In both regions, slaves switched between different varieties of language, employed words in artful and inventive ways, and pronounced words in similar fashion.

Slaves employed varieties of language in different contexts. They switched registers within the same language and switched codes—that is, between languages. One obstacle that faced modern investigators of Gullah throws light on the earlier contact period. So adept were modern Gullah-speakers in passing from creole to Standard English when the situation merited it that they fooled putative analysts of their speech patterns for a long time. Bilingualism, so common to their African heritage, was second nature to them. No doubt many eighteenth-century slaves had honed a similar facility. As a young adult, Ned, the Angolan who ran away in 1741, spoke "good English when he pleases." By implication, he spoke some other form of language the rest of the time. That many slaves, particularly in the Chesapeake, spoke an English that whites could readily understand cannot, therefore, preclude the possibility that they spoke a creole among themselves. In short, the languages both Chesapeake and Lowcountry slaves spoke among themselves might have been far more alike than the ones they spoke to whites.[30]

The artfulness of black speech made a significant impression on whites. Bryan Edwards said of Jamaican slaves that they "convey much strong meaning in a short compass" and acknowledged his surprise at the "figurative expressions" and "pointed sentences" of which slaves were capable. As illustration, he related a story of a slave whose sleep was interrupted; before returning to his slumbers, the bondman exclaimed, "Sleep hab no Massa!" In South Carolina, St. George Tucker witnessed the return of his brother, Tudor, to his Dorchester

---

29. Hasell to SPG, Mar. 12, 1712, A7/400–401; Arwin and Rugge, *SCG*, Dec. 2, 1777 (Scipio); Magretta D. Schutt, *Charleston Courier*, July 20, 1803 (Dinah). For "correct" or "proper" English, see Daniel Stewart, *SCG and CJ*, July 7, 1772; Workhouse, *State Gaz of SC*, July 25, 1785; Andrew Pleym, ibid., June 28, 1787; and Cotton M. Stevens, *City Gaz*, Sept. 18, 1790. For fluent speakers of more than one European language, see John Davison, *SCG*, Aug. 25, 1759; John Dutarque, Jr., ibid., July 2, 1763; Samuel Warner, *SC and AGG*, Apr. 18, 1764, supplement; and John Rains, *SCG*, July 13, 1765.

30. Turner, *Africanisms*, 11–14; the reference to Ned is in note 12, above. On switching registers and codes, see J. A. Fishman, "The Sociology of Language," in Pier Paolo Giglioli, ed., *Language and Social Context: Selected Readings* (Harmondsworth, Eng., 1972), 45–58; C. A. Ferguson, "Diglossia," ibid., 232–251; and M.A.K. Halliday, *Language as Social Semiotic: The Social Interpretation of Language and Meaning* (London, 1978), 35.

plantation, where one slave "expressed himself in a most energetical Metaphor—approaching his Master he accosted him in these Words—Aw, Mawser, me hungry for see You!" St. George Tucker was amused at the "droll Idiom he had introduced in our language." John Davis admired the way Lowcountry blacks "endure execration without emotion, for they say, 'when Mossa curse, he break no bone.'" A slave belonging to James Habersham was anxious that his master "wanted to sell him *softly*"—that is, without the slave's "Consent and knowledge." Habersham "Perfectly understood his meaning" and assured the slave that he had no such intention. A South Carolina slave told a minister that his religious address had a significant impact, for he and other slaves had returned home "and did not even give sleep to their eyes . . . till they had settled every quarrel among themselves."[31]

Inventiveness in religious language elicited special comment. In mid-eighteenth-century Virginia, the Reverend Samuel Davies noted how blacks "express the sensations of their minds so much in the language of simple nature, and with such genuine indications of Sincerity." In early-nineteenth-century Virginia, the Reverend Henry Boehm heard a memorable conversion experience by a black man, who began, "'Bredren, I cannot exactly tell it, but when I was converted two suns rose dat morning sartin.'" Boehm was moved to describe this as "a beautiful figure." Boehm also described preaching from Luke 9:62 on putting the hand to the plow. The "colored people are fond of figures," he observed condescendingly, and "a circle of smiles passed over their black faces" as he told them of the plowman who looked backward, only to make a crooked furrow. But he was surprised later to hear a black man reinterpret the image. "I have put my hand to the Gospel plow," the man declared, "and I am determined to plow my furrow clean up to glory." A Virginia slave addressed John Miller "in a most eloquent manner," and, among many of his remarks, one in particular struck home, for the slave observed "that what I had spoken had passed through his heart like a plough."[32]

Masters had reason to rue the story-telling capacities of some of their slaves.

---

31. Bryan Edwards, *The History, Civil and Commercial, of the British Colonies in the West Indies*, II (Dublin, 1793), 78–79; St. George Tucker's Journal to Charlestown, Apr. 14, 1777, Tucker-Coleman Papers, typescript, CW; Davis, *Travels*, 100; *The Letters of Hon. James Habersham, 1756–1775*, GHS, *Collections*, VI (Savannah, Ga., 1904), 242; Elhanan Winchester, *The Reigning Abominations, Especially the Slave Trade . . .* (London, 1788), 26. See also Roger D. Abrahams, *The Man-of-Words in the West Indies* (Baltimore, 1983).

32. Samuel Davies, *Letters from the Rev. Samuel Davies, etc. Shewing the State of Religion in Virginia, Particularly among the Negroes* (London, 1757), 10; J. B. Wakeley, *The Patriarch of One Hundred Years: Being Reminiscences, Historical and Biographical, of Rev. Henry Boehm . . .* (New York, 1875), 212–213; Jasper W. Cross, ed., "John Miller's Missionary Journal—1816–1817: Religious Conditions in the South and Midwest," *Journal of Presbyterian History*, XLVII (1969), 230.

In the Lowcountry, a few of these accomplished narrators were Africans. The Workhouse jailer became exasperated at Bambara Jemmy, who "seems to have several stories, and tells them different ways," and the master of Coromantee Jockey warned of this fifty-two-year-old slave's ability to "tell a fine story, and make any person believe he is an honest fellow." In most cases, however, these slaves were creoles. Brutus was "never at a Loss for a plausible Tale"; Stepney could "very readily invent" one; Cuffy could relate "a story very compleatly to serve himself"; and Bob's abilities were put most pejoratively, for he could "invent a Lye as soon as he pleases." Perhaps the most striking testimonial, however, was Joseph Child's description of Moll, who had "a most artful knack of framing and delivering a story." In the Chesapeake, Harry was "very subtle and insinuating"; Emanuel, a creole, spoke "remarkably well and has a great knack of insinuation"; Toby was "seldom at a Loss for Words to make out a plausible Tale." Most notable, perhaps, was a waiting man named Christmas, who spoke "with great Propriety, and is so artful that he can invent a Plausible Tale at a Moment's Warning."[33]

Slaves were also said to be great cursers. Bondpeople were, as one master said of his South Carolina slave, "much addicted to swearing." According to Charles Woodmason, slaves "copied [swearing] from their Masters." "How horrid this Crime is in White Men and Christians every thinking Mind must acknowledge," Woodmason expostulated, "but when the tremendous Name of the Almighty [is] prophan'd and abus'd by Negroes Ignorant possibly of the Crime [it] is certainly most shocking." Virginia slaves were little different, it would seem. Thomas Jefferson observed that his slave Sandy "in his conversation swears much," and Peter Deadfoot was "apt to speak quick, swear, and with dreadful curses upon himself, in defence of his innocence, if taxed with a fault."[34]

A number of explanations for these related features of black verbal art may be offered. The most condescending is the "baby talk" theory. Novice or unlearned speakers of a language employed words in unusual and incongruous ways. Even some masters, however, failed to subscribe completely to this the-

---

33. Workhouse, *SCG and CJ*, Dec. 3, 1771 (Jemmy); Joseph Maybank, *SC and AGG*, July 9, 1778 (Jockey); Henry Yonge, *SCG*, Nov. 3, 1746 (Brutus); Rawlins Lowndes, ibid., Sept. 30, 1756 (Stepney); Robert Raper, *SC and AGG*, Mar. 18, 1779 (Cuffy); Daniel O'Neill, *SCG*, July 28, 1779 (Bob); Joseph Child, ibid., Nov. 8, 1751 (Moll); Theodorick Bland, *VaG* (P and D), July 14, 1774 (Harry); John Fox, *VaG* (Rind), Apr. 19, 1770 (Emanuel); Anthony Thornton, Jr., *VaG* (P and D), Feb. 20, 1772 (Toby); James Mercer, ibid., Mar. 19, 1772 (Christmas).

34. Montmollin Caravan and Co., *City Gaz*, Jan. 9, 1800; Richard J. Hooker, ed., *The Carolina Backcountry on the Eve of the Revolution: The Journal and Other Writings of Charles Woodmason, Anglican Itinerant* (Chapel Hill, N.C., 1953), 121; Thomas Jefferson, *VaG* (P and D), Sept. 14, 1769; Thomas Mason, *VaG* (Rind), Sept. 22, 1768.

ory, occasionally complimenting inventive black speakers. Second, class can be invoked. Thorstein Veblen, for instance, has distinguished between the cumbrous and archaic speech of an upper class and the more forcible and direct speech of the lower orders. Similarly, Basil Bernstein has delineated two codes—one elaborated and abstract, the other restricted and concrete—that also can be related to class. The directness and concreteness of black speech may, therefore, owe something to lower-class speech in general. Third, by using words in unfamiliar ways, by maintaining a somewhat separate lexicon, and by swearing profusely, slaves might have been creating antilanguages, somewhat like those associated with certain minority religious groups or the cant of beggars and thieves. Finally, the tradition of eloquence in oral African cultures was probably influential. Proverbs, for example, are a highly prestigious form of speech in many African societies (whereas, in English, eighteenth-century opinion turned sharply against their use). African American speech seems to have been peppered with proverbs, a significant continuity with an African past. The verbal dexterity of Caribbean and North American blacks, evident in their rapping, rhyming, and playing the dozens, suggests another continuity. These different, though complementary, ways of explaining a cultural trait serve as a good example of how difficult it is to trace origins, yet how much simpler it is to recognize creativity.[35]

Finally, although it is extremely difficult to know how slaves spoke, fleeting references suggest common patterns. Perhaps the distinctive pronunciation of certain vowels and the use of particular tonal patterns, identified as unique to Gullah-speakers in the twentieth century, also applied to many slaves two centuries earlier. The few descriptions of slave speech indicate that the addition of a vowel or the dropping of a consonant was a widespread feature of black pronunciation. In addition, masters in both regions occasionally described slaves as speaking "thickly" or "hoarsely." Whether this signified a distinctive intonation is difficult to say, but it resembles a distinctive quality of black singing, which has been described as "hoarse," "rough," or "guttural." Furthermore, distinctive forms of pitch may be suggested by, for example, Glasgow's speaking "with a squeaking Voice in common" with other Igbos or native-born Peter having a "Squeel in his Speech." Perhaps this is a reference to

35. Thorstein Veblen, *The Theory of the Leisure Class: An Economic Study in the Evolution of Institutions* (New York, 1934 [orig. publ. 1899]), 398–400; Basil Bernstein, *Class, Codes, and Control*, 3 vols. (London, 1971–1975); Halliday, *Language as Social Semiotic*, chap. 9; Peter Burke, "Languages and Anti-Languages in Early Modern Italy," *History Workshop*, XI (1981), 24–32; Ruth Finnegan, *Oral Literature in Africa* (Oxford, 1970); Joyce Penfield, *Communicating with Quotes: The Igbo Case* (Westport, Conn., 1983); James Obelkevich, "Proverbs and Social History," in Burke and Porter, eds., *Social History of Language*, 57–59.

the use of falsetto common to African American speech patterns. It may also be traced to particular social groups in Africa, for, among the Wolof, pitch is an important social indicator, with nobles speaking in low-pitched, quiet voices and commoners speaking in high-pitched, loud voices. Moreover, a slave was occasionally said to speak "quick" or talk "very fast," a common description of creole-speakers throughout British America. Finally, perhaps the drawl often associated with southern speech can be traced to slaves, for a few African Americans were said to speak in a "drawling tone" or to have "a drawling speech." If these are African influences, then they point to deep-level continuities, not so much what was spoken but how it was said—phonology rather than lexicon.[36]

Language formation among blacks in both the Lowcountry and the Chesapeake was far more complicated than the linear, two-step model of pidgin followed by creole would imply. Many stages of linguistic development were present in both regions. African languages, a pidgin or pidgins, certainly a creole in South Carolina and perhaps also in Virginia, Standard English and sometimes other European languages, and all the intermediate steps between these extremes could be heard in both the Chesapeake and the Lowcountry. Moreover, many slaves were undoubtedly conversant in more than one variety of these languages. At the same time, the mixture of these variants differed both across space and over time. African languages were more likely to be heard in the Lowcountry than in the Chesapeake. Furthermore, if a creole existed in eighteenth-century Virginia, it underwent more rapid and extensive decreolization than was the case in South Carolina. Indeed, by the late eighteenth century, perhaps most Virginia slaves spoke a dialectical form of Stan-

---

36. For a few examples of slaves' speaking "hoarsely" or "thickly," see James Parsons and Robert Phils, *SCG*, Oct. 20, 1759; John Fitch, ibid., Jan. 19, 1760; Charles Reeks, *VaG* (P and D), Aug. 1, 1771; and Young Shortt, ibid., Jan. 14, 1773. For "hoarse" singing in blues and jazz, see Harold Courlander, *Negro Folk Music, U.S.A.* (New York, 1963), 24; Wood Furman, *SCG*, Sept. 6, 1770, supplement (Glasgow); William Park, *VaG* (D and H), Dec. 19, 1777 (Peter); and Judith R. Irvine, "Strategies of Status Manipulation in the Wolof Greeting," in Richard Bauman and Joel Sherzer, eds., *Explorations in the Ethnography of Speaking* (Cambridge, 1974), 167–181. For speaking "quickly," see William Coachman, *SCG and CJ*, Oct. 6, 1767; John Paul Grimke, *Gaz of State of SC*, Mar. 17, 1779; Richard Edwards, *VaG* (Rind), Aug. 4, 1768; and William Boswell, ibid.(P and D), Aug. 16, 1770. For a "drawling" speech, see Ferdinando Leigh, *VaG* (Hunter), Nov. 7, 1754; and on the sounds and intonation of modern Gullah, see Turner, *Africanisms*, 240–253. For technical analyses of other creole phonologies, see Hazel Carter, "Suprasegmentals in Guyanese: Some African Comparisons," in Gilbert, ed., *Pidgin and Creole Languages*, 213–263; and Barbara Lalla, "Tracing Elusive Phonological Features of Early Jamaican Creole," in Görlach and Holm, eds., *Focus on the Caribbean*, 117–132.

dard English, whereas, in South Carolina, creole-speakers were probably still in the majority.[37]

As to the relation between language and culture, part of the story is certainly one of catastrophic language loss, which in turn produced and accompanied considerable cultural loss. African vocabularies disappeared almost entirely. Only about 2 percent of the words in the ordinary speech of mid-twentieth-century Gullah-speakers were of African origin. In the eighteenth century, the contribution might have been somewhat greater, but probably not by much. Other English-based Atlantic creoles, such as Krio and Jamaican Creole, contain equally small proportions of African lexical items, whereas such dialects as Belizean and Guyanese, which may be more comparable to the speech of black Virginians, incorporate even fewer African words. The destruction of African vocabularies dramatically demonstrates how language is an enormously effective instrument in the hands of the powerful.[38]

But in neither region would it be true to say that the native languages of African immigrants had been totally supplanted. Rather, Africans retained elements of their grammars, phonology, and even parts of their lexicon in the unique languages that they created and bequeathed to their descendants. Even Chesapeake slaves, who traveled further along the road toward assimilation than their Lowcountry counterparts, spoke English with distinctive tones and idioms that owed much to their African past. Because, therefore, it is inappropriate to speak of the total dismantling of the slaves' indigenous languages, it is equally inappropriate to expect the total destruction of their cultural heritage. In part at least, the powerless can appropriate a dominant language on their own terms.

PLAY

In words, as in the creation of new figures of speech, African Americans demonstrated the importance of expressiveness, improvisation, and creativity in their lives. Playfulness—in the best sense of the word—was central not just to black verbal art but to black culture in general. Fashioning distinctive sartorial styles, forging a particular sense of humor, even walking in a singular way, slaves demonstrated the importance of play in their lives. Play had a more precise meaning in black culture, too, referring to ceremonies of music and dance, often performed at funerals. African American slaves performed most conspicuously when they sang and danced, two activities that permeated their

---

37. Dell Hymes, ed., *Pidginization and Creolization of Languages: Proceedings of a Conference Held at the University of the West Indies, Mona, Jamaica, April 1968* (Cambridge, 1971), 77.

38. Hancock, "Gullah and Barbadian," *Am. Speech*, LV (1980), 21.

everyday existence. Such celebrations were dramatic emblems of a more general cultural style.[39]

Just as African languages can be subdivided almost at will and yet grouped into major families, a comparable variety *and* uniformity characterized the continent's music and dance. Thus, according to Richard Waterman, "Peoples of a large section of Dahomey, for example, manage to do almost entirely without harmony, while the Ashanti, in the neighboring West African territory of the Gold Coast, seem to employ at least two-part and frequently three- and four-part harmony for almost all of their music." In general terms, however, harmony seems to have played a minor role in almost all West African music. Perhaps the most important shared feature of African music was its centrality to everyday life. Olaudah Equiano put it well when he said, "We are almost a nation of dancers, musicians, and poets." More technically, African music is characterized as essentially rhythmic and percussive in its overall effect. As Alan Merriam has pointed out, drumming is important, but "if a single percussion device were to be singled out as most universally used in Africa, we should certainly have to point to handclapping."[40]

The great value Africans attached to music and dance, together with their prowess at both activities, was transferred to the New World. Even Thomas Jefferson acknowledged that in music blacks "are more generally gifted than the whites with accurate ears for tune and time." In South Carolina, James Barclay spoke admiringly of the slaves' "ear for musick." Individual slaves made similar impressions. In the Chesapeake, Peter Brown was "fond of Singing and sings well"; John Jones was "a mighty singer"; Tabby "whistles remark-

---

39. Abrahams, *The Man-of-Words,* 47–54; Price and Price, *Afro-American Arts,* chaps. 3, 6; Mullin, *Africa in America,* 66; James Murray to Sister Clark, Dec. 26, 1755, Robbins Papers, Massachusetts Historical Society, as cited in Sylvia R. Frey, *Water from the Rock: Black Resistance in a Revolutionary Age* (Princeton, N.J., 1991), 41. Murray lived in the Cape Fear region of North Carolina.

40. Richard Alan Waterman, "African Influence on the Music of the Americas," in Sol Tax, ed., *Acculturation in the Americas,* Proceedings and Selected Papers of the Twenty-Ninth International Congress of Americanists, Chicago, 1952, 207–218 (quotation on 208); Paul Edwards, ed., *The Life of Olauda Equiano; or, Gustavus Vassa the African, 1789,* 2 vols. (London, 1969 [orig. publ. 1789]), I, 10; Alan P. Merriam, "The African Idiom in Music," *Journal of American Folklore,* LXXV (1962), 120–130 (quotation on 121); Merriam, "African Music," in William R. Bascom and Melville J. Herskovits, eds., *Continuity and Change in African Cultures* (Chicago, 1959), 49–86; Alan Lomax, "The Homogeneity of African-Afro-American Musical Style," in Norman E. Whitten, Jr., and John F. Szwed, eds., *Afro-American Anthropology: Contemporary Perspectives* (New York, 1970), 181–201. Two general books are particularly helpful: Dena J. Polachek Epstein, *Sinful Tunes and Spirituals: Black Folk Music to the Civil War* (Urbana, Ill., 1977); and Lawrence W. Levine, *Black Culture and Black Consciousness: Afro-American Folk Thought from Slavery to Freedom* (New York, 1977).

ably well"; Tom was notable "for his fine dancing"; and George Lewis was "very fond of dancing." Similarly, in the Lowcountry, Dick was "a remarkable Whistler," and Stepney was "remarkable for being a great dancer and for frequent and loud singing."[41]

Slave dances were often frowned on by whites, particularly when accompanied by the sound of drums, which masters commonly found threatening. In the late seventeenth century or early eighteenth century, "a negro drum from S. Carolina" found its way into the collection of Sir Hans Sloane in London. Whether it was fashioned in the colony or in Africa is not known. In the early-eighteenth-century Lowcountry, the Reverend Francis Le Jau attempted to stamp out the slaves' "feasts, dances, and merry Meetings" conducted on the Sabbath in his neighborhood. If he was successful—and there are grounds for doubt—others apparently failed, for, in 1721, the South Carolina Assembly passed a law to prohibit slave dances, particularly when drumming was featured. And yet, through the 1730s, the attendance of slaves at weekend dances continued to concern whites. Indeed, dancing to drums assumed notoriety during the Stono revolt of 1739, when, after some successes, the rebels "halted in a field, and set to dancing, Singing and beating Drums, to draw more Negroes to them." The following year, South Carolina's ruling authorities passed draconian legislation in an attempt to outlaw slave meetings and the use or ownership of "drums, horns or other loud instruments." And yet also in the same year, George Whitefield witnessed South Carolina slaves dancing around a great fire in the woods.[42]

Slave dances persisted in the Lowcountry throughout the century, though

---

41. Thomas Jefferson, *Notes on the State of Virginia,* ed. William Peden (Chapel Hill, N.C., 1955), 140; Barclay, *Voyages and Travels,* 27; Peterfield Trent, *VaG* (P and D), June 16, 1774 (Peter Brown); Stephen Higgins, *Md Gaz,* Apr. 14, 1746 (John Jones); Sampson Mathews, *VaG or AA,* June 26, 1784 (Tabby); John Scott, *VaG* (P and D), Dec. 1, 1774 (Tom); Robert Rawlings, *VaG and WA,* Sept. 4, 1788 (George Lewis); David Hopkins, *SCG,* May 14, 1772 (Dick); Thomas Patterson, *SC and AGG,* Dec. 30, 1774 (Stepney).

42. Arthur MacGregor, ed., *Sir Hans Sloane: Collector, Scientist, Antiquary, Founding Father of the British Museum* (London, 1994), 234, 243; Rev. Francis Le Jau to SPG, Oct. 20, 1709, A5/49, June 3, 1710, A5/120, Aug. 30, 1712, A7/436–439; Thomas Cooper and David J. McCord, eds., *The Statutes at Large of South Carolina,* 10 vols. (Columbia, S.C., 1836–1841), IX, 639–640 (1721 law), VII, 410 (1740 law); South Carolina Council journal, June 2, 1733, CO5/434, PRO; "An Account of the Negroe Insurrection in South Carolina," in General Oglethorpe to the Accotant, Oct. 9, 1739, in Allan D. Candler et al., eds., *The Colonial Records of the State of Georgia,* XXII, part 2 (Atlanta, Ga., 1913), 234–235; George Whitefield, *A Continuation of the Reverend Mr. Whitefield's Journal, from His Embarking after the Embargo, to His Arrival at Savannah in Georgia* (London, 1740), 78. The law of 1740 echoed earlier Barbadian legislation (Jerome S. Handler and Charlotte J. Frisbie, "Aspects of Slave Life in Barbados: Music and Its Cultural Context," *Caribbean Studies,* XI, no. 4 [1972], 8).

with some modifications. By the second half of the eighteenth century, for example, banjos (a musical instrument with direct African antecedents) became the most common musical accompaniment. In 1749, slaves congregated from a number of Cooper River plantations at dances where banjos were played (marking the first known reference to this instrument on mainland North America). In the early 1770s, James Barclay, an overseer on a Lowcountry plantation, observed that dancing was the slaves' "favourite amusement." Their "instrument of musick," Barclay noted, "is called a Bangier, made of Calabash." To this music, he continued, the slaves danced "pair and pair in their own way, hollowing [sic], shrieking, and making an intolerable noise."[43]

Drums, however, certainly did not disappear. When Barclay described how the "bangier" was played, he described the musician as seated on the ground with it between his feet, upon which he beat "very artfully with two sticks, as we do on a drum." Barclay, in other words, seems to have witnessed drum playing and to have confused it with the most common slave instrument, the "bangier." Significantly, the famous watercolor *The Old Plantation*, which portrays a slave dance in eighteenth-century South Carolina, depicts one slave playing a banjo and another sitting cross-legged; between his thighs is a small drum upon which he is beating with two sticks. In 1805, the tutor in the Georgetown district heard drums as slaves danced for whites during the Christmas holidays—in this context, drumming was not perceived as threatening. Many twentieth-century Georgia blacks recollected hearing drums, particularly at funerals, and some even specialized in making "old time" drums.[44]

Furthermore, as Sidney Mintz has observed, drumming is a remarkably "concealable" Africanism, for not even the instrument is required in order to arrive at the same percussive and rhythmic effect. A motor habit, a learned musical skill, and hands are all that are required. Other percussive devices

43. South Carolina Council Journal, no. 17, part 1, 70, 101; Barclay, *Voyages and Travels*, 27; Abe C. Ravitz, "John Pierpont and the Slaves' Christmas," *Phylon*, XXI (1960), 384. The first reference to a banjo in Barbados was in 1741. For the best discussion of the instrument, see Epstein, *Sinful Tunes and Spirituals*, 33–38; but see also Michael Theodore Coolen, "Senegambian Archetypes for the American Folk Banjo," *Western Folklore*, XLIII (1984), 117–132; and Robert Lloyd Webb, comp., *Ring the Banjar!: The Banjo in America from Folklore to Factory* (Cambridge, Mass., 1984).

44. Barclay, *Voyages and Travels*, 27; Ravitz, "John Pierpont," *Phylon*, XXI (1960), 384. For later drumming, see WPA, Writers' Program, Georgia, *Drums and Shadows: Survival Studies among the Georgia Coastal Negroes* (Athens, Ga., 1940), esp. 62, 71, 76, 91, 101. For slaves named "drummer," see Francis Le Brasseur, *SCG*, Sept. 4, 1736 (boy); and Bendix Waag, ibid., May 15, July 31, 1762 ("Fantee" man). For a description of another African instrument, called the *gambee*, played with two sticks by a Lowcountry African on a voyage from East Florida to the Bahamas, see Johann David Schoepf, *Travels in the Confederation [1783–1784]*, trans. and ed. Alfred J. Morrison, 2 vols. (Philadelphia, 1911), II, 261.

could also be used. No instances of Lowcountry slaves' using rattles, clappers, or rasps have been found, but two fugitives were tambourine players. Moreover, the tutor on the Georgetown plantation recognized the most obvious way in which slaves drummed without drums when he observed that handclapping constituted the basis of the slaves' music. "Patting juba," striking body parts as well as handclapping, was known to early American slaves, even if the term itself was not, so far as is known, current.[45]

Rather than rural slaves coming into Charleston to attend dances, urban slaves apparently tended to venture into the countryside to join those on plantations. In 1765, a runaway slave from Charleston was captured "at a dance up the Path." Seven years later, a white observer, calling himself "The Stranger," described a "Country-Dance" that took place five miles outside town on a Saturday night. About sixty blacks, fifty from Charleston, bearing bottled liquors and an array of food, attended the "entertainment [which] was opened, by the men copying (or *taking off*) the manners of their masters, and the women those of their mistresses . . . to the inexpressible diversion of that company." This group of slaves apparently danced, gamed, and otherwise amused themselves until an hour before daybreak. Such assemblies were common, often attracting as many as two hundred people, this observer learned. Indeed, about thirty years later, a visitor to Beale's wharf in Charleston early one Sunday morning was "astonished to see about forty negroes, men and women, arrive in one boat from Sullivan's Island. Curiosity led [him] to enquire what such a number had been amusing themselves with during the night, and [he] found they had been dancing and carousing from Saturday night, until near sunrise the next morning, to the number, [he] was informed, of about one hundred." These all-night slave dances aroused the indignation of whites throughout the New World.[46]

Unfortunately, little can be discerned about Lowcountry dancing styles. Barclay's observation that slaves danced in pairs is one clue, whereas separate male and female dances observed by "The Stranger" are another. Thomas Butler, a rare Lowcountry slave with a surname, was "the famous Pushing and Dancing Master," his title perhaps suggesting the importance of contest in slave dances. A detailed description of a nineteenth-century slave dance, "the jig," which Henry William Ravenel termed "an African dance," suggests links with

45. Sidney W. Mintz, "Labor Exaction and Cultural Retention in the Antillean Region," in James Schofield Saeger, ed., *Essays on Eighteenth-Century Race Relations in the Americas* (Bethlehem, Pa., 1987), 43; John Connolly, *City Gaz*, June 25, 1799, and Archibald Pagan, *Charleston Courier*, May 7, 1807 (tambourine players); Ravitz, "John Pierpont," *Phylon*, XXI (1960), 384.

46. Arthur Neil, *SCG*, July 20, 1765; "The Stranger," *SCG*, Sept. 17, 1772; a Bye Stander, *Charleston Courier*, Aug. 14, 1804, in Charleston Scrapbook Clippings, USC.

PLATE 20. The Old Plantation. *Artist unknown. Circa 1800. A slave dance in the Lowcountry. Courtesy Abby Aldrich Rockefeller Folk Art Center, Williamsburg*

earlier times. Ravenel described a dance for two, the man leading the woman of his choice, placing himself behind her, the step "a slow shuffling gait" in "artistic style," with the pair "edging along by some unseen exertion of the feet, from one side to the other—sometimes courtesying down and remaining in that posture while the edging motion from one side to the other continued." The female partner "always carried a handkerchief held at arm's length over her head, which was waved in a graceful motion to and fro as she moved." The depiction of the eighteenth-century slave dance in *The Old Plantation* shows two slave women holding handkerchiefs at arm's length, not over their heads, but in front of their bodies. In this depiction, the man seems to be descending to a crouched position while balancing on the soles of his feet, as if courtesying.[47]

47. Thomas Patterson, *SC and AGG*, Dec. 30, 1774; Alexander Vander Dussen, *SCG*, May 26, 1733; Henry William Ravenel, "Recollections of Southern Plantation Life," *Yale Review*, XXV (1935–1936), 768. This was written in 1876 but looks back to the author's childhood and youth. For a similar account of Barbadian slave dancing, see George Pinckard, *Notes on the West Indies*, 2 vols. (London, 1806), I, 264–267, as quoted in Handler and Frisbie, "Aspects of Slave Life in Barbados," *Caribbean Studies*, XI, no. 4 (1972), 30–31. Waving a handkerchief has been interpreted as warding off evil spirits (Mary Arnold Twining, "Movement and Dance on the Sea Islands," *Journal of Black Studies*, XV [1985], 463–479, esp. 467). The *hipsaw* dance was known in 18th-century Jamaica and the 19th-century United States, so it

Interpretations of *The Old Plantation* illustrate the complexity of cultural analysis of slave music and dance in the Lowcountry. One advocate for the Sierra Leonean influence on Gullah culture has argued that this watercolor depicts, not a scarf dance, but rather two women playing the *shagureh,* a women's rattle characteristic of the Mende. Others have argued that the musician at the far right of the picture is playing a Yoruban drum (a *gudugudu*) and have therefore attributed the dance to Yoruban origin. Although African ethnic identity remained meaningful in the Lowcountry, the dance was probably neither completely Sierre Leonean nor completely Yoruban. Rather, what is known of slave musical development elsewhere in the New World, together with the late-eighteenth-century attribution of this painting, argues for syncretism among a variety of musical cultures. Hans Sloane's transcription of three African songs—ostensibly from "Angola," "Papa," and "Koromanti," respectively—in late-seventeenth-century Jamaica is particularly instructive. These songs, on closer inspection, involve a mixture of different African musical styles. A "process of interchange and experimentation," Richard Cullen Rath concludes, had already taken place in African styles of music quite early in a New World setting. Most likely, a similar transformation was even further advanced in late-eighteenth-century South Carolina.[48]

The observation of "The Stranger" that slaves imitated and mocked white dances is our only other important clue to a notable function of slave dances and of slave music in general. Satire continued to be an important feature of slave dances in the Lowcountry, for a South Carolina "strut gal" recollected that, in the 1840s, "us slaves watched white folks' parties where the guests danced a minuet and then paraded in a grand march.... Then we'd do it too, *but we used to mock 'em,* every step." Slaves, in short, were inventive, open to white influences, but always accepting them on their own terms, just as often parodying what they saw as adopting styles wholesale.[49]

Chesapeake slaves also engaged in dances, apparently often accompanied by drums. Thus, in the first decade of the eighteenth century, slaves in Somerset County, Maryland, were said to spend the Sabbath "beating their Negro Drums by which they call considerable Numbers of Negroes together in some

---

might well have been present in 18th-century North America (Frederic G. Cassidy, "'Hipsaw' and 'John Canoe,'" *Am. Speech,* XLI [1966], 46).

48. Joseph A. Opala, *The Gullah: Rice, Slavery, and the Sierra Leone Connection* (Freetown, Sierra Leone, 1986), 9; Marvin L. Michael Kay and Lorin Lee Cary, *Slavery in North Carolina, 1748–1775* (Chapel Hill, N.C., 1995), 182; Richard Cullen Rath, "African Music in Seventeenth-Century Jamaica: Cultural Transit and Transition," *WMQ,* 3d Ser., L (1993), 700–726.

49. Marshall W. Stearns and Jean Stearns, *Jazz Dance: The Story of American Vernacular Dance* (New York, 1968), 22.

Certaine places," presumably to attend dances. At midcentury, the Reverend Thomas Bacon, resident in Maryland, spoke "of that noisy Riot and Drumming, which now seems to be the nightly employment of most Quarters, and in which Men, Women, and Children join, as it were, to strive who shall be the loudest." And in the late colonial period, John F. D. Smyth noted that Virginia slaves danced to the "qua-qua (somewhat resembling a drum)." Most significant, perhaps, an Asante drum made from African woods and decorated with carvings apparently accompanied an African to Virginia. It was collected in the colony and eventually made its way into Hans Sloane's collection in London.[50]

As in the Lowcountry, however, Chesapeake slaves more often than not played the banjo at their dances. The loyalist Jonathan Boucher, recalling his Chesapeake days in the 1760s and 1770s, "well remember[ed], that in Virginia and Maryland the favourite and almost only instrument in use among the slaves ... was a *bandore;* or, as they pronounced the word, *banjer*. Its body was a large hollow gourd, with a long handle attached to it, strung with catgut, and played on with the fingers." In 1774, Nicholas Cresswell attended a "Negro Ball" one Sunday and witnessed "Dancing to the Banjo." A year later, thirty-eight-year-old Charles ran away from his Nansemond County master, carrying his banjo, which he played "exceeding well"; and in 1784, another runaway, Humphrey, born and bred in Essex County, was also said to be "fond of playing on the banjo." At the end of the century, John Bernard heard that blacks would "walk five or six miles after a hard day's work to enjoy the pleasures of flinging about their hands, heads, and legs to the music of a banjo."[51]

---

50. Somerset County Judicials, 1707–1711, 1, MHR, as cited in Russell R. Menard, "The Maryland Slave Population, 1658 to 1730: A Demographic Profile of Blacks in Four Counties," *WMQ*, 3d Ser., XXXII (1975), 37; Thomas Bacon, *Four Sermons, Preached at the Parish Church of St. Peter, in Talbot County, in the Province of Maryland* (London, 1750), 132; Smyth, *A Tour in the United States of North America*, I, 46; Epstein, *Sinful Tunes and Spirituals*, 48; John Michael Vlach, *The Afro-American Tradition in Decorative Arts* (Cleveland, Ohio, 1978), 20–22, but apparently Vlach was wrong to think that the drum was made from American wood: see MacGregor, ed., *Sir Hans Sloane*, 234, 243. The *qua-qua* is described in John Gabriel Stedman, *Narrative of a Five Years Expedition against the Revolted Negroes of Surinam: Transcribed for the First Time from the Original 1790 Manuscript*, ed. Richard Price and Sally Price (Baltimore, 1988 [orig. publ. 1796]), 538–539. One Saturday, Francis Asbury waited for three hours at a ferry in northeastern North Carolina, which led him to observe that the "Negroes were dancing" (Elmer T. Clark et al., eds., *The Journals and Letters of Francis Asbury*, 3 vols. [London, 1958], I, 663–664).

51. Nicholas Cresswell, *The Journal of Nicholas Cresswell, 1774–1777* (New York, 1924), 18–19; John Giles, *VaG* (D and H), Feb. 18, 1775; Giles, ibid. (D and N), Jan. 8, 1780; Pitmon Kidd, *VaG and WA*, May 1, 1784; Jonathan Boucher, *Boucher's Glossary of Archaic and Provincial Words: A Supplement to the Dictionaries of the English Language, Particularly Those of Dr. Johnson and Dr. Webster* ... (London, 1832–1833), xlix; John Bernard, *Retrospec-*

Slaves in the Chesapeake also played other African or African-styled instruments. In 1775, John Harrower heard the balafo, or xylophone, played by a slave. He described the instrument, which he termed "a Barrafou," as "an oblong box with the mouth up and stands on four sticks put in bottom, and cross the [top?] is laid 11 lose sticks upon [which?] he beats." Five years later, a Hessian officer had occasion to note the "native genius" of another Virginia slave, who "put a few brass chords across a piece of wood full of holes, whereby he was able not only to make all kinds of tones, but also truly to play a sort of music, or at least keep rhythm." This slave's children then danced to their father's rhythmic playing. These are two important events: the first an indication that quite complex African instruments could find their way across the Atlantic, either literally or in the minds of slaves, the other a testament to the improvisational skills of an African musician and an important illustration of musical transmission from an African father to his African American children.[52]

Little is known about black styles of dancing in Virginia. John Fanning Watson, an unsympathetic observer of black folkways, described "the steps of actual negro dancing in Virginia" as "a sinking of one or other leg of the body alternately; producing an audible sound of the feet at every step" in strict accordance with every word of a song. He also noted that some "strike the sounds alternately on each thigh." A witness to a slave dance in Prince Edward County, Virginia, in the 1830s saw "Juber clapped to the banjor," and his account bears some resemblance to that of Watson. "The clappers rested the right foot on the heel, and its clap on the floor was in perfect unison with the notes of the banjor, and palms of the hands on the corresponding extremities."[53]

To date, there is evidence of African songs only in the Lowcountry. In 1777,

---

tions of America, 1787–1811, ed. Mrs. Bayle Bernard (New York, 1887), 206. For other 18th-century accounts of Chesapeake slaves' playing the banjo, see Jefferson, *Notes on the State of Virginia*, ed. Peden, 288; and Thomas Fairfax, *Journey from Virginia to Salem, Massachusetts, 1799* (London, 1936), 2.

52. Edward Miles Riley, ed., *The Journal of John Harrower, an Indentured Servant in the Colony of Virginia, 1773–1776* (Williamsburg, Va., 1963), 89; M. D. Learned and C. Grosse, eds., "Tagebuch des Capt. Wiederholdt vom 7 October 1776 bis 7 December 1780," *Americana Germanica*, IV (1901), 51, as cited in Rodney Atwood, *The Hessians: Mercenaries from Hessen-Kassel in the American Revolution* (Cambridge, Mass., 1980), 166. Although no direct evidence exists that the balafo reached South Carolina, the word itself, *bara* or *bala* (from Bambara and Mandinka), was current among Gullah-speakers in the 20th century. It seems likely that the instrument, too, must have been known (Turner, *Africanisms*, 190).

53. [John Fanning Watson], *Methodist Error; or, Friendly, Christian Advice, to Those Methodists, Who Indulge in Extravagant Emotions and Bodily Exercises* (Trenton, N.J., 1819), 30–31; William B. Smith, "The Persimmon Tree and the Beer Dance," *Farmers' Register*, VI (April 1838), 58–61, reproduced in Bruce Jackson, ed., *The Negro and His Folklore in Nineteenth-Century Periodicals* (Austin, Tex., 1967), 6–7.

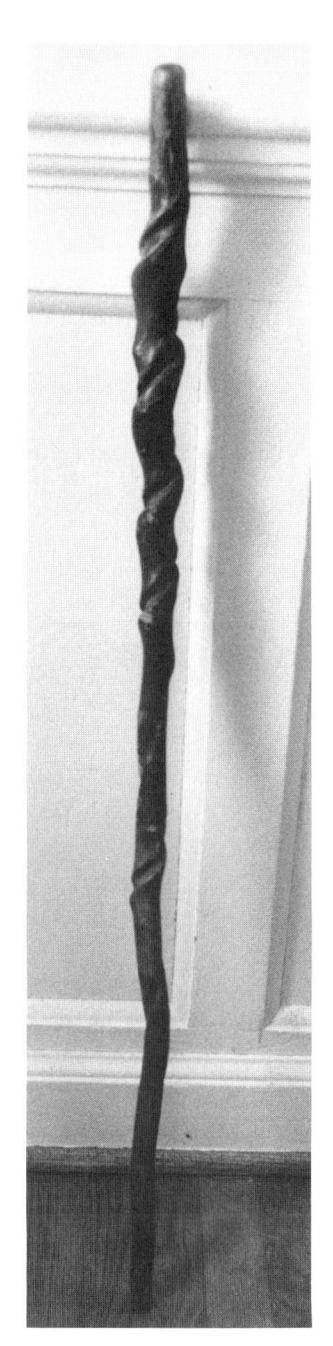

PLATE 21. *Asante Drum; Sweet Gum Cane with Honeysuckle Vine.* The drum, found in Virginia, was made from African woods and presumably transported from Africa on a slave ship (courtesy British Museum). A slave conjurer might have secreted this cane (circa 1796) between the walls of an addition to a plantation house (courtesy Historical Stagville, North Carolina Department of Cultural Resources).

Elkanah Watson listened to four slaves "singing their plaintive African songs in cadence with the oars," as they ferried him across Winyaw Bay. Five years later, when General William Moultrie returned to his South Carolina plantation, his "old Africans joined in a war-song in their own language, of 'welcome the war home.'" For some Africans, the singing of indigenous songs prompted desperate thoughts of returning home. At the turn of the century, an overseer recalled that at night the Africans on his plantation "would begin to sing their native songs, and in a short while would become so wrought up that, utterly oblivious to the dangers involved, they would grasp their bundles of personal effects, swing them on their shoulders, and setting their faces towards Africa, would march down into the water singing as they marched till recalled to their senses only by the drowning of some of their party." In nineteenth-century Georgia, a group of Igbo slaves under the direction of their ethnic leader, and singing homeland songs, marched into the sea and drowned themselves off Saint Simon's Island.[54]

But even where African songs did not survive, African American songs served the same functions as their African antecedents. Satire characterizes much African vocal music, and many slave songs had a satirical and derisive edge. Nicholas Cresswell described Chesapeake slave music as "droll"; slaves' songs, he observed, often addressed "the usage they have received from their Masters and Mistresses in a very satirical style and manner." In early-nineteenth-century Charleston, a traveler noted how slaves composed "their own verse," which "abound[ed] in praise or satire, intended for kind or unkind masters." In song, as in dance, slaves judged their masters. Naturally, slaves had to temper their lampoons, but their songs of praise and flattery, by their very effusiveness, might well have served an ironic purpose. If so, it was lost on William Bartram, who heard Lowcountry slaves chorusing "the virtues and beneficence of their master in songs of their own composition." George Tucker might have been a little closer to the mark when he had a planter in a fictional work say of Virginia corn songs that they expressed "kind and amiable feelings—such as, praise of their master, gratitude for his kindness, thanks for his goodness, praise of one another, and, now and then, a little humorous satire."[55]

54. Elkanah Watson, *Men and Times of the Revolution . . .* , ed. Winslow C. Watson (New York, 1856), 43; Moultrie, *Memoirs*, II, 356; John Spencer Bassett, *Slavery in the State of North Carolina*, Johns Hopkins University Studies in Historical and Political Science, XVII, nos. 7–8 (Baltimore, 1899), 92–93; Writers' Program, *Drums and Shadows*, 150. For 19th-century accounts of boat songs in the Lowcountry, see Epstein, *Sinful Tunes and Spirituals*, 166–172.

55. Cresswell, *Journal*, 19; W[illiam] Faux, *Memorial Days in America . . .* (London, 1823), in Reuben Gold Thwaites, ed., *Early Western Travels, 1748–1846* (Cleveland, Ohio, 1904–1907), XI, 95; "The Stranger," *SCG*, Sept. 17, 1772; Francis Harper, ed., *The Travels of William*

Slave songs were also often antiphonal in style, a marked characteristic of African singing traditions. John Fanning Watson described how "in the blacks' quarter, the coloured people get together, and sing for hours together, short scraps of disjointed affirmations, pledges, or prayers, lengthened out with long repetition *choruses*." The singing of "short scraps" followed by "long choruses" sounds very much like the call-and-response pattern common to much African and African American singing. Watson labeled this form the "merry chorus-manner of the southern harvest field, or husking-frolic methods of the slave blacks."[56]

But if the form and occasional content of slave songs owed much to African traditions, their power drew inspiration from a range of sources—from the tragedy of slavery to Christian influences. The bittersweet quality of slave song is captured in a description of a group of slaves, making the great trek from Virginia to the Southwest, "singing a little wild hymn of sweet and mournful melody." Even more poignant was the response of slaves to a Methodist preacher who asked a group of slaves why they sang "Vain tunes." "To take away trouble," they replied. Moravian visitors to the Bryan plantations in South Carolina in 1741 heard "a slave woman singing a spiritual at the water's edge," her way of "jubilating" at attaining "assurance of the forgiveness of sins and the mercy of God in Christ." Evangelicals were much taken with slaves' religious singing. John Leland found blacks "remarkable for learning a tune" and for having "very melodious voices." Masters, too, remarked on their slaves' penchant for religious song. Daniel and Dinah, from piedmont Virginia, were "much given to singing hymns"; Jack, from South Carolina, enjoyed singing psalms.[57]

Influences from Africa and from the institution of slavery had a significant impact on African American music, but so, of course, did the broader Anglo-American culture. Perhaps the best illustration is the use slaves made of Anglophone musical instruments—a development particularly noticeable in the Chesapeake. The most common instrument among Chesapeake slaves was the fiddle or violin. Some black fiddlers gained renown. When William Fearson's

---

Bartram (New Haven, Conn., 1958), 198; [George Tucker], *The Valley of Shenandoah*, 2 vols. (New York, 1824), II, 116–117. See also William D. Pierson, "Puttin' Down Ole Massa: African Satire in the New World," in Daniel J. Crowley, ed., *African Folklore in the New World* (Austin, Tex., 1977), 20–34.

56. [Watson], *Methodist Error*, 30.

57. [George Tucker], *Letters from Virginia* (Baltimore, 1816), 29; Nathaniel Mills Journal, Apr. 16, 1787, Lovely Lane Museum, Baltimore; George Fenwick Jones et al., eds., Hermann J. Lacher et al., trans., *Detailed Reports on the Salzburger Emigrants Who Settled in America . . . Edited by Samuel Urlsperger*, VIII (Athens, Ga., 1985), 512; Leland, *Virginia Chronicle*, 11; Samuel Hatcher, *VaG or AA*, June 22, 1782; Warden of Workhouse, *SC and AGG*, Sept. 10, 1779.

slave boy ran away, the master eschewed a description because the fugitive was "well known in this City [of Williamsburg] by the name of FIDDLER BILLY"; Hannah looked "a good deal like her father, the well known Fiddler"; and Sy Gilliat, a famous Richmond fiddler, claimed to have played at the governor's palace during Lord Botetourt's tenure. Slave fiddlers earned money. An Eastern Shore fiddler who entertained whites in the 1690s received money and fine cloth for his playing; the owner of mulatto shoemaker Samuel Berry observed, "As he plays on the fiddle, he has many opportunities of changing his dress." Fifty Virginia runaways were said to play the fiddle or violin, and a number carried off fiddles when absenting themselves. Most fiddlers were extremely conversant with white culture: they were invariably described as "smart," "artful," or "likely"; many were skilled—none more so than Sambo, who made fiddles; most were creoles; and a few could read and write. Fiddlers also seem to have relished the social opportunities that their skills presented: Peter "delighted in" fiddling "when he gets any strong drink"; Dick and Daniel played on the fiddle and were good dancers; Bob played the fiddle and was "fond of singing with it."[58]

Chesapeake slaves also became adept at playing other European musical instruments. In 1766, a Virginia master offered for sale a slave who played "extremely well on the French horn," and, seven years later, another Virginian advertised for his well-assimilated African sailor who played the instrument. Two Chesapeake slaves developed their talent outside the region: "a young handsome Negro," recently brought from London, was touted to prospective Virginian owners as a most "genteel" servant and as the possessor of a French horn, upon which he played; and a fugitive from Fauquier County, a Portuguese-speaking slave, born on the island of Saint Jago, could "blow the French horn, play the fiddle, whistles many tunes, well to be heard at a surprising distance, is fond of marches and Church music, particularly of that belonging to the Roman Catholic religion, which he professes." Other Chesapeake slaves learned to play European military instruments. Such was probably the

---

58. Philip Alexander Bruce, *Social Life of Virginia in the Seventeenth Century* . . . (Richmond, Va., 1907), 181–183; William Fearson, *VaG* (P and D), Nov. 4, 1773 (Billy); Thomas Fenner, ibid. (D and H), Oct. 17, 1777 (Hannah); Epstein, *Sinful Tunes and Spirituals,* 115; Judith Harbert, *VaG* (Rind), July 18, 1771 (Samuel Berry); Thomas Pemble, ibid., May 20, 1773 (carrying fiddle). For "smart," "artful," and "likely" fiddlers, see Richard Chilton, *VaG* (P and D), Dec. 21, 1769; Francis Pearce, ibid. (D and N), Feb. 26, 1779; Robert Rawlings, *VaG and WA,* Sept. 4, 1788; and Mark Jackson, *VaG* (P and D), Aug. 18, 1768 (Sambo); for literate fiddlers, see Henry Lee, ibid., Mar. 9, 1769; John Hare, ibid., June 24, 1773; William Green, *VaG* (Purdie), May 9, 1777; William Gregory, ibid. (P and D), May 4, 1769 (Peter); Thomas Ker, *Va Ind Chron,* Jan. 2, 1788 (Dick); Richard Stewart, ibid., Jan. 23, 1788 (Daniel); and Richard Witton, *VaG* (Rind), June 30, 1774 (Bob).

case with Damon, a native West Indian, formerly a sailor, and Dick, a mulatto waiting man, both of whom were drummers, whereas mulatto Charles and Francis, the latter described as an "incomparable house servant," were good fife players.[59]

In South Carolina, some slaves became proficient players of European musical instruments, although not to the degree of their Chesapeake counterparts. Thus, only thirty-one slave runaways were said to play the fiddle or violin. As in the Chesapeake, however, fiddlers in the Lowcountry tended to be well-assimilated creole servants or skilled slaves. In 1767, for instance, a carpenter named Noko was said to play on the violin, something he probably learned from a former owner, Mr. Brownwell, the dancing master in Charleston. Also as in the Chesapeake, Lowcountry fiddlers played at slave dances. In 1800, a South Carolina master noted that his slave man, Tower, was "good at playing on the Fiddle, and usually frequents Negro Dancings for that purpose." Lowcountry slaves might have had greater opportunities to play European military instruments than their Chesapeake counterparts because of the paucity of white labor in some rural areas of South Carolina. Lowcountry slave boys, in particular, were often used as drummers: thus, Prince, a shoemaker, had been "a drummer to one of the companies of the Regiment" in Charleston; fifteen-year-old Peter was "formerly a drummer to the Grenadier Company"; and Quash "carried off with him a drummer's suit of clothes which he formerly wore when a drummer on the Borough Company." The French horn also had military associations, for Charles, a seaman who had sailed twice to England, had acted as "a french-horn man on board the Deal Castle Captain Mantle a privateer."[60]

Musical developments among African American slaves parallel changes in the linguistic realm. A basic musical grammar, as it were, with an emphasis on the importance of music and dance in everyday life and the role of rhythm and percussion in musical style, survived the Middle Passage. Even complex musical instruments made the crossing, although more notable is how slaves

59. *VaG*, Mar. 28, 1766, as cited in Epstein, *Sinful Tunes and Spirituals*, 117; John Goodrich, Jr., *VaG* (P and D), Apr. 8, 1773; William Allason, *VaG or AA*, Nov. 13, 1784; Sarah Gist, *VaG* (Purdie), Apr. 4, 1766 (Damon); George Mason, Jr., *VaG or AA*, Aug. 14, 1784 (Dick); Robert Goode, *Va Ind Chron*, Oct. 22, 1788 (Charles); Halcot B. Pride, *Va Ind Chron and GA*, June 16, 1790 (Francis). I assume that these fifes were European instruments, although cane fifes were common in West Africa and have been found among African Americans (see Vlach, *Afro-American Tradition*, 22–23). See also Bruce A. MacLeod, "Quills, Fifes, and Flutes before the Civil War," *Southern Folklore Quarterly*, XLII (1978), 201–208.

60. Joseph Glover, *SCG and CJ*, July 7, 1767 (Noko); Henry Calder, *City Gaz*, Mar. 29, 1800 (Tower); Henry Middleton, *SCG*, June 23, 1757 (Prince); John M'Call, Jr., *SC and AGG*, Jan. 1, 1778 (Peter); John Postell, *Gaz of State of SC*, Mar. 31, 1779 (Quash); Hugh Hughes, *SCG and CJ*, Jan. 21, 1772 (Charles) (see also Hugh Hughes, *SCG*, Sept. 6, 1770).

adapted traditional instruments, invented new ones, and borrowed Anglo-American ones. These adaptations, inventions, and borrowings, however, were interpreted according to deep-level aesthetic principles that were fundamentally African. Outward forms, whether song lyrics or common musical instruments, were primarily Anglo-American, but underlying principles owed more to African sources. To borrow Melville and Frances Herskovits's words, blacks retained "the inner meanings of traditional modes of behavior while adopting new outer institutional forms." The key elements of traditional music—complex rhythms, percussive qualities, syncopation, and antiphonal patterns—were not alien to Anglo-American musical styles. Indeed, precisely because of this compatibility, African retentions and syncretism were encouraged. But to listen to eighteenth-century whites is to know that their slaves created a distinctive music and dance. In the final analysis, this distinctiveness depended on creativity and innovation far more than on any attachment to an indelible cultural tradition.[61]

Creativity and innovation, expressiveness and improvisation flourished in others areas of black life—in modes of personal adornment and display, in love of humor and folklore, even in motor patterns and gestures. These are small matters, of no great public moment. A particular hairstyle, a joke, a game—these are not the stuff on which great events turn. Artifacts such as these constitute a repository of opportunities that, when infused with meaning, helped create a culture—one in which performance was central. To make sense of these traits is to bear witness to "a remarkable drama of culture-building" by an oppressed people.[62]

In terms of formal recreations, African American life was impoverished. So much was lost in the forced migration—a more extreme version of the diminution that also affected English popular culture in its transference to North America. Moreover, once in America, slaves were hardly in a position to recreate the rich pageantry of their former lives. There is no direct evidence, for instance, that any African American festivals occurred among eighteenth-century Virginia and South Carolina slaves. Ceremonial occasions took place among blacks in the northern colonies and throughout the British Caribbean. Why they failed to materialize in the Lowcountry and Chesapeake is hard to explain. Social control cannot be the whole answer; otherwise, why were they permitted in the West Indies? Perhaps they did occur, but no references have survived? In the nineteenth century, after all, John Canoe or Jonkonnu festi-

---

61. Melville J. Herskovits and Frances S. Herskovits, *Trinidad Village* (New York, 1947), vi; Sidney W. Mintz, *Caribbean Transformations* (Chicago, 1974), 14.

62. Mintz, "Labor Exaction and Cultural Retention," in Saeger, ed., *Essays on Eighteenth-Century Race Relations*, 45.

vals—ritual celebrations permitting a measure of social license and status inversion—were commonplace among slaves in eastern North Carolina and apparently also in Suffolk, Virginia. Can this festival be traced to the previous century? At least one North Carolinian thought so, for she believed that the custom "was introduced into South Carolina by the slaves who accompanied Governor Sir John Yeamans from the Barbadoes." Indeed, she argued, John Canoe festivals "were confined altogether to the low country or tide-water region. The Coonahs were an institution principally known on the South Carolina, Georgia and Florida coast." Perhaps so.[63]

John Canoe festivals are unquestionably a good example of the syncretism of African and Anglo-American traditions that occurred in black culture. The name itself seems to derive from a historical figure on the West African coast. Many of the practices associated with the festival, particularly the animal face masks, the horned headdresses, and the dancing to drums, banjos, and rattles as well as antiphonal singing, suggest African influences. At the same time, the ship or house headdress, which is quite common in many John Canoe festivals, together with some of the costumes and musical accompaniments as well as the timing of the parades, which usually take place at Christmas, suggest Anglo-Saxon influences, particularly the traditions of mummery and morris dancing.[64]

Some popular recreations, at least among Lowcountry slaves, can be traced to Africa. Thus, Charleston blacks played *papaw,* an African dice game. Other

63. Rebecca Cameron, "Christmas at Buchoi, a North Carolina Rice Plantation," *North Carolina Booklet,* XIII (1913), 8, as cited in Richard Walser, "His Worship the John Kuner," *North Carolina Folklore,* XIX (1971), 166–167; Fillmore Norfleet, *Suffolk in Virginia, c. 1795–1840: A Record of Lots, Lives, and Likenesses* (Richmond, Va., 1974), 43, 124n, as cited in Elizabeth A. Fenn, "'A Perfect Equality Seemed to Reign': Slave Society and Jonkonnu," *North Carolina Historical Review,* LXV (1988), 130. Harriet (Brent) Jacobs, *Incidents in the Life of a Slave Girl* (Boston, 1861), 179–180, also mentions seeing "Johnkannaus," perhaps in or near Georgia, suggests one commentator (Cassidy, "'Hipsaw' and 'John Canoe,'" *Am. Speech,* XLI [1966], 47). For other types of festivals in northern mainland colonies, see Joseph P. Reidy, "'Negro Election Day' and Black Community Life in New England, 1750–1860," *Marxist Perspectives,* I, no. 3 (Fall 1978), 102–117; Hubert H. Aimes, "African Institutions in America," *Jour. Am. Folklore,* XVIII (1905), 15–32; Lewis V. Baldwin, "Festivity and Celebration in a Black Methodist Tradition, 1813–1981," *Methodist History,* XX (1982), 183–191; William D. Piersen, *Black Yankees: The Development of an Afro-American Subculture in Eighteenth-Century New England* (Amherst, Mass., 1988), 117–140.

64. Dougald Mac Millan, "John Kuners," *Journal of American Folk-Lore,* XXXIX (1926), 53–57; Ira De A. Reid, "The John Canoe Festival: A New World Africanism," *Phylon,* III (1942), 349–370; Judith Bettelheim, "Jamaican Jonkonnu and Related Caribbean Festivals," in Margaret E. Crahan and Franklin W. Knight, eds., *Africa and the Caribbean: The Legacies of a Link* (Baltimore, 1979), 80–100; Fenn, "'A Perfect Equality Seemed to Reign,'" *N.C. Hist. Rev.,* LXV (1988), 127–153.

South Carolina slaves engaged in athletic contests. In 1805, a tutor in the Georgetown district saw Africans performing "a specimen of the sports and amusements" of their homeland, which involved "jumping, running, and climbing trees." Perhaps the "Calabar" runaway, captured by a South Carolinian in 1766, performed similar feats, for he reported his name as "Jumper," a most appropriate name, observed the Workhouse jailer, "by his actions in jumping and tumbling, which he has showed in the house since he has been with me." Formal contests probably occurred among this region's slaves, for a South Carolina–born slave (but one who had spent much time in the West Indies, where he might have received his injuries) claimed that the wound under his right eye came from "fighting sticks" and the bite on his right breast from "single combat."[65]

Slaves did not have to be athletic to exhibit distinctive forms of physical behavior. Just by their manner of walking, they drew attention to themselves. Some slaves walked with gusto, with an almost exaggerated physicality. Sharper "swings his arms much when walking," Toby was "of a brisk motion," Will walked "remarkably quick," Cuffy "remarkably wide," Dick "very wide at the knees," and Charles "straddles much in his walk." A visitor to Charleston in the early nineteenth century whirled around in "astonishment" at the sight of a "six feet three tall" black man who "came coursing down the side walk with a flourishing gait and swaggering knee." Strutting rather than shuffling, swaggering rather than shambling, some slaves walked in a most unslavelike manner. A "stately" or "strutting" walk, a "proud carriage," carrying the "head high," walking "remarkable grand and strong" or "boldly" represented one small way in which slaves could resist the dehumanization inherent in their status. Other slaves might have succumbed to their stereotype or perhaps parodied it, for some sauntered in a seemingly exaggerated fashion. Primas walked "lazily," Tom had "a clumsey lounging walk," Stephen a "slouching, clumsy gait," and Peter "a very slouching appearance." One master described his slave's gait as "slouch walking." Either by striding forward vigorously or by ambling along slowly, African Americans appear to have carved out some distinctiveness for themselves—and usually provoked their masters into the bargain.[66]

---

65. *Laurens Papers,* VIII, 128; Ravitz, "John Pierpont," *Phylon,* XXI (1960), 384; Workhouse, *SCG and CJ,* May 27, 1766; Workhouse, *City Gaz,* Mar. 20, 1798. Another African runaway had the name Jumper (Lewis Burwell, *VaG* [Parks], Apr. 21, 1738). Occasionally, too, a slave might be said to be "athletic": see, for instance, Stephen St. John, *City Gaz,* May 13, 1789.

66. John Glen, *City Gaz,* Aug. 4, 1797 (Sharper); Benjamin Wimbish, *VaG* (P and D), Apr. 23, 1772 (Toby); Walter Coles, ibid. (D and H), Nov. 13, 1778 (Will); John Mills, *VaG or AA,* Feb. 7, 1784 (Cuffy); Henry Miller, ibid., July 9, 1785 (Dick); Thomas Cowle, *VaG* (Rind), Feb. 22, 1770 (Charles); John Hammond Moore, ed., "The Abiel Abbot Journals: A Yankee

Almost certainly there were distinctive African American gestures, most of which went unnoticed by contemporary whites. However, one body motion did register an impression. A Virginian observed that his African slave Jack "avoids looking in the Face of them he is speaking to as much as possible," and a South Carolinian noted that his creole slave boy "occasionally holds his head away." This aversion of the head is a common gesture among African Americans. A visitor to the British West Indies in the early nineteenth century observed that when "Negroes quarrel, they seldom look each other in the face." The "down looks" that masters commonly ascribed to slaves in both Lowcountry and Chesapeake and that they interpreted as surliness might have owed more to a widespread African imperative of avoiding eye contact in hostile situations. The tenaciousness of this pose is suggested by its continued existence among blacks today. Thus, on the Sea Islands of South Carolina and Georgia, a child will commonly turn his or her head to one side when rebuked by a parent. More generally, it has been argued that black audiences in the United States indicate rejection by turning their heads away, often with eyes closed.[67]

A closely related set of gestures, commonly referred to as "cut-eye" and "suck-teeth," are well known among blacks throughout the Caribbean and the United States. Intended to communicate hostility and disapproval, "cut-eye" consists of a hostile glare, followed by a "cut" of the eyes downward and across the body, and ending with another hostile glance, often with the head turned away, to the accompaniment of a loud "suck-teeth," or a drawing of air through the teeth to produce a sucking sound, a gesture of anger and annoyance. Similar terms for cut-eye have even been found in Haitian Creole ("couper yeux") and Saramaccan ("a ta koti woyo"), suggesting different New World relexifications

---

Preacher in Charleston Society, 1818–1827," *SCHM*, LXVIII (1967), 250–251; William Chapman, *SCG*, June 27, 1761 (stately); John Mullryne, ibid., June 5, 1759 (strutting); William Skinner, *VaG or AA*, Feb. 22, 1786 (proud carriage); James Henry Butler, *Gaz of State of SC*, Oct. 14, 1777 (head high); James Overton, ibid., July 3, 1784 (grand); J. Laval, *City Gaz*, July 3, 1798 (boldly); George Chisolm, *SCG and TDA*, Sept. 5, 1798 (Primas); James Belsches, *VaG* (Purdie), June 19, 1778 (Tom); James Stobo, *SCG*, Oct. 20, 1758 (Stephen); Legare and Burden, *SC State Gaz*, Jan. 18, 1799 (Peter); T. W. Price, *SCG and TDA*, Oct. 5, 1798 (slouch walking).

67. Thomas Poindexter, *VaG* (Rind), Aug. 8, 1766; James Kennedy, *SCG and DA*, Sept. 24, 1785; Charles William Day, *Five Years' Residence in the West Indies*, II (London, 1852), 111–112; Kenneth R. Johnson, "Black Kinesics—Some Non-Verbal Communication Patterns in Black Culture," in J. L. Dillard, ed., *Perspectives on Black English* (The Hague, 1975), 299–300; Robert Farris Thompson and Joseph Cornet, *The Four Moments of the Sun: Kongo Art in Two Worlds* (Washington, D.C., 1981), 169; Annette Powell Williams, "Dynamics of a Black Audience," in Kochman, ed., *Rappin' and Stylin' Out*, 103; Amelia Wallace Vernon, *African Americans at Mars Bluff, South Carolina* (Baton Rouge, La., 1993), 164.

of an expression that existed in African languages or in Proto-Pidgin. Indeed, various West African languages contain direct equivalents for both cut-eye and suck-teeth. Cut-eye is particularly associated with black women.[68]

Distinctive gestures are one way a people can express individuality; personal adornment is another. Slaves created distinctive styles of clothing even though their sartorial resources were highly controlled. In some cases, slaves made a virtue out of this restrictiveness. Planters required slaves to repair and patch their clothes, to make do. Slaves responded by attaching brightly colored cuffs, collars, and edging to otherwise drab jackets, trousers, and petticoats. In South Carolina, Jamey, an "Angolan," decorated the front of his "white negro cloth jacket" with a "slip of blue in the shape of a serpent." In Virginia, Cyrus, the oldest and the apparent leader of a group of twelve runaways, was particularly conspicuous, for he wore "a very remarkable coat, having a great number of patches of different colours." Slaves seem also to have used natural dyes to add a welcome touch of color to their drab uniforms. Thus, a number of Lowcountry slaves wore clothing dyed with red oak bark; an African slave revealed his adaptation to Lowcountry life by wearing "an old white oznabrug shirt and breeches, dyed with indico"; one Virginia slave donned a "Kendal Cotton Jacket and Breeches died with Maple Bark"; and another usually dyed his clothing "with walnut, maple, and other barks."[69]

Whether the use of vegetable dyes owed anything to an African influence is hard to say, but the use of breechcloths or waist ties by men and wraparound skirts by women linked slave dress in the Lowcountry (where this pattern was most clearly evident) to styles found both in Africa and among African Americans in many other parts of the New World. The waist tie is best described by Johann Bolzius, who noted that slave men in South Carolina wore a "cloth rag which hangs from a strap tied round the body." As for Lowcountry slave women, Ebenezer Hazard observed that they usually wore a "coarse Kind of

---

68. John R. Rickford and Angela E. Rickford, "Cut-Eye and Suck-Teeth: African Words and Gestures in New World Guise," *Jour. Am. Folklore*, LXXXIX (1976), 294–309. Africans told a missionary that "they hide their Faces, or cast down their Eyes, when they hear any thing which does not please them" (Thomas Thompson, *An Account of Two Missionary Voyages . . .* [London, 1758], 55.)

69. John Fitts, *SC and AGG*, Dec. 11, 1770 (Jamey); John Payne, *Maryland Journal, and the Baltimore Advertiser*, June 27, 1780, supplement (Cyrus); William Macluer, *SCG*, Aug. 3, 1747, Workhouse, *State Gaz of SC*, July 25, Aug. 25, 1785 (red oak bark); John Brown, *SCG and CJ*, Sept. 17, 1771 (indigo dye); William Slater, *VaG* (D and H), Feb. 4, 1775 (maple bark); Charles Yates, *VaG and WA*, Sept. 20, 1783 (walnut and maple). For patches, cuffs, and trimming, see, for instance, Thomas Stitsmith, *SCG*, Dec. 16, 1732; Commander of Fort Moor, ibid., June 24, 1734; John Cattell, ibid., Jan. 19, 1740; Paul Smiser, ibid., Jan. 10, 1771; Workhouse, *SCG and CJ*, June 25, 1771; William Colvin, *VaG* (D and H), July 31, 1779; and William Nelson, *VaG and WA*, May 15, 1784.

Cloth wrapped round their waists." Scanty clothing can be attributed to inadequate allocations and to an obvious reluctance to wear ill-fitting and heavy-duty garments. But it also represented African and African American cultural preferences. A white South Carolinian recollected how difficult it was to make an old African "wear any clothes at all."[70]

Even the cords used to hold up dresses might have had homeland associations. Olaudah Equiano noted that in his country "none but married women are permitted to wear" a cotton string around the waist. In Virginia, a traveler noted that the slave women wore "loose garments . . . , girt round the waist with a small cord." Photographs of Sea Island women in the early twentieth century show their dresses held up by two separate pieces of string. The lower one tied around the hips had a practical intent, lifting the woman's garments and thereby protecting the dress from contact with dirt. However, these women also spoke of "an African superstition" that the second cord gave the wearer extra strength.[71]

An African influence probably accounts for the high value slaves attached to headgear. As Sidney Mintz has observed, "Throughout Afro-America hats and headgear seem to carry a strong, positive, symbolic meaning," whether manifested on ceremonial occasions (the extravagant headdresses associated with John Canoe festivals, for instance) or used in more prosaic, daily ways. If a belief that heads ought to be covered was African in origin, slaves were certainly not averse to employing conventional Anglo-American forms. Thus, the most common headgear among Chesapeake slaves appears to have been the felt hat, although beaver, straw, raccoon, leather, and fashionable macaroni hats as well as Scotch bonnets, worsted caps, and flapped hats also graced some heads. In the Lowcountry, a similar range of headgear existed, though masters, at least

---

70. "Johann Martin Bolzius Answers a Questionnaire on Carolina and Georgia," trans. and ed. Klaus G. Loewald et al., *WMQ*, 3d Ser., XIV (1957), 236; Hugh Buckner Johnston, ed., "The Journal of Ebenezer Hazard in North Carolina, 1777 and 1778," *N.C. Hist. Rev.*, XXXVI (1959), 364; Rose Ravenel Pringle, *Piazza Tales: A Charleston Memory*, ed. Anthony Harrington (Charleston, S.C., 1952), 15. For more on possible Afro-American preferences for scanty clothing, see Essex County Coroner's Inquest, Nov. 8, 1743, George Baylor Papers, VHS; Jack P. Greene, ed., *The Diary of Landon Carter of Sabine Hall, 1752–1778*, 2 vols. (Charlottesville, Va., 1965), 214–215, 218 (hereafter cited as *Carter Diary*); William Tatham, *Communications concerning the Agriculture and Commerce of the United States of America . . .* (London, 1800), 55; Charles William Janson, *The Stranger in America* (London, 1807), 316.

71. Edwards, ed., *The Life of Olauda Equiano*, I, 9; Robert Sutcliff, *Travels in Some Parts of North America . . .* (New York, 1811), 51–52; Edith M. Dabbs, *Face of an Island . . .* (New York, 1971), photograph of Adelaide Washington and Mrs. Mack; Rupert Sargent Holland, ed., *Letters and Diary of Laura M. Towne . . .* (Cambridge, Mass., 1912), photograph facing 20; Orrin Sage Wightman and Margaret Davis Cate, *Early Days of Coastal Georgia* (St. Simons Island, Ga., 1955), photograph facing 123.

in the first half of the century, more often referred to caps rather than to hats (with round hats becoming most common in the late eighteenth century). Lowcountry slaves were resourceful: one recent immigrant from Senegambia wore "an indigo bag for a cap," and a boy in Charleston wore a raccoon's tail to his hat. What appears to distinguish Lowcountry slaves from their Chesapeake counterparts was the greater popularity of the headkerchiefs that were worn by both men and women, Africans and creoles. In South Carolina, mulatto Judy wore a man's hat tied on her head with a silk handkerchief; Erskyne, an African, reversed the order, wearing a handkerchief tied about his head, upon which sat a round hat; some slaves wore two handkerchiefs, one around their neck or shoulders, the other on their head; most common was the slave who wore a single headcloth, occasionally made of silk, sometimes striped, usually white.[72]

What was important, of course, was not just the headgear but how it was worn. Some South Carolina slave women, particularly in the late eighteenth century, wore their headcloths in inventive ways. Phillis wore a "neck handkerchief" and another "tied round her head as a turban"; Ruth wore a headcloth "in the French fashion"; and Sue had "a remarkable way of tying her handkerchief" so as to expose "the greatest part of her hair above" the bandanna. The jaunty angle at which some slave men wore their hats was surely not accidental. Sharper, an "excessively artful" slave, "commonly" wore his hat "inclined to the right side of his head"; Calais, a painter, simply wore his hat on one side of his head; Caesar, in contrast, "wore a hat, which he is fond of cocking three ways"; and Bacchus, a particularly "cunning" slave, besported "a fine Hat cut and cocked in the Macaroni Figure."[73]

---

72. Mintz, "Labor Exaction and Cultural Retention," in Saeger, ed., *Essays on Eighteenth-Century Race Relations,* 40; John Filbin, *SCG,* Sept. 24, 1753 (Senegambian); Robert Robinson, ibid., June 16, 1777 (boy); William Wilkins, ibid., Feb. 19, 1741 (Judy); Alexander Wylly, ibid., May 10, 1773 (Erskyne); Richard Peake, ibid., Apr. 29, 1745, Mark Tongues, *SC State Gaz,* Mar. 11, 1794, and John Tool, ibid., Jan. 5, 1796 (two handkerchiefs). I count about 50 headkerchiefs among 18th-century South Carolina runaways. They are rarely mentioned among Chesapeake fugitives, who tended to wear felt hats. See also Anna Atkins Simkins, "The Functional and Symbolic Roles of Hair and Headgear among Afro-American Women: A Cultural Perspective" (Ph.D. diss., University of North Carolina, Greensboro, 1982). John Thornton suggests that bareheadedness was "nearly universal" among Africans in the 15th and 16th centuries. He wonders whether covering the head was a sign of Christian conversion, but, if his characterization of early Africans is correct, head covering is perhaps more plausibly of European influence: *Africa and Africans in the Making of the Atlantic World, 1400–1680* (Cambridge, 1992), 233.

73. Thomas W. Bacot, *City Gaz,* May 6, 1797 (Phillis); A. Philson, *SCG and DA,* Aug. 16, 1798 (Ruth); T. W. Price, ibid., Oct. 5, 1798 (Sue); Emanuel Rengil, *City Gaz,* Jan. 10, 1798 (Sharper); J. Wilcox, ibid., Feb. 28, 1799 (Calais); William Dandridge, Jr., *VaG* (Pinkney), Dec. 8, 1774 (Caesar); Gabriel Jones, ibid. (P and D), June 30, 1774 (Bacchus).

Cocking a hat was but one small manifestation of the keen interest slaves exhibited in sartorial expressiveness. In South Carolina, bondwomen and urban slaves drew especial fire for dressing above their station. In 1744, a provincial grand jury identified "Negro women in particular" as the chief culprits in not restraining "themselves in their Cloathing as the Law requires, but dress in Apparel quite gay and beyond their condition." In the early 1770s, other grand juries again complained that "the Law for preventing the excessive and costly apparel of Negroes and other Slaves in this Province (especially in Charlestown) is not being put in force." Women, house servants, and urban residents figure as the most extravagantly dressed Lowcountry slaves. "There is scarce a new mode" of fashion, noted the "Stranger," "which *favourite* black and mulatto *women slaves* are not immediately *enabled* to adopt." Isabella, a needlewomen living on Johns Island, was "very fond of dressing well" and "appeared lately in mourning clothes for the death of her mother." Jenny, an urban house servant, dressed "gay at all times." Ben, an urban sailmaker, apparently excelled his master in dress. Nevertheless, Africans and rural slaves as well as creoles and urban bondmen were able, on Sundays and holidays in particular, to wear dress a little out of the ordinary. Jack, an African, who spoke "indifferent English," yet "affects to dress spruce"; Erskyne, already mentioned for wearing a handkerchief and hat, carried off clothes, some of which, in his master's opinion, were "really too good for any of his colour"; Will, a rural sawyer, went to extreme lengths to display his fashion-consciousness, for he had "the skin of his legs cut in the exact form of ribbed stockings."[74]

In the Chesapeake, too, whites complained, in the words of one correspondent, about "the great Liberties" allowed slaves, "particularly in their Dress." According to this observer, slaves stole "purely to raise Money to buy fine Cloaths, and when dressed in them, make them so bold and impudent that they insult every poor white Person they meet with." Slaves ought to be consigned to "mean Dress" and stripped of any finery, this correspondent continued, for with their "Sunday or Holyday Cloaths on" slaves became as "bold as a Lion." There was no doubt in this man's mind that clothes mattered: "such

---

74. Presentments of the Grand Jury, *SCG*, Nov. 5, 1744; Presentments of the Grand Jury of Charlestown, ibid., May 24, 1773, June 3, 1774; "The Stranger," *SCG*, Sept. 24, 1772; Thomas Farr, *SC and AGG*, Nov. 4, 1780 (Isabella); Joseph Wigfall, *Royal Gaz*, Oct. 24, 1781 (Jenny); Patrick Byrne, *City Gaz*, July 19, 1797 (Ben); James Skirving, *Royal Gaz*, Feb. 23, 1782 (Jack); Alexander Wylly, *SCG*, May 10, 1773 (Erskyne); Robert Johnston, *SC and AGG*, Dec. 24, 1778 (Will). For particularly extravagant dress, see, for instance, M. Gist, *Columbian Herald,* June 18, 1787; Joseph Wigfall, *State Gaz of SC,* Apr. 16, 1789; Rogers, Barker, and Lord, *City Gaz,* Mar. 29, 1797; and for the meanings attached to such dress, Shane White and Graham White, "Slave Clothing and African-American Culture in the Eighteenth and Nineteenth Centuries," *Past and Present,* no. 148 (August 1995), 149–186.

PLATE 22. Preparations for the Enjoyment of a Fine Sunday among the Blacks, Norfolk. Benjamin Henry Latrobe. 1797. The importance of hairdressing and shaving among Virginia blacks. Courtesy Maryland Historical Society

is the Difference fine Cloaths make in the Vulgar," he concluded. One Virginia owner reached a similar conclusion, for, in attempting to restrain his skilled slave's propensity for flight, he confiscated the man's "holiday clothes." However, the bondman, so "extremely fond of dress," ran away anyway and soon, his master had no doubts, supplied himself with a new wardrobe.[75]

As in the Lowcountry, many Chesapeake slaves displayed a strong interest in clothing. Women and waiting men were the most extravagantly dressed, often carrying away great armloads of clothing when making an escape. Road, who went off wearing a homespun striped jacket, a red quilted petticoat, a black silk hat, a pair of leather shoes with wooden heels, a chintz gown, and a black cloak, was said to strive for "gaiety in dress"; Molly had four horse-locks attached to her legs, but that neither stopped her flight nor her donning a pair of high-heeled shoes; mulatto Harry, who traveled widely with his owner, was "very fond of Dress, and cannot bear to go bearfoot." But again, field slaves were not without resources to vary their wardrobe. When, in 1738, three plantation slaves ran away, they wore the standard attire of field hands, but they also "carried with them several Sorts of old Cloaths they had got off their

75. *Md Gaz*, Oct. 18, 1770; Thomson Mason, *VaG* (Rind), Dec. 22, 1768.

Neighbours." Charles ran away immediately after finishing work in the fields and so was wearing only a shirt and trousers. But he then went to his wife's dwelling and equipped himself with many other clothes that he kept there.[76]

Hairstyles also made cultural statements. In the Lowcountry, some Africans continued to braid their hair in homeland fashion. Tobey and Jemmy, two recent "Mandingo" immigrants, were said to have hair "twisted up like twine"; two men and a woman, said to be Kisis, wore plaited hair in their "country manner"; another African had "very bushy hair which he usually ornaments into several small plaits." By the late eighteenth century, if not before, some creoles had adopted this style. Thus, in the late 1790s, Guy braided his hair on each side of his head; Doctor wore his hair "plaited all over his head"; and Ishmael kept his hair "long and plaited." No Chesapeake slaves have been discovered with braided hair, except perhaps Moll, who was said to wear her hair "filleted"—further confirmation of the reduced African influence in that region.[77]

But even those slaves who braided their hair experimented with other styles. Cato's "hair was sometimes platted, at other times queued." A number of other slave men commonly queued their hair or tied it in a club, in the white fashion. In the Chesapeake, Phill and Rochester often wore false queues, and George wore "a long que to his hair." In the Lowcountry, Emanuel "in general" wore his hair queued; Robert "often" queued his hair; and when Plenty ran away, his owner noted that "he begins to screw up his hair into a little queue." Some slaves wore wigs: Jeremy, a Charleston blacksmith, wore one made of sheepskin, Cuffee often wore one, and African Peter made do with an old one. Slave women, such as Road, who wore "her hair combed over a large roll," used artifice to raise their hair high. They, too, occasionally resorted to wigs, for Harriot's hair was "naturally short," but "in general she wears false hair under a

---

76. Josiah Hall, *VaG* (Pinkney), June 15, 1775 (Road); Isacah Isaacs, *VaG or AA*, June 8, 1782 (Molly); Theodorick Bland, *VaG* (P and D), July 14, 1774 (Harry); Nathaniel Harrison, ibid. (Parks), July 21, 1738 (3 slaves); Augustine Moore, ibid. (Purdie), June 23, 1775 (Charles). For particularly well dressed waiting men, often carrying away many types of clothes, see Thomas Huson, *VaG* (P and D), May 26, 1774; Gabriel Jones, ibid., June 30, 1774; John Cooke, ibid. (D and H), Mar. 7, 1777; William Park, ibid., Dec. 19, 1777; and Hamilton Ballantine, ibid. (D and N), May 22, 1779. For well-dressed women, see Allen Freeman, ibid. (Purdie), Apr. 11, 1777; Thomas Fenner, ibid. (D and H), Oct. 17, 1777.

77. Workhouse, *SCG*, Nov. 1, 1759 (Tobey and Jemmy); Workhouse, *SCG and CJ*, June 2, 1772 (three Kisis); John Ward, *City Gaz and DA*, Oct. 26, 1799 (African); Daniel Seiler, *City Gaz*, July 13, 1798 (Guy); P. Neyle, ibid., Sept. 12, 18, 1798 (Doctor); Philip Neyle, ibid., June 7, 1799 (Ishmael); David Gorsuch, *Maryland Journal, and the Baltimore Advertiser*, Apr. 12, 1775 (Moll). For the importance of hair, see Shane White and Graham White, "Slave Hair and African American Culture in the Eighteenth and Nineteenth Centuries," *Journal of Southern History*, LXI (1995), 45–76.

handkerchief." Slaves changed hairstyles. Ben wore his hair long when he ran away; six weeks later, his master speculated that he might have cut it short. In 1782, Walton wore his hear cropped at the front, but, two years later, he combed his hair "very high." In short, slaves were conscious of changing fashion, as Charles Ball noted of a boy who "wore his hair long, on the top of his head, in the fashion of that day." Indeed, when one Lowcountry master advertised for his runaway slave Isaac, he did not describe his hairstyle but simply stated that it was "cut in the present fashion." Similarly, a Chesapeake master pointed out that his slave's hair was "done up in the tastiest manner."[78]

A particularly fashion-conscious slave was a young waiting man named Frank of South Carolina. He had an especially "fancy hair style," for he "would feign dress the wool of his head in a maccaroni taste," teasing it to create "side licks, and a queue." This "maccaroni" style originated in about 1770, when English dandies who had traveled in Italy determined exaggerated pompadours to be the height of fashion. Frank imitated it at least by 1774, only a few years after its invention in England. But when Frank was "too lazy to comb" his hair, his master observed, he tied it with a handkerchief, the distinctive African American headgear. Frank, therefore, personifies rather neatly an alternation of white and black styles.[79]

Shaving part or all of the head, which was certainly not a white fashion, occurred among slaves. It could be involuntary, as when masters shaved a slave's hair as punishment. Hannah had her hair cut "in a Very irregular manner, as a Punishment for Offences," and Peter had all his hair cut off for running away. The shorn head, Orlando Patterson has written, symbolizes loss of virility, power, and freedom and is commonly associated with slaves in many societies. Interestingly, however, some African American slaves voluntarily cropped their hair in varied ways. Charles wore his hair "cut on the Top and turned up before"; Syphax and Joe cropped their hair close at the front

---

78. Richard H. Peyton, *City Gaz*, Nov. 8, 1799 (Cato); Molly Tunstall, *VaG and WA*, Sept. 4, 1784 (Phill); Charles Love, Jr., *Va Ind Chron*, July 2, 1788 (Rochester); Robert Rawlings, *VaG and WA*, Sept. 4, 1788 (George); Humphrey Sommers, *SC and AGG*, Dec. 19, 1776; George Tunno, *State Gaz of SC*, Jan. 4, 1787 (Emanuel); John Crocker, *City Gaz*, Sept. 8, 1788 (Robert); J. Laval, ibid., July 3, 1798 (Plenty); Nicholas Matthison, *SCG*, Nov. 23, 1734 (Jeremy); Mrs. Crosthwaite, *SCG*, Mar. 17, 1757 (Cuffee); John Barkley, *SC and AGG*, Apr. 13, 1770 (Peter); Josiah Hall, *VaG* (Pinkney), June 15, 1775 (Road); William Roper, *City Gaz*, Apr. 20, 1798 (Harriot); James Fraser, *SC and AGG*, July 24, 1777 (Ben); Peterfield Trent, *VaG*, (P and D), Dec. 1, 1774, and *VaG and WA*, Dec. 11, 1784 (Walton); Charles Ball, *Fifty Years in Chains* (New York, 1970), rpt. of *Slavery in the United States: A Narrative of the Life and Adventures of Charles Ball, a Black Man* (New York, 1837), 226; Mathew Brady, *Charleston Courier*, July 2, 1807 (Isaac); John Cockey, *Maryland Journal, and the Baltimore Advertiser*, Nov. 16, 1779.

79. Benjamin Guerard, *SCG and CJ*, Aug. 30, 1774.

and wore it long at the back; Jack wore his hair very long at the front and back and just shaved the top; Sam had "a long Shock of Wool on his Head, which he often shears about the Crown"; Gilbert had the "Top of his head shaved, and . . . combs it back like a Woman"; and fifty-year-old Charles Sellers generally had his whole "head shaved."[80]

In Africa, the shorn head was associated with slaves, but head-shaving also signified important rites de passage. Africans, for instance, might shave a person's head on inclusion or release from a kinship group. Jamaican slaves shaved their heads apparently as a signal of warlike intent and also of mourning. One recent African immigrant in South Carolina, who gave his name as Carolina (the only word of English known to him), had the "top of his head lately shaved," which might have been intended to signify the dramatic caesura that had occurred in his life. Perhaps creoles adopted this form for similar reasons. When, in 1762, John, a Virginia-born mulatto slave living near Beaufort, South Carolina, ran away, his master thought it "probable he will shave his head, wear a Scotch bonnet," and pretend to be free. Or perhaps slaves were creating a form of antilanguage, taking something intended to be shameful and turning it into something positive—a matter of personal style.[81]

Braiding, queuing, and head-shaving were some of the more popular hairstyles among blacks, but most common was the "bushy head of hair." Apparently, many slaves did not (perhaps from white discouragement) wear their hair long, for more than once a slave was described as having hair "thicker and longer than is common for negroes." Nevertheless, "remarkably bushy heads" and "large shocks" of hair were commonplace. In one case, a master associated long hair with an African group, for Sambo (or Sam) had "pretty long" hair,

---

80. Thomas Fenner, *VaG* (D and H), Oct. 17, 1777 (Hannah); Samuel Sherwin, ibid. (Rind), May 9, 1771 (Peter); John Cabell, ibid. (D and H), Dec. 12, 1777 (Charles); Armistead Churchill, ibid. (Hunter), June 12, 1752 (Syphax); John Cobbs, ibid. (P and D), Nov. 9, 1769 (Joe); Joseph Seawell, ibid., July 9, 1767 (Jack); Stafford Lightburn, Jr., ibid., Mar. 7, 1771 (Sam); John Evans, Sr., ibid., July 21, 1774, postscript (Gilbert); Thomas Walker, Jr., *VaG or AA*, July 12, 1783 (Charles Sellers). For head-shaving, see Orlando Patterson, *Slavery and Social Death: A Comparative Study* (Cambridge, Mass., 1982), 60–62; and Mary C. Karasch, *Slave Life in Rio de Janeiro, 1808–1850* (Princeton, N.J., 1987), 224.

81. Workhouse, *SCG and CJ*, Aug. 29, 1769 (Carolina); John Mullryne, *SCG*, July 10, 1762 (John). See also Henry Laurens, ibid., Aug. 27, 1753; and Workhouse, *SCG and CJ*, Sept. 12, 1769. For purposes behind head-shaving, see Robin Horton, "From Fishing Village to City-State: A Social History of New Calabar," in Mary Douglas and Phyllis M. Kaberry, eds., *Man in Africa* (London, 1969), 48; Gerald W. Hartwig, "Changing Forms of Servitude among the Kerebe of Tanzania," in Suzanne Miers and Igor Kopytoff, eds., *Slavery in Africa: Historical and Anthropological Perspectives* (Madison, Wis., 1977), 244; and Mullin, *Africa in America*, 41; Albert J. Raboteau, *A Fire in the Bones: Reflections on African-American Religious History* (Boston, 1995), 154.

"being of the Fulla country." Slaves manipulated their long hair in various ways: some combed their hair forward so that "it peeked over" the forehead; others combed it back to expose the whole face; yet others wore it "remarkably high" or "high before"; and one mulatto man occasionally combed his out "so as to look like a wig." What we now know as the "Afro" hairdo was the most popular style among both Lowcountry and Chesapeake slaves, but it obviously took many forms.[82]

A number of slave men, both recent immigrants and creoles, wore beards to accompany their "bushy" hairdos. But styles varied considerably: "thick" and "strong," "large" and "long," "short" and "small" were adjectives masters commonly employed to describe their slaves' beards. Caesar had a large beard, which "he seldom shaves close"; Adam had a beard that grew largely under his chin; Isaac had "a beard on the tip of his chin"; Abraham wore his beard "halfway down his cheek"; and Titus had "large bunches of beard each side of his face." Some slaves let their hair grow "far down on their cheeks"; others displayed only "temple whiskers"; and Peter let "his Hair grow from his Temples Half Way down his Face, very long and frizzed." Of course, slaves changed styles: James "generally" sported a beard, which indicates that he sometimes cut it off; Harry "generally" wore his beard long, which suggests that he occasionally wore it short. In fact, styles might have varied regionally, too, for the proportion of "smooth-faced" to bearded men among runaway advertisements differed considerably between South Carolina and Virginia. Beards seem to have been more widespread among Lowcountry slaves. Perhaps greater assimilation to white norms increased the number of Chesapeake slaves who preferred the smooth-shaven look.[83]

82. Among 18th-century South Carolina advertisements, I count at least 100 references to "bushy" or "remarkably bushy" heads of hair, much the most widespread description; Thomas Radcliffe, Jr., *Royal Gaz*, Jan. 12, 1782 (Sambo or Sam); James Roulain, *SCG*, Nov. 15, 1770 (combing forward); Miles Brewton, ibid., Feb. 28, 1771 (backward); John Hume, *Gaz of State of SC*, Aug. 4, 1777 (upward); Andrew Bay, ibid., Oct. 22, 1790 (mulatto). Among 18th-century Virginia advertisements, I count about 50 runaway slaves with "bushy" hair, also the most widespread description. For those with longer hair than usual, see Lewis Burwell, *VaG* (D and N), May 1, 1779; John Saunders, ibid., July 24, 1779; and Henry Macon, *VaG or AA*, May 25, 1782.

83. Barnard Elliott, *SCG*, Apr. 24, 1770 (Caesar); John Fox, *VaG* (P and D), July 18, 1771 (Adam); Workhouse, *SCG*, Nov. 22, 1760 (Isaac); Thomas Mill, *SC and AGG*, Mar. 7, 1777 (Abraham); Stephen St. John, *City Gaz*, May 13, 1789 (Titus); John Stuart, *SC and AGG*, July 10, 1767, and James Donnom, *SCG and CJ*, Dec. 22, 1767 (hair down on cheeks); Workhouse, ibid., Aug. 21, 1770, and John Brown, ibid., Nov. 13, 1770 (temple whiskers); Joseph Crenshaw, *VaG* (P and D), May 7, 1772 (Peter); Paul Douxsaint, *SCG and CJ*, Mar. 19, 1771 (James); W. Byrd, *VaG* (P and D), Dec. 3, 1767. In 18th-century South Carolina runaway

A similar disproportion exists in the extent of jewelry wearing among slaves of the two regions. Again, if runaway advertisements are a reliable guide, a number of South Carolina slaves wore jewelry. This practice was closely associated with Africans, for recent immigrants wore a variety of jewelry. The most common forms were glass bead necklaces (referred to once as "negro beads" and once as "Jobs beads"), colored black, red, white, and green, or combinations thereof, but with blue the most popular color. In addition, slaves wore bead earrings, bead armbands, brass wire earrings, iron ring bracelets, and silver or gold earbobs and drops. Some Africans sported ostentatious displays: one man had small wire rings in both of his ears; London had a brass ring and a bead in his left ear; Hannah wore small green beads in each ear as well as a bead necklace; Tabie had five brass rings in one ear and six in the other; Sylvia had a brass ring in one ear and a string of beads in the other; and an eighteen-year-old girl from "Gola" wore five strings of red and blue beads around her neck, a link with two red beads and one green bead in her right ear, and a small iron ring in her left ear. A larger number of African immigrants had either or both of their ears "bored." The few creoles or well-assimilated slaves who wore jewelry invariably displayed an earbob or earring. In this respect, Tenah was typical in sporting gold drops in each ear but unusual in also wearing a necklace of coral with gold in the center. References to jewelry among Chesapeake slaves are rare. As in the Lowcountry, some African immigrants arrived with jewelry—"outlandish" Will had "rings in his ears," and a visitor of two Chesapeake slavers noted that some Africans "had beads about their necks, arms, and Wasts"—but Africans soon disappeared from the scene. Chesapeake creoles, again like their Lowcountry counterparts, seem to have confined their jewelry wearing to earrings and earbobs. Thus, Betty wore silver earrings set with white stones, and Persilla owned several pairs of earbobs.[84]

---

advertisements, I count 182 bearded and 16 "smooth-faced" men. The numbers in colonial Virginia were 25 and 11, respectively. Beards appear to have been uncommon among white men, if runaway advertisements, prints, and portraits are any guide.

84. Workhouse, *SCG and CJ*, Dec. 22, 1772 (negro beads); Workhouse, *State Gaz of SC*, Oct. 9, 1786 (Jobs beads); Workhouse, *SCG*, Sept. 1, 1752 (African man); Workhouse, ibid., Nov. 4, 1756 (London); Workhouse, *SCG and CJ*, Jan. 9, 1770 (Hannah); Workhouse, *SCG*, Apr. 7, 1772 (Tabie); Workhouse, *SCG and CJ*, June 2, 1772 (Sylvia); Workhouse, *State Gaz of SC*, July 21, 1785 ("Gola" girl); Edward Neufville, *City Gaz*, Mar. 9, 1799 (Tenah); Harden Perkins, *VaG or AA*, Dec. 21, 1782 (Will); Gregory A. Stiverson and Patrick H. Butler III, eds., "Virginia in 1732: The Travel Journal of William Hugh Grove," *VMHB*, LXXXV (1977), 31; Hardin Burnley, *VaG* (P and D), May 12, 1774, postscript (Betty); William Colvin, ibid. (D and N), July 31, 1779 (Persilla). From 18th-century South Carolina newspapers, I count 53 runaway slaves who wore some form of jewelry and 118 who had their ears bored. Of the 171,

One final aspect of appearance that speaks to the importance of playfulness concerns demeanor. Masters, it is well known, often spoke of their slaves' "down looks," their "surly" and "insolent" countenances. Less well noted, but as thoroughly documented, are testimonials to the slaves' cheerful appearance and love of humor. Masters described slaves who "generally" laughed when they spoke, who were "apt to grin," who scarcely ever spoke "without grinning," who frequently smiled when spoken to, who had "a pleasing smile when spoken to," who showed their teeth when laughing, who laughed "heartily," who were "fond of laughing," or who simply had smiling, agreeable, pleasing countenances. These descriptions reflect close observation: when Sophia laughed, her eyes were closed; Will spoke "generally with a grinning smile, especially when answering a question"; and Lewis had a "peculiar smiling and insinuating way of speaking." Many such slaves were Africans, who might have been signifying, on the surface at least, a willingness to accept their status. Among Yoruba slaves, "a cheerful nature, a jocular disposition, wit and humor and playfulness, . . . and readiness to oblige, went a long way to insure a slave against ill-treatment." Others were creoles who must have realized that cheerfulness was no guarantee against ill-treatment but nevertheless put a cheerful face on a bleak situation. Of course, the laughter might have been derisive, as appears to have been the case with Hector, who "when spoken to will hold up his head and laugh seemingly like a rogue." Whatever the intent, humor was a way to deny the dehumanization inherent in slavery.[85]

Closely associated with this playful demeanor was the slaves' love of mimicry and humorous stories. Creole Bob could "mimick the Back Wood or Northward Languages," whereas Dick was more ambitious, for he "sometimes affect[ed] to speak broad Scotch or Northumberland dialect." In 1772, "The Stranger," who observed a gathering of South Carolina slaves, heard them telling "some highly curious anecdotes" that proved highly diverting to the assembled company. Unfortunately, nothing has survived about the content of such anecdotes or stories—at least from the eighteenth century. Almost certainly, the animal fables, trickster tales, proverbs, and riddles—all the varied

---

136 were males, and 35 were females (roughly the same proportion as in the runaway group as a whole). In ethnicity, 151 were Africans, often recent immigrants; the other 20 were either creoles or well-assimilated Africans. I count only 5 Virginia slaves (4 women, 1 man) as wearing jewelry. See also Karasch, *Slave Life*, 224–226.

85. Cotton Stevens, *State Gaz of SC,* Mar. 21, 1791 (Sophia); George Turberville, *VaG* (Purdie), Mar. 15, 1776 (Will); John Pryor, *VaG or AA,* May 10, 1786 (Lewis); Joseph Watson, *SCG and DA,* Nov. 7, 1798 (Hector). For a few examples of many such descriptions, see John Stith, *VaG* (Hunter), May 9, 1751; Archibald Cary, ibid. (Purdie), Mar. 7, 1766; William Watts, ibid. (P and D), Aug. 16, 1770; Henry Bedon, *SCG,* Oct. 29, 1750; Workhouse, ibid., July 31, 1762; and Daniel Gardner, ibid., Nov. 14, 1771.

expressions of black verbal art, found in such abundance in the nineteenth century—existed in this earlier period, but to date no substantive details have been found.[86]

From nineteenth-century recollections, old Africans often told tales about their homeland, usually about their capture or the animals of the "old country." Charles Ball remembered African stories "fraught with demons, miracles, and murders." Henry W. Ravenel had vivid childhood memories of old Africans telling him of "lions and tigers, and alligators, and monkeys—of the great snakes, 'as big as your body, sir,' that could crush and swallow a man or a horse," as well as of the "middle passage." In the 1870s, an elderly freedman recollected how his African-born grandfather had told him a variety of animal stories. This African also provided a narrative of his capture, telling of how the whites came ashore in a small boat, hired young boys with pieces "ob red flannel" and other inducements, and then held them as slaves once aboard the slaver. Apart from content, many observers were impressed by the inventiveness and dramatic manner of these black storytellers as well as the full involvement of their audience in their recitations. These were obviously important performances, and they usually assumed an antiphonal structure common to black religious meetings and much African American music-making.[87]

Play or performance, then, infused African American culture in both the Chesapeake and the Lowcountry. This cultural focus took different forms in the two regions, with Lowcountry slaves exhibiting more obvious African patterns, evident in everything from clothing to jewelry, than their Chesapeake counterparts. More generally, both regional cultures were impoverished in formal recreations. But this very diminution encouraged more informal creativity. Precisely because, as Mintz and Price have argued, slavery involved "the relentless assault on personal identity, the stripping away of status and rank, the treatment of people as nameless ciphers," its victims cultivated "an enhanced appreciation for exactly those most personal, most human characteristics which differentiate one individual from another." Ironically, a system that aimed at dehumanizing its victims helped create a people keenly interested in fashion, intensely aware of personal style, and fervently committed to expressiveness in their everyday life.[88]

---

86. Henry Reeves, *SCG*, Nov. 14, 1775 (Bob); Andrew Robertson, *SC and AGG*, Jan. 29, 1768 (Dick); "The Stranger," *SCG*, Sept. 17, 1772.

87. Ball, *Fifty Years in Chains*, 201 (see also 19, 167–186); Ravenel, "Recollections," *Yale Review*, XXV (1935–1936), 750; A.M.H. Christensen, *Afro-American Folk Lore: Told Round Cabin Fires on the Sea Islands of South Carolina* (New York, 1969 [orig. publ. 1892]), 4–5, as cited in Levine, *Black Culture*, 86–87.

88. Mintz and Price, *An Anthropological Approach*, 26.

Wide differences separated the religious ideas and practices of the varying African cultures from which slaves to British North America were drawn. There were, as Terence Ranger points out, "major differences in the ways in which African societies explain evil or conceive salvation; ... major differences in the role allocated to a creator divinity; the absence or presence of prophetism or spirit possession; and so on. These differences resulted in sharply contrasting styles of thought and action from one African society to another." Assumptions about the timelessness or uniformity of West African religion must be strenuously rejected. Slaves from some cultures most likely had available to them certain forms of spiritual adaptation not available to slaves from other cultures.[89]

At the same time, a great diversity of religious forms seems to have coexisted with certain widely shared, basic principles. Most basic, perhaps, West African cultures drew no neat distinction between the sacred and secular, whereas in Anglo-American culture the Reformation had radically assaulted, if not totally dismantled, the established balance between the sacred and the profane. If the supernatural and everyday inexorably grew apart in Anglo-American culture, they formed an integrated system in West African cultures. More specifically, slaves from many African cultures, as Mintz and Price observe, shared basic assumptions "about the nature of causality and the ability of divination to reveal specific causes, about the active role of the dead in the lives of the living, about the responsiveness of [most] deities to human actions, about the close relationship between social conflict and illness or misfortune." An extraordinary diversity of form went hand in hand with some fundamental similarities in basic beliefs.[90]

Robin Horton has boldly proceeded to outline an overall religious system common to most, if not all, traditional African religions. The core of traditional cosmology, Horton argues, was a system of "unobservable personal beings" whose activities were supposed to make meaningful the events of the ordinary, everyday world. This system had two tiers: in the first were the lesser spirits, those who were mainly concerned with the affairs of the local community or, to use Horton's phrase, the microcosm. In the second tier was a supreme being concerned with the world as a whole—the macrocosm. Traditional African cosmologies saw a rich proliferation of ideas about the lesser spirits and their modes of action. Most events, fortunate or unfortunate, were

---

89. T. O. Ranger, "Recent Developments in the Study of African Religious and Cultural History and Their Relevance for the Historiography of the Diaspora," *Ufahamu*, IV (1973), 21.
90. Mintz and Price, *An Anthropological Approach*, 23.

attributed to their agency. Ideas about the supreme being tended to be much less developed. In fact, many African peoples believed in, not one, but two supreme creators, and some had no concept of a creator, whether single or dual, at all. Most high gods were usually thought to be otiose, remote, and detached, though ultimately responsible for the design and preservation of the universe. According to the eighteenth-century traveler William Bosman, West Africans on the Slave Coast had "a faint Idea of the True God"; they believed in a high god but did not worship him. For most Africans, then, belief in a supreme being or beings was peripheral rather than central to religious life; the creator or creators inspired less awe than apathy; and the aim of religious life was, not to commune with spiritual beings, but to explain, predict, and control worldly events. Horton's explanation for this emphasis is that, in premodern Africa, most events affecting the life of an individual occurred within the microcosm of the local community, which was largely insulated from the wider world. As such, the activity of the spirits demanded most attention.[91]

Horton's ingenious and sophisticated scheme may in fact be too schematic. Insofar as it emphasizes the microcosmic focus of African religion, it probably underestimates the extent to which precolonial Africans were always part of a macrocosm, were already familiar with sweeping change. They traded, hunted, traveled, and constantly encountered visitors. Without doubt, local religion—especially beliefs about the power of the ancestors, the living dead, to influence the fate of their descendants, which necessarily centered on the homestead and village—was paramount. But, as Terence Ranger has argued, precolonial Africans often belonged to a variety of "overlapping networks of religious relationship." They could express control of the household through a localized African cult, carry tribute to a distant shrine, belong to a hunter's guild, and be a member of a spirit possession cult with links to men and women who lived along a trading route. Rather than a model of a total organic collectivity, Ranger posits one of "creative and resilient pluralism." African religions, Ranger states, were "multilayered and dynamic, with a history of contradiction, contestation, and innovation." Yet, no matter whether Horton or Ranger has best captured the precise relation between the local and the general in indigenous African religions, both emphasize the inherent potential for change within those religions. In their different ways, both Horton and Ranger stress the remarkable adaptability of African religions, their responsiveness to new ideas, their capacity to

91. Robin Horton, "African Conversion," *Africa,* XLI (1971), 85–108; William Bosman, *A New and Accurate Description of the Coast of Guinea* . . . (London, 1967 [orig. publ. 1704]), 368a. For another use of Horton's argument, see Monica Shuler, "Afro-American Slave Culture," in Michael Craton, ed., *Roots and Branches: Current Directions in Slave Studies* (Toronto, 1979), 121–137.

balance continuity and change. As Richard Gray puts it, "The approach of most Africans to supernatural powers was pragmatic and experimental."[92]

A major development that took place in the metaphysics of the slave community, in response to the enforced coexistence with other African groups and to the grave, everyday problems of dealing with harsh taskmasters, was an expanded role for the realm of lesser spirits, particularly those deemed useful in injuring others. Melville Herskovits, who pioneered so many of the most fruitful avenues of African American research, wondered whether in the New World "African religion goes underground, and manifests itself in an increase of magic (especially black magic)." This development occurred in the slave cultures of both Virginia and South Carolina to a degree. Not all resort to magic was to injure people—for a spectrum of activities, from outright sorcery to folk healing, from witchcraft to divination, certainly existed—but the dominant trend may be labeled a shift from "saints" (the benevolent lesser spirits so prominent in traditional cosmologies) to "sorcery" (the harming of others by secretive means).[93]

Anglo-Americans described slaves' attempts to harm others by secretive means as either "poisoning" or "conjuring." Even granting the white predilection to see malevolence behind what might have been innocent black actions, many slaves clearly believed in conjuring, often resorted to it, and on occasion sought to harm others by it. The slaves' alleged use of poisons against the white community gained most notoriety. In eighteenth-century Virginia, at least 175 slaves were brought before the county courts on charges of poisoning, and a large proportion had white masters or overseers as their ostensible targets. The revulsion felt by whites is captured in some of the sentences. In Orange County, a slave woman named Eve, found guilty of poisoning her master, was drawn on a hurdle to the place of execution and there burnt at the stake. Threats, not just actions, were also frightening. Chesterfield County magistrates, for example, took seriously Sharper's threats to "administer divers Poisonous Drugs to his said Master and Mistress." In one dramatic case, white Virginians seemed keen to keep a poisoning quiet, perhaps for fear of encouraging others. Thus, a report emanating from Alexandria that four slaves had

---

92. Terence Ranger, "The Local and the Global in Southern African Religious History," in Robert W. Hefner, ed., *Conversion to Christianity: Historical and Anthropological Perspectives on a Great Transformation* (Berkeley, Calif., 1993), 65–98 (quotations on 73–75); Richard Gray, *Black Christians and White Missionaries* (New Haven, Conn., 1990), 4.

93. Melville J. Herskovits, *The New World Negro: Selected Papers in Afroamerican Studies*, ed. Frances S. Herskovits (Bloomington, Ind., 1966), 22; Ranger, "Recent Developments," *Ufahamu*, IV (1973), 24; Elliott J. Gorn, "Black Magic: Folk Beliefs of the Slave Community," in Ronald L. Numbers and Todd L. Savitt, eds., *Science and Medicine in the Old South* (Baton Rouge, La., 1989), 295–326.

been executed for poisoning whites (with their heads placed on the courthouse chimneys) and that another four were expected to meet the same fate cannot be verified from local records. It surfaces in newspapers as far away as Pennsylvania and Georgia.[94]

In South Carolina, white fears of black poisonings appear to have been even more intense than in Virginia. In 1741, a newspaper report claimed that a sinister drug had been used by a "Negro Doctor" to poison a white infant. The black was burned at the stake. Three years later, a black man was hanged in chains on a gibbet near Dorchester for allegedly poisoning his master. In 1749, the "horrid practice of poisoning White People," another editorial expostulated, led to several executions "by burning, gibbeting, [and] hanging." That same year, the *South-Carolina Gazette* printed a letter from Dr. Milward to the president of the Royal Society on "Indian or Negro poison" in the West Indies, indicating the extent of the interest in the matter. Two years later, the minister of Saint George Dorchester saw at close quarters "the horrid practice of [slaves'] poisoning their Masters or those set over them." Five or six slaves were condemned to die, he continued, "altho' 40 or 50 more were privy to it." Suspected poisoning scares recurred throughout the century—in 1761, for example, slaves reportedly had "begun again the hellish practice of poisoning"— and whites retaliated savagely, gibbeting and burning alive the suspects.[95]

94. Trial of Eve, Jan. 23, 1746, Orange County Court Order Book, no. 4, 454–455, VSL; A. G. Grinnan, "The Burning of Eve in Virginia," *VMHB*, III (1896), 308–310 (see also trial of Hampton and Sambo, May 24, 1756, Bedford County Court Order Book, no. 1A, 165); trial of Sharper, Feb. 13, 1752, Chesterfield County Court Order Book, no. 1, 175–176 (see also trial of Joyce, July 21, 1766, Essex County Court Order Book, no. 26, 356); the Alexandria case is reported in *Pennsylvania Gazette*, Dec. 31, 1767, and *Ga Gaz*, Mar. 30, 1768, but is not mentioned in town and county records of extant Virginia newspapers: Thomas Milton Preisser, "Eighteenth-Century Alexandria, Virginia, before the Revolution, 1749–1776" (Ph.D. diss., College of William and Mary, 1977), 96. I count 175 slaves accused of poisoning in the court records (up to c. 1780) of 22 Virginia counties, and in the auditor's papers, legislative petitions, and executive papers of the state (c. 1777–1800), all located in the VSL. Of the 175, 143 were men, 32 women. See also Philip J. Schwarz, *Twice Condemned: Slaves and the Criminal Laws of Virginia, 1705–1865* (Baton Rouge, La., 1988), 92–113. For a good description of white hysteria concerning alleged slave poisonings, see Yvan Debbasch, "Le crime d'empoisonnement aux îles pendant la période esclavagiste," *Revue française d'histoire d'Outre-Mer*, L (1963), 137–188. I use the term *poison* because this is the one employed by white contemporaries.

95. *SCG*, Aug. 15, 1741, July 30, 1744, Oct. 30, 1749, July 24, 1749; Rev. William Coles to SPG, Dec. 2, 1751, B19/141; *SCG*, Jan. 17, 1761. For other cases, see South Carolina Commons House Journal, Feb. 20, 1753, no. 27, part 1, 205, and Apr. 10, 1753, part 2, 415; South Carolina Council Journal, Aug. 24, 1753, no. 21, part 2, 598, and box 3, Parish Transcripts, NYHS; John Bartram, "Diary of a Journey through the Carolinas, Georgia, and Florida, from July 1, 1765, to April 10, 1766," ed. Francis Harper, American Philosophical Society, *Transactions*, N.S.,

Poisonings, however, were as much, if not more, directed inwardly at blacks as targeted outwardly against whites. Indeed, some observers thought that poisonings of whites were infrequent. A French visitor to Virginia during the Revolutionary war was poorly informed when he reported, "We never hear in this country of masters poisoned by their negroes," but he was undoubtedly correct when he claimed that the practice was much more extensive in the French West Indies. Peter Kalm observed that the "dangerous art of poisoning" was well known among North American blacks and that they used it primarily against one another. When "a negro feels himself poisoned and can recollect the enemy," Kalm explained, "he goes to him, and endeavors by money and entreaties to move him to deliver him from its effects." According to Kalm, the "negroes commonly employ it on such of their brethren as behave well [toward the whites], are beloved by their masters, and separate, as it were, from their countrymen, or do not like to converse with them. They have likewise often other reasons for their enmity; but there are few examples of their having poisoned their masters."[96]

Intrablack conflict, stemming perhaps from frictions among African ethnic groups or between Africans and creoles or perhaps from the natural stresses to which all slave communities were subject, lay at the heart of many poisonings. Tangled webs of claims and counterclaims, all pointing to serious divisions among blacks, characterize a number of poisonings. Thus, many whites in Louisa County believed that a slave named Peter had prepared substances as an "Ostentatious charade to increase his Credit with Those Negroes who had pressed him to Destroy . . . their Enemies," when in fact his supposed clients hoped to betray him "as a person Guilty of poisoning and conjuring." Likewise, blacks and whites came to the defense of Roger, a Pittsylvania County

---

XXXIII (1942–1944), 22; *SCG and CJ,* Aug. 1, 1769, *SCG,* extraordinary, Aug. 1, 1769, and ibid., Aug. 17, 1769; petition of Joseph Warnock of St. Thomas, planter, Feb. 11, 1785, House of Representatives Petitions, SCDAH; Ulrich Bonnell Phillips, *Life and Labor in the Old South* (Boston, 1929), 166; petition of John Jordan, Jan. 25, 1791, Senate Petitions, SCDAH; and J. H. Easterby, *History of the St. Andrew's Society of Charleston, South Carolina, 1729–1929* (Charleston, S.C., 1929), 39–40. Slave crime records have not survived for colonial South Carolina, so this investigation relies on newspaper reports, legislative, executive records, and so on.

96. J. G. Shea, ed., *The Operations of the French Fleet under the Count de Grasse in 1781–2, as Described in Two Contemporaneous Journals* (New York, 1864), 87; Adolph B. Benson, ed., *Peter Kalm's Travels in North America* (New York, 1937 [orig. publ. 1770]), 210. Of the 71 colonial Virginia court cases in which the identity of the victim is recorded, 40 were white, 31 black. In another 32, the victim was unidentified. I suspect that many of the unidentified victims were black, especially since the defendants in such cases were more often acquitted—indeed, acquittal rates matched those where there were known black victims. Cf. Schwarz, *Twice Condemned,* 96.

slave accused of poisoning, on the grounds that his chief accuser, a slave named Matt, had vengeful motives. But another white resident strongly asserted Roger's guilt, claiming that the slave had a long history as a poisoner, extending back to Dinwiddie County "near Twenty years ago." He even alleged that Roger had poisoned several of his own slaves and recalled hearing Roger's "master and mistress [say] at several times as he has poison'd as they believe 18 or 20 Slaves for them." Wherever the truth lay, Peter and Roger aroused strong and contrasting feelings from their fellow slaves, not to mention whites.[97]

Intrablack poisonings were more extensive than court records indicate—for many cases never came to trial. Twice in the 1760s, Colonel James Gordon of Lancaster County heard allegations of poisoning among his slaves. Gordon took no legal action in either case. In 1764, an overseer of George Washington's slaves reported that one of his charges lay close to death, apparently poisoned. A week later, the overseer was adamant that there had been foul play, but the bondman had recovered (perhaps because the overseer had used a "negro doctor"), and the matter was dropped. Henry Muhlenberg noted the hard luck story of a beginning Georgia planter whose key purchase, a slave woman, had been poisoned by other slaves—but there is no evidence of a trial. Similarly, an East Florida manager reported "a most shocking affair" on his plantation. Two slave brothers had died suddenly within days of one another "in great agonys and with all the Symptoms of Poison." Two slave men and a woman on the same plantation stood accused of the crime; indeed, one of the men, perhaps out of remorse, had attempted suicide. The overseer predicted, "It will be a difficult matter to come at the truth where none but Negroes are concerned." He was right, for, two months later, no culprit had been found.[98]

Blacks and whites alike testified to the important role of the dispenser

97. Petition of Thomas Johnson, Jr., et al., Aug. 11, 1783, Executive Papers, August–October 1783 (trial of Peter); depositions of Mary Brown, Chiner, Jack, and Dall, May 9, 1787, and letters of S. Williams and Jeremiah White (Roger's owner), May 1787, ibid., April–May 1787, VSL. Roger's history as a poisoner can be traced at least to 1782, for in that year he received 39 lashes and had his ears cut off for a poisoning offense (Pittsylvania County Court Order Book, no. 4, 406; thanks to Michael L. Nicholls for this reference).

98. "Journal of Col. James Gordon," *WMQ*, 1st Ser., XI (1902–1903), 224, XII (1903–1904), 2–3; Joseph Valentine to George Washington, July 29, Aug. 6, 1764, Custis Papers, VHS; Henry Melchior Muhlenberg, *The Journals of Henry Melchior Muhlenberg*, trans. Theodore G. Tappert and John W. Doberstein, 2 vols. (Philadelphia, 1942–1958), II, 638; David Yeats to Governor James Grant, June 1, Aug. 10, 1780, 0771/250, Papers of General James Grant of Ballindalloch. See also List of Edmund Jenings's slaves at Beverdam Quarter, King William County, Dec. 16, 1712, Francis Porteus Corbin Papers, Duke; South Carolina Council Journal, June 11, 1752, box 3, Parish Transcripts; and Commons House Journal, Feb. 20, 28, 1753, no. 28, part 1, 197, 250; *Laurens Papers*, V, 123; John Price to Joseph Duval, May 1786, Executive Papers.

of poisons (or medicines or charms) within the slave community. In the Chesapeake, at least one conjurer was brought to trial. Tom, a Caroline County slave, was accused of causing the death of another slave, Joe, by administering "several poisonous powders, roots, herbs and simples." Acquitted of this offense, Tom was transported for giving "powder to other Negroes." More often, however, the role of the conjurer became apparent only when his or her clients came before the courts. Thus, seventy-six Spotsylvania County residents sought a pardon for two slave blacksmiths accused of poisoning their master on the grounds that these "orderly well behaved" men had been duped by "a Negro wench, or Conjurer" belonging to a neighboring planter. Similarly, a Fauquier County slave accused of arson elicited the support of neighboring whites because his chief accuser was "a notorious Villan," a slave named Ben, who "pretend[ed] to be a conjurer or fortune teller." Three slave men accused of murdering a white overseer in Powhatan County revealed the crucial role of Pompey, a neighbor's slave, who was "reputed among the Negroes as a Conjurer." The plotters had frequently consulted Pompey, "relied much on [his] art . . . to prevent detection," and had even paid him a fee. Henry Knight's observation that Virginia slaves were "very superstitious" and relied on "their poison-doctors, and their conjurers" was well founded.[99]

Black conjurers played similar behind-the-scenes, and occasionally starring, roles in the Lowcountry. A Mr. Vaughan, a South Carolina carpenter, experienced what he believed to be a poisoning in his "family." One slave man died within a few hours, and a slave woman and Vaughan's wife also fell ill. After a search, "poisonous herbs and roots" were found in the pockets of an "old Negro fellow named Doctor Jack." When the wife of Thomas Miles of Stono fell seriously ill, it turned out that the poison had been furnished by a slave man belonging to another owner. James Sand, his wife, and their child were allegedly poisoned by Dolly, at the behest of mulatto Dick, but the supplier was Liverpoole, described as "a Negro Doctor," who belonged to another master. At the trial of three of John Colhoun's slaves, evidence came to light of the role of Captain McCaleb's "Old Jack" and Colhoun's "Old Hazard" in dispensing poisons. In fact, one of the accused slaves said that Hazzard "gave him a small root and directed him to give it to his master and said Twou'd kill him." Most revealing was the case involving a slave named John, executed on suspicion of poisoning a white. Apparently, John had boasted to other slaves of

---

99. Trial of Tom, Caroline County Court Order Book, 1740–1746, 288–290; petition of Spotsylvania County residents, Dec. 20, 1795, Executive Papers, December 1795; depositions of Epaphroditus Timberlake, June 6, 1791, and William Pickett, June 30, 1791 (also see that of Charles Marshall, n.d., ibid., May–August 1791); petition of Bentley Crump et al., n.d., ibid., May–June 1794; Knight, *Letters*, 75.

going "to a free school to learn To Conjure sixteen years." Nat, a fellow slave, testified that John had told him "that he could give poison that [Nat's] father Could not Cure." The court acknowledged that "Nat's father is allowd to be one of the most skilful doctors in these pa[r]ts of a negro—also in Conjuration" while other slaves told of being rubbed by John and falling ill, of resorting to an "old Negro Conjurer" to ward off John's powers, and of hearing John wish for a "Rattle snakes head [so that] he Could do well Enough."[100]

The spatial distribution of poisoning cases in Virginia, together with the advanced age of many conjurers, suggests an African influence. At least two-thirds of the slaves accused of poisoning resided in the piedmont. This high concentration in a region where numbers of Africans lived, together with stray scraps of information such as a suspect's African name, make the connection plausible. Further, an offhand remark by Edmund Pendleton suggests such a link in the contemporary mind. In 1777, when referring to the atrocities perpetrated by the British army, Pendleton exclaimed that they had descended to the "low, mean, petiful, skulking, perfidious, wicked, Italian and African business of Poisoning."[101]

In South Carolina, the connection between Africa and poisoning was drawn rather more authoritatively. In 1752, nine months after arriving in the colony, the physician Dr. Alexander Garden observed that "the Negroe slaves here seem to be but too well acquainted with the Vegetable poisons (whether they gain that knowledge in this province or before they leave Africa I know not, tho' I imagine the Latter)." He also noted that a native African had revealed an antidote for poisons three years earlier. After a further three years in the colony, Garden saw little to change his mind about an African provenance for the slaves' knowledge of poisons, for he now "greatly . . . suspect[ed] that the Negroes bring their knowledge of the Poisonous Plants, which they use here, with them from their own Country." In the early nineteenth century, a respectable South Carolina doctor raised the possibility with his patient that he might

100. South Carolina Council Journal, Jan. 22, 1747, box 2, Parish Transcripts; ibid., Nov. 7, 1749, no. 17, part 1, 677, also box 2, Parish Transcripts; *SCG and CJ*, Aug. 1, 1769, *SCG*, Extraordinary, Aug. 1, 1769, and ibid., Aug. 17, 1769; court of Justices and Freeholders at the plantation of John E. Colhoun, Aug. 13, 1795, John Ewing Colhoun Papers, USC; petition of Leroy Beauford, General Assembly, Petitions, 1800, no. 174, SCDAH.

101. David John Mays, ed., *The Letters and Papers of Edmund Pendleton, 1734–1803*, 2 vols. (Charlottesville, Va., 1967), I, 216. For the elderly, see Muhlenberg, *Journals*, II, 585; *SCG*, July 30, 1744; petition in respect of Cate belonging to Betty Lewis, June 20, 1786, Executive Papers. I count four African names among alleged poisoners from piedmont Virginia: Obee, Mazar, Okie, and Mustapha. On the regional distribution, see Schwarz, *Twice Condemned*, 110. My analysis of Virginia court cases was weighted toward the piedmont, i.e., 15 piedmont and 7 tidewater counties constituted my colonial sample, and, of the 175 slaves I counted, 84% were from the piedmont.

be suffering from "what was called African poisoning" or "tricking." The doctor had failed with previous patients who had then been "perfectly cured by applying to an old African." The cure involved "art," not medicine.[102]

The slaves' apparent skill in using poison confirmed whites' beliefs in the alien origins of the practice. Even Garden, who thought that the label "poison" was indiscriminately applied to many untreatable illnesses, was impressed by the slaves' abilities. He believed their administration of poison "so certain . . . as to render the use of Medicines entirely ineffectual even when given by the ablest practitioners in the province." John Bartram found it "surprising what effect this dreadful poison hath upon all animals either to cause Sudden death or lingering." South Carolinians told him, "A little of the powder laid on the skin will presently eat to the bone." By what he could learn, the powder consisted of "toxicodendron triphilon," which "it's supposed the negroes can cure in time." Thomas Anburey heard from Virginians about the "remarkable" abilities of slaves to cause swift or slow deaths "agreeable to their ideas of revenge." Likewise, the slave poisoner's ability to cause lingering deaths and "never disclose the nature of the poison" most impressed Peter Kalm.[103]

At the same time, this connection to Africa cannot just be taken at face value. Indeed, whether slaves were using poisons on the scale imagined by whites is highly debatable. Presumably, many lingering deaths were not in fact caused by poison. Ascribing a fatality to poison might well have acted, as Dr. Garden perceptively noted, "as good a screen to ignorance [in South Carolina] as ever that of Malignancy was in Britain." The inextricable blend of fantasy and fact concerning the slaves' expertise in roots, poisons, and herbs is captured well in a story related by Sarah Wiggins, a married woman of Dobbs County, North Carolina. She told how, in 1769, a slave named Will had come to her door and offered her a drink of rum, which made her "strangely sick." Will then produced a bottle containing herbs that he said would cure her illness. Instead, the potion intoxicated her "and took away her Senses." Thereafter, Will returned "at different times" with "some Liquid thing to drink which always deprived her of her Senses, and by that means had Carnal knowledge of her Body." Subsequently, she had a child by Will, who threatened to poison

---

102. Garden to Alston, Jan. 21, 1753, Feb. 18, 1756, Laing MSS, III, 375/42, 44, University of Edinburgh (the native African mentioned by Garden was a slave named Caesar, discussed below); James Potter Collins, *A Revolutionary Soldier,* rev. John M. Roberts (Clinton, La., 1859), 141–147, as cited in Mechal Sobel, "Whatever You Do, Treat People Right: Personal Ethics in a Slave Society," in Ted Ownby, ed., *Black and White Cultural Interaction in the Antebellum South* (Jackson, Miss., 1993), 64–69.

103. Garden to Alston, Jan. 21, 1753, Laing MSS, III; Bartram, "Diary," ed. Harper, Am. Phil. Soc., *Trans.,* N.S., XXXIII (1942–1944), 22; Anburey, *Travels,* II, 435; Benson, ed., *Peter Kalm's Travels,* I, 210.

anybody who talked about it. Further, Will boasted that he could use roots and herbs in order to "lye with the best of the Women" in the county. Sarah Wiggins might have fabricated a tale to explain the birth of her mulatto child, but presumably the accusation that Will was knowledgeable about poisons and herbs was eminently believable.[104]

In a few poisonings, whites were involved alongside blacks, which may suggest a fusion of Euro-American and African knowledge, although blacks appear to have been the prime suspects. Thus, in Charles County, Maryland, at midcentury, William Stretton, a white servant, was accused of giving boiled milk to his master that contained "certain Poisonous Herbs and Powders." Apparently, he conspired with two slaves, Anthony "the poison doctor" and Jenny, who seem to have been his suppliers. In 1792, the Reverend James Ireland of Virginia thought that a white woman, probably a servant, and a black slave woman had tried to poison his family. His later mention of a rumor circulating among Virginians "that the negroes had put poison in certain sugars of the West India islands" suggests the most likely object of his suspicions.[105]

Slaves fitted unfamiliar substances and techniques into familiar ways of thinking. The blue color that outlined windows and doors of Lowcountry slave cabins and acted as a protection against evil spirits derived from the scrapings of indigo vats. Blacks acquired knowledge from whites and from Indians. In the late seventeenth century, the Reverend John Clayton heard of "a very strange and extraordinary cure" performed by an Indian on a black slave in Virginia. Perhaps this folk remedy passed into black lore. In South Carolina, Boston King recalled that his mother took care of the sick, "having some knowledge of the virtue of herbs, which she learned from the Indians." Richard Parkinson told of a white conjurer who apparently produced charms that blacks found powerful. Some superstitions held by blacks comported well with those found in the white community and were thereby reinforced. Others might have been derived from whites entirely. When a Virginia master noted that his "travelling servant," a slave named George, was "much afraid of Spirits and being alone in the night," there is no reason to think that this belief was

---

104. Garden to Alston, Feb. 18, 1756, Laing MSS, III; deposition of Sarah Wiggins, Apr. 12, 1772, Slavery Papers Miscellaneous, NCDAH, as cited in Jeffrey J. Crow, *The Black Experience in Revolutionary North Carolina* (Raleigh, N.C., 1977), 38.

105. Maryland Council Proceedings, June 24, 1755, XXXI, 69, and Black Book, IV, 113, VIII, 59, IX, 62, MHR; Jean B. Lee, *The Price of Nationhood: The American Revolution in Charles County* (New York, 1995), 80; *The Life of the Reverend James Ireland . . .* (Winchester, Va., 1819), 199, 204. See also Hunter Dickinson Farish, ed., *Journal and Letters of Philip Vickers Fithian, 1773–1774: A Plantation Tutor of the Old Dominion* (Williamsburg, Va., 1957), 252; and David Curtis Skaggs, ed., *The Poetic Writings of Thomas Cradock, 1718–1770* (East Brunswick, N.J., 1983), 189–190.

African in origin. In the realm of supernatural beliefs, blacks absorbed so much because the additions complemented, or acted in place of, traditional convictions.[106]

Although slave magical practices and beliefs drew on many sources, the African dimension seems most evident in the prevalence of sorcery. In E. E. Evans-Pritchard's classic distinction, both witches and sorcerers seek to injure people, but sorcery is the deliberate attempt by an individual to harm others by secretive means (whether by magic or poison), whereas witchcraft is the unconscious harming of others by magical means. Witchcraft is an inherent quality; sorcery is a deliberate, conscious action. Rarely were eighteenth-century Southern slaves linked to witchcraft, but sorcery was widespread.[107] The most common term for sorcery was *obi* or *obia* (with many other variant spellings), which had multiple African origins, including Efik *ubio* (a charm to cause sickness or death) and Twi *o-bayifo* (sorcerer). The term was current among North American slaves. A Virginia slave accused of poisoning a white was known as Obee. A South Carolina slave, Hector, said to possess magical powers, claimed, "Let the fire kindle as fast as it will, he will Engage by his obias to stiffle and put it out." In Johnston County, North Carolina, Quash, otherwise known as an "Ober Negro," sold "a small mater of truck" or "Ober" to other slaves. In the nineteenth century, W. B. Hodgson, a Georgian who was knowledgeable about African slaves still living in his vicinity, spoke of "the Obi practices and fetish worship, of the Pagan negroes early imported into this country, and of which traditional traces may still be discovered."[108]

---

106. Carl Thomas Julien, *Pee Dee Panorama: Photographs* (Columbia, S.C., 1951), 13; Edmund Berkeley and Dorothy Smith Berkeley, *The Reverend John Clayton: A Parson with a Scientific Mind* (Charlottesville, Va., 1965), 24–25; "Memoirs of the Life of Boston King, a Black Preacher," *Methodist Magazine*, XXI (1798), 105; Richard Parkinson, *A Tour in America, in 1798, 1799, and 1800 . . .* , II (London, 1805), 465; Thomas Miller, *VaG or AA*, Apr. 2, 1785. See also Levine, *Black Culture*, 60; Elliott J. Gorn, "Black Spirits: The Ghostlore of Afro-American Slaves," *American Quarterly*, XXXVI (1984), 549–565; Jon Butler, *Awash in a Sea of Faith: Christianizing the American People* (Cambridge, Mass., 1990), 67–97.

107. E. E. Evans-Pritchard, *Witchcraft, Oracles, and Magic among the Azande* (Oxford, 1937), 21. Alan Macfarlane points out that Evans-Pritchard's distinction does not always apply to societies other than the Azande (*Witchcraft in Tudor and Stuart England* [London, 1970], 310). Yet Macfarlane found the distinction useful when applied to early modern England, and, significantly, Anglo-Americans referred to slaves skilled in administering poisons as "conjurers," not "witches." For a case of witchcraft involving a black girl, see journal of William Colbert, Nov. 27, 1801, IV, 45, Garrett Theological Library, Evanston, Ill.

108. Trial of Obee, July 29, 1778, Spotsylvania County Court Order Book, 1774–1782, 94; testimony of Landgrave John Morton's Hector, South Carolina Council Journal, no. 17, part 1, 139; trial of Harry, Cuff, and Dick, 1768, Johnston County, Miscellaneous Records, NCDAH, as cited in Alan D. Watson, "North Carolina Slave Courts, 1715–1785," *N.C. Hist.*

More important than etymological parallels were the similarities in the practice of *obeah* between mainland and West Indian islands. First, North American conjuring was clearly an individual practice, with "professionals" often receiving payment from clients. Second, the ingredients of fetishes and charms on the mainland—"Scorpions heads, Sarsparilla, spiders, and glass bottles powdered" in one case, "snake and scorpion heads . . . and great quantity of Roots" in another—resemble those employed by obeah-men in Jamaica. Finally, canes or wands embellished with entwined serpents and frogs, important to the ritual practices of both conjurers and obeah-men, have been found on the mainland as well as in the West Indies.[109]

A variety of charms and magical symbols has been found among the debris of slave quarters. At a site in Baltimore County, Maryland, three polygonal objects shaped from glass, earthenware, and wood appear to have been ritual objects. A raccoon *baculum,* or penis bone, recovered from George Washington's Mount Vernon slave quarter, might well have been a fertility symbol; the incision of a line encircling one end suggests that it was hung around the neck by a cord. Blue glass beads, made in Europe but perhaps conceived by Africans and African Americans as having magical properties, have been excavated at various slave sites. On Parris Island, South Carolina, four thousand glass beads were found in a small pit; they might well have played a role in an African American religious ritual. An African cowrie shell has been found along Mulberry Row at Monticello. These items were probably used to ward off the "evil eye." Similarly, three brass amulets shaped like human fists uncovered at the Hermitage plantation in Tennessee and a hand-shaped hook-and-eye discovered at the Charles Calvert home in Annapolis, Maryland, have all been attributed to an African-American interest in hand images, which were thought to confer spiritual power.[110]

Rev., LX (1983), 31; W. B. Hodgson, *The Gospels, Written in the Negro Patois of English, with Arabic Characters, by a Mandingo Slave in Georgia* (New York, 1857), 8. See also Orlando Patterson, *The Sociology of Slavery: An Analysis of the Origins, Development, and Structure of Negro Slave Society in Jamaica* (London, 1967), 188; Cassidy and Le Page, eds., *Dictionary of Jamaican English,* 326; Richard Price, *First-Time: The Historical Vision of an Afro-American People* (Baltimore, 1983), esp. 47, 53–54; and Handler and Lange, *Plantation Slavery in Barbados,* 32–33, 181–182.

109. For the ingredients of charms, see trial of three slaves, Sussex County Court, July 23, 1795, Executive Papers; Wayne County, N.C., trial of 1805, described by I. Slocumb to Thomas Henderson, June 25, 1810, Thomas Henderson Letter Book, NCDAH; James Hugo Johnston, *Race Relations in Virginia and Miscegenation in the South 1776–1860* (Amherst, Mass., 1970), 27.

110. Eric Klingelhofer, "Aspects of Early Afro-American Material Culture: Artifacts from the Slave Quarters at Garrison Plantation, Maryland," *Historical Archaeology,* XXI, no. 2

In South Carolina, a number of African words associated with magic, particularly magic aimed at causing harm, were in use well into the twentieth century. The Hausa word *huduba,* meaning "to arouse resentment," was simplified to *hudu,* meaning "to cause bad luck"; the Mende word *ndzoso,* meaning "spirit or magic," was simplified to *joso,* meaning "charm, witchcraft." Other words with essentially similar meanings were also employed, such as *juju* for "evil spirit," *kafa* for "charm," *moco* for "witchcraft or magic," *wanga* for "charm, witchcraft," and, most famous of all, *wudu* for "sorcery." Perhaps most significantly, some African words that seem to have had benign meanings became associated with sorcery in Gullah. Thus the Ewe word *fufu,* which simply means "dust," became in Gullah "a fine dust used with the intention of bewitching one or causing harm to one." Likewise, the Mende word *gafa,* meaning "spirit, soul, or idol," became for Gullah speakers "evil spirit, or devil." Transferred from the Chesapeake to the Lowcountry, Charles Ball noted the difference when he described cotton slaves as "exceedingly superstitious ... beyond all other people that I have ever known." They "uniformly believe," Ball continued, "in witchcraft, conjuration, and the agency of evil spirits in the affairs of human life."[111]

(1987), 112–119; Dennis J. Pogue, "The Archaeology of Plantation Life: Another Perspective on George Washington's Mount Vernon," *Virginia Cavalcade,* XLI (1991–1992), 79; Charles H. Fairbanks, "The Kingsley Slave Cabins in Duval County, Florida, 1968," *Conference on Historic Site Archaeology Papers,* VII (1972), 90; John Solomon Otto, *Cannon's Point Plantation, 1794–1860: Living Conditions and Status Patterns in the Old South* (Orlando, Fla., 1984), 175; William Hampton Adams, ed., *Historical Archaeology of Plantations at Kings Bay, Camden County, Georgia,* Reports of Investigations, Department of Anthropology, University of Florida (Gainesville, Fla., 1987), 14, 118, 204; Stanley South, *Revealing Santa Elena, 1982,* Research Manuscript Series 88, Institute of Archaeology and Anthropology, University of South Carolina (Columbia, S.C., 1983), 73; Leland Ferguson, *Uncommon Ground: Archaeology and Early African America, 1650–1800* (Washington, D.C., 1992), 116–117; William M. Kelso, "Mulberry Row: Slave Life at Thomas Jefferson's Monticello," *Archaeology,* XXXIX, no. 5 (September–October 1986), 30; Larry McKee, "The Earth Is Their Witness," *Sciences* (March–April 1995), 40; Anne Elizabeth Yentsch, *A Chesapeake Family and Their Slaves: A Study in Historical Archaeology* (Cambridge, 1994), 33; Charles E. Orser, Jr., "The Archaeology of African-American Slave Religion in the Antebellum South," *Cambridge Archaeological Journal,* IV (1994), 33–45.

111. Turner, *Africanisms,* 193–204; Ball, *Fifty Years in Chains,* 165, 260. Nineteenth-century accounts of black superstitions are also insightful; for example, Roland Steiner, "Observations on the Practice of Conjuring in Georgia," *Jour. Am. Folk-Lore,* XIV (1901), 173–180; Jackson, ed., *The Negro and His Folklore,* 134–143, 274–292; and Alan Dundes, ed., *Mother Wit from the Laughing Barrel: Readings in the Interpretation of Afro-American Folklore,* rev. ed. (New York, 1981), 359–387. An account of slave religion on Bull's Island, South Carolina, in 1834 noted that slaves organized their own punishments: "If the crime was of the first magnitude, the perpetrator had to pick up a quart of benne seed ... poured on the ground

Important as the association of sorcery with an African influence clearly was, the practice had to appeal to creoles or it would soon have fossilized. The South Carolina Assembly recognized this danger in 1751 when it made it a capital offense for "any slave [to] teach or instruct another slave in the knowledge of any poisonous root, plant, herb, or other sort of poison whatever." But apparently whites were powerless to halt the dissemination of knowledge. As early as 1724, the minister of Saint James Goose Creek lamented that the "secret poisonings" in his parish stemmed, not from unassimilated Africans, but from those slaves converted to Christianity. A generation later, the minister of Saint George Dorchester was surprised to find a baptized slave accused of poisoning. She told the startled minister "that notwithstanding what was alledged against her, she still hoped to be saved because she believed in Christ." He attributed her optimism to the influence of "our sectaries." Perhaps South Carolina officials showed great wisdom in reimbursing Culcheth Golightly's estate for a whole family of slaves, transported to Jamaica on suspicion of poisoning their master. Diffusion would surely take place within a family, they might have decided.[112]

In piedmont Virginia, one case of poisoning involved the apparent transmission of magical knowledge from African father to African American son. Joe, the son, was found guilty of poisoning. A number of the county's white residents petitioned for a pardon on the grounds that it was Joe's father, a slave with the African name Mazar, who "compounded and administered medicines." Indeed, Joe had once "informed his father who was very Deaf that physic was wanted stronger than some he had given before," but also "cautioned his Father to beware and take care not to take life." Furthermore, Joe's "crime" appeared less heinous to many of his white neighbors because part of the evidence against him lay merely in his prediction that sick people would die on the return of warm weather. At worst, this was little more than harmless fortune-telling.[113]

---

by the priest . . . the rule was, if it was not done in one night, they had to continue until they did it." This black "superstition," as this observer termed it, is important for signifying the supernatural significance of an African cultigen, which still retained its African name (Thos. D. Turpin, "Missionary Intelligence," *Christian Advocate and Journal* [New York], VIII, no. 23 [Jan. 31, 1834], 90).

112. Cooper and McCord, *Statutes at Large,* VII, 423; Rev. Richard Ludlam to SPG, July 12, 1724, B4/181; Rev. William Coles to SPG, Dec. 2, 1751, B19/141; Estate of Culcheth Golightly with Charles Pinckney, May 17, 1750, Inventories, WPA, CXXXIV, 575, SCDAH.

113. Petitions of Thomas Maddux, Obadiah Pettit, John Green, Jr., and F. Brooke, September 1790, Executive Papers, August–November 1790. A possible transmission of knowledge might have occurred among the Jerdone slaves. In 1793, Peg, a Jerdone slave, was convicted of poisoning. She was probably the same slave listed in Jerdone's records as a resident of the Pigeon quarter in 1770 and who had her last child in 1768. Presumably, she

As this case and others indicate, some alleged poisonings probably involved divination or folk medicine as much as sorcery, although the distinction might have escaped many slaves. Some slaves got off lightly in the courts because their putative magical powers were seen as harmless. One slave "latterly pretended to be a fortune teller, for which he receives a dram or some other trifle." Another's credibility as a diviner rose among his fellow blacks when he predicted that a house would be burnt, but a member of the court was skeptical and asked the slave "how he gaind the knowledege, whether by his art as a conjuror or did any Person inform him as so." Both slaves escaped with a whipping. Many slaves were acquitted of the charge of poisoning because, like Dinah of Cumberland County, who administered medicines to her fellow slave Amey, probably to help with Amey's pregnancy, no harm was intended. Some slaves used "poisons" as charms to influence their masters. Peg of Louisa County administered a substance procured from a slave man in the neighborhood "to keep peace in the family, and to make her Master kind to her." Sarah of Prince Edward County put black seeds "resembling Jaucestor seeds" into the peas she prepared for her white family "for the purpose of making her mistress love her." A North Carolina slave, Bristoe, prepared concoctions and supplied roots intended to make one master sell a slave and another owner buy a man's wife. Another North Carolina slave gave a substance to his mistress "to make her better to him"; his supplier also had an interest because the white woman intended to purchase his daughter, and he apparently wanted to influence her conduct toward his loved one.[114]

The boundary between conjuring and folk medicine was porous. In an age

---

was an old woman in 1793. The Jerdone family records also reveal that Barnet, born in 1769 (and, presumably, acquainted with Peg), was transported for attempting to administer poison some time in the 19th century. See Louisa County Court of Oyer and Terminer, Dec. 6, 1793, Executive Papers, and Lists of Slaves, Jerdone Slave Book, VSL.

114. Trial of Bob, June 16, 1764, Chesterfield County Court Order Book, 1759–1767, 542; petition of Charles Marshall and William Pickett, May–August 1791, Executive Papers; trial of Dinah, May 19, 1792, Cumberland Order Book, 1788–1792, 504; petition of John Poindexter, Jr., et al., n.d., and letter of W. O. Callis, Jan. 11, 1794, Executive Papers, January–February 1794; depositions of Elizabeth Young and William Keeling, n.d., ibid., August–September 1794; trial of Bristoe, Oct. 16, 1779, Johnston County Papers, Special Court for Trials of Negroes, 1764–1780, NCDAH, as cited in Crow, *Black Experience*, 38; Pasquotank County Court Minutes, Aug. 2, 1761, and Governor's Office, Committee of Claims Reports, 1760–1764, NCDAH, as cited in Kay and Cary, *Slavery in North Carolina*, 80–81, 107, 154, 186–187. Kay and Cary repeatedly claim that the substance was *touck*, which they interpret as a shortened version of *tuckahoe*, a root. In fact, the word is mentioned four times in the court minutes and is clearly "truck" in three instances (and only once appears, in my view mistakenly, as "touck"). *Truck* is commonly used in conjuring or poisoning cases and is a synonym for odds and ends.

where diseases struck often and mysteriously, a lingering illness could easily be attributed to magic. Particularly was this true when blacks revealed a strong interest in herbs and pharmacopoeia as panaceas for everyday problems. In the early eighteenth century, John Brickell observed that North Carolina slaves gathered snakeroot on Sundays; at midcentury, Dr. Alexander Garden pointedly noted that, were it not for what had been learned from "Negroe Strollers and Old Women," South Carolinians would not "know a Common Dock from a Cabbage Stock"; and, at the end of the century, Benjamin Henry Latrobe learned that "Negro woodmen" in Virginia rubbed swamp plantain onto snakebites. Slaves were undoubtedly well versed in the medicinal powers of various plants.[115]

Some slaves won fame for their healing powers, especially those involving poisons. In 1729, Virginia's ruling authorities freed a "very old" slave, almost certainly an African, because he was known as James Papaw, in order that he might reveal his "many wonderfull cures . . . in the most inveterate venerial Distempers." A resident of New Kent County, James had practiced many years but kept his remedy "a most profound Secrett." In return for his freedom, he revealed his decoction of "Roots and barks," which proved so effective that the following year the colony offered him an annual pension of twenty pounds if he would "make a discovery of other secrets for expelling poison and cure of other diseases." Forty years later, another slave, "Doctor Harry of Caroline," publicized his remedies, also consisting of roots and barks, for "poison, pains in the head, stomach, or belly." Similarly, two South Carolinians gained their freedom for their medicinal abilities. The most notable was sixty-seven-year-old Caesar, a "native of Africa," who in 1749 secured his freedom and a one-hundred-pound annuity for revealing his cures for poison—essentially a concentrate of plantain roots and wild horehound—and for rattlesnake bites. Five years later, Sampson followed in Caesar's footsteps by revealing a cure for snake bites. His treatment included the use of such native herbs as heartsnake root, common polypody, "five fingers," rough spleenwort, small erect clubmoss, and creeping goldilocks, but his fame rested on his going frequently "about with Rattle Snakes in Calabashes," which he would handle, even "put them into his Pockets or Bosom, and sometimes their Heads into his Mouth, without being bitten."[116]

---

115. John Brickell, *The Natural History of North-Carolina* (Dublin, 1737), 275; Dr. Alexander Garden to Dr. Charles Alston, Jan. 21, 1753, Laing MSS, III, 375/42,; Carter et al., eds., *Virginia Journals of Latrobe*, I, 107.

116. James Papaw is mentioned in Governor Gooch to the Secretary of State, June 29, 1729, CO5/1337, fols. 132–133, PRO; H. R. McIlwaine, ed., *Executive Journals of the Council of Colonial Virginia*, IV (Richmond, Va., 1930), 199, 217; and Governor William Gooch to

With less fanfare, a number of other South Carolina slaves practiced as doctors. A few were Africans. In 1749, the master of an Igbo fugitive named Simon, thought to be harbored by slaves on Johns Island, described him as pretending "to be a doctor"; fifteen years later, another Lowcountry master had grounds for being more charitable toward an African doctor, for his fugitive slave was "remarkable for having a bosent [swelling?] which he tried to have cut out, and was cured by a doctor, Guinea born." Other doctors were creoles or highly assimilated slaves. Thus, a South Carolina slave who pretended to be free and from Virginia gave "himself out for a DOCTOR, by the name of Mr. or DOCTOR ANDERSON," and Pero, who spoke French and English, "passe[d] for a Doctor among people of his color" and was thought to practice in town. Although Lowcountry masters often ridiculed these black doctors (the master of Newman, like Simon's owner, described his slave as "pretend-[ing] to be a sort of Doctor"), they also resorted to them for their own slaves. Thus James Hartley's estate recorded a payment of five pounds to "a Negro for curing Sharper of the flux," and DeSaussure and Ford's cash book registered one pound, ten shillings to "a black quack for medicine for Clarinda."[117]

Slave women practiced as nurses, midwives, and doctors in the Lowcountry.

Bishop Gibson, June 29, 1729, XII, 137, Fulham Palace Papers, Lambeth Palace Library, London. Harry's cures are printed in *Virginia Almanac,* 1767, Almanac Collection, CW, and he is probably the same Harry, described as a "Negroe Doctor" (belonging to Michael Yates, the Caroline County physician), who in 1765 administered to three of Colonel Washington's slaves. Yates received three pounds and Harry's ferriage expenses in payment for his slave's services (Joseph Ellyson's receipt, Feb. 6, 1765, Custis Papers). Yates, but not Harry, is mentioned in T. E. Campbell, *Colonial Caroline: A History of Caroline County, Virginia* (Richmond, Va., 1954), 451. For Caesar, see J. H. Easterby and Ruth S. Green, eds., *The Journal of the Commons House of Assembly, March 28, 1749–March 19, 1750,* Colonial Records of South Carolina (Columbia, S.C., 1962), 293, 326; journal of Upper House, May 22, 1750, CO5/461; and, for his will, May 17, 1754, Charleston County Wills, VII, 176–177, SCDAH. His cures were printed and recorded in many places: see *SCG,* May 14, 1750; *London Magazine,* XIX (1750), 367–368; *Gentleman's Magazine, and Historical Quarterly,* XX (1750), 342–343; *Virginia Almanac* (William Hunter), 1753; Robert Jordan Commonplace Book, c. mid-18th century, VHS; Tobler's Almanac, 1759; Taylor's Almanac, 1765, CW. For Sampson, see South Carolina Commons House Journals, Jan. 17, 1754, no. 29, 26, May 9, 1754, no. 29, 369, Mar. 6, 1755, no. 30, part 1, 295, May 16, 1755, no. 30, part 2, 569; *SCG,* Apr. 8, 1756; and certificate no. 1876, marked by Negro Sampson, Aug. 23, 1775, Treasury Receipts, 1774–1778, 280, SCDAH.

117. Jacob Martin, *SCG,* Oct. 9, 1749 (Simon); Robert Ekills, *SC and AGG,* Apr. 18, 1764; Jacob Valk, *Gaz of State of SC,* May 12, 1777 (Mr. Anderson); James George, *City Gaz,* June 19, 1797 (Pero); William Anderson, *SCG,* Nov. 19, 1750 (Newman); administration of James Hartley's estate, July 11, 1758, Inventories, WPA, LXXXVIIA, 210; DeSaussure and Ford Cash Book, Nov. 18, 1797, SCHS. For another slave, "well known in town, especially among the Negroes, being employed by them as a Doctor," see Jacob-Nicholas Schwartzkopff, *SCG,* Jan. 3, 1771.

The advertisement of sale for one South Carolina estate made particular mention of "a wench that has been used to tend sick negroes." Another South Carolina slave woman was said to be "a good midwife and nurse, can weigh out medicines and let blood, which she has done for many years on a plantation." An absentee planter from Georgia entrusted the care of his young slaves and the tending of the sick to a slave woman named Amey. He shipped medicines from England, which she dispensed; indeed, he told his manager that no oversight was necessary, for she would remember "directions how to make use of" them.[118]

In the Chesapeake, slave doctors were also widely used. Planters' accounts are dotted with payments for services rendered. In 1752, William Dabney paid eleven shillings, three pence to John Bates for the use of his "negroe Doctor"; six years later, in Essex County, Lancaster received ten shillings for curing Tom; and, in 1774, William Ennals, a resident of Maryland's Eastern Shore, gave two shillings to his slave Aminta so that she could pass it along to "J. Stevens's Negro for curing her tooth ache." In 1760, Dr. Robertson, who agreed to attend Mr. Chichester as a surgeon, was displeased to find out that "a negro doctor" had been employed before him. Fourteen years later, Charles Yates was even unhappier to find that his recent purchase, a slave man named Harry, had been distempered for many years and "long under the hands of Negro Doctors." The master of the fugitive Sambo happened to mention that his slave "pretends to be a doctor," and the master of runaway Hannah pointed out the resemblance to her father, "Syke's doctor." Jenny, a renowned "Flux Doctor" had "great liberty in going about and attending people sick with the Flux in the Neighbourhood" of Charles County, Maryland. Typically, people directly approached her, not her master, for medical assistance. Some "said she was a witch," once again revealing the fine line between magic and folk healing in eighteenth-century minds.[119]

Although the precise form of medicine these doctors practiced is not known, some slave practitioners had intimate knowledge of Euro-American

---

118. John Ward, *SCG*, Jan. 11, 1768; Colcock and Gibbons, *SC Weekly Gaz*, Dec. 12, 1783; John Channing to Edward Telfair, Aug. 10, 1786, Edward Telfair Papers, Duke. See also John Scott, *SCG*, Nov. 21, 1754; and Downes and Jones, ibid., Feb. 12, 1763.

119. William Dabney Account Book, 1749–1757, 1752, Dabney Family Papers, VHS; accounts of William Daingerfield's estate, Dec. 31, 1758, Essex County Court Order Book, no. 28, 100–104; Memorandum Book, 1771–1774, Apr. 26, 1774, William Ennals Papers, LC; "Journal of Col. James Gordon," *WMQ*, 1st Ser., XI (1902–1903), 197; Charles Yates to Rev. Jno. Dixon, Jan. 11, 1774, Charles Yates Letterbook, microfilm, CW; Alexander Marshall, *VaG* (Royle), Nov. 4, 1763; Thomas Fenner, ibid. (D and H), Oct. 17, 1777; General Court of the Western Shore, Judgement Records (S497), Lib. JG25 (October Term 1794), fols. 251, 253–256, 276, 282, MHR, in Lee, *The Price of Nationhood*, 70–71.

remedies. The medical worldview of eighteenth-century whites penetrated the quarters. In 1776, a slave woman belonging to Robert Carter of Nomini Hall informed him that "she believed Addam's sickness was a return of his dropsical complaint." The following day, Sam, one of Carter's home quarter slaves, "blooded" Adam. In the 1780s, "Tom coachman" had become Carter's chief medical aide. On one occasion, Tom took "about 4 ounces of blood" from a slave and gave him a "Purge of Rhubarb." Nassau, Landon Carter's waiting man, seems to have adhered closely to his master's medical directions. Presumably he learned venesection and cupping from his master, who described his assistant as "the best bleeder about." Another waiting man, twenty-four-year-old Romeo of Westmoreland County, was equally conversant with white ways, being able to read, write, and practice arithmetic. His master described him as especially "fond of prescribing and administering to sick negroes, by which he acquired the nick-name of Doctor among them, a name perhaps he may attempt to pass by" as a fugitive. It would be surprising if Romeo was not aware of many Euro-American medical practices. The slaves who stole garlic "to make necklaces against yellow fever" were presumably inspired in part by European influences.[120]

In other cases, the source of inspiration for black doctors seems less firmly anchored in the Anglo-American tradition. Perhaps such was the case with the "negro doctor" who treated Jupiter when he "unfortunately conceived himself poisoned." He told Jupiter that his prescription would *"kill or cure."* Unfortunately, almost immediately after taking the medicine, Jupiter experienced "a strong convulsion fit" and languished for nine days before dying. According to Jupiter's owner, this was not the first slave to have been killed by this black doctor, although apparently his reputation remained undiminished among the slaves. The distinguished Dr. Galt of Williamsburg encountered an alien medical practice when a slave named Gabriel informed him that his medicines were useless. Gabriel believed that he had been "tricked" and "must have a Negro Doctor" to reverse the illness.[121]

---

120. Robert Carter, Nov. 5–7, 1776, Robert Carter Daybook, XIII, 220–221, Duke; Robert Carter to Dr. Timothy Harrington, Jan. 12, 1787, Robert Carter Letterbook, VII, 172, Duke; John Peck to Robert Carter, Feb. 23, 1787, Carter Family Papers, VHS; Greene, ed., *Carter Diary*, 411, 797 (there are many other references to Nassau's medical duties); Austin Brockebrough, *Va Ind Chron*, Mar. 4, 1789; William Scott Willis, "A Swiss Settler in East Florida: A Letter of Francis Philip Fatio," *Florida Historical Quarterly*, LXIV (1985–1986), 185.

121. Edwin Morris Betts and James Adam Bear, Jr., eds., *The Family Letters of Thomas Jefferson* (Columbia, Mo., 1966), 182–183; [A. D. Galt], *Practical Medicine: Illustrated by Cases of the Most Important Diseases*, ed. John M. Galt (Philadelphia, 1843), 295–296. For related beliefs and practices, see Susan A. McClure, "Parallel Usage of Medicinal Plants by Africans and Their Caribbean Descendants," *Economic Botany*, XXXVI (1982), 291–301.

More important than whether black doctors practiced in the Euro-American mode or incorporated a measure of African knowledge is their popularity among their clients. Robert Carter's slaves can stand as one good example of the strong preference exhibited for medical practitioners from within the black community. In 1781, his slave Michael recommended a slave woman, black Hannah, a resident of Charles County, Maryland, as the best person to cure Suckey, who suffered from fits. Apparently, Hannah traveled "great distances from home to visit sick people." On other occasions—in 1786 and 1788—two more of Carter's slaves, Guy and Kitty, availed themselves (at their initiative, but with Carter's blessing) of the services of a second doctor, David, belonging to William Berry of King George County. Berry noted that the charge for David's services was half a dollar a day, although "what medicine he gives on Sunday is his own charge." During the late 1780s and early 1790s, the slave women of Old Ordinary Plantation resorted to midwife Anne Lucas, a free mulatto "granny," who delivered a number of their babies. In 1790, a fourth healer, Eliza Steptoe's Caesar, took Carter's slave Daniel as his patient. Caesar practiced surgery, because Daniel's disorders called for the cutting of a "seaton" at the back of his neck. Carter's slaves could also resort to a black practitioner from within their own midst. One of Carter's overseers requested the assistance of the Nomini Hall slave Tom Coachman, for "the Black people at this place hath more faith in him as a doctor than any white Doctor."[122]

It is futile, finally, to differentiate too finely between sorcerer, wizard, diviner, and doctor or to search too single-mindedly for pure African "survivals." The term Anglo-Americans used to describe blacks who engaged in magic was itself ambiguous. *Conjurer* derived from "cunning man," who could be both a "wise man" and a "doctor." Similarly, African American culture was above all flexible and adaptive, embodying an amalgam of cultural traditions, many of which were complementary and self-reinforcing. Yet, there can be no doubting the dominance of sorcery in the slave community or its fundamentally African inspiration.[123]

---

122. Robert Carter to Bennett Neal, Sept. 15, 1781, Carter Letterbook, IV, 118–119; Carter to William Berry, July 31, 1786, ibid., VII, 62; Berry to Carter, Aug. 11, 1786, Carter Family Papers; George Randell to Berry, Aug. 18, 1786, Robert Carter Journal, 1784–1789, LC; Carter's Pass to Sampson, Jan. 31, 1788, Carter Letterbook, VIII, 77; Carter to Berry, Feb. 26, 1788, ibid., VIII, 88; Bert Carter to Anne Lucas, Apr. 1, 1790, Carter Family Papers; Elder William Dawson to Carter, July 21, 1788, ibid.; Carter to Dawson, Aug. 20, 1788, Carter Letterbook, VIII, 169; Carter to Mrs. Eliza Steptoe, Jan. 18, 1790, ibid., IX, 91.

123. On cunning folk, see Macfarlane, *Witchcraft*, 115–134; and Keith Thomas, *Religion and the Decline of Magic* (Harmondsworth, Eng., 1973), 252–300. Anglo-Americans could describe doctors as "conjurers": see Greene, ed., *Carter Diary*, 650. A slave belonging to one

In short, the movement from microcosm to macrocosm, from small-scale communities to enforced exchange with much larger communities, did not necessarily diminish the belief of the lesser spirits, as Robin Horton implied. Rather, the benevolent lesser spirits so prominent in traditional cosmologies gave way to a powerful concentration on those means for injuring people, be they white or black. Folk medicine and divination were not unimportant within the slave community, but the practice of sorcery was dominant. Horton acknowledged that one effect of an enlargement of scale might be to see the lesser spirits as "*downright evil*," and, in a further extension of his argument, has noted that an increase in witchcraft accusations might well flow from a weakening of microcosmic boundaries.[124]

In fact, African parallels to this African American development can be found. Geoffrey Parrinder has drawn the comparison both explicitly and somewhat generally, pointing out how magical practices withstood the strain of removal from countryside to town in Africa and multiplied to meet new circumstances. "The same thing happened when African slaves were taken across to America," he continued, for the "gods, and even more the ancestors, were at a discount but magic survived in Voodoo and Obeah." More specific parallels can be sought in the nineteenth-century cults of affliction, movements that represented an intensification and multiplication of alien spirits as Christianity advanced. T. O. Ranger and Isaria Kimambo suggest that these cults were one way of meeting the "macrocosmic challenge." Another, even more germane parallel derives from Gerald Hartwig's study of the Kerebe. The ability to manipulate spiritual forces for socially approved purposes, as in rainmaking and divining, was fundamental to traditional Kerebe life. However, as the Kerebe became involved in the ivory trade—that is, as they left the microcosmic world—sorcery evolved among them. As human-created misfortunes increased, the authority of the elders responsible for clan rituals diminished while the stock of those who could identify people responsible for the misfortune rose.[125]

In some African situations, therefore, as well as in many African American

---

Virginia estate was even named Conjuror (inventory of Ralph Rowzer, Jr., June 9, 1719, Essex County Will Book, no. 3, 99–101, VSL).

124. Horton, "African Conversion," *Africa*, XLI (1971), 102 (emphasis added); Horton, "On the Rationality of African Conversion," part 1, ibid., XLV (1975), 222–223.

125. Geoffrey Parrinder, *African Traditional Religion* (Westport, Conn., 1976 [orig. publ. 1962]), 144; T. O. Ranger and Isaria N. Kimambo, eds., *The Historical Study of African Religion* (Berkeley, Calif., 1972), 16–17; Gerald W. Hartwig, "Long-Distance Trade and the Evolution of Sorcery among the Kerebe," *African Historical Studies*, IV (1971), 505–524. For spirit cults in Brazil, see Roger Bastide, *The African Religions of Brazil: Toward a Sociology of the Interpenetration of Civilizations*, trans. Helen Sebba (Baltimore, 1978 [orig. publ. 1960]).

ones, the resort to magic, particularly sorcery, seemed especially appropriate in new and disorienting conditions. When life appears unusually capricious and unpredictable, conditions are ripe for magical expression. Not that magic will inevitably flourish, of course, but, in the slaves' case, much in their traditions as well as in those of their masters encouraged its spread. The unpredictability of the slave world may also explain why Christianity had little appeal for most eighteenth-century slaves. Until slaves could see that Christianity might symbolize an improvement in the conditions of their daily lives, or until it could serve as an expression of their situation and a message of hope for the future, it was unattractive. The religious worldview of early American slaves was primarily magical, not Christian.

In Africa, Horton argues, the shift from microcosm to macrocosm facilitated conversion to Christianity. The key change in African cosmologies, when faced with the interpretative challenge of large-scale social change, was an expanded place for the supreme being, the underpinner of the macrocosm. Among Africans this took the form of a far more elaborate theory of the supreme being and his ways of working in the world, and a battery of new ritual techniques for approaching him and directing his influence. The acceptance of Christianity or Islam in Africa owed as much to the evolution of traditional cosmologies as to the activities of missionaries.[126] Did anything remotely similar occur among African slaves in North America? Fortunately, a few eighteenth-century Africans described their traditional beliefs once they reached America. Their interrogators tended to be white preachers, who did what missionaries typically do—seek similarities between the alien religion and their own. But the replies seem to have been reported in unvarnished fashion and generally have an authentic ring to them. They merit careful attention.

In the early eighteenth century, the Reverend Francis Varnod, an Anglican

---

126. Horton, "African Conversion," *Africa*, XLI (1971), 100–104. Important modifications or amplifications of Horton's original schema may be found in Humphrey Fisher, "Conversion Reconsidered: Some Historical Aspects of Religious Conversion in Black Africa," *Africa*, XLIII (1973), 27–40; Horton, "On the Rationality of African Conversion," parts 1 and 2, ibid., XLV (1975), 219–235, 373–399; Willy De Craemer et al., "Religious Movements in Central Africa: A Theoretical Study," *Comparative Studies in Society and History*, XVIII (1976), 458–475; J.D.Y. Peel, "Conversion and Tradition in Two African Societies: Ijebu and Buganda," *Past and Present*, no. 77 (November 1977), 108–141; Richard Gray, "Christianity and Religious Change in Africa," *African Affairs*, LXXVII (1978), 89–100; Horton, "Social Psychologies: African and Western," appendix to Meyer Fortes, *Oedipus and Job in West African Religion* (Cambridge, 1983), 41–87; Horton, "Judeo-Christian Spectacles: Boon or Bane to the Study of African Religions?" *Cahiers d'études africaines*, XLVI (1984), 391–436; and Horton, *Patterns of Thought in Africa and the West: Essays on Magic, Religion, and Science* (Cambridge, 1993).

missionary in South Carolina who was sympathetic to slaves, stated emphatically, "Our Negro-Pagans have a Notion of a God." Indeed, he continued, their conception was "of a God that disposes absolutely of all things." As illustration, Varnod reported a conversation with a "Negro Pagan Woman" in which he asked her how she became a slave. Her reply was that "God would have it so and she cou'd not help it." Varnod also heard another African woman "saying the same thing on the account of the death of her husband." These Africans shared (or perhaps it would be more accurate to say, had developed) a fatalistic view of an omnipotent supreme being.[127]

Much later in the century, Jeremiah Norman, a Methodist preacher in North Carolina, described a conversation he had with an "old Negroe man" who gave him an account of "the Worship carryed on in Africa and the manner in which he was taken and brought to America." This African described how a nation would "collect on a large spot of open ground, while thus drawn in a circle 2 men goes round proclaiming to them what they ought to do as their Duty, then making their adoration to that great one above they then return to their respective employments leaving the ruling man to take care of the place and things with those of the children, in such cases they are sometimes routed and taken." Presumably, this was a childhood experience recollected in old age, perhaps insensitively transcribed. Nevertheless, the mention of an "adoration to the great one above" is suggestive, perhaps representing an accurate rendering of an African experience or a selective emphasis brought about by the experience of New World slavery.[128]

Other Africans associated the supreme being with the nonterrestrial. In North Carolina, John Chavis encountered an African woman who discoursed on "the planetary system," arguing that "the sun, moon and stars displayed the glory and majesty of God; that they were created not merely for the benefit of the inhabitants of this world, but for that of the inhabitants of other worlds." Perhaps this was an elaboration of a native belief, for Olaudah Equiano recollected that his people believed "that there is one Creator of all things, and that

---

127. Rev. Francis Varnod to SPG, Apr. 1, 1724, B4/173. Naturally, some questioning elicited little information. In 1742, the Reverend Muhlenberg questioned "a pair of black heathen" in Charleston, South Carolina. He reported that "they knew nothing of the true God, nor of Him whom He sent" (Muhlenberg, *Journals*, I, 58).

128. Jeremiah Norman Diary, July 1796, VII, 237–238, Stephen B. Weeks Collection, UNC. Osifekunde, captured in the early 19th century, delivered a much more penetrating recollection, recalling that his native Ijebu had "knowledge of a single God, superior to all the rest and called *Obba Oloroun,* or king of heaven . . . , the supreme will which created and governs all things." He even remembered a prayer to *Obba Oloroun*. How much this account had been modified by his years in slavery and Europe is impossible to determine (P. C. Lloyd, "Osifekunde of Ijebu," in Philip D. Curtin, ed., *Africa Remembered: Narratives by West Africans from the Era of the Slave Trade* [Madison, Wis., 1967], 274, 276).

he lives in the sun." Not that Equiano's Igbo believed in a remote creator, for he was "girted round with a belt that he may never eat or drink" and "smokes a pipe, which is our own favourite luxury." Nevertheless, Equiano continued, this creator "governs events, especially our deaths or captivity." The importance of this personal god—*chi* in Igbo—may well account for Equiano's later emphasis on personal destiny and divine providence in his autobiography. References in his *Narrative* to "God on the top" and "God on high"—or, as one slave once put it to him, "I must look up to God Mighty in the top for right"— might be no more than conventional Christian pieties, even if idiosyncratically expressed, but perhaps, too, they had their roots in African conceptions of a personal god who was responsible for an individual's fate.[129]

Links to the nonterrestrial are also apparent in surviving African American artifacts that display geometric designs resembling depictions of the cosmos in cruciforms, circles, and pointed stars, traditional among the Bakongo. At Shirley plantation in Virginia, a slave decorated a tobacco pipe with intersecting triangles that seem to have been part of a star; the base of a handpainted pearlware bowl found at an eighteenth-century site in Annapolis, Maryland, had a star motif; and a button, recovered at a slave site in Texas, had a six-sided star carved into its surface. The patterns of lines and crosses that decorate a number of metal spoons from Garrison plantation in Maryland and from Kingsmill plantation in Virginia resemble Bakongo cosmograms. At two sites in Annapolis, Maryland, perforated disks from wood or seed, perhaps representing the sun and thought to signify the shape of the soul, have been found. Probably worn around the neck or ankle, these amulets served as protection. But perhaps the most telling examples are South Carolina earthenware bowls containing marks in the shape of crosses either on the interior or exterior, most of which have been found in rivers adjacent to old rice plantations. These bowls contain clues to their ritual importance: the use of ceramic vessels to invoke the spirits of the Bakongo cosmos that connected the living with the dead; the association with water, which separates the corporeal and spirit worlds in Bakongo cosmology; and the power of the circle to elaborate a

---

129. John Chavis, "Extracts from the Missionary Journals," *Assembly's Missionary Magazine; or, Evangelical Intelligencer*, I, no. 9 (September 1805), 449–450; Edwards, ed., *Life of Equiano*, I, 27; Paul Edwards and Rosalind Shaw, "The Invisible *Chi* in Equiano's *Interesting Narrative*," *Journal of Religion in Africa*, XIX (1989), 146–156. See also Parrinder, *African Traditional Religion*, 38. The "Prayer of an African" that was "taken from the mouth of an African servant in the city of Charleston" seems too formal to be trustworthy, but conceivably the references to the "rising day," "setting sun," and "stars that gild the night"— mentioned in this case as God's wonders that could not be appreciated without gospel teaching—connect to the association of a supreme deity with the nonterrestrial (*Massachusetts Missionary Magazine*, I [August 1803], 160).

religious vision, as in the ring shout, which may explain why the marks were more commonly found on bowls with ring bases than on those with rounded or flattened bases. Possible ritual objects with incised crosses have also been found at early-nineteenth-century slave sites in Kentucky and Tennessee.[130]

Another African with a powerful religious vision was Charles Ball's grandfather, who retained or perhaps broadened his faith in a high god when he came to Maryland. When the old man encouraged Charles's father to run away, he prayed "to the God of his native country to protect his son." Indeed, he prayed every night, "though he said he ought to pray oftener; but that his God would excuse him for the non-performance," because he was now a slave. He was scathing about Christianity, declaring it "altogether false, and indeed, no religion at all." Rather, he lauded his people's faith, "which had been of old time delivered by the true God to a holy man, who was taken up into heaven for that purpose, and after he had received the divine communication, had returned to earth, and spent a hundred years in preaching and imparting the truth which had been revealed to him, to mankind." In spite of his aversion to Christianity, the old man seems to have appropriated some Christian terminology and themes.[131]

Whether these were accurate portrayals of the role of a supreme being in traditional African religions or modifications brought about by the experience of being captured and transferred to the New World is impossible to say. In fact, the situation was even more complex, because some Africans had been exposed to Christianity before they left their homeland, where syncretisms of African high gods with the Christian God had already occurred. Transplanted Africans, then, certainly conceived of a supreme being, in some cases the Christian God or, more likely, an indigenous or syncretized high god, and might have enlarged on this deity's role in response to the wrenching experi-

---

130. Theodore R. Reinhart, ed., *The Archaeology of Shirley Plantation* (Charlottesville, Va., 1984), 22–23; Drake Patten, "Mankala and Minkisi: Possible Evidence of African-American Folk Beliefs and Practices," *African-American Archaeology: Newsletter of the African-American Archaeology Network,* VI (1992), 5–7; Kenneth L. Brown and Doreen C. Cooper, "Structural Continuity in an African-American Slave and Tenant Community," *Historical Archaeology,* XXIV, no. 4 (1990), 16; Klingelhofer, "Aspects of Early Afro-American Material Culture," ibid., XXI, no. 2 (1987), 112–119; "Slave Artifacts under the Hearth," *New York Times,* Aug. 27, 1996; Ferguson, *Uncommon Ground,* 110–116; Sterling Stuckey, *Slave Culture: Nationalist Theory and the Foundations of Black America* (New York, 1987), 11–17; Leland Ferguson, "'The Cross Is a Magic Sign': Marks on Eighteenth-Century Bowls from South Carolina," in Theresa A. Singleton, ed., *"I, Too, Am, America": Contributions to African American Archaeology* (Charlottesville, Va., forthcoming); Amy L. Young, "Religion and Ritual among African American Slaves during the Antebellum Period in Kentucky: An Archaeological Perspective" (MS, 1996).

131. Ball, *Fifty Years in Chains,* 21–22.

ences of becoming New World slaves. If this elaboration took place, it may well explain, at least in part, some slaves' emphasis on the awesome powers of the Creator. Belief in an all-powerful God, like the widespread resort to magic, was a way of making sense of a world over which the individual had little control.[132]

Another possible source of syncretism concerned those African slaves who practiced Islam. Muslims, though a minority of slaves brought to North America, were more numerous in the Lowcountry than in the Chesapeake. Runaways with names like Moosa, Wali, Amadi, and Fatima dot the pages of South Carolina and Georgia newspapers; such prominent slaves as driver Salih Bilali lived in the Lowcountry; reports of practicing Muslims also originated from the region, as in Charles Ball's recollection of "several who must have been, from what I have since learned Mohammedans." Ball particularly recollected a man "who prayed five times every day, always turning his face to the east." Most Muslims in the early Lowcountry seem to have kept to themselves, mixing infrequently with other slaves and maintaining homeland practices. Thus, a Moravian missionary preaching to African slaves in Georgia in 1775 made no headway with David, "a Negro who in his homeland was instructed in the religion of Mahomed and who clings to it very firmly." Occasional mention of "prayer mats, prayer beads, veiling, head coverings, Qur'ans, dietary laws, and ritualized, daily prayer," as Michael A. Gomez observes, denoted "a serious pursuit of Islam" by at least some Lowcountry slaves. Quite possibly, as Gomez further notes, some Islamicized slaves, "while ostensibly practicing Christianity, were in reality reinterpreting Christian dogma in the light of Islamic precepts." Sancho, an African who was captured at about age twelve and after one year in Jamaica reached South Carolina, where he was converted to Methodism by Bishop Asbury, may well personify this process, for he spoke of being "raised by my Parents [in Africa] in the fear of God, the same God that I now adore. My father worship him before me. The name of God was Ala." Sancho seemed to view an Islamic and a Christian God as one seamless whole.[133]

---

132. John Thornton, "The Development of an African Catholic Church in the Kingdom of Kongo, 1491–1750," *Journal of African History,* XXV (1984), 147–167; Thornton, "On the Trail of Voodoo: African Christianity in Africa and the Americas," *Americas,* XLIV (1987–1988), 261–278.

133. Michael A. Gomez, "Muslims in Early America," *Journal of Southern History,* LX (1994), 671–710 (quotations on 698, 707–708); Ball, *Fifty Years in Chains,* 165–167; "Diarium von dem Anfang und Fortgang der Mission der Brn. unter den Negern auf Knoxborough in Georgien vom 1 February 1775 an," European Photostats, LC, as cited by Jon Frederiksen Sensbach, "A Separate Canaan: The Making of an Afro-Moravian World in North Carolina, 1763–1856" (Ph.D. diss., Duke University, 1991), 14; B. G. Martin, "Sapelo Island's Arabic Document: The 'Bilali Diary' in Context," *GHQ,* LXXVII (1994), 589–601; William S. McFeely, *Sapelo's People: A Long Walk into Freedom* (New York, 1994), 34–43; Allen D.

Whatever the source, the importance of a supreme God is evident in the folk memory of South Carolina blacks. In "The King's Buzzard," one of the narrators recalls the story his father told him about an African chief who tricked his people into slavery. The chief in turn was captured and brought to the New World. When he died, neither heaven nor hell had a place for him. As punishment, the "Great Master" decided that the king must wander forever more. Because he had killed people's "sperrits," his spirit, too, "should always travel in de form of a great buzzard." Always solitary, the bird would eat only carrion. Sterling Stuckey has drawn attention to parallel African, particularly Igbo, beliefs, in which the spirit of a deceased murderer returns to earth in animal form. The Creator, or "great Spirit" in Igbo accounts, consigns the transgressor to eternal wandering. An African belief in a great God, translated and domesticated by slavery into "Great Master," apparently remained alive in the oral traditions of Lowcountry blacks.[134]

A remarkable parallel between a Seminole creation myth told to whites in the early nineteenth century and various African creation myths recorded in the eighteenth and nineteenth centuries also provides insight into the prominent position assigned to an omnipotent God. The Florida Seminoles had, of course, an especially close relationship with Lowcountry black slaves who either escaped to or were captured by them. The myth, in its variant forms, has God offering whites and blacks (and Indians in the Seminole version) vocational choices based on various forms of material and literary materials. In the Seminole and an Ashanti version, the choices come in the form of boxes that contain different items. Blacks choose or are left with gold, iron, or tools, thereby consigning themselves to a life of toil; whites gain the knowledge of letters, which they then use to dominate other peoples. As William McLoughlin has observed, the purpose of the myth is clear: "God created blacks at the same time as whites and decreed their separate destinies from the beginning of time."[135]

Austin, *African Muslims in Antebellum America: A Sourcebook* (New York, 1984); Austin, "Islamic Identities in Africans in North America in the Days of Slavery (1731–1865)," *Islam et sociétés au sud du Sahara*, VII (1993), 205–219; Account of Sancho, a former slave, Papers of Hugh A. C. Walker, United Methodist Church Archives, Wofford College, Spartanburg, S.C. For a fugitive named Sambo, a 30-year-old recent African immigrant with a "grave countenance" and ability to write "the Arabic language," see *Charleston Courier*, Feb. 8, 1805.

134. E.C.L. Adams, *Nigger to Nigger* (New York, 1928), 13–15; Stuckey, *Slave Culture*, 4–6; perhaps, too, some 20th-century black South Carolinians' references to a "Great Da," a Dahomean god, is another testament to the tenacity of folk memory: Vernon, *African Americans at Mars Bluff*, 18–19.

135. William G. McLoughlin, "A Note on African Sources of American Indian Racial Myths," *Jour. Am. Folklore*, LXXXIX (1976), 331–335 (quotation on 332). See also Levine, *Black Culture*, 84–86.

A close accompaniment to this view of an omnipotent God was the conception of the Devil as a trickster. In the early eighteenth century, the South Carolina missionary Varnod observed that slaves believed in "a Devil who leads them to do mischief and betrays them." In the early nineteenth century, a North Carolina creation legend popular among slaves told of the Devil's attempt to emulate God's creation of Adam. Lacking clay, the Devil went to the swamp, where he used mud for the body and thick, curly moss for the hair. But he was so disgusted with his creation that he kicked it on the shins and struck it on the nose, thus establishing the physical attributes of black people. Here self-denigration received a religious sanction. Also in the nineteenth century, a French visitor to Monticello recorded a black folktale about the Devil, not the conventional figure, but more of an "African Forest Spirit" who could bring death.[136]

Other slaves, whether African or creole, who had been directly exposed to Christian teachings, understandably viewed God as omnipotent. In South Carolina, William De Brahm encountered a middle-aged African who could cite several scriptural passages from memory. When De Brahm admiringly asked how he did it, the African replied, "I seek God incessantly, have no opportunities to hear of him but in meetings and never miss one if I can help it, there I attend carefully the ministers quotations and god gives me grace to keep them in my heart." In 1774, Daddy Gumby, an extremely elderly slave, perhaps an African, who resided at Nomini Hall in Virginia, expounded on the sins of dishonesty to the plantation tutor, Philip Fithian. The slave had a thoroughly austere and terrifying creed, one no doubt familiar to the stern Presbyterian tutor. "God yonder in Heaven Master will burn *Lyars* with *Fire and Brimstone!*" Gumby declared. "I speak Truth I will not decieve you Men are wicked, Master; look see the Grass is burnt: God burns it to punish us! . . . O! all dry and all burnt."[137]

But is it possible that seemingly conventional Christian accounts, as provided by these two slaves, could have derived from the reinforcement of Afri-

136. Rev. Francis Varnod to SPG, Apr. 1, 1724, B4/173; Levine, *Black Culture*, 84 (see also 94, 96, 102–135); Eugene A. Vail, *De la littérature et des hommes de lettres des Etats-Unis d'Amérique* (Paris, 1841), 321–333, as cited in Mechal Sobel, *The World They Made Together: Black and White Values in Eighteenth-Century Virginia* (Princeton, N.J., 1987), 141–142. See also Genovese, *Roll, Jordan, Roll*, 218–219.

137. John De Brahm's testimony on African Slavery, Aug. 8, 1787, Cox, Parrish, Wharton Papers, HSP; Farish, ed., *Journal and Letters of Philip Vickers Fithian*, 199. Fithian reported Thomas Gumby's age as 94, but a list of slaves in 1775 lists his age as 75. If he was not an African, he was brought up around Africans. For a fuller biography, see John Randolph Barden, "'Flushed with Notions of Freedom': The Growth and Emancipation of a Virginia Slave Community, 1732–1812" (Ph.D. diss., Duke University, 1993), 84–88, and Biographical Data, entries 174, 203, 290, 344, 409, 415, 473.

can and Anglo-American ideas? It is impossible to be certain, but two further clues suggest that such conjectures ought not to be dismissed out of hand. First, in 1789, Job Scott described an evening meeting with a group of blacks near Petersburg, Virginia. They blessed "God in accents bespeaking heart-felt reverence and deep thankfulness of soul," he observed. Their "songs of praise" might have been thoroughly orthodox. But Scott also singled out one black for declaiming, "O may I ever bless and praise my great God, for the great good he has this evening done my soul! for the sweet precious love that I have felt—I never felt such heavenly love before—blessed for ever be the Great God!" This mention of the "Great God" might have been nothing more than rhetorical extravagance, but just possibly it also owed something to African-derived notions of a supreme deity. If so, what Scott took to be the "feeling sensibility" with which blacks returned "thanks to God" might have had more complex origins than he ever suspected.[138]

Second, an observation by Richard Parkinson, who lived among Chesapeake slaves in the last few years of the eighteenth century, may also be significant. At that time, most slaves in the region were creoles; many undoubtedly had been exposed to Christian influence, although few would have experienced much active proselytization. Yet, according to Parkinson, all the slaves he encountered shared "a very great respect for the Deity." He continued: "You cannot give them so great a pleasure as to say at parting with them, 'May God bless you!' in a fervent manner. They will from that expression take off their hats, and in a very solemn manner say, 'Thank you, massa!—I thank you, massa! I thank you more for than if you had given me a dollar.'" This "veneration for their Maker," as Parkinson termed it, may well represent orthodox Christian doctrine, perhaps some "puttin' on ole massa," but conceivably the elaboration of African ideas as well.[139]

The probability of fusion is not to deny that Christianity introduced new concepts to an African religious repertory. Most African cosmologies contain few speculations concerning the nature of life after death. The insistence of Christianity on the fear of hell and the delights of heaven introduced African Americans to radically new conceptions of the afterlife. This novelty certainly

138. Job Scott, *Journal of the Life, Travels, and Gospel Labours*... (New York, 1797), 216–217.
139. Parkinson, *Tour in America*, II, 433. God was viewed reverentially by many West Indian slaves. In a dialogue between two slaves, Cudjoe quoted a proverb, "Da know no hab no tail, Gor-a-mity brush fry," meaning, "If a cow has no tail, God Almighty brushes the flies." This led the hearer to quote another common saying among blacks, which "bespeaks their conviction of the omnipresence of the Deity": "Gor-a-mity nebber shet he yie," meaning, "God Almighty never shuts his eye" ([T. Wentworth], *The West India Sketch Book*, 2 vols. [London, 1834], II, 16–18). The first proverb is still current among the Igbo in Africa (Penfield, *Communicating with Quotes*, 118).

wrought its effect on an "old gray-headed negro" encountered by Andrew Burnaby in the Northern Neck of Virginia. The slave told Burnaby that he "awaited the hour when it please God to call him to another life." Did he not wish for that time, Burnaby inquired, since it would release him from his sufferings? No, the slave replied, for "he was afraid to die." Did this fear stem from a bad conscience, a lack of honesty and fidelity? asked Burnaby. No, insisted the slave, he had done his duty; but he remained fearful, as he had every right to be, for "was not our Saviour himself afraid to die?" The profundity of this remark "sunk deep" into Burnaby's mind. The deathbed remarks of Frank, the daughter of Betty and Old Jack, all slaves of James Gordon, a Northern Neck planter, reveal a more optimistic view of the afterlife. A few hours before expiring, Frank told her mother that she was dying and hoped to see her in heaven. At a revival in Virginia, an old black man had a similarly uplifting message: "Our colour is black, but his blood washes our souls whiter than snow! We shall live among the redeemed forever with the Lord. O! the love of Christ to us poor black people! O! his service is sweet! it is very sweet. Hold on in it, hold on till you get the prize."[140]

Nor is it to deny that many slaves were pious Christians, quite orthodox in their beliefs. Some masters might deride slaves for "pretending" to "the religion the Negroes have of late practiced," as one Virginia master did, but others were more impressed. James Gordon, a New Light himself, "had much conversation" with a neighbor's slave, "whose piety I have great opinion of." A Maryland master even gave his "old Negro woman her liberty *because she had too much religion for him*," a story that made the normally stern Francis Asbury laugh. Even unsympathetic masters had to acknowledge that Christianity was important to some slaves. Gilbert was a Baptist and expected to "show a little of it in Company"; Tom was "fond of talking about Religion"; Will missed "no opportunity of holding forth" on religious subjects; Jack was "remarkable for affecting religious conversation"; Talbot "generally carried about him a new testament or psalter"; Peter was "fond of conversing on religion, and professes to be of the Baptist church"; Cesar was simply "very religious."[141]

---

140. Andrew Burnaby, *Travels through the Middle Settlements in North-America, in the Years 1759 and 1760* . . . , 3d ed. (London, 1798 [orig. publ. 1775]), 66–67; "Journal of Col. James Gordon," *WMQ*, 1st Ser., XI (1902–1903), 227; William Henry Foote, *Sketches of Virginia, Historical and Biographical* (Philadelphia, 1850), 423. See also Abigail Mott, comp., *Biographical Sketches and Interesting Anecdotes of Persons of Color* . . . (New York, 1839), 224. For the discussion of African cosmologies and Christianity's impact, see Gray, "Christianity and Religious Change," *Af. Affairs*, LXXVII (1978), 96–97; Gray, *Black Christians and White Missionaries*, 67–69.

141. "Journal of Col. James Gordon," *WMQ*, 1st Ser., XI (1902–1903), 227; Clark et al., eds., *Journal and Letters of Asbury*, I, 655–656; John Evans, Sr., *VaG* (P and D), postscript,

Granting the novelty of Christianity and the piety, even orthodoxy, of many of its slave adherents, a case can nevertheless be made not only that African slaves were predisposed toward Christianity because of developments within their traditional religious beliefs but also that they infused elements of their traditional religion into Christianity. Slaves, in other words, did not just accept Christianity wholesale, but did so on their own terms. They engaged in what Terence Ranger has called "continuities through substitution." This is not to argue that the story of Afro-American religion is one of bizarre survivals and exotic curiosities. Rather, some African ideas were retained, transformed, and engaged with the new environment while others were discarded.[142]

One area where African ideas merged with the new environment in complicated ways was that of attitudes toward the dead. For West Africans, as Herskovits has observed, "the funeral is the true climax of life, and no belief drives deeper into their thought." The dead played an active role in the lives of the living. In fact, African kin groups are often described as communities of both the living and the dead. As Equiano described his native Igbo, the spirits of "their dear friends or relations, they believe always attend them, and guard them from the bad spirits of their foes." When a Catholic priest told a "Grandee" at Whydah on the African coast that he and his people would burn in hell if they continued in their traditional ways, he received a sharp riposte: "Our Fathers, Grandfathers, to an endless Number, Liv'd as we do, and Worship'd the same Gods as we do; and if they must burn therefore, Patience, we are not better than our Ancestors, and shall comfort our selves with them." No direct evidence exists that elaborate beliefs about dead ancestors or friends survived the Middle Passage—at least among North American slaves. However, the importance of funerals to slaves and their distinctive practices on such occasions suggest some continuity with traditional beliefs.[143]

Slaves clearly attached great significance to funerals. In 1687, Virginia officials thought that slaves had used their funeral gatherings, where they met "in great numbers," to discuss a possible insurrection. In South Carolina, the

---

July 21, 1774 (Gilbert); John Scott, ibid., Dec. 1, 1774 (Tom); John Murchie, ibid., June 13, 1777 (Will); John Nelson, *VaG and WA,* Aug. 6, 1785 (Jack); George Carter, ibid., Mar. 8, 1787 (Talbot); Vincent Redman, *VaG and GA,* Oct. 27, 1790 (Peter); Snowden, Lothrop, and Forrest, *City Gaz,* Apr. 24, 1788 (Cesar). For "pretending" to be religious, see, for example, John Fox, *VaG* (P and D), July 18, 1771; Thomas Bowyer, ibid. (Purdie), Jan. 3, 1777, supplement; and William Green, ibid., May 9, 1777.

142. Ranger, "Recent Developments," *Ufahamu,* IV (1973), 17–34 (quotation on 31).

143. Herskovits, *Myth of the Negro Past,* 63; Edwards, ed., *The Life of Olaudah Equiano,* I, 28. An impressive essay on this subject is Igor Kopytoff, "Ancestors as Elders in Africa," *Africa,* XLI (1971), 129–142; Bosman, *A New and Accurate Description,* 385–386. See also James L. Brain, "Ancestors as Elders in Africa—Further Thoughts," *Africa,* XLIII (1973), 122–133.

importance of slave burials became evident in 1745, when a provincial grand jury warned against the "Ill consequences which may attend the Gathering Together such Great Numbers of Negroes, both in Town and Country, at their Burials, and on the Sabbath Day." At midcentury, an act for keeping the streets of Charleston clean noted that black funeral processions were "frequent" occurrences, often attended by a "great concourse of slaves." In the same year, a provincewide act attempted to confine black funerals to hours of daylight. A quarter-century later, officials in Savannah became concerned at slave funerals in their town. Either because of white restrictions or slave preference, blacks usually presided at these occasions. A twenty-eight-year-old native-born shoemaker, suitably named Moses, officiated "as a reader at negro funerals" in northeastern North Carolina, and Peter was a well-known preacher, "being at Negro funerals both far and near" of Charleston.[144]

According to African, Anglo-American, or a combination of both traditions, liquor was a normal accompaniment at slave funerals. At midcentury in South Carolina, Charles Pinckney simply noted payment of one pound, ten shillings for the making of a coffin and for rum and sugar at the burial of a slave child. Thirty years later in Virginia, Robert Carter adopted a more disapproving stance, when old Nat wished "to buy Brandy to bury his Granddaughter Lucy." Refusing to sell, Carter instead offered the slave a dollar, "telling him he might lay out his Annuity as he pleased." Henry Knight, who visited the Chesapeake in the early nineteenth century, observed that slaves "drink the dead to his new home, which some believe to be in old Guinea."[145]

This belief in a return to Africa was one way for slaves to retain a link to ancestors and friends. In midcentury Delaware, a missionary observed that African slaves had "a notion, that when they die, they are translated to their own countrey, there to live in their former free condition." Some Africans, particularly "Keromantees," he continued, committed suicide calmly and deliberately as a result of their faith. Johann Bolzius saw the same behavior among Lowcountry Africans who "frequently take their own lives out of desperation, with the hope of resurrection in their homeland, and of rejoining their people." The Africans that Charles Ball encountered in the Lowcountry "universally" believed in a return to Africa after death. With this expectation,

---

144. McIlwaine, ed., *Executive Journals,* I, 85–87; South Carolina Council Journal, Apr. 29, 1745, XIV, 192, SCDAH; An Act for Keeping Streets in Charlestown Clean, Acts of the General Assembly, no. 775, 1750, SCDAH; Easterby and Green, eds., *Journal of the Commons House of Assembly, March 28, 1749–March 19, 1750,* 383; *Ga Gaz,* Sept. 14, 1774; William Skinner, *VaG or AA,* Feb. 22, 1786 (Moses); James King, *Charleston Courier,* Dec. 6, 1805 (Peter).

145. Charles Pinckney Account Book, May 1, 1753, Pinckney Family Papers, LC; Robert W. Carter Diaries, Feb. 20, 1785, typescript, CW; Knight, *Letters,* 77.

an African former priest buried his son with a small bow and arrows, a little bag of food, a stick seemingly in the form of an agricultural tool, a piece of cloth "with several curious and strange figures painted on it in blue and red, by which, he said, his relations and countrymen would know the infant to be his son," and a miniature canoe and paddle "with which he said it would cross the ocean to his own country." After casting a lock of his own hair into the grave, the father "then told us the God of his country was looking at him, and was pleased with what he had done."[146]

Mortuary practices also demonstrate the close relation slaves saw between the living and the dead. Ten eighteenth-century blacks buried in a group near Stratford Hall in Virginia were interred in traditional European fashion in coffin and shroud, but three black men wore African-style clothing to the grave. At other sites in the Chesapeake, a string of beads interred with an infant and concentrations of seeds on coffin surfaces suggest African-style burial offerings. At Utopia quarter on the James River in Virginia, a burial ground containing twenty-five individuals has been dated to the first half of the eighteenth century. The burials appear to have been arranged in family groups. Three adults had English clay tobacco pipes placed under their arms, and one was interred with a glass bead necklace around the neck. In the Lowcountry, the African influence in burial goods was more notable. In Liberty County, Georgia, the remains of a plate directly above the head of an early-nineteenth-century slave skeleton accords with the testimony of "a Gullah Negro on the Santee River," who explained "that it was their custom to place the last plate, the last glass and spoon used before death on the grave." A depiction of a black burial, attributed to early-nineteenth-century northern Florida, showing a scaffold, dead animal skin, and a variety of personal possessions, has been linked to a number of precise African traditions. More generally, the broken crockery, upturned bottles, seashells, and particular plants that mark black graves in cemeteries particularly throughout the Lowcountry have African analogues. All of these practices were ways of propitiating the dead, of easing their journey to the spirit world, and of ensuring that they did not return to haunt the living.[147]

---

146. Rev. Philip Reading to Rev. Samuel Smith, Oct. 10, 1748, in Van Horne, ed., *Religious Philanthropy and Colonial Slavery*, 100; "Bolzius Answers a Questionnaire," trans. and ed. Loewald et al., *WMQ*, XIV (1957), 233; Ball, *Fifty Years in Chains*, 265. Serers in Senegambia during the 17th–19th centuries were noted for placing bows and arrows on male burial mounds: Marie-Joss Opper and Howerd Opper, "Diakhite: A Study of the Beads from an Eighteenth–Nineteenth-Century Burial Site in Senegal, West Africa," *Beads: Journal of the Society of Bead Researchers*, I (1989), 5–20, esp. 10.

147. Fraser D. Neiman, *The "Manner House" before Stratford (Discovering the Clifts Plantation)* (Stratford, Va., 1980), 28; Frey, *Water from the Rock*, 40–41; Garrett R. Fesler,

Not all slave funerals, of course, were necessarily influenced by African traditions. Some planters provided the means or the money for coffins and might have been present at funerals, perhaps thereby influencing events. In the late eighteenth century, white evangelicals occasionally preached at slave funerals. One Sunday evening in New Kent County, Virginia, the Reverend James Meacham preached a funeral sermon "over a poor old slave who died in the Lord." He observed the presence of many blacks and "much ingagedness amongst both white and black." Black preachers followed the white evangelicals' lead. In 1793, the Reverend Harry Toulmin, a Unitarian minister, heard a black man introduce "the Calvinistical doctrine" into a funeral sermon that he delivered near Urbanna in Virginia. Although this black preacher also "dwelt with peculiar pleasure" on the spiritual equality of all people and used an "unusually mournful" tone of voice to work the two hundred slaves in "his audience to a wonderful pitch of enthusiasm," the white Virginians in his audience responded "with the most perfect unconcern."[148]

The practice of double funerals may originate in a combination of African customs and the constraints of slavery. On June 8, 1787, Francis Taylor of

---

"Interim Report of Excavations at Utopia Quarter (44JC32): An Eighteenth-Century Slave Complex at Kingsmill on the James in James City County, Virginia" (MS, 1995); David Hurst Thomas et al., "Rich Man, Poor Men: Observations on Three Antebellum Burials from the Georgia Coast," American Museum of Natural History, *Anthropological Papers,* LIV (1977), 393–420, esp. 406–409; Peter A. Brannon, "Central Alabama Negro Superstitions," *Birmingham News,* Jan. 18, 1925, as cited in Robert Farris Thompson, *Flash of the Spirit: African and Afro-American Art and Philosophy* (New York, 1983), 287 (see also 132–145); Elizabeth A. Fenn, "Honoring the Ancestors: Kongo-American Graves in the American South," *Southern Exposure,* XIII, no. 5 (September–October 1985), 42–47; Vlach, *Afro-American Tradition,* 139–147; Thompson and Cornet, *Four Moments of the Sun,* 178–203 (the 19th-century Florida print is reproduced on 191); David R. Roediger, "And Die in Dixie: Funerals, Death, and Heaven in the Slave Community, 1700–1865," *Massachusetts Review,* XXII (1981), 163–183; Cynthia Connor, "'Sleep On and Take Your Rest': Black Mortuary Behavior on the East Branch of the Cooper River, South Carolina" (master's thesis, University of South Carolina, 1989), 21, 57–60, 100–103.

148. Journal of James Meacham, 1792–1794, June 3, 1792 (and also Journal, 1796–1797, Apr. 17, 1797), Duke; Harry Toulmin, *The Western Country in 1793: Reports on Kentucky and Virginia,* ed. Marion Tinling and Godfrey Davies (San Marino, Calif., 1948), 30. For other white evangelicals preaching at black funerals, see journal of William Colbert, Aug. 31, 1794, Garrett Theological Seminary; and journal of William Ormond, Feb. 19, 1797, Duke. For the provisions of coffins for slaves, see estate of Francis Le Jau, Oct. 10, 1766, Feb. 18, 1767, Inventories, &, WPA, 234–243; "Account Book of Cabinetmaker, Thomas Elfe, 1768–1775," *SCHM,* XXXVII (1936), 151, XLI (1941), esp. 18; Robert Carter Waste Book, Dec. 6, 1773, CW; and for a slave's conveying the coffin of his mother to a burial site near her husband, see William Priest, *Travels in the United States of America: Commencing in the Year 1793, and Ending in 1797* (London, 1802), 19–20.

Orange County, Virginia, noted the death of a neighbor's old slave named Judy and the construction of her coffin. A month later, his own slave woman, Betty, died after a long illness. Another three weeks elapsed before the neighborhood slaves gathered one Sunday and had their "funeral over Old Judy and Betty." Seven weeks after her interment, then, Judy received her memorial. The event that Harry Toulmin witnessed near Urbanna also involved two "distinct affairs"—first, the burial, then, three weeks later, the "funeral rites," where slaves paid their "last honors to a deceased acquaintance." Toulmin provided a plausible explanation, attributing this practice to the slaves' inability "to leave home on any other day than Sunday." At the same time, some West African peoples often had two "burials." New World exigencies might have reinforced Old World religious beliefs.[149]

The behavior of slaves at funerals reflected a combination of African traditions and evangelical reinforcement. The physical expressiveness of participants at slave funerals suggests an African influence. One Saturday night in 1775, a literate native-born black man who preached regularly at slave funerals in Lowcountry Georgia presided at one such event where the slaves had "a dance for a fellow that was shot in the Woods." When criticized for his conduct, this preacher justified himself by saying that "it was a custom among the Negroes to make mery for the dead." Twenty years earlier, a Cape Fear observer noted that, one Christmas, the slaves were bereft of "a death to play for." Celebrations of dancing and music—"plays"—were customary at slave funerals. Such expressive behavior disturbed Janet Schaw, a visitor to North Carolina, who described slave funeral rites as "running, jumping, crying and various exercises." The Reverend John Holt Rice was appalled at slave funeral practices in piedmont Virginia. "Instead of the preaching of the Gospel Christ," Rice continued, "there are many remains, I suppose, of the savage customs of Africa. They cry and bawl and howl around the grave and roll in the dirt, and make many expressions of the most frantic grief . . . sometimes the noise that they make may be heard as far as one or two miles." This ethnocentric description nevertheless emphasized the distinctiveness of black funeral behavior.[150]

---

149. Diary of Col. Francis Taylor, June 8, July 7, July 29, 1787, VSL; Toulmin, *The Western Country in 1793,* 29 (see also 21 for a slave buried at 11:00 P.M. on the same day as his body was found).

150. Elizabeth Cosson to the Countess of Huntingdon, Sept. 12, 1775, A 3/4/7; James Murray to "Sister Clark," Dec. 26, 1755, Robbins Papers, Massachusetts Historical Society, as cited in Frey, *Water from the Rock,* 41; [Janet Schaw], *Journal of a Lady of Quality . . .* , ed. Evangeline Walker Andrews and Charles McLean Andrews (New Haven, Conn., 1939), 171; John Holt Rice, "Report to the General Assembly's Committee on Missions, 1809," *Evangelical Intelligencer,* III (1809), 390–391. Distinctive practices that survived into the 20th century also suggest an African influence. See Johnson, *Folk Culture on St. Helena Island,* 172; for a

Highly expressive funeral practices are, however, not far removed from the typical behavior of eighteenth-century evangelicals, white or black. Trembling, quaking bodies and tear-lined faces were characteristic features of revivalist meetings. Indeed, John Lambert thought that black Methodists imitated their white coreligionists, so that "they often fall down in *divine ecstacies,* crying, shouting, bawling, and beating their breasts, until they are ready to faint." Many preachers' comments that single out black behavior—William Colbert's observation that the blacks "shout aloud and may be heard afar off," or Noah Fidler's report that "a black man in the gallery shouted so loud that my voice was almost drowned in the sound," or Francis Asbury's description of "Hundreds of Negroes . . . , with tears streaming down their faces"—may suggest only that blacks could outdo whites, not that they engaged in behavior peculiar to themselves.[151]

At the same time, blacks so often exceeded whites in the expression of their evangelicalism that the question of distinctiveness cannot be so easily dismissed. For instance, Nelson Reed was amazed at one slave woman who fell to the ground "as if she was all but dead" at a morning service. When he returned, after preaching elsewhere, for the evening service, he found her still prostrate. She was unable to talk, and Reed noted uncertainly in his diary, "If there was any good done the Lord take the praise." Similarly, another preacher was unsure how to interpret the behavior of a black man who "for a long time . . . was very attentive, tears flowd freely from his eyes while he stood in silence— after some time he was very much agitated, and gave a most awful shriek, foaming at the mouth and looking frightfully out of his eyes." These dramatic seizures gave the preachers pause, perhaps because this extreme behavior was so unusual. It might have owed more to African patterns of possession trance than to the range of physical responses found in white evangelicalism.[152]

There are indeed occasions when even evangelical preachers sympathetic to black responsiveness noted something extraordinary that either disturbed

---

parallel belief, Ian F. Hancock, "Krio Folk-Beliefs and Dream Interpretations," *Journal of Creole Studies,* I (1977), 82; and Herskovits, *Myth of the Negro Past,* 189.

151. John Lambert, *Travels through Lower Canada and the United States of North America, in the Years 1806, 1807, and 1808* (London, 1810), II, 415; journal of Colbert, May 10, 1790, 9; journal of Rev. Noah Fidler, June 16, 1801, microfilm, LC; Clark et al., eds., *Journal and Letters of Asbury,* I, 222.

152. Diary of Rev. Nelson Reed, Aug. 9, 1778, typescript, Methodist Historical Society, Lovely Lane Museum, Baltimore; journal of Colbert, Sept. 21, 1800. On possession trance, see Erika Bourguignon, "Ritual Dissociation and Possession Belief in Caribbean Negro Religion," in Norman E. Whitten, Jr., and John F. Szwed, eds., *Afro-American Anthropology: Contemporary Perspectives* (New York, 1970), 87–101, esp. 94. See also John Beattie and John Middleton, eds., *Spirit Mediumship and Society in Africa* (London, 1969).

them or led them to view black behavior with disfavor. At an interracial meeting in Surry County, Virginia, the Reverend William Hill observed, with no particular emphasis, that the congregation was "vociferous in their expressions of interest, often entirely drowning the preacher's voice with shouts." He then added that "the Negroes were fanatically wild." Freeborn Garrettson remonstrated with fifty or so blacks in his audience when one woman "fell down, thumped her breast and kicked all over the floor" to the others' approbation. He stopped the proceedings to emphasize that conversion could be accomplished "without falling down or hollering." On one occasion, William Colbert witnessed blacks who "began to shout and jump about" so that his colleague insisted "that the devil was among them"; on another occasion, Colbert himself found the "black people . . . strangely agitated."[153]

What might have been so remarkable was the patterned, choreographed response of the slaves, a characteristic feature of African American possession behavior. This could have been what Thomas Morrell had in mind when he observed that "the people in Virginia are fond of noisy meetings particularly the blacks" and that the blacks' "noise appears too mechanical." Mechanical noise may be another way of describing what Henry Boehm saw only too well—slaves praising "Jesus with their lungs, Hands and feet." Or, as John Leland put it, blacks are "more noisy in time of preaching than the whites, and are more subject to bodily exercise," in which "they often grow extravagant." This behavior separated black from white revivalists.[154]

Charles Colcock Jones, in the nineteenth century, claimed that blacks found "true conversion" through "dreams, visions, trances, voices—all bearing a perfect or striking resemblance to some form or type which has been handed down for generations." This predisposition quite possibly reflected an African influence; perhaps it originated, as Jones speculated, "in the wild fancy of some [black] religious teacher" or, more likely, teachers, who drew inspiration from a variety of cultural traditions. Certainly, Anglo-American religion was thoroughly familiar with visions and voices. Eighteenth-century opponents labeled the phenomenon "enthusiasm." An association with evangelicals helps explain

---

153. William Henry Foote, *Sketches of Virginia, Historical and Biographical*, 2d Ser. (Philadelphia, 1855), 184; journal of Rev. Freeborn Garretson, July 3, 1781, microfilm, Duke; journal of Colbert, July 4, 1790, Apr. 20, 1794. Expressiveness might have been involved in the mid-18th-century decision of a parish vestry in Anne Arundel County, Maryland, to prohibit "negroes from going in among the white people to disturb them, as frequently they have done, and to prevent their going in and out of the church in time of Divine Service, as they often make a practice of it" (Rev. Theodore C. Gambrall, *Church Life in Colonial Maryland* [Baltimore, 1885], 198).

154. Journal of Rev. Thomas Morrell, Dec. 23, 1791, Drew University, Madison, N.J.; journal of Henry Boehm, Jan. 1, 1802, microfilm, Duke; Leland, *Virginia Chronicle*, 12.

this behavior. Hugh Bryan was said to have filled slaves "with a Parcel of Cant-Phrases, Trances, Dreams, Visions, and Revelations." An Anglican minister in South Carolina spoke of blacks' being "taught" enthusiasm, by which they "pretend to see Visions, and Receive Revelations from Heaven." But more important than the source—or, more likely, multiple sources—of this religious pattern among blacks was its very existence. The uses to which blacks put their dreams and voices, and how whites reacted to them, are far more interesting than their precise derivation.[155]

Slaves certainly experienced vivid revelations. In the early 1770s, at age twelve, Boston King, the son of an African father, encountered his first religious impressions. King later recalled that he had a "remarkable dream" at midday while tending cattle. He "dreamt that the world was on fire, and that I saw the supreme Judge descend on his great white Throne! I saw millions of millions of souls; some of whom ascended up to heaven; while others were rejected, and fell into the greatest confusion and despair." From that point, King refrained from swearing and "acknowledged that there was a GOD." At the turn of the century, the Reverend Samuel M'Corkle claimed never to have seen a more intense conversion experience than that of "a stout negro woman" in Rowan County, North Carolina. "It was impossible," he declared, "for my imagination to conceive of her being more tormented had she actually been in hell." She told him that "she saw hell-flames below, herself hung over by a thread, and a sharp, bright sword drawn to cut it through."[156]

Not all whites were as impressed as M'Corkle; in fact, some were unsympathetic to such visions, and others found them downright disturbing. In 1760, Davy, a slave boy, got up in the middle of the night "and said he was struck by the sun down the chimney, and then ran out of the house into the woods." His evangelical master treated the vision as an illness and had the boy bled. After this, the boy "ran out of the kitchen into the chamber and said he saw a great cat with stripes on her head"; again the response was to "quiet" him. Thirty years later, a Methodist minister was equally nonplussed when a "poor black" woman told him that "she sometimes sees something like milk streaming down her breast; at other times something like a cake of ice or snow, and

---

155. Charles Colcock Jones, *The Religious Instruction of the Negroes in the United States* (Savannah, Ga., 1842), 125–126; *SCG*, Apr. 24, 1742; Lewis Jones to SPG, Dec. 27, 1743, B11/26. See also David S. Lovejoy, *Religious Enthusiasm in the New World: Heresy to Revolution* (Cambridge, Mass., 1985); J. S. Mbiti, "God, Dreams, and African Militancy," in J. S. Pobee, ed., *Religion in a Pluralistic Society . . .* (Leiden, 1976), 38–47.

156. "Memoirs of the Life of Boston King," *Methodist Mag.*, XXI (1798), 106; James Hall, *A Narrative of a Most Extraordinary Work of Religion in North Carolina . . .* (Philadelphia, 1801), 36; William Henry Foote, *Sketches of North Carolina, Historical and Biographical . . .* (New York, 1846), 402.

sometimes something like a young child sitting on her shoulder." He was at a loss how to interpret these dreams. A few years later, another minister expressed deep disquiet at the "very strange and ridiculous notions" held by a majority of black converts. "Nothing can persuade them that they have not seen strange sights," he observed, "such as the devil, chasing them with balls of fire; Hell opening to receive them; Jesus dying on the cross for them; and I know not what."[157]

Particularly disturbing to masters were those slaves who imbued their visions and voices with an apocalyptic message. An early example is afforded by the Reverend Francis Le Jau's account of "the best scholar of all the Negroes" in the parish of Saint James Goose Creek, South Carolina. According to the missionary, this slave was "a very sober and honest liver," but, in 1710, he obtained "a Book wherein he read some descriptions of the several judgmts that Chastize Men because of their Sins." This made "an Impression upon his Spirit, and he told his Master abruptly there would be a dismal time and the Moon wou'd be turned into Blood, and there wou'd be dearth of darkness." The slave's words to his master were overheard by another bondman, and before long "it was publickly blazed abroad that an angel came and spake to the Man, he had seen a hand that gave him a Book, he had heard Voices, seen fires." What is most interesting about this event is how quickly the story spread and was embellished by other slaves, suggesting their receptivity to "visions" and "voices."[158]

In 1759, John Pendarvis, a free mulatto; Philip John, a free black; and Caesar, a slave, were accused of inciting an insurrection among the slaves of Saint Helena Parish. The chief witness, Prince, a slave who had belonged to Philip John, claimed that his ex-master came to him and said, "You may go and work where you please, but God Almighty has given me other work to do." Apparently, John spoke of Caesar as the "Headman" and described his own role as that of second-in-command. On a subsequent occasion, Prince reported John's words, as follows:

> That the 17th day of June was fixed upon for killing the Buckraas, but afterwards told him that it was agreed to wait till the Corn was turned down, and the Indians were then to be sent to and they would come and assist in killing all the Buckraas, that the Justices before whom he had been, had taken his paper from him but he did not care if the devil had it for he had another and would go to Charles Town with it and would do the work

---

157. "Journal of Col. James Gordon," *WMQ*, 1st Ser., XI (1902–1903), 204; journal of Colbert, Aug. 24, 1794; "A Sabbath Evening at Mr. Jervas's," *Virginia Religious Magazine*, III (May–June 1807), 169.

158. Rev. Francis Le Jau to SPG, Feb. 1, 10, 1710, A5/82, 98.

God Almighty had set him about, that in six weeks time all the Buckraas would be killed.

John then disappeared into the woods, and rumors circulated that he had been eaten by "Bears or Tygers." But in a week he returned and told his wife that "God Almighty had been with him in the Woods—sometimes before him and sometimes behind him." South Carolina's governor reported that John had attempted

> to Stir up Sedition among the Negroes, by telling them he had seen a Vision, in which it was reveal'd to him that in the Month of September the white People shou'd be all under ground, that the Sword shou'd go through the Land, and it shou'd shine with their blood, that there should be no more white King's Governors or great Men but the Negros shou'd live happily and have Laws of their own.

Christianity took on a prophetic cast for John.[159]

Slaves did not, however, have to experience visions to view Christianity in a revolutionary light. In 1730, in spite of Anglican ministers' teachings that baptism would not alter the slaves' temporal status, a number of black Virginians "were willing," in the words of James Blair, "to fool themselves with a secret fancy . . . that the king designed that all christians should be made free." Slaves "flocked to baptism," but, when their hopes failed to materialize, "they grew angry and saucy, and met in the night time in great numbers, and talked of rising; and in some places of choosing their leaders." After some blacks were imprisoned and whipped, the rumors died down. Yet they persisted, and, some six weeks later, about two hundred blacks gathered one Sunday in Norfolk and Princess Anne Counties in order, it was alleged, to choose their officers. Four ringleaders were hanged for their radical interpretation of baptism.[160]

On the eve of the Revolution, religious slaves in South Carolina preached revolutionary messages in both Charleston and outlying Saint Bartholemew Parish. In late 1774, David Margate, a Methodist preacher, proclaimed:

> The Jews of old treated the Gentiles as Dogs and I am informed the people of this Country use those of my Complection as such[.] I dont mean myself Thank God. I am come from a better Country than this, I mean old En-

---

159. South Carolina Council Journal, no. 28, 105–111; William Henry Lyttleton to the Board of Trade, Sept. 1, 1759, CO5/390, fols. 213–214. A "Philip John, Negro," was married to Rebecca Royal, a black widow, on Apr. 23, 1753 (Joseph W. Barnwell and Mabel L. Webber, eds., "St. Helena's Parish Register," *SCHM*, XXIII [1922], 123).

160. James Blair to Bishop Gibson, May 14, 1731, XII, 163–164, Fulham Palace Papers; Governor Gooch to Bishop Gibson, May 28, 1731, ibid., 169–170. See also James Blair to Bishop Gibson, June 28, 1729, ibid., 135.

gland but let them remember that the Children of Israel were delivered out of the hands of Pharo and he and all his Host were drowned in the Red Sea and God will deliver his own People from Slavery.

David was quickly hustled out of Charleston to the Bethesda orphanage in Georgia. He persisted in his "shocking delusion," as one minister termed it, thinking himself "a second moses . . . called to deliver his people from slavery"—a view of Moses that would be popular among slaves into the nineteenth century. David's "problem," so one of his colleagues surmised, was that "he can't bear to think of any of his own colour being slaves." Only after David was discreetly shipped back to England in May 1775 did the furor subside.[161]

But fresh rumors began to circulate only a month or two later among the slaves proselytized by John Burnett in outlying Saint Bartholomew Parish. Stories about a book that predicted a revolutionary transformation of the world, one in which blacks would be "equally entitled to the good things of this life, in common with the whites," were apparently rife. According to one slave informant, one of the slave leaders, a man named George who belonged to Francis Smith, had declared "that the old king had received a book from our Lord, by which he was to alter the world, (meaning to set the negroes free), but his not doing so, was now gone to hell and in punishment; that the young king, meaning our present one, came up with the book, and was about to alter the world, and set the negroes free."[162]

A major insurrection scare that swept parts of eastern North Carolina and adjoining Virginia counties at the turn of the century seems to have been rooted in the evangelical meetings associated with the Great Revival. Reports circulated that slaves plotted at religious gatherings, that one slave preached with a gun in his pocket, and that the date of the insurrection was set to coincide with the quarterly meeting of the local Baptist association. One slave preacher, Dr. Joe, who also practiced medicine, was acquitted of fomenting rebellion but was prohibited from holding any further religious meetings.[163]

---

161. John Edwards to the Countess of Huntingdon, Jan. 16, 1775, A3/6/10, Countess of Huntingdon's American Papers. See also ibid., Jan. 11, 1775, A3/6/9; William Piercey to the Countess of Huntingdon, Nov. 28, 1774, A4/1/9, Mar. 27, 1775, A4/2/6; presentments of the Grand Jury, *SCG*, Mar. 27, 1775; *Letters of Habersham*, GHS, *Colls.*, VI, 238–244. Habersham reported that David "dropped some unguarded Expressions such as, that he did not doubt; but 'God would send Deliverance to the Negroes, from the power of their Masters, as He freed the Children of Israel from Egyptian Bondage.'" See also Boyd Stanley Schlenther, "'To Convert the Poor People in America': The Bethesda Orphanage and the Thwarted Zeal of the Countess of Huntingdon," *GHQ*, LXXVII (1994), 225–256, esp. 244–245.

162. "Journal of the Council of Safety," July 13–18, 1774, SCHS, *Collections*, II (1858), 37, 43, 50–51, 70–71.

163. Crow, *Black Experience*, 88–89.

A rebellious Christian also seems to have been central to the insurrectionary plans of slaves in Charleston and the surrounding countryside in the early nineteenth century. Apparently, Lowcountry blacks "held nightly assemblies on one of the islands near Charleston, at which, the proceedings were opened and closed by singing" a hymn composed by one of their leaders. The hymn has survived. It emphasizes the oppression endured by blacks, "the toil and sweat" of bound labor, the shame of "wives and daughters" being robbed of their virtue. Its chorus emphasizes unity and draws on America's Revolutionary tradition by encouraging slaves to stand united and seek "death or liberty" as "a band of Patriots joined." Stilted and formal as the language sounds, the hymn contains an occasional echo of authentic folk speech, as when calling on slaves to "wrest the scourge from Buckra's hand." But its most notable features are a strident militancy and the promise of freedom in this world. Sounding a clarion call, "a warlike blast," the hymn exhorts the "Afric clan" to "shake off" chains, raise arms, bare breasts, and "drive each tyrant from the land." Looking to heaven was to see a God "that's always just," an Almighty who would "do the rest" as slaves wrestled with their "white foe."[164]

Clearly, then, a millenarian tradition existed in Afro-American religion. Notions of an imminent, spiritually ordained intervention and deliverance were present. It never spread widely in the eighteenth century, in large part because it was stamped out whenever it surfaced. But the fervent response of some slaves to this message is testament to its power. Another thread that runs through many of these incidents is an uncommon respect for the written word. Time and again are mentioned the talismanic qualities of a book that predicted or prophesied a revolutionary transformation. In many societies that restrict literacy, common folk tend to view books in a reverential, quasi-magical way. The credence attached to prophetic books probably reflects the slaves' essentially magical approach to literacy.[165]

---

164. John Hammond Moore, "A Hymn of Freedom—South Carolina, 1813," *Journal of Negro History*, L (1965), 50–53. John Forsyth, a Presbyterian clergymen who reported the hymn in a letter of 1862, had received a copy about 30 years earlier from the English antislavery missionary George Thompson. Apparently, Thompson gave an account of how the hymn came into his possession that convinced Forsyth of the hymn's "genuineness and authenticity." See also David Waldstreicher, *In the Midst of Perpetual Fetes: The Making of American Nationalism, 1776–1820* (Chapel Hill, N.C., 1997), 316–319, who reprints the song and the popular model on which it was based.

165. Genovese, *Roll, Jordan, Roll*, 272–279; but cf. David E. Stannard, "Time and the Millennium: On the Religious Experience of the American Slave," *Prospects*, II (1976), 349–371. For magical approaches to literacy, see Peter Burke, "The Uses of Literacy in Early Modern Italy," in Burke and Porter, eds., *Social History of Language*, 31–32; Frank Lambert, "'I Saw the Book Talk': Slave Readings of the First Great Awakening," *Journal of Negro*

But it would be misleading to emphasize the revolutionary implications of black Christianity. Rather, religion was a liberating *and* repressive force in slaves' lives. This double-edged quality is captured in a distinctive feature of Afro-American Christianity: black men and women joined evangelical churches in roughly equal numbers. If anything, men predominated—a clear reversal of the typical pattern among whites. What explains it? The general lack of opportunity in slave life provides much of the answer; church membership appealed to men as one of the few available spheres of public activity. By drawing men into the church, evangelicalism both coopted slave leaders and gave them opportunities. The ambivalence is neatly caught in the practice of the Tomahawk Baptist Church of Chesterfield County, which in the late eighteenth century employed at least six slave men to investigate wrongdoing among other slaves. In this case, as in others, assuming positions of leadership meant serving as moral watchdogs of the slave community. An exploration of the roles and characteristics of black preachers, who were almost always men, illuminates the ambivalence at the heart of black Christianity.[166]

Some black preachers were drawn from the humblest ranks of slaves. As one historian of the Baptist denomination observed in the early nineteenth century: "Among the African Baptists in the southern states, here are a multitude of preachers and exhorters, whose names do not appear on the minutes of Associations. They preach principally on the plantations to those of their own colour." David Benedict described their preaching as "broken and illiterate"

History, LXXVII (1992), 185–198. For a secular view of the power of the printed word, see Council Journal, Feb. 6, 1749, 144, SCDAH.

166. Tomahawk Baptist Church Records, June 2, 1799, VBHS. Black membership lists of Baptist churches are rare. I have assembled such information, and occasionally supplemented it with additional members mentioned in the church records, for 15 churches in Virginia, 7 in the piedmont (Birchcreek, Fall Creek, Frying Pan, Ebenezer, Goose Creek, Mill Creek, and Meherrin) and 8 in the tidewater (Potowmack, Chappawamsic, Mill Swamp, Upper King and Queen, South Quay, Morattico, Hartwood, and Antioch). The records cover the period 1766–1804. Although a few churches had more black women than black men members, overall I count 300 men and 279 women. South Carolina Baptist churches tend to be in the backcountry, and records usually begin in the early 19th century. However, of the 72 slaves baptized in the Welsh Neck Church in 1779, 50 were men, and 22 were women. In the first decade of the 19th century, the Big Stephens Creek Baptist Church in Edgefield district listed 35 black men and 26 black women as members, although the Cashaway Baptist Church in Darlington listed 76 black men and 113 black women (the ratio among whites, however, was 2:1 in favor of women). Virginia records can be found in VBHS, the Welsh Neck Church minutes are on microfilm at Duke, and Big Stephens Creek and Cashaway Church records can be seen on microfilm at Furman University. White church membership, from the late 17th through the 18th centuries, tended to be 60–75% female: see, for instance, the essays by Mary Maples Dunn and Gerald F. Moran in Janet Wilson James, ed., *Women in American Religion* (Philadelphia, 1980), 27–65.

but "in many cases highly useful." The Reverend John Holt Rice observed "great numbers of negro preachers" in Virginia but was less sanguine about their influence. "For the most part they are as ignorant as any of their species," he claimed. "And very frequently by their preaching if it may be dignified with the name, they prevent the blacks from attending where they might get instruction."[167]

In one South Carolina parish on the eve of the Revolution, fifteen slaves— all men—were named as preaching "to great crowds of negroes . . . very frequently . . . in the woods and other places." We know a little about five of the fifteen. Shifnal, Quashy, and Jupiter, all belonging to George Austin, were thirty-seven, twenty-three, and twenty-one, respectively. Shifnal was married, the other two were single, and all three were field hands. Ben, belonging to James Parsons, had a wife and three children in 1779; the appraisers of Parson's estate valued this slave family more highly than any other. Pearce, also belonging to Parsons, was single and a cooper. In other words, preaching was available to both single and married, young and old, field hands and artisans—a cross-section of the colony's slave men.[168]

In Virginia, a number of slave fugitives advertised in the local newspapers were preachers. If masters can generally be expected to mention the skills of their runaway slaves, then a number were unskilled. Nat, "a Baptist teacher" from Brunswick County, even suffered the indignity of being ironed to another slave when he absconded. However, most Chesapeake slave preachers tended to be drawn from outside the ranks of ordinary field hands: Primus, who took to preaching when sixteen, and Jemmy, who was "very fond of singing hymns and preaching," were both mulattoes and expected to pass as freemen; Joe, who could "read a little, is fond of singing hymns, and exhorting his brethren of the Ethiopian tribe," and Dick, who could also "read (and took with him his prayer book) . . . [and] may pretend to have a call to preach the gospel," were both house servants. Most were in their twenties or early thirties.[169]

Notable black preachers were even more distanced from the ranks of ordinary slaves. Invariably creoles, these men were well used to the ways of whites and were often literate. Occasionally, their primary constituency was white, as with Jesse Peter or Galphin, who was an admired preacher in late-eighteenth-

---

167. David Benedict, *A General History of the Baptist Denomination in America . . .*, 2 vols. (Boston, 1813), II, 212.

168. "Journal of the Council of Safety," SCHS, *Colls.*, II (1858), 71; inventory of George Austin, Nov. 16, 1774, Inventories, AA, 42–51; inventory of James Parsons, Oct. 23, 1779, Inventories, WPA, XCVIII, 335–337.

169. Turner Bynam, *VaG* (Purdie), May 1, 1778 (Nat); Seth Ward, ibid. (P and D), Feb. 27, 1772 (Primus); David Walker, ibid. (Purdie), Sept. 8, 1775 (Jemmy); John Gordon, ibid., May 29, 1778 (Joe); William Bradley, *VaG and WA*, Apr. 26, 1783 (Dick).

century Georgia, or William Lemon, "a man of colour," who was chosen pastor by the Pettsworth Baptist Church in Gloucester, Virginia. Whites even clubbed together to purchase the freedom of a slave preacher, so that he might use his talents more effectively—a situation likely to foster a sense of obligation on the part of the ex-slave. Thus, in the 1790s, residents of the Eastern Shore in Virginia purchased the freedom of Jacob Bishop, a black preacher, who then oversaw the black wing of the First Baptist Church in Portsmouth.[170]

The most famous eighteenth-century slave preachers had to know how to succeed in a white world. George Liele, born in Virginia about 1750, was manumitted by his Georgia master on the eve of the Revolutionary war. Another of his patrons was Colonel Moses Kirkland, who helped Liele out of prison and provided funds for his transportation to Jamaica. The covenant of the Baptist church, "begun in America, Dec. 1777," and reestablished in Kingston in 1784, was rooted in a deep appreciation of white power. It included stipulations that no slaves could "join the church without first having a few lines from their owners of their good behaviour" and that a disobedient slave would "be dealt with according to the word of God." Andrew Bryan, born in South Carolina and converted by Liele, purchased his freedom some time after the Revolutionary war. In a letter written in 1800, when he was age sixty-three, Andrew Bryan spoke with pride of his family, particularly Hannah, his "pious wife, whose freedom I have obtained," and of his "worldly comforts," for he then owned a house and lot in Savannah, some rental property in the city, a fifty-six-acre tract and buildings four miles outside the city, and eight slaves. Recognizing the one sure way to secure respect, Bryan acquired, in the words of Henry Holcombe, "a handsome estate." David George was another slave who came under the influence of Liele, whom he had known in Virginia, where George was born. After fleeing slavery, taking refuge first among the Creeks and then the Natchez, George was purchased by George Galphin, an Indian trader who lived at Silver Bluff on the Savannah River. George became a privileged slave and waited on his master, whom he found "very kind." During the Revolution, he attached himself to the British and eventually went to Nova Scotia.[171]

---

170. "Letters Showing the Rise and Progress of the Early Negro Churches of Georgia and the West Indies," *Jour. Negro Hist.*, I (1916), 83; Robert B. Semple, *A History of the Rise and Progress of the Baptists in Virginia* (Richmond, Va., 1810), 128, 351–352; Lemuel Burkitt and Jesse Read, *A Concise History of the Kehukee Baptist Association, from Its Original Rise down to 1803* (Philadelphia, 1850), 262–264. Jacob Bishop was probably the black man heard by Richard Dozier in 1789, for he mentioned a slave named Jacob coming from the Eastern Shore to preach at Farnham Meeting House. "A most wonderful preacher," Dozier declared (journal of Dozier, Apr. 27, 1789, VBHS).

171. "Letters Showing the Rise and Progress of the Early Negro Churches," *Jour. Negro Hist.*, I (1916), 69–74, 79–80, 82–83, 86–87; "An Account of the Jamaica Baptists, with

Unlike Liele, Bryan, or George, Harry Hoosier, or "Black Harry," as he was known, was an African and never learned to read or write. In the words of the Reverend Henry Boehm, Hoosier "was very black, an African of the Africans . . . [and] so illiterate he could not read a word." But Harry, too, learned how to succeed in a white world. In 1780, Francis Asbury mused that, if only he had two horses and Harry, he could convert blacks galore in Virginia and the Carolinas. A year later in Fairfax County, Virginia, Harry spoke after Asbury, and "the white people looked on with attention." Indeed, as Thomas Coke mentioned in 1784, white crowds flocked to hear Harry, for he had "amazing power." In the same year, Thomas Haskins called Harry "a wonder of grace" and at a meeting near Quantico observed how he "excited and won the attention and admiration of the audience." In 1790, Richard Dozier heard Harry expound a text in Westmoreland County, Virginia, "all in a clear and most wonderful manner." After listening to several "excellent discourse[s]" from Harry in 1804 and 1805, William Colbert exclaimed, "This is not a man made preacher," and expressed great surprise "to hear a man that cannot read, preach like this man." According to Boehm, Harry "would repeat the hymn as if reading it, and quote his text with great accuracy. His voice was musical, and his tongue as the pen of a ready writer." Although Asbury intended Harry to be useful among blacks—and on occasion some blacks "came a great distance to hear him"—Harry's primary audience appears to have been whites. Asbury once found Harry unwilling to travel to Virginia and feared that "his speaking so much to white people" might have ruined him. Harry seems never to have traveled into the heart of the slaveholding South.[172]

Even slave preachers bent on accommodating themselves to whites fell foul of the authorities. In the Lowcountry, Andrew Bryan was frequently imprisoned and whipped for exhorting blacks during the Revolutionary war. On one occasion, fifty of his congregation "were severely whipped," and Andrew him-

---

Memoirs of Mr. George Liele," *General Baptist Repository*, I (1802), 229–240; Henry Holcombe, *The First Fruits, in a Series of Letters* (Philadelphia, 1812), 116; "An Account of the Life of Mr. David George, from Sierra Leone in Africa . . . ," *Baptist Annual Register*, I (1790–1793), 473–484; Grant Gordon, *From Slavery to Freedom: The Life of David George, Pioneer Baptist Minister* (Hantsport, Canada, 1992); G. A. Rawlyk, *The Canada Fire: Radical Evangelicalism in British North America, 1775–1812* (Kingston, Ont., 1994), 33–43.

172. Wakeley, *The Patriarch of One Hundred Years*, 89–92; Clark et al., eds., *Journal and Letters of Asbury*, I, 362, 403, 413, 494; Thomas Coke, *Extracts of the Journals of the Late Rev. Dr. Coke's Five Visits to America* (Dublin, 1816), 47 (see also 45, 46, 49, 91, 118, 149); journal of Thomas Haskins, Aug. 11, 12, 13, 1783, Nov. 21, 1784, LC; journal of Dozier, Nov. 2, 1790; journal of Colbert, Sept. 15, 1804, Jan. 19, 20, 26, 27, 1805. Harry preached mostly in the northern states, sometimes in the upper Chesapeake, occasionally on the Eastern Shore, but never apparently in lower Virginia or parts further south.

self *"was cut and bled abundantly."* In the mid-1790s, he and his brother Sampson were arrested and charged with plotting a rebellion. In the same decade, the Bush River Baptist Church, located in backcountry South Carolina, followed a common pattern in allowing a slave named Moses to exhort but then silencing him when his preaching gave offense.[173]

In the Chesapeake, much larger numbers of black preachers ran into problems. As early as 1766, Jack from Mecklenburg County appeared to have been "principally concerned in promoting the late disorderly meetings among the Negroes"; one year later, Jupiter received a severe whipping in Sussex County after "having been tried there for stirring up the Negroes to an insurrection, being a great Newlight preacher"; Primus, who had been preaching in Chesterfield County since 1768, was said to have "done much Mischief in the Neighborhood." Perhaps most notable, however, was Gowan Pamphlet, who first began preaching in Middlesex County, Virginia, before the Revolution. He became the pastor of a black Baptist church in Williamsburg that had five hundred members in 1791, when it was admitted into the Dover Association. A respected pillar of the Baptist Association in Virginia, Gowan was still not immune from suspicion. In 1793, leading citizens of South Carolina and Virginia exchanged messages about "black Preacher Gawin," who was thought to have journeyed among Charleston, Richmond, Norfolk, and Yorktown in order to coordinate a general insurrection involving six thousand South Carolina slaves and untold numbers in the major towns of Virginia.[174]

As much as some slaves wished to become orthodox Christians, they were always subject to suspicion, which helps explain why Christianity remained a minority experience within the eighteenth-century black community. By 1790, perhaps eleven thousand Virginia blacks were Methodist or Baptist church members, representing 4 percent of the blacks in the state. Of course, many more blacks went to evangelical meetings or learned something of Christianity than were church members, and it is impressive that the black membership

---

173. "Letters Showing the Rise and Progress of the Early Negro Churches," *Jour. Negro Hist.*, I (1916), 77–78, 82–83; Mary Granger, ed., *Savannah River Plantations* (Savannah, Ga., 1947), 400; J. H. Redding, *Life and Times of Jonathan Bryan, 1708–1788* (Savannah, Ga., 1901), 44; Bush River Baptist Church, Newberry Co., July 21, 1792, Oct. 11, 1794, Oct. 10, 1795, microfilm, Furman University.

174. Robert Munford, *VaG* (Purdie), May 2, 1766 (Jack); George Noble, ibid. (P and D), Oct. 1, 1767 (Jupiter); Seth Ward, ibid. (P and D), Feb. 27, 1772 (Primus). On Pamphlet, see William Nelson, Jr., to Thomas Newton, Aug. 8, 1793, Thomas Newton to Capt. Edward Blake, Aug. 11, 1793, Peter Oram to Col. Vanderhorst, Aug. 16, 1793, South Carolina Senate Messages, SCDAH; William Nelson to Gov. Henry Lee, Aug. 8, 1793, Executive Papers; Semple, *A History*, 114–115; and Asplund's *Register*, 1794, as cited in Luther P. Jackson, "Religious Development of the Negro in Virginia from 1762 to 1860," *Jour. Negro Hist.*, XVI (1931), 189.

in evangelical churches was just over half the size of its white counterpart. Nevertheless, active evangelicalism was the preserve of a small minority of Chesapeake blacks. In the Lowcountry, of course, a mere fraction were church members. Christianity remained a closed book for the vast majority of Lowcountry slaves.[175]

Two broad developments characterized the religious life of slaves in the Chesapeake and Lowcountry. The first and perhaps most important, at least in the eighteenth century, was the enhanced role of magic. Before Christianity penetrated the world of slaves, magical beliefs and practices, particularly those associated with harming individuals, had assumed a prominent place that they would retain even after widespread Christianization. Second, even when African slaves came into contact with Christianity, they did not accept it wholesale. Rather than adding a high god to their pantheon of lesser spirits, they seem to have elaborated on a traditional concept of a supreme being. If this development encouraged Africans and their descendants to adapt Christianity to their needs rather than having it thrust upon them, such discrimination was certainly evident in their distinctive funeral practices, their particularly expressive religious behavior, their apocalyptic visions, and the charisma of some of their preachers.

The religion of slaves in eighteenth-century British America highlights how blacks, laboring under extreme hardships and in radically different settings, managed to preserve some deep-level principles drawn from their African heritage. Much was lost: few priests and almost no collective rituals survived the passage to British North America. One exception seems to have occurred in the household of Jacob Stewart (Jacobo Estuart), a free black from the Lowcountry who lived in Spanish Florida in 1784 and then migrated to New Providence in the Bahamas. He celebrated "Negro rites in the style of Guinea" in his Florida home. Thus, contrary to one interpretation, North American plantation slaves generally could not practice "African religion," nor did they appropriate only those values that could be absorbed into their "Africanity." This is to make excessive claims for the autonomy of slaves and the primacy of their African background. Ultimately, such an argument belittles the slaves' achievements by minimizing the staggering obstacles they faced in forging a culture. "The glory of Afro-Americana," Mintz states, "depended—had to depend—on creativity and innovation far more than on the indelibility of particular culture contents."[176]

---

175. Jackson, "Religious Development," *Jour. Negro Hist.*, XVI (1931), 179–180.
176. Statement of Jacobo Estuart, Census Returns, 1784–1814, bundle 323A, microfilm roll 148, frame 2-91, East Florida Papers, LC (thanks to Patrick Riordan for this reference); and

Opting for the opposite extreme, however, and arguing that North American slaves experienced an "African spiritual holocaust" is no more persuasive. Rather, at the fundamental level of epistemological beliefs, interpersonal relations, and expressive behavior, slaves kept alive a measure of their African "character." They engaged in a process of selective appropriation or structured improvisation in which values and practices were reinterpreted as they were incorporated. At bottom, blacks shared a similar outlook on how the world worked as well as common means of cultural expression, but they borrowed widely, melding older cultural traits with new ones, the mix always varying from place to place, but overall creating a distinctive pattern of their own.[177]

---

see Jane Landers, "Spanish Sanctuary: Fugitives in Florida, 1687–1790," *Florida Hist. Qtly,* LXII (1984), 307; Stuckey, *Slave Culture,* esp. viii, 27; Mintz, *Caribbean Transformations,* 14.

177. Butler, *Awash in a Sea of Faith,* 151. Butler is correct when he argues that "traditional African religious systems as *systems*" were destroyed in North America, but he goes too far in speaking of a holocaust or in saying that slaves were "remarkably bereft of traditional collective religious practice."

And the end of all our exploring

Will be to arrive where we started

And know the place for the first time.

—T. S. Eliot, "Little Gidding"

Coda : Two Mature Slave Societies

The slave societies of the eighteenth-century Chesapeake and Lowcountry matured with basically the same institutional structures and cultural inheritances and were part of the same imperial and, later, national systems, but they differed in their environments, settlement patterns, demographic regimes, crops, labor arrangements, styles of race relations, and regional cultures. Alike, and yet different, the Lowcountry and Chesapeake slave societies provide useful commentaries upon one another. These two slave societies are not so dissimilar as to produce merely predictable contrasts; they are not so alike as to produce only variations on a theme. Rather, each society looks different alongside the other; our understanding of each is enlarged by knowledge of the other.

By the late eighteenth century, the Chesapeake and Lowcountry were the two dominant slave societies on the North American mainland. Never before, or since, has such a large proportion of the mainland's slaves congregated in the two regions. In 1800, a half of all African Americans in the United States—almost 500,000—lived in the Chesapeake. Virginia was the center of black life in North America. Indeed, according to the first census, the pivotal point, or center of gravity, of the United States black population was a location just southwest of Petersburg. Appropriately enough, the Southside, witness to one of the most dynamic expansions of slavery in the eighteenth century, was the epicenter of the new nation's black population. The other great focus of slavery's expansion was the Lower South. In fact, in the last decade of the eighteenth century, this region's black population grew by almost half, more than twice the rate of its Upper South counterpart. By 1800, 350,000 African Americans, more than a third of all those in the United States, lived in the Lower South states of North Carolina, South Carolina, and Georgia. Overall, about nine of ten blacks in the early United States inhabited the Chesapeake and the Lower South.[1]

These two full-fledged regional slave societies had much in common. Both were expansive, restlessly opening up new territory to accommodate rapidly growing slave populations. Both had a majority of native-born slaves, many able to trace descent through six or seven creole generations. Unlike almost all other large-scale slave societies in the New World, both could boast self-reproducing slave populations. Slaves in both regions lived on larger plantations over time, and in many locales they increasingly outnumbered whites. In both regions most enslaved men, women, and children worked on the land, wielding hoes and axes reminiscent of biblical times. In both regions, a sizable and growing minority of slaves, particularly men, worked at crafts, on the water, as supervisors, in manufacturing, and as domestics. North American slaves everywhere lived in societies that increasingly rested on a rationale of racial superiority. One reason African Americans came together is that the deep canyon separating white and black grew ever wider, even as bridges arose to routinize contact across the color line. In spite of powerful obstacles and inherent fragility, family life became more robust for both Chesapeake and Lowcountry slaves. Two-parent families were increasingly the norm. Although fragmentation and conflict were never absent in slave communities, cohesion emerged. Finally, in the major symbolic dimensions of their lives—the way they spoke, the way they danced and made music, and the way they worshiped their gods—African Americans in both regions elaborated similar styles.

In short, a large part of the story of eighteenth-century black life in the Chesapeake and Lowcountry was one of integration, parallels, and intersections. Subject to extraordinary duress and enormous hardships, a people came together. Yet, the theme of convergence is at least matched, and in some respects overshadowed, by that of divergence, contrasts, bifurcations. In many cases, the same forces pulling a people together were also pushing them apart.

Thus, although expansion was basic to both these regional slave societies, profound differences centered on how they expanded. Slaves moved westward in both regions, but by the end of the century a majority of Virginia's slave population lived outside the tidewater in the piedmont and Valley, whereas two-thirds of South Carolina's slave population still lived in the Lowcountry.

1. U.S., Bureau of the Census, *Negro Population, 1790–1915* (Washington, D.C., 1918), 41.

Movement out of the two regions was on markedly different scales. From the first, Chesapeake blacks participated in settling the trans-Appalachian frontier. In 1751 a black slave accompanied Christopher Gist in explorations of the Ohio River territory. A generation later, a slave led Daniel Boone to the body of the pioneer's eldest son, who had been killed by Indians. By the time of the first census about 16,000 slaves, almost all of them from the Chesapeake, lived in Kentucky and Tennessee. In the 1790s the migration quickened, with about one in twelve Chesapeake slaves moving southwest. By the end of the century, 55,000 African Americans, more than 5 percent of the early nation's total, lived in the two trans-Appalachian states. The nation's black population had begun its inexorable—and painful—march south and west. By contrast, very few Lower South slaves moved out of their region during the late eighteenth century. Hundreds moved to Spanish Louisiana (a notable example being Dr. Benjamin Farrar's complement of about 150 slaves), and a few thousand reached the Mississippi Territory. But by the end of the century fewer than 5,000 Lower South slaves had left the region.[2]

The characters of the two regions' slave populations also diverged as much as converged. To be sure, both black populations were more creole than immigrant by the late eighteenth century, but slaves in the Upper South were generally healthier and more fertile than slaves in the Lower South. In 1790 Africans were about a fifth of the Lowcountry's slave population and only a fiftieth of the Chesapeake's. The Lower South imported more Africans in the post-Revolutionary years than ever before—more than 100,000 between 1783 and 1807—whereas the Upper South ended the trade in 1775 and legalized its ban eight years later. Africans entering the Lower South in the early national years contributed to an increasingly black countryside. By the late eighteenth century, most Lowcountry parishes were predominantly black, whereas most Chesapeake counties were predominantly white. In many Lowcountry areas most slaves lived on large plantations, whereas in the Chesapeake most slaves lived on small to middling units. A large part of the Lower South was a black world; most of the Chesapeake was a white world.

Although a majority of Chesapeake and Lowcountry slaves worked in the fields, their laboring experiences contrasted sharply. Late-eighteenth-century

---

2. Marion B. Lucas, *A History of Blacks in Kentucky*, I, *From Slavery to Segregation, 1760–1891* (Frankfort, Ky., 1992), xi; Ellen Eslinger, "The Shape of Slavery on the Kentucky Frontier, 1775–1800," *Register of the Kentucky Historical Society*, XCII (1994), 2; Allan Kulikoff, "Uprooted Peoples: Black Migrants in the Age of the American Revolution, 1790–1820," in Ira Berlin and Ronald Hoffman, eds., *Slavery and Freedom in the Age of the American Revolution* (Charlottesville, Va., 1983), 143–171; Gwendolyn Midlo Hall, *Africans in Colonial Louisiana: The Development of Afro-Creole Culture in the Eighteenth Century* (Baton Rouge, La., 1992), 283.

PLATE 23. A South View of Julianton Plantation, the Property of Francis Levett, Esqr. *John McKinnon. Before 1803. McIntosh Co., Georgia. A large plantation in Lowcountry Georgia. Courtesy Duke University*

South Carolina was a "Rice Thumping Country." With the decline of indigo and incomplete emergence of cotton, rice reigned supreme. Whole areas of the late-eighteenth-century Chesapeake, by contrast, were no longer tobacco country. Tobacco was still the region's primary crop, but in many of the older areas mixed farming held sway. The range of farming activities—tending corn, wheat, small grains, flax, garden produce, and fruit, planting clover, sowing timothy, making hay, raising livestock, and cutting trees—was impressive. Many Chesapeake slaves were farm hands. Diversification was the hallmark of the Chesapeake work routine, specialization the key to the Lowcountry regime; slaves worked by gang in the one region, by task in the other; slave skills increased with a greater range in the Chesapeake, but at a faster pace in the Lowcountry.[3]

In both regions, white society gained greater communal solidarity through the debasement of blacks; nevertheless, the texture of race relations was not uniform. The relationship of masters and slaves was personal in the Chesapeake, regimented in the Lowcountry, evident in everything from the character of the legal code to the nature of health care, from the delegation of command to the pattern of barter, from the degree of interracial sex to the intimacy of religious associations. Greater numbers of nonelite whites in the Chesapeake than in the Lowcountry also shaped the character of the two slave societies. Chesapeake slaves engaged in greater cooperation with, but also encountered more slights from, plain white folk than Lower South slaves. Fewer religious contacts, sexual encounters, and opportunities for recreational fraternization but also more exploitative cohabitations as well as crueler acts of violence occurred across the color line in the Lower than in the Upper South. Overall,

3. Lorena S. Walsh, "Rural African Americans in the Constitutional Era in Maryland, 1776–1810," *MHM,* LXXXIV (1989), 327–341.

slavery was a little less brutal in the Chesapeake than in the Lowcountry because of the personal nature of the Upper South master-slave relationship and the moderating and mediating effects of a large group of plain white folk.

Although the process of transforming a predominantly African into a predominantly creole society was similar in both the Chesapeake and Lowcountry, black society nevertheless developed differently in the two regions. Although sharply divided among themselves, Africans from the same coastal region or of similar ethnic background had more opportunity to band together, shipmates an easier time maintaining contact, and maroons more chance to establish settlements in the Lower than in the Upper South. Conversely, creoles, although subject to internal tensions and conflicts, yet more readily assimilated Africans, developed more cohesion among themselves, and were more conversant with white ways in the Chesapeake than in the Lowcountry. Chesapeake blacks largely incorporated Indians into their society, but Lowcountry blacks often encountered hostility from Indians, particularly tributary and frontier but even from enslaved ones. There were many more free blacks in the Upper than in the Lower South, but, ironically, the gap between slave and free was wider in the Lowcountry than in the Chesapeake.

Urban slavery—which had some uniform features throughout plantation America, in part because it was a minority experience in a predominantly rural world—was more deeply rooted in the Lowcountry than in the Chesapeake. Blacks congregated in larger numbers and in a more confined space in Charleston than anywhere else on the North American mainland. In 1800, the ten thousand or so slaves living in this Lower South city equaled the combined total of slaves living in the five most notable Chesapeake towns: Baltimore, Norfolk, Richmond, Alexandria, and Petersburg. In addition, although attention is often directed at the growing free black population of the urban Chesapeake, the five largest Lower South towns—Charleston, Savannah, Newbern,

Wilmington, and Edenton—had about as many free blacks as their Upper South counterparts. Blacks were a majority in all Lower South towns but in only two Upper South towns: Richmond and Petersburg. In Alexandria and Baltimore, blacks were minorities, less than a quarter of the total population. In short, urban blacks were a greater presence in the Lower than in the Upper South, and Charleston blacks in particular created a rich community life. Black Charlestonians dominated the local economy and put their stamp on the social and cultural fabric of the town in ways unthinkable in the Upper South. In 1790 light-skinned free blacks even created their own Brown Fellowship Society.[4]

The immediate family and enlarged kin group were vital institutions to slaves in both regions, but family life developed differently across the regions. Two-parent families and solitaries were common household forms in the Lowcountry, one-parent families and extended kin networks were widespread in the Chesapeake. Polygyny occurred in the Lower South, necronymic naming and frequent surname use in the Upper South. Although family life was more robust among Chesapeake than Lowcountry slaves, especially through the first three-quarters of the eighteenth century, the balance gradually shifted. By the early national years, the odds on maintaining family ties had significantly worsened for many Chesapeake slaves who made (or saw relatives make) the long and arduous trek westward, were subject to continual hirings, and were dispersed on a master's death among many heirs. In contrast, the odds had significantly improved for many Lowcountry slaves who were tied closely to the coast, lived on large units, and were kept together through being distributed among few heirs. In this respect, at least, slavery was harsher farther north, contrary to popular stereotype.

While Lowcountry and Chesapeake slaves laid the foundations of a single ethnic subculture, they also created two distinct regional cultures. Thus, most Lowcountry slaves spoke a creole, whereas most Chesapeake slaves spoke a dialectical form of Standard English. Upper South slaves incorporated Anglophone instruments into their musical repertoires more readily than their Lower South counterparts. Slaves sported more beards and jewelry in the Lowcountry than in the Chesapeake. Sorcery was practiced more widely among Lower South than Upper South slaves, a millenarian tradition was more notable in Lowcountry than in Chesapeake Christianity, and black evangelicalism was more extensive and popular in Virginia and Maryland than in the Carolinas and Georgia. From what they spoke to what they wore, from the music

---

4. Philip D. Morgan, "Black Life in Eighteenth-Century Charleston," *Perspectives in American History*, N.S., I (1984), 187–232; U.S., Bureau of the Census, *Return of the Whole Number of Persons within the Several Districts of the United States . . . Second Census . . . 1800* (Washington, D.C., 1802), 2H–2P.

they played to the religion they practiced, Lowcountry and Chesapeake blacks created cultural variations on common themes.

A way to encapsulate many of these differences is, as has been argued earlier, to invoke an inverse relationship between material conditions and communal autonomy. It is almost as if a cruel jest, a tragic quirk of fate, were at work. Seemingly, to be overworked and unhealthy was to be less dependent on masters. To be treated brutally was to have more latitude. To work methodically but not frenetically was to have less time to work provision plots. To have sufficient food supplies was to gain less right to hunt, forage, and fish. To receive stingy rations was a spur to engage in independent provisioning and marketing. To be the recipient of a master's solicitude was to have less room for maneuver. There is no sense in asking which of these binary possibilities was better. How does one calibrate degrees of oppression? How does one weigh brutality on a moral index? How does one balance a moral ledger? Is oppression measured in fertility or independence, in hunger or self-esteem? To pose the question is to realize the impossibility of an answer.

The differences in regional experiences are, then, real and palpable. To reemphasize the dual presence of convergence and divergence, the parallels and the contrasts in the experiences of Lowcountry and Chesapeake slaves can be explored through the window of the two most momentous late-eighteenth-century events—the Revolution and westward settlement—that would transform black life well into the nineteenth century.

The expansion of freedom and slavery at the heart of the Revolutionary experience is nowhere better captured than in the Chesapeake region. Freedom dramatically widened for many blacks, as some took advantage of the Revolutionary war to join the British and others benefited from a postwar liberalization of manumission, which led masters—driven by Revolutionary libertarianism, evangelical egalitarianism, and economic necessity—to free slaves in large numbers. Not all manumissions were altruistic. In Baltimore, for example, masters employed offers of delayed manumissions as an incentive to spur production, and a lively market arose in slaves with limited terms to serve who were therefore cheaper than slaves for life. Nevertheless, even with delayed manumissions, the Chesapeake in 1800 had more free blacks than any other region in the nation. The commitment to slavery also deepened. As one historian has noted, "In those Chesapeake districts where most blacks lived, slavery was more deeply rooted when Jefferson stepped down from the presidency than when he composed the Declaration of Independence." More than a thousand white Virginians, particularly from the rapidly expanding Southside, underscored their unreserved commitment to slavery by signing proslavery petitions. In fact, the Chesapeake region embodied the differential growth of freedom and slavery, and began to fragment as a single unit. Blacks gained considerably more freedom in the upper Chesapeake, whereas slavery became more entrenched in the lower Chesapeake. This bifurcation of the region had long-reaching consequences, for, when the Civil War came, Maryland stood with the Union and Virginia with the Confederacy.[5]

Freedom and slavery also expanded in the Lowcountry, but in different ways. The Revolutionary war was more disruptive in South Carolina and Georgia than anywhere else on the mainland. Far more slaves escaped bondage in the Lower South than in the rest of the fledgling nation. South Carolina and Georgia lost almost one-quarter of their pre-Revolutionary slave populations. In one Lowcountry parish, the number of adult slave men nearly halved between 1774 and 1784. A power vacuum arose in the warring countryside. Even blacks who remained at home became, as one Lowcountry mistress observed of her slaves, "insolent and quite their own masters." After the war, many slaves continued to flaunt their increased autonomy. Nevertheless, while some blacks used the war and immediate postwar chaos to effect their escape, broaden their horizons, or gain a political education, many others suffered grievously. Masters hustled their slaves out of the paths of marauding armies; patriots and loyalists confiscated and sold each other's slaves; both belligerents used blacks as bounties for white volunteers; unprincipled men with no loyalty except to themselves used the anarchy of war to kidnap slaves for their own benefit; and many slaves died from malnutrition and rampant disease. The general loss of manpower stiffened slaveholder commitment to bondage, and the postwar Lower South witnessed a huge expansion of slavery, evident in the reopening of the slave trade, a resilient and later booming economy, the massive settlement of the backcountry, and a dramatic growth of large slaveholdings. As slavery tightened its grip on the postwar Lower South, formal freedom expanded little. Manumissions increased, but the Lower South saw much the lowest rate of manumission in mainland America. South Carolina was a bulwark of slavery and would be a driving force in the events leading up to the Civil War.[6]

In spite of the different ways the interrelationship of slavery and freedom worked itself out in the two regions, blacks learned similar lessons from the

---

5. Stephen Whitman, "Diverse Good Causes: Manumission and the Transformation of Urban Slavery," *Social Science History*, XIX (1995), 333–370; Richard S. Dunn, "Black Society in the Chesapeake, 1776–1810," in Berlin and Hoffman, eds., *Slavery and Freedom*, 49–82 (quote on 52); Frederika Teute Schmidt and Barbara Ripel Wilhelm, eds., "Early Proslavery Petitions in Virginia," *WMQ*, 3d Ser., XXX (1973), 133–146.

6. Philip D. Morgan, "Black Society in the Lowcountry," in Berlin and Hoffman, eds., *Slavery and Freedom*, 83–141.

Revolution. As early as 1775, one South Carolina slave had the "audacity," as his master put it, to tell his owner that "he will be free, that he will serve no Man, and that he will be conquered or governed by no Man." In that year, Lowcountry slaves apparently believed that the king intended to set them free. Two years later, Lowcountry slaves' "pride and bearing," their "serenity in the presence of a white man," impressed a visitor to Charleston. Virginia masters observed a difference in their slaves. Too many, noted John Randolph, displayed a proud "sense of their rights, and a contempt for danger." Before the Revolution, slaves "fought [for] freedom merely as a good," George Tucker noted, but "now they also claim it as a right." During Gabriel's conspiracy, Jack Ditcher insisted, "We have as much right to fight for our liberty as any men." Even more striking are the words of another Gabriel conspirator, who defiantly announced: "I have nothing more to offer than what General Washington would have had to offer, had he been taken by the British and put on trial. I have adventured my life in endeavouring to obtain the liberty of my countrymen, and am a willing sacrifice in their cause." In past slave societies—whether Roman, Greek, European, African—slaves had attempted to overthrow slavery, but never before had slaves challenged slavery on the grounds of natural rights. Never before in human history had slaves attacked the general principles justifying their enslavement.[7]

African Americans from both Lowcountry and Chesapeake seem also to have joined forces, even if temporarily and unsuccessfully. In 1793, while walking along a Yorktown street, Gowan Pamphlet, the free black minister of Williamsburg's African Baptist Church, reportedly dropped a letter that mentioned long-laid insurrectionary plans among both Richmond and Norfolk blacks. If the letter was accurate, guns and ammunition were being stockpiled. The letter referred to a "friend in Charleston" who claimed that six thousand Lowcountry slaves had already enlisted. How much of a plot was in the offing, it is impossible to say, but Pamphlet did visit South Carolina, and the governors of South Carolina and Virginia took the rumor seriously. Indeed, the governor of South Carolina reported the strict observance of patrol duty for two weeks after the first report. Perhaps blacks in the two regions were secretly corresponding with one another. Seemingly, then, by the last decade of the eighteenth century, some free blacks and slaves in the towns of Virginia and

7. Joshua Eden, *SCG*, Nov. 7, 1775; Robert A. Olwell, "'Domestick Enemies': Slavery and Political Independence in South Carolina, May 1775–March 1776," *Journal of Southern History*, LV (1989), 21–48, esp. 29, 34; Edward D. Seeber, trans., *On the Threshold of Liberty: Journal of a Frenchman's Tour of the American Colonies in 1777* (Bloomington, Ind., 1959), 14–15; Douglas R. Egerton, "Gabriel's Conspiracy and the Election of 1800," *Jour. So. Hist.*, LVI (1990), 201, 208–209.

South Carolina conceived of themselves as sharing enough of an identity to speak of forming a joint conspiracy.[8]

Such actions and noble words usually got slaves executed, so they constructed their lives in the Revolutionary era in less self-defeating ways. They survived, struggled, and adapted, arguably more important acts than mounting the occasional and unsuccessful revolt. The American Revolution does not represent, as one historian has claimed, "the largest slave uprising" in United States history. The tragedy of the American Revolution is that many more slaves lost their lives, went to the British under duress, or ended up in the Caribbean than escaped to freedom. During the Revolutionary era, the vast majority of slaves continued to build and rebuild their family lives. They increasingly named children for kinfolk, signifying the importance they attached to extended kin. They continued to broaden their economic skills and strive for economic independence. They exercised greater and greater control over their churches, revealing the determination to control their religious lives. And, in the creativity and spontaneity of their worship, speech, dance, music, naming, and clothing, they exhibited their own idea of freedom. It was, and had to be, a freedom of the soul, of words, of play, and of the body. It was a freedom of the spirit, an irrepressible and unquenchable human spirit. In this way, above all, slaves kept alive the deferred promises of the Revolution.[9]

Just as the Revolution reveals in dramatic fashion the process of divergence and convergence among blacks, so, on the frontier, slaves retained some of their old regional ways even as they engaged in new forms of cultural fusion. Some of the frontier differences can be traced to particular regional streams of influence. Thus, Kentucky and Tennessee were largely extensions of the Chesapeake, whereas Mississippi, Louisiana, and Alabama reflected more pronounced Lowcountry influences. For example, Chesapeake slaves took their prior experiences of diversified farming to the Kentucky frontier, and Lowcountry slaves were able at least in part to recreate rice and indigo farming and even their basket-making techniques in Mississippi and Alabama. Gang labor was widespread in Kentucky and Tennessee; tasking, while never common, was

8. William Nelson to Governor Henry Lee, Aug. 8, 1793, Executive Papers, VSL; Lt. Gov. James Wood to Governor William Moultrie, Aug. 14, 1793, and Peter Oram to Governor William Moultrie, Aug. 16, 1793, Governor's Messages, SCDAH; William Moultrie to James Wood, Aug. 29, 1793, William Moultrie Papers, USC. This incident is discussed in detail in James Sidbury, *Ploughshares into Swords: Race, Rebellion, and Identity in Gabriel's Virginia, 1730–1810* (New York, 1997).

9. For works that stress overt resistance, see Sylvia R. Frey, *Water from the Rock: Black Resistance in a Revolutionary Age* (Princeton, N.J., 1991); and Gary B. Nash, *Race and Revolution* (Madison, Wis., 1990), 57.

incorporated into gang routines in the upcountry regions of South Carolina and Georgia as well as in Alabama and Mississippi. One Lowcountry planter who moved to central Georgia tasked his hoe hands but employed gangs in all other plantation work. Slaves encountered legal structures on the frontier that would have been familiar to them. Kentucky generally adopted Virginia slave laws, in some cases not the most up-to-date versions; Tennessee based its code on that of North Carolina; Alabama followed Georgia's example; and Louisiana in 1806 passed legislation based on the South Carolina law of 1740. Whole religious communities moved west. In 1781 more than five hundred Baptists left Spotsylvania County, Virginia, for the Dick's River region of Kentucky. The exodus included many slaves, among them Reverend Joseph Craig's "Uncle Peter," also known as "Old Captain," who transplanted his Virginia Baptist traditions to the West; about the turn of the century he founded the First African Baptist Church in Lexington.[10]

As with this religious community, some slaves moved west in large groups. Atypical though they were, these migrations represented the best possibilities slaves had to sustain links with their past. In 1805 Robert Carter Harrison, for example, migrated from Virginia to Fayette County, Kentucky, with just over one hundred slaves. Although Harrison could not own all his slaves' kinfolk, family separations were at least minimized. Another series of migrations that lasted from 1790 to 1806 moved many members of the Cabell-Breckenridge kin network and their slaves to Kentucky. These piecemeal and drawn-out transfers separated families and caused grief. Thus, in 1804 when an advance party of Cabell Harrison slaves left, it was anticipated that "there will be great crying and morning, children Leaving there mothers, mothers there children, and women there husbands." In this case, the families were reunited two years later. Over time, the serial migration of Cabell-Breckenridge slaves reunited and recombined many immediate families and extended kin on a distant frontier, but that so many slaves had to pass information in letters or by word of mouth

---

10. J. Winston Coleman, Jr., *Slavery Times in Kentucky* (Chapel Hill, N.C., 1940), 3–17; James Benson Sellers, *Slavery in Alabama* (University, Ala., 1950), 7, 69; John Hebron Moore, *The Emergence of the Cotton Kingdom in the Old Southwest: Mississippi, 1770–1860* (Baton Rouge, La., 1988), 4, 75; Dale Rosengarten, "The Lowcountry Basket in a Global Setting," paper presented to the College of Charleston, May 1995, 13–14; Drew Gilpin Faust, *James Henry Hammond and the Old South: A Design for Mastery* (Baton Rouge, La., 1982), 74–75; Joseph P. Reidy, *From Slavery to Agrarian Capitalism in the Cotton Plantation South: Central Georgia, 1800–1880* (Chapel Hill, N.C., 1992), 36; Thomas D. Morris, *Southern Slavery and the Law, 1619–1860* (Chapel Hill, N.C., 1996), 71, 172, 183–184, 218; George W. Ranck, *"The Travelling Church": An Account of the Baptist Exodus from Virginia to Kentucky in 1781 under the Leadership of Rev. Lewis Craig and Capt. William Ellis* (Louisville, Ky., 1910), 22.

between Kentucky and Virginia also indicates how even under optimum conditions westward migration caused heartache and distress. It also of course forced slaves to make new connections.[11]

Similarly, black Christianity on the early national frontier was not simply an extension of an earlier Chesapeake form, even though so many Kentucky blacks came from Virginia. Blacks were a much weaker presence in the Baptist churches of late-eighteenth-century Kentucky than they were in the evangelical churches of Virginia in the same period. The slaves most likely to join a western congregation in the early national era came from larger than average slaveholdings. Apparently, slaves needed to recapture or recreate a sense of community as a condition for the rise of black Christianity on the frontier.[12]

Although regional ways persisted on the frontier, the more notable development was an accelerated cultural convergence. The frontier mixed peoples from all regions. In the 1770s, for example, Virginians, Carolinians, and Georgians, among others, settled the Natchez District. In addition, frontier conditions necessarily wrought much homogeneity. In the trans-Applachian West, slaves lived on small slaveholdings reminiscent of pioneer days on both Chesapeake and Lowcountry seaboards. In 1800 the average slaveholding unit in Kentucky was just four slaves. In the 1790s a slave man formerly from Virginia but then living in a remote part of Kentucky complained to his master, "There are no colored people here, and we have no women to wash for us, on Sundays we stalk about without being able to talk to any one." The master tried to persuade the slave that "in time" he would "have many black people here for neighbors," but the man was impatient and ran away, aiming significantly toward a larger plantation also of former Virginia slaves. On the late-eighteenth-century Tennessee frontier, almost all recorded sales and transfers of slaves were of single men, women, and children, again reminiscent of pioneer days on the coast. Only about half a dozen transactions concerned what might have been nuclear families. Not until 1802 was the term "family" used in a bill of sale for slaves in Davidson County, Tennessee. Early race relations were somewhat fluid on the frontier, where black numbers were small and generally seen as

---

11. Allan Kulikoff, *The Agrarian Origins of American Capitalism* (Charlottesville, Va., 1992), 238; Gail S. Terry, "Sustaining the Bonds of Kinship in a Trans-Appalachian Migration, 1790–1811: The Cabell-Breckenridge Slaves Move West," *VMHB*, CII (1994), 455–476. For messages passed back and forth between Kentucky and Virginia slaves, see Todd Harold Barnett, "The Evolution of 'North' and 'South': Settlement and Slavery on America's Sectional Border, 1650–1810" (Ph.D. diss., University of Pennsylvania, 1993), 300–302. For new family connections that also incorporated memories of the past, see Juliet E. K. Walker, *Free Frank: A Black Pioneer on the Antebellum Frontier* (Lexington, Ky., 1983), 7, 11, 24–25.

12. Ellen Eslinger, "The Beginnings of Afro-American Christianity among Kentucky Baptists," paper presented to The Newberry Library, 1996.

nonthreatening, again recalling the pioneer seaboard. Some frontier slaves had guns; many labored alongside whites, recreating an earlier era of "sawbuck equality"; a significant minority worked together with whites in the frontier lead mines, salt licks, ironworks, and ropewalks; a few slaves even shopped in backcountry stores, purchasing goods on credit as did free consumers; and yet others fraternized openly with poor whites. In 1785 an ordinary keeper in Nashville was indicted for "allowing a number of Negroes to play at fives on the Sabbath."[13]

But the greatest homogenizer in the interior was cotton. From the beginning of the nineteenth century, when about one in ten slaves in the United States grew cotton, the proportion rose to one in three by the middle of the century. In upcountry Georgia, where Chesapeake and Lowcountry planters mingled in the late eighteenth and early nineteenth centuries, the most impressive feature of the agricultural regimen was, not the older traditions these planters incorporated, but rather the new routines they instituted. Frontier slaveowners took advantage of a new situation to organize their laborers into closely supervised gangs, work them extremely long hours, leave them little time to provide for their own subsistence, and hire them (paying cash) on Sundays for yet more field labor. Indeed, the renting of slaves seems to have been extremely common on the labor-starved frontier. Slaves from both Chesapeake and Lowcountry found the work rigorous and unremitting. Charles Ball, a former Chesapeake slave, described labor in the cotton fields as "excessive" and "incessant throughout the year." Cotton picking, while not requiring undue physical strength, demanded a measure of dexterity that Ball could never quite master. The new cotton regimen, which slaves contested and shaped, would in time do as much as any other force to create uniformity in the lives of slaves.[14]

---

13. Robert V. Haynes, *The Natchez District and the American Revolution* (Jackson, Miss., 1976), 13, 18, 30–32; Joan Wells Coward, *Kentucky in the New Republic: The Process of Constitution Making* (Lexington, Ky., 1979); Eslinger, "The Shape of Slavery on the Kentucky Frontier," *Register of Ky. Hist. Soc.*, XCII (1994), 1–23; Barnett, "The Evolution of 'North' and 'South'" (Ph.D. diss., University of Pennsylvania, 1993), 273–274; Fredrika Johanna Teute, "Land, Liberty, and Labor in the Post-Revolutionary Era: Kentucky as the Promised Land" (Ph.D. diss., The Johns Hopkins University, 1988), 209–212; Elizabeth A. Perkins, "The Consumer Frontier: Household Consumption in Early Kentucky," *JAH*, LXXVIII (1991–1992), 487–510, esp. 495–497; Anita S. Goodstein, "Black History on the Nashville Frontier, 1780–1810," *Tennessee Historical Quarterly*, XXXVIII (1979), 401–420.

14. Joseph P. Reidy, "Obligation and Right: Patterns of Labor, Subsistence, and Exchange in the Cotton Belt of Georgia, 1790–1860," in Ira Berlin and Philip D. Morgan, eds., *Cultivation and Culture: Labor and the Shaping of Slave Life in the Americas* (Charlottesville, Va., 1993), 138–154; Steven F. Miller, "Plantation Labor Organization and Slave Life on the Cotton Frontier: The Alabama-Mississippi Black Belt, 1815–1840," ibid., 155–169; John

Even as slaves forged a national subculture, they retained allegiance to distinct regional cultures. Their American experience, particularly in the eighteenth century but also beyond, was profoundly regional. Through events such as the Revolution and westward migration, together with long-range demographic, economic, and social developments, a new people gradually came into being, a new people for whom after many generations in North America the most formative experience would be America itself.

Campbell, "As 'A Kind of Freeman'?: Slaves' Market-Related Activities in the South Carolina Up Country, 1800–1860," ibid., 243–274; Robert William Fogel, *Without Consent or Contract: The Rise and Fall of American Slavery* (New York, 1989), 30.

Acknowledgments

I know many will describe this book as long-awaited. I apologize for its slow appearance, but hope that the final product, which would have been weaker had I published it earlier, will seem worthwhile. Because this book has been so long in the making, I have accumulated many debts, not all of which I can ever hope to repay. To list all of those who have helped me would trespass on the patience of an already overburdened reader. To those who have assisted me, you know who you are, and I am grateful. To any whose feelings are hurt by omission, please forgive the oversight.

But I must thank the many archivists and librarians who have facilitated my research. Particularly helpful to me, and going back in some cases many years, were Nicholas Olsberg, Alexia Halsey, and Charles Lesser at the South Carolina Department of Archives and History, Allen Stokes at the University of South Carolina, Gene Waddell, David Moltke-Hansen, and Alex Moore at the South Carolina Historical Society. Also solicitous were the staffs at the Virginia State Library, the Virginia Historical Society, the University of Virginia Library, the Colonial Williamsburg Foundation Research Department, the Duke University Library, the Southern Historical Collection at the University of North Carolina, Chapel Hill, the North Carolina Division of Archives and History, the Library of Congress, the British Library, the British Public Record Office, and a number of other local libraries and archives too numerous to mention.

Many friends and acquaintances have read parts of my work and have offered useful advice and criticism. I single out for special thanks Tom Doerflinger, Roger Ekirch, Stan Engerman, Eugene Genovese, the late Herbert Gutman, Jerry Handler, Rachel Klein, Drew McCoy, Jim Merrell, Mick Nicholls, Pete Ripley, Jim Sidbury, Scott Strickland, George Terry, and Danny Vickers. I know less well Sidney Mintz and Bernard Bailyn, two scholars not often linked together, but they have both helped me in their different ways, particularly by allowing me to see how history and anthropology can be graciously and powerfully written. Ira Berlin and Richard Dunn read an early version of the whole manuscript and provided invaluable commentary.

I am grateful for the financial support I have received, most notably fellowships from Flinders University of South Australia (where Paul Bourke welcomed me with open arms and a mean tennis game), the (now) Omohundro Institute of Early American History and Culture (a fellowship funded by the Colonial Williamsburg Foundation through the good offices of Cary Carson), the Charles Warren Center at Harvard University (where Bernard Bailyn was an exemplary director), and the National Endowment for the Humanities. I also received travel grants from the Central Research Fund of the University of

London, the Twenty-seven Foundation of the Institute of Historical Research, and the American Association for State and Local History.

Two people have stood by me steadfastly. The first, Jack P. Greene, encouraged me to spend time at The Johns Hopkins University when I was a graduate student and, later, Andrew Mellon teaching fellow. Jack, together with his students and colleagues at Hopkins, was an admirable mentor. I have never ceased to admire Jack's enthusiasm, energy, boundless knowledge, and elephantine memory. Thad Tate has been my other staunch supporter and ally. Ever since I was a fellow and, later, editor of publications at the Institute of Early American History and Culture, Thad has provided calm and wise counsel. The advice, loyalty, and example of these two historians mean more to me than they know.

I have benefited greatly from my association with the Institute of Early American History and Culture, my spiritual home in the United States, to which I have returned. I first met David Ammerman in Williamsburg, we later became colleagues, and then much later he agreed to come out of retirement (as an editor) to shape an unwieldy manuscript. He did an excellent job of coaxing and cajoling me to make it more readable. Although he might still have some doubts about the result, I value his unfailing assistance and close friendship. Other Institute staff, most notably Fredrika Teute and Gil Kelly, provided excellent help at critical stages. Particular mention should go to Laura Jones Dooley, who copyedited meticulously.

I owe my greatest debt to my family. My parents, Edwin and Patricia, have supported me generously through thick and thin. My sons, Gareth and Matthew, have always been a source of pride and joy. My wife, Barbara, whom I met at Cambridge so many years ago, has enriched my life beyond measure. I dedicate this book to her as a token of my appreciation, a poor reward for all she has done for me.

Index

Aberdeen (slave), 528
Abraham (foreman), 327
Abraham (old slave), 337
Abraham (sailor), 341
Abraham (slave), 286
Abraham (slave), 361
Abraham (slave), 531
Abraham (waterman), 340
Abraham (woodworker), 350
Accomac Co., Va., 14
Adair, Douglass, 404
Adam (George Ball's slave), 513
Adam (slave), 213
Adam, Guinea (slave), 185
Adam, Mary (slave), 513
Affey (or Occoe) (African), 455
African Americans. *See* Creoles
African influences: on naming, 21, 451–452, 454–455; on tobacco pipes, 21–22; on ranching, 53; on housing, 118–120; on plants and cuisine, 141–142; on sowing patterns, 150–151; on rice cultivation, 178, 182–183; on skills, 216, 232–236; on fishing, 242–244; on quilting, 248–249; on marketing, 251; on animal tales, 335; on lack of baptisms, 423; on conch, 432; on gaming, 461, 595; on marriage, 534–535; on kinship beliefs, 549, 553–555; on language, 560–573, 575, 578–580; on music, 581–591, 594; on festivals, 595; on athletic contests, 596; on gestures, 597–598; on clothing, 598–600; on hairstyles, 603, 605; on poisoning, 617–618, 620; on magic, 622; on Christianity, 631–638; on attitudes toward the dead, 640–644; on evangelicalism, 644–647; on religion, 657
African slaves, xviii, 2–4, 13, 19–20; naming of, 21, 451–452, 454–455; and pipes, 21–22; and livestock, 53; immigration of, 58–80, 85, 421–422, 460; in the population, 59–62, 80, 95; ethnicity of, 62–77, 455–458; suicide by, 65–66, 456, 590, 641; sales of, 77–79; housing for, 105; yards of, 123; hunting by, 138; and rice techniques, 157–158, 182–183; and tobacco, 189; and head carrying, 200; and time reckoning, 201–202; as domestics, 214; and drivers, 222–224; as sawyers, 228; as blacksmiths, 232; as basketmakers, 232–233; as potters, 235; as woodworkers, 236; as watermen, 243–244; as hawkers, 251; as runaways, 301, 305, 307, 446–451; and transmission of disease, 323, 444–445; resistance by, 330; religious conversion of, 426; and creoles, 459–463, 497; family life of, 503, 505, 523, 530, 535; and languages, 560–566, 575, 577–578; and music, 581–582, 588, 590, 592; and gesture, 597; clothing of, 599; hairstyles of, 603, 605–606; jewelry of, 607; demeanor of, 608; stories of, 609; religion of, 610–612, 630–635, 642; poisoning among, 614; as doctors, 625–626; in late 18th century, 661, 663. *See also* Angola; Asante; Bambara; Bance Island, Sierra Leone; Bight of Benin; Bight of Biafra; Calabar; Chamba; Dyalonke; Ewe; Fulla; Grain Coast; Hausa; Igbos; Kisi; Kongo; Koromanti; Mandingo; Mende; Senegambia; Shipmates; Sierra Leone; Whydah; Windward Coast; Yoruba
African slave trade, 3–4, 58–80, 85, 421–422, 442–446, 448–449, 453
Age: of African immigrants, 70–73; and plantation pyramids, 85–86, 88–91; of skilled workers, 212–218; of drivers, 222–223; of domestics, 246–248, 252–253; and the elderly, 334–337, 348–349, 476; and generations, 473–475; of husbands and wives, 534. *See also* Slave children
Aggy (domestic), 409
Aggy (slave), 247
Aggy, Mammy (slave), 355
Agriculture: diversification of, 5, 45–58, 162–163, 170–175, 178, 206, 361, 662; state of, 27–28. *See also* Corn; Cotton; Indigo; Labor; Rice; Tobacco; Wheat

Aikman, Louisa Susanna, 342
Akin, James, 248, 338
Alabama, 197, 668, 669
Albemarle Co., Va., 168, 465
Albemarle Sound, 413
Alcohol: and interracial drinking, 9; trade in, 16, 131; as reward, 142; excess of, 252, 313, 352, 471; fondness for, 297; and dramshops, 308; and house slaves, 355–357; access to, 413–416, 584, 618; at funerals, 641. *See also* Rum
Alexandria, Va., 201, 232, 252, 314, 372, 409, 419, 612
All Hallow's Parish, Md., 421
Allston, Joseph, 156, 492
Alston, John, 475
Amelia Co., Va., 31, 297, 370, 472, 520, 556
American Revolution, xvii, xviii, 39; and slave trade, 62; and cloth production, 247–248; and master-slave relations, 259, 280n, 283–285, 290, 375, 384–385; and fears of interracial uprisings, 308–309; rumors during, 321; watermen during, 341–342; skilled slaves during, 347; unusual opportunities in, 366; and religious activities, 425–426, 649–650; slaves' communication in, 476; free black loyalist in, 486; expansion of slavery and freedom during, 665–666; lessons from, 667–668
Amherst Co., Va., 303, 396, 448, 480
Ammon (slave), 363
Amory, Rev. Isaac, 422
Amos (slave), 414
Amy (slave), 461
Anaka (slave), 355–356
Anburey, Thomas, 136, 618
Andrew (cooper), 222
Andrew (driver), 225
Anglicans: and murder of slave, 14; on household slavery, 274; and sex with slaves, 401–402, 406–407; and conversion, 420–423, 459–460; on monogamy, 536, 553; on language proficiency, 564, 573–574; on music and dance, 582, 587; on slave religion, 631–632, 637, 647–649. *See also* Religion
Angola: as plantation name, 20; Africans from, 62–64, 65, 67, 68, 72–73; passage times from, 69; runaway slaves from, 228, 446–449, 456; and pottery, 235; market woman from, 251; slaves from, 453–455, 458, 462; washerwoman from, 494; languages of, 563, 565, 567, 575; and clothing, 598. *See also* Kongo
Animals: in diet, 136–140, 151; analogy to humans of, 271–272, 295; tales about, 462–463, 609, 636. *See also* Dogs; Horses; Livestock
Annapolis, Md., 95, 252, 621, 633
Anne Arundel Co., Md., 131, 166, 190, 231, 551
Anne Arundel manor, Md., 111
Anthony (African), 457
Anthony (old slave), 550
Apalachicola, Fla., 483
Argyle (slave), 464
Armistead, Lucy, 392
Aron (slave), 282
Asante, 581, 587, 636
Asbury, Francis: on landscape, 32; on master, 288, 428; and Harry, 430, 655; on slaves and masters, 433, 435, 436, 645; and Sancho, 635
Ash, Richard Cochran, 222
Ashepoo, 49, 481. *See also* Austin, George
Ashepoo River, 159, 339
Ashley River, 159, 252, 381, 496, 521, 529
Ashwell, Anne, 304
Athy (slave), 291
Atkinson, Roger, 170
Attmore, William, 416–417, 458
August (slave), 528
Augusta Co., Va., 486
Austin, George, 49, 157, 184, 223, 454, 653
Axtell, Daniel, 7
Ayres, Robert, 402, 429

Bacchus (African), 460–461
Bacchus (hawker), 251
Bacchus (runaway), 541
Bacchus (waiting man), 246
Backcountry (S.C.), 41, 75, 76, 304–305, 309, 391, 521, 574
Bacon, Rev. Thomas, 274, 587
Bacon's Rebellion, 9, 308

Bagge, Edmund, 220
Bahamas, 657
Bakongo. *See* Angola; Kongo
Balafo, 588. *See also* Music
Ball, Charles: on meat, 137; and hunting, 138; on masters, 269, 298, 318; on theft, 366; on slave purchasing, 375; and Africans, 461–463, 609; family of, 509, 514–515, 537, 539; on family life, 535, 541; on hairstyle, 604; and religion, 622, 634, 635, 641–642; on cotton, 671
Ball, Elias, 270, 361, 362, 453, 492
Ball, Elisha, 454
Ball, John, 291, 363, 378
Ball, Joseph, 106, 113, 122, 132, 282, 329, 509
Ball, Spencer, 118
Ball family, 90, 412, 546, 550
Baltimore, Lord, 10
Baltimore, Md., 252, 372, 486, 665
Baltimore Company ironworks, 230, 535, 537, 544
Baltimore Co., Md., 174, 209, 230–231, 380, 434, 621
Bambara, 53, 563, 577
Bance Island, Sierra Leone, 243
Banister, John, 128
Banjos, 474, 583, 587. *See also* Music
Banneker, Benjamin, 486
Baptists: and scruples about slavery, 17; ministers of, 85, 566; as slaves, 297, 427, 430, 435–436, 552, 639; as masters, 354; and church discipline, 368, 369, 410, 416–417, 420, 431, 652; and proselytization of slaves, 425, 427–428; opposition of, to slavery, 430–431, 433–434; and black preachers, 652–656, 669. *See also* Religion
Barbados, 571, 595
Barber, Billy (slave), 536
Barclay, James, 457–458, 531–533, 569, 581, 583–584
Bart (slave), 475
Bartram, John: on landscape, 28, 32; on cowpens, 52–53; on Koromantees, 66; on slave housing, 121; and rice, 148, 157; and ditching, 196; and poisoning, 618
Bartram, William, 28, 100–101, 138, 397, 590

Baskets, 183n, 199, 232–233, 362
Bastian (slave), 482
Bauer, Carl, 567
Bayard, Francis, 406
Beamer, James, 80
Beatty, Adam, 198
Beaufort, S.C., 367, 397, 414, 521, 605
Beck (slave), 547
Beckey (slave), 462
Beckford, Peter, 177
Bedford Co., Va., 403, 511
Bell, Jane, 496
Bell, Joseph, 412
Bella (slave), 250
Bellinger, Edmund, 53
Belvidere plantation, 246
Ben (African), 457
Ben (African, old), 461
Ben (slave), 214
Ben (slave), 411
Ben (waiting man), 245
Benedict, David, 652
Benehan, Richard, 475
Benni. *See* Sesame
Berkeley Co., Va., 431
Bermuda, 103
Bermuda Hundred, Va., 77
Bernard, John, 417, 587
Bernstein, Basil, 578
Berry, Samuel (slave), 592
Berwick (slave), 537–538
Bess (nanny), 325
Bess (runaway), 537–538
Bethesda Orphanage (Ga.), 253, 337, 348, 650
Betty (African), 449
Betty (mulatto), 462
Betty (runaway), 541
Beverley, William, 85, 127
Bight of Benin, 63, 66, 68, 69, 72–73
Bight of Biafra, 62, 64–65, 67–69, 72–73
Billie (ship carpenter), 230
Billy (carpenter), 351
Billy (foundry worker), 346
Billy (indigo maker), 164, 347
Billy (mulatto), 289–290
Billy (slave), 214–215
Binsaw (slave), 448

INDEX : 677

Bishop, Jacob, 430, 654
Black River, 149, 542
Blair, James, 258
Blair, John, 537
Blakely, George, 314
Bloom Hill plantation, 313
Blount, John G., 292
Blue, Stepney (slave), 496
Boats. *See* Transportation
Bob (ferryman), 460
Bob (slave), 361
Bob (waiting boy), 543–544
Bobb (slave), 415
Body: and head carrying, 198–200; and manner of walking, 200, 596; and athletic contests, 596; and gestures, 597–599; and hairstyles, 603–607; and beards, 606; and jewelry, 607; and evangelical behavior, 645–646. *See also* Clothing
Boehm, Rev. Henry, 576, 646, 655
Bolling, John, 513
Bolling, William, 327
Bolzius, Johann Martin: on population, 39; on housing, 106, 110, 120; on clothing, 126, 133, 598; on diet, 135, 138; on rice cultivation, 148, 186; on work, 196, 198; on slaves' money, 359; on interracial sex, 399, 407; on slave families, 498; on Africans' suicide, 641
Bond, James, 409
Boone, Daniel, 661
Boone, Thomas, 266
Bosman, William, 611
Botetourt, Lord, 592
Botetourt Co., Va., 277
Botsford, Edmund, 186, 202, 383
Boucher, Jonathan, 587
Bourne, Andrew, 315
Boyd, Robert, 338
Brathewaite, Anne, 415
Braudel, Fernand, 149
Bray, James, 219
Breacky (slave), 370
Breckenridge family, 669
Breen, T. H., 13, 20
Bremo Bluff plantation, 119
Brickell, John, 531, 625

Brissot de Warville, Jean-Pierre, 109
Bristol (African), 460
Bristol (runaway), 292
Bristol (woodworker), 349
Bristow, Robert, 332, 444
Brockenbough, Mr., 430
Broughton, Thomas, 409
Brown, William, 375
Brown Fellowship Society, 497, 664
Bruce, Philip, 433–434
Brunswick Co., Va., 540, 653
Brunswick Methodist circuit, 428
Bryan, Andrew, 424, 654, 655
Bryan, Hugh, 423–424, 647
Bryan, Jonathan, 138, 423–424
Bryan family, 591
Buckingham Co., Va., 427
Buckley, Thomas E., 403
Buckner, George, 392
Bull, Mary, 516, 553
Burck, Benjamin, 314
Burnaby, Andrew, 263, 418, 639
Burnett, John, 425, 650
Burwell, James, 556
Burwell family, 10, 21, 522
Bush River Baptist Church, 656
Butler, Nell, 10–11, 523
Butler, Pierce, 149, 156, 291, 517
Butler, Thomas (slave), 584
Butler, William, 87, 150–151, 156
Byrd, Maria, 284–285
Byrd, Mary Willing, 322
Byrd, William, I, 444, 479
Byrd, William, II: on diet, 134; on tobacco, 177; and ironworks, 230; on family, 268, 274, 277; on punishment, 271; on health, 322; house slaves of, 355–356; on effect of slaves, 379; on rebellion, 388
Byrd, William, III, 244, 514, 547

Cabell, William, 247, 361
Cabell family, 669
Caesar (African), 484
Caesar (basketmaker), 233
Caesar (creole), 537
Caesar (free African), 625
Caesar (hawker), 251
Caesar (old slave), 411

Caesar (runaway), 304
Caesar (sawyer), 228
Caesar (slave), 648
Calabar, 62, 65, 69, 223, 447, 448, 462, 596
Calabash, 142
Calvert, Benedict, 164
Calvert, Charles, 621
Calvert Co., Md., 166, 402, 461, 509
Cambridge (waterman), 536
Camden, S.C., 238
Campbell, Colin, 522
Campbell Co., Va., 231
Canoes. *See* Transportation
Cape Fear, N.C., 367, 548, 644
Caribbean, 93, 100, 190, 316, 474, 597. *See also* Barbados; Jamaica; Saint Christopher; Saint Domingue; West Indies
Carolina (slave), 298
Caroline Co., Va., 314, 342, 392, 427, 489, 529, 540, 616, 625
Carr, Peter, 404
Carroll, Charles, 214, 230, 546, 551
Carter, Benjamin, 403–404, 418
Carter, Betty (free black), 486
Carter, Charles, 539
Carter, Harry, 123, 418
Carter, James (slave), 392, 543
Carter, John, 65, 71, 169, 281, 530–531
Carter, Landon: slave housing of, 109, 111, 117; and clothing, 128, 131, 247; and provisioning, 136, 359; and tobacco, 166, 168, 169; and wheat, 171–172, 174; and ganging, 188, 192; conversations of, with slaves, 192–193; and health, 195, 322; slave foremen of, 219, 220, 343; skilled slaves of, 228, 236, 349, 351, 525; on leniency toward slaves, 265; as patriarch, 278, 280–281; as sentimentalist, 293, 359; and Nassau, 312–313, 324, 356–358, 415; and overseer, 314; elderly slaves of, 334–336; runaways of, 378, 390, 465, 475; punishment by, 383; and slaves' access to guns, 390; and slaves' access to alcohol, 415; and slaves' residential loyalties, 475; and slave families, 513, 525, 544, 547, 551–552; and slave names, 550, 555, 557; and slave speech, 572

Carter, Robert, of Nomini Hall: on slaves' privacy, 113; on skilled slaves, 119, 214, 347, 351, 365, 545; and provisioning, 134, 360; on river traffic, 239; on fishing, 242; and textile production, 247; as patriarch, 277, 283–284; and slave's posture, 299; and capture of whites, 312; and health, 322–324, 628, 629; and overseer, 327, 332; elderly slaves of, 335–337; sloop of, 339; domestics of, 354; and slaves' trading, 370; interest of, in mulatto, 400; and recreational activities, 418; religion of, 426; and divisions among slaves, 472; and slave families, 531, 539, 544–545, 549, 551–552; and single male slaves, 535; and slave surnames, 556; on funerals, 641
Carter, Robert "King": on Africans, 65; slave housing of, 114, 117, 122–123; and clothing, 127; and slave occupations, 207–208, 219; punishment by, 267; and overseer, 332; elderly slaves of, 334–335, 459; and purchases of slaves, 379–380; mulatto slaves of, 401; runaway of, 447; and African-creole tensions, 459; and slave–free black relations, 496; and slave families, 503–504, 513, 554; and slave names, 550
Carter, Robert Wormeley, 113, 166, 214–215, 364, 365
Carter's Grove, 522
Carts. *See* Transportation
Cary, Archibald, 388
Cary, Edward, 290, 515
Cassidy, Frederic, 571
Castiglioni, Luigi, 141, 163, 272, 419
Catawbas, 368n, 478, 484
Cate (slave), 512
Catesby, Mark, 134, 141, 150–151
Cato (slave), 298
Catoctin iron furnace, 144, 347
Cattell, Mrs., 406
Cattle. *See* Livestock
Caw, Dr. David, 363
Caw, Thomas, 516
Cecil Co., Md., 421
Chamba, 64. *See also* Gold Coast
Channing, John, 129, 278, 291, 549
Charity (slave), 291

INDEX : 679

Charles (African), 448
Charles (African), 457
Charles (fiddler), 419
Charles (mulatto), 201–202
Charles (slave), 10
Charles City Co., Va., 85, 296
Charles Co., Md., 5, 261, 266, 502, 512, 515, 523, 619, 627, 629
Charleston, S.C.: slaves in, 20; as center, 34; small plantations about, 40, 42, 47; small households in, 41, 42, 47; specialized units near, 55; Africans imported into, 62, 76–77, 444–446, 449; merchant of, 65, 70, 71, 76; countryside around, 84, 338–340, 342, 529; slave housing in, 107; and slave clothing, 132, 601; master in, 183, 344; domestics in, 213, 382; specialized crafts of, 229, 232, 362; marketing in, 235, 250–252, 371; and watercraft services, 238–239; and fishermen, 240–241; kitchens of, 245; slave trips to and from, 280, 323, 357, 364, 381, 536; runaways to and from, 299, 548, 549, 552; slaves and plain folk in, 305–306, 311, 392–393; watch in, 308, 311, 414; fears of insurrection in, 309, 389; hospitals in, 323; self-hiring in, 352; free blacks in, 365, 486, 487, 493, 495; access to guns in, 391; interracial sex in, 407; disorderly houses in, 413–414; and dances, 408, 419, 584; religion in, 424–425, 435–436, 650; Africans and creoles in, 461–462, 466; fighting in, 471; free mulattoes in, 488, 491, 495, 496; slave families in, 517, 542; music in, 590; swaggering slave in, 596; funerals in, 641; insurrectionary scare near, 651
Charleston District, S.C., 373
Charley (slave), 298
Charlotte Co., Va., 248, 426, 538
Charlottesville, Va., 360
Charter group, 19
Chastellux, marquis de, 242
Chavis, John, 632
Cheehaw, S.C., 552
Cheraws District, S.C., 456, 539
Cherokees, 456, 483, 484
Chesapeake region: defined, xvii

Chesterfield Co., Va., 231, 427, 513–514, 528–529, 612, 652, 656
Chickahominy River, 448
Chickasaws, 483
Chloe (slave), 249
Chowan Co., N.C., 369
Christ Church Parish, S.C., 42–43, 108, 113, 228
Christmas (slave), 286, 415
Chubb, Martha, 248
Clarke, Sarah, 400
Clarke, Thomas (mulatto), 400–401
Clarkson, Levinius, 71
Clayton, John, 412, 619
Cleland, Janet, 269
Clifts plantation, 105
Clothing: and cheapness, 14, 102, 126–127, 262; supplies of, 125–127, 280, 290; irregular combinations of, 128–129; and footwear, 129; and headgear, 129–130, 599–600; standardization of, 130, 144; of skilled slaves, 130–131, 144, 246, 355; cast-off, 131–132; scantiness of, 132–133, 372, 398–399, 598–599; making of, 246–249, 361; purchases of, 369, 374, 375; and finery, 376, 396, 601–603; reward of, 385, 470; inventiveness in, 598–599. See also Body
Clusteny, Henry, 409
Coachman, William, 227
Cochran, Robert, 467
Cocke, Thomas, 9
Cockfighting, 418. See also Fowl
Coke, Thomas, 288, 655
Colbert, William, 428–431, 645–646, 655
Cole, Thomas, Jr. (free mulatto), 488
Cole, Thomas, Sr. (free mulatto), 486–487
Colhoun, John Ewing, 470, 616
Colleton, John, 328
Colleton Co., S.C., 368
Colono ware, 234–235. See also Pottery
Combahee River, 110, 157, 159, 306, 367
Comingtee plantation, 453, 454. See also Ball, Elias
Compton, William, 314
Congaree River, 136, 248
Congarees, S.C., 398
Congo. See Kongo

Conjuring, 612, 616–617, 622, 629. *See also* Divination; Magic; Obeah; Poisoning; Sorcery
Connolly, John, 569
Conspiracies: in 17th century, 21; in South Carolina, 56, 186, 239, 303, 389, 474; in American Revolution, 341–342, 495; in Maryland, 460; and betrayal, 470–471; and Gabriel, 471, 533, 667; in Virginia, 277, 473, 479, 493, 532, 656; and religious inspiration, 424–425, 648–651. *See also* Rebellions; Resistance; Stono rebellion
Convicts, 301, 306
Conway, Col. Edwin, 427
Cooke, Henry (free black), 493
Cooper, Ezekiel, 431, 435
Cooper River, 118, 156, 159, 225, 239, 266, 303, 371, 521, 583
Corbin, Richard, 168
Cormack, Alice, 304
Corn, 48–50, 122, 134–136, 362–364, 368–370. *See also* Wheat
Cornwallis, Lord, 277
Coromanti. *See* Koromanti
Cotton, 179–180, 361, 368, 372, 521, 671
Cousens, Frank (free mulatto), 493
Cousins, John (free mulatto), 488
Cox, Charles (slave), 131, 132
Cox, Thomas, 309
Crafts, 53–55, 123. *See also* Slave artisans
Craven Co., S.C., 491
Creeks, 483, 654
Creole language. *See* Language
Creoles: in 17th century, 3–4; and natural increase, 79–95; as skilled slaves, 216–217; as runaways, 305, 307, 460–462, 464–468; and Africans, 454, 459–463; African names of, 454; familiarity of, with whites, 463–467; divisions among, 468–475, 477; cohesion among, 472–477, 497; language of, 566, 573–575, 577; music of, 592–593; clothing of, 600–602; hairstyles of, 603–604; and beards, 606; and jewelry, 607; and sorcery, 623; and Christianity, 653–654; in late 18th century, 661, 663
Cresswell, Nicholas, 396, 409, 587, 590
Crèvecoeur, M. G. J. de, 34, 267, 272, 540

Crokatt, James, 161
Cromwell (slave), 220
Crow, Hugh, 569
Cudgo (slave), 252
Cudjoe (old slave), 335, 474
Cuffee (slave), 527
Cuffy (slave), 225
Cullins, Nathan, 302
Culpeper Co., Va., 427
Culture: defined, xx
Cumba (slave), 448
Cumberland (slave), 500
Cumberland Co., Va., 202, 369, 465, 480, 489, 624
Cumberland Island, Ga., 380
Cupid (brickmaker), 348
Cupid (slave), 412
Cussitaws, 484
Cussos, 482
Custis, John, 127, 140, 187, 212, 253, 323, 402, 528
Cuttino family, 286
Cypress plantation, S.C., 133
Cyrus (slave), 598

Dabney, Charles, 361, 474, 627
Dacon plantation, 337
Daingerfield, William, 452
Dalby, David, 561
Dances: in Charleston, 408; in Chesapeake towns, 416, 494; and cultural diffusion, 418–420; and Kongo, 456; in the Lowcountry, 524; at marriages, 532; cultural significance of, 581–588, 592–593; at funerals, 644. *See also* Music
Dandy (free mulatto), 492
Daniel (carpenter), 323
Daniel (slave), 469
Daniel, John, 229
Daphne (domestic), 249
Dauber (colored), 424
David (chairmaker), 228
David (slave), 469
Davidson Co., Tenn., 670
Davies, Rev. Samuel, 426–427, 576
Davis, Captain, 408
Davis, John, 121, 325, 355, 407, 570, 573, 576
Davy (foreman), 343

INDEX : 681

Davy (slave), 528
Dean Hall plantation, 373
De Brahm, William, 35, 637
Defoe, Daniel, 275
Delaware, 641
Dembo (slave), 343
De St. Julien, Benjamin, 454
DeSaussure family, 525, 626
Dew, Charles, 231
Diamond (slave), 340
Dick (Indian), 481
Dick (Indian), 482
Dick (old slave), 118, 419
Dick (slave), 314
Dick, Alexander (mulatto), 408
Dick, George, 408
Dick, Jenny (free black), 408
Dickie, Rev. Adam, 422
Dickinson, Thomas Cooper, 313
Dido (slave), 453
Diet, 85, 92–93, 102–103, 134–145, 544. *See also* Population; Stature
Digges, Dudley, 320
Digges, Ignatius, 215
Dinah (slave), 467
Dinwiddie Co., Va., 535, 615
Dishman, Peter, 512
Dismal Swamp Land Company, 142, 219, 361, 526–527
Ditcher, Jack, 667
Divination, 616, 624, 630. *See also* Conjuring; Magic; Obeah; Poisoning; Sorcery
Dobbs Co., N.C., 618
Dogs, 138, 286, 299, 331, 375, 390, 412
Donaldson, Jesse (free mulatto), 489
Donaldson, Sarah (free mulatto), 489
Dorchester Co., Md., 308
Dorinda (slave), 453
Douglass, Frederick, 523
Downes, Richard, 55
Downman, Capt. Robert, 220, 331
Dozier, Richard, 430, 655
Drayton, Charles, 233, 302, 331
Drayton, John, 57, 151, 156, 185, 186, 375, 393–394
Drayton, William, 382
Drayton Hall, 302
Drighouse, Azaricum (free mulatto), 486

Drums, 420, 450, 582–587, 589, 593. *See also* Music
Dubose, Samuel, 163
Dudley, John, 314
Duff (slave), 475
Dulany, Daniel, 514
Dumfries, Va., 372
Dunmore, Lord, 283, 388, 493
Dunn, Richard S., 490
Dupont, John, 229
Dutarque, Lewis, 373
Dyalonke, 457
Dyssli, Samuel, 95

Eastern Shore: free blacks on, 16, 485; and grains, 47, 175; and white-black relations, 302, 304; and master-slave exchange, 364, 627; guns among slaves on, 390, 465; and holidays, 413; and dance, 419, 592; slave of, 464; and Indians, 480; slave families on, 554; and purchase of slave's freedom, 654
East Florida: and slave women, 94, 526; indigo in, 162, 163; and tasking, 180; and search for slaves, 182; slave assessment of, 184; and gardens, 186; and slave skills, 216, 348; and search for overseers, 221; sawyers in, 228; and application of the law, 266; dangers in, 279; planters in, 378, 397; interracial sex in, 407, 410; and slave families, 508, 517, 530; slaves sent to, 563; poisoning in, 615
Ebba (old slave), 249
Ebba (young slave), 249
Eddis, William, 85, 95
Edenton, N.C., 413
Edgefield District, S.C., 235, 419–420
Edisto River, 159
Edmondson, John, 114
Edwards, Bryan, 575
Edwards, John, 424
Elizabeth (slave), 409
Elizabeth City Co., Va., 125; and hiring, 175, 352; and slave trials, 273, 468, 472; and slave property, 375; and murder, 396; and disorderly house, 415; and Anglican minister, 423; and divisions of slaves, 515
Elizabeth River, 9

Elliott, Barnard, 393–394
Elliott, Jehu, 223, 554
Elliott, Thomas, 454, 470
Elsey (slave), 250
English, John, 153
Ennals, William, 364, 627
Equiano, Olaudah, 456–457, 581, 599, 632–633, 640
Erskine, David M., 272
Essex Co., Va.: free black in, 15; corn production in, 48; slave households in, 94; bedding in, 114; slave from, 198, 587; slave overseer in, 220; attacks on whites in, 313; preachers in, 428, 430; and divisions of slaves, 512; slave surnames in, 556; and slave doctor, 627
Essig, James D., 434
Esther (slave), 543
Ethnicity. *See* African slaves; Angola; Asante; Bambara; Chamba; Dyalonke; Ewe; Fulla; Germans; Indians; Igbos; Irish; Kongo; Koromanti; Scots; Swiss
Etiwan, 483
Ettwein, John, 422
Eugene (slave), 355
Evangelicalism: 287–288, 420, 423–436, 644–648, 649–657. *See also* Baptists; Methodists; Moravians; Presbyterians; Religion
Evans, Joshua, 85
Evans-Pritchard, E. E., 620
Eve (slave), 612
Eveleigh, Samuel, 482
Ewald, Johann, 567
Ewe, 622
Exeter (slave), 382

Fabian, James, 55
Fairfax Co., Va., 118, 493, 655
Fanny (slave), 510
Farrar, Benjamin, 64, 661
Farquharson, John, 28
Fauquier, Francis, 281, 498, 512–513
Fauquier Co., Va., 489, 592, 616
Fayette Co., Ky., 669
Fearson, William, 591
Feltman, William, 140, 396, 398
Fenwicke, Edward, 228, 417

Ferguson, Henry, 180
Ferguson, Leland, 234
Ferguson's Swamp, S.C., 483
Fiddles, 418–419, 591–593. *See also* Music
Fidler, Noah, 645
Finlay, Hugh, 238, 320
Firth, Raymond, xxiii
Fisher, George, 369
Fithian, Philip Vickers, 117–118, 122–123, 193, 324, 335, 360, 418, 544, 637
Fitzhugh, George, 296
Fitzhugh, Henry, 85
Fitzhugh, William, 80, 401, 512, 556
Flax, 246–247, 361–362
Fleetsbay plantation, 332
Fletchall, Col. Thomas, 309
Flood, William, 493
Florida, 450, 470, 642, 657. *See also* East Florida; Saint Augustine, East Fla.
Flowers, Simon (Indian servant), 481
Flud, William, 447
Fluvanna Co., Va., 119
Fogel, Robert, 190
Folklore, 462–463, 609, 636–637
Fontaine, Rev. Peter, 85
Fooser (slave), 452
Ford, Timothy, 30, 121, 244, 379
Forest quarter, 472
Fork quarter, 474–475
Fortune (slave), 478
Four Holes, S.C., 536
Four Mile Tree plantation, 119
Fowl: and exchange for alcohol, 131, 415; in diet, 139–140; and raising of, 186, 249, 282; trade in, 359–364, 369–372, 374; present of, 474. *See also* Cockfighting; Livestock
Foxcroft, Bridget, 15
Francis, Warwick (slave), 393–394
Frank (runaway), 480
Frank (slave), 469
Frank (slave), 531
Frank (waiting man), 604
Frederick Co., Md., 538
Fredericksburg, Va., 170, 246, 252, 320, 370, 372, 415
Free blacks: in 17th century, 3, 11–12, 14; population of, 15–16, 489–491; in early

South Carolina, 17–18; and support of runaways, 304; as watermen, 341–342; passing as, 349, 350, 461, 483; and self-purchase, 352, 365, 373, 374, 486, 654; and trade with slaves, 369; bequests to, 408–409; and Indians, 479, 480, 484; and separation from slaves, 485–489; and ties with slaves, 489–497; as doctors, 625, 629; and insurrection, 648–649; in late 18th century, 666. *See also* Manumission

Frost, Mrs., 408
Fulla, 606
Fullerton, John, 227

Gabriel: and conspiracy, 471, 533, 667
Gadsden, Christopher, 366
Gaillard family, 550
Galphin, George, 654
Galt, Dr., 628
Gambia. *See* Senegambia
Gang system, 172–174, 179, 187–194, 668, 671. *See also* Task system
Garden, Dr. Alexander, 45, 148, 149, 153, 155, 159, 162, 240, 248, 322, 324, 444, 617–618, 625
Garden, Rev. Alexander, 106, 457
Gardens, 28, 141–142, 186–187, 193–194. *See also* Yards
Garretson, Freeborn, 428, 434, 646
Garrison plantation, 633
Gellner, Ernest, 560
Gender. *See* Sex; Slave boys; Slave girls; Slave men; Slave women
Genovese, Eugene, 194, 258, 313, 353, 395, 557
George (carpenter), 544
George (cooper), 349
George (creole), 464
George (driver), 223
George (foreman), 188, 343
George (indigo maker), 164
George (old slave), 336
George (old slave), 474
George (preacher), 650
George (slave), 370
George (waiting boy), 246
George, David (free black), 198, 192, 459, 654

George, Peter (free black), 14
Georgetown, S.C., 50, 101, 244, 286, 340, 351, 365, 435
Georgetown region, S.C., 41, 149, 185, 265, 351, 367, 415, 521, 583, 584, 596
Georgia: pottery in, 115; hunting in, 138; planters in, 179–180, 223, 476; and wood-carving traditions, 236; orphanage in, 253; slaves as property in, 294; absentee planter in, 345; payments to slaves in, 363; new plantation in, 374; during American Revolution, 384; arming slaves in, 391; interracial sex in, 406; evangelicals in, 423, 435–436; slave conflicts in, 475; runaway from, 529; slave sale to, 539; fatherhood in, 541; slave music in, 590; poisoning in, 615; obeah in, 620; and health care, 627; and Muslim slaves in, 635; slave burial in, 642, 644; upcountry of, 669
Germans, 302, 359, 432, 486, 567, 588
Gervais, John Lewis, 332
Gibb, John, 269
Gibbes, Thomas, Jr., 493
Gibbons, William, 233
Gibby (driver), 338
Gibby (slave), 550
Gibson, Gideon (free mulatto), 488
Gignilliat, Rev. James, 459
Gilbert, William, 423
Gilliat, Sy, 592
Gingaskins, 480
Gist, Christopher, 661
Glasgow (slave), 465
Glasgow (slave), 547
Glasgow (slave), 578
Glaze, Esther, 222
Glen, James, 83, 147
Glen, John, 567
Gloucester, Va., 320, 515, 654
Gloucester Co., Va., 342, 412, 421, 430, 557
Glover, Joseph, 307
Godfrey, William, 332
Godin, Benjamin, 222, 454
Godin, Isaac, 554
Godwyn, Morgan, 313
Gold Coast, 63–69, 72–73, 75–76, 581
Golightly, Culcheth, 623

Gomez, Michael A., 635
Gooch, William, 136, 262, 315
Goochland Co., Va., 108, 421, 452, 473, 488, 493
Goodbe, John (free black), 486
Goose Creek. *See* Saint James Goose Creek Parish, S.C.
Gordon, Adam, 32
Gordon, Alexander, 110, 159
Gordon, James, 139, 426, 615, 639
Gordon, Roderick, 444
Gourdin, Peter, 164, 347
Gowan, Alexander (free black), 487
Gracia Real de Santa Teresa de Mose, 450
Graeme, Mrs., 225
Graham, John, 77, 221, 343, 563
Graham, William, 315
Grain Coast, 449
Grains. *See* Corn; Rice; Wheat
Grant, James, 35, 163–164, 182, 221, 225, 266
Grasher (slave), 13
Gray, James, 154
Gray, Richard, 612
Green, John, 343
Greene, David, 325
Greene, Sarah, 493
Greenhow, John, 369
Gregory, William, 296–297
Grimball, Joshua, 455
Grimes, William, 363
Grove, William Hugh, 121, 125, 132, 134, 140
Guerard, Benjamin, 325
Guerard, John, 65, 67, 70, 76
Guilford Co., N.C., 396
Guinea, 64
Gullah, 465, 565, 567–570, 572, 575, 622, 642
Gumby family (slaves), 334–335, 360, 637
Guns: restrictions on, 8, 389–390; access to, 9, 17–18, 296, 306, 330, 386, 390–391, 398, 465; for hunting, 139, 390, 412; in rice fields, 152; celebratory firing of, 377; and maroons, 450, 465; and frontier, 671
Gutman, Herbert, 549, 551, 557, 558
Guy (slave), 415

Habersham, James, 127, 180, 285–286, 348, 532, 576
Hagar (domestic), 382

Hagar (indigo maker), 164
Halifax Co., Va., 107
Hambleton, William, 221
Hamilton, Alexander, 294
Hammett, William, 435–436
Hampton (slave), 352
Hampton, Va., 339, 464, 496, 536
Hancock, Ian, 571
Handy (slave), 307
Hannah (creole), 307
Hannah (Indian), 481
Hannibal (slave), 277
Hanover Co., Va., 140, 330, 426, 447, 529, 547
Harlitt, Peter (slave), 132
Harman, William (free black), 4, 6
Harrison, Robert Carter, 669
Harrison, Sam (slave), 426
Harrower, John, 246–247, 417, 588
Harry (carpenter), 494
Harry (fiddler), 419
Harry (free black), 491
Harry (runaway), 467
Harry (slave), 469
Harry, Doctor (free), 625
Hart, Oliver, 396
Hartley, James, 363, 626
Hartwig, Gerald, 630
Hartwood Baptist Church, 402
Hasell, Rev. Thomas, 564, 574
Haskins, Thomas, 288, 655
Hausa, 621
Haynes, Isaac, 324
Haynes, Solomon (pilot), 338
Hazard (slave), 324
Hazard, Ebenezer, 51, 132, 279, 302, 399, 408, 598
Head carrying. *See* Body
Health: in Lowcountry, 33; and black immunity, 85; and loss of work, 195; and treatment, 293, 321–325; and slave aide, 356; and inoculation against smallpox, 357; of Africans, 444–445; and Indian doctor, 483; and family traits, 513; and venereal disease, 535, 625; and folk medicine, 624–629. *See also* Slave doctors; Slave midwives; Slave mortality; Slave nurses

INDEX : 685

Hearne, John, 251
Hector (hawker), 251,
Hector (slave), 362
Hemings, Elizabeth (or Betty), 404
Hemings, Sally, 404
Hemp, 54
Henrico Co., Va., 9, 479
Henson, Josiah, 114, 121–122
Hercules (slave), 213
Herskovits, Frances, 594
Herskovits, Melville, 559, 594, 612, 640
Hessians, 567, 588
Hext, Alexander, 222
High Hills of Santee, S.C., 313
Hill, Christopher, 275
Hill, Eliza, 250
Hill, Matthew, 235
Hill, Rev. William, 646
Hinds, Patrick, 425
Hiring, 175, 351–352, 471, 515–516
Hitchens, Edward (mulatto), 402
Hobbes Hole, Va., 306
Hobcaw, S.C., 529
Hodgson, Adam, 118
Hodgson, W. B., 620
Hogs. *See* Livestock
Holcombe, Henry, 654
Holidays: and Christmas, 138, 202, 330, 341, 389, 583, 595; and tobacco cycle, 169–170, 191; regularization of, 195, 215; importance of, 201–202; and New Year's Day, 202, 351; and harvest-home, 387; and interracial socializing, 412–413, 415–416, 418; religious motive of, 423; and Easter Sunday, 429; meetings of slaves on, 524; fine clothing for, 601
Holt, John, 369
Hoomes, John, 339
Hoosier, Harry ("Black Harry"), 430, 655
Horry, Daniel, 323
Horry, Elias, 6
Horry, Peter, 286
Horses, 306, 319, 373–375, 390, 468, 510; racing of, 416–417
Horse Savannah, S.C., 542, 552
Horton, Robin, 610–611, 630, 631
Household slaves. *See* Slave domestics
Housing, 102–124, 144–145, 469

Howell, Sam (free mulatto), 489
Huey, Samuel, 330
Huger, Daniel, 110, 454
Huger, John, 291
Huggins, Joseph, 491
Hughes, Sarah, 175
Hull, Henry, 200
Hunter, Robert, 29, 415
Hunting and fishing, 137–140, 387, 390, 412. *See also* Slave fishermen
Huntington, countess of, 424
Hutson, Richard, 224
Hyde, Benjamin, 396
Hyrne, Edward, 222

Ibo. *See* Igbos
Igbos: in Virginia, 62, 64; and suicide, 65–66, 590; dislike of, 67; as watermen, 243; as runaways, 447, 462, 626; conflict of, with Angolans, 458; speech of, 578; and religious belief, 633, 636, 640
Indentured servants: work of, alongside slaves, 6, 239; blacks as, 8, 11; socializing of, with slaves, 8–9, 302, 303, 306, 367, 416; sex of, with slaves, 10, 17, 400–401, 523; distancing of, from slaves, 14–15, 285, 300; housing for, 105; condition of, compared to slavery, 261, 263n, 271; and poisoning, 619
Indians: as slaves, 6, 479, 481–482; and mats, 114; and baskets, 199; and herbal influence, 222, 619; influence of, on fishing techniques, 242; marriage of, to black slaves, 307, 480, 552; and mustees, 330, 479, 482; arming slaves against, 391; and dislike of blacks, 477–478; population of, 478, 479; relations of, with blacks, 479–480, 482, 485, 493; tributaries among, 478, 480, 482–483. *See also* Catawbas; Cherokees; Chickasaws; Creeks; Cussitaws; Cussos; Etiwans; Gingaskins; Kiawahs; Mattaponys; Muscogulges; Nansemonds; Natchez; Pamunkeys; Seminoles; Tuscaroras; Wawees; Windaws
Indigo, 37, 38n, 148, 159–164, 178, 180, 222, 301, 521
Innes, Stephen, 20

Ireland, James, 427, 619
Irish, 10–11, 297, 305, 306, 313
Ironworks, 136, 144, 230–231, 347. *See also* Baltimore Company ironworks
Isaac (slave), 462
Isaac, Rhys, 475
Ishmael (slave), 241
Islam, 462, 631, 635. *See also* Religion
Isle of Wight Co., Va., 44
Izard, Alice, 249
Izard, Ralph, 77, 223, 248, 280, 336, 344, 347

Jack (African), 457
Jack (boy), 302
Jack (boy), 528
Jack (creole), 462
Jack (driver), 222
Jack (mulatto slave), 215
Jack (old slave), 375
Jack (slave), 113
Jack (slave), 313
Jack, Dr. (slave), 219
Jacksonburgh, S.C., 526
Jacob (slave), 467
Jamaica, 462, 557, 575, 586, 605, 621, 623, 654
James (slave), 227–228
James, Edward, 388–389
James City Co., Va., 278, 329, 428, 468
James Island, S.C., 42–43, 240, 251, 536, 552
Jameson, Aron (slave), 111
James River, 22, 41, 100, 166, 175, 237, 365, 642
Jamieson, James, 162
Jamy, Fork (slave), 314
Janson, Charles, 386–387
Jarrett, Devereaux, 301, 383
Jefferson, Thomas: on slave women, 94, 196, 252–253; and slave cabins, 120; and slave gardening, 140; and wheat harvest, 173; and gangs, 192; on age of slave tradesmen, 214; overseers of, 327; on slaves' tobacco growing, 360; on slavery, 380, 385; greeting of, 383; and interracial sex, 404; on Mattaponys, 480; and free black, 487; on broad marriage, 509; slave families of, 511, 513, 551, 555; on slave speech, 577; on black music, 581

Jehosse plantation, 331
Jelot, Aron, 393
Jemmy (runaway), 291
Jemmy (runaway), 537
Jenings, Edmund, 106, 334, 458
Jenkins, Christopher, 164
Jerdone, Francis, 71
Jeremiah, Thomas (free black), 341–342, 495
Jericho plantation, 330
Jerry (slave), 472
Jesuits, 360. *See also* Religion
Jewelry. *See* Body
Jim (mulatto), 480
Jim (slave), 193
Joe (African), 214
Joe (African), 457
Joe (African), 473
Joe (poisoner), 623
Joe, Dr. (preacher), 650
Joe, Black (slave), 509–510
John (body servant), 355
John (driver), 222
John (sailor), 475
John, Philip (free black), 648–649
John Canoe, 594–595, 599
Johnny, Watboo (patroon), 340
Johns Island, S.C., 224, 228, 417, 481, 516, 542, 567, 601, 626
Johnson, Anthony, 20, 487
Johnson, Joseph, 307
Johnson family (free blacks), 13, 20
Johnston Co., N.C., 620
Johny (slave), 361
Jones, Alexander, 339
Jones, Charles Colcock, 646
Jones, Rev. Hugh, 106, 573
Jones, Jacqueline, 533
Jones, Katherine, 303
Jones, Rev. Lewis, 460
Jones, Thomas, 174–175, 266
Jones family, 546
Jordan, Terry G., 53
Jordan, Winthrop D., xxii, 15
Joshua (old slave), 336
Judah (slave), 509
July (boy), 519
July (slave), 378

INDEX : 687

July (slave), 470
June (slave), 251
Jupiter (old slave), 360
Jupiter (preacher), 653

Kalm, Peter, 614, 618
Kate (runaway), 537
Kate (slave), 515
Keith, Mrs., 351
Kelly, Samuel, 241
Kennedy, James, 229
Kent Co., Md., 209
Kent Island, Md., 431
Kentucky, 165, 634, 661, 668–670
Kerebe, 630
Keswick quarter, 119
Key, Elizabeth, 11
Kiawah, 482
Kimambo, Isaria, 630
Kimber, Edward, 193, 237, 272
King, Boston, 212, 222, 392–393, 543, 619, 647
King and Queen Co., Va., 168, 405, 444, 528
King George Co., Va., 540, 629
Kingroad (slave), 338
Kings Bay plantation, 113
Kingsmill plantation, 116, 633
King William Co., Va., 106, 428, 434, 447, 458, 496, 529, 537
Kinloch, Francis, 184
Kirkland, Moses, 309, 654
Kisi, 448, 603
Kit (slave), 549
Kitty (slave), 127
Knight, Henry, 196, 200, 616, 641
Kobler, John, 430
Kongo, 67, 72, 243, 448, 449, 456, 567; and Bakongo, 633
Koromanti, 64, 66, 447, 565, 577, 641
Kulikoff, Allan, 502

Labor: importance of, xxi; and rice, 149–157; and indigo, 159–164, 178; and tobacco, 164–170, 191; and wheat, 170–175, 178; and rewards, 171, 173n; division of, 173–174, 196–198; pace of, 175–177, 194–195; organization of, 179–194; and disputes, 183–184, 191–193; and seasonal rhythms, 194; regularity of, 195; and head carrying, 198–200; and time reckoning, 201–202; uniformities in, 202–203; and contrasts, 203; demands of, 281–282. *See also* Gang system; Slave skills; Task system
Lambert, John, 199, 380, 645
Lancaster (slave), 240
Lancaster Co., Va., 13, 44, 303, 312, 369, 415, 426–427, 486, 496, 615
Land, xx; and constructed environments, 27–29, 33–34; and natural environment, 29–33; and tobacco, 36; holdings of, 42–44; and swamps, 45n, 155–157; slave assessment of, 184–185; black inscriptions on, 378–379. *See also* Agriculture
Landholdings, 42–44
Langresh, John, 229
Language, xviii, 664; and cursing, 302, 577; effect of, on whites, 325; and stuttering, 353; and figures of speech, 378, 575–576; fluency of, 464–466; and Manding, 480, 561, 563; and Nanticoke, 480; and cultural role, 560; and Africans, 560–566; and Wolof, 561, 579; and pidgins, 562, 579; and creoles, 562, 567, 573, 575, 579–580; and Bambara, 563; and Fulla, 563; and Standard English, 573–575; and dialects, 574, 608; code switching in, 575; and antilanguage, 578; and proverbs, 578; pronunciation of, 578–579; and African words, 622. *See also* Gullah
Lansdowne quarter, 475
Lanter, Peter (free mulatto), 488
Lanter, Reuben (free mulatto), 488
La Rochefoucauld-Liancourt, duc de, 186, 238, 295, 301, 380, 395, 400
Lary, Sarah (free mulatto), 488
Latrobe, Benjamin Henry, 31, 132, 242, 399, 441, 573, 625
Laurens, Henry: on Africans, 66–68; and sale of Africans, 76, 77; on natural increase, 94; and slave clothing, 126, 131–132, 374; and provisioning, 142, 363, 364; on indigo, 162–164, 178; and drivers, 224, 344; and Cuffy, 225; on African skills, 232, 243; as patriarch, 258, 276–280, 283; on slaves' loyalty, 285; as senti-

688 : INDEX

mentalist, 293–294; runaway of, 301; slave messenger of, 319; as doctor, 322; and overseers, 327, 330, 406; elderly slaves of, 335–336, 474; and watermen, 340; and skilled slaves, 347, 348, 350; domestics of, 357–358, 382; and slaves' property, 374–375; slave gardener of, 379; on slave rebelliousness, 389, 397; and slaves' access to alcohol, 414; on Lowcountry irreligion, 422; and free mulatto, 488; and slave families, 507–508, 516–517, 530, 533, 539, 554; and slave surnames, 556–557
Laurens, James, 327, 357, 382
Laurens, John, 355, 382
Laurens, Robert Scipio. *See* Scipio (messenger)
Laws: and early discrimination, 8; early latitude in, 11; as dividing white and black, 13, 15–17, 310; against slave resistance, 21n; and fish market, 240; degradation of slaves by, 263–266; and powers of masters, 275–276; and mercy, 277; administration of, 278, 315; amelioration of, 288–289, 291; on policing, 307; against trading with slaves, 367; and slave livestock, 373–375; on arming and disarming slaves, 389–391; against interracial marriage, 402; against drinking and gambling, 416; and visiting family, 509; against drums, 582; on frontier, 669
Leander (butcher, free black), 352
Leath (slave), 470
Lee, Arthur, 388
Lee, Charles, 321
Lee, Lucinda, 419
Lee, Richard Henry, 364, 381
Lee, William, 127, 247, 287, 427–428
Leftrage, Susan, 402
Le Jau, Rev. Francis, 267, 536, 553, 564, 582, 648
Leland, Rev. John, 85, 572, 591, 646
Lemas (slave), 370
Lemon, William, 430, 654
Lesesne, Daniel, 271–272
Lewis (slave), 430
Lexington, Ky., 669
Liberty Co., Ga., 289, 642

Liele, George, 654
Lightburn, Stafford, 290
Lincoln, Gen. Benjamin, 321
Lister, Edmund, 5
Liston, Lady, 103, 165, 248
Livestock: early importance of, 5; of slaves, 11, 187, 345, 373–375; of free blacks, 12, 14; and cowpens, 20, 53, 214; on plantations, 52–53; on indigo plantations, 163; and wheat cultivation, 171, 174–175; and dairying, 249; killing of, 369, 390; at marriages, 532. *See also* Animals; Fowl; Horses
Lloyd, Edward, IV, 290
Lombardy, 181
Long Bay, S.C., 101, 300
Loudoun Co., Va., 44, 306
Louisa Co., Va., 332, 614, 624
Louisiana, 64, 661, 668
Lowcountry region: defined, xvii
Lowndes, Rawlins, 112, 348
Loyde, Stephen, 400
Lubbar, Jack (slave), 192, 220, 335–336, 343, 473–474
Lucas, Anne (free mulatto), 629
Lucas, Eliza, 141, 320
Lucretia (slave), 362, 516
Lucy (slave), 482
Ludlam, Rev. Richard, 141, 482
Ludwell, Philip, 355
Lumber, 7, 54, 361. *See also* Naval stores; Slave woodworkers
Lunan, Rev. Patrick, 401
Lunenburg Co., Va., 452
Lydia (slave), 535
Lynch, Thomas, 505–506

McBoyd, Sarah, 304
McCarty, William, 324
M'Corkle, Rev. Samuel, 647
McIntosh, Lachlan Bain, 378
McKenzie, John, 222
McLeach, John (free mulatto), 495
McLoughlin, William, 636
McPherson, Captain, 303
McPherson, Christopher (free black), 487
McPherson, Isaac, 221, 393–394, 517
Madagascar, 63, 65n

Madison, James, 485, 487
Madison, Va., 386
Magic, 612, 614, 619, 620, 622, 651, 657. *See also* Conjuring; Divination; Poisoning; Religion; Sorcery
Maize. *See* Corn
Mallory, Mary, 375
Manchester, Va., 529
Mandingo, 447, 448, 457, 480, 603
Mangorike quarter, 475
Manigault, Gabriel, 70, 252
Manigault, Peter, 77
Manuel (slave), 171, 277, 544
Manumission, 11, 15, 18, 175, 269–270, 292–293, 374, 402–405, 408–410, 491, 492, 654. *See also* Free blacks
March (slave), 533
Maree (slave), 361
Margate, David, 424–425, 649–650
Marion, Job, 370
Marketing, 250–252, 358–364, 366–374, 376. *See also* Slave hawkers
Marks, Stuart, 412
Marmaduke (slave), 431
Marmaduke, Vincent, 266
Maroons, 449–451
Martha (slave), 445
Mary (slave), 533
Mary-Ann (slave), 249
Marye, Rev. James, Jr., 564
Maryland: law of, on miscegenation, 15; slave population of, 80, 86; creoles in, 85, 460, 461, 463–465; quarters in, 112; slave diet of, 137; skilled slaves in, 217, 220; masters in, 269, 278, 290–291; ironworks in, 347; livestock in, 369; and slave punishment, 396; mulattoes in, 399, 523; interacial sex in, 402; white-black socializing in, 413, 415–416, 523; religion in, 421, 429, 431, 434, 639; slave plot in, 460; Africans in, 460, 461, 463; mobility of slaves in, 524; slave sold from, 539; slave's letter in, 572–573; dances in, 586–587; religious artifacts in, 633
Mason, George, 212, 355, 380, 512
Masters, xxi–xxii; and dividing poor whites and slaves, 13–16; on Africans, 65–67; on creoles, 83–85; and material treatment, 103, 111, 144; and slaves' right to privacy, 113; siting of houses of, 120; distribution of clothing by, 125–128; and slave rations, 134–138, 142–143; absenteeism of, 181; as bound to slaves, 257–258; and punishment of slaves, 263–267, 282, 392–394; on slaves as family, 268–270, 273–275; kindly feelings of, toward slaves, 269–270, 282–283; as patriarchs, 273–284; as incipient paternalists, 284–296; relations of, with slaves, 296–300, 377–385; relations of, with plain folk, 307–311, 313–316, 366–371, 388–389, 391; and slave messengers, 319–321; and health care, 321–325; relations of, with overseers, 326–334; and elderly slaves, 334–337; and slave watermen, 337–342; and slave drivers and foremen, 342–346; and slave artisans, 346–353; and slave domestics, 353–358; trading of, with slaves, 358–366; and slaves' property, 372–376; and dependency on slaves, 379–382; and slave violence, 386–391, 394–398; and slave families, 499–501, 507–509; and separation of slave families, 512–519; on slaves' speech, 565–567, 573–574, 576–577; on slaves' music, 581–582, 592–593; on slaves' walking, 596; on slaves' gestures, 597; and slaves in late 18th century, 662–663. *See also* Labor; Manumission; Plantations; *individual slaveowners*
Mathews, Gov. John, 371
Mathias (slave), 554
Mattapony River, 341, 536
Mattaponys, 480
Maury, Rev. James, 422–423
Mazar (slave), 623
Mazyck, Ben, 157
Meacham, Rev. James, 288, 430, 433, 643
Mecklenburg Co., Va., 165, 277, 656
Menard, Russell, 86
Mende, 586, 622
Mepkin plantation, 77, 301, 336, 508, 530. *See also* Laurens, Henry
Mercer, James, 286, 290, 327, 328, 359, 364, 415
Mercer, John, 136, 315, 360
Merchant, Thomas, 331

Methodists, 185, 212, 402, 591; sympathy of, for slaves, 287, 314; and black preachers, 309, 424–425, 649–650; dream by, 378; inroads of, among slaves, 427–431, 433–436, 635, 656; conversations of, with slaves, 632, 647. *See also* Religion
Meyer, John, 395–396
Michaux, André, 135, 138
Middlesex Co., Va., 14, 113, 219, 302, 306, 314, 389, 451, 476, 656
Middleton, Thomas, 157
Middleton, William, 159
Migration, 58–80, 85, 93, 519–524, 660, 661. *See also* African slave trade
Miles, Silas, 330
Miles, Thomas, 616
Miller, Rev. John, 576
Milligen-Johnston, George, 33, 135, 146
Milly (slave), 531
Mingo (slave), 431
Mintz, Sidney, xxiii, 553, 583, 599, 609, 610, 657
Miscegenation. *See* Sex
Mississippi Territory, 661, 668, 669
Mitchell, J. and W. B., 225
Molly (slave), 462
Mongon, Philip, 12–13
Montgomery Co., Md., 520
Monticello plantation, 121, 383, 637. *See also* Jefferson, Thomas
Moore, James (slave), 202
Moravians, 200, 300, 370, 422, 432, 434–435, 591, 635. *See also* Religion
Morgan, Edmund S., xv, 266, 271, 278, 310, 558
Morrell, Thomas, 646
Moses (driver), 344
Moses (fiddler), 419
Moses (fisherman), 240
Moses (preacher), 641
Moses (slave), 278
Motley, Mrs., 356
Moultrie, John, 286, 336, 522
Moultrie, William, 296, 568, 590
Mount Vernon plantation, 115, 139, 360, 379, 621. *See also* Washington, George
Muhlenberg, Rev. Henry Melchior, 39, 279, 374, 407, 541, 615

Mulattoes: and sexual encounter, 9; born of slave women, 10; born of white women, 12, 619; among slaves, 14, 289, 380, 479; and voting, 17; among runaways, 132, 306, 307, 460, 462, 464, 465, 555; as waiting men, 214; as skilled slaves, 215, 546, 552; as fishermen, 240; distribution of, 399–410; as preachers, 427, 653; and Indians, 480; as free people, 486, 488–497, 629; and slave women, 536; speech of, 566; as musicians, 592, 593; appearance of, 601, 602, 605, 606. *See also* Sex
Mulberry Row, Monticello, 120, 123, 137, 621
Mulcaster, Frederick George, 378
Mullryne, John, 110
Mungo (slave), 452
Muscogulges, 484
Music, 244, 418–420, 474, 581–584, 586–594. *See also* Dances; Drums
Muslims. *See* Islam
Mustees, 240, 330, 479, 482, 566. *See also* Indians
Myrtle Grove plantation, 95

Nairne, Thomas, 17, 35
Naming, 21, 451–452, 454–455, 546–547, 549–551, 555–558
Nanny (slave), 511
Nanny (slave), 550
Nansemond Co., Va., 401, 431, 587
Nansemond River, 202
Nansemonds, 480
Nanticoke, 480
Nashville, Tenn., 671
Nassau (slave), 312, 324, 356–358, 415, 555, 628
Nat (slave), 653
Natchez, 654
Natchez District, 670
Naval stores, 7, 48, 162
Ned (Angolan), 565, 575
Ned (groom), 245–246
Ned (Indian), 481
Ned (slave), 201
Ned (slave), 493
Ned (slave), 528

INDEX : 691

Nelson, Hugh, 105, 489
Nelson, John, 369
Nelson, William, 174
Nero (mulatto), 545
Nero (slave), 364
New Bern, N.C., 416, 417, 449
New Kent Co., Va., 139, 278, 625, 643
Newton, Abraham, 408
Newton, Thomas, 348
Nicken, Edward (free black), 486
Nichols, William, 215
Niemcewicz, Julian Ursyn, 142
Nimcock (slave), 364
Ninety-Six District, 574
Noah (slave), 419
Nomini Hall plantation, 122–123, 193, 312, 324, 339, 418, 541, 544–545, 637. *See also* Carter, Robert, of Nomini Hall
Nonslaveholders. *See* Indentured servants; Plain folk
Norfolk, Va., 109; shipyards in, 230; water transport in, 238, 339, 341; marketing in, 252; loyalists and slaves in, 270, 375; interracial socializing in, 303, 416; plain folk and slaves in, 311, 369; religion in, 434, 649; free black in, 486; slave wife in, 536
Norfolk Co., Va., 10, 44, 276, 400, 423
Norman, Jeremiah, 430, 632
Northampton Co., N.C., 418, 549
Northampton Co., Va., 4, 5, 12, 14, 402, 486, 487, 494
Northampton Ironworks (Md.), 231
North Carolina: housing in, 119–120; head carrying in, 200; master in, 202; slave weaving in, 248; patroller in, 308; rumors of rebellion in, 309; relations between poor whites and slaves in, 311, 367, 416, 417, 418; slave punishment in, 396; free blacks' trade with Indians in, 479; and slave family, 510, 531; and slave men's purchases, 537; and slave father, 545; runaway from, 548; John Canoe in, 595; and slave magic, 624; and folk medicine, 625; and African religion, 632; creation legend in, 637; funerals in, 641, 644; insurrectionary scare in, 650

Northern Neck (Va.): slave plot in, 21; landscape of, 31; livestock in, 53; creoles in, 80; proportion of slaves in, 100; housing in, 105, 111; planters and farmers of, 174, 400, 475; religion in, 426, 430, 639; slave husband and wife in, 500–501; and brother-sister networks, 548
North Farnham Parish, Va., 421
Northumberland Co., Va., 297, 312, 416
Norton, John, 106, 328
Nottingham Ironworks, 231

Obeah, 620–621. *See also* Conjuring; Divination; Magic; Poisoning; Sorcery
Occoquan Ironworks, 231
Ogeechee River, 446
Ogilvie, George, 95, 149, 517
Ogle, Robert, 423
O'Kelly, James, 433
Okree (free black), 15
Old Town, Va., 402
Olive, Thomas, 327
Orangeburg, S.C., 395, 415
Orange Co., N.C., 475
Orange Co., Va., 473, 488, 493, 531, 564, 612, 644
Orr, Robert, 214
Ortiz, Fernando, 177, 188, 297–298
Orwell, George, 441
Osborne's Warehouse, Va., 77
Oswald, Richard, 49, 216, 232, 243, 330, 508, 517
Ottolenghe, Rev. Joseph, 564
Overseers: and indigo maker, 164, 347; and violence from slaves, 185n, 314, 396; and clashes with slaves, 193; paucity of, 221; humanity of, 286; and master's orders, 293, 322, 364, 459; on Lowcountry estates, 298, 302, 303, 305, 307; on Chesapeake estates, 312; violence of, toward slaves, 315, 320, 392, 393, 431, 551; lack of trust in, 322; and illness of slave, 324; and field hands, 326–334, 368; and drivers, 344; sex of, with slaves, 406; socializing of, with slaves, 415–416; on slave marriages, 532
Oxford Ironworks, 231

692 : INDEX

Page, John, 514
Palmer, Ann, 53
Pamphlet, Gowan, 656, 667
Pamunkey River, 341, 536
Pamunkeys, 480
Papaw, James (free black), 625
Papaw, 461, 595
Parker, Judge, 167–168
Parker, James and Margaret, 270
Parker, John, 271
Parkinson, Richard, 102, 139, 202, 252, 372, 430, 509, 525, 619, 638
Parrinder, Geoffrey, 630
Parris Island, S.C., 621
Parsons, James, 554, 653
Parsons, William, 303
Paternalism, 284–296. *See also* Masters; Patriarchalism
Patillo, Henry, 287
Patriarchalism, xxi, 258–259; and household relations, 268–269, 273–284. *See also* Paternalism
Patrols, 307–308, 311, 374, 388–389, 434, 667
Patt (slave), 527
Patterson, Orlando, xv, 258, 269, 358
Patty (slave), 289–290
Patuxent River, 429
Paul (slave), 224
Pearoe (slave), 362
Pedee plantation, 49, 157. *See also* Austin, George
Pee Dee River, 159, 307, 425
Peg (market woman), 250
Peg (plower), 196
Peg (slave), 364
Peg (slave), 522
Peggy (domestic), 249
Peggy (slave), 409
Peggy (slave), 436
Pendarvis, Catherine Rumph, 488
Pendarvis, James (free mulatto), 488
Pendarvis, John (free mulatto), 648
Pendarvis, Joseph, 488
Pendleton, Edmund, 617
Peronneau, Rose (free black), 408
Perry, Charles, 397
Peter (Angolan), 462
Peter (carpenter), 131

Peter (ditcher), 173, 297
Peter (fiddler), 296–297
Peter (preacher), 641
Peter (slave), 113
Peter (slave), 468
Peter (slave), 614–615
Peter, Jesse, 653
Peter Deadfoot (slave), 346, 577
Petersburg, Va., 77, 170, 372, 417, 446, 511, 638, 659
Pettigrew, Ebenezer, 524
Pettsworth Baptist Church, 654
Pharoah (slave), 471
Pheby (slave), 252
Phil (slave), 537
Philander (slave), 522
Philip (driver), 331
Philip (skilled slave), 482
Phillip, John (free black), 3
Phillippa (slave), 526
Phillips, Ulrich Bonnell, 181
Phillis (slave), 250
Piedmont (N.C.), 416, 432, 434
Piedmont (S.C.), 93
Piedmont (Va.): settlement of, 30; forest of, 31–32; size of plantations in, 41–42; landholdings in, 43; Africans in, 60, 77, 458, 564; movement into, 93, 521, 660; proportion of slaves in, 100; housing in, 111; tobacco in, 165–166; and slave skills, 209; overseer and slaves in, 333; interracial sex in, 403; religion in, 426, 591; free black in, 487; and slave kin networks, 510–511; and slave poisoning, 617, 623; funerals in, 644
Pierce (slave), 303
Pierce, Capt. William, 9
Pierce, Rev. William, 564
Pilmore, Joseph, 185, 300, 434
Pinckney, Mrs., 320
Pinckney, Charles, 641
Pinckney, Charles Cotesworth, 550
Pinckney, Eliza, 249, 320, 325, 375, 424, 567
Pinckney, Thomas, 344
Pinckney, William, 339
Pinckney family, 345, 545, 546
Piper, Harry, 419
Piscataway, Md., 396

INDEX : 693

Pittsylvania Co., Va., 614
Plain folk: and nonslaveholders, 100; and tobacco, 165; and wheat, 173; as artisans, 209, 226, 227; opportunities for, 221; complaints of, 239, 262, 311–312; relation of, to large planters, 260, 315–316, 391; contempt of, for poor, 271; and working alongside slaves, 301; ties of, to slaves, 301–302; and cooperation with slaves, 302–309; and white women's relations to slaves, 303–304; and patrolling, 307–308; antipathy of, toward slaves, 310–312; hostility toward, from slaves, 312–313; and fear of slaves, 313–314; and trading with slaves, 367–370; socializing of, with slaves, 413–416; on frontier, 671. *See also* Indentured servants; Overseers
Plantations: starting costs of, 35–36; labor forces of, 36; capital requirements of, 37–38; profitability of, 38; productivity of, 39; size of, 39–42, 44, 103; landholdings of, 42–44; stability of, 44–45, 110, 158–159; diversification of, 45–58; tools of, 50–51; livestock of, 52–53; crafts of, 53–55; transportation on, 55–57; slave housing of, 104–124; and differential material conditions, 120–121, 144; and differential skill levels, 206, 207, 209, 216–217, 225–226; and slave foremen, 219; and slave watermen, 236–237; and household slaves, 244–245, 249; and slave households, 503–507; and family stability, 513–514, 516–519; on the frontier, 670. *See also* Agriculture; Corn; Cotton; Indigo; Labor; Masters; Rice; Tobacco; Wheat; *individual plantations and owners*
Plows, 51, 169, 171–172, 174n, 175, 196, 206n
Poisoning, 265, 314, 469, 493, 612–619. *See also* Conjuring; Divination; Magic; Obeah; Sorcery
Polidore (slave), 449
Politeness, 474
Polydore (African), 458
Polydore (runaway), 298
Pompey (slave), 616
Ponpon, S.C., 424, 538, 552
Population: proportion of slaves in, 1, 39, 95–101, 661; structure of, 3; free blacks in, 11–12, 16, 489–491; African immigration in, 58–79, 661; natural increase of, 79–95, 101, 143, 163; mulattoes in, 399–400; and number of blacks in 1790 and 1800, 659–660. *See also* African slaves; African slave trade; Age; Creoles; Slave fertility; Slave mortality
Porcher, Philip, 361, 370
Porter, George, 517
Port Royal Island, S.C., 122, 496
Portsmouth, Va., 238, 339, 341, 430, 461, 654
Potatoes, 140
Potomac River, 239, 242, 283, 529
Pottery, 115, 633–634. *See also* Colono ware
Poultry. *See* Fowl
Powhatan Co., Va., 220, 616
Presbyterians, 287, 424, 426–427, 637. *See also* Religion
Price, Richard, xxiii, 553, 609, 610
Primus (slave), 487
Prince (slave), 202
Prince Edward Co., Va., 520, 588, 624
Prince Frederick Parish, S.C., 43, 162
Prince George Co., Va., 31, 289, 427, 472, 535–536, 549
Prince George's Co., Md., 81, 166, 207, 209, 215, 217, 401, 502, 520, 563
Prince George Parish, S.C., 55
Princess Anne Co., Va., 388, 649
Prince William Parish, S.C., 225, 447
Pringle, Robert, 162, 543
Property: of slaves, 11, 113–116, 187, 327, 347, 358–376, 469–470, 537, 538; slaves as, 257–259, 261, 263, 265–266, 271, 273, 294. *See also* Slave internal economy
Provisioning, 48–50, 162, 290, 336, 359–364, 369–373, 375–376. *See also* Corn
Purrysburg, S.C., 238

Quaco (slave), 251
Quakers, 9, 85. *See also* Religion
Quantico, Va., 655
Quash, John (slave), 452
Quashy (slave), 653
Queen Anne Co., Md., 269
Queenstown, Md., 413

694 : INDEX

Quilting. *See* Clothing
Quincy, Josiah, 28, 30, 100, 148, 265, 325, 414
Quomony (slave), 452

Race relations: flexibility of, 8–13, 16–18; hardening of, 13–16; intimacy of, 296–299, 353–358, 436–437; impersonality of, 298–300, 436–437; between plain white folk and blacks, 300–316, 326–334; routinization of, 318–326, 334–353, 358–366; cruelty of, 385–398. *See also* Masters; Paternalism; Patriarchalism; Plain folk; Sex
Rachel (slave), 286
Rachel (slave), 400
Ramsay, David, 28, 84, 95, 135, 296
Randolph, David, 306
Randolph, Edmund, 248, 278, 305
Randolph, John, 355, 667
Randolph, Peter, 514
Randolph, Peyton, 510–511
Randolph, Ryland, 409
Ranger, Terence, 610, 611, 630, 640
Rankin, Rev. Thomas, 429
Raper, Robert, 266, 328
Rappahannock River, 41, 100, 166, 341, 529, 536, 549
Rath, Richard Cullen, 586
Ravenel, Daniel, 344
Ravenel, Henry, 361, 362
Ravenel, Henry William, 584–585, 609
Ravenel family, 90, 516, 546, 550
Read, Elizabeth, 4
Read, William, 331
Rebecca (slave), 490–491
Rebellions, 386, 470, 533. *See also* Conspiracies; Resistance; Stono rebellion
Redfield, Robert, xxiii
Redman, Vincent, 297
Reed, Nelson, 645
Religion: and funerals, 21, 640–645; and Christian stewardship, 274, 281, 287, 293; and access to baptism, 303; and white-black religious contacts, 420–437; and Christian slaves, 468; and language, 576; and music, 591–592; among Africans, 610–612; and Christianity, 631–635, 637–640; and Islam, 631, 635; and views of God, 631–638; and visions, 646–648; and millenarianism, 648–651; character of, 664, 668; on the frontier, 669, 670. *See also* Anglicans; Baptists; Evangelicalism; Islam; Jesuits; Magic; Methodists; Moravians; Quakers; Society for the Propagation of the Gospel
Remington, Margaret, 250
Resistance: definition of, xxii; armed, 9–10, 15, 308–309; in the field, 153–155, 183–184, 191–193, 202, 225; expectations of, 278–279; against plain folk, 313–314; against overseers, 329–332, 368; by skilled slaves, 348–351; by domestics, 355–358; in the marketplace, 366–371; and violence, 385–388, 394–398; by maroons, 450–451; by creoles, 464–467; by free blacks and slaves, 493–494. *See also* Poisoning; Runaways; Slave crime; Stono rebellion
Rhode Island, 136
Rhonnald, Rev. Alexander, 423
Rice, Rev. John Holt, 644, 653
Rice, 33–46; and beginnings of, 7; and land use, 28, 33–34; culture of, 33; and settlement patterns, 34; starting costs of, 35; labor forces of, 36; capital requirements of, 37; profitability of, 38; productivity of, 39; plantation size for, 39–41; landholding size of, 42–43; specialization in, 45–46; as provisions, 49, 135; and seasonal labor patterns, 147–159; and baskets, 153; and machines, 155; and tidewater production, 156–159, 180, 521; and indigo, 162; pace of, 175–177; and tasking, 179–184; slaves' personal, 186–187, 351, 362–364, 368; and master-slave relations, 298
Ricehope plantation, 331
Richardson, Billy, 381
Richardson, John, 369
Richardson, Nancy, 381
Richardson, William, 313, 381
Richmond, Va., 198, 200, 252; cooperation between slaves and plain folk in, 305, 308, 416; hiring in, 352, 557; runaways from, 448; and Gabriel's conspiracy, 471; free blacks and slaves in, 494

INDEX : 695

Richmond Co., Va., 44, 113, 220, 277, 297, 306, 339, 342, 371, 394
Richneck quarter, 329
Riedesel, baroness von, 360
Riggins, James, 429
Ringold, Thomas, 65, 69
Ritson, Anne, 416
River Farm quarter, 118
Rivers, Colonel, 251
Roberts, Easter (free black), 496
Robin (African), 449
Robin (fisherman), 240
Robin (free black), 492
Robin (house servant), 132, 246
Robin (slave), 336
Robinson, John, 55
Roger (slave), 458
Roger (slave), 614–615
Romans, Bernard, 33
Rose (slave), 527
Rose, Elizabeth, 222
Rose, Rev. Robert, 56
Rose, Willie Lee, 300, 519
Ross, David, 231, 531
Ross, John, 410
Rowan Co., N.C., 647
Royal African Company, 78
Rum, 142, 151, 347, 367, 369, 414–416, 532, 641. *See also* Alcohol
Runaways: and castration, 17; mode of escape of, 56–57; speed of escape of, 75–76; in groups, 77–78, 143, 446–451, 460, 462, 466–467; with children, 87–88; large family of, 90; appearance of, 130, 132, 133, 394; and hunting, 138; seasonal patterns of, 151–154, 167; and time reckoning, 201–202; ages of, 212–214, 216; and drivers and foremen, 219, 220, 224, 345; on plantations without whites, 221; sawyers among, 228; brickmaker among, 228; ironworkers among, 231; fishing by, 240–241; as waiting men, 246; as hawkers, 251, 252, 371; master's leniency toward, 266, 291; punishment of, 267, 271, 394, 431; and liberty, 279; evangelical intervention over, 288; advertising of, 290–292, 382; in cooperation with former master, 297; and views of masters, 298–299, 375; and white support of, 301; in cooperation with plain folk, 304–307, 402; capture of, 310, 329–330, 344, 390, 392, 468, 475; and overseer, 327; on South Carolina estates, 331, 344; watermen among, 340–341; skilled slaves among, 348, 349, 351, 417; and stuttering, 353; dream about, 378; destinations of, 383, 413; religion among, 427; Africans among, 446–452; creoles among, 464–468; and Indians, 480–484; and free blacks, 493, 494, 496; and previous owners, 518–519; to avoid transfer, 522; visiting by, 525–530; parents and children among, 541–543, 547; in search of siblings, 548–549; on the frontier, 670. *See also* Resistance
Russell, Alexander, 229
Russell, Jack, 469
Russell, James, 231
Russell, Nathaniel, 71
Russo, Jean B., 226
Rutherford, John, 325

Sabinah (free black), 487
Sabine Hall, 111, 171, 172, 280, 544. *See also* Carter, Landon
Saby (slave), 345
Sacheverelle, Thomas, 352
Saint Andrew Parish, Ga., 330
Saint Andrew Parish, S.C., 43
Saint Augustine, East Fla., 266, 284, 289, 341, 450
Saint Bartholomew Parish, S.C., 406, 409, 425, 487, 649, 650
Saint Christopher, 287, 557
Saint Domingue, 491
Saint George Dorchester Parish, S.C., 40, 162, 374, 421, 552, 575, 613, 623
Saint Helena Island, S.C., 341, 453
Saint Helena Parish, S.C., 217, 406, 423, 424, 496, 648
Saint James Goose Creek Parish, S.C.: large plantations in, 40; large landholdings in, 42–43; runaways from and in, 143, 449, 536, 548; cooper in, 213; hawker from, 252; slaves collecting Spanish moss in, 362; slaves visiting and trading in, 371;

Christians in, 422, 474, 648; robbery in, 482; free black in, 491; poisonings in, 623
Saint John Berkeley Parish, S.C., 30, 40, 53, 161–162, 486, 487, 492, 520, 548
Saint Johns River, 184
Saint Mark's Fort, 484
Saint Mary's Co., Md., 108, 360, 419, 523
Saint Mathew's Parish, S.C., 76
Saint Paul's Parish, S.C., 42–43, 55, 488
Saint Simon's Island, Ga., 590
Saint Stephen Parish, S.C., 548
Saint Thomas and Saint Dennis Parish, S.C., 414, 481, 542
Sally (slave), 501
Saltketchers, S.C., 53, 224
Sam (carpenter), 346
Sam (carpenter), 539
Sam (mulatto), 341
Sam (mulatto), 496
Sam (slave), 332
Sam (slave), 468
Sam (slave), 522
Sambo (African), 453
Sambo (slave), 276
Sampson (African), 307
Sampson (creole), 462
Sampson (doctor), 625
Sampson (runaway), 301
Sampson (slave), 374
Samuel, Johannes, 432
Samuel, Maria, 432
Sancho (African), 635
Sancho (pilot), 342
Sand, James, 616
Sanders, John, 431
Sanders, William, 517
Sandy (slave), 201, 577
Sandy Island plantation, 351
Santee region (S.C.), 374, 447, 481, 521
Santee River, 95, 138, 159, 185, 300, 301, 323, 344, 456, 548, 549, 642
Sapho (slave), 462
Sarah (old slave), 375
Sarah (slave), 511
Savannah, Ga.: cane in, 236; water transport to, 238, 338; marketing in, 345, 363; hiring in, 352; mulatto mistress in, 408; Baptists in, 435; family in, 539, 542, 548; slaves sent from, 563; funerals in, 641; free black in, 654
Savannah River, 159, 233, 304, 339, 450–451, 481, 525, 654
Sawney (slave), 355
Saxby, George, 221
Saxe Gotha, S.C., 424
Schad, Abraham, 327
Schaw, Janet, 141–142, 148, 377, 644
Schneider, Edgar, 572
Schoepf, Johann David: on gardening, 28; on forests, 32; on corn, 49; on diet, 103, 135; on housing, 118; on slaves' love of fire, 122; on work, 146, 160, 164; on acquisition of slaves, 380; on interracial sex, 409–410; on holidays, 413
Schwarz, Philip J., 395
Scipio (African), 307
Scipio (foreman), 136
Scipio (messenger), 319, 357–358, 556
Scipio (waterman), 460
Scots, 132, 306, 574n
Scott, Job, 638
Seabrook, John, 221
Sea Islands (S.C. and Ga.), 151, 162, 178, 180, 571, 597, 599
Selor, Cornelius, 313
Selsdon quarter, 458
Seminoles, 636
Senegambia, 62–69, 72–73, 233, 335, 444, 447–449, 453, 561–562, 567, 600
Sensbach, Jon F., 434–435
Serre, Noah, 455
Servants. *See* Indentured servants
Sesame, 141
Severally, George (free black), 493
Severally, Rose (free black), 493
Sex, 9, 10, 12, 15, 17, 398–412, 618–619. *See also* Mulattoes; Slave boys; Slave girls; Slave men; Slave women
Shadwell (slave), 338
Shammas, Carole, 275
Shaw, Ralph, 262
Shenandoah Valley (Va.), 369, 660
Sheppard, Mosby, 471
Shifnal (slave), 653
Shipmates, 77–79n, 448–449, 459. *See also* African slaves

Shirley plantation, 633
Shrews-Berry (waiting man), 354–355
Sierra Leone, 63–64, 67–69, 72–73, 243, 567, 586
Silkhope plantation, 412
Silver Bluff, S.C., 481, 654
Silvia (slave), 495
Simmons, John, 309
Simmons, Philip, 232
Simon (runaway), 475
Simon (slave), 475
Simpson, William, 539–540
Skilled slaves. See Slave artisans; Slave skills
Skinner, Mary, 402
Skiper, Francis, 400
Slade, Daniel, 227
Slave artisans: absence of, 54; growing numbers of, 55, 204–212; clothing of, 130–131; in wheat harvest, 173; and tending rice, 186; life cycle of, 212–218; apprenticeship of, 214–215, 350, 392–393; as drivers, 222; range of skills of, 225–236; relations of, with masters, 346–353; price for, 351; products of, 365. See also Ironworks; Slave butchers; Slave carpenters; Slave coopers; Slave painters; Slave sawyers; Slave seamstresses; Slave weavers
Slave bakers, 348
Slave basketmakers, 232–233. See also Baskets
Slave blacksmiths, 54, 131, 212, 215, 228, 230, 232, 347, 365, 471, 616
Slave boys: early presence of, 4, 80; among African immigrants, 70–71; growing numbers of, 83; cleaning of swamps by, 149; as plowers, 171; in fields, 197; as domestics, 212, 214; and playing with white boys, 302; property of, 376; as gifts to masters, 380; punishment of, 393; nakedness of, 398–399; and interracial sex, 411; as jockeys, 417; and cockfighting, 418; and parents, 465; separation of, from family, 518–519, 528. See also Slave children; Slave girls
Slave bricklayers, 228, 346, 351, 352
Slave brickmakers, 54, 228–229, 346, 348
Slave butchers, 55, 413

Slave carpenters, 117–118, 131, 214–215, 218, 222, 227, 346–347, 349, 351–352, 365, 525. See also Slave coopers; Slave sawyers; Slave woodworkers
Slave children: early presence of, 3–5; among African immigrants, 58, 70–73; growing numbers of, 79–83, 86–90; death rates of, 91; in the piedmont, 93; in various households, 94; value of, 94; and work, 197–198; carrying of, on back, 200; as domestics, 212, 214, 252–253; and scavenging, 366; play of, with whites, 381; and Anglican minister, 423; separation of, from family, 514–515, 518–519, 528; relations of, with parents, 540–548. See also Slave boys; Slave girls
Slave coopers, 213, 215, 222, 229, 348, 349, 351, 653. See also Slave carpenters; Slave sawyers; Slave woodworkers
Slave crime, 394–398, 468–473, 479, 482, 493–494. See also Slave theft
Slave doctors, 324, 613, 616, 624–629, 650. See also Health; Slave midwives; Slave nurses
Slave domestics: clothing of, 130–133; material conditions of, 144; proportions of, 209–211; ages of, 212–214; numbers and roles of, 244–253; relations of, with masters, 353–358, 381; access of, to cash, 365; manumission of, 409; access of, to liquor, 415; visit of, to parents, 543; as preachers, 653. See also Slave waiting men
Slave drivers, 204, 216, 218–225, 342–346, 384, 392, 393, 470, 475, 492
Slave families: early presence of, 3–4; size of, 89–90; disruptions in, 93; fertility of, 94; in houses, 106, 108; clothing of, 129; transmission of skills by, 216, 228, 243, 347, 545; and drivers, 222–223; and heads of households, 284; separation of, 285, 512–519; and effects on masters, 285–286; and father-child relationship, 287, 374, 540–548; and husband-wife relationship, 304, 329–330, 375, 411, 448, 454, 462, 463, 500–501, 507–510, 530–540, 603; and extended kin, 334–335, 461, 465, 474, 510–511, 549–553, 641; and sibling rela-

tionship, 370, 449, 453–454, 465, 548–549; and family burial, 392; and nuclear form, 462, 465; of Indians and blacks, 480, 482; and free blacks, 487, 493–496; structures of, 498–512; definition of, 499; and runaways, 527–530; African influences on, 549, 553–555; and polygyny, 553–554; and kin terms, 568; character of, 664, 668; on the frontier, 669–670

Slave fertility, 87–90, 92, 94, 621

Slave field hands: and white servants, 8–9; and size of labor force, 35–36; output of, 39; standardized clothing of, 130; material conditions of, 144; and foundation of economies, 146; in rice cultivation, 148–157; in indigo cultivation, 159–163; in tobacco cultivation, 166–170; in wheat cultivation, 170–175; work days of, 176; and tasking, 179–187; and ganging, 187–194; and patterns of labor, 194–203; close ties of, to masters, 296–299; and overseers, 326–334; demotion to, 346; reward to, for loss of Sundays, 366; as preachers, 653

Slave fishermen, 240–243, 251, 361. *See also* Slave watermen

Slave foremen: in the Chesapeake, 7, 204, 208, 216, 218–220, 342–343, 475; in indigo, 164; in gangs, 188; and family, 554. *See also* Slave drivers

Slave girls: early presence of, 4, 80; among African immigrants, 71; growing numbers of, 83; and work, 197, 247, 253, 372; love of, for father, 287; nakedness of, 399; and accusation of master, 410–411; and mother, 544. *See also* Slave boys; Slave children

Slave hawkers, 235, 250–252, 367, 372–373. *See also* Marketing

Slave internal economy, 185–187, 193–194. *See also* Property

Slave jockeys, 417

Slave leatherworkers, 54, 55, 214, 228

Slave men: in 17th century, 2–6, 10; among African immigrants, 70–71; and parity of sexes, 80, 83; life span of, 89, 347; clothing allocations to, 126; and cutting trees, 149; and working on roads, 152, 162; as plowers, 171; in wheat cultivation, 173–174; and working with women, 196; and head carrying, 200; skills of, 205–212; as basketmakers, 233; as domestics, 244–246, 253; as hawkers, 250–252; selling provisions by, 362; in congregations, 426; and attacking women, 472; and Indian women, 482; as runaways, 526–527; and church membership, 652

Slave messengers, 319–321, 357

Slave midwives, 324–325, 377, 627, 629. *See also* Health; Slave doctors; Slave nurses

Slave millers, 131–132, 214

Slave mortality, 89, 91–92, 125, 153, 347, 444–446

Slave nurses, 324–325, 377, 392, 627. *See also* Health; Slave doctors; Slave midwives

Slave painters, 381

Slave pilots, 9, 214, 342

Slave potters, 234–235. *See also* Pottery

Slave preachers, 465, 641, 643, 648–656. *See also* Religion

Slave punishment: killing as, 14, 310–311, 315; castration as, 17, 265; whipping as, 224, 266–267, 288, 383, 387, 389, 431, 501, 655; and the law, 263–265; animality of, 271–272; and patriarchal severity, 275–278, 282–283; moderation in, 290, 292; sale as, 294–295; and household, 355, 357, 358; and personal testimony, 392–394; of runaways, 394

Slaves. *See names of individual slaves*

Slave sawyers, 180, 218, 227–228, 351, 462, 601. *See also* Slave carpenters; Slave coopers; Slave woodworkers

Slave seamstresses, 54, 244, 494. *See also* Slave domestics

Slave skills: in tidewater rice cultivation, 157; in indigo cultivation, 163–164; in wheat cultivation, 173. *See also* Baskets; Colono ware; Ironworks; Music; Pottery; Slave artisans; Slave doctors; Slave domestics; Slave drivers; Slave foremen; Slave hawkers; Slave jockeys; Slave midwives; Slave nurses; Slave pilots; Slave preachers; Slave waiting men; Slave washerwomen; Slave watermen

Slave society: definition of, 1–2, 18–19

INDEX : 699

Slave spinners, 54, 205, 246–249. *See also* Slave domestics
Slave theft, 112–113, 116–117, 266, 273, 339–340, 356, 366, 370–372, 376, 511, 601. *See also* Slave crime
Slave visiting, 387, 524–530. *See also* Runaways
Slave waiting men, 245–246, 354–358, 378, 418, 540, 543–544, 602, 604. *See also* Slave domestics
Slave washerwomen, 244–245, 253, 494. *See also* Slave domestics
Slave watchmen, 390
Slave watermen, 131, 214, 236–244, 266, 310–311, 327, 337–342, 365, 366, 381, 413, 460, 475, 574–575
Slave weavers, 247–248, 383. *See also* Slave domestics
Slave women: early presence of, 2–5, 11; among African immigrants, 70–72; growing numbers of, 79–83; fertility of, 85–90, 93–94; clothing allocations of, 125, 126; in cleaning swamps, 149; in wheat cultivation, 173–174; in rice cultivation, 182–183; work of, with and without men, 196–197; and head carrying, 199, 200; skills of, 205–208; as driver's wife, 222; as basketmakers, 233, 362; as potters, 235; as domestics, 245–253; as hawkers, 250–251; as midwives, 324–325; and overseers, 329, 331; selling provisions by, 362; in congregations, 426; attacking men, 472; as runaways, 526; as strong figures, 532–533; relation of, to men, 533–537; nursing patterns of, 554; gestures of, 598; clothing of, 599, 600, 601, 602; as nurses and doctors, 626–627; church membership of, 652; on the frontier, 670
Slave woodworkers, 54, 180, 205, 227–231, 236. *See also* Slave carpenters; Slave coopers; Slave sawyers
Sloane, Hans, 582, 586, 587
Smith, Josiah, 49–50, 151
Smith, Tamar, 402
Smith, William, 55
Smyth, J. F. D., 30, 87, 111, 143, 168, 568, 572, 587

Smyth, John, 6
Snowden Ironworks, 231
Society for the Propagation of the Gospel, 421, 474. *See also* Religion
Solomon (free black), 489
Solomon (slave), 312
Solomon (slave), 522
Somerset Case, 246, 461
Somerset Co., Md., 489, 586
Somerton (slave), 362
Sorcery, 620–623, 630–631. *See also* Magic
Southampton Co., Va., 303, 418
Southside (Va.), 41, 100, 289, 410, 427, 548, 659, 665
Spencer, William, 428
Spotswood, Alexander, 230
Spotsylvania Co., Va., 556, 616, 669
Spriggs, Thomas, 217
Stafford, Robert, 380
Stafford Co., Va., 170, 402
Stanton, Lucia, 404
Stanyarne, John, 250
Stapleton, John, 217, 453–454
Stark, Bolling, 402
Stature, 93, 143. *See also* Diet; Population
Stead, Mr., 233
Steffen, Charles, 380
Steiner, George, 560
Stepney (old slave), 336, 382
Stepney (slave), 466
Steuart, Charles, 70, 71, 388
Stewart, Jacob (free black), 657
Stokes, Anthony, 186
Stone, John, 483
Stono, S.C., 43, 87, 138, 292, 394, 467, 567, 616
Stono rebellion, 386, 455–456, 470, 582
Stony Creek Independent Church, 424
Stork, William, 182, 348
"Stranger, The," 240–241, 250–251, 414, 584, 585, 601, 608
Stratford Hall, 642
Stretton, William, 619
Strickland, William, 191
Stripes, Francis, 10
Stuart, Rev. James, 83
Stuckey, Sterling, 636
Sue (midwife), 325

700 : INDEX

Sue (slave), 528
Suffolk Co., Va., 595
Sukey (maid), 403–404
Sukey (slave), 193
Sukey (slave), 431–432
Sullivan's Island, S.C., 75, 79, 309, 536, 584
Sunbury, Ga., 289
Surry Co., Va., 14, 20, 119, 392, 452, 460, 548, 646
Surry Methodist circuit, 428
Susie (slave), 286
Sussex Co., Va., 304, 389, 465, 528, 656
Sutcliff, Robert, 198
Sutherland, James, 241
Sutton, John, 369
Swiss, 406, 424
Sylvia (slave), 403

Talbot Co., Md., 209, 226
Tanner, Edward (free black), 487
Tappahanock, Va., 415
Tarr, Edward (free black), 486
Task system: and time for hunting, 138; for cutting trees, 149; for pounding, 153, 180; for ditching, 156; described, 179–187; apportioning of, 344; and overwork, 347; on the frontier, 668–669. *See also* Gang system
Tatham, William, 165, 168, 191, 194, 237, 359, 360
Tayloe, John, 346
Taylor, Col. Francis, 531, 643–644
Taylor, John, 342, 417
Taylor, William, 71
Telfair, Edward, 507
Tennessee, 165, 621, 634, 661, 668–670
Thacker, Henry, 219
Thomas (slave), 423
Thomas, Dalby, 35, 187
Thomas, John, 343
Thomas, John (slave), 545
Thompson, Talbot (free black), 486
Thomson, Hugh, 554
Thornton, John K., 456
Thorpe, Thomas, 512
Time reckoning, 201
Titchy (nurse), 325
Titus (African), 462

Titus (free black), 374
Titus (slave), 138
Tobacco, 33–44; in 17th century, 4–5, 7; and pipes, 6, 21–22, 374, 464, 537, 633, 642; and fields, 28; culture of, 33; and land use, 33–34; and settlement patterns, 34; starting costs of, 35–36; labor forces of, 36; capital requirements of, 36; profitability of, 38; productivity of, 39; plantation size for, 39–42; landholdings of, 42–44; seasonal labor routines of, 164–170; and wheat, 170–171; pace of, 175–177; and ganging, 187–193; and children's work, 198; and master-slave relations, 297–298; slave opinion of, 356; slaves' personal, 360
Tobias, Joseph, 305
Tobit (slave), 538
Toby (African), 457
Toby (runaway), 298
Toby (slave), 314
Toby (slave), 466
Togo (messenger), 320
Tom (boy), 374
Tom (coachman), 628, 629
Tom (conjurer), 616
Tom (foreman), 220
Tom (Jamaican), 462
Tom (old slave), 270
Tom (old slave), 370
Tom (oysterman), 320
Tom (runaway), 266
Tom (runaway), 298–299
Tom (slave), 202
Tom (slave), 374
Tom (slave), 471
Tom (Tom Salter), 220
Tomahawk Baptist Church, 652
Toney (jockey), 417
Tony (patroon), 337
Tony (slave), 474
Topsam (slave), 529
Torrans and Rose partnership, 362
Toulmin, Harry, 109, 643–644
Transportation: by watercraft, 55–57, 169, 236–240, 362, 365, 370, 388, 413, 450–451, 465; by carts and wagons, 56–57, 172, 548; on heads, 198–200

Tuckahoe plantation, 108, 109
Tucker, Frances, 329
Tucker, George, 590, 667
Tucker, St. George, 395, 490, 543, 575–576
Turner, Daniel, 136, 185
Turner, Lorenzo Dow, 567
Turner, Mary, 302
Tuscaroras, 483

Unitarians, 643. *See also* Religion
Urbanna, Va., 464, 536, 643
Urban slavery, 206, 663–664. *See also* Alexandria, Va.; Baltimore, Md.; Charleston, S.C.; Edenton, N.C.; New Bern, N.C.; Norfolk, Va.; Petersburg, Va.; Richmond, Va.; Savannah, Ga.; Williamsburg, Va.; Wilmington, N.C.
Utopia quarter, 642

Vall (slave), 313
Vane, George, 488
Varnod, Rev. Francis, 631–632, 637
Veblen, Thorstein, 578
Venus (domestic), 356
Verrell, John, 528

Waccamaw River, 159
Wachovia, N.C., 432
Wadboo plantation, 328, 340
Waddingham, Samuel, 222
Wadmelaw Island, S.C., 481
Wagons. *See* Transportation
Walker, John, 465
Walsh, Lorena S., 522, 533
Walter, John Alleyne, 338
Walton, Mr., 410–411
Wambaw plantation, 77, 363, 508
Wando River, 303, 449
Wanny (slave), 483
Wappetaw, S.C., 396
Wappo, S.C., 467
Waring, Richard, 392
Warwick Co., Va., 551
Washington, George: on rice rivers, 28–29; and slave housing, 109, 118; and slave possessions, 115; and provisioning, 134, 290, 360; and fishing, 139; and alcohol rations, 142; and livestock, 171; and wheat, 173; work demands of, 191; conversations of, with slaves, 192; and slave foremen, 220, 343; and slave carpenters, 227; and textile production, 247; and health care, 322; and overseers, 333; and domestics, 356; and horse races, 416–417; and dancing, 419; and slave families, 545; and poisoned slave, 615
Washington, Hugh, 329
Washington, Thomas, 215
Washington, D.C., 372, 474
Wat (slave), 284–285
Watboo. *See* Wadboo
Waterman, Richard, 581
Watkins, Katherine, 9, 10
Watson, Elkanah, 122, 241, 412, 418, 590
Watson, John Fanning, 588, 591
Wawees, 479
Wayles, John, 404
Webb, Abimilech (free black), 494
Webb, Jane (free black), 494
Weber, Jacob, 424
Weld, Isaac, 111, 174, 225, 359, 417
Wells, Peter, 9
Wells, Robert, 201
Welsh Neck Baptist Church, 425–426
Welsh Tract, S.C., 447
Wesley, Charles, 380
Wesley, John, 422
West, Benjamin, 272
West, Capt. James, 402
West Indies: early slaves from, 2–3; similarity of, to Lowcountry, 17, 118; immigrants from, 72, 74, 407, 596; minister to, 83–84; and gangs, 181; head carrying in, 200; transportation to, 283, 358; stories about, 287, 613; sugar growing in, 362; gestures in, 597; poisonings in, 614, 619; obeah in, 621. *See also* Barbados; Caribbean; Jamaica
Westmoreland Co., Va., 266, 400, 493, 628, 655
Westover plantation, 242, 244. *See also* Byrd, William, I; Byrd, William, II; Byrd, William, III
West Point, Va., 77
Wheat, 37, 47, 134, 170–175, 178, 190–191. *See also* Corn

Whitaker, Peggy, 402
Whitefield, George, 423, 582
Whitesides, Thomas, 291
Whydah, 66, 640
Wiggins, Sarah, 618–619
Wilcox, Edmund, 361, 364
Wilkinson, Eliza, 321
Will (African), 223
Will (Indian), 481
Will (Mangorike, foreman), 475
Will (old slave), 373–374
Will (slave), 220
Will (slave), 277
William (weaver), 113
Williams, Robert, 338
Williamsburg, Va.: runaways to and from, 87, 246, 452, 515, 551; outbuilding in, 119; and slave nakedness, 132; slave craftsmen in, 214; fears of insurrection in, 309; river traffic of, 341; trading with slaves in, 369; king's coronation in, 377; hanged slave in, 396; slave theft in, 468; king's attorney in, 489; slave separated from mother in, 543–544; and slave doctor, 628; Baptist church in, 656
Williamsburg township, S.C., 415
Williamson, Benjamin, 405
Williamson, Joel, 401
Willis, Francis, 332, 513–514
Willis, Harry, 418
Willoughby (slave), 113
Willtown, S.C., 121, 552
Wilmington, N.C., 367
Winchester, Elhanan, 425–426
Winchester, Elkanah, 380
Windaws, 479
Windward Coast, 63–64, 67–69, 72–73
Winney (slave), 113

Winney (midwife), 324
Winyaw, S.C., 48, 214, 265, 307
Winyaw River, 184, 590
Wise, Charles, 512
Wolf House quarter, 335
Wood, Alexander, 455
Wood, Peter H., 455
Woodford, William, 168
Woodmason, Charles, 120, 160, 577
Woodward, C. Vann, 258
Woolman, John, 132, 498
Wormeley, Ralph, 314
Wormeley family, 219
Wragg, Joseph, 338
Wragg, Samuel, 337
Wright, James, 77, 195
Wright, John, 482
Wright, Robert, 403
Wright, Thomas, 403
Wright Savanna plantation, 332, 363
Wyatt-Brown, Bertram, 442

Yamassee War, 17, 532
Yams, 135, 141
Yards, 122–123. *See also* Gardens
Yates, Charles, 132, 170, 627
Yeats, David, 163
Yeomen farmers. *See* Plain folk
Yeopim Baptist Church, 369
Younhocon, Cris (free black), 496
York Co., Va., 9, 94, 106, 137, 219, 277, 309, 312, 314, 415, 496, 512, 547
York River, 121
Yorktown, Va., 77, 252
Yoruba, 586, 608

Zoar Baptist Church, 431
Zuckerman, Michael, 268, 322